Macroeconomics

Fifth Edition

Olivier Blanchard

Massachusetts Institute of Technology

PEARSON

Prentice
Hall

Pearson Education International

Acquisitions Editor: Chris Rogers
Editorial Director: Sally Yagan
Editor in Chief: Eric Svendsen
Product Development Manager: Ashley Santora
Editorial Assistant: Vanessa Bain
Editorial Project Manager: Mary Kate Murray
Marketing Manager: Andrew Watts
Marketing Assistant: Ian Gold
Permissions Project Manager: Charles Morris
Senior Managing Editor: Judy Leale
Production Project Manager: Carol Samet
Senior Operations Specialist: Arnold Vila
Operations Specialist: Michelle Klein, Carol O'Rourke
Art Director: Steve Frim
Interior Design: Jill Little
Cover Designer: Jill Little
Cover Image: Argosy Illustration
Director, Image Resource Center: Melinda Patelli
Manager, Rights and Permissions: Zina Arabia
Manager, Visual Research: Beth Brenzel
Image Permission Coordinator: Joanne Dippel
Composition: GGS Book Services PMG
Full-Service Project Management: GGS Book Services PMG/Ann Courtney
Printer/Binder: CJ Krehbiel
Typeface: Utopia 10/12

If you purchased this book within the United States or Canada you should be aware that it has been wrongfully imported without the approval of the Publisher or the Author.

Pearson Education Ltd., London
Pearson Education Singapore, Pte.
Pearson Education, Canada, Inc.
Pearson Education–Japan
Pearson Education Australia PTY, Limited

Pearson Education North Asia, Ltd., Hong Kong
Pearson Educación de Mexico, S.A. de C.V.
Pearson Education Malaysia, Pte. Ltd
Pearson Education Upper Saddle River, New Jersey

10 9 8 7 6 5 4 3 2
ISBN-13: 978-0-13-207963-1
ISBN-10: 0-13-207963-1

A Noelle

About the Author

Olivier Blanchard is the Class of 1941 Professor of Economics at MIT. He did his under-graduate work in France and received a Ph.D. in economics from MIT in 1977. He taught at Harvard from 1977 to 1982, and has taught at MIT since 1983. He has frequently received the award for best teacher in the department of economics.

He has done research on many macroeconomic issues, from the effects of fiscal policy, to the role of expectations, to price rigidities, to speculative bubbles, to unemployment in Western Europe, transition in Eastern Europe, and, more recently, on labor market institutions. He has done work for many governments and many international organizations, including the *World Bank*, the *IMF*, the *OECD*, the *EU Commission* and the *EBRD*. He has published more than 160 articles and edited or written more than 15 books, including *Lectures on Macroeconomics* with Stanley Fischer.

He is a research associate of the National Bureau of Economic Research, a fellow of the Econometric Society, a member of the American Academy of Arts and Sciences, and a past vice president of the American Economic Association. He is a member of the French Council of Economic Advisers. He is also the editor of one of the new Journals of the American Economic Association, *AEJ-Macroeconomics*.

He lives in Cambridge, with his wife, Noelle. He has three daughters, Marie, Serena, and Giulia.

Brief Contents

Contents

Contents

8 Contents

Focus Boxes

Preface

I had two main goals in writing this book:

- To make close contact with current macroeconomic events.

  What makes macroeconomics exciting is the light it sheds on what is happening around the world, from the introduction of the euro in western Europe, to the large U.S. current account deficits, to the economic rise of China. These events—and many more—are described in the book, not in footnotes, but in the text or in detailed boxes. Each box shows how you can use what you have learned to get an understanding of these events. My belief is that these boxes not only convey the "life" of macroeconomics, but also reinforce the lessons from the models, making them more concrete and easier to grasp.

- To provide an integrated view of macroeconomics.

  The book is built on one underlying model, a model that draws the implications of equilibrium conditions in three sets of markets: the goods market, the financial markets, and the labor market. Depending on the issue at hand, the parts of the model relevant to the issue are developed in more detail while the other parts are simplified or lurk in the background. But the underlying model is always the same. This way, you will see macroeconomics as a coherent whole, not a collection of models. And you will be able to make sense not only of past macroeconomic events, but also of those that unfold in the future.

Organization

The book is organized around two central parts: a core and a set of three major extensions. An introduction precedes the core. The set of extensions is followed by a review of the role of policy. The book ends with an epilogue. A flowchart on the front endpaper makes it easy to see how the chapters are organized and fit within the book's overall structure.

- Chapters 1 and 2 introduce the basic facts and issues of macroeconomics. Chapter 1 offers a tour of the world, from the United States, to Europe, to China. Some instructors will prefer to cover Chapter 1 later, perhaps after Chapter 2, which introduces basic concepts; articulates the notions of short run, medium run, and long run; and gives the reader a quick tour of the book.

  While Chapter 2 gives the basics of national income accounting, I have put a detailed treatment of national income accounts in Appendix 1 at the end of the book. This decreases the burden on the beginning reader and allows for a more thorough treatment in the appendix.

- Chapters 3 through 13 constitute the **core**.

  Chapters 3 through 5 focus on the **short run**. These three chapters characterize equilibrium in the goods market and in the financial markets, and they derive the basic model used to study short-run movements in output, the *IS–LM* model.

  Chapters 6 through 9 focus on the **medium run**. Chapter 6 focuses on equilibrium in the labor market and introduces the notion of the natural rate of unemployment. Chapters 7 through 9 develop a model based on aggregate demand and aggregate supply, and show how that model can be used to understand movements in activity and movements in inflation, both in the short and in the medium run.

  Chapters 10 through 13 focus on the **long run**. Chapter 10 describes the facts, showing the evolution of output across countries and over long periods of time. Chapters 11 and 12 develop a model of growth and describe how capital accumulation and technological progress determine growth. Chapter 13 focuses on the determinants of technological progress, and on its effects not only in the long run, but also in the short run and in the medium run. This topic is typically not covered in textbooks but is important. And the chapter shows how one can integrate the short run, the medium run, and the long run—a clear example of the payoff to an integrated approach to macroeconomics.

- Chapters 14 through 24 cover the three major **extensions**.

  Chapters 14 through 17 focus on the role of **expectations** in the short run and in the medium run. Expectations play a major role in most economic decisions, and, by implication, play a major role in the determination of output.

  Chapters 18 through 21 focus on the implications of **openness** of modern economies. Chapter 21 focuses on the implications of different exchange rate regimes, from flexible exchange rates, to fixed exchange rates, currency boards, and dollarization.

  Chapters 22 and 23 focus on **pathologies**, times when (macroeconomic) things go very wrong. Chapter 22 looks at depressions and slumps, including the Great Depression in the United States before World War II, and the Japanese economic slump that started in the early 1990s. Chapter 23 looks at episodes of hyperinflation.

- Chapters 24 through 26 return to macroeconomic **policy**. Although most of the first 23 chapters constantly discuss macroeconomic policy in one form or another, the purpose of Chapters 24 through 26 is to tie the threads together. Chapter 24 looks at the role and the limits of macroeconomic policy in general. Chapters 25 and 26 review monetary policy and fiscal policy. Much of Chapter 26 is devoted to recent developments in monetary policy, from inflation targeting to interest rate rules. Some instructors may want to use parts of these chapters earlier. For example, it is easy to move forward the discussion of the government budget constraint in Chapter 26.

- Chapter 27 serves as an **epilogue;** it puts macroeconomics in historical perspective by showing the evolution of macroeconomics in the past 70 years and discussing current directions of research.

Changes from the Fourth to the Fifth Edition

I am repeatedly told by students and teachers alike that the two main strengths of the book are its integrated structure, and its use of examples. Thus, the structure of the fifth edition is the same as that of the fourth edition, and the changes reflect both exciting developments in macroeconomic research as well as important new macroeconomic developments around the world.

The tour of the world in Chapter 1, for example, now goes through China, reflecting the increasing importance of the Chinese economy in the world. Reflecting modern practice in monetary policy, Chapter 4 shows how one can reinterpret the LM relation in terms of an interest rate rule. The treatment of the effects of the price of oil in Chapter 7 has been expanded, reflecting the two major oil price increases the world economy has experienced since the late 1990s. In looking at variations in the unemployment rate across countries, Chapter 8 focuses on European unemployment rather than Japanese unemployment. Chapter 10 has an extended treatment of the relation between measures of the standard of living and measures of happiness; Chapter 13 discusses the role of institutions in allowing and sustaining growth. Both of these topics are the subject of active research in macroeconomics today.

The book also has a number of new Focus boxes (and good cartoons!). Among the new boxes: a box on who holds U.S. currency, in Chapter 4; a box on the effects of oil price increases on output and inflation, in Chapter 7; a new box on European unemployment, in Chapter 8; a box on the sources of growth in China, in Chapter 13; two boxes on the sources and the implications of U.S. current account deficits, in Chapters 19 and 20.

Alternative Course Outlines

Within the book's broad organization, there is plenty of room for alternative course organizations. I have made the chapters shorter than is standard in textbooks, and, in my experience, most chapters can be covered in an hour and a half. A few (Chapters 5 and 7 for example) might require two lectures to sink in.

- Short courses (15 or fewer lectures)

  A short course can be organized around the two introductory chapters and the core. Omitting Chapters 9 and 13 gives a total of 11 lectures. Informal presentations of one or two of the extensions, based for example on Chapter 17 for expectations (which can be taught as a stand-alone), and on Chapter 18 for the open economy, can then follow, for a total of 13 lectures.

  A short course might leave out the study of growth (the long run). In this case, the course can be organized around the introductory chapters, and Chapters 3 through 8 in the core; this gives a total of eight lectures, leaving enough time to cover, for example, Chapter 17 on expectations, Chapters 18 through 20 on the open economy, and Chapter 22 on depressions and slumps, for a total of 13 lectures.

- Longer courses (20 to 25 lectures)

A full-semester course gives more than enough time to cover the core, plus at least two extensions, and the review of policy.

The extensions assume knowledge of the core, but are otherwise mostly self-contained. Given the choice, the order in which they are best taught is probably the order in which they are presented in the book. Having studied the the role of expectations first helps students to understand the interest parity condition, and the nature of exchange rate crises.

One of the choices facing instructors is likely to be whether or not to teach growth (the long run). If growth is taught, there may not be enough time to cover all three extensions and have a thorough discussion of policy. In this case, it may be best to leave out the study of pathologies. If growth is not taught, there should be time to cover most of the other topics in the book.

Features

I have made sure never to present a theoretical result without relating it to the real world. In addition to discussions of facts in the text itself, I have written a large number of **Focus boxes**, which discuss particular macroeconomic events or facts, from the United States or from around the world.

I have tried to re-create some of the student-teacher interactions that take place in the classroom by the use of **margin notes**, running parallel to the text. The margin notes create a dialogue with the reader, to smooth the more difficult passages, and to give a deeper understanding of the concepts and the results derived along the way.

For students who want to explore macroeconomics further, I have introduced the following two features:

- **Short appendixes** to some chapters, which expand on points made within the chapter.

- A **Further Readings** section at the end of each chapter, indicating where to find more information, including a number of key internet addresses.

Each chapter ends with three ways of making sure that the material in the chapter has been digested:

- A **summary** of the chapter's main points.

- A list of **key terms**.

- A series of **end-of-chapter exercises**. "Quick check" exercises are easy, "Dig deeper" exercises are a bit harder, and "Explore further" typically require either access to the Internet or the use of a spreadsheet program.

A list of symbols on the back endpapers makes it easy to recall the meaning of the symbols used in the text.

The Teaching and Learning Package

The book comes with a number of supplements to help both students and instructors.

For Instructors

- **Instructor's Manual**—Written by Mark Moore, of the University of California–Irvine, the Instructor's Manual discusses pedagogical choices, alternative ways of presenting the material, and ways of reinforcing students' understanding. For each chapter in the book, the manual has seven sections: objectives, in the form of a motivating question; why the answer matters; key tools, concepts, and assumptions; summary; pedagogy; extensions; and observations and additional exercises. The Instructor's Manual also includes the answers to all end-of-chapter questions and exercises.

- **Test Item File**—Written by David Findlay, of Colby College, the test bank is completely revised with an additional 25% new multiple-choice questions for each chapter.

- **TestGen**—The printed test bank is designed for use with the computerized TestGen package, which allows instructors to customize, save, and generate classroom tests. The test program permits instructors to edit, add, or delete questions from the test bank edit existing graphics and create new graphics; analyze test results; and organize a database of tests and student results. This software allows for extensive flexibility and ease of use. It provides many options for organizing and displaying tests, along with search and sort features. The software and the test banks can be downloaded from the Instructor's Resource Center. (**www.prenhall.com/blanchard**)

- **Digital Image Library**—We have digitized the complete set of figures, graphs, and charts from the book. These files can be downloaded from the Instructor's Resource Center. (**www.prenhall.com/blanchard**)

- **PowerPoint Lecture Slides**—Created by Fernando and Yvonn Quijano, these electronic slides provide outlines, summaries, equations, and graphs for each chapter, and can be downloaded from the Instructor's Resource Center. (**www.prenhall.com/blanchard**)

For Students

- A **Study Guide**—David Findlay, of Colby College, has again done an outstanding job of writing a student-friendly study guide. Each chapter begins with a presentation of objectives and review. It is organized in the form of a tutorial, covering the important points of the chapter, with learning suggestions along the way. The tutorial is followed by quick self-test questions, review problems, and multiple-choice questions. Solutions are provided for all Study Guide problems.

Acknowledgments and Thanks

This book owes much to many.

I thank Adam Ashcraft, Peter Berger, Peter Benczur, Efe Cakarel, Harry Gakidis, David Hwang, Kevin Nazemi, John Simon, Jianlong Tan, Stacy Tevlin, Gaurav Tewari, Corissa Thompson, and Jeromin Zettelmeyer for their research assistance. I thank the generations of students in 14.02 at MIT who have freely shared their reactions to the book over the years.

I have benefited from comments from many colleagues and friends. Among them are John Abell, Daron Acemoglu, Tobias Adrian, Chuangxin An, Roland Benabou, Samuel Bentolila, and Juan Jimeno (who have adapted the book for a Spanish edition), Francois Blanchard, Roger Brinner, Ricardo Caballero, Wendy Carlin, Martina Copelman, Henry Chappell, Ludwig Chincarini, Daniel Cohen (who has adapted the book for a French edition), Larry Christiano, Bud Collier, Andres Conesa, Peter Diamond, Martin Eichenbaum, Gary Fethke, David Findlay, Francesco Giavazzi, and Alessia Amighini (who have adapted the book for an Italian edition), Andrew Healy, Steinar Holden, Gerhard Illing (who has adapted the book for a German edition), Yannis Ioannides, David Johnson, and Angelo Melino (who have adapted the book for a Canadian edition), P. N. Junankar, Sam Keeley, Bernd Kuemmel, Paul Krugman, Antoine Magnier, Peter Montiel, Bill Nordhaus, Tom Michl, Dick Oppermann, Athanasios Orphanides, Daniel Pirez Enri (who has adapted the book for a Latin American edition), Michael Plouffe, Zoran Popovic, Jim Poterba, Jeff Sheen (who has adapted the book for an Australasian edition), Ronald Schettkat, Watanabe Shinichi (who has adapted the book for a Japanese edition), Francesco Sisci, Brian Simboli, Changyong Rhee, Julio Rotemberg, Robert Solow, Andre Watteyne, and Michael Woodford. I have also benefited from often-stimulating suggestions from my daughters, Serena, Giulia, and Marie; I did not however follow all of them.

I have benefited from comments from many readers, reviewers, and class testers. Among them:

- John Abell, Randolph, Macon Womans' College
- Carol Adams, Cabrillo College
- Gilad Aharonovitz, School of Economic Sciences
- Terence Alexander, Iowa State University
- Roger Aliaga-Diaz, Drexel University
- Robert Archibald, College of William & Mary
- John Baffoe-Bonnie, La Salle University
- Fatolla Bagheri, University of North Dakota
- Stephen Baker, Capital University
- Erol Balkan, Hamilton College
- Jennifer Ball, Washburn University
- Richard Ballman, Augustana College
- King Banaian, St. Cloud State University
- Charles Bean, London School of Economics and Political Science
- Scott Benson, Idaho State University
- Gerald Bialka, University of North Florida
- Robert Blecker, American University
- Scott Bloom, North Dakota State University
- Pim Borren, University of Canterbury, New Zealand
- James Butkiewicz, University of Delaware
- Bruce Carpenter, Mansfield University
- Kyongwook Choi, Ohio University College
- Michael Cook, William Jewell College
- Nicole Crain, Lafayette College

- Rosemary Cunningham, Agnes Scott College
- Evren Damar, Pacific Lutheran University
- Dale DeBoer, University of Colorado at Colorado Springs
- Adrian de Leon-Arias, Universidad de Guadalajara
- Brad DeLong, UC Berkeley
- Wouter Denhaan, UC San Diego
- John Dodge, King College
- F. Trenery Dolbear, Brandeis University
- Patrick Dolenc, Keene State College
- Brian Donhauser, University of Washington
- Michael Donihue, Colby College
- Vincent Dropsy, California State University
- Justin Dubas, St. Norbert College
- Amitava Dutt, University of Notre Dame
- John Edgren, Eastern Michigan University
- Eric Elder, Northwestern College
- Sharon J. Erenburg, Eastern Michigan University
- Antonina Espiritu, Hawaii Pacific University
- J. Peter Federer, Clark University
- Rendigs Fels, Vanderbilt University
- John Flanders, Central Methodist University
- Marc Fox, Brooklyn College
- Yee-Tien (Ted) Fu, Stanford University
- Yee-Tien Fu, National Cheng-Chi University, Taiwan
- Scott Fullwiler, Wartburg College
- Julie Gallaway, University of Missouri–Rolla
- Bodhi Ganguli, Rutgers, The State University of NJ
- Fabio Ghironi, Boston College
- Alberto Gomez-Rivas, University of Houston–Downtown
- Fidel Gonzalez, Sam Houston State University
- Randy Grant, Linfield College
- Alan Gummerson, Florida International University
- Reza Hamzaee, Missouri Western State College
- Michael Hannan, Edinboro University
- Kenneth Harrison, Richard Stockton College
- Thomas Havrilesky, Duke University
- George Heitmann, Muhlenberg College
- Ana Maria Herrera, Michigan State University
- Peter Hess, Davidson College
- Eric Hilt, Wellesley College
- John Holland, Monmouth College
- Mark Hopkins, Gettysburg College
- Takeo Hoshi, University of California, San Diego
- Ralph Husby, University of Illinois, Urbana-Champaign
- Yannis Ioannides, Tufts University
- Aaron Jackson, Bentley College
- Bonnie Johnson, California Lutheran University
- Louis Johnston, College of St. Benedict
- Barry Jones, SUNY Binghamton
- Fred Joutz, George Washington University
- Cem Karayalcin, Florida International University
- Okan Kavuncu, University of California
- Miles Kimball, University of Michigan
- Paul King, Denison University
- Michael Klein, Tufts University
- Todd Knoop, Cornell College
- Paul Koch, Olivet Nazarene University
- Ng Beoy Kui, Nanyang Technical University, Singapore
- Leonard Lardaro, University of Rhode Island
- James Leady, University of Notre Dame
- Charles Leathers, University of Alabama
- Hsien-Feng Lee, National Taiwan University
- Jim Lee, Texas A&M University–Corpus Christi
- John Levendis, Loyola University New Orleans
- Frank Lichtenberg, Columbia University
- Mark Lieberman, Princeton University

- Shu Lin, Florida Atlantic University
- Maria Luengo-Prado, Northeastern University
- Mathias Lutz, University of Sussex
- Bernard Malamud, University of Nevada, Las Vegas
- Ken McCormick, University of Northern Iowa
- William McLean, Oklahoma State University
- B. Starr McMullen, Oregon State University
- Mikhail Melnik, Niagara University
- O. Mikhail, University of Central Florida
- Fabio Milani, University of California, Irvine
- Rose Milbourne, University of New South Wales
- Roger Morefield, University of Saint Thomas
- Shahriar Mostashari, Campbell University
- Eshragh Motahar, Union College
- Nick Noble, Miami University
- Ilan Noy, University of Hawaii
- John Olson, College of St. Benedict
- Brian O'Roark, Robert Morris University
- Jack Osman, San Francisco State University
- Emiliano Pagnotta, Northwestern University
- Andrew Parkes, Mesa State College
- Allen Parkman, University of Mexico
- Jim Peach, New Mexico State University
- Gavin Peebles, National University of Singapore
- Michael Quinn, Bentley College
- Charles Revier, Colorado State University
- Jack Richards, Portland State University
- Raymond Ring, University of South Dakota
- Monica Robayo, University of North Florida
- Malcolm Robinson, Thomas Moore College
- Brian Rosario, University of California, Davis
- Kehar Sangha, Old Dominion University
- Ahmad Saranjam, Bridgewater State College
- Carol Scotese, Virginia Commonwealth University
- John Seater, North Carolina State University
- Peter Sephton, University of New Brunswick
- Ruth Shen, San Francisco State University
- Kwanho Shin, University of Kansas
- Tara Sinclair, The George Washington University
- David Sollars, Auburn University
- Edward Stuart, Northeastern Illinois University
- Abdulhanid Sukaar, Cameron University
- Peter Summers, Texas Tech University
- Mark Thomas, University of Maryland Baltimore County
- Brian Trinque, The University of Texas at Austin
- Marie Truesdell, Marian College
- David Tufte, Southern Utah University
- Abdul Turay, Radford University
- Frederick Tyler, Fordham University
- Pinar Uysal, Boston College
- Evert Van Der Heide, Calvin College
- Kristin Van Gaasbeck, California State University, Sacramento
- Lee Van Scyoc, University of Wisconsin, Oshkosh
- Paul Wachtel, New York University Stern Business School
- Susheng Wang, Hong Kong University
- Donald Westerfield, Webster University
- Christopher Westley, Jacksonville State University
- David Wharton, Washington College
- Jonathan Willner, Oklahoma City University
- Mark Wohar, University of Nebraska, Omaha
- Steven Wood, University of California, Berkeley
- Michael Woodford, Princeton University
- Ip Wing Yu, University of Hong Kong
- Chi-Wa Yuen, Hong Kong University of Science and Technology
- Christian Zimmermann, University of Connecticut

They have helped me beyond the call of duty, and each has made a difference to the book.

I have many people to thank at Prentice Hall, from Stephen Dietrich for convincing me to write this book in the first place, to Chris Rogers, the executive editor for Economics, to Mary Kate Murray, the assistant editor, to Vanessa Bain, the editorial assistant, to Carol Samet, the production editor, and to Andy Watts, the marketing manager for Economics.

I want to single out Steve Rigolosi, the editor for the first edition; Michael Elia, the editor to the second and third edition; and Amy Ray, the editor of the fourth edition. Steve forced me to clarify, Michael forced me to simplify, and Amy forced me to simplify further. Together, they have made all the difference to the process and to the book. I thank all three of them deeply.

At MIT, I continue to thank John Arditi for his absolute reliability.

At home, I continue to thank Noelle for preserving my sanity.

Olivier Blanchard
Cambridge, MIT,
December 2007

Student Subscriptions

Staying on top of current economic issues is critical to understanding and applying macroeconomic theory, in and out of class. Keep your students engaged by packaging a semester-long subscription to the *Wall Street Journal*, the *Financial Times*, or Economist.com with each student text. Simply order one of the following discounted packages through your bookstore:

- Order Package ISBN 0-13-606986-X—To package this textbook with a *15-week* subscription to the *Wall Street Journal* both print and online formats.

- Order Package ISBN 0-13-814681-0—To package this textbook with a *15-week* subscription to the *Financial Times* in student's choice of print or online formats.

- Order Package ISBN 0-13-504295-X—To package this textbook with a *12-week* subscription to Economist.com.

The Wall Street Journal

Global events. Financial markets. Your personal finances. What's the one source that can tell you how all the pieces fit together? the *Wall Street Journal*, the world's most trusted source of vital business news and analysis.

In addition to daily home delivery of the *Wall Street Journal*, students receive all of the benefits of the *Wall Street Journal Online*, including:

- All the news from the *Wall Street Journal*—plus 24-hour-a-day updates

- The ability to search for past *Journal* articles

- Detailed company research providing background, historical and financial information, news articles, and press releases on nearly 30,000 companies

- Powerful personalization features, including online portfolios

- In-depth coverage of technology, and much more

As an adopting professor, you'll receive a free one-year subscription to both the print and online editions of the *Wall Street Journal.**

The Financial Times

Covering far more than just finance, the *Financial Times* is universally acknowledged as the world's leading business newspaper of global affairs. It is the only worldwide daily concentrating on international business, and its team of 600 journalists presents economic and business news from a truly global perspective.

In addition to daily home delivery of the *Financial Times*, students receive all the benefits of FT.com (Level 1) including access to:

- **Exclusive news and commentary**

- **Industry-specific insight and analysis**

- **Surveys/in-depth reports**—industries, countries, and business trends

- **Power search** tool for searching through five years' of archives

- **View print edition**—exclusive previews from the *Financial Times* newspaper

- **PDA access**—download content to your PDA

- **News by email**—news summaries and alerts direct to your inbox

As an adopting professor, you will qualify for a complimentary one-year personal subscription to the *Financial Times.**

Economist.com

Economist.com is the premier online source for the analysis of world business and current affairs, providing

Package adoptions of over 10 copies qualify for complimentary professor subscriptions.

authoritative insight and opinion on international news, world politics, business, finance, science and technology, as well as overviews of cultural trends and regular industry, business, and country surveys.

Economist.com publishes all articles from the *Economist* print edition plus:

- The **Advanced Search** feature retrieves from the Economist.com archives of over 30,000 *Economist* articles and surveys published since May 1997, making our library your personal reference source.

- The **Global Agenda** offers analysis of the international issues and events that matter most, when they matter most: a rolling selection of six to eight editorial briefings on the most important issues and events in global current affairs and business.

- **Country Briefings** offers continuously updated reports, forecasts, economic statistics, news, and analysis on 60 countries around the world.

- **Markets & Data** features global market data and charting, economic indicators from the *Economist*, stock quotes, foreign exchange graphs for 164 countries, currency converter, and our annual favorite: The Big Mac Index.

As an adopting professor, you will qualify for a complimentary six-month personal subscription to Economist.com.

Introduction

The first two chapters of this book introduce you to the issues and the approach of macroeconomics.

Chapter 1

Chapter 1 takes you on a macroeconomic tour of the world, from U.S. trade deficits, to unemployment in Europe, to the implications of the euro, to the extraordinary growth in China.

Chapter 2

Chapter 2 takes you on a tour of the book. It defines the three central variables of macroeconomics: output, unemployment, and inflation. It introduces the three concepts around which the book is organized: the short run, the medium run, and the long run.

THE CORE

What is macroeconomics? The best way to answer is not to give you a formal definition but rather to take you on an economic tour of the world, to describe both the main economic evolutions and the issues that keep macroeconomists and macroeconomic policymakers awake at night.

At the time of this writing (mid-2007), one might think they should be sleeping rather well. Since the early 2000s, the world economy has been steadily growing. World output growth in 2006 was close to 5%, the highest growth rate on record. In the United States, the recession of 2001 gave way to a long expansion. In Europe, economic growth has also increased, although unemployment remains high. The most impressive economic performances have come from poorer countries, in particular China and India, which are growing at close to 10% a year.

Yet, macroeconomists find reasons to worry (after all, it is part of their job description). They worry that the U.S. expansion may soon turn into a recession. They worry that Europe may not be able to achieve low unemployment. They wonder about the sources of growth in China, and they worry that this growth may not be sustainable.

My goal in this chapter is to give you a sense of these evolutions and the issues confronting macroeconomists today. There is no way I can take you on a full world tour, so I shall give you a sense of what is happening in the United States, the European Union, and China:

■ Section 1-1 looks at the United States.

■ Section 1-2 looks at Europe.

■ Section 1-3 looks at China.

■ Section 1-4 concludes and looks ahead.

Read the chapter as you would read an article in a newspaper. Do not worry about the exact meaning of the words, or about understanding all the arguments in detail: The words will be defined, and the arguments will be developed in later chapters. Regard it as background, intended to introduce you to the issues of macroeconomics. If you enjoy reading this chapter, you will probably enjoy reading this book. Indeed, once you have read the book, come back to this chapter; see where you stand on the issues and judge how much progress you have made in your study of macroeconomics. ■

Figure 1-1

The United States

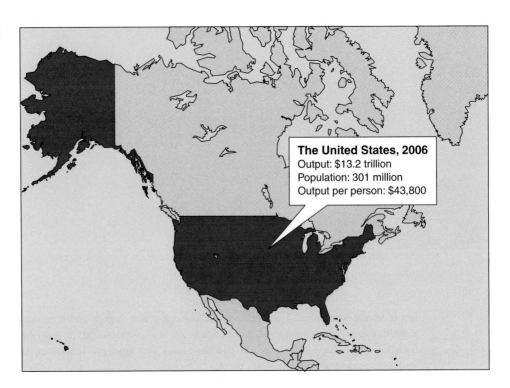

The United States, 2006
Output: $13.2 trillion
Population: 301 million
Output per person: $43,800

1-1 The United States

When macroeconomists study an economy, they first look at three variables:

- *Output*—The level of production of the economy as a whole—and its rate of growth.
- The *unemployment rate*—The proportion of workers in the economy who are not employed and are looking for jobs.
- The *inflation rate*—the rate at which the average price of the goods in the economy is increasing over time.

The basic numbers for the U.S. economy are given in Table 1-1. To put the current numbers in perspective, the first column gives you the average value of the rate of growth of output, the unemployment rate, and the inflation rate in the United States for the period 1970 to 2006. The second column gives you the same three numbers, but for the more recent period 1996 to 2006. The last three columns then give you the numbers for each of the years 2006 to 2008. The numbers for 2006 are actual numbers; the numbers for 2007 and 2008 are forecasts, as of mid-2007.

Table 1-1   Growth, Unemployment, and Inflation in the United States Since 1970

	1970–2006 (average)	1996–2006 (average)	2006	2007	2008
Output growth rate	3.1%	3.4%	3.3%	2.1%	2.5%
Unemployment rate	6.2%	5.0%	4.6%	4.6%	4.8%
Inflation rate	4.0%	2.0%	2.9%	2.6%	2.2%

Output growth rate: annual rate of growth of output (GDP). Unemployment rate: average over the year. Inflation rate: annual rate of change of the price level (GDP deflator).

Source: OECD *Economic Outlook* database, May 2007.

From an economic point of view, there is no question that the past decade has been one of the best decades in recent memory. Look at the column giving the numbers for the period 1996 to 2006:

- The average rate of growth was 3.4% per year, substantially higher than the average growth rate since 1970.
- The average unemployment rate was 5.0%, substantially lower than the average unemployment rate since 1970.
- The average inflation rate was 2.0%, substantially lower than the average inflation rate since 1970.

Growth was not high in every single year: In 2001, the U.S. economy actually went through a short recession—a decrease in output. But for the period as a whole, the U.S. economy had an impressive performance.

In the recent past, however, the U.S. economy has slowed down. Growth is projected to reach only 2.1% in 2007. The forecast for 2008 is of a rebound, but not all macroeconomists agree.

Some believe that the risk of a recession is high. In February 2007, Alan Greenspan, the previous chairman of the Fed (the U.S. central bank, formally known as the *Federal Reserve Board*) and a very influential economist, put the probability of a recession in 2007 at one-third. Those who believe a recession is likely point to what is happening in the housing sector: Housing construction, which was very strong until 2006, has slowed down sharply. Housing prices are decreasing. This decrease in housing prices may lead, they argue, to a decrease in consumption demand: As housing prices fall, consumers will feel poorer and reduce their spending. If this happens, the decrease in demand, from lower housing construction and lower consumption demand, may lead to a recession.

That remark led to a decline in stock market prices of more than 3% in one day.

Others are more optimistic. The decline in housing prices has so far been limited, and consumers have not yet cut their spending. But even if housing prices led to lower housing construction and lower consumption, the Fed could decrease interest rates to stimulate demand and avoid a recession. This is indeed one of the major responsibilities of the Fed, and it is something it has done in the past. Monetary policy is not a magic bullet: In early 2001, feeling that the economy was slowing down, the Fed aggressively decreased interest rates to stimulate demand. This was, however, not enough to avoid a (small) recession; but the recession would have surely been deeper and longer in the absence of the decrease in interest rates.

In the short run, whether or not the expansion will continue is the major issue confronting U.S. policymakers. Looking beyond the short run, however, there are two other issues macroeconomists worry about.

The first concerns productivity. High output growth in the past decade has come largely from high productivity growth. A crucial issue is whether we can count on productivity growth remaining high in the future.

The second concerns the trade deficit. Since the mid-1990s, the trade deficit of the United States—that is, the difference between what the United States imports and what it exports—has steadily increased. The trade deficit is now very large as a proportion of output, and a crucial issue is whether this can go on and for how long.

Let me discuss both issues in turn.

Has the United States Entered a New Economy?

The strong performance of the U.S. economy in the second half of the 1990s led many people to argue that the United States had entered a *New Economy*, in which it could sustain high growth, low unemployment, and low inflation forever. Many of the New

Figure 1-2

Rate of Growth of Output per Hour in the United States since 1970

The average rate of growth of output per hour appears to have increased again since the mid-1990s.

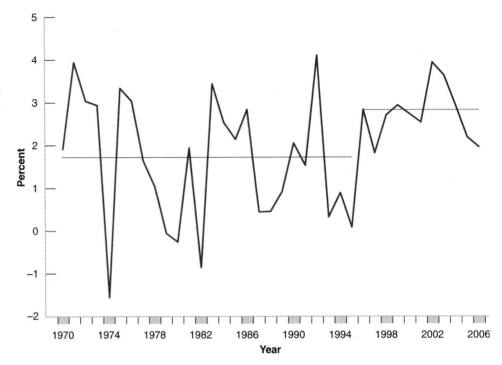

Economy claims had no basis in fact and have proven empty. Recall, for example, the claims of some of the dot-com companies whose share prices rose to astronomical heights, only to collapse in the early 2000s. One claim, however—the claim that the U.S. economy had entered a period of faster technological progress and therefore we can expect higher growth in the future than in the past—is more plausible and worth examining.

The way to examine this claim is to plot the rate of growth of *output per hour worked* since 1970 in the United States. (Output per hour worked, or *output per hour* for short, is also called *productivity*; the rate of growth of output per hour is called the rate of productivity growth.) This is done in Figure 1-2. A look at the figure suggests that the underlying rate of productivity growth may indeed have increased since the mid-1990s: The average annual growth rate for the period 1996 to 2006 (represented by the green horizontal line from 1996 to 2006) was 2.8%, 1% higher than the average of 1.8% for the period 1970 to 1995 (represented by the blue horizontal line from 1970 to 1995).

$(1.01)^{20} - 1.0 = 22\%$; $(1.01)^{50} - 1.0 = 64\%$. **For a review of exponents, see Appendix 2 at ▶ the end of the book.**

A difference in the average growth rate of output per hour of 1% per year might not seem like much, but it is. Think of it this way: A 1% higher annual growth sustained for 20 years implies a 22% higher level of productivity at the end of 20 years; sustained for 50 years, it implies a 64% higher level of productivity after 50 years. Other things equal, an increase in productivity of 64% translates into a 64% increase in output per person, a 64% increase in what economists call the *standard of living*—a very substantial increase.

This discussion might remind you of the controversies surrounding global warming. The world temperature varies a lot from year to year. It took many unusually warm years before scientists became fairly confi-dent that there was indeed ▶ global warming.

Can we be confident that productivity growth will continue in the future at the same higher rate as it has since 1996? Figure 1-2 suggests caution: The rate of produc-tivity growth fluctuates a lot from year to year. The high growth rates since 1996 might just be a series of "lucky" years that won't soon be repeated. Some economists believe that it is indeed too early to tell. Other economists are more optimistic. They believe that the underlying rate of technological progress has indeed increased in the United States, largely as a result of the development and better use of *information technologies*, from computers to faster communication networks. If they are right, it is indeed reasonable to expect higher productivity growth and a faster increase in the standard of living for some time to come.

Should We Worry About the U.S. Trade Deficit?

Since the early 1990s, the United States has consistently bought more goods and services from the rest of the world than it has sold to the rest of the world. Put another way, U.S. imports have consistently exceeded U.S. exports. Not only that, but the difference between imports and exports, which is called the *trade deficit*, has steadily increased and is now very large. Figure 1-3 shows the evolution of the U.S. trade deficit as a proportion of U.S. output since 1990. The deficit, which was equal to $78 billion, or about 1% of U.S. output in 1990, stood at $760 billion, or about 6% of U.S. output in 2006.

If you buy more goods than you sell, then your spending exceeds your income, and you must make up the difference by borrowing. Exactly the same thing is true of a country. Thus, to finance its trade deficit, the United States has been borrowing from the rest of the world. As the trade deficit has increased, so has the amount of borrowing. This should strike you as a bit strange: the richest country in the world, borrowing $760 billion per year from the rest of the world. An obvious question is can this go on? If not, what is likely to happen?

Think again about your own situation. As long as you find people willing to lend to you, you can clearly continue to borrow and thus continue to spend more than your income. But even if you can borrow, it may not be wise to do so: Borrowing more means having to repay more and having less to spend in the future. Again, the same logic applies to a country, in this case the United States.

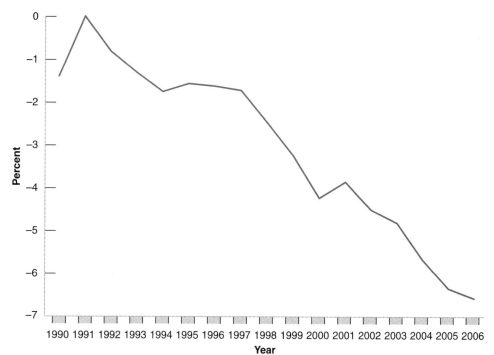

Figure 1-3

The U.S. Trade Deficit since 1990

The trade deficit increased from about 1% of output in 1990 to about 6% of output in 2006.

Can the United States continue to borrow such large amounts in the future? So far, foreigners have been quite willing, indeed often eager, to finance the U.S. trade deficit. They have been willing, for example, to buy U.S. government bonds or to buy shares in the U.S. stock market. The question is whether they will be willing to do so in the future. In the late 1990s, foreigners, who had been willing to lend to a number of Asian countries, suddenly changed their mind, forcing the countries to suddenly eliminate their trade deficits, and causing major economic crises in countries from Thailand to

This crisis is known as the Asian ▶ crisis.

South Korea. The United States is not Thailand, and there is little chance of a similar sudden change of mind on the part of foreigners. But some economists worry that it may be increasingly difficult for the United States to borrow such large amounts from the rest of the world in the future.

Even if the United States can borrow, shouldn't it try to reduce its trade deficit and therefore its borrowing? To answer this question, one must look more closely at who is borrowing—the government, firms, or people. Some economists point to the U.S. government budget deficit, which has increased a lot since 2000, as one of the main causes, and argue that it should be reduced: Budget deficits lead to the accumulation of government debt and the need for higher taxes in the future. Others point to the low saving rate of U.S. consumers as another cause. They worry that U.S. consumers may not be saving enough for their retirement and thus argue for an increase in the private saving rate. Whether budget deficits should be reduced and, if so, how fast; whether private saving should be increased and how; and how these changes would affect the trade deficit are among the most important questions confronting U.S. macroeconomists today.

1-2   The European Union

The original name was the *European Community*, or EC. You may still encounter that name in some documents.

The reason for not giving numbers for the EU27 as a whole is that many of the new members are former communist countries. Data on growth, inflation, and unemployment, pretransition, are often not available or are ▶ not reliable.

In 1957, 6 European countries decided to form a common European market—an economic zone where people and goods could move freely. Since then, 21 more countries have joined, bringing the total to 27. This group is now known as the **European Union (EU)**. The group of 27 countries, sometimes also referred to as the EU27, forms a formidable economic power. As Figure 1-4 shows, their combined output exceeds the output of the United States, and many of them have a standard of living—a level of output per person—not far from that of the United States.

Table 1-2 gives the recent economic performance for the group composed of the five largest EU members: Germany, France, Italy, Spain, and the United Kingdom. Together, these countries account for 75% of the total output of the EU27. The format

Table 1-2   Growth, Unemployment, and Inflation in the Five Major European Countries Since 1970

	1970–2006 (average)	1996–2006 (average)	2006	2007	2008
Output growth rate	2.3%	2.0%	2.7%	2.6%	2.2%
Unemployment rate	7.4%	8.7%	7.6%	7.0%	6.7%
Inflation rate	5.4%	1.8%	1.7%	1.8%	2.2%

Output growth rate: annual rate of growth of output (GDP). Unemployment rate: average over the year. Inflation rate: annual rate of change of the price level (GDP deflator).

Source: OECD *Economic Outlook* database.

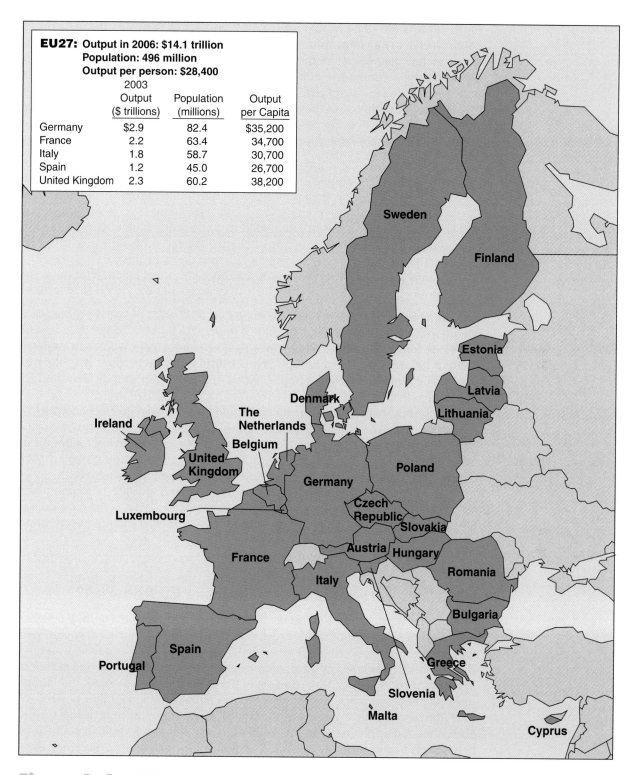

EU27:	Output in 2006: $14.1 trillion		
	Population: 496 million		
	Output per person: $28,400		
	2003		
	Output ($ trillions)	Population (millions)	Output per Capita
Germany	$2.9	82.4	$35,200
France	2.2	63.4	34,700
Italy	1.8	58.7	30,700
Spain	1.2	45.0	26,700
United Kingdom	2.3	60.2	38,200

Figure 1-4

The European Union

of the table is the same format we used for the United States earlier: The first two columns give the average value of the rate of growth of output, the unemployment rate, and the inflation rate for the period 1970 to 2006 and for the period 1996 to 2006. The next three columns give numbers for 2006, 2007, and 2008. The numbers for 2007 and 2008 are forecasts, as of mid-2007.

The main conclusion to draw from Table 1-2 is that the economic performance of these five countries over the past decade has been far less impressive than that of the United States over the same period:

■ Average annual output growth from 1996 to 2006 was only 2.0%. This was 1.4% below the average annual growth rate in the United States over the same period, and it was 0.3% below the average growth rate in the European Union from 1970 to 2006.

■ Low output growth was accompanied by persistently high unemployment. The average unemployment rate from 1996 to 2006 was 8.7%, which is 3.7% higher than the average U.S. unemployment rate over the same period.

■ The only good news was about inflation. Average annual inflation for these countries was 1.8%, much lower than the 5.4% average over the period 1970 to 2006.

The numbers for 2006 and the forecasts for 2007 and 2008 give a more positive picture, however. Output growth for 2007 is forecast to be 2.6%, higher than the corresponding forecast for the United States. And unemployment is forecast to decline. There is indeed a feeling in Europe that the future may be brighter than the recent past, that a number of reforms implemented in the recent past may allow for higher output growth in the future.

At this time, two issues dominate the agenda of European macroeconomists.

The first is, not surprisingly, high unemployment. Although the unemployment rate has come down from its peak in the mid-1990s, it is still very high. Can it be reduced further, say all the way down to the U.S. rate of unemployment? What reforms and what macroeconomic policies would be needed to achieve this?

The second issue is associated with the introduction, in 2002, of a common currency, the *euro*. After five years, many questions remain. What is the euro doing for Europe? What macroeconomic changes has it brought? How should macroeconomic policy be conducted in this new environment?

Let me discuss both issues in turn.

How Can European Unemployment Be Reduced?

High unemployment has not always been the norm in Europe. Figure 1-5 plots the evolution of the unemployment rate, since 1970, in the four largest continental European countries (Germany, France, Italy, and Spain) taken as a whole, and in the United States. Note how low the unemployment rate was in these European countries in the early 1970s. At that time, the talk in the United States was about the European *unemployment miracle*; U.S. macroeconomists actually went to Europe, hoping to discover the secrets of that miracle. By the late 1970s, however, the miracle had vanished. Since then, unemployment in the four largest continental European countries has been much higher than in the United States. And despite a decrease since the late 1990s, it still stood at 8.1% in 2006, nearly 3.5% higher than the unemployment rate in the United States.

Despite a large amount of research, there is no full agreement on the causes of high European unemployment:

Politicians often blame macroeconomic policy. They argue that the monetary policy followed by the European Central Bank has kept interest rates too high, leading

Figure 1-5

**Unemployment Rates:
Continental Europe
Versus the United States
since 1970**

The unemployment rate in the
four largest continental European
countries has gone from being
much lower than the U.S. unemployment rate to being much
higher.

to low demand and high unemployment. According to them, the central bank should decrease interest rates and allow for an increase in demand, and unemployment would decrease.

Most economists believe, however, that the source of the problem is not macroeconomic policy but *labor market institutions*. Too tight a monetary policy, they concede, can indeed lead to high unemployment for some time, but surely not for 20 years. The fact that unemployment has been so high for so long points to problems in the labor market. The challenge is then to identify exactly what these problems are.

Some economists believe the main problem is that European states protect workers too much. To prevent workers from losing their jobs, they make it expensive for firms to lay off workers. One of the results, however, is to deter firms from hiring workers in the first place, and this increases unemployment. To protect workers who become unemployed, they provide generous unemployment insurance. But by doing so, they decrease the incentives for the unemployed to look for jobs; this also increases unemployment. The solution, they argue, is to be less protective, to eliminate these *labor market rigidities* and adopt U.S.-style labor market institutions. This is indeed what the United Kingdom has largely done, and its unemployment rate is low.

Others are more skeptical. They point to the fact that unemployment is not high everywhere in Europe. It is indeed high in the four large continental European countries I focused on in Figure 1-5 (which is precisely why I chose them). But it is low in a number of smaller countries, such as the Netherlands and Denmark, where the unemployment rate is now under 4%. Yet these countries are very different from the United States and provide generous social insurance to workers. This suggests that the problem may lie not so much with the degree of protection but with the way it is implemented. The challenge, these economists argue, is to understand what the Netherlands and Denmark do right. Resolving these questions is one of the major tasks facing European macroeconomists and policymakers today.

What Will the Euro Do for Europe?

In 1999, the European Union started the process of replacing national currencies with one common currency, called the *euro*. Only 11 countries, among them France, Germany, Italy, and Spain, participated at the start; since then, 4 more countries have joined. Some countries, in particular Denmark, Sweden, and the United Kingdom, have decided not to join, but they may do so in the future.

What to call the group of countries that have adopted the euro is not settled. "Euro zone" sounds technocratic. "Euroland" reminds some of Disneyland. "Euro area" seems to be winning, and this is how I shall refer to it in this book.

The transition took place in steps. On January 1, 1999, each of the 11 countries fixed the value of its currency to the euro. For example, 1 euro was set equal to 6.56 French francs, to 166 Spanish pesetas, and so on. From 1999 to 2002, some prices were quoted both in national currency units and in euros, but the euro was not yet used as currency. This happened in 2002, when euro notes and coins replaced national currencies. The 15 countries of the euro area have now become a *common currency* area.

What will the euro do for Europe? Supporters of the euro point first to its enormous symbolic importance. In light of the many past wars between European countries, what better proof that the page has definitely been turned than the adoption of a common currency? They also point to the economic advantages of having a common currency: no more changes in the relative price of currencies for European firms to worry about, no more need to change currencies when traveling between euro countries. Together with the removal of other obstacles to trade between European countries, which has taken place since 1957, the euro will contribute, they argue, to the creation of a large, if not the largest, economic power in the world. There is little question that the move to the euro is indeed one of the main economic events of the start of the twenty-first century.

Others worry that the symbolism of the euro may come with some economic costs. They point out that a common currency means a common monetary policy, and that means the same interest rate across the euro countries. What if, they argue, one country plunges into recession while another is in the middle of an economic boom? The first country needs lower interest rates to increase spending and output; the second country needs higher interest rates to slow down its economy. If interest rates have to be the same in both countries, what will happen? Isn't there a risk that one country will remain in recession for a long time or that the other will not be able to slow down its booming economy?

Throughout the 1990s, the question was: Should Europe adopt the euro? That question is now moot: The euro is here, and it is here to stay. So far, no member country has had to face a severe recession, so the system has not really been tested. The full costs and benefits of the euro remain to be assessed.

1-3 China

China is in the news every day. It is increasingly seen as one of the major economic powers in the world. Is the attention justified? A look at the numbers in Figure 1-6 suggests that it may not be. True, the population of China is enormous, more than four times that of the United States. But its output, expressed in dollars by multiplying the number in yuans (the Chinese currency) by the dollar–yuan exchange rate, is only $2.8 trillion, roughly the same as that of Germany, and less than one-fourth that of the United States. Output per person is only $2,100, roughly one-twentieth of output per person in the United States.

So, why is so much attention paid to China? There are primarily two reasons.

First, let's go back to the number for output per person. When comparing output per person in a rich country such as the United States and a relatively poor country

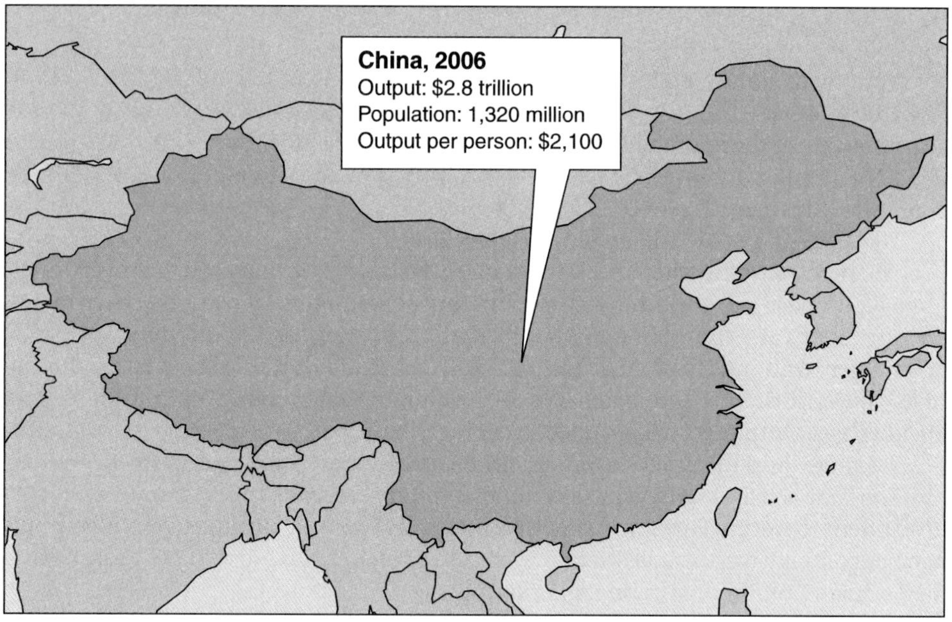

Figure 1-6

China

China, 2006
Output: $2.8 trillion
Population: 1,320 million
Output per person: $2,100

such as China, one has to be careful because many goods are cheaper in poor countries. For example, the price of an average restaurant meal in New York City is about $20; the price of an average restaurant meal in Beijing is about 15 yuans, which at the current exchange rate is about $2. Put another way, the same income (expressed in dollars) buys you much more in Beijing than in New York City. If we want to compare standards of living, we have to correct for these differences; measures that do so are called PPP (for *purchasing power parity*) measures. Using such a measure, output per person in China is estimated to be about $8,000, roughly one-fifth of output per person in the United States. This gives a more accurate picture of the standard of living in China. It is obviously much lower than that of the United States and other rich countries. But it is much higher than suggested by the numbers in Figure 1-6.

Second, and more importantly, China has been growing very fast for more than two decades. This is shown in Table 1-3, which gives output growth and inflation, for the periods 1980 to 2006, 1996 to 2006, and the years 2006 to 2008. The numbers for 2007 and 2008 are forecasts, as of mid-2007.

Note two things about Table 1-3. First, the numbers go back only to 1980, not to 1970, as in the previous tables. The reason is that the pre-1980 numbers are unreliable. Second, the table does not give unemployment rates. Unemployment in poorer countries is difficult to measure because many workers may decide to stay in agriculture

Table 1-3 Growth and Inflation in China Since 1980

	1980–2006	1996–2006	2006	2007	2008
Output growth rate	9.3%	8.8%	10.7%	10.0%	9.5%
Inflation rate	5.4%	3.3%	1.5%	2.5%	2.2%

Output growth rate: annual rate of growth of output (GDP). Inflation rate: annual rate of change of the price level (GDP deflator).

Source: IMF *World Economic Outlook* database.

rather than be unemployed. As a result, official unemployment rates are typically not very informative.

Now, focus on the main feature of the table: the very high growth rate of output since 1980. Since 1980, Chinese output has grown at close to 10% per year, and the forecasts are for more of the same. This is a truly astonishing number. Compare it to the 3.1% number achieved by the U.S. economy over the same period. At that rate, output doubles every 7 years.

These numbers raise many obvious questions.

The first is whether the numbers are for real. Could it be that growth is overstated? After all, China is still a communist country, and government officials may have incentives to overstate the economic performance of their sector or their province. Economists who have looked at this carefully conclude that this is probably not the case. The statistics are not as reliable as they are in richer countries, but there is no obvious bias. Output growth is indeed very high in China.

So where does the growth come from? It clearly comes from two sources.

The first is very high accumulation of capital. The investment rate (the ratio of investment to output) in China is between 40% and 45% of output, a very high number. For comparison, the investment rate in the United States is only 17%. More capital means higher productivity and higher output.

The second is very fast technological progress. The strategy followed by the Chinese government has been to encourage foreign firms to come and produce in China. As foreign firms are typically much more productive than Chinese firms, this has increased productivity and output. Another aspect of the strategy has been to encourage joint ventures between foreign and Chinese firms; making Chinese firms work with and learn from foreign firms has made them much more productive.

When described in this way, achieving high productivity and high output growth appears easy, with easy recipes that every poor country could and should follow. In fact, things are less obvious: China is only one of many countries that have made the transition from central planning to a market economy. Most of those countries, among them Russia and Central European countries, have experienced a large decrease in output at the time of transition. Most still have growth rates far below that of China. In many of these countries, widespread corruption and poor property rights make firms unwilling to invest. So why has China fared so much better? Economists are not sure. Some believe that it is the result of a slower transition: The first Chinese reforms took place, in agriculture, in 1980, and even today, many firms remain owned by the state. Others argue that the fact that the Communist party has remained in control has actually helped the economic transition; tight political control has allowed for better protection of property rights, at least for firms, giving them incentives to invest. Getting the answers to these questions, and thus learning what other poor countries can take from the Chinese experience, can clearly make a huge difference—not only for China but for the rest of the world.

1-4 Looking Ahead

This concludes our world tour. There are many other regions of the world we could have looked at:

- India, another poor and very large country, with a population of 1,100 million people, which, like China, is now growing very fast. In 2006, India's output growth rate was 9.2%.

Where do the data we have examined in this chapter come from? Suppose we wanted to find the numbers for inflation in Germany over the past five years. Fifty years ago, the answer would have been to learn German, find a library with German publications, find the page where inflation numbers were given, write them down, and plot them by hand on a clean sheet of paper. Today, improvements in the collection of data, the development of computers and electronic databases, and access to the Internet make the task much easier.

International organizations now collect data for many countries. For the richest countries, the most useful source is the **Organisation for Economic Co-operation and Development (OECD),** based in Paris. You can think of the OECD as an economic club for rich countries. The complete list of member countries is Australia, Austria, Belgium, Canada, the Czech Republic, Denmark, Finland, France, Germany, Greece, Hungary, Iceland, Italy, Japan, Korea, Luxembourg, Mexico, the Netherlands, New Zealand, Norway, Poland, Portugal, the Slovak Republic, Spain, Sweden, Switzerland, Turkey, the United Kingdom, and the United States. Together, these countries account for about 70% of the world's output. The OECD Economic Outlook, which is published twice a year, contains basic data on inflation, unemployment, and other major variables for member countries, as well as an assessment of their recent macroeconomic performance. The data, often going back to 1960, are available on CD-ROM and on the Internet.

For countries that are not members of the OECD, information is available from other international organizations. The main world economic organization is the **International Monetary Fund (IMF)**. The IMF publishes the monthly International Financial Statistics (IFS), which contains basic macroeconomic information for all IMF members. It also publishes, twice a year, the World Economic Outlook, an assessment of macroeconomic developments in various parts of the world. Both the **World Economic Outlook** and the OECD **Economic Outlook** are precious sources of information.

Because these publications sometimes do not contain sufficient details, you may need to turn to specific country publications. Major countries now produce remarkably clear statistical publications, often with an English translation available. In the United States, an extremely good resource is the **Economic Report of the President**, prepared by the Council of Economic Advisors and published annually. This report has two parts. The first, an assessment of current U.S. events and policy, is often a good read. The second is a set of data for nearly all relevant macroeconomic variables, usually for the entire post–World War II period.

A longer list of data sources, both for the United States and for the rest of the world, as well as instructions on how to access data sources through the Internet, is given in the appendix to this chapter.

FOCUS

- Japan, whose growth performance for the 40 years following World War II was so impressive that it was referred to as an economic miracle but is one of the few rich countries which has done very poorly in the past decade. Since a stock market crash in the early 1990s, Japan has been in a prolonged slump, with average output growth of under 1% per year.

- Latin America, which went from very high to low inflation in the 1990s. Some countries, such as Chile, appear to be in good economic shape. Some, such as Argentina, are struggling. A collapse of its exchange rate and a major banking crisis led to a large decline in output in the early 2000s, from which it is now recovering.

- Central and Eastern Europe, where most countries shifted from central planning to a market system in the early 1990s. In most countries, the shift was characterized by a sharp decline in output at the start of transition. Most countries now have high growth rates; but in a few of them, output is still below its pre-transition level.

- Africa, which has suffered decades of economic stagnation, but where growth has been high since 2000, reaching 5.4% in 2006, and reflecting growth in most of the countries of the continent.

There is a limit, however, to how much you can absorb in this first chapter. Think about the questions to which you have been exposed already:

- What determines expansions and recessions? Can monetary policy be used to prevent a recession in the United States? How will the euro affect monetary policy in Europe?
- Why is inflation so much lower today than it was in the past? Can Europe reduce its unemployment rate? Should the United States reduce its trade deficit?
- Why do growth rates differ so much across countries, even over long periods? Has the United States entered a New Economy, in which growth will be much higher in the future? Can other countries emulate China and grow at the same rate?

The purpose of this book is to give you a way of thinking about these questions. As we develop the tools you need, I shall show you how to use them by returning to these questions and showing you the answers they suggest.

Key Terms

- European Union (EU), 30
- Organization for Economic Co-operation and Development (OECD), 37
- International Monetary Fund (IMF), 37

Questions and Problems

Quick Check

1. Using the information in this chapter, label each of the following statements true, false, or uncertain. Explain briefly.

a. Recently, inflation has been below its historical average in the United States and the European Union.

b. In the 1960s and early 1970s, the United States had a higher rate of unemployment than Europe, but today it has a much lower rate of unemployment.

c. The rate of growth of output per worker in the United States decreased beginning in the mid-1990s.

d. In the mid-1990s, the United States entered a New Economy, in which the growth of output per worker was higher than in the previous two decades and in which similarly high rates of growth (on average) can be expected in the future.

e. China's seemingly high growth rate is a myth, a product solely of misleading official statistics.

f. The European "unemployment miracle" refers to the extremely low rate of unemployment that Europe has been enjoying since the 1980s.

g. The Federal Reserve lowers interest rates when it wants to avoid recession and raises interest rates when it wants to slow the rate of growth in the economy.

h. Even though the United States is the richest country in the world, it borrows hundreds of billions of dollars annually from the rest of the world.

2. Macroeconomic policy in Europe

Beware of simplistic answers to complicated macroeconomic questions. Consider each of the following statements and comment on whether there is another side to the story.

a. There is a simple solution to the problem of high European unemployment: Reduce labor market rigidities.

b. What can be wrong about joining forces and adopting a common currency? The euro is obviously good for Europe.

3. Productivity growth in the United States and China

Productivity growth is at the heart of recent economic developments in the United States and China.

a. How has China achieved high rates of productivity growth in recent decades?

b. How has the United States achieved high rates of productivity growth in the past decade? (You can base your answer on the views of optimists about U.S. productivity growth.)

c. Why do you think your answers to parts (a) and (b) are different? To what degree do you think China's methods of achieving productivity growth are relevant to the United States?

d. Do you think China's experience provides a model for developing countries to follow?

Dig Deeper

4. When will Chinese output catch up with U.S. output?

In 2006, U.S. output was $13.2 trillion, and Chinese output was $2.8 trillion. Suppose that from now on, the output of China grows at an annual rate of 8.8% per year (roughly what it has done during the past decade), while the output of the United States grows at an annual rate of 3.4% per year.

a. Using these assumptions and a spreadsheet, plot U.S. and Chinese output over the next 100 years. How many years will it take for China to have a level of output equal to that of the United States?

b. When China catches the United States in total output, will residents of China have the same standard of living as U.S. residents? Explain.

5. *The New Economy and growth*

The average annual growth rate of output per worker in the United States rose from 2% during the period 1970 to 1995 to 3% for the years 1996 to 2006. This has led to talk of a New Economy and of sustained higher growth in the future than in the past.

a. Suppose output per worker grows at 2% per year. What will output per worker be—relative to today's level—in 5 years? 15 years? 30 years?

b. Suppose output per worker grows instead at 3% per year. What will output per worker be—relative to today's level—in 5 years? 15 years? 30 years?

c. If the United States has really entered a New Economy, and the average annual growth rate of output per worker has increased from 2% per year to 3%, how much higher will the U.S. standard of living be in 5 years, 15 years, and 30 years relative to what it would have been had the United States remained in the Old Economy?

d. Can we be sure the United States has really entered a New Economy, with a permanently higher growth rate? Why or why not?

Explore Further

6. *U.S. postwar recessions*

This question looks at the recessions of the past 40 years. To work this problem, first obtain quarterly data on U.S. output growth for the period 1960 to 2006 from the Web site **www.bea.gov**. Find NIPA Table 1.1.6. (If you are having trouble finding it, enter "NIPA 1.1.6" in the search box at the Web site.) Look at the quarterly data in chained 2000 dollars. Copy the data to your favorite spreadsheet program. Plot the quarterly GDP growth rates from 1960 through 2006. Did any quarters have negative growth? Using the standard definition of recessions as two or more consecutive quarters of negative growth, answer the following questions.

a. How many recessions has the U.S. economy undergone since 1970?

b. How many quarters has each recession lasted?

c. In terms of length and magnitude, which two recessions have been the most severe?

At the time of this writing, the data for 2001 and 2002 did not indicate two consecutive quarters of negative growth. By the traditional definition, therefore, there was not a recession in 2001. However, the National Bureau of Economic Research (NBER), which dates recessions according to a broader set of criteria, does identify the period from March 2001 to November 2001 as a recession. Most macroeconomists rely on the NBER dating of recessions. We will explore the performance of the U.S. economy in 2001 and 2002 in future chapter questions.

7. *From problem 6, write down the quarters during which the U.S. economy has experienced negative output growth since 1970. Go to the Web page of the Bureau of Labor Statistics, **www.bls.gov**. Find the historical data for the A tables (you will be using Table A.1). Retrieve the monthly data series on the unemployment rate for the period 1970 to 2006. Make sure all data series are seasonally adjusted.*

a. Look at each recession since 1970. What was the unemployment rate in the first month of the first quarter of negative growth? What was the unemployment rate in the last month of the last quarter of negative growth? By how much did the unemployment rate increase?

b. Which recession had the largest increase in the rate of unemployment? For comparison, by how much did the unemployment rate increase from January 2001 to January 2002?

We invite you to visit the Blanchard page on the Prentice Hall Web site, at:
www.prenhall.com/blanchard
for this chapter's World Wide Web exercises.

Further Readings

■ This book has a companion Web page (**www. prenhall.com/blanchard**) that is updated regularly. For each chapter, the page offers discussions of current events and includes relevant articles and Internet links. You can also use the page to make comments on the book and engage in discussions with other readers.

■ The best way to follow current economic events and issues is to read *The Economist*, a weekly magazine published in England. The articles in *The Economist* are well informed, well written, witty, and opinionated. Make sure to read it regularly. (You may have purchased this book together with a 12-week subscription to the Web version of *The Economist*. Take advantage of this.)

Appendix: Where to Find the Numbers

This appendix will help you find the numbers you are looking for, whether they deal with inflation in Malaysia last year, consumption in the United States in 1959, or unemployment in Ireland in the 1980s.

For a Quick Look at Current Numbers

- The best source for the most recent numbers on output, unemployment, inflation, exchange rates, interest rates, and stock prices for a large number of countries is the last four pages of *The Economist*, published each week (www.economist.com). This Web site, like most of the following Web sites, contains both information available free to anyone and information available only to subscribers. The 12-week subscription to the Web version of *The Economist* that comes with this book gives you access to all the numbers and all the articles.

- A good source for recent numbers about the U.S. economy is *National Economic Trends*, published monthly by the Federal Reserve Bank of St. Louis (www.research.stlouisfed.org/publications/net/).

For More Detail About the U.S. Economy

- For a detailed presentation of the most recent numbers, look at the *Survey of Current Business*, published monthly by the U.S. Department of Commerce, Bureau of Economic Analysis (www.bea.gov). A user's guide to the statistics published by the Bureau of Economic Analysis is given in the Survey of Current Business, April 1996. It tells you what data are available, in what form, and at what price.

- Once a year, the *Economic Report of the President*, written by the Council of Economic Advisors and published by the U.S. Government Printing Office in Washington, gives a description of current evolutions, as well as numbers for most major macroeconomic variables, often going back to the 1950s. (The report and the statistical tables can be found at www.gpoaccess.gov/eop/.)

- The standard reference for national income accounts is *National Income and Product Accounts of the United States*. Volume 1, 1929–1958, and Volume 2, 1959–1994, published by the U.S. Department of Commerce, Bureau of Economic Analysis (www.bea.gov).

- For data on just about everything, including economic data, a precious source is the *Statistical Abstract of the United States*, published annually by the U.S. Department of Commerce, Bureau of the Census (www.census.gov/prod/www/statistical-abstract.html).

Numbers for Other Countries

The OECD (www.oecd.org) includes most of the rich countries in the world. (The list was given earlier in this chapter.) The OECD puts out three useful publications, all available electronically on the site:

- The first is the *OECD Economic Outlook*, published twice a year. In addition to describing current macroeconomic issues and evolutions, it includes a data appendix, with data for many macroeconomic variables. The data typically go back to the 1980s and are reported consistently, both across time and across countries. A more complete data set is available on CD-ROM that includes most important macroeconomic variables for all OECD countries, typically going back to the 1960s. The data are also available on the OECD site.

- The second is the *OECD Employment Outlook*, published annually. It focuses specifically on labor market issues and numbers.

- Occasionally, the OECD puts together current and past data and publishes the OECD *Historical Statistics*. At this point, the most recent is *Historical Statistics, 1970–2000*, published in 2001.

The main strength of the publications of the International Monetary Fund (IMF, located in Washington, DC) is that they cover most of the countries of the world (www.imf.org). A particularly useful IMF publication is the *World Economic Outlook*, published twice a year, which describes major evolutions in the world and in specific member countries. Selected series associated with the *Outlook* are available on the IMF site (www.imf.org/external/data.htm).

Historical Statistics

For long-term historical statistics for the United States, the basic reference is *Historical Statistics of the United States, Colonial Times to 1970*, Parts 1 and 2, published by the U.S. Department of Commerce, Bureau of the Census (www.census.gov/prod/www/abs/statab.html).

For long-term historical statistics for several countries, a precious data source is Angus Maddison's *Monitoring the World Economy, 1820–1992*, Development Centre Studies, OECD, Paris, 1995. This study gives data going back to 1820 for 56 countries. Two even longer and broader sources are *The World Economy. A Millennial Perspective*, Development Studies, OECD, 2001, and *The World Economy: Historical Statistics*, Development Studies, OECD 2004, both also by Angus Maddison.

Current Macroeconomic Issues

A number of Web sites offer information and commentaries about the macroeconomic issues of the day. In addition to the Web site of *The Economist*, mentioned earlier, two useful sites are:

The Morgan Stanley site, with daily commentaries of macroeconomic events (www.morganstanley.com/views/index.html).

The RGE monitor site maintained by Nouriel Roubini (www.rgemonitor.com) offers an extensive set of links to articles and discussions on macroeconomic issues (by subscription).

Finally, if you still have not found what you are looking for, try a site maintained by Bill Goffe at SUNY (www.rfe.org), which lists not only many more data sources but sources for economic information in general, from working papers, to data, to jokes, to jobs in economics, to blogs.

The words *output, unemployment,* and *inflation* appear daily in newspapers and on the evening news. So when I used them in Chapter 1, you knew roughly what I was talking about. We now need to define them precisely, and this is what I do in the first two sections of this chapter.

■ Section 2–1 focuses on aggregate output and shows how we can look at aggregate output both from the production side and from the income side.

■ Section 2–2 looks at the unemployment rate and the inflation rate.

■ Section 2–3 introduces the three central concepts around which the book is organized:

  ■ The *short run*—What happens to the economy from year to year.

  ■ The *medium run*—What happens to the economy over a decade or so.

  ■ The *long run*—What happens to the economy over a half century or longer.

Building on these three concepts, Section 2–4 gives you a road map to the rest of the book. ■

Economists studying economic activity in the nineteenth century or during the Great Depression had no measure of aggregate activity (*aggregate* is the word macroeconomists use for *total*) on which to rely. They had to put together bits and pieces of information, such as the shipments of iron ore, or sales at some department stores, to try to infer what was happening to the economy as a whole.

It was not until the end of World War II that **national income and product accounts** (or national income accounts, for short) were put together. Measures of aggregate output have been published on a regular basis in the United States since October 1947. (You will find measures of aggregate output for earlier times, but those have been constructed retrospectively.)

Two economists, Simon Kuznets, from Harvard University, and Richard Stone, from Cambridge University, were awarded the Nobel Prize for their contributions to the development of the national income and product accounts—a gigantic intellectual and empirical achievement.

Like any other accounting system, the national income accounts first define concepts and then construct measures corresponding to those concepts. You need only to look at statistics from countries that have not yet developed such accounts to realize how crucial are such precision and consistency. Without them, numbers that should add up do not; trying to understand what is going on feels like trying to balance someone else's checkbook. I shall not burden you with the details of national income accounting here. But because you will occasionally need to know the definition of a variable and how variables relate to each other, Appendix 1 at the end of the book gives you the basic accounting framework used in the United States (and, with minor variations, in most other countries) today. You will find it useful whenever you want to look at economic data on your own.

You may come across another term, gross national product, or GNP. There is a subtle difference between "domestic" and "national," and thus between GDP and GNP. We examine the distinction in Chapter 18 (also in Appendix 1 at the end of the book). For now, ignore it.

GDP: Production and Income

The measure of **aggregate output** in the national income accounts is called the **gross domestic product**, or **GDP** for short. To understand how GDP is constructed, it is best to work with a simple example. Consider an economy composed of just two firms:

In reality, not only are workers and machines required for steel production, but so are electricity, iron, ore, etc. We shall ignore these to keep this example simple.

- ■ Firm 1 produces steel, employing workers and using machines to produce the steel. It sells the steel for $100 to Firm 2, which produces cars. Firm 1 pays its workers $80, leaving $20 in profit to the firm.
- ■ Firm 2 buys the steel and uses it, together with workers and machines, to produce cars. Revenues from car sales are $200. Of the $200, $100 goes to pay for steel and $70 goes to workers in the firm, leaving $30 in profit to the firm.

We can summarize this information in a table:

Steel Company (Firm 1)		
Revenues from sales		$100
Expenses		$ 80
Wages	$80	
Profit		$ 20

Car Company (Firm 2)		
Revenues from sales		$200
Expenses		$170
Wages	$70	
Steel purchases	$100	
Profit		$ 30

An intermediate good is a good used in the production of another good. Some goods can be both final goods and intermediate goods. Potatoes sold directly to consumers are final goods. Potatoes used to produce potato chips are intermediate goods. Can you think of other examples?

Would you define aggregate output in this economy as the sum of the values of all goods produced in the economy—the sum of $100 from the production of steel and $200 from the production of cars, so $300? Or would you define aggregate output as just the value of cars, which is equal to $200?

Some thought suggests that the right answer must be $200. Why? Because steel is an **intermediate good**: It is used up in the production of cars. Once we count the production of cars, we do not want to count the production of the goods that went into the production of those cars.

This motivates the first definition of GDP.

1. GDP is the value of the final goods and services produced in the economy during a given period.

The important word here is *final*. We want to count only the production of **final goods**, not intermediate goods. Using our example, we can make this point in another way. Suppose the two firms merged, so that the sale of steel took place inside the new firm and was no longer recorded. The accounts of the new firm would be given by the following table:

Steel and Car Company	
Revenues from sales	$200
Expenses (wages)	$150
Profit	$ 50

All we would see would be one firm selling cars for $200, paying workers $80 + $70 = $150, and making $20 + $30 = $50 in profits. The $200 measure would remain unchanged—as it should. We do not want our measure of aggregate output to depend on whether firms decide to merge.

This first definition gives us one way to construct GDP: by recording and adding up the production of all final goods—and this is indeed roughly the way actual GDP numbers are put together. But it also suggests a second way of thinking about and constructing GDP.

2. GDP is the sum of value added in the economy during a given period.

The term **value added** means exactly what it suggests. The value added by a firm is defined as the value of its production minus the value of the intermediate goods used in production.

In our two-firms example, the steel company does not use intermediate goods. Its value added is simply equal to the value of the steel it produces, $100. The car company, however, uses steel as an intermediate good. Thus, the value added by the car company is equal to the value of the cars it produces minus the value of the steel it uses in production, $200 − $100 = $100. Total value added in the economy, or GDP, equals $100 + $100 = $200. (Note that aggregate value added would remain the same if the steel and car firms merged and became a single firm. In this case, we would not observe intermediate goods at all—as steel would be produced and then used to produce cars within the single firm—and the value added in the single firm would simply be equal to the value of cars, $200.)

This definition gives us a second way of thinking about GDP. Put together, the two definitions imply that the value of final goods and services—the first definition of GDP—can also be thought of as the sum of the value added by all the firms in the economy—the second definition of GDP.

So far, we have looked at GDP from the *production side*. The other way of looking at GDP is from the *income side*. Let's return to our example and think about the revenues left to a firm after it has paid for its intermediate goods. Some of the revenues go to pay workers—this component is called *labor income*. The rest goes to the firm—that component is called *capital income*, or *profit income*.

Of the $100 of value added by the steel manufacturer, $80 goes to workers (labor income) and the remaining $20 goes to the firm (capital income). Of the $100 of value

Table 2-1 The Composition of GDP by Type of Income, 1960 and 2006

	1960	2006
Labor income	66%	64%
Capital income	26%	29%
Indirect taxes	8%	7%

Source: Survey of Current Business, April 2007.

added by the car manufacturer, $70 goes to labor income and $30 to capital income. For the economy as a whole, labor income is equal to $150 ($80 + $70), and capital income is equal to $50 ($20 + $30). Value added is equal to the sum of labor income and capital income and is equal to $200 ($150 + $50).

This motivates the third definition of GDP.

3. GDP is the sum of incomes in the economy during a given period.

In our example, labor income accounts for 75% of GDP and capital income for 25%. Table 2-1 shows the breakdown of value added among the different types of income in the United States in 1960 and 2006. It includes one category of income we did not have in our example, *indirect taxes,* the revenues paid to the government in the form of sales taxes. (In our example, these indirect taxes were equal to zero.) The table shows that labor income accounts for 64% of U.S. GDP. Capital income accounts for 29%. Indirect taxes account for the remaining 7%. The proportions have not changed much since 1960.

Two lessons to remember:
1. GDP is the measure of ▶ aggregate output, which we can look at from the production side (aggregate production) or the income side (aggregate income).
2. Aggregate production and aggregate income are always equal.

To summarize: You can think about aggregate output—*GDP*—in three different, but equivalent, ways:

■ From the *production side*—GDP equals the value of the final goods and services produced in the economy during a given period.
■ Also from the *production side*—GDP is the sum of value added in the economy during a given period.
■ From the *income side*—GDP is the sum of incomes in the economy during a given period.

Nominal and Real GDP

U.S. GDP was $13,246 billion in 2006, compared to $526 billion in 1960. Was U.S. output really 25 times higher in 2006 than in 1960? Obviously not: Much of the increase reflected an increase in prices rather than an increase in quantities produced. This leads to the distinction between nominal GDP and real GDP.

Nominal GDP is the sum of the quantities of final goods produced multiplied by their current prices. This definition makes clear that nominal GDP increases over time for two reasons:

Warning! People often use ▶ *nominal* to denote small amounts. Economists use *nominal* for variables expressed in current prices. And they surely do not refer to small amounts: The numbers typically run in the billions or trillions of dollars.

■ The production of most goods increases over time.
■ The prices of most goods also increase over time.

If our goal is to measure production and its change over time, we need to eliminate the effect of increasing prices on our measure of GDP. That's why **real GDP** is constructed as the sum of the quantities of final goods multiplied by *constant* (rather than *current*) prices.

If the economy produced only one final good—say, a particular car model—constructing real GDP would be easy: We would use the price of the car in a given year and then use it to multiply the quantity of cars produced in each year. An example will help here. Consider an economy that produces only cars—and to avoid issues we shall tackle later, assume that the same model is produced every year. Suppose the number and the price of cars in three successive years are given by:

Year	Quantity of Cars	Price of Cars	Nominal GDP	Real GDP (in 2000 dollars)
1999	10	$20,000	$200,000	$240,000
2000	12	$24,000	$288,000	$288,000
2001	13	$26,000	$338,000	$312,000

Nominal GDP, which is equal to the quantity of cars multiplied by their price, goes up from $200,000 in 1999 to $288,000 in 2000—a 44% increase—and from $288,000 in 2000 to $338,000 in 2001—a 17% increase.

■ To construct real GDP, we need to multiply the number of cars in each year by a *common* price. Suppose we use the price of a car in 2000 as the common price. This approach gives us, in effect, *real GDP in 2000 dollars.*

■ Using this approach, real GDP in 1999 (in 2000 dollars) equals 10 cars × $24,000 per car = $240,000. Real GDP in 2000 (in 2000 dollars) equals 12 cars × $24,000 per car = $288,000, the same as nominal GDP in 2000. Real GDP in 2001 (in 2000 dollars) is equal to 13 × $24,000 = $312,000. So real GDP goes up from $240,000 in 1999 to $288,000 in 2000—a 20% increase—and from $288,000 in 2000 to $312,000 in 2001—an 8% increase.

■ How different would our results have been if we had decided to construct real GDP using the price of a car in, say, 2001 rather than 2000? Obviously, the level of real GDP in each year would be different (because the prices are not the same in 2001 as in 2000), but its rate of change from year to year would be the same as above.

◄ To be sure, compute real GDP in 2001 dollars and compute the rate of growth from 1999 to 2000 and from 2000 to 2001.

The problem in constructing real GDP in practice is that there is obviously more than one final good. Real GDP must be defined as a weighted average of the output of all final goods, and this brings us to what the weights should be.

The *relative prices* of the goods would appear to be the natural weights. If one good costs twice as much per unit as another, then that good should count for twice as much as the other in the construction of real output. But this raises the question: What if, as is typically the case, relative prices change over time? Should we choose the relative prices of a particular year as weights, or should we change the weights over time? More discussion of these issues, and of the way real GDP is constructed in the United States, is left to the appendix to this chapter. Here, what you should know is that the measure of real GDP in the U.S. national income accounts uses weights that reflect relative prices and that change over time. The measure is called **real GDP in chained (2000) dollars** ("2000" because, as in our earlier example, 2000 is the year when, by construction, real GDP is equal to nominal GDP). It is our best measure of the output of the U.S. economy, and its evolution shows how U.S. output has increased over time.

Figure 2-1 plots the evolution of both nominal GDP and real GDP since 1960. By construction, the two are equal in 2000. The figure shows that real GDP in 2006 was about 4.5 times its level of 1960—a considerable increase, but clearly much less than the 25-fold increase in nominal GDP over the same period. The difference between the two results comes from the increase in prices over the period.

◄ Suppose real GDP were measured in 2006 dollars rather than 2000 dollars. Where would the nominal GDP and real GDP lines on the graph intersect?

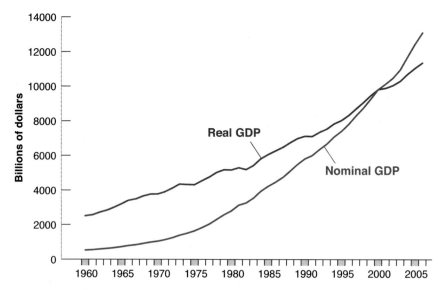

The terms *nominal GDP* and *real GDP* each have many synonyms, and you are likely to encounter them in your readings:

■ Nominal GDP is also called **dollar GDP** or **GDP in current dollars**.
■ Real GDP is also called **GDP in terms of goods, GDP in constant dollars, GDP adjusted for inflation, or GDP in 2000 dollars**—if the year in which real GDP is set equal to nominal GDP is 2000, as is the case in the United States at this time.

In the chapters that follow, unless I indicate otherwise,

■ GDP will refer to *real GDP*, and Y_t will denote *real GDP in year t*.
■ Nominal GDP and variables measured in current dollars will be denoted by a dollar sign in front of them—for example, $\$Y_t$ for nominal GDP in year *t*.

GDP: Level versus Growth Rate

We have focused so far on the level of real GDP. This is an important number, which gives the economic size of a country. A country with twice the GDP of another country is economically twice as big as the other country. Equally important is the level of **real GDP per capita**, the ratio of real GDP to the population of the country. It gives us the average standard of living of the country.

▶ In assessing the performance of the economy from year to year, economists focus, however, on the *rate of growth* of real GDP—**GDP growth**. Periods of positive GDP growth are called **expansions**. Periods of negative GDP growth are called **recessions**.

The evolution of GDP growth in the United States since 1960 is given in Figure 2-2. GDP growth in year *t* is constructed as $(Y_t - Y_{t-1})/Y_{t-1}$. The figure shows how the U.S. economy has gone through a series of expansions, interrupted by short recessions. Look in particular at the past 15 years. Note how a recession in the early 1990s gave way to a long expansion from 1992 to 2000. In 2001, growth was positive but very low. It has increased since then, and the U.S. economy is currently in an expansion.

Warning! One must be careful about how one does the comparison: Recall the discussion in Chapter 1 about the standard of living in China. You'll learn more on this in Chapter 10.

FOCUS

A tough problem in computing real GDP is how to deal with changes in quality of existing goods. One of the most difficult cases is computers. It would clearly be absurd to assume that a personal computer in 2007 is the same good as a personal computer produced in 1981 (the year in which the IBM PC was introduced): The same amount of money can clearly buy much more computing in 2007 than it could in 1981. But how much more? Does a 2007 computer provide 10 times, 100 times, or 1,000 times the computing services of a 1981 computer? How should we take into account the improvements in internal speed, the size of the RAM or of the hard disk, the fact that computers can now access the Internet, and so on?

The approach used by economists to adjust for these improvements is to look at the market for computers and how it values computers with different characteristics in a given year. For example, suppose the evidence from prices of different models on the market shows that people are willing to pay 10% more for a computer with a speed of 3 GHz (3,000 MHz) rather than 2 GHz. (The first edition of this book, published in 1996, compared two computers, with speeds of 50 and 16 MHz. This is a good indication of technological progress.) Suppose new computers this year have a speed of 3 GHz compared to a speed of 2 GHz for new computers last year. And suppose the dollar price of new computers this year is the same as the dollar price of new computers last year. Then, economists in charge of computing the adjusted price of computers will conclude that new computers are in fact 10% cheaper than last year.

This approach, which treats goods as providing a collection of characteristics—here speed, memory, and so on—each with an implicit price, is called **hedonic pricing** (*hedone* means "pleasure" in Greek). It is used by the Department of Commerce—which constructs real GDP—to estimate changes in the prices of complex and fast-changing goods, such as automobiles and computers. Using this approach, the Department of Commerce estimates that, for a given prices, the quality of new computers has increased on average by 18% per year since 1981. Put another way, a typical personal computer in 2007 delivers $1.18^{26} = 74$ times the computing services a typical personal computer delivered in 1981.

Not only do computers deliver more services, they have become cheaper as well: Their dollar price has declined by about 10% per year since 1981. Putting this together with the information in the previous paragraph, this implies that their quality-adjusted price has fallen at an average rate of 18% + 10% = 28% per year. Put another way, a dollar spent on a computer today buys $1.28^{26} = 613$ times more computing services than a dollar spent on a computer in 1981.

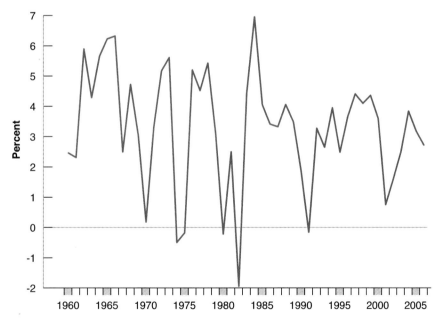

Figure 2-2

Growth Rate of U.S. GDP since 1960

Since 1960, the U.S. economy has gone through a series of expansions, interrupted by short recessions.

The figure raises a small puzzle. Given that GDP growth was positive in 2001, why do macroeconomists refer to the "recession of 2001"? The reason is that they look at GDP growth quarter by quarter rather than year by year. There is no official definition of what constitutes a recession, but the convention is to refer to a recession if the economy goes through at least two consecutive quarters of negative growth. Although GDP growth was positive for 2001 as a whole, it was negative during each of the first three quarters of 2001; thus 2001 qualifies as a (mild) recession.

2-2 The Other Major Macroeconomic Variables

Because it is a measure of aggregate activity, GDP is obviously the most important macroeconomic variable. But two other variables, unemployment and inflation, tell us about other important aspects of how an economy is performing.

The Unemployment Rate

Let's start with some definitions: **Employment** is the number of people who have a job. **Unemployment** is the number of people who do not have a job but are looking for one. The **labor force** is the sum of employment and unemployment:

$$L = N + U$$
$$\text{Labor force} = \text{Employment} + \text{Unemployment}$$

The **unemployment rate** is the ratio of the number of people who are unemployed to the number of people in the labor force:

$$u = \frac{U}{L}$$
$$\text{Unemployment rate} = \text{Unemployment/Labor force}$$

Constructing the unemployment rate is less obvious than you might think. The cartoon below not withstanding, determining whether somebody is employed is straightforward. Determining whether somebody is unemployed is harder. Recall from the definition that, to be classified as unemployed, a person must meet two conditions: that he or she does not have a job, and he or she is looking for one; this second condition is harder to assess.

Until the 1940s in the United States, and until more recently in most other countries, the only available source of data on unemployment was the number of people registered at unemployment offices, and so only those workers who were registered in unemployment offices were counted as unemployed. This system led to a poor measure of unemployment. How many of those looking for jobs actually registered at the unemployment office varied both across countries and across time. Those who had no incentive to register—for example, those who had exhausted their unemployment benefits—were unlikely to take the time to go to the unemployment office, so they were not counted. Countries with less generous benefit systems were likely to have fewer unemployed registering and therefore smaller measured unemployment rates.

Today, most rich countries rely on large surveys of households to compute the unemployment rate. In the United States, this survey is called the **Current Population Survey (CPS)**. It relies on interviews of 50,000 households every month. The survey classifies a person as employed if he or she has a job at the time of the interview; it classifies a person as unemployed if he or she does not have a job *and has been looking for a job in the past four weeks*. Most other countries use a similar definition of unemployment. In the United States, estimates based on the CPS show that, during 2006, an average of 144.4 million people were employed, and 7.0 million people were unemployed, so the unemployment rate was $7.0/(144.4 + 7.0) = 4.6\%$.

Note that only those *looking for a job* are counted as unemployed; those who do not have a job and are not looking for one are counted as **not in the labor force**. When unemployment is high, some of the unemployed give up looking for a job and therefore are no longer counted as unemployed. These people are known as **discouraged workers**. Take an extreme example: If all workers without a job gave up looking for one, the unemployment rate would equal zero. This would make the unemployment rate a very poor indicator of what is happening in the labor market. This example is too extreme; in practice, when the economy slows down, we typically observe both an ◄ increase in unemployment and an increase in the number of people who drop out of the labor force. Equivalently, a higher unemployment rate is typically associated with a lower **participation rate**, defined as the ratio of the labor force to the total population of working age.

At the start of economic reform in Eastern Europe in the early 1990s, unemployment increased dramatically. But equally dramatic was the fall in the participation rate. In Poland in 1990, 70% of the decrease in employment was reflected in early retirements—by people dropping out of the labor force rather than becoming unemployed.

Figure 2-3 shows the evolution of unemployment in the United States since 1960. Since 1960, the U.S. unemployment rate has fluctuated between 3% and 10%, going up during recessions and going down during expansions. Note in particular how much the unemployment rate increased during the recession of the early 1980s, reaching 9.7% in 1982, and how much the unemployment rate decreased during the long expansion of the 1990s, reaching 3.9% in 2000.

Why Do Economists Care About Unemployment?

Economists care about unemployment for two reasons.

Economists care about unemployment because of its direct effects on the welfare of the unemployed. Although unemployment benefits are more generous today than they were during the Great Depression, unemployment is still often associated with financial and psychological suffering. How much suffering depends on the nature of the unemployment. One image of unemployment is that of a stagnant pool, of people remaining unemployed for long periods of time. As you shall see later in this book, this image does not reflect what happens in the United States. In the United States each month, many people become unemployed, and many of the unemployed (on average, 25%–30% of them) find jobs. But even in the United States, some groups (often the ◄ young, the ethnic minorities, and the unskilled) suffer disproportionately from unemployment, remaining chronically unemployed and being more vulnerable to becoming unemployed when the unemployment rate increases.

Things are quite different in Europe. There, the unemployed typically remain unemployed for a long time, and the image of a stagnant pool is much more appropriate.

Figure 2-3

U.S. Unemployment Rate since 1960

Since 1960, the U.S. unemployment rate has fluctuated between 3% and 10%, going down during expansions and going up during recessions.

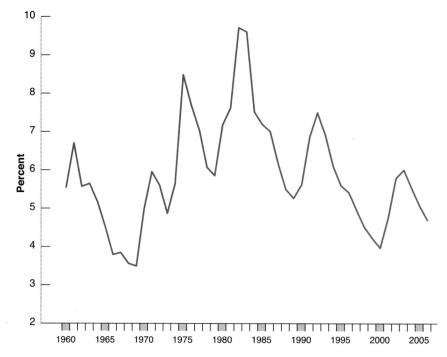

Economists also care about the unemployment rate because it provides a signal that the economy may not be using some of its resources efficiently. Many workers who want to work do not find jobs; the economy is not efficiently utilizing its human resources. From this viewpoint, can very low unemployment also be a problem? The answer is yes. Like an engine running at too high a speed, an economy in which unemployment is very low may be overutilizing its human resources and run into labor shortages. How low is "too low"? This is a difficult question, a question we will take up later in the book. The question came up in 2000 in the United States. At the end of 2000, some economists worried that the unemployment rate, 4% at the time, was indeed too low. So, while they did not advocate triggering a recession, they favored lower (but positive) output growth for some time so as to allow the unemployment rate to increase to a somewhat higher level. It turned out that they got more than they had asked for: a recession rather than a slowdown.

▶ It is probably because of statements like this that economics is known as the "dismal science."

The Inflation Rate

Inflation is a sustained rise in the general level of prices—the **price level**. The **inflation rate** is the rate at which the price level increases. Symmetrically, **deflation** is a sustained decline in the price level. It corresponds to a negative inflation rate.

▶ Deflation is rare, but it happens. Japan has had deflation since the late 1990s.

The practical issue is how to define the price level. Macroeconomists typically look at two measures of the price level, at two *price indexes*: the GDP deflator and the consumer price index.

The GDP Deflator

We saw earlier how increases in nominal GDP can come either from an increase in real GDP or from an increase in prices. Put another way, if we see nominal GDP increase faster than real GDP, the difference must come from an increase in prices.

In 1994, the official unemployment rate in Spain reached 24%. (It has decreased a lot since then, but it still stood at 8% in 2007.) This was roughly the same unemployment rate as the United States in 1933, the worst year of the Great Depression. Yet Spain in 1994 looked nothing like the United States in 1933: There were few homeless people, and most cities looked prosperous. Can we really believe that nearly one-fifth of the Spanish labor force was looking for work?

To answer this, we must first examine how the Spanish unemployment number is put together. Much as in the United States, it comes from a large survey. People are classified as unemployed if they indicate that they are not working but are seeking work.

Can we be sure that people tell the truth? No. Although there is no obvious incentive to lie—answers to the survey are confidential and are not used to determine whether people are eligible for unemployment benefits—those who are working in the underground economy may prefer to play it safe and report that they are unemployed instead.

The size of the **underground economy**—the part of economic activity which is not measured in official statistics, either because the activity is illegal or because firms and workers would rather not report it and thus not pay taxes—is an old issue in Spain. And because of that, we actually know more about the underground economy in Spain than in many other countries: In 1985, the Spanish government tried to find out more and organized a detailed survey of 60,000 individuals. To try to elicit the truth from those interviewed, the questionnaire asked interviewees for an extremely precise account of the use of their time, making it more difficult to misreport. The answers were interesting. The underground economy in Spain—defined as the number of people working without declaring it to the social security administration—accounted for between 10%–15% of employment. But it was composed mostly of people who already had a job and were taking a second or even a third job. The best estimate from the survey was that only about 15% of the unemployed were in fact working. This implied that the unemployment rate, which was officially 21% at the time, was in fact closer to 18%, still a very high number. In short, the Spanish underground economy was significant, but it just was not the case that most of the Spanish unemployed work in the underground economy.

How did the unemployed survive? Did they survive because unemployment benefits were unusually generous in Spain? No. Except for very generous unemployment benefits in two regions, Andalusia and Extremadura—which, not surprisingly, had even higher unemployment than the rest of the country—unemployment benefits were roughly in line with unemployment benefits in other OECD countries. Benefits were typically 70% of the wage for the first 6 months and 60% thereafter. They were given for a period of 4 to 24 months, depending on how long people had worked before becoming unemployed. The 30% of the unemployed who had been unemployed for more than two years did not receive unemployment benefits.

So how did they survive? A key to the answer lies with the Spanish family structure. The unemployment rate was highest among the young: In 1994, it was close to 50% for those between 16 and 19, and it was around 40% for those between 20 and 24. The young typically stay at home until their late 20s and increasingly did so as unemployment increased. Looking at households rather than at individuals, the proportion of households where nobody was employed was less than 10% in 1994; the proportion of households that received neither wage income nor unemployment benefits was around 3%. In short, the family structure and transfers from the rest of the family were the factors that allowed many of the unemployed to survive.

FOCUS

This remark motivates the definition of the GDP deflator. The **GDP deflator** in year t, P_t, is defined as the ratio of nominal GDP to real GDP in year t:

$$P_t = \frac{\text{Nominal GDP}_t}{\text{Real GDP}_t} = \frac{\$Y_t}{Y_t}$$

Note that in the year in which, by construction, real GDP is equal to nominal GDP (2000 at this point in the United States), this definition implies that the price level is equal to 1. This is worth emphasizing: The GDP deflator is what is called an **index number**. Its level is chosen arbitrarily—here it is equal to 1 in 2000—and has no economic interpretation. But its rate of change, $(P_t - P_{t-1})/P_{t-1}$, has a clear economic ◄

Index numbers are often set equal to 100 (in the base year) rather than to 1. If you look at the *Economic Report of the President* (see Chapter 1), you will see that the GDP deflator, reported in Table B3, is equal to 100 for 2000 (the base year), 100.5 in 2001, and so on.

Compute the GDP deflator and the associated rate of inflation from 1999 to 2000 and from 2000 to 2001 in our car example in Section 2-1, when real GDP is constructed using the 2000 price of cars as the common price.

interpretation: It gives the rate at which the general level of prices increases over time—the rate of inflation.

One advantage to defining the price level as the GDP deflator is that it implies a simple relation between *nominal GDP*, *real GDP*, and the *GDP deflator*. To see this, reorganize the previous equation to get:

$$\$Y_t = P_t\, Y_t$$

For a refresher, see Appendix 2, Proposition 7.

Nominal GDP is equal to the GDP deflator multiplied by real GDP. Or, putting it in terms of rates of change, the rate of growth of nominal GDP is equal to the rate of inflation plus the rate of growth of real GDP.

The Consumer Price Index

The GDP deflator gives the average price of output—the final goods *produced* in the economy. But consumers care about the average price of consumption—the goods they *consume*. The two prices need not be the same: The set of goods produced in the economy is not the same as the set of goods purchased by consumers, for two reasons:

- Some of the goods in GDP are sold not to consumers but to firms (machine tools, for example), to the government, or to foreigners.
- And some of the goods bought by consumers are not produced domestically but are imported from abroad.

To measure the average price of consumption or, equivalently, the **cost of living**, macroeconomists look at another index, the **consumer price index**, or **CPI**. The CPI has been in existence since 1917 and is published monthly. (In contrast, numbers for GDP and the GDP deflator are constructed and published only quarterly.)

Do not confuse the CPI with the PPI, or *producer price index*, which is an index of prices of domestically produced goods in manufacturing, mining, agriculture, fishing, forestry, and electric utility industries.

The CPI gives the cost in dollars of a specific list of goods and services over time. The list, which is based on a detailed study of consumer spending, attempts to represent the consumption basket of a typical urban consumer and is updated roughly only once every 10 years.

Each month, Bureau of Labor Statistics (BLS) employees visit stores to find out what has happened to the prices of the goods on the list; prices are collected in 87 cities, from about 23,000 retail stores, car dealerships, gas stations, hospitals, and so on. These prices are then used to construct the CPI.

Like the GDP deflator, the CPI is typically set to 100 rather than to 1 in the base period.

Like the GDP deflator (the price level associated with aggregate output, GDP), the CPI is an index. It is set equal to 1 in the period chosen as the base period, and so its level has no particular significance. The current base period is 1982 to 1984, so the average for the period 1982 to 1984 is equal to 100. In 2006, the CPI was 201.6; thus, it cost roughly twice as much in dollars to purchase the same consumption basket than in 1982 to 1984.

You may wonder how the rate of inflation differs depending on whether the GDP deflator or the CPI is used to measure it. The answer is given in Figure 2-4, which plots the two inflation rates since 1960 for the United States. The figure yields two conclusions:

- The CPI and the GDP deflator move together most of the time. In most years, the two inflation rates differ by less than 1%.
- There are clear exceptions to the first conclusion. In 1979 and 1980, the increase in the CPI was significantly larger than the increase in the GDP deflator. The reason

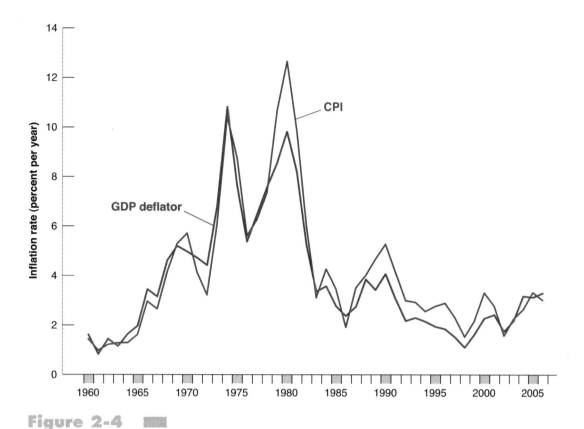

Figure 2-4

U.S. Inflation Rate, Using the CPI and the GDP Deflator, since 1960

The inflation rates, computed using either the CPI or the GDP deflator, are largely similar.

is not hard to find. Recall that the GDP deflator is the price of goods *produced* in the United States, whereas the CPI is the price of goods *consumed* in the United States. That means when the price of imported goods increases relative to the price of goods produced in the United States, the CPI increases faster than the GDP deflator. This is precisely what happened in 1979 to 1980. The price of oil doubled. And although the United States is a producer of oil, it produces much less than it consumes: It was and still is a major oil importer. The result was a large increase in the CPI compared to the GDP deflator.

◀ You may wonder why the effect of the increases in the price of oil since 1999 is much less visible in the figure. The answer: The increases have taken place more slowly over time, and other factors have worked in the opposite direction.

In what follows, I shall typically assume that the two indexes move together, so I do not need to distinguish between them. I shall simply talk about *the price level* and denote it by P_t, without indicating whether I have the CPI or the GDP deflator in mind.

Why Do Economists Care About Inflation?

If a higher inflation rate meant just a faster but proportional increase in all prices and wages—a case called *pure inflation*—inflation would be only a minor inconvenience, as relative prices would be unaffected.

Take, for example, the workers' *real wage*—the wage measured in terms of goods rather than in dollars. In an economy with 10% more inflation, prices would increase by 10% more per year. But wages would also increase by 10% more per year, so real wages would be unaffected by inflation. Inflation would not be entirely irrelevant; people would have to keep track of the increase in prices and wages when making decisions. But this would be a small burden, hardly justifying making control of the inflation rate one of the major goals of macroeconomic policy.

So, why do economists care about inflation? Precisely because there is no such thing as pure inflation:

■ During periods of inflation, not all prices and wages rise proportionately. Because they don't, inflation affects income distribution. For example, retirees in many countries receive payments that do not keep up with the price level, so they lose in relation to other groups when inflation is high. This is not the case in the United States, where Social Security benefits automatically rise with the CPI, protecting retirees from inflation. But during the very high inflation that took place in Russia in the 1990s, retirement pensions did not keep up with inflation, and many retirees were pushed to near starvation.

■ Inflation leads to other distortions. Variations in relative prices also lead to more uncertainty, making it harder for firms to make decisions about the future, such as investment decisions. Some prices, which are fixed by law or by regulation, lag behind others, leading to changes in relative prices. Taxation interacts with inflation to create more distortions. If tax brackets are not adjusted for inflation, for example, people move into higher and higher tax brackets as their nominal income increases, even if their real income remains the same.

> This is known as *bracket creep*. In the United States, the tax brackets are typically adjusted for inflation: If inflation is 5%, tax brackets also go up by 5%—in other words, there is no bracket creep.

If inflation is so bad, does this imply that deflation (negative inflation) is good? The answer is no. First, high deflation (a large negative rate of inflation) would create many of the same problems as high inflation, from distortions to increased uncertainty. Second, as we shall see later in the book, even a low rate of deflation limits the ability of monetary policy to affect output. So what is the "best" rate of inflation? Most macroeconomists believe that the best rate of inflation is a low and stable rate of inflation, somewhere between 0 and 3%. We shall look at the pros and cons of different rates of inflation later in the book.

> Newspapers sometimes confuse deflation and recession. They may happen together, but they are not the same. Deflation is a decrease in the price level. A recession is a decrease in real output.

We have now looked at the main macroeconomic variables: aggregate output, unemployment, and inflation. Clearly, a successful economy is an economy that combines high output growth, low unemployment, and low inflation. Can all these objectives be achieved simultaneously? Is low unemployment compatible with low and stable inflation? Do policymakers have the tools to sustain growth, to achieve low unemployment while maintaining low inflation? These are some of the questions we shall take up as we go through the book. The next two sections give you a road map.

> This has been one of the problems faced by Japan in the past decade. We discuss it in more detail in Chapter 22.

2-3 The Short Run, the Medium Run, and the Long Run

What determines the level of aggregate output in an economy?

■ Reading newspapers suggests a first answer: Movements in output come from movements in the demand for goods. You probably have read news stories that begin like this: "Production and sales of automobiles were higher last month, due to a surge in consumer confidence, which drove consumers to showrooms in record numbers." Stories like this highlight the role demand plays in determining aggregate output; they point to factors that affect demand, ranging from consumer confidence to interest rates.

■ But, surely, no number of Indian consumers rushing to Indian showrooms can increase India's output to the level of output in the United States. This suggests a second answer: What matters when it comes to aggregate output is the supply side—how much the economy can produce. How much can be produced depends on how advanced is the technology of the country, how much capital it is using, and the size and the skills of its labor force. These factors—not consumer confidence—are the fundamental determinants of a country's level of output.

■ The previous argument can be taken one step further: Neither technology, nor capital, nor skills are given. The technological sophistication of a country depends on its ability to innovate and introduce new technologies. The size of its capital stock depends on how much people save. The skills of workers depend on the quality of the country's education system. Other factors are also important: If firms are to operate efficiently, for example, they need a clear system of laws under which to operate and an honest government to enforce those laws. This suggests a third answer: The true determinants of output are factors such as a country's education system, its saving rate, and the quality of its government. If we want to understand what determines the level of output, we must look at these factors.

You might be wondering at this point which of the three answers is right. All three are right. But each applies over a different time frame:

■ In the **short run**, say, a few years, the first answer is the right one. Year-to-year movements in output are primarily driven by movements in demand. Changes in demand, perhaps due to changes in consumer confidence or other factors, can lead to a decrease in output (a recession) or an increase in output (an expansion).

■ In the **medium run**, say, a decade, the second answer is the right one. Over the medium run, the economy tends to return to the level of output determined by supply factors: the capital stock, the level of technology, and the size of the labor force. And, over a decade or so, these factors move sufficiently slowly that we can take them as given.

■ In the **long run**, say, a few decades or more, the third answer is the right one. To understand why China has been able to achieve such a high growth rate since 1980, we must understand why both capital and the level of technology in China are increasing so fast. To do so, we must look at factors such as the education system, the saving rate, and the role of the government.

This way of thinking about the determinants of output underlies macroeconomics, and it underlies the organization of this book.

2-4　A Tour of the Book

This book is organized in three parts: a core, three extensions, and a deeper look at the role of macroeconomic policy. This organization is shown in Figure 2-5. Let me describe it in more detail.

The Core

The core is composed of three parts—the short run, the medium run, and the long run:

■ Chapters 3 to 5 look at how output is determined in the short run. To focus on the role of demand, we assume that firms are willing to supply any quantity at a given price. In other words, we ignore supply constraints.

Figure 2-5

The Organization of the Book

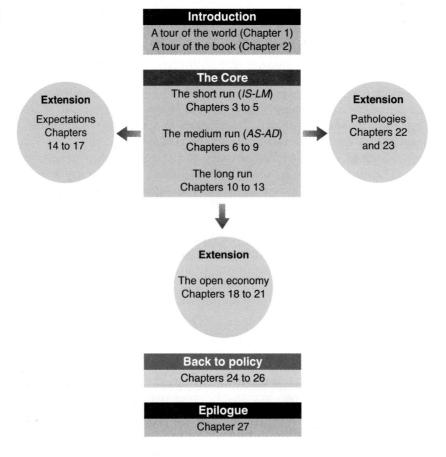

Introduction
A tour of the world (Chapter 1)
A tour of the book (Chapter 2)

The Core
The short run (*IS-LM*)
Chapters 3 to 5

The medium run (*AS-AD*)
Chapters 6 to 9

The long run
Chapters 10 to 13

Extension
Expectations
Chapters
14 to 17

Extension
Pathologies
Chapters 22
and 23

Extension
The open economy
Chapters 18 to 21

Back to policy
Chapters 24 to 26

Epilogue
Chapter 27

Chapter 3 looks at the goods market. Chapter 4 focuses on financial markets. Chapter 5 puts the goods and financial markets together. The resulting framework is known as the *IS–LM* model. Developed in the late 1930s, the *IS–LM* model still provides a simple way of thinking about the determination of output in the short run, and it remains a basic building block of macroeconomics. It also allows for a first pass at studying the effects of fiscal policy and monetary policy on output.

■ Chapters 6 to 9 develop the supply side and look at how output is determined in the medium run.

Chapter 6 introduces the labor market. Chapter 7 puts together goods, financial, and labor markets, and shows you how to think about the determination of output both in the short run and in the medium run. The model developed in Chapter 7 is called the aggregate supply–aggregate demand (*AS–AD*) model of output. Chapters 8 and 9 then show how the *AS–AD* model can be used to think about many issues, such as the relation between output and inflation and the role of monetary and fiscal policy in both the short run and the medium run.

■ Chapters 10 to 13 focus on the long run.

Chapter 10 introduces the relevant facts by looking at the growth of output both across countries and over long periods of time. Chapters 11 and 12 then discuss how both capital accumulation and technological progress determine growth. Chapter 13 looks at the effects of technological progress, in the short, the medium, and the long run.

Extensions

The core chapters give you a way of thinking about how output (and unemployment and inflation) is determined over the short, medium, and long run. However, they leave out several elements, which are explored in three extensions:

- The core chapters ignore the role of *expectations*. But expectations play an essential role in macroeconomics. Nearly all the economic decisions people and firms make—whether to buy a car, whether to buy bonds or to buy stocks, whether to build a new plant—depend on their expectations about future income, future profits, future interest rates, and so on. Fiscal and monetary policy affect economic activity not only through their direct effects but also through their effects on people's and firms' expectations. Chapters 14 to 17 focus on these expectations and their implications for fiscal and monetary policy.
- The core chapters treat the economy as *closed*, ignoring its interactions with the rest of the world. But the fact is, economies are increasingly *open*, trading goods and services and financial assets with one another. As a result, countries are becoming more and more interdependent. The nature of this interdependence and the implications for fiscal and monetary policy are the topics of Chapters 18 to 21.
- The core chapters on the short run and the medium run focus on fluctuations in output—on expansions and on recessions. Sometimes, however, the word *fluctuations* does not accurately capture what is happening when something goes very wrong such as when inflation reaches extremely high rates or, as was the case during the Great Depression, unemployment remains very high for a very long time; or, as in Japan in the 1990s, a country goes through a prolonged economic slump. These *pathologies* are the topics of Chapters 22 and 23.

Back to Policy

Monetary policy and fiscal policy are discussed in nearly every chapter of this book. But once the core and the extensions have been covered, it is useful to go back and put things together in order to assess the role of policy:

- Chapter 24 focuses on general issues of policy, whether macroeconomists really know enough about how the economy works to use policy as a stabilization tool at all, and whether policymakers can be trusted to do what is right.
- Chapters 25 and 26 then return to the role of monetary and fiscal policy.

Epilogue

Macroeconomics is not a fixed body of knowledge. It evolves over time. The final chapter, Chapter 27, looks at the recent history of macroeconomics and how macroeconomists have come to believe what they believe today. From the outside, macroeconomics sometimes looks like a field divided between schools— "Keynesians," "monetarists," "new classicals," "supply-siders," and so on—hurling arguments at each other. The actual process of research is more orderly and more productive than this image suggests. So, as a way to end the book, I identify what I see as the main differences among macroeconomists and the set of propositions that define the core of macroeconomics today.

Summary

- We can think of GDP, the measure of aggregate output, in three equivalent ways: (1) GDP is the value of the final goods and services produced in the economy during a given period; (2) GDP is the sum of value added in the economy during a given period; and (3) GDP is the sum of incomes in the economy during a given period.

- Nominal GDP is the sum of the quantities of final goods produced multiplied by their current prices. This implies that changes in nominal GDP reflect both changes in quantities and changes in prices. Real GDP is a measure of output. Changes in real GDP reflect changes in quantities only.

- A person is classified as unemployed if he or she does not have a job and is looking for one. The unemployment rate is the ratio of the number of people unemployed to the number of people in the labor force. The labor force is the sum of those employed and those unemployed.

- Economists care about unemployment because of the human cost it represents. They also look at unemployment because it sends a signal about how efficiently the economy is using its resources. High unemployment indicates that the economy is not utilizing its human resources efficiently.

- Inflation is a rise in the general level of prices—the price level. The inflation rate is the rate at which the price level increases. Macroeconomists look at two measures of the price level. The first is the GDP deflator, which is the average price of the goods produced in the economy. The second is the CPI, which is the average price of goods consumed in the economy.

- Inflation leads to changes in income distribution. It also leads to distortions and increased uncertainty.

- Macroeconomists distinguish between the short run (a few years), the medium run (a decade), and the long run (a few decades or more). They think of output as being determined by demand in the short run. They think of output as being determined by the level of technology, the capital stock, and the labor force in the medium run. Finally, they think of output as being determined by factors such as education, research, saving, and the quality of government in the long run.

Key Terms

- national income and product accounts, 42
- aggregate output, 42
- gross domestic product (GDP), 42
- gross national product (GNP), 42
- intermediate good, 42
- final good, 43
- value added, 43
- nominal GDP, 44
- real GDP, 44
- real GDP in chained (2000) dollars, 45
- dollar GDP, GDP in current dollars, 46
- GDP in terms of goods, GDP in constant dollars, GDP adjusted for inflation, GDP in 2000 dollars, 46
- real GDP per capita, 46
- GDP growth, 46
- expansion, 46
- recession, 46
- hedonic pricing, 47
- employment, 48
- unemployment, 48
- labor force, 48
- unemployment rate, 48
- Current Population Survey (CPS), 49
- not in the labor force, 49
- discouraged workers, 49
- participation rate, 49
- inflation, 50
- price level, 50
- inflation rate, 50
- deflation, 50
- underground economy, 51
- GDP deflator, 51
- index number, 51
- cost of living, 52
- consumer price index (CPI), 52
- short run, 55
- medium run, 55
- long run, 55
- base year, 61

Questions and Problems

Quick Check

1. Using the information in this chapter, label each of the following statements true, false, or uncertain. Explain briefly.

a. The share of labor income in GDP is much larger than the share of capital income.

b. U.S. GDP was 25 times higher in 2006 than it was in 1960.

c. When the unemployment rate is high, the participation rate is also likely to be high.

d. The rate of unemployment tends to fall during expansions and rise during recessions.

e. If the Japanese CPI is currently at 108 and the U.S. CPI is at 104, then the Japanese rate of inflation is higher than the U.S. rate of inflation.

f. The rate of inflation computed using the CPI is a better index of inflation than the rate of inflation computed using the GDP deflator.

g. The high unemployment rate in Spain is no mystery; it is primarily the result of workers taking jobs in the underground economy instead of taking jobs in the sectors of the economy measured by the official statistics.

2. *During a given year, the following activities occur:*

   i. *A silver mining company pays its workers $400,000 to mine 150 pounds of silver. The silver is then sold to a jewelry manufacturer for $500,000.*

   ii. *The jewelry manufacturer pays its workers $450,000 to make silver necklaces, which the manufacturer sells directly to consumers for $1,500,000.*

   a. Using the "production-of-final-goods" approach, what is GDP in this economy?

   b. What is the value added at each stage of production? Using the "value-added" approach, what is GDP?

   c. What are the total wages and profits earned? Using the income approach, what is GDP?

3. *Suppose you are measuring annual U.S. GDP by adding up the final value of all goods and services produced in the economy. Determine the effect on GDP of each of the following transactions.*

   a. A seafood restaurant buys $100 worth of fish from a fisherman.

   b. A family spends $100 on a fish dinner at a seafood restaurant.

   c. Delta Air Lines buys a new jet from Boeing for $200 million.

   d. The Greek national airline buys a new jet from Boeing for $200 million.

   e. Delta Air Lines sells one of its jets to Denzel Washington for $100 million.

4. *An economy produces three goods: cars, computers, and oranges. Quantities and prices per unit for years 2006 and 2007 are as follows:*

	2006		2007	
	Quantity	Price	Quantity	Price
Cars	10	$2,000	12	$3,000
Computers	4	$1,000	6	$ 500
Oranges	1,000	$ 1	1,000	$ 1

   a. What is nominal GDP in 2006 and in 2007? By what percentage does nominal GDP change from 2006 to 2007?

   b. Using the prices for 2006 as the set of common prices, what is real GDP in 2006 and in 2007? By what percentage does real GDP change from 2006 to 2007?

   c. Using the prices for 2007 as the set of common prices, what is real GDP in 2006 and in 2007? By what percentage does real GDP change from 2006 to 2007?

   d. Why are the two output growth rates constructed in (b) and (c) different? Which one is correct? Explain your answer.

5. *Consider the economy described in problem 4.*

   a. Use the prices for 2006 as the set of common prices to compute real GDP in 2006 and in 2007. Compute the GDP deflator for 2006 and for 2007 and compute the rate of inflation from 2006 to 2007.

   b. Use the prices for 2007 as the set of common prices to compute real GDP in 2006 and in 2007. Compute the GDP deflator for 2006 and for 2007 and compute the rate of inflation from 2006 to 2007.

   c. Why are the two rates of inflation different? Which one is correct? Explain your answer.

6. *Consider the economy described in problem 4.*

   a. Construct real GDP for years 2006 and 2007 by using the average price of each good over the two years.

   b. By what percentage does real GDP change from 2006 to 2007?

   c. What is the GDP deflator in 2006 and 2007? Using the GDP deflator, what is the rate of inflation from 2006 to 2007?

   d. Is this an attractive solution to the problems pointed out in problems 4 and 5 (i.e., two different growth rates and two different inflation rates, depending on which set of prices is used)? (The answer is yes and is the basis for the construction of chained-type deflators. See the appendix to this chapter for more discussion.)

Dig Deeper

7. *Measured and true GDP*

   Suppose that instead of cooking dinner for an hour, you decide to work an extra hour, earning an additional $12. You then purchase some (takeout) Chinese food, which costs you $10.

   a. By how much does measured GDP increase?

   b. Do you think the increase in measured GDP accurately reflects the effect on output of your decision to work? Explain.

8. *Hedonic pricing*

   As the first Focus box in this chapter explains, it is difficult to measure the true increase in prices of goods whose characteristics change over time. For such goods, part of any price increase can be attributed to an increase in quality. Hedonic pricing offers a method to compute the quality-adjusted increase in prices.

   a. Consider the case of a routine medical checkup. Name some reasons you might want to use hedonic pricing to measure the change in the price of this service.

   Now consider the case of a medical checkup for a pregnant woman. Suppose that a new ultrasound method is introduced. In the first year that this method is available, half of doctors offer the new method, and half offer the old method. A checkup using the new method costs 10% more than a checkup using the old method.

   b. In percentage terms, how much of a quality increase does the new method represent over the old method? (Hint: Consider the fact that some women *choose* to see a doctor offering the new method, when they could have chosen to see a doctor offering the old method.)

   Now, in addition, suppose that in the first year the new ultrasound method is available, the price of checkups using the new method is 15% higher than the price of checkups in the previous year (when everyone used the old method).

c. How much of the higher price for checkups using the new method (as compared to checkups in the previous year) reflects a true price increase of checkups and how much represents a quality increase? In other words, how much higher is the quality-adjusted price of checkups using the new method as compared to the price of checkups in the previous year?

In many cases, the kind of information we used in parts (b) and (c) is not available. For example, suppose that in the year the new ultrasound method is introduced, all doctors adopt the new method, so the old method is no longer used. In addition, continue to assume that the price of checkups in the year the new method is introduced is 15% higher than the price of checkups in the previous year (when everyone used the old method). Thus, we observe a 15% price increase in checkups, but we realize that the quality of checkups has increased.

d. Under these assumptions, what information required to compute the quality-adjusted price increase of checkups is lacking? Even without this information, can we say anything about the quality-adjusted price increase of checkups? Is it more than 15%? less than 15%? Explain.

Explore Further

9. *The labor market and the recession of 2001*

   Go to the Web page of the Bureau of Economic Analysis, at www.bea.gov. Find NIPA Table 1.1.6. (NIPA stands for national income and product accounts.) Retrieve the quarterly data in chained 2000 dollars.

   a. Plot the quarterly GDP growth rates from 1999 through 2002. Did any quarters have negative growth?

Go to the Web page of the Bureau of Labor Statistics, www. bls.gov. Retrieve the monthly data series on the participation rate, employment, the employment-to-population ratio, and the unemployment rate for the period 1994 to 2004. Make sure all data series are seasonally adjusted. The data will be easier to interpret if they are presented graphically rather than as tables of numbers. (As of this writing, the BLS website provides the option to show data graphically.)

a. How did the unemployment rate change in 2001 and after? Do you think the unemployment rate tells the whole story about the labor market? How did the participation rate evolve? What might explain the change in the participation rate?

b. Some economists prefer to look at employment as opposed to unemployment. How did the growth of employment after 2001 compare to the growth of employment before 2001? How did the employment-to-population ratio change?

c. The National Bureau of Economic Research (NBER), which dates recessions, identified a recession beginning in March 2001 and ending in November 2001. In other words, according to the NBER, the economy began a recovery in November 2001. Given your answers to parts (b) and (c), do you think the labor market recovered as quickly as GDP? Explain.

For more on NBER recession dating, visit www.nber.org. This site provides a history of recession dates and some discussion of their methodology.

 We invite you to visit the Blanchard page on the Prentice Hall Web Site, at:

www.prenhall.com/blanchard

for this chapter's World Wide Web exercises.

Further Readings

- If you want to learn more about the definitions and the construction of the many economic indicators that are regularly reported on the news—from the help-wanted index to the retail sales index—two easy-to-read references are:

  The Guide to Economic Indicators, 3rd edition, by Norman Frumkin, M.E. Sharpe, New York, 2000.

  The Economist Guide to Economic Indicators, 6th edition, by the staff of *The Economist*, Bloomberg, New York, 2007.

- In 1995, the U.S. Senate set up a commission to study the construction of the CPI and make recommendations about potential changes. The commission concluded that the rate of inflation computed using the CPI was on average about 1% too high. If this conclusion is correct, this implies in particular that real wages (nominal wages divided by the CPI) have grown at 1% more per year than is currently being reported. For more on the conclusions of the commission and some of the exchanges that followed, read

"Consumer Prices, the Consumer Price Index, and the Cost of Living," by Michael Boskin et al, *Journal of Economic Perspectives*, Volume 12, Number 1, Winter 1998, 3–26.

- For a short history of the construction of the National Income Accounts, read "GDP: One of the Great Inventions of the 20th Century," *Survey of Current Business*, January 2000, 1–9 (www.bea.gov/bea/articles/beawide/2000/0100od.pdf).

- For a discussion of some of the problems involved in measuring activity, read "What We Don't Know Could Hurt Us; Some Reflections on the Measurement of Economic Activity," by Katherine Abraham, *Journal of Economic Perspectives*, Volume 19, Number 3, 3–18. To see why it is hard to measure the price level and output correctly, read "Viagra and the Wealth of Nations," by Paul Krugman, 1998 (www.pkarchive.org/theory/viagra.html). (Paul Krugman is an economist at Princeton University and a columnist for the *New York Times*.)

Appendix: The Construction of Real GDP and Chain-Type Indexes

The example I used in the chapter had only one final good—cars—so constructing real GDP was easy. But how do we construct real GDP when there is more than one final good? This appendix gives the answer.

To understand how real GDP in an economy with many final goods is constructed, all you need to do is look at an economy where there are just two final goods. What works for two goods works just as well for millions of goods.

Suppose that an economy produces two final goods, say wine and potatoes:

- In year 0, it produces 10 pounds of potatoes at a price of $1 per pound and 5 bottles of wine at a price of $2 per bottle.
- In year 1, it produces 15 pounds of potatoes at a price of $1 per pound and 5 bottles of wine at a price of $3 per bottle.
- Nominal GDP in year 0 is therefore equal to $20. Nominal GDP in year 1 is equal to $30.

This information is summarized in the following table:

Nominal GDP in Year 0 and in Year 1

	Quantity	Year 0 $ Price	$ Value
Potatoes (pounds)	10	1	10
Wine (bottles)	5	2	10
Nominal GDP			20

	Quantity	Year 1 $ Price	$ Value
Potatoes (pounds)	15	1	15
Wine (bottles)	5	3	15
Nominal GDP			30

The rate of growth of nominal GDP from year 0 to year 1 is equal to ($30 − $20)/$20 = 50%. But what is the rate of growth of real GDP?

Answering this question requires consructing real GDP for each of the two years. The basic idea behind constructing real GDP is to evaluate the quantities in each year, using the *same set of prices*.

Suppose we choose, for example, the prices in year 0. Year 0 is then called the **base year**. In this case, the computation is as follows:

- Real GDP in year 0 is the sum of the quantity in year 0 multiplied by the price in year 0 for both goods: (10 × $1) + (5 × $2) = $20.
- Real GDP in year 1 is the sum of the quantity in year 1 multiplied by the price in year 0 for both goods: (15 × $1) + (5 × $2) = $25.
- The rate of growth of real GDP from year 0 to year 1 is then ($25 − $20)/$20, or 25%.

This answer raises an obvious issue: Instead of using year 0 as the base year, we could have used year 1, or any other year. If, for example, we had used year 1 as the base year, then:

- Real GDP in year 0 would be equal to (10 × $1 + 5 × $3) = $25.
- Real GDP in year 1 would be equal to (15 × $1 + 5 × $3) = $30.
- The rate of growth of real GDP from year 0 to year 1 would be equal to $5 / $25, or 20%.

The answer using year 1 as the base year would therefore be different from the answer using year 0 as the base year. So, if the choice of the base year affects the constructed percentage rate of change in output, which base year should one choose?

Until the mid-1990s in the United States—and still in most countries today—the practice was to choose a base year and change it infrequently, say, every five years or so. For example, in the United States, 1987 was the base year used from December 1991 to December 1995. That is, measures of real GDP published, for example, in 1994 for both 1994 and for all earlier years were constructed using 1987 prices. In December 1995, national income accounts shifted to 1992 as a base year; measures of real GDP for all earlier years were recalculated using 1992 prices.

This practice was logically unappealing. Every time the base year was changed and a new set of prices was used, all past real GDP numbers—and all past real GDP growth rates—were recomputed. Economic history was, in effect, rewritten every five years! Starting in December 1995, the U.S. Bureau of Economic Analysis (BEA)—the government office that produces the GDP numbers—shifted to a new method that does not suffer from this problem.

The method requires four steps:

1. Construct the rate of change of real GDP from year t to year $t + 1$ in two different ways. First, use the prices from year t as the set of common prices. Then, use the prices from year $t + 1$ as the set of common prices.

   For example, the rate of change of GDP from 2006 to 2007 is computed by:
   a. Constructing real GDP for 2006 and real GDP for 2007 using 2006 prices as the set of common prices, and computing a first measure of the rate of growth of GDP from 2006 to 2007.
   b. Constructing real GDP for 2006 and real GDP for 2007 using 2007 prices as the set of common prices, and computing a second measure of the rate of growth of GDP from 2006 to 2007.

2. Construct the rate of change of real GDP as the average of these two rates of change.
3. Construct an index for the level of real GDP by *linking—* or *chaining*—the constructed rates of change for each year.

   The index is set equal to 1 in some arbitrary year. At the time this book was written, the arbitrary year is 2000.

   Given that the constructed rate of change from 2000 to 2001 by the Bureau of Economic Analysis is 0.7%, the index for 2001 equals (1 + .07%) = 1.007. The index for 2002 is then obtained by multiplying the index for 2001 by the rate of change from 2001 to 2002, and so on. (You will find the value of this index—multiplied by 100—in the second column of Table B3 in the *Economic Report of the President*. Check that it is 100 in 2000 and 100.7 in 2001, and so on.)
4. Multiply this index by nominal GDP in 2000 to derive *real GDP in chained (2000) dollars*. As the index is 1 in 2000, this implies that real GDP in 2000 equals nominal GDP in 2000.

Chained refers to the chaining of rates of change described above. (2000) refers to the year where, by construction, real GDP is equal to nominal GDP. (You will find the value of real GDP in chained 2000 dollars in the first column of Table B2 of the *Economic Report of the President*.)

This index is more complicated to construct than the indexes used before 1995. (To make sure you understand the steps, construct real GDP in chained (year 0) dollars for year 1 in our example.) But it is clearly better conceptually:

■ The prices used to evaluate real GDP in two adjacent years are the right prices, namely the average prices for those two years.
■ Because the rate of change from one year to the next is constructed using the prices in those two years rather than the set of prices in an arbitrary base year, history will not be rewritten every five years—as it used to be when, under the previous method for constructing real GDP, the base year was changed.

(For more detail, look at **www.bea.gov/scb/pdf/ NATIONAL/NIPA/1995/0795od.pdf.**)

The Short Run

In the short run, demand determines output. Many factors affect demand, from consumer confidence to fiscal and monetary policy.

Chapter 3

Chapter 3 looks at equilibrium in the goods market and the determination of output. It focuses on the interaction between demand, production, and income. It shows how fiscal policy affects output.

Chapter 4

Chapter 4 looks at equilibrium in financial markets and the determination of the interest rate. It shows how monetary policy affects the interest rate.

Chapter 5

Chapter 5 looks at the goods market and financial markets together. It shows what determines output and the interest rate in the short run. It looks at the roles of fiscal and monetary policy. The model developed in Chapter 5, called the *IS–LM* model, is one of the workhorses of macroeconomics.

CHAPTER 3

When economists think about year-to-year movements in economic activity, they focus on the interactions between *production, income,* and *demand*:

■ Changes in the demand for goods lead to changes in production.

■ Changes in production lead to changes in income.

■ Changes in income lead to changes in the demand for goods.

Nothing makes the point better than the following cartoon:

This chapter looks at these interactions and their implications:

- Section 3-1 looks at the composition of GDP and the different sources of the demand for goods.

- Section 3-2 looks at the determinants of the demand for goods.

- Section 3-3 shows how equilibrium output is determined by the condition that the production of goods must be equal to the demand for goods.

- Section 3-4 gives an alternative way of thinking about the equilibrium, based on the equality of investment and saving.

- Section 3-5 takes a first pass at the effects of fiscal policy on equilibrium output. ■

3-1   The Composition of GDP

The purchase of a machine by a firm, the decision to go to a restaurant by a consumer, and the purchase of combat airplanes by the federal government are clearly very different decisions and depend on very different factors. So, if we want to understand what determines the demand for goods, it makes sense to decompose aggregate output (GDP) from the point of view of the different goods being produced, and from the point of view of the different buyers for these goods.

Output and *production* are synonymous. There is no rule for using one or the other. Use the one that sounds better. ▶

The decomposition of GDP typically used by macroeconomists is shown in Table 3-1 (a more detailed version, with more precise definitions, appears in Appendix 1 at the end of the book):

- First comes **consumption** (which I will denote by the letter C when I use algebra throughout this book). These are the goods and services purchased by consumers, ranging from food to airline tickets, to vacations, to new cars, and so on. Consumption is by far the largest component of GDP. In 2006, it accounted for 70.0% of GDP.

- Second comes **investment** (I), sometimes called **fixed investment** to distinguish it from inventory investment (which we will discuss shortly). Investment is the sum of **nonresidential investment**, the purchase by firms of new plants or new machines (from turbines to computers), and **residential investment**, the purchase by people of new houses or apartments.

Warning! To most people, *investment* refers to the purchase of assets such as gold or shares of General Motors. Economists use *investment* to refer to the purchase of *new capital goods*, such as (new) machines, (new) buildings, or (new) houses. When economists refer to the purchase of gold, or shares of General Motors, or other financial assets, they use the term *financial investment*. ▶

Nonresidential investment and residential investment, and the decisions behind them, have more in common than it might first appear. Firms buy machines or plants to produce output in the future. People buy houses or apartments to get *housing services* in the future. In both cases, the decision to buy depends on the services these goods will yield in the future. Consequently, it makes sense to treat them together. Together, nonresidential and residential investment accounted for 16.3% of GDP in 2006.

- Third comes **government spending** (G). This represents the purchases of goods and services by the federal, state, and local governments. The goods range from airplanes to office equipment. The services include services provided by government employees: In effect, the national income accounts treat the government as buying the services provided by government employees—and then providing these services to the public, free of charge.

Note that G does not include **government transfers**, such as Medicare or Social Security payments, nor interest payments on the government debt. Although these are clearly government expenditures, they are not purchases of goods and services.

Table 3-1

		Billions of Dollars		Percent of GDP	
	GDP (Y)	13,246		100.0	
1	Consumption (C)	9,269		70.0	
2	Investment (I)	2,163		16.3	
	Nonresidential		1,396		10.5
	Residential		767		5.8
3	Government spending (G)	2,528		19.0	
4	Net exports	−763		−5.8	
	Exports (X)		1,466		11.0
	Imports (IM)		−2,229		−16.8
5	Inventory investment	49		0.4	

Table 3-1 The Composition of U.S. GDP, 2006

Source: Survey of Current Business, April 2007, Table 1-1-5.

That is why the number for government spending on goods and services in Table 3-1, 19% of GDP, is smaller than the number for total government spending including transfers and interest payments. That number, in 2006, was 31% of GDP.

■ The sum of lines 1, 2, and 3 gives the *purchases of goods and services by U.S. consumers, U.S. firms, and the U.S. government*. To determine the *purchases of U.S. goods and services*, two more steps are needed:

First, we must subtract **imports** (**IM**), the purchases of foreign goods and services by U.S. consumers, U.S. firms, and the U.S. government.

Second, we must add **exports** (**X**), the purchases of U.S. goods and services by foreigners.

The difference between exports and imports, (**X − IM**), is called **net exports**, or the **trade balance**. If exports exceed imports, the country is said to run a **trade surplus**. If exports are less than imports, the country is said to run a **trade deficit**. In 2006, U.S. exports accounted for 11.0% of GDP. U.S. imports were equal to 16.8% of GDP, so the United States was running a trade deficit equal to 5.8% of GDP.

◄ Exports > Imports
⇔ Trade surplus
Exports < Imports
⇔ Trade deficit

■ So far we have looked at various sources of purchases (sales) of U.S. goods and services in 2006. To determine U.S. production in 2006, we need to take one last step:

In any given year, production and sales need not be equal. Some of the goods produced in a given year are not sold in that year, but in later years. And some of the goods sold in a given year may have been produced in an earlier year. The difference between goods produced and goods sold in a given year—the difference between production and sales, in other words—is called **inventory investment**. If production exceeds sales and firms accumulate inventories as a result, then inventory investment is said to be positive. If production is less than sales, and ◄ firms inventories fall, then inventory investment is said to be negative. Inventory investment is typically small—positive in some years and negative in others. In 2006, inventory investment was positive, equal to just $49 billion. Put another way, production was higher than sales by an amount equal to $49 billion.

Make sure you understand each of these three equivalent ways of stating the relation between production, sales, and inventory investment:
Inventory investment =
Production − Sales
Production =
Sales + Inventory investment
Sales = Production
− Inventory investment

We now have what we need to develop our first model of output determination.

3-2 The Demand for Goods

Denote the total demand for goods by Z. Using the decomposition of GDP we saw in Section 3-1, we can write Z as

$$Z \equiv C + I + G + X - IM$$

This equation is an **identity** (which is why it is written using the symbol ≡ rather than an equals sign). It *defines* Z as the sum of consumption, plus investment, plus government spending, plus exports, minus imports.

Recall that inventory investment is not part of demand.

We now need to think about the determinants of Z. To make the task easier, let's first make a number of simplifications:

A model nearly always starts with *Assume* (or *Suppose*). This is an indication that reality is about to be simplified to focus on the issue at hand.

■ Assume that all firms produce the same good, which can then be used by consumers for consumption, by firms for investment, or by the government. With this (big) simplification, we need to look at only one market—the market for "the" good—and think about what determines supply and demand in that market.

■ Assume that firms are willing to supply any amount of the good at a given price, P. This assumption allows us to focus on the role demand plays in the determination of output. As we shall see later in the book, this assumption is valid only in the short run. When we move to the study of the medium run (starting in Chapter 6), we will abandon it. But for the moment, it will simplify our discussion.

■ Assume that the economy is *closed*—that it does not trade with the rest of the world: Both exports and imports are zero. This assumption clearly goes against the facts: Modern economies trade with the rest of the world. Later on (starting in Chapter 18), we will abandon this assumption as well and look at what happens when the economy is open. But, for the moment, this assumption will also simplify our discussion because we won't have to think about what determines exports and imports.

Under the assumption that the economy is closed, $X = IM = 0$, so the demand for goods, Z, is simply the sum of consumption, investment, and government spending:

$$Z \equiv C + I + G$$

Let's discuss each of these three components in turn.

Consumption (C)

Consumption decisions depend on many factors. The main one is surely income or, more precisely, **disposable income** (Y_D), the income that remains after consumers have received transfers from the government and paid their taxes. When their disposable income goes up, people buy more goods; when it goes down, they buy fewer goods.

Let C denote consumption and Y_D denote disposable income. We can then write:

$$C = C(Y_D)$$
$$(+)\hspace{8cm}(3.1)$$

This is a formal way of stating that consumption, C, is a function of disposable income, Y_D. The function $C(Y_D)$ is called the **consumption function**. The positive sign below Y_D reflects the fact that when disposable income increases, so does consumption. Economists call such an equation a **behavioral equation** to indicate that the equation captures some aspect of behavior—in this case, the behavior of consumers.

I will use functions in this book as a way of representing relations between variables. What you need to know about functions—which is very little—is described in Appendix 2 at the end of the book. That appendix develops the mathematics you need to go through this book. Not to worry: I shall always describe a function in words when I introduce it for the first time.

It is often useful to be more specific about the form of the function. Here is such a case. It is reasonable to assume that the relation between consumption and disposable income is given by the simpler relation:

$$C = c_0 + c_1 Y_D \tag{3.2}$$

In other words, it is reasonable to assume that the function is a **linear relation**. The relation between consumption and disposable income is then characterized by two **parameters**, c_0 and c_1:

- The parameter c_1 is called the **propensity to consume**. (It is also called the *marginal propensity to consume*. I will drop the word *marginal* for simplicity.) It gives the effect an additional dollar of disposable income has on consumption. If c_1 is equal to 0.6, then an additional dollar of disposable income increases consumption by $\$1 \times 0.6 = 60$ cents.

  A natural restriction on c_1 is that it must be positive: An increase in disposable income is likely to lead to an increase in consumption. Another natural restriction is that c_1 must be less than 1: People are likely to consume only part of any increase in disposable income and save the rest.

- The parameter c_0 has a simple interpretation. It is what people would consume if their disposable income in the current year were equal to zero: If Y_D equals zero in equation (3.2), $C = c_0$.

  A natural restriction is that, if current income were equal to zero, consumption would still be positive: With or without income, people still need to eat! This implies that c_0 is positive. How can people have positive consumption if their income is equal to zero? Answer: They dissave. They consume either by selling some of their assets, or by borrowing.

Think about your own consumption behavior. What are ◄ your values of c_0 and c_1?

The relation between consumption and disposable income shown in equation (3.2) is drawn in Figure 3-1. Because it is a linear relation, it is represented by a straight line. Its intercept with the vertical axis is c_0; its slope is c_1. Because c_1 is less than 1, the slope of the line is less than 1: Equivalently, the line is flatter than a 45-degree line. (A refresher on graphs, slopes, and intercepts is given in Appendix 2.)

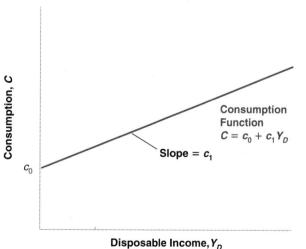

Figure 3-1

Consumption and Disposable Income

Consumption increases with disposable income but less than one for one.

Next, we need to define disposable income, Y_D. Disposable income is given by

$$Y_D \equiv Y - T$$

In the United States, the two major taxes paid by individuals are income taxes and Social Security contributions. The main government transfers are Social Security benefits, Medicare (health care for retirees), and Medicaid (health care for the poor). In 2006, taxes and social contributions paid by individuals were $2,300 billion, and transfers to individuals were $1,600 billion.

where Y is income and T is taxes paid minus government transfers received by consumers. For short, I will refer to T simply as taxes—but remember that it is equal to taxes minus transfers. Note that the equation is an identity, indicated by $\equiv$.

Replacing Y_D in equation (3.2) gives

$$C = c_0 + c_1(Y - T) \qquad (3.3)$$

Equation (3.3) tells us that consumption, C, is a function of income, Y, and taxes, T. Higher income increases consumption, but less than one for one. Higher taxes decrease consumption, also less than one for one.

Investment (*I*)

Models have two types of variables. Some variables depend on other variables in the model and are therefore explained within the model. Variables like these are called **endogenous**. This was the case for consumption above. Other variables are not explained within the model but are instead taken as given. Variables like these are called **exogenous**. This is how we will treat investment here. We will take investment as given and write:

$$I = \bar{I} \qquad (3.4)$$

Endogenous variables— explained within the model Exogenous variables— taken as given.

Putting a bar on investment is a simple typographical way to remind us that we take investment as given.

We take investment as given to keep our model simple. But the assumption is not innocuous. It implies that, when we later look at the effects of changes in production, we will assume that investment does not respond to changes in production. It is not hard to see that this implication may be a bad description of reality: Firms that experience an increase in production might well decide they need more machines and increase their investment as a result. For now, though, we will leave this mechanism out of the model. In Chapter 5 we will introduce a more realistic treatment of investment.

Government Spending (*G*)

The third component of demand in our model is government spending, G. Together with taxes, T, G describes **fiscal policy**—the choice of taxes and spending by the government. Just as we just did for investment, we will take G and T as exogenous. But the reason why we assume G and T are exogenous is different from the reason we assumed investment is exogenous. It is based on two distinct arguments:

Recall, that "taxes" stands for taxes minus government transfers.

■ First, governments do not behave with the same regularity as consumers or firms, so there is no reliable rule we could write for G or T corresponding to the rule we wrote, for example, for consumption. (This argument is not airtight, though. Even if governments do not follow simple behavioral rules as consumers do, a good part of their behavior is predictable. We will look at these issues later, in particular in Chapters 24 to 26. Until then, we will set them aside.)

Because we will (nearly always) take G and T as exogenous, I won't use a bar to denote their values. This will keep the notation lighter.

■ Second, and more importantly, one of the tasks of macroeconomists is to think about the implications of alternative spending and tax decisions. We want to be able to say, "If the government were to choose these values for G and T, this is what would happen." The approach in this book will typically treat G and T as variables chosen by the government and will not try to explain them within the model.

Let's put together the pieces we have introduced so far.

Assuming that exports and imports are both zero, the demand for goods is the sum of consumption, investment, and government spending:

$$Z \equiv C + I + G$$

Replacing C and I from equations (3.3) and (3.4), we get

$$Z = c_0 + c_1(Y - T) + \bar{I} + G \qquad (3.5)$$

The demand for goods, Z, depends on income, Y, taxes, T, investment, $\bar{I}$, and government spending, G.

Let's now turn to **equilibrium** in the goods market and the relation between production and demand. If firms hold inventories, then production need not be equal to demand. For example, firms can satisfy an increase in demand by drawing upon their inventories—by having negative inventory investment. They can respond to a decrease in demand by continuing to produce and accumulating inventories—by having positive inventory investment. Let's first ignore this complication, though, and begin by assuming that firms do not hold inventories. In this case, inventory investment is always equal to zero, and **equilibrium in the goods market** requires that production, Y, be equal to the demand for goods, Z:

◀ Think of an economy that produces only haircuts. There cannot be inventories of haircuts—haircuts produced but not sold?—so production must always be equal to demand.

$$Y = Z \qquad (3.6)$$

This equation is called an **equilibrium condition**. Models include three types of equations: identities, behavioral equations, and equilibrium conditions. You have seen examples of each: The equation defining disposable income is an identity, the consumption function is a behavioral equation, and the condition that production equals demand is an equilibrium condition.

◀ There are three types of equations:
Identities
Behavioral equations
Equilibrium conditions

Replacing demand, Z, in equation (3.6) by its expression from equation (3.5) gives

$$Y = c_0 + c_1(Y - T) + \bar{I} + G \qquad (3.7)$$

Equation (3.7) represents algebraically what we stated informally at the beginning of this chapter:

In equilibrium, production, Y, (the left side of the equation) is equal to demand (the right side). Demand in turn depends on income, Y, which is itself equal to production.

◀ Relate this statement to the cartoon at the start of the chapter.

Note that we are using the same symbol Y for production and income. This is no accident! As you saw in Chapter 2, we can look at GDP either from the production side or from the income side. Production and income are identically equal.

Having constructed a model, we can solve it to look at what determines the level of output—how output changes in response to, say, a change in government spending. Solving a model means not only solving it algebraically but also understanding why the results are what they are. In this book, solving a model also means characterizing the results using graphs— sometimes skipping the algebra altogether—and describing the results and the mechanisms in words. Macroeconomists always use these three tools:

1. **Algebra to make sure that the logic is correct**

2. **Graphs to build the intuition**

3. **Words to explain the results**

Make it a habit to do the same.

Using Algebra

Rewrite the equilibrium equation (3.7):

$$Y = c_0 + c_1 Y - c_1 T + \bar{I} + G$$

Move $c_1 Y$ to the left side and reorganize the right side:

$$(1 - c_1)Y = c_0 + \bar{I} + G - c_1 T$$

Divide both sides by $(1 - c_1)$:

$$Y = \frac{1}{1 - c_1}[c_0 + \bar{I} + G - c_1 T] \tag{3.8}$$

Equation (3.8) characterizes equilibrium output, the level of output such that production equals demand. Let's look at both terms on the right, beginning with the second term:

Autonomous means independent—in this case, independent of output. ▶

- The term $[c_0 + \bar{I} + G - c_1 T]$ is that part of the demand for goods that does not depend on output. For this reason, it is called **autonomous spending**.

  If $T = G$, then $(G - c_1 T) = (T - c_1 T) = (1 - c_1)T > 0.$ ▶

  Can we be sure that autonomous spending is positive? We cannot, but it is very likely to be. The first two terms in brackets, c_0 and $\bar{I}$, are positive. What about the last two, $G - c_1 T$? Suppose the government is running a **balanced budget**—taxes equal government spending. If $T = G$, and the propensity to consume (c_1) is less than one (as we have assumed), then $(G - c_1 T)$ is positive, and so is autonomous spending. Only if the government were running a very large budget surplus—if taxes were much larger than government spending—could autonomous spending be negative. We can safely ignore that case here.

- Turn to the first term, $1/(1 - c_1)$. Because the propensity to consume (c_1) is between zero and one, $1/(1 - c_1)$ is a number greater than one. For this reason, this number, which *multiplies* autonomous spending, is called the **multiplier**. The closer c_1 is to 1, the larger the multiplier.

  What does the multiplier imply? Suppose that, for a given level of income, consumers decide to consume more. More precisely, assume that c_0 in equation (3.3) increases by $1 billion. Equation (3.8) tells us that output will increase by more than $1 billion. For example, if c_1 equals 0.6, the multiplier equals $1/(1 - 0.6) = 1/0.4 = 2.5$, so that output increases by $2.5 \times \$1$ billion $= \$2.5$ billion.

  We have looked at an increase in consumption, but equation (3.8) makes it clear that any change in autonomous spending—from a change in investment, to a change in government spending, to a change in taxes—will have the same qualitative effect: It will change output by more than its direct effect on autonomous spending.

Where does the multiplier effect come from? Looking back at equation (3.7) gives us the clue: An increase in c_0 increases demand. The increase in demand then leads to an increase in production. The increase in production leads to an equivalent increase in income (remember that the two are identically equal). The increase in income further increases consumption, which further increases demand, and so on. The best way to describe this mechanism is to represent the equilibrium using a graph. Let's do that.

Using a Graph

Let's characterize the equilibrium graphically:

■ First, plot production as a function of income.

In Figure 3-2, measure production on the vertical axis. Measure income on the horizontal axis. Plotting production as a function of income is straightforward: Recall that production and income are identically equal. Thus, the relation between them is the 45-degree line, the line with a slope equal to 1.

■ Second, plot demand as a function of income.

The relation between demand and income is given by equation (3.5). Let's rewrite it here for convenience, regrouping the terms for autonomous spending together in the term in parentheses:

$$Z = (c_0 + \bar{I} + G - c_1 T) + c_1 Y \qquad (3.9)$$

Demand depends on autonomous spending and on income—via its effect on consumption. The relation between demand and income is drawn as ZZ in the graph. The intercept with the vertical axis—the value of demand when income is equal to zero—equals autonomous spending. The slope of the line is the propensity to consume, c_1: When income increases by 1, demand increases by c_1. Under the restriction that c_1 is positive but less than 1, the line is upward sloping but has a slope of less than 1.

■ In equilibrium, production equals demand.

Equilibrium output, Y, therefore occurs at the intersection of the 45-degree line and the demand function. This is at point A. To the left of A, demand exceeds production; to the right of A, production exceeds demand. Only at A are demand and production equal.

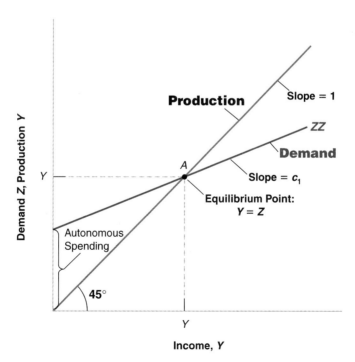

Figure 3-2 ■

Equilibrium in the Goods Market

Equilibrium output is determined by the condition that production be equal to demand.

Suppose that the economy is at the initial equilibrium, represented by point A in the graph, with production equal to Y.

Now suppose c_0 increases by $1 billion. At the initial level of income (the level of income associated with point A), consumers increase their consumption by $1 billion. What happens is shown in Figure 3-3, which builds on Figure 3-2.

Equation (3.9) tells us that, for any value of income, demand is higher by $1 billion. Before the increase in c_0, the relation between demand and income was given by the line ZZ. After the increase in c_0 by $1 billion, the relation between demand and income is given by the line ZZ', which is parallel to ZZ but higher by $1 billion. In other words, the demand curve shifts up by $1 billion. The new equilibrium is at the intersection of the 45-degree line and the new demand relation, at point A'.

Equilibrium output increases from Y not Y'. The increase in output, $(Y' - Y')$, which we can measure either on the horizontal or the vertical axis, is larger than the initial increase in consumption of $1 billion. This is the multiplier effect.

Look at the vertical axis. The distance between Y and Y' on the vertical axis is larger than the distance between A and B—which is equal to $1 billion.

With the help of the graph, it becomes easier to tell how and why the economy moves from A to A'. The initial increase in consumption leads to an increase in demand of $1 billion. At the initial level of income, Y, the level of demand is shown by point B: Demand is $1 billion higher. To satisfy this higher level of demand, firms increase production by $1 billion. This increase in production of $1 billion implies that income increases by $1 billion (recall that income = production), so the economy moves to point C. (In other words, both production and income are higher by $1 billion.) But this is not the end of the story. The increase in income leads to a further increase in demand. Demand is now shown by point D. Point D leads to a higher level of production, and so on, until the economy is at A', where production and demand are again equal. This is therefore the new equilibrium.

We can pursue this line of explanation a bit more, which will give us another way to think about the multiplier:

- The first-round increase in demand, shown by the distance AB in Figure 3-3— equals $1 billion.

Figure 3-3

The Effects of an Increase in Autonomous Spending on Output

An increase in autonomous spending has a more than one-for-one effect on equilibrium output.

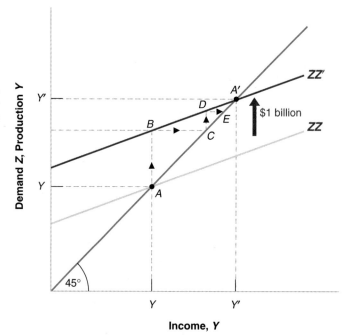

The Short Run   **The Core**

- This first-round increase in demand leads to an equal increase in production, or $1 billion, which is also shown by the distance AB.
- This first-round increase in production leads to an equal increase in income, shown by the distance BC, also equal to $1 billion.
- The second-round increase in demand, shown by the distance CD, equals $1 billion (the increase in income in the first round) multiplied by the propensity to consume, c_1—hence, $\$c_1$ billion.
- This second-round increase in demand leads to an equal increase in production, also shown by the distance CD, and thus an equal increase in income, shown by the distance DE.
- The third-round increase in demand equals $\$c_1$ billion (the increase in income in the second round), multiplied by c_1, the marginal propensity to consume; it is equal to $\$ c_1 \times c_1 = \$c_1^2$ billion, and so on.

Following this logic, the total increase in production after, say, $n + 1$ rounds equals $1 billion multiplied by the sum:

$$1 + c_1 + c_1^2 + \cdots + c_1^n$$

Such a sum is called a **geometric series**. Geometric series frequently appear in this book. A refresher is given in Appendix 2 at the end of the book. One property of geometric series is that, when c_1 is less than 1 (as it is here) and as n gets larger and larger, the sum keeps increasing but approaches a limit. That limit is $1/(1 - c_1)$, making the eventual increase in output $\$1/(1 - c_1)$ billion.

The expression $1/(1 - c_1)$ should be familiar: it is the multiplier, derived another way. This gives us an equivalent but more intuitive way of thinking about the multiplier. We can think of the original increase in demand as triggering successive increases in production, with each increase in production leading to an increase in income, which leads to an increase in demand, which leads to a further increase in production, which leads . . . and so on. The multiplier is the sum of all these successive increases in production.

Trick question: Think about the multiplier as the result of these successive rounds. What would happen in each successive round if c_1, the propensity to consume, were larger than 1?

Using Words

How can we summarize our findings in words?

Production depends on demand, which depends on income, which is itself equal to production. An increase in demand, such as an increase in government spending, leads to an increase in production and a corresponding increase in income. This increase in income leads to a further increase in demand, which leads to a further increase in production, and so on. The end result is an increase in output that is larger than the initial shift in demand, by a factor equal to the multiplier.

The size of the multiplier is directly related to the value of the propensity to consume: The higher the propensity to consume, the higher the multiplier. What is the value of the propensity to consume in the United States today? To answer this question, and more generally to estimate behavioral equations and their parameters, economists use **econometrics**, the set of statistical methods used in economics. To give you a sense of what econometrics is and how it is used, read Appendix 3 at the end of this book. That appendix gives you a quick introduction, along with an application estimating the propensity to consume. The conclusion from the appendix is that, in the United States today, the propensity to consume is around 0.6. In other words, an additional dollar of income leads on average to an increase in consumption of 60 cents. This implies that the multiplier is equal to $1/(1 - c_1) = 1/(1 - 0.6) = 2.5$.

How Long Does It Take for Output to Adjust?

Let's return to our example one last time. Suppose that c_0 increases by \$1 billion. We know that output will increase by an amount equal to $1/(1 - c_1)$ multiplied by \$1 billion. But how long will it take for output to reach this higher value?

Under the assumptions we have made so far, the answer is: Right away! In writing the equilibrium condition (3.6), I have assumed that production is always equal to demand. In other words, I have assumed that production responds to demand instantaneously. In writing the consumption function (3.2), I have assumed that consumption responds to changes in disposable income instantaneously. Under these two assumptions, the economy goes instantaneously from point A to point A' in Figure 3-3: The increase in demand leads to an immediate increase in production, the increase in income associated with the increase in production leads to an immediate increase in demand, and so on. There is nothing wrong in thinking about the adjustment in terms of successive rounds as we did earlier, even though the equations indicate that all these rounds happen at once.

In the model we saw earlier, we ruled out this possibility by assuming that firms did not hold ▶ inventories and so could not rely on drawing down inventories to satisfy an increase in demand.

This instantaneous adjustment isn't really plausible: A firm that faces an increase in demand might well decide to wait before adjusting its production, meanwhile drawing down its inventories to satisfy demand. A worker who gets a pay raise might not adjust her consumption right away. Delays like these imply that the adjustment of output will take time.

Formally describing this adjustment of output over time—that is, writing the equations for what economists call the **dynamics** of adjustment, and solving this more complicated model—would be too hard to do here. But it is easy to do it in words:

- Suppose, for example, that firms make decisions about their production levels at the beginning of each quarter. Once their decisions are made, production cannot be adjusted for the rest of the quarter. If purchases by consumers are higher than production, firms will draw down their inventories to satisfy the purchases. On the other hand, if purchases are lower than production, firms will accumulate inventories.

- Now suppose that consumers decide to spend more, that they increase c_0. During the quarter in which this happens, demand increases, but production—because we assumed it was set at the beginning of the quarter—doesn't yet change. Therefore, income doesn't change either.

- Having observed an increase in demand, firms are likely to set a higher level of production in the following quarter. This increase in production leads to a corresponding increase in income and a further increase in demand. If purchases still exceed production, firms further increase production in the following quarter, and so on.

- In short, in response to an increase in consumer spending, output does not jump to the new equilibrium but rather increases over time from Y to Y'.

  How long this adjustment takes depends on how and how often firms revise their production schedules. If firms adjust their production schedules more frequently in response to past increases in purchases, the adjustment will occur more quickly.

I will often do in this book what I just did here: After we have looked at changes in equilibrium output, I will then describe informally how the economy moves from one equilibrium to the other. This will not only make the description of what happens in the economy feel more realistic, but it will often reinforce your intuition about why the equilibrium changes.

I have focused in this section on increases in demand. But the mechanism, of course, works both ways: Decreases in demand lead to decreases in output. The 1990

In the third quarter of 1990, after the invasion of Kuwait by Iraq but before the beginning of the Persian Gulf War, U.S. GDP growth turned negative and remained negative for the following two quarters.

Column (1) of Table 1 shows the size and the timing of the recession. It gives the change in GDP—in billions of 1992 dollars—for each quarter from the second quarter of 1990, going down the column, to the second quarter of 1991. In 1990:3, 1990:4, and 1991:1, the change in GDP is negative. This episode is known as the 1990 to 1991 recession.

■ Was the recession forecast by economists? The answer is no. Column (2) gives the **forecast error**, the difference between the actual value of GDP and the value of GDP forecast by economists one quarter earlier. A positive forecast error indicates that actual GDP turned out to be higher than was forecast; a negative forecast error indicates that actual GDP turned out to be lower than was forecast. As you can see, the forecast errors were negative during all three quarters of the 1990 to 1991 recession. They were larger than the actual fall in GDP in each of the first two quarters of the recession. What this means is that, at the beginning of each of these two quarters, the forecasts were for positive GDP growth, but growth actually turned out to be negative. For example, the forecast for 1990:4 was for an increase in GDP of $25 billion. The outcome, however, was actually a decrease in GDP of $63 billion. So the forecast error was equal to –$25 billion – $63 billion = –$88 billion.

■ Where did these forecast errors come from? In terms of equation (3.8), which of the determinants of spending was the main culprit? Was it c_0, or $\bar{I}$, or G, or T? Research that has looked at the evolution of each of the components of spending concludes that the main culprit, for the last two quarters of the recession, was an adverse shift in consumption—that is, an unexpected decrease in c_0. Forecast errors for c_0 are shown in column (3). There were two large negative

errors for the last two quarters of the recession, –$37 billion for 1990:4, and –$30 billion for 1991:1.

■ A large decrease in c_0 is a drop in consumption given disposable income. Why did consumption drop so much, given disposable income, in late 1990 and early 1991? The direct cause is shown in column (4) of the table, which shows the value of the **consumer confidence index**. This index is computed from a monthly survey of about 5,000 households. The survey asks consumers how confident they are about both current and future economic conditions, from job opportunities to their expected family income six months ahead. As you can see, there was a very large decrease in the index from the third to the fourth quarter of 1990—from 90 to 61. Consumers lost confidence and cut their consumption, which triggered the recession.

■ This brings us to the last question: Why did consumers lose confidence in late 1990? Why did they become more pessimistic about the future? Even today, economists are not sure. It is more than likely that this change in mood was related to the increasing probability of a war in the Middle East—a war that started in early 1991, after the beginning of the recession. People worried that the United States might get involved in a prolonged and costly war. They also worried that a war in the Middle East could lead to a large increase in oil prices and to a recession: The two previous large increases in oil prices in the 1970s had both been associated with recessions. Whatever the reason, the decrease in consumer confidence was a major factor behind the 1990 to 1991 recession.

Do not conclude that all recessions are caused by a drop in consumption. The recession in 2001 appears to have been caused instead by a drop in investment. We will look at that recession and its causes in more detail in Chapter 5.

Table 1	GDP, Consumption, and Forecast Errors, 1990–1991			
Quarter	(1) Change in Real GDP	(2) Forecast Error for GDP	(3) Forecast Error for c_0	(4) Index of Consumer Confidence
1990:2	19	–17	–23	105
1990:3	–29	–57	–1	90
1990:4	–63	–88	–37	61
1991:1	–31	–27	–30	65
1991:2	27	47	8	77

Columns (1) to (3) are in billions of 1992 dollars.

Source: Olivier Blanchard, "Consumption and the Recession of 1990–1991," *American Economic Review*, May 1993.

to 1991 recession in the United States was largely the result of a sudden drop in consumer confidence, leading to a sharp decrease in consumption, which led, in turn, to a sharp decline in output. The origins of the 1990 to 1991 recession are examined in the Focus box "Consumer Confidence and the 1990 to 1991 Recession."

3-4 Investment Equals Saving: An Alternative Way of Thinking About Goods-Market Equilibrium

Thus far, we have been thinking of equilibrium in the goods market in terms of the equality of the production and the demand for goods. An alternative—but equivalent—way of thinking about equilibrium focuses instead on investment and saving. This is how John Maynard Keynes first articulated this model in 1936, in *The General Theory of Employment, Interest and Money*.

Let's start by looking at saving. **Saving** is the sum of private saving and public saving:

Saving: Private saving + Public saving ▶

■ By definition, **private saving** (S), saving by consumers, is equal to their disposable income minus their consumption:

$$S \equiv Y_D - C$$

Using the definition of disposable income, we can rewrite private saving as income minus taxes minus consumption:

$$S \equiv Y - T - C$$

■ By definition, **public saving** is equal to taxes (net of transfers) minus government spending, $T - G$. If taxes exceed government spending, the government is running a

Public saving ⇔ Budget surplus ▶

budget surplus, so public saving is positive. If taxes are less than government spending, the government is running a **budget deficit**, so public saving is negative.

■ Now return to the equation for equilibrium in the goods market that we derived earlier. Production must be equal to demand, which in turn is the sum of consumption, investment, and government spending:

$$Y = C + I + G$$

Subtract taxes (T) from both sides and move consumption to the left side:

$$Y - T - C = I + G - T$$

The left side of this equation is simply private saving, *(S)*, so

$$S = I + G - T$$

Or, equivalently,

$$I = S + (T - G) \qquad (3.10)$$

■ On the left is investment. On the right is saving, the sum of *private saving* and *public saving*.

Equation (3.10) gives us another way of thinking about equilibrium in the goods market: It says that equilibrium in the goods market requires that investment equal saving—the sum of private and public saving. This way of looking at equilibrium explains why the equilibrium condition for the goods market is called the *IS relation*, which stands for "investment equals saving": What firms want to invest must be equal to what people and the government want to save.

To understand equation (3.10), imagine an economy with only one person who has to decide how much to consume, invest, and save—a "Robinson Crusoe" economy, for example. For Robinson Crusoe, the saving and the investment decisions are one and the same: What he invests (say, by keeping rabbits for breeding rather than having them for dinner), he automatically saves. In a modern economy, however, investment decisions are made by firms, whereas saving decisions are made by consumers and the government. In equilibrium, equation (3.10) tells us all these decisions have to be consistent: Investment must equal saving.

To summarize: There are two equivalent ways of stating the condition for equilibrium in the goods market:

$$\text{Production} = \text{Demand}$$
$$\text{Investment} = \text{Saving}$$

Earlier, we characterized the equilibrium using the first condition, equation (3.6). We now do the same using the second condition, equation (3.10). The results will be the same, but the derivation will give you another way of thinking about the equilibrium:

Note first that *consumption and saving decisions are one and the same*. Given their disposable income, once consumers have chosen consumption, their saving is determined, and vice versa. The way we specified consumption behavior implies that private saving is given by

$$S = Y - T - C$$
$$= Y - T - c_0 - c_1(Y - T)$$

Rearranging, we get

$$S = -c_0 + (1 - c_1)(Y - T) \tag{3.11}$$

In the same way that we called c_1 the propensity to consume, we can call $(1 - c_1)$ the **propensity to save**. The propensity to save tells us how much of an additional unit of income people save. The assumption we made earlier—that the propensity to consume (c_1), is between zero and one implies that the propensity to save $(1 - c_1)$, is also between zero and one. Private saving increases with disposable income, but by less than one dollar for each additional dollar of disposable income.

In equilibrium, investment must be equal to saving, the sum of private and public saving. Replacing private saving in equation (3.10) by its expression from above,

$$I = -c_0 + (1 - c_1)(Y - T) + (T - G)$$

Solving for output,

$$Y = \frac{1}{1 - c_1}[c_0 + I + G - c_1 T] \tag{3.12}$$

Equation (3.12) is exactly the same as equation (3.8). This should come as no surprise. We are looking at the same equilibrium condition, just in a different way. This alternative way will prove useful in various applications later in the book. The Focus box looks at such an application, which was first emphasized by Keynes and is often called the *paradox of saving*.

The Paradox of Saving

As we grow up, we are told about the virtues of thrift. Those who spend all their income are condemned to end up poor. Those who save are promised a happy life. Similarly, governments tell us, an economy that saves is an economy that will grow strong and prosper. The model we have seen in this chapter, however, tells a different and surprising story.

Suppose that, at a given level of disposable income, consumers decide to save more. In other words, suppose consumers decrease c_0, therefore decreasing consumption and increasing saving at a given level of disposable income. What happens to output and to saving?

Equation (3.12) makes it clear that equilibrium output decreases: As people save more at their initial level of income, they decrease their consumption. But this decreased consumption decreases demand, which decreases production.

Can we tell what happens to saving? Let's return to the equation for private saving, equation (3.11) (recall that we assume no change in public saving, so saving and private saving move together):

$$S = -c_0 + (1 - c_1)(Y - T)$$

On the one hand, $-c_0$ is higher (less negative): Consumers are saving more at any level of income; this tends to increase saving. On the other hand, their income, Y, is lower: This decreases saving. The net effect would seem to be ambiguous. In fact, we can tell which way it goes.

To see how, go back to equation (3.10), the equilibrium condition that investment and saving must be equal:

$$I = S + (T - G)$$

By assumption, investment does not change: $I = \bar{I}$. Nor do T or G. So the equilibrium condition tells us that in equilibrium, private saving, S, cannot change either. Although people want to save more at a given level of income, their income decreases by an amount such that their saving is unchanged.

This means that as people attempt to save more, the result is both a decline in output and unchanged saving. This surprising pair of results is known as the **paradox of saving** (or the paradox of thrift).

So should you forget the old wisdom? Should the government tell people to be less thrifty? No. The results of this simple model are of much relevance in the short run. The desire of consumers to save more led to the 1990 to 1991 recession (as we saw in the Focus box earlier in this chapter). But, as we will see later in this book when we look at the medium run and the long run, other mechanisms come into play over time, and an increase in the saving rate is likely to lead over time to higher saving and higher income. A warning remains, however: Policies that encourage saving might be good in the medium run and in the long run, but they can lead to a recession in the short run.

3-5 Is the Government Omnipotent? A Warning

Equation (3.8) implies that the government, by choosing the level of spending, G, or the level of taxes, T, can choose the level of output it wants. If it wants output to be higher by, say, $1 billion, all it needs to do is to increase G by $(1 - c_1)$ billion; this increase in government spending, in theory, will lead to an output increase of $(1 - c_1)$ billion multiplied by $1/(1 - c_1)$, or $1 billion.

For a glimpse at the longer list, go to the Focus box "Fiscal Policy: What You Have Learned and Where" in Chapter 26.

Can governments really choose the level of output they want? Obviously not. There are many aspects of reality that we have not yet incorporated into our model, and all these complicate the government's task. We shall incorporate them in due time. But it is useful to list them briefly here:

- Changing government spending or taxes is not always easy. Getting the U.S. Congress to pass bills always takes time and often becomes a president's nightmare (Chapters 24 and 26).
- We have assumed that investment remained constant. But investment is also likely to respond. And so are imports: Some of the increased demand by consumers and firms will not be for domestic goods but for foreign goods. All these responses are likely to associated with complex, dynamic effects, making it hard for governments to assess them with much certainty (Chapters 5, 18, and 19).

- Anticipations are likely to matter. For example, the reaction of consumers to a tax cut is likely to depend very much on whether they think of the tax cut as transitory or permanent. The more they perceive the tax cut as permanent, the larger will be their consumption response (Chapters 16 and 17).
- Achieving a given level of output can come with unpleasant side effects. Trying to achieve too high a level of output can, for example, lead to increasing inflation and, for that reason, be unsustainable in the medium run (Chapters 7 and 8).
- Cutting taxes or increasing government spending can lead to large budget deficits and an accumulation of public debt. A large debt can have adverse effects in the long run. This is a hot issue in the United States today because the tax cuts implemented by the Bush administration, together with increased spending for the war in Iraq, have led to large deficits and to increasing public debt (Chapters 11 and 26).

In short, the proposition that, by using fiscal policy, the government can affect demand and output in the short run is an important and correct one. But, as we refine our analysis, we will see that the role of the government in general, and the successful use of fiscal policy in particular, become increasingly difficult: Governments will never again have it so good as they had it in this chapter.

Summary

Here's what you should remember about the components of GDP:

- GDP is the sum of consumption, investment, government spending, inventory investment, and exports minus imports.
- Consumption (C) is the purchase of goods and services by consumers. Consumption is the largest component of demand.
- Investment (I) is the sum of nonresidential investment—the purchase of new plants and new machines by firms—and of residential investment—the purchase of new houses or apartments by people.
- Government spending (G) is the purchase of goods and services by federal, state, and local governments.
- Exports (X) are purchases of U.S. goods by foreigners. Imports (IM) are purchases of foreign goods by U.S. consumers, U.S. firms, and the U.S. government.
- Inventory investment is the difference between production and sales. It can be positive or negative.

Here's what you should remember about our first model of output determination:

- In the short run, demand determines production. Production is equal to income. Income in turn affects demand.
- The consumption function shows how consumption depends on disposable income. The propensity to consume describes how much consumption increases for a given increase in disposable income.
- Equilibrium output is the level of output at which production equals demand. In equilibrium, output equals autonomous spending times the multiplier. Autonomous spending is the part of demand that does not depend on income. The multiplier is equal to $1/(1 - c_1)$, where c_1 is the propensity to consume.
- Increases in consumer confidence, investment demand, and government spending, as well as decreases in taxes all increase equilibrium output in the short run.
- An alternative way of stating the goods market equilibrium condition is that investment must be equal to saving—the sum of private and public saving. For this reason, the equilibrium condition is called the IS relation (I for investment, S for saving).

Key Terms

- consumption (C), 66
- investment (I), 66
- fixed investment, 66
- nonresidential investment, 66
- residential investment, 66
- government spending (G), 66
- government transfers, 66
- imports (IM), 67
- exports (X), 67
- net exports (X–IM), 67
- trade balance, 67
- trade surplus, 67

Questions and Problems

Quick Check

1. Using the information in this chapter, label each of the following statements true, false, or uncertain. Explain briefly.

a. The largest component of GDP is consumption.

b. Government spending, including transfers, was equal to 19% of GDP in 2006.

c. The propensity to consume has to be positive, but otherwise it can take on any positive value.

d. *Fiscal policy* describes the choice of government spending and taxes and is treated as exogenous in our goods market model.

e. The equilibrium condition for the goods market states that consumption equals output.

f. An increase of one unit in government spending leads to an increase of one unit in equilibrium output.

g. An increase in the propensity to consume leads to a decrease in output.

2. Suppose that the economy is characterized by the following behavioral equations:

$$C = 180 + 0.8Y_D$$

$$I = 160$$

$$G = 160$$

$$T = 120$$

Solve for the following variables.

a. Equilibrium GDP (Y)

b. Disposable income (Y_D)

c. Consumption spending (C)

3. Use the economy described in problem 2.

a. Solve for equilibrium output. Compute total demand. Is it equal to production? Explain.

b. Assume that G is now equal to 136. Solve for equilibrium output. Compute total demand. Is it equal to production? Explain.

c. Assume that G is equal to 136, so output is given by your answer to (b). Compute private plus public saving. Is the sum of private and public saving equal to investment? Explain.

Dig Deeper

4. The balanced budget multiplier

For both political and macroeconomic reasons, governments are often reluctant to run budget deficits. Here, we examine whether policy changes in G and T that maintain a balanced budget are macroeconomically neutral. Put another way, we examine whether it is possible to affect output through changes in G and T so that the government budget remains balanced.

Start from equation (3.8).

a. By how much does Y increase when G increases by one unit?

b. By how much does Y decrease when T increases by one unit?

c. Why are your answers to (a) and (b) different?

Suppose that the economy starts with a balanced budget: G = T. If the increase in G is equal to the increase in T, then the budget remains in balance. Let us now compute the balanced budget multiplier.

d. Suppose that G and T increase by one unit each. Using your answers to (a) and (b), what is the change in equilibrium GDP? Are balanced budget changes in G and T macroeconomically neutral?

e. How does the specific value of the propensity to consume affect your answer to (a)? Why?

5. Automatic stabilizers

So far in this chapter, we have assumed that the fiscal policy variables G and T are independent of the level of income. In the real world, however, this is not the case. Taxes typically depend on the level of income and so tend to be higher when income is higher. In this problem, we examine how this automatic response of taxes can help reduce the impact of changes in autonomous spending on output.

Consider the following behavioral equations:

$$C = c_0 + c_1 Y_D$$
$$T = t_0 + t_1 Y$$
$$Y_D = Y - T$$

G and I are both constant. Assume that t_1 is between 0 and 1.

a. Solve for equilibrium output.
b. What is the multiplier? Does the economy respond more to changes in autonomous spending when t_1 is 0 or when t_1 is positive? Explain.
c. Why is fiscal policy in this case called an automatic stabilizer?

6. Balanced budget versus automatic stabilizers

It is often argued that a balanced budget amendment would actually be destabilizing. To understand this argument, consider the economy of problem 5.

a. Solve for equilibrium output.
b. Solve for taxes in equilibrium.

Suppose that the government starts with a balanced budget and that there is a drop in c_0.

c. What happens to Y? What happens to taxes?
d. Suppose that the government cuts spending in order to keep the budget balanced. What will be the effect on Y? Does the cut in spending required to balance the budget counteract or reinforce the effect of the drop in c_0 on output? (Don't do the algebra. Use your intuition and give the answer in words.)

7. Investment and income

This problem examines the implications of allowing investment to depend on output. Chapter 5 carries this analysis much further and introduces an essential relation—the effect of the interest rate on investment—not examined in this problem.

a. Suppose the economy is characterized by the following behavioral equations:

$$C = c_0 + c_1 Y_D$$

$$Y_D = Y - T$$

$$I = b_0 + b_1 Y$$

Government spending and taxes are constant. Note that investment now increases with output. (Chapter 5 discusses the reasons for this relation.) Solve for equilibrium output.
b. What is the value of the multiplier? How does the relation between investment and output affect the value of the multiplier? For the multiplier to be positive, what condition must $(c_1 + b_1)$ satisfy? Explain your answers.
c. Suppose that the parameter b_0, sometimes called business confidence, increases. How will equilibrium output be affected? Will investment change by more or less than the change in b_0? Why? What will happen to national saving?

8. Taxes and transfers

Recall that we define taxes, T, as net of transfers. In other words,

$$T = Taxes - Transfer\ payments$$

a. Suppose that the government increases transfer payments to private households, but these transfer payments are not financed by tax increases. Instead, the government borrows to pay for the transfer payments. Show in a diagram (similar to Figure 3-2) how this policy affects equilibrium output. Explain.
b. Suppose instead that the government pays for the increase in transfer payments with an equivalent increase in taxes. How does the increase in transfer payments affect equilibrium output in this case?
c. Now suppose that the population includes two kinds of people: those with high propensity to consume and those with low propensity to consume. Suppose the transfer policy increases taxes on those with low propensity to consume to pay for transfers to people with high propensity to consume. How does this policy affect equilibrium output?
d. How do you think the propensity to consume might vary across individuals according to income? In other words, how do you think the propensity to consume compares for people with high income and people with low income? Explain. Given your answer, do you think tax cuts will be more effective at stimulating output when they are directed toward high-income or toward low-income taxpayers?

Explore Further

9. The paradox of saving revisited

You should be able to complete this question without doing any algebra, although you may find making a diagram helpful for part (a). For this problem, you do not need to calculate the magnitudes of changes in economic variables—only the direction of change.

a. Consider the economy described in problem 8. Suppose that consumers decide to consume less (and therefore to save more) for any given amount of disposable income. Specifically, assume that consumer confidence (c_0) falls. What will happen to output?
b. As a result of the effect on output you determined in part (a), what will happen to investment? What will happen to public saving? What will happen to private saving? Explain. (Hint: Consider the saving-equals-investment characterization of equilibrium.) What is the effect on consumption?
c. Suppose that consumers had decided to increase consumption expenditure, so that c_0 had increased. What would have been the effect on output, investment, and private saving in this case? Explain. What would have been the effect on consumption?

d. Comment on the following logic: "When output is too low, what is needed is an increase in demand for goods and services. Investment is one component of demand, and saving equals investment. Therefore, if the government could just convince households to attempt to save more then investment, and output, would increase. *Output is not the only variable that affects investment. As we develop our model of the economy, we will revisit the paradox of saving in future chapter problems.*

10. Consumer confidence

A box in the text makes reference to the consumer confidence index. Go to the Web site of The Conference Board (www.conference-board.org) and download the latest release of the consumer confidence index. Typically The Conference Board makes the latest release available for free. Ignoring any other factors, do the confidence data suggest higher-than-normal or lower-than-normal output in the near future? Explain.

 We invite you to visit the Blanchard page on the Prentice Hall Web site, at:
www.prenhall.com/blanchard
for this chapter's World Wide Web exercises.

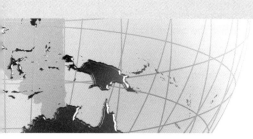

CHAPTER 4

Barely a day goes by without the media speculating whether the Fed (short for Federal Reserve Bank, the U.S central bank) is going to change the interest rate and what the change is likely to do to the economy. Alan Greenspan, the chairman of the Fed from 1987 to 2006, was widely perceived as the most powerful policymaker in the United States, if not in the world (the cartoon below nicely makes the point). His successor, Ben Bernanke, is steadily establishing a similar reputation.

The model of economic activity we developed in Chapter 3 did not include the interest rate, so there was no role for Alan Greenspan or Ben Bernanke there. That was a strong simplification, and it is now time to relax it. This requires that we take two steps:

First, we must look at what determines the interest rate and how the Fed can affect it—the topic of this chapter. Second, we must look at how the interest rate affects demand and output—the topic of the next chapter.

This chapter has four sections:

■ Section 4-1 looks at the demand for money.

■ Section 4-2 assumes that the central bank directly controls the supply of money and shows how the interest rate is determined by the condition that the demand for money be equal to its supply.

■ Section 4-3, an optional section, introduces banks as suppliers of money, revisits interest rates and how they are determined, and describes the role of the central bank in this process.

■ Section 4-4, also an optional section, presents two alternative ways of looking at the equilibrium. One focuses on the federal funds market. The other focuses on the money multiplier. ■

4-1 The Demand for Money

This section looks at the determinants of *the demand for money*. A warning before we start: Words such as *money* or *wealth* have very specific meanings in economics, often not the same meanings as in everyday conversations. The purpose of the Focus box "Semantic Traps: Money, Income, and Wealth" is to help you avoid some of these traps. Read it carefully and come back to it once in a while.

Suppose, as a result of having steadily saved part of your income in the past, your financial wealth today is $50,000. You may intend to keep saving in the future and increase your wealth further, but its value today is given. Suppose also that you only have the choice between two assets, money and bonds:

▶ Make sure you see the difference between the decision about how much to save (a decision that determines how wealth changes over time) and the decision about how to allocate a given stock of wealth between money and bonds.

■ **Money**, which you can use for transactions, pays no interest. In the real world, there are two types of money: **currency**, coins and bills, and **checkable deposits**, the bank deposits on which you can write checks. The distinction between the two will be important when we look at the supply of money. For the moment, however, the distinction does not matter, and we can ignore it.

▶ We will abandon this assumption and look at a larger menu of interest rates when we focus on the role of expectations, beginning in Chapter 14.

■ **Bonds** pay a positive interest rate, i, but they cannot be used for transactions. In the real world, there are many types of bonds, each associated with a specific interest rate. For the time being, we will also ignore this aspect of reality and assume that there is just one type of bond and that it pays, i, the rate of interest.

Assume that buying or selling bonds implies some cost—for example, a phone call to broker and the payment of a transaction fee. How much of your $50,000 should you hold in money and how much in bonds? On the one hand, holding all your wealth in the form of money is clearly very convenient. You won't ever need to call a broker or pay transaction fees. But it also means you will receive no interest income. On the other hand, if you hold all your wealth in the form of bonds, you will earn interest on the full amount, but you will have to call your broker frequently—whenever you need money to take the subway, pay for a cup of coffee, and so on. This is a rather inconvenient way of going through life.

Therefore, it is clear that you should hold both money and bonds. But in what proportions? This depends mainly on two variables:

■ Your *level of transactions*—You'll want to have enough money on hand to avoid having to sell bonds too often. Say, for example, that you typically spend $3,000 per month. In this case, you might want to have, on average, say, two months' worth of spending on hand, or $6,000 in money, and the rest, $50,000 − $6,000 = $44,000 in bonds. If, instead, you typically spend $4,000 per month, you might want to have, say, $8,000 in money and only $42,000 in bonds.

In everyday conversation, we use money to denote many different things. We use it as a synonym for income: "making money." We use it as a synonym for wealth: "She has a lot of money." In economics, you must be more careful. Here is a basic guide to some terms and their precise meanings in economics.

Income is what you earn from working plus what you receive in interest and dividends. It is a **flow**—something expressed in units of time: weekly income, monthly income, or yearly income, for example. J. Paul Getty was once asked what his income was. Getty answered: "$1,000." He meant, but did not say, $1,000 per minute!

Saving is the part of after-tax income that you do not spend. It is also a flow. If you save 10% of your income, and your income is $3,000 per month, then you save $300 per month. **Savings** (plural) is sometimes used as a synonym for wealth—the value of what you have accumulated over time. To avoid confusion, I will not use *savings* in this book.

Your **financial wealth,** or simply **wealth,** is the value of all your financial assets minus all your financial liabilities. In contrast to income or saving, which are flow variables, financial wealth is a **stock** variable. It is the value of wealth at a given moment in time.

At a given moment in time, you cannot change the total amount of your financial wealth. You can change it only over time as you save or dissave, or as the values of your assets and liabilities change. But you can change the composition of your wealth; you can, for example, decide to pay back part of your mortgage by writing a check against your checking account. This leads to a decrease in your liabilities (a smaller mortgage) and a corresponding decrease in your assets (a smaller checking account balance); but, at that moment, it does not change your wealth.

Financial assets that can be used directly to buy goods are called *money*. Money includes currency and checkable deposits—deposits against which you can write checks. Money is also a stock. Someone who is wealthy might have only small money holdings—say, $1,000,000 in stocks but only $500 in a checking account. It is also possible for a person to have a large income but only small money holdings—say, an income of $10,000 monthly but only $1,000 on his checking account.

Investment is a term economists reserve for the purchase of new capital goods, from machines to plants to office buildings. When you want to talk about the purchase of shares or other financial assets, you should refer them as a financial investment.

Learn how to be economically correct:

Do not say "Mary is making a lot of money"; say "Mary has a high income."
Do not say "Joe has a lot of money"; say "Joe is very wealthy."

■ The *interest rate on bonds*—The only reason to hold any of your wealth in bonds is that they pay interest. If bonds paid zero interest, you would want to hold all your wealth in the form of money because it's more convenient.

The higher the interest rate, the more you will be willing to deal with the hassle and the costs associated with buying and selling bonds. If the interest rate is very high, you might even decide to squeeze your money holdings to an average of only two weeks' worth of spending, or $1,500 (assuming that your monthly spending is $3,000). This way, you will be able to keep, on average, $48,500 in bonds and earn more interest as a result.

Let's make this last point more concrete. Many of you probably do not hold bonds; few of you have a broker. However, many of you likely do hold bonds indirectly if you have a money market account with a financial institution. **Money market funds** (the full name is *money market mutual funds*) pool together the funds of many people. The funds are then used to buy bonds—typically government bonds. Money market funds pay an interest rate close to but slightly below the interest rate on the bonds they hold—the difference coming from the administrative costs of running the funds and from their profit margins.

When the interest rate on these funds reached 14% per year in the early 1980s (a very high interest rate by today's standards), many people who had previously kept their wealth in their checking accounts (which paid little or no interest) realized how much interest they could earn by moving some of it into money market accounts instead. As a result, accounts like these became very popular. Since then, however, interest rates have fallen. In 2006, the average interest rate paid by money market funds was only 4.7%. This is better than zero—the rate paid on many checking accounts—but is much less attractive than the rate in the early 1980s. As a result, people are now less careful about putting as much as they can in their money market funds. Put another way, for a given level of transactions, people now keep more of their wealth in money than they did in the early 1980s.

Deriving the Demand for Money

Let's go from this discussion to an equation describing the demand for money.

Denote the amount of money people want to hold—their *demand for money*—by M^d. (The superscript d stands for *demand*.) The demand for money in the economy as a whole is just the sum of all the individual demands for money by the people in the economy. Therefore, it depends on the overall level of transactions in the economy and on the interest rate. The overall level of transactions in the economy is hard to measure, but it is likely to be roughly proportional to nominal income (income measured in dollars). If nominal income were to increase by 10%, it is reasonable to think that the dollar value of transactions in the economy would also increase by roughly 10%. We can write the relation between the demand for money, nominal income, and the interest rate as

▶

$$M^d = \$Y \, L(i)$$
$$(-)$$
(4.1)

where $\$Y$ denotes nominal income. Read this equation in the following way: *The demand for money, M^d, is equal to nominal income, $\$Y$, times a function of the interest rate, i, with the function denoted by $L(i)$.* The minus sign under i in $L(i)$ captures the fact that the interest rate has a negative effect on money demand: An increase in the interest rate *decreases* the demand for money, as people put more of their wealth into bonds.

Equation (4.1) summarizes what we have discussed so far:

- First, the demand for money increases in proportion to nominal income. If nominal income doubles, increasing from $\$Y$ to $\$2Y$, then the demand for money also doubles, increasing from $\$Y L(i)$ to $2 \$Y L(i)$.
- Second, the demand for money depends negatively on the interest rate. This is captured by the function $L(i)$ and the negative sign underneath: An increase in the interest rate decreases the demand for money.

The relation between the demand for money, nominal income, and the interest rate implied by equation (4.1) is shown in Figure 4-1. The interest rate, i, is measured on the vertical axis. Money, M, is measured on the horizontal axis.

The relation between the demand for money and the interest rate *for a given level of nominal income, $\$Y$,* is represented by the M^d curve. The curve is downward sloping: The lower the interest rate (the lower i), the higher the amount of money people want to hold (the higher M).

For a given interest rate, an increase in nominal income increases the demand for money. In other words, an increase in nominal income shifts the demand for money to the right, from M^d to $M^{d'}$. For example, at interest rate i, an increase in nominal income from $\$Y$ to $\$Y'$ increases the demand for money from M to M'.

Revisit Chapter 2's example of an economy composed of a steel company and a car company. Calculate the total value of transactions in that economy. If the steel and the car companies doubled in size, what would happen to transactions and to GDP?

What matters here is nominal income—income in dollars, not real income. If real income does not change but prices double, leading to a doubling of nominal income, people will need to hold twice as much money to buy the same consumption basket.

Who Holds U.S. Currency?

According to household surveys, in 2006, the average U.S. household held $1,600 in currency (dollar bills and coins). Multiplying by the number of households in the U.S. economy (about 110 million), this implies that the total amount of currency held by U.S. households was around $170 billion.

According to the Federal Reserve Board, however—which issues the dollar bills and therefore knows how much is in circulation, the amount of currency in circulation was actually much higher, $750 billion. Here lies the puzzle: If it was not held by households, where was all this currency?

Clearly some currency was held by firms rather than by households. And some was held by those involved in the underground economy or in illegal activities. When dealing with drugs, dollar bills, not checks, are the way to settle accounts. Surveys of firms and IRS estimates of the underground economy suggest, however, that this can only account for another $80 billion at the most. This leaves $500 billion, or 66% of the total, unaccounted for. So where was it? The answer: abroad, held by foreigners:

A couple of countries, Ecuador and El Salvador, have actually adopted the dollar as their own currency. So people in those countries use dollar bills for transactions. But these two countries are just too small to explain the puzzle.

So where are all these dollar bills? In a number of countries that have suffered from high inflation in the past, people have learned that their domestic currency may quickly become worthless, and they see dollars as a safe and convenient asset. This is the case, for example, in Argentina and Russia. Estimates by the U.S. Treasury suggest that Argentina holds more than $50 billion in dollar bills, Russia more than $80 billion—so together they have more than the holdings of U.S. households.

In yet other countries, people who have emigrated to the United States bring home U.S. dollar bills; or tourists pay some transactions in dollars, and the bills stay in that country. This is the case, for example, in Mexico and Thailand.

The fact that foreigners hold such a high proportion of the dollar bills in circulation has two main macroeconomic implications. First, the rest of the world, by being willing to hold U.S. currency, is making in effect an interest-free loan to the United States of $500 billion. Second, while we shall think of money demand (which includes both currency and checkable deposits) as being determined by the interest rate and the level of transactions in the country, it is clear that U.S. money demand also depends on other factors. Can you guess, for example, what would happen to U.S. money demand if the degree of civil unrest increased in the rest of the world?

FOCUS

Figure 4-1

The Demand for Money

For a given level of nominal income, a lower interest rate increases the demand for money. At a given interest rate, an increase in nominal income shifts the demand for money to the right.

M^d (for nominal income $\$Y$)

$M^{d\prime}$ (for $\$Y\prime > \$Y$)

Interest rate, i

i

M $M\prime$

Money, M

Having looked at the demand for money, we now look at the supply of money and then at the equilibrium.

In the real world, there are two types of money: checkable deposits, which are supplied by banks, and currency, which is supplied by the central bank. In this section, we will assume that checkable deposits do not exist—that the only money in the economy is currency. In the next section, we will reintroduce checkable deposits and look at the role banks play. Introducing banks makes the discussion more realistic, but it also makes the mechanics of money supply more complicated. It is better to build up the discussion in two steps.

Money Demand, Money Supply, and the Equilibrium Interest Rate

Suppose the central bank decides to supply an amount of money equal to M, so

$$M^s = M$$

> **Throughout this section, "money" stands for "central bank money," or "currency."** ▶

The superscript s stands for *supply*. (Let's disregard, for the moment, the issue of how exactly the central bank supplies this amount of money. We shall return to it in a few paragraphs.)

Equilibrium in financial markets requires that money supply be equal to money demand, that $M^s = M^d$. Then, using $M^s = M$ and equation (4.1) for money demand, the equilibrium condition is

$$\text{Money supply} = \text{Money demand}$$

$$M = \$Y\, L(i) \tag{4.2}$$

This equation tells us that the interest rate, i, must be such that, given their income, $\$Y$, people are willing to hold an amount of money equal to the existing money supply, M.

> **As for the IS relation, the name of the LM relation is more than 50 years old. The letter L stands for *liquidity*: Economists use liquidity as a measure of how easily an asset can be exchanged for money. Money is *fully liquid*; other assets less so. We can think of the demand for money as a demand for liquidity. The letter M stands for *money*. The demand for liquidity must equal the supply of money.** ▶

This equilibrium relation is called the **LM relation**.

This equilibrium condition is represented graphically in Figure 4-2. As in Figure 4-1, money is measured on the horizontal axis, and the interest rate is measured on the vertical axis. The demand for money, M^d, drawn for a given level of nominal income, $\$Y$, is downward sloping: A higher interest rate implies a lower demand for money. The supply of money is drawn as the vertical line denoted M^s: The money supply equals M and is independent of the interest rate. Equilibrium occurs at point A, and the equilibrium interest rate is given by i.

Now that we have characterized the equilibrium, we can look at how changes in nominal income or changes in the money supply by the central bank affect the equilibrium interest rate:

■ Figure 4-3 shows the effects of an increase in nominal income on the interest rate.

Figure 4-3 replicates Figure 4-2, and the initial equilibrium is at point A. An increase in nominal income from $\$Y$ to $\$Y'$ increases the level of transactions, which increases the demand for money at any interest rate. The money demand curve *shifts* to the right, from M^d to $M^{d'}$. The equilibrium moves from A up to A', and the equilibrium interest rate increases from i to i'.

In words: *An increase in nominal income leads to an increase in the interest rate.* The reason: At the initial interest rate, the demand for money exceeds the supply. An increase in the interest rate is needed to decrease the amount of money people want to hold and to reestablish equilibrium.

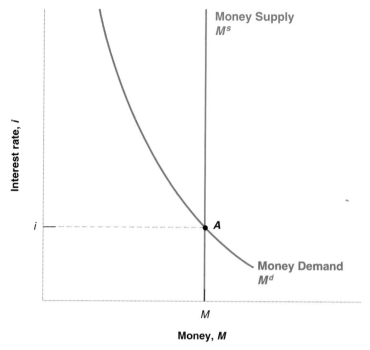

Figure 4-2

The Determination of the Interest Rate

The interest rate must be such that the supply of money (which is independent of the interest rate) is equal to the demand for money (which does depend on the interest rate).

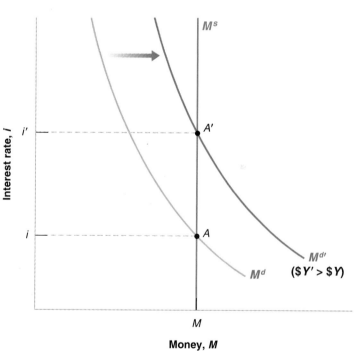

Figure 4-3

The Effects of an Increase in Nominal Income on the Interest Rate

An increase in nominal income leads to an increase in the interest rate.

■ Figure 4-4 shows the effects of an increase in the money supply on the interest rate.
   The initial equilibrium is at point A, with interest rate, i. An increase in the money supply, from $M^s = M$ to $M^{s\prime} = M\prime$, leads to a shift of the money supply curve to the right, from M^s to $M^{s\prime}$. The equilibrium moves from A down to $A\prime$; the interest rate decreases from i to $i\prime$.

***The Effects of an Increase
in the Money Supply on
the Interest Rate***

An increase in the supply of
money leads to a decrease in
the interest rate.

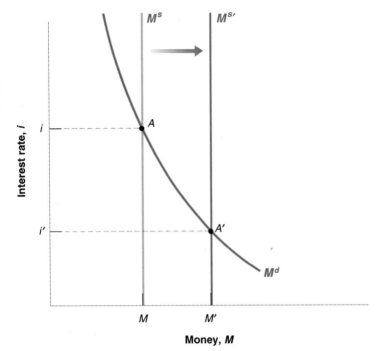

In words: *An increase in the supply of money by the central bank leads to a decrease in the interest rate.* The decrease in the interest rate increases the demand for money, so it equals the now larger money supply.

Monetary Policy and Open Market Operations

We can get a better understanding of the results in Figures 4-3 and 4-4 by looking more closely at how the central bank actually changes the money supply and what happens when it does so.

Open Market Operations

In modern economies, the way central banks change the supply of money is by buying or selling bonds in the bond market. If a central bank wants to increase the amount of money in the economy, it buys bonds and pays for them by creating money. If it wants to decrease the amount of money in the economy, it sells bonds and removes from circulation the money it receives in exchange for the bonds. These actions are called **open market operations** because they take place in the "open market" for bonds.

> The balance sheet of a bank (or a firm, or an individual) is a list of its assets and liabilities at a point in time. The assets are the sum of what the bank owns and what is owed to it by others. The liabilities are what the bank owes to others.

The balance sheet of the central bank is given in Figure 4-5. The assets of the central bank are the bonds it holds in its portfolio. Its liabilities are the stock of money in the economy. Open market operations lead to equal changes in assets and liabilities.

If the central bank buys, say, $1 million worth of bonds, the amount of bonds it holds is higher by $1 million, and so is the amount of money in the economy. Such an operation is called an **expansionary open market operation** because the central bank increases (*expands*) the supply of money.

If the central bank sells $1 million worth of bonds, both the amount of bonds held by the central bank and the amount of money in the economy are lower by $1 million. Such an operation is called a **contractionary open market operation** because the central bank decreases (*contracts*) the supply of money.

Figure 4-5 ▨

(a)

Balance Sheet

Assets	Liabilities
Bonds	Money (currency)

(b)

The Effects of an Expansionary Open-Market Operation

Assets	Liabilities
Change in bond holdings: +$1 million	Change in money stock: +$1 million

The Balance Sheet of the Central Bank and the Effects of an Expansionary Open Market Operation

The assets of the central bank are the bonds it holds. The liabilities are the stock of money in the economy. An open market operation in which the central bank buys bonds and issues money increases both assets and liabilities by the same amount.

Bond Prices and Bond Yields

We have focused so far on the interest rate on bonds. In fact, what is determined in bond markets is not interest rates but bond *prices*; the interest rate on a bond can then be inferred from the price of the bond. Understanding this relation between the interest rate and bond prices will prove useful both here and later in this book:

■ Suppose the bonds in our economy are one-year bonds—bonds that promise a payment of a given number of dollars, say $100, one year from now. In the United States, bonds issued by the government promising payment in a year or less are called **Treasury bills**, or **T-bills**. Let the price of a bond today be $\$P_B$, where the subscript B stands for *bond*. If you buy the bond today and hold it for a year, the rate of return on holding the bond for a year is $(\$100 - \$P_B)/\$P_B$. Therefore, the interest rate on the bond is given by

▸ *The interest rate is what you get for the bond a year from now ($100) minus what you pay for the bond today ($\$P_B$), divided by the price of the bond today ($\$P_B$).*

$$i = \frac{\$100 - \$P_B}{\$P_B}$$

If $\$P_B$ is $95, the interest rate equals $5/$95 = 0.053, or 5.3% per year. If $\$P_B$ is $90, the interest rate is 11.1% per year. *The higher the price of the bond, the lower the interest rate.*

■ If we are given the interest rate, we can figure out the price of the bond using the same formula. Reorganizing the formula above, the price today of a one-year bond paying $100 a year from today is given by

$$\$P_B = \frac{\$100}{1 + i}$$

The price of the bond today is equal to the final payment divided by 1 plus the interest rate. If the interest rate is positive, the price of the bond is less than the final payment. The higher the interest rate, the lower the price today. When newspapers write that "bond markets went up today," they mean that *the prices of* ◂ *bonds went up* and therefore that *interest rates went down.*

▸ *In Japan today, the one-year interest rate is (nearly) equal to zero. If a one-year Japanese government bond promises 100 yen in one year, for what price will it sell today?*

We are now ready to return to the effects of an open market operation.

Consider first an expansionary open market operation, in which the central bank buys bonds in the bond market and pays for them by creating money. As the central bank buys bonds, the demand for bonds goes up, increasing their price. Conversely, the interest rate on bonds goes down.

Consider instead a contractionary open market operation, in which the central bank decreases the supply of money. It sells bonds in the bond market. This leads to a decrease in their price and an increase in the interest rate.

Let's summarize what we have learned so far in this chapter:

- The interest rate is determined by the equality of the supply of money and the demand for money.
- By changing the supply of money, the central bank can affect the interest rate.
- The central bank changes the supply of money through open market operations, which are purchases or sales of bonds for money.
- Open market operations in which the central bank increases the money supply by buying bonds lead to an increase in the price of bonds and a decrease in the interest rate.
- Open market operations in which the central bank decreases the money supply by selling bonds lead to a decrease in the price of bonds and an increase in the interest rate.

Let me take up two more issues before moving on.

Choosing Money or Choosing the Interest Rate?

I have described the central bank as choosing the money supply and letting the interest rate be determined at the point where money supply equals money demand. Instead, I could have described the central bank as choosing the interest rate and then adjusting the money supply so as to achieve that interest rate.

To see this, return to Figure 4-4. Figure 4-4 shows the effect of a decision by the central bank to increase the money supply from M^s to $M^{s'}$, causing the interest rate to fall from i to i'. However, I could have described the figure in terms of the central bank's decision to lower the interest rate from i to i' by increasing the money supply from M^s to $M^{s'}$.

Suppose nominal income increases, as in Figure 4-3, and that the central bank ▶ wants to keep the interest rate unchanged. How does it need to adjust the money supply?

Why is it useful to think about the central bank as choosing the interest rate? Because this is what modern central banks, including the Fed, typically do. They typically think about the interest rate they want to achieve and then move the money supply so as to achieve it. This is why, when you listen to the news, you do not hear: "The Fed decided to increase the money supply today." Instead you hear: "The Fed decided to decrease the interest rate today." The way the Fed did it was by increasing the money supply appropriately.

Money, Bonds, and Other Assets

We have been looking at an economy with only two assets: money and bonds. This is obviously a much simplified version of actual economies, with their many financial assets and many financial markets. But, as you will see in later chapters, the basic lessons we have just learned apply very generally. The only change we will have to make is to replace "interest rate" in our conclusions with "short-term interest rate." You will see that the short-term interest rate is determined by the condition we just discussed—the equilibrium between money supply and money demand. The central bank can, through open market operations, change the short-term interest rate; and open market operations are indeed the basic tool used by most modern central banks, including the Fed, to affect interest rates.

The complication: The short-term interest rate—the rate directly controlled by the Fed—is not the only interest rate that affects spending. The determination of other interest rates and asset prices (such as stock prices) is the topic of Chapter 15.

You can skip the next two sections and still go through most of the arguments in the rest of the book. If you do, let me give you the bottom line: Even in this more complicated case, the central bank can, by changing the amount of central bank money, control the interest rate.

There is one dimension, however, in which our model must be extended. We have assumed that all money in the economy consists of currency supplied by the central bank. In the real world, money includes not only currency but also checkable deposits. Checkable deposits are supplied not by the central bank but by (private) banks. How the presence of banks and checkable deposits changes our conclusions is the topic of the next section.

The Short Run   **The Core**

To understand what determines the interest rate in an economy with both currency and checkable deposits, we must first look at what banks do.

What Banks Do

Modern economies are characterized by the existence of many types of **financial intermediaries**—institutions that receive funds from people and firms and use those funds to buy financial assets or to make loans to other people and firms. The assets of these institutions are the financial assets they own and the loans they have made. Their liabilities are what they owe to the people and firms from whom they have received funds.

Banks are one type of financial intermediary. What makes banks special—and the reason we focus on banks here rather than on financial intermediaries in general—is that their liabilities are money: People can pay for transactions by writing checks up to the amount of their account balance. Let's look more closely at what banks do:

The balance sheet of *banks* is shown in Figure 4-6(b):

- Banks receive funds from people and firms who either deposit funds directly or have funds sent to their checking accounts (via direct deposit of their paychecks, for example). At any point in time, people and firms can write checks or withdraw up to the full amount of their account balances. The liabilities of the banks are therefore equal to the value of these *checkable deposits*.

- Banks keep as **reserves** some of the funds they receive. The reserves are held partly in cash and partly in an account the banks have at the central bank, which they can draw on when they need to. Banks hold reserves for three reasons:

  On any given day, some depositors withdraw cash from their checking accounts, while others deposit cash into their accounts. There is no reason for the inflows and outflows of cash to be equal, so the bank must keep some cash on hand.

  In the same way, on any given day, people with accounts at the bank write checks to people with accounts at other banks, and people with accounts at other banks write checks to people with accounts at the bank. What the bank, as a result of these transactions, owes the other banks can be larger or smaller than what the other banks owe to it. For this reason, also, the bank needs to keep reserves.

  The first two reasons imply that the banks would want to keep some reserves even if they were not required to do so. In addition, banks are subject to reserve requirements, which say that they must hold reserves in some proportion of

> This balance sheet is a much-simplified version of the actual balance sheets of banks. Banks have other types of liabilities in addition to checkable deposits, and they are engaged in more activities than just holding bonds or making loans. But these complications are not relevant here, so we ignore them.

(a) **Central Bank**

Assets	Liabilities
Bonds	Central Bank Money = Reserves + Currency

(b) **Banks**

Assets	Liabilities
Reserves Loans Bonds	Checkable deposits

Figure 4-6

The Balance Sheet of Banks and the Balance Sheet of the Central Bank, Revisited

*This section is optional.

Bank Runs

Is bank money (checkable deposits) just as good as central bank money (currency)? To answer this question, we must look at what banks do with the funds they receive from depositors and at the distinction between making loans and holding bonds.

Making a loan to a firm or buying a government bond are more similar than they may seem. In one case, the bank lends to a firm. In the other, the bank lends to the government. This is why, for simplicity, I have assumed in the text that banks hold only bonds.

But, in one respect, making a loan is very different from buying a bond. Bonds, especially government bonds, are very liquid: If need be, they can be sold easily in the bond market. Loans, on the other hand, are often not liquid at all. Calling them back may be impossible. Firms have probably already used their loans to buy inventories or new machines, so they no longer have the cash on hand. Likewise, individuals likely have used their loans to purchase cars, houses, or other things. The bank could in principle sell the loans to a third party to get cash. However, selling them might be very difficult because potential buyers would know little about how reliable the borrowers are.

This fact has one important implication: take a healthy bank, a bank with a portfolio of good loans. Suppose rumors start that the bank is not doing well and some loans will not be repaid. Believing that the bank may fail, people with deposits at the bank will want to close their accounts and withdraw cash. If enough people do so, the bank will run out of reserves. Given that the loans cannot be called back, the bank will not be able to satisfy the demand for cash, and it will have to close.

Conclusion: Fear that a bank will close can actually cause it to close—even if all its loans are good. The financial history of the United States up to the 1930s is full of such **bank runs**. One bank fails for the right reason (because it has made bad loans). This, then, causes depositors at other banks to panic and withdraw money from their banks, forcing them to close. You have probably seen *It's a Wonderful Life,* an old movie with James Stewart, that runs on TV every year around Christmas. After another bank in Stewart's town fails, depositors at the savings and loan he manages get scared and want to withdraw their money, too. Stewart successfully persuades them this is not a good idea. *It's a Wonderful Life* has a happy ending. But in real life, most bank runs didn't.

What can be done to avoid bank runs? The United States has dealt with this problem since 1934 with **federal deposit insurance**. The U.S. government insures each account up to a ceiling of $100,000. As a result, there is no reason for depositors to run and withdraw their money. Today, healthy banks do not fail.

Federal deposit insurance leads, however, to problems of its own. Depositors, who do not have to worry about their deposits, no longer look at the activities of the banks in which they have their accounts. Banks may then misbehave, by making loans they wouldn't have made in the absence of deposit insurance. (There will be more on this when we discuss the economic problems in Japan in Chapter 22.)

An alternative to federal insurance, which has been often discussed but never implemented, is called **narrow banking**. Narrow banking would restrict banks to holding liquid and safe government bonds, such as T-bills. Loans would have to be made by financial intermediaries other than banks. This would eliminate bank runs as well as the need for federal insurance.

---

their checkable deposits. In the United States, reserve requirements are set by the Fed. The actual **reserve ratio**—the ratio of bank reserves to bank checkable deposits—is about 10% in the United States today. Banks can use the other 90% to make loans or buy bonds.

■ Loans represent roughly 70% of banks' nonreserve assets. Bonds account for the rest, 30%. The distinction between bonds and loans is unimportant for our purpose—which is to understand how the money supply is determined. For this reason, to keep the discussion simple, I will assume that banks do not make loans and that they hold only reserves and bonds as assets. But the distinction between loans and bonds is important for other purposes, from the possibility of "bank runs" to the role of federal deposit insurance. These topics are explored in the Focus box "Bank Runs."

Figure 4-6(a) returns to the balance sheet of the central bank, in an economy in which there are banks. It is very similar to the balance sheet of the central bank we saw in Figure 4-5. The asset side is the same as before: The assets of the central bank are the bonds it holds. The liabilities of the central bank are the money it has issued, **central bank money**. The new feature is that not all of central bank money is held as currency by the public. Some of it is held as reserves by banks.

The Supply and the Demand for Central Bank Money

The easiest way to think about how the interest rate in this economy is determined is by thinking in terms of the supply and the demand for *central bank money*:

- The demand for central bank money is equal to the demand for currency by people plus the demand for reserves by banks.
- The supply of central bank money is under the direct control of the central bank.
- The equilibrium interest rate is such that the demand and the supply for central bank money are equal.

Figure 4-7 shows the structure of the demand and the supply of central bank money in more detail. (Ignore the equations for the time being. Just look at the boxes.) Start on the left side. The demand for money by people is for both checkable deposits and currency. Because banks have to hold reserves against checkable deposits, the demand for checkable deposits leads to a demand for reserves by banks. Conse- ◄ quently, the demand for central bank money is equal to the demand for reserves by banks plus the demand for currency. Go to the right side: The supply of central bank money is determined by the central bank. Look at the equal sign: The interest rate must be such that the demand and the supply of central bank money are equal.

We now go through each of the boxes in Figure 4-7 and ask:

- What determines the demand for checkable deposits and the demand for currency?
- What determines the demand for reserves by banks?

> Be careful to distinguish among:
> Demand for money (demand for currency and checkable deposits)
> Demand for bank money (demand for checkable deposits)
> Demand for central bank money (demand for currency by people and demand for reserves by banks)

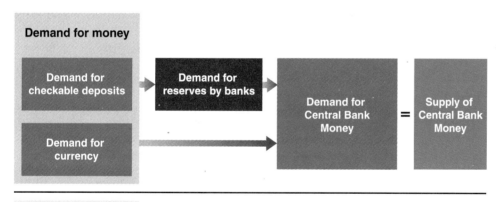

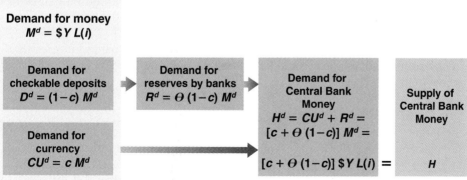

Figure 4-7

Determinants of the Demand and the Supply of Central Bank Money

- What determines the demand for central bank money?
- How does the condition that the demand and the supply of central money be equal determine the interest rate?

The Demand for Money

When people can hold both currency and checkable deposits, the demand for money involves *two* decisions. First, people must decide how much money to hold. Second, they must decide how much of this money to hold in currency and how much to hold in checkable deposits.

It is reasonable to assume that the overall demand for money (currency plus checkable deposits) is given by the same factors as before. People will hold more money the higher the level of transactions and the lower the interest rate on bonds. We can assume that overall money demand is given by the same equation as before (equation (4.1)):

$$M^d = \$Y\, L(i)$$
$$(-)$$

(4.3)

That brings us to the second decision: How do people decide how much to hold in currency and how much in checkable deposits? Currency is more convenient for small transactions and also more convenient for illegal transactions. Checks are more convenient for large transactions. Holding money in your checking account is safer than holding cash.

Let's assume that people hold a fixed proportion of their money in currency—call this proportion c—and, by implication, hold a fixed proportion $(1 - c)$ in checkable deposits. (In the United States, people hold 40% of their money in the form of currency, so $c = 0.4$.) Call the demand for currency CU^d (CU for currency, and d for demand). Call the demand for checkable deposits D^d (D for deposits, and d for demand). The two demands are given by

$$CU^d = c\, M^d$$

(4.4)

$$D^d = (1 - c)\, M^d$$

(4.5)

Equation (4.4) shows the first component of the demand for central bank money— the demand for currency by the public. Equation (4.5) shows the demand for checkable deposits.

We now have a description of the first box, "Demand for money," on the left side of Figure 4-7: Equation (4.3) shows the overall demand for money. Equations (4.4) and (4.5) show the demand for checkable deposits and the demand for currency, respectively.

The demand for checkable deposits leads to a demand by banks for reserves, the second component of the demand for central bank money. To see how, let's turn to the behavior of banks.

The Demand for Reserves

The larger the amount of checkable deposits, the larger the amount of reserves the banks must hold, for both precautionary and regulatory reasons. Let θ (the Greek lowercase letter theta) be the reserve ratio, the amount of reserves banks hold per dollar of checkable deposits. Let R denote the reserves of banks. Let D denote the

The Short Run   **The Core**

dollar amount of checkable deposits. Then, by the definition of θ, the following relation holds between R and D:

$$R = \theta D \qquad (4.6)$$

We saw earlier that in the United States today, the reserve ratio is roughly equal to 10%. Thus, θ is roughly equal to 0.1.

If people want to hold D^d in deposits, then, from equation (4.6), banks must hold θD^d in reserves. Combining equations (4.5) and (4.6), the second component of the demand for central bank money—the demand for reserves by banks—is given by

$$R^d = \theta (1 - c)M^d \qquad (4.7)$$

We now have the equation corresponding to the second box, "Demand for reserves by banks," on the left side of Figure 4-7.

The Demand for Central Bank Money

Call H^d the demand for central bank money. This demand is equal to the sum of the demand for currency and the demand for reserves:

$$H^d = CU^d + R^d \qquad (4.8)$$

Replace CU^d and R^d with their expressions from equations (4.4) and (4.7) to get

$$H^d = cM^d + \theta(1 - c)M^d = [c + \theta(1 - c)]M^d$$

Finally, replace the overall demand for money, M^d, with its expression from equation (4.3) to get:

$$H^d = [c + \theta(1 - c)] \; \$YL(i) \qquad (4.9)$$

This gives us the equation corresponding to the third box, "Demand for Central Bank Money," on the left side of Figure 4-7.

The Determination of the Interest Rate

We are now ready to characterize the equilibrium. Let H be the supply of central bank money. H is directly controlled by the central bank; just like in the previous section, the central bank can change the amount of H through open market operations. The equilibrium condition is that the supply of central bank money be equal to the demand for central bank money:

$$H = H^d \qquad (4.10)$$

Or, using equation (4.9):

$$H = [c + \theta(1 - c)]\$Y \; L(i) \qquad (4.11)$$

The supply of central bank money (the left side of equation (4.11)) is equal to the demand for central bank money (the right side of equation (4.11)), which is equal to the term in brackets multiplied by the overall demand for money.

Look at the term in brackets more closely. Suppose that people held only currency, so $c = 1$. Then, the term in brackets would be equal to 1, and the equation would be

◄ Suppose banks doubled the number of locations of ATMs, making them more convenient to use for their customers. What would happen to the demand for central bank money?

exactly the same as equation (4.2) in Section 4-2 (with the letter H replacing the letter M on the left side, but H and M both stand for the supply of central bank money). In this case, people would hold only currency, and banks would play no role in the supply of money. We would be back to the case we looked at in Section 4-2.

Assume instead that people did not hold currency at all, but held only checkable deposits, so $c = 0$. Then, the term in brackets would be equal to θ. Suppose, for example, that $\theta = 0.1$, so that the term in brackets was equal to 0.1. Then, the demand for central bank money would be equal to one-tenth of the overall demand for money. This is easy to understand: People would hold only checkable deposits. For every dollar people wanted to hold, banks would need to have 10 cents in reserves. In other words, the demand for reserves would be one-tenth of the overall demand for money.

Leaving aside these two extreme cases, note that as long as people hold some checkable deposits (so that $c < 1$), the term in brackets is less than one. This means the demand for central bank money is less than the overall demand for money. This is due to the fact that the demand for reserves by banks is only a fraction of the demand for checkable deposits.

We can represent the equilibrium condition, equation (4.11), graphically, and we do this in Figure 4-8. The figure looks the same as Figure 4-2, but with central bank money rather than money on the horizontal axis. The interest rate is measured on the vertical axis. The demand for central bank money, $CU^d + R^d$, is drawn for a given level of nominal income. A higher interest rate implies a lower demand for central bank money for two reasons: (1) The demand for currency by people goes down; (2) the demand for checkable deposits by people also goes down. This leads to lower demand for reserves by banks. The supply of money is fixed and is represented by a vertical line at H. Equilibrium is at point A, with interest rate, i.

The effects of either changes in nominal income or changes in the supply of central bank money are qualitatively the same as in the previous section. In particular, an increase in the supply of central bank money leads to a shift in the vertical supply line to the right. This leads to a lower interest rate. As before, an increase in central bank

Figure 4-8

Equilibrium in the Market for Central Bank Money and the Determination of the Interest Rate

The equilibrium interest rate is such that the supply of central bank money is equal to the demand for central bank money.

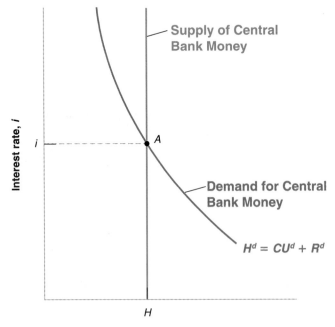

The Short Run   **The Core**

money leads to a decrease in the interest rate. Conversely, a decrease in central bank money leads to an increase in the interest rate.

◀ Suppose people get worried about the possibility of bank runs and decide to hold a higher proportion of money in the form of currency. If the central bank keeps the money supply constant, what will happen to the interest rate?

4-4 Two Alternative Ways of Looking at the Equilibrium*

In Section 4-3, we looked at the equilibrium through the condition that the supply and the demand of central bank money be equal. There are two other ways of looking at the equilibrium. While they are all equivalent, each provides a different way of thinking about the equilibrium, and going through each one will strengthen your understanding of how monetary policy affects the interest rate.

The Federal Funds Market and the Federal Funds Rate

Instead of thinking in terms of the supply and the demand for central bank money, we can think in terms of the supply and the demand for bank reserves.

The supply of reserves is equal to the supply of central bank money, H, minus the demand for currency by the public, CU^d. The demand for reserves by banks is R^d. So the equilibrium condition that the supply and the demand for bank reserves be equal is given by

$$H - CU^d = R^d$$

Notice that if we move CU^d from the left side to the right side and use the fact that the demand for central bank money, H^d, is given by $H^d = CU^d + R^d$, then this equation is equivalent to $H = H^d$. In other words, looking at the equilibrium in terms of the supply and the demand for reserves is equivalent to looking at the equilibrium in terms of the supply and the demand for central bank money—the approach we followed in Section 4-3.

Nevertheless, this alternative way of looking at the equilibrium is attractive because, in the United States, there is indeed an actual market for bank reserves, where the interest rate moves up and down to balance the supply and demand for reserves. This market is called the **federal funds market**. Banks that have excess reserves at the end of the day lend them to banks that have insufficient reserves. In equilibrium, the total demand for reserves by all banks taken together, R^d, must be equal to the supply of reserves to the market, $H - CU^d$—the equilibrium condition stated earlier.

The interest rate determined in this market is called the **federal funds rate**. ◀ Because the Fed can in effect choose the federal funds rate it wants by changing the supply of central bank money, H, the federal funds rate is typically thought of as the main indicator of U.S. monetary policy. This is why so much attention is focused on it and why changes in the federal funds rate typically make front-page news.

In short, the Fed determines the federal funds rate. It does so by intervening in the federal funds market.

The Supply of Money, the Demand for Money, and the Money Multiplier

We have seen how we can think of the equilibrium in terms of the equality of the supply and demand of central bank money, or in terms of the equality of the supply and demand of reserves. There is yet another way of thinking about the equilibrium, which is sometimes very useful. We can think about the equilibrium in terms of the equality

*This section is optional.

Remember: All three ways are
equivalent in the sense that ▶
they yield the same answer. But
each gives us a different way
of thinking about the answer
and strengthens our intuition.

of the overall supply and the overall demand for money (currency and checkable deposits).

To derive an equilibrium condition in terms of the overall supply and the overall demand for money, start with the equilibrium condition (4.11) (which states that the supply of central bank money must equal the demand for central bank money) and divide both sides by $[c + \theta(1 - c)]$:

$$\frac{1}{[c + \theta(1 - c)]}H = \$Y \ L(i) \qquad (4.12)$$

Supply of money = Demand for money

The right side of equation (4.12) is the overall demand for money (currency plus checkable deposits). The left side is the overall supply of money (currency plus checkable deposits). Basically the equation says that, in equilibrium, the overall supply and the overall demand of money must be equal:

- If you compare equation (4.12) with equation (4.2), the equation characterizing the equilibrium in an economy without banks, you will see that the only difference is that the overall supply of money is not equal just to central bank money but to central bank money multiplied by a constant term $1/(c + \theta(1 - c))$.

  Notice also that because $(c + \theta(1 - c))$ is less than one, its inverse—the constant term on the left of the equation—is greater than one. For this reason, this constant term is called the **money multiplier**. The overall supply of money is therefore equal to central bank money multiplied by the money multiplier. If the money multiplier is 4, for example, then the overall supply of money is equal to 4 times the supply of central bank money.

- To reflect the fact that the overall supply of money depends in the end on the amount of central bank money, central bank money is sometimes called **high-powered money** (this is where the letter H we used to denote central bank money comes from), or the **monetary base**. The term *high powered* reflects the fact that increases in H lead to more than one-for-one increases in the overall money supply and are therefore high powered. In the same way, the term *monetary base* reflects the fact that the overall money supply depends ultimately on a "base"— the amount of central bank money in the economy.

The presence of a multiplier in equation (4.12) implies that a given change in central bank money has a larger effect on the money supply—and in turn a larger effect on the interest rate—in an economy with banks than in an economy without banks. To understand why, it is useful to return to the description of open market operations, this time in an economy with banks.

Understanding the Money Multiplier

To make things easier, let's consider a special case where people hold only checkable deposits, so $c = 0$. In this case, the multiplier is $1/\theta$. In other words, an increase of a dollar of high-powered money leads to an increase of $1/\theta$ dollars in the money supply. Assume further that $\theta = 0.1$, so that the multiplier equals $1/0.1 = 10$. The purpose of what follows is to help you understand where this multiplier comes from and, more generally, how the initial increase in central bank money leads to a tenfold increase in the overall money supply.

Suppose the Fed buys \$100 worth of bonds in an open market operation. It pays the seller—call him seller 1—\$100. To pay the seller, the Fed creates \$100 in central bank money. The increase in central bank money is \$100. When we looked earlier at the effects of an open market operation in an economy in which there were no banks, this was the end of the story. Here, it is just the beginning:

- Seller 1 (who, we have assumed, does not want to hold any currency) deposits the $100 in a checking account at his bank—call it bank A. This leads to an increase in checkable deposits of $100.
- Bank A keeps $100 times 0.1 = $10 in reserves and buys bonds with the rest, $100 times 0.9 = $90. It pays $90 to the seller of those bonds—call her seller 2.
- Seller 2 deposits $90 in a checking account in her bank—call it bank B. This leads to an increase in checkable deposits of $90.
- Bank B keeps $90 times 0.1 = $9 in reserves and buys bonds with the rest, $90 times 0.9 = $81. It pays $81 to the seller of those bonds—call him seller 3.
- Seller 3 deposits $81 in a checking account in his bank—call it bank C.
- And so on.

By now, the chain of events should be clear. What is the eventual increase in the money supply? The increase in checkable deposits is $100 when seller 1 deposits the proceeds of his sale of bonds in bank A, plus $90 when seller 2 deposits the proceeds of her sale of bonds in bank B, plus $81 when seller 3 does the same, and so on. Let's write the sum as:

$$\$100 \ (1 + 0.9 + 0.9^2 + \cdots)$$

The series in parentheses is a geometric series, so its sum is equal to $1/(1 - 0.9) = 10$. (See Appendix 2 at the end of this book for a refresher on geometric series.) The money supply increases by $1,000—10 times the initial increase in central bank money.

This derivation gives us another way of thinking about the money multiplier: We can think of the ultimate increase in the money supply as the result of *successive rounds of purchases of bonds*—the first started by the Fed in its open market operation, and the following rounds by banks. Each successive round leads to an increase in the money supply, and eventually the increase in the money supply is equal to 10 times the initial increase in the central bank money. Note the parallel between our interpretation of the money multiplier as the result of successive purchases of bonds and the interpretation of the goods market multiplier (Chapter 3) as the result of successive rounds of spending. Multipliers can often be derived as the sum of a geometric series and interpreted as the result of successive rounds of decisions. This interpretation often gives a better understanding of how the process works.

Summary

- The demand for money depends positively on the level of transactions in the economy and negatively on the interest rate.
- The interest rate is determined by the equilibrium condition that the supply of money be equal to the demand for money.
- For a given supply of money, an increase in income leads to an increase in the demand for money and an increase in the interest rate. An increase in the supply of money leads to a decrease in the interest rate.
- The central bank changes the supply of money through open market operations.

- Expansionary open market operations, in which the central bank increases the money supply by buying bonds, lead to an increase in the price of bonds and a decrease in the interest rate.
- Contractionary open market operations, in which the central bank decreases the money supply by selling bonds, lead to a decrease in the price of bonds and an increase in the interest rate.
- When money includes both currency and checkable deposits, we can think of the interest rate as being determined by the condition that the supply of central bank money be equal to the demand for central bank money.

- The supply of central bank money is under the control of the central bank. The demand for central bank money depends on the overall demand for money, the proportion of money people keep in currency, and the ratio of reserves to checkable deposits chosen by banks.
- Another, but equivalent, way to think about the determination of the interest rate is in terms of the equality of the supply and demand for bank reserves. The market for bank reserves is called the federal funds market. The interest rate determined in that market is called the federal funds rate.
- Yet another way to think about the determination of the interest rate is in terms of the equality of the overall supply and the overall demand of money. The overall supply of money is equal to central bank money times the money multiplier.

Key Terms

- Federal Reserve Bank (Fed), 85
- money, 86
- currency, 86
- checkable deposits, 86
- bonds, 86
- income, 87
- flow, 87
- saving, 87
- savings, 87
- financial wealth, wealth, 87
- stock, 87
- investment, 87
- financial investment, 87
- money market funds, 87
- *LM* relation, 90
- open market operation, 92
- expansionary, and contractionary, open market operation, 92
- Treasury bill, (T-bill), 93
- financial intermediaries, 95
- (bank) reserves, 95
- reserve ratio, 96
- bank run, 96
- federal deposit insurance, 96
- narrow banking, 96
- central bank money, 97
- federal funds market, 101
- federal funds rate, 101
- money multiplier, 102
- high-powered money, 102
- monetary base, 102

Questions and Problems

Quick Check

1. Using the information in this chapter, label each of the following statements true, false, or uncertain. Explain briefly.

  a. Income and financial wealth are both examples of stock variables.
  b. The term *investment,* as used by economists, refers to the purchase of bonds and shares of stock.
  c. The demand for money does not depend on the interest rate because only bonds earn interest.
  d. About two-thirds of U.S. currency is held outside the United States.
  e. The central bank can increase the supply of money by selling bonds in the market for bonds.
  f. The Federal Reserve can determine the money supply, but it cannot determine interest rates—not even the federal funds rate—because interest rates are determined in the private sector.
  g. Bond prices and interest rates always move in opposite directions.
  h. Since the Great Depression, the United States has used federal deposit insurance to deal with bank runs.

2. Suppose that a person's yearly income is $80,000. Also, suppose that this person's money demand function is given by

$$M^d = \$Y(.30 - i)$$

  a. What is this person's demand for money when the interest rate is 4%? 8%?
  b. Explain how the interest rate affects money demand.
  c. Suppose that the interest rate is 4%. In percentage terms, what happens to this person's demand for money if her yearly income is reduced by 50%?
  d. Suppose that the interest rate is 8%. In percentage terms, what happens to this person's demand for money if her yearly income is reduced by 50%?
  e. Summarize the effect of income on money demand. In percentage terms, how does this effect depend on the interest rate?

3. Suppose that money demand is given by

$$M^d = \$Y(.25 - i)$$

where $Y is $100. Also, suppose that the supply of money is $20.

  a. What is the equilibrium interest rate?

b. If the Federal Reserve Bank wants to increase i by 10 percentage points (e.g., from 2% to 12%), at what level should it set the supply of money?

4. Consider a bond that promises to pay $100 in one year.
   a. What is the interest rate on the bond if its price today is $75? $85? $95?
   b. What is the relation between the price of the bond and the interest rate?
   c. If the interest rate is 8%, what is the price of the bond today?

Dig Deeper

5. The demand for bonds

   In this chapter, you learned that an increase in the interest rate makes bonds more attractive, so it leads people to hold more of their wealth in bonds, as opposed to money.

   However, you also learned that an increase in the interest rate reduces the price of bonds.

   How can an increase in the interest rate make bonds more attractive and reduce their price?

6. Suppose that a person's wealth is $50,000 and that her yearly income is $60,000. Also suppose that her money demand function is given by

$$M^d = \$Y(.35 - i)$$

   a. Derive the demand for bonds. Suppose the interest rate increases by 10 percentage points. What is the effect on the demand for bonds?
   b. What are the effects of an increase in wealth on the demand for money and the demand for bonds? Explain in words.
   c. What are the effects of an increase in income on the demand for money and the demand for bonds? Explain in words.
   d. Consider the statement "When people earn more money, they obviously will hold more bonds." What is wrong with this statement?

7. ATMs and credit cards

   This problem examines the effect of the introduction of ATMs and credit cards on money demand. For simplicity, let's examine a person's demand for money over a period of four days.

   Suppose that before ATMs and credit cards, this person goes to the bank once at the beginning of each four-day period and withdraws from her savings account all the money she needs for four days. Assume that she spends $4 per day.

   a. How much does this person withdraw each time she goes to the bank? Compute this person's money holdings for days 1 through 4 (in the morning, before she spends any of the money she withdraws).
   b. What is the amount of money this person holds, on average?

   Suppose now that with the advent of ATMs, this person withdraws money once every two days.

   c. Recompute your answer to part (a).
   d. Recompute your answer to part (b).

   Finally, with the advent of credit cards, this person pays for all her purchases using her card. She withdraws no money

until the fourth day, when she withdraws the whole amount necessary to pay for her credit card purchases over the previous four days.

   e. Recompute your answer to part (a).
   f. Recompute your answer to part (b).
   g. Based on your previous answers, what do you think has been the effect of ATMs and credit cards on money demand?

8. The money multiplier

   The money multiplier is described in Section 4-4. Assume the following:
   i. The public holds no currency.
   ii. The ratio of reserves to deposits is 0.1.
   iii. The demand for money is given by

$$M^d = \$Y(.8 - 4i)$$

   Initially, the monetary base is $100 billion, and nominal income is $5 trillion.

   a. What is the demand for central bank money?
   b. Find the equilibrium interest rate by setting the demand for central bank money equal to the supply of central bank money.
   c. What is the overall supply of money? Is it equal to the overall demand for money at the interest rate you found in part (b)?
   d. What is the impact on the interest rate if central bank money is increased to $300 billion?
   e. If the overall money supply increases to $3,000 billion, what will be the impact on i? [Hint: Use what you learned in part (c).]

9. Bank runs and the money multiplier

   During the Great Depression, the U.S. economy experienced many bank runs, to the point where people became unwilling to keep their money in banks, preferring to keep it in cash.

   How would you expect such a shift away from checkable deposits toward currency to affect the size of the money multiplier? (To find out what happened to the money multiplier during the Great Depression, go to Chapter 22.)

Explore Further

10. Current monetary policy

   Go to the Web site for the Federal Reserve Board of Governors (**www.federalreserve.gov**) and download the most recent monetary policy press release of the Federal Open Market Committee (FOMC). Make sure you get the most recent FOMC press release and not simply the most recent Fed press release.

   a. What is the current stance of monetary policy? (Note that policy will be described in terms of increasing or decreasing the federal funds rate as opposed to increasing or decreasing the money supply.)
   b. If the federal funds rate has changed recently, what does the change imply about the bond holdings of the Federal Reserve? Has the Fed been increasing or decreasing its bond holdings?

   Finally, you might want to read the explanation of the FOMC for the current policy stance. It may not make much sense now, but keep it in mind for Chapter 5.

We invite you to visit the Blanchard page on the Prentice Hall Web site, at:
www.prenhall.com/blanchard
for this chapter's World Wide Web exercises.

Further Readings

■ For more on financial markets and institutions, read a textbook on money and banking. An excellent one is *Money, the Financial System and the Economy*, by R. Glenn Hubbard, Addison-Wesley, Reading, MA, 2007.

■ The Fed maintains a useful Web site that contains not only data on financial markets but also information on what the Fed does, on recent testimonies by the Fed chairman, and so on (**www.federalreserve.gov**).

Goods and Financial Markets: The *IS–LM* Model

n Chapter 3, we looked at the goods market. In Chapter 4, we looked at financial markets. We now look at goods and financial markets together. By the end of this chapter, you will have a framework to think about how output and the interest rate are determined in the short run.

In developing this framework, we follow a path first traced by two economists, John Hicks and Alvin Hansen, in the late 1930s and the early 1940s. When the economist John Maynard Keynes published his *General Theory* in 1936, there was much agreement that his book was both fundamental and nearly impenetrable. (Try to read it, and you will agree.) There were many debates about what Keynes "really meant." In 1937, John Hicks summarized what he saw as one of Keynes's main contributions: the joint description of goods and financial markets. His analysis was later extended by Alvin Hansen. Hicks and Hansen called their formalization the *IS–LM* model.

Macroeconomics has made substantial progress since the early 1940s. This is why the *IS–LM* model is treated in Chapter 5 rather than in Chapter 27 of this book. (If you had taken this course 40 years ago, you would be nearly done!) But to most economists, the *IS–LM* model still represents an essential building block—one that, despite its simplicity, captures much of what happens in the economy in *the short run*. This is why the *IS–LM* model is still taught and used today.

This chapter has five sections:

■ Section 5-1 looks at equilibrium in the goods market and derives the IS relation.

■ Section 5-2 looks at equilibrium in financial markets and derives the LM relation.

■ Sections 5-3 and 5-4 put the IS and the LM relations together and use the resulting IS—LM model to study the effects of fiscal and monetary policy—first separately, and then together.

■ Section 5-5 introduces dynamics and explores how the IS–LM model captures what happens in the economy in the short run. ■

Let's first summarize what we learned in Chapter 3:

- We characterized equilibrium in the goods market as the condition that production, Y, be equal to the demand for goods, Z. We called this condition the *IS* relation.
- We defined demand as the sum of consumption, investment, and government spending. We assumed that consumption was a function of disposable income (income minus taxes) and took investment spending, government spending, and taxes as given:

$$Z = C(Y - T) + \bar{I} + G$$

  In Chapter 3, we assumed, to simplify the algebra, that the relation between consumption, C, and disposable income, $Y - T$, was linear. Here, we do not make that assumption but use the more general form $C = C(Y - T)$ instead.
- The equilibrium condition was thus given by

$$Y = C(Y - T) + \bar{I} + G$$

- Using this equilibrium condition, we then looked at the factors that moved equilibrium output. We looked in particular at the effects of changes in government spending and of shifts in consumption demand.

The main simplification of this first model was that the interest rate did not affect the demand for goods. Our first task in this chapter is to abandon this simplification and introduce the interest rate in our model of equilibrium in the goods market. For the time being, we focus only on the effect of the interest rate on investment and leave a discussion of its effects on the other components of demand until later.

> We cover much more on the effects of interest rates on both consumption and investment in Chapter 16.

Investment, Sales, and the Interest Rate

In Chapter 3, investment was assumed to be constant. This was for simplicity. Investment is in fact far from constant and depends primarily on two factors:

- The level of sales—Consider a firm facing an increase in sales and needing to increase production. To do so, it may need to buy additional machines or build an additional plant. In other words, it needs to invest. A firm facing low sales will feel no such need and will spend little, if anything, on investment.
- The interest rate—Consider a firm deciding whether to buy a new machine. Suppose that to buy the new machine, the firm must borrow. The higher the interest rate, the less attractive it is to borrow and buy the machine. At a high enough interest rate, the additional profits from using the new machine will not cover interest payments, and the new machine will not be worth buying.

> The argument still holds if the firm uses its own funds: The higher the interest rate, the more attractive it is to lend the funds rather than to use them to buy the new machine.

To capture these two effects, we write the investment relation as follows:

$$I = I(Y, i) \qquad (5.1)$$
$$(+, -)$$

Equation (5.1) states that investment, I, depends on production, Y, and the interest rate, i. (We continue to assume that inventory investment is equal to zero, so sales and production are always equal. As a result, Y denotes sales, and it also denotes production.) The positive sign under Y indicates that an increase in production (equivalently, an increase in sales) leads to an increase in investment. The negative sign under the interest rate, i, indicates that an increase in the interest rate leads to a decrease in investment.

> An increase in output leads to an increase in investment. An increase in the interest rate leads to a decrease in investment.

Determining Output

Taking into account the investment relation (5.1), the condition for equilibrium in the goods market becomes

$$Y = C(Y - T) + I(Y,i) + G \qquad (5.2)$$

Production (the left side of the equation) must be equal to the demand for goods (the right side). Equation (5.2) is our expanded *IS* relation. We can now look at what happens to output when the interest rate changes.

Start with Figure 5-1. Measure the demand for goods on the vertical axis. Measure output on the horizontal axis. For a given value of the interest rate, i, demand is an increasing function of output, for two reasons:

- An increase in output leads to an increase in income and thus to an increase in disposable income. The increase in disposable income leads to an increase in consumption. We studied this relation in Chapter 3.
- An increase in output also leads to an increase in investment. This is the relation between investment and production that we have introduced in this chapter.

In short, an increase in output leads, through its effects on both consumption and investment, to an increase in the demand for goods. This relation between demand and output, for a given interest rate, is represented by the upward-sloping curve, *ZZ*.

Note two characteristics of *ZZ* in Figure 5-1:

- Since we have not assumed that the consumption and investment relations in equation (5.2) are linear, *ZZ* is in general a curve rather than a line. Thus, I have drawn it as a curve in Figure 5-1. All the arguments that follow would apply if we assumed that the consumption and investment relations were linear and that *ZZ* were a straight line.
- I have drawn *ZZ* so that it is flatter than the 45-degree line. Put another way, I have assumed that an increase in output leads to a less than one-for-one increase in demand.

Make sure you understand why the two statements mean ◀ the same thing.

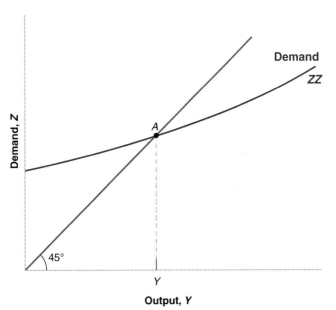

Figure 5-1

Equilibrium in the Goods Market

The demand for goods is an increasing function of output. Equilibrium requires that the demand for goods be equal to output.

In Chapter 3, where investment was constant, this restriction naturally followed from the assumption that consumers spend only part of their additional income on consumption. But now that we allow investment to respond to production, this restriction may no longer hold. When output increases, the sum of the increase in consumption and the increase in investment could exceed the initial increase in output. Although this is a theoretical possibility, the empirical evidence suggests that it is not the case in reality. That's why I will assume that the response of demand to output is less than one-for-one and draw ZZ flatter than the 45-degree line.

Equilibrium in the goods market is reached at the point where the demand for goods equals output—that is, at point A, the intersection of ZZ and the 45-degree line. The equilibrium level of output is given by Y.

So far, what we have done is extend, in straightforward fashion, the analysis of Chapter 3. But we are now ready to derive the IS curve.

Deriving the *IS* Curve

We have drawn the demand relation, ZZ, in Figure 5-1 for a given value of the interest rate. Let's now derive in Figure 5-2 what happens if the interest rate changes.

Suppose that, in Figure 5-2(a), the demand curve is given by ZZ, and the initial equilibrium is at point A. Suppose now that the interest rate increases from its initial value, i, to a new higher value, i'. At any level of output, the higher interest rate leads to lower investment and lower demand. The demand curve ZZ shifts down to ZZ': At a given level of output, demand is lower. The new equilibrium is at the intersection of the lower demand curve, ZZ', and the 45-degree line, at point A'. The equilibrium level of output is now equal to Y'.

Can you show graphically what the size of the multiplier is? (Hint: Look at the ratio of the decrease in equilibrium output to the initial decrease in investment.)

In words: The increase in the interest rate decreases investment. The decrease in investment leads to a decrease in output, which further decreases consumption and investment, through the multiplier effect.

Using Figure 5-2(a), we can find the equilibrium value of output associated with *any* value of the interest rate. The resulting relation between equilibrium output and the interest rate is drawn in Figure 5-2(b).

Figure 5-2(b) plots equilibrium output, Y, on the horizontal axis against the interest rate on the vertical axis. Point A in Figure 5-2(b) corresponds to point A in Figure 5-2(a), and point A' in Figure 5-2(b) corresponds to A' in Figure 5-2(a). The higher interest rate is associated with a lower level of output.

Equilibrium in the goods market implies that an increase in the interest rate leads to a decrease in output. This relation is represented by the downward-sloping *IS* curve.

This relation between the interest rate and output is represented by the downward-sloping curve in Figure 5-2(b). This curve is called the **IS curve**.

Shifts of the *IS* Curve

We have drawn the IS curve in Figure 5-2, taking as given the values of taxes, T, and government spending, G. Changes in either T or G will shift the IS curve. To see how, consider Figure 5-3. In Figure 5-3, the IS curve gives the equilibrium level of output as a function of the interest rate. It is drawn for given values of taxes and spending. Now consider an increase in taxes, from T to T'. At a given interest rate, say i, disposable income decreases, leading to a decrease in consumption, leading in turn to a decrease in the demand for goods and a decrease in equilibrium output. The equilibrium level of output decreases from Y to Y'. Put another way, the IS curve shifts to the left: At a given interest rate, the equilibrium level of output is lower than it was before the increase in taxes.

For a given interest rate, an increase in taxes leads to a decrease in output. In other words, an increase in taxes shifts the *IS* curve to the left.

More generally, any factor that, for a given interest rate, decreases the equilibrium level of output causes the IS curve to shift to the left. We have looked at an increase in

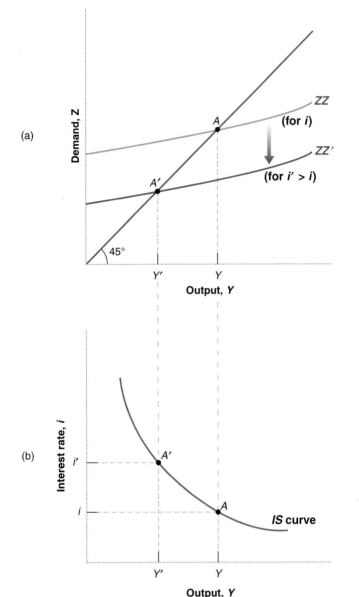

Figure 5-2

(a)

Demand, Z

ZZ
(for *i*)

A

ZZ'

(for *i' > i*)

A'

45°

Y'   Y

Output, **Y**

(b)

Interest rate, *i*

i'   A'

i   A

IS curve

Y'   Y

Output, **Y**

The Derivation of the IS *Curve*

(a) An increase in the interest rate decreases the demand for goods at any level of output, leading to a decrease in the equilibrium level of output.

(b) Equilibrium in the goods market implies that an increase in the interest rate leads to a decrease in output. The *IS* curve is therefore downward sloping.

taxes. But the same would hold for a decrease in government spending or a decrease in consumer confidence (which decreases consumption, given disposable income). Symmetrically, any factor that, for a given interest rate, increases the equilibrium level of output—a decrease in taxes, an increase in government spending, an increase in consumer confidence—causes the *IS* curve to shift to the right.

Let's summarize:

■ Equilibrium in the goods market implies that an increase in the interest rate leads to a decrease in output. This relation is represented by the downward-sloping *IS* curve.

■ Changes in factors that decrease the demand for goods, given the interest rate, shift the *IS* curve to the left. Changes in factors that increase the demand for goods, given the interest rate, shift the *IS* curve to the right.

Suppose the government announces that the Social Security system is in trouble, and it may have to cut retirement benefits in the future. How ◀ are consumers likely to react? What is then likely to happen to demand and output today?

Shifts of the IS Curve

An increase in taxes shifts the
IS curve to the left.

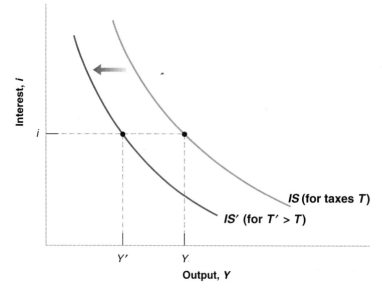

5-2 ■■■ Financial Markets and the LM Relation

Let's now turn to financial markets. We saw in Chapter 4 that the interest rate is determined by the equality of the supply of and the demand for money:

$$M = \$YL(i)$$

The variable M on the left side is the nominal money stock. We will ignore here the
details of the money supply process that we saw in Sections 4-3 and 4-4 and simply
think of the central bank as controlling M directly.

The right side gives the demand for money, which is a function of nominal
income, $\$Y$, and of the nominal interest rate, i. As we saw in Section 4-1, an increase in
nominal income increases the demand for money; an increase in the interest rate
decreases the demand for money. Equilibrium requires that money supply (the left
side of the equation) be equal to money demand (the right side of the equation).

Real Money, Real Income, and the Interest Rate

From Chapter 2: Nominal
GDP = Real GDP multiplied by
the GDP deflator: $\$Y = Y \times P$.
Equivalently: Real GDP =
Nominal GDP divided by the
GDP deflator: $Y = \$Y/P$. ▶

The equation $M = \$YL(i)$ gives a relation between money, nominal income, and the
interest rate. It will be more convenient here to rewrite it as a relation between real
money (that is, money in terms of goods), real income (that is, income in terms of
goods), and the interest rate.

Recall that nominal income divided by the price level equals real income, Y.
Dividing both sides of the equation by the price level, P, gives

$$\frac{M}{P} = YL(i) \qquad (5.3)$$

Hence, we can restate our equilibrium condition as the condition that the *real money
supply*—that is, the money stock in terms of goods, not dollars—be equal to the *real
money demand*, which depends on real income, Y, and the interest rate, i.

The notion of a "real" demand for money may feel a bit abstract, so an example
will help. Think not of your demand for money in general but just of your demand for
coins. Suppose you like to have coins in your pocket to buy two cups of coffee during

the day. If a cup costs $1.20, you will want to keep about $2.40 in coins: This is your nominal demand for coins. Equivalently, you want to keep enough coins in your pocket to buy two cups of coffee. This is your demand for coins in terms of goods—here in terms of cups of coffee.

From now on, I shall refer to equation (5.3) as the *LM relation*. The advantage of writing things this way is that *real income, Y,* appears on the right side of the equation instead of *nominal income, $Y.* And real income (equivalently real output) is the variable we focus on when looking at equilibrium in the goods market. To make the reading lighter, I will refer to the left and right sides of equation (5.3) simply as "money supply" and "money demand" rather than the more accurate but heavier "real money supply" and "real money demand." Similarly, I will refer to income rather than "real income."

Deriving the *LM* Curve

To see the relation between output and the interest rate implied by equation (5.3), let's use Figure 5-4. Look first at Figure 5-4(a). Let the interest rate be measured on the vertical axis and (real) money be measured on the horizontal axis. (Real) money supply is given by the vertical line at M/P and is denoted M^s. For a given level of (real) income, $Y,$ (real) money demand is a decreasing function of the interest rate. It is drawn as the downward-sloping curve denoted M^d. Except for the fact that we measure real rather than nominal money on the horizontal axis, the figure is similar to Figure 4-3 in Chapter 4. The equilibrium is at point A, where money supply is equal to money demand, and the interest rate is equal to i.

Now consider an increase in income from Y to Y', which leads people to increase their demand for money at any given interest rate. Money demand shifts to the right, to $M^{d'}$. The new equilibrium is at A', with a higher interest rate, i'. Why does an increase in income lead to an increase in the interest rate? When income increases, money demand increases; but the money supply is given. Thus, the interest rate must go up until the two opposite effects on the demand for money—the increase in income that leads people to want to hold more money and the increase in the interest rate that leads people to want to hold less money—cancel each other out. At that point, the demand for money is equal to the unchanged money supply, and financial markets are again in equilibrium.

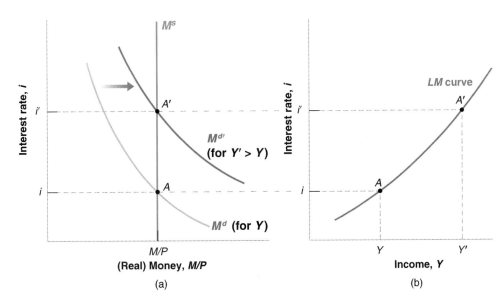

Figure 5-4

The Derivation of the LM *Curve*

(a) An increase in income leads, at a given interest rate, to an increase in the demand for money. Given the money supply, this increase in the demand for money leads to an increase in the equilibrium interest rate.

(b) Equilibrium in the financial markets implies that an increase in income leads to an increase in the interest rate. The *LM* curve is therefore upward sloping.

(a) — **(Real) Money, M/P** — M/P — M^s — A' — A — M$^{d'}$ (for Y' > Y) — M^d (for Y) — Interest rate, i — i' — i

(b) — **Income, Y** — Y — Y' — LM curve — A' — A — Interest rate, i — i' — i

Using Figure 5-4(a), we can find the value of the interest rate associated with *any* value of income for a given money stock. The relation is derived in Figure 5-4(b).

Figure 5-4(b) plots the equilibrium interest rate, i, on the vertical axis against income on the horizontal axis. Point A in Figure 5-4(b) corresponds to point A in Figure 5-4(a), and point A' in Figure 5-4(b) corresponds to point A' in Figure 5-4(a). More generally, equilibrium in financial markets implies that the higher the level of output, the higher the demand for money and, therefore, the higher the equilibrium interest rate.

> Equilibrium in financial markets implies that, for a given money stock, the interest rate is an increasing function of the level of income. This relation is represented by the upward-sloping *LM* curve.

This relation between output and the interest rate is represented by the upward-sloping curve in Figure 5-4(b). This curve is called the **LM curve**. Economists sometimes characterize this relation by saying "higher economic activity puts pressure on interest rates." Make sure you understand the steps behind this statement.

Shifts of the *LM* Curve

> For a given level of output, an increase in the money supply leads to a decrease in the interest rate. In other words, an increase in the money supply shifts the *LM* curve down.

We have derived the *LM* curve in Figure 5-4, taking both the nominal money stock, M, and the price level, P—and, by implication, their ratio, the real money stock, M/P—as given. Changes in M/P, whether they come from changes in the nominal money stock, M, or from changes in the price level, P, will shift the *LM* curve.

> Why do we think about shifts of the *IS* curve to the left or to the right, but about shifts of the *LM* curve up or down? The reason:
>
> We think of the goods market as determining Y given i, so we want to know what happens to Y when an exogenous variable changes. Y is on the horizontal axis and moves right or left.
>
> We think of financial markets as determining i given Y, so we want to know what happens to i when an exogenous variable changes. i is on the vertical axis and moves up or down.

To see how, let us look at Figure 5-5 and consider an increase in the nominal money supply, from M to M'. Given the fixed price level, the real money supply increases from M/P to M'/P. Then, at any level of income, say Y, the interest rate consistent with equilibrium in financial markets is lower, going down from i to, say, i'. The *LM* curve shifts down, from *LM* to *LM'*. By the same reasoning, at any level of income, a decrease in the money supply leads to an increase in the interest rate. It causes the *LM* curve to shift up.

Let's summarize:

- Equilibrium in financial markets implies that, for a given real money supply, an increase in the level of income, which increases the demand for money, leads to an increase in the interest rate. This relation is represented by the upward-sloping *LM* curve.

- An increase in the money supply shifts the *LM* curve down; a decrease in the money supply shifts the *LM* curve up.

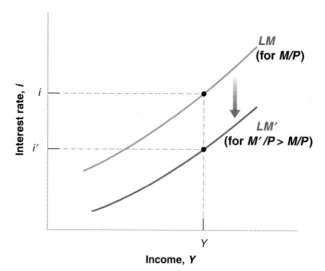

5-3 Putting the *IS* and the *LM* Relations Together

The *IS* relation follows from the condition that the supply of goods must be equal to the demand for goods. It tells us how the interest rate affects output. The *LM* relation follows from the condition that the supply of money must be equal to the demand for money. It tells us how output in turn affects the interest rate. We now put the *IS* and *LM* relations together. At any point in time, the supply of goods must be equal to the demand for goods, and the supply of money must be equal to the demand for money. Both the *IS* and *LM* relations must hold. Together, they determine both output and the interest rate.

$$\text{IS relation:} \qquad Y = C(Y - T) + I(Y, i) + G$$

$$\text{LM relation:} \qquad \frac{M}{P} = Y L(i)$$

Figure 5-6 plots both the *IS* curve and the *LM* curve on one graph. Output—equivalently, production or income—is measured on the horizontal axis. The interest rate is measured on the vertical axis.

Any point on the downward-sloping *IS* curve corresponds to equilibrium in the goods market. *Any point* on the upward-sloping *LM* curve corresponds to equilibrium in financial markets. *Only at point* A are both equilibrium conditions satisfied. That means point A, with the associated level of output, *Y*, and interest rate, *i*, is the overall equilibrium—the point at which there is equilibrium in both the goods market and the financial markets.

The *IS* and *LM* relations that underlie Figure 5-6 contain a lot of information about consumption, investment, money demand, and equilibrium conditions. But you may ask: So what if the equilibrium is at point A? How does this fact translate into anything directly useful about the world? Don't despair: Figure 5-6 holds the answers to many questions in macroeconomics. Used properly, it allows us to study what happens to output and the interest rate when the central bank decides to increase the money stock, or when the government decides to increase taxes, or when consumers become pessimistic about the future, and so on.

Let's now see what the *IS–LM* model can do.

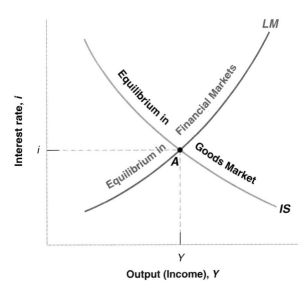

Figure 5-6

The IS–LM *Model*

Equilibrium in the goods market implies that an increase in the interest rate leads to a decrease in output. This is represented by the *IS* curve. Equilibrium in financial markets implies that an increase in output leads to an increase in the interest rate. This is represented by the *LM* curve. Only at point A, which is on both curves, are both goods and financial markets in equilibrium.

Fiscal Policy, Activity, and the Interest Rate

Decrease in $G - T \Leftrightarrow$ Fiscal contraction $\Leftrightarrow$ Fiscal consolidation Increase in $G - T \Leftrightarrow$ Fiscal expansion.

Suppose the government decides to reduce the budget deficit and does so by increasing taxes while keeping government spending unchanged. Such a change in fiscal policy is often called a **fiscal contraction**, or a fiscal **consolidation**. (An *increase* in the deficit, either due to an increase in government spending or to a decrease in taxes, is ▶ called a **fiscal expansion**.) What are the effects of this fiscal contraction on output, on its composition, and on the interest rate?

When you answer this or any other question about the effects of changes in policy, always go through the following three steps:

1. Ask how the change affects equilibrium in the goods market and how it affects equilibrium in the financial markets. Put another way: How does it shift the *IS* and/or the *LM* curve?

2. Characterize the effects of these shifts on the intersection of the *IS* and *LM* curves. What does this do to equilibrium output and the equilibrium interest rate?

And when you feel really confident, put on a bow tie and go explain events on TV. (Why so many TV economists actually wear bow ties is a mystery.) ▶

3. Describe the effects in words.

With time and experience, you will often be able to go directly to step 3. By then, you will be ready to give an instant commentary on the economic events of the day. But until you get to that level of expertise, go step by step:

■ Start with step 1. The first question is how the increase in taxes affects equilibrium in the goods market—that is, how it affects the *IS* curve.

Let's draw, in Figure 5-7(a), the *IS* curve corresponding to equilibrium in the goods market before the increase in taxes. Now take an arbitrary point, *B*, on this *IS* curve. By construction of the *IS* curve, output Y_B and the corresponding interest rate, i_B, are such that the supply of goods is equal to the demand for goods.

At the interest rate, i_B, ask what happens to output if taxes increase from *T* to *T'*. We saw the answer in Section 5-1. Because people have less disposable income, the increase in taxes decreases consumption, and through the multiplier, decreases output. At interest rate i_B, output decreases from Y_B to Y_C. More generally, at *any* interest rate, higher taxes lead to lower output. Consequently, the *IS* curve shifts to the left, from *IS* to *IS'*.

Taxes appear in the *IS* relation $\Leftrightarrow$ Taxes shift the *IS* curve. ▶

Next, let's see if anything happens to the *LM* curve. Figure 5-7(b) draws the *LM* curve corresponding to equilibrium in the financial markets before the increase in taxes. Take an arbitrary point, *F,* on this *LM* curve. By construction of the *LM* curve, the interest rate, i_F, and income, Y_F, are such that the supply of money is equal to the demand for money.

What happens to the *LM* curve when taxes are increased? Nothing. At the given level of income, Y_F, the interest rate at which the supply of money is equal to the demand for money is the same as before, namely i_F. In other words, because taxes do not appear in the *LM* relation, they do not affect the equilibrium condition. They do not affect the *LM* curve.

Taxes do not appear in the LM relation $\Leftrightarrow$ Taxes do not shift the **LM** curve. ▶

Note the general principle here: A curve shifts in response to a change in an exogenous variable only if this variable appears directly in the equation represented by that curve. Taxes enter in equation (5.2), so, when they change, the *IS* curve shifts. But taxes do not enter in equation (5.3), so the *LM* curve does not shift.

A reminder: An exogenous variable is a variable we take ▶ as given, unexplained within the model. Here, taxes is an exogenous variable.

■ Now consider step 2, the determination of the equilibrium. Let the initial equilibrium in Figure 5-7(c) be at point *A*, at the intersection between the initial *IS* curve and the *LM* curve. The *IS* curve is the same as the *IS* curve in Figure 5-7(a), and the *LM* curve is the same as the *LM* curve in Figure 5-7(b).

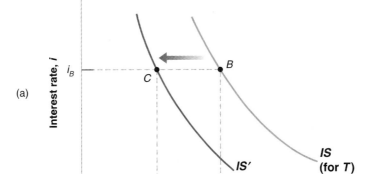

(a)

Figure 5-7 ▨

The Effects of an Increase in Taxes

An increase in taxes shifts the *IS* curve to the left and leads to a decrease in the equilibrium level of output and the equilibrium interest rate.

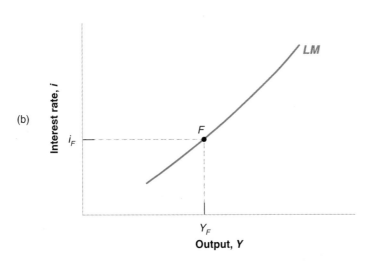

(b)

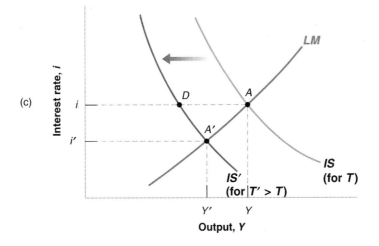

(c)

After the increase in taxes, the *IS* curve shifts to the left—from *IS* to *IS'*. The new equilibrium is at the intersection of the new *IS* curve and the unchanged *LM* curve, or point *A'*. Output decreases from *Y* to *Y'*. The interest rate decreases from *i* to *i'*. Thus, as the *IS* curve *shifts*, the economy *moves along* the *LM* curve, from *A* to *A'*. The reason these words are italicized is that it is important to always distinguish between the *shift of* a curve (here the shift of the *IS* curve) and the *movement along* a curve (here the movement along the *LM* curve). Many mistakes come from not distinguishing between the two.

The increase in taxes shifts the *IS* curve. The *LM* curve does not shift. The economy moves along the *LM* curve. ▶

■ Step 3 is to tell the story in words: The increase in taxes leads to lower disposable income, which causes people to decrease their consumption. This decrease in demand leads, in turn, to a decrease in output and income. At the same time, the decrease in income reduces the demand for money, leading to a decrease in the interest rate. The decline in the interest rate reduces but does not completely offset the effect of higher taxes on the demand for goods.

If the interest rate did not decline, the economy would go from point *A* to point *D* in Figure 5-7(c), and output would be directly below point *D*. Because of the decline in the interest rate—which stimulates investment—the decline in activity is only to point *A'*. ▶

What happens to the components of demand? By assumption, government spending remains unchanged (We have assumed that the reduction in the budget deficit takes place through an increase in taxes.) Consumption surely goes down: Taxes go up and income goes down, so disposable income goes down on both counts. What happens to investment? On the one hand, lower output means lower sales and lower investment. On the other, a lower interest rate leads to higher investment. Without knowing more about the exact form of the investment relation, equation (5.1), we cannot tell which effect dominates. If investment depended only on the interest rate, then investment would surely increase; if investment depended only on sales, then investment would surely decrease. In general, investment depends on both the interest rate and on sales, so we cannot tell. Contrary to what is often stated by politicians, a reduction in the budget deficit does not necessarily lead to an increase in investment. (The Focus box "Deficit Reduction: Good or Bad for Investment?" discusses this in more detail.)

We shall return to the relation between fiscal policy and investment many times in this book, and we shall qualify this first answer in many ways. But the result that *in the short run, a reduction of the budget deficit may decrease investment* will remain.

Monetary Policy, Activity, and the Interest Rate

Increase in *M* ⇔ monetary expansion.
Decrease in *M* ⇔ monetary contraction ⇔ monetary tightening. ▶

An increase in the money supply is called a **monetary expansion**. A decrease in the money supply is called a **monetary contraction**, or **monetary tightening**.

Let's take the case of a monetary expansion. Suppose that the central bank increases nominal money, *M*, through an open market operation. Given our assumption that the price level is fixed, this increase in nominal money leads to a one-for-one increase in real money, *M/P*. Let's denote the initial real money supply by *M/P* and the new higher one by *M'/P*, and let's trace in Figure 5-8 the effects of the money supply increase on output and the interest rate:

For a given price level *P, M* increases by 10% ⇒ *M/P* increases by 10%. ▶

■ Again, step 1 is to see whether and how the *IS* and *LM* curves shift.

Let's look at the *IS* curve first. The money supply does not *directly* affect either the supply of or the demand for goods. In other words, *M* does not appear in the *IS* relation. Thus, a change in *M* does not shift the *IS* curve.

Money does not appear in the *IS* relation ⇔ Money does not shift the *IS* curve. ▶

Money enters the *LM* relation, however, so the *LM* curve shifts when the money supply changes. As we saw in Section 5-2, an increase in the money supply shifts the *LM* curve down, from *LM* to *LM'*: At a given level of income, an increase in money leads to a decrease in the interest rate.

Money appears in the *LM* relation ⇔ Money shifts the *LM* curve. ▶

You may have heard the argument before: "Private saving goes either towards financing the budget deficit or financing investment. It does not take a genius to conclude that reducing the budget deficit leaves more saving available for investment, so investment increases."

This argument sounds simple and convincing. How do we reconcile it with what we just saw—that a deficit reduction may decrease rather than increase investment?

First go back to Chapter 3, equation (3.10). There we learned that we can also think of the goods market equilibrium condition as

$$Investment = Private\ saving + Public\ saving$$
$$I = S + (T - G)$$

In equilibrium, investment is equal to private saving plus public saving. If public saving is positive, the government is said to be running a budget surplus; if public saving is negative, the government is said to be running a budget deficit. So it is true that, given private saving, if the government reduces its deficit—either by increasing taxes or reducing government spending so that $T - G$ goes up—investment must go up: Given S, $T - G$ going up implies that I goes up.

The crucial part of this statement, however, is "given private saving." The point is that a fiscal contraction affects private saving as well: The contraction leads to lower output and therefore to lower income. As consumption goes down by less than income, private saving also goes down. And it may go down by more than the reduction in the budget deficit, leading to a decrease rather than an increase in investment. In terms of the equation: If S decreases by more than $T-G$ increases, then I will decrease, not increase.

To sum up, a fiscal contraction may decrease investment. Or, looking at the reverse policy, a fiscal expansion—a decrease in taxes or an increase in spending—may actually increase investment.

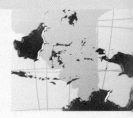

- Step 2 is to see how these shifts affect the equilibrium. The monetary expansion shifts the *LM* curve. It does not shift the *IS* curve. The economy moves along the *IS* curve, and the equilibrium moves from point *A* to point *A'*. Output increases from *Y* to *Y'*, and the interest rate decreases from *i* to *i'*.

The increase in M shifts the LM curve down. It does not shift the IS curve. The economy moves along the IS curve.

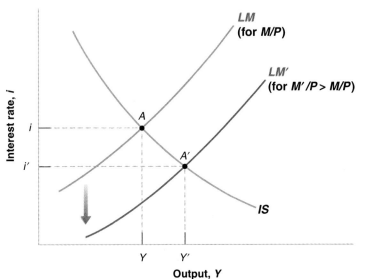

Figure 5-8

The Effects of a Monetary Expansion

A monetary expansion leads to higher output and a lower interest rate.

Table 5-1	The Effects of Fiscal and Monetary Policy			
	Shift of *IS*	Shift of *LM*	Movement in Output	Movement in Interest Rate
Increase in taxes	Left	None	Down	Down
Decrease in taxes	Right	None	Up	Up
Increase in spending	Right	None	Up	Up
Decrease in spending	Left	None	Down	Down
Increase in money	None	Down	Up	Down
Decrease in money	None	Up	Down	Up

■ Step 3 is to say it in words: The increase in money leads to a lower interest rate. The lower interest rate leads to an increase in investment and, in turn, to an increase in demand and output.

In contrast to the case of fiscal contraction, we can tell exactly what happens to the different components of demand after a monetary expansion: Because income is higher and taxes are unchanged, disposable income goes up, and so does consumption. Because sales are higher and the interest rate is lower, investment also unambiguously goes up. So a monetary expansion is more investment friendly than a fiscal expansion.

Let's summarize:

■ You should remember the three-step approach we have developed in this section (characterize the shifts, show the effect on the equilibrium, tell the story in words) to look at the effects of changes in policy on activity and the interest rate. We will use it throughout the book.

■ Table 5-1 summarizes what we have learned about the effects of fiscal and monetary policy. Use the same method to look at changes other than changes in policy. For example, trace the effects of a decrease in consumer confidence through its effect on consumption demand, or, say, the introduction of new, more convenient credit cards through their effect on the demand for money.

5-4 ▬ Using a Policy Mix

We have looked so far at fiscal policy and monetary policy in isolation. Our purpose was to show how each worked. In practice, the two are often used together. The combination of monetary and fiscal policies is known as the **monetary–fiscal policy mix**, or simply the **policy mix**.

Sometimes, the right mix is to use fiscal and monetary policy in the same direction. This was the case, for example, during the recession of 2001 in the United States, when both monetary and fiscal policy were used to fight the recession. The story of the recession and the role of monetary and fiscal policy are described in the Focus box "The U.S. Recession of 2001."

Sometimes, the right mix is to use the two policies in opposite directions—for example, combining a fiscal contraction with a monetary expansion. This was the case in the early 1990s in the United States. When Bill Clinton was elected president in 1992, one of his priorities was to reduce the budget deficit using a combination of cuts in spending and increases in taxes. However, Clinton was worried, that, by itself, such a fiscal contraction would lead to a decrease in demand and trigger another recession. The right strategy was to combine a fiscal contraction (to get rid of the deficit) with a

In 1992, the U.S. economy embarked on a long expansion. For the rest of the decade, GDP growth was positive and high. In 2000, however, signs appeared that the expansion might be coming to an end. GDP growth was negative in the third quarter, although it turned positive again in the fourth quarter. In 2001, GDP growth remained negative for the first three quarters, before becoming positive again in the last quarter. (Figure 1 shows the growth rate of GDP for each quarter from 1999:1 to 2002:4, measured at an annual rate. The shaded area corresponds to the three quarters of negative growth in 2001.) The National Bureau of Economic Research (NBER), a non-profit organization that has traditionally dated U.S. recessions and expansions, concluded that the U.S. economy had indeed had a recession in 2001, starting in March 2001 and ending in December 2001.

What triggered the recession was not, as in 1990 to 1991, a decrease in consumption demand (see the Focus box on the 1990 to 1991 recession in Chapter 4) but a sharp decline in investment demand. Non-residential investment—the demand for plant and equipment by firms—decreased by 4.5% in 2001. The cause was the end of what Alan Greenspan had dubbed a period of "irrational exuberance": During the second part of the 1990s, firms had been extremely optimistic about the future, and the rate of investment had been very high: The average yearly growth rate of investment from 1995 to 2000 exceeded 10%. In 2001, however, it became clear to firms that they had been overly optimistic and had invested too much. This led them to cut back on investment, leading to a decrease in demand and, through the multiplier, a decrease in GDP.

The recession could have been much worse. But it was met by a strong macroeconomic policy response, which certainly limited the depth and the length of the recession.

Take monetary policy first. Starting in early 2001, the Fed, feeling that the economy was slowing down, started increasing the money supply and aggressively decreasing the federal funds rate. (Figure 2 shows the behavior of the federal funds rate from 1999:1 to 2002:4.) It continued to do so throughout the year. The funds rate, which stood at 6.5% in January, stood at less than 2% at the end of the year, a very low level by historical standards.

Now turn to fiscal policy. During the 2000 campaign, then candidate George W. Bush had run on a platform of lower taxes. The argument was that the federal budget was in surplus, and so there was room to reduce tax rates while keeping the budget in balance. When President Bush took office in 2001, and it became clear that the economy was slowing down, he had an additional rationale to cut tax rates, namely the use of lower taxes to increase demand and fight the

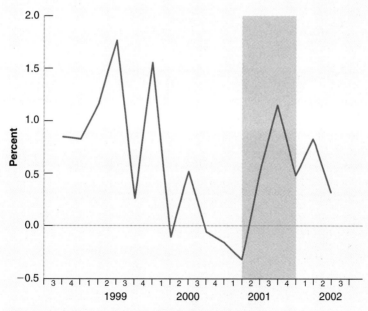

Figure 1   *The U.S. Growth Rate, 1999:1 to 2002:4*

Continued

recession. Both the 2001 and the 2002 budgets included substantial reductions in tax rates. On the spending side, the events of September 11, 2001, led to an increase in spending, mostly on defense and homeland security.

Figure 3 shows the evolution of federal government revenues and spending from 1999:1 to 2002:4, both expressed as ratios to GDP. Note the dramatic decrease in revenues, starting in the third quarter of 2001. Even without decreases in tax rates, revenues would have gone down during the recession: Lower output and lower income mechanically imply lower tax revenues. But, because of the tax cuts, the decrease in revenues in 2001 and 2002 was much larger than can be explained by the recession. Note also the smaller but steady increase in spending, starting around the same time. As a result, the budget surplus—the difference between revenues and spending—went from positive up until 2000 to negative in 2001 and, much more so, in 2002.

The effects of the initial decrease in investment demand and the monetary and fiscal responses can be represented using the *IS–LM* model. In Figure 4, assume that the equilibrium at the end of 2000 is represented by point A, at the intersection of the initial *IS* and initial *LM* curves. The following happened in 2001:

■ The decrease in investment demand led to a sharp shift of the IS curve to the left, from *IS* to *IS″*. Absent

policy reactions, the economy would have been at point $A″$, with output $Y″$.

■ The increase in the money supply led to a downward shift of the *LM* curve, from *LM′* to *LM′*.

■ The decrease in tax rates and the increase in spending both led to a shift of the *IS* curve to the right, from *IS″* to *IS′*.

As a result of the decrease in investment demand and of the two policy responses, the economy in 2001 ended up at point $A′$, with a decrease in output and a much lower interest rate. The output level associated with $A′$ was lower than the output level associated with A—there was a recession—but it was much higher than the output level associated with $A″$, the level that would have prevailed in the absence of policy responses.

Let me end by taking up three questions you are probably asking at this point:

■ Why weren't monetary and fiscal policy used to avoid rather than just limit the size of the recession?
  The reason is that changes in policy affect demand and output only over time (more on this in Section 5-5). Thus, by the time it became clear that the U.S. economy was entering a recession, it was already too late to use policy to avoid it. What the policy did was to reduce both the depth and the length of the recession.

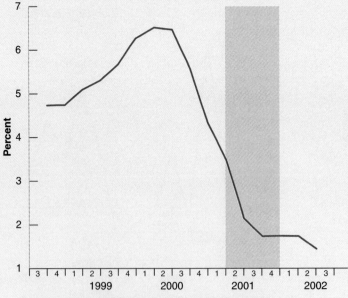

Figure 2   *The Federal Funds Rate, 1999:1 to 2002:4*

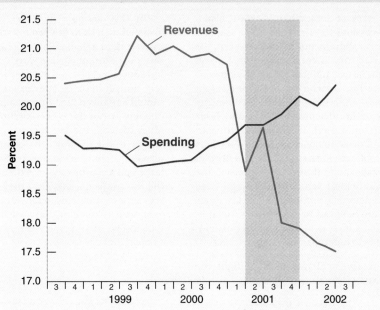

Figure 3 *U.S. Federal Government Revenues and Spending (as Ratios to GDP), 1999:1 to 2002:4*

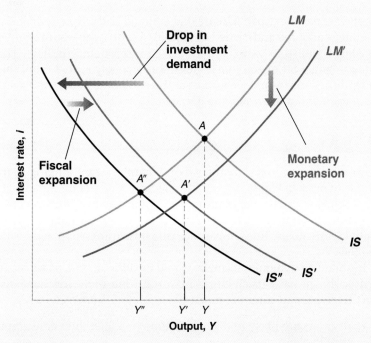

Figure 4 *The U.S. Recession of 2001*

Continued

■ Weren't the events of September 11, 2001, also a cause of the recession?

The answer, in short, is no. As we have seen, the recession started long before September 11, and it ended soon after. Indeed, GDP growth was positive in the last quarter of 2001. One might have expected—and, indeed, most economists expected—the events of September 11 to have large adverse effects on output, leading, in particular, consumers and firms to delay spending decisions until the outlook was clearer. In fact, the drop in spending was short and limited. Decreases in the federal funds rate after September 11—and large discounts by automobile producers in the last quarter of 2001—are believed to have been crucial in maintaining consumer confidence and consumer spending during that period.

■ Was the monetary-fiscal mix used to fight the recession a textbook example of how policy should be conducted?

On this, economists differ. Most economists give high marks to the Fed for strongly decreasing interest rates as soon as the economy slowed down. But most economists are worried that the tax cuts introduced in 2001 and 2002 led to large and persistent budget deficits. They argue that the tax cuts should have been temporary, helping the U.S. economy get out of the recession, but stopping thereafter. Instead, the tax cuts were permanent, and despite the fact that the U.S. economy is now going through a strong expansion, budget deficits are still large and are projected to remain large at least for the rest of the decade. This, they argue, will create very serious problems in the future. Instead, the tax cuts were permanent, and have led to lasting fiscal deficits. We shall return to this issue in depth in Chapter 26.

monetary expansion (to make sure that demand and output remained high). This was the strategy adopted and carried out by Bill Clinton (who was in charge of fiscal policy) and Alan Greenspan (who was in charge of monetary policy). The result of this strategy—and a bit of economic luck—was a steady reduction of the budget deficit (which turned into a budget surplus at the end of the 1990s) and a steady increase in output throughout the rest of the decade.

> Make sure you can tell the story using the *IS–LM* diagram. Which curves shifted? What was the effect on the equilibrium?

5-5   How Does the *IS-LM* Model Fit the Facts?

We have so far ignored dynamics. For example, when looking at the effects of an increase in taxes in Figure 5-7—or the effects of a monetary expansion in Figure 5-8—we made it look as if the economy moved instantaneously from A to A' and as if output went instantaneously from Y to Y'. This is clearly not realistic: The adjustment of output clearly takes time. To capture this time dimension, we need to reintroduce dynamics.

Introducing dynamics formally would be difficult. But, as we did in Chapter 3, we can describe the basic mechanisms in words. Some of the mechanisms will be familiar from Chapter 3, and some are new:

■ Consumers are likely to take some time to adjust their consumption following a change in disposable income.
■ Firms are likely to take some time to adjust investment spending following a change in their sales.
■ Firms are likely to take some time to adjust investment spending following a change in the interest rate.
■ Firms are likely to take some time to adjust production following a change in their sales.

So, with an increase in taxes, it takes some time for consumption spending to respond to the decrease in disposable income, some more time for production to decrease in response to the decrease in consumption spending, yet more time for investment to decrease in response to lower sales, for consumption to decrease in response to the decrease in income, and so on.

With a monetary expansion, it takes some time for investment spending to respond to the decrease in the interest rate, some more time for production to increase in response to the increase in demand, yet more time for consumption and investment to increase in response to the induced change in output, and so on.

Describing precisely the adjustment process implied by all these sources of dynamics is obviously complicated. But the basic implication is straightforward: Time is needed for output to adjust to changes in fiscal and monetary policy. How much time? This question can only be answered by looking at the data and using econometrics.

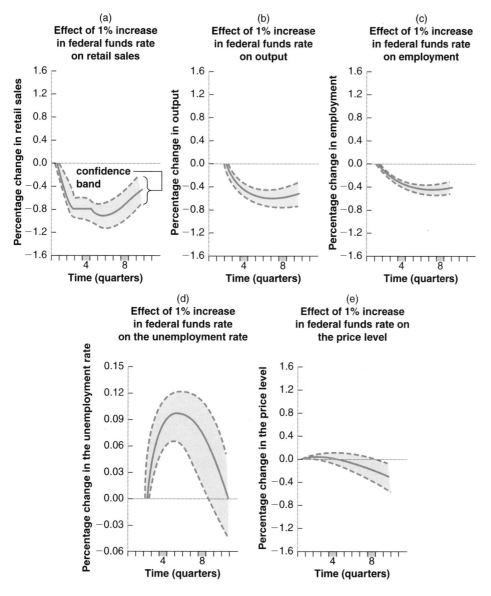

Figure 5-9

The Empirical Effects of an Increase in the Federal Funds Rate

In the short run, an increase in the federal funds rate leads to a decrease in output and to an increase in unemployment, but it has little effect on the price level.

Source: Lawrence Christiano, Martin Eichenbaum, and Charles Evans, "The Effects of Monetary Policy Shocks: Evidence from the Flow of Funds," Review of Economics and Statistics, February 1996.

Figure 5-9 shows the results of such an econometric study, which uses data from the United States from 1960 to 1990.

The study looks at the effects of a decision by the Fed to increase the *federal funds rate* by 1%. It traces the typical effects of such an increase on a number of macroeconomic variables.

We discussed the federal funds market and the federal funds ▶ rate in Section 4-3.

Each panel in Figure 5-9 represents the effects of the change in the interest rate on a given variable. Each panel plots three lines. The solid line in the center of a band gives the best estimate of the effect of the change in the interest rate on the variable we look at in the panel. The two dashed lines and the tinted space between the dashed lines represents a **confidence band**, a band within which the true value of the effect lies with 60% probability:

There is no such thing in econometrics as learning the exact value of a coefficient or the exact effect of one variable on another. Rather, what econometrics does is to provide a best ▶ estimate—here, the solid line—and a measure of confidence we can have in the estimate—here, the confidence band.

■ Figure 5-9(a) shows the effects of an increase in the federal funds rate of 1% on retail sales over time. The percentage change in retail sales is plotted on the vertical axis; time, measured in quarters, is on the horizontal axis.

Focusing on the best estimate—the solid line—we see that the increase in the federal funds rate of 1% leads to a decline in retail sales. The largest decrease in retail sales, –0.9%, is achieved after five quarters.

This explains why monetary policy could not prevent the 2001 recession (see the Focus box earlier in this chapter). At the start of 2001, the Fed starting decreasing the federal funds rate, but it was already too late for these cuts to have much effect in 2001. ▶

■ Figure 5-9(b) shows how lower sales lead to lower output. In response to the decrease in sales, firms cut production, but by less than the decrease in sales. Put another way, firms accumulate inventories for some time. The adjustment of production is smoother and slower than the adjustment of sales. The largest decrease, –0.7%, is reached after eight quarters. In other words, monetary policy works, but it works with long lags. It takes nearly two years for monetary policy to have its full effect on production.

■ Figure 5-9(c) shows how lower output leads to lower employment: As firms cut production, they also cut employment. As with output, the decline in employment is slow and steady, reaching –0.5% after eight quarters. The decline in employment is reflected in an increase in the unemployment rate, shown in Figure 5-9(d).

■ Figure 5-9(e) looks at the behavior of the price level. Remember, one of the *assumptions* of the *IS–LM* model is that the price level is given, and so it does not change in response to changes in demand. Figure 5-9(e) shows that this assumption is not a bad approximation of reality in the short run. The price level is nearly unchanged for the first six quarters or so. Only after the first six quarters does the price level appear to decline. This gives us a strong hint as to why the *IS–LM* model becomes less reliable as we look at the medium run: In the medium run, we can no longer assume that the price level is given, and movements in the price level become important.

Figure 5-9 provides two important lessons. First, it gives us a sense of the dynamic adjustment of output and other variables to monetary policy.

Second, and more fundamentally, it shows that what we observe in the economy is consistent with the implications of the *IS–LM* model. This does not *prove* that the *IS–LM* model is the right model. It may be that what we observe in the economy is the result of a completely different mechanism, and the fact that the *IS–LM* model fits well is a coincidence. But this seems unlikely. The *IS–LM* model looks like a solid basis on which to build when looking at movements in activity in the short run. Later, we will extend the model to look at the role of expectations (Chapters 14 to 17) and the implications of openness in both the goods markets and the financial markets (Chapters 18 to 21). But we must first understand what determines output in the medium run. This is the topic of the next four chapters.

Summary

- The *IS–LM model* characterizes the implications of equilibrium in both the goods and financial markets.
- The *IS* relation and the *IS* curve show the combinations of the interest rate and the level of output that are consistent with equilibrium in the goods market. An increase in the interest rate leads to a decline in output. Consequently, the *IS* curve is downward sloping.
- The *LM* relation and the *LM* curve show the combinations of the interest rate and the level of output consistent with equilibrium in financial markets. Given the real money supply, an increase in output leads to an increase in the interest rate. Consequently, the *LM* curve is upward sloping.
- A fiscal expansion shifts the *IS* curve to the right, leading to an increase in output and an increase in the interest rate. A fiscal contraction shifts the *IS* curve to the left, leading to a decrease in output and a decrease in the interest rate.
- A monetary expansion shifts the *LM* curve down, leading to an increase in output and a decrease in the inter-

est rate. A monetary contraction shifts the *LM* curve up, leading to a decrease in output and an increase in the interest rate.
- The combination of monetary and fiscal policies is known as the monetary–fiscal policy mix, or simply the policy mix. Sometimes monetary and fiscal policy are used in the same direction. This was the case during the 2001 U.S. recession. Sometimes, they are used in opposite directions. Fiscal contraction and monetary expansion can, for example, achieve a decrease in the budget deficit while avoiding a decrease in output.
- The *IS–LM* model appears to describe well the behavior of the economy in the short run. In particular, the effects of monetary policy appear to be similar to those implied by the *IS–LM* model once dynamics are introduced in the model. An increase in the interest rate due to a monetary contraction leads to a steady decrease in output, with the maximum effect taking place after about eight quarters.

Key Terms

- *IS* curve, 110
- *LM* curve, 114
- fiscal contraction, fiscal consolidation, 116
- fiscal expansion, 116
- monetary expansion, 118
- monetary contraction, monetary tightening, 118
- monetary–fiscal policy mix, policy mix, 120
- confidence band, 126

Questions and Problems

Quick Check

1. Using the information in this chapter, label each of the following statements true, false, or uncertain. Explain briefly.

  a. The main determinants of investment are the level of sales and the interest rate.

  b. If all the exogenous variables in the *IS* relation are constant, then a higher level of output can be achieved only by lowering the interest rate.

  c. The *IS* curve is downward sloping because goods market equilibrium implies that an increase in taxes leads to a lower level of output.

  d. If government spending and taxes increase by the same amount, the *IS* curve does not shift.

  e. The *LM* curve is upward sloping because a higher level of the money supply is needed to increase output.

  f. An increase in government spending leads to a decrease in investment.

  g. Government policy can increase output without changing the interest rate only if both monetary and fiscal policy variables change.

2. Consider first the goods market model with constant investment that we saw in Chapter 3. Consumption is given by

$$C = c_0 + c_1(Y - T)$$

and I, G, and T are given.

  a. Solve for equilibrium output. What is the value of the multiplier?

  Now let investment depend on both sales and the interest rate:

$$I = b_0 + b_1 Y - b_2 i$$

  b. Solve for equilibrium output. At a given interest rate, is the effect of a change in autonomous spending bigger than what it was in part (a)? Why? (Assume $c_1 + b_1 < 1$.)
  Next, write the LM *relation as*

$$M/P = d_1 Y - d_2 i$$

  c. Solve for equilibrium output. (Hint: Eliminate the interest rate from the *IS* and *LM* relations.) Derive the multiplier (the effect of a change of one unit in autonomous spending on output).

d. Is the multiplier you obtained in part (c) smaller or larger than the multiplier you derived in part (a)? Explain how your answer depends on the parameters in the behavioral equations for consumption, investment, and money demand.

3. *The response of investment to fiscal policy*

a. Using the *IS–LM* diagram, show the effects on output and the interest rate of a decrease in government spending. Can you tell what happens to investment? Why?

Now consider the following IS–LM *model:*

$$C = c_0 + c_1(Y - T)$$
$$I = b_0 + b_1Y - b_2i$$
$$M/P = d_1Y - d_2i$$

b. Solve for equilibrium output. Assume $c_1 + b_1 < 1$. (Hint: You may want to work through problem 2 if you are having trouble with this step.)

c. Solve for the equilibrium interest rate. (Hint: Use the *LM* relation.)

d. Solve for investment.

e. Under what conditions on the parameters of the model (i.e., c_0, c_1, and so on) will investment increase when G decreases? (Hint: If G decreases by one unit, by how much does I increase? Be careful; you want the change in I to be positive when the change in G is negative.)

f. Explain the condition you derived in part (e).

4. *Consider the following* IS–LM *model:*

$$C = 400 + .25Y_D$$
$$I = 300 + .25Y - 1,500i$$
$$G = 600$$
$$T = 400$$
$$(M/P)^d = 2Y - 12,000i$$

$$M/P = 3,000$$

a. Derive the *IS* relation. (Hint: You want an equation with Y on the left side and everything else on the right.)

b. Derive the *LM* relation. (Hint: It will be convenient for later use to rewrite this equation with i on the left side and everything else on the right.)

c. Solve for equilibrium real output. (Hint: Substitute the expression for the interest rate given by the *LM* equation into the *IS* equation and solve for output.)

d. Solve for the equilibrium interest rate. (Hint: Substitute the value you obtained for Y in part (c) into either the *IS* or *LM* equations and solve for i. If your algebra is correct, you should get the same answer from both equations.)

e. Solve for the equilibrium values of C and I, and verify the value you obtained for Y by adding C, I, and G.

f. Now suppose that the money supply increases to $M/P = 4,320$. Solve for Y, i, C, and I, and describe in words the effects of an expansionary monetary policy.

g. Set *M/P* equal to its initial value of 3,000. Now suppose that government spending increases to $G = 840$. Summarize the effects of an expansionary fiscal policy on Y, i, and C.

Dig Deeper

5. *Investment and the interest rate*

The chapter argues that investment depends negatively on the interest rate because an increase in the cost of borrowing discourages investment. However, firms often finance their investment projects using their own funds.

If a firm is considering using its own funds (rather than borrowing) to finance investment projects, will higher interest rates discourage the firm from undertaking these projects? Explain. (Hint: Think of yourself as the owner of a firm that has earned profits and imagine that you are going to use the profits either to finance new investment projects or to buy bonds. Will your decision to invest in new projects in your firm be affected by the interest rate?)

6. *The liquidity trap*

a. Suppose the interest rate on bonds is negative. Will people want to hold bonds or to hold money? Explain.

b. Draw the demand for money as a function of the interest rate for a given level of real income. How does your answer to part (a) affect your answer? (Hint: Show that the demand for money becomes very flat as the interest rate gets very close to zero.)

c. Derive the *LM* curve. What happens to the *LM* curve as the interest rate gets very close to zero? (Hint: It becomes very flat.)

d. Consider your *LM* curve. Suppose that the interest rate is very close to zero, and the central bank increases the supply of money. What happens to the interest rate at a given level of income?

e. Can an expansionary monetary policy increase output when the interest rate is already very close to zero?

The inability of the central bank to reduce the interest rate when it is already very close to zero is known as the *liquidity trap* and was first mentioned by Keynes in 1936 in his General Theory—which laid the foundations of the IS–LM model. As we shall see in Chapter 22, Japan is now in such a liquidity trap. This liquidity trap sharply limits the ability of monetary policy to get Japan out of its economic slump.

7. *Policy mixes*

Suggest a policy mix to achieve each of the following objectives.

a. Increase Y while keeping i constant.

b. Decrease the fiscal deficit while keeping Y constant. What happens to i? to investment?

8. *The Bush–Greenspan policy mix*

In 2001, the Fed pursued a very expansionary monetary policy. At the same time, President George W. Bush pushed through legislation that lowered income taxes.

a. Illustrate the effect of such a policy mix on output.

b. How does this policy mix differ from the Clinton–Greenspan mix?

c. What happened to output in 2001? How do you reconcile the fact that both fiscal and monetary policies were expansionary with the fact that growth was so low in 2002? (Hint: What else happened?)

9. The (less paradoxical) paradox of saving

A chapter problem at the end of Chapter 3 considered the effect of a drop in consumer confidence on private saving and investment, when investment depended on output but not the interest rate. Here, we consider the same experiment in the context of the IS–LM framework, in which investment depends on the interest rate and output.

a. Suppose households attempt to save more, so that consumer confidence falls. In an IS–LM diagram, show the effect of the fall in consumer confidence on output and the interest rate.

b. How will the fall in consumer confidence affect consumption, investment, and private saving? Will the attempt to save more necessarily lead to more saving? Will this attempt necessarily lead to less saving?

Explore Further

10. The Clinton–Greenspan policy mix

As described in the chapter, during the Clinton administration, the policy mix changed toward more contractionary fiscal policy and more expansionary monetary policy. This question explores the implications of this change in the policy mix, in theory and fact.

a. Suppose G falls, T rises, and M increases and that this combination of policies has no effect on output. Show the effects of these policies in an IS–LM diagram. What happens to the interest rate? What happens to investment?

b. Go to the Web site of the Economic Report of the President (**www.gpoaccess.gov/eop/**). Look at Table B-79 in the statistical appendix. What happened to federal receipts (tax revenues), federal outlays, and the budget deficit as a percentage of GDP over the period 1992 to 2000? (Note that federal outlays include transfer payments, which would be excluded from the variable G, as we define it in our IS–LM model. Ignore the difference.)

c. The Federal Reserve Board of Governors posts the recent history of the federal funds rate at **www.federalreserve. gov/fomc/fundsrate.htm**. Look at the years between 1992 and 2000. When did monetary policy become more expansionary?

d. Go to Table B-2 of the Economic Report of the President and collect data on real GDP and real gross domestic investment for the period 1992 to 2000. Calculate investment as a percentage of GDP for each year. What happened to investment over the period?

e. Finally, go to Table B-31 and retrieve data on real GDP per capita (in chained 2000 dollars) for the period. Calculate the growth rate for each year. What was the average annual growth rate over the period 1992 to 2000? In Chapter 10, you will learn that the average annual growth rate of U.S. real GDP per capita was 2.6% between 1950 and 2004. How did growth between 1992 and 2000 compare to the postwar averages?

11. Consumption, investment, and the recession of 2001

This question asks you to examine the movements of investment and consumption before, during, and after the recession of 2001. It also asks you to consider the response of investment and consumption to the events of September 11, 2001.

Go to the Web site of the Bureau of Economic Analysis (**www.bea.gov**). Find the NIPA tables, in particular the quarterly versions of Table 1.1.1, which shows the percentage change in real GDP and its components, and Table 1.1.2, which shows the contribution of the components of GDP to the overall percentage change in GDP. Table 1.1.2 weighs the percentage change of the components by their size. Investment is more variable than consumption, but consumption is much bigger than investment, so smaller percentage changes in consumption can have the same impact on GDP as much larger percentage changes in investment. Note that the quarterly percentage changes are annualized (i.e., expressed as annual rates). Get quarterly data on real GDP, consumption, gross private domestic investment, and non-residential fixed investment for the years 1999 to 2002 from Tables 1.1.1 and 1.1.2.

a. Identify the quarters of negative growth in 2000 and 2001.

b. Track consumption and investment around 2000 and 2001. From Table 1.1.1, which variable had the bigger percentage change around this time? Compare non-residential fixed investment with overall investment. Which variable had the bigger percentage change?

c. From Table 1.1.2, get the contribution to GDP growth of consumption and investment for 1999 to 2001. Calculate the average of the quarterly contributions for each variable for each year. Now calculate the change in the contribution of each variable for 2000 and 2001 (i.e., subtract the average contribution of consumption in 1999 from the average contribution of consumption in 2000, subtract the average contribution of consumption in 2000 from the average contribution of consumption in 2001, and do the same for investment for both years). Which variable had the bigger fall in contribution to growth? What do you think was the proximate cause of the recession of 2001? (Was it a fall in investment demand or a fall in consumption demand?)

d. Now look at what happened to consumption and investment in the third and fourth quarters of 2001 and in the first two quarters of 2002, after the events of September 11. Does the drop in investment at the end of 2001 make sense to you? How long did the drop in investment last? What happened to consumption around this time? How do you explain, in particular, the change in consumption in the fourth quarter of 2001? Did the events of September 11, 2001, cause the recession of 2001? Use the discussion in the chapter and your own intuition as guides in answering these questions.

We invite you to visit the Blanchard page on the Prentice Hall Web site, at:
www.prenhall.com/blanchard
for this chapter's World Wide Web exercises.

Further Readings

- A description of the U.S. economy, from the period of "irrational exuberance" to the 2001 recession and the role of fiscal and monetary policy is given by Paul Krugman, in *The Great Unraveling*, W.W. Norton, New York, 2003. (Warning: Krugman does not like the Bush administration or its policies!)

Appendix: An Alternative Derivation of the *LM* Relation as an Interest Rate Rule:

In this chapter, we derived the *LM* relation under the assumption that *the money stock remained constant*. This gave us the positive relation between the interest rate and income shown, for example, in Figure 5-4(b).

As we discussed in Chapter 4, however, the assumption that the central bank keeps the money stock constant and lets the interest rate adjust when income changes is not a good description of what modern central banks do. Most central banks think instead in terms of setting the interest rate and adjusting the money stock so as to achieve the interest rate they want. Thus, we may want to derive the *LM* relation under the alternative assumption that the central bank sets the interest rate and adjusts the money supply as needed to achieve that goal.

To see what this implies, turn to Figure 1(a). Like Figure 5-4(a), it plots money supply and money demand, with the interest rate on the vertical axis, and money on the horizontal axis. The money supply is given by the vertical line M^s, and money demand is given by the downward-sloping curve M^d. The initial equilibrium is at point A, with the interest rate, i_A.

Now consider an increase in income that shifts money demand from M^d to $M^{d'}$. If the central bank does not change the money supply, then the equilibrium will move from A to B, and the interest rate will increase from i_A to i_B. The implied *LM* curve, *LM*, the relation between the interest rate and income, is drawn in Figure 1(b). It is exactly the same as in Figure 5-4(a).

Suppose however that the central bank wants to keep the interest rate constant in the face of the increase in income. Can it do it? Yes. How can it do it? By increasing the money supply in response to the increase in income, from M^s to $M^{s'}$. If it does so, the interest rate will remain constant. The equilibrium will move from A to D, and the interest rate will remain constant, at i_A. The resulting *LM* curve, denoted by LM' in Figure 1(b), will be horizontal: In response to the

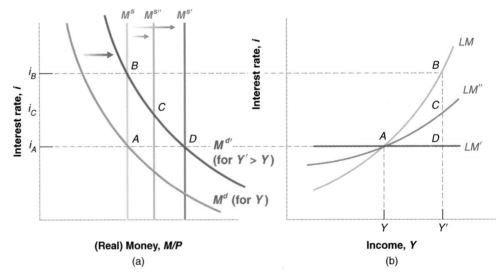

Figure 1

The LM *Relation as an Interest Rate Rule*

(a) Depending on whether and by how much the central bank increases the money supply in response to a shift in money demand coming from changes in income, the interest rate may remain constant, increase a little, or increase a lot.

(b) We can think of the *LM* curve as showing whether and by how much the central bank allows the interest rate to increase in response to increases in income.

increase in income, the central bank will adjust the money supply so as to keep the interest rate constant.

This may be too extreme a policy. Perhaps the central bank wants to allow the interest rate to increase, but by less than it would if the central bank kept the money supply constant. For example, in response to the increase in income, the central bank may choose to increase the money supply by $M^{s''} < M^{s'}$. In this case, the equilibrium will move from A to C, and the interest rate will increase from i_A to i_C. The resulting LM curve, denoted by LM'' in Figure 1(b), will be upward sloping but flatter than LM.

To summarize: The LM relation we derived in the text gave us the relation between the interest rate and income for a *given money supply*. The LM relation derived in the appendix gives us the relation between the interest rate and income when the central bank follows a *given interest rule* and lets the money supply adjust as needed. Its slope then depends on how much the central bank increases the interest rate in response to increases in income.

Which LM relation should you use? It depends on the question at hand. Take, for example, the case of an increase in the deficit, shifting the IS curve to the right. You might want to know what would happen to output and the interest rate if the central bank money supply remained constant, in which case you would use the LM relation derived in the text. But you might know, for example, that the central bank is likely to keep the interest rate constant, in which case you would use the LM relation derived in this appendix—in this particular case, a horizontal LM curve. (Under which of the two assumptions will fiscal policy have the strongest effect on output?)

Key Term

■ interest rate rule, 130

The Medium Run

In the medium run, the economy returns to a level of output associated with the natural rate of unemployment.

THE CORE

Chapter 6

Chapter 6 looks at equilibrium in the labor market. It derives the natural rate of unemployment—the unemployment rate to which the economy tends to return in the medium run. Associated with the natural rate of unemployment is a natural level of output.

Chapter 7

Chapter 7 looks at equilibrium in all three markets—goods, financial, and labor—together. It shows that, while output typically deviates from the natural level of output in the short run, it returns to the natural level in the medium run. The model developed in Chapter 7 is called the *AS–AD* model, and, together with the *IS–LM* model, it is one of the workhorses of macroeconomics.

Chapter 8

Chapter 8 looks more closely at the relation between inflation and unemployment, a relation known as the Phillips curve. It shows that, in the United States today, low unemployment leads to an increase in inflation; high unemployment leads to a decrease in inflation.

Chapter 9

Chapter 9 looks at the determination of output, unemployment, and inflation and the effects of money growth. In the short run, decreases in money growth can trigger a recession. In the medium run, however, they are neutral; they have no effect on unemployment or output but are reflected one-for-one in changes in the rate of inflation.

The Labor Market

hink about what happens when firms respond to an increase in demand by increasing production: Higher production leads to higher employment. Higher employment leads to lower unemployment. Lower unemployment leads to higher wages. Higher wages increase production costs, leading firms to increase prices. Higher prices lead workers to ask for higher wages. Higher wages lead to further increases in prices, and so on.

So far, we have simply ignored this sequence of events: By assuming a constant price level, we have in effect assumed that firms were able and willing to supply any amount of output at a given price level. So long as our focus was on the *short run*, this assumption was acceptable. But as our attention turns to the *medium run*, we must now abandon this assumption, explore how prices and wages adjust over time, and explore how this, in turn, affects output. This will be our task in this and the next three chapters.

At the center of the sequence of events described here is the *labor market*, the market in which wages are determined. This chapter focuses on the labor market. It has six sections:

- Section 6-1 provides an overview of the labor market.

- Section 6-2 focuses on unemployment, how it moves over time, and how its movements affect individual workers.

- Sections 6-3 and 6-4 look at wage and price determination.

- Section 6-5 looks at equilibrium in the labor market. It characterizes the *natural rate of unemployment*, the rate of unemployment to which the economy tends to return in the medium run.

- Section 6-6 gives a map of where we will be going next. ■

6-1 █ A Tour of the Labor Market

The total U.S. population in 2006 was 301.0 million (Figure 6-1). Excluding those who were either under working age (under 16), in the armed forces, or behind bars, the number of people potentially available for civilian employment, the **noninstitutional civilian population**, was 228.0 million.

The civilian labor force—the sum of those either working or looking for work—was only 151.4 million. The other 77.4 million people were **out of the labor force**, neither working in the marketplace nor looking for work. The **participation rate**, defined as the ratio of the labor force to the noninstitutional civilian population, was therefore 151.4/228.0, or 66%. The participation rate has steadily increased over time, reflecting mostly the increasing participation rate of women: In 1950, one woman out of three was in the labor force; now the number is close to two out of three.

Of those in the labor force, 144.4 million were employed, and 7.0 million were unemployed—looking for work. The **unemployment rate**, defined as the ratio of the unemployed to the labor force, was therefore 7.0/151.4 = 4.6%.

Work in the home, such as ▶ cooking or raising children, is not classified as work in the official statistics. This is a reflection of the difficulty of measuring these activities—not a value judgment about what constitutes work and what doesn't.

The Large Flows of Workers

To get a sense of what a given unemployment rate implies for individual workers, consider the following analogy. Take an airport full of passengers. It may be crowded because many planes are coming and going, and many passengers are quickly moving in and out of the airport. Or it may be crowded because bad weather is delaying flights and passengers are stuck, waiting for the weather to improve. The number of passengers in the airport will be high in both cases, but their plights are quite different. Passengers in the second scenario are likely to be much less happy.

█ **Figure 6-1**

Population, Labor Force, Employment, and Unemployment in the United States (in millions), 2006

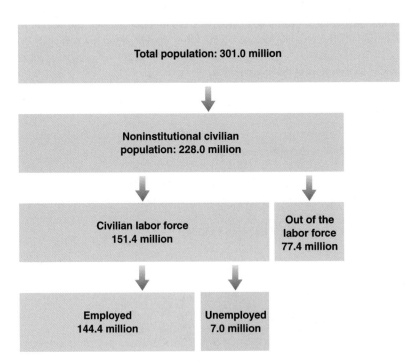

In the same way, a given unemployment rate may reflect two very different realities. It may reflect an active labor market, with many **separations** and many **hires**, and so with many workers entering and exiting unemployment; or it may reflect a sclerotic labor market, with few separations, few hires, and a stagnant unemployment pool.

Finding out which reality hides behind the aggregate unemployment rate requires data on the movements of workers. These data are available in the United States from a monthly survey called the **Current Population Survey (CPS)**. Average monthly flows, computed from the CPS for the United States from 1996 to 2003, are reported in Figure 6-2. (For more on the ins and outs of the CPS, see the Focus box "The Current Population Survey.")

Figure 6-2 has three striking features:

■ The flows of workers in and out of employment are very large.

On average, there are 7.4 million separations each month in the United States (out of an employment pool of 122 million): 2.8 million workers move directly from one job to another (shown by the circular arrow at the top of the figure). Another 1.8 million move from employment to unemployment (shown by the arrow from employment to unemployment). And 2.8 million move from employment out of the labor force (shown by the arrow from employment to out of the labor force).

■ Why are there so many separations each month? About three-fourths of all separations are **quits**—workers leaving their jobs for a better alternative. The remaining one-fourth are **layoffs**. Layoffs come mostly from changes in employment levels across firms: The slowly changing aggregate employment numbers hide a reality of continual job destruction and job creation across firms. At any given time, some firms are suffering decreases in demand and decreasing their employment; other firms are enjoying increases in demand and increasing employment.

■ The flows in and out of unemployment are large relative to the number of unemployed:

The average monthly flow out of unemployment each month is 2.8 million: 1.4 million people get a job, and 1.4 million stop searching for one and drop out of

Sclerosis, a medical term, means hardening of tissue. By analogy, it is used in economics to describe markets that function poorly and have few transactions. ◀

The numbers for employment, unemployment, and those out of the labor force in Figure 6-1 refer to 2006. The numbers for ◀ the same variables in Figure 6-2 refer to averages from 1996 to 2003. This is why they are different.

Put another, and perhaps more dramatic, way: On average, every day in the United States, ◀ 50,000 workers become unemployed.

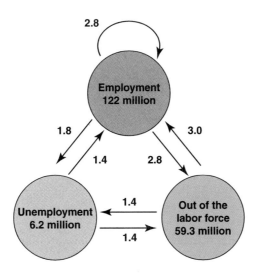

Figure 6-2

Average Monthly Flows Between Employment, Unemployment, and Nonparticipation in the United States, 1996–2003

(1) The flows of workers in and out of employment are large. (2) The flows in and out of unemployment are large relative to the number of unemployed. (3) There are also large flows in and out of the labor force, much of it directly to and from employment.

The average duration of unemployment equals the inverse of the proportion of unemployed leaving unemployment each month. To see why, consider an example. Suppose the number of unemployed is constant and equal to 100, and each unemployed person remains unemployed for two months. So, at any given time, there are 50 people who have been unemployed for one month and 50 who have been unemployed for two months. Each month, the 50 unemployed who have been unemployed for two months leave unemployment. In this example, the proportion of unemployed leaving unemployment each month is 50/100, or 50%. The duration of unemployment is two months—the inverse of 1/50%.

the labor force. Put another way, the proportion of unemployed leaving unemployment equals 2.8/6.2 or about 45% each month. Put yet another way, the average **duration of unemployment**—the average length of time people spend unemployed—is between two and three months.

This fact has an important implication. You should not think of unemployment in the United States as a stagnant pool of workers waiting indefinitely for jobs. For most (but obviously not all) of the unemployed, being unemployed is more a quick transition than a long wait between jobs. In this respect, the United States is unusual among rich countries: As we will see in Chapter 13, the average duration of unemployment is much longer in Western Europe.

■ The flows in and out of the labor force are also surprisingly large: Each month, 4.2 million workers drop out of the labor force (2.8 plus 1.4), and a slightly larger number join the labor force (3.0 plus 1.4).

You might have expected these two flows to be composed, on one side, of those finishing school and entering the labor force for the first time and, on the other side, of workers going into retirement. But each of these two groups actually represents a small fraction of the total flows. Each month, only about 400,000 new people enter the labor force, and about 250,000 retire. But the actual flows in and out of the labor force are 8.4 million (2.8 + 1.4 + 3.0 + 1.4), or more than 10 times larger.

What this fact implies is that many of those classified as "out of the labor force" are in fact willing to work and move back and forth between participation and nonparticipation. Indeed, among those classified as out of the labor force, nearly 5 million report that although they are not looking, they "want a job." What they really mean by this statement is unclear, but the evidence is that many do take jobs when offered to them.

Working in the opposite direction: Some of the unemployed may be unwilling to accept any job offered to them and should probably not be counted as unemployed because they are not really looking for a job.

This fact has another important implication. The sharp focus on the unemployment rate by economists, policymakers, and news media is partly misdirected. Some of the people classified as "out of the labor force" are very much like the unemployed. They are in effect **discouraged workers**. And while they are not actively looking for a job, they will take one if they find one. This is why economists sometimes focus on the **non-employment** rate, the ratio of population minus employment to population, rather than the unemployment rate. I will follow tradition in this book and focus on the unemployment rate, but you should keep in mind that the unemployment rate is not the best estimate of the number of people available for work.

6-2 Movements in Unemployment

Let's now look at movements in unemployment. Figure 6-3 shows the average value of the U.S. unemployment rate for each year since 1948. The shaded areas represent years during which there was a recession.

Figure 6-3 has two important features:

The evolution of the unemployment rate has been very different in Western Europe. As we saw in Chapter 1, it steadily increased from the 1960s to the late 1990s, and it remains high today. We'll cover this further in Chapters 8 and 13.

■ Until the mid-1980s, it looked as if the U.S. unemployment rate was on an upward trend, from an average of 4.5% in the 1950s to 4.7% in the 1960s, 6.2% in the 1970s, and 7.3% in the 1980s. Since then, however, the unemployment rate has steadily declined. In the 1990s, the average unemployment rate stood at 5.2%. This decrease has led a number of economists to conclude that the trend has been reversed and that the U.S. economy is likely to operate at a lower average unemployment rate in the future than in the past 20 years. We will return to this issue in Chapter 8.

The Current Population Survey (CPS) is the main source of statistics on the labor force, employment, participation, and earnings in the United States.

When the CPS began in 1940, it was based on interviews of 8,000 households. The sample has grown considerably, and now more than 50,000 households are interviewed every month. The households are chosen so that the sample is representative of the U.S. population. Each household stays in the sample for four months, leaves the sample for the following eight months, then comes back for another four months before leaving the sample permanently.

The survey is now based on computer-assisted interviews. Interviews are either done in person, in which case interviewers use laptop computers, or by phone. Some questions are asked in every survey. Other questions are specific to a particular survey and are used to find out about particular aspects of the labor market.

The Labor Department uses these data to compute and publish numbers on employment, unemployment, and participation by age, sex, education, and industry. Economists use these data, which are available in large computer files, in two ways.

The first way economists use these data is to get snapshots of how things are at various points in time, to answer such questions as: What is the distribution of wages for Hispanic-American workers with only primary education, and how does it compare with the same distribution 10 or 20 years ago?

The second way, of which Figure 6-2 is an example, is to exploit the fact that the survey follows people through time. By looking at the same people in two adjacent months, economists can find out, for example, how many of those who were unemployed last month are employed this month. This number gives them an estimate of the probability that somebody unemployed in a given month finds a job in the following month.

For more on the CPS, you can go to the CPS home page (www.bls.gov/cps/).

■ Leaving aside these trend changes, year-to-year movements in the unemployment rate are closely associated with recessions and expansions. Look, for example, at the last three peaks in unemployment. The most recent, at 6%, was associated with the recession of 2001. (Note that the peak in unemployment actually took place in 2003, two years after the recession. We will look at this episode, which at the time was known as the "jobless recovery," in Chapter 13.) The previous peak, at 7.5%, was associated with the 1990 to 1991 recession. The peak before that, in which unemployment reached 9.7% (a postwar high), was during the recession of 1982.

◀ The average unemployment rate for the year is 9.7%. The unemployment rate actually reached 10.8% in November 1982.

How do these fluctuations in the *aggregate unemployment rate* affect *individual workers*? This is an important question because the answer determines two effects:

■ The effect of movements in the aggregate unemployment rate on the welfare of individual workers
■ The effect of the aggregate unemployment rate on wages

Let's start by asking how firms can decrease their employment in response to a decrease in demand. They can hire fewer new workers, or they can lay off the workers they currently employ. Typically, firms prefer to slow or stop the hiring of new workers first, relying on quits and retirements to achieve a decrease in employment. But doing only this may not be enough if the decrease in demand is large, so firms may then have to lay off workers.

Figure 6-3

*Movements in the U.S.
Unemployment Rate
Since 1948*

Since 1948, the average yearly
U.S. unemployment rate has
fluctuated between 3% and 10%.

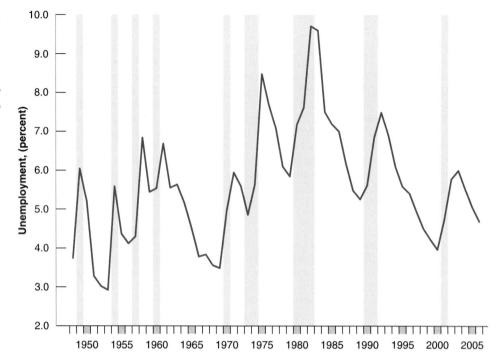

Now think about the implications for both employed and unemployed workers:

- If the adjustment takes place through fewer hires, the chance that an unemployed worker will find a job diminishes. Fewer hires means fewer job openings; higher unemployment means more job applicants. Fewer openings and more applicants combine to make it harder for the unemployed to find jobs.
- If the adjustment takes place instead through higher layoffs, then employed workers are at a greater risk of losing their jobs.

In general, as firms do both, higher unemployment is associated with both a lower chance of finding a job if a person is unemployed and a higher chance of losing it if a person is already employed. Figures 6-4 and 6-5 show these two effects at work in the United States over the period 1968 to 1999.

Figure 6-4 plots two variables against time: the unemployment rate (measured on the left vertical axis); and the proportion of unemployed workers finding a job each month (measured on the right vertical axis). This proportion is constructed by dividing the flow from unemployment to employment during each month by the number of unemployed at the beginning of the month. To show the relation between the two variables more clearly, the proportion of unemployed finding jobs is plotted on an inverted scale. Be sure you see that on the right vertical scale, the proportion is lowest at the top and highest at the bottom.

The relation between movements in the proportion of unemployed workers finding jobs and the unemployment rate is striking: Periods of higher unemployment are associated with much lower proportions of unemployed workers finding jobs. At the peak of the 1980 to 1982 recession, for example, the proportion of workers finding jobs was down to about 16% per month, compared to an average value of 25% over the whole period.

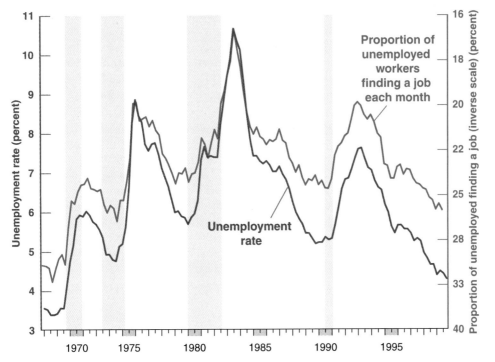

Figure 6-4

The Unemployment Rate and the Proportion of Unemployed Finding Jobs, 1968–1999

When unemployment is high, the proportion of unemployed finding jobs is low. Note that the scale on the right is an inverse scale.

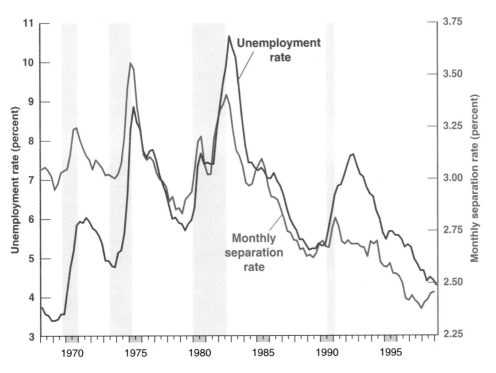

Figure 6-5

The Unemployment Rate and the Monthly Separation Rate from Employment, 1968–1999

When unemployment is high, a higher proportion of workers lose their jobs.

To be precise, we only learn from Figure 6-5 that, when unemployment is higher, separations are higher. Separations equal quits plus layoffs. We know from other sources that quits are lower when unemployment is high: It is more attractive to quit when there are plenty of jobs. So, if separations go up and quits go ▶ down, this implies that layoffs (which equal separations minus quits) go up even more than separations.

Similarly, Figure 6-5 plots two variables against time: the unemployment rate (measured on the left vertical axis) and the monthly separation rate from employment (measured on the right vertical axis). The monthly separation rate is constructed by dividing the flow from employment (to unemployment and to out of the labor force) during each month by the number of employed at the beginning of the month. The relation between the separation rate and the unemployment rate plotted in Figure 6-5 is less tight than the relation plotted in Figure 6-4, but it is nevertheless quite visible. Higher unemployment implies a higher separation rate—that is, a higher chance of employed workers losing their jobs.

To summarize, when unemployment is high, workers are worse off in two ways:

■ Employed workers face a higher probability of losing their jobs.
■ Unemployed workers face a lower probability of finding a job; equivalently, they can expect to remain unemployed for a longer time.

6-3 Wage Determination

Having looked at unemployment, let's turn to wage determination and to the relation between wages and unemployment.

Wages are set in many ways. Sometimes they are set through **collective bargaining**—that is, bargaining between firms and unions. In the United States, however, collective bargaining plays a limited role, especially outside the manufacturing sector. Today, fewer than 15% of U.S. workers have their wages set by collective bargaining agreements. For the rest, wages are either set by employers or by bargaining between the employer and individual employees. The higher the skills needed to do the job, the more likely there is to be bargaining. Wages offered for entry-level jobs at McDonald's are on a take-it-or-leave-it basis. New college graduates, on the other hand, can typically negotiate a few aspects of their compensation. CEOs and baseball stars can negotiate a lot more.

Collective bargaining is bargaining between a union (or a group of unions) and a firm (or a group of firms). ▶

There are also large differences across countries. Collective bargaining plays an important role in Japan and in most European countries. Negotiations may take place at the firm level, at the industry level, or at the national level. Sometimes contract agreements apply only to firms that have signed the agreement. Sometimes they are automatically extended to all firms and all workers in the sector or the economy.

Given these differences across workers and across countries, can we hope to formulate anything like a general theory of wage determination? Yes. Although institutional differences influence wage determination, there are common forces at work in all countries. Two sets of facts stand out:

■ Workers are typically paid a wage that exceeds their **reservation wage**, the wage that would make them indifferent between working or being unemployed. In other words, most workers are paid a high enough wage that they prefer being employed to being unemployed.
■ Wages typically depend on labor market conditions. The lower the unemployment rate, the higher the wages. (I will state this more precisely in the next section.)

To think about these facts, economists have focused on two broad lines of explanation. The first is that even in the absence of collective bargaining, workers have some bargaining power, which they can and do use to obtain wages above their reservation wages. The second is that firms themselves may, for a number of reasons, want to pay wages higher than the reservation wage. Let's look at each explanation in turn.

Bargaining

How much **bargaining power** a worker has depends on two factors. The first is how costly it would be for the firm to replace him, were he to leave the firm. The second is how hard it would be for him to find another job, were he to leave the firm. The more costly it is for the firm to replace the worker, and the easier it is for him to find another job, the more bargaining power he will have. This has two implications:

- How much bargaining power a worker has depends first on the nature of the job. Replacing a worker at McDonald's is not very costly: The required skills can be taught quickly, and typically a large number of willing applicants have already filled out job application forms. In this situation, the worker is unlikely to have much bargaining power. If he asks for a higher wage, the firm can lay him off and find a replacement at minimum cost. In contrast, a highly skilled worker who knows in detail how the firm operates may be very difficult and costly to replace. This gives her more bargaining power. If she asks for a higher wage, the firm may decide that it is best to give it to her.

- How much bargaining power a worker has also depends on labor market conditions. When the unemployment rate is low, it is more difficult for firms to find acceptable replacement workers. At the same time, it is easier for workers to find other jobs. Under these conditions, workers are in a stronger bargaining position and may be able to obtain a higher wage. Conversely, when the unemployment rate is high, finding good replacement workers is easier for firms, while finding another job is harder for workers. Being in a weak bargaining position, workers may have no choice but to accept a lower wage.

Efficiency Wages

Regardless of workers' bargaining power, firms may want to pay more than the reservation wage. They may want their workers to be productive, and a higher wage can help them achieve that goal. If, for example, it takes a while for workers to learn how to do a job correctly, firms will want their workers to stay for some time. But if workers are paid only their reservation wage, they will be indifferent between staying or leaving. In this case, many of them will quit, and the turnover rate will be high. Paying a wage above the reservation wage makes it financially attractive for workers to stay. It decreases turnover and increases productivity.

Behind this example lies a more general proposition: Most firms want their workers to feel good about their jobs. Feeling good promotes good work, which leads to higher productivity. Paying a high wage is one instrument a firm can use to achieve these goals. (See the Focus box "Henry Ford and Efficiency Wages.") Economists call the theories that link the *productivity* or the *efficiency* of workers to the wage they are paid **efficiency wage theories**.

Like theories based on bargaining, efficiency wage theories suggest that wages depend on both the nature of a job and on labor market conditions:

- Firms—such as high-tech firms—that see employee morale and commitment as essential to the quality of their work will pay more than firms in sectors where workers' activities are more routine.

- Labor market conditions will affect the wage. A low unemployment rate makes it more attractive for employed workers to quit: When unemployment is low, it is easy to find another job. That means when unemployment decreases, a firm that wants to avoid an increase in quits will have to increase wages to induce workers to stay with the firm. When this happens, lower unemployment will again lead to higher wages. Conversely, higher unemployment will lead to lower wages.

Before September 11, 2001, the approach to airport security was to hire workers at low wages and accept the resulting high turnover. Now that airport security has become a much higher priority, the approach is to make the jobs more attractive and better paying so as to get more motivated and more competent workers, and reduce turnover.

In 1914, Henry Ford—the builder of the most popular car in the world at the time, the Model T—made a stunning announcement. His company would pay every qualified employee a minimum of $5 per day for an eight-hour day. This was a very large salary increase for most employees, who had been earning an average of $2.30 for a nine-hour day. From the point of view of the Ford company, this increase in pay was far from negligible—it represented about half of the company's profits at the time.

What Ford's motivations were is not entirely clear. Ford himself gave too many reasons for us to know which ones he actually believed. The reason was not that the company had a hard time finding workers at the previous wage. But the company clearly had a hard time retaining workers. There was a very high turnover rate, and there was much dissatisfaction among workers.

Whatever the reasons behind Ford's decision, the results of the wage increase were astounding, as Table 1 shows.

The annual turnover rate (the ratio of separations to employment) plunged from a high of 370% in 1913 to a low of 16% in 1915. (An annual turnover rate of 370% means that, on average, 31% of the company's workers left each month, so that over the course of a year, the ratio of separations to employment was 31% × 12 = 370%.)

The layoff rate collapsed from 62% to nearly 0%. The average rate of absenteeism (not shown in the table), which ran at close to 10% in 1913, was down to 2.5% one year later. There is little question that higher wages were the main source of these changes.

Did productivity at the Ford plant increase enough to offset the cost of increased wages? The answer to this question is less clear. Productivity was much higher in 1914 than in 1913. Estimates of the productivity increases range from 30% to 50%. Despite higher wages, profits were also higher in 1914 than in 1913. But how much of this increase in profits was due to changes in workers' behavior and how much was due to the increasing success of Model T cars is harder to establish.

While the effects support efficiency wage theories, it may be that the increase in wages to $5 per day was excessive, at least from the point of view of profit maximization. But Henry Ford probably had other objectives as well, from keeping the unions out—which he did—to generating publicity for himself and the company—which he also surely did.

Source: Dan Raff and Lawrence Summers, "Did Henry Ford Pay Efficiency Wages?" *Journal of Labor Economics,* October 1987.

Table 1	Annual Turnover and Layoff Rates (%) at Ford, 1913–1915		
	1913	1914	1915
Turnover rate	370	54	16
Layoff rate	62	7	0.1

Wages, Prices, and Unemployment

We capture our discussion of wage determination by using the following equation:

$$W = P^e F(u, z) \qquad (6.1)$$
$$(-, +)$$

The aggregate nominal wage, W, depends on three factors:

- The expected price level, P^e
- The unemployment rate, u
- A catchall variable, z, that stands for all other variables that may affect the outcome of wage setting

Let's look at each factor.

The Expected Price Level

First, ignore the difference between the expected and the actual price levels and ask: Why does the price level affect nominal wages? Because both workers and firms care about *real wages*, not nominal wages:

■ Workers do not care about how many dollars they receive but about how many goods they can buy with those dollars. In other words, they do not care about the nominal wages they receive but about the nominal wages, W, they receive relative to the price of the goods they buy, P. They care about W/P.

■ In the same way, firms do not care about the nominal wages they pay but about the nominal wages, W, they pay relative to the price of the goods they sell, P. So they also care about W/P.

Think of it another way: If workers expect the price level—the price of the goods they buy—to double, they will ask for a doubling of their nominal wage. If firms expect the price level—the price of the goods they sell—to double, they will be willing to double the nominal wage. So, if both workers and firms expect the price level to double, they will agree to double the nominal wage, keeping the real wage constant. This is captured in equation (6.1): A doubling in the expected price level leads to a doubling of the nominal wage chosen when wages are set.

◀ An increase in the expected price level leads to an increase in the nominal wage, in the same proportion.

Return now to the distinction we set aside earlier: Why do wages depend on the *expected price level*, P^e, rather than the *actual price level*, P? Because wages are set in nominal (dollar) terms, and when they are set, the relevant price level is not yet known. For example, in many union contracts in the United States, nominal wages are set in advance for three years. Unions and firms have to decide what nominal wages will be over the following three years based on what they expect the price level to be over those three years. Even when wages are set by firms or by bargaining between the firm and each worker, nominal wages are typically set for a year. If the price level goes up unexpectedly during the year, nominal wages are typically not readjusted. (How workers and firms form expectations of the price level will occupy us for much of the next three chapters; we will leave this issue aside for the moment.)

The Unemployment Rate

Also affecting the aggregate wage in equation (6.1) is the unemployment rate, u. The minus sign under u indicates that an increase in the unemployment rate *decreases* wages.

The fact that wages depend on the unemployment rate was one of the main conclusions of our earlier discussion. If we think of wages as being determined by bargaining, then higher unemployment weakens workers' bargaining power, forcing them to accept lower wages. If we think of wages as being determined by efficiency wage considerations, then higher unemployment allows firms to pay lower wages and still keep workers willing to work.

◀ An increase in unemployment leads to a decrease in the nominal wage.

The Other Factors

The third variable in equation (6.1), z, is a catchall variable that stands for all the factors that affect wages, given the expected price level and the unemployment rate. By convention, I will define z so that an increase in z implies an increase in the wage (hence the positive sign under z in the equation). Our earlier discussion suggests a long list of potential factors here.

◀ By the definition of z, an increase in z leads to an increase in the nominal wage.

Take, for example, **unemployment insurance**—the payment of unemployment benefits to workers who lose their jobs. There are very good reasons why society should provide some insurance to workers who lose their jobs and have a hard time finding new ones. But there is little question that, by making the prospects of unemployment less distressing, more generous unemployment benefits do increase wages at a given unemployment rate. To take an extreme example, suppose unemployment insurance did not exist. Some workers would have little to live on and would be willing to accept very low wages to avoid remaining unemployed. But unemployment insurance does exist, and it allows unemployed workers to hold out for higher wages. In this case, we can think of z as representing the level of unemployment benefits: At a given unemployment rate, higher unemployment benefits increase the wage.

It is easy to think of other factors. An increase in the minimum wage may increase not only the minimum wage itself but also wages just above the minimum wage, leading to an increase in the average wage, W, at a given unemployment rate. Or take an increase in employment protection, which makes it more expensive for firms to lay off workers. Such a change is likely to increase the bargaining power of workers covered by this protection (laying them off and hiring other workers is now more costly for firms), increasing the wage for a given unemployment rate.

We will explore some of these factors as we go along.

6-4 Price Determination

Having looked at wage determination, let's now turn to price determination.

The prices set by firms depend on the costs they face. These costs depend, in turn, on the nature of the **production function**—the relation between the inputs used in production and the quantity of output produced and on the prices of these inputs.

For the moment, we will assume that firms produce goods using labor as the only factor of production. We will write the production function as follows:

$$Y = AN$$

where Y is output, N is employment, and A is labor productivity. This way of writing the production function implies that **labor productivity**—output per worker—is constant and equal to A.

It should be clear that this is a strong simplification. In reality, firms use other factors of production in addition to labor. They use capital—machines and factories. They use raw materials—oil, for example. Moreover, there is technological progress, so that labor productivity, A, is not constant but steadily increases over time. We shall introduce these complications later. We will introduce raw materials in Chapter 7, when we discuss changes in the price of oil. We will focus on the role of capital and technological progress when we turn to the determination of output in the *long run* in Chapters 10 through 13. For the moment, though, this simple relation between output and employment will make our lives easier and still serve our purposes.

Given the assumption that labor productivity, A, is constant, we can make one further simplification. We can choose the units of output so that one worker produces one unit of output—in other words, so that $A = 1$. (This way, we do not have to carry the letter A around, and this will simplify notation.) With this assumption, the production function becomes

$$Y = N \qquad (6.2)$$

The production function, $Y = N$, implies that the cost of producing one more unit of output is the cost of employing one more worker, at wage W. Using the terminology introduced in your microeconomics course: The *marginal cost of production*—the cost of producing one more unit of output—is equal to W.

If there were perfect competition in the goods market, the price of a unit of output would be equal to marginal cost: P would be equal to W. But many goods markets are

> We can use a term from microeconomics here: This assumption implies *constant returns to labor* in production. If firms double the number of workers they employ, they double the amount of output they produce.

not competitive, and firms charge a price higher than their marginal cost. A simple way of capturing this fact is to assume that firms set their prices according to

$$P = (1 + \mu)W \qquad (6.3)$$

where μ is the **markup** of the price over the cost. If goods markets were perfectly competitive, μ would be equal to zero, and the price, P, would simply equal the cost, W. To the extent that they are not competitive, and firms have market power, μ is positive, and the price, P, will exceed the cost, W, by a factor equal to $(1 + \mu)$.

6-5 The Natural Rate of Unemployment

Let's now look at the implications of wage and price determination for unemployment.

For the rest of this chapter, let's do so under the assumption that nominal wages depend on the actual price level, P, rather than on the expected price level, P^e. (Why we make this assumption will become clear soon.) Under this additional assumption, wage setting and price setting determine the equilibrium rate of unemployment. Let's see how.

◄ **The rest of the chapter is based on the assumption that $P^\theta = P$.**

The Wage-Setting Relation

Given the assumption that nominal wages depend on the actual price level, P, rather than on the expected price level, P^e, equation (6.1), which characterizes wage determination, becomes

$$W = PF(u, z)$$

We can divide both sides by the price level:

$$\frac{W}{P} = F(u, z) \atop (-,+) \qquad (6.4)$$

Wage determination implies a negative relation between the real wage, W/P, and the unemployment rate, u: *The higher the unemployment rate, the lower the real wage chosen by wage setters*. The intuition is straightforward: The higher the unemployment rate, the weaker the position of workers in bargaining and the lower the real wage will be.

This relation between the real wage and the rate of unemployment—let's call it the **wage-setting relation**—is drawn in Figure 6-6. The real wage is measured on the vertical axis. The unemployment rate is measured on the horizontal axis. The wage-setting relation is drawn as the downward-sloping curve WS (for wage setting): The higher the unemployment rate, the lower the real wage.

◄ **Wage setters are unions and firms if wages are set by collective bargaining; individual workers and firms if wages are set on a case-by-case basis and firms if wages are set on a take-it-or-leave-it basis.**

The Price-Setting Relation

Let's now look at the implications of price determination. If we divide both sides of the price-determination equation (6.3), by the nominal wage, we get

$$\frac{P}{W} = 1 + \mu \qquad (6.5)$$

The ratio of the price level to the wage implied by the price-setting behavior of firms equals 1 plus the markup. Now invert both sides of this equation to get the implied real wage:

$$\frac{W}{P} = \frac{1}{1 + \mu} \qquad (6.6)$$

Figure 6-6

Wages, Prices, and the Natural Rate of Unemployment

The natural rate of unemployment is the unemployment rate such that the real wage chosen in wage setting is equal to the real wage implied by price setting.

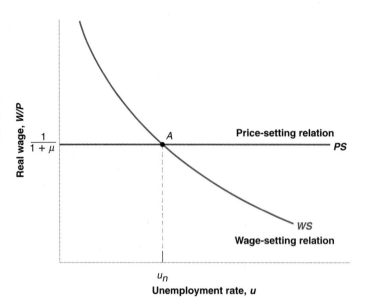

Note what this equation says: *Price-setting decisions determine the real wage paid by firms.* An increase in the markup leads firms to increase their prices, given the wage they have to pay; equivalently, it leads to a decrease in the real wage.

The step from equation (6.5) to equation (6.6) is algebraically straightforward. But how price setting actually determines the real wage paid by firms may not be intuitively obvious. Think of it this way: Suppose the firm you work for increases its markup and therefore increases the price of its product. Your real wage does not change very much: You are still paid the same nominal wage, and the product produced by the firm is at most a small part of your consumption basket.

Now suppose that not only the firm you work for but all the firms in the economy increase their markup. All the prices go up. Even if you are paid the same nominal wage, your real wage goes down. So, the higher the markup set by firms, the lower your (and everyone else's) real wage will be.

The **price-setting relation** in equation (6.6) is drawn as the horizontal line *PS* (for price setting) in Figure 6-6. The real wage implied by price setting is $1/(1 + \mu)$; it does not depend on the unemployment rate.

Equilibrium Real Wages and Unemployment

Equilibrium in the labor market requires that the real wage chosen in wage setting be equal to the real wage implied by price setting. (This way of stating equilibrium may sound strange if you learned to think in terms of labor supply and labor demand in your microeconomics course. The relation between wage setting and price setting on the one hand and labor supply and labor demand on the other is closer than it looks at first and is explored further in the appendix at the end of this chapter.) In Figure 6-6, equilibrium is therefore given by point *A*, and the equilibrium unemployment rate is given by u_n.

We can also characterize the equilibrium unemployment rate algebraically; eliminating *W/P* between equations (6.4) and (6.6) gives

$$F(u_n, z) = \frac{1}{1 + \mu} \qquad (6.7)$$

The equilibrium unemployment rate, u_n, is such that the real wage chosen in wage setting—the left side of equation (6.7)—is equal to the real wage implied by price setting—the right side of equation (6.7).

The equilibrium unemployment rate (u_n) is called the **natural rate of unemployment** (which is why I have used the subscript n to denote it). The terminology has become standard, so I will adopt it, but this is actually a bad choice of words. The word *natural* suggests a constant of nature, one that is unaffected by institutions and policy. As its derivation makes clear however, the "natural" rate of unemployment is anything but natural. The positions of the wage-setting and price-setting curves, and thus the equilibrium unemployment rate, depend on both z and μ. Consider two examples:

Natural, in Webster's dictionary, means "in a state provided by nature, without man-made changes."

- An increase in unemployment benefits—An increase in unemployment benefits can be represented by an increase in z: Because an increase in benefits makes the prospect of unemployment less painful, it increases the wage set by wage setters at a given unemployment rate. So it shifts the wage-setting relation up, from WS to WS' in Figure 6-7. The economy moves along the PS line, from A to A'. The natural rate of unemployment increases from u_n to u'_n.

  An increase in unemployment benefits shifts the wage-setting curve up. The economy moves along the price-setting curve. Equilibrium unemployment increases.

  In words: At a given unemployment rate, higher unemployment benefits lead to a higher real wage. A higher unemployment rate is needed to bring the real wage back to what firms are willing to pay.

  This has led some economists to call unemployment a "discipline device": Higher unemployment is the device that returns wages to the level firms are willing to pay.

- A less stringent enforcement of existing antitrust legislation—To the extent that this allows firms to collude more easily and increase their market power, it leads to an increase in their markup—an increase in μ. The increase in μ implies a decrease in the real wage paid by firms, and so it shifts the price-setting relation down, from PS to PS' in Figure 6-8. The economy moves along WS. The equilibrium moves from A to A', and the natural rate of unemployment increases from u_n to u'_n.

  An increase in the markup shifts the price-setting line down. The economy moves along the wage-setting curve. Equilibrium unemployment increases.

  In words: By letting firms increase their prices given the wage, less stringent enforcement of antitrust legislation leads to a decrease in the real wage. Higher unemployment is required to make workers accept this lower real wage, leading to an increase in the natural rate of unemployment.

Factors such as the generosity of unemployment benefits or antitrust legislation can hardly be thought of as the result of nature. Rather, they reflect various characteristics of the structure of the economy. For that reason, a better name for the equilibrium

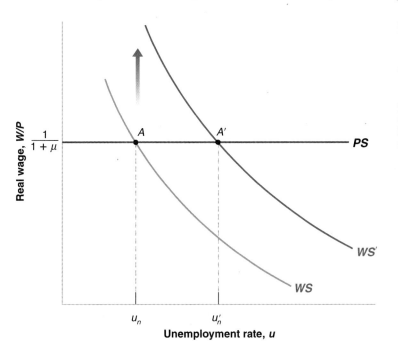

Figure 6-7

Unemployment Benefits and the Natural Rate of Unemployment

An increase in unemployment benefits leads to an increase in the natural rate of unemployment.

Markups and the Natural Rate of Unemployment

An increase in markups decreases the real wage and leads to an increase in the natural rate of unemployment.

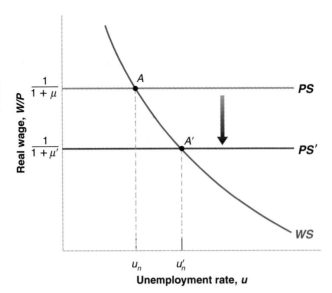

This name has been suggested ▶ by Edmund Phelps from Columbia University. Phelps was awarded the Nobel Prize in 2006. For more on some of his contributions, see Chapters 8 and 27.

rate of unemployment would be the **structural rate of unemployment**, but so far the name has not caught on.

From Unemployment to Employment

Associated with the natural rate of unemployment is a **natural level of employment**, the level of employment that prevails when unemployment is equal to its natural rate.

Let's review the relation between unemployment, employment, and the labor force. Let U denote unemployment, N denote employment, and L the labor force. Then:

$$u \equiv \frac{U}{L} = \frac{L - N}{L} = 1 - \frac{N}{L}$$

The first step follows from the definition of the unemployment rate, u. The second follows from the fact that, from the definition of the labor force, the level of unemploy-
$L = N + U \Rightarrow U = 2 - N$ ▶ ment, U, equals the labor force, L, minus employment, N. The third step follows from simplifying the fraction. Putting all three steps together: The unemployment rate, u, equals 1 minus the ratio of employment, N, to the labor force, L.

Rearranging to get employment in terms of the labor force and the unemployment rate gives:

$$N = L(1 - u)$$

Employment, N, is equal to the labor force, L, times 1 minus the unemployment rate, u.

So, if the natural rate of unemployment is u_n, and the labor force is equal to L, the natural level of employment, N_n, is given by

$$N_n = L(1 - u_n)$$

For example, if the labor force is 150 million and the natural rate of unemployment is 5%, then the natural level of employment is $150 \times (1 - .05) = 142.5$ million.

From Employment to Output

Finally, associated with the natural level of employment is the **natural level of output**, the level of production when employment is equal to the natural level of employment. Given the production function we have used in this chapter ($Y = N$), the natural level of output, Y_n, is easy to derive. It is given by

$$Y_n = N_n = L(1 - u_n)$$

Using equation (6.7) and the relations between the unemployment rate, employment, and the output we just derived, the natural level of output satisfies the following equation:

$$F\left(1 - \frac{Y_n}{L}, z\right) = \frac{1}{1 + \mu} \qquad (6.8)$$

The natural level of output, Y_n, is such that, at the associated rate of unemployment ($u_n = 1 - Y_n/L$), the real wage chosen in wage setting—the left side of equation (6.8)—is equal to the real wage implied by price setting—the right side of equation (6.8). As you will see, equation (6.8) will turn out to be very useful in Chapter 7. Make sure you understand it.

We have gone through many steps in this section. Let's summarize: assume that the expected price level is equal to the actual price level. Then:

- The real wage chosen in wage setting is a decreasing function of the unemployment rate.
- The real wage implied by price setting is constant.
- Equilibrium in the labor market requires that the real wage chosen in wage setting be equal to the real wage implied by price setting.
- This determines the equilibrium unemployment rate.
- This equilibrium unemployment rate is known as the natural rate of unemployment.
- Associated with the natural rate of unemployment are a natural level of employment and a natural level of output.

6-6 Where We Go from Here

We have just seen how equilibrium in the labor market determines the equilibrium unemployment rate (which we have called the natural rate of unemployment), which in turn determines the level of output (which we have called the natural level of output).

So, you may ask, what did we do in the previous three chapters? If equilibrium in the labor market determines the unemployment rate, and by implication, the level of output, why did we spend so much time looking at the goods and financial markets? What about our earlier conclusions that the level of output was determined by factors such as monetary policy, fiscal policy, consumer confidence, and so on—all factors that do not enter equation (6.8) and therefore do not affect the natural level of output?

The key to the answer is simple:

- We have derived the natural rate of unemployment and the associated levels of employment and output under two assumptions. First, we have assumed equilibrium in the labor market. Second, we have assumed that the price level was equal to the expected price level.
- However, there is no reason for the second assumption to be true in the *short run*. The price level may well turn out to be different from what was expected when nominal wages were set. Hence, in the short run, there is no reason for unemployment to be equal to the natural rate, or for output to be equal to its natural level.

In the short run, the factors that determine movements in output are the factors we focused on ▶ in the preceding three chapters: monetary policy, fiscal policy, and so on.
In the medium run, output tends to return to the natural level, and the factors that determine ▶ output are the factors we have focused on in this chapter.

As we will see in Chapter 7, the factors that determine movements in output *in the short run* are indeed the factors we focused on in the preceding three chapters: monetary policy, fiscal policy, and so on. Your time (and mine) was not wasted.

■ Expectations are unlikely to be systematically wrong (say, too high or too low) forever. That is why, in the medium run, unemployment tends to return to the natural rate, and output tends to return to the natural level. *In the medium run*, the factors that determine unemployment and output are the factors that appear in equations (6.7) and (6.8).

Developing these answers in detail will be our task in the next three chapters.

Summary

■ The labor force consists of those who are working (employed) and looking for work (unemployed). The unemployment rate is equal to the ratio of the number of unemployed to the number in the labor force. The participation rate is equal to the ratio of the labor force to the working-age population.

■ The U.S. labor market is characterized by large flows between employment, unemployment, and "out of the labor force." Each month, on average, about 45% of the unemployed move out of unemployment, either to take a job or to drop out of the labor force.

■ Unemployment is high in recessions and low in expansions. During periods of high unemployment, the probability of losing a job increases, and the probability of finding a job decreases.

■ Wages are set unilaterally by firms or through bargaining between workers and firms. They depend negatively on the unemployment rate and positively on the expected price level. The reason wages depend on the expected price level is that they are typically set in nominal terms for some period of time. During that time, even if the price level turns out to be different from what was expected, wages are typically not readjusted.

■ The price set by firms depends on the wage and on the markup of prices over wages. The higher the markup chosen by firms, the higher the price, given the wage, and thus the lower the real wage implied by price-setting decisions.

■ Equilibrium in the labor market requires that the real wage chosen in wage setting be equal to the real wage implied by price setting. Under the additional assumption that the expected price level is equal to the actual price level, equilibrium in the labor market determines the unemployment rate. This unemployment rate is known as the *natural rate of unemployment*.

■ In general, the actual price level may turn out to be different from the price level expected by wage setters. Therefore, the unemployment rate need not be equal to the natural rate.

■ The coming chapters will show that in the short run, unemployment and output are determined by the factors we focused on in the previous three chapters, but, in the medium run, unemployment tends to return to the natural rate, and output tends to return to its natural level.

Key Terms

- non-institutional civilian population, 136
- labor force; out of the labor force, 136
- participation rate, 136
- unemployment rate, 136
- separations, hires, 137
- Current Population Survey (CPS), 137
- quits, layoffs, 137
- duration of unemployment, 138
- discouraged workers, 138
- non-employment rate, 138
- collective bargaining, 142
- reservation wage, 142
- bargaining power, 143
- efficiency wage theories, 143
- unemployment insurance, 145
- production function, 146
- labor productivity, 146
- markup, 147
- wage-setting relation, 147
- price-setting relation, 148
- natural rate of unemployment, 149
- structural rate of unemployment, 150
- natural level of employment, 150
- natural level of output, 151

Quick Check

1. Using the information in this chapter, label each of the following statements true, false, or uncertain. Explain briefly.

a. Since 1950, the participation rate in the United States has remained roughly constant at 60%.

b. Each month, the flows into and out of employment are very small compared to the size of the labor force.

c. Fewer than 10% of all unemployed workers exit the unemployment pool each year.

d. The unemployment rate tends to be high in recessions and low in expansions.

e. Most workers are typically paid their reservation wage.

f. Workers who do not belong to unions have no bargaining power.

g. It may be in the best interest of employers to pay wages higher than their workers' reservation wage.

h. The natural rate of unemployment is unaffected by policy changes.

2. Answer the following questions using the information provided in this chapter.

a. As a percentage of the employed workers, what is the size of the flows into and out of employment (i.e., hires and separations) each month?

b. As a percentage of the unemployed workers, what is the size of the flows from unemployment into employment each month?

c. As a percentage of the unemployed, what is the size of the total flows out of unemployment each month? What is the average duration of unemployment?

d. As a percentage of the labor force, what is the size of the total flows into and out of the labor force each month?

e. What percentage of flows into the labor force do new workers entering the labor force constitute?

3. The natural rate of unemployment

   Suppose that the markup of goods prices over marginal cost is 6%, and that the wage-setting equation is $W = P(1 - u)$, where u is the unemployment rate.

a. What is the real wage, as determined by the price-setting equation?

b. What is the natural rate of unemployment?

c. Suppose that the markup of prices over costs increases to 12%. What happens to the natural rate of unemployment? Explain the logic behind your answer.

Dig Deeper

4. Reservation wages

   In the mid-1980s, a famous supermodel once said that she would not get out of bed for less than $10,000 (presumably per day).

a. What is your own reservation wage?

b. Did your first job pay more than your reservation wage at the time?

c. Relative to your reservation wage at the time you accept each job, which job pays more: your first one or the one you expect to have in 10 years?

d. Explain your answers to parts (a) through (c) in terms of the efficiency wage theory.

5. The existence of unemployment

a. Suppose the unemployment rate is very low. How easy is it for firms to find workers to hire? How easy is it for workers to find jobs? What do your answers imply about the relative bargaining power of workers and firms when the unemployment rate is very low? What do your answers imply about what happens to the wage as the unemployment rate gets very low?

b. Given your answer to part (a), why is there unemployment in the economy? (What would happen to real wages if the unemployment rate were equal to zero?)

6. Bargaining power and wage determination

   Even in the absence of collective bargaining, workers do have some bargaining power that allows them to receive wages higher than their reservation wage. Each worker's bargaining power depends both on the nature of the job and on the economy-wide labor market conditions. Let's consider each factor in turn.

a. Compare the job of a delivery person and a computer network administrator. In which of these jobs does a worker have more bargaining power? Why?

b. For any given job, how do labor market conditions affect a worker's bargaining power? Which labor market variable would you look at to assess labor market conditions?

c. Suppose that for given labor market conditions [the variable you identified in part (b)], worker bargaining power throughout the economy increases. What effect would this have on the real wage in the medium run? in the short run? What determines the real wage in the model described in this chapter?

7. The informal labor market

   You learned in Chapter 2 that informal work at home (e.g., preparing meals, taking care of children) is not counted as part of GDP. Such work also does not constitute employment in labor market statistics. With these observations in mind, consider two economies, each with 100 people, divided into 25 households, each composed of four people. In each household, one person stays at home and prepares the food, two people work in the non-food sector, and one person is unemployed. Assume that the workers outside food preparation produce the same actual and measured output in both economies.

   In the first economy, EatIn, the 25 food-preparation workers (one per household) cook for their families at home and do not work outside the house. All meal are prepared and eaten at home. The 25 food preparation workers in this economy do not seek work in the formal labor market (and when asked, they say they are not looking for work). In the second economy, EatOut, the 25 food *preparation workers are employed by restaurants. All meals are purchased in restaurants.*

a. Calculate measured employment and unemployment and the measured labor force for each economy. Calculate the measured unemployment rate and participation rate for each economy. In which economy is measured GDP higher?

b. Suppose now that EatIn's economy changes. A few restaurants open, and the food-preparation workers in 10 households take jobs restaurants. The members of these 10 households now eat all of their meals in restaurants. The food preparation workers in the remaining 15 households continue to work at home and do not seek jobs in the formal sector. The members of these 15 households continue to eat all of their meals at home. Without calculating the numbers, what will happen to measured employment and unemployment and to the measured labor force, unemployment rate, and participation rate in EatIn? What will happen to measured GDP in EatIn?

c. Suppose that you want to include work at home in GDP and the employment statistics. How would you measure the value of work at home in GDP? How would you alter the definitions of *employment, unemployment,* and *out of the labor force*?

d. Given your new definitions in part (c), would the labor market statistics differ for EatIn and EatOut? Assuming that the food produced by these economies has the same value, would measured GDP in these economies differ? Under your new definitions, would the experiment in part (b) have any effect on the labor market or GDP statistics for EatIn?

Explore Further

8. *Unemployment spells and long-term unemployment*
   According to the data presented in this chapter, about 45% of unemployed workers leave unemployment each month.

a. What is the probability that an unemployed worker will still be unemployed after one month? two months? six months?

   Now consider the composition of the unemployment pool. We will use a simple experiment to determine the proportion of the unemployed who have been unemployed six months or more. Suppose the number of unemployed work-

ers is constant and equal to x *(where* x *is some constant). Each month, 45% of the unemployed find jobs, and an equivalent number of previously employed workers become unemployed.*

b. Consider the group of x workers who are unemployed this month. After a month, what percentage of this group will still be unemployed? (Hint: If 45% of unemployed workers find jobs every month, what percentage of the original x unemployed workers did not find jobs in the first month?)

c. After a second month, what percentage of the original x unemployed workers has been unemployed for at least two months? [Hint: Given your answer to part (b), what percentage of those unemployed for at least one month do not find jobs in the second month?] After the sixth month, what percentage of the original x unemployed workers has been unemployed for at least six months? *This percentage applies to the economy at any time (remember that we started with an arbitrary month). Under our assumptions, the percentage of the unemployed who have been unemployed six months or more is constant.*

d. Using Table B-44 of the *Economic Report of the President* (**www.access.gpo.gov/eop/**), compute the proportion of unemployed who have been unemployed six months or more (27 weeks or more) for each year between 1996 and 2003. How do these numbers compare with the answer you obtained in part (c)? Can you guess what may account for the difference between the actual numbers and the answer you obtained in this problem? (Hint: Suppose that the probability of exiting unemployment goes down the longer you are unemployed.)

9. *Go to the Web site maintained by the U.S. Bureau of Labor Statistics* (**www.bls.gov**). *Find the latest Employment Situation Summary. Look under the link "National Employment."*

a. What are the latest monthly data on the size of the U.S. civilian labor force, on the number of unemployed, and on the unemployment rate?

b. How many people are employed?

c. Compute the change in the number of unemployed from the first number in the table to the most recent month in the table. Do the same for the number of employed workers. Is the decline in unemployment equal to the increase in employment? Explain in words.

We invite you to visit the Blanchard page on the Prentice Hall Web site, at:
www.prenhall.com/blanchard
for this chapter's World Wide Web exercises.

Further Readings

■ A further discussion of unemployment along the lines of this chapter is given by Richard Layard, Stephen Nickell, and Richard Jackman, in *The Unemployment Crisis*, Oxford University Press, Oxford, UK, 1994.

Appendix: Wage and Price Setting Relations versus Labor Supply and Labor Demand

If you have taken a microeconomics course, you have probably seen a representation of labor market equilibrium in terms of labor supply and labor demand. You may therefore be asking: How does the representation in terms of wage setting and price setting relate to the representation of the labor market I saw in that course?

In an important sense, the two representations are similar. To see why, let's redraw Figure 6-6 in terms of the real wage on the vertical axis and the level of *employment* (rather than the unemployment rate) on the horizontal axis. We do this in Figure 1.

Employment, N, is measured on the horizontal axis. The level of employment must be somewhere between zero and L, the labor force: Employment cannot exceed the number of people available for work—that is, the labor force. For any employment level, N, unemployment is given by $U = L - N$. Knowing that, we can measure unemployment by starting from L and *moving to the left* on the horizontal axis: Unemployment is given by the distance between L and N. The lower is employment, N, the higher is unemployment, and by implication the higher is the unemployment rate, u.

Let's now draw the wage-setting and price-setting relations and characterize the equilibrium:

- An increase in employment (a movement to the right along the horizontal axis) implies a decrease in unemployment and therefore an increase in the real wage chosen in wage setting. Thus, the wage-setting relation is now *upward sloping:* Higher employment implies a higher real wage.

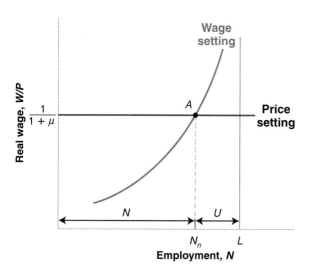

Figure 1 *Wage and Price Setting and the Natural Level of Employment*

- The price-setting relation is still a horizontal line, at $W/P = 1/(1 + \mu)$.
- The equilibrium is given by point A, with natural employment level, N_n, and an implied natural unemployment rate equal to $u_n = (L - N_n)/L$.

In Figure 1, the wage-setting relation looks like a labor supply relation. As the level of employment increases, the real wage paid to workers increases as well. For that reason, the wage-setting relation is sometimes called the "labor supply" relation (in quotes).

What we have called the price-setting relation looks like a flat labor demand relation. The reason it is flat rather than downward sloping has to do with our simplifying assumption of constant returns to labor in production. Had we assumed, more conventionally, that there were decreasing returns to labor in production, our price-setting curve would, like the standard labor demand curve, be downward sloping: As employment increased, the marginal cost of production would increase, forcing firms to increase their prices, given the wages they pay. In other words, the real wage implied by price setting would decrease as employment increased.

In a number of ways, however, the two approaches are different:

- The standard labor supply relation gives the wage at which a given number of workers are willing to work: The higher the wage, the larger the number of workers who are willing to work.

  In contrast, the wage corresponding to a given level of employment in the wage-setting relation is the result of a process of bargaining between workers and firms, or unilateral wage setting by firms. Factors such as the structure of collective bargaining or the use of wages to deter quits affect the wage-setting relation. In the real world, they seem to play an important role. Yet they play no role in the standard labor supply relation.
- The standard labor demand relation gives the level of employment chosen by firms at a given real wage. It is derived under the assumption that firms operate in competitive goods and labor markets and therefore take wages and prices—and, by implication, the real wage—as given.

  In contrast, the price-setting relation takes into account the fact that in most markets, firms actually set prices. Factors such as the degree of competition in the goods market affect the price-setting relation by affecting the markup. But these factors aren't considered in the standard labor demand relation.
- In the labor supply–labor demand framework, those unemployed are *willingly unemployed*: At the equilibrium real wage, they prefer to be unemployed rather than work.

In contrast, in the wage setting–price setting framework, unemployment is likely to be involuntary. For example, if firms pay an efficiency wage—a wage above the reservation wage—workers would rather be employed than unemployed. Yet, in equilibrium, there is still involuntary unemployment. This also seems to capture reality better than does the labor supply–labor demand framework.

These are the three reasons I have relied on the wage-setting and price-setting relations rather than on the labor supply–labor demand approach to characterize equilibrium in this chapter.

Putting All Markets Together: The AS–AD Model

I n Chapter 5, we looked at the determination of output in the short run. In Chapter 6, we looked at the determination of output in the medium run. We are now ready to put the two together and look at the determination of output in both the short run and the medium run.

To do so, we use the equilibrium conditions for *all* the markets we have looked at so far— the goods and financial markets in Chapter 5, and the labor market in Chapter 6. Then, using these equilibrium conditions, we derive two relations:

The first relation, which we call the *aggregate supply relation*, captures the implications of equilibrium in the labor market; it builds on what you saw in Chapter 6.

The second relation, which we call the *aggregate demand relation*, captures the implications of equilibrium in both the goods market and financial markets; it builds on what you saw in Chapter 5.

Combining these two relations gives us the *AS–AD* model (for aggregate supply–aggregate demand). This chapter presents the basic version of the model. When confronted with a macro-economic question, this is the version I typically use to organize my thoughts. For some questions, however (in particular, for the study of inflation), the basic *AS–AD* model must be extended. That is what we will do in the next two chapters.

This chapter is organized as follows:

■ Section 7-1 derives the aggregate supply relation, and Section 7-2 derives the aggregate demand relation.

■ Section 7-3 combines the two relations to characterize equilibrium output in the short run and in the medium run.

■ Sections 7-4 to 7-6 show how we can use the model to look at the dynamic effects of monetary policy, of fiscal policy, and of changes in the price of oil.

■ Section 7-7 summarizes. ■

7-1 Aggregate Supply

The **aggregate supply relation** captures the effects of output on the price level. It is derived from the behavior of wages and prices we described in Chapter 6.

In Chapter 6, we derived the following equation for wage determination [equation (6.1)]:

$$W = P^e F(u, z)$$

The nominal wage, W, set by wage setters, depends on the expected price level, P^e; on the unemployment rate, u; and on the catchall variable, z, for all the other factors that affect wage determination, from unemployment benefits to the form of collective bargaining.

Also in Chapter 6, we derived the following equation for price determination [equation (6.3)]:

$$P = (1 + \mu)W$$

The price, P, set by firms (equivalently, the price level) is equal to the nominal wage, W, multiplied by 1 plus the markup, μ.

We then used these two relations together with the additional assumption that the actual price level was equal to the expected price level. Under this additional assumption, we derived the natural rate of unemployment and, by implication, the natural level of output.

The difference in this chapter is that we will not impose this additional assumption. (It will turn out that the price level is equal to the expected price level in the medium run but will typically not be equal to the expected price level in the short run.) Without this additional assumption, the price-setting relation and the wage-setting relation give us a relation, which we now derive, between the price level, the output level, and the expected price level.

The first step is to eliminate the nominal wage, W, between the two equations. Replacing the nominal wage in the second equation above by its expression from the first gives

$$P = P^e(1 + \mu) F(u, z) \tag{7.1}$$

The price level, P, depends on the expected price level, P^e, on the unemployment rate, u (as well as on the markup, μ, and on the catchall variable, z; but we will assume that both μ and z are constant here).

The second step is to replace the unemployment rate, u, with its expression in terms of output. To replace u, recall the relation between the unemployment rate, employment, and output we derived in Chapter 6:

$$u = \frac{U}{L} = \frac{L-N}{L} = 1 - \frac{N}{L} = 1 - \frac{Y}{L}$$

The first equality follows from the definition of the unemployment rate. The second equality follows from the definition of unemployment ($U \equiv L - N$). The third equality just simplifies the fraction. The fourth equality follows from the specification of the production function, which says that to produce one unit of output requires one worker, so that $Y = N$. What we get then is

$$u = 1 - \frac{Y}{L}$$

In words: For a given labor force, the higher the output, the lower the unemployment rate.

The Medium Run **The Core**

Replacing u with $1 - (Y/L)$ in equation (7.1) gives us the *aggregate supply relation,* or AS *relation*:

$$P = P^e(1 + \mu) F\left(1 - \frac{Y}{L}, z\right) \tag{7.2}$$

The price level, P, depends on the expected price level, P^e, and the level of output, Y (and also on the markup, μ; the catchall variable, z; and the labor force, L, which we take as constant here). The AS relation has two important properties.

The first property of the AS relation is that *an increase in output leads to an increase in the price level*. This is the result of four underlying steps:

1. An increase in output leads to an increase in employment.
2. The increase in employment leads to a decrease in unemployment and therefore to a decrease in the unemployment rate.
3. The lower unemployment rate leads to an increase in the nominal wage.
4. The increase in the nominal wage leads to an increase in the prices set by firms and therefore to an increase in the price level.

The second property of the AS relation is that *an increase in the expected price level leads, one-for-one, to an increase in the actual price level*. For example, if the expected price level doubles, the price level will also double. This effect works through wages:

1. If wage setters expect the price level to be higher, they set a higher nominal wage.
2. The increase in the nominal wage leads to an increase in costs, which leads to an increase in the prices set by firms and a higher price level.

The relation between the price level, P, and output, Y, for a given value of the expected price level, P^e, is represented by the AS curve in Figure 7-1. The AS curve has three properties that will prove useful in what follows:

■ The aggregate supply curve is upward sloping. Put another way, an increase in output, Y, leads to an increase in the price level, P. You saw why earlier.
■ The aggregate supply curve goes through point A, where $Y = Y_n$ and $P = P^e$. Put another way: When output, Y, is equal to the natural level of output, Y_n, the price level, P, turns out to be exactly equal to the expected price level, P^e.

◀ A better name would be the "labor market relation." But because the relation looks graphically like a supply curve (there is a positive relation between output and the price), it is called the "aggregate supply relation." I will follow tradition.

◀ An increase in Y leads to an increase in P.

An increase in P^e leads to an increase in P.

◀ Put informally: High economic activity puts pressure on prices.

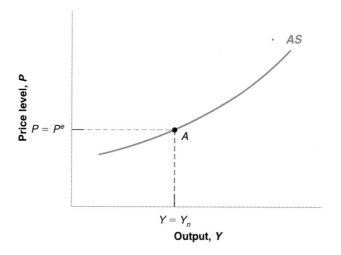

Figure 7-1

The Aggregate Supply Curve

Given the expected price level, an increase in output leads to an increase in the price level. If output is equal to the natural level of output, the price level is equal to the expected price level.

Figure 7-2

The Effect of an Increase in the Expected Price Level on the Aggregate Supply Curve

An increase in the expected price level shifts the aggregate supply curve up.

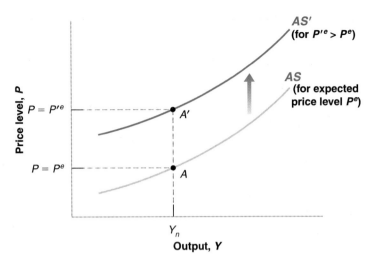

How do we know this? From the definition of the natural level of output in Chapter 6. Recall that we defined the natural rate of unemployment (and, by implication, the natural level of output) as the rate of unemployment (and, by implication, the level of output) that prevails if the price level and the expected price level are equal. This property—that the price level equals the expected price level when output is equal to the natural level of output—has two straightforward implications:

When output is above the natural level of output, the price level is higher than expected. In Figure 7-1, if Y is to the right of Y_n, P is higher than P^e. Conversely, when output is below the natural level of output, the price level is lower than expected. In Figure 7-1, if Y is to the left of Y_n, P is lower than P^e.

■ An increase in the expected price level, P^e, shifts the aggregate supply curve up. Conversely, a decrease in the expected price level shifts the aggregate supply curve down.

This third property is shown in Figure 7-2. Suppose the expected price level increases from P^e to P'^e. At a given level of output, and, correspondingly, at a given unemployment rate, the increase in the expected price level leads to an increase in wages, which leads in turn to an increase in prices. So, at any level of output, the price level is higher: The aggregate supply curve shifts up. In particular, instead of going through point A (where $Y = Y_n$ and $P = P^e$), the aggregate supply curve now goes through point A' (where $Y = Y_n$, $P = P'^e$).

> *Recall that when output equals the natural level of output, the price level turns out to be equal to the expected price level.* ▶

Let's summarize:

■ Starting from wage determination and price determination in the labor market, we have derived the *aggregate supply relation.*
■ This relation implies that for a given expected price level, the price level is an increasing function of the level of output. It is represented by an upward-sloping curve, called the *aggregate supply curve.*
■ Increases in the expected price level shift the aggregate supply curve up; decreases in the expected price level shift the aggregate supply curve down.

7-2 Aggregate Demand

The **aggregate demand relation** captures the effect of the price level on output. It is derived from the equilibrium conditions in the goods and financial markets described in Chapter 5.

In Chapter 5, we derived the following equation for goods market equilibrium [equation (5.2)]:

$$Y = C(Y - T) + I(Y, i) + G$$

Equilibrium in the goods market requires that output equal the demand for goods—the sum of consumption, investment, and government spending. This is the *IS* relation.

Also in Chapter 5, we derived the following equation for equilibrium in financial markets [equation (5.3)]:

$$\frac{M}{P} = YL(i)$$

Equilibrium in financial markets requires that the supply of money equal the demand for money. This is the *LM* relation.

Recall that what appears on the left side of the *LM* equation is the real money stock, M/P. We focused in Chapter 5 on changes in the real money stock that came from changes in nominal money, M, made by the Fed. But changes in the real money stock, M/P, can also come from changes in the price level, P. A 10% increase in the price level, P, has the same effect on the real money stock as a 10% decrease in the stock of nominal money, M: Either leads to a 10% decrease in the real money stock.

Using the *IS* and *LM* relations, we can derive the relation between the price level and the level of output implied by equilibrium in the goods and financial markets. We do this in Figure 7-3:

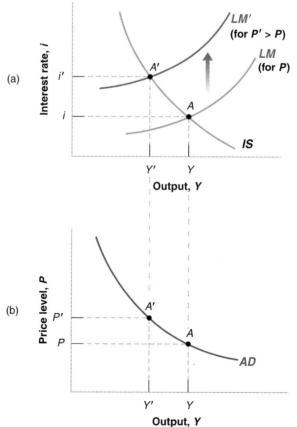

Figure 7-3

The Derivation of the Aggregate Demand Curve

An increase in the price level leads to a decrease in output.

- Figure 7-3(a) draws the *IS* curve and the *LM* curve. The *IS* curve is drawn for given values of *G* and *T*. It is downward sloping: An increase in the interest rate leads to a decrease in output. The *LM* curve is drawn for a given value of *M/P*. It is upward sloping: An increase in output increases the demand for money, and the interest rate increases so as to maintain equality of money demand and the (unchanged) money supply. The point at which the goods market and the financial market are both in equilibrium is at the intersection of the *IS* curve and the *LM* curve, at point *A*.

  Now consider the effects of an increase in the price level from *P* to *P'*. Given the stock of nominal money, *M*, the increase in the price level, *P*, decreases the real money stock, *M/P*. This implies that the *LM* curve shifts up: At a given level of output, the lower real money stock leads to an increase in the interest rate. The economy moves along the *IS* curve, and the equilibrium moves from *A* to *A'*. The interest rate increases from *i* to *i'*, and output decreases from *Y* to *Y'*. In short: The increase in the price level leads to a decrease in output.

  In words: The increase in the price level leads to a decrease in the real money stock. This monetary contraction leads to an increase in the interest rate, which leads in turn to a lower demand for goods and lower output.

A better name would be the "goods market and financial markets relation." But because it is a long name, and because the relation looks graphically like a demand curve (that is, a negative relation between output and the price), it is called the "aggregate demand relation." I will, again, follow ▶ tradition.

- This negative relation between output and the price level is drawn as the downward-sloping curve *AD* in Figure 7-3(b). Points *A* and *A'* in Figure 7-3(b) correspond to points *A* and *A'* in Figure 7-3(a). An increase in the price level from *P* to *P'* leads to a decrease in output from *Y* to *Y'*. This curve is called the *aggregate demand curve*. The underlying negative relation between output and the price level is called the *aggregate demand relation*.

  Any variable other than the price level that shifts either the IS *curve or the* LM *curve also shifts the aggregate demand relation.*

  Take, for example, an increase in government spending, *G*. At a given price level, the level of output implied by equilibrium in the goods and the financial markets is higher: In Figure 7-4, the aggregate demand curve shifts to the right, from *AD* to *AD'*.

Recall that open-market operations are the means through which the Fed changes the ▶ nominal money stock.

  Or take a contractionary, open market operation—a decrease in *M*. At a given price level, the level of output implied by equilibrium in the goods and the financial

Figure 7-4

Shifts of the Aggregate Demand Curve

At a given price level, an increase in government spending increases output, shifting the aggregate demand curve to the right. At a given price level, a decrease in nominal money decreases output, shifting the aggregate demand curve to the left.

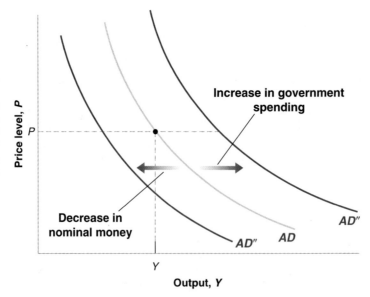

markets is lower. In Figure 7-4, the aggregate demand curve shifts to the left, from AD to AD''.

We can represent what we have just discussed by the following aggregate demand relation:

$$Y = Y\left(\frac{M}{P}, G, T\right)$$

$$(+, +, -)$$

(7.3)

Output, Y, is an increasing function of the real money stock, M/P; an increasing function of government spending, G; and a decreasing function of taxes, T.

Given monetary and fiscal policy—that is, given M, G, and T—an increase in the price level, P, leads to a decrease in the real money stock, M/P, which leads to a decrease in output. This is the relation captured by the AD curve in Figure 7-3(b).

Let's summarize:

- Starting from the equilibrium conditions for the goods and financial markets, we have derived the *aggregate demand relation*.
- This relation implies that the level of output is a decreasing function of the price level. It is represented by a downward-sloping curve, called the *aggregate demand curve*.
- Changes in monetary or fiscal policy—or, more generally, in any variable other than the price level that shifts the IS or the LM curves—shift the aggregate demand curve.

7-3 Equilibrium in the Short Run and in the Medium Run

The next step is to put the AS and the AD relations together. From Sections 7-1 and 7-2, the two relations are given by

AS relation: $$P = P^e(1 + \mu)F\left(1 - \frac{Y}{L}, z\right)$$

AD relation: $$Y = Y\left(\frac{M}{P}, G, T\right)$$

For a given value of the expected price level, P^e (which enters the aggregate supply relation), and for given values of the monetary and fiscal policy variables M, G, and T (which enter the aggregate demand relation), these two relations determine the equilibrium value of output, Y, and the price level, P.

Note that the equilibrium depends on the value of P^e. The value of P^e determines the position of the aggregate supply curve (go back to Figure 7-2), and the position of the aggregate supply curve affects the equilibrium. In the short run, we can take P^e, the price level expected by wage setters when they last set wages, as given. But over time, P^e is likely to change, shifting the aggregate supply curve, and changing the equilibrium. With this in mind, we first characterize equilibrium in the short run—that is, taking P^e as given. We then look at how P^e changes over time and how that change affects the equilibrium.

Equilibrium in the Short Run

The short-run equilibrium is characterized in Figure 7-5:

- The aggregate supply curve, AS, is drawn for a given value of P^e. It is upward sloping: The higher the level of output, the higher the price level. The position of the curve depends on P^e. Recall from Section 7-1 that, when output is equal to the

The Short-Run Equilibrium

The equilibrium is given by the intersection of the aggregate supply curve and the aggregate demand curve. At point A, the labor market, the goods market, and financial market are all in equilibrium.

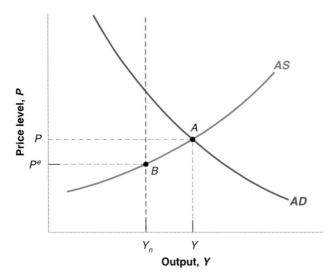

natural level of output, the price level is equal to the expected price level. This means that, in Figure 7-5, the aggregate supply curve goes through point B: If $Y = Y_n$, then $P = P^e$.

■ The aggregate demand curve, AD, is drawn for given values of M, G, and T. It is downward sloping: The higher the price level, the lower the level of output.

The equilibrium is given by the intersection of the AS and AD curves at point A. By construction, at point A, the goods market, the financial markets, and the labor market are *all* in equilibrium. The fact that the labor market is in equilibrium is because point A is on the aggregate supply curve. The goods and financial markets are in equilibrium because point A is on the aggregate demand curve. The equilibrium level of output and price level are given by Y and P.

There is no reason, in general, why equilibrium output, Y, should be equal to the natural level of output, Y_n. Equilibrium output depends both on the position of the aggregate supply curve (and therefore on the value of P^e) and on the position of the aggregate demand curve (and therefore on the values of M, G, and T). As I have drawn the two curves, Y is greater than Y_n: In other words, the equilibrium level of output exceeds the natural level of output. But I could clearly have drawn the AS and the AD curves so that equilibrium output, Y, was smaller than the natural level of output, Y_n.

Figure 7-5 gives us our first important conclusion: In the *short run*, there is no reason output should equal the natural level of output. Whether it does depends on the specific values of the expected price level and the values of the variables affecting the position of aggregate demand.

We must now ask: What happens over time? More precisely, suppose that in the short run, output is above the natural level of output—as is the case in Figure 7-5. What will happen over time? Will output eventually return to the natural level of output? If so, how? These are the questions we take up in the rest of the section.

From the Short Run to the Medium Run

To think about what happens over time, consider Figure 7-6. The curves denoted AS and AD are the same as in Figure 7-5, and so the short-run equilibrium is at point A—which corresponds to point A in Figure 7-5. Output is equal to Y and is higher than the natural level of output, Y_n.

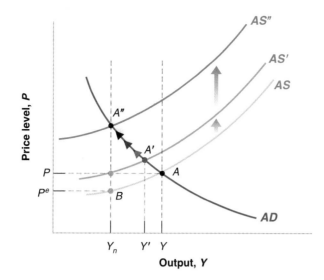

Figure 7-6

The Adjustment of Output over Time

If output is above the natural level of output, the *AS* curve shifts up over time until output has fallen back to the natural level of output.

At point *A*, output exceeds the natural level of output. So we know from Section 7-1 that the price level is higher than the expected price level—higher than the price level wage setters expected when they set nominal wages.

The fact that the price level is higher than wage setters expected is likely to lead them to revise upward their expectations of what the price level will be in the future. ◄ So, next time they set nominal wages, they are likely to make their decision based on a higher expected price level, say based on P'^e, where $P'^e > P^e$.

This increase in the expected price level implies that in the next period, the aggregate supply curve shifts up, from *AS* to *AS'*: At a given level of output, wage setters expect a higher price level. They set a higher nominal wage, which in turn leads firms to set a higher price. The price level therefore increases.

This upward shift in the *AS* curve implies that the economy moves up along the *AD* curve. The equilibrium moves from *A* to *A'*. Equilibrium output decreases from *Y* to *Y'*.

The adjustment does not end at point *A'*. At *A'*, output, *Y'*, still exceeds the natural level of output, Y_n, so the price level is still higher than the expected price level. Because of this, wage setters are likely to continue to revise upward their expectation of the price level.

This means that as long as equilibrium output exceeds the natural level of output, Y_n, the expected price level increases, shifting the *AS* curve upward. As the *AS* curve shifts upward and the economy moves up along the *AD* curve, equilibrium output continues to decrease.

Does this adjustment eventually come to an end? Yes. It ends when the *AS* curve has shifted all the way to *AS''*, when the equilibrium has moved all the way to *A''*, and the equilibrium level of output is equal to Y_n. At *A''*, equilibrium output is equal to the natural level of output, so the price level is equal to the expected price level. At this point, wage setters have no reason to change their expectations; the *AS* curve no longer shifts, and the economy stays at *A''*.

In words: As long as output exceeds the natural level of output, the price level turns out to be higher than expected. This leads wage setters to revise their expectations of the price level upward, leading to an increase in the price level. The increase in the price level leads to a decrease in the real money stock, which leads to an increase in the interest rate, which leads to a decrease in output. The adjustment stops when output is equal to the natural level of output. At that point, the price level is equal to

If you live in an economy where the inflation rate is typically positive, then, even if the price level this year turns out to be equal to what you expected, you may still take into account the presence of inflation and expect the price level to be higher next year. In this chapter, we look at an economy in which there is no steady inflation. We will focus on the dynamics of output and inflation in the next two chapters.

the expected price level, expectations no longer change, and output remains at the natural level of output. Put another way, in the *medium run*, output returns to the natural level of output.

We have looked at the dynamics of adjustment, starting from a case in which initial output was higher than the natural level of output. Clearly, a symmetric argument holds when initial output is below the natural level of output. In this case, the price level is lower than the expected price level, leading wage setters to lower their expectations of the price level. Lower expectations of the price level cause the *AS* curve to shift down and the economy to move down the *AD* curve until output has increased back to the natural level of output.

Let's summarize:

Short run: $Y \neq Y_n$ ▶

- In the *short run*, output can be above or below the natural level of output. Changes in any of the variables that enter either the aggregate supply relation or the aggregate demand relation lead to changes in output and to changes in the price level.

Medium run: $Y - Y_n$ ▶

- In the *medium run*, output eventually returns to the natural level of output. The adjustment works through changes in the price level. When output is above the natural level of output, the price level increases. The higher price level decreases demand and output. When output is below the natural level of output, the price level decreases, increasing demand and output.

The best way to more fully understand the *AS–AD* model is to use it to look at the dynamic effects of changes in policy or in the economic environment. In the next three sections, we focus on three such changes: The first two—a change in the stock of nominal money and a change in the budget deficit—are old favorites by now. The third, which we could not examine until we had developed a theory of wage and price determination, is an increase in the price of oil.

We will take up the more difficult question of the effects of a change in the rate of money growth—rather than a change in the level of money—in the next two chapters.

7-4 ▏ The Effects of a Monetary Expansion

What are the short-run and medium-run effects of an expansionary monetary policy, ▶ say of an increase in the level of nominal money from M to M'?

The Dynamics of Adjustment

We think of shifts in the *AD* curve as shifts to the right or to the left because we think of the *AD* relation as telling us what output is for a given price level. We then ask: At a given price level does output increase (a shift to the right) or decrease (a shift to the left)? We think of shifts in the *AS* curve as shifts up or down because we think of the *AS* relation as telling us what the price level is for a given level of output. We then ask: At a given ▶ output level, does the price level increase (a shift up) or decrease (a shift down)?

Look at Figure 7-7. Assume that before the change in nominal money, output is at its natural level. Aggregate demand and aggregate supply cross at point *A*, the level of output at *A* equals Y_n, and the price level equals P.

Now consider an increase in nominal money. Recall the specification of aggregate demand from equation (7.3):

$$Y = Y\left(\frac{M}{P}, G, T\right)$$

For a given price level, P, the increase in nominal money, M, leads to an increase in the real money stock, M/P, leading to an increase in output. The aggregate demand curve shifts to the right, from *AD* to *AD'*. In the short run, the economy goes from point *A* to *A'*. Output increases from Y_n to Y', and the price level increases from P to P'.

Over time, the adjustment of price expectations comes into play. As output is higher than the natural level of output, the price level is higher than wage setters

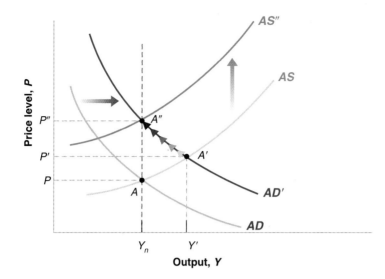

Figure 7-7

The Dynamic Effects of a Monetary Expansion

A monetary expansion leads to an increase in output in the short run but has no effect on output in the medium run.

expected. They then revise their expectations, which causes the aggregate supply curve to shift up over time. The economy moves up along the aggregate demand curve, *AD'*. The adjustment process stops when output has returned to the natural level of output. At that point, the price level is equal to the expected price level. In the medium run, the aggregate supply curve is given by *AS''*, and the economy is at point *A''*: Output is back to Y_n, and the price level is equal to *P''*.

We can actually pin down the exact size of the eventual increase in the price level. If output is back to the natural level of output, the real money stock must also be back to its initial value. In other words, the proportional increase in prices must be equal to the proportional increase in the nominal money stock: If the initial increase in nominal money is equal to 10%, then the price level ends up 10% higher.

Go back to equation (7.3): If *Y* is unchanged (and *G* and *T* are also unchanged), then *M/P* must also be unchanged.

If *M/P* is unchanged, it must be that *M* and *P* both increase in the same proportion.

Going Behind the Scenes

To get a better sense of what is going on, it is useful to go behind the scenes to see what happens not only to output and to the price level but also to the interest rate. We can do this by looking at what happens in terms of the *IS–LM* model.

Figure 7-8(a) reproduces Figure 7-7 (leaving out the *AS''* curve to keep things simple) and shows the adjustment of output and the price level in response to the increase in nominal money. Figure 7-8(b) shows the adjustment of output and the interest rate by looking at the same adjustment process but in terms of the *IS–LM* model.

Look first at Figure 7-8(b). Before the change in nominal money, the equilibrium is given by the intersection of the *IS* and *LM* curves—that is, at point *A*, which corresponds to point *A* in Figure 7-8(a). Output is equal to the natural level of output, Y_n, and the interest rate is given by *i*.

The short-run effect of the monetary expansion is to shift the *LM* curve down from *LM* to *LM'*, moving the equilibrium from point *A* to point *A'*, which corresponds to point *A'* in Figure 7-8(a). The interest rate is lower, and output is higher.

Note that there are two effects at work behind the shift from *LM* to *LM'*: One is due to the increase in nominal money. The other, which partly offsets the first, is due to the increase in the price level. Let's look at these two effects more closely:

■ If the price level did not change, the increase in nominal money would shift the *LM* curve down to *LM''*. So, if the price level did not change—as was our

The Dynamic Effects of a Monetary Expansion on Output and the Interest Rate

The increase in nominal money initially shifts the *LM* curve down, decreasing the interest rate and increasing output. Over time, the price level increases, shifting the *LM* curve back up until output is back at the natural level of output.

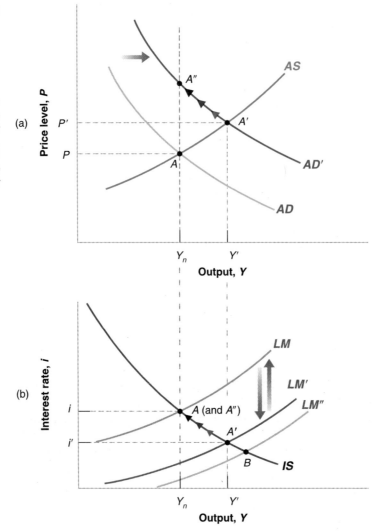

Why only partially? Suppose the price level increased in the same proportion as the increase in nominal money, leaving the real money stock ▶ unchanged. If the real money stock were unchanged, output would remain unchanged as well. But if output were unchanged, the price level would not increase, contradicting our premise.

assumption in Chapter 5—the equilibrium would be at the intersection of *IS* and *LM″*, or point *B*.

■ But even in the short run, the price level increases—from *P* to *P′* in Figure 7-8(a). This increase in the price level shifts the *LM* curve upward from *LM″* to *LM′*, partially offsetting the effect of the increase in nominal money.

■ The net effect of these two shifts—down from *LM* to *LM″* in response to the increase in nominal money, and up from *LM″* to *LM′* in response to the increase in the price level—is a shift of the *LM* curve from *LM* to *LM′*, and the equilibrium is given by *A′*.

Over time, the fact that output is above its natural level implies that the price level continues to increase. As the price level increases, it further reduces the real money stock and shifts the *LM* curve back up. The economy moves along the *IS* curve: The interest rate increases, and output declines. Eventually, the *LM* curve returns to where it was before the increase in nominal money.

The economy ends up at point *A*, which corresponds to point *A″* in Figure 7-8(a): The increase in nominal money is exactly offset by a proportional increase in the price level. The real money stock is therefore unchanged. With the real money stock unchanged, output is back to its initial value, Y_n, which is the natural level of output, and the interest rate is also back to its initial value, i.

The Neutrality of Money

Let's summarize what we have just discussed about the effects of monetary policy:

■ In the *short run*, a monetary expansion leads to an increase in output, a decrease in the interest rate, and an increase in the price level.

How much of the effect of a monetary expansion falls initially on output and how much on the price level depends on the slope of the aggregate supply curve. In Chapter 5, we assumed that the price level did not respond at all to an increase in output; we assumed in effect that the aggregate supply curve was flat. Although we intended this as a simplification, empirical evidence does show that the initial effect of changes in output on the price level is quite small. We saw this when we looked at estimated responses to changes in the federal funds rate in Figure 5-9: Despite the change in output, the price level remained practically unchanged for nearly a year.

■ Over time, the price level increases, and the effects of the monetary expansion on output and on the interest rate disappear. *In the medium run, the increase in nominal money is reflected entirely in a proportional increase in the price level. The increase in nominal money has no effect on output or on the interest rate.* (How long it takes in reality for the effects of money on output to disappear is the topic of the Focus box "How Long Lasting Are the Real Effects of Money?") Economists refer to the absence of a medium-run effect of money on output and on the interest rate by saying that money is neutral in the medium run.

Actually, the way the proposition is typically stated is that money is neutral in the *long run*. This is because many economists use "long run" to refer to what I call in this book ◄ the "medium run."

The **neutrality of money** in the medium run does not mean that monetary policy cannot or should not be used to affect output. An expansionary monetary policy can, for example, help the economy move out of a recession and return more quickly to the natural level of output. As we saw in Chapter 5, this is exactly the way monetary policy was used to fight the 2001 recession. But it is a warning that monetary policy cannot sustain higher output forever.

7-5   A Decrease in the Budget Deficit

The policy we just looked at—a monetary expansion—led to a shift in aggregate demand coming from a shift in the *LM* curve. Let's now look at the effects of a shift in aggregate demand coming from a shift in the *IS* curve.

Recall from Chapter 5 that a reduction in the budget deficit ◄ is also called a fiscal contraction, or a fiscal consolidation.

Suppose the government is running a budget deficit and decides to reduce it by decreasing its spending from G to G' while leaving taxes, T, unchanged. How will this affect the economy in the short run and in the medium run?

Assume that output is initially at the natural level of output so that the economy is at point A in Figure 7-9: output equals Y_n. The decrease in government spending from G to G' shifts the aggregate demand curve to the left, from AD to AD': For a given price level, output is lower. In the short run, the equilibrium moves from A to A'; output decreases from Y_n to Y', and the price level decreases from P to P'.

The initial effect of the deficit reduction triggers lower output. We first derived this result in Chapter 3, and it holds here as well.

What happens over time? As long as output is below the natural level of output, we know that the aggregate supply curve keeps shifting down. The economy moves down along the aggregate demand curve, AD', until the aggregate supply curve is given by AS'' and the economy reaches point A''. By then, the recession is over, and output is back at Y_n.

To determine how long lasting the real effects of money are, economists use **macroeconometric models**. These models are larger-scale versions of the aggregate supply and aggregate demand model in this chapter.

The model we examine in this box was built in the early 1990s by John Taylor at Stanford University.

The Taylor model is substantially larger than the model we studied in this chapter. On the aggregate supply side, it has separate equations for price and for wage setting. On the demand side, it has separate equations for consumption, for investment, for exports, and for imports. (Recall that, so far, we have assumed that the economy is closed, so we have ignored exports and imports altogether.) In addition, instead of looking at just one country, as we have done here, it looks at eight countries (the United States and seven major OECD countries) and solves for equilibrium in all eight countries simultaneously. Each equation, for each country, is estimated using econometrics and allows for a richer dynamic structure than the equations we have relied on in this chapter.

The implications of the model for the effects of money on output are shown in Figure 1. The simulation looks at the effects of an increase in nominal money of 3%, taking place over four quarters—0.1% in the first quarter, another 0.6% in the second, another 1.2% in the third, and another 1.1% in the fourth. After these four step increases, nominal money remains at its new higher level forever.

The effects of money on output reach a maximum after three quarters. By then, output is 1.8% higher than it would have been without the increase in nominal money. Over time, however, the price level increases, and output returns to the natural level of output. In year 4, the price level is up by 2.5%, while output is up by only 0.3%. Therefore, the Taylor model suggests that it takes roughly four years for output to return to its natural level or, put another way, four years for changes in nominal money to become neutral.

Do all macroeconometric models give the same answer? No. Because they differ in the way they are constructed, in the way variables are chosen, and in the way equations are estimated, their answers are different. But most of them have the following implications in common: The effects of an increase in money on output build up for one to two years and then decline over time. (For a sense of how the answers differ across models, see the Focus box "Twelve Macroeconometric Models" in Chapter 24.)

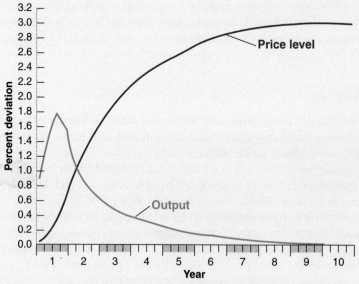

Figure 1 *The Effects of an Expansion in Nominal Money in the Taylor Model*

Source: Figure 1 is reproduced from John Taylor, Macroeconomic Policy in a World Economy, *W.W. Norton, New York, 1993, Figure 5-1A, p. 138.*

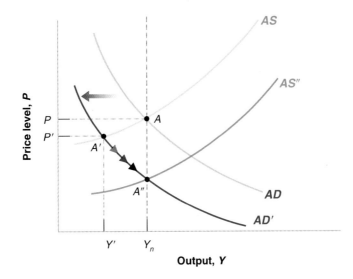

Figure 7-9

The Dynamic Effects of a Decrease in the Budget Deficit

A decrease in the budget deficit leads initially to a decrease in output. Over time, however, output returns to the natural level of output.

Like an increase in nominal money, a reduction in the budget deficit does not affect output forever. Eventually, output returns to its natural level. But there is an important difference between the effects of a change in money and the effects of a change in the deficit. At point A'', not everything is the same as before: Output is back to the natural level of output, but the price level and the interest rate are lower than before the shift. The best way to see why is to look at the adjustment in terms of the ◄ underlying IS–LM model.

Deficit Reduction, Output, and the Interest Rate

Figure 7-10(a) reproduces Figure 7-9, showing the adjustment of output and the price level in response to the increase in the budget deficit (but leaving out AS'' to keep things visually simple). Figure 7-10(b) shows the adjustment of output and the interest rate by looking at the same adjustment process, but in terms of the IS–LM model.

Look first at Figure 7-10(b). Before the change in fiscal policy, the equilibrium is given by the intersection of the IS curve and the LM curve, at point A—which corresponds to point A in Figure 7-10(a). Output is equal to the natural level of output, Y_n, and the interest rate is given by i.

As the government reduces the budget deficit, the IS curve shifts to the left, to IS'. If the price level did not change (the assumption we made in Chapter 5), the economy would move from point A to point B. But because the price level declines in response to the decrease in output, the real money stock increases, leading to a partially offsetting shift of the LM curve, down to LM'. So the initial effect of deficit reduction is to move the economy from point A to point A' (which corresponds to point A' in Figure 7-10(a)). Both output and the interest rate are lower than before the fiscal contraction. Note that, just as was the case in Chapter 5, we cannot tell whether investment increases or decreases in the short run: Lower output decreases investment, but the lower interest rate increases investment.

So long as output remains below the natural level of output, the price level continues to decline, leading to a further increase in the real money stock. The LM curve continues to shift down. In Figure 7-10(b), the economy moves down from point A' along IS' and eventually reaches A'' (which corresponds to A'' in Figure 7-10(a)). At A'', the LM curve is given by LM''.

At A'', output is back at the natural level of output, but the interest rate is lower than it was before deficit reduction, down from i to i''. The composition of output is

The fact that the price level decreases along the way may seem strange: We rarely observe deflation (although recall the case of Japan, from Chapter 2). This result comes from the fact that we are looking at an economy in which money growth is zero (we are assuming that M is constant, not growing), and so there is no inflation in the medium run. When we introduce money growth in the next chapter, we will see that a recession typically leads to a decrease in inflation, not to a decrease in the price level.

The Dynamic Effects of a Decrease in the Budget Deficit on Output and the Interest Rate

A deficit reduction leads in the short run to a decrease in output and to a decrease in the interest rate. In the medium run, output returns to its natural level, while the interest rate declines further.

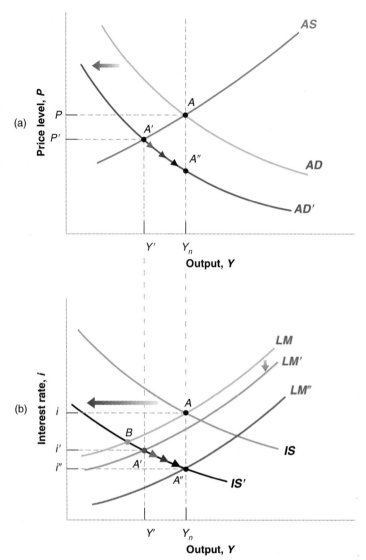

also different: To see how and why, let's rewrite the *IS* relation, taking into account that at A'', output is back at the natural level of output, so that $Y = Y_n$:

$$Y_n = C(Y_n - T) + I(Y_n, i) + G$$

Because income, Y_n, and taxes, T, are unchanged, consumption, C, is the same as before the deficit reduction. By assumption, government spending, G, is lower than before. Therefore, investment, I, must be higher than before the deficit reduction—higher by an amount exactly equal to the decrease in G. Put another way, in the medium run, a reduction in the budget deficit unambiguously leads to a decrease in the interest rate and an increase in investment.

Budget Deficits, Output, and Investment

Let's summarize what we have just discussed about the effects of fiscal policy:

■ In the *short run*, a budget deficit reduction, if implemented alone—that is, without an accompanying change in monetary policy—leads to a decrease in output and may lead to a *decrease* in investment. Note the qualification "without an accompanying change in monetary policy": In principle, these adverse short-run effects on output can be avoided by using the right monetary–fiscal mix. What is needed is for the central bank to increase the money supply enough to offset the adverse effects of the decrease in government spending on aggregate demand. This is what happened in the United States in the 1990s. As the Clinton administration reduced budget deficits, the Fed made sure that, even in the short-run, the deficit reduction did not lead to a recession and lower output.

◄ Recall the discussion of the policy mix in Chapter 5.

◄ Go back to Figure 7-10. What would the Fed need to do in order to avoid a decrease in output in response to the fiscal contraction?

■ In the *medium run*, output returns to the natural level of output, and the interest rate is lower. In the medium run, a deficit reduction leads unambiguously to an *increase* in investment.

■ We have not taken into account so far the effects of investment on capital accumulation and the effects of capital on production (we will do so in Chapter 10 and beyond when we look at the long run). But it is easy to see how our conclusions would be modified if we did take into account the effects on capital accumulation. In the long run, the level of output depends on the capital stock in the economy. So if a lower government budget deficit leads to more investment, it will lead to a higher capital stock, and the higher capital stock will lead to higher output.

Everything we have just said about the effects of deficit reduction would apply equally to measures aimed at increasing private (rather than public) saving. An increase in the saving rate increases output and investment in the medium run and in the long run. But it may also create a recession and a decrease in investment in the short run.

Disagreements among economists about the effects of measures aimed at increasing either public saving or private saving often come from differences in time frames. Those who are concerned with short-run effects worry that measures to increase saving, public or private, might create a recession and decrease saving and investment for some time. Those who look beyond the short run see the eventual increase in saving and investment and emphasize the favorable medium-run and long-run effects on output.

Effects of a deficit reduction:
Short run: Y decreases, I increases or decreases
Medium run: Y unchanged, I increases
Long run: Y increases, I increases

7-6 Changes in the Price of Oil

We have looked so far at the effects of variables that shift the aggregate demand curve: an increase in the money supply and a reduction in the budget deficit. Now that we have formalized the supply side, we can look at the effects of variables that shift the aggregate supply curve. An obvious candidate is the price of oil. Increases in the price of oil have often made the news in the recent past, and for good reasons: The price of oil, which stood around $13 per barrel at the start of 1999, stands at the time of writing, around $80. What effects such an increase is likely to have on the economy is clearly of much current concern to policymakers.

This is not the first time the world economy has experienced a sharp increase in the price of oil. In the 1970s, the formation of OPEC (the Organization of Petroleum Exporting Countries), a cartel of oil producers, together with disruptions due to wars and revolutions in the Middle East, led to two sharp increases in the price of oil, the first one in 1973 to 1975, the second in 1979 to 1981. Figure 7-11 plots the real price of oil, defined as the ratio of the price of crude petroleum to the GDP deflator, since 1970 (the ratio is set to 100 in 1970). As the figure shows, by 1981, the real price of oil reached nearly six times its level in 1970. This high price did not last very long. From 1982 until the late 1990s, the OPEC cartel became steadily weaker, unable to enforce the production quotas it had set for its members. By 1998, the real price of oil was roughly back to its 1970 level. Since then, however, the combination of the Iraq war and a steady increase in the demand for oil by fast-growing countries such as China and India, have led to large increases in prices, to levels close to those of the early 1980s.

At the time of writing (mid-2007), the price of oil in dollars is nearly twice as high as it was in 1981. But because the price level has increased over time, the real price of oil is still lower ◄ than it was in 1981.

Figure 7-11

The Real Price of Oil Since 1970

There were two sharp increases in the relative price of oil in the 1970s, followed by a decrease until the 1990s, and a large increase since then.

Each of the two large price increases of the 1970s was associated with a sharp recession and a large increase in inflation—a combination macroeconomists call **stagflation**, to capture the combination of *stag*nation and in*flation* that characterized these episodes. The obvious worry is that the recent price of oil may trigger another such episode. So far, it has not happened, and we shall reexamine the issue shortly. First, we must understand the effects of the price of oil in our model.

Note that we face a serious problem in using the model to think about the macroeconomic effects of an increase in the price of oil: The price of oil appears neither in our aggregate supply relation nor in our aggregate demand relation! The reason is that, until now, we have assumed that output was produced using only labor. One way to extend our model would be to recognize explicitly that output is produced using labor and other inputs (including energy) and then figure out what effect an increase in the price of oil has on the price set by firms and on the relation between output and employment. An easier way, and the way we will go, is simply to capture the increase in the price of oil by an increase in μ—the markup of the price over the nominal wage. The justification is straightforward: Given wages, an increase in the price of oil increases the cost of production, forcing firms to increase prices.

We can then track the dynamic effects of an *increase in the markup* on output and the price level. It will be easiest here to work backward in time, first asking what happens in the medium run and then working out the dynamics of adjustment from the short run to the medium run.

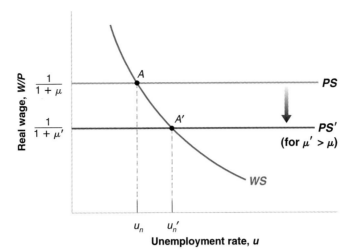

Figure 7-12

The Effects of an Increase in the Price of Oil on the Natural Rate of Unemployment

An increase in the price of oil leads to a lower real wage and a higher natural rate of unemployment.

Effects on the Natural Rate of Unemployment

What happens to the natural rate of unemployment when the price of oil increases? Figure 7-12 reproduces the characterization of labor market equilibrium from Chapter 6. The wage-setting curve is downward sloping. The price-setting relation is represented by the horizontal line at $W/P = 1/(1 + \mu)$. The initial equilibrium is at point A, and the initial natural unemployment rate is u_n. An increase in the markup leads to a downward shift of the price-setting line, from PS to PS': The higher the markup, the lower the real wage implied by price setting. The equilibrium moves from A to A'. The real wage is lower. The natural unemployment rate is higher: Getting workers to accept the lower real wage requires an increase in unemployment.

◄ Do not be confused: u and μ are not the same; u is the unemployment rate, and μ is the markup.

The increase in the natural rate of unemployment leads to a decrease in the natural level of employment. If we assume that the relation between employment and output is unchanged—that is, that each unit of output still requires one worker in addition to the energy input—then the decrease in the natural level of employment leads to an identical decrease in the natural level of output. Putting things together: An increase in the price of oil leads to a decrease in the natural level of output.

The Dynamics of Adjustment

Let's now turn to dynamics. Suppose that before the increase in the price of oil, the aggregate demand curve and the aggregate supply curve are given by AD and AS, respectively, so the economy is at point A in Figure 7-13, with output at the natural level of output, Y_n, and, by implication, $P = P^e$.

We have just established that the increase in the price of oil decreases the natural level of output. Call this lower level Y_n'. We now want to know what happens in the short run and how the economy moves from Y_n to Y_n'.

To think about the short run, recall that the aggregate supply relation is given by

$$P = P^e(1 + \mu) F\left(1 - \frac{Y}{L}, z\right)$$

Recall that we capture the effect of an increase in the price of oil by an increase in the markup, μ. So, in the short run (given P^e), the increase in the price of oil shows up as an increase in the markup, μ. This increase in the markup leads firms to increase their prices, resulting in an increase in the price level, P, at any level of output, Y. The aggregate supply curve shifts up.

The Dynamic Effects of an Increase in the Price of Oil

An increase in the price of oil leads, in the short run, to a decrease in output and an increase in the price level. Over time, output decreases further, and the price level increases further.

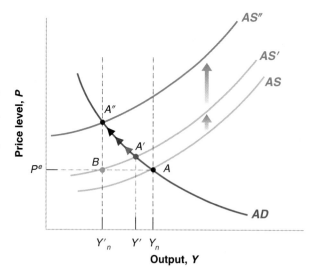

We can be more specific about the size of the shift, and knowing the size of this shift will be useful in what follows. We know from Section 7-1 that the aggregate supply curve always goes through the point such that output equals the natural level of output and the price level equals the expected price level. Before the increase in the price of oil, the aggregate supply curve in Figure 7-13 goes through point A, where output equals Y_n and the price level is equal to P^e. After the increase in the price of oil, the new aggregate supply curve goes through point B, where output equals the new lower natural level of output, Y_n', and the price level equals the expected price level, P^e. The aggregate supply curve shifts from AS to AS'.

Does the aggregate demand curve shift as a result of the increase in the price of oil? Maybe. There are many channels through which demand might be affected at a given price level: The higher price of oil may lead firms to change their investment plans, canceling some investment projects and/or shifting to less energy-intensive equipment. The increase in the price of oil also redistributes income from oil buyers to oil producers. Oil producers may spend less than oil buyers, leading to a decrease in consumption demand. Let's take the easy way out: Because some of the effects shift the aggregate demand curve to the right and others shift the aggregate demand curve to the left, let's simply assume that the effects cancel each other out and that aggregate demand does not shift.

> This was the case in the 1970s. The OPEC countries realized that high oil revenues might not last forever. Many of them saved a large proportion of the income from oil revenues.

Under this assumption, in the short run, only the AS shifts. The economy therefore moves along the AD curve, from A to A'. Output decreases from Y_n to Y'. The increase in the price of oil leads firms to increase their prices. This increase in the price level then decreases demand and output.

What happens over time? Although output has fallen, the natural level of output has fallen even more: At point A', output, Y', is still above the new natural level of output, Y_n', the aggregate supply curve continues to shift up. The economy therefore moves over time along the aggregate demand curve, from A' to A''. At point A'', output, Y', is equal to the new lower natural level of output, Y_n', and the price level is higher than before the oil shock: Shifts in aggregate supply affect output not only in the short run but in the medium run as well.

Do these implications fit what we have observed in response to increases in the price of oil, both in the 1970s and recently? The answer is given by Figure 7-14, which plots the evolution of the real price of oil and inflation—using the CPI—and Figure 7-15, which plots the evolution of the real price of oil and the unemployment rate, in the United States since 1970.

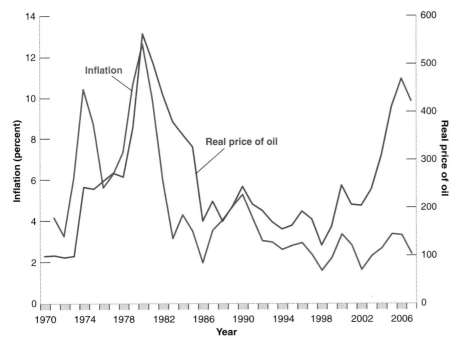

Figure 7-14

Oil Price Increases and Inflation in the United States Since 1970

The oil price increases of the 1970s were associated with large increases in inflation. But this has not been the case for the recent oil price increases.

Figure 7-15

Oil Price Increases and Unemployment in the United States Since 1970

The oil price increases of the 1970s were associated with large increases in unemployment. But this has not been the case for the recent oil price increases.

The question triggered by Figures 7-14 and 7-15 is an obvious one: Why is it that oil price increases were associated with stagflation in the 1970s but have had so little apparent effect on the economy in the 2000s?

A first line of explanation is that other shocks besides just the increase in the price of oil were at work in the 1970s and in the 2000s. In the 1970s, not only did the price of oil increase, so did the prices of many other raw materials. This implies that the aggregate supply relation shifted up by more than implied by just the increase in the price of oil. In the 2000s, many economists believe that, partly because of globalization and foreign competition, U.S. workers became weaker in bargaining. If true, this implies that, while the increase in oil prices shifted the aggregate supply curve up, the decrease in bargaining power of workers shifted it down, dampening or even eliminating the adverse effects of the oil price increase on output and the price level.

Econometric studies suggest, however, that more was at work, and that, even after controlling for the presence of these other factors, the effects of the price of oil have changed since the 1970s. Figure 1 shows the effects of a 100% increase in the price of oil on output and the price level, estimated using data from two different periods. The black and brown lines show the effects of an increase in the price of oil on the CPI and on GDP, based on data from 1970:1 to 1986:4; the blue and pink lines do the same, but based on data from 1987:1 to 2006:4 (the time scale on the horizontal axis is in quarters). The figure suggests two main conclusions. First, in both periods, as predicted by our model, the increase in the price of oil leads to an increase in the CPI and a decrease in GDP. Second, the effects of the increase in the price of oil on both the CPI and GDP have become smaller, roughly half of what they were earlier.

Why have the adverse effects of the increase in the price of oil become smaller? This is still very much a topic of research. But, at this stage, two hypotheses appear plausible.

The first hypothesis is that, today, U.S. workers are less powerful in bargaining than they were in the 1970s. Thus, as the price of oil has increased, workers have been more willing to accept a reduction in wages, limiting the upward shift in the aggregate supply curve and thus limiting the adverse effect on the price level and on output. (Make sure you understand this statement, using Figure 7-13.)

The second hypothesis concerns monetary policy. When the price of oil increased in the 1970s, people started expecting much higher prices, and P^e increased a lot. The result was a further shift of the aggregate supply curve, leading to a larger increase in the price level and a larger decrease in output. Today, monetary policy is very different from what it was in the 1970s, and expectations are that the Fed will not let the increase in the price of oil lead to a higher price level. Thus, P^e has barely increased, leading to a smaller shift of the aggregate supply curve, and thus a smaller effect on output and the price level, than in the 1970s. (Again, make sure you understand this statement, using Figure 7-13.)

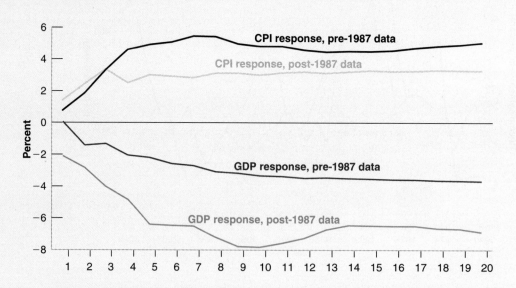

Figure 1   *The Effects of a 100% Increase in the Price of Oil on the CPI and on GDP*

The effects of an increase in the price of oil on output and the price level are much smaller than they used to be.

First, the good news (for our model, although not for the U.S. economy): Note how both the first and the second large increases in the price of oil were followed by major increases in inflation and in unemployment. This fits our analysis perfectly. Then, the bad news (for our model): Note how the increase in the price of oil since the late 1990s has not been associated—at least so far—with either an increase in inflation or an increase in unemployment. In light of what happened in the 1970s, this lack of an effect has come as a surprise to macroeconomists. The state of research and the various hypotheses being explored are discussed in the Focus box "Oil Price Increases: Why Are the 2000s So Different from the 1970s?"

7-7   Conclusions

This chapter has covered a lot of ground. Let me repeat some key ideas and develop some of the earlier conclusions.

The Short Run Versus the Medium Run

One message of this chapter is that changes in policy and changes in the economic environment—from changes in consumer confidence to changes in the price of oil—typically have different effects in the short run than in the medium run. We looked at the effects of a monetary expansion, a deficit reduction, and an increase in the price of oil. The main results are summarized in Table 7-1. A monetary expansion, for example, affects output in the short run but not in the medium run. In the short run, a reduction in the budget deficit decreases output and decreases the interest rate, and it may decrease investment. But in the medium run, the interest rate decreases, and output returns to the natural level of output, so investment increases. An increase in the price of oil decreases output not only in the short run but also in the medium run. And so on.

This difference between the short-run effects and the medium-run effects of policies is one of the reasons economists disagree in their policy recommendations. Some economists believe the economy returns quickly to its medium-run equilibrium, so they emphasize medium-run implications of policy. Others believe the adjustment mechanism through which output returns to the natural level of output can be very slow, so they put more emphasis on the short-run effects of policy. They are more willing to use active monetary policy or fiscal policy to get out of a recession, even if money is neutral in the medium run and budget deficits have adverse implications in the long run.

> We will return to these issues many times in this book. See the discussion of the Great Depression and of the current situation in Japan in Chapter 22, and see Chapters 24 to 26 ◄ on policy.

Shocks and Propagation Mechanisms

This chapter also gives you a general way of thinking about **output fluctuations** (sometimes called **business cycles**)—movements in output around its trend (a trend that we have ignored so far but on which we will focus in Chapters 10 to 13).

Table 7-1	**Short-Run Effects and Medium-Run Effects of a Monetary Expansion, a Budget Deficit Reduction, and an Increase in the Price of Oil on Output, the Interest Rate, and the Price Level**					
	Short Run			**Medium Run**		
	Output Level	Interest Rate	Price Level	Output Level	Interest Rate	Price Level
Monetary expansion	Increase	Decrease	Increase (small)	No change	No change	Increase
Deficit reduction	Decrease	Decrease	Decrease (small)	No change	Decrease	Decrease
Increase in oil price	Decrease	Increase	Increase	Decrease	Increase	Increase

The economy is constantly hit by **shocks** to aggregate supply, or to aggregate demand, or to both. These shocks may be shifts in consumption coming from changes in consumer confidence, shifts in investment, shifts in the demand for money, changes in oil prices, and so on. Or they may come from changes in policy—from the introduction of a new tax law, to a new program of infrastructure investment, to a decision by the central bank to fight inflation by tightening the money supply.

▶ How to define *shocks* is harder than it looks. Suppose a failed economic program in an Eastern European country leads to political chaos in that country, which leads to increased risk of nuclear war in the region, which leads to a fall in consumer confidence in the United States, which leads to a recession in the United States. What is the "shock"? the failed program? the fall of democracy? the increased risk of nuclear war? or the decrease in consumer confidence? In practice, we have to cut the chain of causation somewhere. Thus, we may refer to the drop in consumer confidence as the shock, ignoring its underlying causes.

Each shock has dynamic effects on output and its components. These dynamic effects are called the **propagation mechanism** of the shock. Propagation mechanisms are different for different shocks. The effects of a shock on activity may be largest at the beginning of the shock and then decrease over time. Or the effects may build up for a while and then decrease and disappear. We saw, for example, that the effects of an increase in money on output reach a peak after six to nine months and then slowly decline afterward, as the price level eventually increases in proportion to the increase in nominal money. Some shocks have effects even in the medium run. This is the case for any shock that has a permanent effect on aggregate supply, such as a permanent change in the price of oil.

Fluctuations in output come from the continual appearance of new shocks, each with its propagation mechanism. At times, some shocks are sufficiently bad or come in sufficiently bad combinations that they create a recession. The two recessions of the 1970s were due largely to increases in the price of oil; the recession of the early 1980s was due to a sharp contraction in money; the recession of the early 1990s was due primarily to a sudden decline in consumer confidence; the recession of 2001 was due to a sharp drop in investment spending. What we call *economic fluctuations* are the result of these shocks and their dynamic effects on output.

Where We Go from Here: Output, Unemployment, and Inflation

In developing the model of this chapter, we assumed that the nominal money stock was constant. That is, although we considered the effects of a one-time change in the level of nominal money (in Section 7-4), we did not allow for sustained nominal money growth. We are now ready to relax this assumption and allow for nominal money growth. Only by considering positive nominal money growth can we explain why inflation is typically positive and think about the relation between economic activity and inflation. Movements in unemployment, output, and inflation are the topics of the next two chapters.

Summary

■ The model of aggregate supply and aggregate demand describes the movements in output and the price level when account is taken of equilibrium in the goods market, the financial market, and the labor market.

■ The aggregate supply relation captures the effects of output on the price level. It is derived from equilibrium in the labor market. It is a relation between the price level, the expected price level, and the level of output. An increase in output decreases unemployment; the decrease in unemployment increases wages and, in turn, increases the price level. An increase in the expected price level leads, one-for-one, to an increase in the actual price level.

■ The aggregate demand relation captures the effects of the price level on output. It is derived from equilibrium in goods and financial markets. An increase in the price level decreases the real money stock, increasing the interest rate and decreasing output.

■ In the short run, movements in output come from shifts in either aggregate demand or aggregate supply. In the medium run, output returns to the natural level of output, which is determined by equilibrium in the labor market.

■ An expansionary monetary policy leads in the short run to an increase in the real money stock, a decrease in the interest rate, and an increase in output. Over time, the price level increases, and the real money stock decreases until output has returned to its natural level. In the medium run, money does not affect output, and changes in money are reflected in proportional increases in the price level. Economists refer to this fact by saying that, in the medium run, money is neutral.

■ A reduction in the budget deficit leads in the short run to a decrease in the demand for goods and therefore to a decrease in output. Over time, the price level decreases, leading to an increase in the real money stock and a decrease in the interest rate. In the medium run, output increases back to the natural level of output, but the interest rate is lower, and investment is higher.

■ An increase in the price of oil leads, in both the short run and the medium run, to a decrease in output. In the short run, it leads to an increase in the price level, which decreases the real money stock and leads to a contraction of demand and output. In the medium run, an

increase in the price of oil decreases the real wage paid by firms, increases the natural rate of unemployment, and therefore decreases the natural level of output.

■ The difference between short-run effects and medium-run effects of policies is one of the reasons economists disagree in their policy recommendations. Some economists believe the economy adjusts quickly to its medium-run equilibrium, so they emphasize medium-run implications of policy. Others believe the adjustment mechanism through which output returns to the natural level of output is a slow process at best, so they put more emphasis on the short-run effects of policy.

■ Economic fluctuations are the result of a continual stream of shocks to aggregate supply or to aggregate demand and of the dynamic effects of each of these shocks on output. Sometimes the shocks are sufficiently adverse, alone or in combination, that they lead to a recession.

Key Terms

■ aggregate supply relation, 158
■ aggregate demand relation, 160
■ neutrality of money, 169
■ macroeconometric models, 170

■ stagflation, 174
■ output fluctuations, business cycles, 179
■ shocks, 180
■ propagation mechanism, 180

Questions and Problems

Quick Check

1. Using the information in this chapter, label each of the following statements true, false, or uncertain. Explain briefly.

a. The aggregate supply relation implies that an increase in output leads to a decrease in the price level.

b. The aggregate demand relation slopes down because at a higher price level, consumers wish to purchase fewer goods.

c. The natural level of output can be determined by looking at the aggregate supply relation alone.

d. Expansionary monetary policy has no effect on the level of output in the short run.

e. In the absence of changes in fiscal or monetary policy, the economy will always remain at the natural level of output.

f. The neutrality of money in the medium run does not mean that monetary policy cannot or should not be used to affect output.

g. In the short run, a reduction in the budget deficit decreases output and decreases the interest rate.

2. Supply shocks and the medium run

Consider an economy with output equal to the natural level of output. Now suppose there is an increase in unemployment benefits.

a. Using the model developed in this chapter, show the effects of an increase in unemployment benefits on the position of the AD and AS curves in the short run and in the medium run.

b. How will the increase in unemployment benefits affect

output and the price level in the short run and in the medium run?

3. Spending shocks and the medium run

Suppose the economy begins with output equal to its natural level. Then, there is a reduction in income taxes.

a. Using the AS–AD model developed in this chapter, show the effects of a reduction in income taxes on the position of the AD, AS, IS, and LM curves in the medium run.

b. What happens to output, the interest rate, and the price level in the medium run? What happens to consumption and investment in the medium run?

4. The neutrality of money

a. In what sense is money neutral? How is monetary policy useful if money is neutral?

b. Fiscal policy, like monetary policy, cannot change the natural level of output. Why then is monetary policy considered neutral but fiscal policy is not?

c. Discuss the statement "Because neither fiscal nor monetary policy can affect the natural level of output, it follows that, in the medium run, the natural level of output is independent of all government policies."

Dig Deeper

5. The paradox of saving, one last time

In chapter problems at the end of Chapters 3 and 5, we examined the paradox of saving in the short run, under different assumptions about the response of investment to output and the interest rate. Here we consider the issue one last time in the context of the AS–AD model.

Suppose the economy begins with output equal to its natural level. Then there is a decrease in consumer confidence, as households attempt to increase their saving, for a given level of disposable income.

a. In AS–AD and IS–LM diagrams, show the effects of the decline in consumer confidence in the short run and the medium run. Explain why curves shift in your diagrams.

b. What happens to output, the interest rate, and the price level in the short run? What happens to consumption, investment, and private saving in the short run? Is it possible that the decline in consumer confidence will actually lead to a fall in private saving in the short run?

c. Repeat part (b) for the medium run. Is there any paradox of saving in the medium run?

6. Suppose that the interest rate has no effect on investment.

a. Can you think of a situation in which this may happen?

b. What does this imply for the slope of the IS curve?

c. What does this imply for the slope of the LM curve?

d. What does this imply for the slope of the AD curve?

Continue to assume that the interest rate has no effect on investment. Assume that the economy starts at the natural level of output. Suppose there is a shock to the variable z, so that the AS curve shifts up.

e. What is the short-run effect on output and the price level? Explain in words.

f. What happens to output and the price level over time? Explain in words.

7. You learned in problem 6 (on the liquidity trap) in Chapter 5 that money demand becomes very flat at low interest rates. For this problem, consider the money demand function to be horizontal at a zero nominal interest rate.

a. Draw the LM curve. How does the slope of the curve change when the interest rate rises above zero?

b. Draw the IS curve. Does the shape of the curve change (necessarily) when the interest rate falls below zero?

c. Draw the AD curve? (Hint: From the IS–LM diagram, think about the price level at which the interest rate is zero. How does the AD curve look above this price level? How does the AD curve look below this price level?)

d. Draw the AD and AS curves and assume that equilibrium is at a point where output is below the natural level of output and where the interest rate is zero. Suppose the central bank increases the money supply. What will be the effects on output in the short run and in the medium run? Explain in words.

8. Supply shocks and demand management

Assume that the economy starts at the natural level of output. Now suppose there is an increase in the price of oil.

a. In an AS–AD diagram, show what happens to output and the price level in the short run and the medium run.

b. What happens to the unemployment rate in the short run? in the medium run?

Suppose that the Federal Reserve decides to respond immediately to the increase in the price of oil. In particular, suppose that the Fed wants to prevent the unemployment rate from changing in the short run, after the increase in the price of oil. Assume that the Fed changes the money supply once—immediately after the increase in the price of oil— and then does not change the money supply again.

c. What should the Fed do to prevent the unemployment rate from changing in the short run? Show how the Fed's action, combined with the decline in business confidence, affects the AD–AS diagram in the short run and the medium run.

d. How do output and the price level in the short run and the medium run compare to your answers from part (a)?

e. How do the short-run and medium-run unemployment rates compare to your answers from part (b)?

9. Demand shocks and demand management

Assume that the economy starts at the natural level of output. Now suppose there is a decline in business confidence, so that investment demand falls for any interest rate.

a. In an AD–AS diagram, show what happens to output and the price level in the short run and the medium run.

b. What happens to the unemployment rate in the short run? in the medium run?

Suppose that the Federal Reserve decides to respond immediately to the decline in business confidence in the short run. In particular, suppose that the Fed wants to prevent the unemployment rate from changing in the short run after the decline in business confidence.

a. What should the Fed do? Show how the Fed's action, combined with the decline in business confidence, affects the AD–AS diagram in the short run and the medium run.

b. How do short-run output and the short-run price level compare to your answers from part (a)?

c. How do the short-run and medium-run unemployment rates compare to your answers from part (b)?

10. Based on your answers to problems 8 and 9 and the material from the chapter, comment on the following statement:

The Federal Reserve has the easiest job in the world. All it has to do is conduct expansionary monetary policy when the unemployment rate increases and contractionary monetary policy when the unemployment rate falls.

11. Taxes, oil prices, and workers

Everyone in the labor force is concerned with two things: whether they have a job and, if so, their after-tax income from the job (i.e., their after-tax real wage). An unemployed worker may also be concerned with the availability and amount of unemployment benefits, but we will leave that issue aside for this problem.

a. Suppose there is an increase in oil prices. How will this affect the unemployment rate in the short run and the medium run? How about the real wage (W/P)?

b. Suppose there is a reduction in income taxes. How will this affect the unemployment rate in the short run and the medium run? How about the real wage? For a given worker, how will after-tax income be affected?

c. According to our model, what policy tools does the government have available to increase the real wage?

d. During 2003 and 2004, oil prices increased more or less at the same time that income taxes were reduced. A popular joke at the time was that people could use their tax refunds to pay for the higher gas prices. How do your answers to this problem make sense of this joke?

Explore Further

12. *Adding energy prices to the* AS *curve*

   In this problem, we incorporate the price of energy inputs (e.g., oil) explicitly into the AS curve.

   Suppose the price-setting equation is given by

$$P = (1 + \mu) \, W^a \, P_E^{1-a}$$

where P_E *is the price of energy resources and* $0 < a < 1$. *Ignoring a multiplicative constant,* $W^a \, P_E^{1-a}$ *is the marginal cost function that would result from the production technology,* $Y = N^a E^{1-a}$, *where* N *is employed labor and* E *represents units of energy resources used in production. As in the text, the wage-setting relation is given by*

$$W = P^e F(u, z)$$

   Make sure to distinguish between P_E, *the price of energy resources, and* P^e, *the expected price level for the economy as a whole.*

a. Substitute the wage-setting relation into the price-setting relation to obtain the aggregate supply relation.

b. Let $x \equiv P_E/P$, the real price of energy. Observe that $P \times x = P_E$ and substitute for P_E in the AS relation you derived in part (a). Solve for P to obtain

$$P = P^e (1 + \mu)^{1/a} F(u,z) \, x^{(1-a)/a}$$

c. Graph the AS relation from part (b) for a given P^e and a given x.

d. Suppose that $P = P^e$. How will the natural rate of unemployment change if x, the real price of energy, increases? [Hint: You can solve the AS equation for x to obtain the answer, or you can reason it out. If $P = P^e$, how must $F(u, z)$ change when x increases to maintain

the equality in part (b)? How must u change to have the required effect on $F(u, z)$?]

e. Suppose that the economy begins with output equal to the natural level of output. Then the real price of energy increases. Show the short-run and medium-run effects of the increase in the real price of energy in an AD–AS diagram.

The text suggests that a change in expectations about monetary policy may help explain why increases in oil prices over the past few years have had less of an adverse effect on the economy than the oil price shocks of the 1970s. Let us examine how such a change in expectations would alter the effect of an oil price shock.

f. Suppose there is an increase in the real price of energy. In addition, despite the increase in the real price of energy, suppose that the expected price level (i.e., P^e) does not change. After the short-run effect of the increase in the real price of energy, will there be any further adjustment of the economy over the medium run? In order for the expected price level not to change, what monetary action must wage setters be expecting after an increase in the real price of energy?

13. *Growth and fluctuations: some economic history*

   When economists think about history, fluctuations often stand out—oil shocks and stagflation in the 1970s, a recession followed by a long expansion in the 1980s, a recession followed by an extraordinary low-unemployment, low-inflation boom in the 1990s. This question puts these fluctuations into some perspective.

   *Go to the Web site of the Bureau of Economic Analysis (**www.bea.gov**) and retrieve the quarterly version of NIPA Table 1.1.6, real GDP in chained (2000) dollars. Get real GDP for the fourth quarter of 1959, 1969, 1979, 1989, and 1999 and for the fourth quarter of the most recent year available.*

a. Using the real GDP numbers for 1959 and 1969, calculate the decadal growth rate of real GDP for the 1960s. Do the same for the 1970s, 1980s, and 1990s and for the available years of the most recent decade.

b. How does growth in the 1970s compare to growth in the later decades? How does growth in the 1960s compare to the later decades? Which decade looks most unusual?

We invite you to visit the Blanchard page on the Prentice Hall Web site, at:
www.prenhall.com/blanchard
for this chapter's World Wide Web exercises.

The Natural Rate of Unemployment and the Phillips Curve

n 1958, A. W. Phillips drew a diagram plotting the rate of inflation against the rate of unemployment in the United Kingdom for each year from 1861 to 1957. He found clear evidence of a negative relation between inflation and unemployment: When unemployment was low, inflation was high, and when unemployment was high, inflation was low, often even negative.

Two years later, Paul Samuelson and Robert Solow replicated Phillips's exercise for the United States, using data from 1900 to 1960. Figure 8-1 reproduces their findings, using CPI inflation as a measure of the inflation rate. Apart from the period of very high unemployment during the 1930s (the years from 1931 to 1939 are denoted by triangles and are clearly to the right of the other points in the figure), there also appeared to be a negative relation between inflation and unemployment in the United States.

This relation, which Samuelson and Solow labeled the **Phillips curve**, rapidly became central to macroeconomic thinking and policy. It appeared to imply that countries could choose between different combinations of unemployment and inflation. A country could achieve low unemployment if it were willing to tolerate higher inflation, or it could achieve price-level stability—zero inflation—if it were willing to tolerate higher unemployment. Much of the discussion about macroeconomic policy became a discussion about which point to choose on the Phillips curve.

In the 1970s, however, the relation broke down. In the United States and most other OECD countries, there was both high inflation *and* high unemployment, clearly contradicting the original Phillips curve. A relation reappeared, but it reappeared as a relation between the unemployment rate and the *change* in the inflation rate. Today in the United States, high unemployment leads not to low inflation but to a decrease in inflation over time. Conversely, low unemployment doesn't lead to high inflation but to an increase in inflation over time.

The purpose of this chapter is to explore the mutations of the Phillips curve and, more generally, to understand the relation between inflation and unemployment. You will see that what Phillips discovered was the aggregate supply relation and that the mutations of the Phillips curve came from changes in the way people and firms formed expectations.

The chapter has three sections:

■ Section 8-1 shows how we can think of the aggregate supply relation as a relation between inflation, expected inflation, and unemployment.

Figure 8-1

*Inflation versus
Unemployment in the
United States, 1900 to 1960*

During the period 1900 to 1960 in the United States, a low unemployment rate was typically associated with a high inflation rate, and a high unemployment rate was typically associated with a low or negative inflation rate.

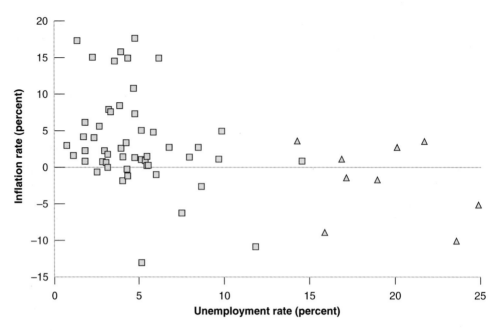

■ Section 8-2 uses this relation to interpret the mutations in the Phillips curve over time.

■ Section 8-3 further discusses the relation between unemployment and inflation across countries and over time. ■

8-1 Inflation, Expected Inflation, and Unemployment

Our first step will be to show that the aggregate supply relation we derived in Chapter 7 can be rewritten as a relation between *inflation, expected inflation*, and the *unemployment rate*.

We then replaced the unemployment rate by its expression in terms of output to obtain a relation between the price level, the expected price level, and output. We do not need to take that step here.

Let's go back to the aggregate supply relation between the price level, the expected price level, and the unemployment rate we derived in Chapter 7 [equation (7.1)]:

$$P = P^e(1 + \mu)F(u, z)$$

Recall that the function, F, captures the effects on the wage of the unemployment rate, u, and of the other factors that affect wage setting, represented by the catchall variable, z. It will be convenient here to assume a specific form for this function:

The function, F, comes from the wage-setting relation, equation (6.1):

$$W = P^eF(u, z).$$

$$F(u, z) = 1 - \alpha u + z$$

This captures the notion that the higher the unemployment rate, the lower the wage; and the higher z (for example, the more generous unemployment benefits are), the higher the wage. The parameter α (the Greek lowercase letter alpha) captures the strength of the effect of unemployment on the wage.

Replace the function, F, by this specific form in the aggregate supply relation above:

$$P = P^e(1 + \mu)(1 - \alpha u + z) \tag{8.1}$$

Finally, let π denote the inflation rate and π^e denote the expected inflation rate. Then, equation (8.1) can be rewritten as

$$\pi = \pi^e + (\mu + z) - \alpha u \tag{8.2}$$

Deriving equation (8.2) from equation (8.1) is not difficult, but it is tedious, so it is left to an appendix at the end of this chapter. What is important is that you understand each of the effects at work in equation (8.2):

■ *An increase in expected inflation, π^e, leads to an increase in actual inflation, π.*

From now on, to lighten your reading, I often refer to the *inflation rate* simply as *inflation* and to the *unemployment rate* simply as *unemployment*.

To see why, start from equation (8.1). An increase in the expected price level, P^e, leads, one for one, to an increase in the actual price level, P: If wage setters expect a higher price level, they set a higher nominal wage, which leads to an increase in the price level.

Now note that, given last period's price level, a higher price level this period implies a higher rate of increase in the price level from last period to this period—that is, higher inflation. Similarly, given last period's price level, a higher expected price level this period implies a higher expected rate of increase in the price level from last period to this period—that is, higher expected inflation. So the fact that an increase in the expected price level leads to an increase in the actual price level can be restated as: An increase in expected inflation leads to an increase in inflation.

Increase in π^e ⇒ Increase in π

■ *Given expected inflation, π^e, an increase in the markup, μ, or an increase in the factors that affect wage determination—an increase in z—leads to an increase in inflation, π.*

From equation (8.1): Given the expected price level, P^e, an increase in either μ or z increases the price level, P. Using the same argument as in the previous bullet to restate this proposition in terms of inflation and expected inflation: Given expected inflation, π^e, an increase in either μ or z leads to an increase in inflation π.

Increase in μ or z ⇒ Increase in π

■ *Given expected inflation, π^e, an increase in the unemployment rate, u, leads to a decrease in inflation, π.*

From equation (8.1): Given the expected price level, P^e, an increase in the unemployment rate, u, leads to a lower nominal wage, which leads to a lower price level, P. Restating this in terms of inflation and expected inflation: Given expected inflation, π^e, an increase in the unemployment rate, u, leads to a decrease in inflation, π.

Increase in u ⇒ Decrease in π

We need one more step before we return to a discussion of the Phillips curve: When we look at movements in inflation and unemployment in the rest of the chapter, it will often be convenient to use time indexes so that we can refer to variables such as inflation, or expected inflation, or unemployment, in a specific year. So we rewrite equation (8.2) as:

$$\pi_t = \pi_t^e + (\mu + z) - \alpha u_t \qquad (8.3)$$

The variables π_t, π_t^e, and u_t refer to inflation, expected inflation, and unemployment in year t. Be sure you see that there are no time indexes on μ and z. This is because we shall typically think of both μ and z as constant while we look at movements in inflation, expected inflation, and unemployment over time.

8-2 The Phillips Curve

Now let's look at the relation between unemployment and inflation as it was first discovered by Phillips, Samuelson, and Solow, around 1960.

The Early Incarnation

Imagine an economy where inflation is positive in some years, negative in others, and is on average equal to zero. This is not the way things are in the United States today: The last year inflation was negative—when there was deflation, in other words—was

1955. In that year, inflation was –0.3%. But as we will see later in this chapter, average inflation *was* close to zero during much of the period Phillips, Samuelson, and Solow were looking at.

In such an environment, how will wage setters choose nominal wages for the coming year? With the average inflation rate equal to zero in the past, it is reasonable for wage setters to expect that inflation will be equal to zero over the next year as well. So, let's assume that expected inflation is equal to zero—that $\pi_t^e = 0$. Equation (8.3) then becomes

$$\pi_t = (\mu + z) - \alpha u_t \tag{8.4}$$

This is precisely the negative relation between unemployment and inflation that Phillips found for the United Kingdom and that Solow and Samuelson found for the United States. The story behind it is simple: Given the expected price level, which workers simply take to be last year's price level, lower unemployment leads to a higher nominal wage. A higher nominal wage leads to a higher price level. Putting the steps together, lower unemployment leads to a higher price level this year relative to last year's price level—that is, to higher inflation. This mechanism has sometimes been called the **wage–price spiral**, an expression that captures well the basic mechanism at work:

- Low unemployment leads to a higher nominal wage.
- In response to the higher nominal wage, firms increase their prices and the price level increases.
- In response to the higher price level, workers ask for a higher nominal wage the next time the wage is set.
- The higher nominal wage leads firms to further increase their prices. As a result, the price level increases further.
- In response to this further increase in the price level, workers, when they set the wage again, ask for a further increase in the nominal wage.

And so the race between prices and wages results in steady wage and price inflation.

Mutations

The combination of an apparently reliable empirical relation together with a plausible story to explain it led to the adoption of the Phillips curve by macroeconomists and policymakers. During the 1960s, U.S. macroeconomic policy was aimed at maintaining unemployment in a range that appeared consistent with moderate inflation. And, throughout the 1960s, the negative relation between unemployment and inflation provided a reliable guide to the joint movements in unemployment and inflation.

Figure 8-2 plots the combinations of the inflation rate and the unemployment rate in the United States for each year from 1948 to 1969. Note how well the Phillips relation held during the long economic expansion that lasted during most of the 1960s. During the years 1961 to 1969, denoted by black diamonds in the figure, the unemployment rate declined steadily from 6.8% to 3.4%, and the inflation rate steadily increased from 1.0% to 5.5%. Put informally, from 1961 to 1969, the U.S. economy moved up along the Phillips curve.

Around 1970, however, the relation between the inflation rate and the unemployment rate, so visible in Figure 8-2, broke down. Figure 8-3 shows the combination of the inflation rate and the unemployment rate in the United States for each year since 1970. The points are scattered in a roughly symmetric cloud: There is no visible relation between the unemployment rate and the inflation rate.

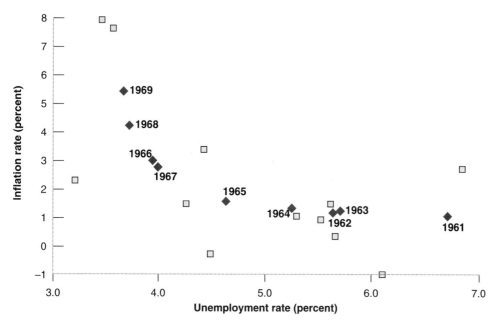

Figure 8-2

Inflation versus Unemployment in the United States, 1948 to 1969

The steady decline in the U.S. unemployment rate throughout the 1960s was associated with a steady increase in the inflation rate.

Why did the original Phillips curve vanish? There are two main reasons:

■ The United States was hit twice in the 1970s by large increases in the price of oil (see Chapter 7). The effect of these increases in non-labor costs was to force firms to increase their prices relative to the wages they were paying—in other words, to increase the markup, μ. As shown in equation (8.3), an increase in μ leads to an increase in inflation, even at a given rate of unemployment, and this happened twice in the 1970s. But the main reason for the breakdown of the Phillips curve relation was the second reason.

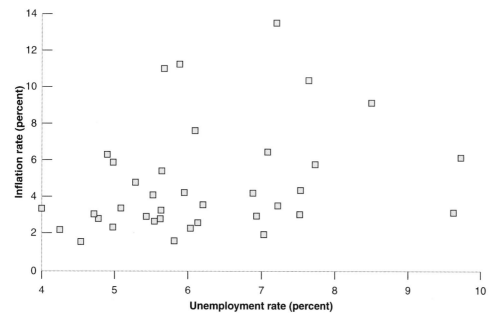

Figure 8-3

Inflation versus Unemployment in the United States Since 1970

Beginning in 1970, the relation between the unemployment rate and the inflation rate disappeared in the United States.

Figure 8-4

U.S. Inflation since 1900

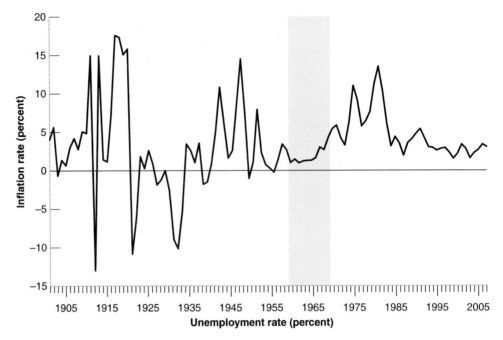

- Wage setters changed the way they formed their expectations. This change came, in turn, from a change in the behavior of inflation. Look at Figure 8-4, which shows the U.S. inflation rate since 1900. Starting in the 1960s (the decade shaded in the figure), you can see a clear change in the behavior of the rate of inflation. First, rather than being sometimes positive and sometimes negative, as it had been for the first part of the century, the rate of inflation became consistently positive. Second, inflation became more persistent: High inflation in one year became more likely to be followed by high inflation the next year.

   The persistence of inflation led workers and firms to revise the way they formed their expectations. When inflation is consistently positive year after year, expecting that the price level this year will be the same as the price level last year—which is the same as expecting zero inflation—becomes systematically incorrect; worse, it becomes foolish. People do not like to make the same mistake repeatedly. So, as inflation became consistently positive and more persistent, when people formed expectations, they started to take into account the presence and the persistence of inflation. This change in expectation formation changed the nature of the relation between unemployment and inflation.

   Let's look at the argument in the previous paragraph more closely. First, suppose expectations of inflation are formed according to

$$\pi_t^e = \theta\pi_{t-1} \tag{8.5}$$

   The value of the parameter θ (the Greek lowercase theta) captures the effect of last year's inflation rate, π_{t-1}, on this year's expected inflation rate, π_t^e. The higher the value of θ, the more last year's inflation leads workers and firms to revise their expectations of what inflation will be this year. We can think of what happened in the 1970s as an increase in the value of θ over time:

- As long as inflation was low and not very persistent, it was reasonable for workers and firms to ignore past inflation and to assume that the price level this year would be roughly the same as price level last year. For the period that Samuelson and Solow had looked at, θ was close to zero, and expectations were roughly given by $\pi_t^e = 0$.

- As inflation became more persistent, workers and firms started changing the way they formed expectations. They started assuming that if inflation was high last year, inflation was likely to be high this year as well. The parameter θ, the effect of last year's inflation rate on this year's expected inflation rate, increased. The evidence suggests that, by the mid-1970s, people formed expectations by expecting this year's inflation rate to be the same as last year's inflation rate—in other words, that θ was now equal to 1.

Think about how *you* form expectations. What do you expect inflation to be next year? How did you come to this ◀ conclusion?

Now turn to the implications of different values of θ for the relation between inflation and unemployment. To do so, replace equation (8.5) in equation (8.3):

$$\pi_t = \overbrace{\theta\pi_{t-1}}^{\pi_t^e} + (\mu + z) - \alpha u_t$$

- When θ equals 0, we get the original Phillips curve, a relation between the inflation rate and the unemployment rate:

$$\pi_t = (\mu + z) - \alpha u_t$$

- When θ is positive, the inflation rate depends not only on the unemployment rate but also on last year's inflation rate:

$$\pi_t = \theta\pi_{t-1} + (\mu + z) - \alpha u_t$$

- When θ equals 1, the relation becomes (moving last year's inflation rate to the left side of the equation)

$$\pi_t - \pi_{t-1} = (\mu + z) - \alpha u_t \qquad (8.6)$$

So, when $\theta = 1$, the unemployment rate affects not the *inflation rate* but rather the *change in the inflation rate*: High unemployment leads to decreasing inflation; low unemployment leads to increasing inflation.

This discussion is the key to what happened from 1970 onward. As θ increased from 0 to 1, the simple relation between the unemployment rate and the inflation rate disappeared. This disappearance is what we saw in Figure 8-3. But a new relation emerged, this time between the unemployment rate and the change in the inflation rate—as predicted by equation (8.6). This relation is shown in Figure 8-5, which plots the change in the inflation rate versus the unemployment rate observed for each year since 1970. The figure shows a clear negative relation between the unemployment rate and the change in the inflation rate. The line that best fits the scatter of points for the period 1970 to 2006 is given by

This line, called a regression line, is obtained using econometrics. (See Appendix 3 at the end of the book.) Note that the line does not fit the cloud of points very tightly. There are years when the change in inflation is much larger than implied by the line, and years when the ◀ change in inflation is much smaller than implied by the line. We return to this point later.

$$\pi_t - \pi_{t-1} = 4.4\% - 0.73\, u_t \qquad (8.7)$$

The line is drawn in Figure 8-5. For low unemployment, the change in inflation is positive. For high unemployment, the change in inflation is negative. This is the form the Phillips curve relation between unemployment and inflation takes today.

To distinguish it from the original Phillips curve [equation (8.4)], equation (8.6)—or its empirical counterpart, equation (8.7)—is often called the **modified Phillips curve**, or the **expectations-augmented Phillips curve** (to indicate that π_{t-1} stands for expected inflation), or the **accelerationist Phillips curve** (to indicate that a low unemployment rate leads to an increase in the inflation rate and thus *an acceleration* of the price level). I will simply call equation (8.6) the Phillips curve and refer to the earlier incarnation, equation (8.4), as the *original* Phillips curve.

Original Phillips curve:
Increase in $u_t \Rightarrow$
       Lower inflation
Modified Phillips curve:
Increase in $u_t \Rightarrow$
       Decreasing inflation ◀

Figure 8-5

Change in Inflation versus Unemployment in the United States Since 1970

Since 1970, there has been a negative relation between the unemployment rate and the change in the inflation rate in the United States.

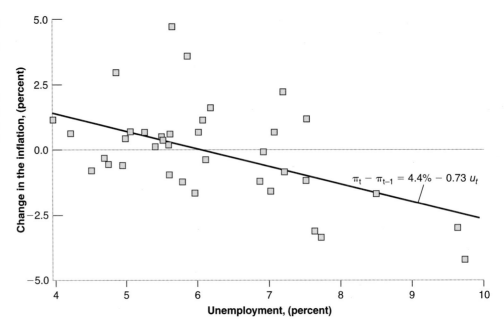

Back to the Natural Rate of Unemployment

The history of the Phillips curve is closely related to the discovery of the concept of the natural unemployment rate that we introduced in Chapter 6.

The original Phillips curve implied that there was no such thing as a natural unemployment rate: If policymakers were willing to tolerate a higher inflation rate, they could maintain a lower unemployment rate forever.

In the late 1960s, while the original Phillips curve still gave a good description of the data, two economists, Milton Friedman and Edmund Phelps, questioned the existence of such a trade-off between unemployment and inflation. They questioned it on logical grounds, arguing that such a trade-off could exist only if wage setters systematically underpredicted inflation and that they were unlikely to make the same mistake forever. Friedman and Phelps also argued that if the government attempted to sustain lower unemployment by accepting higher inflation, the trade-off would ultimately disappear; the unemployment rate could not be sustained below a certain level, a level they called the "natural rate of unemployment." Events proved them right, and the trade-off between the unemployment rate and the infla-tion rate indeed disappeared. (See the Focus box "Theory ahead of Facts: Milton Friedman and Edmund Phelps.") Today, most economists accept the notion of a *natural rate of unemployment*—subject to the many caveats we will see in the next section.

Friedman was awarded the Nobel Prize in 1976. Phelps was awarded the Nobel Prize in 2006.

Let's make explicit the connection between the Phillips curve and the natural rate of unemployment.

By definition (see Chapter 6), the natural rate of unemployment is the unemploy-ment rate such that the actual price level is equal to the expected price level. Equivalently, and more conveniently here, the natural rate of unemployment is the unemployment rate such that the actual inflation rate is equal to the expected infla-tion rate. Denote the natural unemployment rate by u_n (where the index, n, stands for *natural*). Then, imposing the condition that actual inflation and expected inflation be the same ($\pi_t = \pi_t^e$) in equation (8.3) gives

$$0 = (\mu + z) - \alpha u_n$$

Solving for the natural rate, u_n:

$$u_n = \frac{\mu + z}{\alpha} \qquad (8.8)$$

The higher the markup, μ, or the higher the factors that affect wage setting, z, the higher the natural rate of unemployment.

Now rewrite equation (8.3) as

$$\pi_t - \pi_t^e = -\alpha\left(u_t - \frac{\mu + z}{\alpha}\right)$$

Note from equation (8.8) that the fraction on the right side is equal to u_n, so we can rewrite the equation as

$$\pi_t - \pi_t^e = -\alpha(u_t - u_n) \qquad (8.9)$$

If—as is the case in the United States today—the expected rate of inflation (π_t^e) is well approximated by last year's inflation rate, π_{t-1}, the equation finally becomes

$$\pi_t - \pi_{t-1} = -\alpha(u_t - u_n) \qquad (8.10)$$

Equation (8.10) is an important relation, for two reasons:

- It gives us another way of thinking about the *Phillips curve* as a relation between the actual unemployment rate, u_t, the natural unemployment rate, u_n, and the change in the inflation rate, $\pi_t - \pi_{t-1}$.

  The change in the inflation rate depends on the difference between the actual and the natural unemployment rates. When the actual unemployment rate is higher than the natural unemployment rate, the inflation rate decreases; when the actual unemployment rate is lower than the natural unemployment rate, the inflation rate increases.

  ◀ $u_t < u_n \Rightarrow \pi_t > \pi_{t-1}$
  ◀ $u_t > u_n \Rightarrow \pi_t < \pi_{t-1}$

- It also gives us another way of thinking about the *natural rate of unemployment*:

  The natural rate of unemployment is the rate of unemployment required to keep the inflation rate constant. This is why the natural rate is also called the **non-accelerating inflation rate of unemployment (NAIRU)**.

◀ Calling the natural rate "the non-accelerating–inflation rate of unemployment" is actually wrong. It should be called "the non-increasing inflation rate of unemployment," or NIIRU. But NAIRU has now become so standard that it is too late to change it.

What has been the natural rate of unemployment in the United States since 1970? Put another way: What has been the unemployment rate that, on average, has led to constant inflation?

To answer this question, all we need to do is to return to equation (8.7), the estimated relation between the change in inflation and the unemployment rate since 1970. Setting the change in inflation equal to zero in that equation implies a value for the natural unemployment rate of $4.4\%/0.73 = 6\%$. In words: The evidence suggests that, since 1970 in the United States, the average rate of unemployment required to keep inflation constant has been equal to 6%.

◀ From 1997 to 2006, the average unemployment rate was 4.9%. Yet the inflation rate was roughly the same in 2006 as in 1997. This suggests the U.S. natural rate of unemployment is now lower than 6%. More on this in the next section.

8-3 A Summary and Many Warnings

Let's summarize what we have discussed so far:

- The aggregate supply relation is well captured in the United States today by a relation between the change in the inflation rate and the deviation of the unemployment rate from the natural rate of unemployment [equation (8.8)].
- When the unemployment rate exceeds the natural rate of unemployment, the inflation rate decreases. When the unemployment rate is below the natural rate of unemployment, the inflation rate increases.

FOCUS

Economists are usually not very good at predicting major changes before they happen, and most of their insights are derived after the fact. Here is an exception.

In the late 1960s—precisely as the original Phillips curve relation was working like a charm—two economists, Milton Friedman and Edmund Phelps, argued that the appearance of a trade-off between inflation and unemployment was an illusion.

Here are a few quotes from Milton Friedman. About the Phillips curve, he said:

> Implicitly, Phillips wrote his article for a world in which everyone anticipated that nominal prices would be stable and in which this anticipation remained unshaken and immutable whatever happened to actual prices and wages. Suppose, by contrast, that everyone anticipates that prices will rise at a rate of more than 75% a year—as, for example, Brazilians did a few years ago. Then, wages must rise at that rate simply to keep real wages unchanged. An excess supply of labor [by this, Friedman means high unemployment] will be reflected in a less rapid rise in nominal wages than in anticipated prices, not in an absolute decline in wages.

He went on:

> To state [my] conclusion differently, there is always a temporary trade-off between inflation and unemployment; there is no permanent trade-off. The temporary trade-off comes not from inflation per se, but from a rising rate of inflation.

He then tried to guess how much longer the apparent trade-off between inflation and unemployment would last in the United States:

> But how long, you will say, is "temporary"? . . . I can at most venture a personal judgment, based on some examination of the historical evidence, that the initial effect of a higher and unanticipated rate of inflation lasts for something like two to five years; that this initial effect then begins to be reversed; and that a full adjustment to the new rate of inflation takes as long for employment as for interest rates, say, a couple of decades.

Friedman could not have been more right. A few years later, the original Phillips curve started to disappear, in exactly the way Friedman had predicted.

Source: Milton Friedman, "The Role of Monetary Policy," American Economic Review, Volume 58, Number 1, March 1968, 1–17. (The article by Phelps, "Money–Wage Dynamics and Labor–Market Equilibrium," Journal of Political Economy, August 1968, 678–711, made many of the same points more formally.)

This relation has held quite well since 1970. But evidence from its earlier history, as well as evidence from other countries, point to the need for a number of warnings. All of them are on the same theme: The relation between inflation and unemployment can and does vary across countries and time.

Variations in the Natural Rate across Countries

Recall from equation (8.8) that the natural rate of unemployment depends on all the factors that affect wage setting, represented by the catchall variable, z; the markup set by firms, μ; and the response of inflation to unemployment, represented by α. If these factors differ across countries, there is no reason to expect all countries to have the same natural rate of unemployment. And natural rates indeed differ across countries, sometimes considerably.

In Chapter 1, we saw that countries such as Germany and France suffer from high unemployment. Because their inflation rates are stable, we can, relying on the argument just developed, reach a stronger conclusion: This high unemployment reflects a high natural rate of unemployment, not a deviation of the unemployment rate from the natural rate. This in turn tells us where we should look for explanations: in the factors determining the wage-setting and the price-setting relations.

Is it easy to identify the relevant factors? One often hears the statement that one of the main problems of Europe is its *labor market rigidities*. These rigidities, the argument goes, are responsible for its high unemployment. While there is some truth to this statement, the reality is more complex. The Focus box "What Explains European Unemployment?" discusses these issues further.

What Explains European Unemployment?

What do critics have in mind when they talk about the "labor market rigidities" afflicting Europe? They have in mind in particular:

■ A generous system of unemployment insurance—The replacement rate—that is, the ratio of unemployment benefits to the after-tax wage—is often high in Europe, and the duration of benefits—the period of time for which the unemployed are entitled to receive benefits—often runs in years.

   Some unemployment insurance is clearly desirable. But generous benefits may increase unemployment in at least two ways: They decrease the incentives the unemployed have to search for jobs. They may also increase the wage that firms have to pay. Recall our discussion of efficiency wages in Chapter 6: The higher unemployment benefits are, the higher the wages firms have to pay in order to motivate and keep workers.

■ A high degree of employment protection—By employment protection, economists have in mind the set of rules that increase the cost of layoffs for firms. These range from high severance payments to the need for firms to justify layoffs, to the possibility for workers to appeal the decision and have it reversed.

   The purpose of employment protection is to decrease layoffs and thus to protect workers from the risk of unemployment. What it does, however, is also increase the cost of labor for firms, thus reducing hires and making it harder for the unemployed to get jobs. The evidence suggests that, while employment protection does not necessarily increase unemployment, it changes its nature: The flows in and out of unemployment decrease, but the average duration of unemployment increases. Such long duration increases the risk that the unemployed lose skills and morale, decreasing their employability.

■ Minimum wages—Most European countries have national minimum wages. In some countries, the ratio of the minimum wage to the median wage can be quite high. High minimum wages clearly run the risk of decreasing employment for the least skilled workers, thus increasing their unemployment rate.

■ Bargaining rules—In most European countries, labor contracts are subject to extension agreements. A contract agreed to by a subset of firms and unions can be automatically extended to all firms in the sector. This considerably reinforces the bargaining power of unions because it reduces the scope for competition by non-unionized firms. As we saw in Chapter 6, stronger bargaining power on the part of the unions may result in higher unemployment: Higher unemployment is needed to reconcile the demands of workers with the wages paid by firms.

Do these labor market institutions really explain high unemployment in Europe? Is the case open and shut? Not quite. Here it is important to recall two important facts.

Fact 1: As we saw in Chapter 1, unemployment was not always high in Europe. Recall the evolution of unemployment shown in Figure 1-5: In the 1960s, the unemployment rate in the four major continental European countries was lower than that in the United States, around 2% to 3%. The natural rate in these countries today is around 8% to 9%. How do we explain this increase?

One hypothesis is that institutions were different then and that labor market rigidities have appeared only in the past 40 years. This turns out not to be the case, however. It is true that, in response to the adverse shocks of the 1970s (in particular the two recessions following the increases in the price of oil), many European governments increased the generosity of unemployment insurance and the degree of employment protection. But, even in the 1960s, European labor market institutions looked nothing like U.S. labor market institutions. Social protection was higher in Europe, yet unemployment was lower.

A different line of explanation focuses on the interaction between institutions and shocks. Some labor market institutions may be benign in some environments and very costly in others. Take employment protection. If competition between firms is limited, the need to adjust employment in each firm may be limited as well, and so the cost of employment protection may be low. But if competition, either from other domestic firms or from foreign firms, increases, the cost of employment protection may become very high. Firms that cannot adjust their labor force quickly may simply be unable to compete and may go out of business. Thus, even if employment protection rules do not change, higher competition can lead to a higher natural rate.

Fact 2: Many European countries actually have low unemployment. This is shown in Figure 1, which gives the unemployment rate for 15 European countries (the 15 members of the European Union before the increase in membership to 27). In all these countries, inflation is stable, so the unemployment rate is roughly equal to the natural rate. The unemployment rate is high in the 4 large continental countries; this is indeed why I focused on them in Chapter 1. But note how low the unemployment rate is in some other countries—in particular, Denmark, Ireland, and the Netherlands.

Is it the case that these low-unemployment countries have low benefits, low employment protection, and weak unions? Things are unfortunately not so simple: Countries such as Ireland and the United Kingdom indeed have labor market institutions that resemble those of the United States: limited benefits, low employment protection, and weak unions. But countries such as Denmark and the Netherlands have a high degree of

Continued

social protection—in particular, high unemployment benefits and strong unions.

So what is one to conclude? An emerging consensus among economists is that the devil is in the details: Generous social protection is consistent with low unemployment. But it has to be provided efficiently. For example, unemployment benefits can be generous, as long as the unemployed are, at the same time, forced to take jobs if such jobs are available. Some employment protection—for example, in the form of generous severance payments—may not prevent low unemployment as long as firms do not face the prospect of long administrative or judicial uncertainty when they lay off workers. Countries such as Denmark appear to have been more successful in achieving these goals. Creating incentives for the unemployed to take jobs, and simplifying the rules of employment protection are on the reform agenda of many European governments. One may hope they will lead to a decrease in the natural rate in the future.

Note: For more, read Olivier Blanchard, "European Unemployment. The Evolution of Facts and Ideas," Economic Policy, *Volume 1, 2006, 1–54.*

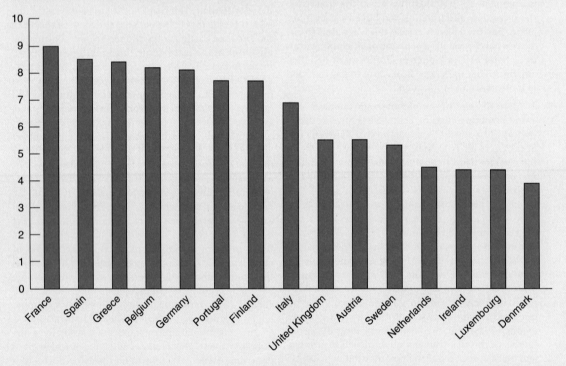

Figure 1   *Unemployment Rates in 15 European Countries, 2006*

Variations in the Natural Rate over Time

In writing equation (8.6) and estimating equation (8.7), we treated $\mu + z$ as a constant. But there are good reasons to believe that μ and z vary over time. The degree of monopoly power of firms, the structure of wage bargaining, the system of unemployment benefits, and so on, are likely to change over time, leading to changes in either μ or z and, by implication, changes in the natural rate of unemployment.

Changes in the natural unemployment rate over time are hard to measure. The reason is, again, that we do not observe the natural rate, only the actual rate. But broad evolutions can be established by comparing average unemployment rates, say across decades. Using this approach, we just saw how the natural rate of unemployment had increased in Europe since the 1960s, and discussed some reasons why this might be.

The Medium Run   **The Core**

Despite an average since unemployment rate under 5% over the past decade, the inflation rate is roughly the same today as it was a decade ago, around 3%.

This combination of low unemployment and stable inflation has led some economists to proclaim the emergence of a "new labor market" where unemployment can be kept much lower than before without risk of increasing inflation—an economy with a much lower natural rate of unemployment. What should we make of this claim? Has the natural rate of unemployment fallen? And if it has, why?

Let us first look at the relation between the change in the inflation rate and the unemployment rate in the past decade. Figure 1 replicates Figure 8-5, with the points corresponding to the years since 1997 indicated by black diamonds. The line drawn in the figure shows the historical relation between the change in the inflation rate and the unemployment rate, based on observations from 1970 to 2006 [equation (8.7)]. Note that, since 1997, all the points except one (corresponding to the year 2003) lay on or below the line: In other words, given the unemployment rate, the change in the inflation rate in each of these years, except one, has been less than would have been predicted by the average relation between the change in the inflation rate and the unemployment rate for the period 1970 to 2006.

Does this mean the relation between the change in the inflation rate and the unemployment rate has shifted—that the line corresponding to the past decade is lower than the line drawn in the figure? Figure 1 makes it clear that the relation between the change in the inflation rate and the unemployment rate has never been tight. There have been many years since 1970 when the change in inflation was much larger or much smaller than predicted by the line. It would have been wrong to conclude, in each of those years, that the natural rate of unemployment had dramatically decreased or increased. The favorable outcomes since 1997 could represent a series of lucky breaks, with the underlying relation between the change in inflation and unemployment remaining the same as before. But nine lucky breaks out of 10 years is not very likely. Instead, the evidence points to a downward shift in the relation, implying a decrease in the rate of unemployment corresponding to zero inflation. In other words, the natural rate of unemployment fell.

Does the decrease in the natural rate of unemployment reflect the emergence of a "new labor market"? The most extreme claims that, in a new global economy, we should no longer expect any relation between unemployment and inflation have no basis either in fact or in theory: In a tight labor market, firms still need to increase wages to attract and keep workers, and wage increases

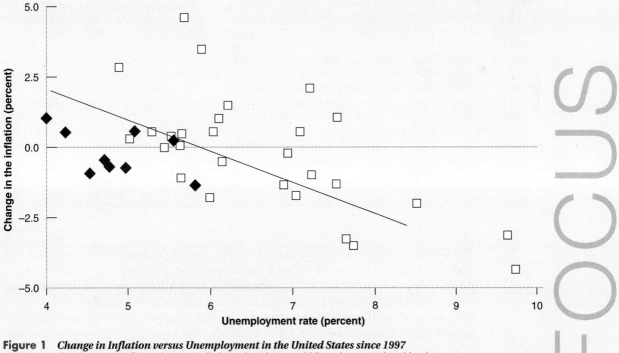

Figure 1 *Change in Inflation versus Unemployment in the United States since 1997*
Since 1997, the change in inflation has typically been less than would have been predicted by the average relation between inflation and unemployment for the period 1970 to 2003.

Continued

still lead to price increases. But the argument that globalization can lower the natural rate of unemployment is not without merit: Stronger competition between U.S. and foreign firms might lead to a decrease in monopoly power and a decrease in the markup. Also, the fact that firms can more easily move some of their operations abroad surely makes them stronger when bargaining with their workers. There is indeed some evidence that unions in the U.S. economy are becoming weaker: The unionization rate in the United States, which stood at 25% in the mid-1970s, is below 15% today. So, part of the decrease in the natural rate may come from globalization.

Part of the decrease, however, seems attributable to other factors. Among them:

■ The aging of the U.S. population—The proportion of young workers (workers between the ages of 16 and 24) fell from 24% in 1980 to 14% in 2006. (This reflects the end of the baby boom, which ended in the mid-1960s.) Young workers tend to start their working life by going from job to job and typically have a higher unemployment rate than older workers. So, a decrease in the proportion of young workers leads to a decrease in the overall unemployment rate. Estimates are that this effect could account for a decrease in the natural unemployment rate of up to 0.6% since 1980.

■ The increase in the prison population—The proportion of the population in prison or in jail has tripled in the past 20 years in the United States. In 1980, 0.3% of the U.S. population of working age was in prison. In 2006, the proportion had increased to 1.0%. Because many of those in prison would likely have been unemployed were they not incarcerated, this is likely to have had an effect on the unemployment rate. Estimates are that this effect could account for a decrease in the natural unemployment rate of up to 0.2% since 1980.

■ The increase in the number of workers on disability—A relaxation of eligibility criteria since 1984 has led to a steady increase in the number of workers receiving disability insurance, from 2.2% of the working-age population in 1984 to 3.8% in 2006. It is again likely that,

absent changes in the rules, some of the workers on disability insurance would have been unemployed instead. Estimates are that this effect could account for a decrease in the natural rate of up to 0.6% since 1980.

■ The increase in temporary help employment—In 1980, employment by temporary help agencies accounted for less than 0.5% of total U.S. employment. Today, it accounts for more than 2%. This is also likely to have reduced the natural rate of unemployment. In effect, it allows many workers to look for jobs while being employed rather than unemployed. Estimates are that this could account for a 0.3% decrease in the natural unemployment rate in the 1990s.

■ The unexpectedly high rate of productivity growth since the end of the 1990s—As you saw in Chapter 1, productivity growth has been very high in the United States since the mid-1990s. This had been expected neither by firms nor by workers. Given nominal wage inflation, the higher productivity growth led to a smaller increase in costs, which led to lower inflation. There is little question that this is part of the reason why, despite low unemployment, there was so little increase in inflation at the end of the 1990s.

Will the natural rate of unemployment remain low in the future? It depends on the relative contribution of the factors we just listed. Globalization, demographics, prisons, and temporary help agencies are probably here to stay. The effects of high productivity growth on the natural unemployment rate may not stay: Productivity growth may slow down. Even if it does not, higher productivity growth is likely to be reflected in higher wage increases. (We return to this issue in Chapter 13.)

To summarize: Today, the natural unemployment rate in the United States is probably below 5%, lower than it was in the 1970s and the 1980s. Some of the decrease in the natural unemployment rate is likely to be permanent; some is not.

Note: For more, read Lawrence Katz and Alan Krueger, "The High-Pressure U.S. Labor Market of the 1990s," Brookings Papers on Economic Activity, Volume 1, 1999, 1–87.

The U.S. natural rate has moved much less than that in Europe. Nevertheless, it is also far from constant. We saw in Chapter 6 that, from the 1950s to the 1980s, the U.S. unemployment rate fluctuated around a slowly increasing trend: Average unemployment was 4.5% in the 1950s, and it was 7.3% in the 1980s. Since 1990, the trend appears to have been reversed, with an average unemployment rate of 5.7% in the 1990s and (so far) an average unemployment rate of 5.1% in the 2000s. This has led a number of economists to conclude that the U.S. natural rate of unemployment has fallen. Whether this is the case is discussed in the Focus box "Has the U.S. Natural Rate of Unemployment Rate Fallen since the Early 1990s and, If So, Why?" The conclusion is that the natural rate has indeed fallen. It is probably close to 5% today.

Refer to Figure 6-3. ▶

High Inflation and the Phillips Curve Relation

Recall how, in the 1970s, the U.S. Phillips curve changed as inflation became more persistent and wage setters changed the way they formed inflation expectations. The lesson is a general one: The relation between unemployment and inflation is likely to change with the level and the persistence of inflation. Evidence from countries with high inflation confirms this lesson. Not only does the way workers and firms form their expectations change, but so do institutional arrangements.

When the inflation rate becomes high, inflation also tends to become more variable. As a result, workers and firms become more reluctant to enter into labor contracts that set nominal wages for a long period of time: If inflation turns out to be higher than expected, real wages may plunge, and workers will suffer a large cut in their living standard. If inflation turns out to be lower than expected, real wages may go up sharply. Firms may not be able to pay their workers. Some may go bankrupt.

For this reason, the terms of wage agreements change with the level of inflation. Nominal wages are set for shorter periods of time, down from a year to a month or even less. **Wage indexation**, a provision that automatically increases wages in line with inflation, becomes more prevalent.

These changes lead in turn to a stronger response of inflation to unemployment. To see this, an example based on wage indexation will help. Imagine an economy that has two types of labor contracts. A proportion, λ (the Greek lowercase letter lambda), of labor contracts is indexed: Nominal wages in those contracts move one for one with variations in the actual price level. A proportion, $1 - \lambda$, of labor contracts is not indexed: Nominal wages are set on the basis of expected inflation.

Under this assumption, equation (8.9) becomes

$$\pi_t = [\lambda\pi_t + (1 - \lambda)\pi_t^e] - \alpha(u_t - u_n)$$

The term in brackets on the right reflects the fact that a proportion, λ, of contracts is indexed and thus responds to actual inflation, π_t, and a proportion, $1 - \lambda$, responds to expected inflation, π_t^e. If we assume that this year's expected inflation is equal to last year's actual inflation, $\pi_t^e = \pi_{t-1}$, we get

$$\pi_t = [\lambda\pi_t + (1 - \lambda)\pi_{t-1}] - \alpha(u_t - u_n) \qquad (8.11)$$

When $\lambda = 0$, all wages are set on the basis of expected inflation—which is equal to last year's inflation, π_{t-1}—and the equation reduces to equation (8.10):

$$\pi_t - \pi_{t-1} = -\alpha(u_t - u_n)$$

When λ is positive, however, a proportion, λ, of wages is set on the basis of actual inflation rather than expected inflation. To see what this implies, reorganize equation (8.11): Move the term in brackets to the left, factor $(1 - \lambda)$ on the left of the equation, and divide both sides by $1-\lambda$, to get

$$\pi_t - \pi_{t-1} = -\frac{\alpha}{1 - \lambda}(u_t - u_n)$$

Wage indexation increases the effect of unemployment on inflation. The higher the proportion of wage contracts that are indexed—the higher λ—the larger the effect

More concretely: When inflation runs, on average, at 3% per year, wage setters can be confident that inflation will be between 1% and 5%. When inflation runs, on average, at 30% per year, wage setters can be confident inflation will be between 20% and 40%. In the first case, the real wage may end up 2% higher or lower than expected when the wage setters set the nominal wage. In the second case, it may end up 10% higher or lower than expected. There is much more uncertainty in the second case.

the unemployment rate has on the change in inflation—the higher the coefficient $\alpha/(1-\lambda)$.

The intuition is as follows: Without wage indexation, lower unemployment increases wages, which in turn increases prices. But because wages do not respond to prices right away, there is no further increase in prices within the year. With wage indexation, however, an increase in prices leads to a further increase in wages within the year, which leads to a further increase in prices, and so on, so that the effect of unemployment on inflation within the year is higher.

If, and when, λ gets close to 1—which is when most labor contracts allow for wage indexation—small changes in unemployment can lead to very large changes in inflation. Put another way, there can be large changes in inflation with nearly no change in unemployment. This is what happens in countries where inflation is very high: The relation between inflation and unemployment becomes more and more tenuous and eventually disappears altogether.

High inflation is the topic of ▶ Chapter 23.

Deflation and the Phillips Curve Relation

We have just looked at what happens to the Phillips curve when inflation is very high. Another issue is what happens when inflation is low, and possibly negative—when there is deflation.

The motivation for asking the question is given by an aspect of Figure 8-1 we mentioned at the start of the chapter but then left aside. In that figure, note how the points corresponding to the 1930s (they are denoted by triangles) lie to the right of the others. Not only is unemployment unusually high—this is no surprise because we are looking at the years corresponding to the Great Depression—but, *given the high unemployment rate*, the inflation rate is surprisingly high. In other words, given the very high unemployment rate, we would have expected not merely deflation but a large rate of deflation. In fact, deflation was limited, and from 1934 to 1937, inflation was actually positive.

How do we interpret this fact? There are two potential explanations.

One explanation is that the Great Depression was associated with an increase not only in the actual unemployment rate but also in the natural unemployment rate. This seems unlikely. Most economic historians see the Depression primarily as the result of a large adverse shift in aggregate demand leading to an increase in the actual unemployment rate over the natural rate of unemployment rather than an increase in the natural rate of unemployment itself.

For more on the Great Depression, see Chapter 22. ▶

The other explanation is that, when the economy starts experiencing deflation, the Phillips curve relation breaks down. One possible reason is the reluctance of workers to accept decreases in their nominal wages. Workers will unwittingly accept a cut in their real wages that occurs when their nominal wages increase more slowly than inflation. However, they are likely to fight the same cut in their real wages if it results from an overt cut in their nominal wages. If this argument is correct, this implies that the Phillips curve relation between the change in inflation and unemployment may disappear or at least become weaker when the economy is close to zero inflation.

Consider two scenarios. In one, inflation is 4%, and your nominal wage goes up by 2%. In the other, inflation is 0%, and your nominal wage is cut by 2%. Which do you dislike most? ▶ You should be indifferent between the two: In both cases, your real wage goes down by 2%. There is some evidence, however, that most people find the first scenario less painful. More on this in Chapter 25.

This issue is a crucial one at this stage because, in many countries, inflation is now very low. Inflation has actually been negative in Japan since the late 1990s. What happens to the Phillips curve relation in this environment of low inflation or even deflation is one of the developments closely watched by macroeconomists

For more on the Japanese economic slump, see Chapter 22. ▶

today.

Summary

- The aggregate supply relation can be expressed as a relation between inflation, expected inflation, and unemployment. Given unemployment, higher expected inflation leads to higher inflation. Given expected inflation, higher unemployment leads to lower inflation.

- When inflation is not very persistent, expected inflation does not depend very much on past inflation. Thus, the aggregate supply relation becomes a relation between inflation and unemployment. This is what Phillips in the United Kingdom and Solow and Samuelson in the United States discovered when they looked, in the late 1950s, at the joint behavior of unemployment and inflation.

- As inflation became more persistent in the 1970s and 1980s, expectations of inflation became based more and more on past inflation. In the United States today, the aggregate supply relation takes the form of a relation ___ nd the change in inflation. ___ to decreasing inflation; low ___ reasing inflation. ___ t rate is the unemployment ___ rate remains constant. When ___ rate exceeds the natural rate ___ lation rate decreases; when

the actual unemployment rate is less than the natural unemployment rate, the inflation rate increases.

- The natural rate of unemployment depends on many factors that differ across countries and can change over time. This is why the natural rate of unemployment varies across countries: It is much higher in Europe than in the United States. This is also why the natural unemployment rate varies over time: In Europe, the natural unemployment rate has increased a lot since the 1960s. In the United States, the natural unemployment rate increased by 1% to 2% from the 1960s to the 1980s, and appears to have decreased since then.

- Changes in the way the inflation rate varies over time affect the way wage setters form expectations and also how much they use wage indexation. When wage indexation is widespread, small changes in unemployment can lead to very large changes in inflation. At high rates of inflation, the relation between inflation and unemployment disappears altogether.

- At very low or negative rates of inflation, the Phillips curve relation appears to become weaker. During the Great Depression, even very high unemployment led only to limited deflation. The issue is important because many countries have low inflation today.

- non-accelerating inflation rate of unemployment (NAIRU), 193
- wage indexation, 199

___ s-augmented, or accelera-

Problems

Quick Check

1. Using the information in this chapter, label each of the following statements true, false, or uncertain. Explain briefly.

a. The original Phillips curve is the negative relation between unemployment and inflation first observed in the United Kingdom.

b. The original Phillips curve relation has proven to be very stable across countries and over time.

c. The aggregate supply relation is consistent with the Phillips curve as observed before the 1970s, but not since.

d. Policymakers can exploit the inflation–unemployment trade-off only temporarily.

e. In the late 1960s, the economists Milton Friedman and Edmund Phelps said that policymakers could achieve as low a rate of unemployment as they wanted.

f. The expectations-augmented Phillips curve is consistent with workers and firms adapting their expectations after the macroeconomic experience of the 1960s.

2. Discuss the following statements.

a. The Phillips curve implies that when unemployment is high, inflation is low, and vice versa. Therefore, we may experience either high inflation or high unemployment, but we will never experience both together.

b. As long as we do not mind having high inflation, we can achieve as low a level of unemployment as we want. All we have to do is increase the demand for goods and services by using, for example, expansionary fiscal policy.

3. Oil shocks, inflation, and unemployment
   Suppose that the Phillips curve is given by

$$\pi_t - \pi_t^e = 0.08 + 0.1\,\mu_t - 2\,u_t$$

where μ is the markup of prices over wages. Suppose that μ is initially equal to 20%, but that as a result of a sharp increase in oil prices, μ increases to 40% in year t and after.

a. Why would an increase in oil prices result in an increase in μ?

b. What is the effect of the increase in μ on the natural rate of unemployment? Explain in words.

4. Mutations of the Phillips curve

Suppose that the Phillips curve is given by

$$\pi_t = \pi_t^e + 0.2 - 2u_t$$

a. What is the natural rate of unemployment?
   Assume,

$$\pi_t^e = \theta \, \pi_{t-1}$$

and suppose that θ is initially equal to 0. Suppose that the rate of unemployment is initially equal to the natural rate. In year t, the authorities decide to bring the unemployment rate down to 6% and hold it there forever.

b. Determine the rate of inflation in years $t, t + 1, t + 2$, and $t + 5$.

c. Do you believe the answer given in (b)? Why or why not? (Hint: Think about how people are likely to form expectations of inflation.)
   Now suppose that in year t + 5, θ increases from 0 to 1. Suppose that the government is still determined to keep u at 6% forever.

d. Why might θ increase in this way?

e. What will the inflation rate be in years $t + 5, t + 6$, and $t + 7$?

f. Do you believe the answer given in (e)? Why or why not?

Dig Deeper

5. The price of oil declined substantially in the 1990s.

a. Can the fall in the price of oil help explain the evidence (presented in this chapter) on inflation and unemployment in the 1990s?

b. What was the likely effect of the fall in the price of oil on the natural rate of unemployment?

6. The macroeconomic effects of the indexation of wages

Suppose that the Phillips curve is given by

$$\pi_t - \pi_t^e = 0.1 - 2u_t$$

where

$$\pi_t^e = \pi_{t-1}$$

Suppose that inflation in year $t - 1$ is zero. In year t, the authorities decide to keep the unemployment rate at 4% forever.

a. Compute the rate of inflation for years $t, t + 1, t + 2$, and $t + 3$.
   Now suppose that half the workers have indexed labor contracts.

b. What is the new equation for the Phillips curve?

c. Recompute your answer to part (a).

d. What is the effect of wage indexation on the relation between π and u?

7. Supply shocks and wage flexibility

Suppose that the Phillips curve is given by

$$\pi_t - \pi_{t-1} = -\alpha(u_t - u_n)$$

where $u_n = (\mu + z)/\alpha$.

Recall that this Phillips curve was derived in this chapter under the assumption that the wage bargaining equation took the form

$$W = P^e(1 - \alpha u_t + z)$$

We can think of α as a measure of wage flexibility—the higher is α, the greater is the response of the wage to a change in the unemployment rate, a u_t.

a. Suppose $\mu = 0.03$ and $z = 0.03$. What is the natural rate of unemployment if $\alpha = 1$? if $\alpha = 2$? What is the relation between α and the natural rate of unemployment? Interpret your answer.
   In Chapter 7, the text suggested that a reduction in the bargaining power of workers may have something to do with the economy's relatively mild response to the increases in oil prices in the past few years as compared to the economy's response to increases in oil prices in the 1970s. One manifestation of a reduction in worker bargaining power could be an overall increase in wage flexibility, i.e., an increase in α.

b. Suppose that as a result of an oil price increase, μ increases to 0.06. What is the new natural rate of unemployment if $\alpha = 1$? if $\alpha = 2$? Would an increase in wage flexibility tend to weaken the adverse effect of an oil price increase?

Explore Further

8. Estimating the natural rate of unemployment
   To answer this question, you will need data on the annual U.S. unemployment and inflation rates since 1970, which can be obtained from the Web site of the Bureau of Labor Statistics (**www.bls.gov**).
   Retrieve the data for the civilian unemployment rate. This is a monthly series, so use the year's average for a given year's unemployment rate. In addition, retrieve the data for the consumer price index (CPI), all urban consumers. Again, you can use the average monthly CPI for each year. The BLS provides this number as its annual CPI.

a. Define the inflation rate in year t as the percentage change in the CPI between year $t - 1$ and year t. Compute the inflation rate for each year and the change in the inflation rate from one year to the next.

b. Plot the data for all the years since 1970 on a diagram, with the change in inflation on the vertical axis and the rate of unemployment on the horizontal axis. Is your graph similar to Figure 8-5?

c. Using a ruler, draw the line that appears to fit best the points in the figure. Approximately what is the slope of the line? What is the intercept? Write down the corresponding equation.

d. According to your analysis in (b), what has been the natural rate of unemployment since 1970?

9. *Changes in the natural rate of unemployment*

a. Repeat problem 8, but now draw separate graphs for the period 1970 to 1990 and the period since 1990.

b. Do you find that the relation between inflation and unemployment is different in the two periods? If so, how has the natural rate of unemployment changed?

We invite you to visit the Blanchard page on the Prentice Hall Web site, at:
www.prenhall.com/blanchard
for this chapter's World Wide Web exercises.

Appendix: From the Aggregate Supply Relation to a Relation Between Inflation, Expected Inflation, and Unemployment

This appendix shows how to go from the relation between the price level, the expected price level, and the unemployment rate given by equation (8.1):

$$P = P^e(1 + \mu)(1 - \alpha u + z)$$

to the relation between inflation, expected inflation, and the unemployment rate given by equation (8.2):iii

$$\pi = \pi^e + (\mu + z) - \alpha u$$

First, introduce time subscripts for the price level, the expected price level, and the unemployment rate, so P_t, P_t^e, and u_t refer to the price level, the expected price level, and the unemployment rate in year t, retrospectively. Equation (8.1) becomes

$$P_t = P_t^e(1 + \mu)(1 - \alpha u_t + z)$$

Next, go from an expression in terms of price levels to an expression in terms of inflation rates. Divide both sides by last year's price level, P_{t-1}:

$$\frac{P_t}{P_{t-1}} = \frac{P_t^e}{P_{t-1}}(1 + \mu)(1 - \alpha u_t + z) \qquad (8A.1)$$

Take the fraction P_t/P_{t-1} on the left side and rewrite it as

$$\frac{P_t}{P_{t-1}} = \frac{P_t - P_{t-1} + P_{t-1}}{P_{t-1}} = 1 + \frac{P_t - P_{t-1}}{P_{t-1}} = 1 + \pi_t$$

where the first equality follows from adding and subtracting P_{t-1} in the numerator of the fraction, the second equality follows from the fact that $P_{t-1}/P_{t-1} = 1$, and the third follows from the definition of the inflation rate $(\pi_t \equiv (P_t - P_{t-1})/P_{t-1})$.

Do the same for the fraction P_t^e/P_{t-1} on the right side, using the definition of the expected inflation rate $(\pi_t^e \equiv (P_t^e - P_{t-1})/P_{t-1})$:

$$\frac{P_t^e}{P_{t-1}} = \frac{P_t^e - P_{t-1} + P_{t-1}}{P_{t-1}} = 1 + \frac{P_t^e - P_{t-1}}{P_{t-1}} = 1 + \pi_t^e$$

Replacing P_t/P_{t-1} and P_t^e/P_{t-1} in equation (8A.1) with the expressions we have just derived:

$$(1 + \pi_t) = (1 + \pi_t^e)(1 + \mu)(1 - \alpha u_t + z)$$

This gives us a relation between inflation, π_t, expected inflation, π_t^e, and the unemployment rate (u_t). The remaining steps make the relation look more friendly: Divide both sides by $(1 + \pi_t^e)(1 + \mu)$:

$$\frac{(1 + \pi_t)}{(1 + \pi_t^e)(1 + \mu)} = 1 - \alpha u_t + z$$

As long as inflation, expected inflation, and the markup are not too large, a good approximation to the left side of this equation is given by $1 + \pi_t - \pi_t^e - \mu$ (see Propositions 3 and 6 in Appendix 2 at the end of the book). Replacing in the equation above and rearranging gives

$$\pi_t = \pi_t^e + (\mu + z) - \alpha u_t$$

Dropping the time indexes, this is equation (8.2) in the text. With the time indexes kept, this is equation (8.3) in the text.

The inflation rate, π_t, depends on the expected inflation rate, π_t^e, and the unemployment rate, u_t. The relation also depends on the markup, μ, on the factors that affect wage setting, z, and on the effect of the unemployment rate on wages, α.

Inflation, Activity, and Nominal Money Growth

At the end of the 1970s, inflation in the United States reached 14% per year. In October 1979, the Fed decided to reduce inflation and, to do so, embarked on a major monetary contraction. Five years later, and after the deepest recession of the postwar period, inflation was down to 4% per year. It has remained under 4% since.

Why did the Fed decide to reduce inflation? How did it do it? Why was there a recession? More generally, what are the effects of nominal money growth on inflation and output? Our treatment of expectations in Chapter 7 was too simple to allow us to take up these questions. But, with our discussion of expectations and the introduction of the Phillips curve relation in Chapter 8, we now have the tools we need to answer them. This is what we do in this chapter:

■ Section 9-1 extends the model of Chapter 7 and looks at the three relations between output, unemployment, and inflation: Okun's law, the Phillips curve, and the aggregate demand relation.

■ Section 9-2 looks at the effects of money growth on output, unemployment, and inflation, in both the short and the medium run.

■ Section 9-3 revisits disinflation, looking at the trade-off between unemployment and inflation and looking at how credibility of the central bank affects the adjustment of the economy to a decrease in nominal money growth. ■

In Chapter 7, we examined the behavior of two variables: output and the price level. We characterized the economy by two relations: an aggregate supply relation and an aggregate demand relation. In this chapter, we extend the model of Chapter 7 to examine three variables: output, unemployment, and inflation. We characterize the economy by three relations:

- A relation between *output growth* and the *change in unemployment*, called Okun's law.
- A relation between *unemployment, inflation*, and *expected inflation*. This is the Phillips curve relation we developed in Chapter 8.
- An aggregate demand relation between *output growth, money growth*, and *inflation*. This relation follows from the aggregate demand relation we derived in Chapter 7.

In this section, we look at each of these relations on its own. In Section 9-2, we put them together and show their implications for movements in output, unemployment, and inflation.

Okun's Law

We discussed the relation between output and unemployment in Chapter 6. We did so, however, under two convenient but restrictive assumptions. We assumed that output moved one-for-one with employment, so changes in output led to equal changes in employment. We also assumed that the labor force was constant, so changes in

> We assumed that $Y = N$ was that L (the labor force) was constant.

employment were reflected one-for-one in opposite changes in unemployment.

We must now move beyond these assumptions. To see why, let's see what they imply for the relation between the rate of output growth and the unemployment rate. If output and employment moved together, a 1% increase in output would lead to a 1% increase in employment. And if movements in employment were reflected in opposite movements in unemployment, the 1% increase in employment would lead to a decrease of 1% in the unemployment rate. Let u_t denote the unemployment rate in year t, u_{t-1} the unemployment rate in year $t - 1$, and g_{yt} the growth rate of output from year $t - 1$ to year t. Then, under these two assumptions, the following relation would hold:

$$u_t - u_{t-1} = -g_{yt} \qquad (9.1)$$

In words: The change in the unemployment rate would be equal to the negative of the growth rate of output. If output growth is, say, 4% for a year, then the unemployment rate should decline by 4% in that year.

> The relation is named after Arthur Okun, an economist and an adviser to President Kennedy, who first characterized and interpreted this relation.

Contrast this with the actual relation between output growth and the change in the unemployment rate, a relation called **Okun's law**. Figure 9-1 plots the change in the unemployment rate against the rate of output growth for each year since 1970. It also plots the regression line that best fits the scatter of points. The equation corresponding to the line is given by

$$u_t - u_{t-1} = -0.4(g_{yt} - 3\%) \qquad (9.2)$$

Like equation (9.1), equation (9.2) shows a negative relation between the change in unemployment and output growth. But it differs from equation (9.1) in two ways:

> If $g_{yt} > 3\%$, then $u_t < u_{t-1}$
> If $g_{yt} < 3\%$, then $u_t > u_{t-1}$
> If $g_{yt} = 3\%$, then $u_t = u_{t-1}$

- Annual output growth has to be at least 3% to prevent the unemployment rate from rising. This is because of two factors we have neglected so far: labor force growth and labor productivity growth.

  To maintain a constant unemployment rate, employment must grow at the same rate as the labor force. Suppose the labor force grows at 1.7% per year; then

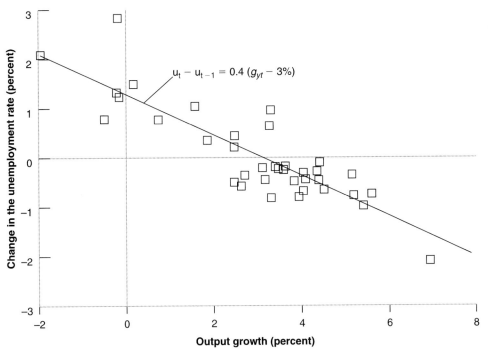

Figure 9-1

Changes in the Unemployment Rate versus Output Growth in the United States since 1970

High output growth is associated with a reduction in the unemployment rate; low output growth is associated with an increase in the unemployment rate.

employment must grow at 1.7% per year. If, in addition, labor productivity—output per worker—grows at 1.3% per year, this implies that output must grow at 1.7% + 1.3% = 3% per year. In other words, just to maintain a constant unemployment rate, output growth must be equal to the sum of labor force growth and labor productivity growth.

In the United States, the sum of the rate of labor force growth and of labor productivity growth has been roughly equal to 3% per year on average since 1960, and this is why the number 3% appears on the right side of equation (9.2). I shall call the rate of output growth needed to maintain a constant unemployment rate the **normal growth rate** in the following text.

■ The coefficient on the right side of equation (9.2) is −0.4, compared to −1.0 in equation (9.1). Put another way, output growth 1% above normal leads only to a 0.4% reduction in the unemployment rate in equation (9.2) rather than a 1% reduction in equation (9.1). There are two reasons:

Suppose productivity growth increases from 1.3% to 2.3%. What is now the growth rate of output required to maintain a constant unemployment rate? More on this when we discuss the U.S. "jobless recovery" of 2002 to 2004 in Chapter 13.

1. Firms adjust employment less than one-for-one in response to deviations of output growth from normal. More specifically, output growth 1% above normal for one year leads to only a 0.6% increase in the employment rate.

   Employment responds less than one-for-one to movements in output.

   One reason is that some workers are needed, no matter what the level of output. The accounting department of a firm, for example, needs roughly the same number of employees whether the firm is selling more or less than normal.

   Another reason is that training new employees is costly; for this reason, firms prefer to keep current employees rather than lay them off when output is lower than normal and to ask them to work overtime rather than hire new employees when output is higher than normal. In bad times, firms in effect hoard labor—the labor they will need when times are better; this behavior of firms is therefore called **labor hoarding**.

2. An increase in the employment rate does not lead to a one-for-one decrease in the unemployment rate. More specifically, a 0.6% increase in the employment rate leads to only a 0.4% decrease in the unemployment rate. The reason is that

   Employment responds less than one-for-one to movements in output.

labor force participation increases. When employment increases, not all the new jobs are filled by the unemployed. Some of the jobs go to people who were classified as *out of the labor force*, meaning they were not actively looking for jobs. Also, as labor market prospects improve for the unemployed, some discouraged workers—who were previously classified as out of the labor force—decide to start actively looking for jobs and become classified as unemployed. For both reasons, unemployment decreases less than employment increases.

Putting the two steps together: Unemployment responds less ▶ than one-for-one to movements in employment, which itself responds less than one-for-one to movements in output.

Let's write equation (9.2) using letters rather than numbers. Let $\bar{g}_y$ denote the normal growth rate (about 3% per year for the United States). Let the coefficient β (the Greek lowercase beta) measure the effect of output growth above normal on the change in the unemployment rate. As you saw in equation (9.2), in the United States, β equals 0.4. The evidence for other countries is given in the Focus box "Okun's Law across Countries." We can then write:

$$u_t - u_{t-1} = -\beta(g_{yt} - \bar{g}_y) \tag{9.3}$$

Output growth above normal leads to a decrease in the unemployment rate; output growth below normal leads to an increase in the unemployment rate.

Okun's law:
$g_{yt} > \bar{g}_y \Rightarrow u_t < u_{t-1}$
$g_{yt} < \bar{g}_y \Rightarrow u_t > u_{t-1}$

The Phillips Curve

We saw in Chapter 8 that the aggregate supply relation can be expressed as a relation between inflation, expected inflation, and unemployment [equation (8.7)], the *Phillips curve*:

$$\pi_t = \pi_t^e - \alpha(u_t - u_n) \tag{9.4}$$

Inflation depends on expected inflation and on the deviation of unemployment from the natural rate of unemployment.

We then argued that in the United States today, expected inflation is well approximated by last year's inflation. This means we can replace π_t^e with π_{t-1}. With this assumption, the relation between inflation and unemployment takes the form

$$\pi_t - \pi_{t-1} = -\alpha(u_t - u_n) \tag{9.5}$$

Phillips curve:
$u_t < u_n \Rightarrow \pi_t > \pi_{t-1}$
$u_t > u_n \Rightarrow \pi_t < \pi_{t-1}$

Unemployment below the natural rate leads to an increase in inflation; unemployment above the natural rate leads to a decrease in inflation. The parameter α gives the effect of unemployment on the change in inflation. We saw in Chapter 8 that, since 1970 in the United States, the natural unemployment rate has been on average equal to 6%, and α has been equal to 0.73. This value of α means that an unemployment rate of 1% above the natural rate for one year leads to a decrease in the inflation rate of about 0.73%.

The Aggregate Demand Relation

The third relation we will need is a relation between output growth, money growth, and inflation. We will now see that it follows from the aggregate demand relation we derived in Chapter 7.

In Chapter 7, we derived the aggregate demand relation as a relation between the level of output and the real money stock, government spending, and taxes [equation (7.3)], based on equilibrium in both goods and financial markets:

$$Y_t = Y\left(\frac{M_t}{P_t}, G_t, T_t\right)$$

Note that I have added time indexes, which we did not need in Chapter 7 but will need in this chapter. To simplify things, we will make two further assumptions here.

Okun's Law across Countries

The coefficient β in Okun's law gives the effect on the unemployment rate of deviations of output growth from normal. A value of β of 0.4 tells us that output growth 1% above the normal growth rate for one year decreases the unemployment rate by 0.4%.

The coefficient β depends in part on how firms adjust their employment in response to fluctuations in their production. This adjustment of employment depends in turn on such factors as the internal organization of firms and the legal and social constraints on hiring and firing. As these differ across countries, we would therefore expect the coefficient β to differ across countries, and indeed it does. Table 1 gives the estimated coefficient β for a number of countries.

The first column gives estimates of β based on data from 1960 to 1980. The United States has the highest coefficient, 0.39, followed by Germany, 0.20; the United Kingdom, 0.15; and Japan, 0.02.

The ranking in the 1960 to 1980 column fits well with what we know about the behavior of firms and the structure of firing/hiring regulations across countries. Japanese firms have traditionally offered a high degree of job security to their workers, so variations in Japan's output have little effect on employment and, by implication, little effect on unemployment. So it is no surprise that β is smallest in Japan. It is no surprise either that β is largest in the United States, where there are few social and legal constraints on firms' adjustment of employment. A high degree of employment protection (see Chapter 8) explains why the coefficients estimated for the two European countries are in between those of Japan and the United States.

The last column gives estimates based on data from 1981 to 2006. The coefficient is nearly unchanged for the United States, but it becomes higher for the other three countries. This again fits with what we know about firms and regulations. Increased competition in goods markets since the early 1980s has led firms in these countries to reconsider and reduce their commitment to job security. And, at the urging of firms, legal restrictions on hiring and firing have been weakened in many countries. Both factors have led to a larger response of employment to fluctuations in output, thus to a larger value of β.

Table 1	Okun's Law Coefficients across Countries and Time	
Country	1960 to 1980	1981 to 2006
United States	0.39	0.42
Germany	0.20	0.29
United Kingdom	0.15	0.51
Japan	0.02	0.11

FOCUS

First, to focus on the relation between the real money stock and output, we will ignore changes in factors other than real money here and write the aggregate demand relation simply as

$$Y_t = Y\left(\frac{M_t}{P_t}\right)$$

Second, we shall assume a linear relation between real money balances and output and rewrite the aggregate demand relation further as

$$Y_t = \gamma \frac{M_t}{P_t} \tag{9.6}$$

where γ (the Greek lowercase gamma) is a positive parameter. This equation states that the demand for goods, and thus output, is proportional to the real money stock. You should keep in mind, however, that behind this simple relation hides the mechanism you saw in the *IS–LM* model:

- An increase in the real money stock leads to a decrease in the interest rate.
- The decrease in the interest rate leads to an increase in the demand for goods and, therefore, to an increase in output.

If a variable is the ratio of two variables, its growth rate is equal to the difference between the growth rates of these two variables. (See Proposition 8 in Appendix 2 at the end of the book.) So if $Y = \gamma M/P$ and γ is constant, $g_y = g_m - \pi$.

Equation (9.6) gives a relation between *levels*—the output level, the level of money, and the price level. We need to go from this relation to a relation between *growth rates*—the growth rate of output, the growth rate of money, and the inflation rate (the growth rate of the price level). Fortunately, this is easy:

Let g_{yt} be the growth rate of output. Let π_t be the growth rate of the price level—the rate of inflation—and g_{mt} be the growth rate of nominal money. Then, from equation (9.6), it follows that

$$g_{yt} = g_{mt} - \pi_t \tag{9.7}$$

Aggregate demand relation:
$g_{mt} > \pi_t \implies g_{yt} > 0$
$g_{mt} < \pi_t \implies g_{yt} < 0$

If nominal money growth exceeds inflation, real money growth is positive, and so is output growth. If nominal money growth is less than inflation, real money growth is negative, and so is output growth. In other words, given inflation, expansionary monetary policy (high nominal money growth) leads to high output growth; contractionary monetary policy (low nominal money growth) leads to low, possibly negative, output growth.

9-2 The Effects of Money Growth

Let's collect the three relations between inflation, unemployment, and output growth we have just derived:

■ Okun's law relates the change in the unemployment rate to the deviation of output growth from normal [equation (9.3)]:

$$u_t - u_{t-1} = -\beta(g_{gt} - \bar{g}_y)$$

■ The Phillips curve—equivalently the aggregate supply relation—relates the change in inflation to the deviation of the unemployment rate from the natural rate [equation (9.5)]:

$$\pi_t - \pi_{t-1} = -\alpha(u_t - u_n)$$

■ The aggregate demand relation relates output growth to the difference between nominal money growth and inflation [equation (9.7)]:

$$g_{yt} = g_{mt} - \pi_t$$

These three relations are shown in Figure 9-2. Start on the left and follow the arrows. Through aggregate demand, nominal money growth and inflation determine output

Figure 9-2

Output Growth, Unemployment, Inflation, and Nominal Money Growth

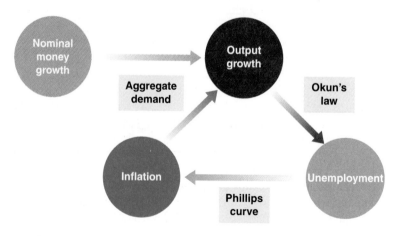

growth. Through Okun's law, output growth determines the change in unemployment. And through the Phillips curve relation, unemployment determines the change in inflation.

Our task now is to see what these three relations imply for the effects of nominal money growth on output, unemployment, and inflation. The easiest way to proceed is to work backward in time—that is, to start by looking at the medium run (by looking at where the economy ends up when all the dynamics have worked themselves out) and then to turn to the dynamics themselves (that is, to see how the economy gets there).

The Medium Run

Assume that the central bank maintains a constant growth rate of nominal money, call it $\bar{g}_m$. In this case, what will be the values of output growth, unemployment, and inflation in the *medium run?*

- In the medium run, the unemployment rate must be constant: The unemployment rate cannot increase or decrease forever. Putting $u_t = u_{t-1}$ in Okun's law implies that $g_{yt} = \bar{g}_y$. In the medium run, output must grow at its normal rate of growth, $\bar{g}_y$. ◄ **Medium run:** $g_y = \bar{g}_y$
- With nominal money growth equal to $\bar{g}_m$ and output growth equal to $\bar{g}_y$, the aggregate demand relation implies that inflation is constant and satisfies

$$\bar{g}_y = \bar{g}_m - \pi$$

Moving π to the left and $\bar{g}_y$ to the right gives an expression for inflation:

$$\pi = \bar{g}_m - \bar{g}_y \qquad (9.8)$$

In the medium run, inflation must be equal to nominal money growth minus normal output growth. If we define **adjusted nominal money growth** as equal to nominal money growth minus normal output growth, equation (9.8) can be stated as: *In the medium run, inflation equals adjusted nominal money growth.* ◄ **Medium run:** $\pi = \bar{g}_m - \bar{g}_y$

The way to think about this result is as follows: A growing level of output implies a growing level of transactions and thus a growing demand for real money. So, if output is growing at 3%, the real money stock must also grow at 3% per year. If the nominal money stock grows at a rate different from 3% per year, the difference must show up in inflation (or deflation). For example, if nominal money growth is 8% per year, then inflation must be equal to 5% per year.

- If inflation is constant, then inflation this year is equal to inflation last year: $\pi_t = \pi_{t-1}$. Putting $\pi_t = \pi_{t-1}$ in the Phillips curve implies that $u_t = u_n$. *In the medium run, the unemployment rate must be equal to the natural rate of unemployment.* ◄ **Medium run:** $u = u_n$

Let's summarize: In the medium run, output growth is equal to the normal growth rate. Unemployment is equal to the natural rate. And both are independent of nominal money growth. Nominal money growth affects only inflation.

These results are the natural extension of the results we derived in Chapter 7. There, we saw that *changes in the level of nominal money* were neutral in the medium run: They had no effect on either output or unemployment but were reflected one-for-one in changes in the price level. We see here that a similar neutrality result applies to *changes in the growth rate of nominal money:* Changes in nominal money growth have no effect on output or unemployment in the medium run but are reflected one-for-one in changes in the rate of inflation.

Another way to state this last result is that the only determinant of inflation in the medium run is nominal money growth. Milton Friedman put it this way: *Inflation is always and everywhere a monetary phenomenon.* Unless they lead to higher nominal money growth, factors such as the monopoly power of firms, strong unions, strikes, fiscal deficits, the price of oil, and so on, have no effect on inflation *in the medium run.* ◄ The word *unless* is important. During episodes of very high inflation (see Chapter 23), fiscal deficits often lead to nominal money creation and to higher nominal money growth.

The Short Run

Let's now turn to dynamics. Suppose that the economy is initially at its medium-run equilibrium: Unemployment is equal to the natural rate. Output growth is equal to the normal growth rate. The inflation rate is equal to adjusted nominal money growth.

Suppose that the central bank decides to decrease nominal money growth. We saw earlier that, in the medium run, lower money growth will lead to lower inflation and unchanged output growth and unemployment. The question now is: What will happen in the short run?

Just by looking at our three relations, we can tell the beginning of the story:

Lower g_m ⇒ Lower $g_m - \pi$
⇒ Lower g_y

- Look at the the aggregate demand relation—Given the initial rate of inflation, lower nominal money growth leads to lower real nominal money growth and thus to a decrease in output growth.

Lower g_y ⇒ Higher u

- Now, look at Okun's law—Output growth below normal leads to an increase in unemployment.

Higher u ⇒ Lower π

- Now, look at the Phillips curve relation—Unemployment above the natural rate leads to a decrease in inflation.

So we have our first result: Tighter monetary policy leads initially to lower output growth and lower inflation. If tight enough, it may lead to negative output growth and thus to a recesssion. What happens between this initial response and the medium run (when unemployment returns to the natural rate)? The answer depends on the path of monetary policy, and the best way to show what happens is to work out a simple example.

Suppose the economy starts in year 0 in medium-run equilibrium. Assume that normal output growth is 3%, the natural unemployment rate is 6%, and nominal money growth is 8%. Inflation is therefore equal to nominal money growth minus output growth, $8\% - 3\% = 5\%$. Real money growth is equal to nominal money growth minus inflation, $8\% - 5\% = 3\%$.

Suppose that the central bank decides to tighten monetary policy in the following way: It decides to decrease real money growth relative to trend by 2.5% in year 1 and to increase it relative to trend by 2.5% in year 2. (Why 2.5%? To make the arithmetic simple, as will be clear later on.) The path of the relevant macroeconomic variables is given in Table 9-1:

> It would be more natural to describe monetary policy in terms of what happens to nominal money growth. The algebra would get more complicated, however. For our purposes, it is easier to describe it in terms of what happens to real money growth. We can do so without loss of generality: Given the inflation rate, the central bank can always choose nominal money growth to achieve the real money growth it wants.

- Line 1 shows the path of real money growth. In year 0 (before the change in policy), real money growth is equal to 3%. Under the assumptions we have just made, the change in monetary policy leads to real money growth of 0.5% (2.5% below normal) in year 1, 5.5% (2.5% above normal) in year 2, and 3% thereafter.
- Line 2 shows the path of output growth. From the aggregate demand relation, real money growth of 0.5% in year 1 leads to output growth of 0.5% (2.5% below

Table 9-1	The Effects of a Monetary Tightening		Year 0	Year 1	Year 2	Year 3
1	Real money growth %	$(g_m - \pi)$	3.0	0.5	5.5	3.0
2	Output growth %	(g_y)	3.0	0.5	5.5	3.0
3	Unemployment rate %	(u)	6.0	7.0	6.0	6.0
4	Inflation rate %	(π)	5.0	4.0	4.0	4.0
5	(Nominal money growth) %	(g_m)	8.0	4.5	9.5	7.0

normal); real money growth of 5.5% in year 2 leads to output growth of 5.5% (2.5% above normal); thereafter, output growth is equal to the normal growth rate, 3%.

- Line 3 shows the path of the unemployment rate. Okun's law implies that output growth of 2.5% below normal for one year leads to an increase in the unemployment rate of 1 percentage point (2.5% multiplied by 0.4, the coefficient in Okun's law). So, in year 1, the unemployment rate increases from 6% to 7%. In year 2, output growth of 2.5% above normal for one year leads to a decrease in the unemployment rate of 1 percentage point. So, in year 2, the unemployment rate decreases from 7% back to 6%. The unemployment rate remains equal to 6% thereafter.

- Line 4 shows the path of the inflation rate. For this computation, let's assume that α is equal to 1.0 rather than its estimated value of 0.73 that we saw in Chapter 8. This assumption will simplify our computations. From the Phillips curve relation, an unemployment rate of 7%, which is 1% above the natural rate, leads to a decrease in inflation from 5% to 4% in year 1. In year 2 and thereafter, the unemployment rate is equal to the natural rate, and, therefore, inflation remains constant at 4%.

- For completeness, line 5 shows the behavior of nominal money growth consistent with the path of real money growth we assumed in line 1. Nominal money growth is equal to real money growth plus inflation. Adding the numbers for real money growth in line 1 and for inflation in line 4 gives the numbers in line 5. This implies a decrease in the rate of nominal money growth from 8% to 4.5% in year 1, an increase to 9.5% in year 2, and a decrease to 7% thereafter.

In words: In the short run, monetary tightening leads to a slowdown in growth and a temporary increase in unemployment. In the medium run, output growth returns to normal, and the unemployment rate returns to the natural rate. Money growth and inflation are both permanently lower.

▶ Put less formally: The temporary increase in unemployment buys a permanent decrease in inflation.

9-3 Disinflation

To better understand the mechanics and the implications of our model, let's return to a situation not unlike that faced by the Fed in 1979: The economy is in medium-run equilibrium: Unemployment is at the natural rate of unemployment; output growth is equal to the normal growth rate. The inflation rate is equal to adjusted nominal money growth. The rate of nominal money growth and, by implication, the inflation rate, are high however, and there is a consensus among policymakers that inflation must be reduced.

▶ At this point, you might ask: What is so bad about high inflation if growth is proceeding at a normal rate, and unemployment is at the natural rate of unemployment? To answer, we need to discuss the costs of inflation. We shall do so in Chapter 23.

We know from the previous section that lower inflation requires lower money growth. We also know that lower money growth implies an increase in unemployment for some time. For the central bank, the question now is: Having decided to act, at what pace should it proceed?

A First Pass

A first pass at the answer can be given by using the Phillips curve relation [equation (9.5)]:

$$\pi_t - \pi_{t-1} = -\alpha(u_t - u_n)$$

The relation makes it clear that **disinflation**—the decrease in inflation—can only be obtained at the cost of higher unemployment: For the left side of the equation to be negative—that is, for inflation to decrease—the term $(u_t - u_n)$ must be positive. In other words, the unemployment rate must exceed the natural rate.

The equation, however, has a stronger and more striking implication: The total amount of unemployment required for a given decrease in inflation does not depend on the speed at which disinflation is achieved. In other words, disinflation can be

▶ Make sure to distinguish between
Deflation: Decrease in the price level (equivalently, negative inflation)
Disinflation: Decrease in the inflation rate

achieved quickly, at the cost of high unemployment for a few years. Or, alternatively, it can be achieved more slowly, with a smaller increase in unemployment spread over many years. In both cases, the total amount of unemployment, summed over the years, will be the same.

Let's see why. First, define a **point-year of excess unemployment** as the difference between the actual and the natural unemployment rates of 1 percentage point for one year. While the expression may sound a bit strange, the concept is simple: For example, if the natural rate of unemployment is 6%, an unemployment rate of 8% four years in a row corresponds to 4 times $(8 - 6) = 8$ point-years of excess unemployment.

Now look at a central bank that wants to reduce inflation by x percentage points. To make things simpler, let's use specific numbers: Assume that the central bank wants to reduce inflation from 14% to 4%, so that x is equal to 10. Let's also make the convenient, if not quite correct, assumption that α equals 1; again, this will simplify computations:

- Suppose the central bank wants to achieve the reduction in inflation in one year. Equation (9.5) tells us that what is required is one year of unemployment at 10% above the natural rate. In this case, the right side of the equation is equal to –10%, and the inflation rate decreases by 10% within a year.
- Suppose the central bank wants to achieve the reduction in inflation over two years. Equation (9.5) tells us that what is required is 2 years of unemployment at 5% above the natural rate. During each of the 2 years, the right side of the equation is equal to –5%, so the inflation rate decreases by 5% each year, thus by $2 \times 5\% = 10\%$ over 2 years.
- By the same reasoning, reducing inflation over 5 years requires 5 years of unemployment at 2% above the natural rate $(5 \times 2\% = 10\%)$; reducing inflation over 10 years requires 10 years of unemployment at 1% above the natural rate $(10 \times 1\% = 10\%)$, and so on.

Note that in each case the number of point-years of excess unemployment required to decrease inflation is the same, namely ten: 1 year times 10% excess unemployment in the first scenario, 2 years times 5% in the second, 10 years times 1% in the last. The implication is straightforward: The central bank can choose the distribution of excess unemployment over time, but it cannot change the total number of point-years of excess unemployment.

We can state this conclusion another way: Define the **sacrifice ratio** as the number of point-years of excess unemployment needed to achieve a decrease in inflation of 1%:

$$\text{Sacrifice ratio} = \frac{\text{Point-years of excess unemployment}}{\text{Decrease in inflation}}$$

Equation (9.5) then implies that this ratio is independent of policy and simply equal to $(1/\alpha)$.

If the sacrifice ratio is constant, does this mean that the speed of disinflation is irrelevant? No. Suppose that the central bank tried to achieve the decrease in inflation in one year. As you have just seen, this would require an unemployment rate of 10% above the natural rate for one year. With a natural unemployment rate of 6%, this would require increasing the actual unemployment rate to 16% for one year. From Okun's law, using a value of 0.4 for β and a normal output growth rate of 3%, output growth would have to satisfy

$$u_t - u_{t-1} = -\beta(g_{yt} - \bar{g}_y)$$
$$16\% - 6\% = -0.4(g_{yt} - 3\%)$$

This implies a value for $g_{yt} = -(10\%)/0.4 + 3\% = -22\%$. In words, output growth would have to equal –22% for a year! In comparison, the largest negative growth rate ever in the United States in the twentieth century was –15%. It occurred in 1931, during the Great Depression. It is fair to say that macroeconomists do not know with great confidence what would happen if monetary policy were aimed at inducing such a large negative growth rate. But they would surely be unwilling to try. The increase in the overall unemployment rate would lead to extremely high unemployment rates for some groups—specifically the young and the unskilled, whose unemployment typically increases more than the average unemployment rate. The associated sharp drop in output would most likely also lead to a large number of bankruptcies. This suggests that the central bank will want to go more slowly and to achieve disinflation over a number of years rather than do it all in one year.

The analysis we have just developed is close to the type of analysis economists at the Fed were conducting in the late 1970s. The econometric model they used, as well as most econometric models in use at the time, shared our simple model's property that policy could change the timing but not the number of point-years of excess unemployment. I shall call this the *traditional approach* in the following text. The traditional approach was challenged, however, by two separate groups of macroeconomists. The focus of both groups was the role of expectations and how changes in expectation formation might affect the unemployment cost of disinflation. But despite this common focus, they reached quite different conclusions.

Expectations and Credibility: The Lucas Critique

The conclusions of the first group were based on the work of Robert Lucas and Thomas Sargent, then at the University of Chicago. In what has become known as the **Lucas critique**, Lucas pointed out that when trying to predict the effects of a major policy change—such as the change considered by the Fed at the time—it could be very misleading to take as given the relations estimated from past data.

Robert Lucas was awarded the Nobel Prize in 1995 and is still at the University of Chicago. Thomas Sargent is now at New York University.

In the case of the Phillips curve, taking equation (9.5) as given was equivalent to assuming that wage setters would keep expecting inflation in the future to be the same as it was in the past, that the way wage setters formed their expectations would not change in response to the change in policy. This was an unwarranted assumption, Lucas argued: Why shouldn't wage setters take policy changes directly into account? If wage setters believed that the Fed was committed to lowering inflation, they might well expect inflation to be lower in the future than in the past. If they lowered their expectations of inflation, then actual inflation would decline without the need for a protracted recession.

The logic of Lucas's argument can be seen by returning to equation (9.4), the Phillips curve with expected inflation on the right:

$$\pi_t = \pi_t^e - \alpha(u_t - u_n)$$

If wage setters kept forming expectations of inflation by looking at the previous year's inflation (if $\pi_t^e = \pi_{t-1}$), then the only way to decrease inflation would be to accept higher unemployment for some time; we explored the implications of this assumption in the preceding subsection.

If $\pi_t^e = \pi_{t-1}$, the Phillips curve is given by
$\pi_t - \pi_{t-1} = -\alpha(u_t - u_n)$
To achieve $\pi_t < \pi_{t-1}$, it must be that $u_t > u_n$.

But if wage setters could be convinced that inflation was indeed going to be lower than in the past, they would decrease their expectations of inflation. This would in turn reduce actual inflation, without any change in the unemployment rate. For example, if wage setters were convinced that inflation, which had been running at 14% in the past, would be only 4% in the future, and if they formed their expectations accordingly, then inflation would fall to 4% *even if unemployment remained at the natural rate of unemployment*:

$$\pi_t = \pi_t^e - \alpha(u_t - u_n)$$
$$4\% = 4\% - 0\%$$

Nominal money growth, inflation, and expected inflation could all be reduced without the need for a recession. Put another way, decreases in nominal money growth could be neutral not only in the medium run but also in the short run.

Lucas and Sargent did not believe that disinflation could really take place without some increase in unemployment. But Sargent, looking at the historical evidence on the end of several very high inflations, concluded that the increase in unemployment could be small. The sacrifice ratio—the amount of excess unemployment needed to achieve disinflation—might be much lower than suggested by the traditional approach. The essential ingredient of successful disinflation, he argued, was **credibility** of monetary policy—the belief by wage setters that the central bank was truly committed to reducing inflation. Only credibility would cause wage setters to change the way they formed their expectations. Furthermore, he argued, a clear and quick disinflation program was much more likely to be credible than a protracted one that offered plenty of opportunities for reversal and political infighting along the way.

The *credibility view* is that fast disinflation is likely to be more credible than slow disinflation. Credibility decreases the unemployment cost of disinflation. So the central bank should go for fast disinflation.

Nominal Rigidities and Contracts

Fischer is now the Governor of the Central Bank of Israel. Taylor was undersecretary for international affairs in the G. W. Bush administration and is now a professor at Stanford University. More on both in Chapter 28.

A contrary view was taken by Stanley Fischer, then from MIT, and John Taylor, then at Columbia University. Both emphasized the presence of **nominal rigidities**, meaning that, in modern economies, many wages and prices are set in nominal terms for some time and are typically not readjusted when there is a change in policy.

Fischer argued that even with credibility, too rapid a decrease in nominal money growth would lead to higher unemployment. Even if the Fed fully convinced workers and firms that nominal money growth was going to be lower, the wages set before the change in policy would still reflect the expectations of inflation prior to the policy change. In effect, inflation would already be built into existing wage agreements and could not be reduced instantaneously and without cost. At the very least, Fischer said, a policy of disinflation should be announced sufficiently in advance of its actual implementation to allow wage setters to take it into account when setting wages.

Taylor's argument went one step further. An important characteristic of wage contracts, he argued, is that they are not all signed at the same time. Instead, they are staggered over time. He showed that this **staggering of wage decisions** imposed strong limits on how fast disinflation could proceed without triggering higher unemployment, even if the Fed's commitment to inflation was fully credible. Why the limits? If workers cared about their wage relative to the wages of other workers, each wage contract would choose a wage not very different from the wages in the other contracts in force at the time. Too rapid a decrease in nominal money growth would therefore not lead to a proportional decrease in inflation. As a result, the real money stock would decrease, triggering a recession and an increase in the unemployment rate.

Taking into account the time pattern of wage contracts in the United States, Taylor then showed that, under full credibility of monetary policy, there *was* a path of disinflation consistent *with no increase in unemployment*. This path is shown in Figure 9-3.

In Figure 9-3, disinflation starts in quarter 1 and lasts for 16 quarters. Once it is achieved, the inflation rate, which started at 10%, is 3%. The striking feature is how slowly disinflation proceeds at the beginning. One year (four quarters) after the announcement of the change in policy, inflation is still 9.9%. But then disinflation

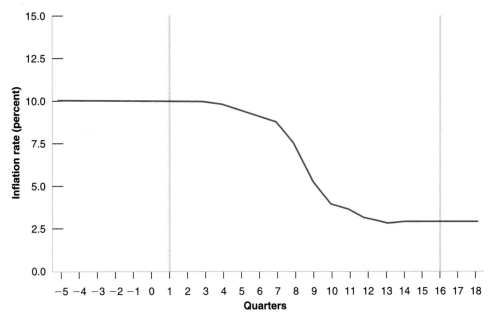

Figure 9-3

Disinflation without Unemployment in the Taylor Model

If wage decisions are staggered, disinflation must be phased in slowly to avoid an increase in unemployment.

proceeds more quickly. By the end of the third year, inflation is down to 4%, and by the end of the fourth year, the desired disinflation is achieved.

The reason for the slow decrease in inflation at the beginning—and, behind the scenes, for the slow decrease in nominal money growth—is straightforward: Wages in force at the time of the policy change are the result of decisions made before the policy change occurred. Because of this, the path of inflation in the near future is largely predetermined. If nominal money growth were to decrease sharply, inflation could not fall very much right away, and the result would be a decrease in real money and a recession. So the best policy is for the Fed to proceed slowly at the beginning of the process while announcing it will proceed faster in the future. This announcement leads new wage settlements to take into account the new policy. When most wage decisions in the economy are based on decisions made after the change in policy, disinflation can proceed much more quickly. This is what happens in the third year following the policy change.

Like Lucas and Sargent, Taylor did not believe that disinflation could really be implemented without an increase in unemployment. For one thing, he realized that the path of disinflation drawn in Figure 9-3 might not be credible. Announcing this year that the Fed will decrease nominal money growth two years from now is likely to cause a serious credibility problem. Wage setters are likely to ask: If the decision has been made to disinflate, why does the central bank want to wait two years? Without credibility, inflation expectations might not change, defeating the hope of disinflation without an increase in the unemployment rate. But Taylor's analysis had two clear messages. First, like Lucas and Sargent, Taylor's analysis emphasized the role of expectations. Second, it suggested that a slow but credible disinflation might have a cost lower than the one implied by the traditional approach.

The *nominal rigidities view* is that many wages are set in nominal terms, sometimes for many years. The way to decrease the unemployment cost of disinflation is to give wage setters time to take into account the change in policy. So the central bank should go ◀ for slow disinflation.

Who turned out to be right? The traditional approach, the Sargent–Lucas approach, or the Fischer–Taylor approach? The answer is given in the Focus box "U.S. Disinflation, 1979–1985," and is easy to summarize: The disinflation of about 10% triggered a deep recession and about 12 point-years of excess unemployment. In other words, there were no obvious credibility gains, and the sacrifice ratio turned out to be roughly what was predicted by the traditional approach.

Was this outcome due to a lack of credibility of the change in monetary policy or to the fact that credibility is not enough to substantially reduce the cost of disinflation?

In 1979, U.S. unemployment was 5.8%, roughly equal to the natural rate at the time. GDP growth was 2.5%, roughly equal to the normal growth rate. The inflation rate (measured using the CPI), however, was a high 13.3%. The question the Federal Reserve faced was no longer whether it should reduce inflation but how fast it should reduce it. In August 1979, President Carter appointed Paul Volcker as chairman of the Federal Reserve Board. Volcker, who had served in the Nixon administration, was considered an extremely qualified chairman who would and could lead the fight against inflation.

In October 1979, the Fed announced a number of changes in its operating procedures. In particular, it indicated that it would shift from targeting a given level of the short-term interest rate to targeting the growth rate of nominal money.

This change would hardly seem to be the stuff of history books. The Fed made no announcement of a major battle against inflation, nor of a targeted path of disinflation, nor of various other ambitious-sounding plans. Nevertheless, financial markets widely interpreted this technical change as a sign of a major shift in monetary policy. In particular, the change was interpreted as

indicating that the Fed had become committed to reduce money growth and inflation and that, if needed, it would let interest rates increase, perhaps to very high levels.

Over the following seven months, the Fed let the federal funds rate increase by more than 6 percentage points, from 11.4% in September 1979 to 17.6% in April 1980. But then there was a halt, followed by a rapid reversal. By July 1980, the rate was back down to 9%, dropping 8.6 percentage points in four months. This roller-coaster movement of the federal funds rate is shown in Figure 1, which plots the federal funds rate and the inflation rate, measured as the rate of change of the CPI over the previous 12 months, for the period January 1979 to December 1984.

The reason the Fed lowered the federal funds rate in mid-1980 was because signs were accumulating that the economy was entering a sharp recession. In March 1980, believing that high consumer spending was one of the causes of inflation, the Carter administration had imposed controls on consumer credit—limits on how much consumers could borrow to buy some durable goods. The effect of these controls turned out to be much larger than the Carter administration had anticipated. The combination of the fear of a sharp recession

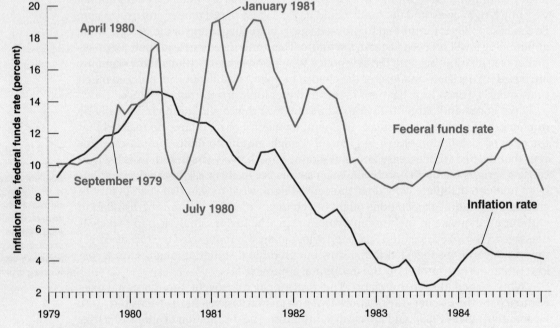

Figure 1 *The Federal Funds Rate and Inflation, 1979 to 1984*
A sharp increase in the federal funds rate from September 1979 to April 1980 was followed by a sharp decline in mid-1980 and then a second and sustained increase from January 1981 on, lasting for most of 1981 and 1982.

Table 1	Inflation and Unemployment, 1979 to 1985						
		1979	1980	1981	1982	1983	1984	1985
1	GDP growth (%)	2.5	−0.5	1.8	−2.2	3.9	6.2	3.2
2	Unemployment rate (%)	5.8	7.1	7.6	9.7	9.6	7.5	7.2
3	CPI inflation (%)	13.3	12.5	8.9	3.8	3.8	3.9	3.8
4	Cumulative unemployment		1.0	2.6	6.3	9.9	11.4	12.6
5	Cumulative disinflation		0.8	4.4	9.5	9.5	9.4	9.5
6	Sacrifice ratio		1.25	0.59	0.66	1.04	1.21	1.32

Cumulative unemployment is the sum of point-years of excess unemployment from 1980 on, assuming a natural rate of unemployment of 6.0%. Cumulative disinflation is the difference between inflation in a given year and inflation in 1979. The sacrifice ratio is the ratio of cumulative unemployment to cumulative disinflation.

and the political pressure coming from the proximity of presidential elections was enough to lead the Fed to decrease interest rates sharply.

By the end of 1980, with the economy apparently in recovery, the Fed again increased the federal funds rate sharply. Cumulative increases in the federal funds rate of 3 percentage points just before the 1980 election surely did not improve Carter's reelection prospects. By January 1981, the rate was back up to 19%.

By the end of 1981, signs accumulated that the very high interest rates were triggering a second recession. The Fed decided not to repeat its 1980 mistake of abandoning its disinflation target in the face of a recession. In contrast to its actions in 1980, it kept interest rates high. The federal funds rate was decreased to 12.3% in December 1981 but then increased back to 14.9% in April 1982.

Was the commitment of the Fed to disinflation credible, in the sense defined by Lucas and Sargent? Paul Volcker had credibility when he became the Fed chairman. However, the credibility of the Fed's disinflation stance was surely eroded by the Fed's behavior in 1980. Credibility was progressively reestablished in 1981 and 1982, especially when, despite clear indications that the economy was in recession, the Fed increased the federal funds rate in the spring of 1982.

Did this credibility of the Fed—to the extent that it was present—lead to a more favorable trade-off between unemployment and disinflation than implied by the traditional approach? Table 1 gives the relevant numbers.

The upper half of the table makes clear that there was no credibility miracle: Line 2 shows that disinflation was

associated with substantial unemployment. The average unemployment rate was above 9% in both 1982 and 1983, peaking at 10.8% in December 1982.

The answer to whether the unemployment cost was lower than implied by the traditional approach is given in the bottom half of the table. Under the traditional approach, each point of disinflation is predicted to require about $(1/\alpha) = 1/0.73 = 1.36$ point-years of excess unemployment. Line 4 computes the cumulative number of point-years of excess unemployment from 1980 onward, assuming a natural rate of unemployment of 6%. Line 5 computes cumulative disinflation— the decrease in inflation starting from its 1979 level. Line 6 gives the sacrifice ratio, the ratio of the cumulative point-years of unemployment above the natural rate of unemployment to cumulative disinflation.

The table shows there were no obvious "credibility gains." By 1982, the sacrifice ratio looked quite attractive: The cumulative decrease in inflation since 1979 was nearly 9.5%, at a cost of 6.3 point-years of unemployment—a sacrifice ratio of 0.66, relative to the sacrifice ratio of 1.36 predicted by the traditional approach. But by 1985, the sacrifice ratio had reached 1.32. A 10% disinflation had been achieved with 13.2 point-years of excess unemployment, an outcome close to the outcome predicted by the traditional approach.

In short: The U.S. disinflation of the early 1980s was associated with a substantial increase in unemployment. The Phillips curve relation between the change in inflation and the deviation of the unemployment rate from the natural rate proved more robust than many economists had anticipated.

One way of learning more is to look at other disinflation episodes. This is the approach followed by Laurence Ball, from The Johns Hopkins University, who estimated sacrifice ratios for 65 disinflation episodes in 19 OECD countries over the past 30 years. He reached three main conclusions:

■ Disinflations typically lead to a period of higher unemployment. Put another way, even if a decrease in nominal money growth is neutral in the medium run, unemployment increases for some time before returning to the natural rate of unemployment.

■ Faster disinflations are associated with smaller sacrifice ratios. This conclusion provides some evidence to support the expectation and credibility effects emphasized by Lucas and Sargent.

■ Sacrifice ratios are smaller in countries that have shorter wage contracts. This provides some evidence to support Fischer and Taylor's emphasis on the structure of wage settlements.

Let's summarize: Policymakers face a trade-off between unemployment and inflation. In particular, to permanently lower inflation requires higher unemployment for some time. One might have hoped that, with credible policies, the trade-off would be much more favorable. The evidence can be read as saying that credibility gains may be present, but they are small.

We shall return to the role of credibility in monetary policy in Chapter 25.

Summary

■ Three relations link inflation, output, and unemployment:
  1. Okun's law, which relates the change in the unemployment rate to the deviation of the rate of growth of output from the normal growth rate. In the United States today, output growth of 1% above normal for a year leads to a decrease in the unemployment rate of about 0.4%.
  2. The aggregate supply relation—the Phillips curve—which relates the change in the inflation rate to the deviation of the actual unemployment rate from the natural rate of unemployment. In the United States today, an unemployment rate 1% below the natural rate of unemployment for a year leads to an increase in inflation of about 1%.
  3. The aggregate demand relation, which relates the rate of growth of output to the rate of growth of real money. The growth rate of output is equal to the growth rate of nominal money minus the rate of inflation. Given nominal money growth, higher inflation leads to a decrease in output growth.

■ In the medium run, the unemployment rate is equal to the natural rate of unemployment, and output grows at its normal growth rate. Nominal money growth determines the inflation rate: A 1% increase in nominal money growth leads to a 1% increase in the inflation rate. As Milton Friedman put it: Inflation is always and everywhere a monetary phenomenon.

■ In the short run, a decrease in nominal money growth leads to a slowdown in growth and an increase in unemployment for some time.

■ Disinflation (a decrease in the inflation rate) can be achieved only at the cost of more unemployment. How much unemployment is required is a controversial issue. The traditional approach assumes that people do not change the way they form expectations when monetary policy changes, so the relation between inflation and unemployment is unaffected by the change in policy. This approach implies that disinflation can be achieved by a short but large increase in unemployment or by a longer and smaller increase in unemployment. But policy cannot affect the total number of point-years of excess unemployment.

■ An alternative view is that, if the change in monetary policy is credible, expectation formation may change, leading to a smaller increase in unemployment than predicted by the traditional approach. In its extreme form, this alternative view implies that if policy is fully credible, it can achieve disinflation at no cost in unemployment. A less extreme form recognizes that while expectation formation may change, the presence of nominal rigidities is likely to result in some increase in unemployment, but less than that implied by the traditional approach.

■ The U.S. disinflation of the early 1980s, during which inflation fell by approximately 10%, was associated with a large recession. The unemployment cost was close to the predictions of the traditional approach.

Key Terms

Questions and Problems

Quick Check

1. Using the information in this chapter, label each of the following statements true, false, or uncertain. Explain briefly.

a. There is a reliable negative relation between the rate of inflation and the growth rate of output.

b. The U.S. unemployment rate will remain constant as long as there is positive output growth.

c. Many firms prefer to keep workers around when demand is low (rather than lay them off) even if the workers are underutilized.

d. According to Okun's Law, output growth above normal leads to a decrease in the unemployment rate.

e. In the medium run, the unemployment rate must be equal to the natural rate of unemployment.

f. Contrary to the traditional Phillips curve analysis, Taylor's analysis of staggered wage contracts makes the case for a quick approach to disinflation.

g. According to the Phillips curve relation, the sacrifice ratio is dependent on the speed of disinflation.

h. If Lucas and Sargent were right, and if monetary policy was fully credible, there would be no relation between inflation and unemployment—i.e., no Phillips curve relation.

i. Ball's analysis of disinflation episodes provides some support for both the credibility effects of Lucas and Sargent and the wage-contract effects of Fischer and Taylor.

2. As shown by equation (9.2), the estimated Okun's law for the United States is given by

$$u_t - u_{t-1} = -0.4(g_{yt} - 3\%)$$

a. What growth rate of output leads to an increase in the unemployment rate of 1% per year? How can the unemployment rate increase even though the growth rate of output is positive?

b. Suppose output growth is constant for the next four years. What growth rate would reduce the unemployment rate by 2 percentage points over the next four years?

c. How would you expect Okun's law to change if the rate of growth of the labor force was higher by 2 percentage points? How do you expect Okun's law to change if the rate of growth of the labor force increases by 2 percentage points?

3. Suppose that an economy can be described by the following three equations:

$$u_t - u_{t-1} = -0.4(g_{yt} - 3\%) \quad \text{Okun's law}$$
$$\pi_t - \pi_{t-1} = -(u_t - 5\%) \quad \text{Phillips curve}$$
$$g_{yt} = g_{mt} - \pi_t \quad \text{Aggregate demand}$$

a. What is the natural rate of unemployment for this economy?

b. Suppose that the unemployment rate is equal to the natural rate and that the inflation rate is 8%. What is the growth rate of output? What is the growth rate of the money supply?

c. Suppose that conditions are as in (b), when, in year *t*, the authorities use monetary policy to reduce the inflation rate to 4% in year *t* and keep it there. Given this inflation rate and using the Phillips curve, what must happen to the unemployment rate in years $t, t + 1, t + 2$, and so on? Given the unemployment rate and using Okun's law, what must happen to the rate of growth of output in years $t, t + 1, t + 2$, and so on? Given the rate of growth of output and using the aggregate demand equation, what must be the rate of nominal money growth in years $t, t + 1, t + 2$, and so on?

4. Markups, unemployment, and inflation

Suppose that the Phillips curve is given by

$$\pi_t - \pi_{t-1} = -(u_t - 5\%) + 0.1\mu$$

where μ is the markup.

Suppose that unemployment is initially at its natural rate. Suppose now that μ increases as a result of an oil price shock, but that the monetary authority continues to keep the unemployment rate at its previous value.

a. What will happen to inflation?

b. What should the monetary authority do instead of trying to keep the unemployment rate at its previous value?

5. Suppose that you are advising a government that wants to reduce the inflation rate. It is considering two options: a gradual reduction over several years or an immediate reduction.

a. Lay out the arguments for and against each option.

b. Considering only the sacrifice ratio, which option is preferable? Why might you want to consider criteria other than the sacrifice ratio?

c. What particular features of the economy would you want to consider before giving your advice?

Dig Deeper

6. *Credibility and disinflation*

   Suppose that the Phillips curve is given by

   $$\pi_t = \pi_t^e - (u_t - 5\%)$$

   and expected inflation is given by

   $$\pi_t^e = \pi_{t-1}$$

a. What is the sacrifice ratio in this economy?

   Suppose that unemployment is initially equal to the natural rate and $\pi = 12\%$. The central bank decides that 12% inflation is too high and that, starting in year t, it will maintain the unemployment rate 1 percentage point above the natural rate of unemployment until the inflation rate has decreased to 2%.

b. Compute the rate of inflation for years $t, t + 1, t + 2$, and so on.

c. For how many years must the central bank keep the unemployment rate above the natural rate of unemployment? Is the implied sacrifice ratio consistent with your answer to (a)?

   Now suppose that people know that the central bank wants to lower inflation to 2%, but they are not sure about the central bank's willingness to accept an unemployment rate above the natural rate of unemployment. As a result, their expectation of inflation is a weighted average of the target of 2% and last year's inflation—i.e,

   $$\pi_t^e = \lambda\, 2\% + (1 - \lambda)\pi_{t-1}$$

   where λ is the weight they put on the central bank's target of 2%.

d. Let $\lambda = 0.25$. How long will it take before the inflation rate is equal to 2%? What is the sacrifice ratio? Why is it different from the answer in (c)?

   Suppose that after the policy has been in effect for one year, people believe that the central bank is indeed committed to reducing inflation to 2%. As a result, they now set their expectations according to

   $$\pi_t^e = 2\%$$

e. From what year onward can the central bank let the unemployment rate return to the natural rate? What is the sacrifice ratio now?

f. What advice would you give to a central bank that wants to lower the rate of inflation by increasing the rate of unemployment as little and for as short a time period as possible?

7. *The effects of a permanent decrease in the rate of nominal money growth*

   Suppose that the economy can be described by the following three equations:

$u_t - u_{t-1} = -0.4(g_{yt} - 3\%)$	Okun's law
$\pi_t - \pi_{t-1} = -(u_t - 5\%)$	Phillips curve
$g_{yt} = g_{mt} - \pi_t$	Aggregate demand

a. Reduce the three equations to two by substituting g_{yt} from the aggregate demand equation into Okun's law.

   Assume initially that $u_t = u_{t-1} = 5\%$, $g_{mt} = 13\%$, and $\pi_t = 10\%$. Now suppose that money growth is permanently reduced from 13% to 3%, starting in year t.

b. Compute (using a calculator or a spreadsheet program) unemployment and inflation in year $t, t + 1, \ldots, t + 10$.

c. Does inflation decline smoothly from 10% to 3%? Why or why not?

d. Compute the values of the unemployment rate and the inflation rate in the medium run.

Explore Further

8. *Go the Web site of the Bureau of Labor Statistics (*www.bls.gov*) and retrieve monthly data on the level of employment and unemployment for 2001. You will notice that the level of unemployment rose in every month of 2001.*

a. Did the level of employment rise in any month(s) in 2001?

b. How is it possible that both employment and unemployment could rise in the same month?

9. *Go to the Web site of the Bureau of Economic Analysis (*www.bea.gov*) and retrieve quarterly data on real chained gross domestic product for 2002 and 2003. Go to the Web site of the Bureau of Labor Statistics (*www.bls.gov*) and retrieve data on monthly unemployment rates and monthly employment levels for 2002 and 2003.*

a. Was output growth positive throughout 2002 and 2003?

b. What happened to the unemployment rate over the period January 2002 to June 2003?

c. How do you reconcile your answers to parts (a) and (b)?

d. Now consider the employment level. Compare the monthly employment levels from September 2002 and December 2002. What happened to employment over the last quarter of 2002?

e. Was output growth positive in the last quarter of 2002?

f. How do you reconcile your answers to parts (d) and (e)?

We invite you to visit the Blanchard page on the Prentice Hall Web site, at:
www.prenhall.com/blanchard
for this chapter's World Wide Web exercises.

Further Readings

■ A description of U.S. monetary policy in the 1980s is given by Michael Mussa in Chapter 2 of Martin Feldstein, ed., *American Economic Policy in the 1980s*, University of Chicago Press and NBER, Chicago, 1994, pp. 81–164. One of the comments on the chapter is by Paul Volcker, who was chairman of the Fed from 1979 to 1987.

The Long Run

The next four chapters focus on the long run. In the long run, what dominates is not fluctuations, but growth. So now we need to ask: What determines growth?

Chapter 10

Chapter 10 looks at the facts of growth. It first documents the large increase in output that has taken place in rich countries over the past 50 years. Then, taking a wider look, it shows that, on the scale of human history, such growth is a recent phenomenon. And it is not a universal phenomenon: Some countries are catching up, but many poor countries are suffering from no or low growth.

Chapter 11

Chapter 11 focuses on the role of capital accumulation in growth. It shows that capital accumulation cannot by itself sustain growth, but that it does affect the level of output. A higher saving rate typically leads to lower consumption initially but to more consumption in the long run.

THE CORE

Chapter 12 ▬▬

Chapter 12 turns to technological progress. It shows how, in the long run, the growth rate of an economy is determined by the rate of technological progress. It looks at the role of R&D in generating such progress. It returns to the facts of growth presented in Chapter 10 and shows how to interpret those facts in the light of the theory developed in Chapters 10 to 12.

Chapter 13 ▬▬

Chapter 13 (an optional chapter) looks at various issues raised by technological progress—in the short, the medium, and the long run. It discusses the relation between technological progress, unemployment, and wage inequality in the short run and the medium run. It also discusses the role of institutions in sustaining technological progress and growth in the long run.

The Facts of Growth

ur perceptions of how the economy is doing are often dominated by year-to-year fluctuations in economic activity. A recession leads to gloom, and an expansion leads to optimism. But if we step back to take a look at activity over longer periods—say over many decades—the picture changes. Fluctuations fade. *Growth*—the steady increase in aggregate output over time—dominates the picture.

Figure 10-1 shows the evolution of U.S. GDP (in 2000 dollars) since 1890. The years from 1929 to 1933 correspond to the large decrease in output during the Great Depression, and the years 1980 to 1982 correspond to the largest postwar recession. Note how small these two episodes appear compared to the steady increase in output over the past 100 years. The cartoon makes the same point about growth and fluctuations in an even more obvious way.

We now shift our focus from fluctuations to growth. Put another way, we turn from the study of the determination of output in the *short run and medium run*—where fluctuations dominate—to the determination of output in the *long run*—where growth dominates. Our goal is to understand what determines growth, why some countries are growing while others are not, and why some countries are rich while many others are still poor.

■ Section 10-1 discusses a central measurement issue: how to measure the standard of living.

■ Section 10-2 looks at growth in the United States and other rich countries over the past 50 years.

■ Section 10-3 takes a broader look at growth across both time and space.

■ Section 10-4 gives a primer on growth and introduces the framework that will be developed in the next chapters. ■

CHAPTER 10

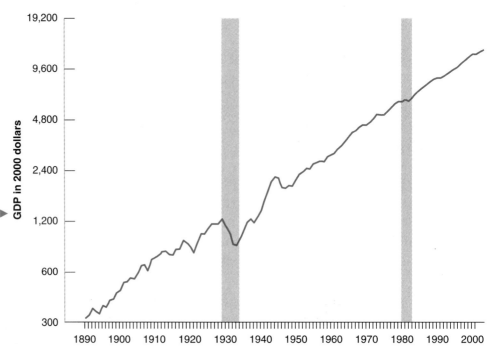

■■■ Figure 10-1

U.S. GDP since 1890

Aggregate U.S. output has increased by a factor of 42 since 1890.

Source: 1890 to 1947: Historical Statistics of the United States; 1948 to 2006: National Income and Product Accounts.

The scale used to measure GDP on the vertical axis in Figure 10-1 is called a logarithmic scale. The defining characteristic of a logarithmic scale is that the same proportional increase in a variable is represented by the same distance on the vertical axis. For more discussion, see Appendix 2 at the end of the book. ▶

▮▯▮▮ Measuring the Standard of Living

The reason we care about growth is that we care about the **standard of living**. Looking across time, we want to know by how much the standard of living has increased. Looking across countries, we want to know how much higher the standard of living is in one country than in another. Thus, the variable we want to focus on and compare either over time or across countries is **output per person** rather than *output* itself.

Output per person is also called *output per capita* (*capita* means "head" in Latin). Given that output and income are always equal, it is also called *income per person*, or *income per capita*. ▶

A practical problem then arises: How do we compare output per person across countries? Countries use different currencies, so output in each country is expressed in terms of its own currency. A natural solution is to use exchange rates: When comparing, say, the output per person of India to the output per person of the United States, we can compute Indian GDP per person in rupees, use the exchange rate to get Indian GDP per person in dollars, and compare it to U.S. GDP per person in dollars. This simple approach will not do, however, for two reasons:

■ Exchange rates can vary a lot (more on this in Chapters 18 to 21). For example, the dollar increased and then decreased in the 1980s by roughly 50% vis-à-vis the currencies of the trading partners of the United States. But, surely, the standard of living in the United States did not increase by 50% and then decrease by 50% compared to the standard of living of its trading partners during the decade. Yet this is the conclusion we would reach if we were to compare GDP per person using exchange rates.

■ The second reason goes beyond fluctuations in exchange rates. In 2006, GDP per person in India, using the current exchange rate, was $790, compared to $44,000 in the United States. Surely no one could live on $790 per year in the United States. But people live on it—admittedly, not very well—in India, where the prices of basic goods—those goods needed for subsistence—are much lower than in the United States. The level of consumption of the average person in India, who consumes mostly basic goods, is not 56 (44,700 divided by 790) times smaller than

Recall a similar discussion in Chapter 1, when looking at output per person in China. ▶

"It's true, Caesar. Rome is declining, but I expect it to pick up in the next quarter."

that of the average person in the United States. This point applies to other countries besides the United States and India: In general, the lower a country's output per person, the lower the prices of food and basic services in that country.

So, when we focus on comparing standards of living, we get more meaningful comparisons by correcting for the two effects we just discussed—variations in exchange rates, and systematic differences in prices across countries. The details of construction are complicated, but the principle is simple: The numbers for GDP—and hence for GDP per person—are constructed using a common set of prices for all countries. Such adjusted real GDP numbers, which you can think of as measures of **purchasing power** across time or across countries, are called **purchasing power parity (PPP)** numbers. Further discussion is given in the Focus box "The Construction of PPP Numbers."

When comparing rich versus poor countries, the differences between PPP numbers and the numbers based on current exchange rates can be very large. Return to the comparison between India and the United States. We saw that, at current exchange rates, the ratio of GDP per person in the United States to GDP per person in India was 56. Using PPP numbers, the ratio is "only" 12. Although this is still a large difference, it is much smaller than the ratio we obtained using current exchange rates. Differences between PPP numbers and numbers based on current exchange rate are typically smaller when making comparisons among rich countries. Based on the numbers we saw in Chapter 1— those numbers were constructed using current exchange rates—GDP per person in the United States in 2006 was equal to 125% of the GDP per person in Germany. Based on PPP numbers, GDP per person in the United States is in fact equal to 138% of GDP per person in Germany. More generally, PPP numbers suggest that the United States still has the highest GDP per person among the world's major countries.

Let me end this section with three remarks before we move on and look at growth:

◄ The bottom line: When comparing standard of living across countries, make sure to use PPP numbers.

- What matters for people's welfare is their consumption rather than their income. One might therefore want to use *consumption per person* rather than output per

Consider two countries—let's call them the United States and Russia, although I am not attempting to fit the characteristics of those two countries very closely:

In the United States, annual consumption per person equals $20,000. People in the United States each buy two goods: Every year, they buy a new car for $10,000 and spend the rest on food. The price of a yearly bundle of food in the United States is $10,000.

In Russia, annual consumption per person equals 60,000 rubles. People there keep their cars for 15 years. The price of a car is 300,000 rubles, so individuals spend on average 20,000 rubles—300,000/15—per year on cars. They buy the same yearly bundle of food as their U.S. counterparts, at a price of 40,000 rubles.

Russian and U.S. cars are of identical quality, and so are Russian and U.S. food. (You may dispute the realism of these assumptions. Whether a car in country X is the same as a car in country Y is very much the type of problem confronting economists constructing PPP measures.) The exchange rate is such that $1 is equal to 30 rubles. What is consumption per person in Russia relative to consumption per person in the United States?

One way to answer is by taking consumption per person in Russia and converting it into dollars, using the exchange rate. Using that method, Russian consumption per person in dollars is $2,000 (60,000 rubles divided by the exchange rate, 30 rubles to the dollar). According to these numbers, consumption per person in Russia is only 10% of U.S. consumption per person.

Does this answer make sense? True, Russian consumers are poorer than U.S. consumers, but food is much cheaper in Russia. A U.S. consumer spending all of his $20,000 on food would buy 2 bundles of food ($20,000/$10,000). A Russian consumer spending all of his 60,000 rubles on food would buy 1.5 bundles of food (60,000 rubles/40,000 rubles). In terms of food bundles, the difference looks much smaller between U.S. and Russian consumption per person. And given that one-half of consumption in the United States and two-thirds of consumption in Russia go to spending on food, this seems like a relevant computation.

Can we improve on our initial answer? Yes. One way is to use the same set of prices for both countries and then measure the quantities of each good consumed in each country using this common set of prices. Suppose we use U.S. prices. In terms of U.S. prices, annual consumption per person in the United States is obviously still $20,000. What is it in Russia? Every year, the average Russian buys approximately 0.07 car (one car every 15 years) and 1 bundle of food. Using U.S. prices—specifically, $10,000 for a car and $10,000 for a bundle of food—gives Russian consumption per person as $[(0.07 \times \$10,000) + (1 \times \$10,000)] = [\$700 + \$10,000] = \$10,700$. So, using U.S. prices to compute consumption in both countries puts annual Russian consumption per person at $10,700/$20,000 = 53.5% of annual U.S. consumption per person, a better estimate of relative standards of living than we obtained using our first method (which put the number at only 10%).

This type of computation—the construction of variables across countries using a common set of prices—underlies PPP estimates. Rather than use U.S. dollar prices, as in our example (why use U.S. rather than Russian or, for that matter, French prices?), these estimates use average prices across countries. These average prices are called *international dollar prices*. Many of the estimates we use in this chapter are the result of an ambitious project known as the "Penn World Tables." (Penn stands for the University of Pennsylvania, where the project is taking place.) Led by three economists—Irving Kravis, Robert Summers, and Alan Heston—over the course of more than 40 years, researchers working on the project have constructed PPP series not only for consumption (as we just did in our example) but, more generally, for GDP and its components, going back to 1950, for most countries in the world.

For more on the construction of PPP numbers, go to the Web site **pwt.econ.upenn.edu.** (In the Penn tables, what is the ratio of Russian PPP GDP per person to U.S. PPP GDP per person?) The IMF and the World Bank also construct their own sets of PPP numbers. The IMF numbers are easily available on the IMF Web site, **www.imf.org**.

---

person as a measure of the standard of living. (This is indeed what we do in the Focus box "The Construction of PPP Numbers.") Because the ratio of consumption to output is rather similar across countries, the ranking of countries is roughly the same whether we use consumption per person or output per person.

■ Thinking about the production side, one may be interested in differences in productivity rather than in differences in the standard of living across countries. In this case, the appropriate measure is *output per worker*—or, even better, *output per hour worked* if the information about total hours worked is available—rather than output per person. Output per person and output per worker (or per hour) will differ to the extent that the ratio of the number of workers (or hours) to

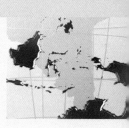

Economists often take for granted that higher output per person means higher utility and increased happiness. The evidence on direct measures of happiness, however, points to a more complex picture.

Looking at Growth and Happiness across Countries

Figure 1 shows the results of a study of happiness in 81 countries in the late 1990s. In each country, a sample of people were asked two questions. The first one was: "Taking all things together, would you say you are very happy, quite happy, not very happy, not at all happy?" The second was: "All things considered, how satisfied are you with your life as a whole these days?" with answers on a scale ranging from 1 (dissatisfied) to 10 (satisfied). The measure on the vertical axis in Figure 1 is constructed as the average of the percentage of people declaring themselves very happy or happy in answer to the first question and the percentage of people answering 6 or more to the second question. The measure of income per person on the horizontal axis is the level of income per person, measured at PPP prices, in 1999 dollars. (The levels of income per person used in the figure were constructed by the World Bank.) The figure suggests three conclusions.

First, most of the countries with very low happiness levels are the eastern European countries, which in the 1990s were suffering from the collapse of the communist regimes and the difficult transition to capitalism.

Second, and leaving those countries aside, there appears to be a positive relation between happiness and the level of income per person. Happiness is lower in poor countries than in rich ones.

Third, looking at rich countries—the countries with PPP output per person above $20,000 (in 1999 dollars), there appears to be little relation between the level of income per person and happiness. (To see that, cover the left side of the figure, and just look at the right side.) For this set of countries, higher income per person does not seem to be associated with greater happiness.

Looking at Growth and Happiness Over Time

One may reasonably argue that comparing happiness across countries is difficult. Different cultures may have different notions of what happiness is. Some countries may be chronically happier or unhappier than others. For this reason, it may be more informative to look at what happens to happiness over time in a given country. This can be done for the United States, where the

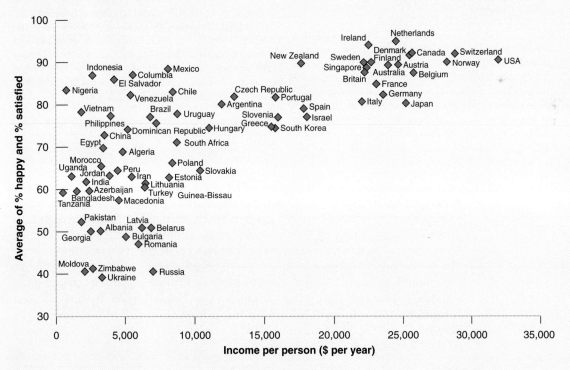

Figure 1 *Happiness and Income per Person across Countries*

Source: "World Values Survey, 1999–2000 Wave."

Continued

Table 1	Distribution of Happiness in the United States Over Time (percent)	
	1975	1996
Very happy	32	31
Pretty happy	55	58
Not too happy	13	11

Table 2	Distribution of Happiness in the United States across Income Groups (percent)	
	Top Quarter	Bottom Quarter
Very happy	37	16
Pretty happy	57	53
Not too happy	6	31

General Social Survey has asked the following question since the early 1970s: "Taken all together, how would you say things are these days—would you say you are very happy, pretty happy, or not too happy?" Table 1 gives the proportion of answers in each category given in 1975 and in 1996.

The numbers in the table are striking. During those 21 years, output per person increased by more than 60%, but there was basically no change in the distribution of happiness. In other words, a higher standard of living was not associated with an increase in self-reported happiness. Evidence from Gallup polls over the past 60 years confirms the finding: The proportion of people defining themselves as "very happy" is the same as it was in the early 1950s.

Looking at Growth and Happiness across Individuals

Do the conclusions in the preceding section mean that "money" (more properly "income") does not bring happiness? The answer is no. If one looks across individuals at any point in time, rich people are likely to report themselves as happier than poor people. This is shown in Table 2, which is again constructed using the answers to the General Social Survey and gives the distribution of happiness for different income groups in the United States in 1998.

The results are again striking: The proportion of "very happy" people is much higher among the rich (the people in the top quarter of the income distribution) than among the poor (the people in the bottom quarter of the income distribution). And the reverse holds for the proportion of "not too happy" people: The proportion is much lower among the rich than among the poor.

What conclusions can we draw from all this evidence? At low levels of output per person, say up to $20,000 or about half of the current U.S. level, increases in output per person lead to increases in happiness. At higher levels, however, the relation appears to be much weaker. Happiness appears to depend more on people's relative incomes. If this is indeed the case, it has important implications for economic policy, at least in rich countries. Growth, and therefore policies that stimulate growth, may not be the key to happiness.

Source: Richard Layard, Happiness. Lessons from a New Science, *Penguin Books, New York, 2005.*

population differs across countries. Most of the difference between output per person in the United States and in Germany we noted earlier comes, for example, from differences in hours worked per person rather than from differences in productivity. Put another way, German workers are about as productive as their U.S. counterparts. However, they work fewer hours, so their standard of living is lower.

■ The reason we ultimately care about the standard of living is presumably that we care about happiness. One may therefore ask the obvious question: Does a higher standard of living lead to greater happiness? The answer is given in the Focus box "Growth and Happiness." The answer: Yes, at least for countries with output per person below $20,000, or roughly half of the U.S. level. The relation appears much weaker, however, for richer countries.

10.2 Growth in Rich Countries since 1950

In this section, let's start by looking at growth in rich countries since 1950. In the next section, we shall look further back in time and across a wider range of countries.

The Long Run **The Core**

Table 10-1	The Evolution of Output per Person in Four Rich Countries since 1950			
	Annual Growth Rate Output per Person (%)	**Real Output per Person (2000 dollars)**		
	1950–2004	1950	2004	2004/1950
France	3.3	5,920	26,168	4.4
Japan	4.6	2,187	24,661	11.2
United Kingdom	2.7	8,091	26,762	3.3
United States	2.6	11,233	36,098	3.2
Average	3.5	6,875	28,422	3.9

Source: Penn World Tables (**pwt.econ.upenn.edu**). The average in the last line is a simple (unweighted) average.

Table 10-1 shows the evolution of output per person (GDP, measured at PPP prices, divided by population) for France, Japan, the United Kingdom, and the United States, since 1950. I have chosen these four countries not only because they are some of the world's major economic powers but because what has happened to them is broadly representative of what has happened in other advanced countries over the past half century or so.

Table 10-1 yields two main conclusions:

- There has been a large increase in output per person.
- There has been convergence of output per person across countries.

Let's look at each of these points in turn.

The Large Increase in the Standard of Living since 1950

Look at the last column of Table 10-1. Since 1950, output per person has increased by a factor of 3.2 in the United States, by a factor of 4.4 in France, and by a factor of 11.2 in Japan.

These numbers show what is sometimes called the *force of compounding*. In a different context, you have probably heard how saving even a little while you are young will build to a large amount by the time you retire. For example, if the interest rate is 4.6% per year, an investment of $1, with the proceeds reinvested every year, will grow to about $11 in 54 years ($[1 + 0.046]^{54} = 11.3$ dollars). The same logic applies to growth rates. The average annual growth rate in Japan over the period 1950 to 2004 was equal to 4.6%. This high growth rate has led to an 11-fold increase in real output per person in Japan over the period.

◀ Most of the increase in Japan took place before 1990. Since then, Japan has been in a prolonged economic slump, with very low growth. More on this in Chapter 22.

Clearly, a better understanding of growth, if it leads to the design of policies that stimulate growth, can have a very large effect on the standard of living. Suppose we could find a policy measure that permanently increased the growth rate by 1% per year. This would lead, after 40 years, to a standard of living 48% higher than it would have been without the policy—a substantial difference.

◀ $1.01^{40} - 1 = 1.48 - 1 = 48\%$.

◀ Unfortunately, policy measures with such magical results have proven difficult to discover!

The Convergence of Output per Person since 1950

The second and third columns of Table 10-1 show that the levels of output per person have converged (become closer) over time: The numbers for output per person are much more similar in 2004 than they were in 1950. Put another way, those countries that were behind have grown faster, reducing the gap between them and the United States.

Figure 10-2

Growth Rate of GDP per Person since 1950 versus GDP per Person in 1950, OECD Countries

Countries with lower levels of output per person in 1950 have typically grown faster.

Source: Penn World Tables. The Czech Republic, Hungary, and Poland are not included because of missing data.

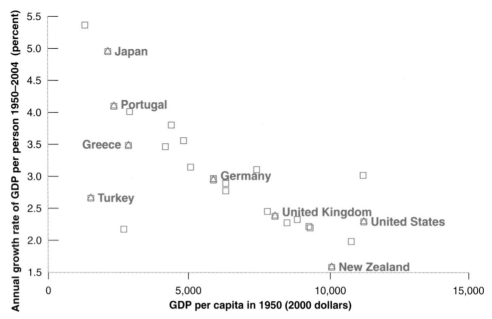

From the Focus box in Chapter 1: The OECD (which stands for Organisation for Economic Co-operation and Development) is an international organization that includes most of the world's rich economies. The complete list is given in Chapter 1.

In 1950, output per person in the United States was roughly twice the level of output per person in France and more than four times the level of output per person in Japan. From the perspective of Europe or Japan, the United States was seen as the land of plenty, where everything was bigger and better. Today these perceptions have faded, and the numbers explain why. Using PPP numbers, U.S. output per person is still the highest, but, in 2004, it was only 40% above the average output per person in the other three countries; a much smaller difference than in the 1950s.

This **convergence** of levels of output per person across countries is not specific to the four countries we are looking at. It extends to the set of OECD countries. This is shown in Figure 10-2, which plots the average annual growth rate of output per person since 1950 against the initial level of output per person in 1950 for the set of countries that are members of the OECD today. There is a clear negative relation between the initial level of output per person and the growth rate since 1950: Countries that were behind in 1950 have typically grown faster. The relation is not perfect: Turkey, which had roughly the same low level of output per person as Japan in 1950, has had a growth rate equal to only about half that of Japan. But the relation is clearly there.

Some economists have pointed to a problem in graphs like Figure 10-2. By looking at the set of countries that are members of the OECD today, what we have done in effect is to look at a club of economic winners: OECD membership is not officially based on economic success, but economic success is surely an important determinant of membership. But when you look at a club whose membership is based on economic success, you will find that those who came from behind had the fastest growth: This is precisely why they made it into the club! The finding of convergence could come in part from the way we selected the countries in the first place.

So a better way of looking at convergence is to define the set of countries we look at not on the basis of where they are today—as we did in Figure 10-2 by taking today's OECD members—but on the basis of where they were in, say, 1950. For example, we can look at all countries that had an output per person of at least one-fourth of U.S. output per person in 1950 and then look for convergence within that group. It turns out that most of the countries in that group have indeed converged, and therefore convergence is not solely an OECD phenomenon. However, a few countries—Uruguay,

Argentina, and Venezuela among them—have not converged. In 1950, those three countries had roughly the same output per person as France. In 2004, they had fallen far behind; their level of output per person stood only between one-fourth and one-half of the French level.

10-3 A Broader Look at Growth across Time and Space

In the previous section, we focused on growth over the past 50 years in rich countries. Let's now put this in context by looking at the evidence over both a much longer time span and a wider set of countries.

Looking at Growth across Two Millennia

Has output per person in the currently rich economies always grown at rates similar to the growth rates in Table 10-1? No. Estimates of growth are clearly harder to construct as we look further back in time. But there is agreement among economic historians about the main evolutions over the past 2,000 years.

From the end of the Roman Empire to roughly the year 1500, there was essentially no growth of output per person in Europe: Most workers were employed in agriculture, in which there was little technological progress. Because agriculture's share of output was so large, inventions with applications outside agriculture could contribute little to overall production and output. Although there was some output growth, a roughly proportional increase in population led to roughly constant output per person.

This period of stagnation of output per person is often called the *Malthusian era*. Thomas Robert Malthus, an English economist, argued at the end of the 18th century that this proportional increase in output and population was not a coincidence. Any increase in output, he argued, would lead to a decrease in mortality, leading to an increase in population until output per person was back to its initial level. Europe was in a **Malthusian trap**, unable to increase its output per person.

Eventually, Europe was able to escape that trap. From about 1500 to 1700, growth of output per person turned positive, but it was still small—only around 0.1% per year. It then increased to 0.2% per year from 1700 to 1820. Starting with the Industrial Revolution, growth rates increased, but from 1820 to 1950, the growth rate of output per person in the United States was still only 1.5% per year. On the scale of human history, therefore, sustained growth of output per person—especially the high growth rates we have seen since 1950—is definitely a recent phenomenon.

Looking at Growth across Many Countries

We have seen how output per person has converged among OECD countries. But what about other countries? Are the poorest countries also growing faster? Are they converging toward the United States, even if they are still far behind?

The answer is given in Figure 10-3, which plots, for 70 countries, the annual growth rate of output per person since 1960 against output per person in 1960.

The striking feature of Figure 10-3 is that there is no clear pattern: It is not the case that, in general, countries that were behind in 1960 have grown faster. Some have, but clearly many have not.

The cloud of points in Figure 10-3 hides, however, a number of interesting patterns that appear when we put countries into different groups. Note that we have used different symbols in the figure: The diamonds represent OECD countries, the squares

> ◄ The numbers for 1950 are missing for too many countries to use 1950 as the initial year, as we did in Figure 10-2.

Figure 10-3

Growth Rate of GDP per Person since 1960 versus GDP per Person in 1960 (2000 dollars) for 70 Countries

There is no clear relation between the growth rate of output per person since 1960 and the level of output per person in 1960.

Source: See Figure 10-2.

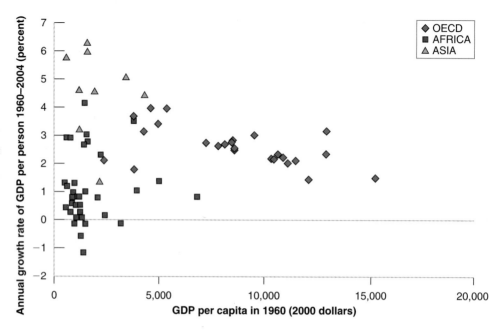

represent African countries, and the triangles represent Asian countries. Looking at patterns by groups yields three main conclusions:

1. The picture for the OECD countries (that is, for the rich countries) is much the same as in Figure 10-2, which looks at a slightly longer period of time (from 1950 onward rather than from 1960). Nearly all start at high levels of output per person (say, at least one-third of the U.S. level in 1960), and there is clear evidence of convergence.

2. Convergence is also visible for most Asian countries: All the countries with growth rates above 4% over the period are in Asia. Japan was the first to grow and now has the highest level of output per person in Asia. But a number of other Asian countries (represented by triangles) are trailing it closely. Starting in the 1960s, four countries—Singapore, Taiwan, Hong Kong, and South Korea, a group of countries sometimes called the **four tigers**—started catching up quickly. In 1960, their average output per person was about 16% of the U.S. level; by 2004, it had increased to 65% of the U.S. level. More recently, the major story has been China—both because of its very high growth rates and because of its sheer size. Over the period, growth of output per person in China has been 5.6%. But because it started very low, its output per person is still only about 20% of the U.S. level. (Economies with high growth rates but low output per person are often called **emerging economies,** a term I use in the remainder of the book.)

3. The picture is very different, however, for African countries. Convergence is certainly not the rule in Africa. Most African countries (represented by squares) were very poor in 1960, and many have had negative growth of output per person—an absolute decline in their standard of living—since then. Even in the absence of major wars, output per person has declined at 1.1% per year in Madagascar (the lowest square in the figure). Output per person in Niger stands at 60% of its 1960 level.

Looking further back in time, a picture emerges. For much of the first millennium, and until the fifteenth century, China probably had the world's highest level of output per person. For a couple centuries, leadership moved to the cities of northern Italy. But until the nineteenth century, differences across countries were typically much smaller than they are today. Starting in the nineteenth century, a number of countries, first in western Europe and then in North and South America, started growing faster than others. Since then, a number of other countries, most notably in Asia, have started growing fast and are converging. Many others, mainly in Africa, are not.

Our main focus in this chapter and the next is primarily on growth in rich and emerging countries. We do not take on some of the wider challenges raised by the facts we have just seen, such as why growth of output per person started in earnest in the nineteenth century or why Africa has so far failed to achieve steady growth. Doing so would take us too far into economic history and *development economics*. But these facts put into perspective the two basic facts we discussed earlier when looking at the OECD: Neither growth nor convergence is a historical necessity.

10.4 Thinking about Growth: A Primer

To think about growth, economists use a framework developed originally by Robert Solow, from MIT, in the late 1950s. The framework has proven sturdy and useful, and we will use it here. This section provides an introduction. Chapters 11 and 12 provide a more detailed analysis, first of the role of capital accumulation and then of the role of technological progress in the process of growth.

The Aggregate Production Function

The starting point of any theory of growth must be an **aggregate production function**, a specification of the relation between aggregate output and the inputs in production.

The aggregate production function we introduced in Chapter 6 to study the determination of output in the short run and the medium run took a particularly simple form. Output was simply proportional to the amount of labor used by firms—specifically, it was proportional to the number of workers employed by firms [equation (6.2)]. As long as our focus was on fluctuations in output and employment, the assumption was acceptable. But now that our focus has shifted to growth, that assumption will no longer do: It implies that output per worker is constant, ruling out growth (or at least growth of output per worker) altogether. It is time to relax it. From now on, we will assume that there are two inputs—capital and labor—and that the relation between aggregate output and the two inputs is given by

$$Y = F(K, N) \tag{10.1}$$

As before, Y is aggregate output. K is capital—the sum of all the machines, plants, and office buildings in the economy. N is labor—the number of workers in the economy. The function F, which tells us how much output is produced for given quantities of capital and labor, is the *aggregate production function*.

This way of thinking about aggregate production is an improvement on our treatment in Chapter 6. But it should be clear that it is still a dramatic simplification of reality. Surely, machines and office buildings play very different roles in production and should be treated as separate inputs. Surely, workers with Ph.D.s are different from high school dropouts; yet by constructing the labor input as simply the *number* of workers in the economy, we treat all workers as identical. We will relax some of these simplifications later. For the time being, equation (10.1), which emphasizes the role of both labor and capital in production, will do.

The next step must be to think about where the aggregate production function, F, which relates output to the two inputs, comes from. In other words, what determines how much output can be produced for given quantities of capital and labor? The answer: the **state of technology**. A country with more advanced technology will

As briefly discussed in Chapter 1, in recent years, many African countries have grown at higher rates than they did in the past. It is much too early to conclude that they are on a steady growth path.

◄ The distinction between *growth theory* and *development economics* is fuzzy. A rough distinction: Growth theory takes many of the institutions of a country (for example, its legal system, its form of government) as given. Development economics asks what institutions are needed to sustain steady growth and how they can be put in place.

◄ Solow's article "A Contribution to the Theory of Economic Growth," appeared in 1956. Solow was awarded the Nobel Prize in 1987 for his work on growth.

The aggregate production function is

$$Y = F(K, N)$$

Aggregate output, Y, depends on the aggregate capital stock, K, and aggregate employment, N.

The function, F, depends on the state of technology. The higher the state of technology, the higher $F(K, N)$ for a given K and a given N.

produce more output from the same quantities of capital and labor than will an economy with primitive technology.

How should we define the *state of technology*? Should we think of it as the list of blueprints defining both the range of products that can be produced in the economy and the techniques available to produce them? Or should we think of it more broadly, including not only the list of blueprints but also the way the economy is organized—from the internal organization of firms, to the system of laws and the quality of their enforcement, to the political system, and so on? In Chapters 11 and 12, I will have in mind the narrower definition—the set of blueprints. In Chapter 13, however, I will consider the broader definition and return to what we know about the role of the other factors, from legal institutions to the quality of government.

Returns to Scale and Returns to Factors

Now that we have introduced the aggregate production function, the next question is: What restrictions can we reasonably impose on this function?

Consider first a thought experiment in which we double both the number of workers and the amount of capital in the economy. What do you expect will happen to output? A reasonable answer is that output will double as well: In effect, we have cloned the original economy, and the clone economy can produce output in the same way as the original economy. This property is called **constant returns to scale**: If the scale of operation is doubled—that is, if the quantities of capital and labor are doubled—then output will also double:

$$2Y = F(2K, 2N)$$

Or, more generally, for any number x (this will be useful later on),

$$xY = F(xK, xN) \qquad (10.2)$$

Constant returns to scale:
$F(xK, xN) = xY.$

We have just looked at what happens to production when *both* capital and labor are increased. Let's now ask a different question: What should we expect to happen if *only one* of the two inputs in the economy—say capital—is increased?

Output here is secretarial services. The two inputs are secretaries and computers. The production function relates secretarial services to the number of secretaries and the number of computers.

Surely output will increase. That part is clear. But it is also reasonable to assume that the same increase in capital will lead to smaller and smaller increases in output as the level of capital increases. In other words, if there is little capital to start with, a little more capital will help a lot. If there is a lot of capital to start with, a little more capital may make little difference. Why? Think, for example, of a secretarial pool, composed of a given number of secretaries. Think of capital as computers. The introduction of the first computer will substantially increase the pool's production because some of the most time-consuming tasks can now be done automatically by the computer. As the number of computers increases and more secretaries in the pool get their own computers, production will further increase, although perhaps by less per additional computer than was the case when the first one was introduced. Once each and every secretary has a PC, increasing the number of computers further is unlikely to increase production very much, if at all. Additional computers might simply remain unused and left in their shipping boxes and lead to no increase in output.

Even under constant returns to scale, there are decreasing returns to each factor, keeping the other factor constant:

- There are decreasing returns to capital: Given labor, increases in capital lead to smaller and smaller increases in output.
- There are decreasing returns to labor: Given capital, increases in labor lead to smaller and smaller increases in output.

We shall refer to the property that increases in capital lead to smaller and smaller increases in output as **decreasing returns to capital** (a property that will be familiar to those who have taken a course in microeconomics).

A similar argument applies to the other input, labor. Increases in labor, given capital, lead to smaller and smaller increases in output. (Return to our example and think of what happens as you increase the number of secretaries for a given number of computers.) There are **decreasing returns to labor** as well.

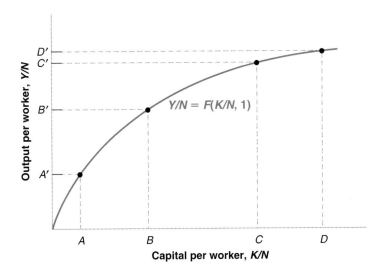

Figure 10-4 ▨

Output and Capital per Worker

Increases in capital per worker lead to smaller and smaller increases in output per worker.

Output per Worker and Capital per Worker

The production function we have written down, together with the assumption of constant returns to scale, implies that there is a simple relation between *output per worker* and *capital per worker*. To see this, set $x = 1/N$ in equation (10.2), so that

$$\frac{Y}{N} = F\left(\frac{K}{N}, \frac{N}{N}\right) = F\left(\frac{K}{N}, 1\right) \tag{10.3}$$

Note that *Y/N* is output per worker, and *K/N* is capital per worker. So equation (10.3) says that the amount of output per worker depends on the amount of capital per worker. This relation between output per worker and capital per worker will play a central role in the following text, so let's look at it more closely.

The relation is drawn in Figure 10-4. Output per worker *(Y/N)* is measured on the vertical axis, and capital per worker *(K/N)* is measured on the horizontal axis. The relation between the two is given by the upward-sloping curve. As capital per worker increases, so does output per worker. Note that the curve is drawn so that increases in capital lead to smaller and smaller increases in output. This follows from the property that there are *decreasing returns to capital:* At point *A*, where capital per worker is low, an increase in capital per worker, represented by the horizontal distance, *AB*, leads to an increase in output per worker equal to the vertical distance *A′B′*. At point *C*, where capital per worker is larger, the same increase in capital per worker, represented by the horizontal distance, *CD* (where the distance *CD* is equal to the distance *AB*), leads to a much smaller increase in output per worker, only *C′D′*. This is just like our secretarial pool example, where additional computers had less and less impact on total output.

> Make sure you understand what is behind the algebra. Suppose capital and the number of workers both double. What happens to output per ◄ worker?

> Increases in capital per worker lead to smaller and smaller increases in output per worker as the level of capital per ◄ worker increases.

The Sources of Growth

We are now ready to return to our basic question: Where does growth come from? Why does output per worker—or output per person, if we assume that the ratio of workers to the population as a whole remains constant—go up over time? Equation (10.3) gives a first answer:

■ Increases in output per worker *(Y/N)* can come from increases in capital per worker *(K/N)*. This is the relation we just looked at in Figure 10-4. As *K/N* increases—that is, as we move to the right on the horizontal axis—*Y/N* increases.

> Increases in capital per worker: movements along the production ◄ tion function.

The Effects of an Improvement in the State of Technology

An improvement in technology shifts the production function up, leading to an increase in output per worker for a given level of capital per worker.

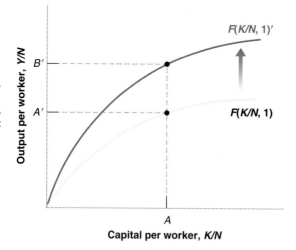

Improvements in the state of technology shift the production function up. ▶

■ Increases in output per worker can also come from improvements in the state of technology that shift the production function, F, and lead to more output per worker given capital per worker. This is shown in Figure 10-5. An improvement in the state of technology shifts the production function up, from $F(K/N, 1)$ to $F(K/N, 1)'$. For a given level of capital per worker, the improvement in technology leads to an increase in output per worker. For example, for the level of capital per worker corresponding to point A, output per worker increases from A' to B'. (To go back to our secretarial pool example, a reallocation of tasks within the pool may lead to better division of labor and an increase in the output per secretary.)

Hence, we can think of growth as coming from **capital accumulation** and from **technological progress**—the improvement in the state of technology. We will see, however, that these two factors play very different roles in the growth process:

■ Capital accumulation *by itself* cannot sustain growth. A formal argument will have to wait until Chapter 11. But you can already see the intuition behind this from Figure 10-5. Because of decreasing returns to capital, sustaining a steady increase in output per worker will require larger and larger increases in the level of capital per worker. At some stage, the economy will be unwilling or unable to save and invest enough to further increase capital. At that stage, output per worker will stop growing.

   Does this mean that an economy's **saving rate**—the proportion of income that is saved—is irrelevant? No. It is true that a higher saving rate cannot permanently increase the *growth rate* of output. But a higher saving rate can sustain a higher *level* of output. Let me state this in a slightly different way. Take two economies that differ only in their saving rates. The two economies will grow at the same rate, but at any point in time, the economy with the higher saving rate will have a higher level of output per person than the other. How this happens, how much the saving rate affects the level of output, and whether a country such as the United States (which has a very low saving rate) should try to increase its saving rate are topics we take up in Chapter 11.

■ Sustained growth requires sustained technological progress. This really follows from the previous proposition: Given that the two factors that can lead to an increase in output are capital accumulation and technological progress, if capital accumulation cannot sustain growth forever, then technological progress must be the key to growth. And it is. We will see in Chapter 12 that the economy's rate of growth of output per person is eventually determined by its rate of technological progress. This is very important. It means that in the long run, an economy that sustains a higher rate of technological progress will eventually overtake all other economies. This, of course, raises yet another question: What determines the rate of technological progress? Recall the two definitions of the state of technology we discussed earlier: a narrow definition, namely the set of blueprints available to the economy; and a broader definition, which captures how the economy is organized, from the nature of institutions to the role of the government. What we know about the determinants of technological progress narrowly defined—the role of fundamental and applied research, the role of patent laws, the role of education and training—will be taken up in Chapter 12. The role of broader factors will be discussed in Chapter 13.

◀ Following up on the distinction introduced earlier between growth theory and development economics: Chapter 12 will deal with technological progress from the viewpoint of growth theory, and Chapter 13 will come closer to development economics.

Summary

- Over long periods, fluctuations in output are dwarfed by growth—the steady increase of aggregate output over time.
- When looking at growth in four rich countries (France, Japan, the United Kingdom, and the United States) since 1950, two main facts emerge:

  1. All four countries have experienced strong growth and a large increase in the standard of living. Growth from 1950 to 2004 increased real output per person by a factor of 3.2 in the United States and by a factor of 11.2 in Japan.
  2. The levels of output per person across the four countries have converged over time. Put another way, countries that were behind have grown faster, reducing the gap between them and the current leader, the United States.

- When looking at the evidence across a broader set of countries and a longer period, the following facts emerge:

  1. On the scale of human history, sustained output growth is a recent phenomenon.
  2. The convergence of levels of output per person is not a worldwide phenomenon. Many Asian countries are rapidly catching up, but most African countries have both very low levels of output per person and low growth rates.

- To think about growth, economists start from an aggregate production function, relating aggregate output to two factors of production: capital and labor. How much output is produced, given these inputs, depends on the state of technology.
- Under the assumption of constant returns, the aggregate production function implies that increases in output per worker can come either from increases in capital per worker or from improvements in the state of technology.
- Capital accumulation by itself cannot permanently sustain growth of output per person. Nevertheless, how much a country saves is very important because the saving rate determines the *level* of output per person, if not its growth rate.
- Sustained growth of output per person is ultimately due to technological progress. Perhaps the most important question in growth theory is what determines technological progress.

Key Terms

- growth, 227
- logarithmic scale, 228
- standard of living, 228,
- output per person, 228
- purchasing power, purchasing power parity (PPP), 229
- convergence, 234
- Malthusian trap, 235
- four tigers, 236
- emerging economies, 236
- aggregate production function, 237
- state of technology, 237
- constant returns to scale, 238
- decreasing returns to capital, 238
- decreasing returns to labor, 238
- capital accumulation, 240
- technological progress, 240
- saving rate, 240

Questions and Problems

Quick Check

1. Using the information in this chapter, label each of the following statements true, false, or uncertain. Explain briefly.

a. On a logarithmic scale, a variable that increases at 5% per year will move along an upward-sloping line with a slope of 0.05.

b. The price of food is higher in poor countries than it is in rich countries.

c. Evidence suggests that happiness in rich countries increases with output per person.

d. In virtually all the countries of the world, output per person is converging to the level of output per person in the United States.

e. For about 1,000 years after the fall of the Roman Empire, there was essentially no growth in output per person in Europe, because any increase in output led to a proportional increase in population.

f. Capital accumulation does not affect the level of output in the long run; only technological progress does.

g. The aggregate production function is a relation between output on one hand and labor and capital on the other.

2. Assume that the average consumer in Mexico and the average consumer in the United States buy the quantities and pay the prices indicated in the following table:

	Food		Transportation Services	
	Price	Quantity	Price	Quantity
Mexico	10 pesos	800	30 pesos	300
United States	$2	2,000	$3	3,000

a. Compute U.S. consumption per capita in dollars.

b. Compute Mexican consumption per capita in pesos.

c. Suppose that 1 dollar is worth 10 pesos. Compute Mexico's consumption per capita in dollars.

d. Using the purchasing power parity method and U.S. prices, compute Mexican consumption per capita in dollars.

e. Under each method, how much lower is the standard of living in Mexico than in the United States? Does the choice of method make a difference?

3. Consider the production function $Y = \sqrt{K}\sqrt{N}$.

a. Compute output when $K = 49$ and $N = 81$.

b. If both capital and labor double, what happens to output?

c. Is this production function characterized by constant returns to scale? Explain.

d. Write this production function as a relation between output per worker and capital per worker.

e. Let $K/N = 4$. What is Y/N? Now double K/N to 8. Does Y/N double as a result?

f. Does the relation between output per worker and capital per worker exhibit constant returns to scale?

g. Is your answer in (f) the same as your answer in (c)? Why or why not?

h. Plot the relation between output per worker and capital per worker. Does it have the same general shape as the relation in Figure 10-4? Explain.

Dig Deeper

4. The growth rates of capital and output

Consider the production function given in problem 3. Assume that N is constant and equal to 1. Note that if $z = x^a$, then $g_z \approx a\, g_x$, where g_z and g_x are the growth rates of z and x.

a. Given the growth approximation here, derive the relation between the growth rate of output and the growth rate of capital.

b. Suppose we want to achieve output growth equal to 2% per year. What is the required rate of growth of capital?

c. In (b), what happens to the ratio of capital to output over time?

d. Is it possible to sustain output growth of 2% forever in this economy? Why or why not?

5. Between 1950 and 1973, France, Germany, and Japan all experienced growth rates that were at least 2 percentage points higher than those in the United States. Yet the most important technological advances of that period were made in the United States. How can this be?

Explore Further

6. Convergence in two sets of countries

Go to the Web site containing the Penn World Table (**pwt.econ.upenn.edu**) and collect data on real GDP per person (chained series) from 1951 to the most recent year available for the United States, France, Belgium, Italy, Argentina, Venezuela, Chad, and Madagascar.

a. Define for each country for each year the ratio of its real GDP to that of the United States for that year (so that this ratio will be equal to 1 for the United States for all years).

b. In one graph, plot the ratios for France, Belgium, and Italy over the period for which you have data. Does your graph support the notion of convergence among France, Belgium, Italy, and the United States?

c. Draw a graph with the ratios for Argentina, Venezuela, Chad, and Madagascar. Does your new graph support the notion of convergence among Argentina, Venezuela, Chad, Madagascar, and the United States?

7. Convergence between Japan and the United States since 1950

Go to the Web site containing the Penn World Table (**pwt.econ.upenn.edu**) and collect data on the annual growth rate of GDP per person for the United States and Japan from 1951 to the most recent year available. In addition, collect the numbers for real GDP per person (chained series) for the United States and Japan in 1973.

a. Compute the average annual growth rates of GDP per person for the United States and Japan for three time periods: 1951 to 1973, 1974 to the most recent year available, and 1991 to the most recent year available. Did the level of real output per person in Japan tend to converge to the level of real output per person in the United States in each of these three periods? Explain.

b. Suppose that in every year since 1973, Japan and the United States had each achieved their average annual growth rates for the period 1951 to 1973. How would real GDP per person compare in Japan and the United States today (i.e., in the most recent year available in the Penn World Table)?

8. *Growth successes and failures*

   *Go to the Web site containing the Penn World Table (***pwt. econ.upenn.edu***) and collect data on real GDP per capita (chained series) for 1970 for all available countries. Do the same for a recent year of data, say one year before the most recent year available in the Penn World Table. (If you choose the most recent year available, the Penn World Table may not have the data for some countries relevant to this question.)*

   a. Rank the countries according to GDP per person in 1970. List the countries with the 10 highest levels of GDP per person in 1970. Are there any surprises?

b. Carry out the analysis in part (a) for the most recent year for which you collected data. Has the composition of the 10 richest countries changed since 1970?

c. For each of the 10 countries you listed in part (b), divide the recent level of GDP per capita by the level in 1970. Which of these countries has had the greatest proportional increase in GDP per capita since 1970?

d. Carry out the exercise in part (c) for all the countries for which you have data. Which country has had the highest proportional increase in GDP per capita since 1970? Which country had the smallest proportional increase? What fraction of countries have had negative growth since 1970?

e. Do a brief Internet search on either the country from part (c) with the greatest increase in GDP per capita or the country from part (d) with the smallest increase. Can you ascertain any reasons for the economic success, or lack of it, for this country?

We invite you to visit the Blanchard page on the Prentice Hall Web site, at:

www.prenhall.com/blanchard

for this chapter's World Wide Web exercises.

Further Readings

■ Brad deLong has a number of fascinating articles on growth on his Web page (**http://econ161.berkeley.edu/**). Read, in particular, "Berkeley Faculty Lunch Talk: Themes of 20th Century Economic History," which covers many of the themes of this chapter.

■ A broad presentation of facts about growth is given by Angus Maddison in *The World Economy. A Millenium Perspective*, OECD, Paris, 2001. The associated site

www.theworldeconomy.org has a large number of facts and data on growth over the past two millenia.

■ Chapter 3 in *Productivity and American Leadership* by William Baumol, Sue Anne Batey Blackman, and Edward Wolff (MIT Press, Cambridge, MA, 1989) gives a vivid description of how life has been transformed by growth in the United States since the mid-1880s.

Saving, Capital Accumulation, and Output

Since 1950, the U.S. **saving rate**—the ratio of saving to GDP—has averaged only 17%, compared to 24% in Germany and 30% in Japan. Can this explain why the U.S. growth rate has been lower than the rates in most other OECD countries in the past 50 years? Would increasing the U.S. saving rate lead to sustained higher U.S. growth in the future?

I already gave the basic answer to these questions at the end of Chapter 10: The answer is no. Over long periods—an important qualification to which we will return—an economy's growth rate does not depend on its saving rate. It does not appear that lower U.S. growth in the past 50 years comes primarily from a low saving rate. Nor should we expect that an increase in the saving rate will lead to sustained higher U.S. growth.

This conclusion does not mean, however, that we should not be concerned about the low U.S. saving rate. Even if the saving rate does not permanently affect the growth rate, it does affect the level of output and the standard of living. An increase in the saving rate would lead to higher growth for some time, and eventually to a higher standard of living in the United States.

This chapter focuses on the effects of the saving rate on the level and the growth rate of output:

- Sections 11-1 and 11-2 look at the interactions between output and capital accumulation, and the effects of the saving rate.

- Section 11-3 plugs in numbers to give a better sense of the magnitudes involved.

- Section 11-4 extends the discussion to take into account not only physical, but also human capital. ■

At the center of the determination of output in the long run are two relations between output and capital:

■ The amount of capital determines the amount of output being produced.
■ The amount of output determines the amount of saving and, in turn, the amount of capital accumulated over time.

Together, these two relations, which are represented in Figure 11-1, determine the evolution of output and capital over time. The green arrow captures the first relation, from capital to output. The blue and purple arrows capture the two parts of the second relation, from output to saving and investment, and from investment to the change in the capital stock. Let's look at each relation in turn.

The Effects of Capital on Output

We started discussing the first of these two relations, the effect of capital on output, in Section 10-3. There we introduced the aggregate production function and you saw that, under the assumption of constant returns to scale, we can write the following relation between output and capital per worker:

$$\frac{Y}{N} = F\left(\frac{K}{N}, 1\right)$$

Output per worker, Y/N, is an increasing function of capital per worker, K/N. Under the assumption of decreasing returns to capital, the effect of a given increase in capital per worker on output per worker decreases as the ratio of capital per worker gets larger. When capital per worker is already very high, further increases in capital per worker have only a small effect on output per worker.

To simplify notation, we will rewrite this relation between output and capital per worker simply as

$$\frac{Y}{N} = f\left(\frac{K}{N}\right)$$

where the function f represents the same relation between output and capital per worker as the function F:

$$f\left(\frac{K}{N}\right) \equiv F\left(\frac{K}{N}, 1\right)$$

Suppose, for example, that the function F has the "double square root" form, $F(K, N) = \sqrt{K}\sqrt{N}$, so

$$Y = \sqrt{K}\sqrt{N}$$

Divide both sides by N, so

$$Y/N = \sqrt{K}\sqrt{N}/N$$

Note that $\sqrt{N}/N = \sqrt{N}/(\sqrt{N}\sqrt{N}) = 1/\sqrt{N}$. Replacing in the preceding equation:

$$Y/N = \sqrt{K}/\sqrt{N} = \sqrt{K/N}$$

So, in this case, the function f giving the relation between ▶ output per worker and capital per worker is simply the square root function:

$$f(K/N) = \sqrt{K/N}$$

Figure 11-1

Capital, Output, and Saving/Investment

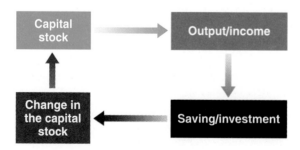

In this chapter, we make two further assumptions:

■ The first assumption is that the size of the population, the participation rate, and the unemployment rate, are all constant. This implies that employment, N, is also constant. To see why, go back to the relations we saw in Chapter 2 and again in Chapter 6 between population, the labor force, unemployment, and employment:

The labor force is equal to population times the participation rate. So if population is constant and the participation rate is constant, the labor force is also constant. Employment, in turn, is equal to the labor force times 1 minus the unemployment rate. If, for example, the size of the labor force is 100 million, and the unemployment rate is 5%, then employment is equal to 95 million [100 million times (1–.05)]. So, if the labor force is constant and the unemployment rate is constant, employment is also constant.

Under these assumptions, output per worker, output per person, and output itself, all move proportionately. Although I usually refer to movements in output or capital *per worker*, to lighten the text, I shall sometimes just talk about movements in output or capital, leaving out the "per worker" or "per person" qualification.

The reason for assuming that N is constant is to make it easier to focus on how capital accumulation affects growth: If N is constant, the only factor of production that changes over time is capital. The assumption is not very realistic, however, so we will relax it in the next two chapters. In Chapter 12, we will allow for steady population and employment growth. In Chapter 13, we will see how we can integrate our analysis of the long run—which ignores fluctuations in employment—with our earlier analysis of the short run and medium run—which focused precisely on these fluctuations in employment (and the associated fluctuations in output and unemployment). But both steps are better left to later.

■ The second assumption is that there is no technological progress, so the production function f (or, equivalently, F) does not change over time. Again, the reason for making this assumption—which is obviously contrary to reality—is to focus just on the role of capital accumulation. In Chapter 12, we will introduce technological progress and see that the basic conclusions we derive here about the role of capital in growth also hold when there is technological progress. Again, this step is better left to later.

With these two assumptions, our first relation between output and capital per worker, from the production side, can be written as

$$\frac{Y_t}{N} = f\left(\frac{K_t}{N}\right) \qquad (11.1)$$

where I have introduced time indexes for output and capital—but not for labor, N, which we assume to be constant and so does not need a time index.

In words: Higher capital per worker leads to higher output per worker.

> In the United States in 2003, output per person (in 2000 PPP dollars) was \$34,875; output per worker was much higher, at \$67,865. (From these two numbers, can you derive the ratio of employment to population?)

> From the production side: The level of capital per worker determines the level of output per worker.

The Effects of Output on Capital Accumulation

To derive the second relation, between output and capital accumulation, we proceed in two steps:

1. We derive the relation between output and investment.

2. We derive the relation between investment and capital accumulation.

As we will see in Chapter 19, saving and investment need not be equal in an open economy. A country can save less than it invests and borrow the difference from the rest of the world. This is indeed the case ▶ for the United States today.

This assumption is again at odds with the situation in the United States today, where, as ▶ we saw in Chapter 1, the government is running a budget deficit. In other words, in the United States, public saving is negative.

You have now seen two specifications of saving behavior (equivalently consumption behavior): one for the short run in Chapter 3, and one for the long run in this chapter. You may wonder how the two specifications relate to each other and ▶ whether they are consistent. The answer is yes. A full discussion is given in Chapter 16.

Output and Investment

To derive the relation between output and investment, we make three assumptions:

■ We continue to assume that the economy is closed. As we saw in Chapter 3 [equation (3.10)], this means that investment, I, is equal to saving—the sum of private saving, S, and public saving, $T - G$.

$$I = S + (T - G)$$

■ To focus on the behavior of private saving, we assume that public saving, $T - G$, is equal to zero. (We will relax this assumption later, when we focus on the effects of fiscal policy on growth.) With this assumption, the previous equation becomes

$$I = S$$

Investment is equal to private saving.

■ We assume that private saving is proportional to income, so

$$S = sY$$

The parameter s is the saving rate. It has a value between 0 and 1. This assumption captures two basic facts about saving. First, the saving rate does not appear to systematically increase or decrease as a country becomes richer. Second, richer countries do not appear to have systematically higher or lower saving rates than poorer ones.

Combining these two relations, and introducing time indexes, gives a simple relation between investment and output:

$$I_t = sY_t$$

Investment is proportional to output: Higher output implies higher saving, and so, higher investment.

Investment and Capital Accumulation

Recall: Flows are variables that have a time dimension (that is, they are defined per unit of time); stocks are variables that ▶ do not have a time dimension (they are defined at a point in time). Output, saving, and investment are flows. Employment and capital are stocks.

The second step relates investment, which is a flow (the new machines produced and new plants built during a given period), to capital, which is a stock (the existing machines and plants in the economy at a point in time).

Think of time as measured in years, so t denotes year t, $t + 1$ denotes year $t + 1$, and so on. Think of the capital stock as being measured at the beginning of each year, so K_t refers to the capital stock at the beginning of year t, K_{t+1} to the capital stock at the beginning of year $t + 1$, and so on.

Assume that capital depreciates at rate δ (the lowercase Greek letter delta) per year: That is, from one year to the next, a proportion, δ, of the capital stock breaks down and becomes useless. Equivalently, a proportion $(1 - \delta)$ of the capital stock remains intact from one year to the next.

The evolution of the capital stock is then given by

$$K_{t+1} = (1 - \delta)K_t + I_t$$

The capital stock at the beginning of year $t + 1$, K_{t+1}, is equal to the capital stock at the beginning of year t which is still intact in year $t + 1$, $(1 - \delta)K_t$, plus the new capital stock put in place during year t (that is, investment during year t, I_t).

We can now combine the relation between output and investment and the relation between investment and capital accumulation to obtain the second relation we need in order to think about growth: the relation from output to capital accumulation.

Replacing investment by its expression previously and dividing both sides by N (the number of workers in the economy) gives

$$\frac{K_{t+1}}{N} = (1 - \delta)\frac{K_t}{N} + s\frac{Y_t}{N}$$

In words: Capital per worker at the beginning of year $t + 1$ is equal to capital per worker at the beginning of year t, adjusted for depreciation, plus investment per worker during year t, which is equal to the saving rate times output per worker during year t.

Expanding the term $(1 - \delta)K_t/N$ to $K_t/N - \delta K_t/N$, moving K_t/N to the left, and reorganizing the right side, we have

$$\frac{K_{t+1}}{N} - \frac{K_t}{N} = s\frac{Y_t}{N} - \delta\frac{K_t}{N} \qquad (11.2)$$

In words: The change in the capital stock per worker—represented by the difference between the two terms on the left—is equal to saving per worker—represented by the first term on the right—minus depreciation—represented by the second term on the right. This equation gives us the second relation between output and capital per worker. ◀ From the saving side: The level of output per worker determines the change in the level of capital per worker over time.

11-2 The Implications of Alternative Saving Rates

We have derived two relations:

■ From the production side, we have seen in equation (11.1) how capital determines output.
■ From the saving side, we have seen in equation (11.2) how output in turn determines capital accumulation.

We can now put the two relations together and see how they determine the behavior of output and capital over time.

Dynamics of Capital and Output

Replacing output per worker, Y_t/N, in equation (11.2) by its expression in terms of capital per worker from equation (11.1) gives

$$\underbrace{\frac{K_{t+1}}{N} - \frac{K_t}{N}}_{\substack{\text{Change in capital} \\ \text{from year } t \text{ to year } t + 1}} = \underbrace{sf\left(\frac{K_t}{N}\right)}_{\substack{\text{Investment} \\ \text{during year } t}} - \underbrace{\delta\frac{K_t}{N}}_{\substack{\text{Depreciation} \\ \text{during year } t}} \qquad (11.3)$$

This relation describes what happens to capital per worker. The change in capital per worker from this year to next year depends on the difference between two terms:

■ Investment per worker, the first term on the right—The level of capital per worker this year determines output per worker this year. Given the saving rate, output per worker determines the amount of saving per worker and thus the investment per worker this year. ◀ $K_t/N \Rightarrow f(K_t/N) \Rightarrow sf(K_t/N)$
■ Depreciation per worker, the second term on the right—The capital stock per worker determines the amount of depreciation per worker this year. ◀ $K_t/N \Rightarrow \delta K_t/N$

If investment per worker exceeds depreciation per worker, the change in capital per worker is positive: Capital per worker increases.

If investment per worker is less than depreciation per worker, the change in capital per worker is negative: Capital per worker decreases.

Figure 11-2

Capital and Output Dynamics

When capital and output are low, investment exceeds depreciation, and capital increases. When capital and output are high, investment is less than depreciation, and capital decreases.

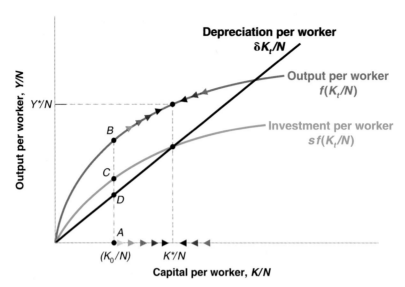

Given capital per worker, output per worker is then given by equation (11.1):

$$\frac{Y_t}{N} = f\left(\frac{K_t}{N}\right)$$

Equations (11.3) and (11.1) contain all the information we need to understand the dynamics of capital and output over time. The easiest way to interpret them is to use a graph. We do this in Figure 11-2, where output per worker is measured on the vertical axis, and capital per worker is measured on the horizontal axis.

In Figure 11-2, look first at the curve representing output per worker, $f(K_t/N)$, as a function of capital per worker. The relation is the same as in Figure 10-5: Output per worker increases with capital per worker, but—because of decreasing returns to capital—the effect is smaller the higher the level of capital per worker.

Now look at the two curves representing the two components on the right of equation (11.3):

■ The relation representing investment per worker, $sf(K_t/N)$, has the same shape as the production function except that it is lower by the factor s (the saving rate). Suppose the level of capital per worker is equal to K_0/N in Figure 11-2. Output per worker is then given by the vertical distance *AB*, and investment per worker is given by the vertical distance *AC*, which is equal to s times the vertical distance *AB*. Thus, just like output per worker, investment per worker increases with capital per worker, but by less and less as capital per worker increases. When capital per worker is already very high, the effect of a further increase in capital per worker on output per worker and, by implication, on investment per worker, is very small.

To make the graph easier to read, I have assumed an unrealistically high saving rate. (Can you tell roughly what value I have assumed for s? What would be a plausible value for s?) ▶

■ The relation representing depreciation per worker, $\delta K_t/N$, is a straight line. Depreciation per worker increases in proportion to capital per worker, so the relation is represented by a straight line with slope equal to δ. At the level of capital per worker K_0/N, depreciation per worker is given by the vertical distance *AD*.

The change in capital per worker is given by the difference between investment per worker and depreciation per worker. At K_0/N, the difference is positive; investment per worker exceeds depreciation per worker by an amount represented by the vertical distance $CD = AC - AD$, so capital per worker increases. As we move to the right along the horizontal axis and look at higher and higher levels of capital per worker, investment increases by less and less, while depreciation keeps increasing in proportion to capital. For some level of capital per worker, K^*/N, in Figure 11-2, investment is just enough to cover depreciation, and capital per worker remains constant. To the left of K^*/N, investment exceeds depreciation, and capital per worker increases. This is indicated by the arrows pointing to the right along the curve representing the production function. To the right of K^*/N, depreciation exceeds investment, and capital per worker decreases. This is indicated by the arrows pointing to the left along the curve representing the production function.

When capital per worker is low, capital per worker and output per worker increase over time. When capital per worker is high, capital per worker and output per worker ◀ decrease over time.

Characterizing the evolution of capital per worker and output per worker over time is now easy. Consider an economy that starts with a low level of capital per worker—say, K_0/N in Figure 11-2. Because investment exceeds depreciation at this point, capital per worker increases. And because output moves with capital, output per worker increases as well. Capital per worker eventually reaches K^*/N, the level at which investment is equal to depreciation. Once the economy has reached the level of capital per worker K^*/N, output per worker and capital per worker remain constant at Y^*/N and K^*/N, their long-run equilibrium levels.

Think, for example, of a country that loses part of its capital stock, say as a result of bombing during a war. The mechanism we have just seen suggests that, if the country has suffered larger capital losses than population losses, it will come out of the war with a low level of capital per worker—that is, at a point to the left of K^*/N. The country will then experience a large increase in both capital per worker and output per worker for some time. This describes well what happened after World War II to countries that had proportionately larger destructions of capital than losses of human lives (see the Focus box "Capital Accumulation and Growth in France in the Aftermath of World War II").

What does the model predict for post-war growth if a country suffers proportional losses in population and in capital? Do you find this answer convincing? What elements may be ◀ missing from the model?

If a country starts instead from a high level of capital per worker—that is, from a point to the right of K^*/N—then depreciation will exceed investment, and capital per worker and output per worker will decrease: The initial level of capital per worker is too high to be sustained, given the saving rate. This decrease in capital per worker will continue until the economy again reaches the point where investment is equal to depreciation and capital per worker is equal to K^*/N. From then on, capital per worker and output per worker will remain constant.

Steady-State Capital and Output

Let's look more closely at the levels of output per worker and capital per worker to which the economy converges in the long run. The state in which output per worker and capital per worker are no longer changing is called the **steady state** of the economy. Setting the left side of equation (11.3) equal to zero (in steady state, by definition, the change in capital per worker is 0), the steady-state value of capital per worker, K^*/N, is given by

$$sf\left(\frac{K^*}{N}\right) = \delta\frac{K^*}{N} \qquad (11.4)$$

The steady-state value of capital per worker is such that the amount of saving per worker (the left side) is just sufficient to cover depreciation of the capital stock per worker (the right side).

K^*/N is the long-run level of ◀ capital per worker.

Given steady-state capital per worker, K^*/N, the steady-state value of output per worker, Y^*/N, is given by the production function

$$\frac{Y^*}{N} = f\left(\frac{K^*}{N}\right) \qquad (11.5)$$

We now have all the elements we need to discuss the effects of the saving rate on output per worker, both over time and in steady state.

Capital Accumulation and Growth in France in the Aftermath of World War II

When World War II ended in 1945, France had suffered some of the heaviest losses of all European countries. The losses in lives were large. More than 550,000 people had died, out of a population of 42 million. Relatively speaking, though, the losses in capital were much larger: It is estimated that the French capital stock in 1945 was about 30% below its pre-war value. A vivid picture of the destruction of capital is provided by the numbers in Table 1.

The model of growth we have just seen makes a clear prediction about what will happen to a country that loses a large part of its capital stock: The country will experience high capital accumulation and output growth for some time. In terms of Figure 11-2, a country with capital per worker initially far below K^*/N will grow rapidly as it converges to K^*/N and output per worker converges to Y^*/N.

This prediction fares well in the case of postwar France. There is plenty of anecdotal evidence that small increases in capital led to large increases in output. Minor repairs to a major bridge would lead to the reopening of the bridge. Reopening of the bridge would significantly shorten the travel time between two cities, leading to much lower transport costs. The lower

transport costs would then enable a plant to get much-needed inputs, increase its production, and so on.

More convincing evidence, however, comes directly from actual aggregate output numbers. From 1946 to 1950, the annual growth rate of French real GDP was a very high 9.6% per year. This led to an increase in real GDP of about 60% over the course of five years.

Was all the increase in French GDP due to capital accumulation? The answer is no. There were other forces at work in addition to the mechanism in our model. Much of the remaining capital stock in 1945 was old. Investment had been low in the 1930s (a decade dominated by the Great Depression) and nearly nonexistent during the war. A good portion of the postwar capital accumulation was associated with the introduction of more modern capital and the use of more modern production techniques. This was another reason for the high growth rates of the postwar period.

Source: Gilles Saint-Paul, "Economic Reconstruction in France, 1945–1958," in Rudiger Dornbusch, Willem Nolling, and Richard Layard, eds, Postwar Economic Reconstruction and Lessons for the East Today, MIT Press, Cambridge, MA, 1993.

Table 1	Proportion of the French Capital Stock Destroyed by the End of World War II					
Railways	Tracks	6%	Rivers	Waterways		86%
	Stations	38%		Canal locks		11%
	Engines	21%		Barges		80%
	Hardware	60%	Buildings	(numbers)		
Roads	Cars	31%		Dwellings	1,229,000	
	Trucks	40%		Industrial	246,000	

Source: See source note for this box.

The Saving Rate and Output

Let's return to the question asked at the beginning of the chapter: How does the saving rate affect the growth rate of output per worker? Our analysis leads to a three-part answer:

1. *The saving rate has no effect on the long-run growth rate of output per worker, which is equal to zero.*

This conclusion is rather obvious: We have seen that, eventually, the economy converges to a constant level of output per worker. In other words, in the long run, the growth rate of output is equal to zero, no matter what the saving rate.

There is, however, a way of thinking about this conclusion that will be useful when we introduce technological progress in Chapter 12. Think of what would be needed to sustain a constant positive growth rate of output per worker in the long run. Capital per worker would have to increase. Not only that, but, because of decreasing returns to capital, it would have to increase faster than output per worker. This implies that each year, the economy would have to save a larger and larger fraction of its output and dedicate it to capital accumulation. At some point, the fraction of output it would need to save would be greater than one—which is clearly impossible. This is why it is impossible to sustain a constant positive growth rate forever. In the long run, capital per worker must be constant, and so output per worker must be constant, too.

2. Nonetheless, *the saving rate determines the level of output per worker in the long run*. Other things equal, countries with a higher saving rate will achieve higher output per worker in the long run.

   Figure 11-3 illustrates this point. Consider two countries with the same production function, the same level of employment, and the same depreciation rate, but different saving rates, say s_0 and $s_1 > s_0$. Figure 11-3 draws their common production function, $f(K_t/N)$, and the functions showing saving/investment per worker as a function of capital per worker for each of the two countries, $s_0 f(K_t/N)$ and $s_1 f(K_t/N)$. In the long run, the country with saving rate s_0 will reach the level of capital per worker K_0/N and output per worker Y_0/N. The country with saving rate s_1 will reach the higher levels K_1/N and Y_1/N.

3. *An increase in the saving rate will lead to higher growth of output per worker for some time, but not forever.*

   This conclusion follows from the two propositions we just discussed. From the first, we know that an increase in the saving rate does not affect the long-run *growth rate of output per worker*, which remains equal to zero. From the second, we know that an increase in the saving rate leads to an increase in the long-run *level of output per worker*. It follows that, as output per worker increases to its new higher level in response to the increase in the saving rate, the economy will go through a period of positive growth. This period of growth will come to an end when the economy reaches its new steady state.

   We can use Figure 11-3 again to illustrate this point. Consider a country that has an initial saving rate of s_0. Assume that capital per worker is initially equal to K_0/N, with associated output per worker Y_0/N. Now consider the effects of an increase in the saving rate from s_0 to s_1. The function giving saving/investment per worker as a function of capital per worker shifts upward from $s_0 f(K_t/N)$ to $s_1 f(K_t/N)$.

Some economists argue that the high output growth achieved by the Soviet Union from 1950 to 1990 was the result of such a steady increase in the saving rate over time, which could not be sustained forever. Paul Krugman has used the term *Stalinist growth* to denote this type of growth—growth resulting from a higher and higher saving rate over time.

Note that the first proposition is a statement about the growth rate of output per worker. The second proposition is a statement about the level of output per worker.

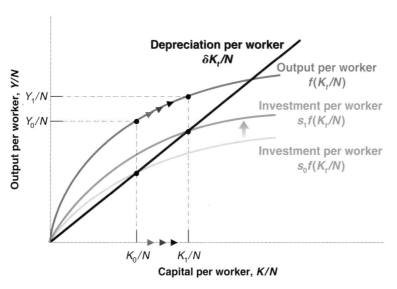

Figure 11-3

The Effects of Different Saving Rates

A country with a higher saving rate achieves a higher steady-state level of output per worker.

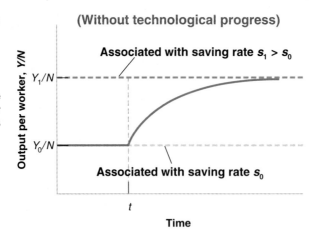

Figure 11-4

The Effects of an Increase in the Saving Rate on Output per Worker

An increase in the saving rate leads to a period of higher growth until output reaches its new, higher steady-state level.

At the initial level of capital per worker, K_0/N, investment exceeds depreciation, so capital per worker increases. As capital per worker increases, so does output per worker, and the economy goes through a period of positive growth. When capital per worker eventually reaches K_1/N, however, investment is again equal to depreciation, and growth ends. From then on, the economy remains at K_1/N, with associated output per worker Y_1/N. The movement of output per worker is plotted against time in Figure 11-4. Output per worker is initially constant at level Y_0/N. After the increase in the saving rate, say, at time t, output per worker increases for some time until it reaches the higher level of output per worker, Y_1/N, and the growth rate returns to zero.

We have derived these three results under the assumption that there was no technological progress, and, therefore, no growth of output per worker in the long run. But, as we will see in Chapter 12, the three results extend to an economy in which there is technological progress. Let me briefly indicate how.

An economy in which there is technological progress has a positive growth rate of output per worker, even in the long run. This long-run growth rate is independent of the saving rate—the extension of the first result just discussed. The saving rate affects the level of output per worker, however— the extension of the second result. An increase in the saving rate leads to growth greater than the steady-state growth rate for some time until the economy reaches its new higher path—the extension of our third result.

These three results are illustrated in Figure 11-5, which extends Figure 11-4 by plotting the effect that an increase in the saving rate has on an economy with positive technological progress. The figure uses a logarithmic scale to measure output per worker: Consequently an economy in which output per worker grows at a constant rate is represented by a line with slope equal to that growth rate. At the initial saving rate, s_0, the economy moves along AA. If, at time t, the saving rate increases to s_1, the economy experiences higher growth for some time until it reaches its new higher path, BB. On path BB, the growth rate is again the same as before the increase in the saving rate (that is, the slope of BB is the same as the slope of AA).

The Saving Rate and Consumption

> Recall that saving is the sum of private plus public saving. Recall also: Public saving ⟺ Budget surplus; Public dissaving ⟺ Budget deficit.

Governments can affect the saving rate in various ways. First, they can vary public saving. Given private saving, positive public saving—a budget surplus, in other words—leads to higher overall saving. Conversely, negative public saving—a budget deficit—leads to lower overall saving. Second, governments can use taxes to affect private saving. For example, they can give tax breaks to people who save, making it more attractive to save, thus increasing private saving.

> See the discussion of logarithmic scales in Appendix 2.

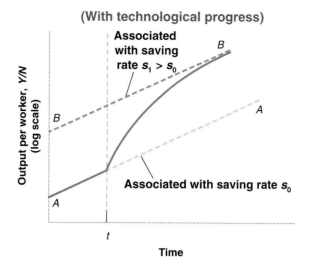

(With technological progress)

Figure 11-5 ▬

The Effects of an Increase in the Saving Rate on Output per Worker in an Economy with Technological Progress

An increase in the saving rate leads to a period of higher growth until output reaches a new, higher path.

What saving rate should governments aim for? To think about the answer, we must shift our focus from the behavior of *output* to the behavior of *consumption*. The reason: What matters to people is not how much is produced but how much they consume.

It is clear that an increase in saving must come initially at the expense of lower consumption (except when I think it helpful, I drop *per worker* in this subsection and just refer to consumption rather than consumption per worker, capital rather than capital per worker, and so on.): A change in the saving rate this year has no effect on capital this year and, consequently, no effect on output and income *this year*. So an increase in saving comes initially with an equal decrease in consumption.

Does an increase in saving lead to an increase in consumption in the long run? Not necessarily. Consumption may decrease not only initially but also in the long run. You may find this surprising. After all, we know from Figure 11-3 that an increase in the saving rate always leads to an increase in the level of *output* per worker. But output is not the same as consumption. To see why, consider what happens for two extreme values of the saving rate:

◄ *Because we assume that employment is constant, we are ignoring the short-run effect of an increase in the saving rate on output we focused on in Chapter 3. In the short run, not only does an increase in the saving rate reduce consumption given income, but it may also create a recession and decrease income further. We will return to a discussion of short-run and long-run effects of changes in saving at various points in the book. See, for example, Chapters 17 and 26.*

- An economy in which the saving rate is (and has always been) 0 is an economy in which capital is equal to zero. In this case, output is also equal to zero, and so is consumption. A saving rate equal to zero implies zero consumption in the long run.
- Now consider an economy in which the saving rate is equal to one: People save all their income. The level of capital, and thus output, in this economy will be very high. But because people save all their income, consumption is equal to zero. What happens is that the economy is carrying an excessive amount of capital: Simply maintaining that level of output requires that all output be devoted to replacing depreciation! A saving rate equal to one also implies zero consumption in the long run.

These two extreme cases mean that there must be some value of the saving rate between zero and one that maximizes the steady-state level of consumption. Increases in the saving rate below this value lead to a decrease in consumption initially but to an increase in consumption in the long run. Increases in the saving rate beyond this value decrease consumption not only initially but also in the long run. This happens because the increase in capital associated with the increase in the saving rate leads to only a small increase in output—an increase that is too small to cover the

The Effects of the Saving Rate on Steady-State Consumption per Worker

An increase in the saving rate leads to an increase and then to a decrease in steady-state consumption per worker.

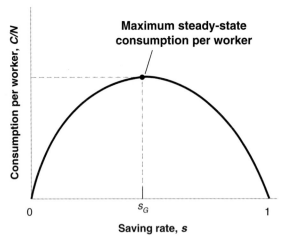

increased depreciation: In other words, the economy carries too much capital. The level of capital associated with the value of the saving rate that yields the highest level of consumption in steady state is known as the **golden-rule level of capital**. Increases in capital beyond the golden-rule level reduce consumption.

This argument is illustrated in Figure 11-6, which plots consumption per worker in steady state (on the vertical axis) against the saving rate (on the horizontal axis). A saving rate equal to zero implies a capital stock per worker equal to zero; a level of output per worker equal to zero, and, by implication, a level of consumption per worker equal to zero. For s between zero and s_G (G for golden rule), a higher saving rate leads to higher capital per worker, higher output per worker, and higher consumption per worker. For s larger than s_G, increases in the saving rate still lead to higher values of capital per worker and output per worker; but they now lead to lower values of consumption per worker: This is because the increase in output is more than offset by the increase in depreciation due to the larger capital stock. For $s = 1$, consumption per worker is equal to zero. Capital per worker and output per worker are high, but all the output is used just to replace depreciation, leaving nothing for consumption.

If an economy already has so much capital that it is operating beyond the golden rule, then increasing saving further will decrease consumption not only now but also later. Is this a relevant worry? Do some countries actually have too much capital? The empirical evidence indicates that most OECD countries are actually far below their golden-rule level of capital. Increasing their saving rate would lead to higher consumption in the future.

This means that, in practice, governments face a trade-off: An increase in the saving rate leads to lower consumption for some time but higher consumption later. So what should governments do? How close to the golden rule should they try to get? It depends on how much weight they put on the welfare of current generations—who are more likely to lose from policies aimed at increasing the saving rate—versus the welfare of future generations—who are more likely to gain. Enter politics: Future generations do not vote. This means that governments are unlikely to ask current generations to make large sacrifices, which in turn means that capital is likely to stay far below its golden-rule level. These intergenerational issues are at the forefront of the current debate on Social Security reform in the United States. The Focus box "Social Security, Saving, and Capital Accumulation in the United States" explores this further.

Social Security was introduced in the United States in 1935. The goal of the program was to make sure the elderly would have enough to live on. Over time, Social Security has become the largest government program in the United States. Benefits paid to retirees now exceed 4% of GDP. For two-thirds of retirees, Social Security benefits account for more than 50% of their income. There is little question that, on its own terms, the Social Security system has been a great success, decreasing poverty among the elderly. There is also little question that it has led to a lower U.S. saving rate and therefore lower capital accumulation and lower output per person in the long run.

To understand why, we must take a theoretical detour. Think of an economy in which there is no social security system—one where workers have to save to provide for their own retirement. Now, introduce a Social Security system that collects taxes from workers and distributes benefits to the retirees. It can do so in one of two ways:

■ One way is by taxing workers, investing their contributions in financial assets, and paying back the principal plus the interest to the workers when they retire. Such a system is called a **fully funded system**: At any time, the system has funds equal to the accumulated contributions of workers, from which it will be able to pay out benefits to these workers when they retire.

■ The other way is by taxing workers and redistributing the tax contributions as benefits to the current retirees. Such a system is called a **pay-as-you-go system**: The system pays benefits out "as it goes" that is, as it collects them through contributions.

From the point of view of workers, the two systems are broadly similar. In both cases, the workers pay contributions when they work and receive benefits when they retire. What they receive, however, is slightly different in each case:

■ What retirees receive in a fully funded system depends on the rate of return on the financial assets held by the fund.

■ What retirees receive in a pay-as-you-go system depends on demographics—the ratio of retirees to workers—and on the evolution of the tax rate set by the system.

From the point of view of the economy, however, the two systems have very different implications:

■ In the fully funded system, workers save less because they anticipate receiving benefits when they are old. The Social Security system saves on their behalf, by investing their contributions in financial assets. The presence of a Social Security system changes the composition of overall saving: Private saving goes down, and public saving goes up. But, to a first approximation, it has no effect on total saving and therefore no effect on capital accumulation.

■ In the pay-as-you-go system, workers also save less because they again anticipate receiving benefits when they are old. But, now, the Social Security system does not save on their behalf. The decrease in private saving is not compensated by an increase in public saving. Total saving goes down, and so does capital accumulation.

Most actual Social Security systems are somewhere between pay-as-you-go and fully funded systems. When the U.S. system was set up in 1935, the intention was to partially fund it. But this did not happen: Rather than being invested, contributions from workers were used to pay benefits to the retirees, and this has been the case ever since. Today, because contributions have slightly exceeded benefits since the early 1980s, the Social Security Administration has built a **trust fund**. But this trust fund is far smaller than the value of benefits promised to current contributors when they retire. The U.S. system is basically a pay-as-you-go system, and this has probably contributed to the lower U.S. saving rate over the past 70 years.

In this context, some economists and politicians have suggested that the United States should shift back to a fully funded system. One of their arguments is that the U.S. saving rate is indeed too low and that funding the Social Security system would increase it. Such a shift could be achieved by investing, from now on, tax contributions in financial assets rather than distributing them as benefits to retirees. Under such a shift, the Social Security system would steadily accumulate funds and would eventually become fully funded. Martin Feldstein, an economist at Harvard and an advocate of such a shift, has concluded that it could lead to a 34% increase of the capital stock in the long run.

How should we think about such a proposal? It would probably have been a good idea to fully fund the system at the start: The United States would have a higher saving rate. The U.S. capital stock would be higher, and output and consumption would also be higher. But we cannot rewrite history. The existing system has promised benefits to retirees, and these promises have to be honored. This means that, under the proposal we just described, current workers would, in effect, have to contribute twice—once to fund the system and finance their own retirement and then to finance the benefits owed to current retirees. This would impose a disproportionate cost on current workers. The practical implication is that, if it is to happen, the move to a fully funded system will have to be very slow, so that the burden of adjustment does not fall too much on one generation relative to the others.

Continued

FOCUS

The debate is likely to be with us for some time. In assessing proposals from the administration or from Congress, ask yourself how they deal with the issue we just discussed. Take, for example, the proposal to allow workers, from now on, to make contributions to personal accounts instead of to the Social Security system, and to be able to draw from these accounts when they retire. By itself, this proposal would clearly increase private saving: Workers will be saving more. But its ultimate effect on saving depends on how the benefits already promised to current workers and retirees by the Social Security system are financed. If, as is the case under some proposals, these benefits are financed not through additional taxes but through debt finance, then the increase in private saving will be offset by an increase in deficits, an increase in public saving: The shift to personal accounts will not increase the U.S. saving rate. If, instead, these benefits are financed through higher taxes, then the U.S. saving rate will increase. But, in that case, current workers will have to both contribute to their personal accounts and pay the higher taxes. They will indeed pay twice.

To follow the debate on Social Security, look at the site run by the (non-partisan) Concord Coalition (**www.concordcoalition.org/issues/socsec/**). (We shall return to these issues in Chapter 26.)

11-3 Getting a Sense of Magnitudes

How big an impact does a change in the saving rate have on output in the long run? For how long and by how much does an increase in the saving rate affect growth? How far is the United States from the golden-rule level of capital? To get a better sense of the answers to these questions, let's now make more specific assumptions, plug in some numbers, and see what we get.

Assume that the production function is

$$Y = \sqrt{K}\sqrt{N} \tag{11.6}$$

> Check that this production function exhibits both constant returns to scale and decreasing returns to either capital or labor.

Output equals the product of the square root of capital and the square root of labor. (A more general specification of the production function, known as the Cobb-Douglas production function, and its implications for growth are given in the appendix to the chapter.)

Dividing both sides by N (because we are interested in output per worker), we get

$$\frac{Y}{N} = \frac{\sqrt{K}\sqrt{N}}{N} = \frac{\sqrt{K}}{\sqrt{N}} = \sqrt{\frac{K}{N}}$$

> The second equality follows from $\sqrt{N}/N = \sqrt{N}/(\sqrt{N}\sqrt{N})$ $= 1/\sqrt{N}.$

Output per worker equals the square root of capital per worker. Put another way, the production function, f, relating output per worker to capital per worker, is given by

$$f\left(\frac{K_t}{N}\right) = \sqrt{\frac{K_t}{N}}$$

Replacing $f(K_t/N)$ with $\sqrt{K_t/N}$ in equation (11.3), we have

$$\frac{K_{t+1}}{N} - \frac{K_t}{N} = s\sqrt{\frac{K_t}{N}} - \delta\frac{K_t}{N} \tag{11.7}$$

This equation describes the evolution of capital per worker over time. Let's look at what it implies.

The Effects of the Saving Rate on Steady-State Output

How big an impact does an increase in the saving rate have on the steady-state level of output per worker?

Start with equation (11.7). In steady state, the amount of capital per worker is constant, so the left side of the equation equals zero. This implies

$$s\sqrt{\frac{K^*}{N}} = \delta\frac{K^*}{N}$$

(I have dropped time indexes, which are no longer needed because in steady state, K/N is constant. The * is to remind you that we are looking at the steady-state value of capital.) Square both sides:

$$s^2\frac{K^*}{N} = \delta^2\left(\frac{K^*}{N}\right)^2$$

Divide both sides by K/N and change the order of the equality:

$$\frac{K^*}{N} = \left(\frac{s}{\delta}\right)^2 \qquad\qquad (11.8)$$

Steady-state capital per worker is equal to the square of the ratio of the saving rate to the depreciation rate.

From equations (11.6) and (11.8), steady-state output per worker is given by

$$\frac{Y^*}{N} = \sqrt{\frac{K^*}{N}} = \sqrt{\left(\frac{s}{\delta}\right)^2} = \frac{s}{\delta} \qquad\qquad (11.9)$$

Steady-state output per worker is equal to the ratio of the saving rate to the depreciation rate.

A higher saving rate and a lower depreciation rate both lead to higher steady-state capital per worker [equation (11.8)] and higher steady-state output per worker [equation (11.9)]. To see what this means, let's look at a numerical example. Suppose the depreciation rate is 10% per year, and suppose the saving rate is also 10%. Then, from equations (11.8) and (11.9), steady-state capital per worker and output per worker are both equal to 1. Now suppose that the saving rate doubles, from 10% to 20%. It follows from equation (11.8) that in the new steady state, capital per worker increases from 1 to 4. And from equation (11.9), output per worker doubles, from 1 to 2. Thus, doubling the saving rate leads, in the long run, to doubling the output per worker: This is a large effect.

The Dynamic Effects of an Increase in the Saving Rate

We have just seen that an increase in the saving rate leads to an increase in the steady-state level of output. But how long does it take for output to reach its new steady-state level? Put another way, by how much and for how long does an increase in the saving rate affect the growth rate?

To answer these questions, we must use equation (11.7) and solve it for capital per worker in year 0, in year 1, and so on.

Suppose that the saving rate, which had always been equal to 10%, increases in year 0 from 10% to 20% and remains at this higher value forever after. In year 0, nothing happens to the capital stock. (Recall that it takes one year for higher saving and higher investment to show up in higher capital.) So, capital per worker remains equal to the steady-state value associated with a saving rate of 0.1. From equation (11.8),

$$\frac{K_0}{N} = (0.1/0.1)^2 = 1^2 = 1$$

In year 1, equation (11.7) gives

$$\frac{K_1}{N} - \frac{K_0}{N} = s\sqrt{\frac{K_0}{N}} - \delta\frac{K_0}{N}$$

The Dynamic Effects of an
Increase in the Saving
Rate from 10% to 20% on
the Level and the Growth
Rate of Output per Worker

It takes a long time for output to
adjust to its new, higher level after
an increase in the saving rate. Put
another way, an increase in the
saving rate leads to a long period
of higher growth.

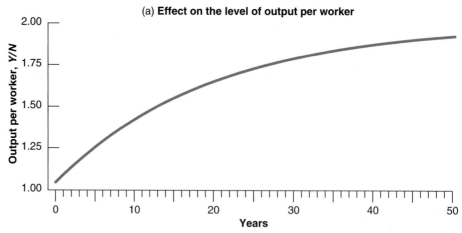

(a) **Effect on the level of output per worker**

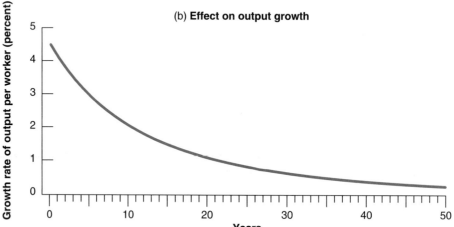

(b) **Effect on output growth**

With a depreciation rate equal to 0.1 and a saving rate now equal to 0.2, this equation implies

$$\frac{K_1}{N} - 1 = [(0.2)(\sqrt{1})] - [(0.1)1]$$

so

$$\frac{K_1}{N} = 1.1$$

In the same way, we can solve for K_2/N, and so on. When we have determined the values of capital per worker in year 0, year 1, and so on, we can then use equation (11.6) to solve for output per worker in year 0, year 1, and so on. The results of this computation are presented in Figure 11-7. Figure 11-7 (a) plots the *level* of output per worker against time. Y/N increases over time from its initial value of 1 in year 0 to its steady-state value of 2 in the long run. Figure 11-7 (b) gives the same information in a different way, plotting instead the *growth rate* of output per worker against time. As Figure 11-7 (b) shows, growth of output per worker is highest at the beginning and then decreases over time. As the economy reaches its new steady state, growth of output per worker returns to zero.

▶ The difference between investment and depreciation is greatest at the beginning. This is
why capital accumulation, and,
by implication, output growth
are highest at the beginning.

Figure 11-7 clearly shows that the adjustment to the new, higher long-run equilibrium takes a long time. It is only 40% complete after 10 years, and it is 63% complete after 20 years. Put another way, the increase in the saving rate increases the growth rate of output per worker for a long time. The average annual growth rate is 3.1% for the first 10 years, and it is 1.5% for the next 10. Although the changes in the saving rate have no effect on growth in the long run, they do lead to higher growth for a long time.

Let's go back to the question raised at the beginning of the chapter: Can the low saving/investment rate in the United States explain why the U.S. growth rate has been so low—relative to the rates of other OECD countries—since 1950? The answer would be yes if the United States had a higher saving rate in the past and *if this saving rate had fallen substantially in the past 50 years.* If this were the case, it could explain the period of lower growth in the United States in the past 50 years along the lines of the mechanism in Figure 11-7 (with the sign reversed, as we would be looking at a decrease—not an increase—in the saving rate). But this is not the case: The U.S. saving rate has been low for a long time. Low saving cannot explain the poor U.S. growth performance over the past 50 years.

The U.S. Saving Rate and the Golden Rule

What is the saving rate that would maximize steady-state consumption per worker? Recall that, in steady state, consumption is equal to what is left after enough is put aside to maintain a constant level of capital. More formally, in steady state, consumption per worker is equal to output per worker minus depreciation per worker:

$$\frac{C}{N} = \frac{Y}{N} - \delta\frac{K}{N}$$

Using equations (11.8) and (11.9) for the steady-state values of output per worker and capital per worker, consumption per worker is thus given by

$$\frac{C}{N} = \frac{s}{\delta} - \delta\left(\frac{s}{\delta}\right)^2 = \frac{s(1-s)}{\delta}$$

Using this equation together with equations (11.8) and (11.9), Table 11-1 gives the steady-state values of capital per worker, output per worker, and consumption per worker for different values of the saving rate (and for a depreciation rate equal to 10%).

Steady-state consumption per worker is largest when s equals one-half. In other words, the golden-rule level of capital is associated with a saving rate of 50%. Below that level, increases in the saving rate lead to an increase in long-run consumption per

Table 11-1	The Saving Rate and the Steady-State Levels of Capital, Output, and Consumption per Worker		
Saving Rate s	Capital per Worker (K/N)	Output per Worker (Y/N)	Consumption per Worker (C/N)
0.0	0.0	0.0	0.0
0.1	1.0	1.0	0.9
0.2	4.0	2.0	1.6
0.3	9.0	3.0	2.1
0.4	16.0	4.0	2.4
0.5	25.0	5.0	2.5
0.6	36.0	6.0	2.4
—	—	—	—
1.0	100.0	10.0	0.0

Check your understanding of the issues: Using the equations in this section, argue the pros ▶ and cons of policy measures aimed at increasing the U.S. saving rate.

worker. We saw earlier that the average U.S. saving rate since 1950 has been only 17%. So we can be quite confident that, at least in the United States, an increase in the saving rate would increase both output per worker and consumption per worker in the long run.

11.4 Physical versus Human Capital

We have concentrated so far on physical capital—machines, plants, office buildings, and so on. But economies have another type of capital: the set of skills of the workers in the economy, or what economists call **human capital**. An economy with many highly skilled workers is likely to be much more productive than an economy in which most workers cannot read or write.

Over the past two centuries, the increase in human capital has been as large as the increase in physical capital. At the beginning of the Industrial Revolution, only 30% of the population of the countries that constitute the OECD today knew how to read. Today, the literacy rate in OECD countries is above 95%. Schooling was not compulsory prior to the Industrial Revolution. Today it is compulsory, usually until age 16. Still, there are large differences across countries. Today, in OECD countries, nearly 100% of children get a primary education, 90% get a secondary education, and 38% get a higher education. The corresponding numbers in poor countries, countries with GDP per person below $400, are 95%, 32%, and 4%, respectively.

Even this comparison may be misleading because the quality of education can be quite different across countries. ▶

How should we think about the effect of human capital on output? How does the introduction of human capital change our earlier conclusions? These are the questions we take up in this last section.

Extending the Production Function

The most natural way of extending our analysis to allow for human capital is to modify the production function relation (11.1) to read

$$\frac{Y}{N} = f\left(\frac{K}{N}, \frac{H}{N}\right) \qquad (11.10)$$

$$(+, +)$$

Note that we are using the same symbol, H, to denote the ▶ monetary base in Chapter 4 and human capital in this chapter. Both uses are traditional. Do not be confused.

The level of output per worker depends on both the level of physical capital per worker, K/N, and the level of human capital per worker, H/N. As before, an increase in capital per worker, K/N, leads to an increase in output per worker. And an increase in the average level of skill, H/N, also leads to more output per worker. More skilled workers can do more complex tasks; they can deal more easily with unexpected complications. All this leads to higher output per worker.

We assumed earlier that increases in physical capital per worker increased output per worker but that the effect became smaller as the level of capital per worker increased. We can make the same assumption for human capital per worker: Think of increases in H/N as coming from increases in the number of years of education. The evidence is that the returns to increasing the proportion of children acquiring a primary education are very large. At the very least, the ability to read and write allows people to use equipment that is more complicated and more productive. For rich countries, however, primary education and secondary education are no longer the relevant margin: Most children now get both. The relevant margin is now higher education. I am sure it will come as good news to you that the evidence shows that higher education increases a person's skills, at least as measured by the increase in the wages of those who acquire it. But, to take an extreme example, it is not clear that forcing everyone to acquire an advanced college degree would increase aggregate output very

We look at this evidence in Chapter 13. ▶

much. Many people would end up overqualified and probably more frustrated rather than more productive.

How should we construct the measure for human capital, H? The answer is: very much the same way we construct the measure for physical capital, K. To construct K, we just add the values of the different pieces of capital, so that a machine that costs $2,000 gets twice the weight of a machine that costs $1,000. Similarly, we construct the measure of H such that workers who are paid twice as much get twice the weight. Take, for example, an economy with 100 workers, half of them unskilled and half of them skilled. Suppose the relative wage of the skilled workers is twice that of the unskilled workers. We can then construct H as $[(50 \times 1) + (50 \times 2)] = 150$. Human capital per worker, H/N, is then equal to $150/100 = 1.5$.

The rationale for using relative wages as weights is that they reflect relative marginal products. A worker who is paid three times as much as another is assumed to have a marginal product that is three times higher.

Human Capital, Physical Capital, and Output

How does the introduction of human capital change the analysis of the previous sections?

Our conclusions about *physical capital accumulation* remain valid: An increase in the saving rate increases steady-state physical capital per worker and therefore increases output per worker. But our conclusions now extend to *human capital accumulation* as well. An increase in how much society "saves" in the form of human capital—through education and on-the-job training—increases steady-state human capital per worker, which leads to an increase in output per worker. Our extended model gives us a richer picture of how output per worker is determined. In the long run, it tells us, output per worker depends on both how much society saves and how much it spends on education.

An issue, however, is whether relative wages accurately reflect relative marginal products. To take a controversial example: In the same job, with the same seniority, women still often earn less than men. Is it because their marginal product is lower? Should they be given a lower weight than men in the construction of human capital?

What are the relative importance of human capital and physical capital in the determination of output per worker? A place to start is to compare how much is spent on formal education to how much is invested in physical capital. In the United States, spending on formal education is about 6.5% of GDP. This number includes both government expenditures on education and private expenditures by people on education. It is between one-third and one-half of the gross investment rate for physical capital (which is around 16%). But this comparison is only a first pass. Consider the following complications:

- Education, especially higher education, is partly consumption—done for its own sake—and partly investment. We should include only the investment part for our purposes. However, the 6.5% number in the preceding paragraph includes both.
- At least for post-secondary education, the opportunity cost of a person's education are his or her foregone wages while acquiring the education. Spending on education should include not only the actual cost of education but also this opportunity cost. The 6.5% number does not include this opportunity cost.

How large is your opportunity cost relative to your tuition?

- Formal education is only part of education. Much of what we learn comes from on-the-job training, formal or informal. Both the actual costs and the opportunity costs of on-the-job training should also be included. The 6.5% number does not include the costs associated with on-the-job training.
- We should compare investment rates net of depreciation. Depreciation of physical capital, especially of machines, is likely to be higher than depreciation of human capital. Skills deteriorate, but they generally do so only slowly. And unlike physical capital, they deteriorate less quickly the more they are used.

For all these reasons, it is difficult to come up with reliable numbers for investment in human capital. Recent studies conclude that investment in physical capital and in education play roughly similar roles in the determination of output. This implies that output per worker depends roughly equally on the amount of physical capital and the amount of human capital in the economy. Countries that save more and/or spend more on education can achieve substantially higher steady-state levels of output per worker.

Endogenous Growth

We have mentioned Lucas once already in connection with the Lucas critique in Chapter 9.

Note what the conclusion we just reached said and did not say. It said that a country that saves more or spends more on education will achieve a *higher level* of output per worker in steady state. It did not say that by saving or spending more on education, a country can sustain permanently *higher growth* of output per worker.

This conclusion, however, has been challenged in the past two decades. Following the lead of Robert Lucas and Paul Romer, researchers have explored the possibility that the joint accumulation of physical capital and human capital might actually be enough to sustain growth. Given human capital, increases in physical capital will run into decreasing returns. And given physical capital, increases in human capital will also run into decreasing returns. But, these researchers have asked, what if both physical and human capital increase in tandem? Can't an economy grow forever just by having steadily more capital and more skilled workers?

Models that generate steady growth even without technological progress are called **models of endogenous growth** to reflect the fact that in those models—in contrast to the model we saw in earlier sections of this chapter—the growth rate depends, even in the long run, on variables such as the saving rate and the rate of spending on education. The jury on this class of models is still out, but the indications so far are that the conclusions we drew earlier need to be qualified, not abandoned. The current consensus is as follows:

- Output per worker depends on the level of both physical capital per worker and human capital per worker. Both forms of capital can be accumulated—one through physical investment and the other through education and training. Increasing either the saving rate and/or the fraction of output spent on education and training can lead to much higher levels of output per worker in the long run. However, given the rate of technological progress, such measures do not lead to a permanently higher growth rate.
- Note the qualifier in the last proposition: *given the rate of technological progress*. Is technological progress unrelated to the level of human capital in the economy? Can't a better-educated labor force lead to a higher rate of technological progress? These questions take us to the topic of the next chapter: the sources and the effects of technological progress.

Summary

- In the long run, the evolution of output is determined by two relations. (To make the reading of this summary easier, I omit *per worker* in what follows.) First, the level of output depends on the amount of capital. Second, capital accumulation depends on the level of output, which determines saving and investment.
- The interactions between capital and output imply that, starting from any level of capital (and ignoring technological progress, the topic of Chapter 12), an economy converges in the long run to a *steady-state* (constant)

level of capital. Associated with this level of capital is a steady-state level of output.
- The steady-state level of capital and, thus, the steady-state level of output depend positively on the saving rate. A higher saving rate leads to a higher steady-state level of output; during the transition to the new steady state, a higher saving rate leads to positive output growth. But (again ignoring technological progress) in the long run, the growth rate of output is equal to zero and so does not depend on the saving rate.

■ An increase in the saving rate requires an initial decrease in consumption. In the long run, the increase in the saving rate may lead to an increase or a decrease in consumption, depending on whether the economy is below or above the *golden-rule level of capital*, the level of capital at which steady-state consumption is highest.

■ Most countries typically have a level of capital below the golden-rule level. Thus, an increase in the saving rate leads to an initial decrease in consumption followed by an increase in consumption in the long run. When considering whether to adopt policy measures aimed at changing a country's saving rate, policymakers must decide how much weight to put on the welfare of current generations versus the welfare of future generations.

■ While most of the analysis of this chapter focuses on the effects of physical capital accumulation, output depends on the levels of both physical *and* human capital. Both forms of capital can be accumulated—one through investment and the other through education and training. Increasing the saving rate and/or the fraction of output spent on education and training can lead to large increases in output in the long run.

Key Terms

- saving rate, 245
- steady state, 251
- golden-rule level of capital, 256
- fully funded system, 257
- pay-as-you-go system, 257
- trust fund, 257
- human capital, 262
- models of endogenous growth, 264

Questions and Problems

Quick Check

1. Using the information in this chapter, label each of the following statements true, false, or uncertain. Explain briefly.
   a. The saving rate is always equal to the investment rate.
   b. A higher investment rate can sustain higher growth of output forever.
   c. If capital never depreciated, growth could go on forever.
   d. The higher the saving rate, the higher consumption in steady state.
   e. We should transform Social Security from a pay-as-you-go system to a fully funded system. This would increase consumption both now and in the future.
   f. The U.S. capital stock is far below the golden-rule level. The government should give tax breaks for saving because the U.S. capital stock is far below the golden-rule level.
   g. Education increases human capital and thus output. It follows that governments should subsidize education.

2. In Chapter 3 we saw that an increase in the saving rate can lead to a recession in the short run (i.e., the paradox of saving). We examined the issue in the medium run in a chapter problem at the end of Chapter 7. We can now examine the long-run effects of an increase in saving.

   Using the model presented in this chapter, what is the effect of an increase in the saving rate on output per worker likely to be after one decade? After five decades?

3. Consider the following statement: "The Solow model shows that the saving rate does not affect the growth rate in the long run, so we should stop worrying about the low U.S. saving rate. Increasing the saving rate wouldn't have any important effects on the economy." Do you agree or disagree?

Dig Deeper

4. Suppose the United States moved from the current pay-as-you-go Social Security system to a fully funded one, and financed the transition without additional government borrowing. How would the shift to a fully funded system affect the level and the rate of growth of output per worker in the long run?

5. Discuss how the level of output per person in the long run would likely be affected by each of the following changes:
   a. The right to exclude saving from income when paying income taxes.
   b. A higher rate of female participation in the labor market (but constant population).

6. Suppose that the production function is given by

$$Y = 0.5\sqrt{K}\sqrt{N}$$

   a. Derive the steady-state levels of output per worker and capital per worker in terms of the saving rate, s, and the depreciation rate, δ.
   b. Derive the equation for steady-state output per worker and steady-state consumption per worker in terms of s and δ.
   c. Suppose that $\delta = 0.05$. With your favorite spreadsheet software, compute steady-state output per worker and steady-state consumption per worker for $s = 0$, $s = 0.1$, $s = 0.2$, ..., $s = 1$. Explain the intuition behind your results.
   d. Use your favorite spreadsheet software to graph the steady-state level of output per worker and the steady-state level of consumption per worker as a function of the saving rate (i.e., measure the saving rate on the

horizontal axis of your graph and the corresponding values of output per worker and consumption per worker on the vertical axis).

e. Does the graph show that there is a value of s that maximizes output per worker? Does the graph show that there is a value of s that maximizes consumption per worker? If so, what is this value?

7. *The Cobb-Douglas production function and the steady state. This problem is based on the material in the chapter appendix. Suppose that the economy's production function is given by*

$$Y = K^\alpha N^{1-\alpha}$$

and assume that $\alpha = 1/3$.

a. Is this production function characterized by constant returns to scale? Explain.

b. Are there decreasing returns to capital?

c. Are there decreasing returns to labor?

d. Transform the production function into a relation between output per worker and capital per worker.

e. For a given saving rate, s, and depreciation rate, δ, give an expression for capital per worker in the steady state.

f. Give an expression for output per worker in the steady state.

g. Solve for the steady-state level of output per worker when $s = 0.32$ and $\delta = 0.08$.

h. Suppose that the depreciation rate remains constant at $\delta = 0.08$, while the saving rate is reduced by half, to $s = 0.16$. What is the new steady-state output per worker?

8. *Continuing with the logic from problem 7, suppose that the economy's production function is given by* $Y = K^{1/3}N^{2/3}$ *and that both the saving rate, s, and the depreciation rate, δ, are equal to 0.10.*

a. What is the steady-state level of capital per worker?

b. What is the steady-state level of output per worker?

Suppose that the economy is in steady state and that, in period t, the depreciation rate increases permanently from 0.10 to 0.20.

c. What will be the new steady-state levels of capital per worker and output per worker?

d. Compute the path of capital per worker and output per worker over the first three periods after the change in the depreciation rate.

9. *Deficits and the capital stock*

For the production function, $Y = \sqrt{K}\sqrt{N}$, equation (11.8) gives the solution for the steady-state capital stock per worker.

a. Retrace the steps in the text that derive equation (11.8).

b. Suppose that the saving rate, s, is initially 18% per year, and the depreciation rate, δ, is 8%. What is the steady-state capital stock per worker? What is steady-state output per worker?

c. Suppose that there is a government deficit of 6% of GDP and that the government eliminates this deficit. Assume that private saving is unchanged so that national saving increases to 24%. What is the new steady-state capital stock per worker? What is the new steady-state output per worker? How does this compare to your answer to part (b)?

Explore Further

10. *U.S. saving*

This question follows the logic of problem 9 to explore the implications of the U.S. budget deficit for the long-run capital stock. The question assumes that the United States will have a budget deficit over the life of this edition of the text.

a. Go to the most recent *Economic Report of the President* (**www.gpoaccess.gov/eop/**). From Table B-32, get the numbers for gross national saving for the most recent year available. From Table B-1, get the number for U.S. GDP for the same year. What is the national saving rate, as a percentage of GDP? Using the depreciation rate and the logic from problem 9, what would be the steady-state capital stock per worker? What would be steady-state output per worker?

b. In Table B-79 of the *Economic Report of the President*, get the number for the federal budget deficit as a percentage of GDP for the year corresponding to the data from part (a). Again using the reasoning from problem 9, suppose that the federal budget deficit was eliminated and there was no change in private saving. What would be the effect on the long-run capital stock per worker? What would be the effect on long-run output per worker?

We invite you to visit the Blanchard page on the Prentice Hall Web site, at:
www.prenhall.com/blanchard
for this chapter's World Wide Web exercises.

Further Readings

- The classic treatment of the relation between the saving rate and output is by Robert Solow, *Growth Theory: An Exposition*, Oxford University Press, New York, 1970.
- An easy-to-read discussion of whether and how to increase saving and improve education in the United

States is given in Memoranda 23 to 27 in Charles Schultze (the Chairman of the Council of Economic Advisers during the Carter administration), *Memos to the President: A Guide Through Macroeconomics for the Busy Policymaker*, Brookings Institution, Washington, DC, 1992.

Appendix: The Cobb-Douglas Production Function and the Steady State

In 1928, Charles Cobb (a mathematician) and Paul Douglas (an economist, who went on to become a U.S. senator) concluded that the following production function gave a very good description of the relation between output, physical capital, and labor in the United States from 1899 to 1922:

$$Y = K^\alpha N^{1-\alpha} \tag{11A.1}$$

with α being a number between 0 and 1. Their findings proved surprisingly robust. Even today, the production function (11A.1), now known as the **Cobb-Douglas production function**, still gives a good description of the relation between output, capital, and labor in the United States, and it has become a standard tool in the economist's toolbox. (Verify for yourself that it satisfies the two properties we discussed in the text: constant returns to scale and decreasing returns to capital and to labor.)

The purpose of this appendix is to characterize the steady state of an economy when the production function is given by (11A.1). (All you need in order to follow the steps is knowledge of the properties of exponents.)

Recall that, in steady state, saving per worker must be equal to depreciation per worker. Let's see what this implies:

■ To derive saving per worker, we must derive first the relation between output per worker and capital per worker implied by equation (11A.1). Divide both sides of equation (11A.1) by N:

$$Y/N = K^\alpha N^{1-\alpha}/N$$

Using the properties of exponents:

$$N^{1-\alpha}/N = N^{1-\alpha}N^{-1} = N^{-\alpha}$$

so, replacing in the preceding equation, we get:

$$Y/N = K^\alpha N^{-\alpha} = (K/N)^\alpha$$

Output per worker, Y/N, is equal to the ratio of capital per worker, K/N, raised to the power α.

Saving per worker is equal to the saving rate times output per worker, so using the previous equation, it is equal to

$$s(K^*/N)^\alpha$$

■ Depreciation per worker is equal to the depreciation rate times capital per worker:

$$\delta(K^*/N)$$

■ The steady-state level of capital, K^*, is determined by the condition that saving per worker be equal to depreciation per worker, so

$$s(K^*/N)^\alpha = \delta(K^*/N)$$

To solve this expression for the steady-state level of capital per worker, K^*/N, divide both sides by $(K^*/N)^\alpha$:

$$s = \delta(K^*/N)^{1-\alpha}$$

Divide both sides by δ and change the order of the equality:

$$(K^*/N)^{1-\alpha} = s/\delta$$

Finally, raise both sides to the power $1/(1 - \alpha)$:

$$(K^*/N) = (s/\delta)^{1/(1-\alpha)}$$

This gives us the steady-state level of capital per worker.

From the production function, the steady-state level of output per worker is then equal to

$$(Y^*/N) = (K/N)^\alpha = (s/\delta)^{\alpha/(1-\alpha)}$$

Let's see what this last equation implies:

■ In the text, we actually worked with a special case of equation (11A.1), the case where $\alpha = 0.5$. (Taking a variable to the power 0.5 is the same as taking the square root of the variable.) If $\alpha = 0.5$, the preceding equation means

$$Y^*/N = s/\delta$$

Output per worker is equal to the ratio of the saving rate to the depreciation rate. This is the equation we discussed in the text. A doubling of the saving rate leads to a doubling in steady-state output per worker.

■ The empirical evidence suggests, however, that if we think of K as physical capital, α is closer to one-third than to one-half. Assuming that $\alpha = 1/3$, then $\alpha(1 - \alpha) = (1/3)/(1 - (1/3)) = (1/3)/(2/3) = 1/2$, and the equation for output per worker yields

$$Y^*/N = (s/\delta)^{1/2} = \sqrt{s/\delta}$$

This implies smaller effects of the saving rate on output per worker than was suggested by the computations in the text. A doubling of the saving rate, for example, means that output per worker increases by a factor of $\sqrt{2}$ or only about 1.4 (put another way, a 40% increase in output per worker).

■ There is, however, an interpretation of our model in which the appropriate value of α is close to 1/2, so the computations in the text are applicable. If, along the lines of Section 11-4, we take into account human capital as well as physical capital, then a value of α around 1/2 for the contribution of this broader definition of capital to output is, indeed, roughly appropriate. Thus, one interpretation of the numerical results in Section 11-3 is that they show the effects of a given saving rate, but that saving must be interpreted to include saving in both physical capital and human capital (more machines and more education).

Key Term

■ Cobb-Douglas production function, 245

Technological Progress and Growth

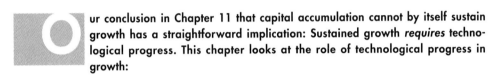

ur conclusion in Chapter 11 that capital accumulation cannot by itself sustain growth has a straightforward implication: Sustained growth *requires* technological progress. This chapter looks at the role of technological progress in growth:

■ Section 12-1 looks at the respective role of technological progress and capital accumulation in growth. It shows how, in steady state, the rate of growth of output per person is simply equal to the rate of technological progress. This does not mean, however, that the saving rate is irrelevant. The saving rate affects the level of output per person—but not its rate of growth.

■ Section 12-2 turns to the determinants of technological progress, focusing in particular on the role of research and development (R&D).

■ Section 12-3 returns to the facts of growth presented in Chapter 10 and interprets them in the light of what we have learned in this and the previous chapter. ■

In an economy in which there is both capital accumulation and technological progress, at what rate will output grow? To answer this question, we need to extend the model developed in Chapter 11 to allow for technological progress. To introduce technological progress into the picture, we must first revisit the aggregate production function.

Technological Progress and the Production Function

Technological progress has many dimensions:

The average number of items carried by a supermarket increased from 2,200 in 1950 to 45,500 in 2005. To get a sense of what this means, see Robin Williams (who plays an immigrant from the Soviet Union) in the supermarket scene in the movie *Moscow on the Hudson*. ▶

- It can lead to larger quantities of output for given quantities of capital and labor. Think of a new type of lubricant that allows a machine to run at a higher speed and to therefore produce more.
- It can lead to better products. Think of the steady improvement in car safety and comfort over time.
- It can lead to new products. Think of the introductions of CD players, fax machines, cell phones, and flat-screen monitors.
- It can lead to a larger variety of products. Think of the steady increase in the number of breakfast cereals available at your local supermarket.

As you saw in the Focus box "Real GDP, Technological Progress, and the Price of Computers" in Chapter 2, thinking of products as providing a number of underlying services is the method used to construct the price index for computers. ▶

These dimensions are more similar than they appear. If we think of consumers as caring not about the goods themselves but about the services these goods provide, then they all have something in common: In each case, consumers receive more services. A better car provides more safety, a new product such as a fax machine or a new service such as the Internet provides more information services, and so on. If we think of output as the set of underlying services provided by the goods produced in the economy, we can think of technological progress as leading to increases in output for given amounts of capital and labor. We can then think of the *state of technology* as a variable that tells us how much output can be produced from given amounts of capital and labor at any time. If we denote the state of technology by A, we can rewrite the production function as

For simplicity, we ignore human capital here. We return to it later in the chapter. ▶

$$Y = F(K, N, A)$$
$$(+, +, +)$$

This is our extended production function. Output depends on both capital and labor, K and N, and on the state of technology, A: Given capital and labor, an improvement in the state of technology, A, leads to an increase in output.

It will be convenient to use a more restrictive form of the preceding equation, however, namely

$$Y = F(K, AN) \qquad (12.1)$$

This equation states that production depends on capital and on labor multiplied by the state of technology. Introducing the state of technology in this way makes it easier to think about the effect of technological progress on the relation between output, capital, and labor. Equation (12.1) implies that we can think of technological progress in two equivalent ways:

- Technological progress *reduces* the number of workers needed to produce a given amount of output. Doubling A produces the same quantity of output with only half the original number of workers, N.

■ ✗ Technological progress *increases* the output that can be produced with a given number of workers. We can think of AN as the amount of **effective labor** in the economy. If the state of technology, A, doubles, it is as if the economy had twice as many workers. In other words, we can think of output being produced by two factors: capital, K, and effective labor, AN.

◀ *AN is also sometimes called labor in efficiency units. The use of "efficiency" for "efficiency units" here and for "efficiency wages" in Chapter 6 is a coincidence: The two notions are unrelated.*

What restrictions should we impose on the extended production function (12.1)? We can build directly here on our discussion in Chapter 10.

Again, it is reasonable to assume constant returns to scale: *For a given state of technology, A, doubling both the amount of capital, K, and the amount of labor, N, is likely to lead to a doubling of output:*

$$2Y = F(2K, 2AN)$$

More generally, for any number x,

$$xY = F(xK, xAN)$$

It is also reasonable to assume decreasing returns to each of the two factors—capital and effective labor. Given effective labor, an increase in capital is likely to increase output, but at a decreasing rate. Symmetrically, given capital, an increase in effective labor is likely to increase output, but at a decreasing rate.

Per worker: divided by the number of workers, N.
Per effective worker: divided by the number of effective workers, AN—the number of workers, N, times the state of ◀ *technology, A.*

It was convenient in Chapter 11 to think in terms of output *per worker* and capital *per worker*. That was because the steady state of the economy was a state where output *per worker* and capital *per worker* were constant. It is convenient here to look at output *per effective worker* and capital *per effective worker*. The reason is the same: As we shall soon see, in steady state, output *per effective worker* and capital *per effective worker* are constant.

To get a relation between output per effective worker and capital per effective worker, take $x = 1/AN$ in the preceding equation. This gives

$$\frac{Y}{AN} = F\left(\frac{K}{AN}, 1\right)$$

Or, if we define the function f so that $f(K/AN) \equiv F(K/AN, 1)$:

$$\frac{Y}{AN} = f\left(\frac{K}{AN}\right) \tag{12.2}$$

◀ *Suppose that F has the "double square root" form:*
$$Y = F(K, AN) = \sqrt{K}\sqrt{AN}$$
Then
$$\frac{Y}{AN} = \frac{\sqrt{K}\sqrt{AN}}{AN} = \frac{\sqrt{K}}{\sqrt{AN}}$$
So the function f is simply the square root function:
$$f(K/AN) = \sqrt{\frac{K}{AN}}$$

In words: *Output per effective worker* (the left side) is a function of *capital per effective worker* (the expression in the function on the right side).

The relation between output per effective worker and capital per effective worker is drawn in Figure 12-1. It looks very much the same as the relation we drew in Figure 11-2 between output per worker and capital per worker in the absence of technological progress. There, increases in K/N led to increases in Y/N, but at a decreasing rate. Here, increases in K/AN lead to increases in Y/AN, but at a decreasing rate.

Interactions between Output and Capital

We now have the elements we need to think about the determinants of growth. Our analysis will parallel the analysis of Chapter 11. There we looked at the dynamics of *output per worker* and *capital per worker*. Here we look at the dynamics of *output per effective worker* and *capital per effective worker*.

The simple key to understanding the results in this section is that the results we derived for output per worker in Chapter 11 still hold in this chapter, but now for output per effective worker. For example, in Chapter 11, we saw that output per worker was constant in steady state. In this chapter, we shall see that output per effective worker is constant in ◀ *steady state. And so on.*

**Output per Effective
Worker versus Capital
per Effective Worker**

Because of decreasing returns to
capital, increases in capital per
effective worker lead to smaller
and smaller increases in output
per effective worker.

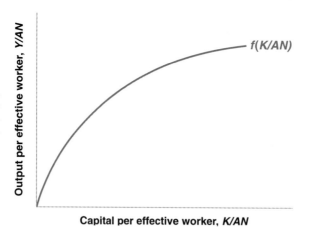

In Chapter 11, we characterized the dynamics of output and capital per worker
using Figure 11-2. In that figure, we drew three relations:

■ The relation between output per worker and capital per worker.
■ The relation between investment per worker and capital per worker.
■ The relation between depreciation per worker—equivalently, the investment per
  worker needed to maintain a constant level of capital per worker—and capital per
  worker.

The dynamics of capital per worker and, by implication, output per worker were
determined by the relation between investment per worker and depreciation per worker.
Depending on whether investment per worker was greater or smaller than depreciation
per worker, capital per worker increased or decreased over time, as did output per worker.

We shall follow the same approach in building Figure 12-2. The difference is that we
focus on output, capital, and investment *per effective worker* rather than per worker:

■ The relation between output per effective worker and capital per effective worker
  was derived in Figure 12-1. This relation is repeated in Figure 12-2: Output per effective worker increases with capital per effective worker, but at a decreasing rate.

■ **Figure 12-2**

**The Dynamics of Capital
per Effective Worker and
Output per Effective
Worker**

Capital per effective worker and
output per effective worker converge to constant values in the
long run.

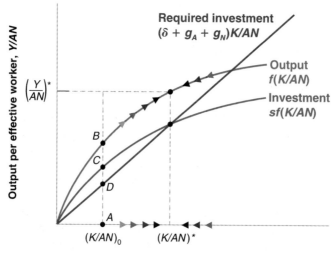

■ Under the same assumptions as in Chapter 11—that investment is equal to private saving, and the private saving rate is constant—investment is given by

$$I = S = sY$$

Divide both sides by the number of effective workers, AN, to get

$$\frac{I}{AN} = s\frac{Y}{AN}$$

Replacing output per effective worker, Y/AN, by its expression from equation (12.2) gives

$$\frac{I}{AN} = sf\left(\frac{K}{AN}\right)$$

The relation between investment per effective worker and capital per effective worker is drawn in Figure 12-2. It is equal to the upper curve—the relation between output per effective worker and capital per effective worker—multiplied by the saving rate, s. This gives us the lower curve.

■ Finally, we need to ask what level of investment per effective worker is needed to maintain a given level of capital per effective worker.

In Chapter 11, for capital to be constant, investment had to be equal to the depreciation of the existing capital stock. Here, the answer is slightly more complicated: Now that we allow for technological progress (so A increases over time), the number of effective workers, AN, increases over time. Thus, maintaining the same ratio of capital to effective workers, K/AN, requires an increase in the capital stock, K, proportional to the increase in the number of effective workers, AN. Let's look at this condition more closely.

Let δ be the depreciation rate of capital. Let the rate of technological progress be equal to g_A. Let the rate of population growth be equal to g_N. If we assume that ◀ the ratio of employment to the total population remains constant, the number of workers, N, also grows at annual rate g_N. Together, these assumptions imply that the growth rate of effective labor, AN, equals $g_A + g_N$. For example, if the number ◀ of workers is growing at 1% per year and the rate of technological progress is 2% per year, then the growth rate of effective labor is equal to 3% per year.

These assumptions imply that the level of investment needed to maintain a given level of capital per effective worker is therefore given by

$$I = \delta K + (g_A + g_N)K$$

Or, equivalently,

$$I = (\delta + g_A + g_N)K \tag{12.3}$$

An amount, δK, is needed just to keep the capital stock constant. If the depreciation rate is 10%, then investment must be equal to 10% of the capital stock just to maintain the same level of capital. And an additional amount, $(g_A + g_N)K$, is needed to ensure that the capital stock increases at the same rate as effective labor. If effective labor increases at 3% per year, for example, then capital must increase by 3% per year to maintain the same level of capital per effective worker. Putting δK and $(g_A + g_N)K$ together in this example: If the depreciation rate is 10% and the growth rate of effective labor is 3%, then investment must equal 13% of the capital stock to maintain a constant level of capital per effective worker.

In Chapter 11, we assumed $g_A = 0$ and $g_N = 0$. Our focus in this chapter is on the implications of technological progress, $g_A > 0$. But once we allow for technological progress, introducing population growth, $g_N > 0$, is straightforward. Thus, I allow for both $g_A > 0$ and $g_N > 0$.

The growth rate of the product of two variables is the sum of the growth rates of the two variables. See Proposition 7 in Appendix 2 at the end of the book.

Dividing the previous expression by the number of effective workers to get the amount of investment per effective worker needed to maintain a constant level of capital per effective worker gives

$$\frac{I}{AN} = (\delta + g_A + g_N)\frac{K}{AN}$$

The level of investment per effective worker needed to maintain a given level of capital per effective worker is represented by the upward-sloping line "Required investment" in Figure 12-2. The slope of the line equals $(\delta + g_A + g_N)$.

Dynamics of Capital and Output

We can now give a graphical description of the dynamics of capital per effective worker and output per effective worker.

Consider a given level of capital per effective worker, say $(K/AN)_0$ in Figure 12-2. At that level, output per effective worker equals the vertical distance AB. Investment per effective worker is equal to AC. The amount of investment required to maintain that level of capital per effective worker is equal to AD. Because actual investment exceeds the investment level required to maintain the existing level of capital per effective worker, K/AN increases.

Hence, starting from $(K/AN)_0$, the economy moves to the right, with the level of capital per effective worker increasing over time. This goes on until investment per effective worker is just sufficient to maintain the existing level of capital per effective worker, until capital per effective worker equals $(K/AN)^*$.

In the long run, capital per effective worker reaches a constant level, and so does output per effective worker. Put another way, the steady state of this economy is such that *capital per effective worker and output per effective worker are constant and equal to $(K/AN)^*$ and $(Y/AN)^*$, respectively.*

This implies that, in steady state, output, Y, is growing at the same rate as effective labor, AN (so that the ratio of the two is constant). Because effective labor grows at rate $(g_A + g_N)$, output growth in steady state must also equal $(g_A + g_N)$. The same reasoning applies to capital: Because capital per effective worker is constant in steady state, capital is also growing at rate $(g_A + g_N)$.

> If Y/AN is constant, Y must grow at the same rate as AN. So it must grow at rate $g_A + g_N$.

Stated in terms of capital or output per effective worker, these results seem rather abstract. But it is straightforward to state them in a more intuitive way, and this gives us our first important conclusion:

> *In steady state, the growth rate of output equals the rate of population growth* (g_N) *plus the rate of technological progress* (g_A). *By implication, the growth rate of output is independent of the saving rate.*

To strengthen your intuition, let's go back to the argument we used in Chapter 11 to show that, in the absence of technological progress and population growth, the economy could not sustain positive growth forever:

■ The argument went as follows: Suppose the economy tried to sustain positive output growth. Because of decreasing returns to capital, capital would have to grow faster than output. The economy would have to devote a larger and larger proportion of output to capital accumulation. At some point, there would be no more output to devote to capital accumulation. Growth would come to an end.

■ Exactly the same logic is at work here. Effective labor grows at rate $(g_A + g_N)$. Suppose the economy tried to sustain output growth in excess of $(g_A + g_N)$. Because of decreasing returns to capital, capital would have to increase faster than output. The economy would have to devote a larger and larger proportion of

Table 12-1	The Characteristics of Balanced Growth	
		Rate of growth of:
1	Capital per effective worker	0
2	Output per effective worker	0
3	Capital per worker	g_A
4	Output per worker	g_A
5	Labor	g_N
6	Capital	$g_A + g_N$
7	Output	$g_A + g_N$

output to capital accumulation. At some point, this would prove impossible. Thus the economy cannot permanently grow faster than $(g_A + g_N)$.

We have focused on the behavior of aggregate output. To get a sense of what happens not to aggregate output but rather to the standard of living over time, we must look instead at the behavior of output per worker (not output per *effective* worker). ◄ Because output grows at rate $(g_A + g_N)$ and the number of workers grows at rate g_N, output per worker grows at rate g_A. In other words, *when the economy is in steady state,* ◄ *output per worker grows at the rate of technological progress.*

Because output, capital, and effective labor all grow at the same rate, $(g_A + g_N)$, in steady state, the steady state of this economy is also called a state of **balanced growth**: In steady state, output and the two inputs, capital and effective labor, grow "in balance," at the same rate. The characteristics of balanced growth will be helpful later in the chapter and are summarized in Table 12-1.

On the balanced growth path (equivalently: in steady state, or in the long run):

- *Capital per effective worker* and *output per effective worker* are constant; this is the result we derived in Figure 12-2.
- Equivalently, *capital per worker* and *output per worker* are growing at the rate of technological progress, g_A.
- Or, in terms of labor, capital, and output: *Labor* is growing at the rate of population growth, g_N; *capital* and *output* are growing at a rate equal to the sum of population growth and the rate of technological progress $(g_A + g_N)$.

The standard of living is given by output per worker (or, more accurately, output per person), not output per effective worker.

The growth rate of Y/N is equal to the growth rate of Y minus the growth rate of N (see Proposition 8 in Appendix 2 at the end of the book). So the growth rate of Y/N is given by $(g_Y - g_N) = (g_A + g_N) - g_N = g_A$.

The Effects of the Saving Rate

In steady state, the growth rate of output depends *only* on the rate of population growth and the rate of technological progress. Changes in the saving rate do not affect the steady-state growth rate. But changes in the saving rate do increase the steady-state level of output per effective worker.

This result is best seen in Figure 12-3, which shows the effect of an increase in the saving rate from s_0 to s_1. The increase in the saving rate shifts the investment relation up, from $s_0 f(K/AN)$ to $s_1 f(K/AN)$. It follows that the steady-state level of capital per effective worker increases from $(K/AN)_0$ to $(K/AN)_1$, with a corresponding increase in the level of output per effective worker from $(Y/AN)_0$ to $(Y/AN)_1$.

Following the increase in the saving rate, capital per effective worker and output per effective worker increase for some time, as they converge to their new higher

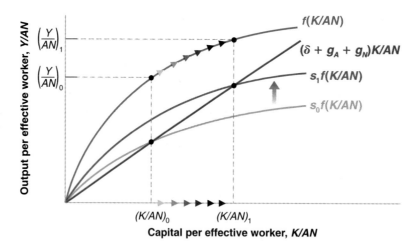

An increase in the saving rate leads to an increase in the steady-state levels of output per effective worker and capital per effective worker.

Figure 12-4 is the same as Figure 11-5, which anticipated the derivation presented here.

For a description of logarithmic scales, see Appendix 2 at the end of the book.

When a logarithmic scale is used, a variable growing at a constant rate moves along a straight line. The slope of the line is equal to the rate of growth of the variable.

▶ level. Figure 12-4 plots output against time. Output is measured on a logarithmic
▶ scale. The economy is initially on the balanced growth path AA: Output is growing at
rate $(g_A + g_N)$—so the slope of AA is equal to $(g_A + g_N)$. After the increase in the saving rate at time t, output grows faster for some period of time. Eventually, output ends
up at a higher level than it would have been without the increase in saving. But its
growth rate returns to $g_A + g_N$. In the new steady state, the economy grows at the
same rate, but on a higher growth path, BB. BB, which is parallel to AA, also has a
▶ slope equal to $(g_A + g_N)$.

Let's summarize: In an economy with technological progress and population
growth, output grows over time. In steady state, output *per effective worker* and capital
per effective worker are constant. Put another way, output *per worker* and capital *per
worker* grow at the rate of technological progress. Put yet another way, output and capital grow at the same rate as effective labor and, therefore, at a rate equal to the growth
rate of the number of workers plus the rate of technological progress. When the economy is in steady state, it is said to be on a *balanced growth path*.

The rate of output growth in steady state is independent of the saving rate.
However, the saving rate affects the steady-state level of output per effective worker.
Increases in the saving rate lead, for some time, to an increase in the growth rate above
the steady-state growth rate.

The increase in the saving rate leads to higher growth until the economy reaches its new, higher, balanced growth path.

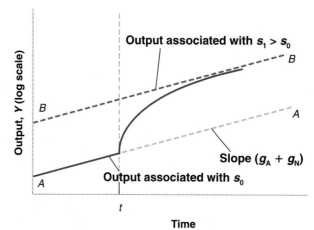

The Long Run   **The Core**

12-2 The Determinants of Technological Progress

We have just seen that the growth rate of output per worker is ultimately determined by the rate of technological progress. This leads naturally to the next question: What determines the rate of technological progress? We now take up this question.

"Technological progress" brings to mind images of major discoveries: the invention of the microchip, the discovery of the structure of DNA, and so on. These discoveries suggest a process driven largely by scientific research and chance rather than by economic forces. But the truth is that most technological progress in modern economies is the result of a humdrum process: the outcome of firms' **research and development (R&D)** activities. Industrial R&D expenditures account for between 2% and 3% of GDP in each of the four major rich countries we looked at in Chapter 10 (the United States, France, Japan, and the United Kingdom). About 75% of the roughly 1 million U.S. scientists and researchers working in R&D are employed by firms. U.S. firms' R&D spending equals more than 20% of their spending on gross investment and more than 60% of their spending on net investment—gross investment less depreciation.

Firms spend on R&D for the same reason they buy new machines or build new plants: to increase profits. By increasing spending on R&D, a firm increases the probability that it will discover and develop a new product. (I use *product* as a generic term to denote new goods or new techniques of production.) If a new product is successful, the firm's profits will increase. There is, however, an important difference between purchasing a machine and spending more on R&D. The difference is that the outcome of R&D is fundamentally *ideas*. And, unlike a machine, an idea can potentially be used by many firms at the same time. A firm that has just acquired a new machine does not have to worry that another firm will use that particular machine. A firm that has discovered and developed a new product can make no such assumption.

This last point implies that the level of R&D spending depends not only on the **fertility** of the research process—how spending on R&D translates into new ideas and new products—but also on the **appropriability of research** results—the extent to which firms benefit from the results of their own R&D. Let's look at each aspect in turn.

The Fertility of the Research Process

If research is very fertile—that is, if R&D spending leads to many new products—then, other things equal, firms will have strong incentives to spend on R&D; R&D spending and, by implication, technological progress will be high. The determinants of the fertility of research lie largely outside the realm of economics. Many factors interact here.

The fertility of research depends on the successful interaction between basic research (the search for general principles and results) and applied research and development (the application of these results to specific uses and the development of new products). Basic research does not lead, by itself, to technological progress. But the success of applied research and development depends ultimately on basic research. Much of the computer industry's development can be traced to a few breakthroughs, from the invention of the transistor to the invention of the microchip. Indeed, the recent increase in productivity growth in the United States, which we discussed in Chapter 1, is widely attributed to the diffusion across the U.S. economy of the breakthroughs in information technology. (This is explored further in the Focus box "Information Technology, the New Economy, and Productivity Growth.")

Some countries appear to be more successful than others at basic research; other countries are more successful at applied research and development. Studies point to differences in the education system as one of the reasons. For example, it is often

Information Technology, the New Economy, and Productivity Growth

Average annual productivity growth in the United States from 1996 to 2006 reached 2.8%—a high number relative to the anemic 1.8% average achieved from 1970 to 1995. This has led some to proclaim an **information technology revolution**, announce the dawn of a **New Economy**, and forecast a long period of high productivity growth in the future.

What should we make of these claims? Research to date gives reasons both for optimism and for caution. It suggests that the recent high productivity growth is indeed linked to the development of information technologies. It also suggests that a sharp distinction must be drawn between what is happening in the information technology (IT) sector—the sector that produces computers, computer software and software services, and communications equipment—and the rest of the economy—which uses this information technology:

■ In the IT sector, technological progress has indeed been proceeding at an extraordinary pace.

In 1965, researcher Gordon Moore, who later founded Intel Corporation, predicted that the number of transistors in a chip would double every 18 to 24 months, allowing for steadily more powerful computers. As shown in Figure 1, this relation—now known as **Moore's law**—has held extremely well over time. The first logic chip produced in 1971 had 2,300 transistors; the Pentium 4, released in 2000, had 42 million. (The Intel Core 2, released in 2006, and thus not included in the figure, has 291 million.)

Although it has proceeded at a less extreme pace, technological progress in the rest of the IT sector has also been very high. And the share of the IT sector in GDP is steadily increasing, from 3% of GDP in 1980 to 7% today. This combination of high technological progress in the IT sector and of an increasing IT share has led to a steady increase in the economy-wide rate of technological progress. This is one of the factors behind the high productivity growth in the United States since the mid-1990s.

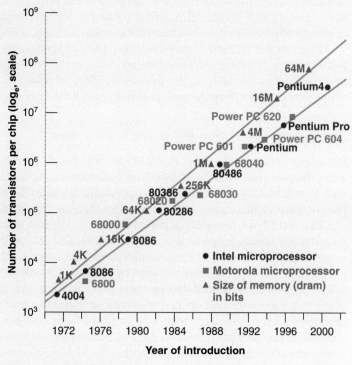

Figure 1 *Moore's Law: Number of Transistors per Chip, 1970 to 2000*

Source: Dale Jorgenson, **post.economics.harvard.edu/faculty/jorgenson/papers/aea5.ppt**.

In the non-IT sector—the "old economy," which still accounts for more than 90% of the U.S. economy—however, there is little evidence of a parallel technological revolution:

■ On the one hand, the steady decrease in the price of IT equipment (reflecting technological progress in the IT sector) has led firms in the non-IT sector to increase their stock of IT capital. This has led to an increase in the ratio of capital per worker and an increase in productivity growth in the non-IT sector.

Let's go through this argument a bit more formally. Go back to equation (12.2), which shows the relation of output per effective worker to the ratio of capital per effective worker:

$$Y/AN = f(K/AN)$$

Think of this equation as giving the relation between output per effective worker and capital per effective worker in the non-IT sector. The evidence is that the decrease in the price of IT capital has led firms to increase their stock of IT capital and, by implication, their overall capital stock. In other words, K/AN has increased in the non-IT sector, leading to an increase in Y/AN.

■ On the other hand, the IT revolution does not appear to have had a major direct effect on the pace of technological progress in the non-IT sector. You have surely heard claims that the information technology revolution was forcing firms to drastically reorganize, leading to large gains in productivity. Firms may be reorganizing, but so far, there is little evidence that this is leading to large gains in productivity: Measures of technological progress show only a small rise in the rate of technological progress in the non-IT sector from the post-1970 average.

In terms of the production function relation we just discussed, there is no evidence that the technological revolution has led to a higher rate of growth of A in the non-IT sector.

Are there reasons to expect productivity growth to be higher in the future than in the past 25 years? The answer is yes: The factors we have just discussed are here to stay. Technological progress in the IT sector is likely to remain high, and the share of IT is likely to continue to increase. Moreover, firms in the non-IT sector are likely to further increase their stock of IT capital, leading to further increases in productivity.

How high can we expect productivity growth to be in the future? Probably not as high as it was from 1996 to 2006, but according to some estimates, we can expect it to be perhaps 0.5 percentage points higher than its post-1970 average. This may not be the miracle some have claimed, but if sustained, it is an increase that will make a substantial difference to the U.S. standard of living in the future.

Note: For more on these issues, read "Information Technology and the U.S. Economy," by Dale Jorgenson, American Economic Review, *Volume 91, Number 1, March 2001, 1–32.*

argued that the French higher education system, with its strong emphasis on abstract thinking, produces researchers who are better at basic research than at applied research and development. Studies also point to the importance of a "culture of entrepreneurship," in which a big part of technological progress comes from the ability of entrepreneurs to organize the successful development and marketing of new products—a dimension where the United States appears to be better than most other countries.

It takes many years, and often many decades, for the full potential of major discoveries to be realized. The usual sequence is that a major discovery leads to the exploration of potential applications, then to the development of new products, and, finally, to the adoption of these new products. The Focus box "The Diffusion of New Technology: Hybrid Corn" shows the results of one of the first studies of this process of the diffusion of ideas. Closer to us is the example of personal computers. Twenty years after the commercial introduction of personal computers, it often seems as if we have just begun discovering their uses.

An age-old worry is that research will become less and less fertile—that most major discoveries have already taken place and that technological progress will now slow down. This fear may come from thinking about mining, where higher-grade mines were exploited first, and we have had to exploit lower- and lower-grade mines. But this is only an analogy, and so far there is no evidence that it is correct.

◀ In Chapter 11, we looked at the role of human capital as an input in production: More educated people can use more complex machines, or handle more complex tasks. Here, we see a second role of human capital: better researchers and scientists, and, by implication, a higher rate of technological progress.

New technologies are not developed or adopted overnight. One of the first studies of the diffusion of new technologies was carried out in 1957 by Zvi Griliches, a Harvard economist, who looked at the diffusion of hybrid corn in different states in the United States.

Hybrid corn is, in the words of Griliches, "the invention of a method of inventing." Producing hybrid corn entails crossing different strains of corn to develop a type of corn adapted to local conditions. The introduction of hybrid corn can increase the corn yield by up to 20%.

Although the idea of hybridization was first developed at the beginning of the twentieth century, the first commercial application did not take place until the 1930s in the United States. Figure 1 shows the rate at which hybrid corn was adopted in a number of U.S. states from 1932 to 1956.

The figure shows two dynamic processes at work. One is the process through which hybrid corn appropriate to each state were discovered. Hybrid corn became available in southern states (Texas and Alabama) more than 10 years after it had become available in northern states (Iowa, Wisconsin, and Kentucky). The other is the speed at which hybrid corn was adopted within each state. Within eight years of its introduction, practically all corn in Iowa was hybrid corn. The process was much slower in the South. More than 10 years after its introduction, hybrid corn accounted for only 60% of total acreage in Alabama.

Why was the speed of adoption higher in Iowa than in the South? Griliches's article showed that the reason was economic: The speed of adoption in each state was a function of the profitability of introducing hybrid corn. And profitability was higher in Iowa than in the southern states.

Source: Zvi Griliches, "Hybrid Corn: An Exploration in the Economics of Technological Change," Econometrica, Volume 25, Number 4, October 1957.

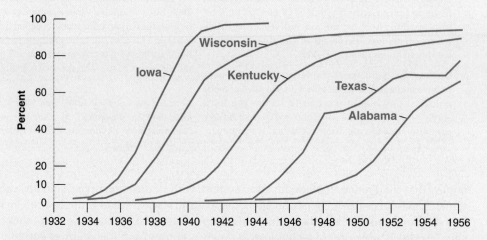

Figure 1 *Percentage of Total Corn Acreage Planted with Hybrid Seed, Selected U.S. States, 1932 to 1956*

Source: See source note for this box.

The Appropriability of Research Results

The second determinant of the level of R&D and of technological progress is the degree of *appropriability* of research results. If firms cannot appropriate the profits from the development of new products, they will not engage in R&D, and technological progress will be slow. Many factors are also at work here.

The nature of the research process itself is important. For example, if it is widely believed that the discovery of a new product by one firm will quickly lead to the discovery of an even better product by another firm, there may be little payoff to being first. In other words, a highly fertile field of research may not generate high levels of R&D because no company will find the investment worthwhile. This example is extreme but revealing.

Even more important is the legal protection given to new products. Without such legal protection, profits from developing a new product are likely to be small. Except in rare cases where the product is based on a trade secret (such as Coca-Cola), it will generally not take long for other firms to produce the same product, eliminating any advantage the innovating firm may have had initially. This is why countries have patent laws. A **patent** gives a firm that has discovered a new product—usually a new technique or device—the right to exclude anyone else from the production or use of the new product for some time.

How should governments design patent laws? On the one hand, protection is needed to provide firms with the incentives to spend on R&D. On the other, once firms have discovered new products, it would be best for society if the knowledge embodied in those new products were made available to other firms and to people without restrictions. Take, for example, biogenetic research. Only the prospect of large profits is leading bioengineering firms to embark on expensive research projects. Once a firm has found a new product, and the product can save many lives, it would clearly be best to make it available at cost to all potential users. But if such a policy was systematically followed, it would eliminate incentives for firms to do research in the first place. So, ◄ patent law must strike a difficult balance. Too little protection will lead to little R&D. Too much protection will make it difficult for new R&D to build on the results of past R&D and may also lead to little R&D. (The difficulty of designing good patent or copy- ◄ right laws is illustrated in the cartoon about cloning.)

Countries that are less technologically advanced than others often have poorer patent protection. China, for example, is a country with poor enforcement of patent

This type of dilemna is known as "time inconsistency." We shall see other examples and discuss it at length in Chapter 25.

The issues go beyond patent laws. To take two controversial examples: Should Microsoft be kept in one piece or broken up to stimulate R&D? Should the government impose caps on the prices of AIDS drugs?

© Chappatte-*www.globecartoon.com*

rights. Our discussion helps explain why. These countries are typically users rather than producers of new technologies. Much of their improvement in productivity comes not from inventions within the country but from the adaptation of foreign technologies. In this case, the costs of weak patent protection are small because there would be few domestic inventions anyway. But the benefits of low patent protection are clear: Domestic firms can use and adapt foreign technology without having to pay royalties to the foreign firms that developed the technology—which is good for the country.

12-3 The Facts of Growth Revisited

We can now use the theory we have developed in this chapter and Chapter 11 to interpret some of the facts we saw in Chapter 10.

Capital Accumulation versus Technological Progress in Rich Countries since 1950

Suppose we observe an economy with a high growth rate of output per worker over some period of time. Our theory implies that this fast growth may come from two sources:

- It may reflect a high rate of technological progress under balanced growth.
- It may reflect instead the adjustment of capital per effective worker, K/AN, to a higher level. As we saw in Figure 12-4, such an adjustment leads to a period of higher growth, even if the rate of technological progress has not increased.

Can we tell how much of the growth comes from one source and how much comes from the other? Yes. If high growth reflects high balanced growth, output per worker should be growing at a rate *equal* to the rate of technological progress (see Table 12-1, line 4). If high growth reflects instead the adjustment to a higher level of capital per effective worker, this adjustment should be reflected in a growth rate of output per worker that *exceeds* the rate of technological progress.

Let's apply this approach to interpret the facts about growth in rich countries we saw in Table 10-1. This is done in Table 12-2, which gives, in column 1, the average rate of growth of output per worker ($g_Y - g_N$) and, in column 2, the average rate of technological progress, g_A, since 1950, for each of the four countries—France, Japan, the

Table 12-2	Average Annual Rates of Growth of Output per Worker and Technological Progress in Four Rich Countries since 1950	
	Rate of Growth of Output per Worker (%) 1950 to 2004	Rate of Technological Progress (%) 1950 to 2004
France	3.2	3.1
Japan	4.2	3.8
United Kingdom	2.4	2.6
United States	1.8	2.0
Average	2.9	2.9

Sources: 1950 to 1970: Angus Maddison, *Dynamic Forces in Capitalist Development,* Oxford University Press, New York, 1991. 1970 to 2004: OECD *Economic Outlook* database. "Average" is a simple average of the growth rates in each column.

United Kingdom, and the United States—we looked at in Table 10-1. (Note one difference between Tables 10-1 and 12-2: As suggested by the theory, Table 12-2 looks at the growth rate of output per worker, while Table 10-1, which focuses on the standard of living, looks at the growth rate of output per person. The differences are small.) The rate of technological progress, g_A, is constructed using a method introduced by Robert Solow; the method and the details of construction are given in the appendix to this chapter.

The table leads to two conclusions. First, growth since 1950 has been a result of rapid technological progress, not unusually high capital accumulation. This conclusion follows from the fact that, in all four countries, the growth rate of output per worker (column 1) has been roughly equal to the rate of technological progress (column 2). This is what we would expect when countries are growing along their balanced growth path.

Note what this conclusion does not say: It does not say that capital accumulation was irrelevant. Capital accumulation was such as to allow these countries to maintain a roughly constant ratio of output to capital and achieve balanced growth. What it says is that, over the period, growth did not come from an unusual increase in capital accumulation, it came from an increase in the ratio of capital to output.

Second, convergence of output per worker across countries has come from higher technological progress, rather than from faster capital accumulation, in the countries that started behind. This conclusion follows from the ranking of the rates of technological progress across the four countries in the second column, with Japan at the top, and the United States at the bottom.

This is an important conclusion. One can think, in general, of two sources of convergence between countries. First, poorer countries are poorer because they have less capital to start with. Over time, they accumulate capital faster than the others, generating convergence. Second, poorer countries are poorer because they are less technologically advanced than the others. Over time, they become more sophisticated, either by importing technology from advanced countries or developing their own. As technological levels converge, so does output per worker. The conclusion we can draw from Table 12-2 is that, in the case of rich countries, the more important source of convergence in this case is clearly the second one.

Capital Accumulation versus Technological Progress in China since 1980

Going beyond growth in OECD countries, one of the striking facts in Chapter 10 was the high growth rates achieved by a number of Asian countries. This raises again the same questions we just discussed: Do these high growth rates reflect fast technological progress, or do they reflect unusually high capital accumulation?

To answer the questions, I shall focus on China because of its size and because of the astonishingly high output growth rate, nearly 10%, it has achieved since the early 1980s. Table 12-3 gives the average rate of growth, g_Y, the average rate of growth of output per worker, $g_Y - g_N$, and the average rate of technological progress, g_A, for the period 1983 to 2003. The fact that the last two numbers are nearly equal yields a very

In the United States, for example, the ratio of employment to population increased from 38% in 1950 to 51% in 2006. This represents an increase of 0.18% per year. Thus, in the United States, output per person has increased 0.18% more per year than output per worker—a small difference, relative to the numbers in the table.

What would have happened to the growth rate of output per worker if these countries had had the same rate of technological progress but no capital accumulation during the period?

While the table looks at only four countries, a similar conclusion holds when one looks at the set of all OECD countries. Convergence is mainly due to the fact that countries that were behind in 1950 have had higher rates of technological progress since then.

Warning: Chinese data for output, employment, and the capital stock (the latter is needed to construct g_A) are not as reliable as similar data for OECD countries. Thus, the numbers in the table should be seen as more tentative than the numbers in Table 12-2.

Table 12-3	Average Annual Rate of Growth of Output per Worker and Technological Progress in China, 1983 to 2003	
Rate of Growth of Output (%)	Rate of Growth of Output per Worker (%)	Rate of Technological Progress (%)
9.7	8.0	8.2

Source: OECD Economic Survey of China, 2005.

clear conclusion: Growth in China since the early 1980s has been nearly balanced, and the high growth of output per worker reflects a high rate of technological progress, 8.2% per year on average.

This is an important conclusion, showing the crucial role of technological progress in explaining China's growth. But, just as in our discussion of OECD countries, it would be wrong to conclude that capital accumulation is irrelevant. To sustain balanced growth at such a high growth rate, the Chinese capital stock has had to increase at the same rate as output. This in turn has required a very high investment rate. To see what investment rate was required, go back to equation (12.3) and divide both sides by output, Y, to get

Recall, from Table 12-1: Under balanced growth, $g_K = g_Y = g_A + g_N$.

$$\frac{I}{Y} = (\delta + g_A + g_N)\frac{K}{Y}$$

Let's plug in numbers for China for the period 1983 to 2003. The estimate of δ, the depreciation rate of capital in China, is 5% a year. As we just saw, the average value of g_A for the period was 8.2%. The average value of g_N, the rate of growth of employment, was 1.7%. The average value of the ratio of capital to output was 2.6. This implies a ratio of investment to output of $(5\% + 9.2\% + 1.7\%) \times 2.6 = 41\%$. Thus, to sustain balanced growth, China has had to invest 41% of its output, a very high investment rate in comparison to, say, the U.S. investment rate. So capital accumulation plays an important role in explaining Chinese growth; but it is still the case that sustained growth has come from a high rate of technological progress.

This ratio indeed is very close to the ratio one gets by looking directly at investment and output in the Chinese national income accounts.

How has China been able to achieve such technological progress? A closer look at the data suggests two main channels. First, China has transferred labor from the countryside, where productivity is very low, to industry and services in the cities, where productivity is much higher. Second, China has imported the technology of more technologically advanced countries. It has, for example, encouraged the development of joint ventures between Chinese firms and foreign firms. Foreign firms have come up with better technologies, and over time, Chinese firms have learned how to use them.

This leads to a general point: The nature of technological progress is likely to be different in more and less advanced economies. The more advanced economies, being by definition at the **technological frontier**, need to develop new ideas, new processes, and new products. They need to innovate. The countries that are behind can instead improve their level of technology by copying and adapting the new processes and products developed in the more advanced economies. They need to imitate. The further behind a country is, the larger the role of imitation relative to innovation. As imitation is likely to be easier than innovation, this can explain why convergence, both within the OECD and in the case of China and other countries, typically takes the form of **technological catch-up**. It raises, however, yet another question: If imitating is so easy, why is it that so many other countries do not seem to be able to do the same and grow? This points to the broader aspects of technology we discussed earlier in the chapter. Technology is more than just a set of blueprints. How efficiently the blueprints can be used and how productive an economy is depend on its institutions, on the quality of its government, and so on. We shall return to this issue in the next chapter.

Summary

- When we think about the implications of technological progress for growth, it is useful to think of technological progress as increasing the amount of effective labor available in the economy (that is, labor multiplied by the state of technology). We can then think of output as being produced with capital and effective labor.

- In steady state, output *per effective worker* and capital *per effective worker* are constant. Put another way, output *per worker* and capital *per worker* grow at the rate of technological progress. Put yet another way, output and capital grow at the same rate as effective labor, thus at a rate equal to the growth rate of the number of workers plus the rate of technological progress.
- When the economy is in steady state, it is said to be on a balanced growth path. Output, capital, and effective labor are all growing "in balance"—that is, at the same rate.
- The rate of output growth in steady state is independent of the saving rate. However, the saving rate affects the steady-state level of output per effective worker. And increases in the saving rate will lead, for some time, to an increase in the growth rate above the steady-state growth rate.

- Technological progress depends on both (1) the fertility of research and development—how spending on R&D translates into new ideas and new products—and (2) the appropriability of the results of R&D—the extent to which firms benefit from the results of their R&D.
- When designing patent laws, governments must balance their desire to protect future discoveries and provide incentives for firms to do R&D with their desire to make existing discoveries available to potential users without restrictions.
- France, Japan, the United Kingdom, and the United States have experienced roughly balanced growth since 1950: Growth of output per worker has been roughly equal to the rate of technological progress. The same is true of China. Growth in China is roughly balanced, sustained by a high rate of technological progress and a high investment rate.

Key Terms

- effective labor, or labor in efficiency units, 271
- balanced growth, 275
- research and development (R&D), 277
- fertility of research, 277
- appropriability of research, 277
- information technology revolution, 278
- New Economy, 278
- Moore's law, 278
- patent, 281
- technology frontier, 284
- technological catch-up, 284

Questions and Problems

Quick Check

1. Using the information in this chapter, label each of the following statements true, false, or uncertain. Explain briefly.

a. The widespread decline in R&D spending seems to have driven the decline in technological progress over the last 30 years.

b. If the rate of technological progress increases, the investment rate (the ratio of investment to output) must decrease in order to keep capital per effective worker constant.

c. In steady state, output per worker grows at the rate of population growth.

d. In steady state, output per effective worker grows at the rate of technological progress.

e. Writing the production function in terms of capital and effective labor implies that as the level of technology increases by 5%, the number of workers required to achieve the same level of output decreases by 5%.

f. The fact that one cannot patent a theorem implies that private firms will not engage in basic research.

g. In the steady state, the growth rate of output is independent of the saving rate.

h. Even if the potential returns from R&D spending are identical to the potential returns from investing in a new machine, R&D spending is much riskier for firms than investing in new machines.

2. Sources of technological progress: economic leaders versus developing countries

a. Where does technological progress come from for the economic leaders of the world?

b. Do developing countries have other alternatives to the sources of technological progress you mentioned in part (a)?

c. Do you see any reasons developing countries may choose to have poor patent protection? Are there any dangers in such a policy (for developing countries)?

3. R&D and growth

a. Why is the amount of R&D spending important for growth? How do the appropriability and fertility of research affect the amount of R&D spending?

How do each of the policy proposals listed in (b) through (e) affect the appropriability and fertility of research, R&D spending in the long run, and output in the long run?

b. An international treaty that ensures that each country's patents are legally protected all over the world.

c. Tax credits for each dollar of R&D spending.

d. A decrease in funding of government-sponsored conferences between universities and corporations.

e. The elimination of patents on breakthrough drugs, so the drugs can be sold at low cost as soon as they are available.

Dig Deeper

4. For each of the economic changes listed in (a) and (b), assess the likely impact on the growth rate and the level of output over the next five years and over the next five decades.

a. a permanent reduction in the rate of technological progress.

b. a permanent reduction in the saving rate.

5. Measurement error, inflation, and productivity growth

Suppose that there are only two goods produced in an economy: haircuts and banking services. Prices, quantities, and the number of workers occupied in the production of each good for year 1 and for year 2 are given below:

| | | Year 1 | | | Year 2 | |
	P1	Q1	W1	P2	Q2	W2
Haircut	10	100	50	12	100	50
Banking	10	200	50	12	230	60

a. What is nominal GDP in each year?

b. Using year 1 prices, what is real GDP in year 2? What is the growth rate of real GDP?

c. What is the rate of inflation using the GDP deflator?

d. Using year 1 prices, what is real GDP per worker in year 1 and year 2? What is labor productivity growth between year 1 and year 2 for the whole economy?

Now suppose that banking services in year 2 are not the same as banking services in year 1. Year 2 banking services include telebanking that year 1 banking services did not include. The technology for telebanking was available in year 1, but the price of banking services with telebanking in year 1 was $13, and no one chose to purchase this package. However, in year 2, the price of banking services with telebanking was $12, and everyone chose to have this package (i.e., in year 2 no one chose to have the year 1 banking services package without telebanking). (Hint: Assume that there are now two types of banking services: those with telebanking and those without. Rewrite the preceding table but now with three goods: haircuts and the two types of banking services.)

e. Using year 1 prices, what is real GDP for year 2? What is the growth rate of real GDP?

f. What is the rate of inflation using the GDP deflator?

g. What is labor productivity growth between year 1 and year 2 for the whole economy?

h. Consider this statement: "If banking services are mismeasured—for example, by not taking into account the introduction of telebanking—we will overestimate inflation and underestimate productivity growth." Discuss this statement in light of your answers to parts (a) through (g).

6. Discuss the potential role of each of the factors listed in (a) through (g) on the steady-state level of output per worker. In each case, indicate whether the effect is through

A, through K, through H, or through some combination of A, K, and H.

a. geographic location

b. education

c. protection of property rights

d. openness to trade

e. low tax rates

f. good public infrastructure

g. low population growth

7. Suppose that the economy's production function is

$$Y = \sqrt{K}\sqrt{AN}$$

that the saving rate, s, is equal to 16%, and that the rate of depreciation, δ, is equal to 10%. Suppose further that the number of workers grows at 2% per year and that the rate of technological progress is 4% per year.

a. Find the steady-state values of the variables listed in (i) through (v).

i. The capital stock per effective worker.

ii. Output per effective worker.

iii. The growth rate of output per effective worker.

iv. The growth rate of output per worker.

v. The growth rate of output.

b. Suppose that the rate of technological progress doubles to 8% per year. Recompute the answers to part (a). Explain.

c. Now suppose that the rate of technological progress is still equal to 4% per year, but the number of workers now grows at 6% per year. Recompute the answers to (a). Are people better off in (a) or in (c)? Explain.

Explore Further

8. Growth accounting

The appendix to this chapter shows how data on output, capital, and labor can be used to construct estimates of the rate of growth of technological progress. We modify that approach in this problem to examine the growth of capital per worker. The function

$$Y = K^{1/3}(AN)^{2/3}$$

gives a good description of production in rich countries. Following the same steps as in the appendix, you can show that

$$(2/3)\,g_A = g_Y - (2/3)\,g_N - (1/3)\,g_K$$
$$= (g_Y - g_N) - (1/3)\,(g_K - g_N)$$

where g_x denotes the growth rate of x.

a. What does the quantity $g_Y - g_N$ represent? What does the quantity $g_K - g_N$ represent?

b. Rearrange the preceding equation to solve for the growth rate of capital per worker.

c. Look at Table 12-2 in the chapter. Using your answer to part (b), substitute in the average annual growth rate of output per worker and the average annual rate of technological progress for the United States for the period 1950 to 2004 to obtain a crude measure of the average annual growth of capital per worker. (Strictly speaking, we should construct these measures individually for every year, but we limit ourselves to readily available data in this problem.) Do the same for the other countries listed in Table 12-2. How does the average growth of capital per worker compare across the countries in Table 12-2? Do the results make sense to you? Explain.

 We invite you to visit the Blanchard page on the Prentice Hall Web site, at:
www.prenhall.com/blanchard
for this chapter's World Wide Web exercises.

Further Readings

- For more on growth, both theory and evidence, read Charles Jones, *Introduction to Economic Growth*, 2nd ed., Norton, New York, 2002. Jones's Web page, **emlab. berkeley.edu/users/chad/**, is a useful portal to the research on growth.
- For more on patents, see the *Economist* survey on *Patents and Technology*, October 20, 2005.

On two issues I have not explored in the text:
- Growth and global warming—Read the *Stern Review on the Economics of Climate Change*, 2006. You can find it at **www.hm-treasury.gov.uk/independent_reviews/ stern_review_economics_climate_change/stern_ review_report.cfm**. (The report is very long. Read just the executive summary.)
- Growth and the environment—Read the *Economist* survey on *The Global Environment; The Great Race*, July 4, 2002.

Appendix: Constructing a Measure of Technological Progress

In 1957, Robert Solow devised a way of constructing an estimate of technological progress. The method, which is still in use today, relies on one important assumption: that each factor of production is paid its marginal product.

Under this assumption, it is easy to compute the contribution of an increase in any factor of production to the increase in output. For example, if a worker is paid $30,000 a year, the assumption implies that her contribution to output is equal to $30,000. Now suppose that this worker increases the number of hours she works by 10%. The increase in output coming from the increase in her hours will therefore be equal to $30,000 × 10%, or $3,000.

Let us write this more formally. Denote output by Y, labor by N, and the real wage by W/P. Then, we just established the change in output is equal to the real wage multiplied by the change in labor:

$$\Delta Y = \frac{W}{P}\Delta N$$

Divide both sides of the equation by Y, divide and multiply the right side by N, and reorganize:

$$\frac{\Delta Y}{Y} = \frac{WN}{PY}\frac{\Delta N}{N}$$

Note that the first term on the right, WN/PY, is equal to the share of labor in output—the total wage bill in dollars divided by the value of output in dollars. Denote this share by α. Note that $\Delta Y/Y$ is the rate of growth of output and denote it by g_Y. Note similarly that $\Delta N/N$ is the rate of change of the labor input and denote it by g_N. Then the previous relation can be written as

$$g_Y = \alpha g_N$$

More generally, this reasoning implies that the part of output growth attributable to growth of the labor input is equal to α times g_N. If, for example, employment grows by 2%, and the share of labor is 0.7, then the output growth due to the growth in employment is equal to 1.4% (0.7 × 2%).

Similarly, we can compute the part of output growth attributable to growth of the capital stock. Because there are only two factors of production, labor and capital, and because the share of labor is equal to α, the share of capital in income must be equal to $1 - \alpha$. If the growth rate of capital is equal to g_K, then the part of output growth attributable to growth of capital is equal to $1 - \alpha$ times g_K. If, for example, capital grows by 5%, and the share of capital is 0.3, then the output growth due to the growth of the capital stock is equal to 1.5% (0.3 × 5%).

Putting the contributions of labor and capital together, the growth in output attributable to growth in both labor and capital is equal to $\alpha g_N + (1 - \alpha)g_K$.

We can then measure the effects of technological progress by computing what Solow called the *residual*, the excess of actual growth of output, g_Y, over the growth attributable to growth of labor and the growth of capital, $\alpha g_N + (1 - \alpha)g_K$:

$$\text{Residual} \equiv g_Y - [\alpha g_N + (1 - \alpha)g_K]$$

This measure is called the **Solow residual**. It is easy to compute: All we need to know to compute it are the growth rate of output, g_Y, the growth rate of labor, g_N, and the growth rate of capital, g_K, together with the shares of labor, α and capital, $1 - \alpha$.

To continue with our previous numeric examples, suppose employment grows by 2%, the capital stock grows by

5%, and the share of labor is 0.7 (and so the share of capital is 0.3). Then the part of output growth attributable to growth of labor and growth of capital is equal to 2.9% ($0.7 \times 2\%$ + $0.3 \times 5\%$). If output growth is equal, for example, to 4%, then the Solow residual is equal to 1.1% ($4\% - 2.9\%$).

The **Solow residual** is sometimes called the **rate of growth of total factor productivity (or the rate of TFP growth**, for short). The use of *total factor productivity* is to distinguish it from the *rate of growth of labor productivity*, which is defined as $g_Y - g_N$, the rate of output growth minus the rate of labor growth.

The Solow residual is related to the rate of technological progress in a simple way. The residual is equal to the share of labor times the rate of technological progress:

$$\text{Residual} = \alpha g_A$$

I shall not derive this result here. But the intuition for this relation comes from the fact that what matters in the production function $Y = F(K, AN)$ [equation (12.1)] is the product of the state of technology and labor, AN. We saw that to get the contribution of labor growth to output growth, we must multiply the growth rate of labor by its share. Because N and A enter the production function in the same way, it is clear that to get the contribution of technological progress to output growth, we must also multiply it by the share of labor.

If the Solow residual is equal to 0, so is technological progress. To construct an estimate of g_A, we must construct the Solow residual and then divide it by the share of labor. This is how the estimates of g_A presented in the text are constructed.

In the numerical example we saw earlier, the Solow residual is equal to 1.1%, and the share of labor is equal to 0.7. So the rate of technological progress is equal to 1.6% ($1.1\%/0.7$).

Keep straight the definitions of productivity growth you have seen in this chapter:

■ Labor productivity growth (equivalently: the rate of growth of output per worker), $g_Y - g_N$
■ The rate of technological progress, g_A

In steady state, labor productivity growth, $g_Y - g_N$, equals the rate of technological progress, g_A. Outside steady state, they need not be equal: An increase in the ratio of capital per effective worker, due, for example, to an increase in the saving rate, will cause $g_Y - g_N$ to be higher than g_A for some time.

Key Term

■ Solow residual, or rate of growth of total factor productivity, or rate of TFP growth, 288

Source: Robert Solow, "Technical Change and the Aggregate Production Function," *Review of Economics and Statistics*, 1957, 312–320.

Technological Progress: The Short, the Medium, and the Long Run

CHAPTER 13

We spent much of Chapter 12 celebrating the merits of technological progress. In the long run, technological progress, we argued, is the key to increases in the standard of living. Popular discussions of technological progress are often blamed for higher unemployment and for higher income inequality. Are these fears groundless? This is the first issue we take up in this chapter. We proceed in three steps:

■ Section 13-1 looks at the short-run response of output and unemployment to increases in productivity. Even if, in the long run, the adjustment to technological progress is through increases in output rather than increases in unemployment, the question remains: How long will this adjustment take? The section concludes that the answer is ambiguous: In the short run, increases in productivity sometimes decrease unemployment, and sometimes increase it.

■ Section 13-2 looks at the medium-run response of output and unemployment to increases in productivity. It concludes that neither the theory nor the evidence supports the fear that faster technological progress leads to more unemployment. If anything, the effect seems to go the other way: In the medium run, increases in productivity growth appear to be associated with lower unemployment.

■ Section 13-3 focuses on the distribution effects of technological progress. Along with technological progress comes a complex process of job creation and job destruction. For those who lose their jobs, or for those who have skills that are no longer in demand, technological progress can indeed be a curse, not a blessing: As consumers, they benefit from the availability of new and cheaper goods. As workers, they may suffer from prolonged unemployment and have to settle for lower wages when taking a new job. Section 13-3 discusses these effects and looks at the evidence.

Another theme of Chapter 12 was that, for countries behind the technological frontier, technological progress is more about imitation as it is about innovation. This makes it sound easy, and the experience of countries such as China reinforces this impression. But, if it is that easy, why are so many other countries unable to achieve sustained technological progress and growth? This is the second issue we take up in this chapter.

■ In Section 13-4, we return to the long run and discuss why some countries are able to achieve steady technological progress and others do not. We look at the role of institutions, from property rights to the efficiency of government, in sustaining growth. ■

13-1 Productivity, Output, and Unemployment in the Short Run

In Chapter 12, we represented technological progress as an increase in A, the *state of technology*, in the production function

$$Y = F(K, AN)$$

What matters for the issues we shall be discussing in this chapter is technological progress, not capital accumulation. So, for simplicity, we will ignore capital for now and assume that output is produced according to the following production function:

$$Y = AN \qquad (13.1)$$

Under this assumption, output is produced using only labor, N, and each worker produces A units of output. Increases in A represent technological progress.

A has two interpretations here. One is indeed as the state of technology. The other is as labor productivity (output per worker), which follows from the fact that $Y/N = A$. So, when referring to increases in A, I shall use *technological progress* and (labor) *productivity growth* interchangeably.

Rewrite equation (13.1) as

$$N = Y/A \qquad (13.2)$$

Employment is equal to output divided by productivity. Given output, the higher the level of productivity, the lower the level of employment. This naturally leads to the question: When productivity increases, does output increase enough to avoid a decrease in employment? In this section we look at the short-run responses of output, employment, and unemployment. In the next, we look at their medium-run responses and, in particular, at the relation between the natural rate of unemployment and the rate of technological progress.

> "Output per worker" (Y/N) and "the state of technology" (A) are in general not the same. Recall from Chapter 12 that an increase in output per worker may come from an increase in capital per worker, even if the state of technology has not changed. They are the same here because, in writing the production function as equation (13.1), we ignore the role of capital in production.

Technological Progress, Aggregate Supply, and Aggregate Demand

The right model to use when thinking about the short- and medium-run responses of output to a change in productivity in the short run is the model that we developed in Chapter 7. Recall its basic structure:

■ Output is determined by the intersection of the aggregate supply curve and the aggregate demand curve.

■ The *aggregate supply* relation gives the price level for a given level of output. The aggregate supply curve is upward sloping: An increase in the level of output leads to an increase in the price level. Behind the scenes, the mechanism is as follows: An increase in output leads to a decrease in unemployment. The decrease in unemployment leads to an increase in nominal wages, which in turn leads to an increase in prices—an increase in the price level.

■ The *aggregate demand* relation gives output for a given price level. The aggregate demand curve is downward sloping: An increase in the price level leads to a decrease in the demand for output. The mechanism behind the scenes is as follows: An increase in the price level leads to a decrease in the real money stock. The decrease in the real money stock in turn leads to an increase in the interest rate. The increase in the interest rate then leads to a decrease in the demand for goods, decreasing output.

The aggregate supply curve is drawn as *AS* in Figure 13-1. The aggregate demand curve is drawn as *AD*. The intersection of the aggregate supply curve and the aggregate demand curve gives the level of output, *Y*, consistent with equilibrium in labor, goods, and financial markets. Given the equilibrium level of output, *Y*, the level of employment is determined by $N = Y/A$. The higher the level of productivity, the smaller the number of workers needed to produce a given level of output.

Suppose productivity increases from level *A* to level *A′*. What happens to output and to employment and unemployment in the short run? The answer depends on how the increase in productivity shifts the aggregate supply curve and the aggregate demand curve.

◄ A and A' refer to levels of productivity here, not points on the graph. (To avoid confusion, points in the graph are denoted B and B'.)

Take the aggregate supply curve first. The effect of an increase in productivity is to decrease the amount of labor needed to produce a unit of output, reducing costs for firms. This leads firms to reduce the price they charge at any level of output. As a result, the aggregate supply curve shifts down, from *AS* to *AS′* in Figure 13-2.

Now take the aggregate demand curve. Does an increase in productivity increase or decrease the demand for goods at a given price level? There is no general answer because productivity increases do not appear in a vacuum; what happens to aggregate demand depends on what triggered the increase in productivity in the first place:

- Take the case where productivity increases come from the widespread implementation of a major invention. It is easy to see how such a change may be associated with an increase in demand at a given price level. The prospect of higher growth in the future leads consumers to feel more optimistic about the future, so they increase their consumption given their current income. The prospect of higher profits in the future, as well as the need to put the new technology in place, may also lead to a boom in investment. In this case, the demand for goods increases at a given price level; the aggregate demand curve shifts to the right.

◄ Recall our discussion of such major inventions in Chapter 12.

◄ This argument points to the role of expectations in determining consumption and investment, something we have not yet studied but will in Chapter 16.

- Now take the case where productivity growth comes not from the introduction of new technologies but from the more efficient use of existing technologies. One of the implications of increased international trade has been an increase in foreign competition. This competition has forced many firms to cut costs by reorganizing production and eliminating jobs (this is often called "downsizing"). When such reorganizations are the source of productivity growth, there is no presumption that aggregate demand will

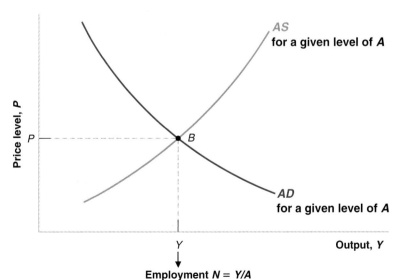

Figure 13-1

Aggregate Supply and Aggregate Demand for a Given Level of Productivity

The aggregate supply curve is upward sloping: An increase in output leads to an increase in the price level. The aggregate demand curve is downward sloping: An increase in the price level leads to a decrease in output.

Figure 13-2

The Effects of an Increase in Productivity on Output in the Short Run

An increase in productivity shifts the aggregate supply curve down. It has an ambiguous effect on the aggregate demand curve, which may shift either to the left or to the right. In this figure, we assume that it shifts to the right.

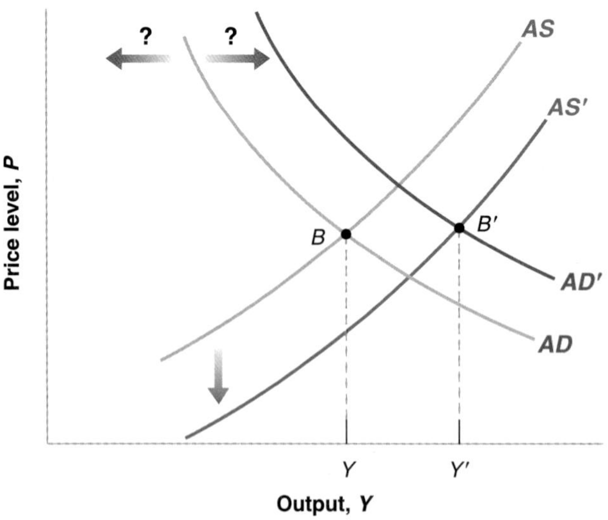

increase: Reorganization of production may require little or no new investment. Increased uncertainty and job security worries faced by workers might cause them to want to save more and so to reduce consumption spending given their current income. In this case, aggregate demand may shift to the left rather than to the right.

Let's assume the more favorable case (more favorable from the point of view of output and employment)—namely the case where the aggregate demand curve shifts to the right. When this happens, the increase in productivity shifts the aggregate supply curve down, from AS to AS', and shifts the aggregate demand curve to the right, from AD to AD'. These shifts are drawn in Figure 13-2. Both shifts contribute to an increase in equilibrium output, from Y to Y'. In this case, the increase in productivity unambiguously leads to an increase in output. In words: Lower costs and high demand combine to create an economic boom.

Even in this case, we cannot tell however what happens to employment without having more information. To see why, note that equation (13.2) implies the following relation:

> % change in employment = % change in output – % change in productivity

Thus, what happens to employment depends on whether output increases proportionately more or less than productivity. If productivity increases by 2%, it takes an increase in output of at least 2% to avoid a decrease in employment—that is, an increase in unemployment. And without a lot more information about the slopes and the size of the shifts of the AS and AD curves, we cannot tell whether this condition is satisfied in Figure 13-2. In the short run, an increase in productivity may or may not lead to an increase in unemployment. Theory alone cannot settle the issue.

The Empirical Evidence

Can empirical evidence help us decide whether, in practice, productivity growth increases or decreases employment? At first glance, it would seem to. Look at Figure 13-3, which plots the behavior of labor productivity and the behavior of output for the U.S. business sector since 1960.

The figure shows a strong positive relation between year-to-year movements in output growth and productivity growth. Furthermore, the movements in output are typically larger than the movements in productivity. This would seem to imply that, when productivity growth is high, output increases by more than enough to avoid any adverse effect on employment. But this conclusion would be wrong. The reason is

Start from the production function $Y = AN$. From Proposition 7 in Appendix 2 at the end of the book, this relation implies that $g_Y = g_A + g_N$. Or, equivalently, $g_N = g_Y - g_A$.

The discussion has assumed that macroeconomic policy was given. But by shifting the aggregate demand curve, fiscal policy and monetary policy can clearly affect the outcome. Suppose you were in charge of monetary policy in this economy: What level of output would you try to achieve? This was one of the main questions the Fed faced in the 1990s.

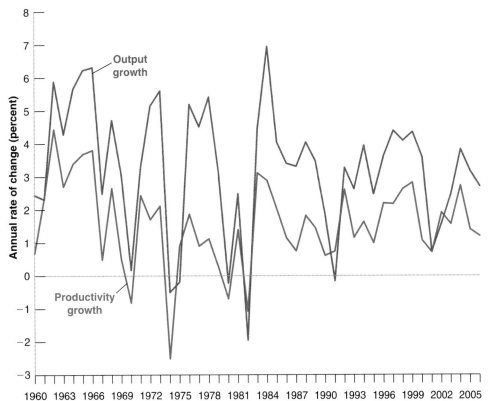

Figure 13-3 ▬

Labor Productivity and Output Growth in the United States since 1960

There is a strong positive relation between output growth and productivity growth. But the causality runs from output growth to productivity growth, not the other way around.

Source: U.S. Department of Labor; Bureau of Labor Statistics.

that, *in the short run*, the causal relation runs mostly the other way, from output growth to productivity growth. That is, in the short run, output growth leads to productivity growth, not the other way around.

We saw why when we discussed Okun's law in Chapter 9: In bad times, firms hoard labor—they keep more workers than they need for current production. When the demand for goods increases for any reason, firms respond partly by increasing employment and partly by having currently employed workers work harder. This is why increases in output lead to increases in productivity. And this is what we see in Figure 13-3: High output growth leads to higher productivity growth. This is not the relation we are after. Rather, we want to know what happens to output and unemployment when there is an *exogenous* change in productivity—a change in productivity that comes from a change in technology, not from the response of firms to movements in output. Figure 13-3 does not help us much here. And the conclusion from the research that has looked at the effects of exogenous movements in productivity growth on output is that the data give an answer just as ambiguous as the answer given by the theory:

- Sometimes increases in productivity lead to increases in output sufficient to maintain or even increase employment in the short run.
- Sometimes they do not, and unemployment increases in the short run.

13-2 Productivity and the Natural Rate of Unemployment

We have looked so far at *short-run* effects of a change in productivity on output and, by implication, on unemployment. In the medium run, we know the economy tends to return to the natural level of unemployment. Now we must ask: Is the natural rate of unemployment itself affected by changes in productivity?

Correlation versus causality: If we see a positive correlation between output growth and productivity growth, should we conclude that high productivity growth leads to high output growth, or that high output growth leads to high productivity growth?

Since the beginning of the Industrial Revolution, workers have worried that technological progress would eliminate jobs and increase unemployment. In early nineteenth-century England, groups of workers in the textile industry, known as the Luddites, destroyed the new machines that they saw as a direct threat to their jobs. Similar movements took place in other countries. *Saboteur* comes from one of the ways French workers destroyed machines: by putting their sabots (their heavy wooden shoes) into the machines.

The theme **technological unemployment** typically resurfaces whenever unemployment is high. During the Great Depression, adherents to a movement called the *technocracy movement* argued that high unemployment came from the introduction of machinery and that things would only get worse if technological progress were allowed to continue. In the late 1990s, France passed a law reducing the normal workweek from 39 down to 35 hours. One of the reasons invoked was that, because of technological progress, there was no longer enough work for all workers to have full-time jobs. Thus the proposed solution: Have each worker work fewer hours (at the same hourly wage) so that more of them could be employed.

In its crudest form, the argument that technological progress must lead to unemployment is obviously false. The very large improvements in the standard of living that advanced countries have enjoyed during the twentieth and twenty-first centuries have come with large *increases* in employment and no systematic increase in the unemployment rate. In the United States, output per person has increased by a factor of 7 since 1900 and, far from declining, employment has increased by a factor of 5 (reflecting a parallel increase in the size of the U.S. population). Nor, looking across countries, is there any evidence of a systematic positive relation between the unemployment rate and the level of productivity. Japan and the United States, two of the countries with the highest levels of productivity, have two of the lowest unemployment rates among OECD countries.

A more sophisticated version of the argument cannot, however, be dismissed so easily. Perhaps periods of *fast technological progress* are associated with a *higher natural rate* of unemployment, and periods of *slower progress* are associated with a *lower natural rate* of unemployment.

To think about the issues, we can use the model we developed in Chapter 6. Recall from Chapter 6 that we can think of the natural rate of unemployment (the *natural rate*, for short, in what follows) as being determined by two relations: the price-setting relation and the wage-setting relation. Our first step must be to think about how changes in productivity affect each of these two relations.

Price Setting and Wage Setting Revisited

Consider price setting first:

■ From equation (13.1), each worker produces A units of output. Put another way, producing 1 unit of output requires $1/A$ workers.
■ If the nominal wage is equal to W, the nominal cost of producing 1 unit of output is therefore equal to $(1/A)W = W/A$.
■ If firms set their price equal to $1 + \mu$ times cost (where μ is the markup), the price level is given by

$$\text{Price setting:} \quad P = (1 + \mu)\frac{W}{A} \qquad (13.3)$$

Equation (6.3): $P = (1+\mu)W$ ▶ The only difference between this equation and equation (6.3) is the presence of the productivity term, A (which we had implicitly set to 1 in Chapter 6). An increase in productivity decreases costs, which decreases the price level, given the nominal wage.

Turn to wage setting. The evidence suggests that other things equal, wages are typically set to reflect the increase in productivity over time. If productivity has been growing at 2% per year on average for some time, then wage contracts will build in a wage increase of 2% per year. This suggests the following extension of our earlier wage-setting equation (6.1)

◀ Equation (6.1): $W = P^e F(u,z)$

$$\text{Wage setting:} \qquad W = A^e P^e F(u, z) \qquad (13.4)$$

Look at the three terms on the right of equation (13.4):

■ Two of them, P^e and $F(u, z)$ should be familiar from equation (6.1). Workers care about real wages, not nominal wages, so wages depend on the (expected) price level, P^e. Wages depend (negatively) on the unemployment rate, u, and on institutional factors captured by the variable z.

■ The new term is A^e: Wages now also depend on the expected level of productivity, A^e. If workers and firms both expect productivity to increase, they will incorporate those expectations into the wages set in bargaining.

Think of workers and firms setting the wage so as to divide (expected) output between workers and firms according to their relative bargaining power. If both sides expect higher productivity and, therefore, higher output, this will be reflected in ◀ the bargained wage.

The Natural Rate of Unemployment

We can now characterize the natural rate. Recall that the natural rate is determined by the price-setting and wage-setting relations and the additional condition that expectations be correct. In this case, this condition requires that expectations of *both* prices *and* productivity be correct, so $P^e = P$ and $A^e = A$.

The price-setting equation determines the real wage paid by firms. Reorganizing equation (13.3), we can write

$$\frac{W}{P} = \frac{A}{1 + \mu} \qquad (13.5)$$

The real wage paid by firms, W/P, increases one-for-one with productivity A: The higher the level of productivity, the lower the price set by firms, given the nominal wage, and therefore the higher the real wage paid by firms.

This equation is represented in Figure 13-4. The real wage is measured on the vertical axis. The unemployment rate is measured on the horizontal axis. Equation (13.5)

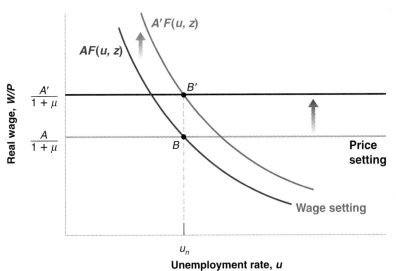

Figure 13-4 ■

The Effects of an Increase in Productivity on the Natural Rate of Unemployment

An increase in productivity shifts both the wage and the price-setting curves by the same proportion and thus has no effect on the natural rate.

is represented by the lower horizontal line at $W/P = A/(1 + \mu)$: The real wage implied by price setting is independent of the unemployment rate.

Turn to the wage-setting equation. Under the condition that expectations are correct—so both $P^e = P$ and $A^e = A$—the wage-setting equation (13.4) becomes

$$\frac{W}{P} = A F(u, z) \qquad (13.6)$$

The real wage, W/P, implied by wage bargaining depends on both the level of productivity and the unemployment rate. For a given level of productivity, equation (13.6) is represented by the lower downward-sloping curve in Figure 13-4: The real wage implied by wage setting is a decreasing function of the unemployment rate.

The reason for using B rather than A to denote the equilibrium: We are already using the letter A to denote the level of productivity.

Equilibrium in the labor market is given by point B, and the natural rate is equal to u_n. Let's now ask what happens to the natural rate in response to an increase in productivity. Suppose that A increases by 3%, so the new level of productivity, A', equals 1.03 times A:

- From equation (13.5), we see that the real wage implied by price setting is now higher by 3%: The price-setting curve shifts up.
- From equation (13.6), we see that at a given unemployment rate, the real wage implied by wage setting is also higher by 3%: The wage-setting curve shifts up.
- Note that, at the initial unemployment rate, u_n, both curves shift up by the same amount, namely 3% of the initial real wage. That is why the new equilibrium is at B', directly above B: The real wage is higher by 3%, and the natural rate remains the same.

The intuition for this result is straightforward: A 3% increase in productivity leads firms to reduce prices by 3%, given wages, leading to a 3% increase in real wages. This increase exactly matches the increase in real wages from wage bargaining at the initial unemployment rate. Real wages increase by 3%, and the natural rate remains the same.

We have looked at a one-time increase in productivity, but the argument we have developed also applies to productivity growth. Suppose that productivity steadily increases, so that each year, A increases by 3%. Then, each year, real wages will increase by 3%, and the natural rate will remain unchanged.

The Empirical Evidence

We have just derived two strong results: The natural rate should depend neither on the level of productivity nor on the rate of productivity growth. How do these two results fit the facts?

An obvious problem in answering this question is that we do not observe the natural rate. But, as we did in Chapter 8, we can work around this problem by looking at the relation between average productivity growth and the average unemployment rate over decades. Because the actual unemployment rate moves around the natural rate, looking at the average unemployment rate over a decade should give us a good estimate of the natural rate for that decade. Looking at average productivity growth over a decade also takes care of another problem we discussed earlier: Although changes in labor hoarding can have a large effect on year-to-year changes in labor productivity, these changes in labor hoarding are unlikely to make much difference when we look at average productivity growth over a decade.

Figure 13-5 plots the average U.S. labor productivity growth and the average unemployment rate during each decade from 1890 to 2000. At first glance, there seems to be little relation between the two. But it is possible to argue that the decade of the Great Depression (the 1930s) is so different that it should be left aside. If we ignore the 1930s, then a relation—although, not a very strong one—emerges between productivity growth and the unemployment rate. But it is the *opposite* of the relation predicted by those who believe in technological unemployment:

The Long Run   **The Core**

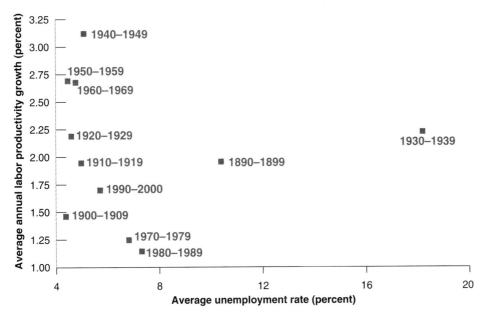

Figure 13-5 ▦

Productivity Growth and Unemployment— Averages by Decade, 1890 to 2000

There is little relation between the 10-year averages of productivity growth and the 10-year averages of the unemployment rate. If anything, higher productivity growth is associated with lower unemployment.

Source: U.S. Bureau of the Census, Historical Statistics of the United States.

Periods of *high productivity growth*, like the 1940s to the 1960s, have been associated with *a lower unemployment rate*. Periods of *low productivity growth*, such as the United States saw in the 1970s and 1980s, have been associated with *a higher unemployment rate*.

Can the theory we have developed be extended to explain this inverse relation in the medium run between productivity growth and unemployment? The answer is yes. To see why, we must look more closely at how expectations of productivity are formed.

Up to this point, we have looked at the rate of unemployment that prevails when *both* price expectations *and* expectations of productivity are correct. However, the evidence suggests that it takes a very long time for expectations of productivity to adjust to the reality of lower productivity growth. When productivity growth slows down for any reason, it takes a long time for society in general, and for workers in particular, to adjust their expectations. In the meantime, workers keep asking for wage increases that are no longer consistent with the new lower rate of productivity growth.

To see what this implies, let's look at what happens to the unemployment rate when price expectations are correct (that is, $P^e = P$), but expectations of productivity (A^e) may not be (that is, A^e may not be equal to A). In this case, the relations implied by price setting and wage setting are

$$\text{Price setting:} \qquad \frac{W}{P} = \frac{A}{1 + \mu}$$

$$\text{Wage setting:} \qquad \frac{W}{P} = A^e \, F(u, z)$$

Suppose productivity growth declines: A increases more slowly than before. If expectations of productivity growth adjust slowly, then A^e will increase for some time by more than A does. What will then happen to unemployment is shown in Figure 13-6. If A^e increases by more than A, the wage-setting relation will shift up by more than the price-setting relation. The equilibrium will move from B to B', and the natural rate will increase from u_n to u'_n. The natural rate will remain higher until expectations of productivity have adjusted to the new reality—that is, until A^e and A are again equal. In words: After the slowdown in productivity growth, workers will ask for larger wage increases than firms are able to give. This will lead to a rise in unemployment. As workers eventually adjust their expectations, unemployment will fall back to its original level.

◀ The price-setting relation shifts up by a factor A. The wage-setting relation shifts up by a factor A^e. If $A^e > A$, the price-setting relation shifts up by less than the wage-setting relation shifts up.

The Effects of a Decrease in Productivity Growth on the Unemployment Rate When Expectations of Productivity Growth Adjust Slowly

If it takes time for workers to adjust their expectations of productivity growth, a slowdown in productivity growth will lead to an increase in the natural rate for some time.

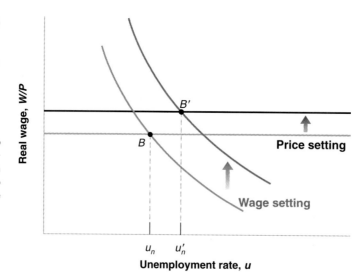

Let's summarize what we have seen in this section and the preceding section. There is not much support, either in theory or in the data, for the idea that faster productivity growth leads to higher unemployment:

■ In the short run, there is no reason to expect, nor does there appear to be, a systematic relation between movements in productivity growth and movements in unemployment.

■ In the medium run, if there is a relation between productivity growth and unemployment, it appears to be an inverse relation. Lower productivity growth leads to higher unemployment. Higher productivity growth leads to lower unemployment.

These two points are nicely illustrated by what has happened in the United States since the mid-1990s, as discussed in the Focus box "The New Economy, the U.S. Expansion of the 1990s, and the Jobless Recovery of the Early 2000s."

Given the evidence discussed so far, where do fears of technological unemployment come from? They probably come from the dimension of technological progress we have neglected so far, **structural change**—the change in the structure of the economy induced by technological progress. For some workers—those with skills no longer in demand—structural change may indeed mean unemployment, or lower wages, or both.

▇▇▇ Technological Progress, Churning, and Distribution Effects

Technological progress is a process of structural change. This theme was central to the work of Joseph Schumpeter, a Harvard economist who, in the 1930s, emphasized that the process of growth was fundamentally a process of **creative destruction**. New goods are developed, making old ones obsolete. New techniques of production are introduced, requiring new skills and making some old skills less useful. The essence of this **churning** process is nicely reflected in the following quote from a president of the Federal Reserve Bank of Dallas in his introduction to a report titled *The Churn*:

Robert McTeer, *The Churn: The Paradox of Progress*, Federal Reserve Bank of Dallas, Dallas, 1993.

My grandfather was a blacksmith, as was his father. My dad, however, was part of the evolutionary process of the churn. After quitting school in the seventh grade to work for the sawmill, he got the entrepreneurial itch. He rented a shed and opened a filling station to service the cars that had put his dad out of business. My dad was successful, so he bought some land on the top of a hill, and built a truck stop. Our truck stop was

We saw in Section 13-1 how an increase in the rate of technological progress can lead, in the short run, either to an increase or to a decrease in unemployment. Quite nicely—for our purposes—the past decade in the United States provides us with an example of each type.

1. During the U.S. expansion of the second half of the 1990s, the increase in productivity growth was accompanied with a larger increase in output growth and a steady decrease in unemployment.

   Table 1 gives the basic numbers. Productivity growth was unusually high from 1996 to 2000, averaging 2.5%. We saw the reasons in Chapter 12: rapid technological progress in the information technology (IT) sector and rapid accumulation of IT capital in the rest of the economy.

   Output growth was even higher, averaging 4.1% over the same period, reflecting the fact that the period was one of high optimism on the part of both firms and consumers. For firms, the New Economy appeared to promise high profits and thus to justify high rates of investment. For consumers, the rise of the stock market justified high rates of consumption.

   The result of output growth far in excess of productivity growth was a steady decrease in unemployment. The unemployment rate, which was equal to 5.4% in 1996, declined to 4% in 2000, its lowest value in 30 years.

   In short, during the second half of the 1990s, the increase in technological progress led to a large decrease in unemployment.

2. In 2001, the U.S. economy went into recession. We saw the reason in Chapter 5: a sharp fall in investment. Firms concluded that they had invested too much during the second half of the 1990s and decided to cut back on their investment spending.

   By the end of 2001, thanks to a strong fiscal and monetary policy reaction, the recession was over, and output growth was positive in 2002 and 2003. But, to the surprise of most economists—and to the disappointment of the Bush administration—unemployment continued to increase. Indeed, the unemployment rate reached a maximum of 6.3% in June 2003, a full year and a half after the official end of the recession (the number in the table for 2003, 6%, is the average for the year). The recovery was dubbed the **jobless recovery**. Some economists saw it as a puzzle. Others argued that, in the New Economy, employment and output were no longer related. In fact, the explanation was simple, and very much along the lines of the theory developed in Section 13-1. Productivity growth was unusually high in 2002 and 2003, averaging 3.7%. Given this high productivity growth, output growth would have had to be much higher to lead to a decrease in unemployment. But, by then, many firms and consumers had turned skeptical of the New Economy, and despite the good news on productivity growth, they did not want to make the same mistake as in the 1990s. As a result, there was no boom in consumption or investment, and so demand and output growth were not sufficient to increase employment.

   By the beginning of 2004, output growth started exceeding productivity growth, unemployment started decreasing, and talk of a jobless recovery subsided. The period 2002 to 2003 remains, however, a good example of a period in which high productivity growth led to an increase rather than a decrease in unemployment.

3. Section 13-2 argued that an increase in the rate of technological progress was likely to lead to a decrease in the natural rate of unemployment for some time. The last decade also offers useful evidence on this point.

   Look at the numbers for the unemployment rate and the inflation rate in Table 1. During the period 1996 to 2000, the unemployment rate averaged 4.6%, a much lower value than its average value of 6% over the past 30 years. Yet there was no pressure on inflation: The inflation rate (using the GDP deflator) was practically flat during the period. This strongly suggests that, during that period, the natural unemployment rate was roughly equal to the actual unemployment rate—about 4.6%. [Recall from equation (8.10) in Chapter 8 that a flat inflation rate implies that the actual unemployment rate is equal to the natural unemployment rate.]

Table 1	Selected Macroeconomic Variables in the United States, 1996 to 2003							
	1996	1997	1998	1999	2000	2001	2002	2003
GDP growth (%)	3.6	4.4	4.2	4.4	3.7	0.5	2.2	3.1
Unemployment rate (%)	5.4	4.9	4.5	4.2	4.0	4.8	5.8	6.0
Inflation rate (GDP deflator, %)	1.9	1.9	1.1	1.4	2.2	2.4	1.5	1.7
Labor productivity (%)	1.8	2.2	2.2	2.4	2.6	0.7	3.9	3.4

(Continued)

Why was the natural rate lower during that period? We looked at that question in detail in Chapter 8. One of the factors we discussed there is directly relevant to our discussion here: The increase in the rate of productivity growth was unexpected both by firms and by workers. Given wage inflation, higher productivity growth led to lower price inflation. This is the main reason why, despite low unemployment, there was so little pressure on inflation—put differently, why the natural rate was lower.

Will the U.S. natural rate remain as low as it was at the end of the 1990s? No. As we argued in Chapter 8, some of the factors behind the decrease in the natural rate may remain. But the effect of higher productivity growth will go away. If productivity growth remains higher than in the past, workers will adjust their expectations and ask for higher wage increases. When this happens, the increase in productivity growth will no longer affect the natural rate of unemployment.

extremely successful until a new interstate went through 20 miles to the west. The churn replaced US 411 with Interstate 75, and my visions of the good life faded.

Many professions, such as those of blacksmiths and harness makers, have vanished forever. For example, there were more than 11 million farm workers in the United States at the beginning of the last century; because of very high productivity growth in agriculture, there are fewer than 1 million today. In contrast, there are now more than 3 million truck, bus, and taxi drivers in the United States; there were none in 1900. Similarly, today, there are more than 1 million computer programmers; there were practically none in 1960. Even for those with the right skills, higher technological change increases uncertainty and the risk of unemployment: The firm in which they work may be replaced by a more efficient firm, and the product their firm was selling may be replaced by another product. This tension between the benefits of technological progress for consumers (and, by implication, for firms and their shareholders) and the risks for workers is well captured in the cartoon below.

In Die Weltwoche, © *Chappatte-**www.globecartoon.com***

The Increase in Wage Inequality

For those in growing sectors, or those with the right skills, technological progress leads to new opportunities and higher wages. But for those in declining sectors, or those with skills that are no longer in demand, technological progress can mean the loss of their jobs a period of unemployment, and possibly much lower wages. In the past 25 years in the United States, we have seen a large increase in wage inequality. Most economists believe that one of the main culprits behind this increase is technological change.

Figure 13-7 shows the evolution of relative wages for various groups of workers, by education level, from 1973 to 2005. The figure is based on information about individual workers from the CPS. Each of the lines in the figure shows the evolution of the wages of workers with a given level of education—"some high school," "high school diploma," "some college," "college degree," "advanced degree"—*relative to* the wages of workers who only have high school diplomas. All relative wages are further divided by their values in 1973, so the resulting wage series are all equal to the one in 1973. The figure yields a very striking conclusion.

◀ We described the CPS survey and some of its uses in Chapter 6.

Since the early 1980s, workers with low levels of education have seen their relative wages steadily fall over time, while workers with high levels of education have seen their relative wages steadily rise. At the bottom end of the education ladder, the relative wages of workers who have not completed high school have declined by 15%. This implies that, in many cases, these workers have seen a drop not only in their relative wages but in their absolute real wages as well. At the top end of the education ladder, the relative wages of those with advanced degrees have increased by 25% since the early 1980s. In short, wage inequality has increased a lot in the United States over the past 20 years.

The Causes of Increased Wage Inequality

What are the causes of the increase in wage inequality? There is general agreement that the main factor behind the increase in the wage of high-skill workers relative to the wage of low-skill workers is a steady increase in the demand for high-skill workers relative to the demand for low-skill workers.

Figure 13-7 ▪

Evolution of Relative Wages, by Education Level, 1973 to 2005

Since the early 1980s, the relative wages of workers with a low education level have fallen; the relative wages of workers with a high education level have risen.

Source: Economic Policy Institute Datazone, www.epinet.org.

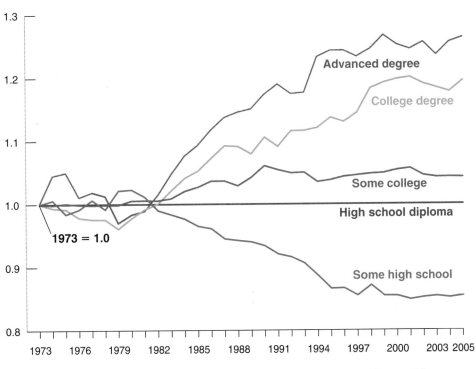

This trend in relative demand is not new; it was already present to some extent in the 1960s and 1970s. But it was offset then by a steady increase in the relative supply of high-skill workers: A steadily larger proportion of children finished high school, went to college, finished college, and so on. Since the early 1980s, relative supply has continued to increase, but not fast enough to match the continuing increase in relative demand. The result has been a steady increase in the relative wage of high-skill workers versus low-skill workers.

What explains this steady shift in relative demand?

Pursuing the effects of international trade would take us too far afield. For a more thorough discussion of who gains and who loses from trade, look at Paul Krugman and Maurice Obstfeld, *International Economics*, 7th ed., HarperCollins, New York, 2007. ▶

■ One line of argument focuses on the role of international trade. Those U.S. firms that employ higher proportions of low-skill workers, the argument goes, are increasingly driven out of markets by imports from similar firms in low-wage countries. Alternatively, to remain competitive, firms must relocate some of their production to low-wage countries. In both cases, the result is a steady decrease in the relative demand for low-skill workers in the United States. There are clear similarities between the effects of trade and the effects of technological progress: While both trade and technological progress are good for the economy as a whole, they lead nonetheless to structural change and make some workers worse off.

There is no question that trade is partly responsible for increased wage inequality. But a closer examination shows that trade accounts for only part of the shift in relative demand. The most telling fact countering explanations based solely on trade is that the shift in relative demand toward high-skill workers appears to be present even in those sectors that are not exposed to foreign competition.

■ The other line of argument focuses on **skill-biased technological progress**. New machines and new methods of production, the argument goes, require more high-skill workers today than in the past. The development of computers requires workers to be increasingly computer literate. The new methods of production require workers to be more flexible and better able to adapt to new tasks. Greater flexibility in turn requires more skills and more education.

Unlike explanations based on trade, skill-biased technological progress can explain why the shift in relative demand appears to be present in nearly all sectors of the economy. At this point, most economists believe that it is the dominant factor in explaining the increase in wage dispersion.

Does all this imply that the United States is condemned to steadily increasing wage inequality? Not necessarily. There are at least three reasons to think that the future may be different from the recent past:

Note that in Figure 13-7, wage ▶ differences have not increased further since 2000. It is, however, too early to know whether this is a change in trends.

■ The trend in relative demand may simply slow down. For example, it is likely that computers will become easier and easier to use in the future, even by low-skill workers. Computers may even replace high-skill workers, those workers whose skills involve primarily the ability to compute or to memorize. Paul Krugman has argued—only partly tongue in cheek—that accountants, lawyers, and doctors may be next on the list of professions to be replaced by computers.

■ Technological progress is not exogenous: This is a theme we explored in Chapter 12. How much firms spend on R&D and in what directions they direct their research depend on expected profits. The low relative wage of low-skill workers may lead firms to explore new technologies that take advantage of the presence of low-skill, low-wage workers. In other words, market forces may lead technological progress to become less skill biased in the future.

■ The relative supply of high-skill versus low-skill workers is also not exogenous. The large increase in the relative wage of more educated workers implies that the returns to acquiring more education and training are higher than they were one or two decades ago. Higher returns to training and education can increase the relative supply of high-skill workers, and, as a result, work to stabilize relative wages.

Many economists believe that policy plays an important role here. It should ensure that the quality of primary and secondary education for the children of low-wage workers does not further deteriorate and that those who want to acquire more education can borrow to pay for it.

13-4 Institutions, Technological Progress, and Growth

To end this chapter, I want to return to the issue raised at the end of the previous chapter: For poor countries, technological progress is more a process of imitation than a process of innovation. China and other Asian countries make it look easy. So, why are so many other countries unable to do the same? As I indicated in Chapter 10, this question takes us from *macroeconomics* to *development economics*, and it would take a textbook in development economics to do it justice. But it is too important a question to leave it aside entirely here.

To get a sense of the issues, compare Kenya and the United States. In 2004, PPP GDP per person in Kenya was about one-thirtieth of PPP GDP per person in the United States. Part of the difference was due to a much lower level of capital per worker in Kenya. The other part of the difference was due to a much lower technological level in Kenya: It is estimated that A, the state of technology in Kenya, is about one-fifteenth of the U.S. level. Why is the state of technology in Kenya so low? Kenya, like most other poor countries, has access to most of the technological knowledge in the world. What prevents it from simply adopting much of the advanced countries' technology and quickly closing much of its technological gap with the United States?

One can think of a number of potential answers, ranging from Kenya's geography and climate to its culture. Most economists believe, however, that the main source of the problem, for poor countries in general and for Kenya in particular, lies in their poor institutions.

What institutions do economists have in mind? At a broad level, the protection of **property rights** may well be the most important. Few individuals are going to create firms, introduce new technologies, and invest, if they expect that profits will be either appropriated by the state, extracted in bribes by corrupt bureaucrats, or stolen by other people in the economy. Figure 13-8 plots PPP GDP per person in 1995 (using a logarithmic scale) for

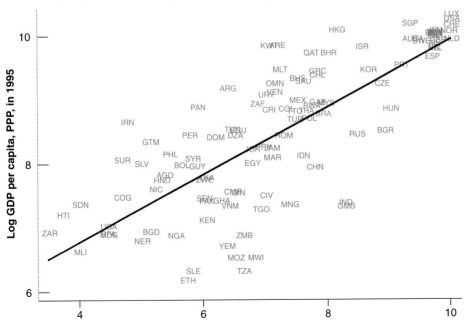

Figure 13-8

Protection from Expropriation and GDP per Person

There is a strong positive relation between the degree of protection from expropriation and the level of GDP per person.

Source: Daron Acemoglu, "Understanding Institutions," Lionel Robbins Lectures, 2004.

The Importance of Institutions: North and South Korea

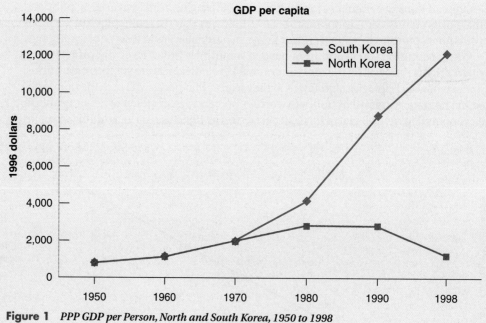

Following the surrender of Japan in 1945, Korea formally acquired its independence, but became divided at the 38th parallel into two zones of occupation, with Soviet armed forces occupying the north, and U.S. armed forces occupying the south. Attempts by both sides to claim jurisdiction over all of Korea triggered the Korean War, which lasted from 1950 to 1953. At the armistice in 1953, Korea became formally divided into two countries, the "Democratic People's Republic of North Korea" in the north and the "Republic of Korea" in the south.

An interesting feature of Korea before separation was its ethnic and linguistic homogeneity. The north and the south were inhabited by essentially the same people, with the same culture and the same religion. Economically, the two regions were also highly similar at the time of separation. PPP GDP per person, in 1996 dollars, was roughly the same, about $700 in both North and South Korea.

Yet, 50 years later, as shown in Figure 1, GDP per person was 10 times higher in South Korea than in North Korea—$12,000 versus $1,100! On the one hand, South

Korea had joined the OECD, the club of rich countries. On the other, North Korea had seen its GDP per person decrease by nearly two-thirds from its peak of $3,000 in the mid-1970s, and it was facing famine on a large scale.

What happened? Institutions and the organization of the economy were dramatically different during that period in South and North Korea. South Korea relied on a capitalist organization of the economy, with strong state intervention, but also private ownership and legal protection of private producers. North Korea relied on central planning. Industries were quickly nationalized. Small firms and farms were forced to join large cooperatives, so they could be supervised by the state. There were no private property rights for individuals. The result was the decline of the industrial sector and the collapse of agriculture. The lesson is sad but transparent: Institutions matter very much for growth.

Source: Daron Acemoglu, "Understanding Institutions," Lionel Robbins Lectures, 2004.

FOCUS

GDP per capita

Figure 1   *PPP GDP per Person, North and South Korea, 1950 to 1998*

Kenya's index is 6. Kenya is below the regression line, which means that Kenya has a lower GDP per person than would be predicted based just on the index.

90 countries against an index measuring the degree of protection from expropriation, constructed for each of these countries by an international business organization. The positive correlation between the two is striking (the figure also plots the regression line): Low protection is associated with a low GDP per person (at the extreme left of the figure are Zaire and Haiti); high protection is associated with a high GDP per person (at the extreme right are the United States, Luxembourg, Norway, Switzerland, and the Netherlands).

What Is Behind Chinese Growth?

From 1949—the year in which the People's Republic of China was established—to the late 1970s, China's economic system was based on central planning. Two major politico-economic reforms, the "Great Leap Forward" in 1958 and the "Cultural Revolution" in 1966, ended up as human and economic catastrophes. Output decreased by 20% from 1959 to 1962, and it is estimated that 25 million people died of starvation during the same period. Output again decreased by more than 10% from 1966 to 1968.

After Chairman Mao's death in 1976, the new leaders decided to progressively introduce market mechanisms in the economy. In 1978, an agricultural reform was put in place, allowing farmers, after satisfying a quota due to the state, to sell their production on rural markets. Over time, farmers obtained increasing rights to the land, and today, state farms produce less than 1% of agricultural output. Outside of agriculture, also starting in the late 1970s, state firms were given increasing autonomy over their production decisions, and market mechanisms and prices were introduced for an increasing number of goods. Private entrepreneurship was encouraged, often taking the form of "Town and Village Enterprises," collective ventures guided by a profit motive. Tax advantages and special agreements were used to attract foreign investors.

The economic effects of these cumulative reforms have been dramatic: Average growth of output per worker increased from 2.5% between 1952 and 1977 to more than 8% since then.

Is such high growth surprising? One could argue that it is not. Looking at the 10-fold difference in productivity between North and South Korea we saw in the previous Focus box, it is clear that central planning is a poor economic system. Thus, it would seem that, by moving from central planning to a market economy, countries could easily experience large increases in productivity. The answer is not so obvious, however, when one looks at the experience of the many countries that, since the late 1980s, have indeed moved away from central planning. In most central European countries, this transition was typically associated initially with a 10% to 20% drop in GDP, and it took five years or more for output to exceed its pre-transition level. In Russia and in the new countries carved out of the former Soviet Union, the drop was even larger and longer lasting. (Most transition countries now have strong growth, although their growth rates are far below China's.)

In central and eastern Europe, the initial effect of transition was a collapse of the state sector, only partially compensated by slow growth of the new private sector. In China, the state sector has declined more slowly, and its decline has been more than compensated by strong private-sector growth. This gives a proximate explanation for the difference between China and the other transition countries. But it still begs the question: How was China able to achieve this smoother transition?

Some observers offer a cultural explanation. They point to the Confucian tradition, based on the teachings of Confucius, which still dominates Chinese values and which emphasizes hard work, respect of one's commitments, and trustworthiness among friends. All these traits, they argue, are the foundations of institutions that allow a market economy to perform well.

Some observers offer an historical explanation. They point to the fact that, in contrast to Russia, central planning in China lasted for only a few decades. Thus, when the shift back to a market economy took place, people still knew how such an economy functioned and adapted easily to the new economic environment.

Most observers point to the strong rule of the Communist party in the process. They point out that, in contrast to central and eastern Europe, the political system did not change, and the government was able to control the pace of transition. It was able to experiment along the way, to allow state firms to continue production while the private sector grew, to guarantee property rights to foreign investors. (In Figure 13-8, China has an index of property rights of 7.7, not far from the value in rich countries.) Foreign investors have brought with them technology from rich countries, and, in time, this knowledge has been transferred to domestic firms. For political reasons, such a strategy was simply not open to governments in central and eastern Europe.

The limits of the Chinese strategy are clear: Property rights are still not well established, and the banking system is still inefficient. So far, however, these problems have not stood in the way of growth.

Note: For more on China's economy, read Gregory Chow, China's Economic Transformation, Blackwell Publishers, New York, 2002. For a comparison between transition in eastern Europe and China, read Jan Svejnar, China in Light of the Performance of Central and East European Economies, IZA Discussion Paper 2791, May 2007.

What does *protection of property rights* mean in practice? It means a good political system, in which those in charge cannot expropriate or seize the property of the citizens. It means a good judicial system, where disagreements can be resolved efficiently and rapidly. Looking at an even finer degree of detail, it means laws against insider trading in the stock market, so people are willing to buy stocks and thereby provide financing to firms; it means clearly written and well-enforced patent laws, so firms have an incentive to do research and develop new products. It means good antitrust laws, so competitive markets do not turn into monopolies with few incentives to introduce new methods of production and new products. And the list obviously goes on. (A particularly clear example of the role of institutions is given in the Focus box "The Importance of Institutions: North and South Korea.")

This still leaves one essential question: Why don't poor countries adopt these good institutions? The answer is that it is hard! Good institutions are complex and difficult for poor countries to put in place. Surely, causality runs both ways in Figure 13-8: Low protection against expropriation leads to low GDP per person. But it is also the case that low GDP per person leads to worse protection against expropriation: Poor countries are often too poor to afford a good judicial system, to maintain a good police force, for example. Thus, improving institutions, and starting a virtuous cycle of higher GDP per person and better institutions, is often very difficult. The fast-growing countries of Asia have succeeded. (The Focus box "What Is Behind Chinese Growth?" explores the case of China in more detail.) So far, much of Africa has been unable to start such a virtuous cycle.

Summary

- People often fear that technological progress destroys jobs and leads to higher unemployment. Theory and evidence suggest that these fears are largely unfounded. There is not much support, either in theory or in the data, for the idea that faster technological progress leads to higher unemployment.

- In the short run, there is no reason to expect, nor does there appear to be, a systematic relation between changes in productivity and movements in unemployment.

- If there is a relation between changes in productivity and movements in unemployment in the medium run, it appears to be an inverse relation: Lower productivity growth appears to lead to higher unemployment; higher productivity growth appears to lead to lower unemployment. An explanation is that it takes high unemployment to reconcile wage demands with lower productivity growth.

- Technological progress is not a smooth process in which all workers are winners. Rather, it is a process of structural change. Even if most people benefit from the increase in the average standard of living, there are losers as well. As new goods and new techniques of production are developed, old goods and old techniques of production become obsolete. Some workers find their skills in higher demand and benefit from technological progress. Others find their skills in lower demand and suffer unemployment and/or reductions in relative wages.

- Wage inequality has increased in the past 25 years in the United States. The real wage of low-skill workers has declined not only relative to the real wage of high-skill workers but also in absolute terms. The two main causes are international trade and skill-biased technological progress.

- Sustained technological progress requires the right institutions. In particular, it requires well-established and well-protected property rights. Without good property rights, a country is likely to remain poor. But, in turn, a poor country may find it difficult to put in place good property rights.

Key Terms

- technological unemployment, 294
- structural change, 298
- creative destruction, 298
- churning, 298
- jobless recovery, 299
- skill-biased technological progress, 302
- property rights, 303

Questions and Problems

Quick Check

1. Using the information in this chapter, label each of the following statements true, false, or uncertain. Explain briefly.

a. The change in employment and output per person in the United States since 1900 lends support to the argument that technological progress leads to a steady increase in employment.

b. Workers benefit equally from the process of creative destruction.

c. In the past two decades, the real wages of low-skill U.S. workers have declined relative to the real wages of high-skill workers.

d. Technological progress leads to a decrease in employment if, and only if, the increase in output is smaller than the increase in productivity.

e. The "jobless recovery" after the recession of 2001 can be explained by unusually high productivity growth unaccompanied by a boom in aggregate demand.

f. The apparent decrease in the natural rate of unemployment in the United States in the second half of the 1990s can be explained by the fact that productivity growth was unexpectedly high during that period.

g. If we could stop technological progress, doing so would lead to a decrease in the natural rate of unemployment.

2. "Higher labor productivity allows firms to produce more goods with the same number of workers and thus to sell the goods at the same or even lower prices. That's why increases in labor productivity can permanently reduce the rate of unemployment without causing inflation." Discuss.

3. Suppose an economy is characterized by the equations below.

$$\text{Price setting:} \quad P = (1 + \mu)(W/A)$$
$$\text{Wage setting:} \quad W = A^e P^e(1 - u)$$

a. Solve for the unemployment rate if $P^e = P$ but A^e does not necessarily equal A. Explain the effects of (A^e/A) on the unemployment rate.

   Now suppose that expectations of both prices and productivity are accurate.

b. Solve for the natural rate of unemployment if the markup is equal to 8%.

c. Does the natural rate of unemployment depend on productivity? Explain.

4. How might policy changes in (a) through (d) affect the wage gap between low-skill and high-skill workers in the United States?

a. increased spending on computers in public schools

b. limits on the numbers of foreign temporary farm workers allowed to enter the United States

c. an increase in the number of public colleges

d. tax credits in Central America for U.S. firms

Dig Deeper

5. Technological progress, agriculture, and employment
"Those who argue that technological progress does not reduce employment should look at agriculture. At the start of the last century, there were more than 11 million farm workers. Today, there are fewer than 1 million. If all sectors start having the productivity growth that took place in agriculture during the twentieth century, nobody will be employed a century from now." Discuss.

6. Productivity and the aggregate supply curve
   Consider an economy in which production is given by

$$Y = AN$$

Assume that price setting and wage setting are described in the equations below.

$$\text{Price setting:} \quad P = (1 + \mu)(W/A)$$
$$\text{Wage setting:} \quad W = A^e P^e(1 - u)$$

   Recall that the relation between employment, N, the labor force, L, and the unemployment rate, u, is given by

$$N = (1 - u)L$$

a. Derive the aggregate supply curve (that is, the relation between the price level and the level of output, given the markup, the actual and expected levels of productivity, the labor force, and the expected price level). Explain the role of each variable.

b. Show the effect of an equiproportional increase in A and A^e (so that A/A^e remains unchanged) on the position of the aggregate supply curve. Explain.

c. Suppose instead that actual productivity, A, increases, but expected productivity, A^e, does not change. Compare the results in this case to your conclusions in part (b). Explain the difference.

7. Skill-biased technological change in the United States and Europe
   This problem uses the labor demand/labor supply framework developed in problem 7 to explore the labor market histories of the United States and Europe.
   The United States: Imagine that there are two labor markets, one for high-skill labor and one for low-skill labor.

a. Suppose there is an increase in demand for high-skill labor and a decrease in demand for low-skill labor. For a given labor force, what happens to the real wage in each sector?

   Europe: Imagine that there are also two labor markets in Europe, but the low-skill labor market has a binding minimum (real) wage. A binding minimum wage means that the equilibrium wage would be lower than the required minimum wage. As a result, employment is determined by the intersection of the minimum wage and the labor demand curve. The difference between labor supply and labor demand at the minimum wage represents unemployment.

b. Consider a decrease in labor demand for low-skill labor in Europe. What will be the effect on the real wage for low-skill workers? What will be the effect on unemployment? Compare these results to those you obtained for the low-skill labor market in part (a) for the United States.

Comparing the Effects:

c. Putting everything together, after an increase in demand for high-skill labor and a fall in demand for low-skill labor, in which economy will the increase in wage inequality be higher? In which economy will the increase in unemployment be higher? (Assume that neither economy has a binding minimum wage in the high-skill labor market.)

d. Although the distinction between the United States and Europe we have drawn in this problem is crude, how does your analysis relate to the labor market histories of these economies over the past two decades?

8. *Technology and the labor market*

In the appendix to Chapter 6, we learned how the wage-setting and price-setting equations could be expressed in terms of labor demand and labor supply. In this problem, we extend the analysis to account for technological change.

Consider the wage-setting equation

$$W/P = F(u, z),$$

as the equation corresponding to labor supply. Recall that for a given labor force, L, *the unemployment rate,* u, *can be written as*

$$u = 1 - N/L,$$

where N *is employment.*

a. Substitute the expression for u into the wage-setting equation.

b. Using the relation you derived in part (a), graph the labor supply curve in a diagram with N on the horizontal axis and W/P, the real wage, on the vertical axis. *We write the price-setting equation as*

$$P = (1 + \mu) MC$$

where MC *is the marginal cost of production. To generalize somewhat our discussion in the text, we shall write* MC = W*MPL, *where* W *is the wage and* MPL *is the marginal product of labor.*

c. Substitute the expression for MC into the price-setting equation and solve for the real wage, W/P. The result is the labor demand relation, with W/P as a function of the MPL and the markup, μ.

In the text, we assumed for simplicity that the MPL *was constant, for a given level of technology. Here, we assume that the* MPL *falls with employment (again for a given level of technology), a more realistic assumption.*

d. Assuming that the MPL falls with employment, graph the labor demand relation you derived in part (c). Use the same diagram you drew for part (b).

e. What happens to the labor demand curve if the level of technology improves? (*Hint*: What happens to MPL when technology improves?) Explain. How is the real wage affected by an increase in the level of technology?

Explore Further

9. *The churn*

The Bureau of Labor Statistics presents a forecast of occupations with the largest job decline and the largest job growth. Examine the tables at **www.bls.gov/emp/emptab4.htm** *(for the largest job decline) and* **www.bls.gov/emp/emptab3.htm** *(for the largest job growth).*

a. Which occupations in decline can be linked to technological change? Which can be linked to foreign competition?

b. Which occupations that are forecast to grow can be linked to technological change? Which can be linked to demographic change—in particular, the aging of the U.S. population?

c. Compare the educational requirements (the last column of the tables) for the occupations in decline and on the rise. Can you see evidence of the effects of technological change?

d. Another development in the U.S. labor market is the increased use of temporary workers. How does this phenomenon fit with the educational requirements of occupations in decline and on the rise?

10. *Real wages*

The chapter presents data on relative wages of high-skill and low-skill workers. In this question, we look at the evolution of real wages.

a. Based on the price-setting equation we use in the book, how should real wages change with technological progress. Explain. Has there been technological progress during the period from 1973 to the present?

b. Go to the Web site of the *Economic Report of the President* (**www.gpoaccess.gov/eop/**) and find Table B-47. Look at the data on average hourly earnings (in non-agricultural industries) in 1982 dollars (i.e., real hourly earnings). How do real hourly earnings in 1973 compare to real hourly earnings in the latest year for which data are available?

c. Given the data on *relative* wages presented in the chapter, what do your results from part (b) suggest about the evolution of *real* wages of low-skill workers since 1973? What do your answers suggest about the strength of the relative decline in demand for low-skill workers?

d. What might be missing from this analysis of worker compensation? Do workers receive compensation in forms other than wages?

The Economic Policy Institute (EPI) publishes detailed information about the real wages of various classes of workers in its publication The State of Working America. *Sometimes, EPI makes data from* The State of Working America *available at* **www.stateofworkingamerica.org**.

We invite you to visit the Blanchard page on the Prentice Hall Web site, at:
www.prenhall.com/blanchard
for this chapter's World Wide Web exercises.

Further Readings

- For more on the process of reallocation that characterizes modern economies, read *The Churn: The Paradox of Progress*, a report by the Federal Reserve Bank of Dallas, 1993.
- For a fascinating account of how computers are transforming the labor market, read Frank Levy and Richard Murnane, *The New Division of Labor: How Computers are Creating the Next Job Market*, Princeton University Press, Princeton, NJ, 2004.

- For the role of institutions in growth, read Abhijit Banerjee and Esther Duflo, "Growth Theory through the Lens of Development Economics," in *Handbook of Economic Growth*, North Holland, Amsterdam, 2005 (read sections 1 to 4 of Chapter 7).
- For more on institutions and growth, read Daron Acemoglu, *Understanding Institutions*, 2004 (**cep.lse.ac.uk/events/lionel_robbins.asp**)

Expectations

The next four chapters represent the first major extension of the core. They look at the role of expectations in output fluctuations.

Chapter 14

Chapter 14 introduces two important concepts. The first is the distinction between the real interest rate and the nominal interest rate. The second is the concept of expected present discounted value. The chapter ends by discussing the "Fisher hypothesis," the proposition that, in the medium run, nominal interest rates fully reflect inflation and money growth.

Chapter 15

Chapter 15 focuses on the role of expectations in financial markets. It first looks at the determination of bond prices and bond yields. It shows how we can learn about the course of expected future interest rates by looking at the yield curve. It then turns to stock prices, and shows how they depend on expected future dividends and interest rates. Finally, it discusses whether stock prices always reflect fundamentals, or may instead reflect bubbles or fads.

Chapter 16 ▬▬▬

Chapter 16 focuses on the role of expectations in consumption and investment decisions. The chapter shows how consumption depends partly on current income, partly on human wealth, and partly on financial wealth. It shows how investment depends partly on current cash flow, and partly on the expected present value of future profits.

Chapter 17 ▬▬▬

Chapter 17 looks at the role of expectations in output fluctuations. Starting from the *IS–LM* model, it modifies the description of goods market equilibrium (the *IS* relation) to reflect the effect of expectations on spending. It revisits the effects of monetary and fiscal policy on output. It shows for example, that, in contrast to the results derived in the core, a fiscal contraction can sometimes increase output, even in the short run.

A consumer who considers buying a new car must ask: Can I safely take a new car loan? How much of a wage raise can I expect over the next few years? Is a recession coming? How safe is my job?

A manager who observes an increase in current sales must ask: Is this a temporary boom that I should try to meet with the existing production capacity? Or is it likely to last, in which case I should order new machines?

A pension fund manager who observes a boom in the stock market must ask: Are stock prices going to increase further, or is the boom likely to fizzle? Does the increase in stock prices reflect expectations of firms' higher profits in the future? Do I share those expectations? Should I move some of my funds into or out of the stock market?

These examples make clear that many economic decisions depend not only on what is happening today but also on expectations of what will happen in the future. Indeed, some decisions should depend very little on what is happening today. For example, why should an increase in sales today—if it is not accompanied by expectations of continued higher sales in the future—cause a firm to alter its investment plans? The new machines may not be in operation before sales have returned to normal. By then, they may sit idle, gathering dust.

Until now, we have not paid systematic attention to the role of expectations in goods and financial markets. We ignored expectations in our construction of both the *IS–LM* model and the aggregate demand component of the *AS–AD* model that builds on the *IS–LM* model. When looking at the goods market, we assumed that consumption depended on current income and that investment depended on current sales. When looking at financial markets, we lumped assets together and called them "bonds"; we then focused on the choice between bonds and money, and ignored the choice between bonds and stocks, the choice between short-term bonds and long-term bonds, and so on. We introduced these simplifications to build the intuition for the basic mechanisms at work. It is now time to think about the role of expectations in economic fluctuations. We shall do it in this and the next three chapters.

This chapter lays the groundwork and introduces two key concepts:

■ Section 14-1 examines the distinction between the *real* interest rate and the *nominal* interest rate.

■ Sections 14-2 and 14-3 build on this distinction to revisit the effects of money growth on interest rates. They lead to a surprising but important result: Higher money growth leads to *lower* nominal interest rates in the short run but to *higher* nominal interest rates in the medium run.

■ Section 14-4 introduces the second concept: the concept of *expected present discounted value.* ■

14-1 Nominal versus Real Interest Rates

In January 1981, the *one-year T-bill rate*—the interest rate on one-year government bonds—was 12.6%. In January 2006, the one-year T-bill rate was only 4.5%. Although most of us cannot borrow at the same interest rate as the government, the interest rates we face as consumers were also substantially lower in 2006 than in 1981. It was much cheaper to borrow in 2006 than it was in 1981.

Or was it? In 1981, inflation was around 12%. In 2006, inflation was around 2%. This would seem relevant: The interest rate tells us how many dollars we shall have to pay in the future in exchange for having 1 more dollar today.

But we do not consume dollars. We consume goods.

When we borrow, what we really want to know is how many goods we will have to give up in the future in exchange for the goods we get today. Likewise, when we lend, we want to know how many goods—not how many dollars—we will get in the future for the goods we give up today. The presence of inflation makes the distinction important. What is the point of receiving high interest payments in the future if inflation between now and then is so high that we are unable to buy more goods then?

This is where the distinction between nominal interest rates and real interest rates comes in:

Nominal interest rate: The interest rate in terms of dollars. ▶

■ Interest rates expressed in terms of dollars (or, more generally, in units of the national currency) are called **nominal interest rates**. The interest rates printed in the financial pages of newspapers are nominal interest rates. For example, when we say that the one-year T-bill rate is 4.5%, we mean that for every dollar the government borrows by issuing one-year T-bills, it promises to pay 1.045 dollars in one year. More generally, if the nominal interest rate for year t is i_t, borrowing 1 dollar this year requires you to pay $1 + i_t$ dollars next year. (I use interchangeably *this year* for *today* and *next year* for *one year from today*.)

Real interest rate: The interest ▶ **rate in terms of a basket of goods.**

■ Interest rates expressed *in terms of a basket of goods* are called **real interest rates**. If we denote the real interest rate for year t by r_t, then, by definition, borrowing the equivalent of one basket of goods this year requires you to pay the equivalent of $1 + r_t$ baskets of goods next year.

What is the relation between nominal and real interest rates? How do we go from nominal interest rates—which we do observe—to real interest rates—which we typically do not observe? The intuitive answer: We must adjust the nominal interest rate to take into account expected inflation.

Let's go through the step-by-step derivation.

Assume that there is only one good in the economy, bread (we shall add jam and other goods later). Denote the one-year nominal interest rate, in terms of dollars, by i_t: If you borrow 1 dollar this year, you will have to repay $1 + i_t$ dollars next year. But you are not interested in dollars. What you really want to know is: If you borrow enough to eat 1 more pound of bread this year, how much will you have to repay, in terms of pounds of bread, next year?

Expectations   **Extensions**

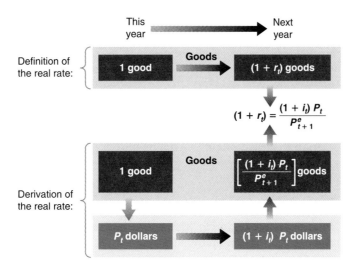

Figure 14-1

Definition and Derivation of the Real Interest Rate

Figure 14-1 helps us derive the answer. The top part repeats the definition of the one-year real interest rate. The bottom part shows how we can derive the one-year real interest rate from information about the one-year nominal interest rate and the price of bread:

■ Start with the arrow pointing down in the lower left of Figure 14-1. Suppose you want to eat 1 more pound of bread this year. If the price of a pound of bread this year is P_t dollars, to eat 1 more pound of bread, you must borrow P_t dollars.

■ If i_t is the one-year nominal interest rate—the interest rate in terms of dollars—and if you borrow P_t dollars, you will have to repay $(1 + i_t)P_t$ dollars next year. This is represented by the arrow from left to right at the bottom of Figure 14-1.

■ What you care about, however, is not dollars but pounds of bread. Thus, the last step involves converting dollars back to pounds of bread next year. Let P_{t+1}^e be the price of bread you expect for next year. (The superscript e indicates that this is an expectation: You do not know yet what the price of bread will be next year.) How much you expect to repay next year, in terms of pounds of bread, is therefore equal to $(1 + i_t)P_t$ (the number of dollars you have to repay next year) divided by P_{t+1}^e (the price of bread in terms of dollars expected for next year), so $(1 + i_t)P_t/P_{t+1}^e$. This is represented by the arrow pointing up in the lower right of Figure 14-1.

> If you have to pay \$10 next year, and you expect the price of bread next year to be \$2 per pound, you expect to have to repay the equivalent of 10/2 = 5 pounds of bread next year. This is why we divide the dollar amount $(1+i_t)\,P_t$ by the expected price of bread next year, P_{t+1}^e.

Putting together what you see in the top part and what you see in the bottom part of Figure 14-1, it follows that the one-year real interest rate, r_t, is given by

$$1 + r_t = (1 + i_t)\frac{P_t}{P_{t+1}^e} \tag{14.1}$$

This relation looks intimidating. Two simple manipulations make it look friendlier:

■ Denote expected inflation between t and $t + 1$ by π_{t+1}^e. Given that there is only one good—bread—the expected rate of inflation equals the expected change in the dollar price of bread between this year and next year, divided by the dollar price of bread this year:

$$\pi_{t+1}^e = \frac{(P_{t+1}^e - P_t)}{P_t} \tag{14.2}$$

> Add 1 to both sides in (14.2):
> $$1 + \pi_{t+1}^e = 1 + \frac{(P_{t+1}^e - P_t)}{P_t}$$
> Reorganize:
> $$1 + \pi_{t+1}^e = \frac{P_{t+1}^e}{P_t}$$
> Take the inverse on both sides:
> $$\frac{1}{1 + \pi_{t+1}^e} = \frac{P_t}{P_{t+1}^e}$$

Using equation (14.2), rewrite P_t/P_{t+1}^e in equation (14.1) as $1/(1 + \pi_{t+1}^e)$. Replace ◀ Replace in (14.1). in (14.1) to get

See Proposition 6 in Appendix 2 at the end of the book. Suppose $i = 10\%$ and $\pi^e = 5\%$. The exact relation (14.3) gives $r_t = 4.8\%$. The approximation given by equation (14.4) gives 5%—close enough.

The approximation can be quite bad, however, when i and ▶ π^e are high. If $i = 100\%$ and $\pi^e = 80\%$, the exact relation gives $r = 11\%$, but the approximation gives $r = 20\%$—a big difference.

$$(1 + r_t) = \frac{1 + i_t}{1 + \pi^e_{t+1}} \tag{14.3}$$

One plus the real interest rate equals the ratio of 1 plus the nominal interest rate, divided by 1 plus the expected rate of inflation.

■ Equation (14.3) gives us the *exact* relation of the real interest rate to the nominal interest rate and expected inflation. However, when the nominal interest rate and expected inflation are not too large—say, less than 20% per year—a close approximation to this equation is given by the simpler relation

$$r_t \approx i_t - \pi^e_{t+1} \tag{14.4}$$

Equation (14.4) is simple. Remember it. It says that *the real interest rate is (approximately) equal to the nominal interest rate minus expected inflation.* [In the rest of the book, I often treat the relation (14.4) as if it were an equality. Remember, however, that it is only an approximation.]

Note some of the implications of equation (14.4):

■ When expected inflation equals 0, the nominal and the real interest rates are equal.
■ Because expected inflation is typically positive, the real interest rate is typically lower than the nominal interest rate.
■ For a given nominal interest rate, the higher the expected rate of inflation, the lower the real interest rate.

The case where expected inflation happens to be equal to the nominal interest rate is worth looking at more closely. Suppose the nominal interest rate and expected inflation both equal 10%, and you are the borrower. For every dollar you borrow this year, you will have to repay 1.10 dollars next year. But dollars will be worth 10% less in terms of bread next year. So, if you borrow the equivalent of 1 pound of bread, you will have to repay the equivalent of 1 pound of bread next year: The real cost of borrowing—the real interest rate—is equal to 0. Now suppose you are the lender: For every dollar you lend this year, you will receive 1.10 dollars next year. This looks attractive, but dollars next year will be worth 10% less in terms of bread. If you lend the equivalent of 1 pound of bread this year, you will get the equivalent of 1 pound of bread next year: Despite the 10% nominal interest rate, the real interest rate is equal to 0.

We have assumed so far that there is only one good—bread. But what we have done generalizes easily to many goods. All we need to do is to substitute the *price level*—the price of a basket of goods—for the price of bread in equation (14.1) or equation (14.3). If we use the consumer price index (CPI) to measure the price level, the real interest rate tells us how much consumption we must give up next year to consume more today.

Nominal and Real Interest Rates in the United States since 1978

Let us return to the question at the start of this section. We can now restate it as follows: Was the *real interest rate* lower in 2006 than it was in 1981? More generally, what has happened to the real interest rate in the United States since the early 1980s?

The answer is shown in Figure 14-2, which plots both nominal and real interest rates since 1978. For each year, the nominal interest rate is the one-year T-bill rate at the beginning of the year. To construct the real interest rate, we need a measure of expected inflation—more precisely, the rate of inflation expected as of the beginning

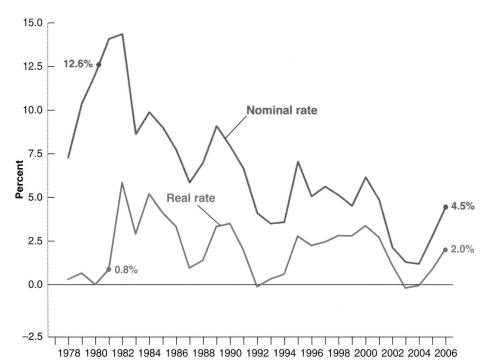

Figure 14-2

Nominal and Real One-Year T-bill Rates in the United States since 1978

Although the nominal interest rate has declined considerably since the early 1980s, the real interest rate was actually higher in 2006 than in 1981.

of each year. Figure 14-2 uses, for each year, the forecast of inflation for that year published at the end of the previous year by the OECD. For example, the forecast of inflation used to construct the real interest rate for 2006 is the forecast of inflation published by the OECD in December 2005—2.2%.

Note that the real interest rate ($i - \pi^e$) is based on *expected* inflation. If actual inflation turns out to be different from expected inflation, the realized real interest rate ($i - \pi$) will be different from the real interest rate. For this reason, the real interest rate is sometimes called the *ex-ante* real interest rate. (*Ex-ante* means "before the fact." Here it means before inflation is known.) The realized real interest rate is called the *ex-post* real interest rate. (*Ex-post* means "after the fact." Here it means after inflation is known.)

Figure 14-2 shows the importance of adjusting for inflation. Although the nominal interest was much lower in 2006 than it was in 1981, the real interest rate was actually *higher* in 2006 than it was in 1981: 2.0% in 2006 versus 0.8% in 1981. Put another way, despite the large decline in nominal interest rates, borrowing was actually more expensive in 2006 than it was 1981. This is due to the fact that inflation (and, with it, expected inflation) has steadily declined since the early 1980s.

Note the large decline in both the nominal and the real interest rates from 2000 to 2004. This reflects the decision of the Fed to cut nominal interest rates starting in early 2001 in order to limit the recession and help the recovery. See the Focus box on the U.S. recession ◄ in Chapter 5.

14-2 Nominal and Real Interest Rates and the IS-LM Model

In the *IS–LM* model we developed in Chapter 5, "the" interest rate came into play in two places: It affected investment in the *IS* relation, and it affected the choice between money and bonds in the *LM* relation. Which interest rate—nominal or real—were we talking about in each case?

■ Take the *IS* relation first. Our discussion in Section 14-1 makes it clear that firms, in deciding how much investment to undertake, care about the *real interest rate*: Firms produce goods. They want to know how much they will have to repay, not in

I shall ignore time subscripts here; they are not needed for ▶ this and the next section.

terms of dollars but in terms of goods. So what belongs in the *IS* relation is the real interest rate. Let r denote the real interest rate. The *IS* relation must therefore be modified as follows:

$$Y = C(Y - T) + I(Y, r) + G$$

Investment spending, and thus the demand for goods, depends on the *real* interest rate.

For the time being, we shall ▶ focus only on how the interest rate affects investment. In Chapters 16 and 17, you shall see how the real interest rate affects both investment and consumption decisions.

■ Now turn to the *LM* relation. When we derived the *LM* relation, we assumed that the demand for money depended on the interest rate. But were we referring to the nominal interest rate or the real interest rate? The answer is: to the *nominal interest rate*. Remember why the interest rate affects the demand for money. When people decide whether to hold money or bonds, they take into account the opportunity cost of holding money rather than bonds—the opportunity cost is what they give up by holding money rather than bonds. Money pays a zero nominal interest rate. Bonds pay a nominal interest rate of i. Hence, the opportunity cost of holding money is equal to the difference between the interest rate from holding bonds minus the interest from holding money, so $i - 0 = i$, which is just the nominal interest rate. Therefore, the *LM* relation is still given by

$$\frac{M}{P} = Y L(i)$$

Putting together the IS relation above with this equation and the relation between the real interest rate and the nominal interest rate, the extended *IS–LM* model is given by

IS relation: $Y = C(Y - T) + I(Y, r) + G$

LM relation: $\dfrac{M}{P} = Y L(i)$

Real interest rate: $r = i - \pi^e$

Note the immediate implications of these three relations:

Interest rate in the *LM* relation: Nominal interest rate, *i*.
▶

■ The interest rate directly affected by monetary policy (the interest rate that enters the *LM* equation) is the nominal interest rate.
■ The interest rate that affects spending and output (the rate that enters the *IS* relation) is the real interest rate.

Interest rate in the *IS* relation: ▶ Real interest rate, *r*.

■ The effects of monetary policy on output therefore depend on how movements in the nominal interest rate translate into movements in the real interest rate. To explore this question further, the next section looks at how an increase in money growth affects the nominal interest rate and the real interest rate, both in the short run and in the medium run.

14-3 Money Growth, Inflation, and Nominal and Real Interest Rates

The Fed's decision to allow for higher money growth is the main factor behind the decline in interest rates in the past six months (circa 1991).

The two economists were Alan Blinder, from Princeton, and Janet Yellen, then from Berkeley. More on Alan Blinder in a Focus box in Chapter 24.
▶

The nomination to the Board of the Federal Reserve of two left-leaning economists, both perceived to be soft on inflation, has led financial markets to worry about higher money growth, higher inflation, and higher interest rates in the future (circa May 1994).

These two quotes are made up, but they are composites of what was written at the time. Which one is right? Does higher money growth lead to lower interest rates, or does higher money growth lead to higher interest rates? The answer: Both!

There are two keys to the answer: One is the distinction we just introduced between the real and the nominal interest rate. The other is the distinction we developed in the core between the short run and the medium run. As you shall see, the full answer is

- Higher money growth leads to lower nominal interest rates in the short run but to higher nominal interest rates in the medium run.
- Higher money growth leads to lower real interest rates in the short run but has no effect on real interest rates in the medium run.

The purpose of this section is to develop this answer and explore its implications.

Revisiting the *IS–LM* Model

We have derived three equations—the *IS* relation, the *LM* relation, and the relation between the real and the nominal interest rates. It will be more convenient to reduce them to two equations. To do so, replace the real interest rate in the *IS* relation with the nominal interest rate minus expected inflation: $r = i - \pi^e$. This gives:

$$IS: \quad Y = C(Y - T) + I(Y, i - \pi^e) + G$$

$$LM: \quad \frac{M}{P} = Y\, L(i)$$

These two equations are the same as in Chapter 5, with just one difference: Investment spending in the *IS* relation depends on the real interest rate, which is equal to the nominal interest rate minus expected inflation.

The associated *IS* and *LM* curves are drawn in Figure 14-3, for given values of P, M, G, and T, and for a given expected rate of inflation, π^e:

- The *IS* curve is still downward sloping. For a given expected rate of inflation π^e, the nominal interest rate and the real interest rate move together. So, a decrease in

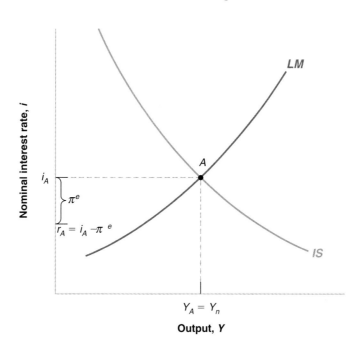

Figure 14-3

Equilibrium Output and Interest Rates

The equilibrium level of output and the equilibrium nominal interest rate are given by the intersection of the *IS* curve and the *LM* curve. The real interest rate equals the nominal interest rate minus expected inflation.

the nominal interest rate leads to an equal decrease in the real interest rate, leading to an increase in spending and in output.

■ The *LM* curve is upward sloping. Given the money stock, an increase in output, which leads to an increase in the demand for money, requires an increase in the nominal interest rate.

■ The equilibrium is at the intersection of the *IS* curve and the *LM* curve, point *A*, with output level, Y_A, and nominal interest rate, i_A. Given the nominal interest rate, the real interest rate, r_A, is given by $r_A = i_A - \pi^e$.

Nominal and Real Interest Rates in the Short Run

Assume that the economy is initially at the natural rate of output, so $Y_A = Y_n$. Now suppose the central bank increases the rate of growth of money. What happens to output, to the nominal interest rate, and to the real interest rate *in the short run*?

One of the lessons from our analysis of monetary policy in the core is that, in the short run, the faster increase in nominal money will not be matched by an equal increase in the price level. In other words, the higher rate of growth of nominal money will lead, in the short run, to an increase in the real money stock, *M/P*. This is all we need to know for our purposes. What happens to output and to interest rates in the short run is shown in Figure 14-4.

The increase in the real money stock causes a shift in the *LM* curve down, from *LM* to *LM′*: For a given level of output, the increase in the real money stock leads to a decrease in the nominal interest rate. If we assume—as seems reasonable—that people and firms do not revise their expectations of inflation immediately, the *IS* curve does not shift: Given expected inflation, a given nominal interest rate corresponds to the same real interest rate and to the same level of spending and ▶ output.

> Can you tell what happens if, in addition, people revise their expectations of inflation upward?

The economy moves down the *IS* curve, and the equilibrium moves from *A* to *B*. Output is higher: The nominal interest rate is lower, and given expected inflation, so is ▶ the real interest rate.

> In the short run, when the rate of money growth increases, *M/P* increases. Both *i* and *r* ▶ decrease, and *Y* increases.

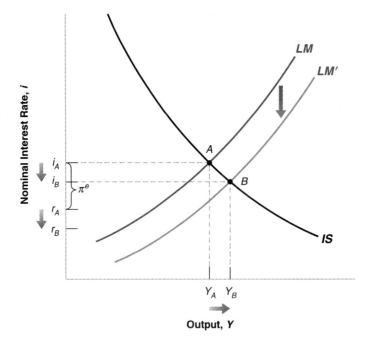

Expectations   **Extensions**

Let's summarize: In the short run, the increase in nominal money growth leads to an increase in the real money stock. This increase in real money leads to a decrease in both the nominal and the real interest rates and to an increase in output.

Go back to our first quote: The goal of the Fed, circa 1991, was precisely to achieve this outcome. Worried that the recession might get worse, the Fed increased money growth to decrease the real interest rate and increase output. (It worked, reducing the length and depth of the recession.)

Nominal and Real Interest Rates in the Medium Run

Turn now to the *medium run*. Suppose that the central bank increases the rate of money growth permanently. What will happen to output and to nominal and real interest rates in the medium run?

To answer that question, we can rely on two of the central propositions we derived in the core:

■ In the medium run, output returns to the natural level of output, Y_n. (We spent ◄ For a refresher, go back to Chapter 6, Section 6-5. Chapters 10 to 13 looking at growth. For simplicity, here we will ignore output growth and assume that Y_n, the natural level of output, is constant over time.)

This has a straightforward implication for what happens to the real interest rate. To see why, return to the *IS* equation:

$$Y = C(Y - T) + I(Y, r) + G$$

One way of thinking about the *IS* relation is that it tells us, for given values of G and T, what real interest rate, r, is needed to sustain a given level of spending and so a given level of output, Y. If, for example, output is equal to the natural level of output, Y_n, then, for given values of G and T, the real interest rate must be such that

$$Y_n = C(Y_n - T) + I(Y_n, r) + G$$

Since we used the word *natural* to denote the level of output in the medium run, let's similarly call this value of the real interest rate the *natural real interest rate* and denote it by r_n. Then, our earlier proposition that, in the medium run, output returns to its natural level, Y_n, has a direct implication for the real interest rate:

This is what the rate was called by Wicksell, a Swedish economist, at the turn of the twentieth century.

> *In the medium run, the real interest rate returns to the natural interest rate,* r_n. *It is independent of the rate of money growth.*

■ In the medium run, the rate of inflation is equal to the rate of money growth minus the rate of growth of output.

For a refresher, go back to ◄ Chapter 9, Section 9-2.

The intuition for this is simple: A growing level of output implies a growing level of transactions and thus a growing demand for real money. If output is growing at 3% per year, the real money stock must also grow at 3% per year. If the nominal money stock grows at a rate different from 3% per year, the difference must show up in inflation (or deflation). For example, if nominal money growth is 10% per year, then inflation must be equal to 7% per year.

If we assume, as we have done here, that output growth is equal to zero, this proposition takes an even simpler form: In the medium run, the rate of inflation is equal to the rate of nominal money growth.

In the medium run (if $g_y = 0$), ◄ $\pi = g_m$.

This proposition, together with the previous result about the real interest rate, has a straightforward implication for what happens to the nominal interest rate in the medium run. To see why, recall the relation between the nominal interest rate and the real interest rate:

$$i = r + \pi^e$$

We saw that in the medium run, the real interest rate equals the natural interest rate, r_n. Also in the medium run, expected inflation is equal to actual inflation (people cannot have incorrect expectations of inflation forever). It follows that

$$i = r_n + \pi$$

Now, because, in the medium run, inflation is equal to money growth, we get

$$i = r_n + g_m$$

In the medium run, the nominal interest rate is equal to the natural real interest rate plus the rate of money growth. So an increase in money growth leads to an equal increase in the nominal interest rate.

Let's summarize: In the medium run, money growth does not affect the real interest rate, but it affects both inflation and the nominal interest rate one-for-one.

A permanent increase in nominal money growth of, say, 10%, is eventually reflected in a 10% increase in the inflation rate and a 10% increase in the nominal interest rate—leaving the real interest rate unchanged. This result—that, in the medium run, the nominal interest rate increases one-for-one with inflation—is known as the **Fisher effect**, or the **Fisher hypothesis**, after Irving Fisher, an economist at Yale University who first stated it and its logic at the beginning of the twentieth century.

▶

This result underlies the second quote we saw at the beginning of the section: If financial investors were worried that the appointment of new board members at the Fed might lead to higher money growth, they were right to expect higher nominal interest rates in the future.

From the Short Run to the Medium Run

We have now seen how to reconcile the two quotes at the beginning of the section: An increase in monetary growth (a monetary expansion) leads to *a decrease* in nominal interest rates in the short run, but it leads to *an increase* in nominal interest rates in the medium run.

What happens, however, between the short run and the medium run? A full characterization of the movements of the real interest rate and the nominal interest rate over time would take us beyond what we can do here. But the basic features of the adjustment process are easy to describe.

In the short run, the real interest rate and the nominal interest rate both go down. Why don't they stay down forever? Let me first state the answer in short: Low interest rates lead to higher demand, which leads to higher output, which eventually leads to higher inflation; higher inflation leads in turn to a decrease in the real money stock and an increase in interest rates.

Now, here is the answer step-by-step:

■ As long as the real interest rate is below the natural real interest rate—that is, the value corresponding to the natural level of output—output is higher than the natural level of output, and unemployment is below its natural rate.

■ From the Phillips curve relation, we know that as long as unemployment is below the natural rate of unemployment, inflation increases.

▶

■ As inflation increases, it eventually becomes higher than nominal money growth, leading to negative real money growth. When real money growth turns negative, the nominal interest rate starts increasing. And, given expected inflation, so does the real interest rate.

- In the medium run, the real interest rate increases back to its initial value. Output is then back to the natural level of output, unemployment is back to the natural rate of unemployment, and inflation is no longer changing. As the real interest rate converges back to its initial value, the nominal interest rate converges to a new higher value, equal to the real interest rate plus the new, higher, rate of nominal money growth.

Figure 14-5 summarizes these results by showing the adjustment over time of the real interest rate and the nominal interest rate to an increase in nominal money growth from, say, 0% to 10%, starting at time t. Before time t, both interest rates are constant and equal to each other. The real interest rate is equal to r_n. The nominal interest rate is also equal to r_n (as inflation and expected inflation are equal to zero).

At time t, the rate of money growth increases from 0% to 10%. The increase in the rate of nominal money growth leads, for some time, to an increase in the real money stock and to a decrease in the nominal interest rate. As expected inflation increases, the decrease in the real interest rate is larger than the decrease of the nominal interest rate.

Eventually, the nominal interest rate and the real interest rate start increasing. In the medium run, the real interest rate returns to its initial value. Inflation and expected inflation converge to the new rate of money growth—in this case, 10%. The result is that the nominal interest rate converges to a value equal to the real interest rate plus 10%.

Evidence on the Fisher Hypothesis

There is plenty of evidence that a monetary expansion decreases nominal interest rates in the short run (see, for example, Chapter 5, Section 5-5). But how much evidence is there for the Fisher hypothesis, the proposition that, in the medium run, increases in inflation lead to one-for-one increases in nominal interest rates?

Economists have tried to answer this question by looking at two types of evidence. One is the relation between nominal interest rates and inflation *across countries.*

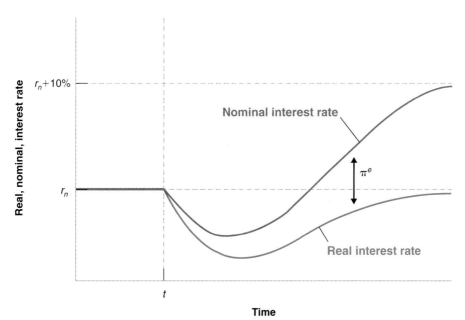

Figure 14-5

The Adjustment of the Real and the Nominal Interest Rates to an Increase in Money Growth

An increase in money growth leads initially to decreases in both the real and the nominal interest rates. Over time, however, the real interest rate returns to its initial value, and the nominal interest rate converges to a new higher value, equal to the initial value plus the increase in money growth.

Figure 1 plots nominal interest rate–inflation pairs for eight Latin American countries (Argentina, Bolivia, Chile, Ecuador, Mexico, Peru, Uruguay, and Venezuela) for 1992 and 1993—a period of high inflation in Latin America. Because the Brazilian numbers would dwarf those from other countries, they are not included in the figure. (In 1992, Brazil's annual inflation rate was 1,008%, and its nominal interest rate was 1,560%. In 1993, its inflation was 2,140%, and its nominal interest rate was 3,240%!) The numbers for inflation refer to the rate of change of the consumer price index. The numbers for nominal interest rates refer to the "lending rate." The exact definition of the lending rate varies with each country, but you can think of it as corresponding to the prime interest rate in the United States—the rate charged to borrowers with the best credit rating.

Note the wide range of inflation rates, from 10% to about 100%. This is precisely why I have chosen to present numbers from Latin America in the early 1990s. With this much variation in inflation, we can learn a lot about the relation between nominal interest rates and inflation. And the figure indeed shows a clear relation between inflation and nominal interest rates. The line drawn in the figure plots what the nominal interest rate should be under the Fisher hypothesis, assuming an underlying real interest rate of 5%, so that $i = 5\% + \pi$. The slope of the line is 1: Under the Fisher hypothesis, a 1% increase in inflation should be reflected in a 1% increase in the nominal interest rate.

As you can see, the line fits reasonably well, and roughly half of the points are above the line, and the other half are below. The Fisher hypothesis appears roughly consistent with the cross-country evidence from Latin America in the early 1990s.

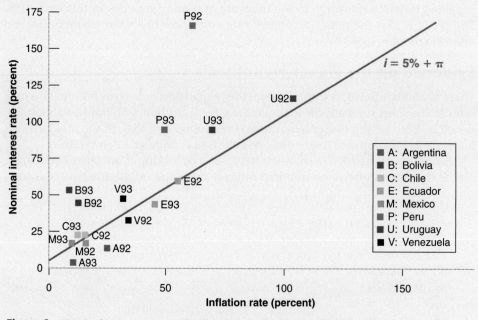

Figure 1 *Nominal Interest Rates and Inflation in Latin America, 1992 to 1993*

Because the relation holds only in the medium run, we should not expect inflation and nominal interest rates to be close to each other in any one country at any one time, but the relation should hold on average. This approach is explored further in the Focus box "Nominal Interest Rates and Inflation across Latin America in the Early 1990s," which looks at Latin American countries during a period when they had high inflation and finds substantial support for the Fisher hypothesis.

The other type of evidence is the relation between the nominal interest rate and inflation over time in a given country. Again, the Fisher hypothesis does not imply that

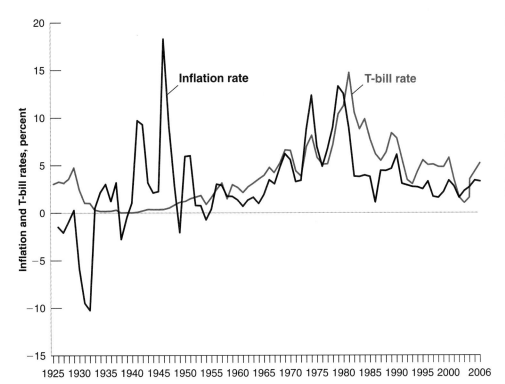

Figure 14-6 ■■■

*The Three-Month
Treasury Bill Rate and
Inflation since 1927*

The increase in inflation from
the early 1960s to the early
1980s was associated with an
increase in the nominal interest
rate. The decrease in inflation
since the mid-1980s has been
associated with a decrease in
the nominal interest rate.

the two should move together from year to year. But it does suggest that the long
swings in inflation should eventually be reflected in similar swings in the nominal
interest rate. To see these long swings, we need to look at as long a period of time as we
can. Figure 14-6 looks at the nominal interest rate and inflation in the United States
since 1927. The nominal interest rate is the three-month Treasury bill rate, and inflation is the rate of change of the CPI.

Figure 14-6 has at least three interesting features:

■ The steady increase in inflation from the early 1960s to the early 1980s was associated with a roughly parallel increase in the nominal interest rate. The decrease in
  inflation since the mid-1980s has been associated with a decrease in the nominal
  interest rate. This evidence supports the Fisher hypothesis.
■ Evidence of the short-run effects that we discussed earlier is also easy to see. The
  nominal interest rate lagged behind the increase in inflation in the 1970s, while
  the disinflation of the early 1980s was associated with an initial *increase* in the
  nominal interest rate, followed by a much slower decline in the nominal interest
  rate than in inflation.
■ The other episode of inflation, during and after World War II, underscores the
  importance of the "medium run" qualifier in the Fisher hypothesis. During that
  period, inflation was high but short-lived. And it was gone before it had time to be
  reflected in a higher nominal interest rate. The nominal interest rate remained
  very low throughout the 1940s.

This was the result of a deliber-
ate policy by the Fed to maintain a very low nominal interest
rate, to reduce interest payments on the large government
debt created during World
◀ War II.

More careful studies confirm our basic conclusion. The Fisher hypothesis that, in
the medium run, increases in inflation are reflected in a higher nominal interest rate,
appears to fit the data quite well. But the adjustment takes a long time. The data confirm the conclusion reached by Milton Friedman, which we quoted in a Focus box in
Chapter 8, that it typically takes a "couple of decades" for nominal interest rates to
reflect the higher inflation rate.

Let me now turn to the second key concept introduced in this chapter: the concept of expected present discounted value.

Let's return to the example of the manager considering whether to buy a new machine. On the one hand, buying and installing the machine involves a cost today. On the other, the machine allows for higher production, higher sales, and higher profits in the future. The question facing the manager is whether the value of these expected profits is higher than the cost of buying and installing the machine. This is where the concept of expected present discounted value comes in handy: The **expected present discounted value** of a sequence of future payments is the value today of this expected sequence of payments. Once the manager has computed the expected present discounted value of the sequence of profits, her problem becomes simple: She compares two numbers, the expected present discounted value and the initial cost. If the value exceeds the cost, she should go ahead and buy the machine. If it does not, she should not.

As for the real interest rate, the practical problem is that expected present discounted values are not directly observable. They must be constructed from information on the sequence of expected payments and expected interest rates. Let's first look at the mechanics of construction.

Computing Expected Present Discounted Values

If the one-year nominal interest rate is i_t, lending 1 dollar this year implies getting back $1 + i_t$ dollars next year. Equivalently, borrowing 1 dollar this year implies paying back $1 + i_t$ dollars next year. In this sense, 1 dollar this year is worth $1 + i_t$ dollars next year. This relation is represented graphically in the first line of Figure 14-7.

Turn the argument around and ask: How much is 1 dollar *next year* worth this year? The answer, shown in the second line of Figure 14-7, is $1/(1 + i_t)$ dollars. Think of it this way: If you lend $1/(1 + i_t)$ dollars this year, you will receive $1/(1 + i_t)$ times $(1 + i_t) = 1$ dollar next year. Equivalently, if you borrow $1/(1 + i_t)$ dollars this year, you will have to repay exactly 1 dollar next year. So, 1 dollar next year is worth $1/(1 + i_t)$ dollars this year.

More formally, we say that $1/(1 + i_t)$ is the *present discounted value* of 1 dollar next year. The word *present* comes from the fact that we are looking at the value of a payment next year in terms of dollars *today*. The word *discounted* comes from the fact that the value next year is discounted, with $1/(1 + i_t)$ being the **discount factor**. (The one-year nominal interest rate, i_t, is sometimes called the **discount rate**).

Because the nominal interest rate is always positive, the discount factor is always less than 1: A dollar next year is worth less than 1 dollar today. The higher the nominal interest rate, the lower the value today of 1 dollar received next year. If $i = 5\%$, the value this year of 1 dollar next year is $1/1.05 \approx 95$ cents. If $i = 10\%$, the value today of 1 dollar next year is $1/1.10 \approx 91$ cents.

Now apply the same logic to the value today of a dollar received *two years from now*. For the moment, assume that current and future one-year nominal interest rates

i_t: discount rate. $1/(1 + i_t)$: discount factor. If the discount rate goes up, the discount factor goes down.

Figure 14-7

Computing Present Discounted Values

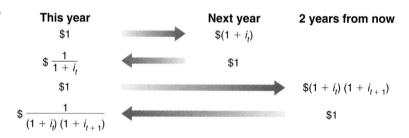

This year	Next year	2 years from now
$1	$(1 + i_t)	
$\dfrac{1}{1 + i_t}$	$1	
$1		$(1 + i_t)(1 + i_{t+1})$
$\dfrac{1}{(1 + i_t)(1 + i_{t+1})}$		$1

are known with certainty. Let i_t be the nominal interest rate for this year and i_{t+1} be the one-year nominal interest rate next year.

If, today, you lend 1 dollar for two years, you will get $(1 + i_t)(1 + i_{t+1})$ dollars two years from now. Put another way, 1 dollar today is worth $(1 + i_t)(1 + i_{t+1})$ dollars two years from now. This relation is represented in the third line of Figure 14-7.

What is 1 dollar two years from now worth today? By the same logic as before, the answer is $1/(1 + i_t)(1 + i_{t+1})$ dollars: If you lend $1/[(1 + i_t)(1 + i_{t+1})]$ dollars this year, you will get exactly 1 dollar in two years. So, the *present discounted value of 1 dollar two years from now* is equal to $1/[(1 + i_t)(1 + i_{t+1})]$ dollars. This relation is shown in the last line of Figure 14-7. If, for example, the one-year nominal interest rate is the same this year and next, equal to 5%—so $i_t = i_{t+1} = 5\%$—then the present discounted value of 1 dollar in two years is equal to $1/(1.05)^2$, or about 91 cents today.

The General Formula

It is now easy to derive the present discounted value for the case where both payments and interest rates can change over time.

Consider a sequence of payments in dollars, starting today and continuing into the future. Assume for the moment that both future payments and future interest rates are known with certainty. Denote today's payment by $\$z_t$, the payment next year by $\$z_{t+1}$, the payment two years from today by $\$z_{t+2}$, and so on.

The present discounted value of this sequence of payments—that is, the value in today's dollars of the sequence of payments—which we shall call $\$V_t$, is given by

$$\$V_t = \$z_t + \frac{1}{(1 + i_t)}\$z_{t+1} + \frac{1}{(1 + i_t)(1 + i_{t+1})}\$z_{t+2} + \ldots$$

Each payment in the future is multiplied by its respective discount factor. The more distant the payment, the smaller the discount factor, and thus the smaller today's value of that distant payment. In other words, future payments are discounted more heavily, so their present discounted value is lower.

We have assumed that future payments and future interest rates were known with certainty. Actual decisions, however, have to be based on expectations of future payments rather than on actual values for these payments. In our earlier example, the manager cannot be sure how much profit the new machine will actually bring; nor does she know what interest rates will be in the future. The best she can do is get the most accurate forecasts she can and then compute the *expected present discounted value* of profits, based on these forecasts.

This statement ignores an important issue—risk. If people dislike risk, the value of an uncertain (and therefore risky) payment now or in the future will be lower than the value of a riskless payment, even if both have the same expected value. We ignore this effect here but return to it briefly in Chapter 15. For a full treatment, you would have to take a course in finance.

How do we compute the expected present discounted value when future payments and interest rates are uncertain? We do this basically in the same way as before but by replacing the *known* future payments and *known* interest rates with *expected* future payments and *expected* interest rates. Formally, we denote expected payments next year by $\$z^e_{t+1}$, expected payments two years from now by $\$z^e_{t+2}$, and so on. Similarly, we denote the expected one-year nominal interest rate next year by i^e_{t+1}, and so on (the one-year nominal interest rate this year, i_t, is known today, so it does not need a superscript e). The expected present discounted value of this expected sequence of payments is given by

$$\$V_t = \$z_t + \frac{1}{(1 + i_t)}\$z^e_{t+1} + \frac{1}{(1 + i_t)(1 + i^e_{t+1})}\$z^e_{t+2} + \ldots \qquad (14.5)$$

"Expected present discounted value" is a heavy expression. Instead, for short, I will often just use **present discounted value**, or even just **present value**. Also, it is convenient to have a shorthand way of writing expressions like equation (14.5). To denote the present value of an expected sequence for $z, I write $V(\$z_t)$, or just $V(\$z)$.

Using Present Values: Examples

Equation (14.5) has two important implications:

$z or future $z^e increase
⇒ $V increases

■ The present value depends positively on today's actual payment and expected future payments. An increase in either today's $z or any future $z^e leads to an increase in the present value.

i or future i^e increase
⇒ $V decreases

■ The present value depends negatively on current and expected future interest rates. An increase in either current i or in any future i^e leads to a decrease in the present value.

Equation (14.5) is not simple, however, and so it will help to go through some examples.

Constant Interest Rates

To focus on the effects of the sequence of payments on the present value, assume that interest rates are expected to be constant over time, so that $i_t = i^e_{t+1} = \ldots$, and denote their common value by i. The present value formula—equation (14.5)—becomes

The weights correspond to the terms of a geometric series. See the discussion of geometric series in Appendix 2 at the end of the book.

Note: $1/(1 + i)^n = (1/(1 + i))^n$

$$\$V_t = \$z_t + \frac{1}{(1 + i)} \$z^e_{t+1} + \frac{1}{(1 + i)^2} \$z^e_{t+2} + \ldots \qquad (14.6)$$

In this case, the present value is a *weighted sum* of current and expected future payments, with weights that decline *geometrically* through time. The weight on a payment this year is 1, the weight on the payment n years from now is $1/(1 + i)^n$. With a positive interest rate, the weights get closer and closer to zero as we look further and further into the future. For example, with an interest rate equal to 10%, the weight on a payment 10 years from today is equal to $1/(1 + 0.10)^{10} = 0.386$, so that a payment of $1,000 in 10 years is worth $386 today. The weight on a payment in 30 years is $1/(1 + 0.10)^{30} = .057$, so that a payment of $1,000 30 years from today is worth only $57 today!

Constant Interest Rates and Payments

In some cases, the sequence of payments for which we want to compute the present value is simple. For example, a typical fixed-rate 30-year mortgage requires constant dollar payments over 30 years. Consider a sequence of equal payments—call them $z without a time index—over n years, including this year. In this case, the present value formula in equation (14.6) simplifies to

$$\$V_t = \$z \left[1 + \frac{1}{(1 + i)} + \ldots + \frac{1}{(1 + i)^{n-1}} \right]$$

Because the terms in the expression in brackets represent a geometric series, we can compute the sum of the series and get

By now, geometric series should not hold any secret, and you should have no problem deriving this relation. But if you do, see Appendix 2 at the end of the book.

$$\$V_t = \$z \frac{1 - [1/(1 + i)^n]}{1 - [1/(1 + i)]}$$

Suppose you have just won $1 million from your state lottery and have been presented with a 6-foot $1,000,000 check on TV. Afterward, you are told that, to protect you from your worst spending instincts as well as from your many new "friends," the state will pay you the million dollars in equal yearly installments of $50,000 over the next 20 years. What is the present value of your prize today? Taking, for example, an interest rate of 6% per year, the preceding equation gives $V = \$50{,}000(.688)/(.057) =$ $608,000. Not bad, but winning the prize did not make you a millionaire.

What is the present value if i equals 4%? 8%? (Answers: $706,000, $530,000.)

Constant Interest Rates and Payments, Forever

Let's go one step further and assume that payments are not only constant but go on forever. Real-world examples are hard to come by for this case, but one example comes from nineteenth-century England, when the government issued *consols*, bonds paying a fixed yearly amount forever. Let $z be the constant payment. Assume that payments start next year rather than right away, as in the previous example (this makes for simpler algebra). From equation (14.6), we have

Most consols were bought back by the British government at the end of the nineteenth century and early twentieth century. A few are still around.

$$\$V_t = \frac{1}{(1+i)}\$z + \frac{1}{(1+i)^2}\$z + \ldots$$

$$= \frac{1}{(1+i)}\left[1 + \frac{1}{(1+i)} + \ldots\right]\$z$$

where the second line follows by factoring out $1/(1+i)$. The reason for factoring out $1/(1+i)$ should be clear from looking at the term in brackets: It is an infinite geometric sum, so we can use the property of geometric sums to rewrite the present value as

$$\$V_t = \frac{1}{(1+i)}\frac{1}{1-(1/(1+i))}\$z$$

Or, simplifying (the steps are given in the application of Proposition 2 in Appendix 2 at the end of the book),

$$\$V_t = \frac{\$z}{i}$$

The present value of a constant sequence of payments, $z, is simply equal to the ratio of $z to the interest rate, i. If, for example, the interest rate is expected to be 5% per year forever, the present value of a consol that promises $10 per year forever equals $10/.05 = $200. If the interest rate increases and is now expected to be 10% per year forever, the present value of the consol decreases to $10/.10 = $100.

Zero Interest Rates

Because of discounting, computing present discounted values typically requires the use of a calculator. There is, however, a case where computations simplify. This is the case where the interest rate is equal to zero: If $i = 0$, then $1/(1+i)$ equals 1, and so does $(1/(1+i)^n)$ for any power n. For that reason, the present discounted value of a sequence of expected payments is just the *sum* of those expected payments. Because the interest rate is in fact typically positive, assuming that the interest rate is 0 is only an approximation. But it is a very useful one for back-of-the-envelope computations.

Nominal versus Real Interest Rates and Present Values

So far, we have computed the present value of a sequence of dollar payments by using interest rates in terms of dollars—nominal interest rates. Specifically, we have written equation (14.5) as

$$\$V_t = \$z_t + \frac{1}{(1+i_t)}\$z_{t+1}^e + \frac{1}{(1+i_t)(1+i_{t+1}^e)}\$z_{t+2}^e + \ldots$$

where i_t, i_{t+1}^e, ... is the sequence of current and expected future nominal interest rates, and $\$z_t$, $\$z_{t+1}^e$, $\$z_{t+2}^e$, ... is the sequence of current and expected future dollar payments.

Suppose we want to compute instead the present value of a sequence of *real* payments—that is, payments in terms of a basket of goods rather than in terms of dollars. Following the same logic as before, we need to use the right interest rates for this case: namely interest rates in terms of the basket of goods—*real interest rates*. Specifically, we can write the present value of a sequence of real payments as

$$V_t = z_t + \frac{1}{(1 + r_t)} z_{t+1}^e + \frac{1}{(1 + r_t)(1 + r_{t+1}^e)} z_{t+2}^e + \cdots \tag{14.7}$$

The proof is given in the appendix to this chapter. Go through it to test your understanding of the two tools introduced in this chapter: real interest rates versus nominal interest rates, and expected present values.

where r_t, r_{t+1}^e, ... is the sequence of current and expected future real interest rates, z_t, z_{t+1}^e, z_{t+2}^e, ... is the sequence of current and expected future real payments, and V_t is the real present value of future payments.

These two ways of writing the present value turn out to be equivalent. That is, the real value obtained by constructing $\$V_t$ using equation (14.5) and dividing by P_t, the price level, is equal to the real value V_t obtained from equation (14.7), so

$$\$V_t / P_t = V_t$$

In words: We can compute the present value of a sequence of payments in two ways. One way is to compute it as the present value of the sequence of payments expressed in dollars, discounted using nominal interest rates, and then divided by the price level today. The other way is to compute it as the present value of the sequence of payments expressed in real terms, discounted using real interest rates. The two ways give the same answer.

Do we need both formulas? Yes. Which one is more helpful depends on the context.

Take bonds, for example. Bonds typically are claims to a sequence of nominal payments over a period of years. For example, a 10-year bond might promise to pay $50 each year for 10 years, plus a final payment of $1,000 in the last year. So when we look at the pricing of bonds in Chapter 15, we shall rely on equation (14.5), which is expressed in terms of dollar payments, rather than on equation (14.7), which is expressed in real terms.

But sometimes, we have a better sense of future expected real values than of future expected dollar values. You might not have a good idea of what your dollar income will be in 20 years: Its value depends very much on what happens to inflation between now and then. But you might be confident that your nominal income will increase by at least as much as inflation—in other words, that your real income will not decrease. In this case, using equation (14.5), which requires you to form expectations of future dollar income, will be difficult. However, using equation (14.7), which requires you to form expectations of future real income, may be easier. For this reason, when we discuss consumption and investment decisions in Chapter 16, we shall rely on equation (14.7) rather than equation (14.5).

Summary

■ The nominal interest rate tells you how many dollars you need to repay in the future in exchange for one dollar today.

■ The real interest rate tells you how many goods you need to repay in the future in exchange for one good today.

■ The real interest rate is approximately equal to the nominal interest rate minus expected inflation.

■ Investment decisions depend on the real interest rate. The choice between money and bonds depends on the nominal interest rate. Thus, the real interest rate enters the *IS* relation, while the nominal interest rate enters the *LM* relation.

■ In the short run, an increase in money growth decreases both the nominal interest rate and the real interest rate. In the medium run, an increase in money growth has no effect on the real interest rate, but it increases the nominal interest rate one-for-one.

■ The proposition that, in the medium run, changes in inflation are reflected one-for-one in changes in the nominal interest rate is known as the Fisher effect or the Fisher hypothesis. The empirical evidence suggests that, while it takes a long time, changes in inflation are eventually reflected in changes in the nominal interest rate.

■ The expected present discounted value of a sequence of payments equals the value this year of the expected sequence of payments. It depends positively on current and future expected payments and negatively on current and future expected interest rates.

■ When discounting a sequence of current and expected future nominal payments, one should use current and expected future nominal interest rates. In discounting a sequence of current and expected future real payments, one should use current and expected future real interest rates.

Key Terms

- nominal interest rate, 314
- real interest rate, 314
- Fisher effect, Fisher hypothesis, 322
- expected present discounted value, 326
- discount factor, 326
- discount rate, 326
- present discounted value, 327
- present value, 327

Questions and Problems

Quick Check

1. Using the information in this chapter, label each of the following statements true, false, or uncertain. Explain briefly.

a. As long as inflation remains roughly constant, the movements in the real interest rate are roughly equal to the movements in the nominal interest rate.

b. If inflation turns out to be higher than expected, the realized real cost of borrowing turns out to be lower than the real interest rate.

c. Looking across countries, the real interest rate is likely to vary much less than the nominal interest rate.

d. The real interest rate is equal to the nominal interest rate divided by the price level.

e. In the medium run, the real interest rate is not affected by money growth.

f. The Fisher effect states that in the medium run, the nominal interest rate is not affected by money growth.

g. The experience of Latin American countries in the early 1990s supports the Fisher hypothesis.

h. The value today of a nominal payment in the future cannot be greater than the nominal payment itself.

i. The real value today of a real payment in the future cannot be greater than the real payment itself.

2. For which of the problems listed in (a) through (c) would you want to use real payments and real interest rates, and for which would you want to use nominal payments and nominal interest rates, to compute the expected present discounted value? In each case, explain why.

a. Estimating the present discounted value of the profits from an investment in a new machine.

b. Estimating the present value of a 20-year U.S. government bond.

c. Deciding whether to lease or buy a car.

3. Nominal and real interest rates around the world.

a. Can the nominal interest rate ever be negative? Explain.

b. Can the real interest rate ever be negative? Under what circumstances can it be negative? If so, why not just hold cash instead of bonds?

c. What are the effects of a negative real interest rate on borrowing and lending?

d. Find a recent issue of *The Economist* and look at the tables in the back (titled "Economic Indicators and Financial Indicators"). Use the three-month money market rate as the nominal interest rate and the most recent three-month rate of change in consumer prices as the expected rate of inflation (both are in annual terms). Which countries have the lowest nominal interest rates? Which countries have the lowest real interest rates? Are these real interest rates close to being negative?

4. Compute the real interest rate using the exact formula and the approximation formula for each set of assumptions listed in (a) through (c).

a. $i = 6\%$; $\pi^e = 3\%$

b. $i = 16\%$; $\pi^e = 12\%$

c. $i = 58\%$; $\pi^e = 42\%$

5. Regular IRAs versus Roth IRAs

You want to save $2,000 today for retirement in 40 years. You have to choose between two plans listed in (i) and (ii).

i. Pay no taxes today, put the money in an interest-yielding account, and pay taxes equal to 25% of the total amount withdrawn at retirement. (In the United States, such an account is known as a regular individual retirement account [IRA].)

ii. Pay taxes equivalent to 20% of the investment amount today, put the remainder in an interest-yielding account, and pay no taxes when you withdraw your funds at retirement. (In the United States, this is known as a Roth IRA.)

a. What is the expected present discounted value of each of these plans if the interest rate is 1%? 10%?

b. Which plan would you choose in each case?

6. *The Fisher hypothesis*

a. What is the Fisher hypothesis?

b. Does the experience of Latin American countries in the 1990s support or refute the Fisher hypothesis? Explain.

c. Look at the figure in the Focus box on Latin America. Note that the line drawn through the scatter of points does not go through the origin. Does the "Fisher effect" suggest that it should go through the origin? Explain.

d. Consider this statement: "If the Fisher hypothesis is true, then changes in the growth rate of the money stock translate one-for-one into changes in i, and the real interest rate is left unchanged. Thus, there is no room for monetary policy to affect real economic activity." Discuss.

7. *Approximating the price of long-term bonds*

The present value of an infinite stream of dollar payments of \$z (that starts next year) is \$z / i when the nominal interest rate, i, is constant. This formula gives the price of a consol—a bond paying a fixed nominal payment each year, forever. It is also a good approximation for the present discounted value of a stream of constant payments over long but not infinite periods, as long as i is constant. Let's examine how close the approximation is.

a. Suppose that $i = 10\%$. Let \$z = 100. What is the present value of the consol?

b. If $i = 10\%$, what is the expected present discounted value of a bond that pays \$z over the next 10 years? 20 years? 30 years? 60 years? (Hint: Use the formula from the chapter but remember to adjust for the first payment.)

c. Repeat the calculations in (a) and (b) for $i = 2\%$ and $i = 5\%$.

Dig Deeper

8. *When looking at the short run in Section 14-2, we showed how an increase in nominal money growth led to higher output, a lower nominal interest rate, and a lower real interest rate.*

The analysis in the text (as summarized in Figure 14-5) assumed that expected inflation, π^e, did not change in the short run. Let us now relax this assumption and assume that in the short run, both money growth and expected inflation increase.

a. Show the effect on the *IS* curve. Explain in words.

b. Show the effect on the *LM* curve. Explain in words.

c. Show the effect on output and on the nominal interest rate. Could the nominal interest rate end up higher—not lower—than before the change in money growth? Why?

d. Even if what happens to the nominal interest rate is ambiguous, can you tell what happens to the real interest rate? (Hint: What happens to output relative to Figure 14-4? What does this imply about what happens to the real interest rate?)

Explore Further

9. *Inflation-indexed bonds*

Some bonds issued by the U.S. Treasury make payments indexed to inflation. These inflation-indexed bonds compensate investors for inflation. Therefore, the current interest rates on these bonds are real interest rates—interest rates in terms of goods. These interest rates can be used, together with nominal interest rates, to provide a measure of expected inflation. Let's see how.

Go to the Web site of the Federal Reserve Board and get the most recent statistical release listing interest rates (**www. federalreserve.gov/releases/h15/Current**). Find the current nominal interest rate on Treasury securities with a five-year maturity. Now find the current interest rate on "inflation-indexed" Treasury securities with a five-year maturity. What do you think participants in financial markets think the average inflation rate will be over the next five years?

We invite you to visit the Blanchard page on the Prentice Hall Web site, at:
www.prenhall.com/blanchard
for this chapter's World Wide Web exercises.

Appendix: Deriving the Expected Present Discounted Value Using Real or Nominal Interest Rates

This appendix shows that the two ways of expressing present discounted values, equations (14.5) and (14.7), are equivalent.

Equation (14.5) gives the present value as the sum of current and future expected *nominal payments*, discounted using current and future expected *nominal interest rates*:

$$\$V_t = \$z_t + \frac{1}{1 + i_t}\$z_{t+1}^e + \frac{1}{(1 + i_t)(1 + i_{t+1}^e)}\$z_{t+2}^e + \ldots \quad (14.5)$$

Equation (14.7) gives the present value as the sum of current and future expected *real payments*, discounted using current and future expected *real interest rates*:

$$V_t = z_t + \frac{1}{1 + r_t}z_{t+1}^e + \frac{1}{(1 + r_t)(1 + r_{t+1}^e)}z_{t+2}^e + \ldots \quad (14.7)$$

Divide both sides of equation (14.5) by the current price level, P_t. So:

$$\frac{\$V_t}{P_t} = \frac{\$z_t}{P_t} + \frac{1}{1 + i_t}\frac{\$z_{t+1}^e}{P_t}$$

$$+ \frac{1}{(1 + i_t)(1 + i_{t+1}^e)}\frac{\$z_{t+2}^e}{P_t} + \ldots \quad (14.A1)$$

Let's look at each term on the right side of equation (14.A1) and show that it is equal to the corresponding term in equation (14.7):

■ Take the first term, $\$z_t/P_t$. Note that $\$z_t/P_t = z_t$, the real value of the current payment. So, this term is the same as the first term on the right of equation (14.7).
■ Take the second term:

$$\frac{1}{1 + i_t}\frac{\$z_{t+1}^e}{P_t}$$

Multiply the numerator and the denominator by P_{t+1}^e, the price level expected for next year, to get

$$\frac{1}{1 + i_t}\frac{P_{t+1}^e}{P_t}\frac{\$z_{t+1}^e}{P_{t+1}^e}$$

Note that the fraction on the right, $\$z_{t+1}^e/P_{t+1}^e$, is equal to z_{t+1}^e, the expected real payment at time $t + 1$. Note that the fraction in the middle, P_{t+1}^e/P_t, can be rewritten as $1 + [(P_{t+1}^e - P_t)/P_t]$, thus, using the definition of expected inflation, as $(1 + \pi_{t+1}^e)$.

Using these two results, rewrite the second term as

$$\frac{(1 + \pi_{t+1}^e)}{(1 + i_t)}z_{t+1}^e$$

Recall the relation between the real interest rate, the nominal interest rate, and expected inflation, in equation (14.3) $[1 + r_t = (1 + i_t)/(1 + \pi_{t+1}^e)]$. Using this relation in the previous equation gives

$$\frac{1}{(1 + r_t)}z_{t+1}^e$$

This term is the same as the second term on the right side of equation (14.7).
■ The same method can be used to rewrite the other terms; make sure that you can derive the next one.

We have shown that the right side of equations (14.7) and (14.A1) are equal to each other. It follows that the terms on the left side are equal, so

$$V_t = \frac{\$V_t}{P_t}$$

This says that the present value of current and future expected *real payments*, discounted using current and future expected *real interest rates* [the term on the left side of equation (14.7)] is equal to the present value of current and future expected *nominal payments*, discounted using current and future expected *nominal interest rates*, divided by the current price level [the term on the left side of equation (14.A1)].

Financial Markets and Expectations

I n our first pass at financial markets in Chapter 4, we assumed that there were only two assets: money and one type of bond—a one-year bond. We now look at an economy with a richer and more realistic menu of non-money assets: short-term bonds, long-term bonds, and stocks.

Our focus throughout this chapter is on the role expectations play in the determination of bond and stock prices. (The reason this belongs in a macroeconomics textbook: As you will see, not only are these prices affected by current and expected future activity, but they in turn affect decisions that affect current activity. Understanding their determination is central to understanding fluctuations.)

■ Section 15-1 looks at the determination of bond prices and bond yields. It shows how bond prices and yields depend on current and expected future short-term interest rates. It then shows how we can use the yield curve to learn about the expected course of future short-term interest rates.

■ Section 15-2 looks at the determination of stock prices. It shows how stock prices depend on current and expected future profits as well as on current and expected future interest rates. It then discusses how movements in economic activity affect stock prices.

■ Section 15-3 discusses fads and bubbles in the stock market—episodes in which stock prices appear to move for reasons unrelated to either profits or interest rates. ■

15-1 Bond Prices and Bond Yields

Bonds differ in two basic dimensions:

- **Default risk**, the risk that the issuer of the bond (which could be a government or a company) will not pay back the full amount promised by the bond.
- **Maturity**, the length of time over which the bond promises to make payments to the bondholder. A bond that promises to make one payment of $1,000 in six months has a maturity of six months; a bond that promises $100 per year for the next 20 years and a final payment of $1,000 at the end of those 20 years has a maturity of 20 years. Maturity is the more important dimension for our purposes, and we shall focus on it here.

Bonds of different maturities each have a price and an associated interest rate, called the *yield to maturity*, or simply the *yield*. Yields on bonds with a short maturity, typically a year or less, are called *short-term interest rates*. Yields on bonds with a longer maturity are called *long-term interest rates*.

On any given day, we observe the yields on bonds of different maturities, and we can trace graphically how the yield depends on the maturity of a bond. This relation between maturity and yield is called the **yield curve**, or the **term structure of interest rates** (where the word *term* is synonymous with maturity). Figure 15-1 gives, for example, the term structure on U.S. government bonds on November 1, 2000, and the term structure on U.S. government bonds on June 1, 2001. The choice of the two dates is not accidental; why I chose them will become clear shortly.

Note how, on November 1, 2000, the yield curve was slightly downward sloping, declining from a three-month interest rate of 6.2% to a 30-year interest rate of 5.8%. In other words, long-term interest rates were slightly lower than short-term interest rates. Note how, seven months later, on June 1, 2001, the yield curve was sharply upward sloping, increasing from a three-month interest rate of 3.5% to a 30-year interest rate of 5.7%. In other words, long-term interest rates were now much higher than short-term interest rates.

Why was the yield curve downward sloping in November 2000 but upward sloping in June 2001? Put another way, why were long-term interest rates slightly lower than short-term interest rates in November 2000 but higher than short-term interest rates in June 2001? What were financial market participants thinking at each date? To

Do not worry: I am just introducing the terms here. They will be defined and explained in this section.

Term structure ≡ Yield curve ▶

To find out what the term structure of interest rates is at the time you read this chapter, look for "Treasury Bonds, Notes and Bills" in the "Money & Investing" section of the paper version of the Wall Street Journal. In the online version, click Markets Data Center, then Bonds, Rates, Credit Markets, then Bond Yields, then Treasury Issues.

Figure 15-1

U.S. Yield Curves: November 1, 2000, and June 1, 2001

The yield curve, which was slightly downward sloping in November 2000, was sharply upward sloping seven months later.

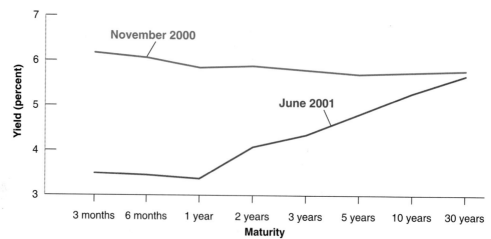

Expectations **Extensions**

Understanding the basic vocabulary of financial markets will help make them less mysterious. Here is a basic vocabulary review:

■ Bonds are issued by governments or by firms. If issued by the government or government agencies, bonds are called **government bonds**. If issued by firms (corporations), they are called **corporate bonds**.

■ In the United States, bonds are rated for their default risk (the risk that they will not be repaid) by two private firms, Standard & Poor's (S&P) and Moody's Investors Service. Moody's **bond ratings** range from Aaa for bonds with nearly no risk of default, such as U.S. government bonds, to C for bonds whose default risk is high. A lower rating typically implies that the bond has to pay a higher interest rate, or else investors will not buy it. The difference between the interest rate paid on a given bond and the interest rate paid on the bond with the highest (best) rating is called the **risk premium** associated with the given bond. Bonds with high default risk are sometimes called **junk bonds**.

■ Bonds that promise a single payment at maturity are called **discount bonds**. The single payment is called the **face value** of the bond.

■ Bonds that promise multiple payments before maturity and one payment at maturity are called **coupon bonds**. The payments before maturity are called **coupon payments**. The final payment is called the face value of the bond. The ratio of coupon payments to the face value is called the **coupon rate**. The **current yield** is the ratio of the coupon payment to the price of the bond.

For example, a bond with coupon payments of $5 each year, a face value of $100, and a price of $80 has a coupon rate of 5% and a current yield of $5/80 = 0.0625 = 6.25\%$. From an economic viewpoint, neither the coupon rate nor the current yield are interesting measures. The correct measure of the interest rate on a bond is its yield to maturity, or simply yield; you can think of it as roughly the average interest rate paid by the bond over its **life**. (The life of a bond is the amount of time left until the bond matures.) We shall define the yield to maturity more precisely later in this chapter.

■ U.S. government bonds range in maturity from a few days to 30 years. Bonds with a maturity of up to a year when they are issued are called **Treasury bills**, or **T-bills**. They are discount bonds, so they make only one payment at maturity. Bonds with a maturity of 1 to 10 years when they are issued are called **Treasury notes**. Bonds with a maturity of 10 or more years when they are issued are called **Treasury bonds**. Both Treasury notes and Treasury bonds are coupon bonds.

■ Bonds are typically nominal bonds: They promise a sequence of fixed nominal payments—payments in terms of domestic currency. There are, however, other types of bonds. Among them are **indexed bonds**, bonds that promise payments adjusted for inflation rather than fixed nominal payments. Instead of promising to pay, say, $100 in a year, a one-year indexed bond promises to pay $100 $(1 + \pi)$, whatever π, the rate of inflation that will take place over the coming year, turns out to be. Because they protect bondholders against the risk of inflation, indexed bonds are popular in many countries. They play a particularly important role in the United Kingdom, where, over the past 20 years, people have increasingly used them to save for retirement. By holding long-term indexed bonds, people can make sure that the payments they receive when they retire will be protected from inflation. Indexed bonds (called inflation-indexed bonds) were introduced in the United States in 1997. They account for less than 10% of U.S. government bonds at this point, but their role will surely increase in the future.

answer these questions, and more generally to think about the determination of the yield curve and the relation between short-term interest rates and long-term interest rates, we proceed in two steps:

1. We derive *bond prices* for bonds of different maturities.

2. We go from bond prices to *bond yields* and examine the determinants of the yield curve and the relation between short-term and long-term interest rates.

Bond Prices as Present Values

Note that both bonds are *discount bonds* (see the Focus box "The Vocabulary of Bond Markets").

In much of this section, we shall look at just two types of bonds: a bond that promises one payment of $100 in one year—a one-year bond, and a bond that promises one payment of $100 in two years—a two-year bond. When you understand how their prices and yields are determined, it will be easy to generalize the results to bonds of any maturity. We shall do so later.

Let's start by deriving the prices of the two bonds:

■ Given that the one-year bond promises to pay $100 next year, it follows from Section 14-2 that its price, call it $\$P_{1t}$, must be equal to the present value of a payment of $100 next year. Let the current one-year nominal interest rate be i_{1t}. Note that I now denote the one-year interest rate in year t by i_{1t} rather than simply by i_t, as I did in earlier chapters. This is to make it easier for you to remember that it is the *one-year* interest rate. So,

$$\$P_{1t} = \frac{\$100}{1 + i_{1t}} \tag{15.1}$$

We already saw this relation in Chapter 4, Section 4-2.

The price of the one-year bond varies inversely with the current one-year nominal interest rate.

■ Given that the two-year bond promises to pay $100 in two years, its price, call it $\$P_{2t}$, must be equal to the present value of $100 two years from now:

$$\$P_{2t} = \frac{\$100}{(1 + i_{1t})(1 + i^e_{1t+1})} \tag{15.2}$$

where i_{1t} denotes the one-year interest rate this year, and i^e_{t+1} denotes the one-year rate expected by financial markets for next year. The price of the two-year bond depends inversely on both the current one-year rate and the one-year rate expected for next year.

Arbitrage and Bond Prices

Before exploring further the implications of equations (15.1) and (15.2), let us look at an alternative derivation of equation (15.2). This alternative derivation will introduce you to the important concept of *arbitrage*.

Suppose you have a choice between holding one-year bonds or two-year bonds and what you care about is how much you will have one year from today. Which bonds should you hold?

■ Suppose you hold one-year bonds. For every dollar you put in one-year bonds, you will get $(1 + i_{1t})$ dollars next year. This relation is represented in the first line of Figure 15-2.

■ Suppose you hold two-year bonds. Because the price of a two-year bond is $\$P_{2t}$, every dollar you put in two-year bonds buys you $\$1/\$P_{2t}$ bonds today.

When next year comes, the bond will have only one more year before maturity. Thus, one year from today, the two-year bond will be a one-year bond. Therefore, the price at which you can expect to sell it next year is $\$P^e_{1t+1}$, which is the expected price of a one-year bond next year.

So for every dollar you put in two-year bonds, you can expect to receive $\$1/\$P_{2t}$ times $\$P^e_{1t+1}$, or, equivalently, $\$P^e_{1t+1}/\$P_{2t}$ dollars next year. This is represented in the second line of Figure 15-2.

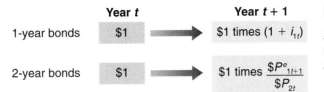

	Year t		Year $t + 1$
1-year bonds	$1	➡	$1 times $(1 + i_{1t})$
2-year bonds	$1	➡	$1 times $\dfrac{\$P^e_{1t+1}}{\$P_{2t}}$

Figure 15-2

Returns from Holding One-Year and Two-Year Bonds for One Year

Which bonds should you hold? Suppose you, and other financial investors, care *only* about the expected return. (This assumption is known as the **expectations hypothesis**. It is a strong simplification: You, and other financial investors, are likely to care not only about the expected return but also about the risk associated with holding each bond. If you hold a one-year bond, you know with certainty what you will get next year. If you hold a two-year bond, the price at which you will sell it next year is uncertain; holding the two-year bond is risky. We will disregard this for now but briefly discuss it in the appendix to this chapter.)

Under the assumption that you, and other financial investors, care only about expected return, it follows that the two bonds must offer the same expected one-year return. Suppose this condition was not satisfied. Suppose that, for example, the one-year return on one-year bonds was lower than the expected one-year return on two-year bonds. In this case, no one would want to hold the existing supply of one-year bonds, and the market for one-year bonds could not be in equilibrium. Only if the expected one-year return is the same on both bonds will financial investors be willing to hold both one-year bonds and two-year bonds.

If the two bonds offer the same expected one-year return, it follows from Figure 15-2 that

$$1 + i_{1t} = \frac{\$P^e_{1t+1}}{\$P_{2t}} \tag{15.3}$$

The left side of equation (15.3) gives the return per dollar from holding a one-year bond for one year; the right side gives the expected return per dollar from holding a two-year bond for one year. I shall call equations such as (15.3)—equations which state that the expected returns on two assets must be equal—**arbitrage** relations. We can rewrite equation (15.3) as

$$\$P_{2t} = \frac{\$P^e_{1t+1}}{1 + i_{1t}} \tag{15.4}$$

◀ I use *arbitrage* to denote the proposition that expected returns on two assets must be equal. Some economists reserve *arbitrage* for the narrower proposition that *riskless* profit opportunities do not go unexploited.

Arbitrage implies that the price of a two-year bond today is the present value of the expected price of the bond next year. This raises the next question: What does the expected price of one-year bonds next year, $\$P^e_{1t+1}$, depend on?

The answer is straightforward: Just as the price of a one-year bond this year depends on this year's one-year interest rate, the price of a one-year bond next year will depend on the one-year interest rate next year. Writing equation (15.1) for next year, year $(t + 1)$, and denoting expectations in the usual way, we get

$$\$P^e_{1t-1} = \frac{\$100}{(1 + i^e_{1t+1})}$$

The price of the bond next year is expected to equal the final payment, $100, discounted by the one-year interest rate expected for next year.

Replacing $\$P^e_{1t+1}$ by $100/(1 + i^e_{1t+1})$ in equation (15.4) gives

$$\$P_{2t} = \frac{\$100}{(1 + i_{1t})(1 + i^e_{1t+1})} \tag{15.5}$$

This expression is the same as equation (15.2). What we have shown is that arbitrage between one- and two-year bonds implies that the price of two-year bonds is the *present value* of the payment in two years, namely $100, discounted using current and next year's expected one-year interest rates.

From Bond Prices to Bond Yields

Having looked at bond prices, we now go on to bond yields. The basic point: Bond yields contain the same information about future expected interest rates as bond prices. They just do so in a much clearer way.

To begin, we need a definition of the yield to maturity: The **yield to maturity** on an *n*-year bond, or, equivalently, the **n-year interest rate**, is defined as the constant annual interest rate that makes the bond price today equal to the present value of future payments on the bond.

This definition is simpler than it sounds. Take, for example, the two-year bond we introduced earlier. Denote its yield by i_{2t}, where the subscript 2 reminds us that this is the yield to maturity on a two-year bond, or, equivalently, the two-year interest rate. Following the definition of the yield to maturity, this yield is the constant annual interest rate that would make the present value of $100 in two years equal to the price of the bond today. So, it satisfies the following relation:

$$\$P_{2t} = \frac{\$100}{(1 + i_{2t})^2} \tag{15.6}$$

$90 = $100/(1 + i_{2t})^2 \Rightarrow$
$(1 + i_{2t})^2 = $100/$90 \Rightarrow$
$(1 + i_{2t}) = \sqrt{\$100/\$90} \Rightarrow$
$i_{2t} = 5.4\%$

Suppose the bond sells for $90 today. Then, the two-year interest rate, i_{2t}, is given ▶ by $\sqrt{100/90} - 1$, or 5.4%. In other words, holding the bond for two years—until maturity—yields an interest rate of 5.4% per year.

What is the relation of the two-year interest rate to the current one-year interest rate and the expected one-year interest rate? To answer this question, look at equations (15.6) and (15.5). Eliminating $\$P_{2t}$ between the two gives

$$\frac{\$100}{(1 + i_{2t})^2} = \frac{\$100}{(1 + i_{1t})(1 + i^e_{1t+1})}$$

Rearranging, we have

$$(1 + i_{2t})^2 = (1 + i_{1t})(1 + i^e_{1t+1})$$

This gives us the exact relation between the two-year interest rate, i_{2t}, the current one-year interest rate, i_{1t}, and next year's expected one-year interest rate, i^e_{t+1}. A useful approximation to this relation is given by

$$i_{2t} \approx \frac{1}{2}(i_{1t} + i^e_{1t+1}) \tag{15.7}$$

Equation (15.7) simply says that *the two-year interest rate is (approximately) the average of the current one-year interest rate and next year's expected one-year interest rate.*

We have focused on the relation between the prices and yields of one-year and two-year bonds, but our results can be generalized to bonds of any maturity. For instance, we could look at bonds with maturities shorter than a year. To take an example: The yield on a bond with a maturity of six months is (approximately) equal to the average of the current three-month interest rate and next quarter's expected three-month interest rate. Or, we could look instead at bonds with maturities longer than two years. For example, the yield on a 10-year bond is (approximately) equal to the average of the current one-year interest rate and the one-year interest rates expected for the next nine years.

The general principle is clear: Long-term interest rates reflect current and future expected short-term interest rates.

Interpreting the Yield Curve

The relations we just derived tell us what we need to interpret the slope of the yield curve. By looking at yields for bonds of different maturities, we can infer what financial markets expect short-term interest rates will be in the future.

Suppose we want to find out, for example, what financial markets expect the one-year interest rate to be one year from now. All we need to do is to look at the yield on a two-year bond, i_{2t}, and the yield on a one-year bond, i_{1t}. From Equation (15.7), multiplying both sides by 2 and reorganizing, we get

$$i^e_{1t+1} = 2i_{2t} - i_{1t} \qquad (15.8)$$

The one-year interest rate expected for next year is equal to twice the yield on a two-year bond minus the current one-year interest rate. Take, for example, the yield curve for June 1, 2001, shown in Figure 15-1.

On June 1, 2001, the one-year interest rate, i_{1t}, was 3.4%, and the two-year interest rate, i_{2t}, was 4.1%. From equation (15.8), it follows that, on June 1, 2001, financial markets expected the one-year interest rate one year later—that is, the one-year interest rate on June 1, 2002—to equal $2 \times 4.1\% - 3.4\% = 4.8\%$—that is, 1.4% higher than the one-year interest rate on June 1, 2001. In words: On June 1, 2001, financial markets expected the one-year interest rate to be substantially higher one year later.

More generally: When the yield curve is upward sloping—that is, when long-term interest rates are higher than short-term interest rates—financial markets expect short-term rates to be higher in the future. When the yield curve is downward sloping—that is, when long-term interest rates are lower than short-term interest rates—financial markets expect short-term interest rates to be lower in the future.

The Yield Curve and Economic Activity

We can now return to our earlier question: Why did the yield curve go from being downward sloping in November 2000 to being upward sloping in June 2001? Put another way, why did long-term interest rates go from being lower than short-term interest rates in November 2000 to much higher than short-term interest rates in June 2001?

First, the answer in short: Because an unexpected slowdown in economic activity in the first half of 2001 led to a sharp decline in short-term interest rates. And because, even as the slowdown was taking place, financial markets expected output to recover and expected short-term interest rates to return to higher levels in the future, leading long-term interest rates to fall by much less than short-term interest rates.

To go through the answer step-by-step, let's use the *IS–LM* model we developed in Chapter 5. We can think of the interest rate measured on the vertical axis as a short-term nominal interest rate. And to keep things simple, let's assume that expected inflation is equal to 0, so we do not have to worry about the distinction between the nominal and real interest rates we introduced in Chapter 14. This distinction is not central here.

In November 2000, economic indicators suggested that, after many years of high growth, the U.S. economy had started to slow down. This slowdown was perceived as largely for the better: Most economists believed output was above the natural level of output (equivalently, that the unemployment rate was below the natural rate), so a mild slowdown was desirable. And the forecasts were indeed for a mild slowdown, or what is called a **soft landing** of output back to the natural level of output.

We shall extend the *IS–LM* model in Chapter 17 to explicitly take into account what we have learned about the role of expectations on decisions. For the moment, the basic *IS–LM* model will do.

It would be easy (and more realistic) to allow for constant but positive (rather than zero) expected inflation. The conclusions would be the same.

You may want to reread the Focus box "The U.S. Recession of 2001" in Chapter 5.

Figure 15-3

The U.S. Economy as of November 2000

In November 2000, the U.S. economy was operating above the natural level of output. Forecasts were for a "soft landing," a return of output to the natural level of output, and a small decrease in interest rates.

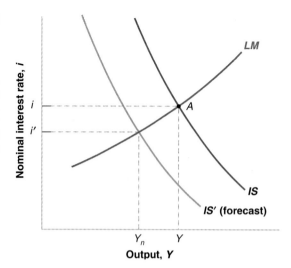

The economic situation at the time is represented in Figure 15-3. The U.S. economy was at a point such as A, with interest rate, i, and output, Y. The level of output, Y, was believed to be above the natural level of output, Y_n. The forecasts were that the IS curve would gradually shift to the left, from IS to IS', leading to a return of output to the natural level of output, Y_n, and a small decrease in the interest rate, from i to i'. This small expected decrease in the interest rate was the reason the yield curve was slightly downward sloping in November 2000.

Forecasts for a mild slowdown turned out, however, to be too optimistic. Beginning in late 2000, the economic situation was worse than had been forecast. What happened is represented in Figure 15-4. There were two major developments:

■ The adverse shift in spending was stronger than had been expected. Instead of shifting from IS to IS' as forecast (see Figure 15-3), the IS curve shifted by much more, from IS to IS'' in Figure 15-4. Had monetary policy remained unchanged, the economy would have moved along the LM curve, and the equilibrium would have

Figure 15-4

The U.S. Economy from November 2000 to June 2001

From November 2000 to June 2001, an adverse shift in spending, together with a monetary expansion, combined to lead to a decrease in the short-term interest rate.

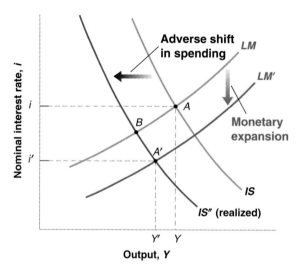

Expectations   **Extensions**

moved from *A* to *B*, leading to a decrease in output and a decrease in the short-term interest rate.

- There was more at work, however. Realizing that the slowdown was stronger than it had anticipated, the Fed shifted in early 2001 to a policy of monetary expansion, leading to a downward shift in the *LM* curve. As a result of this shift in the *LM* curve, the economy was, in June 2001, at a point like *A′*—rather than at a point like *B*. Output was higher and the interest rate lower than they would have been in the absence of the monetary expansion.

In words: The decline in short-term interest rates—and therefore the decline at the short-term end of the yield curve from November 1, 2000, to June 1, 2001—was the result of an unexpectedly large adverse shift in spending, combined with a strong response by the Fed aimed at limiting the size of the decrease in output. This still leaves one question: Why was the yield curve upward sloping in June 2001? Equivalently: Why were long-term interest rates higher than short-term interest rates?

To answer this question, we must look at what the markets *expected* to happen to the U.S. economy in the future, as of June 2001. This is represented in Figure 15-5. Financial markets expected two main developments:

- They expected a pickup in spending—a shift of the *IS* curve to the right, from *IS* to *IS′*. The reasons: Some of the factors that had contributed to the adverse shift in the first half of 2001 were expected to turn more favorable. Investment spending was expected to pick up. Also, the tax cut passed in May 2001, to be implemented over the rest of the year, was expected to lead to higher consumption spending.
- They also expected that, once the *IS* curve started shifting to the right and output started to recover, the Fed would start shifting back to a tighter monetary policy. In terms of Figure 15-5, they expected the *LM* curve to shift up.

As a result of both shifts, financial markets expected the U.S. economy to move from point *A* to point *A′;* they expected both output to recover and short-term interest rates to increase. The anticipation of higher short-term interest rates was the reason long-term interest rates remained high and the reason the yield curve was upward sloping in June 2001.

Note that the yield curve in June 2001 was nearly flat for maturities up to one year. This tells us that financial markets did not expect interest rates to start rising until a year hence—that is, before June 2002. Did they turn out to be right? Not quite. The Fed

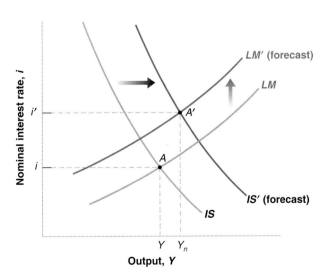

Figure 15-5 ▨

The Expected Path of the U.S. Economy as of June 2001

In June 2001, financial markets expected stronger spending and tighter monetary policy to lead to higher short-term interest rates in the future.

did not increase the short-term interest rate until June 2004—fully two years later than financial markets had anticipated.

Let's summarize. We have seen in this section how bond prices and bond yields depend on current and future expected interest rates. By looking at the yield curve, we (and everybody else in the economy, from people to firms) learn what financial markets expect interest rates to be in the future.

15-2 The Stock Market and Movements in Stock Prices

So far, we have focused on bonds. But while governments finance themselves by issuing bonds, the same is not true of firms. Firms raise funds in two ways: through **debt finance**—bonds and loans; and through **equity finance**, issuing **stocks**—or **shares**, as stocks are also called. Instead of paying predetermined amounts as bonds do, stocks pay **dividends** in an amount decided by the firm. Dividends are paid from the firm's profits. Typically, dividends are less than profits, as firms retain some of their profits to finance their investment. But dividends move with profits: When profits increase, so do dividends.

Another and better-known index is the *Dow Jones Industrial*, an index of stocks of industrial firms only, and therefore less representative of the average price of stocks than is the S&P index. Similar indexes exist for other countries. The *Nikkei index* reflects movements in stock prices in Tokyo, and the *FT* and *CAC* indexes reflect stock price movements in London and Paris, respectively. ▶

Our focus in this section is on the determination of stock prices. As a way of introducing the issues, let's look at the behavior of an index of U.S. stock prices, the *Standard & Poor's 500 Composite Index* (or the S&P index for short) from 1980 to 2006. Movements in the S&P index measure movements in the average stock price of 500 large companies.

Figure 15-6 plots the real stock price index, constructed by dividing the S&P index by the CPI for each quarter, and normalizing so the index is equal to 1 in the first quarter of 1990. The striking feature of the figure is obviously the sharp rise of the index during the 1990s, from 1.0 in 1990:1 to 3.24 in 2000:3, followed by a sharp fall in the early 2000s, from 3.24 in 2000:3 down to 1.78 in 2003:1. At the time of this writing (mid-2007), the index has partially recovered but is still below its 2000 peak. Why the long rise in the 1990s? Why the sharp fall in the 2000s? More generally, what determines the movement in stock prices, and how do stock prices respond to changes in the

Figure 15-6

Standard & Poor's Composite Index, in Real Terms, since 1980

Note the sharp increase in stock prices in the 1990s, followed by the sharp decrease in the early 2000s.

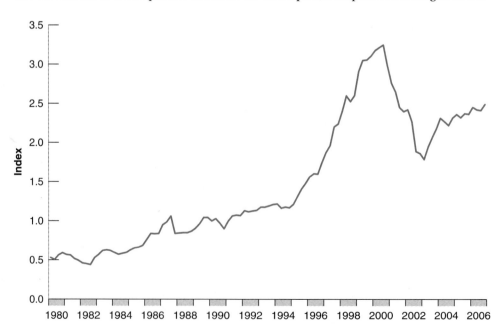

economic environment and macroeconomic policy? These are the questions we take up in this and the next section.

Stock Prices as Present Values

What determines the price of a stock that promises a sequence of dividends in the future? By now, I am sure the material in Chapter 14 has become second nature, and you already know the answer: The stock price must equal the present value of future expected dividends.

Let $\$Q_t$ be the price of the stock. Let $\$D_t$ denote the dividend this year, $\$D^e_{t+1}$ the expected dividend next year, $\$D^e_{t+2}$ the expected dividend two years from now, and so on.

Suppose we look at the price of the stock after the dividend has been paid this year—this price is known as the *ex-dividend price*—so that the first dividend to be paid after the purchase of the stock is next year's dividend. (This is just a matter of convention; we could alternatively look at the price before this year's dividend has been paid. What term would we have to add?) The price of the stock is then given by

$$\$Q_t = \frac{\$D^e_{t+1}}{1 + i_{1t}} + \frac{\$D^e_{t+2}}{(1 + i_{1t})(1 + i^e_{1t+1})} + \cdots \qquad (15.9)$$

The price of the stock is equal to the present value of the dividend next year, discounted using the current one-year interest rate, plus the present value of the dividend two years from now, discounted using both this year's one-year interest rate and next-year's expected one-year interest rate, and so on.

As in the case of long-term bonds, the present value relation in equation (15.9) can be derived from arbitrage—in this case, the condition that the expected return per dollar from holding a stock for one year must be equal to the return from holding a one-year bond. The derivation is given in the appendix to this chapter. (Going through the appendix will improve your understanding of the relation between arbitrage and present values, but it can be skipped without harm.)

Equation (15.9) gives the stock price as the present value of *nominal* dividends, discounted by *nominal* interest rates. From Chapter 14, we know we can rewrite this equation to express the *real* stock price as the present value of *real* dividends, discounted by *real* interest rates. So we can rewrite the real stock price as

$$Q_t = \frac{D^e_{t+1}}{(1 + r_{1t})} + \frac{D^e_{t+2}}{(1 + r_{1t})(1 + r^e_{i_{1t+1}})} + \cdots \qquad (15.10)$$

Q_t and D_t, without a dollar sign, denote the real price and real dividends at time t. The *real stock price is the present value of future real dividends, discounted by the sequence of one-year real interest rates.*

This relation has two important implications:

■ Higher expected future real dividends lead to a higher real stock price.
■ Higher current and expected future one-year real interest rates lead to a lower real stock price.

Let's now see what light this relation sheds on movements in the stock market.

Two equivalent ways of writing the stock price:
■ The nominal stock price equals the expected present discounted value of future nominal dividends, discounted by current and future nominal interest rates.
■ The real stock price equals the expected present discounted value of future real dividends, discounted by current and future real interest rates.

The Stock Market and Economic Activity

Figure 15-6 shows the large movements in stock prices over the past 26 years. It is not unusual for the price index to go up or down by 15% within a year. In 1997, the stock market went up by 24% (in real terms); in 2001, it went down by 22%. Daily movements of 2% or more are not unusual. What causes these movements?

The first point to be made is that these movements should be, and they are for the most part, unpredictable. The reason is best understood by thinking in terms of the choice people have between stocks and bonds. If it were widely believed that, a year from now, the price of a stock was going to be 20% higher than today's price, holding the stock for a year would be unusually attractive, much more attractive than holding short-term bonds. There would be a very large demand for the stock. Its price would increase *today* to the point where the expected return from holding the stock was back in line with the expected return on other assets. In other words, the expectation of a high stock price next year would lead to a high stock price today.

▶ There is indeed a saying in economics that it is a sign of a *well-functioning stock market* that movements in stock prices are unpredictable. The saying is too strong: At any moment, a few financial investors might have better information or simply be better at reading the future. If they are only a few, they may not buy enough of the stock to bid its price all the way up today. Thus, they may get large expected returns. But the basic idea is nevertheless right. The financial market gurus who regularly predict large imminent movements in the stock market are quacks. Major movements in stock prices cannot be predicted.

If movements in the stock market cannot be predicted, if they are the result of news, where does this leave us? We can still do two things:

- We can do Monday-morning quarterbacking, looking back and identifying the news to which the market reacted.
- We can ask what-if questions. For example: What would happen to the stock market if the Fed were to embark on a more expansionary policy or if consumers were to become more optimistic and increase spending?

Let us look at two what-if questions, using the *IS–LM* model. To simplify, let's assume, as we did earlier, that expected inflation equals 0, so that the real interest rate and the nominal interest rate are equal.

A Monetary Expansion and the Stock Market

Suppose the economy is in a recession, and the Fed decides to adopt a more expansionary monetary policy. The increase in money shifts the *LM* curve down in Figure 15-7, and equilibrium output moves from point A to point A'. How will the stock market react?

The answer depends on what participants in the stock market expected monetary policy to be before the Fed's move. If they fully anticipated the expansionary policy, then the stock market will not react: Neither its expectations of future dividends nor its expectations of future interest rates are affected by a move it had already anticipated. Thus, in equation (15.9), nothing changes, and stock prices will remain the same.

Suppose instead that the Fed's move is at least partly unexpected. In that case, stock prices will increase. They increase for two reasons: First, a more expansionary monetary policy implies lower interest rates for some time. Second, it also implies higher output for some time (until the economy returns to the natural level of output) and, therefore, higher dividends. As equation (15.9) tells us, both lower interest rates

▶ and higher dividends—current and expected—will lead to an increase in stock prices.

[Margin notes]

You may have heard the proposition that stock prices follow a **random walk**. This is a technical term, but with a simple interpretation: Something—it can be a molecule or the price of an asset—follows a random walk if each step it takes is as likely to be up as it is to be down. Its movements are therefore unpredictable.

On September 30, 1998, the Fed lowered the target federal funds rate by 0.5%. This decrease was expected by financial markets, though, so the Dow Jones index remained roughly unchanged (actually, it went down 28 points for the day).

Less than a month later, on October 15, 1998, the Fed lowered the target federal funds rate again, that time by 0.25%. In contrast to the September cut, that move by the Fed came as a complete surprise to financial markets. As a result, the Dow Jones index increased by 330 points on that day, an increase of more than 3%.

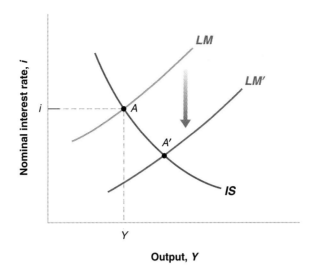

Figure 15-7

*An Expansionary
Monetary Policy and
the Stock Market*

A monetary expansion de-
creases the interest rate and increases output. What it does to
the stock market depends on
whether financial markets anticipated the monetary expansion.

An Increase in Consumer Spending and the Stock Market

Now consider an unexpected shift of the *IS* curve to the right, resulting, for example,
from stronger-than-expected consumer spending. As a result of the shift, output in
Figure 15-8(a) increases from *A* to *A'*.

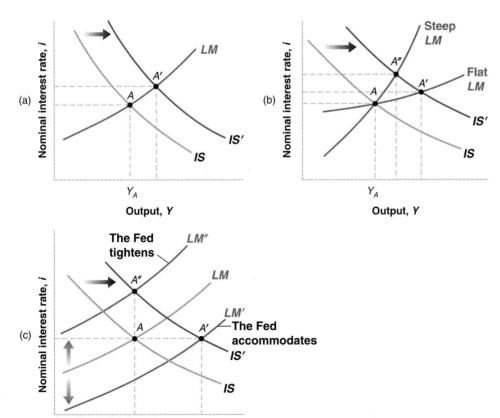

Figure 15-8

*An Increase in
Consumption Spending
and the Stock Market*

Panel (a): The increase in consumption spending leads to a
higher interest rate and a higher
level of output. What happens
to the stock market depends on
the slope of the *LM* curve and on
the Fed's behavior.

Panel (b): If the *LM* curve is steep,
the interest rate increases a lot,
and output increases little. Stock
prices go down. If the *LM* curve is
flat, the interest rate increases little, and output increases a lot.
Stock prices go up.

Panel (c): If the Fed accommo-
dates, the interest rate does not
increase, but output does. Stock
prices go up. If the Fed decides
instead to keep output constant,
the interest rate increases, but
output does not. Stock prices go
down.

Will stock prices go up? You might be tempted to say yes: A stronger economy means higher profits and higher dividends for some time. But this answer is incomplete, for at least two reasons.

First, the answer ignores the effect of higher activity on interest rates: The movement along the *LM* curve implies an increase in both output and interest rates. Higher output leads to higher profits and, therefore, higher stock prices. Higher interest rates lead to lower stock prices. Which of the two effects—higher profits or higher interest rates—dominates? The answer depends on the slope of the *LM* curve. This is shown in Figure 15-8(b). A very flat *LM* curve leads to a movement from *A* to *A'*, with small increases in interest rates, large increases in output, and therefore an increase in stock prices. A very steep *LM* curve leads to a movement from *A* to *A''*, with large increases in interest rates, small increases in output, and therefore a decrease in stock prices.

Second, the answer ignores the effect of the shift in the *IS* curve on the Fed's behavior. In practice, this is the effect that financial investors often care about the most. After receiving the news of unexpectedly strong economic activity, the main question on Wall Street is: How will the Fed react?

- Will the Fed accommodate the shift in the *IS* curve? That is, will the Fed increase the money supply in line with money demand so as to avoid an increase in the interest rate?

    Fed accommodation corresponds to a downward shift of the *LM* curve, from *LM* to *LM'* in Figure 15-8(c). In this case, the economy will go from point *A* to point *A'*. Stock prices will increase, as output is expected to be higher and interest rates are not expected to increase.

- Will the Fed instead keep the same monetary policy, leaving the *LM* curve unchanged? In that case, the economy will move along the *LM* curve. As we saw earlier, what happens to stock prices is ambiguous. Profits will be higher, but so will interest rates.

Another way of thinking about what happens is to think of the *LM* relation of an interest rate rule, as presented in the appendix to Chapter 5. Depending on how much the Fed increases the interest rate in response to the increase in output, the news will lead to an increase or a decrease in the stock market. ▶

- Or will the Fed worry that an increase in output above Y_A may lead to an increase in inflation? This will be the case if the economy is already close to the natural level of output—if, in Figure 15-8(c), Y_A is close to Y_n. In this case, a further increase in output would lead to an increase in inflation, something that the Fed wants to avoid. A decision by the Fed to counteract the rightward shift of the *IS* curve with a monetary contraction causes the *LM* curve to shift up, from *LM* to *LM''*, so the economy goes from *A* to *A''*, and output does not change. In that case, stock prices will surely go down: There is no change in expected profits, but the interest rate is now likely to be higher for some time.

Let's summarize: Stock prices depend very much on current and future movements in activity. But this does not imply any simple relation between stock prices and output. How stock prices respond to a change in output depends on (1) what the market expected in the first place, (2) the source of the shocks behind the change in output, and (3) how the market expects the central bank to react to the output change.

15-3 Bubbles, Fads, and Stock Prices

Do all movements in stock prices result from news about future dividends or interest rates? Many economists doubt it. They point to Black October in 1929, when the U.S. stock market fell by 23% in two days, and to October 19, 1987, when the Dow Jones index fell by 22.6% in a single day. They point to the amazing rise in the Nikkei index (an index of Japanese stock prices) from around 13,000 in 1985 to around 35,000 in 1989, followed by a decline back to 16,000 by 1992. In each of these cases, they point to a lack of obvious news, or at least of news important enough to cause such enormous movements.

Here are some quotes from the *Wall Street Journal* from April 1997 to August 2001. Try to make sense of them, using what you've just learned:

■ April 1997. Good news on the economy, leading to an increase in stock prices:

"Bullish investors celebrated the release of market-friendly economic data by stampeding back into stock and bond markets, pushing the Dow Jones Industrial Average to its second-largest point gain ever and putting the blue-chip index within shooting distance of a record just weeks after it was reeling."

■ December 1999. Good news on the economy, leading to a decrease in stock prices:

"Good economic news was bad news for stocks and worse news for bonds. . . . The announcement of

stronger-than-expected November retail-sales numbers wasn't welcome. Economic strength creates inflation fears and sharpens the risk that the Federal Reserve will raise interest rates again."

■ September 1998. Bad news on the economy, leading to an decrease in stock prices:

"Nasdaq stocks plummeted as worries about the strength of the U.S. economy and the profitability of U.S. corporations prompted widespread selling."

■ August 2001. Bad news on the economy, leading to an increase in stock prices:

"Investors shrugged off more gloomy economic news, and focused instead on their hope that the worst is now over for both the economy and the stock market. The optimism translated into another 2% gain for the Nasdaq Composite Index."

Reprinted by permission of TMS Reprints

FOCUS

Instead, they argue that stock prices are not always equal to their **fundamental value**, defined as the present value of expected dividends given in equation (15.10), and that stocks are sometimes underpriced or overpriced. Overpricing eventually comes to an end, sometimes with a crash, as in October 1929, or with a long slide, as in the case of the Nikkei index.

Under what conditions can such mispricing occur? The surprising answer is that it can occur even when investors are rational and when arbitrage holds. To see why, consider the case of a truly worthless stock (that is, the stock of a company that all financial investors know will never make profits and will never pay dividends). Putting D^e_{t+1}, D^e_{t+2}, and so on, equal to 0 in equation (15.10) yields a simple and unsurprising answer: The fundamental value of such a stock is equal to 0.

◄ Recall: Arbitrage is the condition that the expected rates of return on two financial assets are equal.

◄ The example is obviously extreme, but it makes the point most simply.

FOCUS

Tulipmania in Holland

In the seventeenth century, tulips became increasingly popular in western European gardens. A market developed in Holland for both rare and common forms of tulip bulbs.

The episode called the "tulip bubble" took place from 1634 to 1637. In 1634, the price of rare bulbs started increasing. The market went into a frenzy, with speculators buying tulip bulbs in anticipation of even higher prices later. For example, the price of a bulb called "Admiral Van de Eyck," increased from 1,500 guineas in 1634 to 7,500 guineas in 1637, equal to the price of a house at the time. There are stories about a sailor mistakenly eating bulbs, only to realize the cost of his "meal" later. In early 1637, prices increased faster. Even the prices of some common bulbs exploded, rising by a factor of up to 20 in January. But in February 1637, prices collapsed. A few years later, bulbs were trading for roughly 10% of their value at the peak of the bubble.

The MMM Pyramid in Russia

In 1994 a Russian "financier," Sergei Mavrody, created a company called MMM and proceeded to sell shares, promising shareholders a rate of return of at least 3,000% per year!

The company was an instant success. The price of MMM shares increased from 1,600 rubles (then worth $1) in February to 105,000 rubles (then worth $51) in July. And by July, according to the company claims, the number of shareholders had increased to 10 million.

The trouble was that the company was not involved in any type of production and held no assets, except for its 140 offices in Russia. The shares were intrinsically worthless. The company's initial success was based on a standard pyramid scheme, with MMM using the funds from the sale of new shares to pay the promised returns on the old shares. Despite repeated warnings by government officials, including Boris Yeltsin, that MMM was a scam and that the increase in the price of shares was a bubble, the promised returns were just too attractive to many Russian people, especially in the midst of a deep economic recession.

The scheme could work only as long as the number of new shareholders—and thus new funds to be distributed to existing shareholders—increased fast enough. By the end of July 1994, the company could no longer make good on its promises, and the scheme collapsed. The company closed. Mavrody tried to blackmail the government into paying the shareholders, claiming that not doing so would trigger a revolution or a civil war. The government refused, leaving many shareholders angry at the government rather than at Mavrody. Later on in the year, Mavrody actually ran for Parliament, as a self-appointed defender of the shareholders who had lost their savings. He won!

Source: The Tulipmania account is taken from Peter Garber, "Tulipmania," Journal of Political Economy, *June 1989, 535–560.*

Might you nevertheless be willing to pay a positive price for this stock? Maybe. You might if you expect the price at which you can sell the stock next year to be higher than this year's price. And the same applies to a buyer next year: He may well be willing to buy at a high price if he expects to sell at an even higher price in the following year. This process suggests that stock prices may increase just because investors expect them to. Such movements in stock prices are called **rational speculative bubbles**: Financial investors might well be behaving rationally as the bubble inflates. Even those investors who hold the stock at the time of the crash, and therefore sustain a large loss, may also have been rational. They may have realized there was a chance of a crash, but they thought there was also a chance that the bubble would continue and they could sell at an even higher price.

In a speculative bubble, the price of a stock is higher than its fundamental value. Investors are willing to pay a high price for the stock, in the anticipation of being able to resell the stock at an even higher price.

To make things simple, our example assumes the stock to be fundamentally worthless. But the argument is general and applies to stocks with a positive fundamental value as well: People might be willing to pay more than the fundamental value ▶ of a stock if they expect its price to further increase in the future. And the same argument applies to other assets, such as housing, gold, and paintings. Two such bubbles are described in the Focus box "Famous Bubbles: From Tulipmania in Seventeenth-Century Holland to Russia in 1994."

Are all deviations from fundamental values in financial markets rational bubbles? Probably not. The fact is that many financial investors are not rational. An increase in stock prices in the past, say due to a succession of good news, often creates excessive optimism. If investors simply extrapolate from past returns to predict future returns, a stock may become "hot" (high priced) for no reason other than the fact that its price has increased in the past. Such deviations of stock prices from their fundamental value are called **fads**. We are all aware of fads outside the stock market; there are good reasons to believe they exist in the stock market as well.

Let's now go back to the facts we saw in Figure 15-6, and ask: Was the large increase in the stock market in the 1990s due to fundamentals or to a bubble?

There is no question that there was much good news in the 1990s. After the 1990 to 1991 recession, the U.S. economy went through a long expansion—an expansion that lasted much longer than most economists and financial investors had anticipated. With the long expansion came high profits and high dividends—much higher than had been expected as of 1990. As we saw in Chapter 13, the New Economy was not all hype; the rate of technological progress increased, promising higher growth and higher profits for firms in the future. The natural rate of unemployment decreased (partly, as we discussed in Chapter 14, for the same reasons), allowing the Fed to keep interest rates low for most of the decade. This good news should have led to higher-than-expected stock prices—and indeed it did!

But did this good news justify the tripling of the stock price index that actually occurred? At the time, many economists were—and still are—doubtful. They point to the evolution of the NASDAQ, an index that includes mostly high-tech stocks. The NASDAQ went from 400 in 1990 to 3,900 in 2000, only to fall back to 1,350 in 2003. They point to the increasing number of individuals who would buy stocks on the Internet, without knowing anything about the stock itself, only in anticipation of selling it the next day at a higher price. Indeed, in 1997, Alan Greenspan spoke of *irrational exuberance*, warning that stock prices were probably too high.

The third edition of this text, written in 2001, included a box called: "Is the Stock Market Overvalued?" It concluded that it indeed was.

Another way of looking at the question is to ask: Was the sharp decline of the stock market in the early 2000s associated with bad news on fundamentals or the bursting of a bubble? Most of the evidence points primarily to the bursting of a bubble. As we saw in Chapter 14, the news on productivity growth has continued to be good. Under this interpretation, some of the increase in the 1990s was indeed unjustified, and this is what led to the sharp correction in the early 2000s. After that correction, however, the level of the index still stood at more than twice its value in 1990, reflecting the improvement in fundamentals.

Greenspan appeared to change his mind later and to conclude that fundamentals were good enough to justify the stock price increases. Whatever the reason, he did not reiterate his warning.

We have focused in this chapter on how news about economic activity affects bond and stock prices. But bond and stock markets are more than just a sideshow. They affect economic activity by influencing consumption and investment spending. There is little question, for example, that the decline in the stock market was one of the factors behind the 2001 recession. Most economists also believe that the stock market crash of 1929 was one of the sources of the Great Depression and that the large decline in the Nikkei index is one of the causes of the long Japanese slump in the 1990s. These interactions between bond and stock markets, expectations, and economic activity are the topics of the next two chapters.

See Chapter 22.

Summary

- Arbitrage between bonds of different maturities implies that the price of a bond is the present value of the payments on the bond, discounted using current and expected short-term interest rates over the life of the bond. Hence, higher current or expected short-term interest rates lead to lower bond prices.

- The yield to maturity on a bond is (approximately) equal to the average of current and expected short-term interest rates over the life of a bond.

- The slope of the yield curve—equivalently, the term structure—tells us what financial markets expect to happen to short-term interest rates in the future.

A downward-sloping yield curve (when long-term interest rates are lower than short-term interest rates) implies that the market expects a decrease in short-term interest rates; an upward-sloping yield curve (when long-term interest rates are higher than short-term interest rates) implies that the market expects an increase in short-term rates.

■ The fundamental value of a stock is the present value of expected future real dividends, discounted using current and future expected one-year real interest rates. In the absence of bubbles or fads, the price of a stock is equal to its fundamental value.

■ An increase in expected dividends leads to an increase in the fundamental value of stocks; an increase in current and expected one-year interest rates leads to a decrease in their fundamental value.

■ Changes in output may or may not be associated with changes in stock prices in the same direction. Whether they are depends on (1) what the market expected in the first place, (2) the source of the shocks, and (3) how the market expects the central bank to react to the output change.

■ Stock prices can be subject to bubbles and fads that cause a stock price to differ from its fundamental value. Bubbles are episodes in which financial investors buy a stock for a price higher than its fundamental value, anticipating to resell it at an even higher price. Fads are episodes in which, for reasons of fashion or overoptimism, financial investors are willing to pay more for a stock than its fundamental value.

Key Terms

Questions and Problems

Quick Check

1. Using the information in this chapter, label each of the following statements true, false, or uncertain. Explain briefly.

a. Junk bonds are bonds nobody wants to hold.

b. The price of a one-year bond decreases when the nominal one-year interest rate increases.

c. Given the Fisher hypothesis, an upward-sloping yield curve may indicate that financial markets are worried about inflation in the future.

d. Long-term interest rates typically move more than short-term interest rates.

e. An equal increase in expected inflation and nominal interest rates at all maturities should have no effect on the stock market.

f. A monetary expansion will lead to an upward-sloping yield curve.

g. A rational investor should never pay a positive price for a stock that will never pay dividends.

h. The strong performance of the U.S. stock market in the 1990s reflects the strong performance of the U.S. economy during that period.

2. Determine the yield to maturity of each of the following bonds:

a. A discount bond with a face value of $2,000, a maturity of four years, and a price of $1,700.

b. A discount bond with a face value of $2,000, a maturity of five years, and a price of $1700.

c. A discount bond with a face value of $2,000, a maturity of five years, and a price of $1,750.

3. Using the IS–LM model, determine the impact on stock prices of each of the policy changes described in (a) through (c). If the effect is ambiguous, explain what additional information would be needed to reach a conclusion.

  a. An unexpected expansionary monetary policy with no change in fiscal policy.

  b. A fully expected expansionary monetary policy with no change in fiscal policy.

  c. A fully expected expansionary monetary policy together with an unexpected expansionary fiscal policy.

4. *Suppose that the annual interest rate this year is 5%, and financial market participants expect the annual interest rate to increase to 5.5% next year, to 6% two years from now, and to 6.5% three years from now. Determine the yield to maturity on each of the following bonds.*

  a. A one-year bond.

  b. A two-year bond.

  c. A three-year bond.

Dig Deeper

5. *Money growth and the yield curve*

    In Chapter 14, we examined the effects of an increase in the growth rate of money on interest rates and inflation.

  a. Draw the path of the nominal interest rate following an increase in the growth rate of money. Suppose that the lowest point in the path is reached after one year and that the long-run values are achieved after three years.

  b. Show the yield curve just after the increase in the growth rate of money, one year later, and three years later.

6. *Interpreting the yield curve*

  a. What is the current price of the stock if the real interest rate is expected to remain constant at 5%? at 8%?

  b. What does a steep yield curve imply about future inflation?

7. *Stock prices and the risk premium*

    This problem is based on the appendix to the chapter.

    Suppose a share is expected to pay a dividend of $1,000 next year, and the real value of dividend payments is expected to increase by 3% per year forever after.

  a. What is the current price of the stock if the real interest rate is expected to remain constant at 5%? at 8%?

    Now suppose that people require a risk premium to hold stocks (as described in the appendix).

  b. Redo the calculations in part (a) if the required risk premium is 8%.

  c. Redo the calculations in part (a) if the required risk premium is 4%.

  d. What do you expect would happen to stock prices if the risk premium decreased unexpectedly? Explain in words.

Explore Further

8. *The Volcker disinflation and the term structure*

    In the late 1970s, the U.S. inflation rate reached double digits. Paul Volcker was appointed chairman of the Federal Reserve Board in 1979. Volcker was considered the right person to lead the fight against inflation. In this problem, we will use yield curve data to judge whether the financial markets were indeed expecting Volcker to succeed in reducing the inflation rate.

    *Go to the data section of the Web site of the Federal Reserve Bank of St. Louis (**www.research.stlouisfed.org/fred2**). Go to "Consumer Price Indexes (CPI)" and download monthly data on the seasonally adjusted CPI for all urban consumers for the period 1970 to today. Import it into your favorite spreadsheet program. Similarly, under "Interest Rates" and then "Treasury Constant Maturity," find and download the monthly series for "1-Year Treasury Constant Maturity Rate" and "30-Year Treasury Constant Maturity Rate" into your spreadsheet.*

  a. How can the Fed reduce inflation? How would this policy affect the nominal interest rate?

  b. For each month, compute the annual rate of inflation as the percentage change in the CPI from last year to this year (i.e., over the preceding 12 months). In the same graph, plot the rate of inflation and the one-year interest rate from 1970 to today. When was the rate of inflation the highest?

  c. For each month, compute the difference (called the *spread*) between the yield on the 30-year T-bond and the one-year T-bill. Plot it in the same graph with the one-year interest rate.

  d. What does a declining spread imply about the expectations of financial market participants? As inflation was increasing in the late 1970s, what was happening to the one-year T-bill rate? Were financial market participants expecting that trend to continue?

    In October 1979, the Fed announced several changes in its operating procedures that were widely interpreted as a commitment to fighting inflation.

  e. Using the interest rate spread that you computed in part (c) for October 1979, do you find any evidence of such an interpretation by financial market participants? Explain.

    In early 1980, it became obvious that the United States was falling into a sharp recession. The Fed switched to an expansionary monetary policy from April to July 1980 in order to boost the economy.

  f. What was the effect of the policy switch on the one-year interest rate?

  g. From April to July 1980, did financial markets expect the change in policy to last? Explain. Were financial market participants' expectations correct?

9. *Go to the Web site cited in problem 8 and find the most recent observation on the term structure of interest rates ranging from three months to 30 years.*

    Is the term structure upward sloping, downward sloping, or flat? Why?

10. *Do a news search on the Internet about the most recent Federal Open Market Committee (FOMC) meeting.*

  a. What did the FOMC decide about the interest rate?

  b. What happened to stock prices on the day of the announcement?

  c. To what degree do you think financial market participants were surprised by the FOMC's announcement? Explain.

We invite you to visit the Blanchard page on the Prentice Hall Web site, at:
www.prenhall.com/blanchard
for this chapter's World Wide Web exercises.

Further Readings

- There are many bad books written about the stock market. A good one, and one that is fun to read, is Burton Malkiel, *A Random Walk Down Wall Street*, 9th ed., Norton, New York, 2006.

- An account of historical bubbles is given by Peter Garber in "Famous First Bubbles," *Journal of Economic Perspectives*, Spring 1990, 35–54.

Appendix: Arbitrage and Stock Prices

This appendix has two parts.

The first part of this appendix shows that, in the absence of rational speculative bubbles, arbitrage between stocks and bonds implies that the price of a stock is equal to the expected present value of dividends.

The second part of this appendix shows how to modify the arbitrage relation to take into account the fact that financial investors care about risk. It then shows how the presence of risk modifies the present value relation between stock prices and dividends.

Arbitrage and Stock Prices

You face the choice of investing either in one-year bonds or in stocks for a year. What should you choose?

- Suppose you decide to hold one-year bonds. Then, for every dollar you put in one-year bonds, you will get $(1 + i_{1t})$ dollars next year. This payoff is represented in the upper line of Figure 1.
- Suppose you decide instead to hold stocks for a year. This implies buying a stock today, receiving a dividend next year, and then selling the stock. As the price of a stock is $\$Q_t$, every dollar you put in stocks buys you $\$1/\$Q_t$ stocks. And for each stock you buy, you expect to receive $(\$D^e_{t+1} + \$Q^e_{t+1})$, the sum of the expected dividend and the stock price next year. Therefore, for every dollar you put in stocks, you expect to receive $(\$D^e_{t+1} + \$Q^e_{t+1})/\$Q_t$. This payoff is represented in the lower line of Figure 1.

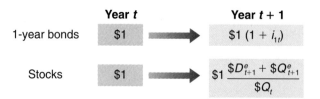

Figure 1 *Returns from Holding One-Year Bonds or Stocks for One Year*

Let's use the same arbitrage argument we used for bonds earlier. Assume that financial investors care only about expected rates of return. Equilibrium then requires that the expected rate of return from holding stocks for one year be the same as the rate of return on one-year bonds:

$$\frac{(\$D^e_{t+1} + \$Q^e_{t+1})}{\$Q_t} = 1 + i_{1t}$$

Rewrite this equation as

$$\$Q_t = \frac{\$D^e_{t+1}}{(1 + i_{1t})} + \frac{\$Q^e_{t+1}}{(1 + i_{1t})} \quad (15.A1)$$

Arbitrage implies that the price of the stock today must be equal to the present value of the expected dividend plus the present value of the expected stock price next year.

The next step is to think about what determines $\$Q^e_{t+1}$, the expected stock price next year. Next year, financial investors will again face a choice between stocks and one-year bonds. Thus, the same arbitrage relation will hold. Writing the previous equation, but now for time $t + 1$, and taking expectations into account, gives

$$\$Q^e_{t+1} = \frac{\$D^e_{t+2}}{(1 + i^e_{1t+1})} + \frac{\$Q^e_{t+2}}{(1 + i^e_{1t+1})}$$

The expected price next year is simply the present value next year of the sum of the expected dividend and price two years from now. Replacing the expected price $\$Q^e_{t+1}$ in equation 15.A1 gives

$$\$Q_t = \frac{\$D^e_{t+1}}{(1 + i_{1t})} + \frac{\$D^e_{t+2}}{(1 + i_{1t})(1 + i^e_{1t+1})} + \frac{\$Q^e_{t+2}}{(1 + i_{1t})(1 + i^e_{1t+1})}$$

The stock price is the present value of the expected dividend next year, plus the present value of the expected dividend two years from now, plus the expected price two years from now.

If we replace the expected price in two years by the present value of the expected price and dividends in three years, and so on for n years, we get

$$\$Q_t = \frac{\$D^e_{t+1}}{(1 + i_{1t})} + \cdots + \frac{\$D^e_{t+n}}{(1 + i_{1t})\dots(1 + i^e_{1t+n-1})}$$

$$+ \frac{\$Q^e_{t+n}}{(1 + i_{1t})\dots(1 + i^e_{1t+n-1})} \quad (15.A2)$$

Look at the last term in equation (15.A2)—the present value of the expected price in n years. As long as people do not expect the stock price to explode in the future, then, as we keep replacing Q^e_{t+n} and n increases, this term will go to 0. To see why, suppose the interest rate is constant and equal to i. The last term becomes

$$\frac{\$Q^e_{t+n}}{(1 + i_{1t})\dots(1 + i^e_{1t+n-1})} = \frac{\$Q^e_{t+n}}{(1 + i)^n}$$

Suppose further that people expect the price of the stock to converge to some value, call it $\$\overline{Q}$, in the far future. Then, the last term becomes

$$\frac{\$Q^e_{t+n}}{(1 + i)^n} = \frac{\$\overline{Q}}{(1 + i)^n}$$

If the interest rate is positive, this expression goes to 0 as n becomes large. Equation 15.A2 reduces to equation (15.9) in the text: The price today is the present value of expected future dividends.

(A subtle point: The condition that people expect the price of the stock to converge to some value over time seems reasonable. And, indeed, most of the time, it is likely to be satisfied. However, when prices are subject to rational bubbles [see Section 15-3], people are expecting large increases in the stock price in the future, and the condition that the expected stock price does not explode is not satisfied. This is why, when there are bubbles, the argument just given fails, and the stock price is no longer equal to the present value of expected dividends.)

An Extension to the Present Value Formula to Account for Risk

In this chapter and Chapter 14, we have assumed that people care only about expected return and do not take risk into account. Put another way, we have assumed that people are **risk neutral**. In fact, most people are **risk averse**. They care both about expected return—which they like—and risk—which they dislike.

Most of **finance theory** is indeed concerned with how people make decisions when they are risk averse and what risk aversion implies for asset prices. Exploring these issues would take us too far from our purpose. But we can nevertheless explore a simple extension of our framework that captures the fact that people are risk averse and shows how to modify the arbitrage and the present value relations.

If people perceive stocks to be more risky than bonds, and if people dislike risk, they are likely to require a *risk premium* to hold stocks rather than bonds. In the case of stocks, this risk premium is called the **equity premium**. Denote it by θ (the Greek lowercase letter theta). If θ is, for example, 5%, then people will hold stocks only if the expected rate of return on stocks exceeds the expected rate of return on short-term bonds by 5% per year.

In that case, the arbitrage equation between stocks and bonds becomes

$$\frac{\$D^e_{t+1} + \$Q^e_{t+1}}{\$Q_t} = 1 + i_{1t} + \theta$$

The only change is the presence of θ on the right side of the equation. Going through the same steps as before (replacing Q^e_{t+1} by its expression at time $t + 1$, and so on), the stock price equals

$$\$Q_t = \frac{\$D^e_{t+1}}{(1 + i_{1t} + \theta)} + \cdots$$

$$+ \frac{\$D^e_{t+n}}{(1 + i_{1t} + \theta)\cdots(1 + i^e_{1t+n-1} + \theta)} + \cdots$$

The stock price is still equal to the present value of expected future dividends. But the discount rate here equals the interest rate plus the equity premium. Note that the higher the premium, the lower the stock price. Over the past 100 years in the United States, the average equity premium has been equal to roughly 5%. But (in contrast to the assumption we made earlier, where we took θ to be constant) it is not constant. For example, the equity premium appears to have decreased since the early 1950s, from around 7% to less than 3% today. The variation in the equity premium is another source of fluctuations in stock prices.

Key Terms

- risk neutral, 355
- risk averse, 355
- finance theory, 355
- equity premium, 355

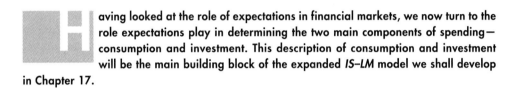

Expectations, Consumption, and Investment

aving looked at the role of expectations in financial markets, we now turn to the role expectations play in determining the two main components of spending—consumption and investment. This description of consumption and investment will be the main building block of the expanded *IS–LM* model we shall develop in Chapter 17.

■ Section 16-1 looks at consumption and shows how consumption decisions depend, not only on a person's current income, but also on her expected future income and on financial wealth.

■ Section 16-2 turns to investment and shows how investment decisions depend on current and expected profits and on current and expected real interest rates.

■ Section 16-3 looks at the movements in consumption and investment over time and shows how to interpret those movements in light of what you learned in this chapter. ■

CHAPTER 16

16-1 Consumption

How do people decide how much to consume and how much to save? Until now, we have assumed that consumption and saving depended only on current income. By now, you realize that they depend on much more, particularly on expectations about the future. We now explore how those expectations affect the consumption decision.

Friedman received the Nobel Prize in Economics in 1976; Modigliani received the Nobel ▶ Prize in Economics in 1985.

The theory of consumption on which this section is based was developed independently in the 1950s by Milton Friedman of the University of Chicago, who called it the **permanent income theory of consumption**, and by Franco Modigliani of MIT, who called it the **life cycle theory of consumption**. Each chose his label carefully. Friedman's "permanent income" emphasized that consumers look beyond current income. Modigliani's "life cycle" emphasized that consumers' natural planning horizon is their entire lifetime.

From Chapter 3: Consumption spending accounts for 70% of total spending in the United ▶ States.

The behavior of aggregate consumption has remained a hot area of research ever since, for two reasons: One is simply the sheer size of consumption as a component of GDP and, therefore, the need to understand movements in consumption. The other is the increasing availability of large surveys of individual consumers, such as the PSID described in the Focus box "Up Close and Personal: Learning from Panel Data Sets." These surveys, which were not available when Friedman and Modigliani developed their theories, have allowed economists to steadily improve their understanding of how consumers actually behave. This section summarizes what we know today.

The Very Foresighted Consumer

Let's start with an assumption that will surely—and rightly—strike you as extreme but will serve as a convenient benchmark. We'll call it the theory of the *very foresighted consumer*. How would a very foresighted consumer decide how much to consume? He would proceed in two steps:

With a slight abuse of language, I use *housing wealth* to refer not only to housing but also to the other goods that the consumer may own, from cars ▶ to paintings and so on.

1. He would add up the value of the stocks and bonds he owns, the value of his checking and savings accounts, the value of the house he owns minus the mortgage still due, and so on. This would give him an idea of his **financial wealth** and his **housing wealth**. He would also estimate what his after-tax labor income was likely to be over his working life and compute the present value of expected after-tax labor income. This would give him an estimate of what economists call his **human wealth**—in contrast with his **nonhuman wealth**, defined as the sum of financial wealth and housing wealth.

Human wealth + Nonhuman wealth = Total wealth ▶

2. Adding his human wealth and nonhuman wealth, he would have an estimate of his **total wealth**. He would then decide how much to spend out of this total wealth. A reasonable assumption is that he would decide to spend a proportion of his total wealth such as to maintain roughly the same level of consumption each year throughout his life. If that level of consumption was higher than his current income, he would then borrow the difference. If it was lower than his current income, he would instead save the difference.

Let's write this formally. What we have described is a consumption decision of the form

$$C_t = C(\text{Total wealth}_t) \qquad (16.1)$$

where C_t is consumption at time t, and (Total wealth$_t$) is the sum of nonhuman wealth (financial plus housing wealth) and human wealth at time t (the expected present value, as of time t, of current and future after-tax labor income).

This description contains much truth: Like the foresighted consumer, we surely do think about our wealth and our expected future labor income in deciding how

Expectations   **Extensions**

Panel data sets are data sets that show the value of one or more variables for many individuals or many firms over time. I described one such survey, the Current Population Survey (CPS), in Chapter 6. Another is the Panel Study of Income Dynamics (PSID).

The PSID was started in 1968, with approximately 4,800 families. Interviews of these families have been conducted every year since and are still continuing. The survey has grown as new individuals have joined the original families surveyed, either by marriage or by birth. Each year, the survey asks people about their income, wage rate, number of hours worked, health, and food consumption. (The focus on food consumption is because one of the survey's initial aims was to better understand the living conditions of poor families. The survey would be more useful if it asked about all of consumption rather than just food consumption. Unfortunately, it does not.)

By providing nearly four decades of information about individuals and their extended families, the survey has allowed economists to ask and answer questions for which there was previously only anecdotal evidence. Among the many questions for which the PSID has been used are:

- How much does (food) consumption respond to transitory movements in income—for example, to the loss of income from becoming unemployed?

- How much risk sharing is there within families? For example, when a family member becomes sick or unemployed, how much help does he or she get from other family members?

- How much do people care about staying geographically close to their families? When someone becomes unemployed, for example, how does the probability that he will migrate to another city depend on the number of his family members living in the city where he currently lives?

FOCUS

much to consume today. But one cannot help but think that it assumes too much computation and foresight on the part of the typical consumer.

To get a better sense of what that description implies and what is wrong with it, let's apply this decision process to the problem facing a typical U.S. college student.

An Example

Let's assume that you are 19 years old, with three more years of college before you start your first job. You may be in debt today, having taken out a loan to go to college. You may own a car and a few other worldly possessions. For simplicity, let's assume that your debt and your possessions roughly offset each other, so that your nonhuman wealth is equal to zero. Your only wealth, therefore, is your human wealth, the present value of your expected after-tax labor income.

You expect your starting annual salary in three years to be around $40,000 (in 2000 dollars) and to increase by an average of 3% per year in real terms, until your retirement at age 60. About 25% of your income will go to taxes.

You are welcome to use your own numbers and see where ◀ the computation takes you.

Building on what you saw in Chapter 14, let's compute the present value of your labor income as the value of *real* expected after-tax labor income, discounted using *real* interest rates [equation (14.7)]. Let Y_{Lt} denote real labor income in year t. Let T_t denote real taxes in year t. Let $V(Y_{Lt}^e - T_t^e)$ denote your human wealth—that is, the expected present value of your after-tax labor income—expected as of year t.

To make the computation simple, assume that the real interest rate equals zero— so the expected present value is simply the sum of expected labor income over your working life and is therefore given by

$$V(Y_{Lt}^e - T_t^e) = (\$40,000)(0.75)[1 + (1.03) + (1.03)^2 + \dots + (1.03)^{38}]$$

The first term ($40,000) is your initial level of labor income, in year 2000 dollars.

The second term (0.75) comes from the fact that, because of taxes, you keep only 75% of what you earn.

The third term, $[1 + (1.03) + (1.03)^2 + \dots + (1.03)^{38}]$, reflects the fact that you expect your real income to increase by 3% per year for 39 years (you will start earning income at age 22 and work until age 60).

Using the properties of geometric series to solve for the sum in brackets gives

$$V(Y_{Lt}^e - T_t^e) = (\$40,000)(0.75)(72.2) = \$2,166,000$$

The computation of the consumption level you can sustain is made easier by our assumption that the real interest rate equals 0. In this case, if you consume one less good today, you can consume exactly one more good next year, and the condition you ▶ must satisfy is simply that the sum of consumption over your lifetime is equal to your wealth. So, if you want to consume a constant amount each year, you just need to divide your wealth by the remaining number of years you expect to live.

Your wealth today, the expected value of your lifetime after-tax labor income, is around $2 million.

How much should you consume? You can expect to live about 16 years after you retire, so that your expected remaining life today is 58 years. If you want to consume the same amount every year, the constant level of consumption that you can afford equals your total wealth divided by your expected remaining life, or $2,166,000/ 58 = $37,344 per year. Given that your income until you get your first job is equal to 0, you will have to borrow $37,344 per year for the next three years, and you will begin to save when you get your first job.

Toward a More Realistic Description

Your first reaction to this computation may be that it is a stark and slightly sinister way of summarizing your life prospects. You might be more in agreement with the retirement plans described in the cartoon below.

Your second reaction may be that while you agree with most of the ingredients that went into the computation, you surely do not intend to borrow $37,344 × 3 = $112,032 over the next three years. For example:

1. You might not want to plan for constant consumption over your lifetime. Instead you may be quite happy to defer higher consumption until later. Student life usually does not leave much time for expensive activities. You may want to defer trips to the Galápagos Islands to later in life. You also have to think about the additional expenses that will come with having children, sending them to nursery school, summer camp, college, and so on.

2. You might find that the amount of computation and foresight involved in the computation we just went through far exceeds the amount you use in your own decisions. You may never have thought until now about exactly how much income you are going to make and for how many years. You might feel that most consumption decisions are made in a simpler, less forward-looking fashion.

3. The computation of total wealth is based on forecasts of what is expected to happen. But things can turn out better or worse. What happens if you become unemployed or sick? How will you pay back what you borrowed? You might want to be prudent, making sure that you can adequately survive even the worst outcomes, and thus decide to borrow much less than $112,032.

4. Even if you decide to borrow $112,032, you might have a hard time finding a bank willing to lend it to you. Why? The bank may worry that you are taking on a commitment you will not be able to afford if times turn bad and that you may not be able or willing to repay the loan.

These reasons, all good ones, suggest that to characterize consumers' actual behavior, we must modify the description we gave earlier. The last three reasons in particular suggest that consumption depends not only on total wealth but also on current income.

Take the second reason: You may, because it is a simple rule, decide to let your consumption follow your income and not think about what your wealth might be. In that case, your consumption will depend on your current income, not on your wealth.

Now take the third reason: It implies that a safe rule may be to consume no more than your current income. This way, you do not run the risk of accumulating debt that you cannot repay if times turn bad.

Or take the fourth reason: It implies that you may have little choice anyway. Even if you wanted to consume more than your current income, you might be unable to do so because no bank will give you a loan.

If we want to allow for a direct effect of current income on consumption, what measure of current income should we use? A convenient measure is after-tax labor income, which we introduced when we defined human wealth. This leads to a consumption function of the form

$$C_t = C(\text{Total wealth}_t, Y_{Lt} - T_t)$$
$$(\qquad + \quad , \quad + \quad)$$

(16.2)

In words: *Consumption is an increasing function of total wealth and of current after-tax labor income. Total wealth is the sum of nonhuman wealth—financial wealth plus housing wealth—and human wealth—the present value of expected after-tax labor income.*

How much does consumption depend on total wealth (and therefore on expectations of future income), and how much does it depend on current income? The evidence is that most consumers look forward, in the spirit of the theory developed by Modigliani and Friedman. (See the Focus box "Do People Save Enough for Retirement?") But some consumers, especially those who have temporarily low income and poor access to credit, are likely to consume their current income, regardless of what they expect will happen to them in the future. A worker who becomes unemployed and has no financial wealth may have a hard time borrowing to maintain her level of consumption, even if she is fairly confident that she will soon find another job. Consumers who are richer and have easier access to credit are more likely to give more weight to the expected future and to try to maintain roughly constant consumption over time.

Putting Things Together: Current Income, Expectations, and Consumption

Let's go back to what motivates this chapter—the importance of expectations in the determination of spending. Note first that, with consumption behavior described by equation (16.2), expectations affect consumption in two ways:

- Expectations affect consumption directly through *human wealth*: To compute their human wealth, consumers have to form their own expectations about future labor income, real interest rates, and taxes.

- Expectations affect consumption indirectly, through *nonhuman wealth*—stocks, bonds, and housing. Consumers do not need to do any computation here and can just take the value of these assets as given. As you saw in Chapter 15, the computation is, in effect, done for them by participants in financial markets: The price of their stocks, for example, itself depends on expectations of future dividends and interest rates.

This dependence of consumption on expectations has, in turn, two main implications for the relation between consumption and income:

1. *Consumption is likely to respond less than one-for-one to fluctuations in current income.* When deciding how much to consume, a consumer looks at more than his current income. If he concludes that the decrease in his income is permanent, he

How expectations of higher output in the future affect consumption today:
Expected future output increases
⇒ Expected future labor income increases
⇒ Human wealth increases
⇒ Consumption increases.
Expected future output increases
⇒ Expected future dividends increase
⇒ Stock prices increase
⇒ Nonhuman wealth increases
⇒ Consumption increases. ▶

Expectations   **Extensions**

How carefully do people look forward when making consumption and saving decisions? One way to answer this question is to look at how much people save for retirement.

Table 1, taken from a study by Steven Venti, from Dartmouth, and David Wise, from Harvard, based on a panel data set called the Survey of Income and Program Participation gives the basic numbers. The table shows the mean level and the composition of (total) wealth for people between 65 and 69 years in 1991—so, most of them retired.

The first three components of wealth capture the various sources of retirement income. The first is the present value of Social Security benefits. The second is the value of the retirement plans provided by employers. And the third is the value of personal retirement plans. The last three components include the other assets held by consumers, such as bonds, stocks, and housing.

A mean wealth of $314,000 is substantial (for comparison, U.S. per-person personal consumption at the time of the study, 1991, was $16,000). It gives an image of forward-looking individuals making careful saving decisions and retiring with enough wealth to enjoy a comfortable retirement.

We must be careful, however: The high average may hide important differences across individuals. Some individuals may save a lot, others little. Another study, by Scholz, Seshadri, and Khitatrakun, from the University of Wisconsin, sheds light on this aspect. The study is based on another panel data set, called the *Health and Retirement Study*. The panel consists of 7,000 households whose heads of household were between 51 and 61 years at the time of the first interview in 1992, and which have been interviewed every two years since. The panel contains information about the level and the composition of wealth for each household, as well as on its labor income (if the individuals in the household have not yet retired). Based on this information, the authors construct a target level of wealth for each household—i.e., the wealth level that each household should have if it wants to maintain a roughly constant level of consumption after retirement. The authors then compare the actual wealth level to the target level for each household.

The first conclusion of their study is similar to the conclusion reached by Venti and Wise: On average, people save enough for retirement. More specifically, the authors find that more than 80% of households have wealth above the target level. Put the other way around, only 20% of households have wealth below the target. But these numbers hide important differences across income levels.

Among those in the top half of the income distribution, more than 90% have wealth that exceeds the target, often by a large amount. This suggests that these households plan to leave bequests and so save more than what is needed for retirement.

Among those in the bottom 20% of the income distribution, however, fewer than 70% have wealth above the target. For the 30% of households below the target, the difference between actual and target wealth is typically small. But the relatively large proportion of individuals with wealth below the target suggests that there are a number of individuals who, through bad planning or bad luck, do not save enough for retirement. For most of these individuals, nearly all their wealth comes from the present value of Social Security benefits (the first component of wealth in Table 1), and it is reasonable to think that the proportion of people with wealth below target would be even larger if Social Security did not exist. This is indeed what the Social Security system was designed to do: To make sure that people have enough to live on when they retire. In that regard, it appears to be a success.

Table 1	Mean Wealth of People, Age 65 to 69, in 1991 (in thousands of 1991 dollars)
Social Security pension	$100
Employer-provided pension	62
Personal retirement assets	11
Other financial assets	42
Home equity	65
Other equity	34
Total	$314

Source: Venti and Wise, Table A1. Used by permission of the author.

Sources: Steven Venti and David Wise, "The Wealth of Cohorts: Retirement and Saving and the Changing Assets of Older Americans," in Sylvester Schieber and John B. Shoven (eds.), Public Policy Toward Pensions, *MIT Press, Cambridge, MA, 1997; and John Scholz, Ananth Seshadri, and Surachai Khitatrakun, "Are Americans Saving 'Optimally' for Retirement?"* Journal of Political Economy, *Volume 114, 2006, 4.*

Go back to the two consumption functions we used in the core:

Looking at the short run (Chapter 3), we assumed $C = c_0 + c_1 Y$ (ignoring taxes here). This implied that, when income increased, consumption increased less than proportionately with income (C/Y went down). This was appropriate because our focus was on fluctuations, on transitory movements in income.

Looking at the long run (Chapter 10), we assumed that $S = sY$ or, equivalently, $C = (1 - s)Y$. This implied that when income increased, consumption increased proportionately with income (C/Y remained the same). This was appropriate because our focus was on permanent—long-run—movements in income.

What does this suggest happens ▶ to the saving rate in a recession?

is likely to decrease consumption one-for-one with the decrease in income. But if he concludes that the decrease in his current income is transitory, he will adjust his consumption by less. In a recession, consumption adjusts less than one-for-one to decreases in income. This is because consumers know that recessions typically do not last for more than a few quarters and that the economy will eventually return to the natural level of output. The same is true in expansions: Faced with an unusually rapid increase in income, consumers are unlikely to increase consumption by as much as income. They are likely to assume that the boom is transitory and that things will return to normal.

2. *Consumption may move even if current income does not change.* The election of a charismatic president who articulates the vision of an exciting future might lead people to become more optimistic about the future in general and about their own future income in particular, leading them to increase consumption even if their current income does not change. You saw in Chapter 3 that the U.S. recession of 1990 to 1991 was caused in large part by a large decrease in consumption, caused in turn by a large decrease in consumer confidence. Even today, economists are not sure why people suddenly became so pessimistic. But they did, and their expectations of the future turned somber. Consumer pessimism was one of the main causes of the 1990 to 1991 recession.

One of the main worries macroeconomists had after the events of September 11 was that we would see a repeat of 1990 to 1991: Consumers would become pessimistic, and consumption would drop, leading to a deeper recession. As you saw in Chapter 5, this was not the case. Although consumer confidence fell in the months following September 11, 2001, the fall was much smaller than in 1990 to 1991, and it did not derail the recovery.

16-2 Investment

How do firms make investment decisions? In our first pass at the answer in Chapter 5, we took investment to depend on the current interest rate and the current level of sales. We refined that answer in Chapter 14 by pointing out that what mattered was the real interest rate, not the nominal interest rate. It should now be clear that investment decisions, just as consumption decisions, depend on more than current sales and the current real interest rate. They also depend very much on expectations of the future. We now explore how those expectations affect investment decisions.

Just like the basic theory of consumption, the basic theory of investment is straightforward. A firm deciding whether to invest—say, whether to buy a new machine—must make a simple comparison. The firm must first compute the present value of profits it can expect from having this additional machine. It must then compare the present value of profits to the cost of buying the machine. If the present value exceeds the cost, the firm should buy the machine—invest; if the present value is less than the cost, then the firm should not buy the machine—not invest. This, in a nutshell, is the theory of investment. Let's look at it in more detail.

Investment and Expectations of Profit

Let's go through the steps a firm must take to determine whether to buy a new machine. (Although I refer to a machine, the same reasoning applies to the other components of investment—the building of a new factory, the renovation of an office complex, and so on.)

Depreciation

To compute the present value of expected profits, a firm must first estimate how long a machine will last. Most machines are like cars. They can last nearly forever, but as time passes, they become more and more expensive to maintain and less and less reliable.

Assume that a machine loses its usefulness at rate δ (the Greek lowercase letter delta) per year. A machine that is new this year is worth only $(1 - \delta)$ machines next year, $(1 - \delta)^2$ machines in two years, and so on. The *depreciation rate*, δ, measures how much usefulness the machine loses from one year to the next. What are reasonable values for δ? This is a question that the statisticians in charge of computing how the U.S. capital stock changes over time have had to answer. Based on their studies of depreciation of specific machines and buildings, they use numbers between 4% and 15% for machines and between 2% and 4% for buildings and factories.

> If the firm has a large number of machines, we can think of δ as the proportion of machines that die every year. (Think of lightbulbs—which work perfectly until they die.) If the firm starts the year with K working machines and does not buy new ones, it will have only $K(1 - \delta)$ machines left one year later, and so on.

The Present Value of Expected Profits

The firm must then compute the present value of expected profits.

To capture the fact that it takes some time to put machines in place (and even more time to build a factory or an office building), let's assume that a machine bought in year t becomes operational—and starts depreciating—only one year later, in year $t + 1$. Denote profit per machine in real terms by Π.

> This is an uppercase Greek pi as opposed to the lowercase Greek pi, which we use to denote inflation.

If the firm buys a machine in year t, the machine will generate its first profit in year $t + 1$; denote this expected profit by Π^e_{t+1}. The present value, in year t, of this expected profit in year $t + 1$, is given by

$$\frac{1}{1 + r_t} \Pi^e_{t+1}$$

This term is represented by the arrow pointing left in the upper line of Figure 16-1. Because we are measuring profit in real terms, we are using real interest rates to discount future profits. This is one of the lessons we learned in Chapter 14.

Denote expected profit per machine in year $t + 2$ by Π^e_{t+2}. Because of depreciation, only $(1 - \delta)$ of the machine is left in year $t + 2$, so the expected profit from the machine is equal to $(1 - \delta)\Pi^e_{t+2}$. The present value of this expected profit as of year t is equal to

$$\frac{1}{(1 + r_t)(1 + r^e_{t+1})} (1 - \delta)\Pi^e_{t+2}$$

This computation is represented by the arrow pointing left in the lower line of Figure 16-1.

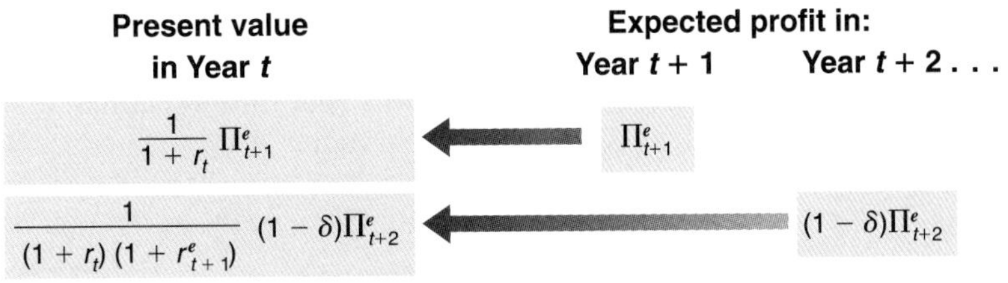

Present value in Year t		Expected profit in:	
		Year $t + 1$	Year $t + 2$ ...
$\frac{1}{1 + r_t} \Pi^e_{t+1}$	←	Π^e_{t+1}	
$\frac{1}{(1 + r_t)(1 + r^e_{t+1})} (1 - \delta)\Pi^e_{t+2}$	←		$(1 - \delta)\Pi^e_{t+2}$

Figure 16-1

Computing the Present Value of Expected Profits

The same reasoning applies to expected profits in the following years. Putting the pieces together gives us *the present value of expected profits* from buying the machine in year t, which we shall call $V(\Pi_t^e)$:

$$V(\Pi_t^e) = \frac{1}{1 + r_t} \Pi_{t+1}^e + \frac{1}{(1 + r_t)(1 + r_{t+1}^e)} (1 - \delta)\Pi_{t+2}^e + \dots \qquad (16.3)$$

The expected present value is equal to the discounted value of expected profit next year, plus the discounted value of expected profit two years from now (taking into account the depreciation of the machine), and so on.

The Investment Decision

The firm must decide whether to buy the machine. This decision depends on the relation between the present value of expected profits and the price of the machine. To simplify notation, let's assume that the real price of a machine—that is, the machine's price in terms of the basket of goods produced in the economy—equals 1. What the firm must then do is to compare the present value of profits to 1.

If the present value is less than 1, the firm should not buy the machine: If it did, it would be paying more for the machine than it expects to get back in profits later. If the present value exceeds 1, the firm has an incentive to buy the new machine.

Let's now go from this one-firm, one-machine example to investment in the economy as a whole.

Let I_t denote aggregate investment. Denote profit per machine or, more generally, profit per unit of capital (where capital includes machines, factories, office buildings, and so on) for the economy as a whole by Π_t. Denote the expected present value of profit per unit of capital by $V(\Pi_t^e)$, as defined as in equation (16.3).

Our discussion suggests an investment function of the form

$$I_t = I[V(\Pi_t^e)] \qquad (16.4)$$
$$(\ + \ )$$

In words: *Investment depends positively on the expected present value of future profits (per unit of capital). The higher the current or expected profits, the higher the expected present value and the higher the level of investment. The higher the current or expected real interest rates, the lower the expected present value, and thus the lower the level of investment.*

If the present value computation the firm has to make strikes you as quite similar to the present value computation we saw in Chapter 15 for the fundamental value of a stock, you are right. This relation was first explored by James Tobin, from Yale University, who argued that, for this reason, there should indeed be a tight relation

▶ between investment and the value of the stock market. His argument and the evidence for it are presented in the Focus box "Investment and the Stock Market."

Tobin received the Nobel Prize in Economics in 1981.

A Convenient Special Case

Before exploring further implications and extensions of equation (16.4), we'll go through a special case where the relation between investment, profit, and interest rates becomes very simple.

Suppose firms expect both future profits (per unit of capital) and future interest rates to remain at the same level as today, so that

$$\Pi_{t+1}^e = \Pi_{t+2}^e = \dots = \Pi_t$$

and

$$r_{t+1}^e = r_{t+2}^e = \dots = r_t$$

Expectations   **Extensions**

Suppose a firm has 100 machines and 100 shares outstanding—1 share per machine. Suppose the price per share is $2, and the purchase price of a machine is only $1. Obviously, the firm should invest—buy a new machine—and finance it by issuing a share: Each machine costs the firm $1 to purchase, but stock market participants are willing to pay $2 for a share corresponding to this machine when it is installed in the firm.

This is an example of a more general argument made by Tobin that there should be a tight relation between the stock market and investment. When deciding whether to invest, he argued, firms might not need to go through the type of complicated computation you saw in the text. In effect, the stock price tells firms how much the stock market values each unit of capital already in place. The firm then has a simple problem: Compare the purchase price of an additional unit of capital to the price the stock market is willing to pay for it. If the stock market value exceeds the purchase price, the firm should buy the machine; otherwise, it should not.

Tobin then constructed a variable corresponding to the value of a unit of capital in place relative to its purchase price and looked at how closely it moved with investment. He used the symbol q to denote the variable,

and the variable has become known as **Tobin's q**. Its construction is as follows:

1. Take the total value of U.S. corporations, as assessed by financial markets. That is, compute the sum of their stock market value (the price of a share times the number of shares). Compute also the total value of their bonds outstanding (firms finance themselves not only through stocks but also through bonds). Add together the values of stocks and bonds.
2. Divide this total value by the value of the capital stock of U.S. corporations at replacement cost (the price firms would have to pay to replace their machines, their plants, and so on).

The ratio gives us, in effect, the value of a unit of capital in place relative to its current purchase price. This ratio is Tobin's q. Intuitively, the higher q, the higher the value of capital relative to its current purchase price, and the higher investment should be. (In the example at the start of the box, Tobin's q is equal to 2, so the firm should definitely invest.)

How tight is the relation between Tobin's q and investment? The answer is given in Figure 1, which plots two variables for each year from 1960 to 1999 for the United States.

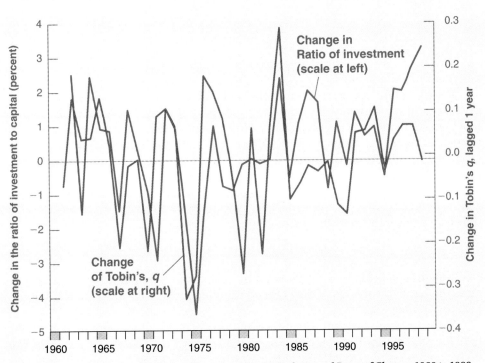

Figure 1 *Tobin's q versus the Ratio of Investment to Capital: Annual Rates of Change, 1960 to 1999*

Measured on the left vertical axis is the change in the ratio of investment to capital.

Measured on the right vertical axis is the change in Tobin's *q*. This variable has been lagged once. For 1987, for example, the figure shows the change in the ratio of investment to capital for 1987 and the change in Tobin's *q* for 1986—that is, a year earlier. The reason for presenting the two variables this way is that the strongest relation in the data appears to be between investment this year and Tobin's *q* last year. Put another way, movements in investment this year are more closely associated with movements in the stock market last year than with movements in the stock market this year; a plausible explanation is that it takes time for firms to make investment decisions, build new factories, and so on.

Figure 1 shows that there is a clear relation between Tobin's *q* and investment. This is probably not because firms blindly follow the signals from the stock market, but because investment decisions and stock market prices depend very much on the same factors—expected future profits and expected future interest rates.

Economists call such expectations—expectations that the future will be like the present—**static expectations.** Under these two assumptions, equation (16.3) becomes

$$V(\Pi_t^e) = \frac{\Pi_t}{r_t + \delta} \tag{16.5}$$

The present value of expected profits is simply the ratio of the profit rate—that is, profit per unit of capital—to the sum of the real interest rate and the depreciation rate. (The derivation is given in the appendix to this chapter.)

Replacing (16.5) in equation (16.4), investment is

$$I_t = I\left(\frac{\Pi_t}{r_t + \delta}\right) \tag{16.6}$$

Investment is a function of the ratio of the profit rate to the sum of the interest rate and the depreciation rate.

> Such arrangements exist. For example, many firms lease cars and trucks from leasing companies.

The sum of the real interest rate and the depreciation rate is called the **user cost**, or the **rental cost, of capital**. To see why, suppose the firm, instead of buying the machine, rented it from a rental agency. How much would the rental agency have to charge per year? Even if the machine did not depreciate, the agency would have to ask for an interest charge equal to r_t times the price of the machine (we have assumed the price of a machine to be 1 in real terms, so r_t times 1 is just r_t): The agency has to get at least as much from buying and then renting the machine out as it would from, say, buying bonds. In addition, the rental agency would have to charge for depreciation, δ times the price of the machine, 1. Therefore:

$$\text{Rental cost} = (r_t + \delta)$$

Even though firms typically do not rent the machines they use, $(r_t + \delta)$ still captures the implicit cost—sometimes called the *shadow cost*—to the firm of using the machine for one year.

The investment function given by equation (16.6) then has a simple interpretation: *Investment depends on the ratio of profit to the user cost. The higher the profit, the higher the level of investment. The higher the user cost, the lower the level of investment.*

This relation between profit, the real interest rate, and investment hinges on a strong assumption: that the future is expected to be the same as the present. It is a useful relation to remember—and one that macroeconomists keep handy in their toolbox.

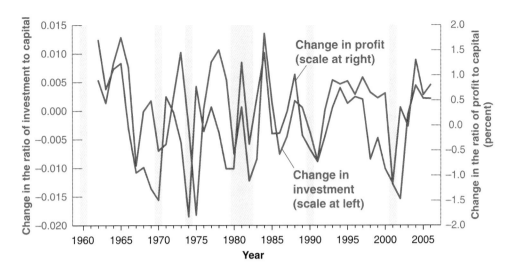

Figure 16-2 ▬

*Changes in Investment
and Changes in Profit
in the United States
since 1960*

Investment and profit move very
much together.

It is time, however, to relax this assumption and return to the role of expectations in
determining investment decisions.

Current versus Expected Profit

The theory we have developed implies that investment should be forward looking and
should depend primarily on *expected future profits*. [Under our assumption that it
takes a year for investment to generate profits, current profit does not even appear in
equation (16.3).] One striking empirical fact about investment, however, is how
strongly it moves with fluctuations in *current profit*.

This relation is shown in Figure 16-2, which plots yearly changes in investment
and profit since 1960 for the U.S. economy. Profit is constructed as the ratio of the sum
of *after-tax profits plus interest payments paid by U.S. non-financial corporations*,
divided by their capital stock. Investment is constructed as the ratio of *fixed non-
residential investment* to the *fixed non-residential capital stock*. The shaded areas in
the figure represent years in which there was a recession—a decline in output for at
least two consecutive quarters of the year.

► For definitions of all these
terms, see Appendix 1 on
national income accounts at the
end of the book.

There is a clear positive relation between changes in investment and changes in
current profit in Figure 16-2. Is this relation inconsistent with the theory we have just
developed, which holds that investment should be related to the present value of
expected future profits rather than to current profit? Not necessarily:

If firms expect future profits to move very much like current profit, then the present value of those future profits will move very much like current profit, and so will
investment.

Economists who have looked at the question more closely have concluded, however, that the effect of current profit on investment is stronger than would be predicted
by the theory we have developed so far. How they have gathered some of the evidence is
described in the Focus box "Profitability versus Cash Flow." On the one hand, some
firms with highly profitable investment projects but low current profits appear to be
investing too little. On the other hand, some firms that have high current profit appear
sometimes to invest in projects of doubtful profitability. In short, current profit appears
to affect investment, even after controlling for the expected present value of profits.

Why does current profit play a role in the investment decision? The answer lurks
in Section 16-1, where we discussed why consumption depends directly on current

How much does investment depend on the expected present value of future profits, and how much does it depend on current profit? In other words, which is more important for investment decisions—**profitability** (the expected present discounted value of future profits) or **cash flow** (current profit, the net flow of cash the firm is receiving now)?

The difficulty in answering this question is that, most of the time, cash flow and profitability move together. Firms that do well typically have both large cash flows and good future prospects. Firms that suffer losses often also have poor future prospects.

The best way to isolate the effects of cash flow and profitability on investment is to identify times or events when cash flow and profitability move in different directions and then to look at what happens to investment. This is the approach taken by Owen Lamont, an economist at Yale University. An example will help you understand Lamont's strategy.

Think of two firms, A and B. Both firms are involved in steel production. Firm B is also involved in oil exploration.

Suppose there is a sharp drop in the price of oil, leading to losses in oil exploration. This shock decreases firm B's cash flow. If the losses in oil exploration are large enough to offset the profits from steel production, firm B might even show an overall loss.

The question we can now ask is: As a result of the fall in the price of oil, will firm B invest less in its steel operation than firm A does? If only the profitability of steel production matters, there is no reason for firm B to invest less in its steel operation than firm A. But if current cash flow also matters, the fact that firm B has a lower cash flow may prevent it from investing as much as firm A in its steel operation. Looking at investment in the steel operations of the two firms can tell us how much investment depends on cash flow versus profitability.

This is the empirical strategy followed by Lamont. He focused on what happened in 1986 when the price of oil in the United States dropped by 50%, leading to large losses in oil-related activities. He then looked at whether firms that had substantial oil activities cut investment in their non-oil activities relatively more than other firms in the same non-oil activities. He concludes that they did. He found that for every $1 decrease in cash flow due to the decrease in the price of oil, investment spending in non-oil activities was reduced by 10 to 20 cents. In short: Current cash flow matters.

Source: Owen Lamont, "Cash Flow and Investment: Evidence from Internal Capital Markets," Journal of Finance, *March 1997.*

income. Some of the reasons we used to explain the behavior of consumers also apply to firms:

- If its current profit is low, a firm that wants to buy new machines can get the funds it needs only by borrowing. It may be reluctant to borrow: Although expected profits might look good, things may turn bad, leaving the firm unable to repay the debt. But if current profit is high, the firm might be able to finance its investment just by retaining some of its earnings and without having to borrow. The bottom line is that higher current profit may lead the firm to invest more.
- Even if the firm wants to invest, it might have difficulty borrowing. Potential lenders may not be convinced that the project is as good as the firm says it is, and they may worry that the firm will be unable to repay. If the firm has large current profits, it does not have to borrow and so does not need to convince potential lenders. It can proceed and invest as it pleases, and it is more likely to do so.

In summary, to fit the investment behavior we observe in practice, the investment equation is better specified as

$$I_t = I[V(\Pi_t^e), \Pi_t]$$
$$(\ +\ \ \ ,+\ )$$

(16.7)

In words: *Investment depends both on the expected present value of future profits and on the current level of profit.*

Profit and Sales

Let's take stock of where we are. We have argued that investment depends on both current and expected profit or, more specifically, current and expected profit per unit of capital. We need to take one last step: What determines profit per unit of capital? Answer: Primarily two factors: (1) the level of sales and (2) the existing capital stock. If sales are low relative to the capital stock, profits per unit of capital are likely to be low as well.

Let's write this more formally. Ignore the distinction between sales and output and let Y_t denote output—equivalently, sales. Let K_t denote the capital stock at time t. Our discussion suggests the following relation:

$$\Pi_t = \Pi\left(\underset{(+)}{\frac{Y_t}{K_t}}\right) \qquad (16.8)$$

Profit per unit of capital is an increasing function of the ratio of sales to the capital stock. For a given capital stock, the higher the sales, the higher the profit per unit of capital. For given sales, the higher the capital stock, the lower the profit per unit of capital.

How well does this relation hold in practice? Figure 16-3 plots yearly changes in profit per unit of capital (measured on the right vertical axis) and changes in the ratio of output to capital (measured on the left vertical axis) for the United States since 1960. As in Figure 16-2, profit per unit of capital is defined as the sum of after-tax profits plus interest payments by U.S. non-financial corporations, divided by their capital stock, measured at replacement cost. The ratio of output to capital is constructed as the ratio of GDP to the aggregate capital stock.

The figure shows that there is a tight relation between changes in profit per unit of capital and changes in the ratio of output to capital. Given that most of the year-to-year changes in the ratio of output to capital come from movements in output, and most of the year-to-year changes in profit per unit of capital come from movements in profit (capital moves slowly over time; the reason is that capital is large compared to yearly investment, so even large movements in investment lead to small changes in the capital stock), we can state the relation as follows: Profit decreases in recessions and increases in expansions.

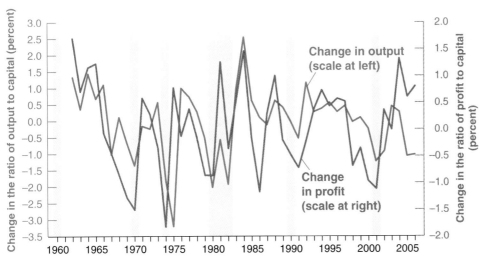

Figure 16-3

Changes in Profit per Unit of Capital versus Changes in the Ratio of Output to Capital in the United States since 1960

Profit per unit of capital and the ratio of output to capital move largely together.

Why is this relation between output and profit relevant here? Because it implies a link between *current output and expected future output* on the one hand and *investment* on the other: Current output affects current profit, expected future output affects expected future profit, and current and expected future profits affect investment. For example, the anticipation of a long, sustained economic expansion leads firms to expect high profits, now and for some time in the future. These expectations in turn lead to higher investment. The effect of current and expected output on investment, together with the effect of investment on demand and output, will play a crucial role when we return to the determination of output in Chapter 17.

High expected output ⇒ High expected profit ⇒ High investment today.

16-3 The Volatility of Consumption and Investment

You will surely have noticed the similarities between our treatment of consumption and of investment behavior in Sections 16-1 and 16-2:

- Whether consumers perceive current movements in income to be transitory or permanent affects their consumption decisions. The more transitory consumers expect a current increase in income to be, the less they will increase their consumption.

- In the same way, whether firms perceive current movements in sales to be transitory or permanent affects their investment decisions. The more transitory firms expect a current increase in sales to be, the less they revise their assessment of the present value of profits, and thus the less likely they are to buy new machines or build new factories. This is why, for example, the boom in sales that happens every year between Thanksgiving and Christmas does not lead to a boom in investment every year in December. Firms understand that this boom is transitory.

In the United States, retail sales are 24% higher on average in December than in other months. In France and Italy, sales are 60% higher in December.

But there are also important differences between consumption decisions and investment decisions:

- The theory of consumption we developed implies that when faced with an increase in income consumers perceive as permanent, they respond with at most an equal increase in consumption. The permanent nature of the increase in income implies that they can afford to increase consumption now and in the future by the same amount as the increase in income. Increasing consumption more than one-for-one would require cuts in consumption later, and there is no reason for consumers to want to plan consumption this way.

- Now consider the behavior of firms faced with an increase in sales they believe to be permanent. The present value of expected profits increases, leading to an increase in investment. In contrast to consumption, however, this does not imply that the increase in investment should be at most equal to the increase in sales. Rather, once a firm has decided that an increase in sales justifies the purchase of a new machine or the building of a new factory, it may want to proceed quickly, leading to a large but short-lived increase in investment spending. This increase in investment spending may exceed the increase in sales.

  More concretely, take a firm that has a ratio of capital to its annual sales of, say, 3. An increase in sales of $10 million this year, if expected to be permanent, requires the firm to spend $30 million on additional capital if it wants to maintain the same ratio of capital to output. If the firm buys the additional capital right away, the increase in investment spending this year will equal *three times* the increase in sales. Once the capital stock has adjusted, the firm will return to its normal pattern of investment. This example is extreme because firms are unlikely to adjust their capital stock right away. But even if they do adjust their capital stock more slowly, say over a few years, the increase in investment might still exceed the increase in sales for a while.

We can tell the same story in terms of equation (16.8). Because we make no distinction here between output and sales, the initial increase in sales leads to an equal increase in output, Y, so that Y/K—the ratio of the firm's output to its existing capital stock—also increases. The result is higher profit, which leads the firm to undertake more investment. Over time, the higher level of investment leads to a higher capital stock, K, so that Y/K decreases back to normal. Profit per unit of capital returns to normal, and so does investment. Thus, in response to a permanent increase in sales, investment may increase a lot initially and then return to normal over time.

These differences suggest that investment should be more volatile than consumption. How much more? The answer is given in Figure 16-4, which plots yearly rates of change in U.S. consumption and investment since 1960. The shaded areas are years during which the U.S. economy was in recession. To make the figure easier to interpret, both rates of change are plotted as deviations from the average rate of change so that they are, on average, equal to zero.

The figure yields three conclusions:

■ Consumption and investment usually move together: Recessions, for example, are typically associated with decreases in *both* investment and consumption. Given our discussion, which has emphasized that consumption and investment depend largely on the same determinants, this should not come as a surprise.

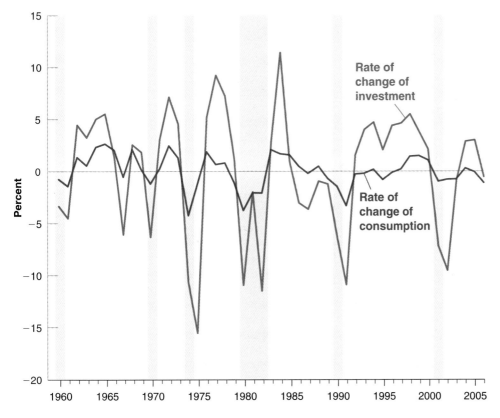

Figure 16-4 ▦

Rates of Change of Consumption and Investment since 1960

Relative movements in investment are much larger than relative movements in consumption.

> Relative movements in *I* are larger than relative movements in *C*. But, because *I* accounts only for 16% of GDP and *C* accounts for 70%, absolute movements in *I* and *C* are of roughly equal magnitude. ▶

■ Investment is much more volatile than consumption. Relative movements in investment range from –16% to 12%, while relative movements in consumption range only from –4% to 3%.

■ Because the level of investment is much smaller than the level of consumption (recall that investment accounts for 16% of GDP versus 70% for consumption), changes in investment from one year to the next end up being of the same overall magnitude as changes in consumption. In other words, both components contribute roughly equally to fluctuations in output over time.

Summary

■ Consumption depends on both wealth and current income. Wealth is the sum of nonhuman wealth (financial wealth and housing wealth) and human wealth (the present value of expected after-tax labor income).

■ The response of consumption to changes in income depends on whether consumers perceive these changes as transitory or permanent.

■ Consumption is likely to respond less than one-for-one to movements in income. Consumption might move even if current income does not change.

■ Investment depends on both current profit and the present value of expected future profits.

■ Under the simplifying assumption that firms expect profits and interest rates to be the same in the future as they are today, we can think of investment as depending on the ratio of profit to the user cost of capital, where the user cost is the sum of the real interest rate and the depreciation rate.

■ Movements in profit are closely related to movements in output. Hence, we can think of investment as depending indirectly on current and expected future output movements. Firms that anticipate a long output expansion, and thus a long sequence of high profits, will invest. Movements in output that are not expected to last will have a small effect on investment.

■ Investment is much more volatile than consumption. But, because investment accounts only for 16% of GDP and consumption accounts for 70%, movements in investment and consumption are of roughly equal magnitude.

Key Terms

- permanent income theory of consumption, 358
- life cycle theory of consumption, 358
- financial wealth, 358
- housing wealth, 358
- human wealth, 358
- nonhuman wealth, 358
- total wealth, 358

- panel data sets, 359
- Tobin's *q*, 367
- static expectations, 368
- user cost of capital, or rental cost of capital, 368
- profitability, 370
- cash flow, 370

Questions and Problems

Quick Check

1. Using the information in this chapter, label each of the following statements true, false, or uncertain. Explain briefly.

a. For a typical college student, human wealth and nonhuman wealth are approximately equal.

b. Natural experiments, such as retirement, do not suggest that expectations of future income are a major factor affecting consumption.

c. Buildings and factories depreciate much faster than machines do.

d. A high value for Tobin's q indicates that the stock market believes that capital is overvalued, and thus investment should be lower.

e. Economists have found that the effect of current profit on investment can be fully explained by the effect of current profit on expectations of future profits.

f. Data from the past three decades in the United States suggest that corporate profits are closely tied to the business cycle.

g. Changes in consumption and investment typically occur in the same direction and at roughly the same magnitude.

2. A pretzel manufacturer is considering buying another pretzel-making machine that costs $100,000. The machine will depreciate by 8% per year. It will generate real profits equal to $18,000 next year, $18,000(1 – 8%) two years from now (that is, the same real profits but adjusted for depreciation), $18,000(1 – 8%)^2 three years from now, and so on. Determine whether the manufacturer should buy the machine if the real interest rate is assumed to remain constant at each rate in (a) through (c).

  a. 5%

  b. 10%

  c. 15%

3. Suppose that at age 21, you have just finished college and have been offered a job with a starting salary of $45,000. Your salary will remain constant in real terms. However, you have also been admitted to a professional school. The school can be completed in two years. Upon graduation, you expect your starting salary to be 10% higher in real terms and to remain constant in real terms thereafter. The tax rate on labor income is 30%.

  a. If the real interest rate is zero and you expect to retire at age 59 (i.e., if you do not go to professional school, you expect to work for 38 years total), what is the maximum you should be willing to pay in tuition to attend this professional school?

  b. What is your answer to part (a) if you expect to pay 25% in taxes?

4. A consumer has nonhuman wealth equal to $100,000. She earns $40,000 this year and expects her salary to rise by 5% in real terms each year for the following two years. She will then retire. The real interest rate is equal to 0% and is expected to remain at 0% in the future. Labor income is taxed at a rate of 25%.

  a. What is this consumer's human wealth?

  b. What is her total wealth?

  c. If she expects to live for seven more years after retiring and wants her consumption to remain the same (in real terms) every year from now on, how much can she consume this year?

  d. If she received a bonus of $20,000 in the current year only, with all future salary payments remaining as stated earlier, by how much could this consumer increase consumption now and in the future?

  e. Suppose now that at retirement, Social Security will start paying benefits each year equal to 60% of this consumer's earnings during her last working year. Assume that benefits are not taxed. How much can she consume this year and still maintain constant consumption over her lifetime?

Dig Deeper

5. Individual saving and aggregate capital accumulation

    Suppose that every consumer is born with zero financial wealth and lives for three periods: youth, middle age, and old age. Consumers work in the first two periods and retire in the last one. Their income is $5 in the first period, $25 in the second, and $0 in the last one. Inflation and expected inflation are equal to zero, and so is the real interest rate.

  a. What is the present discounted value of labor income at the beginning of life? What is the highest sustainable level of consumption such that consumption is equal in all three periods?

  b. For each age group, what is the amount of saving that allows consumers to maintain the constant level of consumption you found in part (a)? (*Hint*: Saving can be a negative number if the consumer needs to borrow in order to maintain a certain level of consumption.)

  c. Suppose there are *n* people born each period. What is total saving in the economy? (*Hint*: Add up the saving of each age group. Remember that some age groups may have negative saving.) Explain.

  d. What is total financial wealth in the economy? (*Hint*: Compute the financial wealth of people at the beginning of the first period of life, the beginning of the second period, and the beginning of the third period. Add the three numbers. Remember that people can be in debt, so financial wealth can be negative.)

6. Borrowing constraints and aggregate capital accumulation

    Continue with the setup from problem 5 but suppose now that restrictions on borrowing do not allow young consumers to borrow. If we call the sum of income and total financial wealth "cash on hand," then the borrowing restriction means that consumers cannot consume more than their cash on hand. In each age group, consumers compute their total wealth and then determine their desired level of consumption as the highest level that allows their consumption to be equal in all three periods. However, if at any time, desired consumption exceeds cash on hand, then consumers are constrained to consume exactly their cash on hand.

  a. Calculate consumption in each period of life. Compare this answer to your answer to part (a) of problem 5, and explain any differences.

  b. Calculate total saving for the economy. Compare this answer to your answer to part (c) of problem 5, and explain any differences.

  c. Derive total financial wealth for the economy. Compare this answer to your answer to part (d) of problem 5, and explain any differences.

  d. Consider the following statement: "Financial liberalization may be good for individual consumers, but it is bad for overall capital accumulation." Discuss.

7. Saving with uncertain future income.

    Consider a consumer who lives for three periods: youth, middle age, and old age. When young, the consumer earns $20,000 in labor income. Earnings during middle age are uncertain; there is a 50% chance that the consumer will earn $40,000 and a 50% change that the consumer will earn $100,000. When old, the consumer spends savings accumulated during the previous periods. Assume that *inflation, expected inflation, and the real interest rate equal zero. Ignore taxes for this problem.*

a. What is the expected value of earnings in the middle period of life? Given this number, what is the present discounted value of expected lifetime labor earnings? If the consumer wishes to maintain constant expected consumption over her lifetime, how much will she consume in each period? How much will she save in each period?

b. Now suppose the consumer wishes, above all else, to maintain a minimum consumption level of $20,000 in each period of her life. To do so, she must consider the worst outcome. If earnings during middle age turn out to be $40,000, how much should the consumer spend when she is young to guarantee consumption of at least $20,000 in each period? How does this level of consumption compare to the level you obtained for the young period in part (a)?

c. Given your answer in part (b), suppose that the consumer's earnings during middle age turn out to be $100,000. How much will she spend in each period of life? Will consumption be constant over the consumer's lifetime? (*Hint:* When the consumer reaches middle age, she will try to maintain constant consumption for the last two periods of life, as long as she can consume at least $20,000 in each period.)

d. What effect does uncertainty about future labor income have on saving (or borrowing) by young consumers?

Explore Further

8. *The movements of consumption and investment*

Go to the latest *Economic Report of the President* (**www.gpoaccess.gov/eop/**) *and find Table B-2 ("Real GDP") in the Statistical Appendix. Note that you can download the statistical appendix separately in a spreadsheet, which will be easier to work with than a PDF file.*

Retrieve annual data for the years 1959 to the present date for personal consumption expenditures and gross private domestic investment. Note that the data are in real terms.

a. On average, how much larger is consumption than investment?

b. Compute the change in the levels of consumption and investment from one year to the next, and graph them for the period 1959 to the present date. Are the year-to-year changes in consumption and investment of similar magnitude?

c. What do your answers in parts (a) and (b) imply about the average annual percentage changes of consumption and investment? Is this implication consistent with Figure 16-4?

9. *Consumer confidence and disposable income*

Go to the Web site of the University of Michigan Survey of Consumers (**www.sca.isr.umich.edu**), and download data on the quarterly Index of Consumer Sentiment from 1960 to the present day. We will use this data series as our measure of consumer confidence. Now, go to the Web site of the Bureau of Economic Analysis (**www.bea.gov**), and find the quarterly version of Table 2-1. The last row of the table gives the percentage change in real personal disposable income. (The quarterly percentage changes are annualized.) Obtain this data for 1960 to the present day.

a. Before you look at the data, can you think of any reasons to expect consumer confidence to be related to disposable income? Can you think of reasons why consumer confidence would be unrelated to disposable income?

b. Calculate the average quarterly percentage change in personal disposable income over the entire period, and subtract this average from each quarterly observation of the percentage change in personal disposable income. Use this new data series as your measure of the quarterly change in personal disposable income. Now calculate the quarterly change in consumer confidence as the quarter-to-quarter change in the Index of Consumer Sentiment. Plot the change in consumer confidence against the change in personal disposable income (the measure you constructed in this part). Is there a clear relation (positive or negative) between the two variables? If you believe there is a relation, is it very tight? In other words, are there many observations that deviate greatly from the average relation?

c. Look at the data for the third quarter of 2001 and the first quarter of 2002. What happened to personal disposable income during these two quarters? What happened to consumer confidence? Why do you think consumer confidence behaved differently in these two time periods?

 We invite you to visit the Blanchard page on the Prentice Hall Web site, at:
www.prenhall.com/blanchard
for this chapter's World Wide Web exercises.

Appendix: Derivation of the Expected Present Value of Profits under Static Expectations

You saw in equation (16.3) that the expected present value of profits is given by

$$V(\Pi_t^e) = \frac{1}{1 + r_t}\Pi_{t+1}^e + \frac{1}{(1 + r_t)(1 + r_{t+1}^e)}(1 - \delta)\Pi_{t+2}^e + \ldots$$

If firms expect both future profits (per unit of capital) and future interest rates to remain at the same level as today, so that $\Pi_{t+1}^e = \Pi_{t+2}^e = \ldots = \Pi_t$, and $r_{t+1}^e = r_{t+2}^e = \ldots = r_t$, the equation becomes

$$V(\Pi_t^e) = \frac{1}{1 + r_t}\Pi_t + \frac{1}{(1 + r_t)^2}(1 - \delta)\Pi_t + \ldots$$

Factoring out $[1/(1 + r_t)]\Pi_t$,

$$V(\Pi_t^e) = \frac{1}{1 + r_t}\Pi_t\left(1 - \frac{1 - \delta}{1 + r_t} + \ldots\right) \qquad (16.A1)$$

The term in parentheses in this equation is a geometric series, a series of the form $1 + x + x^2 + \ldots$. So, from Proposition 2 in Appendix 2 at the end of the book

$$(1 + x + x^2 + \ldots) = \frac{1}{1 - x}$$

Here x equals $(1 - \delta)/(1 + r_t)$, so

$$\left(1 + \frac{1 - \delta}{1 + r_t} + \left(\frac{1 - \delta}{1 + r_t}\right)^2 + \ldots\right) = \frac{1}{1 - (1 - \delta)/(1 + r_t)}$$
$$= \frac{1 + r_t}{r_t + \delta}$$

Replacing in equation (16. A1) gives

$$V(\Pi_t^e) = \frac{1}{1 + r_t}\frac{1 + r_t}{r_t + \delta}\Pi_t$$

Simplifying gives equation (16.5) in the text:

$$V(\Pi_t^e) = \frac{\Pi_t}{(r_t + \delta)}$$

Expectations, Output, and Policy

n Chapter 15, we looked at how expectations affect bond and stock prices. In Chapter 16, we examined how expectations affect consumption decisions and investment decisions. In this chapter, we put together the pieces and take another look at the effects of monetary and fiscal policy:

■ Section 17-1 draws the major implication of what we have learned, namely that expectations of both future output and future interest rates affect current spending and therefore current output.

■ Section 17-2 looks at monetary policy. It shows how the effects of monetary policy depend crucially on how expectations respond to policy: Monetary policy directly affects only the short-term interest rate. What happens to spending and output then depends on how changes in the short-term interest rate lead people and firms to change their expectations of future interest rates and future income, and, by implication, lead them to change their decisions.

■ Section 17-3 turns to fiscal policy. It shows how, in sharp contrast to the simple model you saw in the core, a fiscal contraction may, under some circumstances, lead to an increase in output, even in the short run. Again, how expectations respond to policy is central to the story. ■

CHAPTER 17

Let's review what we have learned, and then examine how we should modify the characterization of goods and financial markets—the *IS–LM* model—we developed in the core.

Expectations, Consumption, and Investment Decisions

The theme of Chapter 16 was that both consumption and investment decisions depend very much on expectations of future income and interest rates. The channels through which expectations affect consumption and investment spending are summarized in Figure 17-1.

Note the many channels through which expected future variables affect current decisions, both directly and through asset prices:

- An increase in current and expected future after-tax real labor income and/or a decrease in current and expected future real interest rates increase human wealth (the expected present discounted value of after-tax real labor income), which in turn leads to an increase in consumption.

- An increase in current and expected future real dividends and/or a decrease in current and expected future real interest rates increase stock prices, which lead to an increase in nonhuman wealth and, in turn, to an increase in consumption.

- A decrease in current and expected future nominal interest rates leads to an increase in bond prices, which leads to an increase in nonhuman wealth and, in turn, to an increase in consumption.

- An increase in current and expected future real after-tax profits and/or a decrease in current and expected future real interest rates increase the present value of real after-tax profits, which leads, in turn, to an increase in investment.

> Note that in the case of bonds, it is nominal rather than real interest rates which matter because bonds are claims to dollars rather than goods in the future. ▶

Expectations and the *IS* Relation

A model that gave a detailed treatment of consumption and investment along the lines suggested in Figure 17-1 would be very complicated. It can be done—and indeed it is done in the large empirical models that macroeconomists build to understand the economy and analyze policy; but this is not the place for such complication. We want to capture the essence of what you have learned so far, how consumption and investment depend on expectations of the future—without getting lost in the details.

■ Figure 17-1

Expectations and Spending: The Channels

Expectations affect consumption and investment decisions, both directly and through asset prices.

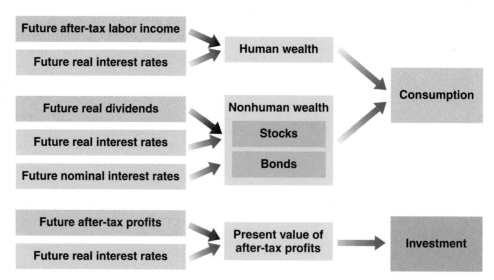

To do so, let me make a major simplification. Let me reduce the present and the future to only two periods: (1) a *current* period, which you can think of as the current year and (2) a *future* period, which you can think of as all future years lumped together. This way, we do not have to keep track of expectations about each future year.

Having made this assumption, the question becomes: How should we write the *IS* relation for the current period? Earlier, we wrote the following equation for the *IS* relation:

$$Y = C(Y - T) + I(Y, r) + G$$

We assumed that consumption depended only on current income and that investment depended only on current output and the current real interest rate. We now want to modify this to take into account how expectations affect both consumption and investment. We proceed in two steps.

First, we simply rewrite the equation in more compact form, but without changing its content. For that purpose, let's define aggregate private spending as the sum of consumption and investment spending:

$$A(Y, T, r) \equiv C(Y - T) + I(Y, r)$$

where *A* stands for **aggregate private spending**, or, simply, **private spending**. With this notation, we can rewrite the *IS* relation as

$$Y = A(Y,\ T,\ r) + G$$
$$(+, -, -) \qquad\qquad (17.1)$$

The properties of aggregate private spending, *A*, follow from the properties of consumption and investment that we derived in earlier chapters:

- Aggregate private spending is an increasing function of income, *Y*: Higher income (equivalently, output) increases consumption and investment.
- Aggregate private spending is a decreasing function of taxes, *T*: Higher taxes decrease consumption.
- Aggregate private spending is a decreasing function of the real interest rate, *r*: A higher real interest rate decreases investment.

The first step only simplified notation. The second step is to extend equation (17.1) to take into account the role of expectations. The natural extension is to allow spending to depend not only on current variables but also on their expected values in the future period:

$$Y = A(Y, T, r, Y'^e, T'^e, r'^e) + G$$
$$(+, -, -, +,\ -,\ -) \qquad\qquad (17.2)$$

Primes denote future values, and the superscript *e* denotes an expectation, so Y'^e, T'^e, and r'^e denote future expected income, future expected taxes, and the future expected real interest rate, respectively. The notation is a bit heavy, but what it captures is straightforward:

- Increases in either current or expected future income increase private spending.
- Increases in either current or expected future taxes decrease private spending.
- Increases in either the current or expected future real interest rate decrease private spending.

With the goods market equilibrium now given by equation (17.2), Figure 17-2 shows the new *IS* curve for the current period. As usual, to draw the curve, we take all

This way of dividing time between "today" and "later" is the way many of us organize our lives: Think of "things to do today" versus "things that can wait."

See the equation for the *IS* relation on p. 296 in Chapter 14, which itself extended equation (5.2) in Chapter 5 to allow for a distinction between the real and nominal interest rates.

The reason for doing this is to group together the two components of demand, *C* and *I*, that both depend on expectations. We continue to treat *G*, government spending, as exogenous—unexplained within our model.

Notation:
Primes stand for values of the variables in the future period. The superscript *e* stands for "expected."

Y or Y'^e increases $\Rightarrow$ *A* increases

T or T'^e increases $\Rightarrow$ *A* decreases

r or r'^e increases $\Rightarrow$ *A* decreases

The New IS Curve

Given expectations, a decrease
in the real interest rate leads to
a small increase in output: The
IS curve is steeply downward
sloping. Increases in government spending or in expected
future output shift the IS curve to
the right. Increases in taxes, in
expected future taxes, or in the
expected future real interest rate
shift the IS curve to the left.

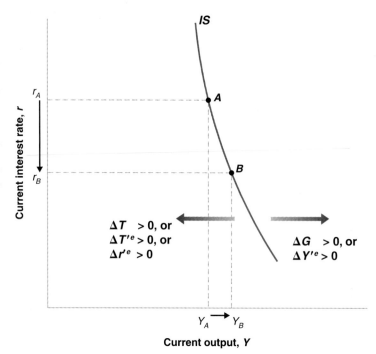

variables other than current output, Y, and the current real interest rate, r, as given.
Thus, the IS curve is drawn for given values of current and future expected taxes, T and
T'^e, for given values of expected future output, Y'^e, and for given values of the expected
future real interest rate, r'^e.

The new IS curve, based on equation (17.2), is still downward sloping, for the same
reason as in Chapter 5: A decrease in the current real interest rate leads to an increase
in spending. This increase in spending leads, through a multiplier effect, to an
increase in output. We can say more, however: The new IS curve is much steeper than
the IS curve we drew in earlier chapters. Put another way, *everything else the same*, a
large decrease in the current interest rate is likely to have only a small effect on equilibrium output.

To see why the effect is small, take point A on the IS curve in Figure 17-2, and
consider the effects of a decrease in the real interest rate, from r_A to r_B. The effect of the
decrease in the real interest rate on output depends on the strength of two effects: the
effect of the real interest rate on spending given income and the size of the multiplier.
Let's examine each one:

Suppose you have a 30-year
loan, and the one-year interest
rate goes down from 5% to
2%. All future one-year rates
remain the same. By how much
will the 30-year interest rate
come down? (Answer: from 5%
to 4.9%. If you got the answer
wrong, go back to the discussion of the relation between
short-term interest rates and
long-term interest rates in
Chapter 15.)   ▶

■ A decrease in the current real interest rate, *given unchanged expectations of the
future real interest rate*, does not have much effect on spending. We saw why in the
previous chapters: A change in only the current real interest rate does not lead to
large changes in present values and, therefore, does not lead to large changes in
spending. For example, firms are not likely to change their investment plans very
much in response to a decrease in the current real interest rate if they do not
expect future real interest rates to be lower as well.

■ The multiplier is likely to be small. Recall that the size of the multiplier depends
on the size of the effect a change in current income (output) has on spending. But
a change in current income, *given unchanged expectations of future income*, is
unlikely to have a large effect on spending. The reason: Changes in income that
are not expected to last have only a limited effect on either consumption or

investment. Consumers who expect their income to be higher only for a year will increase consumption—but by much less than the increase in their income. Firms that expect sales to be higher only for a year are unlikely to change their investment plans much, if at all.

Suppose a firm decides to give all employees a one-time bonus of $10,000. The employees do not expect it to happen again. By how much will they increase their consumption this year? (If you need to, look at the discussion of consumption behavior in Chapter 16.)

Putting things together, a large decrease in the current real interest rate—from r_A to r_B in Figure 17-2—leads to only a small increase in output, from Y_A to Y_B. Put another way: The *IS* curve, which goes through points *A* and *B*, is steeply downward sloping.

A change in any variable in equation (17.2) other than Y and r shifts the *IS* curve:

- Changes in current taxes, T, or in current government spending, G, shift the *IS* curve.
   An increase in current government spending increases spending at a given interest rate, shifting the *IS* curve to the right; an increase in taxes shifts the *IS* curve to the left. These shifts are represented in Figure 17-2.
- Changes in expected future variables also shift the *IS* curve.
   An increase in expected future output, Y'^e, shifts the *IS* curve to the right: Higher expected future income leads consumers to feel wealthier and spend more; higher expected future output implies higher expected profits, leading firms to invest more. Higher spending by consumers and firms leads, through the multiplier effect, to higher output. Similarly, an increase in expected future taxes leads consumers to decrease their current spending and shifts the *IS* curve to the left. And an increase in the expected future real interest rate decreases current spending, also leading to a decrease in output, shifting the *IS* curve to the left. These shifts are also represented in Figure 17-2.

The LM Relation Revisited

The *LM* relation we derived in Chapter 4 and have used until now was given by

$$\frac{M}{P} = Y L(i) \qquad (17.3)$$

where *M/P* is the supply of money, and $Y L(i)$ is the demand for money. Equilibrium in financial markets required that the supply of money be equal to the demand for money. The demand for money depended on real income and on the short-term nominal interest rate—the opportunity cost of holding money. We derived this demand for money before thinking about expectations. Now that we have thought about them, the question is whether we should modify equation (17.3). The answer—I am sure this will be good news—is no.

Think of your own demand for money. How much money you want to hold today depends on your *current* level of transactions, not on the level of transactions you expect next year or the year after; there will be ample time for you to adjust your money balances to your transaction level if and when it changes in the future. And the opportunity cost of holding money today depends on the *current* nominal interest rate, not on the expected nominal interest rate next year or the year after. If short-term interest rates were to increase in the future, increasing the opportunity cost of holding money then, the time to reduce your money balances would be then, not now.

So, in contrast to the consumption decision, the decision about how much money to hold is myopic, depending primarily on current income and the current short-term nominal interest rate. We can still think of the demand for money as depending on the current level of output and the current nominal interest rate, and we can use equation (17.3) to describe the determination of the nominal interest rate in the current period.

Let's summarize. We have seen that expectations about the future play a major role in spending decisions. This implies that expectations enter the *IS* relation: Private spending depends not only on current output and the current real interest rate but also on expected future output and the expected future real interest rate. In contrast, the decision about how much money to hold is largely myopic: The two variables entering the *LM* relation are still current income and the current nominal interest rate.

17-2 Monetary Policy, Expectations, and Output

In the basic *IS–LM* model we developed in Chapter 5, there was only one interest rate, *i*, which entered both the *IS* relation and the *LM* relation. When the Fed expanded the money supply, "the" interest rate went down, and spending increased. From the previous three chapters, you have learned that there are in fact many interest rates and that we must keep two distinctions in mind:

1. The distinction between the nominal interest rate and the real interest rate

2. The distinction between current and expected future interest rates

The interest rate that enters the *LM* relation, which is the interest rate that the Fed affects directly, is the *current nominal interest rate*. In contrast, spending in the *IS* relation depends on both *current and expected future real interest rates*. Economists sometimes state this distinction even more starkly by saying that, while the Fed controls the *short-term nominal interest rate*, what matters for spending and output is the *long-term real interest rate*. Let's look at this distinction more closely.

From the Short Nominal Rate to Current and Expected Real Rates

Expected current inflation: inflation expected, as of today, for the current period (the current year).

Recall from Chapter 14 that the real interest rate is approximately equal to the nominal interest rate minus expected current inflation:

$$r = i - \pi^e$$

Expected future inflation: inflation expected, as of today, for the future period (all future years).

Similarly, the expected future real interest rate is approximately equal to the expected future nominal interest rate minus expected future inflation:

$$r'^e = i'^e - \pi'^e$$

When the Fed increases the money supply—decreasing the current nominal interest rate, *i*—the effects on the current and the expected future real interest rates depend on two factors:

We explored the role of changing expectations of inflation on the relation between the nominal interest rate and the real interest rate in Chapter 14. Leaving changes in expected inflation aside will keep the analysis simpler here. You have, however, all the elements you need to think through what would happen if we also allowed expectations of current inflation and future inflation to adjust. How would these expectations adjust? Would this lead to a larger or a smaller effect on output in the current period?

■ Whether the increase in the money supply leads financial markets to revise their expectations of the future nominal interest rate, i'^e.
■ Whether the increase in the money supply leads financial markets to revise their expectations of both current and future inflation, π^e and π'^e. If, for example, the change in money leads financial markets to expect more inflation in the future—so π'^e increases—the expected future real interest rate, r'^e, will decrease by more than the expected future nominal interest rate, i'^e.

To keep things simple, I shall ignore here the second factor—the role of changing expectations of inflation—and focus on the first—the role of changing expectations of the future nominal interest rate. Thus I shall assume that expected current inflation and expected future inflation are both equal to 0. In this case, we do not need to distinguish between the nominal interest rate and the real interest rate, as they are equal, and we can use the same letter to denote both. Let *r* denote the current real (and nominal) interest rate, and let r'^e denote the expected future real (and nominal) interest rate.

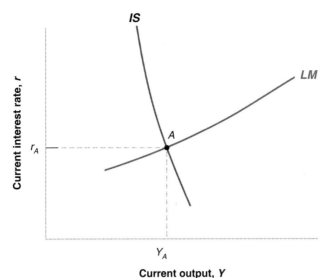

Figure 17-3

The New IS–LM

The *IS* curve is steeply downward sloping. Other things equal, a change in the current interest rate has a small effect on output. The *LM* curve is upward sloping. The equilibrium is at the intersection of the *IS* and *LM* curves.

With this simplification, we can rewrite the *IS* and *LM* relations in equations (17.2) and (17.3) as

◄ The *IS* relation is the same as equation (**17.2**). The *LM* relation is now in terms of the real interest rate—which, here, is equal to the nominal interest rate.

$$IS: \quad Y = A(Y, T, r, Y'^e, T'^e, r'^e) + G \quad\quad (17.4)$$

$$LM: \quad \frac{M}{P} = YL(r) \quad\quad (17.5)$$

The corresponding *IS* and *LM* curves are drawn in Figure 17-3. The vertical axis measures the current interest rate, r; the horizontal axis measures current output, Y. The *IS* curve is steeply downward sloping. We saw the reason earlier: For given expectations, a change in the current interest rate has a limited effect on spending, and the multiplier is small. The *LM* is upward sloping: An increase in income leads to an increase in the demand for money; given the supply of money, the result is an increase in the interest rate. Equilibrium in goods and financial markets implies that the economy is at point *A*, on both the *IS* and the *LM* curves.

There is no need to distinguish ► here between the real interest rate and the nominal interest rate: Given 0 expected inflation, they are the same.

Monetary Policy Revisited

Now suppose the economy is in recession, and the Fed decides to increase the money supply.

Assume first that this expansionary monetary policy does not change expectations of either the future interest rate or future output. In Figure 17-4, the *LM* curve shifts down, from *LM* to *LM"*. (Because I have already used primes to denote future values of the variables, I use double primes, such as in *LM"*, to denote shifts in curves in this chapter.) The equilibrium moves from point *A* to point *B*, with higher output and a lower interest rate. The steep *IS* curve, however, implies that the increase in the money supply has only a small effect on output: Changes in the current interest rate, unaccompanied by changes in expectations, have only a small effect on spending and, in turn, a small effect on output.

Given expectations, an increase in the money supply leads to a shift in the *LM* curve and a movement down the steep *IS* curve. The result is a large decrease in r and a small ◄ increase in Y.

Is it reasonable, however, to assume that expectations are unaffected by an expansionary monetary policy? Isn't it likely that, as the Fed lowers the current interest rate, financial markets now anticipate lower interest rates in the future as well,

The Effects of an Expansionary Monetary Policy

The effects of monetary policy on output depend very much on whether and how monetary policy affects expectations.

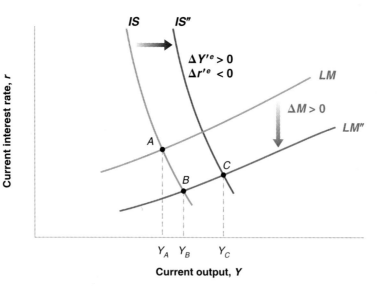

If the increase in money leads to an increase in Y'^e and a decrease in r^e, the IS curve shifts to the right, leading to a larger increase in Y.

This is why macroeconomists ▶ working on monetary policy often argue that the task of a central bank is not only to adjust the short-term nominal interest rate but also to "manage expectations" so as to lead to predictable effects of changes in this interest rate on the economy. More on this in Chapter 25.

along with higher future output stimulated by this lower future interest rate? What happens if they do? At a given current interest rate, prospects of a lower future interest rate and of higher future output both increase spending and output; they shift the IS curve to the right, from IS to IS". The new equilibrium is given by point C. Thus, while the direct effect of the monetary expansion on output is limited, the full effect, once changes in expectations are taken into account, is much larger.

You have just learned an important lesson: The effects of monetary policy—the effects of any type of macroeconomic policy, for that matter—depend crucially on its ▶ effect on expectations:

■ If a monetary expansion leads financial investors, firms, and consumers to revise their expectations of future interest rates and output, then the effects of the monetary expansion on output may be very large.
■ If expectations remain unchanged, the effects of the monetary expansion on output will be small.

We can link this discussion to our discussion in Chapter 15 about the effects of changes in monetary policy in the stock market. Many of the same issues were present there. If, when the change in monetary policy takes place, it comes as no surprise to investors, firms, and consumers, then expectations will not change. The stock market will react only a little, if at all. And demand and output will change only a little, if at all. But if the change comes as a surprise and is expected to last, expectations of future output will go up, expectations of future interest rates will come down, the stock market will boom, and output will increase.

At this stage, you may have become very skeptical that macroeconomists can say much about the effects of policy, or the effects of other shocks: If the effects depend so much on what happens to expectations, can macroeconomists have any hope of predicting what will happen? The answer is yes.

Saying that the effect of a particular policy depends on its effect on expectations is not the same as saying that anything can happen. Expectations are not arbitrary. The manager of a mutual fund who must decide whether to invest in stocks or bonds, the firm thinking about whether to build a new plant, the consumer thinking about how much she should save for retirement, all give a lot of thought to what might happen in the future. We can think of each of them as forming expectations

Most macroeconomists today routinely solve their models under the assumption of rational expectations. This was not always the case. The past 35 years in macroeconomic research are often called the "rational expectations revolution."

The importance of expectations is an old theme in macroeconomics. But until the early 1970s, macroeconomists thought of expectations in one of two ways:

■ One was as **animal spirits** (from an expression Keynes introduced in the *General Theory* to refer to movements in investment that could not be explained by movements in current variables). In other words, shifts in expectations were considered important but were left unexplained.

■ The other was as the result of simple, backward-looking rules. For example, people were often assumed to have static expectations—that is, to expect the future to be like the present (we used this assumption when discussing the Phillips curve in Chapter 8 and when exploring investment decisions in Chapter 16). Or people were assumed to have **adaptive expectations**: If, for example, their forecast of a given variable in a given period turned out to be too low, people were assumed to "adapt" by raising their expectation for the value of the variable for the following period. For example, seeing an inflation rate higher than they had expected led people to revise upward their forecast of inflation in the future.

In the early 1970s, a group of macroeconomists led by Robert Lucas (at the University of Chicago) and Thomas Sargent (then at the University of Chicago, and now at New York University) argued that these assumptions did not reflect the way people form expectations. (Robert Lucas received the Nobel Prize in 1995 for his work on expectations.) They argued that, in thinking about the effects of alternative policies, economists should assume that people have rational expectations, that people look into the future and do the best job they can in predicting it. This is not the same as assuming that people know the future, but rather that they use the information they have in the best possible way.

Using the popular macroeconomic models of the time, Lucas and Sargent showed how replacing traditional assumptions about expectations formation by the assumption of rational expectations could fundamentally alter the results. We saw, for example, in Chapter 9 how Lucas challenged the notion that disinflation necessarily required an increase in unemployment for some time. Under rational expectations, he argued, a credible disinflation policy might be able to decrease inflation without any increase in unemployment. More generally, Lucas' and Sargent's research showed the need for a complete rethinking of macroeconomic models under the assumption of rational expectations, and this is what happened over the next two decades.

Most macroeconomists today use rational expectations as a working assumption in their models and analyses of policy. This is not because they believe that people always have rational expectations. Surely there are times when people, firms, or financial market participants lose sight of reality and become too optimistic or too pessimistic. (Recall our discussion of the Internet bubble in Chapter 15.) But these are more the exception than the rule, and it is not clear that economists can say much about those times anyway. When thinking about the likely effects of a particular economic policy, the best assumption to make seems to be that financial markets, people, and firms will do the best they can to work out its implications. Designing a policy on the assumption that people will make systematic mistakes in responding to it is unwise.

So why did it take until the 1970s for rational expectations to become a standard assumption in macroeconomics? Largely because of technical problems. Under rational expectations, what happens today depends on expectations of what will happen in the future. But what happens in the future also depends on what happens today. Solving such models is hard. The success of Lucas and Sargent in convincing most macroeconomists to use rational expectations comes not only from the strength of their case but also from showing how it could actually be done. Much progress has been made since in developing solution methods for larger and larger models. Today, a number of large macroeconometric models are solved under the assumption of rational expectations. (The simulation of the Taylor model presented in the Focus box on monetary policy in Chapter 7 was derived under rational expectations. You will see another example in Chapter 24.)

about the future by assessing the likely course of future expected policy and then working out the implications for future activity. If they do not do it themselves (surely most of us do not spend our time solving macroeconomic models before making decisions), they do so indirectly by watching TV and reading newsletters and newspapers, which in turn rely on the forecasts of public and private forecasters.

Economists refer to expectations formed in this forward-looking manner as **rational expectations**. The introduction of the assumption of rational expectations is one of the most important developments in macroeconomics in the past 35 years. It has largely shaped the way macroeconomists think about policy. It is discussed further in the Focus box "Rational Expectations."

We could go back and think about the implications of rational expectations in the case of a monetary expansion we have just studied. It will be more fun to do this in the context of a change in fiscal policy, and this is what we now turn to.

17-3 Deficit Reduction, Expectations, and Output

Recall the conclusions we reached in the core about the effects of a budget deficit reduction:

We discussed the short-run and medium-run effects of changes in fiscal policy in Section 7-5. We discussed the long-run effects of changes in fiscal policy in Section 11-2. ▶

■ In the long run, a reduction in the budget deficit is likely to be beneficial for the economy. In the medium run, a lower budget deficit implies higher saving and higher investment. In the long run, higher investment translates into higher capital and thus higher output.

■ In the short run, however, a reduction in the budget deficit, unless it is offset by a monetary expansion, leads to lower spending and to a contraction in output.

It is this adverse short-run effect which—in addition to the unpopularity of increases in taxes and reductions in government programs—often deters governments from tackling their budget deficits: Why take the risk of a recession now for benefits that will accrue only in the future?

In the recent past, however, a number of economists have argued that a deficit reduction might actually increase output even in the *short run*. Their argument: If people take into account the future beneficial effects of deficit reduction, their expectations about the future might improve enough to lead to an increase—rather than a decrease—in current spending, thereby increasing current output. This section presents their argument more formally. The Focus box "Can a Budget Deficit Reduction Lead to an Output Expansion? Ireland in the 1980s" reviews some of the supporting evidence.

Assume that the economy is described by equation (17.4) for the *IS* relation and equation (17.5) for the *LM* relation. Now suppose the government announces a program to reduce the deficit, through decreases both in current spending, G, and in future spending, G^e. What will happen to output *this period*?

The Role of Expectations about the Future

Suppose first that expectations of future output, Y'^e, and of the future interest rate, r'^e, do not change. Then, we get the standard answer: The decrease in government spending in the current period leads to a shift of the *IS* curve to the left and so to a decrease in equilibrium output.

The crucial question, therefore, is what happens to expectations. To answer, let us go back to what we learned in the core about the effects of a deficit reduction in the medium run and the long run:

■ In the medium run, a deficit reduction has no effect on output. It leads, however, to a lower interest rate and to higher investment. These were two of the main lessons of Chapter 7.

Let's review the logic behind each one:

Recall that, when we look at the medium run, we ignore the effects of capital accumulation on output. So, in the medium run, the natural level of output depends on the level of productivity (taken as given) and on the natural level of employment. The natural level of employment depends in turn on the natural rate of unemployment. If spending by the government on goods and services does not affect the natural rate of unemployment—and there is no obvious reason why it should—then changes in spending will not affect the natural level of output. Therefore, a deficit reduction has no effect on the level of output in the medium run.

Now recall that output must be equal to spending and that spending is the sum of public spending and private spending. Given that output is unchanged and that public spending is lower, private spending must therefore be higher. Higher private spending requires a lower equilibrium interest rate. The lower interest rate leads to higher investment and thus to higher private spending, which offsets the decrease in public spending and leaves output unchanged.

◀ In the medium run: Output, Y, does not change, and investment, I, is higher.

- In the long run—that is, taking into account the effects of capital accumulation on output—higher investment leads to a higher capital stock, and, therefore, a higher level of output.

◀ In the long run: I increases $\Rightarrow K$ increases $\Rightarrow Y$ increases.

This was the main lesson of Chapter 11. The higher the proportion of output saved (or invested; investment and saving must be equal for the goods market to be in equilibrium in a closed economy), the higher the capital stock and thus the higher the level of output in the long run.

We can think of our *future period* as including both the medium run and the long run. If people, firms, and financial market participants have *rational expectations*, then, in response to the announcement of a deficit reduction, they will expect these developments to take place in the future. Thus, they will revise their expectation of future output, Y'^e, up, and their expectation of the future interest rate, r'^e, down.

The way this is likely to happen: Forecasts by economists will show that these lower deficits are likely to lead to higher output and lower interest rates in the future. In response to these forecasts, long-term interest rates will decrease, and the ◀ stock market will increase. People and firms, reading these forecasts and looking at bond and stock prices, will revise their spending plans and increase spending.

Back to the Current Period

We can now return to the question of what happens *this period* in response to the announcement and start of the deficit reduction program. Figure 17-5 draws the *IS*

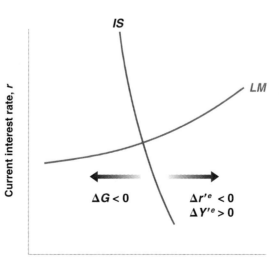

Figure 17-5 ▨

The Effects of a Deficit Reduction on Current Output

When account is taken of its effect on expectations, the decrease in government spending need not lead to a decrease in output.

Ireland went through two major deficit reduction programs in the 1980s:

1. The first program was started in 1982. In 1981, the budget deficit had reached a very high 13.0% of GDP. Government debt, the result of the accumulation of current and past deficits, was 77% of GDP, also a very high level. The Irish government clearly had to regain control of its finances. Over the next three years, it embarked on a program of deficit reduction, based mostly on tax increases. This was an ambitious program: Had output continued to grow at its normal growth rate, the program would have reduced the deficit by 5% of GDP.

   The results, however, were dismal. As shown in line 2 of Table 1, output growth was low in 1982 and negative in 1983. Low output growth was associated with a major increase in unemployment, from 9.5% in 1981 to 15% in 1984 (line 3). Because of low output growth, tax revenues—which depend on the level of economic activity—were lower than anticipated. The actual deficit reduction, shown in line 1, was only 3.5% of GDP. And the result of continuing high deficits and low GDP growth was a further increase in the ratio of debt to GDP to 97% in 1984.

2. A second attempt to reduce budget deficits was made starting in February 1987. At the time, things were still very bad. The 1986 deficit was 10.7% of GDP; debt stood at 116% of GDP, a record high in Europe at the time. This new program of deficit reduction was different from the first. It was focused more on reducing the role of government and cutting government spending than on increasing taxes. The tax increases in the program were achieved through a tax reform widening the tax base—increasing the number of households paying taxes—rather than through an increase in the

marginal tax rate. The program was again very ambitious: Had output grown at its normal rate, the reduction in the deficit would have been 6.4% of GDP.

The results of the second program could not have been more different from the results of the first. 1987 to 1989 were years of strong growth, with average GDP growth exceeding 5%. The unemployment rate was reduced by 2%. Because of strong output growth, tax revenues were higher than anticipated, and the deficit was reduced by nearly 9% of GDP.

A number of economists have argued that the striking difference between the results of the two programs can be traced to the different reaction of expectations in each case. The first program, they argue, focused on tax increases and did not change what many people saw as too large a role of government in the economy. The second program, with its focus on cuts in spending and on tax reform, had a much more positive impact on expectations and, therefore, a positive impact on spending and output.

Are these economists right? One variable, the household saving rate—defined as disposable income minus consumption, divided by disposable income—strongly suggests that expectations are an important part of the story. To interpret the behavior of the saving rate, recall the lessons from Chapter 16 about consumption behavior. When disposable income grows unusually slowly or goes down—as it does in a recession—consumption typically slows down or declines by less than disposable income because people expect things to improve in the future. Put another way, when the growth of disposable income is unusually low, the saving rate typically comes down. Now look (in line 4) at what happened from 1981 to 1984: Despite low growth throughout the period and

and *LM* curves for the current period. In response to the announcement of the deficit reduction, there are now three factors shifting the *IS* curve:

- Current government spending, *G*, goes down, leading the *IS* curve to shift to the left. At a given interest rate, the decrease in government spending leads to a decrease in total spending and to a decrease in output. This is the standard effect of a reduction in government spending, and it is the only one taken into account in the basic *IS–LM* model.
- Expected future output, Y'^e, goes up, leading the *IS* curve to shift to the right. At a given interest rate, the increase in expected future output leads to an increase in private spending, increasing output.
- The expected future interest rate goes down, leading the *IS* curve to shift to the right. At a given current interest rate, a decrease in the future interest rate stimulates spending and increases output.

Table 1	Fiscal and other Macroeconomic Indicators, Ireland, 1981 to 1984 and 1986 to 1989							
	1981	**1982**	**1983**	**1984**	**1986**	**1987**	**1988**	**1989**
1 Budget deficit (% of GDP)	−13.0	−13.4	−11.4	−9.5	−10.7	−8.6	−4.5	−1.8
2 Output growth rate (%)	3.3	2.3	−0.2	4.4	−0.4	4.7	5.2	5.8
3 Unemployment rate (%)	9.5	11.0	13.5	15.0	17.1	16.9	16.3	15.1
4 Household saving rate (% of disposable income)	17.9	19.6	18.1	18.4	15.7	12.9	11.0	12.6

Source: OECD *Economic Outlook*, June 1998.

a recession in 1983, the household saving rate actually increased slightly during that period. Put another way, people reduced their consumption by more than the reduction in their disposable income. The reason must be that they were very pessimistic about the future.

Now turn to the period 1986 to 1989. During that period, economic growth was unusually strong. By the same argument as in the previous paragraph, we would have expected consumption to increase less strongly, and thus the saving rate to increase. Instead, the saving rate dropped sharply, from 15.7% in 1986 to 12.6% in 1989. Consumers must have become much more optimistic about the future to increase their consumption by more than the increase in their disposable income.

The next question is whether this difference in the adjustment of expectations over the two episodes can be attributed fully to the differences in the two fiscal programs. The answer is surely no. Ireland was changing in many ways at the time of the second fiscal program. Productivity was increasing much faster than real wages, reducing the cost of labor for firms. Attracted by tax breaks, low labor costs, and an educated labor force,

many foreign firms were relocating to Ireland and building new plants. These factors played a major role in the expansion of the late 1980s. Irish growth has been very strong ever since, with average output growth exceeding 6% since 1990. Surely, this long expansion is due to many factors. Nevertheless, the change in fiscal policy in 1987 probably played an important role in convincing people, firms (including foreign firms), and financial markets that the government was regaining control of its finances. And the fact remains that the substantial deficit reduction of 1987 to 1989 was accompanied by a strong output expansion, not by the recession predicted by the basic *IS–LM* model.

Note: For a more detailed discussion, look at Francesco Giavazzi and Marco Pagano, "Can Severe Fiscal Contractions Be Expansionary? Tales of Two Small European Countries," NBER Macroeconomics Annual, 1990, 75–110.

A survey of what we have learned by looking at programs of deficit reduction around the world is given in John McDermott and Robert Wescott, "An Empirical Analysis of Fiscal Adjustments," International Monetary Fund working paper, June 1996.

What is the net effect of these three shifts in the *IS* curve? Can the effect of expectations on consumption and investment spending offset the decrease in government spending? Without much more information about the exact form of the *IS* and *LM* relations and about the details of the deficit reduction program, we cannot tell which shifts will dominate and whether output will go up or down. But our analysis tells us that both cases are possible—that output may go up in response to the deficit reduction. And it gives us a few hints as to when this might happen:

■ Note that the smaller the decrease in current government spending, G, the smaller the adverse effect on spending today. Note also that the larger the decrease in expected future government spending, G'^e, the larger the effect on expected future output and interest rates, thus the larger the favorable effect on spending today. This suggests that **backloading** the deficit reduction program toward the future, with small cuts today and larger cuts in the future, is more likely to lead to an increase in output.

- On the other hand, backloading raises other issues. Announcing the need for painful cuts in spending, and then leaving them to the future is likely to decrease the program's **credibility**—the perceived probability that the government will do what it has promised when the time comes to do it.

- The government must play a delicate balancing act: enough cuts in the current period to show a commitment to deficit reduction and enough cuts left to the future to reduce the adverse effects on the economy in the short run.

More generally, our analysis suggests that anything in a deficit reduction program that improves expectations of how the future will look is likely to make the short-run effects of deficit reduction less painful. Let me give two examples:

- Measures that are perceived by firms and financial markets as reducing some of the distortions in the economy may improve expectations and make it more likely that output increases in the short run. Take, for example, unemployment benefits. You saw in Chapter 6 that lower unemployment benefits lead to a decline in the natural rate of unemployment, resulting in a higher natural level of output. So, a reform of the social insurance system, which includes a reduction in the generosity of unemployment benefits, is likely to have two effects on spending and thus on output in the short run:

  An adverse effect on the consumption of the unemployed—Lower unemployment benefits will reduce their income and their consumption.

  A positive effect on spending through expectations—The anticipation of higher output in the future may lead to both higher consumption and higher investment.

  If the second effect dominates, the outcome might be an increase in overall spending, increasing output not only in the medium run but also in the short run. (An important caveat: Even if a reduction in unemployment benefits increases output, this surely does not imply that unemployment benefits should be eliminated. Even if aggregate income goes up, we must worry about the effects on the distribution of income: The consumption of the unemployed goes down, and the pain associated with being unemployed goes up.)

As you will see in Chapter 23, a very large deficit often leads to very high money creation and, soon after, to very high inflation. Very high inflation leads not only to economic trouble but also to political instability. ▶

- Or take an economy where the government has, in effect, lost control of its budget: Government spending is high, tax revenues are low, and the deficit is very large. In such an environment, a credible deficit reduction program is also more likely to increase output in the short run. Before the announcement of the program, people may have expected major political and economic trouble in the future. The announcement of a program of deficit reduction may well reassure them that the government has regained control and that the future is less bleak than they anticipated. This decrease in pessimism about the future may lead to an increase in spending and output, even if taxes are increased as part of the deficit reduction program.

Let's summarize. A program of deficit reduction may increase output even in the short run. Whether it does depends on many factors, in particular:

- The credibility of the program—Will spending be cut or taxes increased in the future, as announced?

- The timing of the program—How large are spending cuts in the future relative to current spending cuts?

Note how far we have moved from the results of Chapter 3, where, by choosing spending and taxes wisely, the government could achieve any level of output it wanted. Here, even the direction of the effect of a deficit reduction on output is ambiguous.

- The composition of the program—Does the program remove some of the distortions in the economy?

- The state of government finances in the first place—How large is the initial deficit? Is this a "last chance" program? What will happen if it fails?

This gives you a sense of both the importance of expectations in determining the ▶ outcome and the complexities involved in the use of fiscal policy in such a context.

Summary

- Spending in the goods market depends on current and expected future output and on current and expected future real interest rates.
- Expectations affect demand and, in turn, affect output: Changes in expected future output or in the expected future real interest rate lead to changes in spending and in output today.
- By implication, the effects of fiscal and monetary policy on spending and output depend on how the policy affects expectations of future output and real interest rates.
- Rational expectations is the assumption that people, firms, and participants in financial markets form expectations of the future by assessing the course of future expected policy and then working out the implications for future output, future interest rates, and so on. Although it is clear that most people do not go through this exercise themselves we can think of them as doing so indirectly by relying on the predictions of public and private forecasters.

- Although there are surely cases in which people, firms, or financial investors do not have rational expectations, the assumption of rational expectations seems to be the best benchmark to evaluate the potential effects of alternative policies. Designing a policy on the assumption that people will make systematic mistakes in responding to it would be unwise.
- Changes in the money supply affect the short-term nominal interest rate. Spending depends instead on current and expected future real interest rates. Thus, the effect of monetary policy on activity depends crucially on whether and how changes in the short-run nominal interest rate lead to changes in currrent and expected future real interest rates.
- A budget deficit reduction may lead to an increase rather than a decrease in output. This is because expectations of higher output and lower interest rates in the future may lead to an increase in spending that more than offsets the reduction in spending coming from the direct effect of the deficit reduction on total spending.

Key Terms

- aggregate private spending, or private spending, 381
- animal spirits, 387
- adaptive expectations, 387
- rational expectations, 388
- backloading 391
- credibility, 392

Questions and Problems

Quick Check

1. Using the information in this chapter, label each of the following statements true, false, or uncertain. Explain briefly.

a. Changes in the current one-year real interest rate are likely to have a much larger effect on spending than changes in expected future one-year real interest rates.

b. The introduction of expectations in the goods market model makes the IS curve flatter, although it is still downward sloping.

c. Current money demand depends on current and expected future nominal interest rates.

d. The rational expectations assumption implies that consumers take into account the effects of future fiscal policy on output.

e. Expected future fiscal policy affects expected future economic activity but not current economic activity.

f. Depending on its effect on expectations, a fiscal contraction may actually lead to an economic expansion.

g. Ireland's experience with deficit reduction programs in 1982 and 1987 provides strong evidence against the hypothesis that deficit reduction can lead to an output expansion.

2. For each of the changes in expectations in (a) through (d), determine whether there is a shift in the IS curve, the LM curve, both curves, or neither. In each case, assume that expected current and future inflation are equal to zero and that no other exogenous variable is changing.

a. a decrease in the current money supply

b. an increase in the expected future real interest rate

c. an increase in expected future income

d. an increase in expected future taxes

3. During the late 1990s, many observers claimed that the United States had transformed into a New Economy, and this justified the very high values for stock prices observed at the time.

a. Discuss how the belief in the New Economy, combined with the increase in stock prices, affected consumption spending.

b. Stock prices subsequently decreased. Discuss how this might have affected consumption.

4. A new president, who promised during the campaign that she would cut taxes, has just been elected. People trust that she will keep her promise, but expect that the tax cuts will be implemented only in the future. Determine the *impact of the election on current output, the current interest rate, and current private spending under each of the assumptions in (a) through (c). In each case, indicate what you think will happen to Y'^e, r'^e, and T'^e, and then how these changes in expectations affect output today.*

a. The Fed will not change its policy.

b. The Fed will act to prevent any change in future output.

c. The Fed will act to prevent any change in the future interest rate.

5. *Consider the following statement. "The rational expectations assumption is unrealistic because, essentially, it amounts to the assumption that every consumer has perfect knowledge of the economy." Discuss.*

Dig Deeper

6. *The Clinton deficit reduction package*

In 1992, the U.S. deficit was $290 billion. During the presidential campaign, the large deficit emerged as a major issue. When President Clinton won the election, deficit reduction was the first item on the new administration's agenda.

a. What does deficit reduction imply for the medium run and the long run? What are the advantages of reducing the deficit?

In the final version passed by Congress in August 1993, the deficit reduction package included a reduction of $20 billion in its first year, increasing gradually to $131 billion four years later.

b. Why was the deficit reduction package backloaded? What are the advantages and disadvantages of this approach to deficit reduction?

In February 1993, President Clinton presented the budget in his State of the Union address. He asked Alan Greenspan, the Fed chairman, to sit next to First Lady Hillary Clinton during the delivery of the address.

c. What was the purpose of this symbolic gesture? How can the Fed's decision to use expansionary monetary policy in the future affect the short-run response of the economy?

7. *A new Federal Reserve chairman*

Suppose, in a hypothetical economy, that the chairman of the Fed unexpectedly announces that he will retire in one year. At the same time, the president announces her nominee to replace the retiring Fed chair. Financial market participants expect the nominee to be confirmed by Congress. They also believe that the nominee will conduct a more contractionary monetary policy in the future. In other words, market participants expect the money supply to fall in the future.

a. Consider the present to be the last year of the current Fed chair's term and the future to be the time after that. Given that monetary policy will be more contractionary in the future, what will happen to future interest rates and future output (at least for a while, before output returns to potential GDP)? Given that these changes in future output and future interest rates are predicted, what will happen to output and the interest rate in the present? What will happen to the yield curve

on the day of the announcement that the current Fed chair will retire in a year?

Now suppose that instead of making an unexpected announcement, the Fed chair is required by law to retire in one year (there are limits on the term of the Fed chair), and financial market participants have been aware of this for some time. Suppose, as in part (a), that the president nominates a replacement who is expected to conduct a more contractionary monetary policy than the current Fed chair.

b. Suppose financial market participants are not surprised by the president's choice. In other words, market participants had correctly predicted who the president would choose as nominee. Under these circumstances, is the announcement of the nominee likely to have any effect on the yield curve?

c. Suppose instead that the identity of the nominee is a surprise and that financial market participants had expected the nominee to be someone who favored an even more contractionary policy than the actual nominee. Under these circumstances, what is likely to happen to the yield curve on the day of the announcement? (*Hint:* Be careful. Compared to what was expected, is the actual nominee expected to follow a more contractionary or more expansionary policy?)

d. On October 24, 2005, Ben Bernanke was nominated to succeed Alan Greenspan as chairman of the Federal Reserve. Do an Internet search and try to learn what happened in financial markets on the day the nomination was announced. Were financial market participants surprised by the choice? If so, was Bernanke believed to favor policies that would lead to higher or lower interest rates (as compared to the expected nominee) over the next three to five years? (You may also do a yield curve analysis of the kind described in problem 8 for the period around Bernanke's nomination. If you do this, use one-year and five-year interest rates.)

Explore Further

8. *Deficits and interest rates*

The dramatic change in the U.S. budget position after 2000 (from a surplus to a large and continuing deficit) has reinvigorated the debate about the effect of fiscal policy on interest rates. This problem asks you to review theory and evidence on this topic.

a. Review what theory predicts about fiscal policy and interest rates. Suppose there is an increase in government spending and a decrease in taxes. Use an *IS–LM* diagram to show what will happen to the nominal interest rate in the short run and the medium run. Assuming that there is no change in monetary policy, what does the *IS–LM* model predict will happen to the yield curve immediately after an increase in government spending and a decrease in taxes?

During the first term of the G. W. Bush administration, the actual and projected federal budget deficits increased dramatically. Part of the increase in the deficit can be attributed to the recession of 2001. However, deficits and projected deficits continued to increase even after the recession had ended.

The following table provides budget projections produced by the Congressional Budget Office (CBO) over the period August 2002 to January 2004. These projections are for the total federal budget deficit, so they include Social Security, which was running a surplus over the period. In addition, each projection assumes that current policy (as of the date of the forecast) continues into the future.

Date of Forecast	Projected Five-Year Deficit (as % of Five-Year GDP)
August 2002	−0.4
January 2003	−0.2
August 2003	−2.3
January 2004	−2.3

b. Go to the Web site of the Federal Reserve Bank of St. Louis (**research.stlouisfed.org/fred2/**). Under "Interest Rates" and then "Treasury Constant Maturity," obtain the data for "3-Month Constant Maturity Treasury Yield" and "5-Year Constant Maturity Treasury Yield" for each of the months in the table shown here. For each month, subtract the three-month yield from the five-year yield to obtain the interest rate spread. What happened to the interest rate spread as the budget picture worsened over the sample period? Is this result consistent with your answer to part (a)?

The analysis you carried out in this problem is an extension of work by William C. Gale and Peter R. Orszag. See "The Economic Effects of Long-Term Fiscal Discipline," Brookings Institution, December 17, 2002. Figure 5 in this paper relates interest rate spreads to CBO five-year projected budget deficits from 1982 to 2002.

We invite you to visit the Blanchard page on the Prentice Hall Web site, at:

www.prenhall.com/blanchard

for this chapter's World Wide Web exercises.

The Open Economy

The next four chapters represent the second major extension of the core. They look at the implications of openness—the fact that most economies trade both goods and assets with the rest of the world.

EXTENSIONS

Chapter 18

Chapter 18 discusses the implications of openness in goods markets and financial markets. Openness in goods markets allows people to choose between domestic goods and foreign goods. An important determinant of their decisions is the real exchange rate—the relative price of domestic goods in terms of foreign goods. Openness in financial markets allows people to choose between domestic assets and foreign assets. This imposes a tight relation between the exchange rate, both current and expected, and domestic and foreign interest rates—a relation known as the interest parity condition.

Chapter 19

Chapter 19 focuses on equilibrium in the goods market in an open economy. It shows how the demand for domestic goods now depends on the real exchange rate. It shows how fiscal policy affects both output and the trade balance. It discusses the conditions under which a real depreciation improves the trade balance and increases output.

Chapter 20 ▬▬

Chapter 20 characterizes the equilibrium of goods and financial markets in an open economy. In other words, it gives an open economy version of the *IS–LM* model we saw in the core. It shows how, under flexible exchange rates, monetary policy affects output not only through its effect on the interest rate but also through its effect on the exchange rate. It shows how fixing the exchange rate also implies giving up the ability to change the interest rate.

Chapter 21 ▬▬

Chapter 21 looks at the properties of different exchange rate regimes. It first shows how, in the medium run, the real exchange rate can adjust even under a fixed exchange rate regime. It then looks at exchange rate crises under fixed exchange rates and at movements in exchange rates under flexible exchange rates. It ends by discussing the pros and cons of various exchange rate regimes, including the adoption of a common currency such as the euro.

Openness in Goods and Financial Markets

CHAPTER 18

We have assumed until now that the economy was *closed*—that it did not interact with the rest of the world. I started this way to keep things simple and build up your intuition for the basic macroeconomic mechanisms. We are now ready to relax this assumption. Understanding the macroeconomic implications of openness will occupy us for this and the next three chapters.

"Openness" has three distinct dimensions:

1. **Openness in goods markets**—The ability of consumers and firms to choose between domestic goods and foreign goods. In no country is this choice completely free of restrictions: Even the countries most committed to free trade have **tariffs**—taxes on imported goods—and **quotas**—restrictions on the quantity of goods that can be imported—on at least some foreign goods. At the same time, in most countries, average tariffs are low and getting lower.

2. **Openness in financial markets**—The ability of financial investors to choose between domestic assets and foreign assets. Until recently, even some of the richest countries in the world, such as France and Italy, had **capital controls**—restrictions on the foreign assets their domestic residents could hold and the domestic assets foreigners could hold. These restrictions are rapidly disappearing. As a result, world financial markets are becoming more and more closely integrated.

3. **Openness in factor markets**—The ability of firms to choose where to locate production, and of workers to choose where to work. Here also, trends are clear. Multinational companies operate plants in many countries and move their operations around the world to take advantage of low costs. Much of the debate about the **North American Free Trade Agreement (NAFTA)**, signed in 1993 by the United States, Canada, and Mexico centered on how it would affect the relocation of U.S. firms to Mexico. Similar fears now center around China. And immigration from low-wage countries is a hot political issue in countries from Germany to the United States.

In the short run and in the medium run—the focus of this and the next three chapters—openness in factor markets plays less of a role than openness in either goods markets or financial markets. Thus, I shall ignore openness in factor markets and focus on the implications of the first two dimensions of openness here.

■ Section 18-1 looks at openness in goods markets, the determinants of the choice between domestic goods and foreign goods, and the role of the real exchange rate.

■ Section 18-2 looks at openness in financial markets, the determinants of the choice between domestic assets and foreign assets, and the role of interest rates and exchange rates.

■ Section 18-3 gives the map to the next three chapters. ■

18-1 Openness in Goods Markets

Let's start by looking at how much the United States sells to and buys from the rest of the world. Then we will be better able to think about the choice between domestic goods and foreign goods and the role of the relative price of domestic goods in terms of foreign goods—the real exchange rate.

Exports and Imports

From Chapter 3: The trade balance is the difference between exports and imports:
If exports exceed imports, there is a trade surplus (equivalently, a positive trade balance).
If imports exceed exports, there is a trade deficit (equivalently, a negative trade balance). ▶

Figure 18-1 plots the evolution of U.S. exports and U.S. imports, as ratios to GDP, since 1960. ("U.S. exports" means exports *from* the United States; "U.S. imports" means imports *to* the United States.) The figure suggests two main conclusions:

■ The U.S. economy is becoming more open over time. Exports and imports, which were equal to 5% of GDP during the 1960s, now are equal to about 14% of GDP (11% for exports, 17% for imports). In other words, the United States trades more than twice as much (relative to its GDP) with the rest of the world as it did just 40 years ago.
■ Although imports and exports have broadly followed the same upward trend, they have also diverged for long periods of time, generating sustained trade surpluses and trade deficits. Two episodes stand out:
    The large trade deficits of the mid-1980s—The ratio of the trade deficit to GDP reached 3% in 1986 and then decreased to 1% in the early 1990s.

▨ Figure 18-1

U.S. Exports and Imports as Ratios of GDP since 1960

Since 1960, exports and imports have more than doubled in relation to GDP.

The large and increasing trade deficits since the mid-1990s—The ratio of the trade deficit to GDP reached 5.9% in 2006, an historical record.

Understanding the sources and implications of these trade deficits is a central issue in macroeconomics today, and one to which we shall return later.

Given all the talk in the media about *globalization*, a volume of trade (measured by the average of the ratios of exports and imports to GDP) around 14% of GDP might strike you as small. However, the volume of trade is not necessarily a good measure of openness. Many firms are exposed to foreign competition but, by being competitive and keeping their prices low enough, these firms are able to retain their domestic market share and limit imports. This suggests that a better index of openness than export or import ratios is the proportion of aggregate output composed of **tradable goods**— ◄ goods that compete with foreign goods in either domestic markets or foreign markets. Estimates are that tradable goods represent about 60% of aggregate output in the United States today.

Tradable goods: Cars, computers, and so on. Nontradable goods: Housing, most medical services, haircuts, and so on.

With exports around 11% of GDP, it is true that the United States has one of the smallest ratios of exports to GDP among the rich countries of the world. Table 18-1 gives ratios for a number of OECD countries.

For more on the OECD and for the list of member countries, ◄ see Chapter 1.

The United States is at the low end of the range of export ratios. Japan's ratio is roughly twice as large, the United Kingdom's is three times as large, and Germany's is nearly five times as large. And the smaller European countries have even larger ratios, from 54% in Switzerland to 92% in Belgium. (Belgium's 92% ratio of exports to GDP raises an odd possibility: Can a country have exports larger than its GDP? In other words, can a country have an export ratio greater than 1? The answer is yes. The reason is given in the Focus box "Can Exports Exceed GDP?")

Do these numbers indicate that the United States has more trade barriers than, say, the United Kingdom or Belgium? No. The main factors behind these differences are geography and size. Distance from other markets explains a good part of the low Japanese ratio. Size also matters: The smaller the country, the more it must specialize in producing and exporting only a few products and rely on imports for other products. Belgium can hardly afford to produce the range of goods produced by the United States, a country roughly 40 times its economic size.

Iceland is both isolated and small. What would you expect its export ratio to be? (Answer: ◄ 43%.)

The Choice between Domestic Goods and Foreign Goods

How does openness in goods markets force us to rethink the way we look at equilibrium in the *goods market*?

Until now, when we were thinking about consumers' decisions in the goods market, we focused on their decision to save or to consume. When goods markets are open, domestic consumers face a second decision: whether to buy domestic goods or to buy foreign goods. Indeed, all buyers—including domestic and foreign firms and ◄ governments—face a similar decision. This decision has a direct effect on domestic output: If buyers decide to buy more domestic goods, the demand for domestic goods

In a closed economy, people face one decision:
  Save or buy (consume).
In an open economy, they face two decisions:
  Save or buy.
  Buy domestic or buy foreign.

Table 18-1	Ratios of Exports to GDP for Selected OECD Countries, 2006		
Country	Export Ratio (%)	Country	Export Ratio (%)
United States	11	Switzerland	54
Japan	18	Austria	62
United Kingdom	30	Netherlands	80
Germany	48	Belgium	92

Source: OECD Economic Outlook *Database.*

Can a country have exports larger than its GDP—that is, can it have an export ratio greater than 1?

It would seem that the answer must be no: A country cannot export more than it produces, so the export ratio must be less than 1. Not so. The key to the answer is to realize that exports and imports may include exports and imports of intermediate goods.

Take, for example, a country that imports intermediate goods for $1 billion. Suppose it then transforms them into final goods using only labor. Say labor is paid $200 million and that there are no profits. The value of these final goods is thus equal to $1,200 million. Assume that $1 billion worth of final goods is exported and the rest, $200 million, is consumed domestically.

Exports and imports therefore both equal $1 billion. What is GDP in this economy? Remember that GDP is value added in the economy (see Chapter 2). So, in this example, GDP equals $200 million, and the ratio of exports to GDP equals $1,000/$200 = 5.

Hence, exports can exceed GDP. This is actually the case for a number of small countries where most economic activity is organized around a harbor and import–export activities. This is even the case for small countries such as Singapore where manufacturing plays an important role. In 2005, the ratio of exports to GDP in Singapore was 243%!

increases, and so does domestic output. If they decide to buy more foreign goods, then foreign output increases instead of domestic output.

Central to the decision of whether to buy domestic goods or foreign goods is the price of domestic goods relative to foreign goods. We call this relative price the **real exchange rate**. The real exchange rate is not directly observable, and you will not find it in newspapers. What you will find in newspapers are *nominal exchange rates*, the relative prices of currencies. We start by looking at nominal exchange rates and then see how we can use them to construct real exchange rates.

Nominal Exchange Rates

Nominal exchange rates between two currencies can be quoted in one of two ways:

- As the price of the domestic currency in terms of the foreign currency—If, for example, we look at the United States and the United Kingdom and think of the dollar as the domestic currency and the pound as the foreign currency, we can express the nominal exchange rate as the price of a dollar in terms of pounds. In July 2007, the exchange rate defined this way was 0.50. In other words, 1 dollar was worth 0.50 pounds.
- As the price of the foreign currency in terms of the domestic currency—Continuing with the same example, we can express the nominal exchange rate as the price of a pound in terms of dollars. In July 2007, the exchange rate defined this way was 2.0. In other words, 1 pound was worth 2.0 dollars.

Either definition is fine; the important thing is to remain consistent. In this book, I adopt the first definition: I define the **nominal exchange rate** as *the price of the domestic currency in terms of foreign currency* and denote it by E. When looking, for example, at the exchange rate between the United States and the United Kingdom (from the viewpoint of the United States, so the dollar is the domestic currency), E denotes the price of a dollar in terms of pounds (so, for example, E was 0.50 in July 2007).

Exchange rates between the dollar and most foreign currencies change every day and every minute of the day. These changes are called *nominal appreciations* or *nominal depreciations—appreciations* or *depreciations* for short:

■ An **appreciation** of the domestic currency is an increase in the price of the domestic currency in terms of a foreign currency. Given our definition of the exchange rate, an appreciation corresponds to an *increase* in the exchange rate.

■ A **depreciation** of the domestic currency is a decrease in the price of the domestic currency in terms of a foreign currency. So, given our definition of the exchange rate, a depreciation of the domestic currency corresponds to a decrease in the exchange rate, E.

You may have encountered two other words to denote movements in exchange rates: "revaluations" and "devaluations." These two terms are used when countries operate under **fixed exchange rates**—a system in which two or more countries maintain a constant exchange rate between their currencies. Under such a system, increases in the exchange rate—which are infrequent by definition—are called **revaluations** (rather than appreciations). Decreases in the exchange rate are called **devaluations** (rather than depreciations).

Figure 18-2 plots the nominal exchange rate between the dollar and the pound since 1970. Note the two main characteristics of the figure:

■ *The trend increase in the exchange rate*—In 1970, 1 dollar was worth only 0.41 pounds. In 2006, 1 dollar was worth 0.54 pounds. Put another way, there was an appreciation of the dollar vis-à-vis the pound over the period.

> Warning: There is no agreed-upon rule among economists or among newspapers as to which of the two definitions to use. You will encounter both. Always check which definition is used.

> ◀ E: Nominal exchange rate— Price of domestic currency in terms of foreign currency. (From the point of view of the United States looking at the United Kingdom, the price of a dollar in terms of pounds.)
> Appreciation of the domestic currency ⇔ Increase in the price of the domestic currency in terms of foreign currency ⇔ Increase in the exchange rate.

> ◀ Depreciation of the domestic currency ⇔ Decrease in the price of the domestic currency in terms of foreign currency ⇔ Decrease in the exchange rate.

> We shall discuss fixed exchange rates in Chapter 20.

The Nominal Exchange Rate between the Dollar and the Pound since 1970

Although the dollar has appreciated relative to the pound over the past four decades, this appreciation has come with large swings in the nominal exchange rate between the two currencies, especially in the 1980s.

- *The large fluctuations in the exchange rate*—In the space of less than 10 years in the 1980s, the value of the dollar increased from 0.42 pounds in 1981 to 0.89 pounds in 1985, only to go back down to 0.54 pounds by early 1988. Put another way, there was a very large appreciation of the dollar in the first half of the 1980s, followed by a large depreciation later in the decade.

If we are interested, however, in the choice between domestic goods and foreign goods, the nominal exchange rate gives us only part of the information we need. Figure 18-2, for example, tells us only about movements in the relative price of the two currencies, the dollar and the pound. To U.S. tourists thinking of visiting the United Kingdom, the question is not only how many pounds they will get in exchange for their dollars, but how much goods will cost in the United Kingdom relative to how much they cost in the United States. This takes us to our next step—the construction of real exchange rates.

From Nominal to Real Exchange Rates

How can we construct the real exchange rate between the United States and the United Kingdom—the price of U.S. goods in terms of British goods?

Suppose the United States produced only one good, a Cadillac 2007 STS, and the United Kingdom also produced only one good, a Jaguar S-type luxury sedan. (This is one of those "Suppose" statements that run completely against the facts, but we shall become more realistic shortly.) Constructing the real exchange rate, the price of the U.S. goods (Cadillacs) in terms of British goods (Jaguars), would be straightforward. We would express both goods in terms of the same currency and then compute their relative price.

> If we expressed both in terms of dollars instead, we would get the same result for the real exchange rate.

Suppose, for example, we expressed both goods in terms of pounds. Then:

- The first step would be to take the price of a Cadillac in dollars and convert it to a price in pounds. The price of a Cadillac in the United States is $40,000. A dollar is worth 0.50 pounds, so the price of a Cadillac in pounds is is $40,000 × 0.50 = £20,000.
- The second step would be to compute the ratio of the price of the Cadillac in pounds to the price of the Jaguar in pounds. The price of a Jaguar in the United Kingdom is £30,000. So the price of a Cadillac in terms of Jaguars—that is, the real exchange rate between the United States and the United Kingdom—would be £20,000/£30,000 = 0.66.

The example is straightforward, but how do we generalize it? The United States and the United Kingdom produce more than Cadillacs and Jaguars, and we want to construct a real exchange rate that reflects the relative price of *all* the goods produced in the United States in terms of *all* the goods produced in the United Kingdom.

The computation we just went through tells us how to proceed. Rather than use the price of a Jaguar and the price of a Cadillac, we must use a price index for all goods produced in the United Kingdom and a price index for all goods produced in the United States. This is exactly what the GDP deflators we introduced in Chapter 2 do: They are, by definition, price indexes for the set of final goods and services produced in the economy.

Let P be the GDP deflator for the United States, P^* be the GDP deflator for the United Kingdom (as a rule, I shall denote foreign variables with an asterisk), and E be the dollar–pound nominal exchange rate. Figure 18-3 goes through the steps needed to construct the real exchange rate:

1. The price of U.S. goods in dollars is P. Multiplying it by the exchange rate, E—the price of dollars in terms of pounds—gives us the price of U.S. goods in pounds, EP.

Figure 18-3

The Construction of the Real Exchange Rate

2. The price of British goods in pounds is P^*. The *real exchange rate*, the price of U.S. goods in terms of British goods, which we shall call ϵ (the Greek lowercase epsilon), is thus given by

$$\epsilon = \frac{EP}{P^*} \qquad (18.1)$$

The real exchange rate is constructed by multiplying the domestic price level by the nominal exchange rate and then dividing by the foreign price level—a straightforward extension of the computation we made in our Cadillac/Jaguar example.

Note, however, an important difference between our Cadillac/Jaguar example and this more general computation. Unlike the price of Cadillacs in terms of Jaguars, the real exchange rate is an index number: That is, its level is arbitrary and, therefore, uninformative. It is uninformative because the GDP deflators used to construct the real exchange rate are themselves index numbers; as we saw in Chapter 2, they are equal to 1 (or 100) in whatever year is chosen as the base year.

But all is not lost. Although the level of the real exchange rate is uninformative, the rate of change of the real exchange rate is informative: If, for example, the real exchange rate between the United States and the United Kingdom increases by 10%, this tells us U.S. goods are now 10% more expensive relative to British goods than they were before.

Like nominal exchange rates, real exchange rates move over time. These changes are called *real appreciations* or *real depreciations*:

■ An increase in the real exchange rate—that is, an increase in the relative price of domestic goods in terms of foreign goods—is called a **real appreciation**.
■ A decrease in the real exchange rate—that is, a decrease in the relative price of domestic goods in terms of foreign goods—is called a **real depreciation**.

Figure 18-4 plots the evolution of the real exchange rate between the United States and the United Kingdom since 1970, constructed using equation (18.1). For convenience, it also reproduces the evolution of the nominal exchange rate from Figure 18-2. The GDP deflators have both been set equal to 1 in the first quarter of 2000, so the nominal exchange rate and the real exchange rate are equal in that quarter by construction. Note the two main characteristics of Figure 18-4:

■ While the nominal exchange rate went up during the period, the real exchange rate went down: In 1970, the real exchange rate was equal to 1.66; in 2006, it was down to 0.87.

How do we reconcile the fact that there was both a nominal appreciation (of the dollar relative to the pound) and a real depreciation (of U.S. goods relative to British goods) during the period? To see why, return to the definition of the real exchange rate:

$$\epsilon = E \frac{P}{P^*}$$

◄ ϵ: Real exchange rate—Price of domestic goods in terms of foreign goods. (For example, from the point of view of the United States looking at the United Kingdom, the price of U.S. goods in terms of British goods.)

Real appreciation Increase in the price of the domestic goods in terms of foreign goods ⇔ Increase in the real exchange rate.

◄ Real depreciation Decrease in the price of the domestic goods in terms of foreign goods ⇔ Decrease in the real exchange rate.

Except for the difference in trend reflecting higher average inflation in the United Kingdom than in the United States, the nominal and the real exchange rates have moved largely together since 1970.

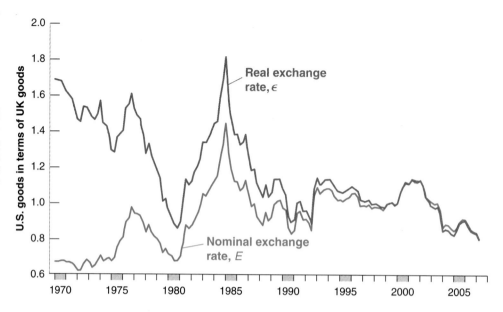

Two things have happened since 1970:

First, E has increased: The dollar has gone up in terms of pounds—this is the nominal appreciation we saw earlier.

Second, P/P^* has decreased. The price level has increased less in the United States than in the United Kingdom. Put another way, over the period, average inflation has been lower in the United States than in the United Kingdom.

The resulting decrease in P/P^* has been larger than the increase in E, leading to a decrease in ϵ, a real depreciation—a decrease in the relative price of domestic goods in terms of foreign goods.

To get a better understanding of what happened, let's go back to our U.S. tourists thinking about visiting the United Kingdom. They find that they can buy more pounds per dollar than in 1970 *(E* has increased). Does this imply that their trip will be cheaper? No. When they arrive in the United Kingdom, they will discover that the prices of goods in the United Kingdom have increased much more than the prices of goods in the United States *(P** has increased more than *P,* so *P/P** has declined), and this more than cancels the increase in the value of the dollar in terms of pounds. They will find that their trip will actually be more expensive (in terms of U.S. goods) than it was in 1970. In other words, they will find that there has been a real depreciation.

Can there be a real appreciation with no nominal appreciation?

Can there be a nominal appreciation with no real appreciation? (The answer to both questions: Yes.)

There is a general lesson here. Over long periods of time, differences in inflation rates across countries can lead to very different movements in nominal exchange rates and real exchange rates. We shall return to this issue in Chapter 20.

- The large fluctuations in the nominal exchange rate we saw in Figure 18-2 also show up in the real exchange rate. This not surprising: Year-to-year movements in the price ratio, P/P^*, are typically small compared to the often-sharp movements in the nominal exchange rate, E. Thus, from year to year, or even over the course of a few years, movements in the real exchange rate, ϵ, tend to be driven mostly by movements in the nominal exchange rate, E. Note that, since the early 1990s, the nominal exchange rate and the real exchange rate have moved nearly together. This reflects the fact that, since the mid-1980s, inflation rates have been very similar—and low—in both countries.

If inflation rates were exactly equal, P/P^* would be constant, and ϵ and E would move together exactly.

From Bilateral to Multilateral Exchange Rates

We need to take one last step. We have so far concentrated on the exchange rate between the United States and the United Kingdom. But the United Kingdom is just one of many countries the United States trades with.

Table 18-2 shows the geographic composition of U.S. trade for both exports and imports. The main message of the table is that the United States does most of its trade with three sets of countries. The first includes its neighbors to the north and to the south: Canada and Mexico. Trade with Canada and Mexico accounts for 22% of U.S. exports and 20% of U.S. imports. The second includes the countries of Western Europe, which account for 29% of U.S. exports and 25% of U.S. imports. The third includes the Asian countries, including Japan and China, which, together, account for 23% of U.S. exports and 33% of U.S. imports.

How do we go from **bilateral exchange rates**, like the real exchange rate between the United States and the United Kingdom we focused on earlier, to **multilateral exchange rates** that reflect this composition of trade? The principle we want to use is simple, even if the details of construction are complicated: We weigh each country by how much each country trades with the United States and how much it competes with the United States in other countries. The variable constructed in this way is called the **multilateral real U.S. exchange rate**, or the U.S. real exchange rate for short.

◄ *Bi* means two. *Multi* means many.

◄ These are all equivalent names for the relative price of U.S. goods in terms of foreign goods:
- The real multilateral U.S. exchange rate
- The U.S. trade-weighted real exchange rate
- The U.S. effective real exchange rate

Figure 18-5 shows the evolution of this multilateral real exchange rate, the price of U.S goods in terms of foreign goods, since 1973. Like the bilateral real exchange rates we saw a few pages earlier, it is an index number. So its level is also arbitrary; here it is set equal to 1 in the first quarter of 2000.

The most striking aspect of the figure is something we saw earlier, when looking at the bilateral exchange rate between the United States and the United Kingdom in Figure 18-4: the large swing in the real exchange rate in the 1980s. U.S. goods were about 40% more expensive relative to foreign goods in the mid-1980s than they were at either the beginning or the end of the decade. In other words, there was a large real appreciation in the first half of the 1980s, followed by a roughly equal real depreciation in the second half. This large swing, which, as we have seen, has its origins in the movement of the nominal exchange rate, is so striking that it has been given various names, from the "dollar cycle" to the more graphic "dance of the dollar."

◄ The figure begins in 1973 because this multilateral real exchange rate, which is constructed by the Federal Reserve Board, is available only from 1973 on.

Note the similar, but smaller, movements of the dollar from the mid-1990s on, including an increase of 25% from 1995 to 2001 and a decrease since then. Many economists wonder whether we are in the middle of a second large swing, a second dollar cycle. In the coming chapters, we shall return to these swings, look at where they come from, and see what effects they have on the trade deficit and economic activity.

Table 18-2	The Country Composition of U.S. Exports and Imports, 2006	
	Proportion of Exports to (%)	Proportion of Imports from (%)
Canada	14	12
Mexico	8	8
European Union	29	25
China	3	13
Japan	6	9
Rest of Asia*	14	11
Others	26	22

*Asia, excluding Japan and China.
Source: *Survey of Current Business*, April 2007, Table F3.

The U.S. Multilateral Real Exchange Rate since 1973

The large real appreciation of U.S. goods in the first half of the 1980s was followed by a large real depreciation in the second half of the 1980s. This large swing in the 1980s is sometimes called the "dance of the dollar."

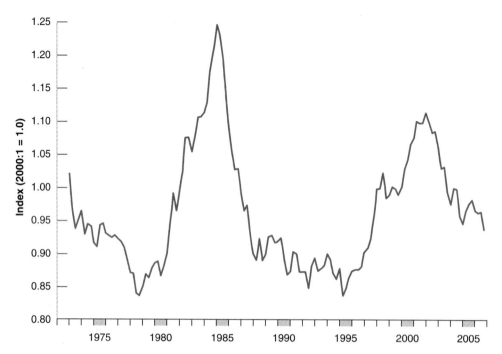

18-2 Openness in Financial Markets

Openness in financial markets allows financial investors to hold both domestic assets and foreign assets, to diversify their portfolios, to speculate on movements in foreign interest rates versus domestic interest rates, to speculate on movements in exchange rates, and so on.

Diversify and speculate they do. Given that buying or selling foreign assets implies buying or selling foreign currency—sometimes called **foreign exchange**—the volume of transactions in foreign exchange markets gives us a sense of the importance of international financial transactions. In 2005, for example, the recorded *daily* volume of foreign exchange transactions in the world was $1.9 trillion, of which 90%—about $1.7 trillion—involved dollars on one side of the transaction.

To get a sense of the magnitude of these numbers, the sum of U.S. exports and imports in 2005 totaled $3.3 trillion *for the year*, or about $9 billion per day. Suppose the only dollar transactions in foreign exchange markets had been, on one side, by U.S. exporters selling their foreign currency earnings, and on the other side by U.S. importers buying the foreign currency they needed to buy foreign goods. Then, the volume of transactions involving dollars in foreign exchange markets would have been $9 billion per day, or about 0.5% of the actual daily total volume of dollar transactions ($1.7 trillion) involving dollars in foreign exchange markets. This computation tells us that most of the transactions are associated not with trade but with purchases and sales of financial assets. Moreover, the volume of transactions in foreign exchange markets is not only high but also rapidly increasing. The volume of foreign exchange transactions has more than doubled since 2001. Again, this increase in activity reflects mostly an increase in financial transactions rather than an increase in trade.

For a country as a whole, openness in financial markets has another important implication. It allows the country to run trade surpluses and trade deficits. Recall that a country running a trade deficit is buying more from the rest of the world than it is selling to the rest of the world. In order to pay for the difference between what it buys and what it sells, the country must borrow from the rest of the world. It borrows by

Daily volume of foreign exchange transactions with dollars on one side of the transaction: $1.7 trillion. Daily volume of trade of the United States with the rest of the world: $9 billion (0.5% of the volume of foreign exchange transactions).

making it attractive for foreign financial investors to increase their holdings of domestic assets—in effect, to lend to the country.

Let's start by looking more closely at the relation between trade flows and financial flows. When this is done, we shall look at the determinants of these financial flows.

The Balance of Payments

A country's transactions with the rest of the world, including both trade flows and financial flows, are summarized by a set of accounts called the **balance of payments**. Table 18-3 presents the U.S. balance of payments for 2006. The table has two parts, separated by a line. Transactions are referred to as being either **above the line** or **below the line**.

The Current Account

The transactions above the line record payments to and from the rest of the world. They are called **current account** transactions:

■ The first two lines record the exports and imports of goods and services. Exports lead to payments from the rest of the world, and imports lead to payments to the rest of the world. In 2006, imports exceeded exports, leading to a U.S. trade deficit of $763 billion—roughly 5.8% of U.S. GDP.

■ Exports and imports are not the only sources of payments to and from the rest of the world. U.S. residents receive **investment income** on their holdings of foreign assets, and foreign residents receive U.S. investment income on their holdings of U.S. assets. In 2006, U.S. investment income received from the rest of the world was $620 billion, and investment income paid to foreigners was $629 billion, for a net balance of −$9 billion.

■ Finally, countries give and receive foreign aid; the net value of these payments is recorded as **net transfers received**. These net transfers amounted in 2006 to −$84 billion. This negative amount reflects the fact that, in 2006, the United States was—as it has traditionally been—a net donor of foreign aid.

Table 18-3 The U.S. Balance of Payments, 2006 (in billions of U.S. dollars)		
Current account		
Exports	1,437	
Imports	2,200	
Trade balance (deficit = −) (1)		−763
Investment income received	620	
Investment income paid	629	
Net investment income (2)		−9
Net transfers received (3)		−84
Current account balance (deficit = −) (1) + (2) + (3)		−856
Capital account		
Increase in foreign holdings of U.S. assets (4)	1,764	
Increase in U.S. holdings of foreign assets (5)	1,049	
Capital account balance (deficit = −) (4)−(5)		715
Statistical discrepancy		141

Source: *Survey of Current Business,* April 2007. All numbers are in billions of dollars.

The sum of net payments to and from the rest of the world is called the **current account balance**. If net payments from the rest of the world are positive, the country is running a **current account surplus**; if they are negative, the country is running a **current account deficit**. Adding all payments to and from the rest of the world, net payments from the United States to the rest of the world were equal in 2006 to $-\$763 - \$9 - \$84 = -\$856$ billion. Put another way, in 2006, the United States ran a current account deficit of \$856 billion—roughly 6.4% of its GDP.

Can a country have:
   A trade deficit and no current account deficit?
   A current account deficit and no trade deficit?
(The answer to both questions: Yes.)

The Capital Account

The fact that the United States had a current account deficit of \$856 billion in 2006 implies that it had to borrow \$856 billion from the rest of the world—or, equivalently, that net foreign holdings of U.S. assets had to increase by \$856 billion. The numbers below the line describe how this was achieved. Transactions below the line are called **capital account** transactions.

Similarly, if you spend more than you earn, you have to finance the difference.

The increase in foreign holdings of U.S. assets was \$1,764 billion: Foreign investors, be they foreign private investors, foreign governments, or foreign central banks, bought \$1,764 billion worth of U.S. stocks, U.S. bonds, and other U.S. assets. At the same time, there was an increase in U.S. holdings of foreign assets of \$1,049 billion: U.S. investors, private and public, bought \$1,049 billion worth of foreign stocks, bonds, and other assets. The result was an increase in net U.S foreign indebtedness (the increase in foreign holdings of U.S. assets minus the increase in U.S. holdings of foreign assets), also called **net capital flows**, to the United States of $\$1,764 - \$1,049 = \$715$ billion. Another name for net capital flows is the **capital account balance**: Positive net capital flows are called a **capital account surplus**; negative net capital flows are called a **capital account deficit**. So, put another way, in 2006, the United States ran a capital account surplus of \$715 billion.

A country that runs a current account deficit must finance it through positive net capital flows. Equivalently, it must run a capital account surplus.

Shouldn't net capital flows (equivalently, the capital account surplus) be exactly equal to the current account deficit (which we saw earlier was equal to \$856 billion in 2006)? In principle, yes; in practice, no.

The numbers for current and capital account transactions are constructed using different sources; although they should give the same answers, they typically do not. In 2006, the difference between the two—the **statistical discrepancy**—was \$141 billion, about 20% of the current account balance. This is yet another reminder that, even for a rich country such as the United States, economic data are far from perfect. (This problem of measurement manifests itself in another way as well. The sum of the current account deficits of all the countries in the world should be equal to 0: One country's deficit should show up as a surplus for the other countries taken as a whole. However, this is not the case in the data: If we just add the published current account deficits of all the countries in the world, it would appear that the world is running a large current account deficit!)

Some economists speculate that the explanation lies in unrecorded trade with the Martians. Most others believe that mismeasurement is the explanation.

Now that we have looked at the current account, we can return to an issue we touched on in Chapter 2: the difference between GDP, the measure of output we have used so far, and GNP, another measure of aggregate output. This is done in the Focus box "GDP versus GNP: The Example of Kuwait."

The Choice between Domestic and Foreign Assets

Openness in financial markets implies that people (or financial institutions that act on their behalf) face a new financial decision: whether to hold domestic assets or foreign assets.

It would appear that we actually have to think about at least *two* new decisions, the choice of holding domestic *money* versus foreign *money*, and the choice of holding

Should value added in an open economy be defined as

■ The value added domestically (that is, within the country), or

■ The value added by domestically owned factors of production?

The two definitions are not the same: Some domestic output is produced with capital owned by foreigners, while some foreign output is produced with capital owned by domestic residents.

The answer is that either definition is fine, and economists use both. **Gross domestic product (GDP)**, the measure we have used so far, corresponds to value added domestically. **Gross national product (GNP)** corresponds to the value added by domestically owned factors of production. To go from GDP to GNP, one must start from GDP, add factor payments received from the rest of the world, and subtract factor payments paid to the rest of the world. Put another way, GNP is equal to GDP plus net factor payments from the rest of the world. While GDP is now the measure most commonly mentioned, GNP was widely used until the early 1990s, and you will still encounter it in newspapers and academic publications.

For most countries, the difference between GNP and GDP is typically small because factor payments to and from the rest of the world roughly cancel one another. For the United States in 2006, the difference between GDP and GNP was $30 billion—about 0.2% of GDP. (This is an unusually small number by historical standards. But, for the United States, the difference between GDP and GNP has never exceeded 1% of GDP.)

There are a few exceptions. Among them is Kuwait. When oil was discovered in Kuwait, Kuwait's government decided that a portion of oil revenues would be saved and invested abroad rather than spent, so as to provide future

Kuwaiti generations with investment income when oil revenues came to an end. Kuwait ran a large current account surplus, steadily accumulating large foreign assets. As a result, it now has large holdings of foreign assets and receives substantial investment income from the rest of the world. Table 1 gives GDP, GNP, and net factor payments for Kuwait from 1989 to 1994.

Note how much larger GNP is compared to GDP throughout the period. Note also how net factor payments decreased after 1989. This is because Kuwait had to pay its allies for part of the cost of the 1990 to 1991 Gulf War and pay for reconstruction after the war. It did so by running a current account deficit—that is, by decreasing its net holdings of foreign assets. This in turn led to a decrease in the income it earned from foreign assets and, by implication, a decrease in its net factor payments.

Since the Gulf War, Kuwait has rebuilt a sizable net foreign asset position. Net income from abroad now exceeds 10% of GDP.

Table 1	GDP, GNP, and Net Factor Payments in Kuwait, 1989 to 1994		
Year	GDP	GNP	Net Factor Payments
1989	7,143	9,616	2,473
1990	5,328	7,560	2,232
1991	3,131	4,669	1,538
1992	5,826	7,364	1,538
1993	7,231	8,386	1,151
1994	7,380	8,321	941

Note: All numbers are in millions of Kuwaiti dinars. 1 dinar = $3.67 (2007).
Source: IMF International Financial Statistics.

FOCUS

domestic *interest-paying assets* versus foreign *interest-paying assets*. But remember why people hold money: to engage in transactions. For someone who lives in the United States and whose transactions are mostly or fully in dollars, there is little point in holding foreign currency: Foreign currency cannot be used for transactions in the United States, and if the goal is to hold foreign assets, holding foreign currency is clearly less desirable than holding foreign bonds, which pay interest. This leaves us ◄ with only one new choice to think about, the choice between domestic interest-paying assets and foreign interest-paying assets.

Let's think of these assets for now as domestic one-year bonds and foreign one-year bonds. Consider, for example, the choice between U.S. one-year bonds and U.K. one-year bonds, from your point of view, as a U.S. investor:

■ Suppose you decide to hold U.S. bonds.

Let i_t be the one-year U.S. nominal interest rate. Then, as Figure 18-6 shows, for every 1 dollar you put in U.S. bonds, you will get $1 + i_t$ dollars next year. (This is represented by the arrow pointing to the right at the top of the figure.)

Two qualifications, from Chapter 4:

Foreigners involved in illegal activities often hold dollars because dollars can be exchanged easily and cannot be traced.

In times of very high inflation, people sometimes switch to a foreign currency, often the dollar, for use even in some domestic transactions.

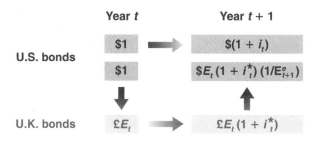

- Suppose you decide instead to hold U.K. bonds.

    To buy U.K. bonds, you must first buy pounds. Let E_t be the nominal exchange rate between the dollar and the pound. For every 1 dollar, you get E_t pounds. (This is represented by the arrow pointing downward in the figure.)

    Let i_t^* denote the one-year nominal interest rate on U.K. bonds (in pounds). When next year comes, you will have $E_t(1 + i_t^*)$ pounds. (This is represented by the arrow pointing to the right at the bottom of the figure.)

    You will then have to convert your pounds back into dollars. If you expect the nominal exchange rate next year to be E_{t+1}^e, each pound will be worth $(1/E_{t+1}^e)$ dollars. So you can expect to have $E_t(1 + i_t^*)(1/E_{t+1}^e)$ dollars next year for every 1 dollar you invest now. (This is represented by the arrow pointing upward in the figure.) We shall look at the expression we just derived in more detail soon. But note its basic implication already: In assessing the attractiveness of U.K. versus U.S. bonds, you cannot look just at the U.K. interest rate and the U.S. interest rate; you must also assess what you think will happen to the dollar/pound exchange rate between this year and next.

The decision about whether to invest abroad or at home depends on more than interest rates. It also depends on the expected movements in the exchange rate in the future. ▶

Let's now make the same assumption we made in Chapter 14 when discussing the choice between short-term bonds and long-term bonds or between bonds and stocks. Let's assume that you and other financial investors care only about the expected rate of return and therefore want to hold only the asset with the highest expected rate of return. In that case, if both U.K. bonds and U.S. bonds are to be held, they must have the same expected rate of return. In other words, because of arbitrage, the following relation must hold:

The word *uncovered* is to distinguish this relation from another relation called the *covered interest parity* condition. The covered interest parity condition is derived by looking at the following choice:

Buy and hold U.S. bonds for one year. Or buy pounds today, buy one-year U.K. bonds with the proceeds, and agree to sell the pounds for dollars a year ahead at a predetermined price, called the *forward exchange rate*.

The rate of return on these two alternatives, which can both be realized at *no risk today*, must be the same. The covered interest parity condition is a *riskless arbitrage* condition. ▶

$$(1 + i_t) = (E_t)(1 + i_t^*)\left(\frac{1}{E_{t+1}^e}\right)$$

Reorganizing, we have

$$(1 + i_t) = (1 + i_t^*)\left(\frac{E_t}{E_{t+1}^e}\right) \tag{18.2}$$

Equation (18.2) is called the **uncovered interest parity relation**, or simply the **interest parity condition**.

The assumption that financial investors will hold only the bonds with the highest expected rate of return is obviously too strong, for two reasons:

Whether holding U.K. bonds or U.S. bonds is more risky actually depends on which investors we are looking at. Holding U.K. bonds is more risky from the point of view of U.S. investors. Holding U.S. bonds is more risky from the point of view of British investors. (Why?) ▶

- It ignores transaction costs. Going into and out of U.K. bonds requires three separate transactions, each with a transaction cost.
- It ignores risk. The exchange rate a year from now is uncertain; holding U.K. bonds is therefore more risky, in terms of dollars, than holding U.S. bonds.

But as a characterization of capital movements among the major world financial markets (New York, Frankfurt, London, and Tokyo), the assumption is not far off. Small changes in interest rates and rumors of impending appreciation or depreciation can lead to movements of billions of dollars within minutes. For the rich countries of the world, the arbitrage assumption in equation (18.2) is a good approximation of reality. Other countries whose capital markets are smaller and less developed, or countries that have various forms of capital controls, have more leeway in choosing their domestic interest rate than is implied by equation (18.2). We shall return to this issue at the end of Chapter 20.

Interest Rates and Exchange Rates

Let's get a better sense of what the interest parity condition implies. First, rewrite E_t/E_{t+1}^e as $1/(1 + (E_{t+1}^e - E_t)/E_t)$. Replacing in equation (18.2) gives

$$(1 + i_t) = \frac{(1 + i_t^*)}{[1 + (E_{t+1}^e - E_t)/E_t]} \qquad (18.3)$$

This gives us a relation between the domestic nominal interest rate, i_t, the foreign nominal interest rate, i_t^*, and the expected rate of appreciation of the domestic currency, $(E_{t+1}^e - E_t)/E_t$. As long as interest rates or the expected rate of depreciation are not too large—say below 20% per year—a good approximation to this equation is given by

> This follows from Proposition 3 in Appendix 2 at the end of the book.

$$i_t \approx i_t^* - \frac{E_{t+1}^e - E_t}{E_t} \qquad (18.4)$$

This is the form of the *interest parity* condition you must remember: Arbitrage by investors implies that *the domestic interest rate must be equal to the foreign interest rate minus the expected appreciation rate of the domestic currency.*

Note that the expected appreciation rate of the domestic currency is also the expected depreciation rate of the foreign currency. So equation (18.4) can be equivalently stated as saying that *the domestic interest rate must be equal to the foreign interest rate minus the expected depreciation rate of the foreign currency.*

> If the dollar is expected to appreciate by 3% vis-à-vis the pound, then the pound is expected to depreciate by 3% vis-à-vis the dollar.

Let's apply this equation to U.S. bonds versus U.K. bonds. Suppose the one-year nominal interest rate is 2.0% in the United States, and it is 5.0% in the United Kingdom. Should you hold U.K. bonds or U.S. bonds? The answer:

■ It depends whether you expect the pound to depreciate vis-à-vis the dollar over the coming year by more or less than the difference between the U.S. interest rate and the U.K. interest rate, 3.0% in this case (5.0% − 2.0%).
■ If you expect the pound to depreciate by more than 3.0%, then, despite the fact that the interest rate is higher in the United Kingdom than in the United States, investing in U.K. bonds is less attractive than investing in U.S. bonds. By holding U.K. bonds, you will get higher interest payments next year, but the pound will be worth less in terms of dollars next year, making investing in U.K. bonds less attractive than investing in U.S. bonds.
■ If you expect the pound to depreciate by less than 3.0% or even to appreciate, then the reverse holds, and U.K. bonds are more attractive than U.S. bonds.

Looking at it another way: If the uncovered interest parity condition holds, and the U.S. one-year interest rate is 3% lower than the U.K. interest rate, it must be that financial investors are expecting on average an appreciation of the dollar vis-à-vis the pound over the coming year of about 3%, and this is why they are willing to hold U.S. bonds despite their lower interest rate. (Another application of the uncovered interest parity condition is provided in the Focus box "Buying Brazilian Bonds.")

Let's go back to September 1993 because the very high interest rate in Brazil at the time helps make the point I want to get across here. Brazilian bonds are paying a monthly interest rate of 36.9%. This seems very attractive compared to the annual rate of 3% on U.S. bonds—corresponding to a monthly interest rate of about 0.2%. Shouldn't you buy Brazilian bonds?

The discussion in this chapter tells you that, to decide, you need one more crucial element: the expected rate of depreciation of the cruzeiro (the name of the Brazilian currency at the time; the currency is now called the real) in terms of dollars.

You need this information because, as we saw in equation (18.3), the return in dollars from investing in Brazilian bonds for a month is equal to 1 plus the Brazilian interest rate, divided by 1 plus the expected rate of depreciation of the cruzeiro relative to the dollar:

$$\frac{1 + i_t^*}{[1 + (E_{t+1}^e - E_t)/E_t]}$$

What rate of depreciation of the cruzeiro should you expect over the coming month? A reasonable assumption is to expect the rate of depreciation during the coming month to be equal to the rate of depreciation during last month. The dollar was worth 100,000 cruzeiros at the end of July 1993, and it was worth 134,600 cruzeiros at the end of August 1993, so the rate of appreciation of the dollar vis-à-vis the cruzeiro—equivalently, the rate of depreciation of the cruzeiro vis-à-vis the dollar—in August was 34.6%. If depreciation is expected to continue at the same rate in September as it did in August, the expected return from investing in Brazilian bonds for a month is

$$\frac{1.369}{1.346} = 1.017$$

The expected rate of return in dollars from holding Brazilian bonds is only (1.017 − 1) = 1.7% per month, not the 36.9% per month that initially looked so attractive. Note that 1.7% per month is still much higher than the monthly interest rate on U.S. bonds (about 0.2%). But think of the risk and the transaction costs—all the elements we ignored when we wrote the arbitrage condition. When these are taken into account, you may well decide to keep your funds out of Brazil.

The arbitrage relation between interest rates and exchange rates, either in the form of equation (18.2) or equation (18.4), will play a central role in the following chapters. It suggests that, unless countries are willing to tolerate large movements in their exchange rates, domestic and foreign interest rates are likely to move very much together. Take the extreme case of two countries that commit to maintaining their bilateral exchange rates at a fixed value. If markets have faith in this commitment, they will expect the exchange rate to remain constant, and the expected depreciation will be equal to zero. In this case, the arbitrage condition implies that interest rates in the two countries will have to move exactly together. Most of the time, as we shall see, governments do not make such absolute commitments to maintain the exchange rate, but they often do try to avoid large movements in the exchange rate. This puts sharp limits on how much they can allow their interest rates to deviate from interest rates elsewhere in the world.

How much do nominal interest rates actually move together in major countries? Figure 18-7 plots the three-month nominal interest rate in the United States and the three-month nominal interest rate in the United Kingdom (both expressed at annual rates) since 1970. The figure shows that the movements are related but not identical. Interest rates were very high in both countries in the early 1980s, and they were high

If $E_{t+1}^e = E_t$, then the interest parity condition implies that $i_t = i_t^*$. ▶

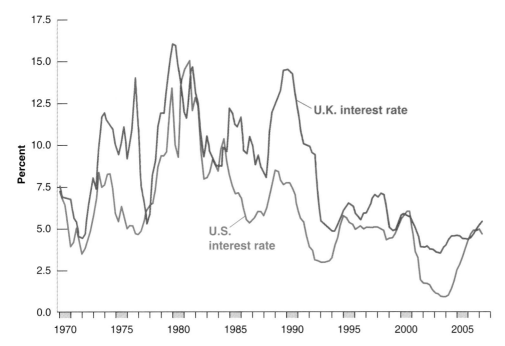

Figure 18-7 ▬

Three-Month Nominal Interest Rates in the United States and in the United Kingdom since 1970

U.S. and U.K. nominal interest rates have largely moved to-gether over the past 38 years.

again—although much more so in the United Kingdom than in the United States—in the late 1980s. They have been low in both countries since the mid-1990s. At the same time, differences between the two have sometimes been quite large: In 1990, for example, the U.K. interest rate was nearly 7% higher than the U.S. interest rate. In the coming chapters, we shall return to why such differences emerge and what their implications may be.

Meanwhile, do the following: Look at the back pages of a recent issue of *The Economist* for short-term interest rates in different countries relative to the United States. Assume that ◀ uncovered interest parity holds. Which currencies are expected to appreciate against the dollar?

18-3 Conclusions and a Look Ahead

We have now set the stage for the study of the open economy:

- Openness in goods markets allows people and firms to choose between domestic goods and foreign goods. This choice depends primarily on the *real exchange rate*—the relative price of domestic goods in terms of foreign goods.
- Openness in financial markets allows investors to choose between domestic and foreign assets. This choice depends primarily on their relative rates of return, which depend on domestic and foreign interest rates, and on the expected rate of appreciation of the domestic currency.

In Chapter 19, we look at the implications of openness in goods markets. Chapter 20 brings in openness in financial markets. In Chapter 21, we discuss the pros and cons of different exchange rate regimes.

Summary

- Openness in goods markets allows people and firms to choose between domestic goods and foreign goods. Openness in financial markets allows financial investors to hold domestic financial assets or foreign financial assets.

- The nominal exchange rate is the price of the domestic currency in terms of foreign currency. From the viewpoint of the United States, the nominal exchange rate between the United States and the United Kingdom is the price of a dollar in terms of pounds.

- A nominal appreciation (an appreciation, for short) is an increase in the price of the domestic currency in terms of foreign currency. In other words, it corresponds to an increase in the exchange rate. A nominal depreciation (a depreciation, for short) is a decrease in the price of the domestic currency in terms of foreign currency. It corresponds to a decrease in the exchange rate.

- The real exchange rate is the relative price of domestic goods in terms of foreign goods. It is equal to the nominal exchange rate times the domestic price level divided by the foreign price level.

- A real appreciation is an increase in the relative price of domestic goods in terms of foreign goods—i.e., an increase in the real exchange rate. A real depreciation is a decrease in the relative price of domestic goods in terms of foreign goods—i.e., a decrease in the real exchange rate.

- The multilateral real exchange rate, or real exchange rate for short, is a weighted average of bilateral real exchange rates, with the weight for each foreign country equal to its share in trade.

- The balance of payments records a country's transactions with the rest of the world. The current account balance is equal to the sum of the trade balance, net investment income, and net transfers the country receives from the rest of the world. The capital account balance is equal to capital flows from the rest of the world minus capital flows to the rest of the world.

- The current account and the capital account are mirror images of each other. Leaving aside statistical problems, the current account plus the capital account must sum to zero. A current account deficit is financed by net capital flows from the rest of the world, thus by a capital account surplus. Similarly, a current account surplus corresponds to a capital account deficit.

- Uncovered interest parity, or interest parity for short, is an arbitrage condition which states that the expected rates of return in terms of domestic currency on domestic bonds and foreign bonds must be equal. Interest parity implies that the domestic interest rate approximately equals the foreign interest rate minus the expected appreciation rate of the domestic currency.

Key Terms

Quick Check

1. *Using the information in this chapter, label each of the following statements true, false, or uncertain. Explain briefly.*

   a. If there are no statistical discrepancies, countries with current account deficits must receive net capital inflows.

   b. While the export ratio can be larger than one—as it is in Singapore—the same cannot be true of the ratio of imports to GDP.

   c. That a rich country like Japan has such a small ratio of imports to GDP is clear evidence of an unfair playing field for U.S. exporters to Japan.

   d. Uncovered interest parity implies that interest rates must be the same across countries.

   e. If the dollar is expected to appreciate against the yen, uncovered interest parity implies that the U.S. nominal interest rate will be greater than the Japanese nominal interest rate.

   f. Given the definition of the exchange rate adopted in this chapter, if the dollar is the domestic currency and the euro the foreign currency, a nominal exchange rate of 0.75 means that 0.75 dollars is worth 0.75 euros.

   g. A real appreciation means that domestic goods become less expensive relative to foreign goods.

2. *Consider two fictional economies, one called the domestic country and the other the foreign country. Given the transactions listed in (a) through (g), construct the balance of payments for each country. If necessary, include a statistical discrepancy.*

   a. The domestic country purchased $125 in oil from the foreign country.

   b. Foreign tourists spent $30 on domestic ski slopes.

   c. Foreign investors were paid $20 in dividends from their holdings of domestic equities.

   d. Domestic residents gave $30 to foreign charities.

   e. Domestic businesses borrowed $75 from foreign banks.

   f. Foreign investors purchased $20 of domestic government bonds.

   g. Domestic investors sold $60 of their holdings of foreign government bonds.

3. *Consider two bonds, one issued in euros (€) in Germany, and one issued in dollars ($) in the United States. Assume that both government securities are one-year bonds— paying the face value of the bond one year from now. The exchange rate, E, stands at 1 dollar = 0.75 euros.*

   The face values and prices on the two bonds are given by

	Face Value	Price
United States	$10,000	$9,615.38
Germany	€10,000	€9,433.96

   a. Compute the nominal interest rate on each of the bonds.

   b. Compute the expected exchange rate next year consistent with uncovered interest parity.

   c. If you expect the dollar to depreciate relative to the euro, which bond should you buy?

   d. Assume that you are a U.S. investor. You exchange dollars for euros and purchase the German bond. One year from now, it turns out that the exchange rate, E, is actually 0.72 (1 dollar = 0.72 euros). What is your realized rate of return in dollars compared to the realized rate of return you would have made had you held the U.S. bond?

   e. Are the differences in rates of return in (d) consistent with the uncovered interest parity condition? Why or why not?

Dig Deeper

4. *The exchange rate and the labor market*

   Suppose the domestic currency depreciates (E falls). Assume that P and P* remain constant.

   a. How does the nominal depreciation affect the relative price of domestic goods (i.e., the real exchange rate)? Given your answer, what effect would a nominal depreciation likely have on (world) demand for domestic goods? on the domestic unemployment rate?

   b. Given the foreign price level, P*, what is the price of foreign goods in terms of domestic currency? How does a nominal depreciation affect the price of foreign goods in terms of domestic currency? How does a nominal depreciation affect the domestic consumer price index? (*Hint*: Remember that domestic consumers buy foreign goods (imports) as well as domestic goods.)

   c. If the nominal wage remains constant, how does a nominal depreciation affect the real wage?

   d. Comment on the following statement. "A depreciating currency puts domestic labor on sale."

5. *Consider a world with three equal-sized economies (A, B, and C) and three goods (clothes, cars, and computers). Assume that consumers in all three economies want to spend an equal amount on all three goods.*

   The value of production of each good in the three economies is given below.

	A	B	C
CLOTHES	10	0	5
CARS	5	10	0
COMPUTERS	0	5	10

   a. What is GDP in each economy? If the total value of GDP is consumed and no country borrows from abroad, how much will consumers in each economy spend on each of the goods?

   b. If no country borrows from abroad, what will be the trade balance in each country? What will be the pattern of trade in this world (i.e., which good will each country export and to whom)?

c. Given your answer to part (b), will country A have a zero trade balance with country B? with country C? Will any country have a zero trade balance with any other country?

d. The United States has a large trade deficit. It has a trade deficit with each of its major trading partners, but the deficit is much larger with some countries (e.g., China) than with others. Suppose the United States eliminates its overall trade deficit (with the world as a whole). Do you expect it to have a zero trade balance with every one of its trading partners? Does the especially large trade deficit with China necessarily indicate that China does not allow U.S. goods to compete on an equal basis with Chinese goods?

Explore Further

6. Retrieve the nominal exchange rates between Japan and the United States from the Internet. A useful and free Canadian site that allows you to construct graphs online is the Pacific Exchange Rate Service (**fx.sauder.ubc.ca**), provided by Werner Antweiler at the Sauder School of Business, University of British Columbia.

 a. Plot the yen versus the dollar since 1979. During which times period(s) did the yen appreciate? During which period(s) did the yen depreciate?

 b. Given the current Japanese slump (although there are some encouraging signs at the time of this writing), one way of increasing demand would be to make Japanese goods more attractive. Does this require an appreciation or a depreciation of the yen?

 c. What has happened to the yen during the past few years? Has it appreciated or depreciated? Is this good or bad for Japan?

7. Saving and investment throughout the world
   Retrieve the most recent World Economic Outlook (WEO) from the Web site of the International Monetary Fund (**www.imf.org**). In the Statistical Appendix, find the table titled "Summary of Sources and Uses of World Saving," which lists saving and investment (as a percentage of GDP) around the world. Use the data for the most recent year available to answer parts (a) and (b).

 a. Does world saving equal investment? (You may ignore small statistical discrepancies.) Offer some intuition for your answer.

 b. How does U.S. saving compare to U.S. investment? How is the United States able to finance its investment? (We explain this explicitly in the next chapter, but your intuition should help you figure it out now.)

8. Retrieve the most recent World Economic Outlook (WEO) from the Web site of the International Monetary Fund (**www.imf.org**). In the Statistical Appendix, find the table titled "Balances on Current Account," which lists current account balances around the world. Use the data for the most recent year available to answer parts (a) through (c).

 a. Note the sum of current account balances around the world. As noted in the chapter, the sum of current account balances should equal zero. What does this sum actually equal? Why does this sum indicate some mismeasurement (i.e., if the sum were correct, what would it imply)?

 b. Which regions of the world are borrowing and which are lending?

 c. Compare the U.S. current account balance to the current account balances of the other advanced economies. Is the United States borrowing only from advanced economies?

 d. The statistical tables in the WEO typically project data for two years into the future. Look at the projected data on current account balances. Do your answers to parts (b) and (c) seem likely to change in the near future?

 We invite you to visit the Blanchard page on the Prentice Hall Web site, at:
www.prenhall.com/blanchard
for this chapter's World Wide Web exercises.

Further Readings

■ If you want to learn more about international trade and international economics, read the very good textbook by Paul Krugman and Maurice Obstfeld, *International Economics, Theory and Policy*, 7th ed., Pearson Addison-Wesley, New York, 2007.

■ If you want to know current exchange rates between nearly any pair of currencies in the world, look at the currency converter at **www.oanda.com**.

The Goods Market in an Open Economy

A t the time of this writing, countries around the world are worried about the risk of a U.S. recession. Their worries are not for the United States but for themselves. To them, a U.S. recession means lower exports to the United States, a deterioration of their trade position, and weaker growth at home.

Are their worries justified? Does the U.S. economy really drive other economies? Could a U.S. recession really throw other countries in recession? To answer these questions, we must expand our treatment of the goods market in Chapter 3 to take into account openness in goods markets. This is what we do in this chapter:

■ Section 19-1 characterizes equilibrium in the goods market for an open economy.

■ Sections 19-2 and 19-3 show the effects of domestic shocks and foreign shocks on the domestic economy's output and trade balance.

■ Sections 19-4 and 19-5 look at the effects of a real depreciation on output and the trade balance.

■ Section 19-6 gives an alternative description of the equilibrium, which shows the close connection between saving, investment, and the trade balance. ■

CHAPTER 19

When we were assuming that the economy was closed to trade, there was no need to distinguish between the *domestic demand for goods* and the *demand for domestic goods*: They were clearly the same thing. Now, we must distinguish between the two. Some domestic demand falls on foreign goods, and some of the demand for domestic goods comes from foreigners. Let's look at this distinction more closely.

"The domestic demand for goods" and "the demand for domestic goods" sound close but are not the same. Part of domestic demand falls on foreign goods. Part of foreign demand falls on domestic goods. ▶

The Demand for Domestic Goods

In an open economy, the **demand for domestic goods** is given by

$$Z \equiv C + I + G - IM/\epsilon + X \qquad (19.1)$$

The first three terms—consumption, C, investment, I, and government spending, G—constitute the **domestic demand for goods**. If the economy were closed, $C + I + G$ would also be the demand for domestic goods. This is why, until now, we have only looked at $C + I + G$. But now we have to make two adjustments:

In Chapter 3, I ignored the real exchange rate and subtracted *IM*, not *IM/ε*. But that was a cheat; I did not want to have to talk about the real exchange rate—and complicate matters—so early in the book. ▶

- First, we must subtract imports—that part of the domestic demand that falls on foreign goods rather than on domestic goods.

    We must be careful here: Foreign goods are different from domestic goods, so we cannot just subtract the quantity of imports, IM. If we were to do so, we would be subtracting apples (foreign goods) from oranges (domestic goods). We must first express the value of imports in terms of domestic goods. This is what IM/ϵ in equation (19.1) stands for: Recall from Chapter 18 that ϵ, the real exchange rate, is defined as the price of domestic goods in terms of foreign goods. Equivalently, $1/\epsilon$ is the price of foreign goods in terms of domestic goods. So $IM(1/\epsilon)$—or, equivalently, IM/ϵ—is the value of imports in terms of domestic goods.

Domestic demand for goods, $C + I + G$
    Minus domestic demand for foreign goods (imports), IM/ϵ ▶
    Plus foreign demand for domestic goods (exports), X
    Equals demand for domestic goods, $C + I + G - IM/\epsilon + X$.

- Second, we must add exports—that part of the demand for domestic goods that comes from abroad. This is captured by the term X in equation (19.1).

The Determinants of *C, I,* and *G*

Having listed the five components of demand, our next task is to specify their determinants. Let's start with the first three: C, I, and G. Now that we are assuming that the economy is open, how should we modify our earlier descriptions of consumption, investment, and government spending? The answer: Not very much, if at all. How much consumers decide to spend still depends on their income and their wealth. While the real exchange rate surely affects the *composition* of consumption spending between domestic goods and foreign goods, there is no obvious reason why it should affect the overall *level* of consumption. The same is true of investment: The real exchange rate may affect whether firms buy domestic machines or foreign machines, but it should not affect total investment.

This is good news because it implies that we can use the descriptions of consumption, investment, and government spending that we developed earlier. Therefore,

$$\text{Domestic demand:} \quad C + I + G = C(Y - T) + I(Y,\ r) + G$$
$$(\ +\ ) \qquad (+,-)$$

We assume that consumption depends positively on disposable income, $Y - T$, and that investment depends positively on production, Y, and negatively on the real interest rate, r. We continue to take government spending, G, as given. We leave aside the refinements introduced in Chapters 14 to 17, where we looked at how expectations affect spending. We want to take things one step at a time to understand the effects of opening the economy; we shall reintroduce some of those refinements later.

The Determinants of Imports

Imports are the part of domestic demand that falls on foreign goods. What do they depend on? They clearly depend on domestic income: Higher domestic income leads to a higher domestic demand for all goods, both domestic and foreign. So a higher domestic income leads to higher imports. Imports also clearly depend on the real exchange rate—the price of domestic goods in terms of foreign goods. The more expensive domestic goods are relative to foreign goods—equivalently, the cheaper foreign goods are relative to domestic goods—the higher the domestic demand for foreign goods. So a higher real exchange rate leads to higher imports. Thus, we write imports as

Recall the discussion at the start of the chapter: Countries in the rest of the world worry about a U.S. recession. The reason: A U.S. recession means a decrease in the U.S. demand for foreign goods.

$$IM = IM(Y, \ \epsilon) \\ (+, +)$$

(19.2)

- An increase in domestic income, Y (equivalently, an increase in domestic output—income and output are still equal in an open economy), leads to an increase in imports. This positive effect of income on imports is captured by the positive sign under Y in equation (19.2).
- An increase in the real exchange rate, ϵ, leads to an increase in imports, IM. This positive effect of the real exchange rate on imports is captured by the positive sign under ϵ in equation (19.2). (As ϵ goes up, note that IM goes up, but $1/\epsilon$ goes down, so what happens to IM/ϵ, the *value* of imports in terms of domestic goods, is ambiguous. We will return to this point shortly.)

The Determinants of Exports

Exports are the part of foreign demand that falls on domestic goods. What do they depend on? They depend on foreign income: Higher foreign income means higher foreign demand for all goods, both foreign and domestic. So higher foreign income leads to higher exports. Exports also depend on the real exchange rate: The higher the price of domestic goods in terms of foreign goods, the lower the foreign demand for domestic goods. In other words, the higher the real exchange rate, the lower the exports.

Let Y^* denote foreign income (equivalently, foreign output). We therefore write exports as

Recall that asterisks refer to foreign variables.

$$X = X(Y^*, \ \epsilon) \\ (+, \ -)$$

(19.3)

- An increase in foreign income, Y^*, leads to an increase in exports.
- An increase in the real exchange rate, ϵ, leads to a decrease in exports.

Putting the Components Together

Figure 19-1 puts together what we have learned so far. It plots the various components of demand against output, keeping constant all other variables (the interest rate, taxes, government spending, foreign output, and the real exchange rate) that affect demand.

In Figure 19-1(a), the line DD plots domestic demand, $C + I + G$, as a function of output, Y. This relation between demand and output is familiar from Chapter 3. Under our standard assumptions, the slope of the relation between demand and output is positive but less than 1. An increase in output—equivalently, an increase in income—increases demand but less than one-for-one. (In the absence of good reasons to the

Figure 19-1

The Demand for Domestic Goods and Net Exports

Panel (a): The domestic demand for goods is an increasing function of income (output).

Panels (b) and (c): The demand for domestic goods is obtained by subtracting the value of imports from domestic demand and then adding exports.

Panel (d): The trade balance is a decreasing function of output.

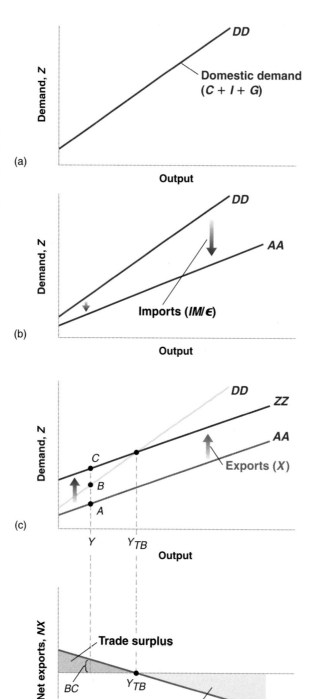

contrary, I draw the relation between demand and output, and the other relations in this chapter, as lines rather than curves. This is purely for convenience, and none of the discussions that follow depend on this assumption.)

To arrive at the demand for domestic goods, we must first *subtract imports*. This is done in Figure 19-1(b), and it gives us the line *AA*. The line *AA* represents the domestic demand for domestic goods. The distance between *DD* and *AA* equals the value of imports, IM/ϵ. Because the quantity of imports increases with income, the distance between the two lines increases with income. We can establish two facts about line AA, which will be useful later in the chapter:

◀ For a given real exchange rate ϵ, IM/ϵ—the value of imports in terms of domestic goods— moves exactly with IM—the quantity of imports.

- AA is flatter than DD: As income increases, some of the additional domestic demand falls on foreign goods rather than on domestic goods. In other words, as income increases, the domestic demand for domestic goods increases less than total domestic demand.
- As long as some of the additional demand falls on domestic goods, AA has a positive slope: An increase in income leads to some increase in the demand for domestic goods.

Finally, we must *add exports*. This is done in Figure 19-1(c), and it gives us the line ZZ, which is above AA. The line ZZ represents the demand for domestic goods. The distance between ZZ and AA equals exports. Because exports do not depend on domestic income (they depend on foreign income), the distance between ZZ and AA is constant, which is why the two lines are parallel. Because AA is flatter than DD, ZZ is also flatter than DD.

From the information in Figure 19-1(c), we can characterize the behavior of net exports—the difference between exports and imports $(X - IM/\epsilon)$—as a function of output. At output level Y, for example, exports are given by the distance AC and imports by the distance AB, so net exports are given by the distance BC.

This relation between net exports and output is represented as the line NX (for Net eXports) in Figure 19-1(d). Net exports are a decreasing function of output: As output increases, imports increase, and exports are unaffected, so net exports decrease. Call Y_{TB} (TB for trade balance) the level of output at which the value of imports equals the value of exports, so that net exports are equal to 0. Levels of output above Y_{TB} lead to higher imports and to a trade deficit. Levels of output below Y_{TB} lead to lower imports and to a trade surplus.

◀ Recall that *net exports* is synonymous with *trade balance*. Positive net exports correspond to a trade surplus, whereas negative net exports correspond to a trade deficit.

19-2 Equilibrium Output and the Trade Balance

The goods market is in equilibrium when domestic output equals the demand—both domestic and foreign—for domestic goods:

$$Y = Z$$

Collecting the relations we derived for the components of the demand for domestic goods, Z, we get

$$Y = C(Y - T) + I(Y, r) + G - IM(Y, \epsilon)/\epsilon + X(Y^*, \epsilon) \qquad (19.4)$$

This equilibrium condition determines output as a function of all the variables we take as given, from taxes to the real exchange rate to foreign output. This is not a simple relation; Figure 19-2 represents it graphically, in a more user-friendly way.

In Figure 19-2(a), demand is measured on the vertical axis, and output (equivalently production or income) is measured on the horizontal axis. The line ZZ plots demand as a function of output; this line simply replicates the line ZZ in Figure 19-1; ZZ is upward sloping but with slope less than 1.

Equilibrium output is at the point where demand equals output, at the intersection of the line ZZ and the 45-degree line: point A in the figure, with associated output level Y.

Figure 19-2(b) replicates Figure 19-1(d), drawing net exports as a decreasing function of output. There is, in general, no reason why the equilibrium level of output, Y, should be the same as the level of output at which trade is balanced, Y_{TB}. As I have

The equilibrium level of output is given by the condition $Y = Z$. The level of output at which there is trade balance is given by the condition $X = IM/\epsilon$. These are two different ◀ conditions.

Figure 19-2

Equilibrium Output and Net Exports

The goods market is in equilibrium when domestic output is equal to the demand for domestic goods. At the equilibrium level of output, the trade balance may show a deficit or a surplus.

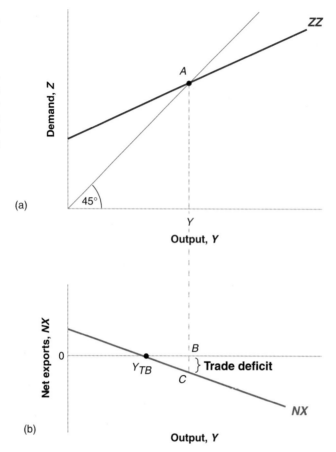

(a)

(b)

drawn the figure, equilibrium output is associated with a trade deficit, equal to the distance *BC*. Note that I could have drawn it differently, so equilibrium output was associated instead with a trade surplus.

We now have the tools needed to answer the questions we asked at the beginning of this chapter.

19-3 Increases in Demand, Domestic or Foreign

How do changes in demand affect output in an open economy? Let's start with an old favorite—an increase in government spending—and then turn to a new exercise, the effects of an increase in foreign demand.

Increases in Domestic Demand

As in the core, we start with the goods market; the conclusions we derive here will still largely ▶ be correct when we introduce financial markets and labor markets later on.

Suppose the economy is in a recession, and the government decides to increase government spending in order to increase domestic demand and output. What will be the effects on output and on the trade balance?

The answer is given in Figure 19-3. Before the increase in government spending, demand is given by *ZZ* in Figure 19-3(a), and the equilibrium is at point *A*, where output equals *Y*. Let's assume that trade is initially balanced—even though, as we have seen, there is no reason this should be true in general. So, in Figure 19-3(b), $Y = Y_{TB}$.

What happens if the government increases spending by ΔG? At any level of output, demand is higher by ΔG, shifting the demand relation up by ΔG, from *ZZ* to *ZZ'*. The equilibrium point moves from *A* to *A'*, and output increases from *Y* to *Y'*. The increase

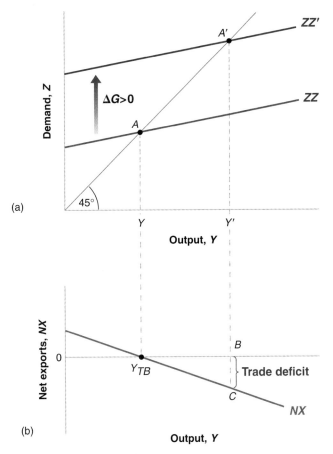

Figure 19-3 ▦

The Effects of an Increase in Government Spending

An increase in government spending leads to an increase in output and to a trade deficit.

in output is larger than the increase in government spending: There is a multiplier effect.

So far, the story sounds the same as the story for a closed economy in Chapter 3. However, there are two important differences:

■ There is now an effect on the trade balance. Because government spending enters neither the exports relation nor the imports relation directly, the relation between net exports and output in Figure 19-3(b) does not shift. So the increase in output from Y to Y' leads to a *trade deficit* equal to BC: Imports go up, and exports do not change.

■ Not only does government spending now generate a trade deficit, but the effect of government spending on output is smaller than it would be in a closed economy. Recall from Chapter 3 that the smaller the slope of the demand relation, the smaller the multiplier (for example, if ZZ were horizontal, the multiplier would be 1). And recall from Figure 19-1 that the demand relation, ZZ, is flatter than the demand relation in a closed economy, DD. This means the *multiplier is smaller in an open economy*.

The trade deficit and the smaller multiplier have the same cause: Because the economy is open, an increase in demand now falls not only on domestic goods but also on foreign goods. So, when income increases, the effect on the demand for domestic goods is smaller than it would be in a closed economy, leading to a smaller multiplier. And, because some of the increase in demand falls on imports—and exports are unchanged—the result is a trade deficit.

◀ Starting from trade balance, an increase in government spending leads to a trade deficit.

An increase in government spending increases output. The multiplier is smaller than in a closed economy.

The smaller multiplier and the trade deficit have the same cause: Some domestic demand falls on foreign goods.

These two implications are important. In an open economy, an increase in domestic demand has a smaller effect on output than in a closed economy, and it has an adverse effect on the trade balance. Indeed, the more open the economy, the smaller the effect on output and the larger the adverse effect on the trade balance. Take Belgium, for example. As we saw in Chapter 18, Belgium's ratio of imports to GDP is very high. When domestic demand increases in Belgium, most of the increase in demand is likely to result in an increase in the demand for foreign goods rather than in an increase in the demand for domestic goods. The effect of an increase in government spending is therefore likely to be a large increase in Belgium's trade deficit and only a small increase in its output, making domestic demand expansion a rather unattractive policy for Belgium. Even for the United States, which has a much lower import ratio, an increase in demand will be associated with a worsening of the trade balance.

Increases in Foreign Demand

Consider now an increase in foreign output—that is, an increase in Y^*. This could be due to an increase in foreign government spending, G^*—the policy change we just analyzed, but now taking place abroad. But we do not need to know where the increase in Y^* comes from to analyze its effects on the U.S. economy.

Figure 19-4 shows the effects of an increase in foreign activity on domestic output and the trade balance. The initial demand for domestic goods is given by ZZ in Figure 19-4(a). The equilibrium is at point A, with output level Y. Let's again assume

Figure 19-4

The Effects of an Increase in Foreign Demand

An increase in foreign demand leads to an increase in output and to a trade surplus.

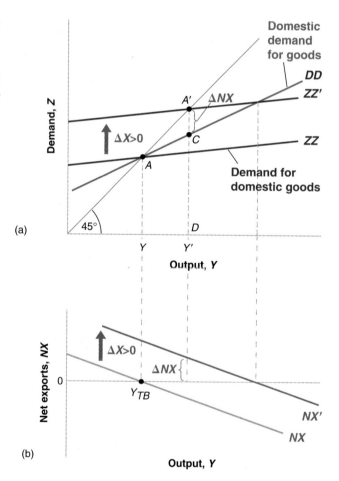

(a)

(b)

that trade is balanced, so that in Figure 19-4(b), the net exports associated with Y equal 0 ($Y = Y_{TB}$).

It will be useful here to refer to the line that shows the *domestic demand for goods*, $C + I + G$, as a function of income. This line is drawn as DD. Recall from Figure 19-1 that DD is steeper than ZZ. The difference between ZZ and DD equals net exports, so that if trade is balanced at point A, ZZ and DD intersect at point A.

◀ **DD is the domestic demand for goods. ZZ is the demand for domestic goods. The difference between the two is equal to the trade deficit.**

Now consider the effects of an increase in foreign output, ΔY^* (for the moment, ignore the line DD; we only need it later). Higher foreign output means higher foreign demand, including higher foreign demand for U.S. goods. So the direct effect of the increase in foreign output is an increase in U.S. exports by some amount, which we shall denote by ΔX:

- For a given level of output, this increase in exports leads to an increase in the demand for U.S. goods by ΔX, so the line showing the demand for domestic goods as a function of output shifts up by ΔX, from ZZ to ZZ'.
- For a given level of output, net exports go up by ΔX. So the line showing net exports as a function of output in Figure 19-4(b) also shifts up by ΔX, from NX to NX'.

The new equilibrium is at point A' in Figure 19-4(a), with output level Y'. The increase in foreign output leads to an increase in domestic output. The channel is clear: Higher foreign output leads to higher exports of domestic goods, which increases domestic output and the domestic demand for goods through the multiplier.

Y^* directly affects exports and so enters the relation between the demand for domestic goods and output. An increase in Y^* shifts ZZ up.

What happens to the trade balance? We know that exports go up. But could it be that the increase in domestic output leads to such a large increase in imports that the trade balance actually deteriorates? No: The trade balance must improve. To see why, note that when foreign demand increases, the demand for domestic goods shifts up from ZZ to ZZ'; but the line DD, which gives the *domestic demand for goods* as a function of output, does not shift. At the new equilibrium level of output, Y', domestic ◀ demand is given by the distance DC, and the demand for domestic goods is given by DA'. Net exports are therefore given by the distance CA'—which, because DD is necessarily below ZZ', is necessarily positive. Thus, while imports increase, the increase does not offset the increase in exports, and the trade balance improves.

Y^* does not affect either domestic consumption, domestic investment, or domestic government spending directly, and so it does not enter the relation between the domestic demand for goods and output. An increase in Y^* does not shift DD.

An increase in foreign output increases domestic output and ◀ improves the trade balance.

Fiscal Policy Revisited

We have derived two basic results so far:

- An increase in domestic demand leads to an increase in domestic output but leads also to a deterioration of the trade balance. (We looked at an increase in government spending, but the results would have been the same for a decrease in taxes, an increase in consumer spending, and so on.)
- An increase in foreign demand (which could come from the same types of changes taking place abroad) leads to an increase in domestic output and an improvement in the trade balance.

These results, in turn, have a number of important implications.

First, and most obviously, they imply that shocks to demand in one country affect all other countries. The stronger the trade links between countries, the stronger the interactions, and the more countries will move together. This implication seems indeed to be consistent with the facts. For example, most OECD countries experienced a strong economic expansion in the second half of the 1990s, followed by a slowdown or an outright recession in the early 2000s. Trade links were probably not the only reason for these common movements. It could be that most countries moved together partly because they were experiencing the same domestic shocks. For example, many countries went through the same "irrational exuberance" cycle and the same investment

See the Focus box in Chapter 5 on the role of investment spending in the U.S. boom and bust.

boom and bust as the United States. But the available evidence suggests that trade links also played an important role.

Second, these interactions very much complicate the task of policymakers, especially in the case of fiscal policy. Let's explore this argument more closely.

Start with the following observation: Governments do not like to run trade deficits, and for good reasons. The main reason is that a country that consistently runs a trade deficit accumulates debt vis-à-vis the rest of the world, and therefore has to pay steadily higher interest payments to the rest of the world. Thus, it is no wonder that countries prefer increases in foreign demand (which improve the trade balance) to increases in domestic demand (which worsen the trade balance).

But these preferences can have disastrous implications. Consider a group of countries, all doing a large amount of trade with each other, so that an increase in demand in any one country falls largely on the goods produced in the other countries. Suppose all these countries are in recession, and each has roughly balanced trade to start. In this case, each country might be very reluctant to take measures to increase domestic demand. Were it to do so, the result might be a small increase in output but also a large trade deficit. Instead, each country might just wait for the other countries to increase their demand. This way, it gets the best of both worlds, higher output and an improvement in its trade balance. But if all the countries wait, nothing will happen, and the recession may last a long time.

Is there a way out of this situation? There is—at least in theory. If all countries coordinate their macroeconomic policies so as to increase domestic demand simultaneously, each can increase demand and output without increasing its trade deficit (vis-à-vis the others; their combined trade deficit with respect to the rest of the world will still increase). The reason is clear: The coordinated increase in demand leads to increases in both exports and imports in each country. It is still true that domestic demand expansion leads to larger imports; but this increase in imports is offset by the increase in exports, which comes from the foreign demand expansions.

Coordination is a word governments often invoke. The seven major countries of the world—the so-called **G7** (the United States, Japan, France, Germany, the United Kingdom, Italy, and Canada; the "G" stands for "group")—meet regularly to discuss their economic situation; the communiqué at the end of the meeting rarely fails to mention coordination. But the evidence is that there is in fact very limited macro–coordination among countries. Here are some reasons:

■ *Some countries might have to do more than others and may not want to do so.* Suppose that only some countries are in recession. Countries that are not in recession will be reluctant to increase their own demand; but if they do not, the countries that expand will run trade deficits vis-à-vis countries that do not.

   Or suppose some countries are already running large budget deficits. These countries will not want to cut taxes nor increase spending further, as doing so would further increase their deficits. They will ask other countries to take on more of the adjustment. Those other countries may be reluctant to do so.

■ *Countries have a strong incentive to promise to coordinate and then not deliver on that promise.* Once all countries have agreed, say, to an increase in spending, each country has an incentive not to deliver, so as to benefit from the increase in demand elsewhere and thereby improve its trade position. But if each country cheats, or does not do everything it promised, there will be insufficient demand expansion to get out of the recession.

These reasons are far from abstract concerns. Countries in the European Union, which are highly integrated with one another, have in the past 30 years often suffered from such coordination problems. In the late 1970s, a bungled attempt at coordination left most countries wary of trying again. In the early 1980s, an attempt by France to go at it alone led to a large French trade deficit and eventually to a change in policy. Thereafter, most countries decided that it was better to wait for an increase in foreign demand than to increase their own demand. There has been very little coordination of fiscal policy since then in Europe.

◀ European countries embarked on fiscal expansion "too late." By the time they increased spending, their economies were already recovering, and there was no longer a need for higher government spending.

19-4 Depreciation, the Trade Balance, and Output

Suppose the U.S. government takes policy measures that lead to a depreciation of the dollar—a decrease in the nominal exchange rate. (We shall see in Chapter 20 how it can do this by using monetary policy. For the moment, we will assume the government can simply choose the exchange rate.)

Recall that the real exchange rate is given by

$$\epsilon \equiv \frac{E\,P}{P^*}$$

The real exchange rate, ϵ (the price of domestic goods in terms of foreign goods), is equal to the nominal exchange rate, E (the price of domestic currency in terms of foreign currency), times the domestic price level, P, divided by the foreign price level, P^*. In the short run, we can take the two price levels, P and P^*, as given. This implies that the nominal depreciation is reflected one-for-one in a real depreciation. More concretely, if the dollar depreciates vis-à-vis the yen by 10% (a 10% nominal depreciation), and if the price levels in Japan and the United States do not change, U.S. goods will be 10% cheaper compared to Japanese goods (a 10% real depreciation).

How will this real depreciation affect the U.S. trade balance and U.S. output?

◀ Given P and P^*, increases $\Rightarrow$ $\epsilon \equiv EP/P^*$ increases

◀ In Chapter 21, we shall look at the effects of a nominal depreciation when we allow the price level to adjust over time. You will see that a nominal depreciation leads to a real depreciation in the short run but not in the medium run.

Depreciation and the Trade Balance: The Marshall–Lerner Condition

Return to the definition of net exports:

$$NX \equiv X - IM/\epsilon$$

Replace X and IM by their expressions from equations (19.2) and (19.3):

$$NX = X(Y^*, \epsilon) - IM(Y, \epsilon)/\epsilon$$

Because the real exchange rate, ϵ, enters the right side of the equation in three places, this makes it clear that the real depreciation affects the trade balance through three separate channels:

- *Exports, X, increase*—The real depreciation makes U.S. goods relatively less expensive abroad. This leads to an increase in foreign demand for U.S. goods—an increase in U.S. exports.
- *Imports, IM, decrease*—The real depreciation makes foreign goods relatively more expensive in the United States. This leads to a shift in domestic demand toward domestic goods and to a decrease in the quantity of imports.
- *The relative price of foreign goods in terms of domestic goods, 1/e, increases*—This increases the import bill, IM/ϵ. The same quantity of imports now costs more to buy (in terms of domestic goods).

For the trade balance to improve following a depreciation, exports must increase enough and imports must decrease enough to compensate for the increase in the price of imports. The condition under which a real depreciation leads to an increase in

More concretely, if the dollar depreciates vis-à-vis the yen by 10%:

U.S. goods will be cheaper in Japan, leading to a larger quantity of U.S. exports to Japan.

Japanese goods will be more expensive in the United States, leading to a smaller quantity of imports of Japanese goods to the United States.

◀ Japanese goods will be more expensive, leading to a higher import bill for a given quantity of imports of Japanese goods to the United States.

net exports is known as the **Marshall–Lerner condition**. (It is derived formally in the appendix at the end of the chapter.) It turns out—with a complication we will state when we introduce dynamics later in this chapter—that this condition is satisfied in reality. So, for the rest of this book, we shall assume that a real depreciation— a decrease in ϵ—leads to an increase in net exports—an increase in NX.

The Effects of a Depreciation

We have looked so far at the *direct* effects of a depreciation on the trade balance—that is, the effects *given U.S. and foreign output*. But the effects do not end there. The change in net exports changes domestic output, which affects net exports further.

Because the effects of a real depreciation are very much like those of an increase in foreign output, we can use Figure 19-4, the same figure that we used to show the effects of an increase in foreign output earlier.

Just like an increase in foreign output, a depreciation leads to an increase in net exports (assuming, as we do, that the Marshall–Lerner condition holds), at any level of output. Both the demand relation [ZZ in Figure 19-4(a)] and the net exports relation [NX in Figure 19-4(b)] shift up. The equilibrium moves from A to A', and output increases from Y to Y'. By the same argument we used earlier, the trade balance improves: The increase in imports induced by the increase in output is smaller than the direct improvement in the trade balance induced by the depreciation.

Let's summarize: *The depreciation leads to a shift in demand, both foreign and domestic, toward domestic goods. This shift in demand leads in turn to both an increase in domestic output and an improvement in the trade balance.*

Although a depreciation and an increase in foreign output have the same effect on domestic output and the trade balance, there is a subtle but important difference between the two. A depreciation works by making foreign goods relatively more expensive. But this means that given their income, people—who now have to pay more to buy foreign goods because of the depreciation—are worse off. This mecha-nism is strongly felt in countries that go through a large depreciation. Governments trying to achieve a large depreciation often find themselves with strikes and riots in the streets, as people react to the much higher prices of imported goods. This was, for example, the case in Mexico, where the large depreciation of the peso in 1994 to 1995—from 29 cents per peso in November 1994 to 17 cents per peso in May 1995—led to a large decline in workers' living standards and to social unrest.

Combining Exchange Rate and Fiscal Policies

Suppose output is at its natural level, but the economy is running a large trade deficit. The government would like to reduce the trade deficit while leaving output unchanged. What should it do?

A depreciation alone will not do: It will reduce the trade deficit, but it will also increase output. Nor will a fiscal contraction work: It will reduce the trade deficit, but it will decrease output. What should the government do? The answer: Use the right com-bination of depreciation and fiscal contraction. Figure 19-5 shows what this combina-tion should be.

Suppose the initial equilibrium in Figure 19-5(a) is at A, associated with output Y. At this level of output, there is a trade deficit, given by the distance BC in Figure 19-5(b). If the government wants to eliminate the trade deficit without changing output, it must do two things:

■ It must achieve a depreciation sufficient to eliminate the trade deficit at the initial level of output. The depreciation must be such as to shift the net exports relation from NX to NX' in Figure 19-5(b).

Figure 19-5

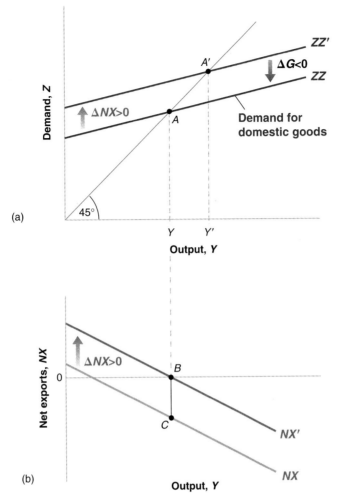

Reducing the Trade Deficit without Changing output

To reduce the trade deficit without changing output, the government must both achieve a depreciation and decrease government spending.

The problem is that this depreciation, and the associated increase in net exports, also shifts the demand relation in Figure 19-5(a) from *ZZ* to *ZZ'*. In the absence of other measures, the equilibrium would move from *A* to *A'*, and output would increase from *Y* to *Y'*.

■ In order to avoid the increase in output, the government must reduce government spending so as to shift *ZZ'* back to *ZZ*. This combination of a depreciation and a fiscal contraction leads to the same level of output and an improved trade balance.

There is a general point behind this example: To the extent that governments care about *both* the level of output and the trade balance, they have to use *both* fiscal policy and exchange rate policies. We just saw one such combination. Table 19-1 gives some others, depending on the initial output and trade situation. Consider, for example, the top-right corner of the table: Initial output is too low (put another way, unemployment is too high), and the economy has a trade deficit. A depreciation will help on both the

A general lesson: If you want to achieve two targets (here, output and trade balance), you need two instruments (here, fiscal policy and the exchange rate).

Table 19-1	Exchange Rate and Fiscal Policy Combinations	
Low output	ϵ? G↑	ϵ↓ G?
High output	ϵ↑ G?	ϵ? G↓

trade and the output fronts: It reduces the trade deficit and increases output. But there is no reason for the depreciation to achieve both the correct increase in output and the elimination of the trade deficit. Depending on the initial situation and the relative effects of the depreciation on output and the trade balance, the government may need to complement the depreciation with either an increase or a decrease in government spending. This ambiguity is captured by the question mark in the box. Make sure that you understand the logic behind each of the other three cases.

19-5 Looking at Dynamics: The J-Curve

We have ignored dynamics so far in this chapter. It is time to reintroduce them. The dynamics of consumption, investment, sales, and production we discussed in Chapter 3 are as relevant to an open economy as they are to a closed economy. But there are additional dynamic effects as well, which come from the dynamics of exports and imports. I focus on these effects here.

Return to the effects of the exchange rate on the trade balance. I argued earlier that a depreciation leads to an increase in exports and to a decrease in imports. But this does not happen overnight. Think of the dynamic effects of, say, a 10% dollar depreciation.

In the first few months following the depreciation, the effect of the depreciation is likely to be reflected much more in prices than in quantities. The price of imports in the United States goes up, and the price of U.S. exports abroad goes down. But the quantity of imports and exports is likely to adjust only slowly: It takes a while for consumers to realize that relative prices have changed, it takes a while for firms to shift to less expensive suppliers, and so on. So a depreciation may well lead to an initial deterioration of the trade balance; ϵ decreases, but neither X nor IM adjusts very much initially, leading to a decline in net exports $(X - IM/\epsilon)$.

As time passes, the effects of the change in the relative prices of both exports and imports become stronger. Less expensive U.S. goods cause U.S. consumers and firms to decrease their demand for foreign goods: U.S. imports decrease. Less expensive U.S. goods abroad lead foreign consumers and firms to increase their demand for U.S. goods: U.S. exports increase. If the Marshall–Lerner condition eventually holds—and we have argued that it does—the response of exports and imports eventually becomes stronger than the adverse price effect, and the eventual effect of the depreciation is an improvement of the trade balance.

Figure 19-6 captures this adjustment by plotting the evolution of the trade balance against time in response to a real depreciation. The pre-depreciation trade deficit is OA. The depreciation initially *increases* the trade deficit to OB: ϵ decreases, but neither IM nor X changes right away. Over time, however, exports increase and imports

Margin notes (left column):

Even these prices may adjust slowly: Consider a dollar depreciation. If you are an exporter to the United States, you may want to increase your dollar price less than implied by the exchange rate. In other words, you may ▶ decrease your markup in order to remain competitive with your U.S. competitors. If you are a U.S. exporter, you may decrease your price in foreign currency abroad by less than implied by the exchange rate. In other words, you may increase your markup.

The response of the trade balance to the real exchange rate:
Initially: X, IM unchanged, ϵ decreases. $\Rightarrow (X - IM/\epsilon)$ decreases.
Eventually:
X increases, IM decreases, ϵ decreases $\Rightarrow (X - IM/\epsilon)$ increases.

Figure 19-6

The J-Curve

A real depreciation leads initially to a deterioration and then to an improvement of the trade balance.

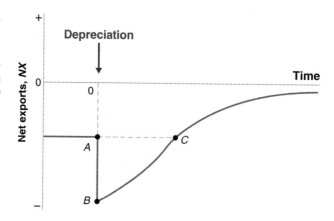

The Open Economy   **Extensions**

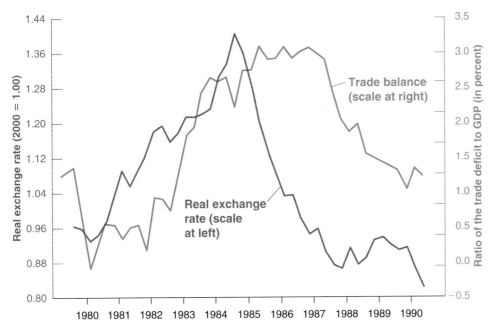

Figure 19-7 ▤

The Real Exchange Rate and the Ratio of the Trade Deficit to GDP: United States, 1980 to 1990

The real appreciation and depreciation of the dollar in the 1980s were reflected in increasing and then decreasing trade deficits. There were, however, substantial lags in the effects of the real exchange rate on the trade balance.

decrease, reducing the trade deficit. Eventually (if the Marshall–Lerner condition is satisfied), the trade balance improves beyond its initial level; this is what happens from point *C* on in the figure. Economists refer to this adjustment process as the **J-curve** because—admittedly, with a bit of imagination—the curve in the figure resembles a "J": first down, then up.

The importance of the dynamic effects of the real exchange rate on the trade balance was seen in the United States in the mid-1980s: Figure 19-7 plots the U.S. trade deficit against the U.S. real exchange rate in the 1980s. As we saw in Chapter 18, the period from 1980 to 1985 was one of sharp real appreciation, and the period from 1985 to 1988 one of sharp real depreciation. Turning to the trade deficit, which is expressed as a ratio to GDP, two facts are clear:

1. Movements in the real exchange rate were reflected in parallel movements in net exports. The appreciation was associated with a large increase in the trade deficit, and the later depreciation was associated with a large decrease in the trade balance.

2. There were, however, substantial lags in the response of the trade balance to changes in the real exchange rate. Note how from 1981 to 1983, the trade deficit remained small while the dollar was appreciating. And note how the steady depreciation of the dollar from 1985 onward was not reflected in an improvement in the trade balance before 1987: The dynamics of the J-curve were very much at work during both episodes.

The delays in 1985 to 1988 were unusually long, prompting some economists at the time to question whether there was still a relation between the real exchange rate and the trade balance. In retrospect, we can see that the relation was still there—the delays were just ◀ longer than usual.

In general, the econometric evidence on the dynamic relation between exports, imports, and the real exchange rate suggests that in all OECD countries, a real depreciation eventually leads to a trade balance improvement. But it also suggests that this process takes some time, typically between six months and a year. These lags have implications not only for the effects of a depreciation on the trade balance but also for the effects of a depreciation on output. If a depreciation initially decreases net exports, it also initially exerts a contractionary effect on output. Thus, if a government relies on a depreciation both to improve the trade balance and to expand domestic output, the effects will go the "wrong" way for a while.

19-6 Saving, Investment, and the Trade Balance

You saw in Chapter 3 how we could rewrite the condition for equilibrium in the goods market as the condition that investment was equal to saving—the sum of private saving and public saving. We can now derive the corresponding condition for the open economy and show how useful this alternative way of looking at the equilibrium can be.

Start from our equilibrium condition:

$$Y = C + I + G - IM/\epsilon + X$$

Subtract $C + T$ from both sides and use the fact that private saving is given by $S = Y - C - T$ to get

$$S = I + G - T - IM/\epsilon + X$$

Use the definition of net exports, $NX \equiv X - IM/\epsilon$, and reorganize, to get:

$$NX = S + (T - G) - I \qquad (19.5)$$

This condition says that, in equilibrium, the trade balance, NX, must be equal to saving—private saving, S, and public saving, $T - G$—minus investment, I. It follows that *a trade surplus must correspond to an excess of saving over investment; a trade deficit must correspond to an excess of investment over saving.*

One way of getting more intuition for this relation is to go back to the discussion of the current account and the capital account in Chapter 18. There we saw that a trade surplus implies net lending from the country to the rest of the world, and a trade deficit implies net borrowing by the country from the rest of the world. So, consider a country that invests more than it saves, so that $S + (T - G) - I$ is negative. That country must be borrowing the difference from the rest of the world; it must therefore be running a trade deficit.

Note some of the things that equation (19.5) says:

■ An increase in investment must be reflected in either an increase in private saving or public saving, or in a deterioration of the trade balance (a smaller trade surplus or a larger trade deficit).
■ An increase in the budget deficit must be reflected in either an increase in private saving, a decrease in investment, or a deterioration of the trade balance.
■ A country with a high saving rate (private plus public) must have either a high investment rate or a large trade surplus.

Note also, however, what equation (19.5) *does not say*. It does not say, for example, whether a budget deficit will lead to a trade deficit, or, instead, to an increase in private saving, or to a decrease in investment. To find out what happens in response to a budget deficit, we must explicitly solve for what happens to output and its components, using the assumptions that we have made about consumption, investment, exports, and imports. We can do so using either equation (19.1)—as we have done throughout this chapter—or equation (19.5), as the two are equivalent. However, let me strongly recommend that you use equation (19.1). Using equation (19.5) can, if you are not careful, be very misleading. To see how misleading it can be, consider, for example, the following argument (which is so common that you may have read something similar in newspapers):

> It is clear that the United States cannot reduce its large trade deficit (currently around 6% of GDP) through a depreciation. Look at equation (19.5). It shows that the trade deficit is equal to investment minus saving. Why should a depreciation affect either saving or investment? So how can a depreciation affect the trade deficit?

Figure 18-1 in the previous chapter showed the evolution of U.S. exports and imports as ratios to GDP since 1960. And their recent evolution is quite striking: Since 1996, the ratio of exports to GDP has remained flat, while the ratio of imports to GDP has rapidly increased. As a result, the trade deficit increased from $104 billion, or 1.2% of U.S. GDP in 1996, to $763 billion, or 5.9% of U.S. GDP in 2006.

The current account deficit (which is equal to the trade deficit minus net income from abroad) increased to $856 billion, or 6.4% of GDP in 2006. Put another way, the United States borrowed $856 billion from the rest of the world in 2006. This is a very large amount. It represents about 50% of the world's net saving (saving net of depreciation). And the notion that the world's richest economy is borrowing so much from the rest of the world is quite surprising. It raises two main questions: Where do these deficits come from? And what do they imply for the future? Let's take up each question in turn.

Where Does the Trade Deficit, and By Implication the Current Account Deficit, Come From?

Three factors appear to have played roughly equal roles in the increase in the current account deficit since the mid-1990s.

The first has been the high U.S. growth rate since the mid-1990s, relative to the growth rates of some of its main trading partners. Table 1 gives the average annual growth rate for the United States, the European Union, and Japan for three periods: 1991 to 1995, 1996 to 2000, and 2001 to 2006. Since 1996, U.S. growth has been much higher than growth in Europe and Japan. The U.S. performance from 1996 to 2000 reflects the New Economy boom, which we have discussed at many points in the book. U.S. growth has decreased since 2001 (recall that the United States went through a recession in 2001), but it has remained higher than growth in Europe and Japan.

Higher growth does not necessarily lead to a higher trade deficit. If the main source of the increase in demand and growth in a country is an increase in foreign demand, the country can grow fast and maintain trade balance, or even sustain a trade surplus. In the case of the United States since the mid-1990s, however, the main source of increased demand has been domestic demand, with high consumption demand as the main factor behind the sustained expansion. Thus, higher growth has come with an increasing trade deficit.

The second factor is shifts in the export and import functions—that is, changes in exports or in imports due neither to changes in activity nor to changes in the exchange rate. The evidence is that these shifts have played an important role as well, explaining up to one-third of the increase in the trade deficit. At a given level of income and a given exchange rate, U.S. consumers, for example, buy a higher proportion of foreign goods—say more foreign cars and fewer domestic cars.

The third factor has been the evolution of the exchange rate. Even if, at a given real exchange rate, growth leads to an increase in the trade deficit, a real depreciation can help maintain trade balance by making domestic goods more competitive. But just the opposite has happened to the U.S. real exchange rate: From 1996 to 2002, the United States experienced a large real appreciation, not a real depreciation. Go back to Figure 18-5, which gives the evolution of the U.S. effective real exchange rate. From the second quarter of 1995 to the first quarter of 2002, the real exchange rate index increased from 0.83 to 1.11, a real appreciation of more than 30%. Since then, the dollar has depreciated, and, at the end of 2006, the index stood at 0.94, still higher than its 1995 value.

Why was the dollar so strong until 2002, in the face of a large current account deficit? A full discussion will have to wait until the next chapter, when we look at the link between financial decisions and the exchange rate. But, in short, the answer is that there was a very high demand for U.S. assets on the part of foreign investors. This demand was enough to drive the dollar up and, in doing so, to increase the trade and the current account deficits. Since the beginning of 2002, the dollar has depreciated, but, because of the two other factors listed—growth differentials and shifts in relative demand for domestic and foreign goods—and because

Table 1	Average Annual Growth Rates in the United States, the European Union, and Japan since 1991 (percent per year)		
United States	2.5	4.1	3.4
European Union	2.1	2.6	1.6
Japan	1.5	1.5	1.6

(Continued)

FOCUS

of the lags in the adjustment of exports and imports to the real exchange rate—the J curve—the trade deficit has continued to increase.

This is a good place to make sure we can tell the story in terms of saving and investment, along the lines of Section 19-6. Figure 1 gives the evolution of U.S. net saving (that is, U.S. saving net of depreciation) and U.S. net investment (U.S. investment net of depreciation) as ratios to GDP, since 1996, and it tells a clear story: The increase in the trade deficit (which, as you will recall, is equal to the difference between investment and saving) has come primarily from a decrease in the ratio of saving to GDP. And, if one looks closely, it is clear that this decrease in saving has come mostly from a decrease in private saving, S, rather than an increase in the budget deficit, $G - T$: The ratio of the budget deficit to GDP is roughly the same in 2006 as it was in 1996, and the ratio of private saving to GDP is more than 3 percentage points lower in 2006 than it was in 1996. Thus, another way of describing what lies behind the trade deficit is that U.S. consumers are saving substantially less than they were 10 years ago. Should they be saving more? We discussed this in Chapter 16. The answer: Most of them appear to be saving enough.

What Happens Next?

Should we expect the large trade deficit and current account deficit to naturally disappear in the future? At an unchanged real exchange rate, the answer is probably no.

If there were good reasons to expect U.S. trading partners to experience much higher growth than the United States over the coming decade, then we could expect to see the same process we saw in the past 10 years but this time in reverse: Lower growth in the United States than in the rest of the world would lead to a steady reduction in the trade deficit. There are few reasons, however, to expect such a scenario. Although the United States cannot expect to replicate the growth rates of the late 1990s, there is also no reason to expect much lower growth than average over the coming decade. And, while growth has increased in Europe and Japan, sustained higher growth in Europe and Japan than in the United States seems unlikely.

Can we expect the shifts in exports and imports to reverse themselves, leading to an improvement in the trade balance without the need for a depreciation? The source of the shifts is poorly understood, so one must be careful in predicting what might happen. But

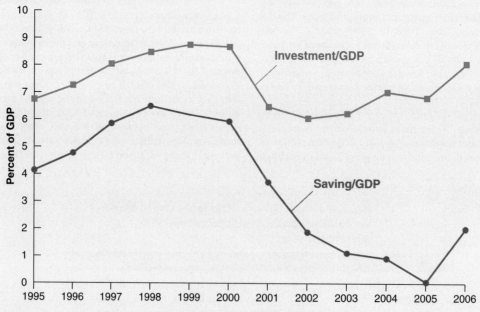

Figure 1   *U.S. Net Saving and Net Investment since 1996 (percent of GDP)*

there does not appear to be any particular reason to think that, for example, U.S. consumers will shift back from foreign cars to U.S. cars. Put another way, there is no particular reason to expect that the trade deficit will narrow by itself, without a depreciation of the dollar.

Will the dollar depreciate further, leading eventually to a reduction in the trade and current account deficits? The answer is: Probably. While financial investors have been willing to lend to the United States until now, there are many reasons to think that they will be reluctant to lend at the current levels of $800 billion or so per year. (More on this in the Focus box "Sudden Stops, the Strong Dollar, and the Limits to the Interest Parity Condition" in Chapter 20.)

These arguments have three implications:

■ The U.S. trade and current account deficits will decline in the future.

■ This decline is unlikely to happen without a real depreciation. How large a depreciation? Estimates range from 20% to 40% from where we are today—in short, a substantial further real depreciation.

■ When will this depreciation take place? This is a hard question to answer. It will take place when foreign investors become reluctant to lend to the United States at the rate of $800 billion or so per year.

Let's go back to the issues discussed in Table 19-1: A depreciation on such a scale will have major effects on the demand for goods both in the United States and abroad.

The depreciation will increase the demand for U.S. goods. If, when the depreciation takes place, U.S. output is already close to its natural level, the risk is that the depreciation will lead to too high a level of demand and too high a level of output. If this happens, it will require a decrease in domestic demand. This may come either from a decrease in spending by consumers or firms or from a reduction in government spending. If the U.S. government succeeds in achieving a smooth depreciation and the decrease in domestic spending, the outcome can be sustained U.S. growth and a reduction of the U.S. trade deficit.

The depreciation will decrease the demand for foreign goods. By the same argument, this may require foreign governments to implement policies to sustain their own demand and output. This would ordinarily call for a fiscal expansion, but it might not be the right solution in this case. A number of countries, such as France and Japan, are already running large budget deficits. For the reasons we saw in Chapter 17, increasing these deficits further may be difficult and even dangerous. If fiscal policy cannot be used to sustain demand and output, a strong dollar depreciation might therefore trigger a recession in those countries.

In short, a smooth reduction of the U.S. trade deficit will require the combination of a dollar depreciation and spending changes both in the United States and abroad. This can be achieved, but it may not be easy.

The argument might sound convincing, but we know it is wrong. We showed earlier that a depreciation leads to an improvement in a country's trade position. So what is wrong with the argument? A depreciation actually affects saving and investment: It does so by affecting the demand for domestic goods, thereby increasing output. Higher output leads to an increase in saving over investment or, equivalently, to a decrease in the trade deficit.

A good way of making sure that you understand the material in this section is to go back and look at the various cases we have considered, from changes in government spending, to changes in foreign output, to combinations of depreciation and fiscal contraction, and so on. Trace what happens in each case to each of the four components of equation (19.5): private saving, public saving (equivalently, the budget surplus), investment, and the trade balance. Make sure, as always, that you can tell the ◀ story in words.

Suppose, for example, that the U.S. government wants to reduce the trade deficit without changing the level of output, so it uses a combination of depreciation and fiscal contraction. What happens to private saving, public saving, and investment?

A good way of making sure you understand the material in the whole chapter is to read the Focus box "The U.S. Trade Deficit: Origins and Implications." It will show you how the concepts we have developed in this chapter can be used to understand the origins and implications of what is probably, at this point, one of the main issues facing policymakers, not only in the United States but also in the rest of the world.

Summary

- In an open economy, the demand for domestic goods is equal to the domestic demand for goods (consumption plus investment plus government spending) minus the value of imports (in terms of domestic goods) plus exports.

- In an open economy, an increase in domestic demand leads to a smaller increase in output than it would in a closed economy because some of the additional demand falls on imports. For the same reason, an increase in domestic demand also leads to a deterioration of the trade balance.

- An increase in foreign demand leads, as a result of increased exports, to both an increase in domestic output and an improvement of the trade balance.

- Because increases in foreign demand improve the trade balance and increases in domestic demand worsen the

trade balance, countries might be tempted to wait for increases in foreign demand to move them out of a recession. When a group of countries is in recession, coordination can, in principle, help them get out of it.

- If the Marshall–Lerner condition is satisfied—and the empirical evidence indicates that it is—a real depreciation leads to an improvement in net exports.

- A real depreciation leads first to a deterioration of the trade balance and then to an improvement. This adjustment process is known as the J-curve.

- The condition for equilibrium in the goods market can be rewritten as the condition that saving (public and private) minus investment must be equal to the trade balance. A trade surplus corresponds to an excess of saving over investment. A trade deficit corresponds to an excess of investment over saving.

Key Terms

- demand for domestic goods, 420
- domestic demand for goods, 420
- coordination, G7, 428

- Marshall–Lerner condition, 430
- J-curve, 433

Questions and Problems

Quick Check

1. *Using the information in this chapter, label each of the following statements true, false, or uncertain. Explain briefly.*

   a. The current U.S. trade deficit is the result of unusually high investment, not the result of a decline in national saving.

   b. The national income identity implies that budget deficits cause trade deficits.

   c. Opening the economy to trade tends to increase the multiplier because an increase in expenditure leads to more exports.

   d. If the trade deficit is equal to zero, then the domestic demand for goods and the demand for domestic goods are equal.

   e. A real depreciation leads to an immediate improvement in the trade balance.

   f. A small open economy can reduce its trade deficit through fiscal contraction at a smaller cost in output than can a large open economy.

   g. The current high U.S. trade deficit is solely the result of a real appreciation of U.S. goods between 1995 and 2002.

2. *Real and nominal exchange rates and inflation*

   Using the definition of the real exchange rate (and Propositions 7 and 8 in Appendix 2 at the end of the book), you can show that

   $$\frac{(\epsilon_t - \epsilon_{t-1})}{\epsilon_{t-1}} = \frac{(E_t - E_{t-1})}{E_{t-1}} + \pi_t - \pi_t^*$$

   In words, the percentage real appreciation equals the percentage nominal appreciation plus the difference between domestic and foreign inflation.

   a. If domestic inflation is higher than foreign inflation, but the domestic country has a fixed exchange rate, what happens to the real exchange rate over time? Assume that the Marshall–Lerner condition holds. What happens to the trade balance over time? Explain in words.

   b. Suppose the real exchange rate is constant—say, at the level required for net exports (or the current account) to equal zero. In this case, if domestic inflation is higher than foreign inflation, what must happen to the nominal exchange rate over time?

3. *Reproduce the results in Table 19-1.*

4. *Japan's slump and the U.S. economy*

   a. In 2006, Japanese spending on U.S. goods accounted for 6% of U.S. exports (see Table 18-2), and U.S. exports amounted to 11% of U.S. GDP (see Table 18-1). What was the share of Japanese spending on U.S. goods relative to U.S. GDP?

   b. Assume that the multiplier in the United States is 2.5 and that Japan's slump has reduced output there by 3% (relative to its natural level). Given your answer to part (a), what is the impact on U.S. GDP of the Japanese slump?

   c. If the Japanese slump also leads to a slowdown of the other economies that import goods from the United

States, the effect could be larger. To put a bound to the size of the effect, assume that U.S. exports fall by 3% (as a result of changes in foreign output) in one year. What is the impact of a 3% fall in exports on U.S. GDP?

d. Comment on this statement. "Unless there is a strong and sustained recovery in Japan, U.S. growth will grind to a halt."

Dig Deeper

5. Eliminating a trade deficit

a. Consider an economy with a trade deficit ($NX < 0$) and with output equal to its natural level. Suppose that, even though output may deviate from its natural level in the short run, it returns to its natural level in the medium run. Assume that the natural level is unaffected by the real exchange rate. What must happen to the real exchange rate over the medium run to eliminate the trade deficit (i.e., to increase NX to 0)?

b. Now write down the national income identity. Assume again that output returns to its natural level in the medium run. If NX increases to 0, what must happen to domestic demand ($C + I + G$) in the medium run? What government policies are available to reduce domestic demand in the medium run? Identify which components of domestic demand each of these policies affect.

6. Net exports and foreign demand

a. Suppose there is an increase in foreign output. Show the effect on the domestic economy (i.e., replicate Figure 19-4). What is the effect on domestic output? On domestic net exports?

b. If the interest rate remains constant, what will happen to domestic investment? If taxes are fixed, what will happen to the domestic budget deficit?

c. Using equation (19.5), what must happen to private saving? Explain.

d. Foreign output does not appear in equation (19.5), yet it evidently affects net exports. Explain how this is possible.

7. Multipliers, openness, and fiscal policy

Consider an open economy characterized by the equations below.

$$C = c_0 + c_1(Y - T)$$
$$I = d_0 + d_1Y$$
$$IM = m_1Y$$
$$X = x_1Y^*$$

The parameters m_1 and x_1 are the propensities to import and export. Assume that the real exchange rate is fixed at a value of 1 and treat foreign income, Y^*, as fixed. Also assume that taxes are fixed and that government purchases are exogenous (i.e., decided by the government). We explore the effectiveness of changes in G under alternative assumptions about the propensity to import.

a. Write the equilibrium condition in the market for domestic goods and solve for Y.

b. Suppose government purchases increase by one unit. What is the effect on output? (Assume that $0 < m_1 < c_1 + d_1 < 1$. Explain why.)

c. How do net exports change when government purchases increase by one unit?

Now consider two economies, one with $m_1 = 0.5$ and the other with $m_1 = 0.1$. Each economy is characterized by $(c_1 + d_1) = 0.6$.

d. Suppose one of the economies is much larger than the other. Which economy do you expect to have the larger value of m_1? Explain.

e. Calculate your answers to parts (b) and (c) for each economy by substituting the appropriate parameter values.

f. In which economy will fiscal policy have a larger effect on output? In which economy will fiscal policy have a larger effect on net exports?

8. Policy coordination and the world economy

Consider an open economy in which the real exchange rate is fixed and equal to one. Consumption, investment, government spending, and taxes are given by

$$C = 10 + 0.8(Y - T), \quad I = 10, \quad G = 10, \quad \text{and} \quad T = 10$$

Imports and exports are given by

$$IM = 0.3\,Y \quad and \quad X = 0.3\,Y^*$$

where Y^* denotes foreign output.

a. Solve for equilibrium output in the domestic economy, given Y^*. What is the multiplier in this economy? If we were to close the economy—so exports and imports were identically equal to zero—what would the multiplier be? Why would the multiplier be different in a closed economy?

b. Assume that the foreign economy is characterized by the same equations as the domestic economy (with asterisks reversed). Use the two sets of equations to solve for the equilibrium output of each country. [Hint: Use the equations for the foreign economy to solve for Y^* as a function of Y and substitute this solution for Y^* in part (a).] What is the multiplier for each country now? Why is it different from the open economy multiplier in part (a)?

c. Assume that the domestic government, G, has a target level of output of 125. Assuming that the foreign government does not change G^*, what is the increase in G necessary to achieve the target output in the domestic economy? Solve for net exports and the budget deficit in each country.

d. Suppose each government has a target level of output of 125 and that each government increases government spending by the same amount. What is the common increase in G and G^* necessary to achieve the target output in both countries? Solve for net exports and the budget deficit in each country.

e. Why is fiscal coordination, such as the common increase in G and G^* in part (d), difficult to achieve in practice?

Explore Further

9. The U.S. trade deficit and investment

a. Define national saving as private saving plus the government surplus—i.e., as $S + T - G$. Now, using equation (19.5), describe the relation between the trade deficit and the difference between national saving and domestic investment.

b. Go the statistical tables of the most recent *Economic Report of the President* (**www.gpoaccess.gov/eop/**). In Table B-2, "Real GDP," retrieve annual data for GDP, gross domestic investment, and net exports from 1980 to the most recent year available. (If the Net Exports column is blank, obtain net exports by subtracting imports from exports for each year.) Divide gross domestic investment and net exports by GDP for each year to express their values as a percentage of GDP.

c. The United States last had a trade surplus in 1981. Subtract the value of net exports (as a percentage of GDP) in 1981 from the value of net exports (as a percentage of GDP) in the most recent year available. Do the same for gross domestic investment. Has the decline in net exports been matched by an equivalent increase in investment? What do your calculations imply about the change in national saving between 1981 and the present?

d. When the United States began experiencing trade deficits during the 1980s, some officials in the Reagan administration argued that the trade deficits reflected attractive investment opportunities in the United States. Consider three time periods: 1981 to 1990, 1990 to 2000, and 2000 to the present. Apply the analysis of part (c) to each of these time periods (i.e., calculate the change in net exports and gross domestic investment as a percentage of GDP). How does the change in net exports compare to the change in investment during each period? How did national saving change during each period?

e. Is a trade deficit more worrisome when not accompanied by a corresponding increase in investment? Explain your answer.

We invite you to visit the Blanchard page on the Prentice Hall Web site, at:
www.prenhall.com/blanchard
for this chapter's World Wide Web exercises.

Further Readings

- A good discussion of the relation among trade deficits, budget deficits, private saving, and investment is given in Barry Bosworth, *Saving and Investment in a Global Economy*, Brookings Institution, Washington, DC, 1993.

- A good discussion of the U.S. trade deficit and its implications for the future is given in William Cline, *The United States as a Debtor Nation*, Peterson Institute, Washington, DC, 2005.

Appendix: Derivation of the Marshall–Lerner Condition

Start from the definition of net exports:

$$NX \equiv X - IM/\epsilon$$

Assume trade to be initially balanced, so that $NX = 0$ and $X = IM/\epsilon$, or, equivalently, $\epsilon X = IM$. The Marshall–Lerner condition is the condition under which a real depreciation, a decrease in ϵ, leads to an increase in net exports.

To derive this condition, first multiply both sides of the equation above by ϵ to get

$$\epsilon NX = \epsilon X - IM$$

Now consider a change in the real exchange rate of $\Delta\epsilon$. The effect of the change in the real exchange rate on the left side of the equation is given by $(\Delta\epsilon) NX + \epsilon(\Delta NX)$. Note that, if trade is initially balanced, $NX = 0$, so the first term in this expression is equal to zero, and the effect of the change on the left side is simply given by $\epsilon(\Delta NX)$. The effect of the change in the real exchange rate on the right side of the equation is given by $(\Delta\epsilon)X + \epsilon(\Delta X) - (\Delta IM)$. Putting the two sides together gives

$$\epsilon(\Delta NX) = (\Delta\epsilon)X + \epsilon(\Delta X) - (\Delta IM)$$

Divide both sides by ϵX to get:

$$\frac{\epsilon(\Delta NX)}{\epsilon X} = \frac{(\Delta\epsilon)X}{\epsilon X} + \frac{\epsilon(\Delta X)}{\epsilon X} - \frac{\Delta(IM)}{\epsilon X}$$

Simplify and use the fact that, if trade is initially balanced, $\epsilon X = IM$, to replace ϵX by IM in the last term on the right. This gives

$$\frac{\Delta NX}{X} = \frac{\Delta\epsilon}{\epsilon} + \frac{\Delta X}{X} - \frac{\Delta IM}{IM}$$

The change in the trade balance (as a ratio to exports) in response to a real depreciation is equal to the sum of three terms:

- The first term is equal to the proportional change in the real exchange rate. It is negative if there is a real depreciation.
- The second term is equal to the proportional change in exports. It is positive if there is a real depreciation.
- The third term is equal to minus the proportional change in the imports. It is positive if there is a real depreciation.

The Marshall–Lerner condition is the condition that the sum of these three terms be positive. If it is satisfied, a real depreciation leads to an improvement in the trade balance.

A numerical example will help here. Suppose that a 1% depreciation leads to a proportional increase in exports of 0.9% and to a proportional decrease in imports of 0.8%. (Econometric evidence on the relation of exports and imports to the real exchange rate suggest that these are indeed reasonable numbers.) In that case, the right-hand side of the equation is equal to $-1\% + 0.9\% - (-0.8\%) = 0.7\%$. Thus, the trade balance improves: The Marshall–Lerner condition is satisfied.

Output, the Interest Rate, and the Exchange Rate

I n Chapter 19, we treated the exchange rate as one of the policy instruments available to the government. But the exchange rate is not a policy instrument. Rather, it is determined in the foreign exchange market—a market where, as you saw in Chapter 18, there is an enormous amount of trading. This fact raises two obvious questions: What determines the exchange rate? How can policymakers affect it?

These questions motivate this chapter. More generally, we examine the implications of equilibrium in both the goods market and financial markets, including the foreign exchange market. This allows us to characterize the joint movements of output, the interest rate, and the exchange rate in an open economy. The model we develop is an extension to the open economy of the *IS–LM* model you saw in Chapter 5 and is known as the **Mundell-Fleming model**— after the two economists, Robert Mundell and Marcus Fleming, who first put it together in the 1960s. (The model presented here retains the spirit of the original Mundell-Fleming model but differs in its details.)

■ Section 20-1 looks at equilibrium in the goods market.

■ Section 20-2 looks at equilibrium in financial markets, including the foreign exchange market.

■ Section 20-3 puts the two equilibrium conditions together and looks at the determination of output, the interest rate, and the exchange rate.

■ Section 20-4 looks at the role of policy under flexible exchange rates.

■ Section 20-5 looks at the role of policy under fixed exchange rates. ■

20-1 Equilibrium in the Goods Market

Equilibrium in the goods market was the focus of Chapter 19, where we derived the equilibrium condition [equation (19.4)]:

$$Y = C(Y - T) + I(Y, r) + G - IM(Y, \epsilon)/\epsilon + X(Y^*, \epsilon)$$
$$\quad\quad (+) \quad\quad (+,-) \quad\quad\quad\quad (+,+) \quad\quad (+, -)$$

Goods market equilibrium (IS): ▶
Output = Demand for domestic goods.

For the goods market to be in equilibrium, output (the left side of the equation) must be equal to the demand for domestic goods (the right side of the equation). The demand for domestic goods is equal to consumption, C, plus investment, I, plus government spending, G, minus the value of imports, IM/ϵ, plus exports, X:

- Consumption, C, depends positively on disposable income, $Y - T$.
- Investment, I, depends positively on output, Y, and negatively on the real interest rate, r.
- Government spending, G, is taken as given.
- The quantity of imports, IM, depends positively on both output, Y, and the real exchange rate, ϵ. The value of imports in terms of domestic goods is equal to the quantity of imports divided by the real exchange rate.
- Exports, X, depend positively on foreign output, Y^*, and negatively on the real exchange rate, ϵ.

It will be convenient in what follows to regroup the last two terms under "net exports," defined as exports minus the value of imports:

$$NX(Y, Y^*, \epsilon) \equiv X(Y^*, \epsilon) - IM(Y, \epsilon)/\epsilon$$

I shall assume, throughout the chapter, that the Marshall-Lerner condition holds. Under this condition, an increase ▶ in the real exchange rate—a real appreciation—leads to a decrease in net exports (see Chapter 19).

It follows from our assumptions about imports and exports that net exports, NX, depend on domestic output, Y, foreign output, Y^*, and the real exchange rate, ϵ: An increase in domestic output increases imports, thus decreasing net exports. An increase in foreign output increases exports, thus increasing net exports. An increase in the real exchange rate leads to a decrease in net exports.

Using this definition of net exports, we can rewrite the equilibrium condition as

$$Y = C(Y - T) + I(Y, \ r) + G + NX(Y, Y^*, \epsilon)$$
$$\quad (\ + \ ) \quad\quad (+,-) \quad\quad\quad\quad (-, +, -)$$
(20.1)

For our purposes, the main implication of equation (20.1) is that both the real interest rate and the real exchange rate affect demand and, in turn, equilibrium output:

- An increase in the real interest rate leads to a decrease in investment spending and, as a result, to a decrease in the demand for domestic goods. This leads, through the multiplier, to a decrease in output.
- An increase in the real exchange rate leads to a shift in demand toward foreign goods and, as a result, to a decrease in net exports. The decrease in net exports decreases the demand for domestic goods. This leads, through the multiplier, to a decrease in output.

For the remainder of the chapter, I shall make two simplifications to equation (20.1):

- Given our focus on the short run, we assumed in our previous treatment of the *IS–LM* model that the (domestic) price level was given. I shall make the same assumption here and extend this assumption to the foreign price level, so the real exchange rate, $\epsilon \equiv EP/P^*$, and the nominal exchange rate, E, move together.

A decrease in the nominal exchange rate—a nominal depreciation—leads, one-for-one, to a decrease in the real exchange rate—a real depreciation. Conversely, an increase in the nominal exchange rate—a nominal appreciation—leads, one-for-one, to an increase in the real exchange rate—a real appreciation. If, for notational convenience, we choose P and P^*, so that $P/P^* = 1$ (and we can do so because both are index numbers), then $\epsilon = E$, and we can replace ϵ by E in equation (20.1).

◀ First simplification:
$P = P^* = 1$, so $\epsilon = E$.

- Because we take the domestic price level as given, there is no inflation, neither actual nor expected. Therefore, the nominal interest rate and the real interest rate are the same, and we can replace the real interest rate, r, in equation (20.1) by the nominal interest rate, i.

Second simplification:
◀ $\pi^e = 0$, so $r = i$.

With these two simplifications, equation (20.1) becomes

$$Y = C(Y - T) + I(Y, i) + G + NX(Y, Y^*, E) \qquad (20.2)$$
$$\quad\ \ (\ +\ )\quad\ (+,-)\qquad\qquad\ (-, +, -)$$

In words: Goods market equilibrium implies that output depends negatively on both the nominal interest rate and the nominal exchange rate.

20-2 Equilibrium in Financial Markets

When we looked at financial markets in the *IS–LM* model, we assumed that people chose between only two financial assets, money and bonds. Now that we are looking at a financially open economy, we must also take into account the fact that people have a choice between domestic bonds and foreign bonds. Let's consider each choice in turn.

We leave aside the other choices—between short-term and long-term bonds, and between short-term bonds and ◀ stocks—studied in Chapter 15.

Money versus Bonds

When we looked at the determination of the interest rate in the *IS–LM* model in Chapter 5, we wrote the condition that the supply of money be equal to the demand for money as

$$\frac{M}{P} = Y L(i) \qquad (20.3)$$

We took the real supply of money [the left side of equation (20.3)] as given. We assumed that the real demand for money [the right side of equation (20.3)] depended on the level of transactions in the economy, measured by real output, Y, and on the opportunity cost of holding money rather than bonds—that is, the nominal interest rate on bonds, i.

How should we change this characterization now that the economy is open? You will like the answer: Not very much, if at all.

In an open economy, the demand for domestic money is still mostly a demand by domestic residents. There is not much reason for, say, the residents of Japan to hold euro currency or demand deposits. Transactions in Japan require payment in yen, not in euros. If residents of Japan want to hold euro-denominated assets, they are better off holding euro bonds, which at least pay a positive interest rate. And the demand for money by domestic residents in any country still depends on the same factors as before: their level of transactions, which we measure by domestic real output, and the opportunity cost of holding money, the nominal interest rate on bonds.

A qualification from Chapter 4 with respect to the demand for U.S. currency: A good proportion of U.S. currency is actually held abroad. The two major reasons are (1) the dollars used for illegal transactions abroad and (2) dollars used for domestic transactions in countries with high inflation. I shall ◀ ignore this qualification here.

Therefore, we can still use equation (20.3) to think about the determination of the nominal interest rate in an open economy. The interest rate must be such that the supply of money and the demand for money are equal. An increase in the money supply leads to a decrease in the interest rate. An increase in money demand, say as a result of an increase in output, leads to an increase in the interest rate.

Financial markets equilibrium.
◀ Condition 1 (*LM*):
Supply of money = Demand for money.

Domestic Bonds versus Foreign Bonds

As we look at the choice between domestic bonds and foreign bonds, we shall rely on the assumption we introduced in Chapter 18: Financial investors, domestic or foreign, go for the highest expected rate of return. This implies that, in equilibrium, both domestic bonds and foreign bonds must have the same expected rate of return; otherwise, investors would be willing to hold only one or the other, but not both, and this could not be an equilibrium. (Like most other economic relations, this relation is only an approximation to reality and does not always hold. More on this in the Focus box "Sudden Stops, the Strong Dollar, and Limits to the Interest Parity Condition" at the end of this section.)

As we saw in Chapter 18 [equation (18.2)], this assumption implies that the following arbitrage relation—the *interest parity condition*—must hold:

$$(1 + i_t) = (1 + i_t^*)\left(\frac{E_t}{E_{t+1}^e}\right)$$

The presence of E_t comes from the fact that, in order to buy the foreign bond, you must first exchange domestic currency for foreign currency. The presence of E_{t+1}^e comes from the fact that, in order to bring the funds back next period, you will have to exchange foreign currency for domestic currency.

where i_t is the domestic interest rate, i_t^* is the foreign interest rate, E_t is the current exchange rate, and E_{t+1}^e is the future expected exchange rate. The left side gives the return, in terms of domestic currency, from holding domestic bonds. The right side gives the expected return, also in terms of domestic currency, from holding foreign bonds. In equilibrium, the two expected returns must be equal.

Multiply both sides by E_{t+1}^e and reorganize, to get

$$E_t = \frac{1 + i_t}{1 + i_t^*} E_{t+1}^e \qquad (20.4)$$

For now, we shall take the expected future exchange rate as given and denote it as $\overline{E}^e$ (we shall relax this assumption in Chapter 21). Under this assumption, and dropping time indexes, the interest parity condition becomes

$$E = \frac{1 + i}{1 + i^*} \overline{E}^e \qquad (20.5)$$

This relation tells us that the current exchange rate depends on the domestic interest rate, on the foreign interest rate, and on the expected future exchange rate:

■ An increase in the domestic interest rate leads to an increase in the exchange rate.
■ An increase in the foreign interest rate leads to a decrease in the exchange rate.
■ An increase in the expected future exchange rate leads to an increase in the current exchange rate.

This relation plays a central role in the real world and will play a central role in this chapter. To understand the relation further, consider the following example.

Consider financial investors—investors, for short—choosing between U.S. bonds and Japanese bonds. Suppose that the one-year interest rate on U.S. bonds is 5% and the one-year interest rate on Japanese bonds is also 5%. Suppose that the current exchange rate is 100 (1 dollar is worth 100 yen), and the expected exchange rate a year from now is also 100. Under these assumptions, both U.S. and Japanese bonds have the same expected return in dollars, and the interest parity condition holds.

Suppose that investors now expect the exchange rate to be 10% higher a year from now, so E^e is now equal to 110. At an unchanged current exchange rate, U.S. bonds are now much more attractive than Japanese bonds: U.S. bonds offer an interest rate of 5%

in dollars. Japanese bonds still offer an interest rate of 5% in yen, but yen a year from today are now expected to be worth 10% less in terms of dollars. In terms of dollars, the return on Japanese bonds is therefore 5% (the interest rate) – 10% (the expected depreciation of the yen relative to the dollar), or −5%.

So what will happen? At the initial exchange rate of 100, investors want to shift out of Japanese bonds into U.S. bonds. To do so, they must first sell Japanese bonds for yen, then sell yen for dollars, and then use the dollars to buy U.S. bonds. As investors sell yen and buy dollars, the dollar appreciates. By how much? Equation (20.5) gives us the answer: $E = (1.05/1.05)110 = 110$. The current exchange rate must increase in the same proportion as the expected future exchange rate. Put another way, the dollar must appreciate today by 10%. When it has appreciated by 10%, so $E = \bar{E}^e = 110$, the expected returns on U.S. and Japanese bonds are again equal, and there is equilibrium in the foreign exchange market.

Suppose instead that, as a result of a U.S. monetary contraction, the U.S. interest rate increases from 5% to 8%. Assume that the Japanese interest rate remains unchanged at 5%, and that the expected future exchange rate remains unchanged at 100. At an unchanged current exchange rate, U.S. bonds are now again much more attractive than Japanese bonds. U.S. bonds yield a return of 8% in dollars. Japanese bonds give a return of 5% in yen and—because the exchange rate is expected to be the same next year as it is today—an expected return of 5% in dollars as well.

So what will happen? Again, at the initial exchange rate of 100, investors want to shift out of Japanese bonds into U.S. bonds. As they do so, they sell yen for dollars, and the dollar appreciates. By how much? Equation (20.5) gives the answer: $E = (1.08/1.05)100 \approx 103$. The current exchange rate increases by approximately 3%. Why 3%? Think of what happens when the dollar appreciates. If, as we have assumed, investors do not change their expectation of the future exchange rate, then the more the dollar appreciates today, the more investors expect it to depreciate in the future (as it is expected to return to the same value in the future). When the dollar has appreciated by 3% today, investors expect it to depreciate by 3% during the coming year. Equivalently, they expect the yen to appreciate vis-à-vis the dollar by 3% over the coming year. The expected rate of return in dollars from holding Japanese bonds is therefore 5% (the yen interest rate) + 3% (the expected yen appreciation), or 8%. This expected rate of return is the same as the rate of return on holding U.S. bonds, so there is equilibrium in the foreign exchange market.

◀ Make sure you understand the argument. Why doesn't the dollar appreciate by, say, 20%?

Note that our argument relies heavily on the assumption that, when the interest rate changes, the expected exchange rate remains unchanged. This implies that an appreciation today leads to an expected depreciation in the future—because the exchange rate is expected to return to the same, unchanged, value. We shall relax the assumption that the future exchange rate is fixed in Chapter 21. But the basic conclusion will remain: *An increase in the domestic interest rate relative to the foreign interest rate leads to an appreciation.*

Figure 20-1 plots the relation between the domestic interest rate, i, and the exchange rate, E, implied by equation (20.5)—the interest parity relation. The relation is drawn for a given expected future exchange rate, $\bar{E}^e$, and a given foreign interest rate, i^*, and is represented by an upward-sloping line: The higher the domestic interest rate, the higher the exchange rate. Equation (20.5) also implies that when the domestic interest rate is equal to the foreign interest rate ($i = i^*$), the exchange rate is equal to the expected future exchange rate ($E = \bar{E}^e$). This implies that the line corresponding to the interest parity condition goes through point A in the figure.

◀ What happens to the line if i^* increases? What happens to the line if $\bar{E}^e$ increases?

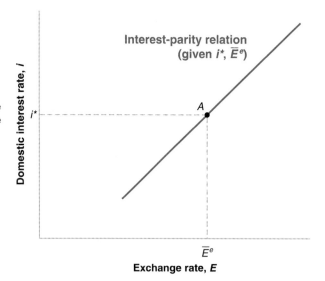

***The Relation between the
Interest Rate and the
Exchange Rate Implied
by Interest Parity***

A higher domestic interest rate
leads to a higher exchange
rate—an appreciation.

20-3 Putting Goods and Financial Markets Together

We now have the elements we need to understand the movements of output, the interest rate, and the exchange rate.

Goods market equilibrium implies that output depends, among other factors, on the interest rate and the exchange rate:

$$Y = C(Y - T) + I(Y, i) + G + NX(Y, Y^*, E)$$

The interest rate, in turn, is determined by the equality of money supply and money demand:

$$\frac{M}{P} = YL(i)$$

And the interest parity condition implies a negative relation between the domestic interest rate and the exchange rate:

$$E = \frac{1 + i}{1 + i^*}\bar{E}^e$$

Together, these three relations determine output, the interest rate, and the exchange rate. Working with three relations is not very easy. But we can easily reduce them to two by using the interest parity condition to eliminate the exchange rate in the goods market equilibrium relation. Doing this gives us the following two equations, the open-economy versions of our familiar *IS* and *LM* relations:

$$IS: \quad Y = C(Y - T) + I(Y, i) + G + NX\left(Y, Y^*, \frac{1 + i}{1 + i^*}\bar{E}^e\right)$$

$$LM: \frac{M}{P} = YL(i)$$

Take the *IS* relation first and consider the effects of an increase in the interest rate on output. An increase in the interest rate now has two effects:

■ The first effect, which was already present in a closed economy, is the direct effect on investment: A higher interest rate leads to a decrease in investment, a decrease in the demand for domestic goods, and a decrease in output.

The interest parity condition assumes that financial investors care only about expected returns. As we discussed in Chapter 18, investors care not only about returns but also about risk and about liquidity—how easy it is to buy or sell an asset.

Much of the time, we can ignore these other factors. Sometimes, however, these factors play a big role in investors' decisions and in determining exchange rate movements.

Perceptions of risk often play an important role in the decisions of large financial investors—for example, pension funds—to invest or not to invest at all in a country. Sometimes the perception that risk has decreased leads many foreign investors to simultaneously buy assets in a country, leading to a large increase in demand for the assets of that country. Sometimes the perception that risk has increased leads the same investors to want to sell all the assets they have in that country, no matter what the interest rate. These episodes, which have affected many Latin American and Asian emerging economies, are known as **sudden stops**. During these episodes, the interest parity condition fails, and the exchange rate may decrease a lot, without any change in domestic or foreign interest rates.

Large countries can also be affected. For example, the appreciation of the dollar in the 1990s—which, as we saw in Chapter 19, is one of the causes of the large U.S. trade deficit—came not so much from an increase in U.S. interest rates over foreign interest rates, as from an increased foreign demand for dollar assets at a given interest rate. Many private foreign investors want to have some proportion of their wealth in U.S. assets: They perceive U.S. assets as being relatively safe. Many foreign central banks want to hold a large proportion of their reserves in U.S. T-bills. The reason they do so is because the T-bill market is very liquid, so they can buy and sell T-bills without affecting the price. This very high demand for U.S. assets, at a given interest rate, was behind the "strong dollar" in the 1990s. Even while U.S. interest rates are relatively low, foreign investors are still eager to increase their holdings of U.S. assets, and thus to finance the large U.S. trade deficit. How long they are willing to do so will determine what happens to the dollar and to the U.S. trade balance.

■ The second effect, which is present only in the open economy, is the effect through the exchange rate: An increase in the domestic interest rate leads to an increase in the exchange rate—an appreciation. The appreciation, which makes domestic goods more expensive relative to foreign goods, leads to a decrease in net exports and, therefore, to a decrease in the demand for domestic goods and a decrease in output.

Both effects work in the same direction: An increase in the interest rate decreases demand directly and indirectly—through the adverse effect of the appreciation on demand.

The *IS* relation between the interest rate and output is drawn in Figure 20-2(a), for given values of all the other variables in the relation—namely T, G, Y^*, i^*, and $\bar{E}^e$. The *IS* curve is downward sloping: An increase in the interest rate leads to lower output. The curve looks very much the same in an open economy as in a closed economy, but it hides a more complex relation than before: The interest rate affects output not only directly but also indirectly through the exchange rate.

> An increase in the interest rate leads, both directly and indirectly (through the exchange rate), to a decrease in output.

The *LM* relation is exactly the same in an open economy as in a closed economy. The *LM* curve is upward sloping. For a given value of the real money stock, (M/P), an increase in output leads to an increase in the demand for money and to an increase in the equilibrium interest rate.

The IS–LM *Model in an Open Economy*

An increase in the interest rate reduces output both directly and indirectly (through the exchange rate): The *IS* curve is downward sloping. Given the real money stock, an increase in output increases the interest rate: The *LM* curve is upward sloping.

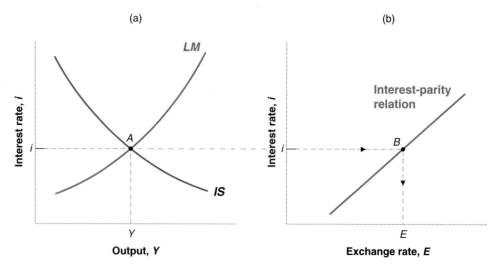

(a)

(b)

Equilibrium in the goods and financial markets is attained at point A in Figure 20-2(a), with output level Y and interest rate i. The equilibrium value of the exchange rate cannot be read directly from the graph. But it is easily obtained from Figure 20-2(b), which replicates Figure 20-1, and gives the exchange rate associated with a given interest rate. The exchange rate associated with the equilibrium interest rate, i, is equal to E.

Let's summarize: We have derived the *IS* and the *LM* relations for an open economy.

■ The *IS* curve is downward sloping: An increase in the interest rate leads directly and indirectly (through the exchange rate) to a decrease in demand and a decrease in output.

■ The *LM* curve is upward sloping: An increase in income increases the demand for money, leading to an increase in the equilibrium interest rate.

Equilibrium output and the equilibrium interest rate are given by the intersection of the *IS* and the *LM* curves. Given the foreign interest rate and the expected future exchange rate, the equilibrium interest rate determines the equilibrium exchange rate.

20-4 ▓ The Effects of Policy in an Open Economy

Having derived the *IS–LM* model for the open economy, we now put it to use and look at the effects of policy.

The Effects of Fiscal Policy in an Open Economy

Let's look again at a change in government spending. Suppose that, starting from a balanced budget, the government decides to increase defense spending without raising taxes and so runs a budget deficit. What happens to the level of output? To the composition of output? To the interest rate? To the exchange rate?

The answers are given in Figure 20-3. The economy is initially at point A. The increase in government spending by, say, $\Delta G > 0$, increases output at a given interest rate, shifting the *IS* curve to the right, from *IS* to *IS'* in Figure 20-3(a). Because government spending does not enter the *LM* relation, the *LM* curve does not shift. The new equilibrium is at point A', with a higher level of output and a higher interest rate. In Figure 20-3(b), the higher interest rate leads to an increase in the exchange rate—an

An increase in government spending shifts the *IS* curve to the right. It shifts neither the ▶ *LM* curve nor the interest-parity line.

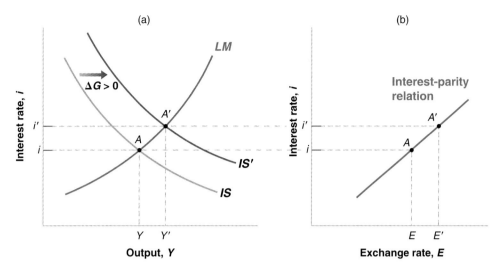

Figure 20-3

The Effects of an Increase in Government Spending

An increase in government spending leads to an increase in output, an increase in the interest rate, and an appreciation.

appreciation. So *an increase in government spending leads to an increase in output, an increase in the interest rate, and an appreciation.*

In words: An increase in government spending leads to an increase in demand, leading to an increase in output. As output increases, so does the demand for money, leading to upward pressure on the interest rate. The increase in the interest rate, which makes domestic bonds more attractive, leads to an appreciation. The higher interest rate and the appreciation both decrease the domestic demand for goods, offsetting some of the effect of government spending on demand and output.

Can we tell what happens to the various components of demand?

■ Clearly, consumption and government spending both go up. Consumption goes up because of the increase in income, and government spending goes up by assumption.

■ What happens to investment is ambiguous. Recall that investment depends on both output and the interest rate: $I = I(Y, i)$. On the one hand, output goes up, leading to an increase in investment. But on the other, the interest rate also goes up, leading to a decrease in investment. Depending on which of these two effects dominates, investment can go up or down. In short: The effect of government spending on investment is ambiguous in a closed economy; it remains ambiguous in an open economy.

■ Recall that net exports depend on domestic output, foreign output, and the exchange rate: $NX = NX(Y, Y^*, E)$. Thus, both the increase in output and the appreciation combine to decrease net exports: The increase in output increases imports, and the appreciation decreases exports and increases imports. As a result, the budget deficit leads to a deterioration of the trade balance. If trade is balanced to start, then the budget deficit leads to a trade deficit. Note that, while an increase in the budget deficit increases the trade deficit, the effect is far from mechanical. It works through the effect of the budget deficit on output and on the exchange rate, and, in turn, on the trade deficit.

The Effects of Monetary Policy in an Open Economy

Now that we have looked at fiscal policy, we look at our other favorite policy experiment, a monetary contraction. Look at Figure 20-4(a). At a given level of output, a decrease in the money stock by, say, $\Delta M < 0$, leads to an increase in the interest rate: The *LM* curve shifts up, from *LM* to *LM'*. Because money does not directly enter the *IS* relation, the *IS* curve does not shift. The equilibrium moves from point *A* to point *A'*. In Figure 20-4(b), the increase in the interest rate leads to an appreciation.

A monetary contraction shifts the *LM* curve up. It shifts neither the *IS* curve nor the interest-parity curve.

Figure 20-4

The Effects of a Monetary Contraction

A monetary contraction leads to a decrease in output, an increase in the interest rate, and an appreciation.

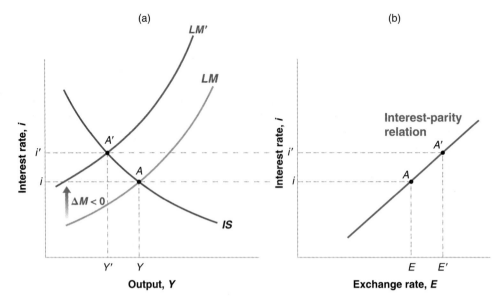

So *a monetary contraction leads to a decrease in output, an increase in the interest rate, and an appreciation.* The story is easy to tell. A monetary contraction leads to an increase in the interest rate, making domestic bonds more attractive and triggering an

◄ Can you tell what happens to consumption, to investment, and to net exports?

appreciation. The higher interest rate and the appreciation both decrease demand and output.

This version of the *IS–LM* model for the open economy was first put together in the 1960s by the two economists we mentioned at the outset of the chapter, Robert Mundell,

◄ Robert Mundell was awarded the Nobel Prize in Economics in 1999.

at Columbia University, and Marcus Fleming, at the International Monetary Fund. How well does the Mundell–Fleming model fit the facts? The answer is: Typically very well, and this is why the model is still very much in use today. (To test the predictions of the model, one could hardly design a better experiment than the sharp monetary and fiscal policy changes the U.S. economy went through in the late 1970s and early 1980s. This is the topic taken up in the Focus box "Monetary Contraction and Fiscal Expansion: The United States in the Early 1980s." The Mundell–Fleming model and its predictions pass with flying colors.)

20-5 Fixed Exchange Rates

We have assumed so far that the central bank chose the money supply and let the exchange rate freely adjust in whatever manner was implied by equilibrium in the foreign exchange market. In many countries, this assumption does not reflect reality: Central banks act under implicit or explicit exchange rate targets and use monetary policy to achieve those targets. The targets are sometimes implicit, sometimes explicit; they are sometimes specific values, sometimes bands or ranges. These exchange rate arrangements (or *regimes*, as they are called) have many names. Let's first see what the names mean.

Pegs, Crawling Pegs, Bands, the EMS, and the Euro

At one end of the spectrum are countries with flexible exchange rates, such as the United States or Japan. These countries do not have explicit exchange rate targets. Although their central banks probably do not ignore movements in the exchange rate, they have shown themselves to be quite willing to let their exchange rates fluctuate considerably.

At the other end are countries that operate under *fixed exchange rates*. These countries maintain a fixed exchange rate in terms of some foreign currency. Some **peg** their currency to the dollar. For example, from 1991 to 2001, Argentina pegged its currency, the peso, at the highly symbolic exchange rate of 1 dollar for 1 peso (more on this in Chapter 21). Other countries used to peg their currency to the French franc (most of these are former French colonies in Africa); as the French franc has been replaced by the euro, they are now pegged to the euro. Still other countries peg their currency to a basket of foreign currencies, with the weights reflecting the composition of their trade.

Like the "dance of the dollar" in the 1980s (see Chapter 18), there was a "dance of the yen" in the 1990s. The yen appreciated sharply in the first half of the 1990s, and then depreciated sharply later in the decade.

The label "fixed" is a bit misleading: It is not the case that the exchange rate in countries with fixed exchange rates never actually changes. But changes are rare. An extreme case involves the African countries pegged to the French franc. When their exchange rates were readjusted in January 1994, it was the first adjustment in 45 years! Because these changes are rare, economists use specific words to distinguish them from the daily changes that occur under flexible exchange rates. A decrease in the exchange rate under a regime of fixed exchange rates is called a *devaluation* rather than a depreciation, and an increase in the exchange rate under a regime of fixed exchange rates is called a *revaluation* rather than an appreciation.

Between these extremes are countries with various degrees of commitment to an exchange rate target. For example, some countries operate under a **crawling peg**. The name describes it well: These countries typically have inflation rates that exceed the U.S. inflation rate. If they were to peg their nominal exchange rate against the dollar, the more rapid increase in their domestic price level above the U.S. price level would lead to a steady real appreciation and rapidly make their goods uncompetitive. To avoid this effect, these countries choose a predetermined rate of depreciation against the dollar. They choose to "crawl" (move slowly) vis-à-vis the dollar.

Recall the definition of the real exchange rate, $\epsilon = EP/P^*$.

If domestic inflation is higher than foreign inflation:
P increases faster than P^*
If E is fixed, EP/P^* steadily increases
Equivalently: There is a steady real appreciation. Domestic goods become steadily more expensive relative to foreign goods.

Yet another arrangement is for a group of countries to maintain their bilateral exchange rates (the exchange rate between each pair of countries) within some bands. Perhaps the most prominent example was the **European Monetary System (EMS)**, which determined the movements of exchange rates within the European Union from 1978 to 1998. Under the EMS rules, member countries agreed to maintain their exchange rate vis-à-vis the other currencies in the system within narrow limits, or **bands**, around a **central parity**—a given value for the exchange rate. Changes in the central parity and devaluations or revaluations of specific currencies could occur, but only by common agreement among member countries. After a major crisis in 1992, which led a number of countries to drop out of the EMS altogether, exchange rate adjustments became more and more infrequent, leading a number of countries to move one step further and adopt a common currency, the **euro**. The conversion from domestic currencies to the euro began January 1, 1999, and was completed in early 2002. We shall return to the implications of the move to the euro in Chapter 21.

We will look at the 1992 crisis in Chapter 21.

You can think of countries adopting a common currency as adopting an extreme form of fixed exchange rates: Their "exchange rate" is fixed at one-to-one between any pair of countries.

We shall discuss the pros and cons of different exchange regimes in Chapter 21. But first, we must understand how pegging the exchange rate affects monetary policy and fiscal policy. This is what we do in the rest of this section.

Pegging the Exchange Rate and Monetary Control

Suppose a country decides to peg its exchange rate at some chosen value, call it $\bar{E}$. How does it actually achieve this? The government cannot just announce the value of the exchange rate and stand there. Rather, it must take measures so that its chosen exchange rate will prevail in the foreign exchange market. Let's look at the implications and mechanics of pegging.

FOCUS

The early 1980s in the United States were dominated by sharp changes in both monetary policy and fiscal policy.

We already discussed the origins of the change in monetary policy in Chapter 9. By the late 1970s, the chairman of the Fed, Paul Volcker, concluded that U.S. inflation was too high and had to be reduced. Starting in late 1979, Volcker embarked on a path of sharp monetary contraction, realizing that it might lead to a recession in the short run but lower inflation in the medium run.

The change in fiscal policy was triggered by the election of Ronald Reagan in 1980. Reagan was elected on the promise of more conservative policies, namely a scaling down of taxation and the government's role in economic activity. This commitment was the inspiration for the *Economic Recovery Act* of August 1981. Personal income taxes were cut by a total of 23%, in three install-ments from 1981 to 1983. Corporate taxes were also reduced. These tax cuts were not, however, accompanied by corresponding decreases in government spending, and the result was a steady increase in budget deficits, which reached a peak in 1983, at 5.6% of GDP. Table 1 gives spending and revenue numbers for 1980 to 1984.

What were the Reagan administration's motivations for cutting taxes without implementing corresponding cuts in spending? They are still being debated today, but there is agreement that there were two main motivations.

One motivation came from the beliefs of a fringe, but influential, group of economists called the **supply siders**, who argued that a cut in tax rates would cause people and firms to work much harder and more productively and that the resulting increase in activity would actually lead to an increase, not a decrease, in tax revenues.

Table 1	The Emergence of Large U.S. Budget Deficits, 1980 to 1984				
	1980	**1981**	**1982**	**1983**	**1984**
Spending	22.0	22.8	24.0	25.0	23.7
Revenues	20.2	20.8	20.5	19.4	19.2
Personal taxes	9.4	9.6	9.9	8.8	8.2
Corporate taxes	2.6	2.3	1.6	1.6	2.0
Budget surplus (−: deficit)	−1.8	−2.0	−3.5	−5.6	−4.5

Note: Numbers are for fiscal years, which start in October of the previous calendar year. All numbers are expressed as a percent-age of GDP.
Source: Historical Tables, Office of Management and Budget.

Whatever the merits of the argument appeared to be then, it proved wrong: Even if some people did work harder and more productively after the tax cuts, tax rev-enues decreased, and the fiscal deficit increased.

The other motivation was more cynical. It was a bet that the cut in taxes, and the resulting increase in deficits, would scare Congress into cutting spending, or, at the very least, into not increasing spending further. This motiva-tion turned out to be partly right; Congress found itself under enormous pressure not to increase spending, and the growth of spending in the 1980s was surely lower than it would have been otherwise. Nonetheless, the adjust-ment of spending was not enough to offset the shortfall in taxes and avoid the rapid increase in deficits.

Pegging or no pegging, the exchange rate and the nominal interest rate must sat-isfy the interest parity condition:

$$(1 + i_t) = (1 + i_t^*)\left(\frac{E_t}{E_{t+1}^e}\right)$$

Now suppose a country pegs the exchange rate at $\bar{E}$, so the current exchange rate $E_t = \bar{E}$. If financial and foreign exchange markets believe that the exchange rate will remain pegged at this value, then their expectation of the future exchange rate, E_{t+1}^e, is also equal to $\bar{E}$, and the interest parity relation becomes

$$(1 + i_t) = (1 + i_t^*) \Rightarrow i_t = i_t^*$$

In words: If financial investors expect the exchange rate to remain unchanged, they will require the same nominal interest rate in both countries. *Under a fixed exchange rate and perfect capital mobility, the domestic interest rate must be equal to the foreign interest rate.*

Whatever the reason for the deficits, the effects of the monetary contraction and fiscal expansion were in line with what the Mundell–Fleming model predicts. Table 2 gives the evolution of the main macroeconomic variables from 1980 to 1984.

From 1980 to 1982, the evolution of the economy was dominated by the effects of the monetary contraction. Interest rates, both nominal and real, increased sharply, leading to both a large dollar appreciation and a recession. The goal of lowering inflation was achieved; by 1982, inflation was down to about 4%, down from 12.5% in 1980. Lower output and the dollar appreciation had opposing effects on the trade balance (lower output leading to lower imports and an improvement in the trade balance; the appreciation of the dollar leading to a deterioration in the trade balance), resulting in little change in the trade deficit before 1982.

From 1982 on, the evolution of the economy was dominated by the effects of the fiscal expansion. As our model predicts, these effects were strong output growth, high interest rates, and further dollar appreciation. The effects of high output growth and the dollar appreciation were an increase in the trade deficit to 2.7% of GDP by 1984. By the mid-1980s, the main macroeconomic policy issue had become the **twin deficits**, the budget deficit and the trade deficit. The twin deficits were to remain one of the central macroeconomic issues throughout the 1980s and early 1990s.

Table 2 Major U.S. Macroeconomic Variables, 1980 to 1984					
	1980	1981	1982	1983	1984
GDP growth (%)	−0.5	1.8	−2.2	3.9	6.2
Unemployment rate (%)	7.1	7.6	9.7	9.6	7.5
Inflation (CPI) (%)	12.5	8.9	3.8	3.8	3.9
Interest rate (nominal) (%)	11.5	14.0	10.6	8.6	9.6
(real) (%)	2.5	4.9	6.0	5.1	5.9
Real exchange rate	85	101	111	117	129
Trade surplus (2: deficit) of GDP)	−0.5	−0.4	−0.6	−1.5	−2.7

Note: Inflation: rate of change of the CPI. The nominal interest rate is the three-month T-bill rate. The real interest rate is equal to the nominal rate minus the forecast of inflation by DRI, a private forecasting firm. The real exchange rate is the trade-weighted real exchange rate, normalized so that 1973 = 100.

This condition has one further important implication. Return to the equilibrium condition that the supply of money and demand for money be equal. Now that $i = i^*$, this condition becomes

$$\frac{M}{P} = YL(i^*) \qquad (20.6)$$

Suppose an increase in domestic output increases the demand for money. In a closed economy, the central bank could leave the money stock unchanged, leading to an increase in the equilibrium interest rate. In an open economy, and under flexible exchange rates, the central bank can still do the same: The result will be both an increase in the interest rate and an appreciation. But under fixed exchange rates, the central bank cannot keep the money stock unchanged. If it did, the domestic interest rate would increase above the foreign interest rate, leading to an appreciation. To maintain the exchange rate, the central bank must increase the supply of money in line with the increase in the demand for money so the equilibrium interest rate does not change. Given the price level, P, nominal money, M, must adjust so that equation (20.6) holds.

Under a fixed exchange rate regime such as the European Monetary System (EMS) (let's ignore here the degree of flexibility that was afforded by the bands), no individual country can change its interest rate if the other countries do not change theirs as well. So how do interest rates actually change? Two arrangements are possible. One is for all the member countries to coordinate changes in their interest rates. Another is for one of the countries to take the lead and for the other countries to follow—this is, in effect, what happened in the EMS, with Germany as the leader.

During the 1980s, most European central banks shared similar goals and were happy to let the Bundesbank (the German central bank) take the lead. But in 1990, German unification led to a sharp divergence in goals between the Bundesbank and the central banks of the other EMS countries. Large budget deficits, triggered by transfers to people and firms in Eastern Germany, together with an investment boom, led to a large increase in demand in Germany. The Bundesbank's fear that this shift would generate too strong an increase in activity led it to adopt a restrictive monetary policy. The result was strong growth in Germany together with a large increase in interest rates.

This may have been the right policy mix for Germany. But for the other European countries, this policy mix was much less appealing. They were not experiencing the same increase in demand, but to stay in the EMS, they had to match German interest rates. The net result was a sharp decrease in demand and output in the other countries. These results are presented in Table 1, which gives nominal interest rates, real interest rates, inflation rates, and GDP growth from 1990 to 1992 for Germany and for two of its EMS partners, France and Belgium.

Note first how the high German nominal interest rates were matched by both France and Belgium. In fact, nominal interest rates were actually higher in France than in Germany in all three years! This is because France needed higher interest rates than Germany to maintain the Deutsche mark/franc parity. The reason is that financial markets were not sure that France would actually keep the parity of the franc vis-à-vis the Deutsche mark. Worried about a possible devaluation of the franc, financial investors asked for a higher interest rate on French bonds than on German bonds.

Although France and Belgium had to match—or, as we have just seen, more than match—German nominal rates, these two countries had less inflation than Germany. The result was very high real interest rates, much higher than the rate in Germany: In both France and Belgium, average real interest rates from 1990 to 1992 were close to 7%. And in both countries, the period 1990 to 1992 was characterized by slow growth and rising unemployment. Unemployment in France in 1992 was 10.4%, up from 8.9% in 1990. The corresponding numbers for Belgium were 12.1% and 8.7%.

A similar story was unfolding in the other EMS countries. By 1992, average unemployment in the European Union, which had been 8.7% in 1990, had increased to 10.3%. The effects of high real interest rates on spending were not the only source of this slowdown, but they were the main one.

These results depend very much on the interest rate parity condition, which in turn depends on the assumption of perfect capital mobility—that financial investors go for the highest expected rate of return. The case of fixed exchange rates with imperfect capital mobility, which is more relevant for middle-income countries, such as in Latin America or Asia, is treated in the appendix to this chapter.

Let's summarize: *Under fixed exchange rates, the central bank gives up monetary policy as a policy instrument.* With a fixed exchange rate, the domestic interest rate must be equal to the foreign interest rate. And the money supply must adjust so as to maintain the interest rate.

Fiscal Policy under Fixed Exchange Rates

If monetary policy can no longer be used under fixed exchange rates, what about fiscal policy? To answer this question, we use Figure 20-5.

Figure 20-5 starts by replicating Figure 20-3(a), which we used earlier to analyze the effects of fiscal policy under flexible exchange rates. In that case, we saw that a fiscal expansion ($\Delta G > 0$) shifted the IS curve to the right. Under flexible exchange rates, the money stock remained unchanged, leading to a movement in the equilibrium from point A to point B, with an increase in output from Y_A to Y_B, an increase in the interest rate, and an appreciation.

However, under fixed exchange rates, the central bank cannot let the currency appreciate. Because the increase in output leads to an increase in the demand for money, the central bank must accommodate this increased demand for money by

By 1992, an increasing number of countries were wondering whether to keep defending their EMS parity or to give it up and lower their interest rates. Worried about the risk of devaluations, financial markets started to ask for higher interest rates in countries where they thought devaluations were more likely. The result was two major exchange rate crises, one in the fall of 1992 and the other in the summer of 1993. By the end of these two crises, two countries, Italy and the United Kingdom, had left the EMS. We shall look at these crises, their origins, and their implications in Chapter 21.

Table 1	Interest Rates and Output Growth: Germany, France, and Belgium, 1990 to 1992					
	Nominal Interest Rates (percent)			Inflation (percent)		
	1990	1991	1992	1990	1991	1992
Germany	8.5	9.2	9.5	2.7	3.7	4.7
France	10.3	9.6	10.3	2.9	3.0	2.4
Belgium	9.6	9.4	9.4	2.9	2.7	2.4
	Real Interest Rates (percent)			GDP Growth (percent)		
	1990	1991	1992	1990	1991	1992
Germany	5.7	5.5	4.8	5.7	4.5	2.1
France	7.4	6.6	7.9	2.5	0.7	1.4
Belgium	6.7	6.7	7.0	3.3	2.1	0.8

Note: The nominal interest rate is the short-term nominal interest rate. The real interest rate is the realized real interest rate over the year—that is, the nominal interest rate minus actual inflation over the year. All rates are annual.
Source: OECD *Economic Outlook.*

increasing the money supply. In terms of Figure 20-5, the central bank must shift the *LM* curve down as the *IS* curve shifts to the right so as to maintain the same interest rate, and thus, the same exchange rate. The equilibrium therefore moves from *A* to *C*, with higher output, Y_C, and unchanged interest and exchange rates. So, *under fixed exchange rates, fiscal policy is more powerful than it is under flexible exchange rates. This is because fiscal policy triggers monetary accommodation.*

As this chapter comes to an end, a question should have started to form in your mind: Why would a country choose to fix its exchange rate? You have seen a number of reasons why this appears to be a bad idea:

◀ Is the effect of fiscal policy stronger in a closed economy or in an open economy with fixed exchange rates? (*Hint:* The answer is ambiguous.)

■ By fixing the exchange rate, a country gives up a powerful tool for correcting trade imbalances or changing the level of economic activity.
■ By committing to a particular exchange rate, a country also gives up control of its interest rate. Not only that, but the country must match movements in the foreign interest rate, at the risk of unwanted effects on its own activity. This is what happened in the early 1990s in Europe. Because of the increase in demand due to the reunification of West and East Germany, Germany felt it had to increase its interest rate. To maintain their parity with the Deutsche mark, other countries in the

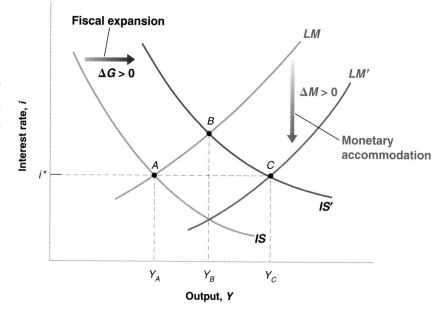

■ Figure 20-5

The Effects of a Fiscal Expansion under Fixed Exchange Rates

Under flexible exchange rates, a fiscal expansion increases output from Y_A to Y_B. Under fixed exchange rates, output increases from Y_A to Y_C.

European Monetary System were forced to also increase their interest rates, something that they would rather have avoided. (This is the topic of the Focus box "German Unification, Interest Rates, and the EMS.")

■ Although the country retains control of fiscal policy, one policy instrument may not be enough. As you saw in Chapter 19, for example, a fiscal expansion can help the economy get out of a recession, but only at the cost of a larger trade deficit. And a country that wants, for example, to decrease its budget deficit cannot, under fixed exchange rates, use monetary policy to offset the contractionary effect of its fiscal policy on output.

So why do some countries fix their exchange rate? Why have 15 European countries—with more to come—adopted a common currency? To answer these questions, we must do some more work. We must look at what happens not only in the short run—which is what we did in this chapter—but also in the medium run, when the price level can adjust. We must look at the nature of exchange rate crises. Once we have done this, we shall then be able to assess the pros and cons of different exchange rate regimes. These are the topics we take up in Chapter 21.

Summary

■ In an open economy, the demand for domestic goods depends on both the interest rate and the exchange rate. An increase in the interest rate decreases the demand for domestic goods. An increase in the exchange rate—an appreciation—also decreases the demand for domestic goods.

■ The interest rate is determined by the equality of money demand and money supply. The exchange rate is determined by the interest parity condition, which states that domestic and foreign bonds must have the same expected rate of return in terms of domestic currency.

■ Given the expected future exchange rate and the foreign interest rate, increases in the domestic interest rate lead

to an increase in the exchange rate—an appreciation. Decreases in the domestic interest rate lead to a decrease in the exchange rate—a depreciation.

■ Under flexible exchange rates, an expansionary fiscal policy leads to an increase in output, an increase in the interest rate, and an appreciation.

■ Under flexible exchange rates, a contractionary monetary policy leads to a decrease in output, an increase in the interest rate, and an appreciation.

■ There are many types of exchange rate arrangements. They range from fully flexible exchange rates to crawling pegs, to fixed exchange rates (or pegs), to the adoption of a common currency. Under fixed exchange rates, a country maintains a fixed exchange rate in terms of a foreign currency or a basket of currencies.

■ Under fixed exchange rates and the interest parity condition, a country must maintain an interest rate equal to the foreign interest rate. The central bank loses the use of monetary policy as a policy instrument. Fiscal policy becomes more powerful than under flexible exchange rates, however, because fiscal policy triggers monetary accommodation and so does not lead to offsetting changes in the domestic interest rate and exchange rate.

Key Terms

- Mundell–Fleming model, 443
- sudden stops, 449
- peg, 453
- crawling peg, 453
- European Monetary System (EMS), 453
- bands, 453
- central parity, 453
- euro, 453
- supply siders, 454
- twin deficits, 455

Questions and Problems

Quick Check

1. Using the information in this chapter, label each of the following statements true, false, or uncertain. Explain briefly.

a. For a given value of the real money stock, an increase in output leads to an increase in the demand for money, and an increase in the equilibrium interest rate.

b. A monetary contraction leads to a decrease in output, a decrease in the interest rate, and an appreciation.

c. Other things equal, the interest parity condition implies that the domestic currency will appreciate in response to an increase in the expected exchange rate.

d. Under fixed exchange rates, fiscal policy is less powerful than it is under flexible exchange rates.

e. If the Japanese interest rate is equal to zero, foreigners will not want to hold Japanese bonds.

f. If financial investors expect the dollar to depreciate against the yen over the coming year, one-year interest rates will be higher in the United States than in Japan. What is the appropriate fiscal-monetary policy mix?

2. In this chapter, we showed that a monetary expansion in an economy operating under flexible exchange rates leads to an increase in output and a depreciation of the domestic currency.

a. How does a monetary expansion (in an economy with flexible exchange rates) affect consumption and investment?

b. How does a monetary expansion (in an economy with flexible exchange rates) affect net exports?

3. Consider an open economy with flexible exchange rates. Suppose output is at the natural level, but there is a trade deficit.

4. Flexible exchange rates and foreign macroeconomic policy
Consider an open economy with flexible exchange rates. Let UIP stand for the uncovered interest parity condition.

a. In an *IS–LM–UIP* diagram, show the effect of an increase in foreign output, Y^*, on domestic output, Y. Explain in words.

b. In an *IS–LM–UIP* diagram, show the effect of an increase in the foreign interest rate, i^*, on domestic output, Y.

Explain in words.

c. Given the discussion of the effects of fiscal policy in this chapter, what effect is a foreign fiscal expansion likely to have on foreign output, Y^*, and on the foreign interest rate, i^*? Given the discussion of the effects of monetary policy in this chapter, what effect is a foreign monetary expansion likely to have on Y^* and i^*?

d. Given your answers to parts (a), (b), and (c), how does a foreign fiscal expansion affect domestic output? How does a foreign monetary expansion affect domestic output? (*Hint:* One of these policies has an ambiguous effect on output.)

Dig Deeper

5. Fixed exchange rates and foreign macroeconomic policy
Consider a fixed exchange rate system, in which a group of countries (called follower countries) peg their currencies to the currency of one country (called the leader country). Since the currency of the leader country is not fixed against the currencies of countries outside the fixed exchange rate system, the leader country can conduct monetary policy as it wishes. For this problem, consider the domestic country to be a follower country and the foreign country to be the leader country.

a. Redo the analysis of problem 4(a).

b. Redo the analysis of problem 4(b).

c. Using your answers to parts (a) and (b) and problem 4(c), how does a foreign monetary expansion (by the leader country) affect domestic output? How does a foreign fiscal expansion (by the leader country) affect domestic output? (You may assume that the effect of Y^* on domestic output is small.) How do your answers differ from those in 4(d)?

6. The exchange rate as an automatic stabilizer
Consider an economy that suffers a fall in business confidence (which tends to reduce investment). Let UIP stand for the uncovered interest parity condition.

a. Suppose the economy has a flexible exchange rate. In

an *IS–LM–UIP* diagram, show the short-run effect of the fall in business confidence on output, the interest rate, and the exchange rate. How does the change in the exchange rate, by itself, tend to affect output? Does the change in the exchange rate dampen (make smaller) or amplify (make larger) the effect of the fall in business confidence on output?

b. Suppose instead the economy has a fixed exchange rate. In an *IS–LM–UIP* diagram, show how the economy responds to the fall in business confidence. What must happen to the money supply in order to maintain the fixed exchange rate? How does the effect on output in this economy, with fixed exchange rates, compare to the effect you found for the economy in part (a), with flexible exchange rates?

c. Explain how the exchange rate acts as an automatic stabilizer in an economy with flexible exchange rates.

Explore Further

7. *Demand for U.S. assets, the dollar, and the trade deficit*

This question explores how an increase in demand for U.S. assets may have slowed the depreciation of the dollar that many economists believe is warranted by the large U.S. trade deficit. Here, we modify the IS–LM–UIP framework (where UIP stands for uncovered interest parity) to analyze the effects of an increase in demand for U.S. assets. Write the uncovered interest parity condition as

$$(1 + i_t) = (1 + i_t^*) \, E_t/E_{t+1}^e - x$$

where the parameter x represents factors affecting the relative demand for domestic assets. An increase in x means that investors are willing to hold domestic assets at a lower interest rate (given the foreign interest rate, and the current and expected exchange rates).

a. Solve the *UIP* condition for the current exchange rate, E_t.

b. Substitute the result from part (a) in the *IS* curve and construct the *UIP* diagram. As in the text, you may assume that P and P^* are constant and equal to one.

c. Suppose that as a result of a large trade deficit in the domestic economy, financial market participants believe that the domestic currency must depreciate in the future. Therefore, the expected exchange rate, E_{t+1}^e, falls. Show the effect of the fall in the expected exchange rate in the *IS–LM–UIP* diagram. What are the effects on the exchange rate and the trade balance? (*Hint*: In analyzing the effect on the trade balance, remember why the *IS* curve shifted in the first place.)

d. Now suppose that the relative demand for domestic assets, *x*, increases. As a benchmark, suppose that the increase in *x* is exactly enough to return the *IS* curve to its original position, before the fall in the expected exchange rate. Show the combined effects of the fall in E_{t+1}^e and the increase in *x* in your *IS–LM–UIP* diagram. What are the ultimate effects on the exchange rate and the trade balance?

e. Based on your analysis, is it possible that an increase in demand for U.S. assets could prevent the dollar from depreciating? Is it possible than an increase in demand for U.S. assets could worsen the U.S. trade balance? Explain your answers.

By the time you read this book, it is possible that relative demand for U.S. assets could be weaker than it is at the time of this writing and that the dollar could be depreciating. Think about how you would use the framework of this problem to assess the current situation.

8. *Expected depreciation of the dollar*

In Chapter 19, the text mentions that the dollar may need to depreciate by as much as 20% to 40% in real terms to achieve a reasonable improvement in the trade balance.

a. Go the Web site of *The Economist* (**www.economist.com**) and find data on 10-year interest rates. Look in the section "Markets & Data" and then the subsection "Economic and Financial Indicators." Look at the interest rates for the United States, Japan, China, Britain, Canada, and the euro area. For each country (treating the euro area as a country), calculate the spreads as that country's interest rate minus the U.S. interest rate.

b. From the uncovered interest parity condition, the spreads from part (a) are the annualized expected appreciation rates of the dollar against other currencies. To calculate the 10-year expected appreciation, you must compound. (So, if *x* is the spread, the 10-year expected appreciation is $[(1 + x)^{10} - 1]$. Be careful about decimal points.) Is the dollar expected to depreciate much in nominal terms against any currency other than the yen?

c. Given your answer to part (b), if we accept that significant real depreciation of the dollar is likely in the next decade, how must it be accomplished? Does your answer seem plausible?

d. What do your answers to parts (b) and (c) suggest about the relative strength of demand for dollar assets, independent of the exchange rate? You may want to review problem 7 before answering this question.

We invite you to visit the Blanchard page on the Prentice Hall Web site, at:
www.prenhall.com/blanchard
for this chapter's World Wide Web exercises.

Further Readings

- A fascinating account of the politics behind fiscal policy under the Reagan administration is given by David Stockman—who was then the director of the Office of Management and Budget (OMB)—*The Triumph of Politics: Why the Reagan Revolution Failed*, Harper & Row, New York, 1986.

- A good book on the evolution of exchange rate arrangements in Europe is Daniel Gros and Niels Thygesen, *European Monetary Integration: From the European Monetary System to Economic and Monetary Union*, 2nd ed. Addison-Wesley-Longman, New York, 1998.

Appendix: Fixed Exchange Rates, Interest Rates, and Capital Mobility

The assumption of perfect capital mobility is a good approximation to what happens in countries with highly developed financial markets and few capital controls, such as the United States, the United Kingdom, Japan, and the euro area. But the assumption is more questionable in countries that have less developed financial markets or have capital controls in place. In those countries, domestic financial investors may have neither the savvy nor the legal right to buy foreign bonds when domestic interest rates are low. The central bank may thus be able to decrease the interest rate while maintaining a given exchange rate.

To look at these issues, we need to have another look at the balance sheet of the central bank. In Chapter 4, we assumed that the only asset held by the central bank was domestic bonds. In an open economy, the central bank actually holds two types of assets: (1) domestic bonds and (2) **foreign exchange reserves**, which we shall think of as foreign currency—although they also take the form of foreign bonds or foreign interest–paying assets. Think of the balance sheet of the central bank as represented in Figure 1.

On the asset side are bonds and foreign exchange reserves, and on the liability side is the monetary base. There are now two ways in which the central bank can change the monetary base: either by purchases or sales of bonds in the bond market or by purchases or sales of foreign currency in the foreign exchange market. (If you did not read Section 4-3 in Chapter 4, replace "monetary base" with "money supply," and you will still get the basic argument.)

Perfect Capital Mobility and Fixed Exchange Rates

Consider the effects of an open market operation under the joint assumptions of perfect capital mobility and fixed exchange rates (the assumptions we made in the last section of this chapter):

- Assume that the domestic interest rate and the foreign interest rate are initially equal, so $i = i^*$. Now suppose the central bank embarks on an expansionary open market operation, buying bonds in the bond market in amount ΔB, and creating money—increasing the monetary base—in exchange. This purchase of bonds leads to a decrease in the domestic interest rate, i. This is, however, only the beginning of the story.

- Now that the domestic interest rate is lower than the foreign interest rate, financial investors prefer to hold foreign bonds. To buy foreign bonds, they must first buy foreign currency. They then go to the foreign exchange market and sell domestic currency for foreign currency.

- If the central bank did nothing, the price of domestic currency would fall, and the result would be a depreciation. Under its commitment to a fixed exchange rate, the central bank cannot allow the currency to depreciate. So it must intervene in the foreign exchange market and sell foreign currency for domestic currency. As it sells foreign currency and buys domestic money, the monetary base decreases.

- How much foreign currency must the central bank sell? It must keep selling until the monetary base is back to its pre–open market operation level, so the domestic interest rate is again equal to the foreign interest rate. Only then are financial investors willing to hold domestic bonds.

How long do all these steps take? Under perfect capital mobility, all this may happen within minutes or so of the original open market operation.

After these steps, the balance sheet of the central bank looks as represented in Figure 2. Bond holdings are up by ΔB, reserves of foreign currency are down by ΔB, and the monetary base is unchanged, having gone up by ΔB in the open market operation and down by ΔB as a result of the sale of foreign currency in the foreign exchange market.

Let's summarize: Under fixed exchange rates and perfect capital mobility, the only effect of the open market operation is to change the *composition* of the central bank's balance sheet but not the monetary base (nor the interest rate).

Assets	Liabilities
Bonds Foreign exchange reserves	Monetary base

Figure 1 *Balance Sheet of the Central Bank*

Assets	Liabilities
Bonds: ΔB	Monetary base $\Delta B - \Delta B$
Reserves: $-\Delta B$	$= 0$

Figure 2 *Balance Sheet of the Central Bank after an Open Market Operation and the Induced Intervention in the Foreign-Exchange Market.*

Imperfect Capital Mobility and Fixed Exchange Rates

Let's now move away from the assumption of perfect capital mobility. Suppose it takes some time for financial investors to shift between domestic bonds and foreign bonds.

Now an expansionary open market operation can initially bring the domestic interest rate below the foreign interest rate. But over time, investors shift to foreign bonds, leading to an increase in the demand for foreign currency in the foreign exchange market. To avoid a depreciation of the domestic currency, the central bank must again stand ready to sell foreign currency and buy domestic currency. Eventually, the central bank buys enough domestic currency to offset the effects of the initial open market operation. The monetary base is back to its pre–open market operation level, and so is the interest rate. The central bank holds more domestic bonds and smaller reserves of foreign currency.

The difference between this case and the case of perfect capital mobility is that, by accepting a loss in foreign exchange reserves, the central bank is now able to decrease interest rates *for some time*. If it takes just a few days for financial investors to adjust, the trade-off can be very unattractive—as many countries, which have suffered large losses in reserves without much effect on the interest rate, have discovered at their expense. But if the central bank can affect the domestic interest rate for a few weeks or months, it may, in some circumstances, be willing to do so.

Now let's deviate further from perfect capital mobility. Suppose that, in response to a decrease in the domestic interest rate, financial investors are either unwilling or unable to move much of their portfolio into foreign bonds. For example, there are administrative and legal controls on financial transactions that make it illegal or very expensive for domestic residents to invest outside the country. This is the relevant case for a number of emerging economies, from Latin America to China.

After an expansionary open market operation, the domestic interest rate decreases, making domestic bonds less attractive. Some domestic investors move into foreign bonds, selling domestic currency for foreign currency. To maintain the exchange rate, the central bank must buy domestic currency and supply foreign currency. However, the foreign exchange intervention by the central bank may now be small compared to the initial open market operation. And if capital controls truly prevent investors from moving into foreign bonds at all, there may be no need at all for such a foreign exchange intervention.

Even leaving this extreme case aside, the net effects of the initial open market operation and the following foreign exchange interventions are likely to be *an increase in the monetary base, a decrease in the domestic interest rate, an increase in the central bank's bond holdings, and some—but limited—loss in reserves of foreign currency.* With imperfect capital mobility, a country has some freedom to move the domestic interest rate while maintaining its exchange rate. This freedom depends primarily on three factors:

- The degree of development of its financial markets and the willingness of domestic and foreign investors to shift between domestic assets and foreign assets.
- The degree of capital controls it is able to impose on both domestic and foreign investors.
- The amount of foreign exchange reserves it holds: The higher the reserves it has, the more it can afford the loss in reserves it is likely to sustain if it decreases the interest rate at a given exchange rate.

Key Term

- foreign-exchange reserves, 461

Exchange Rate Regimes

In July 1944, representatives of 44 countries met in Bretton Woods, New Hampshire, to design a new international monetary and exchange rate system. The system they adopted was based on fixed exchange rates, with all member countries other than the United States fixing the price of their currency in terms of dollars. In 1973, a series of exchange rate crises brought an abrupt end to the system—and an end to what is now called "the Bretton Woods period." Since then, the world has been characterized by many exchange rate arrangements. Some countries operate under flexible exchange rates, some operate under fixed exchange rates, and some go back and forth between regimes. Which exchange rate regime to choose is one of the most debated issues in macroeconomics and, as the cartoon suggests, a decision facing every country in the world.

"Then it's agreed. Until the dollar firms up, we let the clamshell float."

This chapter discusses these issues:

- Section 21-1 looks at the medium run. It shows that, in sharp contrast to the results we derived for the short run in Chapter 20, an economy ends up with the same real exchange rate and output level in the medium run, regardless of whether it operates under fixed exchange rates or flexible exchange rates. This obviously does not make the exchange rate regime irrelevant—the short run matters very much—but it is an important extension and qualification to our previous analysis.

- Section 21-2 takes another look at fixed exchange rates and focuses on exchange rate crises. During a typical exchange rate crisis, a country operating under a fixed exchange rate is forced, often under dramatic conditions, to abandon its parity and to devalue. Such crises were behind the breakdown of the Bretton Woods system. They rocked the European Monetary System in the early 1990s and were a major element of the Asian Crisis of the late 1990s. It is important to understand why they happen and what they imply.

- Section 21-3 takes another look at flexible exchange rates and focuses on the behavior of exchange rates under a flexible exchange rate regime. It shows that the behavior of exchange rates and the relation of the exchange rate to monetary policy are, in fact, more complex than we assumed in Chapter 20. Large fluctuations in the exchange rate, and the difficulty of using monetary policy to affect the exchange rate, make a flexible exchange rate regime less attractive than it appeared to be in Chapter 20.

- Section 21-4 puts all these conclusions together and reviews the case for flexible or fixed rates. It discusses two recent and important developments: the move toward a common currency in Europe, and the move toward strong forms of fixed exchange rate regimes, from currency boards to dollarization. ■

21-1 The Medium Run

When we focused on the short run in Chapter 20, we drew a sharp contrast between the behavior of an economy with flexible exchange rates and an economy with fixed exchange rates:

- Under flexible exchange rates, a country that needed to achieve a real depreciation—for example, to reduce its trade deficit or to get out of a recession—could do so by relying on an expansionary monetary policy to achieve both lower interest and a decrease in the exchange rate—a depreciation.
- Under fixed exchange rates, a country lost both of these instruments: By definition, its nominal exchange rate was fixed and thus could not be adjusted. Moreover, the fixed exchange rate and the interest parity condition implied that the country could not adjust its interest rate; the domestic interest rate had to remain equal to the foreign interest rate.

This appeared to make a flexible exchange rate regime much more attractive than a fixed exchange rate regime: Why should a country give up two macroeconomic instruments? As we now shift focus from the short run to the medium run, you shall see that this earlier conclusion needs to be qualified. Although our conclusions about the short run were valid, we shall see that, in the medium run, the difference between the two regimes fades away. More specifically, in the medium run, the economy reaches the same real exchange rate and the same level of output, whether it operates under fixed or under flexible exchange rates.

The intuition for this result is actually easy to give. Recall the definition of the real exchange rate:

$$\epsilon = \frac{EP}{P^*}$$

The real exchange rate, ϵ, is equal to the nominal exchange rate, E (the price of domestic currency in terms of foreign currency), times the domestic price level, P, divided by the foreign price level, P^*. There are, therefore, two ways in which the real exchange rate can adjust:

- Through a change in the nominal exchange rate, E—This can be done only under flexible exchange rates. And if we assume that the domestic price level, P, and the foreign price level, P^*, do not change in the short run, it is the only way to adjust the real exchange rate in the short run.
- Through a change in the domestic price level, P, relative to the foreign price level P^*—In the medium run, this option is open even to a country operating under a fixed (nominal) exchange rate. And this is indeed what happens under fixed exchange rates: The adjustment takes place through the price level rather than through the nominal exchange rate.

> There are three ways in which a U.S. car can become cheaper relative to a Japanese car: First, through a decrease in the dollar price of the U.S car. Second, through an increase in the yen price of the Japanese car. Third, through a decrease in the nominal exchange rate— a decrease in the value of the dollar in terms of yen. ◄

Let us go through this argument step by step. To begin, let's derive the aggregate demand and aggregate supply relations for an open economy under a fixed exchange rate.

Aggregate Demand Under Fixed Exchange Rates

In an open economy with fixed exchange rates, we can write the aggregate demand relation as

> Recall that the aggregate demand relation captures the effects of the price level on output. It is derived from equilibrium in goods and financial markets. ◄

$$Y = Y\left(\frac{\bar{E}P}{P^*}, G, T\right) \qquad (21.1)$$
$$(-, +, -)$$

Output, Y, depends on the real exchange rate, $\bar{E}P/P^*$ ($\bar{E}$ denotes the fixed nominal exchange rate, and P and P^* denote the domestic and foreign price levels, respectively), government spending, G, and taxes, T. An increase in the real exchange rate—a real appreciation—leads to a decrease in output. An increase in government spending leads to an increase in output; an increase in taxes leads to a decrease in output.

The derivation of equation (21.1) is better left to an appendix at the end of this chapter. The intuition behind the equation is straightforward, however:

Recall that, in a closed economy, the aggregate demand relation took the same form as equation (21.1), except for the presence of the real money stock, M/P, instead of the real exchange rate, $\bar{E}P/P^*$.

> See equation (7.3). ◄

- The reason for the presence of M/P in a closed economy was the following: By controlling the money supply, the central bank could change the interest rate and affect output. In an open economy, and under fixed exchange rates and perfect capital mobility, the central bank can no longer change the interest rate—which is pinned down by the foreign interest rate. Put another way, under fixed exchange rates, the central bank gives up monetary policy as a policy instrument. This is why the money stock no longer appears in the aggregate demand relation.
- At the same time, the fact that the economy is open implies that we must include a variable that we did not include when we looked at the closed economy

earlier: the real exchange rate, $\bar{E}P/P^*$. As we saw in Chapter 20, an increase in the real exchange rate leads to a decrease in the demand for domestic goods and thus a decrease in output. Conversely, a decrease in the real exchange rate leads to an increase in output.

Note that, just as in a closed economy, the aggregate demand relation (21.1) implies a negative relation between the price level and output. But, while the sign of the effect of the price level on output remains the same, the channel is very different:

- In a closed economy, the price level affects output through its effect on the real money stock and, in turn, its effect on the interest rate.
- In an open economy under fixed exchange rates, the price level affects output through its effect on the real exchange rate. Given the fixed nominal exchange rate, $\bar{E}$, and the foreign price level, P^*, an increase in the domestic price level, P, leads to an increase in the real exchange rate, $\bar{E}P/P^*$—a real appreciation. This real appreciation leads to a decrease in the demand for domestic goods and, in turn, to a decrease in output. Put simply: An increase in the price level makes domestic goods more expensive, thus decreasing the demand for domestic goods and, in turn, decreasing output.

> Aggregate demand relation in the open economy under fixed exchange rates: P increases $\Rightarrow$ $\bar{E}P/P^*$ increases $\Rightarrow$ Y decreases.

Equilibrium in the Short Run and in the Medium Run

The aggregate demand curve associated with equation (21.1) is drawn as the *AD* curve in Figure 21-1. It is downward sloping: An increase in the price level decreases output. As always, the relation is drawn for given values of the other variables, in this case for given values of $\bar{E}$, P^*, G, and T.

> Recall that the aggregate supply relation captures the effects of output on the price level. It is derived from equilibrium in labor markets.

For the aggregate supply curve, we rely on the relation we derived in the core. Going back to the *aggregate supply relation* we derived in Chapter 7, equation (7.2),

$$P = P^e(1 + \mu)F\left(1 - \frac{Y}{L}, z\right) \qquad (21.2)$$

■ Figure 21-1

Aggregate Demand and Aggregate Supply in an Open Economy Under Fixed Exchange Rates

An increase in the price level leads to a real appreciation and a decrease in output: The aggregate demand curve is downward sloping. An increase in output leads to an increase in the price level: The aggregate supply curve is upward sloping.

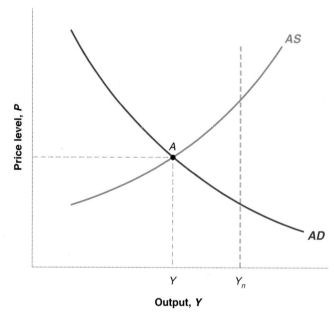

The Open Economy   **Extensions**

The price level, P, depends on the expected price level, P^e, and on the level of output, Y. Recall the two mechanisms at work:

- The expected price level matters because it affects nominal wages, which in turn affect the price level.
- Higher output matters because it leads to higher employment, which leads to lower unemployment, which leads to higher wages, which leads to a higher price level.

◄ Aggregate supply relation: Y increases $\Rightarrow$ P increases.

The aggregate supply curve is drawn as the AS curve in Figure 21-1 for a given value of the expected price level. It is upward sloping: Higher output leads to a higher price level.

The short-run equilibrium is given by the intersection of the aggregate demand curve and the aggregate supply curve, point A in Figure 21-1. As is the case in a closed economy, there is no reason why the short-run equilibrium level of output, Y, should be equal to the natural level of output, Y_n. As the figure is drawn, Y is smaller than Y_n, so output is below the natural level of output.

What happens over time? The basic answer is familiar from our earlier look at adjustment in a closed economy, and is shown in Figure 21-2. As long as output remains below the natural level of output, the aggregate supply shifts down. The reason: When output is below the natural level of output, the price level turns out to be lower than was expected. This leads wage setters to revise their expectation of the price level downward, leading to a lower price level at a given level of output—hence, the downward shift of the aggregate supply curve. So, starting from A, the economy moves over time along the aggregate demand curve until it reaches B. At B, output is equal to the natural level of output. The price level is lower than it was at A; by implication, the real exchange rate is lower than it was at A.

◄ Make sure you understand this step. If you need a refresher, return to Section 7-1.

In words: As long as output is below the natural level of output, the price level decreases. The decrease in the price level over time leads to a steady real depreciation. This real depreciation then leads to an increase in output until output has returned to its natural level.

◄ The result that the price level decreases along the path of adjustment comes from our assumption that the foreign price level is constant. If we had assumed instead that the foreign price level was increasing over time, what would be needed would be for the domestic price level to increase less than the foreign price level or, put another way, for domestic inflation to be lower than foreign inflation for some time.

In the medium run, despite the fact that the nominal exchange rate is fixed, the economy still achieves the real depreciation needed to return output to its natural level. This is an important qualification to the conclusions we reached in the previous chapter—where we were focusing only on the short run:

- In the short run, a fixed nominal exchange rate implies a fixed real exchange rate.
- In the medium run, the real exchange rate can adjust even if the nominal exchange rate is fixed. This adjustment is achieved through movements in the price level.

The Case for and against a Devaluation

The result that, even under fixed exchange rates, the economy returns to the natural level of output in the medium run is important. But it does not eliminate the fact that the process of adjustment may be long and painful. Output may remain too low and unemployment may remain too high for a long time.

Are there faster and better ways to return output to normal? The answer, within the model we have just developed, is a clear yes.

Suppose that the government decides, while keeping the fixed exchange rate regime, to allow for a one-time devaluation. For a given price level, a devaluation (a decrease in the nominal exchange rate) leads to a real depreciation (a decrease in the

Adjustment under Fixed Exchange Rates

The aggregate supply curve shifts down over time, leading to a decrease in the price level, to a real depreciation, and to an increase in output. The process ends when output has returned to its natural level.

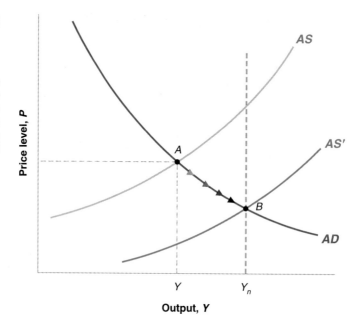

real exchange rate) and, therefore, to an increase in output. In other words, a devaluation shifts the aggregate demand curve to the right: Output is higher at a given price level.

This has a straightforward implication: A devaluation of the right size can take the economy directly from Y to Y_n. This is shown in Figure 21-3. Suppose the economy is initially at A, the same point A as in Figure 21-2. The right size depreciation shifts the aggregate demand curve from AD to AD', moving the equilibrium from A to C. At C, output is equal to the natural level of output, Y_n, and the real exchange rate is the same

Adjustment with a Devaluation

A devaluation of the right size can shift aggregate demand to the right, moving the economy to point C. At point C, output is back to the natural level of output.

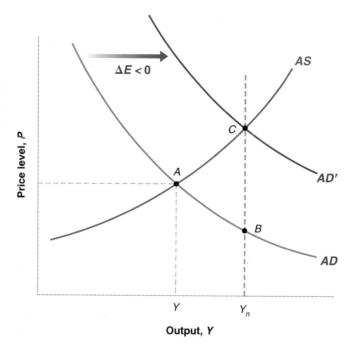

as at *B*. [We know this because output is the same at points *B* and *C*. From equation (21.1), and without changes in *G* or *T*, this implies that the real exchange rate must also be the same.]

That a devaluation of the "right size" can return output to the natural level of output right away sounds too good to be true—and, in reality, it is. Achieving the "right size" devaluation—the devaluation that takes output to Y_n right away—is easier to achieve in a graph than in reality:

- In contrast to our simple aggregate demand relation [see equation (21.1)], the effects of the depreciation on output do not happen right away: As you saw in Chapter 19, the initial effects of a depreciation on output can be contractionary, as people pay more for imports, and the quantities of imports and exports have not adjusted yet.

◄ See Section 19-5 on the J-curve.

- Also, in contrast to our simple aggregate supply relation [see equation (21.2)], there is likely to be a direct effect of the devaluation on the price level. As the price of imported goods increases, the price of a consumption basket increases. This increase is likely to lead workers to ask for higher nominal wages, forcing firms to increase their prices as well.

But these complications do not affect the basic conclusion: A devaluation can hasten the return of output to its natural level. And so, whenever a country under fixed exchange rates faces either a large trade deficit or a severe recession, there is a lot of political pressure either to give up the fixed exchange rate regime altogether, or, at least, to have a one-time devaluation. Perhaps the most forceful presentation of this view was made more than 80 years ago by Keynes, who argued against Winston Churchill's decision to return the British pound in 1925 to its pre–World War I parity with gold. His arguments are presented in the Focus box "The Return of Britain to the Gold Standard: Keynes versus Churchill." Most economic historians believe that history proved Keynes right, and that overvaluation of the pound was one of the main reasons for Britain's poor economic performance after World War I.

Those who oppose a shift to flexible exchange rates or who oppose a devaluation argue that there are good reasons to choose fixed exchange rates and that too much willingness to devalue defeats the purpose of adopting a fixed exchange rate regime in the first place. They argue that too much willingness on the part of governments to consider devaluations actually leads to an increased likelihood of exchange rate crises. To understand their arguments, we now turn to these crises, what triggers them and what their implications might be.

21-2 Exchange Rate Crises under Fixed Exchange Rates

Suppose a country has chosen to operate under a fixed exchange rate. Suppose also that financial investors start believing that there may soon be an exchange rate adjustment—either a devaluation or a shift to a flexible exchange rate regime accompanied by a depreciation.

We just saw why this might be the case:

- The real exchange rate may be too high. Or, put another way, the domestic currency may be overvalued. In this case, a real depreciation is called for. Although this could be achieved in the medium run without a devaluation, financial investors might conclude that the government will take the quickest way out—and devalue.

  Such an overvaluation is likely to happen in a country that pegs its nominal exchange rate to the currency of a country with lower inflation. Higher relative

FOCUS

In 1925, Britain decided to return to the **gold standard**. The gold standard was a system in which each country fixed the price of its currency in terms of gold and stood ready to exchange gold for currency at the stated parity. This system implied fixed exchange rates between countries.

The gold standard had been in place from 1870 until World War I. Because of the need to finance the war, and to do so in part by money creation, Britain suspended the gold standard in 1914. In 1925, Winston Churchill, then Britain's Chancellor of the Exchequer (the English equivalent of Secretary of the Treasury in the United States), decided to return to the gold standard and to return to it at the pre-war parity—that is, at the prewar value of the pound in terms of gold. But because prices had increased faster in Britain than in many of its trading partners, returning to the prewar parity implied a large real appreciation: At the same nominal exchange rate as before the war, British goods were now relatively more expensive relative to foreign goods. (Go back to the definition of the real exchange rate, $\epsilon = EP/P^*$: The price level in Britain, P, had increased more than the foreign price level, P^*. At a given nominal exchange rate, E, this implied that ϵ was higher and that Britain suffered from a real appreciation.)

Keynes severely criticized the decision to return to the pre-war parity. In *The Economic Consequences of Mr. Churchill*, a book he published in 1925, Keynes argued that if Britain were going to return to the gold standard, it should have done so at a lower price of currency in terms of gold—that is, at a lower nominal exchange rate than the pre-war nominal exchange rate. In a newspaper article, he articulated his views as follows:

There remains, however, the objection to which I have never ceased to attach importance, against the return to gold in actual present conditions in view of the possible consequences on the state of trade and employment. I believe that our price level is too high, if it is converted to gold at the par of exchange, in relation to gold prices elsewhere; and if we consider the prices of those articles only which are not the subject of international trade, and of services, i.e. wages, we shall find that these are materially too high—not less than 5 per cent, and probably 10 per cent. Thus, unless the situation is saved by a rise of prices elsewhere, the Chancellor is committing us to a policy of forcing down money wages by perhaps 2 shillings in the Pound.

I do not believe that this can be achieved without the gravest danger to industrial profits and industrial peace. I would much rather leave the gold value of our currency where it was some months ago than embark on a struggle with every trade union in the country to reduce money wages. It seems wiser and simpler and saner to leave the currency to find its own level for some time longer rather than force a situation where employers are faced with the alternative of closing down or of lowering wages, cost what the struggle may.

For this reason, I remain of the opinion that the Chancellor of the Exchequer has done an ill-judged thing—ill judged because we are running the risk for no adequate reward if all goes well.

Keynes's prediction turned out to be right. While other countries were growing, Britain remained in recession for the rest of the decade. Most economic historians attribute a good part of the blame to the initial overvaluation.

Source: "The Nation and Athenaeum," May 2, 1925.

inflation implies a steadily increasing price of domestic goods relative to foreign goods, a steady real appreciation, and so a steady worsening of the trade position. As time passes, the need for an adjustment of the real exchange rate increases, and financial investors become more and more nervous. They start thinking that a devaluation might be coming.

- Internal conditions may call for a decrease in the domestic interest rate. As we have seen, a decrease in the domestic interest rate cannot be achieved under fixed exchange rates. But it can be achieved if the country is willing to shift to a flexible exchange rate regime. If a country lets the exchange rate float and then decreases its domestic interest rate, we know from Chapter 20 that this will trigger a decrease in the nominal exchange rate—a nominal depreciation.

As soon as financial markets believe a devaluation may be coming, maintaining the exchange rate requires an increase—often a large one—in the domestic interest rate. To see this, return to the interest parity condition we derived in Chapter 18:

Because it is more convenient, we use the approximation, equation (18.4), rather than the original interest parity condition, equation (18.2).

$$i_t = i_t^* - \frac{(E_{t+1}^e - E_t)}{E_t} \qquad (21.3)$$

In Chapter 18, we interpreted this equation as a relation between the one-year domestic and foreign nominal interest rates, the current exchange rate, and the expected exchange rate a year hence. But the choice of one year as the period was arbitrary. The relation holds over a day, a week, or a month. If financial markets expect the exchange rate to be 2% lower one month from now, they will hold domestic bonds only if the one-month domestic interest rate exceeds the one–month foreign interest rate by 2% (or, if we express interest rates at an annual rate, if the annual domestic interest rate exceeds the annual foreign interest rate by 2% $\times$ 12 = 24%).

Under fixed exchange rates, the current exchange rate, E_t, is set at some level, say $E_t = \bar{E}$. If markets expect that the parity will be maintained over the period, then $E_{t+1}^e = \bar{E}$, and the interest parity condition simply states that the domestic and the foreign interest rates must be equal.

Suppose, however, that participants in financial markets start anticipating a devaluation—a decrease in the exchange rate. Suppose they believe that, over the coming month, there is a 75% chance the parity will be maintained and a 25% chance there will be a 20% devaluation. The term $(E_{t+1}^e - E_t)/E_t$ in the interest parity equation (21.3), which we assumed equal to 0 earlier, now equals 0.75 $\times$ 0% + 0.25 $\times$ (−20%) = −5% (that is, a 75% chance of no change plus a 25% chance of a devaluation of 20%).

This implies that, if the central bank wants to maintain the existing parity, it must now set a monthly interest rate 5% higher than before—60% higher at an annual rate (12 months $\times$ 5% per month) is the interest differential needed to convince investors to hold domestic bonds rather than foreign bonds! Any smaller interest differential, and investors will not want to hold domestic bonds.

What choices, then, do the government and the central bank have?

- First, the government and the central bank can try to convince markets that they have no intention of devaluing. This is always the first line of defense: Communiqués are issued, and prime ministers go on TV to reiterate their absolute commitment to the existing parity. But words are cheap, and they rarely convince financial investors.

- Second, the central bank can increase the interest rate but by less than would be needed to satisfy equation (21.3)—in our example, by less than 60%. Although domestic interest rates are high, they are not high enough to fully compensate for the perceived risk of devaluation. This action typically leads to a large capital outflow because financial investors still prefer to get out of domestic bonds into foreign bonds. They sell domestic bonds, getting the proceeds in domestic currency. They then go to the foreign exchange market to sell domestic currency for foreign currency in order to buy foreign bonds. If the central bank did not intervene in the foreign exchange market, the large sales of domestic currency for foreign currency would lead to a depreciation. If it wants to maintain the exchange rate, the central bank must therefore stand ready to buy domestic currency and sell foreign currency at the current exchange rate. In doing so, it often loses most of its reserves of foreign currency. (The mechanics of central bank intervention were described in the appendix to Chapter 20.)

- Eventually—after a few hours or a few weeks—the choice for the central bank becomes either to increase the interest rate enough to satisfy equation (21.3), or to validate the market's expectations and devalue. Setting a very high short-term domestic interest rate can have a devastating effect on demand and on output— no firm wants to invest, and no consumer wants to borrow when interest rates are very high. This course of action makes sense only if (1) the perceived probability of a devaluation is small, so the interest rate does not have to be too high, and (2) the government believes markets will soon become convinced that no devaluation is

◀ In most countries, the government is formally in charge of choosing the parity, and the central bank is formally in charge of maintaining it. In practice, choosing and maintaining the parity are joint responsibilities of the government and the central bank.

◀ In the summer of 1998, Boris Yeltsin announced that the Russian government had no intention of devaluing the ruble. Two weeks later, the ruble collapsed.

An example of the problems we discussed in Section 21-2 is the exchange rate crisis that shook the European Monetary System (EMS) in the early 1990s.

At the start of the 1990s, the EMS appeared to work well. The EMS, which had started in 1979, was an exchange rate system based on fixed parities with bands: Each member country (among them, France, Germany, Italy, and, beginning in 1990, the United Kingdom) had to maintain its exchange rate vis-à-vis all other member countries within narrow bands. The first few years had been rocky, with many realignments—adjustment of parities—among member countries. From 1987 to 1992, however, there were only two realignments, and there was increasing talk about narrowing the bands further and even moving to the next stage—to the adoption of a common currency.

In 1992, however, financial markets became increasingly convinced that more realignments were soon to come. The reason was one we have already seen in Chapter 20—namely, the macroeconomic implications of Germany's reunification. Because of the pressure on demand coming from reunification, the Bundesbank (the German central bank) was maintaining high interest rates to avoid too large an increase in output and an increase in inflation in Germany. While Germany's EMS partners needed lower interest rates to reduce the growing unemployment problem, they had to match the German interest rates to maintain their EMS parities. To financial markets, the position of Germany's EMS partners looked increasingly untenable. Lower interest rates outside Germany, and thus devaluations of many currencies vis-à-vis the Deutsche mark, appeared increasingly likely.

Throughout 1992, the perceived probability of a devaluation forced a number of EMS countries to maintain higher nominal interest rates than even those in Germany. Still, the first major crisis did not come until September 1992.

In early September 1992, the belief that a number of countries were soon going to devalue led to speculative attacks on a number of currencies, with financial investors selling in anticipation of an oncoming devaluation. All the lines of defense described earlier were used by the monetary authorities and the governments of the countries under attack. First, solemn communiqués were issued, but with no discernible effect. Then, interest rates were increased. For example, Sweden's overnight interest rate (the rate for lending and borrowing overnight) increased to 500% (expressed at an annual rate)! But interest rates were not increased by enough to prevent capital outflows and large losses of foreign exchange reserves by the central banks under pressure.

At that point, different countries took different courses of action: Spain devalued its exchange rate. Italy and the United Kingdom suspended their participation in the EMS. France decided to tough it out through higher interest rates until the storm was over. Figure 1 shows the evolution of the exchange rates vis-à-vis the Deutsche mark for a number of European countries from January 1992 to December 1993: You can clearly see the effects of the September 1992 crisis and the ensuing depreciations/devaluations.

By the end of September, investors, by and large, believed that no further devaluations were imminent. Some countries were no longer in the EMS. Others had devalued but remained in the EMS, and those that had maintained their parity had shown their determination to stay in the EMS, even if it meant very high interest rates. But the underlying problem—the high German interest rates—was still present, and it was only a matter of time before the next crisis started. In November 1992, further speculation forced a devaluation of the Spanish peseta, the Portuguese escudo, and the Swedish krona. The peseta and the escudo were further devalued in May 1993. In July 1993, after yet another large speculative attack, EMS countries decided to adopt

coming, allowing domestic interest rates to decrease. Otherwise, the only option is to devalue. (All these steps were very much in evidence during the exchange rate crisis that affected much of western Europe in 1992. See the Focus box "The 1992 EMS Crisis.")

To summarize, expectations that a devaluation may be coming can trigger an exchange rate crisis. Faced with such expectations, the government has two options:

- Give in and devalue.
- Fight and maintain the parity, at the cost of very high interest rates and a potential recession. Fighting may not work anyway: The recession may force the government to change policy later on or force the government out of office.

An interesting twist here is that a devaluation can occur even if the belief that a devaluation was coming was initially groundless. In other words, even if the

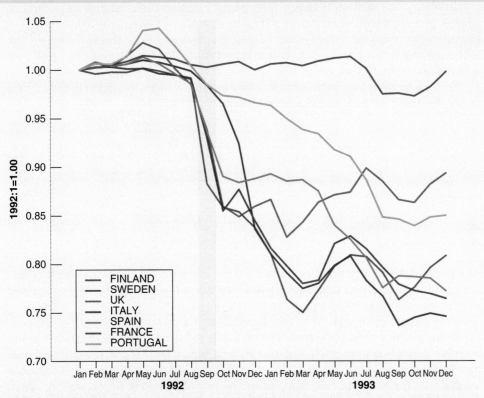

Figure 1 *Exchange Rates of Selected European Countries Relative to the Deutsche Mark, January 1992 to December 1993*

large fluctuation bands (±15%) around central parities, in effect moving to a system that allowed for very large exchange rate fluctuations. This system with wider bands was kept until the adoption of a common currency, the euro, in January 1999.

To summarize: The 1992 EMS crisis resulted from the perception by financial markets that the high interest rates forced by Germany upon its partners under the rules of the EMS were becoming very costly. The belief that some countries might want to devalue or get out of the EMS led investors to ask for even higher interest rates, making it even more costly for those countries to maintain their parity. In the end, some countries could not bear the cost; some devalued, and some dropped out. Others remained in the system—but at a substantial cost in terms of output. (For example, average growth in France from 1990 to 1996 was 1.2%, compared to 2.3% for Germany over the same period.)

government initially has no intention of devaluing, it might be forced to do so if financial markets believe that it will devalue: The cost of maintaining the parity would be a long period of high interest rates and a recession; the government might prefer to devalue instead.

21-3 Exchange Rate Movements under Flexible Exchange Rates

In the model we developed in Chapter 20, there was a simple relation between the interest rate and the exchange rate: The lower the interest rate, the lower the exchange rate. This implied that a country that wanted to maintain a stable exchange rate just had to maintain its interest rate close to the foreign interest rate. A country that wanted to achieve a given depreciation just had to decrease its interest rate by the right amount.

In reality, the relation between the interest rate and the exchange rate is not so simple. Exchange rates often move even in the absence of movements in interest rates. Furthermore, the size of the effect of a given change in the interest rate on the exchange rate is hard to predict. This makes it much harder for monetary policy to achieve its desired outcome.

To see why things are more complicated, we must return once again to the interest parity condition we derived in Chapter 18 [equation (18.2)]:

$$(1 + i_t) = (1 + i_t^*)\left(\frac{E_t}{E_{t+1}^e}\right)$$

As we did in Chapter 20 [equation (20.4)], we multiply both sides by E_{t+1}^e, and reorganize to get

$$E_t = \frac{1 + i_t}{1 + i_t^*} E_{t+1}^e \qquad (21.4)$$

Think of the time period (from t to $t + 1$) as one year. The exchange rate this year depends on the one-year domestic interest rate, the one-year foreign interest rate, and the exchange rate expected for next year.

We assumed in Chapter 20 that the expected exchange rate next year, E_{t+1}^e, was constant. But that was a simplification. The exchange rate expected one year hence is not constant. Using equation (21.4), but now for next year, it is clear that the exchange rate next year will depend on next year's one-year domestic interest rate, the one-year foreign interest rate, the exchange rate expected for the year after, and so on. So, any change in expectations of *current and future* domestic and foreign interest rates, as well as changes in the expected exchange rate in the far future, will affect the exchange rate today.

Let's explore this more closely. Write equation (21.4) for year $t + 1$ rather than for year t:

$$E_{t+1} = \frac{1 + i_{t+1}}{1 + i_{t+1}^*} E_{t+2}^e$$

The exchange rate in year $t + 1$ depends on the domestic interest rate and the foreign interest rate for year $t + 1$, as well as on the expected future exchange rate in year $t + 2$. So, the expectation of the exchange rate in year $t + 1$, held as of year t, is given by

$$E_{t+1}^e = \frac{1 + i_{t+1}^e}{1 + i_{t+1}^{*e}} E_{t\mid 2}^e$$

Replacing E_{t+1}^e in equation (21.4) with this expression gives

$$E_t = \frac{(1 + i_t)(1 + i_{t+1}^e)}{(1 + i_t^*)(1 + i_{t+1}^{*e})} E_{t+2}^e$$

The current exchange rate depends on this year's domestic and foreign interest rates, on next year's expected domestic and foreign interest rates, and on the expected exchange rate two years from now. Continuing to solve forward in time in the same way (by replacing E_{t+2}^e, E_{t+3}^e, and so on until, say, year $t + n$) we get

$$E_t = \frac{(1 + i_t)(1 + i_{t+1}^e)\ldots(1 + i_{t+n}^e)}{(1 + i_t^*)(1 + i_{t+1}^{*e})\ldots(1 + i_{t+n}^{*e})} E_{t+n+1}^e \qquad (21.5)$$

Suppose we take n to be large, say 10 years [equation (21.5) holds for any value of n]. This relation tells us that the current exchange rate depends on two sets of factors:

■ Current and expected domestic and foreign interest rates for each year over the next 10 years.
■ The expected exchange rate 10 years from now.

For some purposes, it is useful to go further and derive a relation between current and expected future domestic and foreign *real* interest rates, the current *real* exchange rate, and the expected future *real* exchange rate. This is done in an appendix to this chapter. (The derivation is not much fun, but it is a useful way of brushing up on the relations between real and nominal interest rates and between real and nominal exchange rates.) Equation (21.5) is sufficient, however, to make the three points I want to make here.

Exchange Rates and the Current Account

Any factor that moves the expected future exchange rate, E_{t+n}^e, moves the current exchange rate, E_t. Indeed, if the domestic interest rate and the foreign interest rate are expected to be the same in both countries from t to $t + n$, the fraction on the right in equation (21.5) is equal to 1, so the relation reduces to $E_t = E_{t+n}^e$. In words: The effect of any change in the expected future exchange rate on the current exchange rate is one-for-one.

If we think of n as large (say 10 years or more), we can think of E_{t+n}^e as the exchange rate required to achieve current account balance in the medium or long run: Countries cannot borrow—run a current account deficit—forever and will not want to lend—run a current account surplus—forever either. Thus, any news that affects forecasts of the current account balance in the future is likely to have an effect on the expected future exchange rate and, in turn, on the exchange rate today. For example, the announcement of a larger-than-expected trade deficit may lead investors to conclude that a depreciation will eventually be needed to reestablish trade balance. Thus, E_{t+n}^e will decrease, leading in turn to a decrease in E_t today.

◄ News about the current account is likely to affect the exchange rate.

Exchange Rates and Current and Future Interest Rates

Any factor that moves current or expected future domestic or foreign interest rates between year t and year $t + n$ moves the current exchange rate, too. For example, given foreign interest rates, an increase in current or expected future domestic interest rates leads to an increase in E_t—an appreciation.

◄ News about current and future domestic and foreign interest rates is likely to affect the exchange rate.

This implies that any variable which causes investors to change their expectations of future interest rates will lead to a change in the exchange rate today. For example, the "dance of the dollar" in the 1980s we discussed in earlier chapters—the sharp appreciation of the dollar in the first half of the decade, followed by an equally sharp depreciation later—can be largely explained by the movement in current and expected future U.S. interest rates relative to interest rates in the rest of the world during that period. During the first half of the 1980s, tight monetary policy and expansionary fiscal policy combined to increase U.S. short-term and long-term interest rates, with the long-term interest rates, with the increase in long-term rates reflecting anticipations of high short-term interest rates in the future. This increase in both current and expected future interest rates was in turn the main cause of the dollar appreciation. Both fiscal and monetary policy were reversed in the second half of the decade, leading to lower U.S. interest rates and a depreciation of the dollar.

◄ See Chapters 18 and 20.

For more on the relation between long-term interest rates and current and expected future short-term interest rates, go back to Chapter 15.

Exchange Rate Volatility

The third implication follows from the first two. In reality, and in contrast to our analysis in Chapter 20, the relation between the interest rate, i_t, and the exchange rate, E_t, is all but mechanical. When the central bank cuts the interest rate, financial markets have to assess whether this action signals a major shift in monetary policy and the cut in the interest rate is just the first of many such cuts, or whether this cut is just a temporary movement in interest rates. Announcements by the central bank may not be very useful: The central bank itself may not even know what it will do in the future. Typically, it will be reacting to early signals, which may be reversed later. Investors also have to assess how foreign central banks will react—whether they will stay put, or follow suit and cut their own interest rates. All this makes it difficult to predict what the effect of the change in the interest rate will be on the exchange rate.

This may remind you of our discussion in Chapter 15 of how monetary policy affects stock prices. This is more than a coincidence: Like stock prices, the exchange rate depends very much on expectations of variables far into the future. How expectations change in response to a change in a current variable (here, the interest rate) very much determines the outcome.

Let's be more concrete. Go back to equation (21.5). Assume that $E^e_{t+n} = 1$. Assume that current and expected future domestic interest rates and current and expected future foreign interest rates are all equal to 5%. The current exchange rate is then given by

$$E_t = \frac{(1.05)^n}{(1.05)^n} 1 = 1$$

Now consider a monetary expansion that decreases the current domestic interest rate, i_t, from 5% to 3%. Will this lead to a decrease in E_t—to a depreciation—and if so by how much? The answer: It depends.

Suppose the interest rate is expected to be lower for just one year, so the $n - 1$ expected future interest rates remain unchanged. The current exchange rate then decreases to

$$E_t = \frac{(1.03)(1.05)^{n-1}}{(1.05)^n} = \frac{1.03}{1.05} = 0.98$$

The expansionary monetary policy leads to a decrease in the exchange rate—a depreciation—of only 2%.

Suppose instead that, when the current interest rate declines from 5% to 3%, investors expect the decline to last for five years (so $i_{t+4} = \ldots = i_{t+1} = i_t = 3\%$). The exchange rate then decreases to

$$E_t = \frac{(1.03)^5(1.05)^{n-5}}{(1.05)^n} = \frac{(1.03)^5}{(1.05)^5} = 0.90$$

The expansionary monetary policy now leads to a decrease in the exchange rate—a depreciation—of 10%, a much larger effect.

You can surely think of yet other outcomes. Suppose investors anticipated that the central bank was going to decrease interest rates, and the actual decrease turns out to be smaller than they anticipated. In this case, the investors will revise their expectations of future nominal interest rates *upward*, leading to an appreciation rather than a depreciation of the currency.

When, at the end of the Bretton Woods period, countries moved from fixed exchange rates to flexible exchange rates, most economists had expected that exchange rates would be stable. The large fluctuations in exchange rates that followed—and have continued to this day—came as a surprise. For some time, these fluctuations were thought to be the result of irrational speculation in foreign exchange markets. It was not until the mid-1970s that economists realized that these large movements could be explained, as we have explained them here, by the rational reaction of financial markets to news about future interest rates and the future exchange rate. This has an important implication: A country that decides to operate under flexible exchange rates must accept the fact that it will be exposed to substantial exchange rate fluctuations over time.

21-4 Choosing between Exchange Rate Regimes

Let us now return to the question that motivates this chapter: Should countries choose flexible exchange rates or fixed exchange rates? Are there circumstances under which flexible rates dominate and others under which fixed rates dominate?

Much of what we have seen in this chapter and Chapter 20 would seem to favor flexible exchange rates:

- Section 21-1 argues that the exchange rate regime may not matter in the medium run. But it does still matter in the short run. In the short run, countries that operate under fixed exchange rates and perfect capital mobility give up two macroeconomic instruments: the interest rate and the exchange rate. This not only reduces their ability to respond to shocks, but can also lead to exchange rate crises.
- Section 21-2 argues that, in a country with fixed exchange rates, the anticipation of a devaluation leads investors to ask for very high interest rates. This in turn makes the economic situation worse and puts more pressure on the country to devalue. This is another argument against fixed exchange rates.
- Section 21-3 introduces one argument against flexible exchange rates—namely that, under flexible exchange rates, the exchange rate is likely to fluctuate a lot and be difficult to control through monetary policy.

On balance, it would therefore appear that, from a macroeconomic viewpoint, flexible exchange rates dominate fixed exchange rates. This indeed appears to be the consensus that has emerged among economists and policymakers. The consensus goes like this: In general, flexible exchange rates are preferable. There are, however, two exceptions: First, when a group of countries is already tightly integrated, a common currency may be the right solution. Second, when the central bank cannot be trusted to follow a responsible monetary policy under flexible exchange rates, a strong form of fixed exchange rates, such as a currency board or dollarization, may provide a solution.

Let me discuss in turn each of these two exceptions.

Common Currency Areas

Countries that operate under a fixed exchange rate regime are constrained to all have the same interest rate. But how costly is that constraint? If the countries face roughly the same macroeconomic problems and the same shocks, they will have chosen similar policies in the first place. Forcing them to have the same monetary policy may not be much of a constraint.

This argument was first explored by Robert Mundell, who looked at the conditions under which a set of countries might want to operate under fixed exchange rates or even adopt a common currency. For countries to constitute an **optimal currency area**, ◄ Mundell argued, they need to satisfy one of two conditions:

This is the same Mundell who put together the Mundell–Fleming model we saw in Chapter 20.

- The countries have to experience similar shocks. We just saw the rationale for this: If they experience similar shocks, then they would have chosen roughly the same monetary policy anyway.
- If the countries experience different shocks, they must have high factor mobility. For example, if workers are willing to move from countries that are doing poorly to countries that are doing well, factor mobility rather than macroeconomic policy

As the European Union celebrated its 30th birthday in 1988, a number of governments decided that the time had come to plan a move to a common currency. They asked Jacques Delors, the president of the European Union, to prepare a report, which he presented in June 1989.

The Delors report suggested moving to a European Monetary Union (EMU) in three stages: Stage I was the abolition of capital controls. Stage II was the choice of fixed parities, to be maintained except for "exceptional circumstances." Stage III was the adoption of a single currency.

Stage I was implemented in July 1990.

Stage II began in 1994, after the exchange rate crises of 1992 to 1993 had subsided. A minor but symbolic decision involved choosing the name of the new common currency. The French liked "Ecu" (European currency unit), which is also the name of an old French currency. But its partners preferred *euro*, and the name was adopted in 1995.

In parallel, EU countries held referendums on whether they should adopt the **Maastricht treaty**. The treaty, negotiated in 1991, set three main conditions for joining the EMU: low inflation, a budget deficit below 3%, and a public debt below 60%. The Maastricht treaty was not very popular and, in many countries, the outcome of the popular vote was close. In France, the treaty passed with only 51% of the votes. In Denmark, the treaty was rejected.

In 1996 and 1997, it looked as if few European countries would satisfy the Maastricht conditions. But a number of countries took drastic measures to reduce their budget deficits. When the time came to decide, in May 1998, which countries would be members of the euro area, 11 countries made the cut: Austria, Belgium, Finland, France, Germany, Italy, Ireland, Luxembourg, the Netherlands, Portugal, and Spain. The United Kingdom, Denmark, and Sweden decided to stay out, at least at the beginning. Greece did not qualify initially and didn't join until 2001. (In 2004, it was revealed that Greece had partly "cooked the books" and understated the size of its budget deficit in order to qualify.)

Stage III began in January 1999. Parities between the 11 currencies and the euro were "irrevocably" fixed. The new **European Central Bank (ECB)** based in Frankfurt became responsible for monetary policy for the euro area.

From 1999 to 2002, the euro existed as a unit of account, but euro coins and bank notes did not exist. In effect, the euro area was still functioning as an area with fixed exchange rates. The next and final step was the introduction of euro coins and bank notes in January 2002. For the first few months of 2002, national currencies and the euro then circulated side by side. Later in the year, national currencies were taken out of circulation.

Today, the euro is the only currency used in the "euro area," as the group of member countries is called.

Note: For more on the euro, go to **www.euro.ecb.int**. *The Wikipedia page on the euro is also very good.*

---

can allow countries to adjust to shocks. When the unemployment rate is high in a country, workers leave that country to take jobs elsewhere, and the unemployment rate in that country decreases back to normal. If the unemployment rate is low, workers come to the country, and the unemployment rate in the country increases back to normal. The exchange rate is not needed.

▶ Each U.S. state could have its own currency that freely floated against other state currencies. But this is not the way things are: The United States is a common currency area, with one currency, the U.S. dollar.

Following Mundell's analysis, most economists believe, for example, that the common currency area composed of the 50 states of the United States is close to an optimal currency area. True, the first condition is not satisfied: Individual states suffer from different shocks. California is more affected by shifts in demand from Asia than the rest of the United States. Texas is more affected by what happens to the price of oil, and so on. But the second condition is largely satisfied. There is considerable labor mobility across states in the United States. When a state does poorly, workers leave that state. When it does well, workers come to that state. State unemployment rates quickly return to normal not because of state-level macroeconomic policy but because of labor mobility.

Clearly, there are also many advantages of using a common currency. For firms and consumers within the United States, the benefits of having a common currency are obvious; imagine how complicated life would be if you had to change currency every time you crossed a state line. The benefits go beyond these lower transaction costs. When prices are quoted in the same currency, it becomes much easier for buyers to compare prices, and competition between firms increases, benefiting consumers.

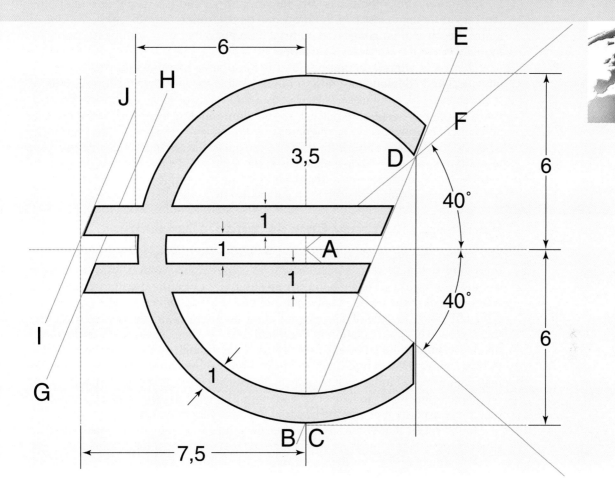

Given these benefits and the limited macroeconomic costs, it makes good sense for the United States to have a single currency.

In adopting the euro, Europe has made the same choice as the United States. When the process of conversion from national currencies to the euro ended in early 2002, the euro became the common currency for 11 European countries. (Look at the Focus box "The Euro: A Short History.") The number of euro countries has now increased to 15. Is the economic argument for this new common currency area as compelling as it is for the United States?

There is little question that a common currency will yield for Europe many of the same benefits that it has for the United States. A report by the European Commission estimates that the elimination of foreign exchange transactions within the euro area will lead to a reduction in costs of 0.5% of the combined GDP of these countries. There are also clear signs that the use of a common currency is already increasing competition. When shopping for cars, for example, European consumers now search for the lowest euro price anywhere in the euro area. This has already led to a decline in the price of cars in a number of countries.

There is, however, less agreement on whether Europe constitutes an optimal common currency area. This is because neither of the two Mundell conditions appears to be satisfied. Although the future may be different, European countries have experienced very different shocks in the past. Recall our discussion of Germany's reunification and how differently it affected Germany and the other European countries.

Furthermore, labor mobility is very low in Europe, and it is likely to remain low. Workers move much less *within* European countries than they do within the United States. Because of language and cultural differences between European countries, mobility *between* countries is even lower.

The risk is, therefore, that one or more euro area members may suffer from a large decline in demand and output but be unable to use either the interest rate or the exchange rate to increase its level of economic activity. As we saw in Section 21-1, the adjustment can still take place in the medium run. But, as we also saw there, this adjustment is likely to be long and painful. At the time of this writing, this is no longer a hypothetical worry: Some euro countries, in particular Portugal, are suffering from low output and a large trade deficit. Without the option of a devaluation, achieving a real depreciation may require many years of high unemployment and downward pressure on wages and prices in Portugal relative to the rest of the euro area.

Hard Pegs, Currency Boards, and Dollarization

The second case for fixed exchange rates is very different from the first. It is based on the argument that there may be times when a country might want to limit its ability to use monetary policy. We shall look at this argument in more detail in Chapter 23, where we look at the dynamics of hyperinflation, and in Chapter 25, where we look at monetary policy in general. The essence of the argument is simple: Look at a country that has had very high inflation in the recent past—perhaps because it was unable to finance its budget deficit by any means other than through money creation, resulting in high money growth and high inflation. Suppose the country decides to reduce money growth and inflation. One way of convincing financial markets that it is serious about doing this is to fix its exchange rate: The need to use the money supply to maintain the parity then ties the hands of the monetary authority.

To the extent that financial markets expect the parity to be maintained, they will stop worrying about money growth being used to finance the budget deficit.

Note the qualifier "to the extent that financial markets expect the parity to be maintained." Fixing the exchange rate is not a magic solution. The country also needs to convince financial investors that not only is the exchange rate fixed today, but it will remain fixed in the future. There are two ways it can do so:

- It can make the fixed exchange rate be part of a more general macroeconomic package. Fixing the exchange rate while continuing to run a large budget deficit will only convince financial markets that money growth will start again and that a devaluation is soon to come.
- It can make it symbolically or technically harder to change the parity, an approach known as a **hard peg**.

  An extreme form of a hard peg is simply to replace the domestic currency with a foreign currency. Because the foreign currency chosen is typically the dollar, this is known as **dollarization**. Few countries are willing, however, to give up their currency and adopt the currency of another country. A less extreme way is the use of a **currency board**. Under a currency board, a central bank stands ready to exchange foreign currency for domestic currency at the official exchange rate set by the government; furthermore, the bank cannot engage in open market operations—that is, buy or sell government bonds.

  Perhaps the best-known example of a currency board is that adopted by Argentina in 1991, but abandoned in a crisis at the end of 2001. The story is told in the Focus box "Argentina's Currency Board." Economists differ on what conclusions one should draw from what happened in Argentina. Some conclude that currency boards are not *hard* enough: They do not prevent exchange rate crises. So, if a

When Israel was suffering from high inflation in the 1980s, an Israeli finance minister proposed such a measure as part of a stabilization program. His proposal was perceived as an attack on the sovereignty of Israel, and he was quickly fired.

When Carlos Menem became president of Argentina in 1989, he inherited an economic mess. Inflation was running at more than 30% per month. Output growth was negative.

Menem and his economy minister, Domingo Cavallo, quickly came to the conclusion that, under these circumstances, the only way to bring money growth—and, by implication, inflation—under control was to peg the peso (Argentina's currency) to the dollar and to do this through a very hard peg. So, in 1991, Cavallo announced that Argentina would adopt a currency board. The central bank would stand ready to exchange pesos for dollars, on demand. Furthermore, it would do so at the highly symbolic rate of 1 dollar for 1 peso.

The creation of a currency board and the choice of a symbolic exchange rate had the same objective: to convince investors that the government was serious about the peg and to make it more difficult for future governments to give up the parity and devalue. By making the fixed exchange rate more credible in this way, the government hoped to decrease the risk of a foreign exchange crisis.

For a while, the currency board appeared to work extremely well. Inflation, which had exceeded 2,300% in 1990, was down to 4% by 1994! This was clearly the result of the tight constraints the currency board put on money growth. Even more impressive, this large drop in inflation was accompanied by strong output growth. Output growth averaged 5% per year from 1991 to 1999.

Beginning in 1999, however, growth turned negative, and Argentina went into a long and deep recession. Was the recession due to the currency board? Yes and no:

- Throughout the second half of the 1990s, the dollar steadily appreciated relative to other major world currencies. Because the peso was pegged to the dollar, the peso also appreciated. By the late 1990s, it was clear that the peso was overvalued, leading to a decrease in demand for goods from Argentina, a decline in output, and an increase in the trade deficit.

- Was the currency board fully responsible for the recession? No. There were other causes. But the currency board made it much harder to fight the recession. Lower interest rates and a depreciation of the peso would have helped the economy recover, but under the currency board, this was not an option.

In 2001, the economic crisis turned into a financial and an exchange rate crisis, along the lines described in Section 21-2:

- Because of the recession, Argentina's fiscal deficit had increased, leading to an increase in government debt. Worried that the government might default on its debt, financial investors started asking for very high interest rates on government bonds, making the fiscal deficit even larger, and, by doing so, further increasing the risk of default.

- Worried that Argentina would abandon the currency board and devalue in order to fight the recession, investors started asking for very high interest rates in pesos, making it more costly for the government to sustain the parity with the dollar and so making it more likely that the currency board would indeed be abandoned.

In December 2001, the government defaulted on part of its debt. In early 2002, it gave up the currency board and let the peso float. The peso sharply depreciated, reaching 3.75 pesos for 1 dollar by June 2002. Many people and firms, given their earlier confidence in the peg, had borrowed in dollars; they found themselves with a large increase in the value of their dollar debts in terms of pesos. Many firms went bankrupt. The banking system collapsed. Despite the sharp real depreciation, which should have helped exports, GDP in Argentina fell by 11% in 2002, and unemployment increased to nearly 20%. In 2003, output growth turned positive, and it has been consistently high since—exceeding 8% per year—and unemployment has decreased. But it took until 2005 for GDP to reach its 1998 level again.

Does this mean that the currency board was a bad idea? Economists still disagree:

- Some economists argue that it was a good idea but that it did not go far enough. They argue that Argentina should have simply dollarized—that is, adopted the dollar outright as its currency—and eliminated the peso altogether. Eliminating the domestic currency would have eliminated the risk of a devaluation. The lesson, they argue, is that even a currency board does not provide a sufficiently hard peg for the exchange rate. Only dollarization will do.

- Other (indeed, most) economists argue that the currency board might have been a good idea at the start, but that it should not have been kept in place for so long. Once inflation was under control, Argentina should have moved from a currency board to a floating exchange rate regime. The problem is that Argentina kept the fixed parity with the dollar for too long, to the point where the peso was overvalued, and an exchange rate crisis was inevitable.

The debate is likely to go on. Meanwhile, Argentina is reconstructing its economy.

Note: For a fascinating, fun, and strongly opinionated book about Argentina's crisis, read Paul Blustein, And the Money Kept Rolling In (and Out). Wall Street, the IMF, and the Bankrupting of Argentina, *New York, Public Affairs, 2005.*

FOCUS

country decides to adopt a fixed exchange rate, it should go all the way and dollarize. Others conclude that adopting a fixed exchange rate is a bad idea. If currency boards are used at all, they should be used only for a short period of time, until the central bank has reestablished its credibility and the country returns to a floating exchange rate regime.

Summary

- Even under a fixed exchange rate regime, countries can adjust their *real* exchange rate in the medium run. They can do this by relying on adjustments in the price level. Nevertheless, the adjustment can be long and painful. Exchange rate adjustments can allow the economy to adjust faster and thus reduce the pain that comes from a long adjustment.

- Exchange rate crises typically start when participants in financial markets believe a currency may soon be devalued. Defending the parity then requires very high interest rates, with potentially large adverse macroeconomic effects. These adverse effects may force the country to devalue, even if there were no initial plans for such a devaluation.

- The exchange rate today depends on both (1) the difference between current and expected future domestic interest rates and current and expected future foreign interest rates and (2) the expected future exchange rate.

  Any factor that increases current or expected future domestic interest rates leads to an increase in the exchange rate today.

  Any factor that increases current or expected future foreign interest rates leads to a decrease in the exchange rate today.

  Any factor that increases the expected future exchange rate leads to an increase in the exchange rate today.

- There is wide agreement among economists that flexible exchange rate regimes generally dominate fixed exchange rate regimes, except in two cases:

  1. When a group of countries is highly integrated and forms an optimal currency area (you can think of a common currency for a group of countries as an extreme form of fixed exchange rates among this group of countries). For countries to form an optimal currency area, they must either face largely similar shocks, or there must be high labor mobility across these countries.

  2. When a central bank cannot be trusted to follow a responsible monetary policy under flexible exchange rates. In this case, a strong form of fixed exchange rates, such as dollarization or a currency board, provides a way of tying the hands of the central bank.

Key Terms

- gold standard, 470
- optimal currency area, 477
- Maastricht treaty, 478
- European Central Bank (ECB), 478
- hard peg, 480
- dollarization, 480
- currency board, 480

Questions and Problems

Quick Check

1. Using the information in this chapter, label each of the following statements true, false, or uncertain. Explain briefly.

a. Britain's return to the gold standard caused years of high unemployment.

b. A sudden fear that a country is going to devalue may force an exchange rate crisis, even if the fear initially had no basis.

c. Because economies tend to return to their natural level of output in the medium run, there is a never a reason to devalue.

d. High labor mobility within Europe makes the euro area a good candidate for a common currency.

e. Changes in the expected level of the exchange rate far in the future have little effect on the current level of the exchange rate.

2. Consider a country operating under fixed exchange rates, with aggregate demand and aggregate supply given by equations (21.1) and (21.2).

$$AD: \quad Y = Y\left(\frac{\bar{E}P}{P^*}, G, T\right)$$

$$AS: \quad P = P^e (1 + \mu) F\left(1 - \frac{Y}{L}, z\right)$$

Assume that the economy is initially in medium-run equilibrium, with a constant price level and output equal to the natural level of output. Foreign output, the foreign price level, and the foreign interest rate are fixed throughout the problem. Assume that expected (domestic) inflation remains constant throughout the problem.

a. Draw an AD–AS diagram for this economy.
b. Now suppose there is an increase in government spending. Show the effects on the AD–AS diagram in the short run and the medium run. How do output and the price level change in the medium run?
c. What happens to consumption in the medium run?
d. What happens to the real exchange rate in the medium run? [*Hint:* Consider the effect on the price level you identified in part (b).] What happens to net exports in the medium run?
e. Given that the exchange rate is fixed, what is the domestic nominal interest rate? Does the increase in government spending affect the domestic nominal interest rate? What happens to the real interest rate in the medium run? (*Hint:* Remember that expected inflation remains constant by assumption.) What happens to investment in the medium run?
f. In a closed economy, how does an increase in government spending affect investment in the medium run? (Refer to Chapter 7 if you need a refresher.)
g. Comment on the following statement. "In a closed economy, government spending crowds out investment. In an open economy with fixed exchange rates, government spending crowds out net exports."

3. Nominal and real interest parity
   In equation (18.4), we wrote the nominal interest parity condition as

$$i_t \approx i_t^* - \frac{E_{t+1}^e - E_t}{E_t}$$

In the appendix to this chapter, we derive a real interest parity condition. We can write the real interest parity condition in a manner analogous to equation (18.4):

$$r_t \approx r_t^* - \frac{(\epsilon_{t+1}^e - \epsilon_t)}{\epsilon_t}$$

a. Interpret this equation. Under what circumstances will the domestic real interest rate exceed the foreign real interest rate?
   Assume that the one-year nominal interest rate is 9% in the domestic economy and 4% in the foreign economy. Also assume that inflation over the coming year is expected to be 4% in the domestic economy and 2% in the foreign economy. Suppose that interest parity holds.
b. What is the expected nominal depreciation of the domestic currency over the coming year?
c. What is the expected real depreciation over the coming year?
d. If you expected a nominal appreciation of the currency over the coming year, should you hold domestic or foreign bonds?

4. Devaluation and interest rates
   Consider an open economy with a fixed exchange rate, $\bar{E}$. Throughout the problem, assume that the foreign interest rate, i*, remains constant.

a. Suppose that financial market participants believe that the government is committed to a fixed exchange rate. What is the expected exchange rate? According to the interest parity condition, what is the domestic interest rate?
b. Suppose that financial market participants do not believe that the government is committed to a fixed exchange rate. Instead, they suspect that the government will either devalue or abandon the fixed exchange rate altogether and adopt a flexible exchange rate. If the government adopts a flexible exchange rate, financial market participants expect the exchange rate to depreciate from its current fixed value, $\bar{E}$. Under these circumstances, how does the expected exchange rate compare to $\bar{E}$? How does the domestic interest rate compare to i*?
c. Suppose that financial market participants feared a devaluation, as in part (b), and a devaluation actually occurs. The government announces that it will maintain a fixed exchange rate regime but changes the level of the fixed exchange rate to $\bar{E}'$, where $\bar{E}' < \bar{E}$. Suppose that financial market participants believe that the government will remain committed to the new exchange rate, $\bar{E}'$, and that there will be no further devaluations. What happens to the domestic interest rate after the devaluation?
d. Does a devaluation necessarily lead to higher domestic interest rates? Does fear of a devaluation necessarily lead to higher domestic interest rates?

Dig Deeper

5. Self-fulfilling exchange rate crises
   Consider an open economy with a fixed exchange rate, $\bar{E}$. Suppose that initially, financial market participants believe that the government is committed to the fixed exchange rate. Suddenly, however, financial market participants become fearful that the government will devalue or allow the exchange rate to float (a decision that everyone believes will cause the currency to depreciate).

a. What happens to the expected exchange rate, E_{t+1}^e? (See your answer to problem 4(b)).
   Suppose that, despite the change in the expected exchange rate, the government keeps the exchange rate fixed today. Let UIP stand for the uncovered interest parity condition.
b. Draw an IS–LM–UIP diagram. How does the change in the expected exchange rate affect the UIP curve? As a result, how must the domestic interest rate change to maintain an exchange rate of $\bar{E}$?
c. Given your answer to part (b), what happens to the domestic money supply if the central bank defends the fixed exchange rate? How does the LM curve shift?
d. What happens to domestic output and the domestic interest rate? Is it possible that a government that was

previously committed to a fixed exchange rate might abandon it when faced with a fear of depreciation (either through devaluation or abandonment of the fixed exchange rate regime)? Is it possible that unfounded fears about a depreciation can create a crisis? Explain your answers.

6. *Exchange rate overshooting*

a. Suppose there is a permanent 10% increase in M in a closed economy. What is the effect on the price level in the medium run? *Hint:* If you need a refresher, review the analysis in Chapter 7.

In a closed economy, we said that money was neutral because in the medium run, a change in the money stock affected only the price level. A change in the money stock did not affect any real variables. A change in the money stock is also neutral in an open economy with flexible exchange rates. In the medium run, a change in the money stock will not affect the real exchange rate, although it will affect the price level and the nominal exchange rate.

b. Consider an open economy with a flexible exchange rate. Write the expression for the real exchange rate. Suppose there is a 10% increase in the money stock and assume that it has the same effect on the price level in the medium run that you found in part (a). If the real exchange rate and the foreign price level are unchanged in the medium run, what must happen to the nominal exchange rate in the medium run?

c. Suppose it takes n years to reach the medium run (and everyone knows this). Given your answer to part (b), what happens to E^e_{t+n} (the expected exchange rate for n periods from now) after a 10% increase in the money stock?

d. Consider equation (21.5). Assume that the foreign interest rate is unchanged for the next n periods. Also assume, for the moment, that the domestic interest rate is unchanged for the next n periods. Given your answer to part (c), what happens to the exchange rate today (at time t) when there is a 10% increase in the money stock?

e. Now assume that after the increase in the money stock, the domestic interest rate falls between time t and time $t + n$. Again assume that the foreign interest rate is unchanged. As compared to your answer to part (d), what happens to the exchange rate today (at time t)? Does the exchange rate move more in the short run than in the medium run?

The answer to part (e) is yes. In this case, the short-run depreciation is greater than the medium-run depreciation. This phenomenon is called overshooting, and may help to explain why the exchange rate is so variable.

7. *Devaluation and credibility*

Consider an open economy with a fixed exchange rate, $\overline{E}$. Suppose that, initially, financial market participants believe that the government is committed to maintaining the fixed exchange rate. Let UIP stand for the uncovered interest parity condition.

Now suppose the central bank announces a devaluation. The exchange rate will remain fixed, but at a new level, $\overline{E}'$, such that $\overline{E}' < \overline{E}$. Suppose that financial market participants believe that there will be no further devaluations and that the government will remain committed to maintaining the exchange rate at $\overline{E}'$.

a. What is the domestic interest rate before the devaluation? If the devaluation is credible, what is the domestic interest rate after the devaluation? (See your answers to problem 4.)

b. Draw an *IS–LM–UIP* diagram for this economy. If the devaluation is credible, how does the expected exchange rate change? How does the change in the expected exchange rate affect the *UIP* curve?

c. How does the devaluation affect the *IS* curve? Given your answer to part (b) and the shift of the *IS* curve, what would happen to the domestic interest rate if there is no change in the domestic money supply?

d. Given your answer to part (c), what must happen to the domestic money supply so that the domestic interest rate achieves the value you identified in part (a)? How does the *LM* curve shift?

e. How is domestic output affected by the devaluation?

f. Suppose that devaluation is not credible in the sense that the devaluation leads financial market participants to expect another devaluation in the future. How does the fear of further devaluation affect the expected exchange rate? How will the expected exchange rate in this case, where devaluation is not credible, compare to your answer to part (b)? Explain in words. Given this effect on the expected exchange rate, what must happen to the domestic interest rate, as compared to your answer to part (a), to maintain the new fixed exchange rate?

Explore Further

8. *Exchange rates and expectations*

In this chapter, we emphasized that expectations have an important effect on the exchange rate. In this problem, we use data to get a sense of how large a role expectations play. Using the results in Appendix 2 at the end of the book, you can show that the uncovered interest parity condition, equation (21.4), can be written as

$$\frac{(E_t - E_{t-1})}{E_{t-1}} \approx (i_t - i_t^*) - (i_{t-1} - i_{t-1}^*) + \frac{(E_t^e - E_{t-1}^e)}{E_{t-1}^e}$$

In words, the percentage change in the exchange rate (the appreciation of the domestic currency) is approximately equal to the change in the interest rate differential (between domestic and foreign interest rates) plus the percentage change in exchange rate expectations (the appreciation of the expected domestic currency value). We shall call the interest rate differential the spread.

a. Go to the Web site of the Bank of Canada (**www.bank-banque-canada.ca**) and obtain data on the monthly one-year Treasury bill rate for the past 10 years. Download the data into a spreadsheet. Now go to the Web site of the Federal Reserve Bank of St. Louis (**research.stlouisfed.org/fred2**) and download data on the monthly U.S. one-year Canadian Treasury bill rate for the same time period. (You may need to look under "Constant Maturity" Treasury securities rather than "Treasury Bills.") For each month, subtract the Canadian interest rate from the U.S. interest rate to calculate the spread. Then, for each month, calculate the change in the spread from the preceding month. (Make sure to convert the interest rate data into the proper decimal form.)

b. At the Web site of the St. Louis Fed, obtain data on the monthly exchange rate between the U.S. dollar and the Canadian dollar for the same period as your data from part (a). Again, download the data into a spreadsheet. Calculate the percentage appreciation of the U.S. dollar for each month. Using the standard deviation function in your software, calculate the standard deviation

of the monthly appreciation of the U.S. dollar. The standard deviation is a measure of the variability of a data series.

c. For each month, subtract the change in the spread [part (a)] from the percentage appreciation of the dollar [part (b)]. Call this difference the *change in expectations*. Calculate the standard deviation of the change in expectations. How does it compare to the standard deviation of the monthly appreciation of the dollar?

There are some complications we do not take into account here. Our interest parity condition does not include a variable that measures relative asset demand. We explored the implications of changes in relative asset demands in problem 7 at the end of Chapter 20. In addition, changes in interest rates and expectations may be related. Still, the gist of this analysis survives in more sophisticated work. In the short run, observable economic fundamentals do not account for much of the change in the exchange rate. Much of the difference must be attributed to changing expectations.

We invite you to visit the Blanchard page on the Prentice Hall Web site, at:
www.prenhall.com/blanchard
for this chapter's World Wide Web exercises.

Appendix 1: Deriving Aggregate Demand under Fixed Exchange Rates

To derive the aggregate demand for goods, start from the condition for goods market equilibrium we derived in Chapter 20, equation (20.1):

$$Y = C(Y - T) + I(Y, r) + G + NX(Y, Y^*, \epsilon)$$

This condition states that, for the goods market to be in equilibrium, output must be equal to the demand for domestic goods—that is, the sum of consumption, investment, government spending, and net exports.

Next, recall the following relations:

■ The real interest rate, r, is equal to the nominal interest rate, i, minus expected inflation, π^e (see Chapter 14):

$$r = i - \pi^e$$

■ The real exchange rate, ϵ, is defined as (see Chapter 18):

$$\epsilon = \frac{EP}{P^*}$$

■ Under fixed exchange rates, the nominal exchange rate, E, is, by definition, fixed. Denote by $\bar{E}$ the value at which the nominal exchange rate is fixed, so:

$$E = \bar{E}$$

■ Under fixed exchange rates and perfect capital mobility, the domestic interest rate, i, must be equal to the foreign interest rate, i^* (see Chapter 18):

$$i = i^*$$

Using these four relations, rewrite equation (21.1) as

$$Y = C(Y - T) + I(Y, i^* - \pi^e) + G + NX\left(Y, Y^*, \frac{\bar{E}P}{P^*}\right)$$

This is a rich—and complicated—equilibrium condition. It tells us that, in an open economy with fixed exchange rates, equilibrium output (or, more precisely, the level of output implied by equilibrium in the goods, financial, and foreign exchange markets) depends on

■ Government spending, G, and taxes, T—An increase in government spending increases output. So does a decrease in taxes.

■ The foreign nominal interest rate, i^*, minus expected inflation, π^e—An increase in the foreign nominal interest rate requires a parallel increase in the domestic nominal interest rate. Given expected inflation, this increase in the domestic nominal interest rate leads to an increase in the domestic real interest rate and then to lower demand and lower output.

- Foreign output, Y^*—An increase in foreign output increases exports and so increases net exports. The increase in net exports increases domestic output.
- The real exchange rate, ϵ, is equal to the fixed nominal exchange rate, $\bar{E}$, times the domestic price level, P, divided by the foreign price level, P^*—A decrease in the real exchange rate—equivalently, a real depreciation—leads to an increase in net exports and so to an increase in output.

We focus in the text on the effects of only three of these variables: the real exchange rate, government spending, and taxes. We therefore write

$$Y = Y\left(\frac{\bar{E}P}{P^*}, G, T\right)$$
$$(-, +, -)$$

All the other variables that affect demand are taken as given and, to simplify notation, are simply omitted from the relation. This gives us equation (21.1) in the text.

Equation (21.1) gives us the *aggregate demand relation*, the relation between output and the price level implied by equilibrium in the goods market and in financial markets.

Note that, in the closed economy, we had to use both the *IS* and the *LM* relations to derive the aggregate demand relation. Under fixed exchange rates, we do not need the *LM* relation. The reason is that the nominal interest rate, rather than being determined jointly by the *IS* and *LM* relations, is determined by the foreign interest rate. (The *LM* relation still holds, but, as we saw in Chapter 20, it simply determines the money stock.)

Appendix 2: The Real Exchange Rate, and Domestic and Foreign Real Interest Rates

We derived in Section 21-3 a relation between the current nominal exchange rate, the current and expected future domestic and foreign nominal interest rates, and the expected future nominal exchange rate [equation (21.5)]. This appendix derives a similar relation but in terms of real interest rates and the real exchange rate. It then briefly discusses how this alternative relation can be used to think about movements in the real exchange rate.

Deriving the Real Interest Parity Condition

Start from the nominal interest parity condition, equation (18.2):

$$(1 + i_t) = (1 + i_t^*)\frac{E_t}{E_{t+1}^e}$$

Recall the definition of the real interest rate from Chapter 14, equation (14.3):

$$(1 + r_t) \equiv \frac{(1 + i_t)}{(1 + \pi_t^e)}$$

where $\pi_t^e \equiv (P_{t+1}^e - P_t)/P_t$ is the expected rate of inflation. Similarly, the foreign real interest rate is given by:

$$(1 + r_t^*) = \frac{(1 + i_t^*)}{(1 + \pi_t^{*e})}$$

where $p_t^{*e} \equiv (P_{t+1}^{*e} - P_t^*)/P_t^*$ is the expected foreign rate of inflation.

Use these two relations to eliminate nominal interest rates in the interest parity condition, so:

$$(1 + r_t) = (1 + r_t^*)\left[\frac{E_t}{E_{t+1}^e}\frac{(1 + \pi_t^{*e})}{(1 + \pi_t^e)}\right] \qquad (21.A1)$$

Note from the definition of inflation that $(1 + \pi_t^e) = P_{t+1}^e/P_t$ and, similarly, $(1 + \pi_t^{*e}) = P_{t+1}^{*e}/P_t^*$.

Using these two relations in the term in brackets gives

$$\frac{E_t}{E_{t+1}^e}\frac{(1 + \pi_t^{*e})}{(1 + \pi_t^e)} = \frac{E_t}{E_{t+1}^e}\frac{P_{t+1}^{*e}P_t}{P_t^*P_{t+1}^e}$$

Reorganizing terms, we have

$$\frac{E_t P_{t+1}^{*e}P_t}{E_{t+1}^e P_t^*P_{t+1}^e} = \frac{E_t P_t/P_t^*}{E_{t+1}^e P_{t+1}^e/P_{t+1}^{*e}}$$

Using the definition of the real exchange rate gives

$$\frac{E_t P_t/P_t^*}{E_{t+1}^e P_{t+1}^e/P_{t+1}^{*e}} = \frac{\epsilon_t}{\epsilon_{t+1}^e}$$

Replacing in equation (21.A1) gives:

$$(1 + r_t) = (1 + r_t^*)\frac{\epsilon_t}{\epsilon_{t+1}^e}$$

Or, equivalently,

$$\epsilon_t = \frac{1 + r_t}{1 + r_t^*}\epsilon_{t+1}^e \qquad (21.A2)$$

The real exchange rate today depends on the domestic and foreign real interest rates this year, and the expected future real exchange rate next year. This equation corresponds to equation (21.4) in the text but now in terms of the real rather than nominal exchange and interest rates.

Solving the Real Interest Parity Condition Forward

The next step is to solve equation (21.A2) forward, in the same way as we did it for equation (21.4). Equation (21.A2) implies that the real exchange rate in year $t + 1$ is given by

$$\epsilon_{t+1} = \frac{1 + r_{t+1}}{1 + r^*_{t+1}} \epsilon^e_{t+2}$$

Taking expectations, as of year t, gives:

$$\epsilon^e_{t+1} = \frac{1 + r^e_{t+1}}{1 + r^{*e}_{t+1}} \epsilon^e_{t+2}$$

Replacing in the previous relation, we have

$$\epsilon_t = \frac{(1 + r_t)(1 + r^e_{t+1})}{(1 + r^*_t)(1 + r^{*e}_{t+1})} \epsilon^e_{t+2}$$

Solving for ϵ^e_{t+2}, and so on gives

$$\epsilon_t = \frac{(1 + r_t)(1 + r^e_{t+1}) \ldots (1 + r^e_{t+n})}{(1 + r^*_t)(1 + r^{*e}_{t+1}) \ldots (1 + r^{*e}_{t+n})} \epsilon^e_{t+n+1}$$

This relation gives the current real exchange rate as a function of current and expected future domestic real interest rates, of current and expected future foreign real interest rates, and of the expected real exchange rate in year $t + n + 1$.

The advantage of this relation over the relation we derived in the text between the nominal exchange rate and nominal interest rates, equation (21.5), is that it is typically easier to predict the future real exchange rate than to predict the future nominal exchange rate. If, for example, the economy suffers from a large trade deficit, we can be fairly confident that there will have to be a real depreciation—that ϵ^e_{t+n+1} will have to be lower. Whether there will be a nominal depreciation—what happens to E_{t+n+1}—is harder to tell: It depends on what happens to inflation, both at home and abroad over the next n years.

Pathologies

Sometimes (macroeconomic) things go very wrong: There is a sharp drop in output. Or unemployment remains high for a long time. Or inflation increases to very high levels. These pathologies are the focus of the next two chapters.

EXTENSIONS

Chapter 22

Chapter 22 looks at depressions and slumps, periods during which output drops far below and stays far below the natural level of output. The chapter discusses the adverse effects of deflation and what happens when an economy is caught in a liquidity trap. It then looks at the Great Depression, what triggered it, what made it so bad, and what eventually led to the recovery. It then turns to the Japanese economic slump, a slump that started in the early 1990s, and from which Japan is slowly emerging today. It shows that many of the factors that contributed to the Great Depression also operated in Japan in the 1990s.

Chapter 23

Chapter 23 looks at episodes of high inflation, from Germany in the early 1920s to Latin America in the 1980s. It shows the role of both fiscal and monetary policy in generating high inflation. Budget deficits can lead to high nominal money growth, and high nominal money growth leads to high inflation. It then looks at how high inflations end, and at the role and the nature of stabilization programs.

Depressions and Slumps

A major theme of this book so far has been that, while economies go through fluctuations in the short run, they return to normal in the medium run. An adverse shock may lead to a recession, but fairly quickly, the economy turns around, and output returns to its natural level.

Most of the time, this is what happens. But once in a while, things go wrong. Output remains far below its natural level for many years. Unemployment remains stubbornly high. Simply put, the economy appears to be stuck, unable to return to normal. The most infamous case is surely that of the Great Depression, which affected most of the world from the late 1920s to the start of World War II. (Although there is no agreed-upon definition, economists use the term **depression** to describe a deep and long-lasting recession.) A more recent case is the Japanese slump that started in the early 1990s, from which Japan is slowly emerging. (Again, while there is no agreed-upon definition, most economists use **slump** to denote a long period of low or no growth, longer than a typical recession but less deep than a depression.)

What goes wrong during such episodes? Are the shocks particularly bad? Do the usual adjustment mechanisms break down? Or are macroeconomic policies particularly misguided? These are the questions we take up in this chapter:

- Section 22-1 looks at two of the central mechanisms in both the Great Depression and the Japanese slump: the adverse effects of deflation and the liquidity trap.

- Section 22-2 gives an account of the Great Depression.

- Section 22-3 gives an account of the Japanese slump. ■

CHAPTER 22

Let's go back to the argument we developed earlier for why output tends to return to its natural level in the medium run. The easiest way to present the argument is in terms of the *IS–LM* graph in Figure 22-1, with the nominal interest rate on the vertical axis and output on the horizontal axis.

The argument we developed in Chapter 7 went like this:

Recall that the natural level of output is the level of output that ▶ prevails when the unemployment rate is equal to the natural unemployment rate. See Chapter 6.

■ Suppose an adverse shock leads to a decrease in output, so the economy is at point *A*, and the level of output, *Y*, is below the natural level of output, Y_n. The nature of the shock is not important here: It could be a decrease in spending by consumers or a decrease in investment spending by firms. What is important is that output is now below the natural level of output.

■ The fact that output is below the natural level of output leads in turn to a decrease in the price level over time. Given the nominal money stock, the decrease in the price level increases the real money stock. This increase in the real money stock shifts the *LM* curve down, leading to a lower interest rate and higher output. After some time, the economy is, for example, at point *B*, with output equal to *Y'*.

■ As long as output remains below its natural level, the price level continues to fall, and the *LM* curve continues to shift down. The economy moves down the *IS* curve until it reaches point *C*, where output is equal to Y_n.

In short: Output below the natural level of output leads to a decrease in the price level, which goes on until the economy has returned to normal.

The argument in Chapter 7 was based on the strong simplifying assumption that the nominal money stock was constant. This implied that, in the medium run, the price level was also constant—that there was no inflation. It also implied that, if output was below the natural level of output, the adjustment of output back to its natural level was achieved through a *decrease* in the price level—something we rarely observe in practice.

Figure 22-1

The Return of Output to Its Natural Level

Low output leads to a decrease in the price level. The decrease in the price level leads to an increase in the real money stock. The *LM* curve shifts down and continues to shift down until output has returned to the natural level of output.

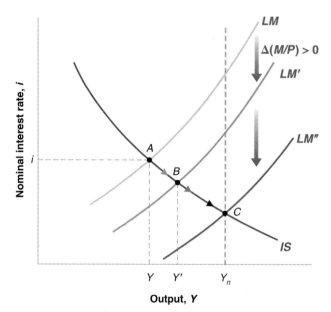

Chapters 8 and 9 presented a more realistic version of the model, which allowed for positive nominal money growth—and so for positive inflation in the medium run. This model gave a richer description of the adjustment of output and inflation to shocks. It delivered, however, the same basic result as the simpler version of the model presented in Chapter 7: The economy tends to return to the natural level of output over time. The argument went as follows:

■ Suppose that, as in Figure 22-1, output is below the natural level of output— or, equivalently, that the unemployment rate is higher than the natural rate of unemployment.

■ With the unemployment rate above the natural rate, inflation falls over time. ◄ This follows from the Phillips curve relation [equation (8.10)]: $u > u_n \Rightarrow \pi_t < \pi_{t-1}$.
Suppose nominal money growth and inflation were initially equal to each other, so real money growth (the difference between nominal money growth and inflation) was initially equal to zero. With inflation falling, and therefore becoming smaller than the rate of nominal money growth, real money growth now turns positive. Equivalently, the real money stock increases. This increase in the real money stock shifts the LM curve down, leading to an increase in output.

■ As long as output is below its natural level, inflation falls, and the LM curve continues to shift down. This goes on until, eventually, output is back to the natural level of output.

It would therefore appear that economies have a strong built-in stabilizing mechanism to get out of recessions:

■ Output below the natural level of output leads to lower inflation.
■ Lower inflation leads in turn to higher real money growth.
■ Higher real money growth leads to an increase in output over time.

The existence of depressions and slumps tells us, however, that this built-in mechanism is not foolproof and that things can clearly go wrong in a number of ways. We now look at two of them: the perverse effects of deflation, and the liquidity trap.

The Nominal Interest Rate, the Real Interest Rate, and Expected Inflation

When we looked at the adjustment of output in Figure 22-1, we ignored the distinction between the nominal interest rate and the real interest rate. This distinction turns out to be important here, so we need to reintroduce it. Recall the following from Chapter 14:

■ What matters for spending decisions, and thus what enters the IS relation, is the *real interest rate*—the interest rate in terms of goods.
■ What matters for the demand for money, and thus what enters the LM relation, is the *nominal interest rate*—the interest rate in terms of dollars.

Recall also the relation between the two interest rates: The real interest rate is equal to the nominal interest rate minus expected inflation.

Let r be the real interest rate, i be the nominal interest rate, ◄ and π^e be expected inflation. Then, from equation (14.4), $r = i - \pi^e$.

What this distinction between the two interest rates implies is shown in Figure 22-2. Suppose the economy is initially at A: Output is initially below the natural level of output. Because output is below the natural level of output, inflation falls. The decrease in inflation now has two effects:

■ The first effect is to increase the real money stock and shift the LM curve down, from LM to LM′. The shift of the LM curve—due to the increase in M/P—is the shift shown in Figure 22-1. This shift of the LM curve leads to an increase in output. If this were the only shift, the economy would go from A to B.

The decrease in inflation leads to an increase in the real money stock. This shifts the LM ◄ curve down.

The Effects of Lower Inflation on Output

When inflation decreases in response to low output, there are two effects: (1) The real money stock increases, leading the *LM* curve to shift down, and (2) expected inflation decreases, leading the *IS* curve to shift to the left. The result may be a further decrease in output.

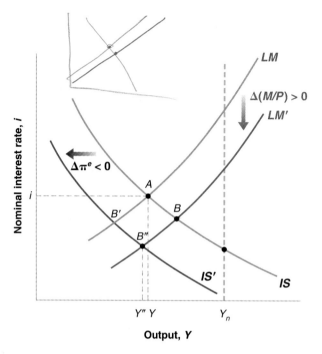

There is, however, now a second effect at work: Suppose the decrease in inflation leads to a decrease in expected inflation. Then, for a given nominal interest rate, the decrease in expected inflation *increases* the real interest rate. The higher real interest rate leads in turn to lower spending and lower output. So, at a given nominal interest rate, the level of output implied by equilibrium in the goods market is lower. The *IS* curve shifts to the left, from *IS* to *IS'*. The shift in the *IS* curve—due to the decrease in π^e—leads to a decrease in output. If this were the only shift, the economy would go from *A* to *B'*.

> The decrease in expected inflation leads to an increase in the real interest rate for a given nominal interest rate. It shifts the *IS* curve to the left.

Does output go up or down as a result of these two shifts? The answer: One cannot tell. The combined effect of the two shifts is to move the economy from *A* to *B"*, with output *Y"*. Whether *Y"* is greater or smaller than *Y* depends on which shift dominates and is, in general, ambiguous.

As I have drawn the figure, *Y"* is smaller than *Y*. In this case, rather than return to its natural level, output declines further away from it: Things get worse rather than better.

A numerical example will help you keep straight the two effects of inflation:

> In Chapter 9, you saw that, in the medium run, inflation is equal to nominal money growth minus normal output growth. This example assumes for simplicity that normal output growth is zero, so inflation and nominal money growth are equal.

■ Suppose nominal money growth, inflation, and expected inflation are all equal to 5% initially. Suppose the nominal interest rate is equal to 7%, so the real interest rate is equal to 7% − 5% = 2%.

■ Suppose that, because output is lower than the natural level of output, inflation decreases from 5% to 3% after a year. Real money growth—nominal money growth minus inflation—is now equal to 5% − 3% = 2%. Equivalently, the real money stock increases by 2%. Suppose this increase in the real money stock leads to a decrease in the nominal interest rate from, say, 7% to 6%. This is the first effect you saw earlier: Lower inflation leads to a higher real money stock, and a lower nominal interest rate.

■ Suppose the decrease in inflation leads people to expect that inflation this year will be 2% lower than it was last year, so expected inflation decreases from 5% to 3%. This implies that, at any given nominal interest rate, the real interest rate increases by 2%. This is the second effect you saw earlier: At a given nominal interest rate, lower expected inflation leads to an increase in the real interest rate.

- Combining the two effects: The nominal interest rate decreases from 7% to 6%. Expected inflation decreases from 5% to 3%. So the real interest rate moves from $7\% - 5\% = 2\%$ to $6\% - 3\% = 3\%$. The net effect of lower inflation is an *increase* in the real interest rate.

We have just looked at what happens at the start of the adjustment process. It is easy to describe a scenario in which things go from bad to worse over time. The decrease in output from Y to Y'' leads to a further decrease in inflation and, so, to a further decrease in expected inflation. This leads to a further increase in the real interest rate, which further decreases output, and so on. In other words, the initial recession can turn into a full-fledged depression, with output continuing to decline rather than returning to the natural level of output. The stabilizing mechanism we described in earlier chapters simply breaks down.

The Liquidity Trap

One reaction to the scenario we just saw is to conclude that, while we should worry about it, it can easily be avoided with the appropriate use of monetary policy: The scenario was derived under the assumption that monetary policy (in our case the rate of growth of nominal money) remained unchanged. But if the central bank were worried about a decrease in output, it would seem that all it would need to do is to embark on an expansionary monetary policy. In terms of Figure 22-2, all the central bank needs to do is to increase the stock of nominal money in order to shift the LM curve down far enough to increase output.

This is clearly the right prescription. But there is a limit to what the central bank can do: It cannot decrease the nominal interest rate below zero. If expected inflation is low or even negative (if people expect a deflation), the implied real interest rate may still not be low enough to get the economy out of a recession. This issue has been at the center of discussions about the Japanese slump. Let's now look at it more closely.

Go back first to our characterization of the demand and the supply of money in Chapter 4. There we drew the demand for money, for a given level of income, as a decreasing function of the nominal interest rate. The lower the nominal interest rate, the larger the demand for money—equivalently, the smaller the demand for bonds. What we did not ask in Chapter 4 is what happens when the interest rate goes down to zero. The answer: Once people hold enough money for transaction purposes, they are then indifferent between holding the rest of their financial wealth in the form of money or in the form of bonds. The reason they are indifferent: Both money and bonds pay the same nominal interest rate: zero. Thus, the demand for money is as shown in Figure 22-3:

◄ Look at Figure 4-1. Note how I avoided the issue by not drawing the demand for money for interest rates close to zero.

- As the nominal interest rate decreases, people want to hold more money (and thus fewer bonds): The demand for money therefore increases.
- As the nominal interest rate becomes equal to zero, people want to hold an amount of money at least equal to the distance OB: This is what they need for transaction purposes. But they are willing to hold even more money (and therefore hold fewer bonds) because they are indifferent between money and bonds. Therefore, the demand for money becomes horizontal beyond point B.

Now consider the effects of an increase in the money supply:

- Consider a case in which the money supply is M^s, so the nominal interest rate consistent with financial market equilibrium is positive and equal to i. (This is the case we considered in Chapter 4.) Starting from that equilibrium in Figure 22-3, an increase in the money supply—a shift of the M^s line to the right—leads to a decrease in the nominal interest rate.

Money Demand, Money Supply, and the Liquidity Trap

When the nominal interest rate is equal to zero, and once people have enough money for transaction purposes, they become indifferent between holding money and holding bonds. The demand for money becomes horizontal. This implies that, when the nominal interest rate is equal to zero, further increases in the money supply have no effect on the nominal interest rate.

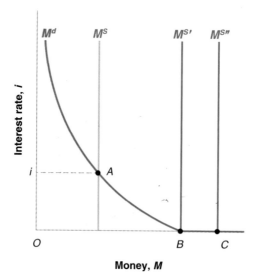

From Chapter 4: The central bank changes the money stock ▶ through open market operations, in which it buys or sells bonds in exchange for money.

■ Now consider a case in which the money supply is $M^{s'}$, so the equilibrium is at point B; or the case where the money supply is $M^{s''}$, so the equilibrium is given at point C. In either case, the initial nominal interest rate is zero. And, in either case, an increase in the money supply has no effect on the nominal interest rate. Think of it this way:

Suppose the central bank increases the money supply. It does so through an open market operation in which it buys bonds and pays for them by creating money. Because the nominal interest rate is zero, people are indifferent to how much money or how many bonds they hold, so they are willing to hold fewer bonds and more money at the same nominal interest rate: zero. The money supply increases but with no effect on the nominal interest rate—which remains equal to zero.

In short: Once the nominal interest rate is equal to zero, expansionary monetary policy becomes powerless. Or to use the words of Keynes, who was the first to point out the problem, the increase in money falls into a **liquidity trap**: People are willing to hold more money (*more liquidity*) at the same nominal interest rate.

Having looked at equilibrium in the financial markets, let's now turn to the *IS–LM* model and see how it must be modified to take into account the liquidity trap.

The derivation of the *LM* curve is shown in the two panels of Figure 22-4. Recall that the *LM* curve gives, for a given real money stock, the relation between the nominal interest rate and the level of income implied by equilibrium in financial markets. To derive the *LM* curve, Figure 22-4(a) looks at equilibrium in the financial markets for a given value of the real money stock and draws three money demand curves, each corresponding to a different level of income:

■ M^d shows the demand for money for a given level of income, Y. The equilibrium is given by point A, with nominal interest rate equal to i. This combination of income, Y, and nominal interest rate, i, gives us the first point on the *LM* curve, point A in Figure 22-4(b).

■ $M^{d'}$ shows the demand for money for a lower level of income, $Y' < Y$. Lower income means fewer transactions, and, therefore, a lower demand for money at any interest rate. In this case, the equilibrium is given by point A', with nominal interest rate equal to i'. This combination of income, Y', and nominal interest rate, i', gives us the second point on the *LM* curve, point A' in Figure 22-4(b).

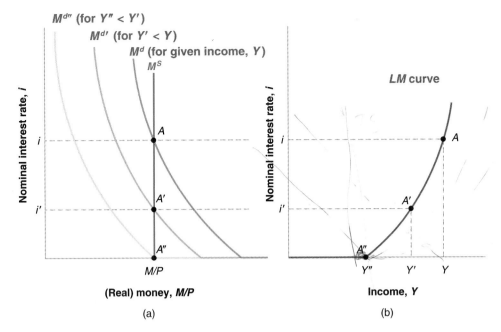

Figure 22-4 ▦

The Derivation of the LM *Curve in the Presence of a Liquidity Trap*

For low levels of output, the *LM* curve is a flat segment, with a nominal interest rate equal to zero. For higher levels of output, it is upward sloping: An increase in income leads to an increase in the nominal interest rate.

(a)

(b)

- $M^{d''}$ gives the demand for money for a still lower level of income, $Y'' < Y'$. In this case, the equilibrium is given by point A'' in Figure 22-4(a), with nominal interest rate equal to zero. Point A'' in Figure 22-4(b) corresponds to A'' in Figure 22-4(a).
- What happens if income decreases below Y'', shifting the demand for money further to the left in Figure 22-4(a)? The intersection between the money supply curve and the money demand curve takes place on the horizontal portion of the money demand curve. The equilibrium remains at A'', and the nominal interest rate remains equal to zero.

So far, the derivation of the *LM* curve is exactly the same as in ◄ Chapter 5. It is only when income is lower than Y'' that things become different.

Let's summarize: In the presence of a liquidity trap, the *LM* curve looks as drawn in Figure 22-4(b). For values of income greater than Y'', it is upward sloping—just as it was in Chapter 5, when we first characterized the *LM* curve. For values of income less than Y'', it is flat at $i = 0$. Intuitively: The nominal interest rate cannot go below zero.

Having derived the *LM* curve in the presence of a liquidity trap, we can look at the properties of the *IS–LM* model modified in this way. Suppose the economy is initially at point A in Figure 22-5. Equilibrium is at point A, at the intersection of the *IS* curve and the *LM* curve, with output Y and nominal interest rate i. And suppose that this level of output is far below the natural level of output, Y_n. The question is: Can monetary policy help the economy return to Y_n?

Suppose the central bank increases the money supply, shifting the *LM* curve from *LM* to *LM′*. The equilibrium moves from point A down to point B. The nominal interest rate decreases from i to zero, and output increases from Y to Y'. Thus, to this extent, expansionary monetary policy can indeed increase output.

What happens, however, if starting from point B, the central bank increases the money supply further, shifting the *LM* curve from *LM′* to, say, *LM″*? The intersection of *IS* and *LM″* remains at point B, and output remains equal to Y'. Expansionary monetary policy no longer has an effect on output; it cannot therefore help output return to Y_n.

In words: When the nominal interest rate is equal to zero, the economy falls in a *liquidity trap:* The central bank can increase *liquidity*—that is, increase the money supply. But this *liquidity* falls into a *trap*: The additional money is willingly held by

The IS–LM *Model and the Liquidity Trap*

In the presence of a liquidity trap, there is a limit to how much monetary policy can increase output. Monetary policy may not be able to increase output back to its natural level.

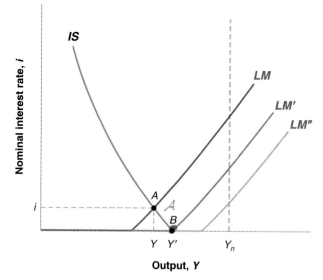

financial investors at an unchanged interest rate, namely zero. If, at this zero nominal interest rate, the demand for goods is still too low, then there is nothing further monetary policy can do to increase output.

Putting Things Together: The Liquidity Trap and Deflation

Just as you may have been skeptical when we were discussing the adverse effects of lower inflation earlier, you may well remain skeptical that the liquidity trap is a serious issue: After all, a zero nominal interest rate is a very low interest rate. Shouldn't a zero nominal interest rate be enough to strongly stimulate spending and avoid a recession?

The answer is no. The key to the answer is again the distinction between the real interest rate and the nominal interest rate. What matters for spending is the real interest rate. What the real interest is, if the nominal interest rate is equal to zero, depends on expected inflation:

$r = i - \pi^e = 0\% - 10\%$
$= -10\%.$

Revisit our discussion of investment decisions in Chapter 16. Why is investment likely to be very high if firms can borrow at a real interest rate of −10%? (*Hint:* To what do firms compare the real interest rate?)

$r = i - \pi^e = 0\% - (-5\%) = 5\%.$

■ Suppose the rate of inflation, actual or expected, is high, say equal to 10%. Then, a zero nominal interest rate corresponds to a real interest rate of −10%. At such a negative real interest rate, consumption and investment spending are likely to be very high, probably high enough to make sure that demand is sufficient to return output to the natural level of output. So, at high inflation, the liquidity trap is unlikely to be a serious problem.

■ Suppose the rate of inflation, actual and expected, is negative—the economy is experiencing deflation. Say the actual and expected rates of inflation are both equal to −5% (equivalently, the rate of deflation is 5%). Then, even if the nominal interest rate were equal to zero, the real interest rate would still be equal to 5%. This real interest rate may still be too high to stimulate spending enough, and, in this case, there is nothing monetary policy can do to increase output.

You can now see how the two mechanisms—the effects of expected inflation on the real interest rate, and the liquidity trap described in this section—can come together to turn recessions into slumps or depressions:

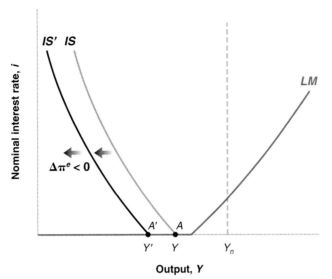

Figure 22-6 ■

The Liquidity Trap and Deflation

Suppose the economy is in a liquidity trap, and there is deflation. Output below the natural level of output leads to more deflation over time, which leads to a further increase in the real interest rate, and leads to a further shift of the IS curve to the left. This shift leads to a further decrease in output, which leads to more deflation, and so on.

■ Suppose the economy has been in a recession for some time, so inflation has steadily decreased and turned into deflation.

■ Suppose monetary policy has decreased the nominal interest rate down to zero. Even at this zero nominal interest rate, expected deflation implies that the real interest rate is still positive.

■ Suppose that, as a result, the economy is at a point such as A in Figure 22-6, at the intersection of the IS and the LM curves. The nominal interest rate is equal to zero, and output, Y, is below the natural level of output, Y_n.

■ There is clearly nothing monetary policy can do in this case to increase output. And things are likely to get worse over time: Because output is below the natural level of output, the rate of deflation, actual and expected, is likely to increase (inflation is likely to become more negative).

■ At a given nominal interest rate, higher expected deflation leads to an increase in the real interest rate; the IS curve shifts to the left in Figure 22-6, from IS to, say, IS', leading to a further decrease in output, from Y down to Y'. This leads to further deflation, which leads to a further increase in the real interest rate, a further decrease in output, and so on.

In words: The economy gets caught in a vicious cycle: Low output leads to more deflation. More deflation leads to a higher real interest rate and even lower output, and there is nothing monetary policy can do about it. The scenario might sound far-fetched, but, as we will now see when we look first at the Great Depression, and then at the Japanese slump, it is far from impossible.

22-2 The Great Depression

In 1929, the U.S. unemployment rate was 3.2%. By 1933, it had increased to 24.9%! One out of every four workers was looking for a job. Not until nine years later, in 1942, was it back down to 4.7%. (Figure 22-7 shows the evolution of the unemployment rate from 1920 to 1950.)

A more complete macroeconomic picture is given in Table 22-1, which shows the evolution of the U.S. unemployment rate, the growth rate of output, the consumer price index, and the money stock from 1929 to 1942.

The U.S. Unemployment Rate, 1920 to 1950

The Great Depression was characterized by a sharp increase in unemployment, followed by a slow decline.

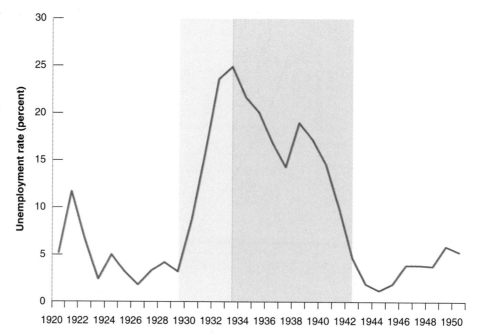

Look first just at output and unemployment. Note, the following:

■   How sharply and how much output declined at the start of the depression. The average annual growth rate from 1929 to 1932 was an astounding –8.6%, leading to an increase in the unemployment rate of more than 20 percentage points (3.2% to 24.9%) in four years.

Table 22-1	U.S. Unemployment, Output Growth, Prices, and Money, 1929 to 1942		
Year	Unemployment Rate (%)	Output Growth Rate (%)	Price Level	Nominal Money Stock
1929	3.2	–9.8	100.0	26.6
1930	8.7	–7.6	97.4	25.7
1931	15.9	–14.7	88.8	24.1
1932	23.6	–1.8	79.7	21.1
1933	24.9	9.1	75.6	19.9
1934	21.7	9.9	78.1	21.9
1935	20.1	13.9	80.1	25.9
1936	16.9	5.3	80.9	29.5
1937	14.3	–5.0	83.8	30.9
1938	19.0	8.6	82.2	30.5
1939	17.2	8.5	81.0	34.1
1940	14.6	16.1	81.8	39.6
1941	9.9	12.9	85.9	46.5
1942	4.7	13.2	95.1	55.3

Note: The price index is normalized to 100 in 1929. The money stock is measured in billions of dollars.

Source: Historical Statistics of the United States, U.S. Department of Commerce.

How long it then took for unemployment to recover. Output growth turned positive in 1933. But in 1941, on the eve of the entry of the United States in World War II, the unemployment rate was still equal to 9.9%.

What triggered the initial increase in unemployment? What made the depression last so long? How did the economy eventually return to low unemployment? These are the questions we take up in the rest of this section.

The Initial Fall in Spending

Popular accounts often say the Great Depression was caused by the stock market crash of 1929. Not so. A recession had actually started before the crash, and other factors played a central role later in the Depression.

Nevertheless, the crash was important. The stock market had boomed from 1921 to 1929. Stock prices had increased much faster than the dividends paid by firms—and as a result, the dividend-price ratio (the ratio of the dividends paid by a stock to the price of the stock) had fallen from 6.5% in 1921 to 3.5% in 1929. On October 28, 1929, the stock market price index dropped from 298 to 260. The next day, it dropped further, to 230. This was a fall of 23% in two days and a drop of 40% from the peak of early September. By November, the index was down to 198. A brief stock market recovery in early 1930 was followed by further declines in stock prices as the depth of the depression became increasingly clear to market participants. By June 1932, the index bottomed out at 47. (The evolution of the index from January 1920 to December 1950 is shown in Figure 22-8.)

Was the October 1929 crash caused by the sudden realization that a depression was coming? There was no major economic news to that effect in October. The source of the crash was almost surely the end of a speculative bubble. Investors who had purchased stocks at high prices, anticipating further price increases in the future, got scared and attempted to sell their stocks. The result was a large drop in prices.

Revisit the discussion of dividends, and prices, and bubbles, and crashes in Section 15-3. ◄

Figure 22-8 ▨

The S&P Composite Index, 1920 to 1950

From September 1929 to June 1932, the stock market index fell from 313 to 47 before it slowly recovered.

The crash not only decreased consumers' wealth, but it also increased their uncertainty about the future. Unsettled by the crash and feeling uncertain about the future, consumers and firms decided to see how things evolved and to postpone purchases of durable goods and investment goods. There was, for example, a large decrease in car sales—the type of purchase that can be easily delayed—in the months just following the crash. Industrial production, which had declined by 1.8% from August to October 1929, declined by 9.8% from October to December and by another 24% from December 1929 to December 1930.

The Contraction in Nominal Money

The impact of the crash was compounded by a major policy mistake: a large decrease in the nominal money stock. The first column of Table 22-2 shows the evolution of the nominal money stock, measured by $M1$. From 1929 to 1933, $M1$ *decreased* from $26.6 billion to $19.2 billion, a decrease of 27%.

Recall that M1 is the sum of currency, travelers' checks, and checkable deposits.

To understand why the nominal money stock went down so much, we must go back to the relation between the nominal money stock and the monetary base we saw in Chapter 4. There, we saw that, in an economy in which some of the money held by people and firms takes the form of bank money, the relation between the money stock, $M1$ (the sum of currency and checkable deposits), and the monetary base, H (currency plus banks' reserves), is given by

$$M1 = H \times \text{Money multiplier}$$

The money multiplier depends in turn on both the reserves banks keep in proportion to their deposits, and the money people keep in the form of currency versus checkable deposits.

The classic treatment is by Milton Friedman and Anna Schwartz, *A Monetary History of the United States, 1867–1960*, (Princeton University Press, Princeton, NJ, 1963).

Now note that from 1929 to 1933, the monetary base, H (shown in the second column of Table 22-2), *increased* from $7.1 to $8.2 billion. This means the decrease in $M1$ did not come from a decrease in the monetary base, but came instead from a decrease in the money multiplier, $M1/H$ (shown in the third column of Table 22-2), which fell from 3.7 in 1929 to 2.4 in 1933. Why did the money multiplier decline so much? The short answer is: Because of bank failures. Here is why: With the large decline in output, more and more borrowers found themselves unable to repay their loans to banks, causing more and more banks to become insolvent and close down. Bank failures increased steadily from 1929 until 1933, when the number of failures reached a peak of 4,000, out of about 20,000 banks in operation at the time.

Table 22-2   Money, Nominal and Real, 1929 to 1933

Year	Nominal Money Stock, M1	Monetary Base, H	Money Multiplier, M1/H	Real Money Stock, M1/P
1929	26.6	7.1	3.7	26.4
1930	25.7	6.9	3.7	26.0
1931	24.1	7.3	3.3	26.5
1932	21.1	7.8	2.7	25.8
1933	19.4	8.2	2.4	25.6

Source: *Historical Statistics of the United States*, U.S. Department of Commerce.

Bank failures had a direct effect on the money supply: Checkable deposits at the failed banks became worthless. But the major effect on the money supply was indirect: Worried that their bank might also fail, many people took their money out of banks and shifted from checkable deposits to currency. The increase in the ratio of currency to deposits led to a decrease in the money multiplier and, therefore, to a decrease in the money supply. Think of the mechanism this way: If people had liquidated *all* of their deposits in exchange for currency, the multiplier would have decreased all the way down to 1. The only money people would have held would have been central bank money. In other words, $M1$ would have been just equal to the monetary base, H. The actual shift was less dramatic; nevertheless, the multiplier dropped from 3.7 in 1929 to 2.4 in 1933, leading to a decrease in the money supply despite an increase in the monetary base.

From Chapter 4: The multiplier is $1/[c + \theta(1 - c)]$ where c is the proportion of money people want to hold as currency, and θ is the ratio of reserves to checkable deposits. The higher c, the lower the multiplier. And, if $c = 1$—if people want to hold only currency—then the multiplier equals 1.

The implication for our purposes is simple: Because of a decrease in the nominal money stock, $M1$, from 1929 to 1933 roughly proportional to the decrease in the price level, the real money stock, $M1/P$ (shown in the fourth column of Table 22-2), remained roughly constant, eliminating one of the mechanisms that could have led to a recovery. In other words, the LM curve remained roughly unchanged—it did not shift down as it would have done if the nominal money stock had remained constant, implying an increase in the real money stock.

This is why Milton Friedman and Anna Schwartz have argued that the Fed was responsible for the depth of the Depression: It was not directly responsible for the decrease in the nominal money supply, but it should have taken steps to offset the decrease in the money multiplier by expanding the monetary base much more than it did.

The Adverse Effects of Deflation

With the fall in spending and the decrease in the nominal money supply, the stage was set for the mechanisms we saw in Section 22-1 to turn the decline in output into a full-fledged depression.

As shown in the first column of Table 22-3, the contraction in nominal money limited the decline in the nominal interest rate. The nominal interest rate, measured by the interest rate on one-year corporate bonds, reached 5.3% in 1929 (up from 4.1% in 1928), only to slowly decline over time, reaching 2.6% in 1933.

At the same time, as shown in the second column of Table 22-3, the result of low output was a strong *deflation*. The rate of deflation—that is, the decrease in the price level—reached 9.2% in 1931, and 10.8% in 1932. If we make the assumption that expected deflation was equal to actual deflation in each year, we can construct a series for the real interest rate. This is done in the last column of Table 22-3, and it gives a

Table 22-3 The Nominal Interest Rate, Inflation, and the Real Interest Rate, 1929 to 1933

Year	One-Year Nominal Interest Rate (%), i	Inflation Rate (%), π	One-Year Real Interest Rate (%), r
1929	5.3	−0.0	5.3
1930	4.4	−2.5	6.9
1931	3.1	−9.2	12.3
1932	4.0	−10.8	14.8
1933	2.6	−5.2	7.8

Source: *Historical Statistics of the United States*, U.S. Department of Commerce.

convincing explanation for why output continued to decline until 1933. The real interest rate reached 12.3% in 1931, 14.8% in 1932, and still a very high 7.8% in 1933. It is no great surprise that, at those interest rates, both consumption and investment demand remained very low, and the depression worsened.

The Recovery

The recovery started in 1933. Except for another sharp decrease in the growth rate of output in 1937 (see Table 22-1), growth was consistently high, running at an average annual rate of 7.7% from 1933 to 1941. Macroeconomists and economic historians have studied the recovery much less than the initial decline, though. And many questions remain.

One of the factors that contributed to the recovery is clear. Following the election of Franklin Roosevelt in 1932, there was a change in monetary policy and a dramatic increase in nominal money growth. From 1933 to 1941, the nominal money stock increased by 140%, and the real money stock increased by 100%. These increases were due to increases in the monetary base, not in the money multiplier. Christina Romer, an economic historian from Berkeley, has argued that if monetary policy had been unchanged from 1933 on, output would have been 25% lower than it actually was in 1937, and 50% lower than it was in 1942. These are very large numbers. Even if we believe these numbers overestimate the effect of monetary policy, the conclusion that monetary policy played an important role in the recovery is still surely warranted.

Christina Romer, "What Ended the Great Depression?" *Journal of Economic History*, December 1992, 757–784.

The role of other factors, from budget deficits to the **New Deal**—the set of programs put in place by the Roosevelt administration to get the U.S. economy out of the Great Depression—is much less clear.

One New Deal program, aimed at improving the functioning of banks, created the *Federal Deposit Insurance Corporation (FDIC)* to insure checkable deposits so as to avoid bank runs and bank failures. And, indeed, there have been few bank failures since 1933.

Other programs included relief and public works programs for the unemployed, as well as a program administered by the **National Recovery Administration (NRA)** to establish "orderly competition" in industry. Economists generally agree that these programs had few direct effects on the recovery. But some economists argue that the indirect effects of these programs—particularly the perception of the government's commitment to getting the economy out of the Depression—were important in changing expectations in 1933 and thereafter. We saw in earlier chapters how important the effects of policy on expectations can be. However, showing their importance in 1933 and later is difficult and remains largely to be done.

The recovery also presents us with a puzzle. In 1933, deflation stopped. The rest of the decade was characterized by small but positive inflation. The CPI was 81.8 in 1940, compared to 75.6 in 1933. The end of deflation probably helped the recovery. The shift from deflation to rough price stability implied much lower real interest rates than had been the case from 1929 until 1933.

The puzzle is *why* deflation ended in 1933: With a large deflation and an all-time-high unemployment rate in 1932, the theory of wage determination we developed in previous chapters implies that there should have been further large wage cuts and further deflation. This is not what happened. As we saw in the Phillips curve diagram constructed for the United States by Samuelson and Solow (Figure 8-1), the years 1933 to 1939 are clear outliers. So why did deflation stop?

■ One proximate cause may be the set of measures taken by the Roosevelt administration. The **National Industrial Recovery Act (NIRA)**, signed in June 1933, asked industries to establish minimum wages and not to take advantage of the high unemployment rate to impose further wage cuts on workers. Economists are usually doubtful that such admonitions to firms have much effect. But the NIRA offered firms a carrot in exchange, in effect lower competition in goods markets—under the guise of "orderly competition"—and, therefore, the potential for higher profits if they complied. The evidence suggests that the NIRA did have an effect on wage setting.

■ Another factor may be that, while unemployment was still high, output growth was high as well. As a result, there were bottlenecks in production, leading firms to increase their prices given wages. Because of the sharp increase in demand, the price of raw materials was also bid up, increasing costs and again forcing firms to increase their prices given wages. In short, the effect of fast growth was to increase prices given wages, thereby reducing the deflationary pressure of unemployment.

■ Yet another factor may be the perception of a "regime change" associated with the election of Roosevelt and its direct effect on inflation expectations. During its first 100 days in office, the Roosevelt administration made clear that it was committed to ending deflation. It replaced the chairman of the Federal Reserve Board, and soon after, the new chairman proceeded to decrease the interest rate. In April 1933, Roosevelt allowed the dollar to float, and the dollar quickly depreciated by 30% or more against other currencies. It is plausible that these changes in policy had an effect on expected inflation, and, in turn, an effect on actual inflation.

> Some economists have argued, however, that the decrease in competition partially explains the weak recovery after 1933. Lower competition, they argued, led to higher markups, a higher ◄ natural rate of unemployment, and a lower natural level of output.

Why should we care about how deflation turned to inflation in the United States in 1933? Because, as you shall see next, the answer is very relevant to Japan today. How to get rid of deflation, and, in so doing, decrease the real interest rate and stimulate growth, is one of the issues confronting Japanese policymakers today.

22-3 The Japanese Slump

From the end of World War II to the beginning of the 1990s, Japan's economic performance was spectacular: From 1950 to 1973, the average growth rate was 7.4% per year. As in other OECD countries, the average growth rate decreased after 1973. But from 1973 to 1991, it was still a very respectable 4% per year, a rate higher than in most other OECD countries. As a result of this growth, Japanese output per person (in PPP prices), which was only 22% of the U.S. level in 1950, had climbed to 84% of the U.S. level in 1990.

> Have you forgotten the defini- tion of GDP in PPP prices? See ◄ Chapter 10.

This high growth came to an abrupt end in the early 1990s. Figure 22-9 shows the evolution of the Japanese growth rate since 1990. From 1992 to 2002, average annual growth was less than 1%—far below what it had been earlier. This long period of low growth is called the *Japanese slump*. This slump was obviously not as sharp and as deep as the Great Depression (recall from Table 22-1 that the average annual growth rate in the United States from 1929 to 1932 was –8.6%), but it was still substantial. Think of it this way: If average output growth between 1992 and 2002 had remained the same as it was during 1973 to 1991, output in Japan would have been roughly 30% higher in 2002 than it actually was.

Since 2003, the growth rate has turned positive. But, unlike in the U.S. recovery from 1933 on, the growth rate in Japan is still much lower than it was before the slump. In the best of cases, it will take many years for the Japanese economy to return to normal.

Figure 22-10 completes the macroeconomic picture by showing the behavior of the unemployment rate and inflation (using the GDP deflator) since 1990.

■■■ **Figure 22-9**

The Japanese Slump: Output Growth since 1990 (percent)

From 1992 to 2002, average GDP growth in Japan was less than 1%.
Note: 2007 data are forecasts as of mid-2007.

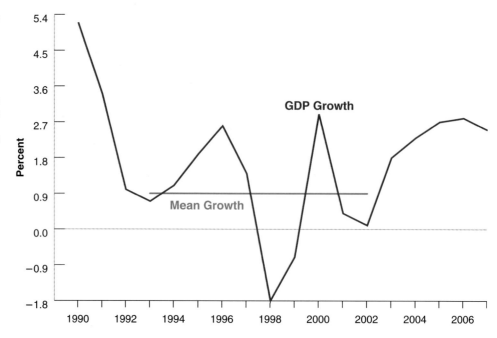

Looking at the unemployment numbers, you might conclude that Japan had in fact not done too badly. True, the unemployment rate increased from 2.1% in 1990 to 5.4% in 2002; it has since declined to around 4%. But even 5.4% is still lower than the average unemployment rate in the United States over the past 40 years, and it is a rate that many European countries can only dream of achieving.

This conclusion would be wrong, however: An unemployment rate of 5% in Japan is the sign of a very depressed labor market. To see why, go back to the discussion in

■ **Figure 22-10**

Unemployment and Inflation in Japan since 1990 (percent)

Low growth in output has led to an increase in unemployment. Inflation has turned into deflation.
Note: 2007 data are forecasts as of mid-2007.

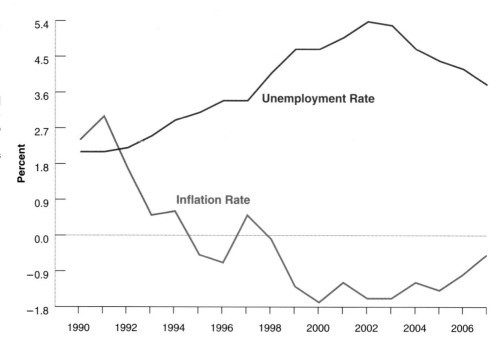

the Focus box: "Okun's Law across Countries" in Chapter 10. We saw there that Japanese firms offer substantial employment protection to their workers. So, when these firms experience a decrease in production, they tend to keep their workers, leading to a small effect of the decrease in output on employment. As a result, low growth has not led to a very large increase in unemployment. But it does not mean that Japan is doing well.

Turn finally to the inflation numbers. Low growth and high unemployment (by Japanese standards) have led to a steady fall in the inflation rate. Since 1995, Japan has had deflation—negative inflation—something that had not been observed in OECD countries since the Great Depression.

The numbers in Table 22-4 raise an obvious set of questions: What triggered Japan's slump? Why did it last so long? Were monetary and fiscal policies misused, or did they fail? What are the factors behind the current recovery? These are the questions we take up in the rest of this section.

The Rise and Fall of the Nikkei

The 1980s were associated with a stock market boom in Japan: The Nikkei index, a broad index of Japanese stock prices, increased from 7,000 in 1980 to 35,000 at the end of 1989—a five-fold increase. Then, within two years, the index fell sharply—down to 16,000 at the end of 1992. It continued to decline throughout the 1990s, reaching a trough of 7,000 in 2003. The index has partially recovered since, and in mid-2007, it stands at 15,000, still less than one-half of its value at the peak.

Why did the Nikkei rise so much in the 1980s and then fall so quickly in the early 1990s? Recall from Chapter 15 there can be two reasons for a stock price to increase:

■ A change in the fundamental value of the stock price, coming, for example, from an increase in current or future expected dividends. Knowing that the stock will pay higher dividends either now or in the future, investors are willing to pay more for the stock today. Consequently, its price goes up.

◄ Recall from Chapter 15 that, in the absence of a speculative bubble, the price of a stock is equal to the expected present value of future dividends.

■ A speculative bubble. Investors buy at a higher price simply because they expect the price to go even higher in the future.

Figure 22-11 shows the evolution of dividends and stock prices in Japan since 1980. The upper line shows the evolution of the stock price index (the Nikkei); the lower line shows the evolution of the corresponding index for dividends. For convenience, both variables are normalized to 1 in 1980. A look at the figure yields a simple

Table 22-4	GDP, Consumption, and Investment Growth in Japan, 1988 to 1993		
Year	GDP (%)	Consumption (%)	Investment (%)
1988	6.5	5.1	15.5
1989	5.3	4.7	15.0
1990	5.2	4.6	10.1
1991	3.4	2.9	4.3
1992	1.0	2.6	–7.1
1993	0.2	1.4	–10.3

Note: Investment is private, fixed, non-residential investment.

Source: OECD *Economic Outlook.*

Figure 22-11

Stock Prices and Dividends in Japan since 1980

The increase in stock prices in the 1980s and the subsequent decrease were not associated with a parallel movement in dividends.

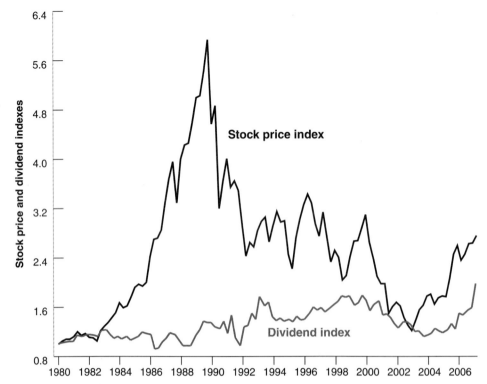

conclusion: While the stock price index increased in the 1980s, the dividend remained flat. This is not necessarily proof that the increase in the Nikkei was a bubble: Investors might have expected large increases in future dividends, even if current dividends were not increasing. But it strongly suggests that the increase in the Nikkei had a large bubble component and that the later fall was largely a bursting of that bubble.

Whatever its origin, the rapid fall in stock prices had a major impact on spending and, in turn, a big impact on output. Table 22-4 shows the evolution of GDP growth, consumption growth, and investment growth from 1988 to 1993. Investment, which had been very strong during the rise of the Nikkei, collapsed. In contrast to the Great Depression—where consumption fell sharply after the stock market crash—consumption was less affected. But the strength in consumption was not enough to avoid a sharp decline in total spending and in GDP growth, from 6.5% in 1999 to 0.2% in 1993.

In short, there is no mystery as to how the Japanese slump started. The more difficult question to answer is why it continued for more than a decade. After all, perhaps the main lesson from the Great Depression was that macroeconomic policies could and should be used to help the economy recover. Were they used in Japan? If so, why did they fail? These are the next two questions we take up.

See the discussion of the effects of stock prices on consumption and investment in both Chapters 16 and 17.

The Failure of Monetary and Fiscal Policy

Monetary policy was used in Japan, but it was used too late. When it was eventually used, it faced the twin problems of the liquidity trap and deflation we discussed in Section 22-1.

The point is made in Figure 22-12, which shows the evolution of the nominal interest rate and the real interest rate in Japan since 1990. (Because we do not observe

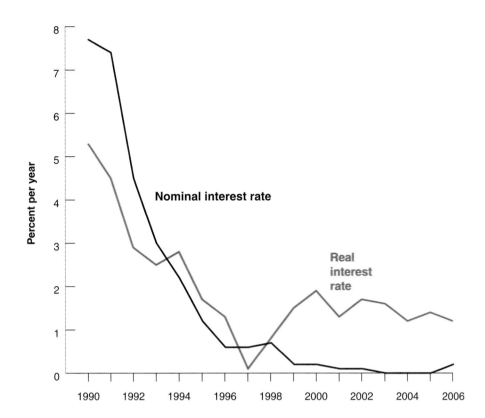

Figure 22-12 ■

The Nominal Interest Rate and the Real Interest Rate in Japan since 1990

Japan has been in a liquidity trap since the mid-1990s: The nominal interest rate has been close to zero, and the inflation rate has been negative. Even at a zero nominal interest rate, the real interest rate has been positive.

expected inflation, I construct the real interest rate as the nominal interest rate minus actual—rather than expected—inflation.)

The nominal interest rate was high in 1990, close to 8%. This was in part because the Bank of Japan (often referred to as the *BoJ*), worried about the rise of the Nikkei, had tried to decrease stock prices by increasing the interest rate. With inflation around 2%, this nominal interest rate implied a real interest rate of about 6%. As growth slowed down, the BoJ cut the nominal interest rate. But it did so slowly, and by 1996, when the nominal interest rate was down to less than 1%, the cumulative effect of low growth was such that inflation had turned to deflation. As a result, the real interest rate was higher than the nominal interest rate. Since the mid-1990s, Japan has been in a liquidity trap. The nominal short-term interest rate has been very close to zero. At the same time, unemployment has remained high, leading to deflation and therefore to a positive real interest rate.

Fiscal policy was used as well. Figure 22-13 shows what has happened to tax revenues and to government spending as a proportion of GDP since 1990. It shows how, as the slump lasted, the Japanese government both decreased taxes and increased spending, with the budget deficit reaching 8% of GDP in 2003. Since then, the deficit has been reduced, but it remains large. Much of the increased spending has taken the form of public work projects, many of them of doubtful usefulness. But from the point of view of increasing demand, one project is as good as another, and so this increase in government spending should have contributed to an overall increase in demand.

Has it? The economists who have looked at this question have concluded that it has, but that it was just not enough to increase spending and output. Put another way, in the absence of increased government spending, output would have declined even more. Could the Japanese government have done more? Probably not. High government spending and low taxes have led to a long string of government deficits and a steady accumulation of government debt. The ratio of government debt to GDP has

◀ Recall that the stock price depends positively on current and expected future dividends, and negatively on current and future interest rates.

◀ A joke circulating in Japan is that, by the time the Japanese economy has recovered, the entire shoreline of the Japanese archipelago will be covered in concrete.

Figure 22-13

Government Spending and Revenues (as a percentage of GDP) in Japan since 1990

Government spending increased and government revenues decreased steadily throughout the 1990s, leading to steadily larger deficits.

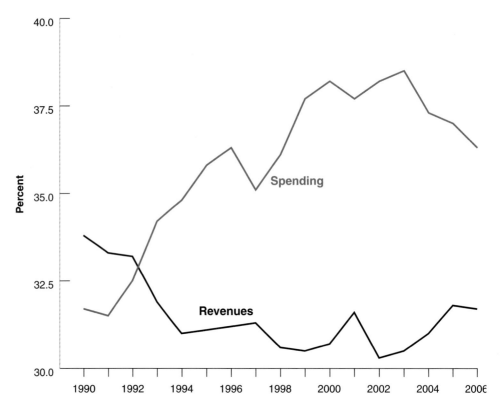

increased from 13.0% of GDP in 1991 to 90% of GDP in 2006. With a near-zero interest rate on government bonds, interest payments on the debt are small. But if the interest rate were to increase in the future, interest payments might represent a very heavy

▶ burden on the government budget. A more expansionary fiscal policy would have led to even higher levels of debt, and the Japanese government became increasingly reluctant to do so as the slump continued.

At an interest rate of 1% per year, a 90% debt-to-GDP ratio results in interest payments equal to 0.9% of GDP. At an interest rate of, say, 6% per year, the same debt-to-GDP ratio results in interest payments equal to 5.4% of GDP, a much heavier interest rate charge for the government.

The Japanese Recovery

Output growth in Japan has increased since 2003, and most economists cautiously predict that the recovery will continue. This raises a final question: What are the factors behind the current recovery? There appear to be two main factors.

A Regime Change in Monetary Policy

In the strange world of the liquidity trap, higher expected inflation is good. At a zero nominal interest rate, higher expected inflation implies a lower real interest rate. A lower real interest rate stimulates spending. Higher spending leads to higher output and lower unemployment.

Note the symmetry with our discussion in Chapter 9 of whether a central bank can achieve disinflation at little or no output cost. The answer there was: If the central bank can credibly convince people that inflation will be lower, it may be able to achieve lower inflation at little output cost.

This suggests that, even if the nominal interest rate is already equal to zero and thus cannot be reduced further, the central bank might still be able to lower the real interest rate by affecting inflation expectations. This may not be easy to do: Suppose the central bank announces an *inflation target*, a rate of inflation it will try to achieve over the next few years. If people believe the announcement, then expected inflation will indeed increase, helping the economy get out of the slump. But if people do not believe

▶ the announcement and continue to expect deflation, then deflation will continue.

Therefore, the advice given to the BoJ by many economists during the second half of the 1990s was that it should try to influence and increase inflation expectations. At worse, this would not work; at best, it might get the economy out of the slump. In 2003, the new chairman of the BoJ decided to follow this advice. He announced that the BoJ was now committed to keeping the nominal interest rate equal to zero until there was strong evidence of sustained inflation. Just like in 1933 in the United States, this statement was perceived as a signal of regime change in monetary policy, and it appears to have changed inflation expectations. Although the current inflation rate is still negative, inflation is now expected to become positive in the future, and the long-term real interest rate has fallen. This appears to be one of the factors behind a strong increase in investment spending since 2003.

The Cleanup of the Banking System

It became clear in the 1990s that the banking system in Japan was in trouble. Largely as a result of the slump in output, many firms were doing poorly, and banks carried on their books many *bad loans*, loans that the borrowers were not able to repay. (Why this was and how it happened are discussed in the Focus box "The Japanese Banking Problem.") Many "bad firms"—firms that were incurring losses and should have closed—continued to be financed by the banks and so continued to operate. At the same time, as a large proportion of bank financing continued to go to the firms with bad loans, "good firms,"—firms with good prospects and good investment projects—could not find financing and thus could not invest. In short, bad loans further depressed investment spending and thus aggregate demand. And, by keeping low-productivity firms afloat, they also reduced aggregate supply.

In such a case, the appropriate policy is clear: Banks that have made too many bad loans should be forced to either close or restructure. Firms that cannot pay their loans should be forced to do the same. These measures achieve two goals: First, they eliminate the bad firms, leading eventually—as these firms are replaced by more productive ones—to higher productivity and to a higher natural level of output. Second, they allow firms with good investment projects to find the funds they need to invest, leading to an increase in investment spending and, therefore, to an increase in demand and output.

It is equally clear, however, that such a policy is politically very risky. Restructuring or closing firms and banks leads initially to layoffs, a politically unpopular outcome, especially when unemployment is already high. For this reason, not much was done to solve the banking problem in Japan in the 1990s. Banks continued to lend to bad firms, and the proportion of bad loans steadily increased. Since 2002, however, the government has put increasing pressure on banks to reduce bad loans, and banks have, in turn, put increasing pressure on bad firms to restructure or close. The proportion of bad loans has been falling, and good firms have been increasingly able to finance investment. This is another factor behind the strong increase in investment spending since 2003.

A number of other factors are also helping Japan recover. In particular, strong output growth in the rest of Asia, particularly in China, has led to strong export growth in Japan. Even if export growth were to fall, however, the regime change in monetary policy, coupled with the cleanup of the banking system, implies that domestic spending might increase enough to sustain growth in the future. This is why most economists are now more optimistic about future growth in Japan than they have been at any other time since 1990.

The Japanese Banking Problem

FOCUS

Like the Great Depression in the United States, the sharp decrease in output growth in Japan in the early 1990s left many firms unable to repay their bank loans.

The situation was made worse by two facts:

First, in the 1980s, the banks had started losing their best borrowers—the large Japanese firms. These large firms increasingly financed themselves by issuing bonds rather than by borrowing from banks. As a result, banks had made loans to more risky borrowers, some of which would have a hard time repaying them even in the absence of a slump.

Second, to make matters worse, many of the firms had used land as collateral ("collateral" is an asset that the borrower promises to give to the bank if the loan is not repaid). The problem is that land prices collapsed along with the stock market in the early 1990s. As a result, the value of that collateral collapsed as well.

During the Great Depression, bad bank loans had led to a series of bank failures and bank runs (see the Focus box "Bank Runs" in Chapter 4). Indeed, one of the lessons of the Great Depression was that, to prevent such bank runs, governments should provide insurance to the depositors. Federal deposit insurance was introduced in 1934 in the United States, and similar insurance systems were later put into place in most other countries, including Japan.

Deposit insurance solves one problem: It eliminates the risk of bank runs. But it creates other problems, which were in evidence in Japan in the 1990s. To understand what these problems are, think of a bank that has the balance sheet described in Figure 1:

- On the asset side, it has one loan for $100.

- On the liability side, it has $50 in deposits.

- The net worth of the bank—the difference between assets and liabilities—is therefore $100 − $50 = $50.

(Note two differences between this balance sheet and the balance sheets we studied in Chapter 4. First, here I ignore reserves. They were important for the arguments developed in Chapter 4; they are not important here. Second, I assumed in Chapter 4 that assets were equal to liabilities—in other words, that net worth was zero. In

reality, net worth is typically positive, and this plays an important role here.)

Now suppose the loan goes bad: The firm to which the loan was made cannot pay any of it back. What should happen?

- The value of the loan is now zero: The bank should write the loan off. The bank still owes $50 in deposits but cannot pay them back. Thus, deposit insurance should pay $50 to the depositors, and the bank should close.

- But that is unlikely to happen. To keep his job, the manager of the bank might pretend that nothing has happened, and the loan is still good. Indeed, he might decide to lend even more to the firm so the firm can repay the old loan. This way, it looks like business as usual. This is clearly throwing good money after bad, but by doing so, the manager buys time and keeps his job, at least for some time.

- Even the owners of the bank might go along. If the bank closes now, they lose everything (net worth is clearly equal to zero). If there is a slight chance that the firm will recover and be able to pay the bank back, they may end up with positive net worth (this is known as "gambling for resurrection"). So, even if the odds of the firm repaying the loan are very low, the bank may continue to lend to the firm.

- Depositors do not care what the bank does: Their deposits are insured, whatever the bank does. Even the bank's regulator, if there is one, might prefer to close his eyes: Acknowledging the existence of bad loans, and the fact that the bank must be closed, might reflect badly on him—again, better to wait.

The result: Banks are likely to renew the bad loans, or even make new loans to the bad firms, at the expense of good firms. And so, the more time passes, the worse the problem of bad loans becomes.

This is exactly what happened in Japan in the 1990s. Until 1993, Japanese banks did not disclose any information about their bad loans. Beginning in 1993, they reluctantly acknowledged the presence of bad loans on their books. The total amount of bad loans (self-reported by banks) steadily increased, from 12 trillion yen in 1993, to 30 trillion yen in 1998, to 44 trillion yen in 2001. But even that amount was far below the true number, and a 2001 estimate by the OECD put the total value of bad loans at more than twice the reported amount. Progress has since been made, the major banks are now healthier, and Japan is slowly taking care of its banking problem.

Assets	Liabilities
Loan: $100	Deposits: $50 Net worth: $50

Figure 1 *The Bank's Balance Sheet*

Pathologies   **Extensions**

Summary

- In general, a recession leads to a decrease in inflation. Given nominal money growth, the decrease in inflation leads to an increase in real money growth, a decrease in the nominal interest rate, and a return of output to its natural level.

- One reason this adjustment mechanism may fail is that the decrease in inflation may lead to an increase in the real interest rate. If the decrease in expected inflation is larger than the decrease in the nominal interest rate, the real interest rate will increase. Because spending depends on the real interest rate, the increase in the real interest rate will lead to a further decrease in output.

- Monetary policy can be used to decrease the nominal interest rate further, which helps increase output. Monetary policy, however, cannot decrease the nominal interest rate below zero. When this happens, the economy is said to be in a liquidity trap.

- The combination of a liquidity trap and deflation can transform a recession into a slump or a depression. If the nominal interest rate is zero, and the economy is experiencing a deflation, the real interest rate is positive and may be too high to lead to an increase in spending and output. Output may continue to decline, leading to higher deflation, a higher real interest rate, and so on.

On the Great Depression in the United States:

- The unemployment rate increased from 3.2% in 1929 to 24.9% in 1933.

- The initial cause of this increase in unemployment was a large adverse shift in demand, brought about by the stock market crash of 1929 and the resulting increase in uncertainty about the future.

- The result of high unemployment was a large deflation from 1929 to 1933.

- The favorable effect of the decrease in the price level on the real money stock was offset by a roughly equal decrease in nominal money. This decrease in nominal money was due to bank failures and a decrease in the money multiplier. The main effect of deflation was a large increase in the real interest rate, leading to a further decrease in demand and output.

- Recovery started in 1933. Average output growth from 1933 to 1941 was high, at 7.7% per year. Unemployment decreased, but it was still equal to 9.9% in 1941. In contrast to the predictions of the Phillips curve, deflation turned into inflation from 1934 on, despite a very high unemployment rate.

- Many questions remain about the recovery. What is clear is that high nominal money growth, leading to high real money growth, was an important factor in the recovery.

On the Japanese slump:

- After a long period of high output growth, Japan has had very low growth since 1992. This period of long growth is called the Japanese slump.

- The slump was triggered by the fall of Japanese stock prices at the end of the 1980s, which led to a sharp decrease in investment spending and, in turn, to a decrease in output.

- Monetary policy was used to try to increase output in the 1990s. But Japan went into a liquidity trap, with a nominal interest rate very close to zero. Because Japan was experiencing deflation, the real interest rate remained positive.

- Fiscal policy was also used to try to increase output in the 1990s. But government debt has increased to 90% of GDP, and the Japanese government has been reluctant to increase its debt much further.

- Since 2003, output growth has been positive, and it appears that Japan is getting out of the slump. The main factors behind this output growth are a change in the monetary policy regime, an improvement in the banking system, and strong export growth.

Key Terms

- depression, 491
- slump, 491
- liquidity trap, 496
- New Deal, 504
- National Recovery Administration (NRA), 504
- National Industrial Recovery Act (NIRA), 504

Questions and Problems

Quick Check

1. Using the information in this chapter, label each of the following statements true, false, or uncertain. Explain briefly.

a. A nominal interest rate of zero should be enough to strongly stimulate spending and avoid a recession.

b. The impact of the stock market crash in 1929 was compounded by a major policy mistake, a large decrease in the nominal money stock.

c. Since the mid 1990s, the nominal short term interest rate in Japan has been very close to zero. At the same time unemployment has remained high, leading to deflation, and therefore a negative real interest rate.

d. The decrease in the unemployment rate explains why deflation ended during the Great Depression.

e. The Japanese slump of the 1990s and 2000s was triggered by the sharp fall of Japanese stock prices at the end of the 1980s.

2. Active monetary policy

a. Consider an economy with output below the natural level of output. How could the central bank use monetary policy to return the economy to its natural level of output? Illustrate your answer in an *IS–LM* diagram.

b. Again suppose that output is below the natural level. This time, however, assume that the central bank does not change monetary policy. Under normal circumstances, how does the economy return to its natural level of output? Illustrate your answer in an *IS–LM* diagram.

c. Considering your answer to part (b), if the central bank does nothing, what is likely to happen to expected inflation? How does this change in expected inflation affect the *IS–LM* diagram? Does output move closer to the natural level?

d. Consider the following policy advice: "Because the economy always returns to the natural level of output on its own, the Fed does not need to concern itself with recessions." Do your answers to parts (a) through (c) support this advice?

3. Monetary versus fiscal policy

a. Consider an economy with output below the natural level and a nominal interest rate equal to zero. Illustrate this economy in an *IS–LM* diagram.

b. Under normal circumstances, how does the economy return to the natural level of output? (Refer to your answer to problem 2(b).) Does this adjustment mechanism work when the nominal interest rate equals zero?

c. Suppose the central bank wants to use monetary policy to return the economy to its natural level of output. Can it do so when the nominal interest rate is equal to zero? What happens if the central bank tries to use expansionary monetary policy? Illustrate your answer in an *IS–LM* diagram.

d. In principle, can fiscal policy be used to restore the economy to its natural level of output when the nominal interest rate equals zero? If so, explain how the appropriate policy affects output. If not, explain why not.

e. Consider the following policy advice: "Because the Fed can act to keep the economy at the natural level of output, the federal government should never use fiscal policy to stimulate the economy." Do your answers to parts (a) through (d) support this advice?

Dig Deeper

4. Long-term unemployment and the natural rate

Suppose that the markup is 5%, so that the price-setting equation is given by

$$\frac{W}{P} = \frac{1}{(1 + 0.05)}$$

Suppose that the wage-setting equation is given by

$$\frac{W}{P} = 1 - (u_S + 0.5\,u_L)$$

where u_S and u_L denote short-term and long-term unemployment rates. In particular, u_S is the number of short-term unemployed, divided by the labor force, and u_L is the number of long-term unemployed, divided by the labor force.

Assume that $u_L = \beta u$ and $u_S = (1 - \beta)u$, where u is the overall unemployment rate and

$$0 < \beta < 1$$

a. According to the wage-setting equation, which type of unemployment has a greater impact on wages—long term or short term? Does this make sense to you? Explain.

b. Derive the natural rate of unemployment. [*Hint:* Substitute $u_L = \beta\,u$ and $u_S = (1 - \beta)\,u$ in the wage-setting equation. The natural rate will depend on β.]

c. Compute the natural rate if $\beta = 0.0, 0.4, 0.8$. Explain.

5. Long-term unemployment and inflation

Recall equation (8.10):

$$\pi_t - \pi_{t-1} = -\alpha(u_t - u_n)$$

a. Interpret the equation. Why does higher unemployment lead to lower inflation, given past inflation? Graph equation (8.10) in a diagram, with the change in inflation on the vertical axis and the unemployment rate on the horizontal axis.

b. Write the overall unemployment rate, u, as $u = u_S + u_L$, with u_S (the short-term unemployment rate) and u_L (the long-term unemployment rate) defined as in problem 4. Using this definition, substitute for u_t in equation (8.10).

c. Now assume that the long-term unemployed have no effect on wage bargaining. Show how equation (8.10) should be modified to fit this assumption.

d. Assume further that $u_L = \beta\,u$ and $u_S = (1 - \beta)\,u$, as in problem 4(b). Substitute the appropriate equality into your revised equation in part (c) to get a relation between the change in inflation and the unemployment rate, u_t. Graph your new equation as in part (a).

e. Suppose the proportion of long-term unemployed in unemployment increases (i.e., β increases). Show what happens to the line you drew in part (d).

f. Look at the line you drew in part (e). Suppose policymakers want to reduce inflation (so that the desired change in inflation is negative). If the proportion of long-term unemployed increases, how will this affect the unemployment rate required to achieve a given reduction in inflation? Does the cost of disinflation increase or decrease?

g. Now suppose that policymakers fear disinflation and are hoping that the inflation rate will increase. Does an increase in the proportion of long-term unemployed tend to imply a larger or smaller increase in inflation? How might your analysis be relevant to our understanding of the recovery from the Great Depression?

Explore Further

6. Japan's future

As we discussed in Chapter 15, the yield curve slopes up (down) when financial market participants expect short-term interest rates to increase (decrease) in the future. Go to the Web site of The Economist *magazine (**www.economist.com**). Find the "Markets & Data" section. In the section "Economic and Financial Indicators," you should be able to obtain three-month, two-year, and 10-year interest rates for Japan.*

a. What is the three-month interest rate in Japan? Is it still near zero? What is the two-year interest rate in Japan? Does the difference between the two-year and three-month interest rates suggest that financial market participants expect Japan to escape the liquidity trap in the near future?

b. Now compare the 10-year interest rate in Japan to the three-month interest rate. Does the difference between these two interest rates suggest that investors expect that Japan will escape the liquidity trap within a decade?

c. Now look at the most recent data on inflation and growth for Japan (probably under the title "Output, Prices, and Jobs" on *The Economist* Web site) and the forecasts for these variables for the near future. Do these data suggest that Japan will soon escape the liquidity trap?

d. Now look at data for economies other than Japan. Consider advanced and emerging economies. Is inflation low or negative (or forecast to be low or negative) in economies other than Japan? If so, look at the growth rates and short-term interest rates for these economies. Are any of these economies close to a liquidity trap?

 We invite you to visit the Blanchard page on the Prentice Hall Web site, at:
www.prenhall.com/blanchard
for this chapter's World Wide Web exercises.

Further Readings

- For more on the Great Depression: Lester Chandler, *America's Greatest Depression,* Harper & Row, New York, 1970, gives the basic facts. So does John A. Garraty, *The Great Depression*, Harcourt Brace Jovanovich, New York, 1986.

- Peter Temin, *Did Monetary Forces Cause the Great Depression?* W.W. Norton, New York, 1976, looks specifically at the macroeconomic issues. So do the articles in a symposium on the Great Depression in the Spring 1993 issue of the *Journal of Economic Perspectives*.

- For a look at the Great Depression in countries besides the United States, read Peter Temin, *Lessons from the Great Depression*, MIT Press, Cambridge, MA, 1989.

- For the argument that the NIRA actually slowed down the recovery, read Harold Cole and Lee Ohanian, "The Great Depression in the United States from a Neoclassical Perspective," *Federal Reserve Bank of Minneapolis Quarterly Review*, Winter 1999.

- A description of the Great Depression through the eyes of those who suffered through it is given in Studs Terkel, *Hard Times: An Oral History of the Great Depression in America*, Pantheon Books, New York, 1970.

- A good book on the Japanese economy, although a bit out of date, is Takatoshi Ito, *The Japanese Economy*, MIT Press, Cambridge, MA, 1992.

- Adam Posen, *Restoring Japan's Economic Growth*, Institute for International Studies, Washington, DC, 1998, discusses the Japanese slump.

- Ben Bernanke, Vincent Reinhart, and Brian Sack, *An Empirical Assessment of Monetary Policy, Alternatives at the Zero Bound*, Brookings Papers on Economic Activity, Washington, DC, 2004, discusses what monetary policy can and cannot do when the economy is in a liquidity trap.

CHAPTER 23

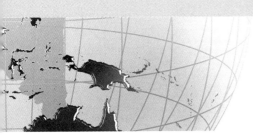

n 1913, the value of all currency circulating in Germany was 6 billion marks. Ten years later, in October 1923, 6 billion marks was barely enough to buy a 1-kilo loaf of rye bread in Berlin. A month later, the price of the same loaf of bread had increased to 428 billion marks.

The German hyperinflation of the early 1920s is probably the most famous hyperinflation. (**Hyperinflation** simply means very high inflation.) But it is not the only one. Table 23-1 summarizes the seven major hyperinflations that followed World War I and World War II. They share a number of features. They were all short (lasting a year or so) but intense, with inflation running at 50% per month or more. In all, the increases in the price levels were staggering. As you can see, the largest price increase actually occured not in Germany, but in Hungary after World War II. What cost 1 Hungarian pengö in August 1945 cost 3,800 trillions of trillions of pengös less than a year later.

Such rates of inflation had not been seen before, nor have they been seen since. The closest in the recent past occured in Bolivia in 1984 and 1985. From January 1984 to September 1985, Bolivian inflation averaged 40% per month—a roughly 1,000-fold increase in the price

517

Table 23-1   Seven Hyperinflations of the 1920s and 1940s

	Beginning	End	P_T/P_0	Average Monthly Inflation Rate (%)	Average Monthly Money Growth (%)
Austria	Oct. 1921	Aug. 1922	70	47	31
Germany	Aug. 1922	Nov. 1923	1.0×10^{10}	322	314
Greece	Nov. 1943	Nov. 1944	4.7×10^{6}	365	220
Hungary 1	Mar. 1923	Feb. 1924	44	46	33
Hungary 2	Aug. 1945	Jul. 1946	3.8×10^{27}	19,800	12,200
Poland	Jan. 1923	Jan. 1924	699	82	72
Russia	Dec. 1921	Jan. 1924	1.2×10^{5}	57	49

Note: P_T/P_0 is the price level in the last month of hyperinflation divided by the price level in the first month.

Source: Philip Cagan, "The Monetary Dynamics of Hyperinflation," in Milton Friedman, ed., *Studies in the Quantity Theory of Money,* University of Chicago Press, Chicago, 1956, Table 1.

level over 21 months. (With an inflation rate of 40% per month, the price level at the end of 21 months is $(1 + 0.4)^{21} = 1,171$ times the price level at the beginning.) But many countries, especially in Latin America, have struggled with prolonged bouts of high inflation. Table 23-2 gives the average monthly inflation rates for four Latin American countries from 1976 to 2000. All four had at least five years with average monthly inflation running above 20% per month. Both Argentina and Brazil had monthly inflation rates in excess of 10% per month for more than a decade. All four countries have now returned to low inflation. Today, inflation is low in nearly all countries. The only exception is Zimbabwe, where, as of mid 2007, the monthly inflation rate was around 25%.

What causes hyperinflations? You saw in Chapter 9 that inflation ultimately comes from nominal money growth. The relation between nominal money growth and inflation is confirmed by the last two columns of Table 23-1. Note how, in each country, high inflation was associated with correspondingly high nominal money growth. Why was nominal money growth so high? The answer turns out to be common to all hyperinflations: Nominal money growth is high because the budget deficit is high. The budget deficit is high because the economy is affected by major shocks that make it difficult or impossible for the government to finance its expenditures in any way other than by money creation.

In this chapter, we look at this answer in more detail, relying on examples from various hyperinflations:

■ Section 23-1 looks at the relation between the budget deficit and money creation.

■ Section 23-2 looks at the relation between inflation and real money balances.

Table 23-2   High Inflation in Latin America, 1976 to 2000

	Average Monthly Inflation Rate, %				
	1976–1980	1981–1985	1986–1990	1991–1995	1996–2000
Argentina	9.3	12.7	20.0	2.3	0.0
Brazil	3.4	7.9	20.7	19.0	0.6
Nicaragua	1.4	3.6	35.6	8.5	0.8
Peru	3.4	6.0	23.7	4.8	0.8

Source: International Financial Statistics, IMF, various issues.

Pathologies   **Extensions**

- Section 23-3 puts the two together and shows how a large budget deficit can lead to high and increasing inflation.

- Section 23-4 looks at how hyperinflations end.

- Section 23-5 draws conclusions from our two chapters on pathologies—depressions and slumps in Chapter 22, and high inflation in this chapter. ■

23-1 Budget Deficits and Money Creation

A government can finance its budget deficit in one of two ways:

- It can borrow, the way you or I would. We borrow by taking out a loan. Governments borrow by issuing bonds.
- It can do something that neither you nor I can do: It can, in effect, finance the deficit by creating money. I say "in effect" because, as you remember from Chapter 4, governments do not create money; the central bank creates money. But with the central bank's cooperation, the government can, in effect, finance itself through money creation: It can issue bonds and ask the central bank to buy them. The central bank then pays the government with money it creates, and the government uses that money to finance its deficit. This process is called **debt monetization**.

Most of the time and in most countries, deficits are financed primarily through borrowing rather than through money creation. But at the start of hyperinflations, two changes usually take place:

- There is a budget crisis. The source is typically a major social or economic upheaval:

   It may be a civil war or a revolution that destroys the state's ability to collect taxes. This was the case, for example, in Nicaragua in the 1980s.

   It may come from the aftermath of a war that leaves the government with both smaller tax revenues and the large expenditures needed for reconstruction. This is what happened in Germany in 1922 and 1923. Burdened with payments for the war (called *war reparations*) it had to pay to Allied forces, Germany had a budget deficit equal to more than two-thirds of its expenditures.

   It may come from a large adverse economic shock—for example, a large decline in the price of a raw material that is both the country's major export and its main source of revenues. As you will see in this chapter's Focus box on the Bolivian hyperinflation, this is what happened in Bolivia in the 1980s. The decline in the price of tin, Bolivia's principal export, was one of the main causes of the Bolivian hyperinflation.

   It may come from a bad policy decision. This is the case for Zimbabwe, where the decision to redistribute land away from white farmers in 2000 led to a catastrophic decline in agricultural output, and, in turn, a large fall of GDP and a large increase in the budget deficit.

- The government becomes increasingly unable to borrow from the public or from abroad to finance its deficit. The reason is the size of the deficit itself. Worried that the government might not be able to repay the debt in the future, potential lenders start asking the government for higher and higher interest rates. Sometimes, foreign lenders decide to stop lending to the government altogether. As a result, the government increasingly turns to the other source of finance—money creation. Eventually, most of the deficit is financed through money creation.

How large is the rate of nominal money growth needed to finance a given amount of revenues?

We are taking a shortcut here. ▶
What should be on the right side
of equation (23.1) is H, the monetary base—that's the money
created by the central bank—
not M, the money stock (which
includes both currency and
checkable deposits). I ignore the
distinction here.

- Let M be the nominal money stock, measured, say, at the end of each month. (In the case of hyperinflation, things change so quickly that it is useful to look at what happens from month to month rather than from quarter to quarter or from year to year.) Let ΔM be the change in the nominal money stock from the end of last month to the end of this month—nominal money creation during the month.
- The revenue, in real terms (that is, in terms of goods), that the government generates by creating an amount of money equal to ΔM is therefore $\Delta M/P$—nominal money creation during the month divided by the price level. This real revenue from money creation is called **seignorage**. The word is revealing: The right to issue money was a precious source of revenue for the "seigneurs" of the past: They could buy the goods they wanted by issuing their own money and using it to pay for the goods.

We can summarize this as follows:

$$\text{Seignorage} = \frac{\Delta M}{P} \qquad (23.1)$$

Seignorage is equal to money creation divided by the price level. To see what rate of nominal money growth is required to generate a given amount of seignorage, note that we can rewrite $\Delta M/P$ as

$$\frac{\Delta M}{P} = \frac{\Delta M}{M}\frac{M}{P}$$

"Real money balances" is just ▶
another name for the real money
stock.

In words: We can think of seignorage ($\Delta M/P$) as the product of the rate of nominal money growth ($\Delta M/M$) and real money balances (M/P). The larger the real money balances held in the economy, the larger the amount of seignorage corresponding to a given rate of nominal money growth. Replacing this expression in equation (23.1) gives

$$\text{Seignorage} = \frac{\Delta M}{M}\frac{M}{P} \qquad (23.2)$$

Remember: Income is a flow. Y
here is real income per month. ▶

This gives us the relation we wanted between seignorage, the rate of nominal money growth, and real money balances. To think about relevant magnitudes, it is convenient to divide both sides of equation (23.2) by real income, Y (measured at a monthly rate):

$$\frac{\text{Seignorage}}{Y} = \frac{\Delta M}{M}\left(\frac{M/P}{Y}\right) \qquad (23.3)$$

Suppose the government is running a budget deficit equal to 10% of real income and decides to finance it through seignorage, so deficit/Y = seignorage/Y = 0.1. Suppose people hold real balances equal to two months of income, so $(M/P)/Y = 2$. This implies that nominal money growth must satisfy

$$\frac{\Delta M}{M} \times 2 = 0.1 \Rightarrow \frac{\Delta M}{M} = 0.05$$

To finance a deficit of 10% of real income through seignorage, the monthly growth rate of nominal money must be equal to 5%.

Does this mean that the government can finance a deficit equal to 20% of real income through a rate of nominal money growth of 10%, a deficit of 40% of real income through a rate of nominal money growth of 20%, and so on? No. As nominal money growth increases, so does inflation. And as inflation increases, the opportunity cost of holding money increases, leading people to reduce their real money balances. In terms of equation (23.2), an increase in nominal money growth $\Delta M/M$ leads to a decrease in real money balances M/P, so that an increase in nominal money growth will generate a less-than-proportional increase in seignorage. What is crucial here is how much people adjust their real money balances in response to inflation, and it is the issue to which we turn next.

Before we do, let's summarize what we learned in this section: Seignorage—the amount of revenues the government gets from money creation—is equal to the product of the rate of nominal money growth and real money balances.

23-2 Inflation and Real Money Balances

What determines the amount of real money balances that people are willing to hold? And how does this amount depend on nominal money growth?

Let's go back to the *LM* relation we derived in Chapter 5:

$$\frac{M}{P} = YL(i)$$
$$(-)$$

Higher real income leads people to hold larger real money balances. A higher nominal interest rate increases the opportunity cost of holding money rather than bonds and leads people to reduce their real money balances.

The equation holds in both stable economic times and times of hyperinflation. But in times of hyperinflation, we can simplify it further. Here's how:

■ First, rewrite the *LM* relation using the relation between the nominal interest rate and the real interest rate, $i = r + \pi^e$:

Recall, from Chapter 14, that $r = i - \pi^e$. Equivalently, $i = r + \pi^e$.

$$\frac{M}{P} = YL(r + \pi^e)$$

Real money balances depend on real income, Y, on the real interest rate, r, and on expected inflation, π^e.

■ Second, note that, while all three variables *(Y, r,* and π^e) vary over time during a hyperinflation, expected inflation is likely to move much more than the other two variables: During a typical hyperinflation, actual inflation—and presumably expected inflation—may move by 20% per month or more from one month to the next.

So it is not a bad approximation to assume that both income and the real interest rate are constant and focus on just the movements in expected inflation. So we write

$$\frac{M}{P} = \overline{Y}L(\overline{r} + \pi^e) \qquad (23.4)$$
$$(\quad - \quad)$$

where the bars over *Y* and *r* mean that we now take both income and the real interest rate as constant. In times of hyperinflation, equation (23.4) tells us we can think of real money balances as depending primarily on the expected rate of inflation. As expected inflation increases and it becomes more and more costly to hold money, people will reduce their real money balances.

In describing the Austrian hyper-inflation of the 1920s, Keynes noted: "In Vienna, during the period of collapse, mushroom exchange banks sprang up at every street corner, where you could change your krone into Zurich francs within a few minutes of receiving them, and so ▶ avoid the risk of loss during the time it would take you to reach your usual bank."

One of the hopes of the European Union is that the euro may ▶ replace the dollar as the foreign currency of choice. (Why would the European Union want this to happen?) If it happens, we may have to speak of "euroization" rather than of "dollarization."

A scatter diagram plots one variable against another. ▶

This decrease in real money balances explains why, in Table 23-1, average inflation is higher-than-average nominal money growth during each of ▶ the seven postwar hyperinflations: That real money balances, M/P, decrease during a hyperinflation implies that prices, P, must increase more than M. In other words, average inflation must be higher than average nominal money growth.

During a hyperinflation, people indeed find many ways to reduce their real money balances. When the monthly rate of inflation is 100%, for example, currency kept for a month will lose half of its real value (because things cost twice as much a month later). **Barter**, the exchange of goods for other goods rather than for money, increases. Payments for wages become much more frequent—often twice weekly. When people are paid, they rush to stores to buy goods. Despite the fact that the government often makes it illegal for its citizens to use currencies other than the one it is printing, people shift to foreign currencies as stores of value. And even if it is illegal, an increasing number of transactions take place in foreign currency. During the Latin American hyperinflations of the 1980s, people shifted to U.S. dollars. The shift to dollars has become so widespread in the world that it has a name: **dollarization** (that is, the use of dollars in another country's domestic transactions).

By how much do real money balances actually decrease as inflation increases? Figure 23-1 examines the evidence from the Hungarian hyperinflation of the early 1920s and provides some insights:

■ Figure 23-1(a) plots real money balances and the monthly inflation rate from November 1922 to February 1924. Note how movements in inflation are reflected in opposite movements in real money balances. The short-lived decline in Hungarian inflation from July to October 1923 is reflected in an equally short-lived increase in real money balances. At the end of the hyperinflation in February 1924, real money balances were roughly half what they had been at the beginning.

■ Figure 23-1(b) presents the same information as Figure 23-1(a), but in the form of a scatter diagram. It plots monthly real money balances on the horizontal axis against inflation on the vertical axis. (We do not observe expected inflation, which is the variable we would like to plot, so I use actual inflation instead.) Note how the points nicely describe a downward-sloping demand for money: As actual inflation—and presumably, expected inflation as well—increases, the demand for money strongly decreases.

Let's summarize what we learned in this section: Increases in expected inflation lead people to decrease their use of money and to decrease their real money balances.

23-3 Deficits, Seignorage, and Inflation

We have derived two relations:

■ The relation between seignorage, nominal money growth, and real money balances [equation (23.2)]. Seignorage is equal to the product of nominal money growth and real money balances.

■ The relation between real money balances and expected inflation [equation (23.4)]. An increase in expected inflation leads people to decrease their real money balances.

Combining the two equations gives

$$\text{Seignorage} = \left(\frac{\Delta M}{M}\right)\left(\frac{M}{P}\right)$$

$$= \left(\frac{\Delta M}{M}\right)\left[\bar{Y}L(\bar{r} + \pi^e)\right] \qquad (23.5)$$

The first line repeats equation (23.2). The second line replaces real money balances by their expression in terms of expected inflation, from equation (23.4).

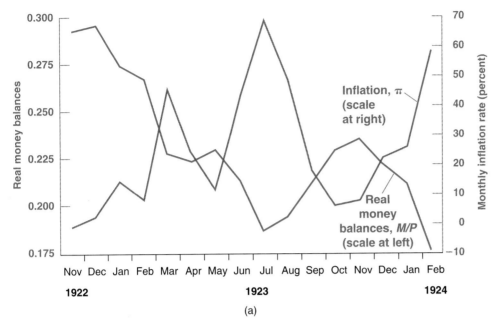

Figure 23-1

Inflation and Real Money Balances in Hungary, November 1922 to February 1924

At the end of the Hungarian hyperinflation, real money balances stood at roughly half their pre-hyperinflation level.

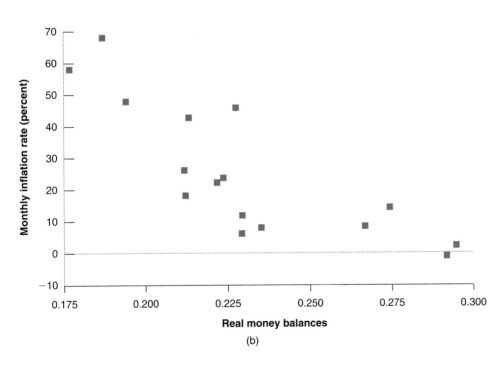

Equation (23.5) gives us what we need to show how the need to finance a large budget deficit through seignorage can lead not only to *high inflation* but also, as is the case during hyperinflations, to *high and increasing inflation.*

The Case of Constant Nominal Money Growth

Suppose the government chooses a *constant* rate of nominal money growth and maintains that rate forever. (Clearly, this is not what happens during hyperinflations, where the rate of nominal money growth typically increases over the course of the hyperinflation; we shall get more realistic later.) How much seignorage will this constant rate of nominal money growth generate?

If nominal money growth is constant forever, then inflation and expected inflation must eventually be constant as well. Assume, for simplicity, that output growth equals zero. Then, actual inflation and expected inflation must both equal nominal money growth:

Recall: In the medium run [equation (9.8)]:

$$\pi = g_m - \bar{g}_Y$$
$$\bar{g}_Y = 0 \Rightarrow \pi = g_m.$$

$$\pi^e = \pi = \frac{\Delta M}{M}$$

Replacing π^e with $\Delta M/M$ in equation (23.5) gives

$$\text{Seignorage} = \frac{\Delta M}{M}\left[\bar{Y} L\left(\bar{r} + \frac{\Delta M}{M}\right)\right] \qquad (23.6)$$

Note that nominal money growth, $\Delta M/M$, enters the equation in two places and has two opposite effects on seignorage:

$\Delta M/M$ increases $\Rightarrow$ Seignorage increases

- Given real money balances, nominal money growth increases seignorage. This effect is captured by the first term in $\Delta M/M$ in equation (23.6).

$\Delta M/M$ increases $\Rightarrow$ π increases $\Rightarrow$ π^e increases $\Rightarrow$ $L(\bar{r} + \pi^e)$ decreases $\Rightarrow$ M/P decreases $\Rightarrow$ Seignorage decreases.

- An increase in nominal money growth increases inflation and therefore decreases real money balances. This effect is captured by $\Delta M/M$ in the second term on the right in equation (23.6).

So the net effect of nominal money growth on seignorage is ambiguous. The empirical evidence is that the relation between seignorage and nominal money growth looks as shown in Figure 23-2.

The relation is hump shaped. When nominal money growth is low—the situation in Europe or the United States today—an increase in nominal money growth leads to a small reduction in real money balances. Thus, higher money growth leads to an increase in seignorage.

When nominal money growth (and therefore inflation) is very high however, the reduction in real money balances induced by higher nominal money growth becomes

Figure 23-2

Seignorage and Nominal Money Growth

Seignorage is first an increasing function, then a decreasing function of nominal money growth.

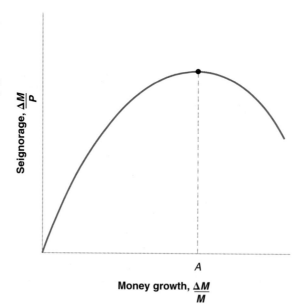

Pathologies   **Extensions**

larger and larger. Eventually, there is a rate of nominal money growth—point *A* in Figure 23-2—beyond which further increases in nominal money growth *decrease* seignorage.

The shape of the relation in Figure 23-2 may look familiar to those of you who have studied the economics of taxation. Income tax revenues equal the *tax rate on income* times income—the *tax base*. At low tax rates, the tax rate has little influence on how much people work, and tax revenues increase with the tax rate. But as tax rates increase further, some people start working less—or stop declaring part of their income—and the tax base decreases. As the income tax reaches very high levels, increases in the tax rate lead to a decline in tax revenues. Obviously, tax rates of 100% lead to no tax revenue at all: Why work if the government takes all your income?

This relation between tax revenues and the tax rate is often called the **Laffer curve**, after the economist Arthur Laffer, who argued in the early 1980s that a cut in U.S. tax rates would lead to more tax revenues. He was clearly wrong about where the United States was on the curve: Tax revenues went down, not up. But the general point still stands: When tax rates are high enough, a further increase in the tax rate can lead to a decrease in tax revenues.

◀ See the Focus box "Monetary Contraction and Fiscal Expansion: The United States in the Early 1980s" in Chapter 20.

There is more than a simple analogy here. Inflation can be thought of as a tax on money balances. The tax rate is the rate of inflation, π, which reduces the real value of money holdings. The tax base is real money balances, M/P. The product of these two variables, $\pi(M/P)$, is called the **inflation tax**. There is a subtle difference with other forms of taxation: What the government receives from money creation at any point in time is not the inflation tax but rather seignorage $(\Delta M/M)$ (M/P). However, the two are closely related. When nominal money growth is constant, inflation must eventually be equal to nominal money growth, so that

◀ If the inflation rate is 5%, you lose 5% of the value of your real money balances. It is as if you were paying a tax of 5% on these balances.

$$
\begin{aligned}
\text{Inflation tax} \ &= \ \pi \left(\frac{M}{P} \right) \\
&= \ \left(\frac{\Delta M}{M} \right) \left(\frac{M}{P} \right) \\
&= \ \text{Seignorage}
\end{aligned}
$$

What rate of nominal money growth leads to the *most seignorage*, and how much seignorage does it generate? These are the questions that Philip Cagan asked in a classic paper on hyperinflation written in 1956. In one of the earliest uses of econometrics, Cagan estimated the relation between the demand for money and expected inflation [equation (23.4)] during each of the hyperinflations in Table 23-1. Then, using equation (23.6), he computed the rate of nominal money growth that maximized seignorage and the associated amount of seignorage. The answers he obtained are given in the first two columns of Table 23-3. The third column repeats the actual nominal money growth numbers from Table 23-1.

Table 23-3 shows something very interesting: In all seven hyperinflations, actual average nominal money growth (column 3) far exceeded the rate of nominal money growth that maximizes seignorage (column 1). Compare the actual rate of nominal money growth in Hungary after World War II, 12,200% per month, to the rate of nominal money growth that would have maximized seignorage, 32% per month. This would seem to be a serious problem for the story we have developed so far. If the reason for money creation was to finance the budget deficit, why was the actual rate of nominal money growth so much higher than the number that maximizes seignorage? The answer lies in the dynamics of the economy's adjustment to high nominal money growth. We now turn to that.

Chapter 23   High Inflation

Table 23-3	Nominal Money Growth and Seignorage		
	Rate of Money Growth Maximizing Seignorage (% per month)	Implied Seignorage (% of output)	Actual Rate of Money Growth (% per month)
Austria	12	13	31
Germany	20	14	314
Greece	28	11	220
Hungary 1	12	19	33
Hungary 2	32	6	12,200
Poland	54	4.6	72
Russia	39	0.5	49

Note: Monthly rate of nominal money growth, in percent.

Source: Philip Cagan, "The Monetary Dynamics of Hyperinflation," in Milton Friedman, ed., *Studies in the Quantity Theory of Money*, University of Chicago Press, Chicago, 1956.

Dynamics and Increasing Inflation

Let's return to the argument we just developed: *If maintained forever*, a higher rate of nominal money growth will *eventually* lead to a proportional increase in both actual inflation and expected inflation and, therefore, to a decrease in real money balances. If nominal money growth is higher than the amount that maximizes seignorage, the increase in nominal money growth will lead to a decrease in seignorage.

The crucial words in the argument are *if maintained forever* and *eventually*. Consider a government that needs to finance a suddenly much larger deficit and decides to do so by creating money. As the rate of money growth increases, it may take a while for inflation and expected inflation to adjust. Even as expected inflation increases, it will take a while longer for people to fully adjust their real money balances: Creating barter arrangements takes time, the use of foreign currencies in transactions develops slowly, and so on.

Let's explore this argument more formally. Recall our equation for seignorage,

$$\text{Seignorage} = \left(\frac{\Delta M}{M}\right)\left(\frac{M}{P}\right)$$

- In the short run, an increase in the rate of nominal money growth, $\Delta M/M$, may lead to little change in real money balances, M/P. Put another way, if it is willing to increase nominal money growth sufficiently, a government will be able to generate nearly any amount of seignorage that it wants *in the short run*, far in excess of the numbers in the second column of Table 23-3.
- Over time, as prices adjust and real money balances decrease, the government will find that the same rate of nominal money growth yields less and less seignorage. (M/P will decrease, leading to lower seignorage for a given rate of nominal money growth, $\Delta M/M$.)
- So, if the government keeps trying to finance a deficit larger than the deficit shown in the second column of Table 23-3 (for example, if Austria tries to finance a deficit that is more than 13% of GDP), it will find that it cannot do so with a constant rate of nominal money growth. The only way it can succeed is by continually

increasing the rate of nominal money growth. This is why actual nominal money growth exceeds the numbers in the first column, and why hyperinflations are nearly always characterized by increasing nominal money growth and inflation.

There is also another effect at work, which we have ignored until now. We have taken the deficit as given. But as the inflation rate becomes very high, the budget deficit typically becomes larger as well. Part of the reason has to do with lags in tax collection. This effect is known as the **Tanzi-Olivera effect**, for Vito Tanzi and Julio Olivera, two economists who have emphasized its importance. As taxes are collected on past nominal income, their real value goes down with inflation. For example, if income taxes are paid this year on income received last year, and if the price level this year is 10 times higher than last year's price level, the actual tax rate is only one-tenth of the official tax rate. Thus, high inflation typically decreases real government revenues, making the deficit problem worse.

The problem is often compounded by other effects on the expenditure side: Governments often try to slow inflation by prohibiting firms under state control from increasing their prices, despite the fact that their costs are increasing with inflation. The direct effect on inflation is small at best, but the firms then run a deficit that must in turn be financed by subsidies from the government, which further increases the budget deficit. As the budget deficit increases, so does the need for more seignorage, and so does the need for even higher nominal money growth.

Hyperinflations and Economic Activity

We have focused so far on movements in nominal money growth and inflation—which clearly dominate the economic scene during a hyperinflation. But hyperinflations affect the economy in many other ways.

Initially, higher nominal money growth may lead to an *increase* in output. It takes some time for increases in nominal money growth to be reflected in inflation, and during that time, the effects of higher nominal money growth are expansionary. As you saw in Chapter 14, an increase in nominal money growth initially *decreases* nominal interest rates and real interest rates, leading to an increase in demand and an increase in output.

But as inflation becomes very high, the adverse effects of inflation dominate:

- The transaction system works less and less well. One famous example of inefficient exchange occurred in Germany at the end of its hyperinflation: People actually had to use wheelbarrows to cart around the huge amounts of currency they needed for their daily transactions.
- Price signals become less and less useful: Because prices change so often, it is difficult for consumers and producers to assess the relative prices of goods and to make informed decisions. The evidence shows that the higher the rate of inflation, the higher the variation in the relative prices of different goods. Thus the price system, which is crucial to the functioning of a market economy, also becomes less and less efficient.
- Swings in the inflation rate become larger. It becomes harder to predict what inflation will be in the near future, whether it will be, say, 500% or 1,000% over the next year. Borrowing at a given nominal interest rate becomes more and more a gamble. If you borrow at, say, 1,000% for a year, you may end up paying a real interest rate of 500% or 0%: A large difference! The result is that borrowing and lending typically come to a near stop in the final months of hyperinflation, leading to a large decline in investment.

◄ This is an "other things being equal" statement. Other things may not be equal. For example, if what is behind the budget deficits and higher money growth is a bad agricultural shock, output is more likely to go down than up.

◄ In the short run: g_m increases $\Rightarrow i$ decreases. Also, g_m increases $\Rightarrow \pi$ increases $\Rightarrow \pi^e$ increases. So $r \equiv i - \pi^e$ decreases for both reasons.

A joke heard in Israel during the high inflation of the 1980s: "Why is it cheaper to take a taxi rather than the bus? Because in the bus, you have to pay the fare at the beginning of the ride. In the taxi, you pay ◄ only at the end."

We have discussed here the costs of very high inflation. The discussion today in OECD countries is about the costs of, say, 4% inflation versus 0%. The issues are quite different in that case, and we return to it in ◄ Chapter 25.

So, as inflation increases and its costs become larger, there is typically an increasing consensus that it should be stopped. This takes us to the next section, how hyperinflations actually end.

23-4 How Do Hyperinflations End?

Hyperinflations do not die a natural death. Rather, they have to be stopped through a **stabilization program**.

The Elements of a Stabilization Program

What needs to be done to end a hyperinflation follows from our analysis of the causes of hyperinflation:

- There must be a fiscal reform and a credible reduction of the government's budget deficit. This reform must take place on both the expenditure side and the revenue side of the budget.

  On the expenditure side, reform typically implies reducing the government subsidies that have often mushroomed during the hyperinflation. Obtaining a temporary suspension of interest payments on foreign debt also helps to decrease expenditures. An important component of stabilization in Germany in 1923 was the reduction in its "reparation payments"—precisely those payments that had triggered the hyperinflation in the first place.

  On the revenue side, what is required is not so much an increase in overall taxation but rather a change in the composition of taxation. This is an important point: As you saw, during a hyperinflation, people are in effect paying a tax—the inflation tax. Stabilization involves replacing the inflation tax with other taxes. The challenge is to put in place and collect these other taxes. This cannot be done overnight, but it is essential that people become convinced that it will be done and that the budget deficit will be reduced.

  > This is what Argentina did in 1991. It adopted a currency board and fixed the exchange rate at 1 dollar for 1 peso. See Chapter 21's discussion of currency boards, and of the evolution of the Argentine economy since 1991. ▶

- The central bank must make a credible commitment that it will no longer automatically monetize the government debt. This credibility can be achieved in a number of ways. The central bank can be prohibited, by decree, from buying any government debt, so that no monetization of the debt is possible. Or the central bank can peg the exchange rate to the currency of a country with low inflation. An even more drastic step is to officially adopt dollarization—that is, making a foreign currency the country's official currency. This step is drastic because it implies giving up seignorage altogether, and it is often perceived as a decrease in the country's independence.

- Are other measures needed as well? Some economists argue that **incomes policies**—that is, wage and/or price guidelines or controls—should be used, in addition to fiscal and monetary measures, to help the economy reach a new lower rate of inflation. Incomes policies, they argue, help coordinate expectations around a new lower rate of inflation. If firms know wages will not increase, they will not increase their prices. If workers know prices will not increase, they will not ask for wage increases, and inflation will be eliminated more easily. Others argue that a credible deficit reduction and central bank independence are all that is required. They argue that the appropriate policy changes, if credible, can lead to dramatic changes in expectations and therefore lead to the elimination of expected and actual inflation nearly overnight. They point to the potential dangers of wage and price controls: The government might end up relying on the controls, and not take the painful but needed fiscal and policy measures to end the hyperinflation. Also, if the structure of relative prices is distorted to begin with, price controls run the risk of maintaining these distortions.

  > This argument was particularly relevant in the stabilizations in Eastern Europe in the early 1990s, where, because of central planning, the initial structure of relative prices was very different from the structure of relative prices in a market economy. Imposing wage or price controls would have prevented relative prices from adjusting to their appropriate market value. ▶

Stabilization programs that do not include incomes policies are called **orthodox**; those that do are called **heterodox** (because they rely on both monetary-fiscal changes and incomes policies). The hyperinflations in Table 23-1 were all ended through orthodox programs. Many of the Latin American stabilizations of the 1980s and 1990s relied instead on heterodox programs.

Can Stabilization Programs Fail?

Can stabilization programs fail? Yes. They can fail, and they often do. Argentina went through five stabilization plans from 1984 to 1989 before succeeding in the early 1990s. Brazil succeeded only in 1995, in its sixth attempt in 12 years.

As we saw in Chapter 21, the instrument used to stabilize inflation in Argentina, a currency board, led to another major macroeconomic crisis 10 years later.

Sometimes failure comes from a botched or half-hearted effort at stabilization. A government puts wage controls in place but does not take the measures needed to reduce the deficit and nominal money growth. Wage controls cannot work if nominal money growth continues, and the stabilization program eventually fails.

Sometimes failure comes from political opposition. If social conflict was one of the causes of the initial budget deficit and thus was at the root of the hyperinflation, it may still be present and just as hard to resolve at the time of stabilization. Those who stand to lose from the fiscal reform needed to reduce the deficit will oppose the stabilization program. Often, workers who perceive an increase in the price of public services or an increase in taxation, but who do not fully perceive the decrease in the inflation tax, will go on strike or even riot, and the stabilization plan will fail.

An example is the failed stabilization attempt in April 1984 in Bolivia described in the Focus box in this chapter.

Failure can also come from the anticipation of failure. Suppose the exchange rate is fixed to the dollar as part of the stabilization program. Also suppose participants in financial markets anticipate that the government will soon be forced to devalue. To compensate for the risk of devaluation, they require very high interest rates to hold domestic bonds rather than U.S. bonds. These very high interest rates then lead to a recession, and the recession forces the government to devalue, validating the markets' initial fears. If, instead, investors believe that the government will maintain the exchange rate, the risk of devaluation will be lower, interest rates will be lower, and the government will be able to proceed with stabilization. To many economists, the successes and failures of stabilization plans often appear to have an element of self-fulfilling prophecy. Even well-conceived plans work only if they are expected to work. In other words, skill, luck, and good public relations, all play a role.

This is a variation on the theme of self-fulfilling exchange rate crises developed in Chapter 21.

The Costs of Stabilization

You saw in Chapter 9 how the U.S. disinflation of the early 1980s was associated with a recession and a large increase in unemployment. Similarly, disinflation in Europe in the 1980s was also associated with a large increase in unemployment. We might therefore expect the much larger disinflations associated with the end of a hyperinflation to be associated with very large recessions or even depressions. This is typically not the case.

To understand why, recall our discussion of disinflation in Section 9-3. We argued that there are three reasons inflation might not decrease as fast as nominal money growth, leading to a recession:

Remember: The rate of real money growth equals the rate of nominal money growth minus the rate of inflation. If inflation decreases by less than nominal money growth, this implies negative real money growth—a decrease in the real money stock. This decrease in the real money stock then leads to high interest rates, which can trigger a recession.

- Wages are typically set in nominal terms for some period of time (up to three years in the United States), and, as a result, many of them are already determined when the decision to disinflate is made.
- Wage contracts are typically staggered, making it difficult to implement a slowdown in all wages at the same time.
- The change in monetary policy may not be fully and instantaneously credible.

In the 1970s, Bolivia achieved strong output growth, in large part because of high world prices for its exports: tin, silver, coca, oil, and natural gas. But by the end of the decade, the economic situation started deteriorating. The price of tin declined. Foreign lending, which had largely financed Bolivia's spending in the 1970s, was sharply curtailed as foreign lenders started worrying about the country's ability to repay its debts. Partly because of this, and partly because of long-running social conflicts, political chaos ensued. From 1979 to 1982, the country had 12 presidents: nine military and three civilian.

When the first freely elected president in 18 years came to power in 1982, he faced a nearly impossible task. U.S. commercial banks and other foreign lenders were running scared. They did not want to make new loans to Bolivia, and they wanted the previous loans to be repaid. Net private (medium-term and long-term) foreign lending to the Bolivian government had fallen from 3.5% of GDP in 1980 to −0.3% in 1982 and to −1.0% in 1983. Because the government had no other choice, it resorted to money creation to finance the budget deficit.

Inflation and Budget Deficits

The next three years were characterized by the interaction of steadily increasing inflation and steadily increasing budget deficits.

Table 1 gives the budget numbers for the period 1981 to 1986. Because of the lags in tax collection, the effect of rising inflation was a sharp reduction in real tax revenues. In addition, the government's attempt to maintain low prices for public services generated large deficits for state-run firms. As these deficits were financed by subsidies from the state, the result was a further increase in Bolivia's budget deficit. In 1984, it reached a staggering 31.6% of GDP.

The result of higher budget deficits and the need for higher seignorage was an increase in nominal money growth and inflation. Inflation, which averaged 2.5% per month in 1981, increased to 7% in 1982 and to 11% in 1983. As shown in Figure 1, which shows Bolivia's monthly inflation rate from January 1984 to April 1986 (the vertical line indicates the beginning of stabilization), inflation kept increasing in 1984 and 1985, reaching 182% in February 1985.

Stabilization

There were many attempts at stabilization in Bolivia along the way. Stabilization programs were launched in November 1982, November 1983, April 1984, August 1984, and February 1985. The April 1984 package was an orthodox program involving a large devaluation, the announcement of a tax reform, and an increase in public-sector prices. But the opposition from trade unions was too strong, and the program was abandoned.

After the election of a new president, yet another attempt at stabilization was made in September 1985. This one proved successful. The stabilization plan was organized around the elimination of the budget deficit. Its main features were:

■ *Fiscal policy*—Public-sector prices were increased; food and energy prices were increased; public-sector wages were frozen; and a tax reform, aimed at reestablishing and broadening the tax base, was announced.

■ *Monetary policy*—The official exchange rate of the peso was adjusted to what the black market rate (the actual exchange rate at which one could exchange pesos for dollars before the stabilization program) had been pre-stabilization. The exchange rate was set at 1.1 million pesos to the dollar, up from 67,000 pesos to the dollar the month before (a 1,600% devaluation). The exchange rate was then left to float, within limits.

Table 1	Central Government Revenues, Expenditures, and the Deficit as a Percentage of Bolivian GDP					
	1981	1982	1983	1984	1985	1986
Revenues	9.4	4.6	2.6	2.6	1.3	10.3
Expenditures	15.1	26.9	20.1	33.2	6.1	7.7
Budget balance (–: deficit)	−5.7	−22.3	−17.5	−31.6	−4.8	2.6

Source: Jeffrey Sachs, "The Bolivian Hyperinflation and Stabilization," National Bureau of Economic Research working paper no. 2073, November 1986, Table 3.

Hyperinflation eliminates the first two problems. During hyperinflation, wages and prices are adjusted so often that both nominal rigidities and the staggering of wage decisions become nearly irrelevant.

But the issue of credibility remains. The fact that even coherent programs might not succeed implies that no program is fully credible from the start. If, for example, the

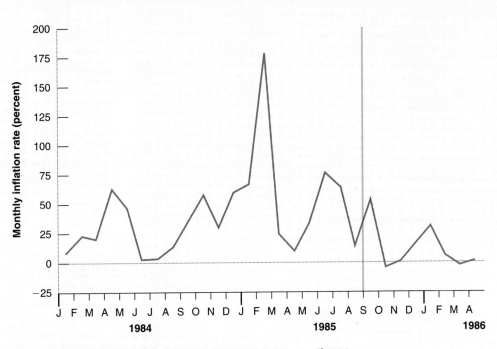

Figure 1 *Bolivian Monthly Inflation Rate, January 1984 to April 1986*

■ *Reestablish international creditworthiness* Negotiations were begun with international organizations and commercial banks to restructure Bolivia's debt. An agreement with its foreign creditors and the IMF was reached nine months later, in June 1986.

As they had in the previous attempt at stabilization, the unions called a general strike. In response, the government declared a state of siege, and the strike ended. After hyperinflation and so many failed attempts to control it, public opinion was clearly in favor of stabilization.

The effects of stabilization plan on inflation were dramatic. By the second week of September, the inflation rate was actually negative! Inflation did not remain negative for very long, but the average monthly rate of inflation was below 2% from 1986 to 1989. As Table 1 shows, the budget deficit was drastically reduced in 1986, and the average deficit was below 5% of GNP for the rest of the decade.

Did stabilization have a negative effect on output? It probably did. Real interest rates remained very high for more than a year after stabilization. The full effect of these high real interest rates on output is hard to establish because, at the same time as stabilization was implemented, Bolivia was hit with further large declines in the prices of tin and natural gas. In addition, a major campaign against narcotics had the effect of disrupting cocoa production. How much of the Bolivian recession of 1986 was due to stabilization and how much was due to these other factors is difficult to assess. The recession lasted a year. Since 1986, output has grown at an average rate of 3% per year, and average inflation has remained under 10%.

Source: The material in this box draws largely from Jeffrey Sachs, "The Bolivian Hyperinflation and Stabilization," National Bureau of Economic Research working paper no. 2073, November 1986. Sachs was one of the architects of the stabilization program. See also Juan Antonio Morales, "The Transition from Stabilization to Sustained Growth in Bolivia," in Michael Bruno, et al., eds., Lessons of Economic Stabilization and Its Aftermath, *MIT Press, Cambridge, MA, 1991.*

government decides to fix the exchange rate, a high interest rate may be needed initially to maintain the parity. Those programs that turn out to be successful are programs where increased credibility leads to lower interest rates over time. But even when credibility is eventually achieved, the initial high interest rate often leads to a recession. Overall, the evidence is that most, but not all, hyperinflations involve some decline in output.

All rich and most middle-income countries in the world have low inflation rates at this point. A few, such as Japan, have deflation. The two middle-income countries with the highest inflation rates as of mid-2007 are Venezuela, with an inflation rate of 20%, and Turkey, with an inflation rate of 13%.

How should a stabilization package be designed in order to reduce this output cost? Should the stabilization program be orthodox or heterodox? Should there be restrictions on nominal money growth, or should the exchange rate be fixed? At this point, few countries are experiencing high inflation, so these questions are not at the top of policymakers' agendas. But, if history is any guide, some countries will again lose control of their budgets, finance the budget deficit through money creation, and experience high inflation, if not hyperinflation. These questions will then surely resurface.

23-5 Conclusions

An underlying theme of the core of this book is that, although output fluctuates around its natural level in the short run, it tends to return to this natural level in the medium run. If the adjustment is too slow, fiscal and monetary policy can be used to help and shape the adjustment. Most of the time, this is indeed what happens. But, as this chapter and Chapter 22 tell us, it does not always happen:

- Sometimes, the adjustment mechanism that is supposed to return the economy to its natural level of output breaks down. An economy in a slump or in a depression experiences deflation, and deflation makes things worse rather than better.
- Monetary and fiscal policies may prove unable to help. In a slump, monetary policy may be constrained by the liquidity trap—the fact that nominal interest rates cannot be negative. Expansionary fiscal policy might not be an option because the budget deficit is very high to start with: The increase in government debt triggered by the high deficits might become a problem in and of itself.
- Governments may lose control of both fiscal policy and monetary policy. Faced with major adverse shocks—war, civil war, a collapse of exports, a social explosion—a government might lose control of its budget, run a large budget deficit, and have no other choice but to finance the deficit through money creation. The result of this loss of control might be high inflation or even hyperinflation.

Summary

- Hyperinflations are periods of high inflation. The most extreme hyperinflations took place after World Wars I and II in Europe. But Latin America has experienced episodes of high inflation as recently as the early 1990s.
- High inflation comes from high nominal money growth. High nominal money growth comes from the combination of large budget deficits and the inability to finance these large budget deficits through borrowing, either from the public or from abroad.
- The revenues from money creation are called seignorage. Seignorage is equal to the product of nominal money growth and real money balances. The smaller real money balances, the higher the required rate of nominal money growth, and therefore the higher the rate of inflation required to generate a given amount of seignorage.
- Hyperinflations are typically characterized by increasing inflation. There are two reasons for this. One is that higher nominal money growth leads to higher inflation,

inducing people to reduce their real money balances, and requiring even higher nominal money growth (and thus leading to even higher inflation) to finance the same real deficit. The other reason is that higher inflation often increases the deficit, which requires higher nominal money growth, and even higher inflation.

- Hyperinflations are ended through stabilization programs. To be successful, stabilization programs must include fiscal measures aimed at reducing the deficit, and monetary measures aimed at reducing or eliminating money creation as a way of financing of the deficit. Some stabilization plans also include wage and price guidelines or controls.
- A stabilization program that imposes wage and price controls without changes in fiscal policy and monetary policy will ultimately fail. But even well-conceived programs do not always succeed. Anticipations of failure may lead to the failure of even a well-conceived plan.

Key Terms

- hyperinflation, 517
- debt monetization, 519
- seignorage, 520
- barter, 522
- dollarization, 522
- Laffer curve, 525

- inflation tax, 525
- Tanzi-Olivera effect, 527
- stabilization program, 528
- incomes policies, 528
- orthodox stabilization program, heterodox stabilization program, 529

Questions and Problems

Quick Check

1. *Using the information in this chapter, label each of the following statements true, false, or uncertain. Explain briefly.*

a. When nominal money growth is constant, inflation must eventually be equal to original money growth so that the inflation tax is equal to seignorage.

b. Most of the time, in most countries, deficits are financed primarily through borrowing rather than money creation.

c. The larger the real money balances held in the economy, the smaller the amount of seignorage corresponding to a given rate of nominal money growth.

d. Increases in expected inflation lead people to decrease their use of money and to decrease their real money balances.

e. Because inflation is generally good for those who borrow money, hyperinflations are the best times to take out large loans.

f. The solution to ending a hyperinflation is to institute a wage and price freeze.

2. *How would each of the policies listed in parts (a) through (c) change the Tanzi-Olivera effect?*

a. requiring monthly instead of yearly income tax payments by households

b. assessing greater penalties for under-withholding of taxes from monthly paychecks

c. decreasing the income tax and increasing the sales tax

3. *Assume that money demand takes the form*

$$\frac{M}{P} = Y[1 - (r + \pi^e)]$$

where Y = 1,000 *and* r = 0.1.

a. Assume that, in the short run, π^e is constant and equal to 25%. Calculate the amount of seignorage for each rate of money growth, $\Delta M/M$, listed below.
  i. 25%
  ii. 50%
  iii. 75%

b. In the medium run, $\pi^e = \pi = \Delta M/M$. Compute the amount of seignorage associated with the three rates of money growth in part (a). Explain why the answers differ from those in part (a).

Dig Deeper

4. *You are the economic advisor to a country experiencing a hyperinflation. Politicians debating the proper course of* stabilization have advocated various positions, listed in statements (a) through (e). Discuss each statement in turn.

a. "This crisis will not end until workers begin to pay their fair share of taxes."

b. "The central bank has demonstrated that it cannot responsibly wield its power to create money, so we have no choice but to adopt a currency board."

c. "Price controls are necessary to end this madness."

d. "Stabilization will be successful only if there is a large recession and if there is a substantial increase in unemployment."

e. "Let's not blame the central bank. The problem is fiscal policy, not monetary policy."

5. *What is the rate of money growth that maximizes seignorage in the economy described in problem 3(b)? (Hint: You learned in problem 3(b) that seignorage, in the medium run, is greater at money growth of 50% than at money growth of 25% or 75%. Start by calculating seignorage for money growth rates near 50%. Increase and then decrease money growth rates by one percentage point until you find the answer.)*

Explore Further

6. *High inflation around the world*

a. Go to the Web site of the IMF (**www.imf.org**) and find the current issue of the *World Economic Outlook*. In the Statistical Appendix, look at the table that lists inflation rates. Find countries that have inflation rates of 10% or higher. Which country has the highest inflation rate, and what is the rate?

b. Find Venezuela in the inflation table. How long has Venezuela had an inflation rate of more than 10%? Look at the projected inflation rates for the current year and the next year. Does inflation show any signs of slowing in Venezuela?

c. Venezuela is an oil producer, so its economy fluctuates with oil prices. Government tax revenues, in particular, depend heavily on the prosperity of the oil industry. With oil prices rising, Venezuela has increased government spending dramatically in recent years. Suppose oil prices fall in the future, but Venezuela does not reduce government spending. How would a fall in oil prices affect the budget deficit in Venezuela? Given the effect on the budget deficit, and following the logic of this chapter, how would a fall in oil prices make a hyperinflation possible in Venezuela?

We invite you to visit the Blanchard page on the Prentice Hall Web site, at:
www.prenhall.com/blanchard
for this chapter's World Wide Web exercises.

Further Readings

- For more on the German hyperinflation, read Steven Webb, *Hyperinflation and Stabilization in the Weimar Republic*, Oxford University Press, New York, 1989.

- Two good reviews of what economists know and don't know about hyperinflation are:
  Rudiger Dornbusch, Federico Sturzenegger, and Holger Wolf, "Extreme Inflation: Dynamics and Stabilization," Brookings Papers on Economic Activity, 1990–2, 1–84.
  Pierre Richard Agenor and Peter Montiel, *Development Macroeconomics,* Princeton University Press, Princeton, NJ, 1995, Chapters 8 to 11. Chapter 8 is easy to read; the other chapters are more difficult.

- The experience of Israel, which went through high inflation and stabilization in the 1980s, is described in Michael Bruno's *Crisis, Stabilization and Economic Reform*, Oxford University Press, New York, 1993, especially Chapters 2 to 5. Bruno was the head of Israel's central bank for most of that period.

- One of the classic articles on how to end hyperinflation is Thomas Sargent, "The Ends of Four Big Inflations," in Robert Hall, ed., *Inflation: Causes and Effects*, NBER and the University of Chicago, Chicago, 1982, 41–97. In that article, Sargent argues that a credible program can lead to stabilization at little or no cost in terms of activity.

- Rudiger Dornbusch and Stanley Fischer, "Stopping Hyperinflations, Past and Present," in *Weltwirtschaftlichers Archiv*, 1986–1, 1–47, gives a very readable description of the end of hyperinflations in Germany, Austria, Poland, and Italy in 1947; Israel in 1985; and Argentina in 1985.

Back to Policy

Nearly every chapter of this book has looked at the role of policy. The next three chapters put it all together.

Chapter 24

Chapter 24 asks two questions: Given the uncertainty about the effects of macroeconomic policy, wouldn't it be better not to use policy at all? And, even if policy can in principle be useful, can we trust policymakers to carry out the right policy? The bottom lines: Uncertainty limits the role of policy. Policymakers do not always do the right thing. But, with the right institutions, policy can help and should be used.

Chapter 25

Chapter 25 looks at monetary policy. It reviews what we have learned, chapter by chapter, and then focuses on two issues. The first is the optimal rate of inflation: High inflation is bad, but how low a rate of inflation should the central bank aim for? The second is the design of policy: Should the central bank target money growth, or should it target inflation? What rule should the central bank use to adjust the interest rate? The chapter ends with a description of the way monetary policy is conducted in the United States today.

Chapter 26 ▬▬▬

Chapter 26 looks at fiscal policy. It reviews what we have learned, and then looks more closely at the implications of the government budget constraint for the relation between debt, spending, and taxes. Next, the chapter considers several issues, from how wars should be financed, to the dangers of accumulating too high a level of debt. It ends with a description of the current budget situation in the United States and, a discussion of the problems on the horizon.

Should Policymakers Be Restrained?

At many points in this book, we have seen how the right mix of fiscal and monetary policy can help a country out of a recession, improve its trade position without increasing activity and igniting inflation, slow down an overheating economy, stimulate investment and capital accumulation, and so on.

These conclusions, however, appear to be at odds with frequent demands that policymakers be tightly restrained: In the United States, there are regular calls for the introduction of a balanced-budget amendment to the Constitution. Such a call was the first item in the "Contract with America," the program drawn by Republicans for the mid-term U.S. elections in 1994, and reproduced in Figure 24-1. In Europe, the countries that adopted the euro signed the "Stability and Growth Pact," which required them to keep their budget deficit under 3% of GDP or else face large fines. Monetary policy is also under fire. For example, the charter of the central bank of New Zealand, written in 1989, defines monetary policy's role as the maintenance of price stability, to the exclusion of any other macroeconomic goal.

This chapter looks at the case for such restraints on macroeconomic policy:

■ Sections 24-1 and 24-2 look at one line of argument, namely that policymakers may have good intentions, but they end up doing more harm than good.

■ Section 24-3 looks at another—more cynical—line, that policymakers do what is best for them, which is not necessarily what is best for the country. ■

CHAPTER 24

House Republican
Contract with America
────

A Program for Accountability

We've listened to your concerns and we hear you loud and clear. If you give us the majority, on the first day of Congress, a Republican House will:

Force Congress to live under the same laws as every other American
Cut one out of three Congressional committee staffers
Cut the Congressional budget

Then, in the first 100 days there will be votes on the following 10 bills:

1. Balanced budget amendment and the line item veto: It's time to force the government to live within its means and restore accountability to the budget in Washington.

2. Stop violent criminals: Let's get tough with an effective, able, and timely death penalty for violent offenders. Let's also reduce crime by building more prisons, making sentences longer and putting more police on the streets.

3. Welfare reform: The government should encourage people to work, not have children out of wedlock.

4. Protect our kids: We must strengthen families by giving parents greater control over education, enforcing child support payments, and getting tough on child pornography.

5. Tax cuts for families: Let's make it easier to achieve the American Dream: save money, buy a home, and send their kids to college.

6. Strong national defense: We need to ensure a strong national defense by restoring the essentials of our national security funding.

7. Raise the senior citizens' earning limit: We can put an end to government age discrimination that discourages seniors from working if they want.

8. Roll back government regulations: Let's slash regulations that strangle small business and let's make it easier for people to invest in order to create jobs and increase wages.

9. Common-sense legal reform: We can finally stop excessive legal claims, frivolous lawsuits, and overzealous lawyers.

10. Congressional term limits: Let's replace career politicians with citizen legislators. After all, politics shouldn't be a lifetime job.
(Please see reverse side to know if the candidate from your district has signed the Contract as of October 5, 1994.)

IF WE BREAK THIS CONTRACT, THROW US OUT, WE MEAN IT.

Figure 24-1

The Contract with America

24-1 Uncertainty and Policy

A blunt way of stating the first argument in favor of policy restraints is that those who know little should do little. The argument has two parts: Macroeconomists, and by implication the policymakers who rely on their advice, know little; they should therefore do little. Let's look at each part separately.

How Much Do Macroeconomists Actually Know?

Macroeconomists are like doctors treating cancer. They know a lot, but there is a lot they don't know.

Take an economy with high unemployment, where the central bank is considering the use of monetary policy to increase economic activity. Think of the sequence of links between an increase in money and an increase in output—all the questions the central bank faces when deciding whether and by how much to increase the money supply:

- Is the current high rate of unemployment above the natural rate of unemployment, or has the natural rate of unemployment itself increased (Chapters 8 and 9)?
- If the unemployment rate is close to the natural rate of unemployment, isn't there a risk that monetary expansion will lead to a decrease in unemployment below the natural rate of unemployment and cause an increase in inflation (Chapters 8 and 9)?

Back to Policy   **Back to Policy**

- By how much will the change in the money supply decrease the short-term interest rate (Chapter 4)? What will be the effect of the decrease in the short-term interest rate on the long-term interest rate (Chapter 15)? By how much will stock prices increase (Chapter 15)? By how much will the currency depreciate (Chapters 20 and 21)?
- How long will it take for lower long-term interest rates and higher stock prices to affect investment and consumption spending (Chapter 16)? How long will it take for the J-curve effects to work themselves out and for the trade balance to improve (Chapter 19)? What is the danger that the effects come too late, when the economy has already recovered?

When assessing these questions, central banks—or macroeconomic policymakers in general—do not operate in a vacuum. They rely in particular on macroeconometric models. The equations in these models show how these individual links have looked in the past. But different models yield different answers. This is because they have different structures, different lists of equations, and different lists of variables.

Figure 24-2 shows an example of this diversity. The example comes from a study commissioned by the Brookings Institution—a research institute in Washington DC—asking the builders of the 12 main macroeconometric models to answer a similar set of questions. (The models are described in the Focus box "Twelve Macroeconometric Models.") The goal of the study was to see how the answers would differ across models. One question was:

Consider a case where the U.S. economy is growing at its normal growth rate, and where unemployment is at its natural rate; call this the *baseline* case. Suppose now, s that over the period of a year, the Fed increases money faster than in the baseline, so that after a year, nominal money is 4% higher than it would have been in the baseline case. From then on, nominal money grows at the same rate as in the baseline case, so the level of nominal money remains 4% higher than it would have been without the change in monetary policy. Suppose further that interest rates in the rest of the world remain unchanged. What will happen to U.S. output?

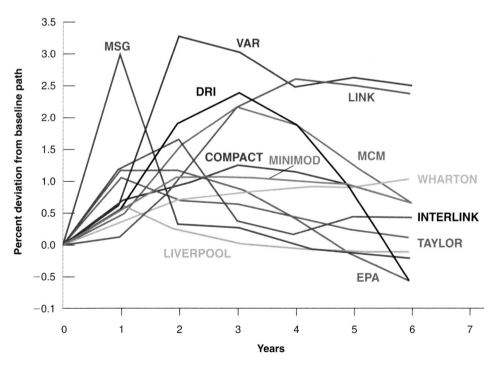

Figure 24-2

The Response of Output to a Monetary Expansion: Predictions from 12 Models

Although all 12 models predict that output will increase for some time in response to a monetary expansion, the range of answers regarding the size and the length of the output response is large.

FOCUS

The Brookings study was done in the late 1980s (to my knowledge, this is the last time such a systematic comparison of a large class of models was made), so some of the models used in the study are no longer in use; others have changed names. The typology presented here remains relevant, however, and reflects the different approaches to modeling followed today:

■ Two models, DRI (Data Resources Incorporated) and WHARTON, were commercial models. Commercial models are used to generate and sell economic forecasts to firms and financial institutions.

■ Five models were used to forecast and help design policy. MCM (for MultiCountry Model) was used by the Federal Reserve Board in Washington, DC, for the conduct of monetary policy; INTERLINK was used by the OECD in Paris; COMPACT was used by the Commission of the European Union in Brussels; and EPA was used by the Japanese Planning Agency. Each of these four models was constructed by one team of researchers doing all the work—that is, building submodels for countries or groups of countries and linking them through trade and financial flows. In contrast, the fifth model, LINK, was composed of individual country models— models constructed in each country by researchers from that country and then linked together by trade and financial relations. The advantage of this approach is that researchers from a particular country are likely to understand that country very well; the disadvantage is that different country models may have quite different structures and may be hard to link to each other.

■ Four models incorporated rational expectations explicitly: the LIVERPOOL model, based in England; MINIMOD, used at the International Monetary Fund; MSG, developed by Warwick McKibbin and Jeffrey Sachs at Harvard University; and the TAYLOR model— which we saw in Section 7-4—developed by John Taylor of Stanford University. Because it is technically difficult to solve for large models under rational expectations, these models are typically smaller models, with less detail than those listed earlier. But they are better at capturing the expectation effects of various policies. Thanks to more and more powerful computers, researchers are building larger and larger models with rational expectations. The modern versions of these models are called **dynamic stochastic general equilibrium—(DSGE) models**, and are the subject of active research. (More on them in Chapter 27.)

■ The last model, VAR (for Vector AutoRegression, the technique of estimation used to build the model), developed by Christopher Sims and Robert Litterman at the University of Minnesota, was very different from the others. VAR models are not structural models but rather statistical summaries of the relations between the different variables, without an explicit economic interpretation. Their strength is in their fit of the data, with a minimum of theoretical restrictions. Their weakness is that they are, essentially, a (very big) black box.

Note: A description of the models and of the study is given in Ralph Bryant, et al., Empirical Macroeconomics for Interdependent Economies, *Brookings Institution, Washington, DC, 1988. The study shows the effects not only of monetary policy but also of fiscal policy.*

Figure 24-2 shows the deviation of output from the baseline predicted by each of the 12 models. All 12 models predict that output increases for some time after the increase in money. After one year, the average deviation of output from the baseline is positive. But the range of answers is large, from nearly no change to close to an increase of 3%; even leaving out the most extreme prediction, the range is still more than 1%. Two years out, the average deviation is 1.2%; again leaving out the most extreme prediction, the range is still 2%. And six years out, the average deviation is 0.6%, and the answers range from −0.3% to 2.5%. In short, if we measure uncertainty by the range of answers from this set of models, there is indeed substantial uncertainty about the effects of policy.

Should Uncertainty Lead Policymakers to Do Less?

Should uncertainty about the effects of policy lead policymakers to do less? In general, the answer is yes. Consider the following example, which builds on the simulations we just looked at.

Suppose the U.S. economy is in recession. The unemployment rate is 7%, and the Fed is considering using monetary policy to expand output. To concentrate on uncertainty about the effects of policy, let's assume that the Fed knows everything else for sure. Based on its forecasts, it *knows* that, absent changes in monetary policy, unemployment will still be 7% next year. It knows that the natural rate of unemployment is 5%, and therefore it knows that the unemployment rate is 2% above the natural rate. And it knows, from Okun's law, that 1% more output growth for a year leads to a 0.4% reduction in the unemployment rate.

Under these assumptions, the Fed knows that if it could use monetary policy to achieve 5% more output growth over the coming year, the unemployment rate a year from now would be lower by 0.4 × 5% = 2%, so would be down to the natural rate of unemployment, 5%. By how much should the Fed increase the money supply?

Taking the average of the responses from the different models in Figure 24-2, an increase in the money supply of 4% leads to a 0.85% increase in output in the first year. Equivalently, a 1% increase in the money supply leads to a 0.85/4 = 0.21% increase in output.

Suppose the Fed takes this average relation as holding with *certainty*. What it should then do is straightforward. To return the unemployment rate to the natural rate in one year requires 5% more output growth. And 5% output growth requires the Fed to increase money by 5%/0.21 = 23.8%. The Fed should therefore increase the money supply by 23.8%. If the economy's response is equal to the *average* response from the 12 models, this increase in money will return the economy to the natural rate of unemployment at the end of the year.

Suppose the Fed actually increases money by 23.8%. But let's now take into account uncertainty, as measured by the *range* of responses of the different models in Figure 24-2. Recall that the range of responses of output to a 4% increase in money after one year varies from 0% to 3%; equivalently, a 1% increase in money leads to a range of increases in output from 0% to 0.75%. These ranges imply that an increase in money of 23.8% leads, across models, to an output response anywhere between 0% and 17.9% (23.8% × 0.75). These output numbers imply, in turn, a decrease in unemployment anywhere between 0% and 7%. Put another way, the unemployment rate a year hence could be anywhere between 7% and 0%!

The conclusion is clear: Given the range of uncertainty about the effects of monetary policy on output, increasing money by 23.8% would be irresponsible. If the effects of money on output are as strong as suggested by one of the 12 models, unemployment by the end of the year could be 5% below the natural rate of unemployment, leading to enormous inflationary pressures. Given this uncertainty, the Fed should increase money by much less than 23.8%. For example, increasing money by 10% leads to a range for unemployment a year hence of 7% to 4%, clearly a safer range of outcomes.

Uncertainty and Restraints on Policymakers

Let's summarize: There is substantial uncertainty about the effects of macroeconomic policy. This uncertainty should lead policymakers to be more cautious and to use less active policy. Policies should be broadly aimed at avoiding prolonged recessions, slowing down booms, and avoiding inflationary pressure. The higher unemployment or

◄ In the real world, of course, the Fed does not know any of these things with certainty. It can only make forecasts. It does not know the exact value of the natural rate of unemployment or the exact coefficient in Okun's law. Introducing these sources of uncertainty would reinforce our basic conclusion.

◄ This example relies on the notion of *multiplicative uncertainty*—that because the effects of policy are uncertain, more active policies lead to more uncertainty. See William Brainard, "Uncertainty and the Effectiveness of Policy," *American Economic Review*, May 1967.

the higher inflation, the more active the policies should be. But they should stop well short of **fine-tuning**, of trying to achieve constant unemployment or constant output growth.

These conclusions would have been controversial 20 years ago. Back then, there was a heated debate between two groups of economists. One group, headed by Milton Friedman from the University of Chicago, argued that because of long and variable lags, activist policy is likely to do more harm than good. The other group, headed by Franco Modigliani from MIT, had just built the first generation of large macroeconometric models and believed that economists' knowledge was becoming good enough to allow for increasing fine-tuning of the economy. Today, most economists recognize that there is substantial uncertainty about the effects of policy. They also accept the implication that this uncertainty should lead to less active policies.

> Note, however, that what we have developed so far is an argument for *self-restraint by* policymakers, not for *restraints on* policymakers. If policymakers understand the implications of uncertainty—and there is no particular reason to think they don't—they will, on their own, follow less active policies. There is no reason to impose further restraints, such as the requirement that money growth be constant or that the budget be balanced. Let's now turn to arguments for restraints *on* policymakers.

Friedman and Modigliani are the same two economists who independently developed the modern theory of consumption we saw in Chapter 16.

24-2 Expectations and Policy

One of the reasons the effects of macroeconomic policy are uncertain is the interaction of policy and expectations. How a policy works, and sometimes whether it works at all, depends not only on how it affects current variables but also on how it affects expectations about the future. (This was the main theme of Chapter 17.) The importance of expectations for policy, however, goes beyond uncertainty about the effects of policy. This brings us to a discussion of *games*.

Until 30 years ago, macroeconomic policy was seen in the same way as the control of a complicated machine. Methods of **optimal control**, developed initially to control and guide rockets, were being increasingly used to design macroeconomic policy. Economists no longer think this way. It has become clear that the economy is fundamentally different from a machine, even from a very complicated one. Unlike a machine, the economy is composed of people and firms who try to anticipate what policymakers will do, and who react not only to current policy but also to expectations of future policy. Hence, macroeconomic policy must be thought of as a **game** between the policymakers and "the economy"—more concretely, the people and the firms in the economy. So, when thinking about policy, what we need is not **optimal control theory** but rather **game theory**.

Even machines are becoming smarter: HAL, the robot in the 1968 movie *2001: A Space Odyssey*, starts anticipating what humans in the spaceship will do. The result is not a happy one. (See the movie.)

Warning: When economists say *game*, they do not mean "entertainment"; they mean **strategic interactions** between **players**. In the context of macroeconomic policy, the players are the policymakers on one side, and people and firms on the other. The strategic interactions are clear: What people and firms do depends on what they expect policymakers to do. In turn, what policymakers do depends on what is happening in the economy.

Game theory has given economists many insights, often explaining how some apparently strange behavior makes sense when one understands the nature of the game being played. One of these insights is particularly important for our discussion of restraints here: Sometimes you can do better in a game by giving up some of your options. To see why, let's start with an example from outside economics—governments' policies toward hostage takers.

Game theory has become an important tool in all branches of economics. Both the 1994 and the 2005 Nobel Prizes in Economics were awarded to game theorists. In 1994, it was awarded to John Nash, from Princeton; John Harsanyi, from Berkeley; and Reinhard Selten, from Germany (John Nash's life is portrayed in the movie *A Beautiful Mind*). In 2005, it was awarded to Robert Aumann, from Israel, and Tom Schelling, from Harvard.

Hostage Takings and Negotiations

Most governments have stated policies that they will not negotiate with hostage takers. The reason for this stated policy is clear: to deter hostage taking by making it unattractive to take hostages.

Suppose, that despite the stated policy, somebody is taken hostage. Now that the hostage taking has taken place anyway, why not negotiate? Whatever compensation the hostage takers demand is likely to be less costly than the alternative—the likelihood that the hostage will be killed. So the best policy would appear to be to announce that you will not negotiate, but if somebody is taken hostage, negotiate.

Upon reflection, it is clear that this would in fact be a very bad policy. Hostage takers' decisions do not depend on the stated policy but on what they expect will actually happen if they take a hostage. If they know that negotiations will actually take place, they will rightly consider the stated policy as irrelevant. And hostage takings will take place.

So what is the best policy? Despite the fact that once hostage takings have taken place, negotiations typically lead to a better outcome, the best policy is for governments to commit *not* to negotiate. By giving up the option to negotiate, they are likely to prevent hostage takings in the first place.

Let's now turn to a macroeconomic example, based on the relation between inflation and unemployment. As you will see, exactly the same logic is involved.

This example was developed by Finn Kydland, from Carnegie Mellon, and Edward Prescott, then from Minnesota and now at Arizona State University, in "Rules Rather than Discretion: The Inconsistency of Optimal Plans," *Journal of Political Economy*, Volume 3, June 1977, 85. Kydland and Prescott were awarded the Nobel Prize in Economics in 2004.

Inflation and Unemployment Revisited

Recall the relation between inflation and unemployment we derived in Chapter 8 [equation (8.9), with the time indexes omitted here for simplicity]:

$$\pi = \pi^e - \alpha(u - u_n) \tag{24.1}$$

Inflation, π, depends on expected inflation, π^e, and on the difference between the actual unemployment rate, u, and the natural unemployment rate, u_n. The coefficient α captures the effect of unemployment on inflation, given expected inflation: When unemployment is above the natural rate, inflation is lower than expected; when unemployment is below the natural rate, inflation is higher than expected.

Suppose the Fed announces it will follow a monetary policy consistent with zero inflation. On the assumption that people believe the announcement, expected inflation, π^e, as embodied in wage contracts is equal to zero, and the Fed faces the following relation between unemployment and inflation:

$$\pi = -\alpha(u - u_n) \tag{24.2}$$

If the Fed follows through with its announced policy, it will choose an unemployment rate equal to the natural rate; from equation (24.2), inflation will be equal to zero, just as the Fed announced and people expected.

Achieving zero inflation and an unemployment rate equal to the natural rate is not a bad outcome. But it would seem that the Fed can actually do even better:

■ Recall from Chapter 8 that in the United States, α is roughly equal to 1. So equation (24.2) implies that, by accepting just 1% inflation, the Fed can achieve an unemployment rate of 1% below the natural rate of unemployment. Suppose the Fed—and everybody else in the economy—finds the trade-off attractive and decides to decrease unemployment by 1% in exchange for an inflation rate of 1%. This incentive to deviate from the announced policy once the other player has made his

A refresher: Given labor market conditions, and given their expectations of what prices will be, firms and workers set nominal wages. Given the nominal wages firms have to pay, firms then set prices. So, prices depend on expected prices and labor market conditions. Equivalently, price inflation depends on expected price inflation and labor market conditions. This is what is captured in equation (24.1).

For simplicity, I assume that the Fed can choose the unemployment rate—and, by implication, the inflation rate—exactly. In doing so, I ignore the uncertainty about the effects of policy. This was the topic of Section 24-1, but it is not central here.

If $\alpha = 1$, equation (24.2) implies $\pi = -(u - u_n)$. If $\pi = 1\%$, then $(u - u_n) = -1\%$.

Remember that the natural rate of unemployment is neither natural nor best in any sense (see Chapters 6 and 8). It may ▶ be reasonable for the Fed and everyone else in the economy to prefer an unemployment rate lower than the natural rate of unemployment.

move—in this case, once wage setters have set the wage—is known in game theory as the **time inconsistency** of optimal policy. In our example, the Fed can improve the outcome this period by deviating from its announced policy of zero inflation: By accepting some inflation, it can achieve a substantial reduction in unemployment.

■ Unfortunately, this is not the end of the story. Seeing that the Fed has increased money by more than it announced it would, wage setters are likely to wise up and begin to expect positive inflation of 1%. If the Fed still wants to achieve an unemployment rate 1% below the natural rate, it will have to achieve 2% inflation. However, if it does achieve 2% inflation, wage setters are likely to increase their expectations of inflation further, and so on.

■ The eventual outcome is likely to be high inflation. Because wage setters understand the Fed's motives, expected inflation catches up with actual inflation, and the Fed will eventually be unsuccessful in its attempt to achieve an unemployment rate below the natural rate. In short, attempts by the Fed to make things better lead in the end to things being worse. The economy ends up with the *same unemployment rate* that would have prevailed if the Fed had followed its announced policy, but with *much higher inflation.*

How relevant is this example? Very relevant. Go back to Chapter 8: We can read the history of the Phillips curve and the increase in inflation in the 1970s as coming precisely from the Fed's attempts to keep unemployment below the natural rate of unemployment, leading to higher and higher expected inflation, and higher and higher actual inflation. In that light, the shift of the original Phillips curve can be seen as the adjustment of wage setters' expectations to the central bank's behavior.

So what is the best policy for the Fed to follow in this case? It is to make a credible commitment that it will not try to decrease unemployment below the natural rate. By giving up the option of deviating from its announced policy, the Fed can achieve unemployment equal to the natural rate of unemployment and zero inflation. The analogy with the hostage-taking example is clear: By credibly committing not to do something that would appear desirable at the time, policymakers can achieve a better outcome: no hostage takings in our earlier example, no inflation here.

Establishing Credibility

How can a central bank credibly commit not to deviate from its announced policy?

One way to establish its credibility is for a central bank to give up—or to be stripped by law of—its policymaking power. For example, the mandate of the central bank can be defined by law in terms of a simple rule, such as setting money growth at 0% forever. (An alternative, which we discussed in Chapter 21, is to adopt a hard peg, such as a currency board or even dollarization: In this case, instead of giving up its ability to use money growth, the central bank gives up its ability to use the exchange rate and the interest rate.)

Such a law surely takes care of the problem of time inconsistency. But the tight restraint it creates comes close to throwing out the baby with the bathwater. We want to prevent the central bank from pursuing too high a rate of money growth in an attempt to lower unemployment below the natural unemployment rate. But—subject to the restrictions discussed in Section 24-1—we still want the central bank to be able to expand the money supply when unemployment is far above the natural rate, and contract the money supply when unemployment is far below the natural rate. Such actions become impossible under a constant-money-growth rule. There are indeed better ways to deal with time inconsistency. In the case of monetary policy, our discussion suggests various ways of dealing with the problem.

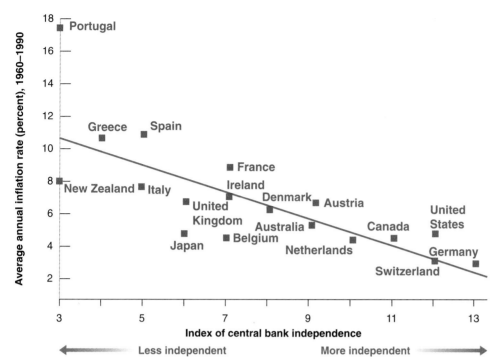

Figure 24-3

Inflation and Central Bank Independence

Across OECD countries, the higher the degree of central bank independence, the lower the rate of inflation.

Source: Vittorio Grilli, Donato Masciandaro, and Guido Tabellini, "Political and Monetary Institutions and Public Financial Policies in the Industrial Countries," *Economic Policy*, October 1991, 341–392.

A first step is to make the central bank independent. Politicians, who face frequent reelections, are likely to want lower unemployment now, even if it leads to inflation later. Making the central bank independent, and making it difficult for politicians to fire the central banker, makes it easier for the central bank to resist the political pressure to decrease unemployment below the natural rate of unemployment.

This may not be enough, however. Even if it is not subject to political pressure, the central bank will still be tempted to decrease unemployment below the natural rate: Doing so leads to a better outcome in the short run. So, a second step is to give incentives to central bankers to take the long view—that is, to take into account the long-run costs from higher inflation. One way of doing so is to give them long terms in office, so they have a long horizon and have an incentive to build credibility.

A third step may be to appoint a "conservative" central banker, somebody who dislikes inflation very much and is therefore less willing to accept more inflation in exchange for less unemployment when unemployment is at the natural rate. When the economy is at the natural rate, such a central banker will be less tempted to embark on a monetary expansion. Thus, the problem of time inconsistency will be reduced.

These are the steps many countries have taken over the past two decades. Central banks have been given more independence. Central bankers have been given long terms in office. And governments typically have appointed central bankers who are more "conservative" than the governments themselves—central bankers who appear to care more about inflation and less about unemployment than the government. (See the Focus box "Was Alan Blinder Wrong in Speaking the Truth?")

Figure 24-3 suggests that this approach has been successful. The vertical axis gives the average annual inflation rates in 18 OECD countries for the period 1960 to 1990. The horizontal axis gives the value of an index of "central bank independence," constructed by looking at a number of legal provisions in the bank's charter—for

In the summer of 1994, President Clinton appointed Alan Blinder, an economist from Princeton, Vice-Chairman (in effect, second in command) of the Federal Reserve Board. A few weeks later, Blinder, speaking at an economic conference, indicated his belief that the Fed has both the responsibility and the ability, when unemployment is high, to use monetary policy to help the economy recover. This statement was badly received. Bond prices fell, and most newspapers ran editorials critical of Blinder.

Why was the reaction of markets and newspapers so negative? It was surely not that Blinder was wrong. There is no doubt that monetary policy can and should help the economy out of a recession. Indeed, the Federal Reserve Bank Act of 1978 requires the Fed to pursue full employment as well as low inflation.

The reaction was negative because, in terms of the argument we developed in the text, Blinder revealed by his words that he was not a conservative central banker, that he cared about unemployment as well as inflation. With the unemployment rate at the time equal to 6.1%, close to what was thought to be the natural rate of unemployment at the time, markets interpreted Blinder's statements as suggesting that he might want to decrease unemployment below the natural rate. Interest rates increased because of higher expected inflation—bond prices decreased.

The moral of the story: Whatever views central bankers may hold, they should try to look and sound conservative. This is why many heads of central banks are reluctant to admit, at least in public, the existence of any trade-off between unemployment and inflation, even in the short run.

A warning: Figure 24-3 shows correlation, not necessarily causality. It may be that countries that dislike inflation tend both to give more independence to their central bankers and have lower inflation. (This is another example of the difference between correlation and causality—discussed in Appendix 3 at the end of the book.)

example, whether and how the government can remove the head of the bank. There is a striking inverse relation between the two variables, as summarized by the regression line: More central bank independence appears to be systematically associated with lower inflation.

Time Consistency and Restraints on Policymakers

Let's summarize what we have learned in this section:

We have examined arguments for putting restraints on policymakers, based on the issue of time inconsistency.

We have looked at the case of monetary policy. But similar issues arise in the context of fiscal policy. For instance, we shall discuss in Chapter 26 the issue of debt repudiation—the option for the government to cancel its debt obligations—and see that the conclusions there are very similar to those in the case of monetary policy.

When issues of time inconsistency are relevant, tight restraints on policymakers—such as a fixed-money-growth rule in the case of monetary policy, or a balanced budget rule in the case of fiscal policy—can provide a rough solution. But the solution has large costs because it prevents the use of macroeconomic policy altogether. Better solutions typically involve designing better institutions (such as an independent central bank or a better budget process) that can reduce the problem of time inconsistency while, at the same time, allowing the use of policy for the stabilization of output.

We have assumed so far that policymakers are *benevolent*—that they try to do what is best for the economy. However, much public discussion challenges that assumption: Politicians or policymakers, the argument goes, do what is best for themselves, and this is not always what is best for the country.

You have heard the arguments: Politicians avoid the hard decisions, they pander to the electorate, partisan politics leads to gridlock, and nothing ever gets done. Discussing the flaws of democracy goes far beyond the scope of this book. What we can do here is to briefly review how these arguments apply to macroeconomic policy and then look at the empirical evidence and see what light it sheds on the issue of policy restraints.

Games between Policymakers and Voters

Many macroeconomic policy decisions involve trading off short-run losses against long-run gains—or, conversely, short-run gains against long-run losses.

Take, for example, tax cuts. By definition, tax cuts lead to lower taxes today. They are also likely to lead to an increase in activity and, therefore, to an increase in pre-tax income, for some time. But unless they are matched by equal decreases in government spending, they lead to a larger budget deficit and to the need for an increase in taxes in the future. If voters are shortsighted, the temptation for politicians to cut taxes may prove irresistible. Politics may lead to systematic deficits, at least until the level of government debt has become so high that politicians are scared into action.

Now move on from taxes to macroeconomic policy in general. Again suppose that voters are shortsighted. If the politicians' main goal is to please voters and get reelected, what better policy than to expand aggregate demand before an election, leading to higher growth and lower unemployment? True, growth in excess of the normal growth rate cannot be sustained, and eventually the economy must return to the natural level of output: Higher growth now must be followed by lower growth later. But with the right timing and shortsighted voters, higher growth can win elections. Thus, we might expect a clear **political business cycle**, with higher growth on average before elections than after elections.

The arguments we have just laid out are familiar; you have heard them before, in one form or another. And their logic is convincing. The question is: How well do they fit the facts?

Take first deficits and debt. The argument above would lead you to expect that budget deficits and high government debt have always been and always will be there. Figure 24-4, which gives the evolution of the ratio of government debt to GDP in the United States since 1900, shows that the reality is more complex.

Look first at the evolution of the ratio of debt to GDP from 1900 to 1980. Note that each of the three buildups in debt was associated with special circumstances: World War I for the first buildup, the Great Depression for the second, and World War II for the third. These were times of unusually high military spending or unusual declines in output. Adverse circumstances—not pandering to voters—were clearly behind the large deficit and the resulting increase in debt during each of these three episodes. Note also how, in each case, the buildup was followed by a steady decrease in debt. In particular, note how the ratio of debt to GDP, which was as high as 130% in 1946, was steadily reduced to a postwar low of 33% in 1979.

The more recent evidence, however, fits the argument of shortsighted voters and pandering politicians much better. Since the early 1980s, large deficits have led to a large increase in the debt-to-GDP ratio. A brief return to budget surpluses at the end of

> From Okun's law, we know that output growth in excess of normal growth leads to a decline in the unemployment rate below the natural rate of unemployment. In the medium run, we know that the unemployment rate must increase back to the natural rate of unemployment. This in turn requires output growth below normal for some time. See ◀ Chapter 9.

> The precise relation between the evolution of deficits, debt, and the ratio of debt to GDP is explored in detail in Chapter 26. For the moment, all you need to know is that deficits ◀ lead to increases in debt.

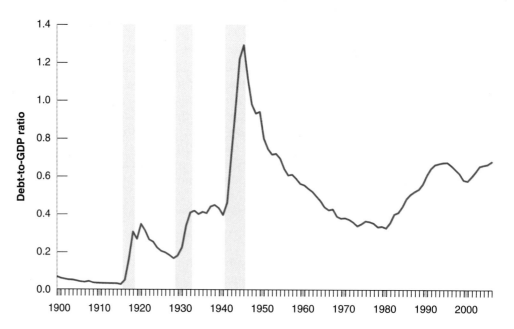

The recession of the early 1980s contributed to the deficits of the early 1980s. The recession of 2001 contributed to the deficits in the early 2000s. In both cases, however, the main cause of the sustained deficits was tax cuts.

the 1990s led to a decrease in the debt ratio for a few years. But, since 2001, deficits have again become large, and the debt-to-GDP ratio is again increasing. In contrast with the earlier three buildups of debt, these increases have not been due primarily to adverse economic conditions or to defense spending. The initial increase in the early 1980s was mostly due to large tax cuts under the Reagan administration. The renewed increase since 2001 is mostly due to the large tax cuts implemented by the Bush administration. Are these tax cuts, and the resulting deficits and increases in debt, best explained by pandering of politicians to shortsighted voters? I argue below that the answer is probably no and that the main explanation lies in a game between political parties rather than in a game between policymakers and voters.

Before I do so, let us return to the political-business-cycle argument, that policymakers try to get high output growth before the elections so they will be reelected. If the political business cycle were important, we would expect to see faster growth before elections than after. Table 24-1 gives average output growth rates for each of the four years of each U.S. administration since President Truman in 1948, distinguishing between Republican and Democratic administrations. Look at the last line: Growth has indeed been highest on average in the last year of an administration. The average difference across years is small however: 3.7% in the last year of an administration versus 3.2% in the first year. (We shall return later in this chapter to the other interesting feature in the table—the difference between Republican and Democratic administrations.)

Table 24-1	Average Growth During Democratic and Republican Administrations (percent per year)				
		Year of the Administration			
	First	Second	Third	Fourth	Average
Democratic	3.4	5.5	4.4	3.5	4.2
Republican	2.9	0.9	2.2	4.0	2.5
Average	3.2	2.9	3.2	3.7	3.3

Back to Policy   **Back to Policy**

There is little evidence of manipulation—or at least of successful manipulation—of the economy to win elections.

Games between Policymakers

Another line of argument shifts the focus from games between politicians and voters to games between policymakers.

Suppose, for example, that the party in power wants to reduce spending but faces opposition to spending cuts in Congress. One way of putting pressure both on Congress and on the future parties in power is to cut taxes and create deficits. As debt increases over time, the increasing pressure to reduce deficits may in turn force Congress and the future parties in power to reduce spending—something they would not have been willing to do otherwise.

This strategy goes by the ugly ◀ name of "Starve the Beast."

Or suppose that, either for the reason we just saw or for any other reason, the country is facing large budget deficits. Both parties in Congress want to reduce the deficit, but they disagree about the way to do it: One party wants to reduce deficits primarily through an increase in taxes; the other wants to reduce deficits primarily through a decrease in spending. Both parties may hold out on the hope that the other side will give in first. Only when debt has increased sufficiently, and it becomes urgent to reduce deficits, will one party give up. Game theorists refer to these situations as **wars of attrition**. The hope that the other side will give in leads to long and often costly delays. Such wars of attrition happen often in the context of fiscal policy, and deficit reduction occurs long after it should.

Wars of attrition arise in other macroeconomic contexts, such as during episodes of hyperinflation. As you saw in Chapter 23, hyperinflations come from the use of money creation to finance large budget deficits. Although the need to reduce those deficits is usually recognized early on, support for stabilization programs—which include the elimination of those deficits—typically comes only after inflation has reached such high levels that economic activity is severely affected.

Another example outside of economics: Think of the 2004 to 2005 NHL lockout in the United States, where the complete season was canceled because owners and players ◀ could not reach an agreement.

These games go a long way in explaining the rise in the ratio of debt to GDP in the United States since the early 1980s. There is little doubt that one of the goals of the Reagan administration, when it decreased taxes from 1981 to 1983, was to slow down the growth of spending. There is also little question that, by mid-1985, there was general agreement among policymakers that the deficits should be reduced. But, because of disagreements between Democrats and Republicans about whether this should happen primarily through tax increases or spending cuts, it was not until the late 1990s that deficit reduction was achieved. The motivation behind the Bush Administration's tax cuts of the early 2000s appears to be very similar to those of the Reagan administration. Now that the deficits are here, it is clear that Republicans would like to reduce them through cuts in non-defense spending, whereas Democrats are more willing to increases taxes. At the time of this writing, all the elements of a war of attrition are in place, and most forecasts are for deficits to continue for the rest of the decade.

See the discussion in the Focus box "Monetary Contraction and Fiscal Expansion: The ◀ United States in the Early 1980s," in Chapter 20.

Another example of games between political parties is the movements in economic activity brought about by the alternation of parties in power. Republicans typically worry more than Democrats about inflation. They worry less than Democrats about unemployment. So we would expect Democratic administrations to show stronger growth—and thus less unemployment and more inflation—than Republican administrations. This prediction appears to fit the facts quite well. Look at Table 24-1 again. Average growth has been 4.2% during Democratic administrations, compared to 2.5% during Republican administrations. The most striking contrast is in the second year, 5.5% during Democratic administrations, compared to 0.9% during Republican administrations.

The Maastricht treaty, negotiated by the countries of the European Union in 1991, set a number of convergence criteria that countries had to meet in order to qualify to join the Euro area. (For more on the history of the euro, see the Focus box "The Euro: A Short History" in Chapter 21.) Among them were two restrictions on fiscal policy. First, the ratio of the country's budget deficit to GDP had to be below 3%. Second, the ratio of the country's debt to GDP had to be below 60%, or at least "approaching this value at a satisfactory pace."

In 1997, would-be members of the Euro area agreed to make some of these criteria permanent. The Stability and Growth Pact (SGP), signed in 1997, required members of the Euro Area to follow these fiscal rules:

- That countries commit to balance their budgets in the medium run. Countries must present programs to the European authorities, specifying their objectives for the current year and following three years in order to show how they are making progress toward their medium-run goal.

- That countries avoid excessive deficits, except under exceptional circumstances. Following the Maastricht treaty criteria, excessive deficits were defined as deficits in excess of 3% of GDP. Exceptional circumstances were defined as declines of GDP larger than 2%.

- That sanctions be imposed on countries that ran excessive deficits. These sanctions could range from 0.2% to 0.5% of GDP—so, for a country like France, up to roughly $10 billion!

Figure 1 plots the evolution of budget deficits since 1990 for the Euro area as a whole. Note how from 1993 to 2000, budget balances went from a deficit of 5.8% of Euro area GDP to a surplus of 0.1%. The performance of some of the member countries was particularly impressive: Greece reduced its deficit from 13.4% of GDP to a reported 1.4% of GDP. (It was discovered in 2004 that the Greek government had cheated in reporting its deficit numbers and that the actual improvement, although impressive, was less than reported; the deficit for 2000 is now estimated to have been 4.1%.) Italy's deficit went from 10.1% of GDP in 1993 to only 0.9% of GDP in 2000.

Was the improvement entirely due to the Maastricht criteria and the SGP rules? Just as in the case of deficit reduction in the United States over the same period, the answer is no: The decrease in nominal interest rates, which decreased the interest payments on the debt, and the strong expansion of the late 1990s both played important roles. But, again as in the United States, the fiscal rules also played a significant role: The carrot—the right to become a member of the Euro Area—was attractive enough to lead a number of countries to take tough measures to reduce their deficits.

Things turned around, however, in 2000. Since 2000, deficits have increased. The ratio of the deficit to GDP for the Euro area increased back to 3.1% in 2003 and now stands at 2.1%. The main reason for the increase has been low output growth since 2001, which has led to low tax revenue growth. Although the deficit for the Euro area as a whole is below the 3% limit, this is not the case for a number of individual countries. The first country to break the limit was Portugal in 2001, with a deficit of 4.4%. The next two were France and Germany, both with deficits in excess of 3% of GDP in 2002. Italy soon followed. In each case, the government of the country decided it was more important to avoid a fiscal contraction, which could lead to even slower output growth, than to satisfy the rules of the SGP.

Faced with clear "excessive deficits" (and without the excuse of exceptional circumstances because output growth in each of these countries was low but positive), European authorities found themselves in a quandary. Starting the excessive deficit procedure against Portugal, a small country, might have been politically feasible, although it is doubtful that Portugal would have ever been willing to pay the fine. Starting the same procedure against the two largest members of the Euro area, France and Germany, proved politically impossible. After an internal fight between the two main European authorities, the European Commission and the European Council—the European Commission wanted to proceed with the excessive deficit procedure, while the European Council, which represents the states, did not—the procedure was suspended.

This raises an intriguing question: Why is the effect so much stronger in the administration's *second* year? The theory of unemployment and inflation we developed in Chapter 9 suggests a possible hypothesis: There are lags in the effects of policy, so it takes about a year for a new administration to affect the economy. And sustaining higher growth than normal for too long would lead to increasing inflation, so even a Democratic administration would not want to sustain higher growth throughout its term. Thus, growth rates tend to be much closer to each other during the second halves of Democratic and Republican administrations—more so than during first halves.

The crisis made it clear that the initial rules were too inflexible. Romano Prodi, the head of the European Commission, admitted to that much. In an interview in October 2002, he stated, "I know very well that the Stability Pact is stupid, like all decisions that are rigid." And the attitudes of both France and Germany showed that the threat to impose large fines on countries with excessive deficits was simply not credible.

For two years, the European Commission therefore explored ways to improve the rules so as to make them more flexible and, by implication, more credible. In 2005, a new, revised SGP was adopted. It keeps the 3% deficit and 60% debt numbers as thresholds, but allows for more flexibility in deviating from the rules.

Growth no longer has to be less than –2% for the rules to be suspended; negative growth, or even prolonged low positive growth, will do. Exceptions can also be made if the deficit comes from structural reforms or for public investment. Fines are gone, and the plan is to rely on early and very public warnings, as well as on peer pressure from other euro area countries. We already saw the potential problems with such proposals earlier in the chapter: Flexible rules are harder to interpret and more prone to disagreements of interpretation. And public warnings and peer pressure only go so far. Finding the right rules is hard, and it is not clear whether and how this new version of the SGP will fare.

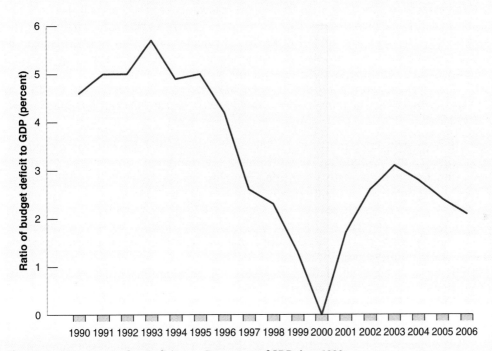

Figure 1   *Euro Area Budget Deficits as a Percentage of GDP since 1990*

Politics and Fiscal Restraints

If politics sometimes lead to long and lasting budget deficits, can rules be put in place to limit these adverse effects?

A constitutional amendment to balance the budget, such as the amendment proposed by the Republicans in 1994 (see Figure 24-1), would surely eliminate the problem of deficits. But, just like a constant money growth rule in the case of monetary policy, it would eliminate the use of fiscal policy as a macroeconomic instrument altogether. This is just too high a price to pay.

A better approach is to put in place rules that put limits on either deficits or debt. This is harder than it sounds. Rules such as limits on the ratio of the deficit to GDP or the ratio of debt to GDP are more flexible than a balanced budget requirement; but they may still not be flexible enough if the economy is affected by particularly bad shocks. This has been made clear by the problems faced by the Stability and Growth Pact; these problems are discussed at more length in the Focus box "The Stability and Growth Pact: A Short History." More flexible or more complex rules, such as rules that allow for special circumstances, or rules that take into account the state of the economy, are harder to design and, especially, harder to enforce. For example, allowing the deficit to be higher if the unemployment rate is higher than the natural rate requires having a simple and unambiguous way of computing the natural rate—a nearly impossible task.

A complementary approach is to put in place mechanisms to reduce deficits, were such deficits to arise. Consider, for example, a mechanism that triggers automatic spending cuts when the deficit gets too large. Suppose the budget deficit is too large, and it is desirable to cut spending across the board by 5%. Members of Congress will find it difficult to explain to their constituency why their favorite spending program was cut by 5%. Now suppose the deficit triggers automatic across-the-board spending cuts of 5% without any congressional action. Knowing that other programs will be cut, members of Congress will accept cuts in their favorite programs more easily. They will also be better able to deflect the blame for the cuts: Members of Congress who succeed in limiting the cuts to their favorite program to, say, 4% (by convincing Congress to make deeper cuts in some other programs in order to maintain the lower overall level of spending) can then return to their constituents and claim that they successfully prevented even larger cuts.

This was indeed the approach which was used to reduce deficits in the United States in the 1990s. The Budget Enforcement Act, passed in 1990 and extended by new legislation in 1993 and 1997, introduced two main rules:

- It imposed constraints on spending. Spending was divided into two categories: discretionary spending (roughly: spending on goods and services, including defense) and mandatory spending (roughly: transfer payments to individuals). Constraints, called **spending caps**, were set on discretionary spending for the following five years. These caps were set in such a way as to require a small but steady decrease in discretionary spending (in real terms). Explicit provisions were made for emergencies. For example, spending on Operation Desert Storm during the Gulf War in 1991 was not subject to the caps.
- It required that a new transfer program could be adopted only if it could be shown that it would not increase deficits in the future (either by raising new revenues or by decreasing spending on an existing program). This rule is known as the pay-as-you-go rule, or the **PAYGO rule**.

The focus on spending rather than on the deficit itself had one important implication. If there was a recession, hence a decrease in revenues, the deficit could increase without triggering a decrease in spending. This happened in 1991 and 1992 when, because of the recession, the deficit increased—despite the fact that spending satisfied the constraints imposed by the caps. This focus on spending had two desirable effects: It allowed for a larger fiscal deficit during a recession—a good thing from the point of view of macroeconomic policy; and it decreased the pressure to break the rules during a recession—a good thing from a political point of view.

By 1998, deficits were gone, and, for the first time in 20 years, the federal budget was in surplus. Not all of the deficit reduction was due to the Budget Enforcement Act rules: A decrease in defense spending due to the end of the Cold War, and a large increase in tax revenues due to the strong expansion of the second half of the 1990s were important factors. But there is wide agreement that the rules played an important role in making sure that decreases in defense spending and increases in tax revenues were used for deficit reduction rather than for increases in other spending programs.

Once budget surpluses appeared, however, Congress became increasingly willing to break its own rules. Spending caps were systematically broken, and the PAYGO rule was allowed to expire in 2002. At the time of this writing, deficits are large and predicted to remain so for many years to come. It is clear that, although spending caps and PAYGO rules were essential in reducing deficits in the 1990s, they did not prevent large deficits from reappearing in the 2000s. This is leading some economists and policymakers to conclude that, in the end, nothing short of a constitutional amendment can do the job of avoiding deficits. The issue is likely to rise again to the forefront of discussions of fiscal policy in the future.

These deficits have led to increasing calls for new rules. In 2007, Congress, under pressure from the newly elected Democratic majority, passed new PAYGO rules. Whether these rules will eliminate the ◀ deficit remains to be seen.

Summary

- The effects of macroeconomic policies are always uncertain. This uncertainty should lead policymakers to be more cautious and to use less active policies. Policies must be broadly aimed at avoiding prolonged recessions, slowing down booms, and avoiding inflationary pressure. The higher the level of unemployment or inflation, the more active the policies should be. But they should stop short of fine-tuning, of trying to maintain constant unemployment or constant output growth.

- Using macroeconomic policy to control the economy is fundamentally different from controlling a machine. Unlike a machine, the economy is composed of people and firms who try to anticipate what policymakers will do, and who react not only to current policy but also to expectations of future policy. In this sense, macroeconomic policy can be thought of as a game between policymakers and people in the economy.

- When playing a game, it is sometimes better for a player to give up some of his or her options. For example, when a hostage taking occurs, it is better to negotiate with the hostage takers than to not negotiate. But a government that credibly commits to not negotiating with hostage takers—a government that gives up the option of negotiation—is actually more likely to deter hostage takings from occurring.

- The same argument applies to various aspects of macroeconomic policy. By credibly committing to not using

monetary policy to decrease unemployment below the natural rate of unemployment, a central bank can alleviate fears that money growth will be high and, in the process, decrease both expected and actual inflation. When issues of time inconsistency are relevant, tight restraints on policymakers—such as a fixed-money-growth rule in the case of monetary policy—can provide a rough solution. But the solution can have large costs if it prevents the use of macroeconomic policy altogether. Better methods typically involve designing better institutions (such as an independent central bank) that can reduce the problem of time inconsistency without eliminating monetary policy as a macroeconomic policy tool.

- Another argument for putting restraints on policymakers is that policymakers may play games either with the public or among themselves, and these games may lead to undesirable outcomes. Politicians may try to fool a shortsighted electorate by choosing policies with short-run benefits but large long-term costs—for example, large budget deficits. Political parties may delay painful decisions, hoping that the other party will make the adjustment and take the blame. In cases like this, tight restraints on policy, such as a constitutional amendment to balance the budget, again provide a rough solution. Better ways typically involve better institutions and better ways of designing the process through which policy and decisions are made.

Key Terms

Quick Check

1. *Using the information in this chapter, label each of the following statements true, false, or uncertain. Explain briefly.*

   a. If the political business cycle was important, we would expect to see faster growth after elections than before.

   b. There is substantial uncertainty about the effects of macroeconomic policies. This should lead policy makers to use less active policies.

   c. Elect a Republican as president if you want low unemployment.

   d. More central bank independence appears to be systematically associated with higher inflation.

   e. Rules such as limits on the ratio of the deficit to GDP or the ratio of debt to GDP are more flexible than a balanced budget requirement.

   f. Governments would be wise to announce a no-negotiation policy with hostage takers.

   g. If hostages are taken, it is clearly wise for governments to negotiate with hostage takers, even if the government has announced a no-negotiation policy.

2. *Implementing a political business cycle*

   You are the economic adviser to a newly elected president. In four years she will face another election. Voters want a low unemployment rate and a low inflation rate. However, you believe that voting decisions are influenced heavily by the values of unemployment and inflation in the last year before the election, and that the economy's performance in the first three years of a president's administration has little effect on voting behavior.

   Assume that inflation last year was 10%, and that the unemployment rate was equal to the natural rate. The Phillips curve is given by

   $$\pi_t = \pi_{t-1} - \alpha(u_t - u_n)$$

   Assume that you can use fiscal and monetary policy to achieve any unemployment rate you want for each of the next four years. Your task is to help the president achieve low unemployment and low inflation in the last year of her administration.

   a. Suppose you want to achieve a low unemployment rate (i.e., an unemployment rate below the natural rate) in the year before the next election (four years from today). What will happen to inflation in the fourth year?

   b. Given the effect on inflation you identified in part (a), what would you advise the president to do in the early years of her administration to achieve low inflation in the fourth year?

   c. Now suppose the Phillips curve is given by

   $$\pi_t = \pi_t^e - \alpha(u_t - u_n)$$

   In addition, assume that people form inflation expectations, π_t^e, based on consideration of the future (as opposed to looking only at inflation last year), and are

aware that the president has an incentive to carry out the policies you identified in parts (a) and (b). Are the policies you described in parts (a) and (b) likely to be successful? Why or why not?

3. *New Zealand rewrote the charter of its central bank in the early 1990s to make low inflation its only goal. Why would New Zealand want to do this?*

4. *Suppose the government amends the constitution to prevent government officials from negotiating with terrorists. What are the advantages of such a policy? What are the disadvantages?*

Dig Deeper

5. *Deficit reduction as a prisoner's dilemma game*

   Suppose there is a budget deficit. It can be reduced by cutting military spending, by cutting welfare programs, or by cutting both. The Democrats have to decide whether to support cuts in welfare programs. The Republicans have to decide whether to support cuts in military spending.

   The possible outcomes are represented in the following table:

		Welfare Cuts	
		Yes	No
Defense Cuts	Yes	$(R = 1, D = -2)$	$(R = -2, D = 3)$
	No	$(R = 3, D = -2)$	$(R = -1, D = -1)$

   The table presents payoffs to each party under the various outcomes. Think of a payoff as a measure of happiness for a given party under a given outcome. If Democrats vote for welfare cuts, and Republicans vote against cuts in military spending, the Republicans receive a payoff of 3, and the Democrats receive a payoff of -2.

   a. If the Republicans decide to cut military spending, what is the best response of the Democrats? Given this response, what is the payoff for the Republicans?

   b. If the Republicans decide not to cut military spending, what is the best response of the Democrats? Given this response, what is the payoff for the Republicans?

   c. What will the Republicans do? What will the Democrats do? Will the budget deficit be reduced? Why or why not? (A game with a payoff structure like the one in this problem, and which produces the outcome you have just described, is known as a *prisoner's dilemma*.) Is there a way to improve the outcome?

6. *Political expectations, inflation, and unemployment*

   Consider a country with two political parties, Democrats and Republicans. Democrats care more about unemployment than Republicans, and Republicans care more about inflation than Democrats. When Democrats are in power, they choose an inflation rate of π_D, and when Republicans are in power, they choose an inflation rate of π_R. We assume that $\pi_D > \pi_R$.

The Phillips curve is given by

$$\pi_t = \pi_t^e - \alpha(u_t - u_n)$$

An election is about to be held. Assume that expectations about inflation for the coming year (represented by π_t^e) are formed before the election. (Essentially, this assumption means that wages for the coming year are set before the election.) Moreover, Democrats and Republicans have an equal chance of winning the election.

a. Solve for expected inflation, in terms of π_D and π_R.

b. Suppose the Democrats win the election and implement their target inflation rate, π_D. Given your solution for expected inflation in part (a), how will the unemployment rate compare to the natural rate of unemployment?

c. Suppose the Republicans win the election and implement their target inflation rate, π_R. Given your solution for expected inflation in part (a), how will the unemployment rate compare to the natural rate of unemployment?

d. Do these results fit the evidence in Table 24-1? Why or why not?

e. Now suppose that everybody expects the Democrats to win the election, and the Democrats indeed win. If the Democrats implement their target inflation rate, how will the unemployment rate compare to the natural rate?

Explore Further

7. *Games, precommitment, and time inconsistency in the news*

Current events offer abundant examples of disputes in which the parties are involved in a game, try to commit themselves to lines of action in advance, and face issues of time inconsistency. Examples arise in the domestic political process, international affairs, and labor-management relations.

a. Choose a current dispute (or one resolved recently) to investigate. Do an Internet search to learn the issues involved in the dispute, the actions taken by the parties to date, and the current state of play.

b. In what ways have the parties tried to precommit to certain actions in the future? Do they face issues of time inconsistency? Have the parties failed to carry out any of their threatened actions?

c. Does the dispute resemble a prisoner's dilemma game (a game with a payoff structure like the one described in problem 6)? In other words, does it seem likely (or did it actually happen) that the individual incentives of the parties will lead them to an unfavorable outcome—one that could be improved for both parties through cooperation? Is there a deal to be made? What attempts have the parties made to negotiate?

d. How do you think the dispute will be resolved (or how has it been resolved)?

 We invite you to visit the Blanchard page on the Prentice Hall Web site, at:
www.prenhall.com/blanchard
for this chapter's World Wide Web exercises.

Further Readings

■ If you want to learn more on these issues, a very useful reference is Alan Drazen, *Political Economy in Macroeconomics*, Princeton University Press, Princeton, NJ, 2000.

■ A leading proponent of the view that governments misbehave and should be tightly restrained is James Buchanan, from George Mason University. Buchanan received the Nobel Prize in 1986 for his work on public

choice. Read, for example, his book with Richard Wagner, *Democracy in Deficit: The Political Legacy of Lord Keynes*, Academic Press, New York, 1977.

■ For an interpretation of the increase in inflation in the 1970s as a result of time inconsistency, see Henry Chappell and Rob McGregor, "Did Time Consistency Contribute to the Great Inflation?" *Economics & Politics*, November 2004.

Monetary Policy: A Summing Up

Nearly every chapter has said something about monetary policy. This chapter puts all these things together and ties up the remaining loose ends.

Let's first briefly review what you have learned (the Focus box "Monetary Policy: What You Have Learned and Where" gives a more detailed summary):

- In the short run, monetary policy affects the level of output as well as its composition:
An increase in money leads to a decrease in interest rates and a depreciation of the currency. Both of these lead to an increase in the demand for goods and an increase in output.

- In the medium run and the long run, monetary policy is neutral:
Changes in either the level or the rate of growth of money have no effect on output or unemployment.
Changes in the level of money lead to proportional increases in prices.
Changes in the rate of nominal money growth lead to corresponding changes in the inflation rate.

With these effects in mind, this chapter looks at the goals and methods of monetary policy today:

- Section 25-1 discusses what inflation rate central banks should try to achieve in the medium run and the long run.

- Section 25-2 discusses how monetary policy should be designed both to achieve this inflation rate in the medium run and the long run, and to reduce output fluctuations in the short run.

- Section 25-3 describes how monetary policy is actually carried out in the United States today. ■

■ In Chapter 4 we looked at the determination of money demand and money supply, as well as the effects of monetary policy on the interest rate.

You saw how an increase in the money supply, achieved through an open market operation, leads to a decrease in the interest rate.

■ In Chapter 5 we looked at the short-run effects of monetary policy on output.

You saw how an increase in money leads, through a decrease in the interest rate, to an increase in spending and to an increase in output.

■ In Chapter 7 we looked at the effects of changes in money on output and prices, not only in the short run but also in the medium run.

You saw that in the medium run, money is neutral: Changes in money are reflected one-for-one in changes in the price level.

■ In Chapter 9 we looked at the relation between nominal money growth, inflation, and unemployment.

You saw that in the medium run, nominal money growth is reflected one-for-one in inflation, leaving the unemployment rate unaffected. You saw that in the short run however, decreases in nominal money growth lead to lower output and higher unemployment for some time.

■ In Chapter 14 we introduced a distinction between the nominal interest rate and the real interest rate.

You saw how higher nominal money growth leads to a lower nominal interest rate and a lower real interest rate in the short run, and to a higher nominal interest rate and an unchanged real interest rate in the medium run.

■ In Chapter 17 we returned to the short-run effects of monetary policy on output, taking into account the effects of monetary policy on expectations.

You saw that monetary policy affects the short-term nominal interest rate, but that spending depends on current and expected future short-term real interest rates. You saw how the effects of monetary policy on output depend on how expectations respond to monetary policy.

■ In Chapter 20 we looked at the effects of monetary policy in an economy open in both goods markets and financial markets.

You saw how, in an open economy, monetary policy affects spending and output, not only through the interest rate, but also through the exchange rate. An increase in money leads to a decrease in the interest rate and to a depreciation, both of which increase spending and output.

■ In Chapter 21 we discussed the pros and cons of different monetary policy regimes, namely flexible exchange rates versus fixed exchange rates.

You saw the pros and cons of adopting a common currency such as the euro, or even giving up monetary policy altogether, through the adoption of a currency board or dollarization.

■ In Chapter 22 we looked at the implications of the liquidity trap, the fact that monetary policy cannot decrease the nominal interest rate below zero.

You saw how the liquidity trap and deflation can combine to turn a recession into a slump or a depression.

■ In Chapter 23 we studied hyperinflations and looked at the conditions under which such episodes arise and eventually end. We focused on the relation between the budget deficit, nominal money growth, and inflation.

You saw how a large budget deficit can lead to high nominal money growth and, in turn, to hyperinflation.

■ In Chapter 24 we looked at the problems facing macroeconomic policy in general, and monetary policy in particular.

You saw that uncertainty about the effects of policy should lead to more cautious policies. You saw that even well-intentioned policymakers may sometimes not do what is best, and that there is a case to be made for putting restraints on policymakers. We also looked at the benefits of having an independent central bank and appointing a conservative central banker.

■ In this chapter we discuss the issues of the optimal inflation rate, the design of monetary policy, and how the Fed actually conducts monetary policy in the United States today.

FOCUS

The five countries with inflation above 5%: Iceland, with 5.8%; Luxembourg, with 7.1%; Mexico, with 6.6%; Norway, with 7.7%; and Turkey, with 13.0%.

25-1 The Optimal Inflation Rate

Table 25-1 shows how inflation has steadily gone down in rich countries since the early 1980s. In 1981, average inflation in OECD countries was 10.5%; in 2006, it was down to 2.2%. In 1981, 2 countries (out of 30) had inflation rates below 5%; in 2006, the number ▶ had increased to 25.

Table 25-1   Inflation Rates in OECD Countries since 1981

Year	1981	1985	1990	1995	2000	2006
OECD average*	10.5%	6.6%	6.2%	5.2%	2.8%	2.2%
Number of countries with inflation below 5%†	2	10	15	21	24	25

* Average of GDP deflator inflation rates, using relative GDPs measured at PPP prices as weights.

† Out of 30 countries.

Does this mean that most central banks have now achieved their goal? Or should they aim for an even lower inflation rate, perhaps 0%? The answer depends on the costs and benefits of inflation.

The Costs of Inflation

We saw in Chapter 23 how very high inflation, say a rate of 30% per month or more, can disrupt economic activity. The debate in OECD countries today, however, is not about the costs of inflation rates of 30% per month or more. Rather, it centers on the advantages of, say, 0% versus 3% inflation per year. Within that range, economists identify four main costs of inflation: (1) shoe-leather costs, (2) tax distortions, (3) money illusion, and (4) inflation variability.

Shoe-Leather Costs

In the medium run, a higher inflation rate leads to a higher nominal interest rate and so to a higher opportunity cost of holding money. As a result, people decrease their money balances by making more trips to the bank—thus the expression **shoe-leather costs**. These trips would be avoided if inflation were lower and people could be doing other things instead, such as working more or enjoying leisure.

From Chapter 14: In the medium run, the real interest rate is not affected by inflation. The increase in inflation is reflected one-for-one in an increase in the nominal interest rate. This is called the Fisher effect.

During hyperinflations, shoe-leather costs can become quite large. But their importance in times of moderate inflation is limited. If an inflation rate of 3% leads people to go to the bank say one more time every month, or to do one more transaction between their money market fund and their checking account every month, this hardly qualifies as a major cost of inflation.

Tax Distortions

The second cost of inflation comes from the interaction between the tax system and inflation.

Consider, for example, the taxation of capital gains. Taxes on capital gains are typically based on the change in the price in dollars of an asset between the time it is purchased and the time it is sold. This implies that the higher the rate of inflation, the higher the tax. An example will make this clear:

- Suppose inflation has been running at $\pi\%$ per year for the past 10 years.
- Suppose you bought your house for $50,000 10 years ago, and you are selling it today for $50,000 \times (1 + \pi\%)^{10}$—so its real value is unchanged.
- If the capital-gains tax is 30%, the *effective tax rate* on the sale of your house—defined as the ratio of the tax you pay to the price for which you sell your house—is

The numerator of the fraction equals the sale price minus the purchase price. The denominator is the sale price.

$$(30\%) \frac{50,000(1 + \pi\%)^{10} - 50,000}{50,000(1 + \pi\%)^{10}}$$

■ Because you are selling your house for the same real price at which you bought it, your real capital gain is zero, so you should not be paying any tax. Indeed, if $\pi = 0$—if there has been no inflation—then the effective tax rate is 0%. But if $\pi = 3\%$, then the effective tax rate is 7.6%: Despite the fact that your real capital gain is zero, you end up paying a high tax.

Some economists argue that the costs of bracket creep were much larger. As tax revenues steadily increased, there was little pressure on the government to control spending. The result, they argue, was an increase in the size of the government in the 1960s and 1970s far beyond what was desirable.

The problems created by the interactions between taxation and inflation extend beyond capital-gains taxes. Although we know that the real rate of return on an asset is the real interest rate, not the nominal interest rate, income for the purpose of income taxation includes nominal interest payments, not real interest payments. Or, to take yet another example, until the early 1980s in the United States, the income levels corresponding to different income tax rates were not increased automatically with inflation. As a result, people were pushed into higher tax brackets as their nominal income—but ▶ not necessarily their real income—increased over time, an effect known as *bracket creep*.

You might argue that this cost is not a cost of inflation per se, but rather the result of a badly designed tax system. In the house example we just discussed, the government could eliminate the problem if it *indexed* the purchase price to the price level—that is, if it adjusted the purchase price for inflation since the time of purchase—and computed the tax on the difference between the sale price and the adjusted purchase price. Under that computation, there would be no capital gains and therefore no capital-gains tax to pay. But because tax codes rarely allow for such systematic adjustment, the inflation rate matters and leads to distortions.

Money Illusion

The third cost of inflation comes from **money illusion**—the notion that people appear to make systematic mistakes in assessing nominal versus real changes. A number of computations that would be simple when prices are stable become more complicated when there is inflation. When they compare their income this year to their income in previous years, people have to keep track of the history of inflation. When they choose between different assets or when they decide how much to consume or save, they have to keep track of the difference between the real interest rate and the nominal interest rate. Casual evidence suggests that many people find these computations difficult and often fail to make the relevant distinctions. Economists and psychologists have gathered more formal evidence, and it suggests that inflation often leads people and firms to make incorrect decisions (see the Focus box "Money Illusion"). If this is the case, then a simple solution is to have zero inflation.

Inflation Variability

The fourth cost comes from the fact that higher inflation is typically associated with *more variable inflation*. And more variable inflation means financial assets such as bonds, which promise fixed nominal payments in the future, become riskier.

Take a bond that pays $1,000 in 10 years. With constant inflation over the next 10 years, not only the nominal value, but also the real value of the bond in 10 years is known with certainty—we can compute exactly how much a dollar will be worth in 10 years. But with variable inflation, the real value of $1,000 in 10 years becomes uncertain. The more variability there is, the more uncertainty it creates. Saving for retirement becomes more difficult. For those who have invested in bonds, lower inflation than they expected means a better retirement; but higher inflation may mean poverty.

A good and sad movie about surviving on a fixed pension in post–World War II Italy is *Umberto D*, made by Vittorio de Sica in 1952.

This is one of the reasons retirees, for whom part of their income is fixed in dollar terms, ▶ typically worry more about inflation than other groups in the population.

You might argue, as in the case of taxes, that these costs are not due to inflation per se, but rather to the financial markets' inability to provide assets that protect their

There is a lot of anecdotal evidence that many people fail to adjust properly for inflation in their financial computations. Recently, economists and psychologists have started looking at money illusion more closely. In a recent study, two psychologists, Eldar Shafir from Princeton and Amos Tversky from Stanford, and one economist, Peter Diamond from MIT, designed a survey aimed at finding how prevalent money illusion is and what causes it. Among the many questions they asked of people in various groups (people at Newark International Airport, people at two New Jersey shopping malls, and a group of Princeton undergraduates) is the following:

Suppose Adam, Ben, and Carl each received an inheritance of $200,000 and each used it immediately to purchase a house. Suppose each sold his house one year after buying it. Economic conditions were, however, different in each case:

■ During the time Adam owned the house, there was a 25% deflation—the prices of all goods and services decreased by approximately 25%. A year after Adam bought the house, he sold it for $154,000 (23% less than what he had paid).

■ During the time Ben owned the house, there was no inflation or deflation—the prices of all goods and services did not change significantly during the year. A year after Ben bought the house, he sold it for $198,000 (1% less than what he had paid).

■ During the time Carl owned the house, there was a 25% inflation—the prices of all goods and services increased by approximately 25%. A year after Carl bought the house, he sold it for $246,000 (23% more than what he had paid).

Please rank Adam, Ben, and Carl in terms of the success of their house transactions. Assign "1" to the person who made the best deal, and "3" to the person who made the worst deal.

In nominal terms, Carl clearly made the best deal, followed by Ben, followed by Adam. But what is relevant is how they did in real terms—adjusting for inflation. In real terms, the ranking is reversed: Adam, with a 2% real gain, made the best deal, followed by Ben (with a 1% loss), followed by Carl (with a 2% loss).

The survey's answers were as follows:

Rank	Adam	Ben	Carl
1st	37%	15%	48%
2nd	10%	74%	16%
3rd	53%	11%	36%

Carl was ranked first by 48% of the respondents, and Adam was ranked third by 53% of the respondents. These answers suggest that money illusion is very prevalent. In other words, people (even Princeton undergraduates) have a hard time adjusting for inflation.

holders against inflation. Rather than issuing only nominal bonds (bonds that promise a fixed nominal amount in the future), governments or firms could also issue *indexed bonds*—bonds that promise a nominal amount adjusted for inflation, so people do not have to worry about the real value of the bond when they retire. Indeed, as we saw in Chapter 15, a number of countries, including the United States, have now introduced such bonds, so people can better protect themselves against movements in inflation.

The Benefits of Inflation

Inflation is actually not all bad. One can identify three benefits of inflation: (1) seignorage, (2) the option of negative real interest rates for macroeconomic policy, and (3) (somewhat paradoxically) the use of the interaction between money illusion and inflation in facilitating real wage adjustments.

Seignorage

Money creation—the ultimate source of inflation—is one of the ways in which the government can finance its spending. Put another way, money creation is an alternative to borrowing from the public or raising taxes.

As you saw in Chapter 23, the government typically does not "create" money to pay for its spending. Rather, the government issues and sells bonds and spends the proceeds. But if the bonds are bought by the central bank, which then creates money

Let H denote the monetary base—the money issued by the central bank. Then

$$\frac{Seignorage}{Y} = \frac{\Delta H}{PY} = \frac{\Delta H}{H}\frac{H}{PY}$$

where $\Delta H/H$ is the rate of growth of the monetary base, and H/PY is the ratio of the monetary base to nominal GDP. ▶

to pay for them, the result is the same: Other things being equal, the revenues from money creation—that is, *seignorage*—allow the government to borrow less from the public or to lower taxes.

How large is seignorage in practice? When looking at hyperinflations in Chapter 23, you saw that seignorage is often an important source of government finance in countries with very high inflation rates. But its importance in OECD economies today, and for the range of inflation rates we are considering, is much more limited. Take the case of the United States. The ratio of the monetary base—the money issued by the Fed (see Chapter 4)—to GDP is about 6%. An increase in nominal money growth of 3% per year (which eventually leads to a 3% increase in inflation) would lead therefore to an increase in seignorage of 3% × 6%, or 0.18% of GDP. This is a small amount of revenues to get in exchange for 3% more inflation.

Therefore, while the seignorage argument is sometimes relevant (for example, in economies that do not yet have a good fiscal system in place), it hardly seems relevant in the discussion of whether OECD countries today should have, say, 0% versus 3% inflation.

The Option of Negative Real Interest Rates

The seignorage argument follows from our discussion of the liquidity trap and its macroeconomic implications in Chapter 22. A numerical example will help here.

From Chapter 14: The natural ▶ real interest rate is the real interest rate implied by equilibrium in the goods market when output is equal to its natural level.

Consider two economies, both with a natural real interest rate equal to 2%.

- In the first economy, the central bank maintains an average inflation rate of 3%, so the nominal interest rate is, on average, equal to 2% + 3% = 5%.
- In the second economy, the central bank maintains an average inflation rate of 0%, so the nominal interest rate is, on average, equal to 2% + 0% = 2%.
- Suppose both economies are hit by a similar adverse shock, which leads, at a given interest rate, to a decrease in spending and a decrease in output in the short run.
- In the first economy, the central bank can decrease the nominal interest rate from 5% to 0%, a decrease of 5%. Under the assumption that expected inflation does not change immediately and remains equal to 3%, the real interest rate decreases from 2% to –3%. This is likely to have a strong positive effect on spending and help the economy recover.
- In the second economy, the central bank can only decrease the nominal interest rate from 2% to 0%, a decrease of 2%. Under the assumption that expected inflation does not change right away and remains equal to 0%, the real interest rate decreases only by 2%, from 2% to 0%. This small decrease in the real interest rate may not increase spending by very much.

In short, an economy with a higher average inflation rate has more scope to use monetary policy to fight a recession. An economy with a low average inflation rate may find itself unable to use monetary policy to return output to the natural level of output. As you saw in Chapter 22, this possibility is far from being just theoretical. Japan faced precisely such a limit on monetary policy, and its recession turned into a slump. In the early 2000s, many economists worried that other countries may also be at risk. Many

The average U.S. short-term nominal rate was only 1.2% in 2003.

As we saw in Chapter 5, in the early 2000s, the Fed decreased the nominal interest rate by 6%. This was still not enough to avoid the 1990–1991 recession.

countries, including the United States, had low inflation and low nominal interest rates. If, for any reason, some of these countries had been faced with further adverse shocks to spending, the room for monetary policy to help avoid a decline in output would clearly have been limited. Fortunately, there were no adverse shocks, and the issue has disappeared from the front pages. It is likely, however, to come back in the future.

Money Illusion Revisited

Paradoxically, the presence of money illusion provides at least one argument *for* having a positive inflation rate.

To see why, consider two situations. In the first, inflation is 3%, and your wage goes up by 1% in nominal terms—in dollars. In the second, inflation is 0%, and your wage goes down by 2% in nominal terms. Both lead to the same 2% decrease in your real wage, so you should be indifferent. The evidence, however, shows that many people will accept the real wage cut more easily in the first case than in the second case.

Why is this example relevant to our discussion? Because, as you saw in Chapter 13, the constant process of change that characterizes modern economies means some workers must sometimes take real pay cuts. Thus, the argument goes, the presence of inflation allows for these downward real-wage adjustments more easily than when there is no inflation. This argument is plausible. Economists have not established its importance; but because so many economies now have very low inflation, we may soon be in a position to test it.

See, for example, the results of a survey of managers by Alan Blinder and Don Choi, in "A Shred of Evidence on Theories of Wage Rigidity," *Quarterly Journal of Economics*, 1990.

A conflict of metaphors: Because inflation makes these real wage adjustments easier to achieve, some economists say inflation "greases the wheels" of the economy. Others, emphasizing the adverse effects of inflation on relative prices, say that inflation "puts sand" in the economy.

The Optimal Inflation Rate: The Current Debate

At this stage, the debate in OECD countries is largely between those who think some inflation (say 3%) is fine and those who want to achieve price stability—that is, 0% inflation.

Those who want an inflation rate around 3% emphasize that the costs of 3% versus 0% inflation are small and that the benefits of inflation are worth keeping. They argue that some of the costs of inflation could be avoided by indexing the tax system and issuing more indexed bonds. They also argue that getting inflation down from its current rate to zero would require some increase in unemployment for some time, and that this transition cost may well exceed the eventual benefits.

Those who want to aim for 0% make the point that 0% is a very different target rate from all others: It corresponds to price stability. This is desirable in itself. Knowing that the price level will be roughly the same in 10 or 20 years as it is today simplifies a number of complicated decisions and eliminates the scope for money illusion. Also, given the time consistency problem facing central banks (discussed in Chapter 24), credibility and simplicity of the target inflation rate are important. Proponents of 0% inflation believe price stability can achieve these goals better than a target inflation rate of 3%.

The debate is not settled. For the time being, most central banks appear to be aiming for low but positive inflation—that is, inflation rates between 2% and 3%.

25-2 The Design of Monetary Policy

Until the 1990s, the design of monetary policy typically centered around nominal money growth. Central banks chose a nominal money growth target for the medium run. And they thought about short-run monetary policy in terms of deviations of nominal money growth from that target. In the past decade, however, this design has evolved. Most central banks have adopted an inflation rate target rather than a nominal money growth rate target. And they think about short-run monetary policy in terms of movements in the nominal interest rate, rather than in terms of movements in the rate of nominal money growth. Let's first look at what they did earlier, before turning to what they do now.

Money Growth Targets and Target Ranges

Until the 1990s, monetary policy in the United States and in other OECD countries was typically conducted as follows:

■ The central bank chose a target rate for nominal money growth corresponding to the inflation rate it wanted to achieve in the medium run. If, for example, it wanted to achieve an inflation rate of 4% and the normal rate of growth of output (the rate of growth implied by the rate of technological progress and the rate of population growth) was 3%, the central bank chose a target rate of nominal money growth of 7%.

■ In the short run, the central bank allowed for deviations of nominal money growth from the target. If, for example, the economy was in a recession, the central bank increased nominal money growth above the target value to allow for a decrease in the interest rate and a faster recovery of output. In an expansion, it might do the reverse to slow down output growth.

■ To communicate to the public both what it wanted to achieve in the medium run and what it intended to do in the short run, the central bank announced a range for the rate of nominal money growth it intended to achieve. Sometimes, this range was presented as a commitment from the central bank; sometimes, it was presented simply as a forecast rather than as a commitment.

Over time, central banks became disenchanted with this way of conducting monetary policy. Let's now look at why.

Money Growth and Inflation Revisited

Recall that inflation and nominal money growth move together during episodes of hyperinflation (Chapter 23).

From Chapter 4: M1 measures the amount of money in the economy and is constructed as the sum of currency and checkable deposits. The Fed does not directly control M1. What it controls is H, the monetary base; but it can choose H to achieve any value of M1 it wants. It is therefore reasonable to think that the Fed controls M1.

The design of monetary policy around nominal money growth is based on the assumption that there is a close relation between inflation and nominal money growth in the medium run. The problem is that, in practice, this relation is not very tight. If nominal money growth is high, inflation will also be high; and if nominal money growth is low, inflation will be low. But the relation is not tight enough that, by choosing a rate of nominal money growth, the central bank can achieve precisely its desired rate of inflation—not even in the medium run.

The relation between inflation and nominal money growth is shown in Figure 25-1, which plots 10-year averages of the inflation rate against 10-year averages of the growth rate of the money stock since 1970 (so the numbers for inflation and for money growth for 2000, for example, are the average inflation rate and the average growth rate of money from 1991 to 2000). The inflation rate is constructed using the CPI as the price index. The growth rate of nominal money is constructed using M1 as the measure for the money stock. The reason for using 10-year averages should be clear: In the short run, changes in nominal money growth affect mostly output, not inflation. It is only in the medium run that a relation between nominal money growth and inflation should emerge. Taking 10-year averages of both nominal money growth and inflation is a way of detecting such a medium-run relation.

Figure 25-1 shows that, for the United States since 1970, the relation between M1 growth and inflation has not been very tight. True, both went up at the beginning of the period, and both have come down since. But note how inflation started declining in the early 1980s, while nominal money growth remained high for another decade and came down only in the 1990s. Average inflation from 1981 to 1990 was down to 4%, while average money growth over the same period was still running at 7.5%. Since 2000, average inflation and average money growth have remained closer, around 2.5%.

Back to Policy   **Back to Policy**

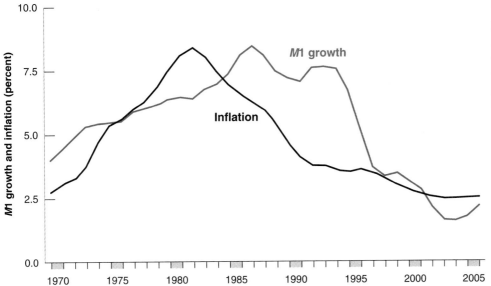

Figure 25-1 ▓

M1 *Growth and Inflation:*
10-Year Averages since
1970

There is no tight relation between
M1 growth and inflation—not
even in the medium run.

Why is the relation between *M*1 growth and inflation not tighter? Because of *shifts in the demand for money.* An example will help. Suppose, as the result of the introduction of credit cards, people decide to hold only half the amount of money they held before; in other words, the real demand for money decreases by half. In the medium run, the real money stock must also decrease by half. For a given nominal money stock, the price level must double. Even if the nominal money stock remains constant, ◄ there is still a period of inflation as the price level doubles. During this period, there is no tight relation between nominal money growth (which is zero) and inflation (which is positive).

Frequent and large shifts in money demand created serious problems for central banks. They found themselves torn between trying to keep a stable target for money growth and staying within announced bands (in order to maintain credibility), or adjusting to shifts in money demand (in order to stabilize output in the short run and inflation in the medium run). Starting in the early 1990s, a dramatic rethinking of monetary policy took place, based instead on inflation targeting rather than money growth targeting, and the use of interest rate rules. Let's look at the way monetary policy is conducted today.

From equation (5.3) (the **LM** equation): The real money supply (the left side) must be equal to the real demand for money (the right side):

$$\frac{M}{P} = Y L(i)$$

If, as a result of the introduction of credit cards, the real demand for money halves, then

$$\frac{M}{P} = \frac{1}{2} Y L(i)$$

For a given level of output and a given interest rate, M/P must also halve. Given M, this implies that P must double.

Inflation Targeting

In many countries, central banks have defined as their primary goal the achievement of a low inflation rate, both in the short run and in the medium run. This is known as **inflation targeting**:

- Trying to achieve a given inflation target *in the medium run* would seem, and indeed is, a clear improvement over trying to achieve a nominal money growth target. After all, in the medium run, the primary goal of monetary policy is to achieve a given rate of inflation. Better to have an inflation rate as the target than a nominal money growth target, which, as we have seen, may not lead to the desired rate of inflation.
- Trying to achieve a given inflation target *in the short run* would appear to be much more controversial. Focusing exclusively on inflation would seem to eliminate any role monetary policy could play in reducing output fluctuations. But, in fact, this

FOCUS

The reason the demand for money shifts over time goes beyond the introduction of credit cards. To understand why, we must challenge an assumption we have maintained until now—namely that there is a sharp distinction between money and other assets. In fact, there are many financial assets that are close to money. They cannot be used for transactions—at least not without restrictions—but they can be exchanged for money at little cost. In other words, these assets are very **liquid**; this makes them attractive substitutes for money. Shifts between money and these assets are the main factor behind shifts in the demand for money.

Take, for example, money market fund shares. Money market funds are financial intermediaries that hold as assets short-maturity securities (typically Treasury bills) and have deposits (or shares, as they are called) as liabilities. The funds pay depositors an interest rate close to the T-bill rate minus the administrative costs of running the fund. Deposits can be exchanged for money on notice and at little cost. Most money market funds allow depositors to write checks but only above a certain amount, typically $500. Because of this restriction, money market funds are not included in $M1$. When these funds were introduced in the mid-1970s, people were able for the first time to hold a very liquid asset while receiving an interest rate close to that on T-bills. Money market funds quickly became very attractive, increasing from nothing in 1973 to $321 billion in 1989. (In comparison, checkable deposits were $280 billion in 1989.) Many people reduced their bank account balances and moved to money market funds. In other words, there was a large negative shift in the demand for money.

The presence of such shifts between money and other liquid assets led central banks to construct and report measures that include not only money but also other liquid assets. These measures are called **monetary aggregates** and come under the names $M2$, $M3$, and so on. In the United States, $M2$—which is also sometimes called **broad money**—includes $M1$ (currency and checkable deposits) plus money market mutual fund shares, money market deposit accounts (the same as money market shares, but issued by banks rather than money market funds), and time deposits (deposits with an explicit maturity of a few months to a few years and with a penalty for early withdrawal). In 2006, $M2$ was $7.0 trillion, compared to $1.3 trillion for $M1$.

The construction of $M2$ and other monetary aggregates would appear to offer a solution to our earlier problem: If most of the shifts in the demand for money are between $M1$ and other assets within $M2$, the demand for $M2$ should be more stable than the demand for $M1$, and so there should be a tighter relation between $M2$ growth and inflation than between $M1$ growth and inflation. If so, the central bank could choose targets for $M2$ growth rather than for $M1$ growth. This is indeed the solution that many central banks adopted. But it did not work well, for two reasons:

■ The relation between $M2$ growth and inflation is no tighter than the relation between $M1$ growth and inflation. This is shown in Figure 1, which plots 10-year averages of the inflation rate and of the rate of growth of $M2$ since 1970. $M2$ growth was nearly 5% above inflation in the early 1970s. This difference disappeared over time, only to reappear and grow in the 2000s. (The same conclusions apply to $M3$ growth.)

is not the case. To see why, return to the Phillips curve relation between inflation, π_t, lagged inflation, π_{t-1}, and the deviation of the unemployment rate, u_t, from the natural rate of unemployment, u_n [equation (8.10)]:

$$\pi_t = \pi_{t-1} - \alpha(u_t - u_n)$$

Let the inflation rate target be π^*. Suppose the central bank could achieve its inflation target exactly in every period. Then the relation would become

$$\pi^* = \pi^* - \alpha(u_t - u_n)$$

$0 = -\alpha(u_t - u_n) \Rightarrow u_t = u_n$ ▶ The unemployment rate, u_t, would always equal u_n, the natural rate of unemployment; by implication, output would always be equal to the natural level of output. In effect, inflation targeting would lead the central bank to act in such a way as to eliminate all deviations of output from its natural level.

The intuition: If the central bank saw that an adverse demand shock were going to lead to a recession, it would know that, absent a monetary expansion, the economy would experience a decline in inflation below the target rate of inflation. To maintain stable inflation, the central bank would then rely on a monetary expansion to avoid the recession. The converse would apply to a favorable

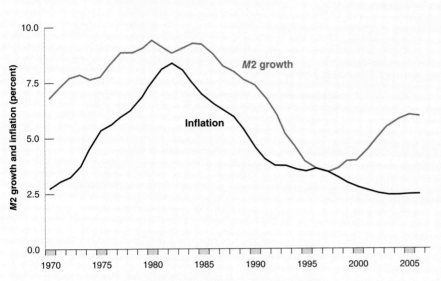

Figure 1 M2 *Growth and Inflation: 10-Year Averages since 1970*

- More importantly, while the central bank controls *M*1, it does not control *M*2. If people shift from T-bills to money market funds, this will increase *M*2—which includes money market funds but does not include T-bills. There is little the central bank can do about this increase in *M*2. Thus, *M*2 is a strange target: It is neither under the direct control of the central bank nor what the central bank ultimately cares about.

In short, the relation between inflation and the growth of monetary aggregates such as *M*2 and *M*3 is no tighter than the relation between inflation and the growth rate of *M*1. And the central bank has little control over the growth of these monetary aggregates anyway. This is why, in most countries, monetary policy has shifted its focus from monetary aggregates—whether it is *M*1, *M*2, or *M*3—to inflation.

demand shock: Fearing an increase in inflation above the target rate, the central bank would rely on a monetary contraction to slow down the economy and keep output at the natural level of output. As a result of this active monetary policy, output would remain at the natural level of output all the time.

The result we have just derived—that inflation targeting eliminates deviations of output from its natural level—is too strong, however, for two reasons:

- The central bank cannot always achieve the rate of inflation it wants in the short run. So suppose that, for example, the central bank was not able to achieve its desired rate of inflation last year, so π_{t-1} is higher than π^*. Then it is not clear that the central bank should try to hit its target this year and achieve $\pi_t = \pi^*$: The Phillips curve relation implies that such a decrease in inflation would require a potentially large increase in unemployment. We return to this issue shortly.
- Like all other macroeconomic relations, the Phillips curve relation above does not hold exactly. It will happen that, for example, inflation increases even when unemployment is at the natural rate of unemployment. In this case, the central bank will face a more difficult choice: whether to keep unemployment at the natural rate and allow inflation to increase, or to increase unemployment above the natural rate to keep inflation in check.

These qualifications are important, but the basic point remains: Inflation targeting makes good sense in the medium run and allows monetary policy to stabilize output around its natural level in the short run.

Interest Rate Rules

Given the discussion so far, the next question is how to achieve the inflation target. In answer to this question, John Taylor, from Stanford University, argued that, because the central bank affects spending through the interest rate, the central bank should think directly in terms of the choice of an interest rate rather than a rate of nominal money growth. He then suggested a rule that the central bank should follow to set the interest rate. This rule, which is now known as the **Taylor rule**, goes as follows:

From Chapter 14: In the medium run, the real interest rate is equal to the natural real interest rate, r_n, so the nominal interest rate moves one-for-one with the inflation rate: If $r_n = 2\%$ and the target inflation rate, $\pi^* = 3\%$, then the target nominal interest rate, $i^* = 2\% + 3\% = 5\%$. If the target inflation rate, π^*, is 0%, then $i^* = 2\% + 0\% = 2\%$.

- Let π_t be the rate of inflation and π^* be the target rate of inflation.
- Let i_t be the nominal interest rate and i^* be the target nominal interest rate—the nominal interest rate associated with the target rate of inflation, π^*, in the medium run.
- Let u_t be the unemployment rate and u_n be the natural unemployment rate.

Think of the central bank as choosing the nominal interest rate, i. (Recall from Chapter 4 that, through open market operations, the central bank can achieve any short-term nominal interest rate that it wants.) Then, Taylor argued, the central bank should adopt the following rule:

$$i_t = i^* + a(\pi_t - \pi^*) - b(u_t - u_n)$$

where a and b are positive coefficients.

Let's look at what the rule says:

- If inflation is equal to target inflation ($\pi_t = \pi^*$) and the unemployment rate is equal to the natural rate of unemployment ($u_t = u_n$), then the central bank should set the nominal interest rate, i_t, equal to its target value, i^*. This way, the economy can stay on the same path, with inflation equal to the target inflation rate and unemployment equal to the natural rate of unemployment.
- If inflation is higher than the target ($\pi_t > \pi^*$), the central bank should increase the nominal interest rate, i_t, above i^*. This higher interest rate will increase unemployment, and this increase in unemployment will lead to a decrease in inflation.

  The coefficient a should therefore reflect how much the central bank cares about unemployment versus inflation. The higher a, the more the central bank will increase the interest rate in response to inflation, the more the economy will slow down, the more unemployment will increase, and the faster inflation will return to the target inflation rate.

Some economists argue that the increase in U.S. inflation in the 1970s was due to the fact that the Fed increased the nominal interest rate less than one-for-one with inflation. The result, they argue, was that an increase in inflation led to a decrease in the real interest rate, which led to higher demand, lower unemployment, more inflation, a further decrease in the real interest rate, and so on.

  In any case, Taylor pointed out, a should be larger than 1. Why? Because what matters for spending is the real interest rate, not the nominal interest rate. When inflation increases, the central bank, if it wants to decrease spending and output, must increase the *real* interest rate. In other words, it must increase the nominal interest rate more than one-for-one with inflation.

- If unemployment is higher than the natural rate of unemployment ($u > u_n$) the central bank should decrease the nominal interest rate. The lower nominal interest rate will increase output, leading to a decrease in unemployment. Like the coefficient a, the coefficient b should reflect how much the central bank cares about unemployment relative to inflation. The higher b, the more the central bank will be willing to deviate from target inflation to keep unemployment close to the natural rate of unemployment.

In stating this rule, Taylor did not argue that it should be followed blindly: Many other events, such as an exchange rate crisis, or the need to change the composition of spending, and thus the mix between monetary policy and fiscal policy, justify changing the nominal interest rate for other reasons than those included in the rule. But, he argued, the rule provided a useful way of thinking about monetary policy: Once the central bank has chosen a target rate of inflation, it should try to achieve it by adjusting the nominal interest rate. The rule it should follow should take into account not only current inflation but also current unemployment.

Since it was first introduced, the Taylor rule has generated a lot of interest, both from researchers and from central banks:

- Interestingly, researchers looking at the behavior of both the Fed in the United States and the Bundesbank in Germany have found that, although neither of these two central banks thought of itself as following a Taylor rule, this rule actually describes their behavior over the past 15 to 20 years quite well.

- Other researchers have explored whether it is possible to improve on this simple rule—for example, whether the nominal interest rate should be allowed to respond not only to current inflation but also to expected future inflation.

- Yet other researchers have discussed whether central banks should adopt an explicit interest rate rule and follow it closely, or whether they should use the rule more informally and feel free to deviate from the rule when appropriate. We shall return to this issue in discussing the behavior of the Fed in the next section.

- In general, most central banks have now shifted from thinking in terms of nominal money growth to thinking in terms of an interest rate rule. Whatever happens to nominal money growth as a result of following such a nominal interest rate rule is increasingly seen as unimportant by both the central banks and financial markets.

25-3 The Fed in Action

Having discussed the design of monetary policy in general, let us end the chapter by looking at how the Fed actually carries out monetary policy in the United States.

> The Fed's Web site (www. federalreserve.gov) gives a lot of information about how the Fed is organized and what it does.

The Mandate of the Fed

The mandate of the Federal Reserve System was last defined in the **Humphrey–Hawkins Act**, passed by Congress in 1978. While the act expired in 2000 and Congress does not appear to be in a hurry to renew or redefine it, it remains a good description of what the Fed takes as its goals:

> Maintain long-run growth of the monetary and credit aggregates commensurate with the economy's long-run potential to increase production, so as to promote effectively the goals of maximum employment, stable prices, and moderate long-term interest rates.

There is one important point behind the heavy official language: The Fed has a mandate not only to achieve low inflation in the medium and long run, but also to stabilize economic activity in the short run.

The Organization of the Fed

The Federal Reserve System has three parts:

- A set of 12 **Federal Reserve Districts**, each with a Federal Reserve District Bank. The main functions of these regional banks are to manage check clearing and to supervise banking and financial activities in the district.

- The **Board of Governors**, located in Washington, DC. The board has seven members, including the chairman of the Fed. Each governor is appointed by the president of the United States for a nonrenewable term of 14 years and must be confirmed by the U.S. Senate. The chairman is appointed by the president for a renewable term of four years. The Board of Governors is in charge of the design of monetary policy.

- The **Federal Open Market Committee (FOMC)** is also located in Washington, DC. The committee has 12 members. Five are Federal Reserve District Bank presidents, and the other seven are the governors. The principle behind this composition is that Federal Reserve Bank presidents are likely to be attuned to the economic situation in their districts and the governors attuned to national trends and evolutions. The main function of the FOMC is to give instructions to the **Open Market Desk**, the office in New York City that is in charge of open market operations—the purchase and sale of bonds by the Fed.

This description might suggest that the Fed is a complex organization with many centers of power. The reality is simpler: The chairman is typically very powerful. And the most important decisions are made by the Federal Open Market Committee.

Note in Figure 24-3 that the United States has the second-highest index of central bank independence.

▶ We discussed in Chapter 24 the importance of central bank independence. The Fed is one of the most independent central banks in the world. The main control lever available to the president and Congress is the nomination and confirmation of the chairman every four years. But during his four-year tenure, the chairman is largely free to choose monetary policy as he thinks best. The Fed's budget is not subject to congressional oversight, so Congress cannot put pressure on the Fed by threatening to cut

Under the Humphrey–Hawkins Act, the chairman had the obligation to testify. Although the act expired in 2000, the tradition continues.

its funding. The chairman of the Fed testifies twice a year in front of Congress to ▶ explain the stance of monetary policy. Members of Congress often complain and grumble about the Fed's decisions, but there is not much they can actually do about it.

The Instruments of Monetary Policy

Recall from Chapter 4 that we can think of the determination of the interest rate in three equivalent ways:

- The supply of central bank money must be equal to the demand for central bank money.
- The supply of reserves, equal to central bank money minus the currency held by people, must be equal to the demand for reserves by banks.
- The supply of money (currency and demand deposits) must be equal to the demand for money.

See Chapter 4 for a review.

You saw in Chapter 4 that we can think of the interest rate as being determined by the ▶ demand for and the supply of central bank money. Recall that the equilibrium condition [equation (4.11)] is given by

$$H = [c + \theta(1 - c)]\$Y L(i) \qquad (25.1)$$

On the left side is H, the supply of central bank money—equivalently, the monetary base. On the right side is the demand for central bank money—the sum of the demand for currency by people, $c\$Y L(i)$, and the demand for reserves by banks, $\theta(1 - c)\$Y L(i)$. Think of it this way:

- Start with $\$Y L(i)$, the overall demand for money (currency and checkable deposits, $M1$). This demand depends on income and the opportunity cost of holding money—the interest rate on bonds.

- The parameter c is the proportion of money people want to hold in the form of currency. So $c \$Y L(i)$ is the demand for currency by people.

- What people do not hold in currency, they hold in the form of checkable deposits. Checkable deposits are therefore a fraction $(1 - c)$ of the overall demand for money, so checkable deposits are equal to $(1 - c) \$Y L(i)$. The parameter θ denotes the ratio of reserves held by banks to checkable deposits. So the demand for reserves by banks is $\theta(1 - c) \$Y L(i)$.

- Adding the demand for currency, $c \$Y L(i)$, and the demand for reserves by banks, $\theta(1 - c) \$Y L(i)$, gives the total demand for central bank money—which is the right side of the equation.

The equilibrium interest rate is then the interest rate at which the supply of, and the demand for, central bank money are equal. The Fed has three instruments at its disposal to affect this interest rate. The first, *reserve requirements,* affects the demand for reserves and, therefore, the demand for central bank money. The other two, *lending to banks* and *open market operations,* affect the supply of central bank money.

Reserve Requirements

The Fed determines **reserve requirements**, the minimum amount of reserves that banks must hold in proportion to checkable deposits. Even without such requirements, banks would want to hold some reserves to be able to satisfy their depositors' demand for cash. But the Fed typically sets reserve requirements above the level that banks would choose. The current requirement is that banks hold reserves equal to 10% of their checkable deposits.

By changing reserve requirements, the Fed changes the amount of reserves banks must hold for a given amount of demand deposits, and, by doing so, it changes the demand for central bank money. An increase in reserve requirements leads to an increase in the demand for central bank money, leading to an increase in the equilibrium interest rate. It works in the other direction as well: A decrease in reserve requirements leads to a decrease in the interest rate.

An increase in reserve requirements by the Fed can force banks to take drastic actions to increase their reserves—for example recalling some of the loans they have made. For this reason, the Fed has become increasingly reluctant to use reserve requirements as a macroeconomic policy instrument, preferring to rely on its other instruments instead.

An increase in θ increases the demand for reserves by banks, increasing the demand for central bank money. Given an unchanged supply, the interest rate must increase.

Lending to Banks

The Fed can also lend to banks (an instrument we ignored in Chapter 4). How much it lends and under what conditions is called the Fed's **discount policy**. The rate at which it lends to banks is called the **discount rate**. When the Fed lends to banks, it is said to lend through the **discount window**.

From the point of view of the Fed, lending to banks is very similar to buying bonds in an open market operation. In both cases, the Fed creates money, thereby increasing H, the monetary base. In both cases, it acquires a claim—on the bank in the case of lending to banks and on the government in the case of an open market operation.

Until the introduction of open market operations in the 1930s, the discount policy was the Fed's main instrument for changing the money supply. But its role has steadily declined in favor of open market operations. The Fed typically discourages banks from borrowing from the discount window except for short-run or seasonal reasons.

Changes in the discount rate still play a role, but mostly as a signal of the Fed's intentions. Financial markets often interpret a decrease in the discount rate as a signal that the Fed is going to follow a more expansionary policy—that it is going to decrease interest rates in the future. Through its effect on expectations of future interest rates, a decrease in the discount rate often leads to a decrease in medium-term and long-term interest rates.

Once upon a time, there must have been an actual window at the central bank where banks would come and borrow funds. This is no longer the case.

From Chapter 15: Medium-term and long-term interest rates are weighted averages of expected short-term interest rates. A decrease in the discount rate, which leads participants in financial markets to expect lower short-term interest rates in the future, leads to a decline in medium-term and long-term interest rates.

Open Market Operations

The Fed's third and main tool is *open market operations,* in which the Fed buys and sells bonds in the bonds market. Open market operations are carried out by the Open Market Desk in New York and are typically conducted in markets for short-term Treasury bills.

When the Fed buys bonds, it pays for them by creating money, increasing H; when it sells bonds, it decreases H. Over the years, the Fed has found using open market

For more on open market operations, go back to Chapter 4.

operations to be the most convenient and flexible way of changing the supply of central bank money and thus of changing the interest rate. Today, open market operations are the main instrument of U.S. monetary policy.

The Implementation of Policy

Most important monetary policy decisions are made at the meetings of the FOMC, which take place about every six weeks. For these meetings, the Fed staff prepares forecasts and simulations of the effects of different monetary policies. The forecasts show what is likely to happen to the economy under unchanged monetary policy and what the major sources of uncertainty appear to be. The simulations show the evolution of the economy under alternative assumptions about monetary policy.

The FOMC then decides on the course of monetary policy. At the end of each meeting, it issues a general directive to the Open Market Desk about what to do during the following six weeks. The conduct of open market operations between FOMC meetings is left to the manager of the Open Market Desk. The manager focuses on the interest rate in the market for central bank money—the *federal funds market*. In that market, banks that have excess reserves (reserves in excess of what they are required to hold) lend overnight to banks that have insufficient reserves. The rate in that market is called the *federal funds rate*. As new information comes in, indicating, for example, that the economy is stronger or weaker than expected, the manager (in consultation with the FOMC members) intervenes so as to change the federal funds rate as he or she sees best until the next FOMC meeting.

So far we have looked at the instruments and methods of monetary policy. This does not tell us what monetary policy the Fed actually follows. Does the Fed have an inflation target, and if so, what is it? Does the Fed follow an interest rate rule, and if so what is the rule?

■ One answer to these two questions is: We do not know. Alan Greenspan, the chairman of the Fed until 2006, never specifically stated an inflation target, nor has his successor, Ben Bernanke. Nor have they ever described the decisions of the Fed in terms of an interest rate rule—or in terms of any other rule, for that matter.

■ Another answer, however, is that, just from observing the behavior of the Fed, we actually know a lot. The evidence strongly suggests that the Fed has, in fact, an implicit inflation target of about 2% to 3%. And it is also clear that the Fed adjusts the federal funds rate in response both to the inflation rate and to deviations of unemployment from the natural rate. Indeed, recall from our earlier discussion that the Taylor rule appears to give a good description of the behavior of the Fed over the past 15 to 20 years.

Does it matter that the Fed has neither an *explicit* inflation target nor an *explicit* interest rate rule? On this question as well, economists disagree:

■ Many economists say: Do not argue with success. And, at the time of this writing, nearly all economists agree that the record of U.S. monetary policy, under both Alan Greenspan and Ben Bernanke, has been outstanding.

Without an explicit inflation target, the Fed has convinced financial markets that it is committed to low inflation, and inflation has indeed remained low.

At the same time, the Fed has shown a willingness to use the nominal interest rate to stabilize activity when it was needed. Figure 25-2 shows the evolution of the federal funds rate since 1987—the year in which Greenspan became chairman of the Fed. Most macroeconomists agree that although the sharp decline in the

Figure 25-2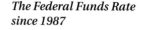

*The Federal Funds Rate
since 1987*

In 1990–1991, and again
in 2001, the Fed dramatically
decreased the federal funds rate
to reduce the depth and length
of the recession.

federal funds rate in the early 1990s, from close to 10% in 1989 to around 3% in
1992, was not enough to avoid a recession, it reduced its depth and its length. In
2001 again, the Fed aggressively cut the federal funds rate, from 7% down to 2% at
the end of the year. Again, although these cuts were not enough to avoid a recession, they clearly limited its depth and its length.

■ Other economists are more skeptical. They argue that it is unwise to have monetary policy depend so much on one individual, that the next chairman of the Fed
may not be able to achieve the same mix of credibility and flexibility. They argue ◀
that improvements in the design of policy, such as the shift to explicit inflation targeting, and a more explicit discussion of interest rules can and should be made.
This debate is likely to be with us for some time to come.

To find out more on how the
personality of Fed chairmen
has affected U.S. monetary pol-
icy, read David and Christina
Romer's "Choosing the Federal
Reserve Chair: Lessons from
History," *Journal of Economic
Perspectives,* Winter 2004.

Summary

On the optimal rate of inflation:

■ Inflation is down to very low levels in most OECD countries. One question facing central banks is whether they
should try to achieve price stability—that is, zero inflation.

■ The main arguments for zero inflation are:

1. Inflation, together with an imperfectly indexed tax
system, leads to tax distortions.

2. Because of money illusion, inflation leads people
and firms to make incorrect decisions.

3. Higher inflation typically comes with higher inflation
variability, creating more uncertainty and making it
more difficult for people and firms to make decisions.

4. As a target, price stability has a simplicity and a credibility that a positive inflation target does not have.

■ There are also arguments for maintaining low but positive inflation:

1. Positive revenues from nominal money growth—
seignorage—allow for decreases in taxes elsewhere in

the budget. However, this argument is quantitatively
unimportant when comparing inflation rates of 0%
versus, say, 3%.

2. Positive actual and expected inflation allow the central bank to achieve negative real interest rates, an
option that can be useful when fighting a recession.

3. Positive inflation allows firms to achieve real wage cuts
when needed without requiring nominal wage cuts.

4. Further decreasing inflation from its current rate to
zero would require an increase in unemployment for
some time, and this transition cost might exceed
whatever benefits come from zero inflation.

On the design of monetary policy:

■ Traditionally, the design of monetary policy was focused
on nominal money growth. But because of the poor
relation between inflation and nominal money growth,
this approach has been abandoned by most central
banks.

- Central banks now typically focus on an inflation rate target rather than a nominal money growth rate target. And they think about monetary policy in terms of determining the nominal interest rate rather than in terms of determining the rate of nominal money growth.
- The Taylor rule gives a useful way of thinking about the choice of the nominal interest rate. The rule states that the central bank should move its interest rate in response to two main factors: the deviation of the inflation rate from the target rate of inflation, and the deviation of the unemployment rate from the natural rate of unemployment. A central bank that follows this rule will stabilize activity and achieve its target inflation rate in the medium run.

On the Fed:

- The Federal Reserve System is composed of three parts: 12 Federal Reserve Districts; a Board of Governors, with seven members, including the chairman; and the Federal Open Market Committee, composed of the seven members of the Board of Governors and five Federal Reserve District Bank presidents. Open market operations are the main instrument of monetary policy. The other two, reserve requirements and discount policy, are used infrequently.
- Decisions about the course of monetary policy are made every six weeks by the Federal Open Market Committee. Daily decisions about open market operations are left to the manager of the Open Market Desk in New York City, in consultation with members of the Federal Open Market Committee.
- The Fed has neither an explicit inflation target nor an explicit interest rate rule. But, in fact, it appears to have an inflation target around 2% to 3%, and to change the nominal interest rate in a manner well described by the Taylor rule.
- Monetary policy has been very successful in the past 20 years. Inflation has remained low. At the same time, the Fed has used monetary policy to stabilize output.

Key Terms

- shoe-leather costs, 559
- money illusion, 560
- inflation targeting, 565
- liquid asset, 566
- monetary aggregates, 566
- broad money (*M*2), 566
- Taylor rule, 568
- Humphrey–Hawkins Act, 569

- Federal Reserve Districts, 569
- Board of Governors, 570
- Federal Open Market Committee (FOMC), 570
- Open Market Desk, 570
- reserve requirements, 571
- discount policy, 571
- discount rate, 571
- discount window, 571

Questions and Problems

Quick Check

1. Using the information in this chapter, label each of the following statements true, false, or uncertain. Explain briefly.

a. The most important argument in favor of a positive rate of inflation in OECD countries is seignorage.

b. The Fed should target *M*2 growth because it moves quite closely with inflation.

c. Fighting inflation should be the Fed's only purpose.

d. Because most people have little trouble distinguishing between nominal and real values, inflation does not distort decision making.

e. The Fed uses reserve requirements as its primary instrument of monetary policy.

f. The higher the inflation rate, the higher the effective tax rate on capital gains.

2. Explain how each of the developments listed in (a) through (d) would affect the demand for M1 and M2.

a. Banks reduce penalties on early withdrawal from time deposits.

b. The government forbids the use of money market funds for check-writing purposes.

c. The government legislates a tax on all ATM transactions.

d. Congress decides to impose a tax on all transactions involving government securities with maturities more than one year.

3. Inflation targets

Consider a central bank that has an inflation target, π^*. The Phillips curve is given by

$$\pi_t - \pi_{t-1} = -\alpha(u_t - u_n)$$

a. If the central bank is able to keep the inflation rate equal to the target inflation rate every period, will there be dramatic fluctuations in unemployment?

b. Is the central bank likely to be able to hit its inflation target every period?

c. Suppose the natural rate of unemployment, u_n, changes frequently. How will these changes affect the central bank's ability to hit its inflation target? Explain.

4. Taxes, inflation, and home ownership

In this chapter, we discussed the effect of inflation on the effective capital-gains tax rate on the sale of a home. In this question, we explore the effect of inflation on another feature of the tax code—the deductibility of mortgage interest.

Suppose you have a mortgage of $60,000. Expected inflation is π^e, and the nominal interest rate on your mortgage is i. Consider two cases.

    i. $\pi^e = 0\%$; $i = 5\%$
    ii. $\pi^e = 10\%$; $i = 15\%$

  a. What is the real interest rate you are paying on your mortgage in each case?
  b. Suppose you can deduct nominal mortgage interest payments from your income before paying income tax (as is the case in the United States). Assume that the tax rate is 20%. So, for each dollar you pay in mortgage interest, you pay 20 cents less in taxes, in effect getting a subsidy from the government for your mortgage costs. Compute, in each case, the real interest rate you are paying on your mortgage, taking into account this subsidy.
  c. Considering only the deductibility of mortgage interest (and not capital-gains taxation), is inflation good for homeowners in the United States?

Dig Deeper

5. Suppose you have been elected to Congress. One day, one of your colleagues makes the following statement:

> The Fed chair is the most powerful economic policy-maker in the United States. We should not turn over the keys to the economy to someone who was not elected and therefore has no accountability. Congress should impose an explicit Taylor rule on the Fed. Congress should choose not only the target inflation rate but the relative weight on the inflation and unemployment targets. Why should the preferences of an individual substitute for the will of the people, as expressed through the democratic and legislative processes?

Do you agree with your colleague? Discuss the advantages and disadvantages of imposing an explicit Taylor rule on the Fed.

6. Inflation targeting and the Taylor rule in the IS–LM model

This problem is based on David Romer's "Short-Run Fluctuations," which is available on his Web site (**emlab. berkeley.edu/users/dromer/index.shtml**). Consider a closed economy in which the central bank follows an interest rate rule. The IS relation is given by

$$Y = C(Y - T) + I(Y, r) + G$$

where r is the real interest rate.

The central bank sets the nominal interest rate according to the rule

$$i = i^* + a(\pi^e - \pi^*) + b(Y - Y_n)$$

where π^e is expected inflation, π^* is the target rate of inflation, and Y_n is the natural level of output. Assume that $a > 1$ and $b > 0$. The symbol i^* is the interest rate the central bank chooses when expected inflation equals the target rate and output equals the natural level. The central bank will increase the nominal interest rate when expected inflation rises above the target or when output rises above the natural level.

(Note that the Taylor rule described in this chapter uses actual inflation instead of expected inflation, and it uses unemployment instead of output. The interest rate rule we use in this problem simplifies the analysis and does not change the basic results.)

Real and nominal interest rates are related by

$$r = i - \pi^e$$

  a. Define the variable r^* as $r^* \equiv i^* - \pi^*$. Use the definition of the real interest rate to express the interest rate rule as

$$r = r^* + (a - 1)(\pi^e - \pi^*) + b(Y - Y_n)$$

    (Hint: Subtract π^* from each side of the nominal interest rate rule and rearrange the right-hand side of the equation.)
  b. Graph the IS relation in a diagram, with r on the vertical axis and Y on the horizontal axis. In the same diagram, graph the interest rate rule (in terms of the real interest rate) you derived in part (a) for given values of π^e, π^*, and Y_n. Call the interest rate rule the monetary policy (MP) relation.
  c. Using the diagram you drew in part (b), show that an increase in government spending leads to an increase in output and the real interest rate in the short run.
  d. Now consider a change in the monetary policy rule. Suppose the central bank reduces its target inflation rate, π^*. How does the fall in π^* affect the MP relation? (Remember that $a > 1$.) What happens to output and the real interest rate in the short run?

7. Consider the economy described in problem 6.
  a. Suppose the economy starts with $Y = Y_n$ and $\pi^e = \pi^*$. Now suppose there is an increase in π^e. Assume that Y_n does not change. Using the diagram you drew in problem 6(b), show how the increase in π^e affects the MP relation. (Again, remember that $a > 1$.) What happens to output and the real interest rate in the short run?
  b. Without attempting to model the dynamics of inflation explicitly, assume that inflation and expected inflation will increase over time if $Y > Y_n$, and that they will decrease over time if $Y < Y_n$. Given the effect on output you found in part (a), will π^e tend to return to the target rate of inflation, π^*, over time?
  c. Redo part (a), but assuming this time that $a < 1$. How does the increase in π^e affect the MP relation when $a < 1$? What happens to output and the real interest rate in the short run?
  d. Again assume that inflation and expected inflation will increase over time if $Y > Y_n$ and that they will decrease

over time if $Y < Y_n$. Given the effect on output you found in part (c), will π^e tend to return to the target rate of inflation, π^*, over time? Is it sensible for the parameter a (in the interest rate rule) to take values less than one?

Explore Further

8. Current monetary policy

Problem 10 in Chapter 4 asked you to consider the current stance of monetary policy. Here, you are asked to do so again, but with the additional understanding of monetary policy you have gained in this and previous chapters.

*Go to the Web site of the Federal Reserve Board of Governors (**www.federalreserve.gov**) and download either* the press release you considered in Chapter 4 (if you did problem 10) or the most recent press release of the Federal Open Market Committee (FOMC).

a. What is the stance of monetary policy, as described in the press release?

b. Is there evidence that the FOMC considers both inflation and unemployment in setting interest rate policy, as would be implied by the Taylor rule?

c. Does any of the language of the press release seem to be aimed at increasing the credibility of the Fed (as committed to low inflation) or at affecting inflation expectations?

We invite you to visit the Blanchard page on the Prentice Hall Web site, at:

www.prenhall.com/blanchard

for this chapter's World Wide Web exercises.

Further Readings

■ "Modern Central Banking," written by Stanley Fischer for the 300th anniversary of the Bank of England (published in Forrest Capie, Stanley Fischer, Charles Goodhart and Norbert Schnadt eds. *The Future of Central Banking*, Cambridge University Press, Cambridge, UK, 1995), provides a nice discussion of the current issues in central banking. (Stanley Fischer is now governor of the Central Bank of Israel.) Read also "What Central Bankers Could Learn from Academics—and Vice Versa," by Alan Blinder, *Journal of Economic Perspectives*, Spring 1997, 3–19.

■ On inflation targeting, read Ben Bernanke and Frederic Mishkin, "Inflation Targeting: A New Framework for Monetary Policy?" *Journal of Economic Perspectives*, Spring 1997. (This article was written by Ben Bernanke before he became chairman of the Fed. Frederic Mishkin, on leave from Columbia University, is currently a member of the Board of Governors of the Federal Reserve.)

■ For more detail on how the Fed operates, read Glenn Hubbard, *Money, the Financial System, and the Economy*, 5th ed. Addison-Wesley, Reading, MA, 2004.

■ For more on monetary policy under Alan Greenspan, read N. Gregory Mankiw, "U.S. Monetary Policy During the 1990s," in *American Economic Policy in the 1990s*, MIT Press, Cambridge, MA, 2001.

■ For a more relaxing read, see Bob Woodward, *Maestro; Greenspan's Fed and the American Boom*, Simon & Schuster, New York, 2001.

Fiscal Policy: A Summing Up

CHAPTER 26

In this chapter, we do for fiscal policy what we did for monetary policy in Chapter 25—review what you have learned and tie up the remaining loose ends.

Let's first review what you have learned (the Focus box "Fiscal Policy: What You Have Learned and Where" gives a more detailed summary):

■ In the short run, a budget deficit (triggered, say, by a decrease in taxes) increases demand and output. What happens to investment spending is ambiguous.

■ In the medium run, output returns to the natural level of output. The interest rate and the composition of spending are different, however. The interest rate is higher, and investment spending is lower.

■ In the long run, lower investment leads to a lower capital stock and, therefore, a lower level of output.

In deriving these conclusions, we did not pay close attention to the government budget constraint—that is, to the relation between debt, deficits, government spending, and taxes. Nevertheless, as, for example, our discussion of fiscal policy in Japan in Chapter 22 made clear, this relation is important: After more than a decade of large budget deficits, government debt in Japan has become very high, and this in turn very much restricts the scope for further use of fiscal policy by the Japanese government. So our main task in this chapter is to look at the government's budget constraint and its implications:

■ Section 26-1 derives the government budget constraint and examines its implications for the relation between budget deficits, the interest rate, the growth rate, and government debt.

■ Section 26-2 examines a number of fiscal policy issues where this constraint plays a central role, from the proposition that deficits do not really matter, to the dangers of accumulating very high levels of public debt.

■ Section 26-3 looks at the current U.S. budget and the issues on the horizon, from the effects of the tax cuts passed by the Bush administration, to the implications of the aging of America. ■

FOCUS

- In Chapter 3 we looked at how government spending and taxes affect demand and output in the short run.

    You saw how, in the short run, a fiscal expansion—increases in government spending or decreases in taxes—increases output.

- In Chapter 5 we looked at the short-run effects of fiscal policy on output and on the interest rate.

    You saw how a fiscal expansion leads to an increase in output and an increase in the interest rate. You also saw how fiscal policy and monetary policy can be used together to affect both the level and the composition of output.

- In Chapter 7 we looked at the effects of fiscal policy in the short run and in the medium run.

    You saw that, in the medium run (that is, taking the capital stock as given), a fiscal expansion has no effect on output but is reflected in a different composition of spending. The interest rate is higher, and investment spending is lower.

- In Chapter 11 we looked at how saving, both private and public, affects the level of capital accumulation and the level of output in the long run.

    You saw how, once capital accumulation is taken into account, a larger budget deficit and, by implication, a lower national saving rate, decrease capital accumulation, leading to a lower level of output in the long run.

- In Chapter 17 we returned to the short-run effects of fiscal policy, taking into account not only its direct effects through taxes and government spending but also its effects on expectations.

    You saw how the effects of fiscal policy depend on expectations of future fiscal policy and future monetary policy. In particular, you saw how a deficit reduction may, in some circumstances, lead to an increase in output, even in the short run.

- In Chapter 19 we looked at the effects of fiscal policy when the economy is open in the goods market.

    You saw how fiscal policy affects both output and the trade balance, and examined the relation between the budget deficit and the trade deficit. You saw how fiscal policy and exchange rate adjustments can be used together to affect both the level of output and its composition.

- In Chapter 20 we looked at the role of fiscal policy in an economy open in both goods markets and financial markets.

    You saw how, when capital is mobile, the effects of fiscal policy depend on the exchange rate regime. Fiscal policy has a stronger effect on output under fixed exchange rates than under flexible exchange rates.

- In Chapter 23 we looked at the relation between fiscal policy, money growth, and inflation.

    You saw how budget deficits must be financed either through borrowing or through money creation. If and when money creation becomes the main source of government finance, the result of large budget deficits is high money growth and high inflation.

- In Chapter 24 we looked at the problems facing fiscal policymakers, from uncertainty about the effects of policy to issues of time consistency and credibility.

    You saw the pros and cons of putting restraints on the conduct of fiscal policy, from spending caps to a constitutional amendment to balance the budget.

- In this chapter we look further at the implications of the budget constraint facing the government and discuss current issues of fiscal policy in the United States.

26-1 The Government Budget Constraint

Suppose that, starting from a balanced budget, the government cuts taxes, creating a budget deficit. What will happen to the debt over time? Will the government need to increase taxes later? If so, by how much?

The Arithmetic of Deficits and Debt

To answer these questions, we must begin with a definition of the budget deficit. We can write the budget deficit in year t as

$$\text{Deficit}_t = rB_{t-1} + G_t - T_t \qquad (26.1)$$

All variables are in real terms:

- B_{t-1} is government debt at the end of year $t - 1$ or, equivalently, at the beginning of year t; r is the real interest rate, which we shall assume to be constant here. Thus rB_{t-1} equals the real interest payments on the government debt in year t.
- G_t is government spending on goods and services during year t.
- T_t is taxes minus transfers during year t.

In words: The budget deficit equals spending, including interest payments on the debt, minus taxes net of transfers.

Do not confuse the words *deficit* and *debt*. (Many journalists and politicians do.) Debt is a *stock*—what the government owes as a result of past deficits. The deficit is a *flow*—how much the government borrows during a given year.

Note two characteristics of equation (26.1):

- We measure interest payments as real interest payments—that is, the product of the *real* interest rate times existing debt—rather than as actual interest payments—that is, the product of the nominal interest rate and the existing debt. As I show in the Focus box "Inflation Accounting and the Measurement of Deficits," this is the correct way of measuring interest payments. Official measures of the deficit, however, use actual (nominal) interest payments and are therefore incorrect. When inflation is high, official measures can be seriously misleading. The correct measure of the deficit is sometimes called the **inflation-adjusted deficit**.
- For consistency with our earlier definition of G as spending on goods and services, G does not include transfer payments. Transfers are instead subtracted from T, so that T stands for *taxes minus transfers*. Official measures of government spending add transfers to spending on goods and services and define revenues as taxes, not taxes net of transfers.

  These are only accounting conventions. Whether transfers are added to spending or subtracted from taxes makes a difference to the measurement of G and T, but clearly does not affect $G - T$ and therefore does not affect the measure of the deficit.

Transfer payments are government transfers to individuals, such as unemployment benefits and Medicare.

The **government budget constraint** simply states that the *change in government debt during year* t is equal to the *deficit during year* t:

$$B_t - B_{t-1} = \text{Deficit}_t$$

If the government runs a deficit, government debt increases. If the government runs a surplus, government debt decreases.

Using the definition of the deficit [equation (26.1)], we can rewrite the government budget constraint as

$$B_t - B_{t-1} = r B_{t-1} + G_t - T_t \qquad (26.2)$$

The government budget constraint links the change in government debt to the initial level of debt (which affects interest payments) and to current government spending and taxes. It is often convenient to decompose the deficit into the sum of two terms:

- Interest payments on the debt, rB_{t-1}.
- The difference between spending and taxes, $G_t - T_t$. This term is called the **primary deficit** (equivalently, $T_t - G_t$ is called the **primary surplus**).

Using this decomposition, we can rewrite equation (26.2) as

Let G represent spending on goods and services; Tr, transfers; and Tax, total taxes. For simplicity, assume interest payments, rB, equal zero, so we can leave them out of the equation. Then,

Deficit = G + Tr − Tax

This can be rewritten in two (equivalent) ways:

Deficit = G − (Tax − Tr)

The deficit equals spending on goods and services minus net taxes—that is, taxes minus transfers. This is the way we write it in the text:

Deficit = (G + Tr) − Tax

The deficit equals total spending—spending on goods and services plus transfers—minus total taxes. This is the way the government reports spending and revenues.

$$\underbrace{B_t - B_{t-1}}_{\text{Change in the debt}} = \underbrace{rB_{t-1}}_{\text{Interest payments}} + \underbrace{(G_t - T_t)}_{\text{Primary deficit}}$$

Inflation Accounting and the Measurement of Deficits

Official measures of the budget deficit are constructed (dropping the time indexes, which are not needed here) as nominal interest payments, iB, plus spending on goods and services, G, minus taxes net of transfers, T:

$$\text{Official measure of the deficit} = iB + G - T$$

This is an accurate measure of the cash flow position of the government. If it is positive, the government is spending more than it receives and must therefore issue new debt. If it is negative, the government buys back previously issued debt.

But it is not an accurate measure of the *change in real debt*—that is, the change in how much the government owes, expressed in terms of goods rather than dollars.

To see why, consider an example. Suppose the official measure of the deficit is equal to zero, so the government neither issues nor buys back debt. Suppose inflation is positive and equal to 10%. Then, at the end of the year, the real value of the debt has decreased by 10%. If we define—as we should—the deficit as the change in the real value of government debt, the government has decreased its real debt by 10% over a year. In other words, it has in fact run a budget surplus equal to 10% times the initial level of debt.

More generally: If B is debt and π is inflation, the official measure of the deficit overstates the correct measure by an amount equal to πB. Put another way, the correct measure of the deficit is obtained by subtracting πB from the official measure:

$$\begin{aligned}\text{Correct measure of the deficit} &= iB + G - T - \pi B \\ &= (i - \pi)B + G - T \\ &= rB + G - T\end{aligned}$$

where $r = i - \pi$ is the (realized) real interest rate. The correct measure of the deficit is then equal to real interest payments plus government spending minus taxes net of transfers—this is the measure we have used in the text.

The difference between the official and the correct measures of the deficit equals πB. So, the higher the rate of inflation, π, or the higher the level of debt, B, the more inaccurate the official measure. In countries in which both inflation and debt are high, the official measure may record a very large budget deficit, when in fact real government debt is decreasing. This is why you should always do the inflation adjustment before deriving conclusions about the position of fiscal policy.

Figure 1 plots the official measure and the inflation-adjusted measure of the (federal) budget deficit for the United States since 1968. The official measure shows a deficit in every year from 1970 to 1997. The inflation-adjusted measure shows instead alternating deficits and surpluses until the late 1970s. However, both measures show how much worse the deficit became after 1980, how things improved in the 1990s, and how they have deteriorated again since 2000. Today, with inflation running at about 2% per year, and the ratio of debt to GDP equal to roughly 40%, the difference between the two measures is roughly equal to 2% × 40%, or 0.8% of GDP. Put another way, an official budget deficit of, say, 2% of GDP corresponds to an actual budget deficit of about (2% − 0.8%) = 1.2% of GDP.

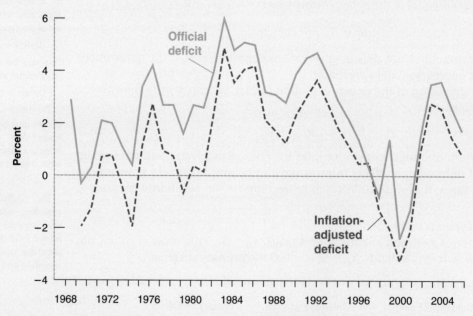

Figure 1   *Official and Inflation-Adjusted Federal Budget Deficits for the United States since 1968*

Or, moving B_{t-1} to the right and reorganizing,

$$B_t = (1 + r) B_{t-1} + \overbrace{G_t - T_t}^{\text{Primary Deficit}} \qquad (26.3)$$

The debt at the end of year t equals $(1 + r)$ times the debt at the end of year $t - 1$, plus the primary deficit during year t, $(G_t - T_t)$. This relation will prove very useful in what follows.

Current versus Future Taxes

Let's look at the implications of a one-year decrease in taxes for the path of debt and future taxes. Start from a situation where, until year 1, the government has balanced its budget, so that initial debt is equal to zero. During year 1, the government decreases taxes by 1 (think 1 billion dollars, for example) for one year. Thus, debt at the end of year 1, B_1, is equal to 1. What happens thereafter?

Full Repayment in Year 2

Suppose the government decides to fully repay the debt during year 2. From equation (26.3), the budget constraint for year 2 is given by

$$B_2 = (1 + r) B_1 + (G_2 - T_2)$$

If the debt is fully repaid during year 2, then the debt at the end of year 2 is equal to zero: $B_2 = 0$. Replacing B_1 with 1 and B_2 with 0 and transposing terms gives

$$T_2 - G_2 = (1 + r)1 = (1 + r)$$

To repay the debt fully during year 2, the government must run a primary surplus equal to $(1 + r)$. It can do so in one of two ways: a decrease in spending or an increase in taxes. I shall assume here and in what follows that the adjustment comes through taxes so that the path of spending is unaffected. It follows that the decrease in taxes by 1 during year 1 must be offset by an increase in taxes by $(1 + r)$ during year 2.

The path of taxes and debt corresponding to this case is given in Figure 26-1(a): If the debt is fully repaid during year 2, the decrease in taxes of 1 in year 1 requires an increase in taxes equal to $(1 + r)$ in year 2.

Full repayment in Year 2:

T_1 decreases by $1 \Rightarrow$
T_2 increases by $(1 + r)$

Full Repayment in Year t

Now suppose the government decides to wait until year t to repay the debt. So, from year 2 to year $t - 1$, the primary deficit is equal to zero—taxes are equal to spending, not including interest payments on the debt.

During year 2, the primary deficit is zero. So, from equation (26.3), debt at the end of year 2 is

$$B_2 = (1 + r)B_1 + 0 = (1 + r)1 = (1 + r)$$

where the second equality uses the fact that $B_1 = 1$.

With the primary deficit still equal to zero during year 3, debt at the end of year 3 is

$$B_3 = (1 + r)B_2 + 0 = (1 + r)(1 + r)1 = (1 + r)^2$$

Solving for debt at the end of year 4 and so on, it is clear that as long as the government keeps a primary deficit equal to zero, debt grows at a rate equal to the interest rate, and thus debt at the end of year $t - 1$ is given by

$$B_{t-1} = (1 + r)^{t-2} \qquad (26.4)$$

Tax Cuts, Debt Repayment, and Debt Stabilization

(a) If the debt is fully repaid during year 2, the decrease in taxes of 1 in year 1 requires an increase in taxes equal to $(1 + r)$ in year 2.
(b) If the debt is fully repaid during year 5, the decrease in taxes of 1 in year 1 requires an increase in taxes equal to $(1 + r)^4$ during year 5.
(c) If the debt is stabilized from year 2 on, then taxes must be permanently higher by r from year 2 on.

(a) Debt Reimbursement in Year 2

Year	0	1	2	3	4	5
Taxes	0	−1	$(1+r)$	0	0	0
End-of-year debt	0 →	1 →	0 →	0 →	0 →	0

(b) Debt Reimbursement in Year 5

Year	0	1	2	3	4	5
Taxes	0	−1	0	0	0	$(1+r)^4$
End-of-year debt	0 →	1 →	$(1+r)$ →	$(1+r)^2$ →	$(1+r)^3$ →	0

(c) Debt Stabilization in Year 2

Year	0	1	2	3	4	5
Taxes	0	−1	r	r	r	r
End-of-year debt	0 →	1 →	1 →	1 →	1 →	1

Despite the fact that taxes are cut only in year 1, debt keeps increasing over time, at a rate equal to the interest rate. The reason is simple: Although the primary deficit is equal to zero, debt is now positive, and so are interest payments on the debt. Each year, the government must issue more debt to pay the interest on existing debt.

In year t, the year in which the government decides to repay the debt, the budget constraint is

$$B_t = (1 + r)B_{t-1} + (G_t - T_t)$$

If debt is fully repaid during year t, then B_t (debt at the end of year t) is zero. Replacing B_t by zero and B_{t-1} by its expression from equation (26.4), gives

$$0 = (1 + r)(1 + r)^{t-2} + (G_t - T_t)$$

Add exponents:
$(1 + r)(1 + r)^{t-2} = (1 + r)^{t-1}$.
See Appendix 2 at the end of this book. ▶

Reorganizing and bringing $G_t - T_t$ to the left implies

$$T_t - G_t = (1 + r)^{t-1}$$

To repay the debt, the government must run a primary surplus equal to $(1 + r)^{t-1}$ during year t. If the adjustment is done through taxes, the initial decrease in taxes of 1 during year 1 leads to an increase in taxes of $(1 + r)^{t-1}$ during year t. The path of taxes and debt corresponding to the case where debt is repaid in year 5 is given in Figure 26-1(b). ▶

Full repayment in year 5:

T_1 decreases by $1 \Rightarrow$
T_5 increases by $(1 + r)^4$

This example yields our first set of conclusions:

■ If government spending is unchanged, a decrease in taxes must eventually be offset by an increase in taxes in the future.
■ The longer the government waits to increase taxes, or the higher the real interest rate, the higher the eventual increase in taxes must be.

Back to Policy **Back to Policy**

Debt Stabilization in Year *t*

We have assumed so far that the government fully repays the debt. Let's now look at what happens to taxes if the government only stabilizes the debt. (Stabilizing the debt means changing taxes or spending so that debt remains constant from then on.)

Suppose the government decides to stabilize the debt from year 2 on. Stabilizing the debt from year 2 on means the debt at the end of year 2 and thereafter remains at the same level as at the end of year 1.

From equation (26.3), the budget constraint for year 2 is

$$B_2 = (1 + r)B_1 + (G_2 - T_2)$$

Under our assumption that debt is stabilized in year 2, $B_2 = B_1 = 1$. Replacing in the preceding equation,

$$1 = (1 + r) + (G_2 - T_2)$$

Reorganizing, and bringing $G_2 - T_2$ to the left side,

$$T_2 - G_2 = (1 + r) - 1 = r$$

To avoid a further increase in debt during year 1, the government must run a primary surplus equal to real interest payments on the existing debt. It must do so in each of the following years as well: Each year, the primary surplus must be sufficient to cover interest payments, leaving the debt level unchanged. The path of taxes and debt is shown in Figure 26-1(c): Debt remains equal to 1 from year 1 on. Taxes are permanently higher from year 1 on, by an amount equal to r; equivalently, from year 1 on, the government runs a primary surplus equal to r.

◄ Stabilizing the debt from year 2 on

T_1 decreases by 1 ⇒ T_2, T_3, . . . increase by r.

The logic of this argument extends directly to the case where the government waits until year *t* to stabilize the debt. Whenever the government stabilizes, it must from then on run a primary surplus sufficient to pay interest on the debt.

This example yields our second set of conclusions:

- The legacy of past deficits is higher government debt.
- To stabilize the debt, the government must eliminate the deficit.
- To eliminate the deficit, the government must run a primary surplus equal to the interest payments on the existing debt. This requires higher taxes forever.

The Evolution of the Debt-to-GDP Ratio

We have focused so far on the evolution of the *level* of debt. But in an economy in which output grows over time, it makes more sense to focus on the *ratio of debt to output*. To see how this change in focus modifies our conclusions, we need to go from equation (26.3) to an equation that gives the evolution of the **debt-to-GDP ratio**—the **debt ratio** for short.

The Arithmetic of the Debt Ratio

Deriving the evolution of the debt ratio takes a few steps. Do not worry: The final equation is easy to understand.

First, divide both sides of equation (26.3) by real output, Y_t, to get

$$\frac{B_t}{Y_t} = (1 + r)\frac{B_{t-1}}{Y_t} + \frac{G_t - T_t}{Y_t}$$

Next rewrite B_{t-1}/Y_t as $(B_t/Y_{t-1})(Y_{t-1}/Y_t)$ (in other words, multiply the numerator and the denominator by Y_{t-1}):

$$\frac{B_t}{Y_t} = (1 + r)\left(\frac{Y_{t-1}}{Y_t}\right)\frac{B_{t-1}}{Y_{t-1}} + \frac{G_t - T_t}{Y_t}$$

Start from $Y_t = (1 + g)Y_{t-1}$. Divide both sides by Y_t to get $1 = (1 + g)Y_{t-1}/Y_t$. Reorganize to get $Y_{t-1}/Y_t = 1/(1 + g)$.

This approximation is derived as Proposition 6 in Appendix 2 at the end of this book.

Note that all the terms in the equation are now in terms of ratios to output, Y. To simplify this equation, assume that output growth is constant and denote the growth rate of output by g, so Y_{t-1}/Y_t can be written as $1/(1 + g)$. And use the approximation $(1 + r)/(1 + g) = 1 + r - g$.

Using these two assumptions, rewrite the preceding equation as

$$\frac{B_t}{Y_t} = (1 + r - g)\frac{B_{t-1}}{Y_{t-1}} + \frac{G_t - T_t}{Y_t}$$

Finally, reorganize to get

$$\frac{B_t}{Y_t} - \frac{B_{t-1}}{Y_{t-1}} = (r - g)\frac{B_{t-1}}{Y_{t-1}} + \frac{G_t - T_t}{Y_t} \qquad (26.5)$$

This took many steps, but the final relation has a simple interpretation: The change in the debt ratio over time (the left side of the equation) is equal to the sum of two terms:

■ The first term is the difference between the real interest rate and the growth rate, times the initial debt ratio.
■ The second term is the ratio of the primary deficit to GDP.

If two variables (here debt and GDP) grow at rates r and g respectively, then their ratio (here the ratio of debt to GDP) will grow at rate $r - g$. See Proposition 8 in Appendix 2 at the end of this book.

Compare equation (26.5), which gives the evolution of the ratio of debt to GDP, to equation (26.2), which gives the evolution of the level of debt itself. The difference is the presence of $r - g$ in equation (26.5) compared to r in equation (26.2). The reason for the difference is simple: Suppose the primary deficit is zero. Debt will then increase at a rate equal to the real interest rate, r. But if GDP is growing as well, the ratio of debt to GDP will grow more slowly; it will grow at a rate equal to the real interest rate minus the growth rate of output, $r - g$.

The Evolution of the Debt Ratio in OECD Countries

Equation (26.5) implies that the increase in the ratio of debt to GDP will be larger:

■ the higher the real interest rate,
■ the lower the growth rate of output,
■ the higher the initial debt ratio,
■ the higher the ratio of the primary deficit to GDP.

For more on the evolution of deficits and debt in Europe since the early 1990s, see the Focus box "The Stability and Growth Pact: A Short History" in Chapter 24. For more on the evolution of U.S. fiscal policy, see the discussion in Chapter 24 and the discussion at the end of this chapter.

This list provides a useful guide to the evolution of the debt-to-GDP ratio over the past four decades in OECD countries. Rather than focus on the OECD as a whole, let me focus on the evolution of the debt ratio in Belgium. While the increase in the debt ratio, which is plotted in Figure 26-2, has been particularly sharp, it shows the factors behind the evolution of the debt ratio in OECD countries in general since the early 1970s.

Figure 26-2 suggests the presence of three distinct regimes:

■ A low and stable debt ratio for most of the 1970s. This might come as a surprise when you recall that much the 1970s were in most OECD countries, including

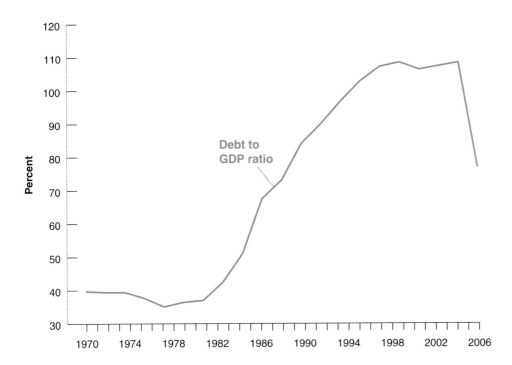

Figure 26-2 ▨

The Belgian Debt Ratio since 1970

Low growth, high interest rates, and primary deficits led to a large increase in the debt ratio from the early 1980s to the mid-1990s. Since then, higher growth, lower interest rates, and primary surpluses have led to a decline in the debt ratio.

Belgium, a period of stagflation—i.e., low growth and high inflation. From equation ◄ (26.5), one would expect low growth to lead to an increase in the debt ratio, both directly, through a higher $r - g$, and indirectly, through a primary deficit, due to lower tax revenues. This was not the case. The adverse effects of growth were indeed present, and Belgium ran primary deficits, but these effects were offset by very low, indeed negative, real interest rates: The nominal interest rate was high, but the inflation rate was even higher, leading to negative values of r. In effect, the Belgian government was able to inflate away part of its debt. The result was a roughly stable debt ratio until the late 1970s.

The main factors behind this stagflation were the increases in the price of oil in 1973–1975 and in 1979–1981. See Chapter 7.

■ A sharp increase in the debt ratio from the early 1980s to the mid-1990s. The reason: Continued low growth and large primary deficits for most of the period, but now combined with high real interest rates, due to disinflation. In most countries, including Belgium, disinflation, which took place in the early 1980s, was associated with a sharp increase in nominal interest rates and thus a sharp increase in r. To avoid an increase in its debt ratio, the Belgian government would have had to run large primary surpluses. Worried about the adverse effects of a fiscal contraction on aggregate demand and on output, it ran large primary deficits instead. The result was a large increase in the debt ratio.

■ A steady decrease in the debt ratio since the mid-1990s. In 1996, the Belgian debt ratio reached 115%! It became clear that a change in fiscal policy was needed. Large primary surpluses, together with the help of higher growth and lower real interest rates, have led to a sharp decrease in the debt ratio. The debt ratio now stands below 80% and continues to decrease.

26-2 Four Issues in Fiscal Policy

Having looked at the mechanics of the government budget constraint, we can now take up four issues in which this constraint plays a central role.

Ricardian Equivalence

How does taking into account the government budget constraint affect the way we should think of the effects of deficits on output?

One extreme view is that when the government budget constraint is taken into account, neither deficits nor debt have an effect on economic activity! This argument is known as the **Ricardian equivalence** proposition. David Ricardo, a nineteenth-century English economist, was the first to articulate its logic. His argument was further developed and given prominence in the 1970s by Robert Barro, then at the University of Chicago, now at Harvard University. For this reason, the argument is also known as the **Ricardo–Barro proposition**.

While Ricardo stated the logic of the argument, he also argued that there were many reasons it would not hold in practice. In contrast, Barro argues that not only is the argument logically correct, but it is also a good description of reality. ▶

The best way to understand the logic of the proposition is to use the example of tax changes from Section 26-1:

■ Suppose that the government decreases taxes by 1 (again think 1 billion dollars) this year. As it does so, it announces that, to repay the debt, it will increase taxes by $(1+r)$ next year. What will be the effect of the initial tax cut on consumption?

See Chapter 16 for a definition of human wealth and a discussion of its role in consumption. ▶

■ One possible answer is: No effect at all. Why? Because consumers realize that the tax cut is not much of a gift: Lower taxes this year are exactly offset, in present value, by higher taxes next year. Put another way, their human wealth—the present value of after-tax labor income—is unaffected. Current taxes go down by 1, but the present value of next year's taxes goes up by $(1 + r)/(1 + r) = 1$, and the net effect of the two changes is exactly equal to zero.

■ Another way of coming to the same answer—this time looking at saving rather than looking at consumption—is as follows: To say that consumers do not change their consumption in response to the tax cut is the same as saying that *private saving increases one-for-one with the deficit*. So the Ricardian equivalence proposition says that if a government finances a given path of spending through deficits, private saving will increase one-for-one with the decrease in public saving, leaving total saving unchanged. The total amount left for investment will not be affected. Over time, the mechanics of the government budget constraint imply that government debt will increase. But this increase will not come at the expense of capital accumulation.

Under the Ricardian equivalence proposition, the long sequence of deficits and the increase in government debt that characterized the OECD until the late 1990s are no cause for worry. As governments were dissaving, the argument goes, people were saving more in anticipation of the higher taxes to come. The decrease in public saving was offset by an equal increase in private saving. Total saving was therefore unaffected, and so was investment. OECD economies have the same capital stock today that they would have had if there had been no increase in debt. High debt is no cause for concern.

How seriously should you take the Ricardian equivalence proposition? Most economists would answer: "Seriously, but not seriously enough to think that deficits and debt are irrelevant." A major theme of this book has been that expectations matter, that consumption decisions depend not only on current income but also on expected future income. If it were widely believed that a tax cut this year is going to be followed by an offsetting increase in taxes *next year*, the effect on consumption would indeed probably be small. Many consumers would save most or all of the tax cut in anticipation of higher taxes next year. (Replace "year" with "month" or "week," and the argument becomes even more convincing.)

Of course, tax cuts rarely come with the announcement of corresponding tax increases a year later. Consumers have to guess when and how taxes will eventually be increased. This fact does not by itself invalidate the Ricardian equivalence argument: No matter when taxes will be increased, the government budget constraint still implies that the present value of future tax increases must always be equal to the decrease in taxes today. Take the second example we looked at in Section 26-1—drawn in Figure 26-1(b)—in which the government waits t years to increase taxes, and so increases taxes by $(1 + r)^{t-1}$. The present value in year 0 of this expected tax increase is $(1 + r)^{t-1}/(1 + r)^{t-1} = 1$—exactly equal to the original tax cut. The change in human ◀ wealth from the tax cut is still zero.

The increase in taxes in t years is $(1 + r)^{t-1}$. The discount factor for a dollar t years from now is $1/(1 + r)^{t-1}$. So the value of the increase in taxes t years from now as of today is $(1 + r)^{t-1}/(1 + r)^{t-1} = 1$.

But insofar as future tax increases appear more distant and their timing more uncertain, consumers are in fact more likely to ignore them. This may be the case because they expect to die before taxes go up, or, more likely, because they just do not think that far into the future. In either case, Ricardian equivalence is likely to fail.

So, it is safe to conclude that budget deficits have an important effect on activity—although perhaps a smaller effect than we thought before going through the Ricardian equivalence argument. In the short run, larger deficits are likely to lead to higher demand and to higher output. In the long run, higher government debt lowers capital accumulation and, as a result, lowers output.

Deficits, Output Stabilization, and the Cyclically Adjusted Deficit

The fact that budget deficits do, indeed, have long-run adverse effects on capital accumulation and, in turn, on output, does not imply that fiscal policy should not be used to reduce output fluctuations. Rather, it implies that deficits during recessions should ◀ be offset by surpluses during booms, so as not to lead to a steady increase in debt.

Note the analogy with monetary policy: The fact that higher money growth leads in the long run to more inflation does not imply that monetary policy should not be used for output stabilization.

◀ Ignore output growth in this section, and so ignore the distinction between stabilizing the debt and stabilizing the debt-to-GDP ratio. (Verify that the argument extends to the case where output is growing.)

To help assess whether fiscal policy is on track, economists have constructed deficit measures that tell what the deficit would be, under existing tax and spending rules, if output were at the natural level of output. Such measures come under many names, ranging from the **full-employment deficit**, to the **midcycle deficit**, to the **standardized employment deficit**, to the **structural deficit** (the term used by the OECD). I shall use **cyclically adjusted deficit**, the term I find the most intuitive.

The cyclically adjusted deficit gives a simple benchmark against which to judge the direction of fiscal policy: If the actual deficit is large but the cyclically adjusted deficit is zero, then current fiscal policy is consistent with no systematic increase in debt over time. The debt will increase as long as output is below the natural level of output; but as output returns to its natural level, the deficit will disappear and the debt will stabilize.

It does not follow that the goal of fiscal policy should be to maintain a cyclically adjusted deficit equal to zero at all times. In a recession, the government may want to run a deficit large enough that even the cyclically adjusted deficit is positive. In that case, the fact that the cyclically adjusted deficit is positive provides a useful warning. The warning is that the return of output to its natural level will not be enough to stabilize the debt: The government will have to take specific measures, from tax increases to cuts in spending, to decrease the deficit at some point in the future.

The theory underlying the concept of cyclically adjusted deficit is simple; the practice of it has proven tricky. To see why, we need to look at how measures of the cyclically adjusted deficit are constructed. Construction requires two steps. First, establish how much lower the deficit would be if output were, say, 1% higher. Second, assess how far output is from its natural level:

- The first step is straightforward. A reliable rule of thumb is that a 1% decrease in output leads automatically to an increase in the deficit of 0.5% of GDP. This increase occurs because most taxes are proportional to output, whereas most government spending does not depend on the level of output. This means that a decrease in output, which leads to a decrease in revenues and not much change in spending, naturally leads to a larger deficit.

If output is, say, 5% below its natural level, the deficit as a ratio to GDP will therefore be about 2.5% larger than it would be if output were at the natural level of output. (This effect of activity on the deficit has been called an **automatic stabilizer**: A recession naturally generates a deficit, and therefore a fiscal expansion, which partly counteracts the recession.)

- The second step is more difficult. Recall from Chapter 6 that the natural level of output is the output level that would be produced if the economy were operating at the natural rate of unemployment. Too low an estimate of the natural rate of unemployment will lead to too high an estimate of the natural level of output, and therefore to too optimistic a measure of the cyclically adjusted deficit.

See our discussion of high European unemployment in Chapter 8. ▶

This difficulty explains in part what happened in Europe in the 1980s. Based on the assumption of an unchanged natural unemployment rate, the cyclically adjusted deficits of the 1980s did not look that bad: If European unemployment had returned to its level of the 1970s, the associated increase in output would have been sufficient to reestablish budget balance in most countries. But, it turned out, much of the increase in unemployment reflected an increase in the natural unemployment rate, and unemployment remained very high during the 1980s. As a result, the decade was characterized by high deficits and large increases in debt ratios in most countries.

Wars and Deficits

Look at the two peaks associated with World War I and World War II in Figure 24–4. ▶

Wars typically bring about large budget deficits. As you saw in Chapter 24, the two largest increases in U.S. government debt in the twentieth century took place during World War I and World War II. We examine the case of World War II further in the Focus box "Deficits, Consumption, and Investment in the United States During World War II."

Is it right for governments to rely so much on deficits to finance wars? After all, war economies are usually operating at low unemployment, so the output stabilization reasons for running deficits we examined earlier are irrelevant. The answer, nevertheless, is yes. In fact, there are two good reasons to run deficits during wars:

- The first is distributional—Deficit finance is a way to pass some of the burden of the war to those alive after the war, and it seems only fair for future generations to share in the sacrifices the war requires.
- The second is more narrowly economic—Deficit spending helps reduce tax distortions.

Let's look at each reason in turn.

Passing on the Burden of the War

Wars lead to large increases in government spending. Consider the implications of financing this increased spending either through increased taxes or through debt. To distinguish this case from our earlier discussion of output stabilization, let's also assume that output is fixed at the natural level of output:

- Suppose the government relies on deficit finance. With government spending sharply up, there will be a very large increase in the demand for goods. Given our assumption that output stays the same, the interest rate will have to increase enough to maintain equilibrium. Investment, which depends on the interest rate, will decrease sharply.

- Suppose instead that the government finances the spending increase through an increase in taxes—say income taxes. Consumption will decline sharply. Exactly how much depends on consumers' expectations: The longer they expect the war to last, the longer they will expect higher taxes to last, and the more they will decrease their consumption. In any case, the increase in government spending will be partly offset by a decrease in consumption. Interest rates will increase by less than they would have increased under deficit spending, and investment will therefore decrease by less.

Assume that the economy is closed, so that $Y = C + I + G$. Suppose that G goes up, and Y remains the same. Then, $C + I$ must go down. If taxes are not increased, most of the decrease will come from a decrease in I. If taxes are increased, most of the decrease will come from a ◄ decrease in C.

In short, for a given output, the increase in government spending requires either a decrease in consumption and/or a decrease in investment. Whether the government relies on tax increases or deficits determines whether consumption or investment does more of the adjustment when government spending goes up.

How does this affect who bears the burden of the war? The more the government relies on deficits, the smaller the decrease in consumption during the war and the larger the decrease in investment. Lower investment means a lower capital stock after the war and, therefore, lower output after the war. By reducing capital accumulation, deficits become a way of passing some of the burden of the war on to future generations.

Reducing Tax Distortions

There is another argument for running deficits, not only during wars but, more generally, in times when government spending is exceptionally high. Think, for example, of reconstruction after an earthquake, or the costs involved in the reunification of Germany in the early 1990s.

See the Focus box "German Unification, Interest Rates, and ◄ the EMS" in Chapter 20.

The argument is as follows: If the government were to increase taxes in order to finance the increase in spending, tax rates would have to be very high. Very high tax rates can lead to very high economic distortions: Faced with very high income tax rates, people work less or engage in illegal, untaxed activities. Rather than moving the tax rate up and down to always balance the budget, it is better (from the point of view of reducing distortions) to maintain a relatively constant tax rate—to *smooth taxes*. **Tax smoothing** implies running large deficits when government spending is exceptionally high and small surpluses the rest of the time.

The Dangers of Very High Debt

You have now seen two costs of high government debt—lower capital accumulation, and higher tax rates and higher distortions. The recent experience of a number of countries with high debt ratios points to yet another cost: High debt can lead to vicious cycles and makes the conduct of fiscal policy extremely difficult.

To see why this is so, return to equation (26.5), which gives the evolution of the debt ratio:

$$\frac{B_t}{Y_t} - \frac{B_{t-1}}{Y_{t-1}} = (r - g)\frac{B_{t-1}}{Y_{t-1}} + \frac{(G_t - T_t)}{Y_t}$$

Take a country with a high debt ratio, say, 100%. Suppose the real interest rate is 3%, and the growth rate is 2%. The first term on the right is $(3\% - 2\%) \times 100\% = 1\%$ of GDP. Suppose further that the government is running a primary surplus of 1%, thus just enough to keep the debt ratio constant (the entire right side of the equation equals $1\% + -1\% = 0\%$).

Now suppose financial investors start requiring a higher interest rate to hold government bonds. This higher interest rate may come from the fact that investors worry

Deficits, Consumption, and Investment in the United States during World War II

FOCUS

In 1939, the share of U.S. government spending on goods and services in GDP was 15%. By 1944, it had increased to 45%! The increase was due to increased spending on national defense, which went from 1% of GDP in 1939 to 36% in 1944.

Faced with such a massive increase in spending, the U.S. government reacted with large tax increases. For the first time in U.S. history, the individual income tax became a major source of revenues; individual income tax revenues, which were 1% of GDP in 1939, increased to 8.5% in 1944. But the tax increases were still far less than the increase in government expenditures. The increase in federal revenues, from 7.2% of GDP in 1939 to 22.7% in 1944, was only a little more than half the increase in expenditures.

The result was a sequence of large budget deficits. By 1944, the federal deficit reached 22% of GDP. The ratio of debt to GDP, already high at 53% in 1939 because of the deficits the government had run during the Great Depression, reached 110%!

Was the increase in government spending achieved at the expense of consumption or private investment?

(As you saw in Chapter 18, it could in principle have come from higher imports and a current account deficit. But the United States had nobody to borrow from during the war. Rather, it was lending to some of its allies: Transfers from the U.S. government to foreign countries were 6% of U.S. GDP in 1944.)

It was met in large part by a decrease in consumption: The share of consumption in GDP fell by 23 percentage points, from 74% to 51%. Part of the decrease in consumption may have been due to anticipation of higher taxes after the war; part of it was due to the unavailability of many consumer durables. Patriotism also probably motivated people to save more and buy the war bonds issued by the government to finance the war.

It was also met, however, by a 6% decrease in the share of (private) investment in GDP—from 10% to 4%. Part of the burden of the war was therefore passed on in the form of lower capital accumulation to those living after the war.

---

that the government won't be able to repay the debt because it won't be able to keep the deficit under control. The specific reason does not matter here. For concreteness, suppose the domestic real interest rate increases from 3% to, say, 12%.

Now assess the fiscal situation: $r - g$ is now 12% − 2% = 10%. With the increase in $r - g$ from 1% to 10%, the government must increase its primary surplus from 1% to 10% of GDP just to keep the debt-to-GDP ratio constant. Now come the potential vicious cycle:

Suppose the government takes steps to avoid an increase in the debt ratio. The spending cuts or tax increases are likely to prove politically costly, generating even more political uncertainty and the need for an even higher interest rate. Also, the sharp fiscal contraction is likely to lead to a recession, decreasing the growth rate. Both the increase in the real interest rate and the decrease in growth further increase $r - g$, making it even harder to stabilize the debt ratio.

Alternatively, suppose the government proves unable or unwilling to increase the primary budget surplus by 9% of GDP. Debt then starts increasing, leading financial markets to become even more worried and require an even higher interest rate. The higher interest rate leads to even larger deficits, an even faster increase in the debt ratio, and so on. At some point, the government has no other option but to default.

In short, the higher the ratio of debt to GDP, the larger the potential for catastrophic debt dynamics. Even if the fear that the government may not fully repay the

Back to Policy   **Back to Policy**

debt was initially unfounded, it can easily become self-fulfilling. The increased interest the government must pay on its debt can lead the government to lose control of its budget, and lead to an increase in debt to a level such that the government is unable to repay the debt, validating the initial fears.

If this reminds you of our discussion of exchange rate crises and the possibility of self-fulfilling crises, you are right. Very much the same mechanisms are at work here: Expectations that a problem may arise lead to the emergence of the problem, validating initial expectations. Indeed, in some crises, both mechanisms are at work. In 1998 in Brazil, fears of a devaluation of the *real* (the Brazilian currency) forced Brazil to increase interest rates to very high levels. These high interest rates led to much larger budget deficits, raising questions about whether the Brazilian government could repay its debt, further increasing interest rates. Eventually, Brazil had no choice but to devalue. It did so in early 1999.

We studied exchange rate crises in Chapter 21.

If a government decides that its debt ratio is too high, how and how fast should it reduce it? It should do so through many years, even many decades, of surpluses. A historical reference here is England in the nineteenth century. By the end of its wars against Napoleon in the early 1800s, England had run up a debt ratio in excess of 200% of GDP. It spent most of the nineteenth century reducing the ratio, so that by 1900, the ratio stood at only 30% of GDP.

The prospect of many decades of fiscal austerity is unpleasant. Thus, when debt ratios are very high, an alternative solution keeps coming up—**debt repudiation**. The argument is simple: Repudiating the debt—canceling it in part or in full—is good for the economy: It allows for a decrease in taxes and thus a decrease in distortions. It decreases the risk of vicious cycles. The problem with this argument is the problem of time inconsistency we studied in Chapter 24: If the government reneges on its promises to repay its debt, it may have great difficulty trying to borrow again for a long time in the future; financial markets will remember what happened and be reluctant to lend again. Taking the easy way out today may be costly in the long run. Debt repudiation is very much a last resort, to be used when everything else has failed.

The argument that debt repudiation is good in the short run is more true if the debt is held by foreigners. If the debt is help by domestic residents, repudiation will be tough on them, and possibly lead to bankruptcies and problems for the financial sector.

26-3 The U.S. Budget: Current Numbers and Future Prospects

We conclude this chapter by looking at current U.S. budget numbers and discussing the issues confronting U.S. fiscal policy, now and in the future.

Current Numbers

If you look at the U.S. budget, you are likely to encounter different numbers for what sounds like the same thing—for example, different numbers for "the U.S. budget deficit." The reason is that there are many different definitions of *expenditures*, *revenues*, and *deficit*:

■ Some numbers refer to the budget of the federal government. Some numbers consolidate the accounts of the federal, state, and local governments. The difference is typically small, however: Most state and local governments operate under rules that prevent them from running deficits, so they typically either run a balanced budget or generate a small surplus. I shall focus here only on the *federal budget*. Even within the federal budget, there are two sets of numbers:

■ One set of numbers is based on the government accounting system; another set of numbers is based on the national income accounting system. The government uses its own accounting system and, because this is the system used to present and discuss the budget in Congress, these are the numbers you are most likely to encounter when reading newspapers. The national income and product accounts (NIPA) use a different accounting system. That system provides a more economically meaningful set of budget numbers.

Here are the main differences between the government numbers and the NIPA numbers:

- The government budget numbers are presented by *fiscal year*. The fiscal year runs from October 1 of the preceding calendar year to September 30 of the current calendar year. The NIPA numbers are typically reported for the calendar year, not the fiscal year. (Given that the NIPA numbers are available for each quarter, it is easy to construct NIPA numbers for each fiscal year.)

- The government budget numbers are presented in two categories: "on-budget" and "off-budget." The most important off-budget item is Social Security. In fiscal year 2006, the on-budget deficit was $434 billion—3.3% of GDP. This deficit was partly offset by an off-budget surplus of $186 billion, leading to a combined deficit of $434 − $186 = $248 billion—1.9% of GDP; the main source of the off-budget surplus was an excess of Social Security taxes over Social Security benefits.

    By separating the Social Security system from the rest of the budget (by putting it in a "lockbox," an expression coined by the Clinton administration), the on-budget/off-budget distinction is supposed to serve a useful political purpose: to make it harder for Congress and the president to use the Social Security surplus to finance the rest of the budget. It is, however, a meaningless distinction from an economic viewpoint. The NIPA measure makes no such distinction; the NIPA deficit corresponds most closely to the sum of the on-budget and off-budget deficits.

So, when you hear a deficit number, ask:
- Federal? or federal, state, and local?
- Fiscal year? or calendar year?
- Government? or NIPA accounts?
- If government accounts, on-budget? off-budget? or the sum of the two? ▶

- The two accounting systems differ in how they treat the sale of government assets. Government accounts treat asset sales as revenues. The NIPA accounts correctly recognize that asset sales bring revenues today but reduce revenues in the future (because the government no longer receives the revenues from these assets); thus asset sales are not included in revenues in the NIPA accounts.

- The two accounting systems differ in the way they treat government investment. Government accounts count all expenditures, including investment purchases, such as aircraft carriers. The NIPA accounts, which measure current rather than capital expenditures, exclude investment but include depreciation on existing government-owned capital.

- The difference between the official and the NIPA measures of the deficit can be positive or negative. In fiscal year 2006, the two measures were close to each other. The official measure of the federal deficit was $248 billion—1.9% of GDP—a bit larger than the NIPA measure of $213 billion—1.7% of GDP.

Finally, you are likely to encounter two numbers for (federal) government debt:

- One is *gross debt*, the sum of the federal government's financial liabilities. When Congress votes to increase the debt ceiling, this is the number to which the ceiling applies. At the end of 2006, gross debt was equal to $8.4 trillion, or 65% of GDP.

- The other, more relevant number is *net debt* or, equivalently, *debt held by the public*. At the end of 2003, net debt was only $4.8 trillion, or 37% of GDP. Where did the difference between gross debt and net debt come from? From holdings of government debt by government agencies; for example, about $2.0 trillion was held by the Social Security Trust Fund. (More on the Trust Fund later in the section.)

Let's now turn to the numbers. Table 26-1 presents the basic budget numbers for fiscal year 2006, using NIPA numbers. The reason for using the fiscal year rather than the calendar year is that budget projections—to which we shall turn later—are

Table 26-1	U.S. Federal Budget Revenues and Expenditures, Fiscal Year 2006 (percent of GDP)		
Revenues	18.9		
Personal taxes		7.9	
Corporate profit taxes		2.9	
Indirect taxes		0.8	
Social insurance contributions		6.8	
Other		1.3	
Expenditures, excluding net interest payments	18.4		
Consumption expenditures		6.1	
Defense			4.1
Nondefense			2.0
Transfers		8.9	
Grants to state/local governments		2.8	
Other		0.7	
Primary surplus (1) (+ sign: surplus)	0.5		
Net interest payments (2)	2.2		
Real interest payments (3)		0.8	
Inflation component		1.4	
Official surplus: (1) minus (2)	−1.7		
Inflation adjusted surplus: (1) minus (3)	−0.3		
Memo item: Debt-to-GDP ratio	37.0		

Source: Survey of Current Business, March 2007, Table 10.

typically framed in terms of fiscal year rather than calendar year numbers. The reason for using NIPA numbers is that they are economically more meaningful.

In 2006, federal revenues were 18.9% of GDP. Expenditures, excluding interest payments, were 18.4% of GDP, so the federal government was running a primary surplus of 0.5% of GDP.

Interest payments on the debt held by the public were 2.2%. The official deficit was therefore equal to −0.5% + 2.2% = 1.7% of GDP. We know, however, that this measure is incorrect (see the Focus box "Inflation Accounting and the Measurement of Deficits"). The correct measure, the sum of the primary deficit plus *real* interest payments, was −0.5% + 0.8% = 0.3%. The federal government was therefore running a deficit of 0.3%.

This is a small deficit, and it would appear that, after the larger deficits of the early 2000s, U.S. fiscal policy is again on track. If one looks forward, however, there are reasons to worry. As Ben Bernanke, the chairman of the Fed, has indicated, what we may be witnessing is the calm before the storm. With this in mind, let's now look at budget projections for the medium run and the long run.

Medium-Run Budget Projections

Figure 26-3 shows the evolution of federal deficits from 2007 to 2017, as projected by the **Congressional Budget Office (CBO)**. The CBO is a nonpartisan agency of Congress that helps Congress assess the costs and the effects of fiscal decisions; among the

Figure 26-3

Deficits Projections: Federal Government Deficit, Fiscal Years 2007 to 2017

Under current fiscal rules, the deficit turns into a surplus by 2012. Under more realistic assumptions about spending and revenues, however, it increases steadily over the period.

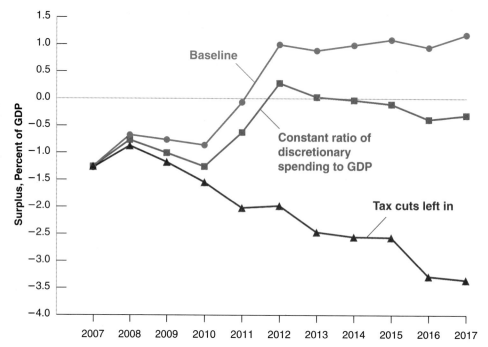

CBO's tasks is preparing projections of revenues, spending, and deficits *under current fiscal rules.* Figure 26-3 presents these projections, as of January 2007. The measure of the deficit is the federal deficit, by fiscal year, using government rather than NIPA conventions.

The blue line shows projected deficits under current rules (these are called **baseline projections**). According to this projection, the future looks good: The deficit turns into a surplus by 2012, and the budget shows a surplus of more than 1% of GDP by 2017. Unfortunately, this projection is misleading. It is based on three assumptions—three budget rules that Congress has said it would follow but is in fact unlikely to follow.

The first assumption is that nominal discretionary spending will increase only at the rate of inflation—in other words, will remain constant in real terms. A more realistic assumption, based on past experience, is that discretionary spending will increase at the same rate as GDP—in other words, that the ratio of discretionary spending to GDP will remain constant. The green line shows what will happen under this alternative assumption. The surplus no longer materializes, and the budget shows a small deficit in 2017.

The second assumption is the provision that most of the tax cuts introduced by the Bush administration in 2001 will expire in 2010. This provision, when passed, was widely seen as a gimmick—that is, only there to make distant deficits look small—and few people believe that this will happen: Most of the tax cuts are likely to be made permanent.

The third assumption is that the rules governing the **alternative minimum tax (AMT)** will not be changed. This alternative tax was introduced to ensure that the richest taxpayers would pay at least some taxes. Because the income threshold at which it is triggered is not indexed to inflation, the number of taxpayers subject to this alternative tax has steadily increased. It is widely believed that the tax will be redefined and the income threshold will be indexed.

The red line shows the projected path of the deficit under the joint assumptions that discretionary spending will increase with nominal GDP, that tax cuts will be

Back to Policy   **Back to Policy**

extended, and that the AMT will be indexed for inflation. Under these assumptions, the deficit grows steadily larger, reaching 3.5% by 2017.

In short, looking at the medium run, the fiscal situation looks less rosy, although not catastrophic. The more serious challenges arise, however, when one looks even further in the future, when one looks to the long run.

The Long-Run Challenges: Low Saving, Aging, and Medical Care

Should we worry if the United States runs budget deficits for the next decade? The answer is yes, for three reasons: low U.S. saving, the aging of America, and the increase in medical costs. Let's look at each in turn.

Deficits and the Low U.S. Saving Rate

The U.S. saving rate is one of the lowest in the OECD: In 2006, it reached a low of 13%, about 7% below the OECD average.

This low saving rate should be a matter of concern. Let's review why. In a closed economy, a low saving rate leads to lower investment and, therefore, to lower capital accumulation and a lower standard of living in the long run. In an open economy, a ◄ **See Chapter 11.** low saving rate might not lead to a lower investment rate because the difference between investment and saving can be financed by running a current account deficit—by borrowing from abroad. This is indeed what is happening in the United States, where the current account deficit is now very large, it was 6.4% in 2006. Even in ◄ **See Chapter 19.** this case, a low saving rate has a long-run cost: The United States is now the largest debtor country in the world, and will have to pay large interest payments to the rest of the world for the indefinite future.

If we believe that the United States is not saving enough, there is a strong argument for taking measures to increase private saving or offsetting low private saving by higher public saving. This is the first argument for running budget surpluses rather than deficits.

Retirement and Medical Care

About half of U.S. federal spending is on **entitlement programs**. These are programs that require the payment of benefits to all who meet the eligibility requirements established by the law. The three largest programs are Social Security (which provides benefits to retirees), Medicare (which provides health care to retirees), and Medicaid (which provides health care to the poor).

Table 26-2 shows actual and projected spending on each of these three programs, under current rules, as a percentage of GDP, from 2005 to 2050.

The numbers are striking: Under current rules, Social Security benefits are projected to increase from 4.2% of GDP in 2005 to 6.2% in 2050. Medicare and Medicaid

They appear under "transfers" in Table 26-1. Spending on these programs is equal to 8% of GDP, or about 40% of total ◄ Federal spending.

Table 26-2	Projected Spending on Social Security, Medicare, and Medicaid (percent of GDP), 2005 to 2050			
	2005	**2010**	**2030**	**2050**
Social Security	4.2	4.2	5.9	6.2
Medicare/Medicaid	4.2	5.0	9.2	12.6
Total	8.4	9.2	15.1	18.8

Source: "The Long-Term Budget Outlook," Congressional Budget Office, December 2005.

benefits are projected to increase from 4.2% to 12.6%. The ratio of entitlement spending to GDP (the sum of the two numbers) is projected, therefore, to increase by 10.4% of GDP over the next 45 years. These projected increases have two main sources:

The problem is not limited to the United States. The increase in the old age dependency ratio is larger in most European countries, and even larger in China—because of China's policy limiting families to only one child. ▶

- The first and main one is the *aging of America*, the rapid increase in the proportion of people over 65 that will take place as the Baby Boom generation begins to reach retirement age, from year 2010 on. The *old age dependency ratio*—the ratio of the population 65 years or older to the population between 20 and 64 years—is projected to increase from about 20% in 1998 to above 40% in 2050. This evolution explains the projected growth in Social Security benefits and some of the increase in Medicare.

- The second source, which explains the rest of the growth of Medicare and all the growth in Medicaid, is the steadily and rapidly increasing cost of health care.

Can these increases in entitlement spending be offset by decreases in other government expenditures? The answer is a clear no. From Table 26-1, you can see that even if *all* expenditures other than transfers were eliminated, there would still not be enough to cover the projected increase in entitlement spending: In 2006, total expenditures, excluding interest payments and transfers, were equal to 9.5% of GDP, less than the 10.4% projected increase in entitlement spending.

It is therefore clear that major changes in entitlement programs will have to take place. Social Security benefits may have to be reduced (relative to projections), and the provision of medical care will have to be limited (again, relative to projections). There is also little doubt that taxes, such as the payroll taxes used to finance Social Security, will have to be increased.

It is also clear that waiting to act until spending starts increasing would be waiting too long. The cut in benefits or the increase in tax rates needed to finance entitlement programs would be too large. Just to finance projected Social Security benefits, the payroll tax rate would have to increase from approximately 12% today to about 20% in 2050. Financing Medicare and Medicaid increases would require further and even larger increases in the tax rate. There is a general agreement that the government should not wait but should start taking measures now.

What should these measures do? They have to combine tax increases and benefit reductions so as to generate surpluses now and accumulate assets in anticipation of future spending. This is the approach that has been taken in dealing with Social Security. Since 1983, Social Security contributions have exceeded Social Security benefits, leading to surpluses and the accumulation of assets in the **Social Security Trust Fund**. Assets in the Trust Fund are now equal to about 15% of GDP.

How does such accumulation help in dealing with future increases in spending? First, decumulation of these assets later on can delay the date at which taxes have to be increased or benefits decreased. If accumulation in the fund is large enough, this can avoid the need for tax increases or benefit cuts altogether. An example will help here. Suppose the real interest rate is 2%. Then, if the Trust Fund accumulated assets in an amount equal to 100% of GDP, real interest payments would be equal to 2% of GDP, an amount sufficient to cover the whole projected increase in Social Security benefits as a percentage of GDP between now and 2050.

For more on current proposals for Social Security reform, see the Focus box "Social Security, Saving, and Capital Accumulation in the United States" in Chapter 11. ▶

Under current projections, the Trust Fund does not come close, however, to reaching such a level. It is projected to reach a peak by 2016, and then to decline and become equal to zero by 2041. So there is a need to do more, not only for Social Security but, as we have seen, for Medicare and Medicaid programs.

Let's summarize: The United States is currently running a budget deficit. While it is not very large, there are three good arguments for reducing it, even for running a substantial surplus: the low U.S. saving rate, the aging of America, and the rapidly increasing cost of medical care.

Summary

- The government budget constraint gives the evolution of government debt as a function of spending and taxes. One way of expressing the constraint is that the change in debt (the deficit) is equal to the primary deficit plus interest payments on the debt. The primary deficit is the difference between government spending on goods and services, G, and taxes net of transfers, T.
- If government spending is unchanged, a decrease in taxes must eventually be offset by an increase in taxes in the future. The longer the government waits to increase taxes or the higher the real interest rate, the higher the eventual increase in taxes.
- The legacy of past deficits is higher debt. To stabilize the debt, the government must eliminate the deficit. To eliminate the deficit, it must run a primary surplus equal to the interest payments on the existing debt.
- Under the Ricardian equivalence proposition, a larger deficit is offset by an equal increase in private saving. Deficits have no effect on demand and on output. The accumulation of debt does not affect capital accumulation. When Ricardian equivalence fails, larger deficits lead to higher demand and higher output in the short

run. The accumulation of debt leads to lower capital accumulation and thus to lower output in the long run.
- To stabilize the economy, the government should run deficits during recessions and surpluses during booms. The cyclically adjusted deficit tells us what the deficit would be, under existing tax and spending rules, if output were at the natural level of output.
- Deficits are justified in times of high spending, such as wars. Relative to an increase in taxes, deficits lead to higher consumption and lower investment during wars. They therefore shift some of the burden of the war from people living during the war to those living after the war. Deficits also help smooth taxes and reduce tax distortions.
- A number of European countries have very high debt-to-GDP ratios. In addition to reducing capital and requiring higher taxes and thus tax distortions, high debt ratios increase the risk of fiscal crises.
- The United States is currently running a budget deficit. While it is not very large, there are three good arguments for reducing it, even for running a substantial surplus: the low U.S. saving rate, the aging of America, and the rapidly increasing cost of medical care.

Key Terms

- inflation-adjusted deficit, 579
- government budget constraint, 579
- primary deficit (primary surplus), 579
- debt-to-GDP ratio, debt ratio, 583
- Ricardian equivalence, Ricardo-Barro proposition, 586
- full-employment deficit, 587
- midcycle deficit, 587
- standardized employment deficit, 587
- structural deficit, 587

- cyclically adjusted deficit, 587
- automatic stabilizer, 588
- tax smoothing, 589
- debt repudiation, 591
- Congressional Budget Office (CBO), 593
- baseline projections, 594
- alternative minimum tax (AMT), 594
- entitlement programs, 595
- Social Security Trust Fund, 596

Questions and Problems

Quick Check

1. Using information in this chapter, label each of the following statements true, false, or uncertain. Explain briefly.

a. Tax smoothing and deficit finance help spread the burden of war across generations.

b. The government should always take immediate action to eliminate a cyclically adjusted budget deficit.

c. If Ricardian equivalence holds, then an increase in income taxes will affect neither consumption nor saving.

d. The ratio of debt to GDP cannot exceed 100%.

e. Because the United States is able to finance investment by borrowing from abroad, the low U.S. saving rate is not a cause for concern.

f. Based on current projections, the Social Security Trust Fund is large enough to pay full benefits (as defined by current law) to retirees for 100 years.

2. Consider the following statement:

"A deficit during a war can be a good thing. First, the deficit is temporary, so after the war is over, the government can go right back to its old level of spending and taxes. Second, given that the evidence supports the Ricardian equivalence proposition, the deficit will stimulate the economy during wartime, helping to keep the unemployment rate low."

Identify the mistakes in this statement. Is anything in this statement correct?

3. Consider an economy characterized by the following facts.

   i. The official budget deficit is 3% of GDP.

   ii. The debt-to-GDP ratio is 100%.

   iii. The nominal interest rate is 8%.

   iv. The inflation rate is 6%.

a. What is the primary deficit/surplus ratio to GDP?
b. What is the inflation-adjusted deficit/surplus ratio to GDP?
c. Suppose that output is 2% below its natural level. What is the cyclically adjusted, inflation-adjusted deficit/surplus ratio to GDP?
d. Suppose instead that output begins at its natural level and that output growth remains constant at the normal rate of 2%. How will the debt-to-GDP ratio change over time?

Dig Deeper

4. Consider the economy described in problem 3 and assume that there is a fixed exchange rate, $\bar{E}$. Suppose that financial investors worry that the level of debt is too high and that the government may devalue to stimulate output (and therefore tax revenues) to help pay down the debt. Financial investors begin to expect a devaluation of 8%. In other words, the expected exchange rate, E^e_{t+1}, decreases by 8% from its previous value of $\bar{E}$.

a. Recall the uncovered interest parity condition:

$$ i_t = i^*_t - \frac{E^e_{t+1} - \bar{E}}{\bar{E}} $$

If the foreign interest rate remains constant at 8%. what must happen to the domestic interest rate when E^e_{t+1} falls by 8%?
b. Suppose that domestic inflation remains the same. What happens to the domestic real interest rate? What is likely to happen to the growth rate?
c. What happens to the official budget deficit? What happens to the inflation-adjusted deficit?
d. Suppose the growth rate decreases from 2% to 0%. What happens to the change in the debt ratio? (Assume that the primary deficit/surplus ratio to GDP is unchanged, even though the fall in growth may reduce tax revenues.)
e. Were the fears of investors justified?

5. Ricardian equivalence and fiscal policy

First consider an economy in which Ricardian equivalence does not hold (i.e., an economy like the one we have described in this book).

a. Suppose the government starts with a balanced budget. Then, there is an increase in government spending, but there is no change in taxes. Show in an IS–LM diagram the effect of this policy on output in the short run. How will the government finance the increase in government spending?
b. Suppose, as in part (a), that the government starts with a balanced budget and then increases government spending. This time, however, assume that taxes increase by the same amount as government spending. Show in an IS–LM diagram the effect of this policy on output in the short run. (It may help to recall the discussion of the multiplier in Chapter 3. Does government spending or tax policy have a bigger multiplier?) How does the output effect compare with the effect in part (a)?

Now suppose Ricardian equivalence holds in this economy. [Parts (c) and (d) do not require use of diagrams.]

c. Consider again an increase in government spending with no change in taxes. How does the output effect compare to the output effects in parts (a) and (b)?
d. Consider again an increase in government spending combined with an increase in taxes of the same amount. How does this output effect compare to the output effects in parts (a) and (b)?
e. Comment on each of the following statements:
   i. "Under Ricardian equivalence, government spending has no effect on output."
   ii. "Under Ricardian equivalence, changes in taxes have no effect on output."

Explore Further

6. Consider an economy characterized by the following facts:
   i. The debt-to-GDP ratio is 40%.
   ii. The primary deficit is 4% of GDP.
   iii. The normal growth rate is 3%.
   iv. The real interest rate is 3%.

a. Using your favorite spreadsheet software, calculate the debt-to-GDP ratio in 10 years, assuming that the primary deficit stays at 4% of GDP each year; the economy grows at the normal growth rate in each year; and the real interest rate is constant, at 3%.
b. Suppose the real interest rate increases to 5%, but everything else remains as in part (a). Calculate the debt-to-GDP ratio in 10 years.
c. Suppose the normal growth rate falls to 1%, and the economy grows at the normal growth rate each year. Everything else remains as in part (a). Calculate the debt-to-GDP ratio in 10 years. Compare your answer to part (b).
d. Return to the assumptions of part (a). Suppose policymakers decide that a debt-to-GDP ratio of more than 50% is dangerous. Verify that reducing the primary deficit to 1% immediately, and maintaining this deficit for 10 years will produce a debt-to-GDP ratio of 50% in 10 years. Thereafter, what value of the primary deficit will be required to maintain the debt-to-GDP ratio of 50%?
e. Continuing with part (d), suppose policymakers wait five years before changing fiscal policy. For five years, the primary deficit remains at 4% of GDP. What is the debt-to-GDP ratio in five years? Suppose that after five years, policymakers decide to reduce the debt-to-GDP ratio to 50%. In years 6 through 10, what constant value of the primary deficit will produce a debt-to-GDP ratio of 50% at the end of year 10?
f. Suppose that policymakers carry out the policy in either parts (d) or (e). If these policies reduce the growth rate of output for a while, how will this affect the size of the reduction in the primary deficit required to achieve a debt-to-GDP ratio of 50% in 10 years?
g. Which policy—the one in part (d) or the one in part (e)—do you think is more dangerous to the stability of the economy?

We invite you to visit the Blanchard page on the Prentice Hall Web site, at:
www.prenhall.com/blanchard
for this chapter's World Wide Web exercises.

Further Readings

- The modern statement of the Ricardian equivalence proposition is Robert Barro's "Are Government Bonds Net Wealth?" *Journal of Political Economy*, December 1974, 1095–1117.
- Each year, the Congressional Budget Office publishes *The Budget and Economic Outlook* (available at **www.cbo.gov**) for the current and future fiscal years.

The document provides a clear and unbiased presentation of the current budget, current budget issues, and budget trends.

- As indicated in Chapter 11, a good site for following current discussions about Social Security reform is the site run by the nonpartisan Concord Coalition (**www.concordcoalition.org/issues/socsec**).

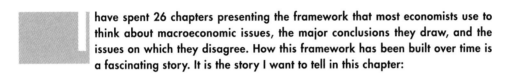

have spent 26 chapters presenting the framework that most economists use to think about macroeconomic issues, the major conclusions they draw, and the issues on which they disagree. How this framework has been built over time is a fascinating story. It is the story I want to tell in this chapter:

■ Section 27-1 starts at the beginning of modern macroeconomics—with Keynes and the Great Depression.

■ Section 27-2 turns to the *neoclassical synthesis*, a synthesis of Keynes' ideas with those of earlier economists—a synthesis that dominated macroeconomics until the early 1970s.

■ Section 27-3 describes the *rational expectations critique*, the strong attack on the neoclassical synthesis that led to a complete overhaul of macroeconomics starting in the 1970s.

■ Section 27-4 gives you a sense of current research developments.

■ Section 27-5 concludes by restating "common beliefs," the set of central propositions on which most macroeconomists agree. ■

27-1 Keynes and the Great Depression

The history of modern macroeconomics starts in 1936, with the publication of Keynes's *General Theory of Employment, Interest, and Money.* As he was writing the *General Theory,* Keynes confided to a friend: "I believe myself to be writing a book on economic theory which will largely revolutionize—not, I suppose at once but in the course of the next ten years—the way the world thinks about economic problems."

Keynes was right. The book's timing was one of the reasons for its immediate success. The Great Depression was not only an economic catastrophe but also an intellectual failure for the economists working on **business cycle theory**—as macroeconomics was then called. Few economists had a coherent explanation for the Depression, either for its depth or for its length. The economic measures taken by the Roosevelt administration as part of the New Deal had been based on instinct rather than on economic theory. The *General Theory* offered an interpretation of events, an intellectual framework, and a clear argument for government intervention.

The *General Theory* emphasized **effective demand**—what we now call *aggregate demand.* In the short run, Keynes argued, effective demand determines output. Even if output eventually returns to its natural level, the process is slow at best. One of Keynes' most famous quotes is "In the long run, we are all dead."

In the process of deriving effective demand, Keynes introduced many of the building blocks of modern macroeconomics:

- The relation of consumption to income, and the multiplier, which explains how shocks to demand can be amplified and lead to larger shifts in output.
- **Liquidity preference** (the term Keynes gave to the demand for money), which explains how monetary policy can affect interest rates and aggregate demand.
- The importance of expectations in affecting consumption and investment, and the idea that *animal spirits* (shifts in expectations) are a major factor behind shifts in demand and output.

The *General Theory* was more than a treatise for economists. It offered clear policy implications, and they were in tune with the times: Waiting for the economy to recover by itself was irresponsible. In the midst of a depression, trying to balance the budget was not only stupid, it was dangerous. Active use of fiscal policy was essential to return the country to high employment.

27-2 The Neoclassical Synthesis

Within a few years, the *General Theory* had transformed macroeconomics. Not everybody was converted, and few agreed with it all. But most discussions became organized around it.

By the early 1950s, a large consensus had emerged, based on an integration of many of Keynes' ideas and the ideas of earlier economists. This consensus was called the **neoclassical synthesis**. To quote from Paul Samuelson, in the 1955 edition of his textbook *Economics*—the first modern economics textbook:

> In recent years, 90 per cent of American economists have stopped being "Keynesian economists" or "Anti-Keynesian economists." Instead, they have worked toward a synthesis of whatever is valuable in older economics and in modern theories of income determination. The result might be called neo-classical economics and is accepted, in its broad outlines, by all but about five per cent of extreme left-wing and right-wing writers.

John Maynard Keynes

Paul Samuelson

The neoclassical synthesis was to remain the dominant view for another 20 years. Progress was astonishing, leading many to call the period from the early 1940s to the early 1970s the golden age of macroeconomics.

Progress on All Fronts

The first order of business after the publication of the *General Theory* was to formalize mathematically what Keynes meant. While Keynes knew mathematics, he had avoided using it in the *General Theory*. One result was endless controversies about what Keynes meant and whether there were logical flaws in some of his arguments.

The *IS–LM* Model

A number of formalizations of Keynes' ideas were offered. The most influential one was the *IS–LM* model, developed by John Hicks and Alvin Hansen in the 1930s and early 1940s. The initial version of the *IS–LM* model—which was actually very close to the version presented in Chapter 5 of this book—was criticized for emasculating many of Keynes' insights: Expectations played no role, and the adjustment of prices and wages was altogether absent. Yet the *IS–LM* model provided a basis from which to start building, and as such it was immensely successful. Discussions became organized around the slopes of the *IS* and *LM* curves, what variables were missing from the two relations, what equations for prices and wages should be added to the model, and so on.

Franco Modigliani

Theories of Consumption, Investment, and Money Demand

Keynes had emphasized the importance of consumption and investment behavior and of the choice between money and other financial assets. Major progress was soon made along all three fronts.

In the 1950s, Franco Modigliani (then at Carnegie Mellon, later at MIT) and Milton Friedman (at the University of Chicago) independently developed the theory of consumption you saw in Chapter 16. Both insisted on the importance of expectations in determining current consumption decisions.

James Tobin, from Yale, developed the theory of investment, based on the relation between the present value of profits and investment. The theory was further developed and tested by Dale Jorgenson, from Harvard. You saw this theory in Chapter 16.

Tobin also developed the theory of the demand for money, and more generally, the theory of the choice between different assets based on liquidity, return, and risk. His work has become the basis not only for an improved treatment of financial markets in macroeconomics, but also for the theory of finance in general.

James Tobin

Growth Theory

In parallel with the work on fluctuations, there was a renewed focus on growth. In contrast to the stagnation in the pre–World War II era, most countries were growing fast in the 1950s and 1960s. Even if they experienced fluctuations, their standard of living was increasing rapidly. The growth model developed by MIT's Robert Solow in 1956, which you saw in Chapters 11 and 12, provided a framework to think about the determinants of growth. It was followed by an explosion of work on the roles saving and technological progress play in determining growth.

Macroeconometric Models

All these contributions were integrated in larger and larger macroeconometric models. The first U.S. macroeconometric model, developed by Lawrence Klein from the University of Pennsylvania in the early 1950s, was an extended *IS* relation, with

Robert Solow

Lawrence Klein

16 equations. With the development of the National Income and Product Accounts (making available better data) and the development of econometrics and computers, the models quickly grew in size. The most impressive effort was the construction of the MPS model (MPS stands for MIT–Penn–SSRC, for the two universities and the research institution—the Social Science Research Council—involved in its construction), developed during the 1960s by a group led by Modigliani. Its structure was an expanded version of the *IS–LM* model, plus a Phillips curve mechanism. But its components—consumption, investment, and money demand—all reflected the tremendous theoretical and empirical progress made since Keynes.

Keynesians versus Monetarists

With such rapid progress, many macroeconomists—those who defined themselves as **Keynesians**—came to believe that the future was bright. The nature of fluctuations was becoming increasingly well understood; the development of models allowed policy decisions to be made more effectively. The time when the economy could be fine-tuned, and recessions all but eliminated, seemed not far in the future.

This optimism was met with skepticism by a small but influential minority, the **monetarists**. The intellectual leader of the monetarists was Milton Friedman. Although Friedman saw much progress being made—and was himself the father of one of the major contributions to macroeconomics, the theory of consumption—he did not share in the general enthusiasm.

Milton Friedman

He believed that the understanding of the economy remained very limited. He questioned the motives of governments as well as the notion that they actually knew enough to improve macroeconomic outcomes.

In the 1960s, debates between Keynesians and monetarists dominated the economic headlines. The debates centered around three issues: (1) the effectiveness of monetary policy versus fiscal policy, (2) the Phillips curve, and (3) the role of policy.

Monetary Policy versus Fiscal Policy

Keynes had emphasized *fiscal* rather than *monetary* policy as the key to fighting recessions—and this had remained the prevailing wisdom. The *IS* curve, many argued, was quite steep: Changes in the interest rate had little effect on demand and output. Thus, monetary policy did not work very well. Fiscal policy, which affects demand directly, could affect output faster and more reliably.

Friedman strongly challenged this conclusion. In their 1963 book *A Monetary History of the United States, 1867–1960*, Friedman and Anna Schwartz painstakingly reviewed the evidence on monetary policy, and the relation between money and output in the United States over a century. Their conclusion was not only that monetary policy was very powerful, but that movements in money explained most of the fluctuations in output. They interpreted the Great Depression as the result of a major mistake in monetary policy, a decrease in the money supply due to bank failures—a decrease that the Fed could have avoided by increasing the monetary base but had not. (We discussed this interpretation in Chapter 22.)

Friedman and Schwartz's challenge was followed by a vigorous debate and by intense research on the respective effects of fiscal policy and monetary policy. In the end, a consensus was reached. Both fiscal policy and monetary policy clearly affected the economy. And if policymakers cared about not only the level but also the composition of output, the best policy was typically a mix of the two.

The Phillips Curve

The second debate focused on the Phillips curve. The Phillips curve was not part of the initial Keynesian model. But because it provided such a convenient (and apparently reliable) way of explaining the movement of wages and prices over time, it had become part of the neoclassical synthesis. In the 1960s, based on the empirical evidence up until then, many Keynesian economists believed that there was a reliable trade-off between unemployment and inflation, even in the long run.

Milton Friedman and Edmund Phelps (from Columbia University) strongly disagreed. They argued that the existence of such a long-run trade-off flew in the face of basic economic theory. They argued that the apparent trade-off would quickly vanish if policymakers actually tried to exploit it—that is, if they tried to achieve low unemployment by accepting higher inflation. As you saw in Chapter 8 when we studied the evolution of the Phillips curve, Friedman and Phelps were definitely right. By the mid-1970s, the consensus was indeed that there was no long-run trade-off between inflation and unemployment.

Edmund Phelps

The Role of Policy

The third debate centered on the role of policy. Skeptical that economists knew enough to stabilize output and that policymakers could be trusted to do the right thing, Friedman argued for the use of simple rules, such as steady money growth (a rule we discussed in Chapter 25). Here is what he said in 1958:

> A steady rate of growth in the money supply will not mean perfect stability even though it would prevent the kind of wide fluctuations that we have experienced from time to time in the past. It is tempting to try to go farther and to use monetary changes to offset other factors making for expansion and contraction . . . The available evidence casts grave doubts on the possibility of producing any fine adjustments in economic activity by fine adjustments in monetary policy—at least in the present state of knowledge. There are thus serious limitations to the possibility of a discretionary monetary policy and much danger that such a policy may make matters worse rather than better.
>
> Political pressures to "do something" in the face of either relatively mild price rises or relatively mild price and employment declines are clearly very strong indeed in the existing state of public attitudes. The main moral to be drawn from the two preceding points is that yielding to these pressures may frequently do more harm than good.

"The Supply of Money and Changes in Prices and Output," ◀ Testimony to Congress, 1958.

As you saw in Chapter 24, this debate on the role of macroeconomic policy has not been settled. The nature of the arguments has changed a bit, but the arguments are still with us today.

27-3 The Rational Expectations Critique

Despite the battles between Keynesians and monetarists, macroeconomics around 1970 looked like a successful and mature field. It appeared to successfully explain events and guide policy choices. Most debates were framed within a common intellectual framework. But within a few years, the field was in crisis. The crisis had two sources.

One was events. By the mid-1970s, most countries were experiencing *stagflation*, a word created at the time to denote the simultaneous existence of high unemployment and high inflation. Macroeconomists had not predicted stagflation. After the fact and after a few years of research, a convincing explanation was provided, based on the effects of adverse supply shocks on both prices and output. (We discussed the effects

Robert Lucas

Thomas Sargent

Robert Barro

of such shocks in Chapter 7.) But it was too late to undo the damage to the discipline's image.

The other was ideas. In the early 1970s, a small group of economists—Robert Lucas from the University of Chicago; Thomas Sargent, then from the University of Minnesota and now at New York University; and Robert Barro, then from University of Chicago and now at Harvard—led a strong attack against mainstream macroeconomics. They did not mince words. In a 1978 paper, Lucas and Sargent stated:

> That the predictions [of Keynesian economics] were wildly incorrect, and that the doctrine on which they were based was fundamentally flawed, are now simple matters of fact, involving no subtleties in economic theory. The task which faces contemporary students of the business cycle is that of sorting through the wreckage, determining what features of that remarkable intellectual event called the Keynesian Revolution can be salvaged and put to good use, and which others must be discarded.

The Three Implications of Rational Expectations

Lucas and Sargent's main argument was that Keynesian economics had ignored the full implications of the effect of expectations on behavior. The way to proceed, they argued, was to assume that people formed expectations as rationally as they could, based on the information they had. Thinking of people as having *rational expectations* had three major implications, all highly damaging to Keynesian macroeconomics.

The Lucas Critique

The first implication was that existing macroeconomic models could not be used to help design policy. Although these models recognized that expectations affect behavior, they did not incorporate expectations explicitly. All variables were assumed to depend on current and past values of other variables, including policy variables. Thus, what the models captured was the set of relations between economic variables as they had held in the past, under past policies. Were these policies to change, Lucas argued, the way people formed expectations would change as well, making estimated relations—and, by implication, simulations generated using existing macroeconometric models—poor guides to what would happen under these new policies. This critique of macroeconometric models became known as the **Lucas critique**. To take again the history of the Phillips curve as an example, the data up to the early 1970s had suggested a trade-off between unemployment and inflation. As policymakers tried to exploit that trade-off, it disappeared.

Rational Expectations and the Phillips Curve

The second implication was that when rational expectations were introduced in Keynesian models, these models actually delivered very un-Keynesian conclusions. For example, the models implied that deviations of output from its natural level were short-lived, much more so than Keynesian economists claimed.

This argument was based on a reexamination of the aggregate supply relation. In Keynesian models, the slow return of output to the natural level of output came from the slow adjustment of prices and wages through the Phillips curve mechanism. An increase in money, for example, led first to higher output and to lower unemployment. Lower unemployment then led to higher nominal wages and to higher prices. The adjustment continued until wages and prices had increased in the same proportion as nominal money, until unemployment and output were both back at their natural levels.

But this adjustment, Lucas pointed out, was highly dependent on wage setters' backward-looking expectations of inflation. In the MPS model, for example, wages responded only to current and past inflation and to current unemployment. But once the assumption was made that wage setters had rational expectations, the adjustment was likely to be much faster. Changes in money, to the extent that they were anticipated, might have no effect on output: For example, anticipating an increase in money of 5% over the coming year, wage setters would increase the nominal wages set in contracts for the coming year by 5%. Firms would in turn increase prices by 5%. The result would be no change in the real money stock and no change in demand or output.

Within the logic of the Keynesian models, Lucas therefore argued, only *unanticipated changes in money* should affect output. Predictable movements in money should have no effect on activity. More generally, if wage setters had rational expectations, shifts in demand were likely to have effects on output for only as long as nominal wages were set—a year or so. Even on its own terms, the Keynesian model did not deliver a convincing theory of the long-lasting effects of demand on output.

Optimal Control versus Game Theory

The third implication was that if people and firms had rational expectations, it was wrong to think of policy as the control of a complicated but passive system. Rather, the right way was to think of policy as a game between policymakers and the economy. The right tool was not *optimal control* but *game theory*. And game theory led to a different vision of policy. A striking example was the issue of *time inconsistency* discussed by Finn Kydland (then at Carnegie Mellon, now at UC Santa Barbara) and Edward Prescott (then at Carnegie Mellon, now at Arizona State University), an issue that we discussed in Chapter 24: Good intentions on the part of policymakers could actually lead to disaster.

Let's summarize: When rational expectations were introduced, Keynesian models could not be used to determine policy; Keynesian models could not explain long-lasting deviations of output from the natural level of output; the theory of policy had to be redesigned, using the tools of game theory.

The Integration of Rational Expectations

As you might have guessed from the tone of Lucas and Sargent's quote, the intellectual atmosphere in macroeconomics was tense in the early 1970s. But within a few years, a process of integration (of ideas, not people, because tempers remained high) had begun, and it was to dominate the 1970s and the 1980s.

Fairly quickly, the idea that rational expectations was the right working assumption gained wide acceptance. This was not because macroeconomists believe that people, firms, and participants in financial markets always form expectations rationally. But rational expectations appears to be a natural benchmark, at least until economists have made more progress in understanding whether, when, and how actual expectations systematically differ from rational expectations.

Work then started on the challenges raised by Lucas and Sargent.

The Implications of Rational Expectations

There was a systematic exploration of the role and implications of rational expectations in goods markets, financial markets, and labor markets. Much of what was discovered has been presented in this book. For example:

- Robert Hall, then from MIT and now at Stanford, showed that if consumers are very foresighted (in the sense defined in Chapter 16), then changes in consumption should be unpredictable: The best forecast of consumption next year would be consumption this year! Put another way, changes in consumption should be

Robert Hall

Rudiger Dornbusch

very hard to predict. This result came as a surprise to most macroeconomists at the time, but it is in fact based on a simple intuition: If consumers are very foresighted, they will change their consumption only when they learn something new about the future. But by definition, such news cannot be predicted. This consumption behavior, known as the **random walk of consumption**, has served as a benchmark in consumption research ever since.

■ Rudiger Dornbusch from MIT showed that the large swings in exchange rates under flexible exchange rates, which had previously been thought of as the result of speculation by irrational investors, were fully consistent with rationality. His argument—which we saw in Chapter 21—was that changes in monetary policy can lead to long-lasting changes in nominal interest rates; changes in current and expected nominal interest rates lead in turn to large changes in the exchange rate. Dornbusch's model, known as the *overshooting* model of exchange rates, has become the benchmark in discussions of exchange rate movements.

Wage and Price Setting

There was a systematic exploration of the determination of wages and prices, going far beyond the Phillips curve relation. Two important contributions were made by Stanley Fischer, then at MIT, now governor of the Central Bank of Israel, and John Taylor, then from Columbia University and now at Stanford. Both showed that the adjustment of prices and wages in response to changes in unemployment can be slow *even under rational expectations.*

Stanley Fischer

Fischer and Taylor pointed out an important characteristic of both wage and price setting, the **staggering** of wage and price decisions. In contrast to the simple story we told earlier, where all wages and prices increased simultaneously in anticipation of an increase in money, actual wage and price decisions are staggered over time. So there is not one sudden synchronized adjustment of all wages and prices to an increase in money. Rather, the adjustment is likely to be slow, with wages and prices adjusting to the new level of money through a process of leapfrogging over time. Fischer and Taylor thus showed that the second issue raised by the rational-expectations critique could be resolved, that a slow return of output to the natural level of output can be consistent with rational expectations in the labor market.

The Theory of Policy

Thinking about policy in terms of game theory led to an explosion of research on the nature of the games being played, not only between policymakers and the economy, but also between policymakers—between political parties, or between the central bank and the government, or between governments of different countries. One of the major achievements of this research was the development of a more rigorous way of thinking about fuzzy notions such as "credibility," "reputation," and "commitment." At the same time, there was a distinct shift in focus from "what governments should do" to "what governments actually do," an increasing awareness of the political constraints that economists should take into account when advising policymakers.

John Taylor

In short: By the end of the 1980s, the challenges raised by the rational-expectations critique had led to a complete overhaul of macroeconomics. The basic structure had been extended to take into account the implications of rational expectations or, more generally, of forward-looking behavior by people and firms. As you have seen, these themes have played a central role in this book.

Since the late 1980s, three groups have dominated the research headlines: the new classicals, the new Keynesians, and the new growth theorists. (Note the generous use of the word *new*. Unlike producers of laundry detergents, economists stop short of using "new and improved." But the subliminal message is the same.)

New Classical Economics and Real Business Cycle Theory

The rational-expectations critique was more than just a critique of Keynesian economics. It also offered its own interpretation of fluctuations. Instead of relying on imperfections in labor markets, on the slow adjustment of wages and prices, and so on, to explain fluctuations, Lucas argued, macroeconomists should see how far they could go in explaining fluctuations as the effects of shocks in competitive markets with fully flexible prices and wages.

This research agenda was taken up by the **new classicals**. The intellectual leader is Edward Prescott, and the models he and his followers have developed are known as **real business cycle (RBC) models**. Their approach has been based on two premises.

The first premise is methodological. Lucas had argued that, in order to avoid earlier pitfalls, macroeconomic models should be constructed from explicit microfoundations—that is, utility maximization by workers, profit maximization by firms, and rational expectations. Before the development of computers, this was hard, if not impossible, to achieve: Models constructed in this way would have been too complex to solve analytically. Indeed, much of the art of macroeconomics was in finding simple shortcuts to capture the essence of a model while keeping the model simple enough to solve. (It still remains the art of writing a good textbook.) The development of computing power has made it possible to solve such models numerically, and an important contribution of RBC theory has been the development of more and more powerful numerical methods of solution, allowing for the development of richer and richer models.

Edward Prescott

The second premise is conceptual. Until the 1970s, most fluctuations had been seen as the result of imperfections, of deviations of actual output from a slowly moving natural level of output. Following up on Lucas' suggestion, Prescott argued in a series of influential contributions that fluctuations could indeed be interpreted as coming from the effects of technological shocks in competitive markets with fully flexible prices and wages. In other words, he argued that movements in actual output could be seen as movements in—rather than as deviations from—the natural level of output. As new discoveries are made, he argued, productivity increases, leading to an increase in output. The increase in productivity leads to an increase in the wage, which makes it more attractive to work, leading workers to work more. Productivity increases therefore lead to increases in both output and employment, just as we observe in the real world.

Not surprisingly, this radical view of fluctuations has been criticized on many fronts. As we discussed in Chapter 12, technological progress is the result of many innovations, each taking a long time to diffuse throughout the economy. It is hard to see how this process could generate anything like the large short-run fluctuations in output that we observe in practice. It is also hard to think of recessions as times of technological *regress*, times in which productivity and output both go down. Finally, as we have seen, there is strong evidence that changes in money, which have no effect on output in RBC models, in fact have strong effects on output in the real world. Still, the conceptual RBC approach has proved useful and influential. It has reinforced an important point: that not all fluctuations in output are deviations of output from its natural level.

New Keynesian Economics

The term **new Keynesians** denotes a loosely connected group of researchers who share a common belief that the synthesis that emerged in response to the rational-expectations critique was basically correct. But they also share the belief that much remains to be learned about the nature of imperfections in different markets and about the implications of those imperfections for macroeconomic fluctuations.

One line of research has focused on the determination of wages in the labor market. We discussed in Chapter 6 the notion of *efficiency wages*—the idea that wages, if perceived by workers as being too low, may lead to shirking by workers on the job, to problems of morale within the firm, to difficulties in recruiting or keeping good workers, and so on. One influential researcher in this area has been George Akerlof from Berkeley, who has explored the role of "norms," the rules that develop in any organization—in this case, the firm—to assess what is fair or unfair. This research has led him and others to explore issues previously left to research in sociology and psychology and to examine their macroeconomic implications.

George Akerlof

Another line of new Keynesian research has explored the role of imperfections in credit markets. Except for a discussion of the role of banks in the Great Depression and in the Japanese slump, I have typically assumed in this book that the effects of monetary policy worked through interest rates, and that firms could borrow as much as they wanted at the market interest rate. In practice, many firms can borrow only from banks. And banks often turn down potential borrowers, despite the willingness of these borrowers to pay the interest rate charged by the bank. Why this happens, and how it affects our view of how monetary policy works, has been the subject of much research, in particular by Ben Bernanke (then from Princeton, and now the chairman of the Fed).

Yet another direction of research is **nominal rigidities**. As we saw earlier in this chapter, Fischer and Taylor have shown that with staggering of wage or price decisions, output can deviate from its natural level for a long time. This conclusion raises a number of questions. If staggering of decisions is responsible, at least in part, for fluctuations, why don't wage setters/price setters synchronize decisions? Why aren't prices and wages adjusted more often? Why aren't all prices and all wages changed, say, on the first day of each week? In tackling these issues, Akerlof and N. Gregory Mankiw (from Harvard University) have derived a surprising and important result, often referred to as the **menu cost** explanation of output fluctuations.

Ben Bernanke

Each wage setter or price setter is largely indifferent as to when and how often he changes his own wage or price (for a retailer, changing the prices on the shelf every day versus every week does not make much of a difference to the store's overall profits). Therefore, even small costs of changing prices—such as the costs involved in printing a new menu, for example—can lead to infrequent and staggered price adjustment. This staggering leads to slow adjustment of the price level and to large aggregate output fluctuations in response to movements in aggregate demand. In short, decisions that do not matter much at the individual level (how often to change prices or wages) lead to large aggregate effects (slow adjustment of the price level and shifts in aggregate demand that have a large effect on output).

New Growth Theory

After being one of the most active topics of research in the 1960s, growth theory went into an intellectual slump. Since the late 1980s, however, growth theory has made a strong comeback. The set of new contributions goes under the name **new growth theory**.

Paul Romer

Two economists, Robert Lucas (the same Lucas who spearheaded the rational-expectations critique) and Paul Romer, then from Berkeley, now at Stanford, have played an important role in defining the issues. When growth theory faded in the late 1960s, two major issues were left largely unresolved. One issue was the role of increasing returns to scale—whether, say, doubling capital and labor can actually cause output to more than double. The other was the determinants of technological progress. These are the two major issues on which new growth theory has concentrated.

The discussion of the effects of R&D on technological progress in Chapter 12 and of the interaction between technological progress and unemployment in Chapter 13 reflect some of the advances made on this front. An important contribution here is the work of Philippe Aghion (from Harvard University) and Peter Howitt (from Brown University) who have developed a theme first explored by Joseph Schumpeter in the 1930s—the notion that growth is a process of *creative destruction*, in which new products are constantly introduced, making old ones obsolete. Institutions that slow this process of reallocation—for example, by making it harder to create new firms or by making it more expensive for firms to lay off workers—may slow down the rate of technological progress and thus decrease growth.

Philippe Aghion

Research has also tried to identify the precise role of specific institutions in determining growth. Andrei Shleifer (from Harvard University) has explored the role of different legal systems in affecting the organization of the economy, from financial markets to labor markets, and, through these channels, the effects of legal systems on growth. Daron Acemoglu (from MIT) has explored how to go from correlations between institutions and growth—democratic countries are on average richer—to causality from institutions to growth—does the correlation tell us that democracy leads to higher output per person, or does it tell us that higher output per person leads to democracy, or that some other factor leads to both more democracy and higher output per person? Examining the history of former colonies, he argues that their growth performance has been very much shaped by the type of institutions put in place by their colonizers, thus showing a strong causal role of institutions on economic performance.

Peter Howitt

Toward an Integration

In the 1980s and 1990s, discussions between these three groups, and in particular between new classicals and new Keynesians, were often heated. New Keynesians would accuse new classicals of relying on an implausible explanation of fluctuations and ignoring obvious imperfections; new classicals would in turn point to the ad hoc nature of some of the new Keynesian models. From the outside—and indeed sometimes from the inside—macroeconomics looked like a battlefield rather than a research field.

Things have very much changed, and a synthesis is emerging. Methodologically, it builds on the RBC approach and its careful description of the optimization problems of people and firms. Conceptually, it recognizes the potential importance, emphasized by the RBC approach and the new growth theory, of changes in the pace of technological progress. But it also allows for many of the imperfections emphasized by the new Keynesians, from the role of bargaining in the determination of wages, to the role of imperfect information in credit and financial markets, to the role of nominal rigidities in creating a role for aggregate demand to affect output. There is no convergence on a single model or on a single list of important imperfections, but there is broad agreement on the framework and on the way to proceed.

A particularly good example of this convergence is shown by the work of Michael Woodford (from Columbia) and of Jordi Gali (from Pompeu Fabra in Catalonia).

Andrei Shleifer

Daron Acemoglu

Michael Woodford

Jordi Gali

Woodford, Gali, and a number of co-authors have developed a model, known as the **new-Keynesian model**, that embodies utility and profit maximization, rational expectations, and nominal rigidities. You can think of it as a high-tech version of the model that was presented in Chapter 17. This model has proven extremely useful and influential in the redesign of monetary policy—from the focus on inflation targeting to the reliance on interest rate rules—which I have described in Chapter 25. It has also led to the development of a class of larger models that build on its simple structure, but allow for a longer menu of imperfections and thus must be solved numerically. These models, which are now used in most central banks, are known as **dynamic stochastic general equilibrium (DSGE) models**. How to specify, to estimate, and to simulate these models is one of the major topics of research in macroeconomics today.

27-5 Common Beliefs

As we come to the end of this brief history of macroeconomics, and to the end of the book, let me restate the basic set of propositions on which most macroeconomists agree:

- In the put short run in quotes, shifts in aggregate demand affect output. Higher consumer confidence, a larger budget deficit, and faster growth of money are all likely to increase output and to decrease unemployment.
- In the medium run, output returns to the natural level of output. This natural level depends on the natural rate of unemployment (which, together with the size of the labor force, determines the level of employment), the capital stock, and the state of technology.
- In the long run, two main factors determine the evolution of the level of output: capital accumulation and the rate of technological progress.
- Monetary policy affects output in the short run, but not in the medium run or the long run. A higher rate of money growth eventually translates one-for-one into a higher rate of inflation.
- Fiscal policy has short-run, medium-run, and long-run effects on output. Higher budget deficits are likely to increase output in the short run. They leave output unaffected in the medium run. And they are likely to decrease capital accumulation and output in the long run.

These propositions leave room for disagreements:

- One is about the length of the "short run," the period of time over which aggregate demand affects output. At one extreme, real business cycle theorists start from the assumption that output is always at the natural level of output: The "short run" is very short! At the other extreme, the study of slumps and depressions (which we explored in Chapter 22) implies that the effects of demand may be extremely long-lasting, that the "short run" may be very long.
- Another is about the role of policy. Although conceptually distinct, this disagreement is largely related to the previous one. Those who believe that output returns quickly to the natural level of output are typically willing to impose tight rules on both monetary and fiscal policy, from constant money growth to the requirement of a balanced budget. Those who believe the adjustment is slow typically believe in the need for more flexible stabilization policies.

Behind these disagreements, there is a largely common framework in which most research is conducted and organized. The framework gives us a way of interpreting events and discussing policy. This is what I have done in this book.

Summary

- The history of modern macroeconomics starts in 1936, with the publication of Keynes' *General Theory of Employment, Interest and Money*. Keynes's contribution was formalized in the *IS–LM* model by John Hicks and Alvin Hansen in the 1930s and early 1940s.

- The period from the early 1940s to the early 1970s can be called the golden age of macroeconomics. Among the major developments were the development of the theories of consumption, investment, money demand, and portfolio choice; the development of growth theory; and the development of large macroeconometric models.

- The main debate during the 1960s was between Keynesians and monetarists. Keynesians believed that developments in macroeconomic theory allowed for better control of the economy. Monetarists, led by Milton Friedman, were more skeptical of the ability of governments to help stabilize the economy.

- In the 1970s, macroeconomics experienced a crisis. There were two reasons. One was the appearance of stagflation, which came as a surprise to most economists. The other was a theoretical attack led by Robert Lucas. Lucas and his followers showed that when rational expectations were introduced, (1) Keynesian models could not be used to determine policy; (2) Keynesian models could not explain long-lasting deviations of output from its natural level; and (3) the theory of policy needed to be redesigned, using the tools of game theory.

- Much of the 1970s and 1980s were spent integrating rational expectations into macroeconomics. As reflected in this book, macroeconomists are now much more aware of the role of expectations in determining the effects of shocks and policy, and of the complexity of policy than they were two decades ago.

- Recent research in macroeconomic theory has proceeded along three lines. New classical economists are exploring the extent to which fluctuations can be explained as movements in the natural level of output, as opposed to movements away from the natural level of output. New Keynesian economists are exploring more formally the role of market imperfections in fluctuations. New growth theorists are exploring the determinants of technological progress. These lines are increasingly overlapping, and a new synthesis appears to be emerging.

- Despite the differences, there exists a set of propositions on which most macroeconomists agree. Two of these propositions are: In the short run, shifts in aggregate demand affect output. In the medium run, output returns to its natural level.

Key Terms

- business cycle theory, 602
- effective demand, 602
- liquidity preference, 602
- neoclassical synthesis, 602
- Keynesians, 604
- monetarists, 604
- Lucas critique, 606
- random walk of consumption, 608
- staggering (of wage and price decisions), 608
- new classicals, 609
- real business cycle (RBC) models, 609
- new Keynesians, 610
- nominal rigidities, 610
- menu cost, 610
- new growth theory, 610
- New-Keynesian model, 612
- DSGE models (dynamic stochastic general equilibrium models), 612

Further Readings

- Two classics are J. M. Keynes, *The General Theory of Employment, Money and Interest*, Macmillan Press, London, 1936, and Milton Friedman and Anna Schwartz, *A Monetary History of the United States, 1867-1960*, Princeton University Press, Princeton, NJ, 1963. Warning: The first makes for hard reading, and the second is a heavy volume.

- For an account of macroeconomics in textbooks since the 1940s, read Paul Samuelson, "Credo of a Lucky Textbook Author," *Journal of Economic Perspectives*, Spring 1997, 153–160.

- In the introduction to *Studies in Business Cycle Theory*, MIT Press, Cambridge, MA, 1981, Robert Lucas develops his approach to macroeconomics and gives a guide to his contributions.

- The paper that launched real business cycle theory is Edward Prescott, "Theory Ahead of Business Cycle Measurement," *Federal Reserve Bank of Minneapolis Review*, Fall 1986, 9–22. It is not easy reading.

- For more on new Keynesian economics, read David Romer, "The New Keynesian Synthesis," *Journal of Economic Perspectives*, Winter 1993, 5–22.

- For more on new growth theory, read Paul Romer, "The Origins of Endogenous Growth," *Journal of Economic Perspectives*, Winter 1994, 3–22.
- For a detailed look at the history of macroeconomic ideas, with in-depth interviews of most of the major researchers, read Brian Snowdon and Howard Vane, "Modern Macroeconomics: Its Origins, Development and Current State," Edward Elgar, England: Cheltenham UK, 2005.
- For two points of view on the state of macroeconomics, read V. V. Chari and Patrick Kehoe, "Macroeconomics in Practice: How Theory is Shaping Policy," and N. Greg Mankiw, "The Macroeconomist as Scientist and Engineer," *Journal of Economic Perspectives*, Fall 2006.

To learn more about macroeconomic issues and theory:
- Most economics journals are heavy on mathematics and are hard to read. But a few make an effort to be more friendly. The *Journal of Economic Perspectives* in particular has nontechnical articles on current economic research and issues. The *Brookings Papers on Economic Activity*, published twice a year, analyze current macroeconomic problems. So does *Economic Policy*, published in Europe, which focuses more on European issues.
- Most regional Federal Reserve Banks publish reviews with easy-to-read articles; these reviews are available free of charge. Among them are the *Economic Review* published by the Cleveland Fed, the *Economic Review* published by the Kansas City Fed, the *New England Economic Review* published by the Boston Fed, and the *Review* published by the Minneapolis Fed.
- More advanced treatments of current macroeconomic theory—roughly at the level of a first graduate course in macroeconomics—are given by David Romer, *Advanced Macroeconomics*, 3rd ed., McGraw-Hill, New York, 2006, and Olivier Blanchard and Stanley Fischer, *Lectures on Macroeconomics*, MIT Press, Cambridge, MA, 1989.

Appendices

APPENDIX 1   An Introduction to National Income and Product Accounts

This appendix introduces the basic structure and the terms used in the national income and product accounts. The basic measure of aggregate activity is gross domestic product, or GDP. The **national income and product accounts (NIPA**, or simply **national accounts)** are organized around two decompositions of GDP.

One decomposes GDP from the *income side:* Who receives what?

The other decomposes GDP from the *production side* (called the *product side* in the national accounts): What is produced, and who buys it?

The Income Side

Table A1-1 looks at the income side of GDP—who receives what.

The top part of the table (lines 1–8) goes from GDP to national income—the sum of the incomes received by the different factors of production:

- The starting point, in line 1, is **gross domestic product (GDP)**.

  GDP is defined as *the market value of the goods and services produced by labor and property located in the United States.*
- The next three lines take us from GDP to **GNP, gross national product** (line 4). GNP is an alternative measure of aggregate output. It is defined as *the market value of the goods and services produced by labor and property supplied by U.S. residents.*

  Until the 1990s, most countries used GNP rather than GDP as the main measure of aggregate activity. The emphasis in the U.S. national accounts shifted from GNP to GDP in 1991. The difference between the two comes from the distinction between "located in the United States" (used for GDP) and "supplied by U.S. residents" (used for GNP). For example, profit from a U.S.-owned plant in Japan is not included in U.S. GDP but is included in U.S. GNP.

  So, to go from GDP to GNP, we must first add **receipts of factor income from the rest of the world**, which is income from U.S. capital or U.S. residents abroad (line 2), and then subtract **payments of factor income to the rest of the world**, which is income received by foreign capital and foreign residents in the United States (line 3).

  In 2006, payments from the rest of the world exceeded receipts to the rest of the world by $30 billion, so GNP was larger than GDP by $30 billion.
- The next step takes us from GNP to **net national product (NNP)** (line 6). The difference between GNP and NNP is the depreciation of capital, called **consumption of fixed capital** in the national accounts.
- Finally, lines 7 and 8 take us from NNP to **national income** (line 8). National income is defined as the *income that originates in the production of goods and services supplied by residents of the United States.* In theory, national income and net national product should be equal. In practice, they typically differ, because they are constructed in different ways.

  Net national product is constructed from the top down, starting from GDP and going through the steps we have just gone through in Table A-1. National income is constructed instead from the bottom up, by adding the different components of factor income (compensation of employees, corporate profits, and so on). If we could measure everything exactly, the two measures would be equal. In practice, the two measures differ, and the difference between the two is called the "statistical discrepancy." In 2003, national income computed from the bottom up (the number in line 8) was larger than the

Table A1-1	GDP: The Income Side, 2006 (billions of dollars)		
From gross domestic product to national income:			
1 **Gross domestic product** (GDP)	13,246		
2 Plus: receipts of factor income from the rest of the world			+666
3 Minus: payments of factor income to the rest of the world			−636
4 Equals: **Gross national product**	13,276		
5 Minus: consumption of fixed capital			−1,577
6 Equals: **Net national product**	11,699		
7 Minus: Statistical discrepancy			3
8 Equals: **National income**	11,702		
The Decomposition of National Income:			
9 Indirect taxes	912		
10 Compensation of employees	7,489		
11 Wages and salaries			6,035
12 Supplements to wages and salaries			1,454
13 Corporate profits and business transfers	1,700		
14 Net interest	509		
15 Proprietors' income	1,015		
16 Rental income of persons	77		

Source: *Survey of Current Business*, April 2007, Tables 1-7-5 and 1-12.

net national product computed from the top down (the number in line 6) by $3 billion. The statistical discrepancy is a useful reminder of the statistical problems involved in constructing the national income accounts.

The bottom part of Table A1-1 (lines 9 to 16) decomposes national income into different types of income:

■ **Indirect taxes** (line 9) are another name for sales taxes. Some of the national income goes directly to the state in the form of sales taxes.

The rest of national income goes either to employees or to firms.

■ **Compensation of employees** (line 10), or labor income, is what goes to employees. It is by far the largest component of national income, accounting for 64% of national income. Labor income is the sum of wages and salaries (line 11) and of supplements to wages and salaries (line 12). These range from employer contributions for social insurance (by far the largest item) to such exotic items as employer contributions to marriage fees to justices of the peace.

■ **Corporate profits and business transfers** (line 13): Profits are revenues minus costs (including interest payments) and minus depreciation. Business transfers, which account for $90 billion out of $1,700 billion, are items such as liability payments for personal injury, and corporate contributions to non-profit organizations.

■ **Net interest** (line 14) is the interest paid by firms minus the interest received by firms, plus interest received from the rest of the world, minus interest paid to the rest of the world. In 2006, most of net interest represented net interest paid by firms: The United States received about as much in interest from the rest of the world as it paid to the rest to the world. So the sum of corporate profits plus net interest paid by firms was approximately $1,700 billion + $509 billion = $2,209 billion, or about 19% of national income.

■ **Proprietors' income** (line 15) is the income received by persons who are self-employed. It is defined as *the income of sole proprietorships, partnerships, and tax-exempt cooperatives.*

■ **Rental income of persons** (line 16) is the income from the rental of real property, minus depreciation on this real property. Houses produce housing services; rental income measures the income received for these services.

Table A1-2	From National Income to Personal Disposable Income, 2006 (billions of dollars)	
1	**National income**	11,702
2	Minus: indirect taxes	−912
3	Minus: corporate profits and business transfers	−1,700
4	Minus: net interest	−509
5	Plus: income from assets	+1,656
6	Plus: personal transfers	+1,602
7	Minus: contributions for social insurance	−956
8	Equals: **Personal income**	10,883
9	Minus: personal tax payments	−1,360
10	Equals: **Personal disposable income**	9,522

Source: *Survey of Current Business*, April 2006, Table 1-7-5, 1-12, and 2-1.

If the national accounts counted only actual rents, rental income would depend on the proportion of apartments and houses that were rented versus those that were owner occupied. For example, if everybody became the owner of the apartment or the house in which he or she lived, rental income would go to zero, and thus measured GDP would drop. To avoid this problem, national accounts treat houses and apartments as if they were all rented out. So, rental income is constructed as actual rents plus *imputed* rents on those houses and apartments that are owner occupied.

Before we move to the product side, Table A1-2 shows how we can go from national income to personal disposable income—the income available to persons after they have received transfers and paid taxes.

■ Not all national income (line 1) is distributed to persons:

Some of the income goes to the state in the form of indirect taxes, so the first step is to subtract indirect taxes. (Line 2 in Table A1-2—equal to line 9 in Table A1-1.)

Some of the corporate profits are retained by firms. Some of the interest payments by firms go to banks, or go abroad. So the second step is to subtract all corporate profits and business transfers (line 3—equal to line 13 in Table A1-1) and all net interest payments (line 4—equal to line 14 in Table A1-1), and add back all income from assets (dividends and interest payments) received by persons (line 5).

■ People receive income not only from production, but also from transfers (line 6). Transfers accounted for $1,602 billion in 2006. From these transfers must

be subtracted personal contributions for social insurance, $956 billion (line 7).

■ The net result of these adjustments is **personal income**, the income actually received by persons (line 8). **Personal disposable income** (line 10) is equal to personal income minus personal tax and nontax payments (line 9). In 2006, personal disposable income was $9,522 billion, or about 72% of GDP.

The Product Side

Table A1-3 looks at the product side of the national accounts—what is produced, and who buys it.

Start with the three components of domestic demand: consumption, investment, and government spending.

■ Consumption, called **personal consumption expenditures** (line 2) is by far the largest component of demand. It is defined as *the sum of goods and services purchased by persons resident in the United States.*

In the same way that national accounts include imputed rental income on the income side, they include imputed housing services as part of consumption. Owners of a house are assumed to consume housing services, for a price equal to the imputed rental income of that house.

Consumption is disaggregated into three components, purchases of **durable goods** (line 3), **nondurable goods** (line 4), and **services** (line 5). Durable goods are commodities that can be stored and have an average life of at least three years; automobile purchases are the largest item here. Nondurable goods are commodities that can be

Table A1-3	GDP: The Product Side, 2006 (billions of dollars)			
1	**Gross domestic product**	13,246		
2	Personal consumption expenditures	9,269		
3	Durable goods		1,070	
4	Nondurable goods		2,715	
5	Services		5,484	
6	Gross private domestic fixed investment	2,163		
7	Nonresidential		1,396	
8	Structures			411
9	Equipment and software			985
10	Residential		767	
11	Government purchases	2,528		
12	Federal		927	
13	National defense			621
14	Nondefense			306
15	State and local		1,601	
16	Net exports	−763		
17	Exports		1,466	
18	Imports		−2,229	
19	Change in business inventories	49		

Source: *Survey of Current Business,* April 2007, Table 1-1-5.

stored but have a life of less than three years. Services are commodities that cannot be stored and must be consumed at the place and time of purchase.

■ Investment, called **gross private domestic fixed investment** (line 6), is the sum of two very different components:

Non-residential investment (line 7) is the purchase of new capital goods by firms. These may be either **structures** (line 8)—mostly new plants—or **equipment and software** (line 9)—such as machines, computers, or office equipment.

Residential investment (line 10) is the purchase of new houses or apartments by persons.

■ **Government purchases** (line 11) equal the purchases of goods by the government plus the compensation of government employees. (The government is thought of as buying the services of the government employees.)

Government purchases equal the sum of purchases by the federal government (line 12) [which themselves can be disaggregated between spending on national defense (line 13) and nondefense spending (line 14)], and purchases by state and local governments (line 15).

Note that government purchases do not include transfers from the government or interest payments on government debt. These do not correspond to purchases of either goods or services and so are not included here. This means that the number for government purchases you see in Table A1-3 is substantially smaller than the number you typically hear for government spending—which includes transfers and interest payments.

■ The sum of consumption, investment, and government purchases gives the demand for goods by U.S. firms, U.S. persons, and the U.S. government. If the United States were a closed economy, this would be the same as the demand for U.S. goods. But because the U.S. economy is open, the two numbers are different. To get to the demand for U.S. goods, we must make two adjustments. First, we must add the foreign purchases of U.S. goods, **exports** (line 17). Second, we must subtract U.S. purchases of foreign goods, **imports** (line 18). In 2006, exports were smaller than imports by $763 billion. Thus, **net exports** (or equivalently the **trade balance**), was equal to –$763 billion (line 16).

Adding consumption, investment, government purchases, and net exports gives the *total purchases of U.S. goods*. Production may, however, be less than purchases if firms satisfy the difference by decreasing inventories. Or production may be greater than purchases, in which case firms are accumulating inventories. The last line of Table A1-3 gives **changes in business inventories** (line 19), also sometimes called (rather misleadingly) "inventory investment." It is defined as the *change in the volume of inventories held by business*. The change in business inventories can be positive or negative. In 2006, it was small and positive: U.S. production was higher than total purchases of U.S. goods by $49 billion.

Warning

National accounts give an internally consistent description of aggregate activity. But underlying these accounts are many choices of what to include and what not to include, where to put some types of income or spending, and so on. Here are three examples:

- Work within the home is not counted in GDP. If, for example, two women decide to babysit each other's child rather than take care of their own child, and pay each other for the babysitting services, measured GDP will go up, while true GDP clearly does not change. The solution would be to count work within the home in GDP, the same way that we impute rents for owner-occupied housing. But, so far, this has not been done.
- The purchase of a house is treated as an investment, and housing services are then treated as part of consumption. Contrast this with the treatment of automobiles. Despite the fact that they provide services for a long time—although not as long a time as houses do—purchases of automobiles are not treated as investment. They are treated as consumption, and appear in the national accounts only in the year in which they are bought.
- Firms' purchases of machines are treated as investment. The purchase of education is treated as consumption of education services. But education is clearly, in part, an investment: People acquire education in part to increase their future income.

The list could go on. However, the point of these examples is not to make you conclude that national accounts are wrong. Most of the accounting decisions you just saw were made for good reasons, often because of data availability or for simplicity. The point is that to use national accounts best, you should understand their logic and also understand the choices that have been made and thus their limitations.

Key Terms

- national income and product accounts (NIPA), national accounts, 615
- gross domestic product (GDP), 615
- gross national product (GNP), 615
- receipts of factor income from the rest of the world, payments of factor income to the rest of the world, 615
- net national product (NNP), 615
- consumption of fixed capital, 615
- national income, 615
- indirect taxes, 616
- compensation of employees, 616
- corporate profits and business transfers, 616
- net interest, 616
- proprietors' income, 616
- rental income of persons, 616
- personal income, 617
- personal disposable income, 617
- personal consumption expenditures, 617
- durable goods, nondurable goods, and services, 617
- gross private domestic fixed investment, 618
- non-residential investment, structures, equipment and software, 618
- residential investment, 618
- government purchases, 618
- exports, imports, 618
- net exports, trade balance, 618
- changes in business inventories, 619

Further Readings

For more details, read "A Guide to the National Income and Product Accounts of the United States," September 2006 (**www.bea.gov/national/pdf/nipaguid.pdf**).

APPENDIX 2   A Math Refresher

This appendix presents the mathematical tools and the mathematical results that are used in this book.

Geometric Series

Definition.   A geometric series is a sum of numbers of the form

$$1 + x + x^2 + \ldots + x^n$$

where x is a number that may be greater or smaller than 1, and x^n denotes x to the power n that is x times itself n times.

Examples of such series are:

■ The sum of spending in each round of the multiplier (Chapter 3). If c is the marginal propensity to consume, then the sum of increases in spending after $n + 1$ rounds is given by

$$1 + c + c^2 + \ldots + c^n$$

■ The present discounted value of a sequence of payments of 1 dollar each year for n years (Chapter 14), when the interest rate is equal to i:

$$1 + \frac{1}{1 + i} + \frac{1}{(1 + i)^2} + \ldots + \frac{1}{(1 + i)^{n-1}}$$

We usually have two questions we want to answer when encountering such a series:

What is the sum?
Does the sum explode as we let n increase, increase, or does it reach a finite limit? If so, what is that limit?

The following propositions tell you what you need to know to answer these questions.

Proposition 1 tells you how to compute the sum.

Proposition 1:

$$1 + x + x^2 + \ldots + x^n = \frac{1 - x^{n+1}}{1 - x} \qquad (A2.1)$$

Here is the proof: Multiply the sum by $(1 - x)$, and use the fact that $x^a x^b = x^{a+b}$ (that is, add exponents when multiplying):

$$(1 + x + x^2 + \ldots + x^n)(1 - x) = 1 + x + x^2 + \ldots + x^n$$
$$- x - x^2 - \ldots - x^n - x^{n+1}$$
$$= 1 \qquad\qquad - x^{n+1}$$

All the terms on the right except for the first and the last cancel. Dividing both sides by $(1 - x)$ gives equation (A2.1).

This formula can be used for any x and any n. If, for example, x is 0.9 and n is 10, then the sum is equal to 6.86. If x is 1.2 and n is 10, then the sum is 32.15.

Proposition 2 tells you what happens as n gets large.

Proposition 2:   If x is less than 1, the sum goes to $1/(1 - x)$ as n gets large. If x is equal to or greater than one, the sum explodes as n gets large.

Here is the proof: If x is less than 1, then x^n goes to 0 as n gets large. Thus, from equation (A2.1), the sum goes to $1/(1 - x)$. If x is greater than 1, then x^n becomes larger and larger as n increases, $1 - x^n$ becomes a larger and larger negative number, and the ratio $(1 - x^n)/(1 - x)$ becomes a larger and larger positive number. Thus, the sum explodes as n gets large.

Application from Chapter 14: Consider the present value of a payment of $1 forever, starting next year, when the interest rate is i. The present value is given by

$$\frac{1}{(1 + i)} + \frac{1}{(1 + i)^2} + \ldots \qquad (A2.2)$$

Factoring out $1/(1 + i)$, rewrite this present value as

$$\frac{1}{(1 + i)}\left[1 + \frac{1}{(1 + i)} + \ldots\right]$$

The term in brackets is a geometric series, with $x = 1/(1 + i)$. As the interest rate, i, is positive, x is less than 1. Applying Proposition 2, when n gets large, the term in brackets equals

$$\frac{1}{1 - \dfrac{1}{(1 + i)}} = \frac{(1 + i)}{(1 + i - 1)} = \frac{(1 + i)}{i}$$

Replacing the term in brackets in the previous equation with $(1 + i)/i$ gives:

$$\frac{1}{(1 + i)}\left[\frac{(1 + i)}{i}\right] = \frac{1}{i}$$

The present value of a sequence of payments of $1 per year forever, starting next year, is equal to $1 divided by the interest rate. If i is equal to 5% per year, the present value equals $1/0.05 = $20.

Useful Approximations

Throughout this book, we use a number of approximations that make computations easier. These approximations are most reliable when the variables x, y, z are small, say between 0% and 10%. The numerical examples in Propositions 3 through 10 are based on the values $x = .05$ and $y = .03$.

Proposition 3:

$$(1 + x)(1 + y) \approx (1 + x + y) \qquad (A2.3)$$

Here is the proof: Expanding $(1 + x)(1 + y)$ gives $(1 + x)(1 + y) = 1 + x + y + xy$. If x and y are small, then the product xy is very small and can be ignored as an approximation (for example, if $x = .05$ and $y = .03$, then $xy = .0015$). So $(1 + x)(1 + y)$ is approximately equal to $(1 + x + y)$.

For the values x and y above, for example, the approximation gives 1.08 compared to an exact value of 1.0815.

Proposition 4:

$$(1 + x)^2 \approx 1 + 2x \qquad (A2.4)$$

The proof follows directly from Proposition 3, with $y = x$. For the value of $x = .05$, the approximation gives 1.10, compared to an exact value of 1.1025.

Application from Chapter 15: From arbitrage, the relation between the two-year interest rate and the current and the expected one-year interest rates is given by

$$(1 + i_{2t})^2 = (1 + i_{1t})(1 + i^e_{1t+1})$$

Using Proposition 4 for the left side of the equation gives

$$(1 + i_{2t})^2 \approx 1 + 2i_{2t}$$

Using Proposition 3 for the right side of the equation gives

$$(1 + i_{1t})(1 + i^e_{1t+1}) \approx 1 + i_{1t} + i^e_{1t+1}$$

Using this expression to replace $(1 + i_{1t})(1 + i^e_{1t+1})$ in the original arbitrage relation gives

$$1 + 2i_{2t} = 1 + i_{1t} + i^e_{1t+1}$$

Or, reorganizing,

$$i_{2t} = \frac{(i_{1t} + i^e_{1t+1})}{2}$$

The two-year interest rate is approximately equal to the average of the current and the expected one-year interest rates.

Proposition 5:

$$(1 + x)^n \approx 1 + nx \qquad (A2.5)$$

The proof follows by repeated application of Propositions 3 and 4. For example, $(1 + x)^3 = (1 + x)^2(1 + x) \approx (1 + 2x)(1 + x)$ by Proposition 4, $\approx (1 + 2x + x) = 1 + 3x$ by Proposition 3.

The approximation becomes worse as n increases, however. For example, for $x = .05$ and $n = 5$, the approximation gives 1.25, compared to an exact value of 1.2763. For $n = 10$, the approximation gives 1.50, compared to an exact value of 1.63.

Proposition 6:

$$\frac{(1 + x)}{(1 + y)} \approx (1 + x - y) \qquad (A2.6)$$

Here is the proof: Consider the product $(1 + x - y)$ $(1 + y)$. Expanding this product gives $(1 + x - y)$ $(1 + y) = 1 + x + xy - y^2$. If both x and y are small, then xy and y^2 are very small, so $(1 + x - y)$ $(1 + y) \approx (1 + x)$. Dividing both sides of this approximation by $(1 + y)$ gives the proposition above.

For the values of $x = .05$ and $y = .03$, the approximation gives 1.02, while the correct value is 1.019.

Application from Chapter 14: The real interest rate is defined by

$$(1 + r_t) = \frac{(1 + i_t)}{(1 + \pi^e_t)}$$

Using Proposition 6 gives

$$(1 + r_t) \approx (1 + i_t - \pi^e_t)$$

Simplifying,

$$r_t \approx i_t - \pi^e_t$$

This gives us the approximation we use at many points in this book: The real interest rate is approximately equal to the nominal interest rate minus expected inflation.

These approximations are also very convenient when dealing with growth rates. Define the rate of growth of x by $g_x \equiv \Delta x / x$, and similarly for z, g_z, y and g_y. The following numerical examples are based on the values $g_x = .05$ and $g_y = .03$.

Proposition 7: If $z = xy$, then

$$g_z \approx g_x + g_y \qquad (A2.7)$$

Here is the proof: Let Δz be the increase in z when x increases by Δx and y increases by Δy. Then, by definition:

$$z + \Delta z = (x + \Delta x)(y + \Delta y)$$

Divide both sides by z.
The left side becomes

$$\frac{z + \Delta z}{z} = \left(1 + \frac{\Delta z}{z}\right)$$

The right side becomes

$$\frac{(x + \Delta x)(y + \Delta y)}{z} = \frac{(x + \Delta x)}{x} \frac{(y + \Delta y)}{y}$$

$$= \left(1 + \frac{\Delta x}{x}\right)\left(1 + \frac{\Delta y}{y}\right)$$

where the first equality follows from the fact that $z = xy$, the second equality from simplifying each of the two fractions.

Using the expressions for the left and right sides gives

$$\left(1 + \frac{\Delta z}{z}\right) = \left(1 + \frac{\Delta x}{x}\right)\left(1 + \frac{\Delta y}{y}\right)$$

Or, equivalently,

$$(1 + g_z) = (1 + g_x)(1 + g_y)$$

From Proposition 3, $(1 + g_z) \approx (1 + g_x + g_y)$, or, equivalently,

$$g_z \approx g_x + g_y$$

For $g_x = 0.05$ and $g_y = 0.03$, the approximation gives $g_z = 8\%$, while the correct value is 8.15%.

Application from Chapter 13: Let the production function be of the form $Y = NA$, where Y is production, N is employment, and A is productivity. Denoting the growth rates of Y, N, and A by g_Y, g_N, and g_A, respectively, Proposition 7 implies

$$g_Y \approx g_N + g_A$$

The rate of output growth is approximately equal to the rate of employment growth plus the rate of productivity growth.

Proposition 8: If $z = x/y$, then

$$g_z \approx g_x - g_y \qquad \text{(A2.8)}$$

Here is the proof: Let Δz be the increase in z, when x increases by Δx and y increases by Δy. Then, by definition:

$$z + \Delta z = \frac{x + \Delta x}{y + \Delta y}$$

Divide both sides by z.
The left side becomes

$$\frac{(z + \Delta z)}{z} = \left(1 + \frac{\Delta z}{z}\right)$$

The right side becomes

$$\frac{(x + \Delta x)}{(y + \Delta y)}\frac{1}{z} = \frac{(x + \Delta x)}{(y + \Delta y)}\frac{y}{x} = \frac{(x + \Delta x)/x}{(y + \Delta y)/y} = \frac{1 + (\Delta x/x)}{1 + (\Delta y/y)}$$

where the first equality comes from the fact that $z = x/y$, the second equality comes from rearranging terms, and the third equality comes from simplifying.

Using the expressions for the left and right sides gives:

$$1 + \Delta z/z = \frac{1 + (\Delta x/x)}{1 + (\Delta y/y)}$$

Or, substituting,

$$1 + g_z = \frac{1 + g_x}{1 + g_y}$$

From Proposition 6, $(1 + g_z) \approx (1 + g_x - g_y)$, or, equivalently,

$$g_z \approx g_x - g_y$$

For $g_x = .05$ and $g_y = .03$, the approximation gives $g_z = 2\%$, while the correct value is 1.9%.

Application from Chapter 9: Let aggregate demand be given by $Y = \gamma M/P$, where Y is output, M is nominal money, P is the price level, and γ is a constant. It follows from Propositions 7 and 8 that:

$$g_Y \approx g_\gamma + g_M - \pi$$

where π is the rate of growth of prices, equivalently the rate of inflation. As γ is constant, g_γ is equal to zero. Thus,

$$g_Y \approx g_M - \pi$$

The rate of output growth is approximately equal to the rate of growth of nominal money minus the rate of inflation.

Functions

I use functions informally in this book, as a way of denoting how a variable depends on one or more other variables.

In some cases, I look at how a variable Y moves with a variable X. I write this relation as

$$Y = f(X)$$
$$(+)$$

A plus sign below X indicates a positive relation: An increase in X leads to an increase in Y. A minus sign below X indicates a negative relation: An increase in X leads to a decrease in Y.

In some cases, I allow the variable Y to depend on more than one variable. For example, I allow Y to depend on X and Z:

$$Y = f(X, Z)$$
$$(+,-)$$

The signs indicate that an increase in X leads to an increase in Y, and that an increase in Z leads to a decrease in Y.

An example of such a function is the investment function (5.1) in Chapter 5:

$$I = I(Y, i)$$
$$(+,-)$$

This equation says that investment, I, increases with production, Y, and decreases with the interest rate, i.

In some cases, it is reasonable to assume that the relation between two or more variables is a **linear relation.** A given increase in X always leads to the same increase in Y. In that case, the function is given by:

$$Y = a + bX$$

This relation can be represented by a line giving Y for any value of X.

The parameter a gives the value of Y when X is equal to zero. It is called the **intercept** because it gives the value of Y when the line representing the relation "intercepts" (crosses) the vertical axis.

The parameter b tells us by how much Y increases when X increases by 1. It is called the **slope** because it is equal to the slope of the line representing the relation.

A simple linear relation is the relation $Y = X$, which is represented by the 45-degree line and has a slope of one. Another example of a linear relation is the consumption function (3.2) in Chapter 3:

$$C = c_0 + c_1 Y_D$$

where C is consumption and Y_D is disposable income. c_0 tells us what consumption would be if disposable income were equal to zero. c_1 tells us by how much consumption increases when income increases by 1 unit; c_1 is called the marginal propensity to consume.

Logarithmic Scales

A variable that grows at a constant growth rate increases by larger and larger increments over time. Take a variable X that grows over time at a constant growth rate, say at 3% per year:

- Start in year 0 and assume that $X = 2$. So a 3% increase in X represents an increase of 0.06 (0.03×2).
- Go to year 20. X is now equal to $2(1.03)^{20} = 3.61$. A 3% increase now represents an increase of 0.11 (0.03×3.61).
- Go to year 100. X is equal to $2(1.03)^{100} = 38.4$. A 3% increase represents an increase of 1.15 (0.03×38.4), so an increase about 20 times larger than in year 0.

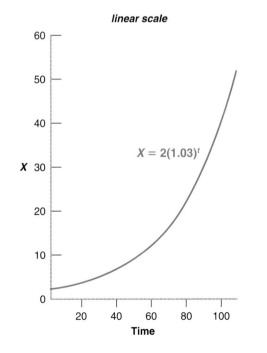

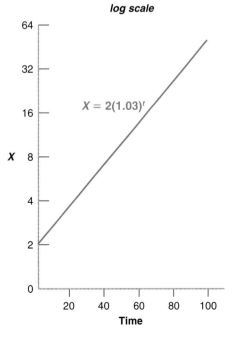

Figure A2-1

(a) The evolution of X using a linear scale.
(b) The evolution of X using a logarithmic scale.

A Math Refresher

If we plot X against time using a standard (linear) vertical scale, the plot looks like Figure A2-1(a). The increases in X become larger and larger over time (0.06 in year 0, 0.11 in year 20, and 1.15 in year 100). The curve representing X against time becomes steeper and steeper.

Another way of representing the evolution of X is to use a *logarithmic scale* to measure X on the vertical axis. The property of a logarithmic scale is that the same *proportional* increase in this variable is represented by the same vertical distance on the scale. So the behavior of a variable such as X, which increases by the same proportional increase (3%) each year, is now represented by a line. Figure A2-1(b) represents the behavior of X, this time using a logarithmic scale on the vertical axis. The fact that the relation is represented by a line indicates that X is growing at a constant rate over time. The higher the rate of growth, the steeper the line.

In contrast to X, economic variables such as GDP do not grow at a constant growth rate every year. Their growth rate may be higher in some decades and lower in others. A recession may lead to a few years of negative growth. Yet, when looking at their evolution over time, it is often more informative to use a logarithmic scale than a linear scale. Let's see why.

Figure A2-2(a) plots real U.S. GDP from 1890 to 2006 using a standard (linear) scale. Because real U.S. GDP is about 46 times bigger in 2006 than in 1890, the same proportional increase in GDP is 46 times bigger in 2006 than in 1890. So the curve representing the evolution of GDP over time becomes steeper and steeper over time. It is very difficult to see from the figure whether the U.S. economy is growing faster or slower than it was 50 years ago or 100 years ago.

Figure A2-2(b) plots U.S. GDP from 1890 to 2006, now using a logarithmic scale. If the growth rate of GDP was the same every year—so the proportional increase in GDP was the same every year—the evolution of GDP would be represented by a line—the same way as the evolution of X was represented by a line in Figure A2-1(b). Because the growth rate of GDP is not constant from year to year—so the proportional increase in GDP is not the same every year—the evolution of GDP is no longer represented by a line. Unlike in Figure A2-2(a), GDP does not explode over time, and the graph is more informative. Here are two examples:

- If, in Figure A2-2(b), we were to draw a line to fit the curve from 1890 to 1929 and another line to fit the curve from 1950 to 2003 [the two periods are separated by the shaded area in Figure A2-2(b)], the two

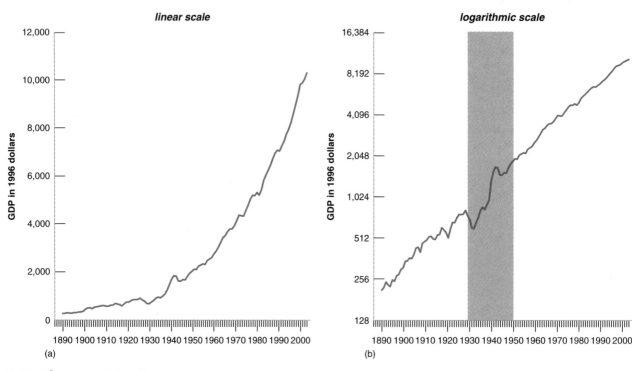

Figure A2-2

(a) U.S. GDP since 1890 using a linear scale. (b) U.S. GDP since 1890 using a logarithmic scale.

lines would have roughly the same slope. What this tells us is that the average growth rate was roughly the same during the two periods.

■ The decline in output from 1929 to 1933 is very visible in Figure A2-2(b). So is the strong recovery of output that follows. By the 1950s, output appears to be back to its old trend line. This suggests that the Great Depression was not associated with a permanently lower level of output.

Note, in both cases, that you could not have derived these conclusions by looking at Figure A2-2(a), but you can derive them by looking at Figure A2-2(b). This shows the usefulness of using a logarithmic scale.

Key Terms

■ linear relation, 623
■ intercept, 623
■ slope, 623

APPENDIX 3 An Introduction to Econometrics

How do we know that consumption depends on disposable income?

How do we know the value of the propensity to consume?

To answer these questions, and more generally, to estimate behavioral relations and find out the values of the relevant parameters, economists use *econometrics*—the set of statistical techniques designed for use in economics. Econometrics can get very technical, but the basic principles behind it are simple.

My purpose in this appendix is to show you these basic principles. I shall do so using as an example the consumption function introduced in Chapter 3, and I shall concentrate on estimating c_1, the propensity to consume out of disposable income.

Changes in Consumption and Changes in Disposable Income

The propensity to consume tells us by how much consumption changes for a given change in disposable income. A natural first step is simply to plot changes in consumption versus changes in disposable income and see how the relation between the two looks. You can see this in Figure A3-1.

The vertical axis in Figure A3-1 measures the annual change in consumption minus the average annual change in consumption, for each year from 1970 to 2006. More precisely, let C_t denote consumption in year t. Let ΔC_t denote $C_t - C_{t-1}$, the change in consumption from year $t-1$ to year t. Let $\overline{\Delta C}$ denote the average annual change in consumption since 1970. The variable measured on the vertical axis is constructed as $\Delta C_t - \overline{\Delta C}$. A positive value of the variable represents an increase in consumption larger than average, while a negative value represents an increase in consumption smaller than average.

Similarly, the horizontal axis measures the annual change in disposable income, minus the average annual change in disposable income since 1970, $\Delta Y_{Dt} - \overline{\Delta Y_D}$.

A particular square in the figure gives the deviations of the change in consumption and disposable income from their respective means for a particular year between 1970 and 2006. In 2006 for example, the change in consumption was higher than average by $50 billion; the change in disposable income was higher than average by $67 billion. (For our purposes, it is not important to know which year each square refers to, just what the set of points in the diagram looks like. So, except for 2006, the years are not indicated on Figure A3-1.)

Figure A3-1 suggests two main conclusions:

- There is a clear positive relation between changes in consumption and changes in disposable income. Most of the points lie in the upper-right and lower-left quadrants of the figure: When disposable income increases by less than average, so typically does consumption.

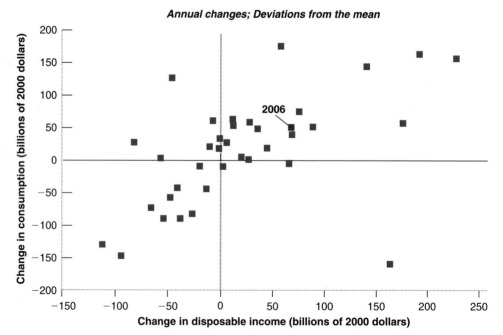

Annual changes; Deviations from the mean

Figure A3-1

Changes in Consumption versus Changes in Disposable income, since 1970

There is a clear positive relation between changes in consumption and changes in disposable income.

The relation between the two variables is good but not perfect. In particular, some points lie in the upper-left quadrant: These points correspond to years when smaller-than-average changes in disposable income were associated with higher-than-average changes in consumption.

Econometrics allows us to state these two conclusions more precisely and to get an estimate of the propensity to consume. Using an econometrics software package, we can find the line that fits the cloud of points in Figure A3-1 best. This line-fitting process is called **ordinary least squares (OLS)**. The estimated equation corresponding to the line is called a **regression** and the line itself is called the **regression line**. The term *least squares* comes from the fact that the line has the property that it minimizes the sum of the squared distances of the points to the line—thus gives the "least" "squares." The word *ordinary* comes from the fact that this is the simplest method used in econometrics.

In our case, the estimated equation is given by

$$(\Delta C_t - \overline{\Delta C}) = 0.77(\Delta Y_{Dt} - \overline{\Delta Y_D}) + \text{residual}$$
$$\overline{R} = 0.58 \qquad\qquad (A3.1)$$

The regression line corresponding to this estimated equation is drawn in Figure A3-2. Equation (A3.1) reports two important numbers (econometrics packages give more information than those reported here; a typical printout, together with further explanations, is given in the Focus box "A Guide to Understanding Econometric Results"):

- The first important number is the estimated propensity to consume. The equation tells us that an increase in disposable income of $1 billion above normal is typically associated with an increase in consumption of $0.77 billion above normal. In other words, the estimated propensity to consume is 0.77. It is positive but smaller than 1.
- The second important number is $\overline{R}^2$, which is a measure of how well the regression line fits:

    Having estimated the effect of disposable income on consumption, we can decompose the change in consumption for each year into that part that is due to the change in disposable income—the first term on the right in equation (A3.1)—and the rest, which is called the **residual**. For example, the residual for 2006 is indicated in Figure A3-2 by the vertical distance from the point representing 2006 to the regression line. (The point representing 2006 happens to be nearly on the regression line, so the vertical distance is very small.)

    If all the points in Figure A3-2 were exactly on the estimated line, all residuals would be 0; all changes in consumption would be explained by changes in disposable income. As you can see, however, this is not the case. $\overline{R}^2$ is a statistic that tells us how well the line fits. $\overline{R}^2$ is always between 0 and 1. A value of 1 would imply that the relation

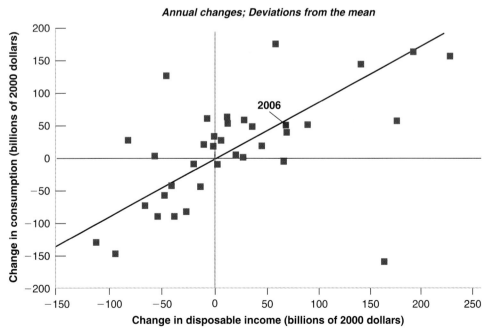

Annual changes; Deviations from the mean

Figure A3-2

Changes in Consumption and Changes in Disposable Income: The Regression Line

The regression line is the line that fits the scatter of points best.

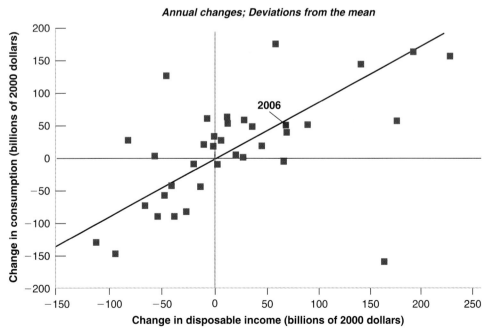

In your readings, you may run across results of estimation using econometrics. Here is a guide, which uses the slightly simplified, but otherwise untouched computer output for equation (A3.1):

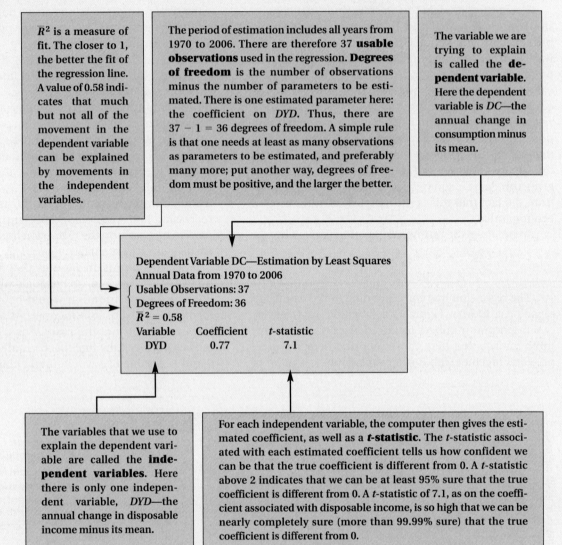

$\overline{R}^2$ is a measure of fit. The closer to 1, the better the fit of the regression line. A value of 0.58 indicates that much but not all of the movement in the dependent variable can be explained by movements in the independent variables.

The period of estimation includes all years from 1970 to 2006. There are therefore 37 **usable observations** used in the regression. **Degrees of freedom** is the number of observations minus the number of parameters to be estimated. There is one estimated parameter here: the coefficient on DYD. Thus, there are $37 - 1 = 36$ degrees of freedom. A simple rule is that one needs at least as many observations as parameters to be estimated, and preferably many more; put another way, degrees of freedom must be positive, and the larger the better.

The variable we are trying to explain is called the **dependent variable**. Here the dependent variable is DC—the annual change in consumption minus its mean.

Dependent Variable DC—Estimation by Least Squares
Annual Data from 1970 to 2006
Usable Observations: 37
Degrees of Freedom: 36
$\overline{R}^2 = 0.58$

Variable	Coefficient	t-statistic
DYD	0.77	7.1

The variables that we use to explain the dependent variable are called the **independent variables.** Here there is only one independent variable, DYD—the annual change in disposable income minus its mean.

For each independent variable, the computer then gives the estimated coefficient, as well as a **t-statistic**. The t-statistic associated with each estimated coefficient tells us how confident we can be that the true coefficient is different from 0. A t-statistic above 2 indicates that we can be at least 95% sure that the true coefficient is different from 0. A t-statistic of 7.1, as on the coefficient associated with disposable income, is so high that we can be nearly completely sure (more than 99.99% sure) that the true coefficient is different from 0.

between the two variables is perfect, that all points are exactly on the regression line. A value of 0 would imply that the computer can see no relation between the two variables. The value of $\overline{R}^2$ of 0.58 in equation (A3.1) is high, but not very high. It confirms the message from Figure A3-2: Movements in disposable income clearly affect consumption, but there is still quite a bit of movement in consumption that cannot be explained by movements in disposable income.

Correlation versus Causality

We have established so far that consumption and disposable income typically move together. More formally, we have seen that there is a positive **correlation**—the technical term for "co-relation"—between annual changes in consumption and annual changes in disposable income. And we have interpreted this relation as showing **causality**—that an increase in disposable income causes an increase in consumption.

We need to think again about this interpretation. A positive relation between consumption and disposable income may reflect the effect of disposable income on consumption. But it may also reflect the effect of consumption on disposable income. Indeed, the model we developed in Chapter 3 tells us that if, for any reason, consumers decide to spend more, then output, and therefore income and, in turn, disposable income will increase. If part of the relation between consumption and disposable income comes from the effect of consumption on disposable income, interpreting equation (A3.1) as telling us about the effect of disposable income on consumption is not right.

An example will help here: Suppose consumption does not depend on disposable income, so that the true value of c_1 is 0. (This is not very realistic, but it will make the point most clearly.) So draw the consumption function as a horizontal line (a line with a 0 slope) in Figure A3-3. Next, suppose that disposable income equals Y_D, so that the initial combination of consumption and disposable income is given by point A.

Now suppose that, because of improved confidence, consumers increase their consumption, so the consumption line shifts up. If demand affects output, then income and, in turn, disposable income, increase, so that the new combination of consumption and disposable income will be given by, say, point B. If, instead, consumers become more pessimistic, the consumption line shifts down, and so does output, leading to a combination of consumption and disposable income given by point D.

If we look at that economy, we observe points A, B, and D. If, as we did earlier, we draw the best-fitting line through these points, we estimate an upward-sloping line, such as CC', and so estimate a positive value for propensity to consume, c_1. Remember, however, that the true value of c_1 is 0. Why do we get the wrong answer—a positive value for c_1 when the true value is 0? Because we interpret the positive relation between disposable income and consumption as showing the effect of disposable income on consumption when, in fact, the relation reflects the effect of consumption on disposable income: Higher consumption leads to higher demand, higher output, and higher disposable income.

There is an important lesson here: *the difference between correlation and causality*. The fact that two variables move together does not imply that movements in the first variable cause movements in the second variable.

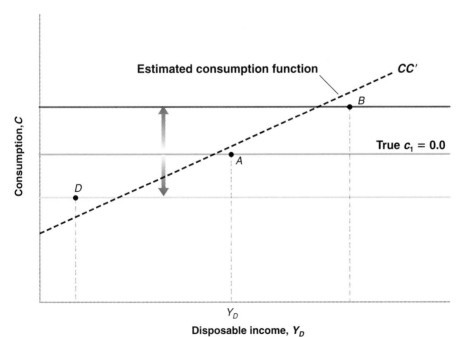

Estimated consumption function

CC'

B

True $c_1 = 0.0$

A

D

Consumption, C

Y_D

Disposable income, Y_D

Figure A3-3 ▬

A Misleading Regression

The relation between disposable income and consumption comes from the effect of consumption on income rather than from the effect of income on consumption.

Perhaps the causality runs the other way: Movements in the second variable cause movements in the first variable. Or perhaps, as is likely to be the case here, the causality runs both ways: Disposable income affects consumption, *and* consumption affects disposable income.

Is there a way out of the correlation-versus-causality problem? If we are interested—and we are—in the effect of disposable income on consumption, can we still learn that from the data? The answer yes, but only by using more information.

Suppose we *knew* that a specific change in disposable income was not caused by a change in consumption. Then, by looking at the reaction of consumption to *this* change in disposable income, we could learn how consumption responds to disposable income; we could estimate the propensity to consume.

This answer would seem to simply assume away the problem: How can we tell that a change in disposable income is not due to a change in consumption? In fact, sometimes we can tell. Suppose, for example, that the government embarks on a major increase in defense spending, leading to an increase in demand and, in turn, an increase in output. In that case, if we see both disposable income and consumption increase, we can safely assume that the movement in consumption reflects the effect of disposable income on consumption, and thus estimate the propensity to consume.

This example suggests a general strategy:

■ Find exogenous variables—that is, variables that affect disposable income but are not in turn affected by it.
■ Look at the change in consumption in response not to all changes in disposable income—as we did in our earlier regression—but in response to those changes in disposable income that can be explained by changes in these exogenous variables.

By following this strategy, we can be confident that what we are estimating is the effect of disposable income on consumption, and not the other way around.

The problem of finding such exogenous variables is known as the **identification problem** in econometrics. These exogenous variables, when they can be found, are called **instruments**. Methods of estimation that rely on the use of such instruments are called **instrumental variable methods**.

When equation (A3.1) is estimated using an instrumental variable method—using current and past changes in government defense spending as the instruments—rather than ordinary least squares, as we did earlier, the estimated equation becomes

$$(\Delta C_t - \overline{\Delta C}) = 0.62(\Delta Y_{Dt} - \overline{\Delta Y_D})$$

Note that the coefficient on disposable income, 0.62, is smaller than 0.77 in equation (A3.1). This decrease in the estimated propensity to consume is exactly what we would expect: Our earlier estimate in equation (A3.1) reflected not only the effect of disposable income on consumption, but also the effect of consumption on disposable income. The use of instruments eliminates this second effect, which is why we find a smaller estimated effect of disposable income on consumption.

This short introduction to econometrics is no substitute for a course in econometrics. But it gives you a sense of how economists use data to estimate relations and parameters, and to identify causal relations between economic variables.

Key Terms

■ ordinary least squares (OLS), 627
■ regression, regression line, 627
■ residual, $\overline{R}^2$, 627
■ dependent variable, independent variables, 628
■ usable observations, degrees of freedom, 628
■ *t*-statistic, 628
■ correlation, causality, 629
■ identification problem, 630
■ instruments, instrumental variable methods, 630

above the line, below the line In the balance of payments, the items in the *current account* are above the line drawn to divide them from the items in the *capital account*, which appear below the line.

accelerationist Phillips curve See *modified Phillips curve.*

adaptive expectations A backward-looking method of forming expectations by adjusting for past mistakes.

adjusted nominal money growth Nominal money growth minus normal output growth.

aggregate demand relation The demand for output at a given price level. It is derived from equilibrium in goods and financial markets.

aggregate output The total amount of output produced in the economy.

aggregate private spending The sum of all nongovernment spending. Also called *private spending.*

aggregate production function The relation between the quantity of aggregate output produced and the quantities of inputs used in production.

aggregate supply relation The price level at which firms are willing to supply a given level of output. It is derived from equilibrium in the labor market.

animal spirits A term introduced by Keynes to refer to movements in investment that could not be explained by movements in current variables.

appreciation (nominal) An increase in the price of domestic currency in terms of foreign currency. Corresponds to an increase in the exchange rate.

appropriability (of research results) The extent to which firms benefit from the results of their research and development efforts.

arbitrage The proposition that the expected rates of return on two financial assets must be equal. Also called *risky arbitrage* to distinguish it from *riskless arbitrage*, the proposition that the actual rates of return on two financial assets must be the same.

Asian crisis The financial and economic crisis in Asia that started in 1997.

Asian miracle The fast growth in many Asian countries over the past 20 to 30 years.

automatic stabilizer The fact that a decrease in output leads, under given tax and spending rules, to an increase in the budget deficit. This increase in the budget deficit in turn increases demand and thus stabilizes output.

autonomous spending The component of the demand for goods that does not depend on the level of output.

balance of payments A set of accounts that summarize a country's transactions with the rest of the world.

balanced budget A budget in which taxes are equal to government spending.

balanced growth The situation in which output, capital, and effective labor all grow at the same rate.

band (for exchange rates) The limits within which the exchange rate is allowed to move under a fixed exchange rate system.

bank reserves Holdings of central bank money by banks. The difference between what banks receive from depositors and what they lend to firms or hold as bonds.

bank run Simultaneous attempts by depositors to withdraw their funds from a bank.

bargaining power The relative strength of each side in a negotiation or a dispute.

barter The exchange of goods for other goods rather than for money.

base year When constructing real GDP by evaluating quantities in different years using a given set of prices, the year to which this given set of prices corresponds.

behavioral equation An equation that captures some aspect of behavior.

bilateral exchange rate The real exchange rate between two countries.

Board of Governors The group of seven members that governs the Federal Reserve System and is in charge of the design of monetary policy.

bond A financial asset that promises a stream of known payments over some period of time.

bond rating The assessment of a bond based on its default risk.

broad money See M2.

budget deficit The excess of government expenditures over government revenues.

business cycle theory The study of macroeconomic fluctuations.

business cycles See *output fluctuations.*

capital account In the balance of payments, a summary of a country's asset transactions with the rest of the world.

capital accumulation Increase in the capital stock.

capital controls Restrictions on the foreign assets domestic residents can hold, and on the domestic assets foreigners can hold.

cash flow The net flow of cash a firm is receiving.

causality A relation between cause and effect.

central bank money Money issued by the central bank. Also known as the *monetary base* and *high-powered money.*

central parity The reference value of the exchange rate around which the exchange rate is allowed to move under a fixed exchange rate system. The center of the *band*.

change in business inventories In the national income and product accounts, the change in the volume of inventories held by businesses.

checkable deposits Deposits at banks and other financial institutions against which checks can be written.

churning The concept that new goods make old goods obsolete, that new production techniques make older techniques and worker skills obsolete, and so on.

collective bargaining Wage bargaining between unions and firms.

compensation of employees In the national income and product accounts, the sum of wages and salaries and of supplements to wages and salaries.

confidence band When estimating the dynamic effect of one variable on another, the range of values where we can be confident the true dynamic effect lies.

Congressional Budget Office (CBO) An office of Congress in charge of constructing and publishing budget projections.

constant returns to scale The proposition that a proportional increase (or decrease) of all inputs leads to the same proportional increase (or decrease) in output.

consumer confidence index An index computed monthly that estimates consumer confidence regarding current and future economic conditions.

consumer price index (CPI) The cost of a given list of goods and services consumed by a typical urban dweller.

consumption (C) Goods and services purchased by consumers.

consumption function A function that relates consumption to its determinants.

consumption of fixed capital Depreciation of capital.

contractionary open-market operation An open-market operation in which the central bank sells bonds to decrease the money supply.

controlled experiment A set of test conditions in which one variable is altered while the others are kept constant.

convergence The tendency for countries with lower output per capita to grow faster, leading to convergence of output per capita across countries.

coordination (of macroeconomic policies between two countries) The joint design of macroeconomic policies to improve the economic situation in the two countries.

corporate bond A bond issued by a corporation.

corporate profits In the national income and product accounts, firms' revenues minus costs (including interest payments) and minus depreciation.

correlation A measure of the way two variables move together. A positive correlation indicates that the two variables tend to move in the same direction. A negative correlation indicates that the two variables tend to move in opposite directions. A correlation of zero indicates that there is no apparent relation between the two variables.

cost of living index The average price of a consumption bundle.

coupon bond A bond that promises multiple payments before maturity and one payment at maturity.

coupon payments The payments before maturity on a coupon bond.

coupon rate The ratio of the coupon payment to the face value of a coupon bond.

crawling peg An exchange rate mechanism in which the exchange rate is allowed to move over time according to a pre-specified formula.

creative destruction The proposition that growth simultaneously creates and destroys jobs.

credibility The degree to which people and markets believe that a policy announcement will actually be implemented and followed through.

credit channel The channel through which monetary policy works by affecting the amount of loans made by banks to firms.

currency Coins and bills.

currency board An exchange rate system in which: (i) the central bank stands ready to buy or sell foreign currency at the official exchange rate; (ii) the central bank cannot engage in open-market operations, that is buy or sell government bonds.

current account In the balance of payments, the summary of a country's payments to and from the rest of the world.

Current Population Survey (CPS) A large monthly survey of U.S. households used, in particular, to compute the unemployment rate.

current yield The ratio of the coupon payment to the price of a coupon bond.

cyclically adjusted deficit A measure of what the government deficit would be under existing tax and spending rules, if output were at its natural level. Also called a *full-employment deficit*, *midcycle deficit*, *standardized employment deficit*, or *structural deficit*.

debt finance Financing based on loans or the issuance of bonds.

debt monetization The printing of money to finance a deficit.

debt ratio See *debt-to-GDP ratio*.

debt repudiation A unilateral decision by a debtor not to repay its debt.

debt-to-GDP ratio The ratio of debt to gross domestic product. Also called simply the *debt ratio*.

decreasing returns to capital The property that increases in capital lead to smaller and smaller increases in output as the level of capital increases.

decreasing returns to labor The property that increases in labor leads to smaller and smaller increases in output as the level of labor increases.

default risk The risk that the issuer of a bond will not pay back the full amount promised by the bond.

deflation Negative inflation.

degrees of freedom The number of usable observations in a *regression* minus the number of parameters to be estimated.

demand deposit A bank account that allows depositors to write checks or get cash on demand, up to an amount equal to the account balance.

demand for domestic goods The demand for domestic goods by people, firms, and governments, both domestic and foreign. Equal to the domestic demand for goods plus net exports.

dependent variable A variable whose value is determined by one or more other variables.

depreciation (nominal) A decrease in the price of domestic currency in terms of a foreign currency. Corresponds to a decrease in the exchange rate.

depreciation rate A measure of how much usefulness a piece of capital loses from one period to the next.

depression A deep and long-lasting recession.

devaluation A decrease in the exchange rate in a fixed exchange rate system.

discount bond A bond that promises a single payment at maturity.

discount factor The value today of a dollar (or other national currency unit) at some time in the future.

discount policy The conditions under which the Fed lends to banks.

discount rate (i) The interest rate used to discount a sequence of future payments. Equal to the nominal interest rate when discounting future nominal payments and to the real interest rate when discounting future real payments. (ii) The interest rate at which the Fed lends to banks.

discount window Metaphorically, the window where the Fed lends to banks. More generally, the means by which the Federal Reserve Bank lends to banks.

discouraged worker A person who has given up looking for employment.

disinflation A decrease in inflation.

disposable income The income that remains once consumers have received transfers from the government and paid their taxes.

dividends The portion of a corporation's profits that the firm pays out each period to its shareholders.

dollar GDP See nominal GDP.

dollarization The use of dollars in domestic transactions in a country other than the United States.

domestic demand for goods The sum of consumption, investment, and government spending.

dual labor market A labor market that combines a primary labor market and a secondary labor market.

durable goods Commodities that can be stored and have an average life of at least three years.

duration of unemployment The period of time during which a worker is unemployed.

dynamic stochastic general equilibrium models (DSGE) Macro models derived from optimization by firms, consumers, and workers.

dynamics Movements of one or more economic variables over time.

econometrics Statistical methods applied to economics.

effective demand Synonym for aggregate demand.

effective labor The number of workers in an economy times the state of technology.

effective real exchange rate See multilateral exchange rate.

efficiency wage The wage at which a worker is performing a job most efficiently or productively.

emerging economies Countries with low output per person, and high growth.

endogenous variable A variable that depends on other variables in a model and is thus explained within the model.

entitlement programs Programs that require the payment of benefits to all who meet the eligibility requirements established by law.

equilibrium The equality between demand and supply.

equilibrium condition The condition that supply be equal to demand.

equilibrium equation An equation that represents an equilibrium condition.

equilibrium in the goods market The condition that the supply of goods be equal to the demand for goods.

equity finance Financing based on the issuance of shares.

equity premium Risk premium required by investors to hold stocks rather than short-term bonds.

euro A European currency that replaced national currencies in 11 countries in 2002 and is now used in 15 countries.

European Central Bank (ECB) The central bank, located in Frankfurt, in charge of determining monetary policy in the euro area.

European Monetary System (EMS) A fixed exchange rate system in place in most of the countries of the European Union from 1978 to 1999.

European Union A political and economic organization of 25 European nations. Formerly called the European Community.

Eurosclerosis A term coined to reflect the belief that Europe suffers from excessive rigidities, especially in the labor market.

exchange rate mechanism (ERM) The rules that determined the bands within which the member countries of the European Monetary System had to maintain their bilateral exchange rate.

exogenous variable A variable that is not explained within a model, but rather, is taken as given.

expansion A period of positive GDP growth.

expansionary open-market operation An open-market operation in which the central bank buys bonds to increase the money supply.

expectations hypothesis The hypothesis that financial investors are risk neutral, which implies that expected returns on all financial assets have to be equal.

expectations-augmented Phillips curve See modified Phillips curve.

expected present discounted value The value today of an expected sequence of future payments. Also called present discounted value or present value.

experiment A test carried out under controlled conditions to assess the validity of a model or hypothesis.

exports (X) The purchases of domestic goods and services by foreigners.

face value (on a bond) The single payment at maturity promised by a discount bond.

fad A period of time during which, for reasons of fashion or over-optimism, financial investors are willing to pay more for a stock than its fundamental value.

Fed accommodation A change in the money supply by the Fed to maintain a constant interest rate in the face of changes in money demand or in spending.

federal deposit insurance Insurance provided by the U.S. government that protects each bank depositor up to $100,000 per account.

federal funds market The market where banks that have excess reserves at the end of the day lend them to banks that have insufficient reserves.

federal funds rate The interest rate determined by equilibrium in the federal funds market. The interest rate affected most directly by changes in monetary policy.

Federal Open Market Committee (FOMC) A committee composed of the seven governors of the Fed, plus five District Bank presidents. The FOMC directs the activities of the Open Market Desk.

Federal Reserve Bank (Fed) The U.S. central bank.

Federal Reserve Districts The 12 regional districts that constitute the Federal Reserve System.

fertility of research The degree to which spending on research and development translates into new ideas and new products.

financial intermediary A financial institution that receives funds from people, firms, or other financial institutions, and uses these funds to make loans or buy financial assets.

financial investment The purchase of financial assets.

financial markets The markets in which financial assets are bought and sold.

financial wealth The value of all of one's financial assets minus all financial liabilities. Sometimes called *wealth*, for short.

fine-tuning A macroeconomic policy aimed at precisely hitting a given target, such as constant unemployment or constant output growth.

fiscal consolidation See *fiscal contraction*.

fiscal contraction A policy aimed at reducing the budget deficit through a decrease in government spending or an increase in taxation. Also called *fiscal consolidation*.

fiscal expansion An increase in government spending or a decrease in taxation, which leads to an increase in the budget deficit.

fiscal policy A government's choice of taxes and spending.

fiscal year An accounting period of 12 months. In the United States, the period from October 1 of the previous calendar year through September 30 of the current calendar year.

Fisher effect or Fisher hypothesis The proposition that, in the long run, an increase in nominal money growth is reflected in an identical increase in both the nominal interest rate and the inflation rate, leaving the real interest rate unchanged.

Fisher hypothesis See *Fisher effect*.

fixed exchange rate An exchange rate between the currencies of two or more countries that is fixed at some level and adjusted only infrequently.

fixed investment See *investment (I)*.

float The exchange rate is said to float when it is determined in the foreign exchange market, without central bank intervention.

floating exchange rate An exchange rate determined in the foreign exchange market without central bank intervention.

flow A variable that can be expressed as a quantity per unit of time (such as income).

forecast error The difference between the actual value of a variable and a forecast of that variable.

foreign direct investment The purchase of existing firms or the development of new firms by foreign investors.

foreign exchange Foreign currency; all currencies other than the domestic currency of a given country.

foreign exchange reserves Foreign assets held by the central bank.

four tigers The four Asian economies of Singapore, Taiwan, Hong Kong, and South Korea.

full-employment deficit See *cyclically adjusted deficit*.

fully funded social security system A retirement system in which the contributions of current workers are invested in financial assets, with the proceeds (principal and interest) given back to the workers when they retire.

fundamental value (of a stock) The present value of expected dividends.

G7 The seven major economic powers in the world: the United States, Japan, France, Germany, the United Kingdom, Italy, and Canada.

game *Strategic interactions* between *players*.

game theory The prediction of outcomes from *games*.

GDP adjusted for inflation See *real GDP*.

GDP deflator The ratio of nominal GDP to real GDP; a measure of the overall price level. Gives the average price of the final goods produced in the economy.

GDP growth The growth rate of real GDP in year t; equal to $(Y_t - Y_{t-1})/Y_{t-1}$.

GDP in chained (2000) dollars See *real GDP*.

GDP in constant dollars See *real GDP*.

GDP in current dollars See *nominal GDP*.

GDP in terms of goods See *real GDP*.

general equilibrium A situation in which there is equilibrium in all markets (goods, financial, and labor).

geometric series A mathematical sequence in which the ratio of one term to the preceding term remains the same. A sequence of the form $1 + c + c^2 + \cdots + c^n$.

gold standard A system in which a country fixed the price of its currency in terms of gold and stood ready to exchange gold for currency at the stated parity.

golden-rule level of capital The level of capital at which steady-state consumption is maximized.

government bond A bond issued by a government or a government agency.

government budget constraint The budget constraint faced by the government. The constraint implies that an excess of spending over revenues must be financed by borrowing, and thus leads to an increase in debt.

government purchases In the national income and product accounts, the sum of the purchases of goods by the government plus compensation of government employees.

government spending (G) The goods and services purchased by federal, state, and local governments.

government transfers Payments made by the government to individuals that are not in exchange for goods or services. Example: Social Security payments.

Great Depression The severe worldwide depression of the 1930s.

gross domestic product (GDP) A measure of aggregate output in the national income accounts. (The market value of the goods and services produced by labor and property located in the United States.)

gross national product (GNP) A measure of aggregate output in the national income accounts. (The market value of the goods and services produced by labor and property supplied by U.S. residents.)

gross private domestic fixed investment In the national income and product accounts, the sum of nonresidential investment and residential investment.

growth The steady increase in aggregate output over time.

hedonic pricing An approach to calculating real GDP that treats goods as providing a collection of characteristics, each with an implicit price.

heterodox stabilization program A stabilization program that includes incomes policies.

high-powered money See *central bank money*.

hires Workers newly employed by firms.

housing wealth The value of the housing stock.

human capital The set of skills possessed by the workers in an economy.

human wealth The labor-income component of wealth.

Humphrey–Hawkins Act A 1978 act of the U.S. Congress defining the goals of monetary policy. It expired in 2000.

hyperinflation Very high inflation.

hysteresis In general, the proposition that the equilibrium value of a variable depends on its history. With respect to unemployment, the proposition that a long period of sustained actual unemployment leads to an increase in the equilibrium rate of unemployment.

identification problem In econometrics, the problem of finding whether correlation between variables X and Y indicates a causal relation from X to Y, or from Y to X, or both. This problem is solved by finding exogenous variables, called *instruments*, that affect X and do not affect Y directly, or affect Y and do not affect X directly.

identity An equation that holds by definition, denoted by the sign $\equiv$.

imports (Q) The purchases of foreign goods and services by domestic consumers, firms, and the government.

income The flow of revenue from work, rental income, interest, and dividends.

incomes policies Government policies that set up wage and/or price guidelines or controls.

independent variable A variable that is taken as given in a relation or in a model.

index number A number, such as the GDP deflator, that has no natural level and is thus set to equal some value (typically 1 or 100) in a given period.

indexed bond A bond that promises payments adjusted for inflation.

indirect taxes Taxes on goods and services. In the United States, primarily sales taxes.

industrial policy A policy aimed at helping specific sectors of an economy.

inflation A sustained rise in the general level of prices.

inflation rate The rate at which the price level increases over time.

inflation targeting The conduct of monetary policy to achieve a given inflation rate over time.

inflation tax The product of the rate of inflation and real money balances.

inflation-adjusted deficit The correct economic measure of the budget deficit: The sum of the *primary deficit* and real interest payments.

instrumental variable methods In econometrics, methods of estimation that use *instruments* to estimate causal relations between different variables.

instruments In econometrics, the exogenous variables that allow the identification problem to be solved.

intercept In a linear relation between two variables, the value of the first variable when the second variable is equal to zero.

interest parity condition See *uncovered interest parity*.

intermediate good A good used in the production of a final good.

International Monetary Fund (IMF) The principal international economic organization. Publishes the *World Economic Outlook* annually and the *International Financial Statistics (IFS)* monthly.

inventory investment The difference between production and sales.

investment (I) Purchases of new houses and apartments by people, and purchases of new capital goods (machines and plants) by firms.

investment income In the current account, income received by domestic residents from their holdings of foreign assets.

IS curve A downward-sloping curve relating output to the interest rate. The curve corresponding to the *IS relation*, the equilibrium condition for the goods market.

IS relation An equilibrium condition stating that the demand for goods must be equal to the supply of goods, or equivalently that investment must be equal to saving. The equilibrium condition for the goods market.

J-curve A curve depicting the initial deterioration in the trade balance caused by a real depreciation, followed by an improvement in the trade balance.

junk bond A bond with a high risk of default.

labor force The sum of those employed and those unemployed.

labor hoarding The practice of retaining workers during a period of low product demand rather than laying them off.

labor in efficiency units See *effective labor*.

labor market rigidities Restrictions on firms' ability to adjust their level of employment.

labor productivity The ratio of output to the number of workers.

Laffer curve A curve showing the relation between tax revenues and the tax rate.

lagged value The value of a variable in the preceding time period.

layoffs Workers who lose their jobs either temporarily or permanently.

leapfrogging Advancing on and then overtaking the leader. Used to describe the process by which economic leadership passes from country to country.

life cycle theory of consumption The theory of consumption, developed initially by Franco Modigliani, which emphasizes that the planning horizon of consumers is their lifetime.

linear relation A relation between two variables such that a one-unit increase in one variable always leads to an increase of *n* units in the other variable.

liquid asset An asset that can be sold easily and at little cost.

liquidity preference The term introduced by Keynes to denote the demand for money.

liquidity trap The case where nominal interest rates are equal to zero, and monetary policy cannot, therefore, decrease them further.

LM curve An upward-sloping curve relating the interest rate to output. The curve corresponding to the *LM relation*, the equilibrium condition for financial markets.

LM relation An equilibrium condition stating that the demand for money must be equal to the supply of money. The equilibrium condition for financial markets.

logarithmic scale A scale in which the same proportional increase is represented by the same distance on the scale, so that a variable that grows at a constant rate is represented by a straight line.

long run A period of time extending over decades.

long-term bond A bond with maturity of 10 years or more.

Lucas critique The proposition, put forth by Robert Lucas, that existing relations between economic variables may change when policy changes. An example is the apparent trade-off between inflation and unemployment, which may disappear if policymakers try to exploit it.

M1 The sum of currency, traveler's checks, and checkable deposits—assets that can be used directly in transactions. Also called *narrow money*.

M2 M1 plus money market mutual fund shares, money market and savings deposits, and time deposits. Also called *broad money*.

M3 A *monetary aggregate* constructed by the Fed that is broader than M2.

Maastricht treaty A treaty signed in 1991 that defined the steps involved in the transition to a common currency for the European Union.

macroeconomics The study of aggregate economic variables, such as production for the economy as a whole, or the average price of goods.

marginal propensity to consume (*mpc* or c_1) The effect on consumption of an additional dollar of disposable income.

marginal propensity to import The effect on imports from an additional dollar in income.

marginal propensity to save The effect on saving of an additional dollar of disposable income. (Equal to one minus the marginal propensity to consume.)

Marshall–Lerner condition The condition under which a real depreciation leads to an increase in net exports.

maturity The length of time over which a financial asset (typically a bond) promises to make payments to the holder.

medium run A period of time between the *short run* and the *long run*.

medium-term bond A bond with a maturity of 1 to 10 years.

menu cost The cost of changing a price.

merchandise trade Exports and imports of goods.

microeconomics The study of production and prices in specific markets.

midcycle deficit See *cyclically adjusted deficit*.

model A conceptual structure used to think about and interpret an economic phenomenon.

models of endogenous growth Models in which accumulation of physical and human capital can sustain growth even in the absence of technological progress.

modified Phillips curve The curve that plots the change in the inflation rate against the unemployment rate. Also called an *expectations-augmented Phillips curve* or an *accelerationist Phillips curve*.

monetarism, monetarists A group of economists in the 1960s, led by Milton Friedman, who argued that monetary policy had powerful effects on activity.

monetary aggregate The market value of a sum of liquid assets. M1 is a monetary aggregate that includes only the most liquid assets.

monetary base See *central bank money*.

monetary contraction A change in monetary policy, which leads to an increase in the interest rate. Also called *monetary tightening*.

monetary expansion A change in monetary policy, which leads to a decrease in the interest rate.

monetary policy The use of the money stock by the central bank to affect interest rates, and by implication, economic activity and inflation.

monetary-fiscal policy mix The combination of monetary and fiscal policies in effect at a given time.

monetary tightening See *monetary contraction*.

money Those financial assets that can be used directly to buy goods.

money illusion The proposition that people make systematic mistakes in assessing nominal versus real changes.

money market funds Financial institutions that receive funds from people and use them to buy short-term bonds.

money multiplier The increase in the money supply resulting from a one-dollar increase in central bank money.

multilateral exchange rate (multilateral real exchange rate) The real exchange rate between a country and its trading partners, computed as a weighted average of bilateral real exchange rates. Also called the *trade-weighted real exchange rate* or *effective real exchange rate*.

multiplier The ratio of the change in an *endogenous variable* to the change in an *exogenous variable* (for example, the ratio of the change in output to a change in autonomous spending).

Mundell–Fleming model A model of simultaneous equilibrium in both goods and financial markets for an open economy.

narrow banking Restrictions on banks that would require them to hold only short-term government bonds.

narrow money See *M1*.

national accounts See *national income and product accounts*.

national income In the United States, the income that originates in the production of goods and services supplied by residents of the United States.

national income and product accounts (NIPA) The system of accounts used to describe the evolution of the sum, the composition, and the distribution of aggregate output.

National Industrial Recovery Act (NIRA) A New Deal program that asked industries to sign codes of behavior, to establish minimum wages, and not to impose further wage cuts.

National Recovery Administration (NRA) The administration in charge of the set of programs designed to help the U.S. economy recover from the Great Depression.

natural experiment A real-world event that can be used to test an economic theory.

natural level of employment The level of employment that prevails when unemployment is equal to its natural rate.

natural level of output The level of production that prevails when employment is equal to its natural level.

natural rate of unemployment The unemployment rate at which price and wage decisions are consistent.

neoclassical synthesis A consensus in macroeconomics, developed in the early 1950s, based on an integration of Keynes' ideas and the ideas of earlier economists.

net capital flows Capital flows from the rest of the world to the domestic economy, minus capital flows to the rest of the world from the domestic economy.

net exports The difference between exports and imports. Also called the *trade balance*.

net interest In the national income and product accounts, the interest paid by firms minus the interest received by firms, plus interest received from the rest of the world minus interest paid to the rest of the world.

net national product (NNP) Gross national product minus capital depreciation.

net transfers received In the current account, the net value of foreign aid received minus foreign aid given.

neutrality of money The proposition that an increase in nominal money has no effect on output or the interest rate, but is reflected entirely in a proportional increase in the price level.

new classicals A group of economists who interpret fluctuations as the effects of shocks in competitive markets with fully flexible prices and wages.

New Deal The set of programs put in place by the Roosevelt administration to get the U.S. economy out of the Great Depression.

New Economy The proposition that rapid technological progress in the information technology sector is fundamentally changing the nature of the U.S. economy.

new growth theory Recent developments in growth theory that explore the determinants of technological progress and the role of increasing returns to scale in growth.

New-Keynesian model Model based on utility maximization, profit maximization, and nominal rigidities.

New Keynesians A group of economists who believe in the importance of nominal rigidities in fluctuations, and who are exploring the role of market imperfections in explaining fluctuations.

nominal exchange rate The price of domestic currency in terms of foreign currency. The number of units of foreign currency you can get for one unit of domestic currency.

nominal GDP The sum of the quantities of final goods produced in an economy times their current price. Also known as *dollar GDP* and *GDP in current dollars.*

nominal interest rate The interest rate in terms of the national currency (in terms of dollars in the United States). It tells us how many dollars one has to repay in the future in exchange for borrowing one dollar today.

nominal rigidities The slow adjustment of nominal wages and prices to changes in economic activity.

nonaccelerating inflation rate of unemployment (NAIRU) The unemployment rate at which inflation neither decreases nor increases. See *natural rate of unemployment.*

nondurable goods Commodities that can be stored but have an average life of less than three years.

nonemployment rate The ratio of population minus employment, to population.

nonhuman wealth The financial and housing component of wealth.

noninstitutional civilian population The number of people potentially available for civilian employment.

nonresidential investment The purchase of new capital goods by firms: *structures* and *producer durable equipment.*

normal growth rate The rate of output growth needed to maintain a constant unemployment rate.

North American Free Trade Agreement (NAFTA) An agreement signed by the United States, Canada, and Mexico in which the three countries agreed to establish all of North America as a free-trade zone.

not in the labor force The number of people who are neither employed nor looking for employment.

n-year interest rate See *yield to maturity.*

Okun's law The relation between GDP growth and the change in the unemployment rate.

Open Market Desk The Federal Reserve agency in charge of open-market operations. Located in New York City.

open-market operation The purchase or sale of government bonds by the central bank for the purpose of increasing or decreasing the money supply.

openness in factor markets The opportunity for firms to choose where to locate production, and for workers to choose where to work and whether or not to migrate.

openness in financial markets The opportunity for financial investors to choose between domestic and foreign financial assets.

openness in goods markets The opportunity for consumers and firms to choose between domestic and foreign goods.

optimal control The control of a system (a machine, a rocket, an economy) by means of mathematical methods.

optimal control theory The set of mathematical methods used for *optimal control.*

ordinary least squares A statistical method to find the best-fitting relation between two or more variables.

Organisation for Economic Co-operation and Development (OECD) An international organization that collects and studies economic data for many countries. Most of the world's rich countries belong to the OECD.

orthodox stabilization program A stabilization program that does not include incomes policies.

output fluctuations Movements in output around its trend. Also called *business cycles.*

output per person A country's gross domestic product divided by its population.

overnight interest rate The interest rate charged in the *federal funds market* for lending and borrowing overnight.

overshooting The large movement in the exchange rate triggered by a monetary expansion or contraction.

panel data set A data set that gives the values of one or more variables for many individuals or many firms over some period of time.

paradox of saving The result that an attempt by people to save more may lead both to a decline in output and to unchanged saving.

parameter A coefficient in a behavioral equation.

participation rate The ratio of the labor force to the noninstitutional civilian population.

patent The legal right granted to a person or firm to exclude anyone else from the production or use of a new product or technique for a certain period of time.

pay-as-you-go Social Security system A retirement system in which the contributions of current workers are used to pay benefits to current retirees.

payments of factor income to the rest of the world In the United States, income received by foreign capital and foreign residents.

peg The exchange rate to which a country commits under a fixed exchange rate system.

permanent income theory of consumption The theory of consumption, developed by Milton Friedman, that emphasizes that people make consumption decisions based not on current income, but on their notion of permanent income.

personal consumption expenditures In the national income and product accounts, the sum of goods and services purchased by persons resident in the United States.

personal disposable income *Personal income* minus personal tax and non-tax payments. The income available to consumers after they have received transfers and paid taxes.

personal income The income actually received by persons.

Phillips curve The curve that plots the relation between movements in inflation and unemployment. The original Phillips curve captured the relation between the inflation rate and the unemployment rate. The *modified Phillips curve* captures the relation between (i) the change in the inflation rate and (ii) the unemployment rate.

players The participants in a *game*. Depending on the context, players may be people, firms, governments, and so on.

point-year of excess employment A difference between the actual unemployment rate and the natural unemployment rate of one percentage point for one year.

policy mix See *monetary-fiscal policy mix*.

political business cycle Fluctuations in economic activity caused by the manipulation of the economy for electoral gain.

post-industrial economies Economies in which the manufacturing sector's share of gross domestic product is small.

present value See *expected present discounted value*.

price level The general level of prices in an economy.

price liberalization The process of eliminating subsidies, decontrolling prices, and allowing them to clear markets.

price-setting relation The relation between the price chosen by firms, the nominal wage, and the markup.

primary deficit Government spending, excluding interest payments on the debt, minus government revenues. (The negative of the *primary surplus*.)

primary labor market A labor market where jobs are good, wages are high, and turnover is low. Contrast to the *secondary labor market*.

primary surplus Government revenues minus government spending, excluding interest payments on the debt.

private saving (S) Saving by the private sector. The value of consumers' disposable income minus their consumption.

private spending See *aggregate private spending*.

privatization The transfer of state-owned firms to private ownership.

producer durable equipment Durable goods such as machines, computers, and office equipment purchased by firms for production purposes.

producer price index (PPI) A price index of domestically produced goods in manufacturing, mining, agricultural, fishing, forestry, and electric utility industries.

production function The relation between the quantity of output and the quantities of inputs used in production.

profitability The expected present discounted value of profits.

propagation mechanism The dynamic effects of a *shock* on output and its components.

proprietors' income In the national income and product accounts, the income of sole proprietorships, partnerships, and tax-exempt cooperatives.

propensity to consume (c_1) The effect of an additional dollar of disposable income on consumption.

propensity to save The effect of an additional dollar of disposable income on saving (equal to one minus the propensity to consume).

public saving Saving by the government; equal to government revenues minus government spending. Also called the *budget surplus*. (A *budget deficit* represents public dissaving.)

purchasing power Income in terms of goods.

purchasing power parity (PPP) A method of adjustment used to allow for international comparisons of GDP.

quits Workers who leave their jobs for better alternatives.

quotas Restrictions on the quantities of goods that can be imported.

$\bar{R}^2$ A measure of fit, between zero and one, from a *regression*. An $\bar{R}^2$ of zero implies that there is no apparent relation between the variables under consideration. An $\bar{R}^2$ of 1 implies a perfect fit: all the *residuals* are equal to zero.

random walk The path of a variable whose changes over time are unpredictable.

random walk of consumption The proposition that, if consumers are foresighted, changes in their consumption should be unpredictable.

rate of growth of multifactor productivity See *Solow residual*.

rational expectations The formation of expectations based on rational forecasts, rather than on simple extrapolations of the past.

rational speculative bubble An increase in stock prices based on the rational expectation of further increases in prices in the future.

real appreciation An increase in the relative price of domestic goods in terms of foreign goods. An increase in the real exchange rate.

real business cycle (RBC) models Economic models that assume that output is always at its natural level. Thus, all output fluctuations are movements of the natural level of output, as opposed to movements away form the natural level of output.

real depreciation A decrease in the relative price of domestic goods in terms of foreign goods. An increase in the real exchange rate.

real exchange rate The relative price of domestic goods in terms of foreign goods.

real GDP A measure of aggregate output. The sum of quantities produced in an economy times their price in a base year. Also known as *GDP in terms of goods, GDP in constant dollars,* or *GDP adjusted for inflation*. The current measure of real GDP in the United States is called *GDP in (chained) 2000 dollars*.

real GDP in chained (2000) dollars See *real GDP*.

real interest rate The interest rate in terms of goods. It tells us how many goods one has to repay in the future in exchange for borrowing the equivalent one good today.

realignment The adjustment of parities in a fixed exchange rate system.

receipts of factor income from the rest of the world In the United States, income received from abroad by U.S. capital or U.S. residents.

recession A period of negative GDP growth. Usually refers to at least two consecutive quarters of negative GDP growth.

regression The output of *ordinary least squares*. Gives the equation corresponding to the estimated relation between variables, together with information about the degree of fit and the relative importance of the different variables.

regression line The best-fitting line corresponding to the equation obtained by using *ordinary least squares*.

rental cost of capital See *user cost*.

rental income of persons In the national income and product accounts, the income from the rental of real property, minus depreciation on this property.

research and development (R&D) Spending aimed at discovering and developing new ideas and products.

reservation wage The wage that would make a worker indifferent between working and being unemployed.

reserve ratio The ratio of bank reserves to checkable deposits.

reserve requirements The minimum amount of reserves that banks must hold in proportion to checkable deposits.

residential investment The purchase of new homes and apartments by people.

residual The difference between the actual value of a variable and the value implied by the *regression line*. Small residuals indicate a good fit.

revaluation An increase in the exchange rate in a fixed exchange rate system.

Ricardian equivalence The proposition that neither government deficits nor government debt have an effect on economic activity. Also called the *Ricardo-Barro proposition*.

Ricardo-Barro proposition See *Ricardian equivalence*.

risk averse A person is risk averse if he/she prefers to receive a given amount for sure to an uncertain amount with the same expected value.

risk neutral A person is risk neutral if he/she is indifferent between receiving a given amount for sure or an uncertain amount with the same expected value.

risk premium The difference between the interest rate paid on a given bond and the interest rate paid on a bond with the highest rating.

riskless arbitrage See *arbitrage*.

risky arbitrage See *arbitrage*.

sacrifice ratio The number of point-years of excess unemployment needed to achieve a decrease in inflation of 1%.

saving The sum of private and public saving, denoted by *S*.

saving rate The proportion of income that is saved.

savings The accumulated value of past saving. Also called *wealth*.

scatter diagram A graphic presentation that plots the value of one variable against the value of another variable.

secondary labor market A labor market where jobs are poor, wages are low, and turnover is high. Contrast to the *primary labor market*.

seignorage The revenues from the creation of money.

separations Workers who are leaving or losing their jobs.

services Commodities that cannot be stored and thus must be consumed at the place and time of purchase.

severance payments Payments made by firms to laid-off workers.

share A financial asset issued by a firm that promises to pay a sequence of payments, called dividends, in the future. Also called *stock*.

shocks Movements in the factors that affect aggregate demand and/or aggregate supply.

shoe-leather costs The costs of going to the bank to take money out of a checking account.

short run A period of time extending over a few years at most.

short-term bond A bond with a maturity of one year or less.

simulation The use of a model to look at the effects of a change in an exogenous variable on the variables in the model.

skill-biased technological progress The proposition that new machines and new methods of production require skilled workers to a greater degree than in the past.

Social Security Trust Fund The funds accumulated by the U.S. Social Security system as a result of surpluses in the past.

slope In a linear relation between two variables, the amount by which the first variable increases when the second increases by one unit.

soft budget constraint The granting of subsidies to firms that make losses, thus decreasing the incentives for these firms to take the measures needed to generate profits.

Solow residual The excess of actual output growth over what can be accounted for by the growth in capital and labor.

stabilization program A government program aimed at stabilizing the economy (typically stopping high inflation).

stagflation The combination of stagnation and inflation.

staggering of wage decisions The fact that different wages are adjusted at different times, making it impossible to achieve a synchronized decrease in nominal wage inflation.

standardized employment deficit See *cyclically adjusted deficit*.

state of technology The degree of technological development in a country or industry.

statistical discrepancy A difference between two numbers that should be equal, coming from differences in sources or methods of construction for the two numbers.

steady state In an economy without technological progress, the state of the economy where output and capital per worker are no longer changing. In an economy with technological progress, the state of the economy where output and capital per effective worker are no longer changing.

stock A variable that can be expressed as a quantity at a point in time (such as wealth). Also a synonym for *share*.

stocks An alternative term for inventories. Also, an alternative term for shares.

strategic interactions An environment in which the actions of one player depend on and affect the actions of another player.

structural deficit See *cyclically adjusted deficit*.

structural rate of unemployment See *natural rate of unemployment*.

structures In the national income and product accounts: plants, factories, office buildings, and hotels.

supply-siders A group of economists in the 1980s who believed that tax cuts would increase activity by enough to increase tax revenues.

Tanzi-Olivera effect The adverse effect of inflation on tax revenues and in turn on the budget deficit.

tariffs Taxes on imported goods.

tax smoothing The principle of keeping tax rates roughly constant, so that the government runs large deficits when government spending is exceptionally high and small surpluses the rest of the time.

Taylor rule A rule, suggested by John Taylor, telling a central bank how to adjust the nominal interest rate in response to deviations of inflation from its target, and of the unemployment rate from the natural rate.

technological progress An improvement in the state of technology.

technological unemployment Unemployment brought about by technological progress.

technology gap The differences between states of technology across countries.

term structure of interest rates See *yield curve*.

time inconsistency In game theory, the incentive for one player to deviate from his previously announced course of action once the other player has moved.

Tobin's q The ratio of the value of the capital stock, computed by adding the stock market value of firms and the debt of firms, to the replacement cost of capital.

total wealth The sum of human wealth and nonhuman wealth.

tradable goods Goods that compete with foreign goods in domestic or foreign markets.

trade balance The difference between exports and imports. Also called *net exports*.

trade deficit A negative trade balance, that is, imports exceed exports.

trade surplus A positive trade balance, that is, exports exceed imports.

trade-weighted real exchange rate See *multilateral exchange rate*.

transfers See *government transfers*.

Treasury bill (T-bill) A U.S. government bond with a maturity of up to one year.

Treasury bond A U.S. government bond with a maturity of 10 years or more.

Treasury note A U.S. government bond with a maturity of one to 10 years.

***t*-statistic** A statistic associated with an estimated coefficient in a regression that indicates how confident one can be that the true coefficient differs from zero.

twin deficits The budget and trade deficits that characterized the United States in the 1980s.

uncovered interest parity An arbitrage relation stating that domestic and foreign bonds must have the same expected rate of return, expressed in terms of a common currency.

underground economy That part of a nation's economic activity that is not measured in official statistics, either because the activity is illegal or because people and firms are seeking to avoid paying taxes.

unemployment rate The ratio of the number of unemployed to the labor force.

union density The proportion of the work force that is unionized.

usable observation An observation for which the values of all the variables under consideration are available for *regression* purposes.

user cost of capital The cost of using capital over a year, or a given period of time. The sum of the real interest rate and the depreciation rate. Also called the *rental cost of capital*.

value added The value a firm adds in the production process, equal to the value of its production minus the value of the intermediate inputs it uses in production.

velocity The ratio of nominal income to money; the number of transactions for a given quantity of money; or the rate at which money changes hands.

wage indexation A rule that automatically increases wages in response to an increase in prices.

wage-price spiral The mechanism by which increases in wages lead to increases in prices, which lead in turn to further increases in wages, and so on.

wage-setting relation The relation between the wage chosen by wage setters, the price level, and the unemployment rate.

war of attrition When both parties to an argument hold their grounds, hoping that the other party will give in.

wealth See *financial wealth*.

yield curve The relation between yield and maturity for bonds of different maturities. Also called the *term structure of interest rates*.

yield to maturity The constant interest rate that makes the price of an *n*-year bond today equal to the present value of future payments. Also called the *n-year interest rate*.

Index

Photo Credits

John Maynard Keynes - Corbis/Bettman

Paul Samuelson - Paul Samuelson

Franco Modigliani - Corbis/Bettman

James Tobin - Yale University Office of Public Affairs

Robert Solow - AP Wide World Photos

Lawrence Klein - Lawrence R. Klein

Milton Friedman - Corbis/Betteman

Edmund Phelps - Edmund S. Phelps

Robert Lucas - Getty Images, Inc., Hulton Archive Photos

Thomas Sargent - Thomas J. Sargent

Robert Barro - Robert J. Barro

Robert Hall - Robert E. Hall

Rudiger Dornbusch - Rudiger Dornbusch

Stanley Fischer - Courtesy International Monetary Fund

John Taylor - John B. Taylor, Stanford University

Edward Prescott - Federal Reserve Bank of Minneapolis

George Akerlof - George A. Akerlof

Ben Bernanke - Benjamin Bernanke

Paul Romer - Paul M. Romer

Philippe Aghion - Philippe Aghion

Peter Howitt - Peter Howitt

Andrei Shleifer - Courtesy of Andrei Shleifer

Daron Acemoglu - Courtesy of Daron Acemoglu

Michael Woodford - Courtesy of Mike Woodford

Jordi Gali - Courtesy of Jordi Gali

Symbols Used in This Book

Symbol	Term	Introduced in Chapter
$(\ )^d$	Superscript ^{d} means demanded	
$(\ )^e$	Superscript ^{e} means expected	
A	Aggregate private spending	17
	Also: Labor productivity/states of technology	6, 12
α	Effect on the inflation rate of the unemployment rate, given expected inflation	8
B	Goverment debt	26
β	Effect of an increase in output growth on the unemployment rate	9
C	Consumption	3
CU	Currency	4
c	Proportion of money held as currency	4
c_0	Consumption when disposable income equals zero	3
c_1	Propensity to consume	3
D	Checkable deposits	4
	Also: Real dividend on a stock	15
$\$D$	Nominal dividend on a stock	15
δ	Depreciation rate	11
E	Nominal exchange rate (price of domestic currency in terms of foreign currency)	18
$\bar{E}$	Fixed nominal exchange rate	20
E^e	Expected future exchange rate	18
ε	Real exchange rate	18
G	Government spending	3
g_A	Growth rate of technological progress	12
g_K	Growth rate of capital	12
g_m	Growth rate of nominal money	9
g_N	Growth rate of population	12
g, g_y	Growth rate of output	9
$\bar{g}_y$	Normal rate of growth of output	9
H	High powered money/monetary base/central bank money	4
	Also: Human capital	11
I	Fixed investment	3
IM	Imports	3
i	Nominal interest rate	4
i_1	One-year nominal interest rate	15
i_2	Two-year nominal interest rate	15
i^*	Foreign nominal interest rate	18
K	Capital stock	10

Symbol	Term	Introduced in Chapter
L	Labor force	2
M	Money stock (nominal)	4
M^d	Money demand (nominal)	4
M^s	Money supply (nominal)	4
μ	Markup of prices over wages	6
N	Employment	2
N_n	Natural level of employment	6
NX	Net exports	19
P	GDP deflator/CPI/price level	2
P^*	Foreign price level	18
π	Inflation	2
Π	Profit per unit of capital	16
Q	Real stock price	15
$\$Q$	Nominal stock price	15
R	Bank reserves	4
r	Real interest rate	14
S	Private saving	3
s	Private saving rate	11
T	Net taxes (taxes paid by consumers minus transfers)	3
Tr	Government transfers	26
θ	Reserve ratio of banks	4
U	Unemployment	2
u	Unemployment rate	2
u_n	Natural rate of unemployment	6
V	Present value of a sequence of real payments z	14
$\$V$	Present value of a sequence of nominal payments $\$z$	14
W	Nominal wage	6
Y	Real GDP/Output/Production	2
$\$Y$	Nominal GDP	2
Y_D	Disposable income	3
Y_L	Labor income	16
Y_n	Natural level of output	6
Y^*	Foreign output	19
X	Exports	3
Z	Demand for goods	3
z	Factors that affect the wage, given unemployment	6
z	Real payment	14
$\$Z$	Nominal payment	14